September 12–16, 2016
Newark, Delaware, USA

I0027583

Association for Computing Machinery

Advancing Computing as a Science & Profession

ICTIR'16

Proceedings of the 2016 ACM

International Conference on the Theory of Information Retrieval

Sponsored by:

ACM SIGIR

Supported by:

University of Delaware, Microsoft Research, and JPMorgan Chase & Co.

**Association for
Computing Machinery**

Advancing Computing as a Science & Profession

The Association for Computing Machinery
2 Penn Plaza, Suite 701
New York, New York 10121-0701

Notice to Past Authors of ACM-Published Articles

ISBN: 978-1-4503-4497-5 (Digital)

ISBN: 978-1-4503-4679-5 (Print)

Additional copies may be ordered prepaid from:

ACM Order Department
PO Box 30777
New York, NY 10087-0777, USA

Phone: 1-800-342-6626 (USA and Canada)
+1-212-626-0500 (Global)
Fax: +1-212-944-1318
E-mail: acmhelp@acm.org
Hours of Operation: 8:30 am – 4:30 pm ET

Printed in the USA

Chairs' Welcome

It is our pleasure to welcome you to the International Conference on the Theory of Information Retrieval (ICTIR), the 6th overall and the second to be fully sponsored by the ACM Special Interest Group on Information Retrieval (SIGIR). We are also happy to welcome you to Delaware and its flagship University. As a land-, sea-, and space-grant institution, UD is the site of groundbreaking research across all disciplines. We believe that the university setting is ideal for stimulating ideas, discussion, and collaborations to come. Plus, as far as we know, this is the first ACM-sponsored conference to be held in Delaware, the so-called "First State" for being the first to ratify the U.S. Constitution in 1787.

The call for papers attracted submissions from all over the world. The program committee reviewed 79 contributions — 44 full papers and 35 short — and accepted a total of 41 papers, all of which will be presented during the conference. We received four excellent tutorial proposals as well, and we hope those will aid in laying down foundational ideas in information retrieval research.

We thank everyone that helped us organize the conference: short paper chairs Fernando Diaz and Stefano Mizzaro, tutorial chair Grace Hui Yang, and the members of the program committee who worked hard to review papers and provide feedback for authors. We also thank our sponsors and supporters: ACM SIGIR, Microsoft Research, J.P. Morgan Chase, and the University of Delaware. Finally, we thank the authors for providing the superb technical content, and our keynote speaker Sandra Carberry for opening the conference.

We hope that you can take some time to explore the University campus, downtown Newark, the Delaware Valley, and the Mid-Atlantic U.S. The University is only two hours away (by train) from both New York City and Washington D.C., and the weather in September is warm and sunny, so you should be able to find plenty to do outside the conference.

Enjoy the conference!

Ben Carterette & Hui Fang
ICTIR'16 General Chairs
University of Delaware, USA

Mounia Lalmas & Jian-Yun Nie
ICTIR'16 Program Chairs
Yahoo! UK & University of Montreal

Table of Contents

Session: Dealing with Bias in IR Evaluation

Session: Word Embedding for IR

Session: Learning to Rank

Session: Exploiting Structure

Session: Query Understanding

Session: Locations and Events

Session: Social Media

Author Index

2016 ACM International Conference on the Theory of Information Retrieval (ICTIR) Organization

General Chairs: Ben Carterette *(University of Delaware, USA)*
Hui Fang *(University of Delaware, USA)*

Program Chairs: Mounia Lalmas *(Yahoo!, UK)*
Jian-Yun Nie *(University of Montreal, Canada)*

Short Paper Chairs: Fernando Diaz *(Microsoft Research, USA)*
Stefano Mizzaro *(University of Udine, Italy)*

Tutorial Chair: Grace Hui Yang *(Georgetown University, USA)*

Local Arrangements Chair: Karankumar Sabhnani *(University of Delaware, USA)*

Volunteer Coordinator: Ashraf Bah *(University of Delaware, USA)*

Registration Co-Chairs: Mustafa Zengin *(University of Delaware, USA)*
Mohammad Alsulmi *(University of Delaware, USA)*

Steering Committee Chair: Leif Azzopardi *(University of Strathclyde, Glasgow, UK)*

Steering Committee: Peter Bruza *(Queensland University of Technology, Australia)*
Susan Dumais *(Microsoft Research, USA)*
Jaap Kamps *(University of Amsterdam, Netherlands)*
Oren Kurland *(Technion, Israel)*
Birger Larson *(Aalborg University, Denmark)*
Don Metzler *(Google, USA)*
Stefan Rueger *(The Open University, UK)*

Program Committee: Enrique Amigó *(UNED, Spain)*
Jaime Arguello *(University of North Carolina at Chapel Hill, USA)*
Leif Azzopardi *(University of Strathclyde, Glasgow, UK)*
Krisztian Balog *(University of Stavanger, Norway)*
Klaus Berberich *(Max Planck Institute for Informatics, Germany)*
Peter Bruza *(Queensland University of Technology, Australia)*
Jamie Callan *(Carnegie Mellon University, USA)*
Claudio Carpineto *(Fondazione Ugo Bordoni, Italy)*
Pablo Castells *(Universidad Autónoma de Madrid, Spain)*
Yi Chang *(Yahoo Research, USA)*
Kevyn Collins-Thompson *(University of Michigan, USA)*
Ronan Cummins *(University of Cambridge, UK)*
Jeffrey Dalton *(Google, USA)*
Gianluca Demartini *(University of Sheffield, UK)*
Thomas Demeester *(Ghent University, Belgium)*

Program Committee (continued):

Ingo Frommholz *(University of Bedfordshire, UK)*
Norbert Fuhr *(University of Duisburg-Essen, Germany)*
Julio Gonzalo *(UNED, Spain)*
Jiafeng Guo *(Institute of Computing Technology, CAS, China)*
Ben He *(University of Chinese Academy of Sciences, China)*
Djoerd Hiemstra *(University of Twente, Netherlands)*
Jimmy Huang *(York University, Canada)*
Hideo Joho *(University of Tsukuba, Japan)*
Jaap Kamps *(University of Amsterdam, Netherlands)*
Jussi Karlgren *(Gavagai & KTH, Sweden)*
Diane Kelly *(University of North Carolina at Chapel Hill, USA)*
Oren Kurland *(Technion, Israel)*
Wai Lam *(The Chinese University of Hong Kong, Hong Kong)*
Birger Larsen *(Aalborg University Copenhagen, Denmark)*
Christina Lioma *(University of Copenhagen, Denmark)*
Yiqun Liu *(Tsinghua University, China)*
Massimo Melucci *(University of Padua, Italy)*
Bhaskar Mitra *(Microsoft, UK)*
Alistair Moffat *(The University of Melbourne, Australia)*
Gabriella Pasi *(Universita degli Studi di Milano Bicocca, Italy)*
Benjamin Piwowarski *(Université Pierre et Marie Curie, France)*
Stefan Rueger *(The Open University, UK)*
Tetsuya Sakai *(Waseda University, Japan)*
Rodrygo Santos *(Universidade Federal de Minas Gerais, Brazil)*
Mark D. Smucker *(University of Waterloo, Canada)*
Benno Stein *(Bauhaus-Universität Weimar, Germany)*
Adith Swaminathan *(Cornell University, USA)*
Theodora Tsikrika *(CERTH, Greece)*
Ellen M. Voorhees *(National Institute of Standards and Technology, USA)*
Bin Wang *(Institute of Information Engineering, Chinese Academy of Sciences, China)*
Ke Zhou *(Yahoo, UK)*
Guido Zuccon *(Queensland University of Technology, Australia)*

ICTIR 2016 Sponsor & Supporters

Sponsor:

Association for
Computing Machinery

Advancing Computing as a Science & Profession

SIGIR
Special Interest Group
on Information Retrieval

Organizer:

UNIVERSITY OF DELAWARE.

Supporters:

Microsoft®
Research

JPMORGAN CHASE & CO.

Advances in Formal Models of Search and Search Behaviour

Full Day Tutorial

Leif Azzopardi
University of Strathclyde
Glasgow, United Kingdom
leifos@acm.org

Guido Zuccon
Queensland University of Technology
Queensland, Australia
g.zuccon@qut.edu.au

ABSTRACT

Searching is performed in the context of a task and as such the value of the information found is with respect to the task. Recently, there has been a drive to developing formal models of information seeking and retrieval that consider the costs and benefits arising through the interaction with the interface/system and the information surfaced during that interaction. In this full day tutorial we will focus on describing and explaining some of the more recent and latest formal models of Information Seeking and Retrieval. The tutorial is structured into two parts. In the first part we will present a series of models that have been developed based on: (i) economic theory, (ii) decision theory (iii) game theory and (iv) optimal foraging theory. The second part of the day will be dedicated to building models where we will discuss different techniques to build and develop models from which we can draw testable hypotheses from. During the tutorial participants will be challenged to develop various formals models, applying the techniques learnt during the day. We will then conclude with presentations on solutions followed by a summary and overview of challenges and future directions. This tutorial is aimed at participants wanting to know more about the various formal models of information seeking, search and retrieval, that have been proposed. The tutorial will be presented at an intermediate level, and is designed to support participants who want to be able to understand and build such models.

Keywords

Search Behaviour, User Models, Retrieval Strategies, Evaluation

1. INTRODUCTION

In the field of Information Retrieval we have developed lots of models - mainly retrieval models for ranking documents. In this tutorial, however, the focus will be on theories that model the interaction between the user and the system,

ICTIR '16 September 12-16, 2016, Newark, DE, USA

© 2016 Copyright held by the owner/author(s).

ACM ISBN 978-1-4503-4497-5/16/09.

DOI: http://dx.doi.org/10.1145/2970398.2970440

thus examining models of interactive information seeking and retrieval. These models not only provide insights into how documents should or could be ranked but also shed light on search behaviours and how the interface/system affects such behaviours. Less attention has been paid to such models but there has been a growing interest in their development. However, building such models introduces numerous complexities and greater appreciation of how people interact with systems. Consequently, developing such models has been hailed as a (somewhat) grand challenge for Interactive Information Retrieval [12]. This is because such models are becoming increasingly important as they form the basis of many performance measures, provide a better understanding of how people interact with such systems, and enable more holistic session/task based evaluation.

The tutorial will be composed of two parts: (1) Theory and (2) Practice. In the theory sessions we will cover how: (i) economic theory, (ii) decision theory (iii) game theory and (iv) optimal foraging theory have been applied to Information Retrieval and Seeking. In the practical sessions we will focus on building various models throughout a series of activities. The day will conclude with a discussion of challenges and future directions.

1.1 Introduction and the Economics of Search

In the first session we will briefly provide the context and motivation for developing formal (by which we mean mathematical) models of Information Seeking and Retrieval (ISR). To begin, we will discuss and describe various conceptual and descriptive models of ISR, including Bates' Berry Picking Model [11] and the ISR framework proposed by Ingwersen and Kalvero [20], along with other such models (e.g. [39, 21, 16]). This will provide the background for the tutorial where we point out the limitations of such models and motivate the need to develop models that are not only descriptive in nature, but predictive and crucially explanatory. To set the context, we will discuss the qualities of information, the poverty of attention, information as a good, and how information can be valued. This is important because information seeking is intrinsically embedded within a task. Following on from this we will review various models based on economics. In this session we will cover:

1. Information as Good and the Value of Information [37].

2. Optimal Search Behaviour and the Pandora's Box Problem [34, 38, 37]

3. Optimal Amount of Information (when to stop and deciding at the margin) [13]

4. Azzopardi's Model of Searching (Assessing vs Querying) [4, 6]

5. Cooper's Model of Searching (User vs System or User vs User) [15].

1.2 Decisions, Games and Foraging

In this session we will consider two contemporary and emerging models (based on Decision Theory and Game Theory) before discussing models based on Information Foraging Theory and then showing how all the models relate together. First we shall show how the PRP can be extended to consider interaction by presenting the Interactive Probability Ranking Principle [18]. Then we will cover the Card Model and the POMPD model. Both of these models are derived from the idea that the user and the system are playing a game - this leads to game theoretic models. Then, we will delve into Information Foraging Theory (IFT), which has become very popular and is often used to motivate experiments, but yet infrequently used in terms of modelling and prediction. Here, we will focus on the patch model, and explain the different implications of the model/theory, and how user behaviour is expected to change under varying circumstances. We will explain how these implications can be generated through a graphical analysis (and for the more math savvy, how they can be analytically derived).

In summary, the topics we shall cover in this session are:

1. Probability Ranking Principle [26].

2. Interactive Probability Ranking Principle [18]

3. Card Model [41, 40]

4. POMPD model [22]

5. Optimal Foraging Theory [33].

6. Information Foraging Theory [24, 25, 29, 30]:
   - Information Scent Model
   - Information Diet Model
   - Information Patch Model
   - Charnov's Marginal Value Theorem [14]

7. IFT Example: Exploration / Exploitation [28, 1]

1.3 A Guide to Modelling

In the third session, we will focus on optimisation models, in general, how to build such models, and how to use them to generate hypotheses using various methods (analytical, graphical and computational) [36, 23]. The essence of such models is to develop a cost function and a gain function given the different interactions that users can perform. Given these functions, it is then possible to establish under what conditions cost is minimized and/or gain is maximized. This section will explore the following topics:

- Decision Making and Optimization Models [19, 23].
- Optimality and Rationality [32, 31, 34].
- What choices are available? What are the limitations?

- What are the interactions, costs and benefits?
- What will vary? Parameters?
- Define the problem and the goal
- Construct a cost and gain function
- What method to choose: analytical, graphically, computational
- Solve, plot, compute
- Draw inferences and generating hypotheses

To help illustrate how to undertake the model building process, we will use an example based on the simple scenario of finding the first highly relevant document in a result list. We will describe how we can characterize the problem, enumerate the different variables, and show how the different variables impact the overall cost and the design of the interface. If time permits, then we will also include some notes on developing simulations to explore such models (i.e., computational approaches).

1.4 Practical Session

The final session of the tutorial will be dedicated to building models. For example, participants will be given a context such as a user trying to find an app on a mobile phone or tablet. The goal here is to find the app that the user wants to use. So the focus will be on building a cost function to model the different ways in which the user can find the app, e.g. search or browse. To add realism to the scenario, we will consider different types of users, ones that can remember where the app is, and those who cant (i.e., best and average/worse cases) as well as consider how screen size and app icon size can be modelled to arrive at an optimal size and layout for such interaction. During the practical session, participants will be encouraged to abstract away the details to form a representation of the problem, and identify the main variables that are likely to influence the interaction (i.e., the number of apps on the phone, the number of apps per screen page, the cost of moving between screens, etc.). These will be used to formulate the costs, then we will be able to reason about when it is better to search for an app and when it is better to browse. We will also consider alternative designs, such as presenting the most used apps first, or a hierarchical browsing structure, and whether they are likely to be more efficient or not, or under what circumstances.

2. INTENDED LEARNING OUTCOMES

By the end of the tutorial, participants should be able to:

- Define and describe the different types of models;
- Explain the rationale for formal models of ISR;
- Define an optimisation model;
- Describe the main contemporary models;
- Explain and infer the predicted user behaviour given the contemporary models;
- Design a formal model and generate hypotheses regarding user behavior.

3. BIOGRAPHY

Leif Azzopardi has been recently awarded a Chancellor's Fellowship at the University of Strathclyde within the Department of Computer and Information Sciences. Prior to this appointment, he was a Senior Lecturer in the School of Computing Science at the University of Glasgow. His research focuses on building formal models for Information Retrieval - usually drawing upon different disciplines for inspiration, such as Quantum Mechanics, Operations Research, Microeconomics, Transportation Planning and Gamification. Central to his research is the theoretical development of statistical language models for Information Retrieval, where his research interests include:

- Models for the retrieval of documents, sentences, experts and other information objects [10, 17];

- Probabilistic models of user interaction and the simulation of users for evaluation [3, 7, 8];

- Microeconomic models of information interaction, specifically how cost and effort affect interaction and performance with search systems [4];

- Methods which assess the impact of search technology on society in application areas such as, search engine bias and the accessibility of e-Government information [9], and;

- Search for fun (i.e. the SINS of users) [5].

He received his Ph.D. in Computing Science from the University of Paisley in 2006, and he received a First Class Honours Degree in Information Science from the University of Newcastle, Australia, 2001. In 2010, he received a Post-Graduate Certificate in Academic Practice and has been lecturing at the University of Glasgow since then. He has given numerous invited talks on Formal Models of Information Seeking and Retrieval throughout the world and lectured at the Information Foraging Summer School (2011, 2012 and 2013) and Symposium of Future Directions in Information Access (2007-2013).

Guido Zuccon is a lecturer within the School of Information Systems at the Queensland University of Technology. His research interests include formal models of search, ranking principles for information retrieval, and retrieval models for health search. Guido has actively contributed to the area of document ranking and search result diversification. During his Ph.D. he performed an extensive analysis of document ranking principles and introduced the quantum probability ranking principle [45, 42] and was the first to empirically evaluate the interactive PRP [43]. His work on formal models of search result diversification based on facility location analysis [44] received the best paper award at ECIR 2013 and then in 2014 he received a best reviewer award at ECIR.

He received a Ph.D. in Computing Science from the University of Glasgow in 2012, and he received a Master in Computer Engineering with summa cum laude from the University of Padua, Italy, in 2007. Before joining the Queensland University of Technology as a lecturer in 2014, he was a postdoctoral research fellow at the CSIRO, Australia.

4. REFERENCES

[1] K. Athukorala, A. Oulasvirta, D. G, J. Vreeken, and G. Jacucci. Narrow or broad?: Estimating subjective specificity in exploratory search. In *Proceedings of the 23rd ACM International Conference on Conference on Information and Knowledge Management*, CIKM '14, pages 819–828, New York, NY, USA, 2014. ACM.

[2] C. W. Axelrod. The economic evaluation of information storage and retrieval systems. *Information Processing & Management*, 13(2):117–124, 1977.

[3] L. Azzopardi. Query side evaluation: an empirical analysis of effectiveness and effort. In *Proceedings of the 32nd international ACM SIGIR conference on Research and development in information retrieval*, pages 556–563. ACM, 2009.

[4] L. Azzopardi. The economics in interactive information retrieval. In *Proc. of the 34th international ACM SIGIR conference*, pages 15–24. ACM, 2011.

[5] L. Azzopardi. Searching for unlawful carnal knowledge. In *Proceedings of the SIGIR Workshop: Search for Fun*, volume 11, pages 17–18, 2011.

[6] L. Azzopardi. Modelling interaction with economic models of search. In *Proc. of the 37th ACM SIGIR Conference*, pages 3–12, 2014.

[7] L. Azzopardi and M. de Rijke. Automatic construction of known-item finding test beds. In *Proceedings of SIGIR '06*, pages 603–604, 2006.

[8] L. Azzopardi, M. de Rijke, and K. Balog. Building simulated queries for known-item topics: an analysis using six european languages. In *Proc. of the 30th annual international ACM SIGIR conference*, pages 455–462. ACM, 2007.

[9] L. Azzopardi and V. Vinay. Retrievability: An evaluation measure for higher order information access tasks. In *Proc. of the 17th ACM CIKM*, pages 561–570, 2008.

[10] K. Balog, L. Azzopardi, and M. de Rijke. Formal models for expert finding in enterprise corpora. In *Proceedings of the 29th Annual International ACM SIGIR Conference on Research and Development in Information Retrieval*, SIGIR '06, pages 43–50, 2006.

[11] M. J. Bates. The design of browsing and berrypicking techniques for the online search interface. *Online Information Review*, 13(5):407–424, 1989.

[12] N. J. Belkin. Some(what) grand challenges for information retrieval. *SIGIR Forum*, 42:47–54, 2008.

[13] U. Birchler and M. Butler. *Information economics*. Routledge, 2007.

[14] E. L. Charnov. Optimal foraging: attack strategy of a mantid. *The American Naturalist*, 110(971):141–151, 1976.

[15] M. D. Cooper. A cost model for evaluating information retrieval systems. *Journal of the American Society for Information Science*, pages 306–312, 1972.

[16] S. Erdelez. Information encountering: a conceptual framework for accidental information discovery. In *Proceedings of an international conference on Information seeking in context*, pages 412–421. Taylor Graham Publishing, 1997.

[17] R. T. Fernández, D. E. Losada, and L. A. Azzopardi. Extending the language modeling framework for

sentence retrieval to include local context. *Information Retrieval*, 14(4):355–389, 2011.

[18] N. Fuhr. A probability ranking principle for interactive information retrieval. *Information Retrieval*, 11(3):251–265, 2008.

[19] F. S. Hillier and G. J. Lieberman. Introduction to operations research. *NY, US*, 2001.

[20] P. Ingwersen and K. Järvelin. *The Turn: Integration of Information Seeking and Retrieval in Context*. Springer-Verlag New York, Inc., 2005.

[21] C. C. Kuhlthau. Developing a model of the library search process: Cognitive and affective aspects. *RQ*, pages 232–242, 1988.

[22] J. Luo, S. Zhang, X. Dong, and H. Yang. *Advances in Information Retrieval: 37th European Conference on IR Research, ECIR 2015*, chapter Designing States, Actions, and Rewards for Using POMDP in Session Search, pages 526–537. 2015.

[23] K. G. Murty. Optimization models for decision making: Volume. *University of Michigan, Ann Arbor*, 2003.

[24] P. Pirolli and S. Card. Information foraging. *Psychological Review*, 106:643–675, 1999.

[25] H. L. Resnikoff, H. Resenikoff, and H. Resnikoff. *The illusion of reality*. Springer-Verlag New York, 1989.

[26] S. E. Robertson. The probability ranking principle in ir. *Journal of documentation*, 33(4):294–304, 1977.

[27] D. H. Rothenberg. An efficiency model and a performance function for an ir system. *Information Storage and Retrieval*, 5(3):109 – 122, 1969.

[28] T. Ruotsalo, K. Athukorala, D. G, K. Konyushkova, A. Oulasvirta, S. Kaipiainen, S. Kaski, and G. Jacucci. Supporting exploratory search tasks with interactive user modeling. In *Proceedings of the 76th ASIS&T Annual Meeting: Beyond the Cloud: Rethinking Information Boundaries*, ASIST '13, pages 39:1–39:10, Silver Springs, MD, USA, 2013. American Society for Information Science.

[29] D. M. Russell, M. J. Stefik, P. Pirolli, and S. K. Card. The cost structure of sensemaking. In *Proceedings of the INTERACT/SIGCHI*, pages 269–276, 1993.

[30] P. E. Sandstrom. An optimal foraging approach to information seeking and use. *The library quarterly*, pages 414–449, 1994.

[31] H. A. Simon. A behavioral model of rational choice. *The quarterly journal of economics*, 69(1):99–118, 1955.

[32] H. A. Simon. Theories of bounded rationality. *Decision and organization*, 1:161–176, 1972.

[33] D. Stephens and J. Krebs. Foraging theory. *Princeton: Princeton University Press*, 1(10):100, 1986.

[34] G. J. Stigler. The economics of information. *The journal of political economy*, 69(3):213–225, 1961.

[35] C. J. van Rijsbergen. *Information Retrieval*. Butterworth, 1979.

[36] H. R. Varian. How to build an economic model in your spare time. *American Economist*, 41:3–10, 1997.

[37] H. R. Varian. Economics and search. *SIGIR Forum*, 33(1):1–5, 1999.

[38] M. L. Weitzman. Optimal search for the best alternative. *Econometrica: Journal of the Econometric Society*, pages 641–654, 1979.

[39] T. D. Wilson. Human information behavior. *Informing science*, 3(2):49–56, 2000.

[40] C. Zhai. Towards a game-theoretic framework for information retrieval. In *Proceedings of the 38th International ACM SIGIR Conference on Research and Development in Information Retrieval*, SIGIR '15, pages 543–543, New York, NY, USA, 2015. ACM.

[41] Y. Zhang and C. Zhai. Information retrieval as card playing: A formal model for optimizing interactive retrieval interface. In *Proceedings of the 38th International ACM SIGIR Conference on Research and Development in Information Retrieval*, SIGIR '15, pages 685–694, New York, NY, USA, 2015. ACM.

[42] G. Zuccon and L. Azzopardi. Using the quantum probability ranking principle to rank interdependent documents. In *Advances in Information Retrieval*, pages 357–369. Springer, 2010.

[43] G. Zuccon, L. Azzopardi, and C. van Rijsbergen. The interactive prp for diversifying document rankings. In *Proceedings of the 34th international ACM SIGIR conference on Research and development in Information Retrieval*, pages 1227–1228. ACM, 2011.

[44] G. Zuccon, L. Azzopardi, D. Zhang, and J. Wang. Top-k retrieval using facility location analysis. In *Proc. of ECIR*, pages 305–316. 2012.

[45] G. Zuccon, L. A. Azzopardi, and K. Rijsbergen. The quantum probability ranking principle for information retrieval. In *Proc. of the 2nd ICTIR*, pages 232–240, 2009.

Utilizing Knowledge Bases in Text-centric Information Retrieval

Laura Dietz
University of New Hampshire
Durham NH, USA
laura.dietz@unh.edu

Alexander Kotov
Wayne State University
Detroit MI, USA
kotov@wayne.edu

Edgar Meij
Bloomberg L.P.
London, United Kingdom
edgar.meij@acm.org

Abstract

General-purpose knowledge bases are increasingly growing in terms of depth (content) and width (coverage). Moreover, algorithms for entity linking and entity retrieval have improved tremendously in the past years. These developments give rise to a new line of research that exploits and combines these developments for the purposes of text-centric information retrieval applications. This tutorial focuses on a) how to retrieve a set of entities for an ad-hoc query, or more broadly, assessing relevance of KB elements for the information need, b) how to annotate text with such elements, and c) how to use this information to assess the relevance of text. We discuss different kinds of information available in a knowledge graph and how to leverage each most effectively.

We start the tutorial with a brief overview of different types of knowledge bases, their structure and information contained in popular general-purpose and domain-specific knowledge bases. In particular, we focus on the representation of entity-centric information in the knowledge base through names, terms, relations, and type taxonomies. Next, we will provide a recap on ad-hoc object retrieval from knowledge graphs as well as entity linking and retrieval. This is essential technology, which the remainder of the tutorial builds on. Next we will cover essential components within successful entity linking systems, including the collection of entity name information and techniques for disambiguation with contextual entity mentions. We will present the details of four previously proposed systems that successfully leverage knowledge bases to improve ad-hoc document retrieval. These systems combine the notion of entity retrieval and semantic search on one hand, with text retrieval models and entity linking on the other. Finally, we also touch on entity aspects and links in the knowledge graph as it can help to understand the entities' context.

This tutorial is the first to compile, summarize, and disseminate progress in this emerging area and we provide both an overview of state-of-the-art methods and outline open research problems to encourage new contributions.

ICTIR '16 September 12-16, 2016, Newark, DE, USA

© 2016 Copyright held by the owner/author(s).

ACM ISBN 978-1-4503-4497-5/16/09.

DOI: http://dx.doi.org/10.1145/2970398.2970441

Presenters

Prof. Dr. Laura Dietz is a professor at University of New Hampshire, where she teaches Information Retrieval and Machine Learning. Before that she was working in the Data and Web Science group at Mannheim University, with Prof. Bruce Croft and Prof. Andrew McCallum at University of Massachusetts, and obtained her Ph.D. from the Max Planck Institute for Informatics. Her research focuses on text processing and information retrieval with knowledge bases. Her scientific contributions span from entity linking to the prediction of influences in citation graphs. In this tutorial, she will cover her seminal publication on entity query feature expansion and her work on finding relevant relations.

Prof. Dr. Alexander Kotov is an Assistant Professor in the Department of Computer Science at Wayne State University. His general research interests lie at the intersection of information retrieval, textual data mining and health informatics. Before joining Wayne State, he was a post-doctoral fellow at Emory University working with Prof. Eugene Agichtein. Dr. Kotov obtained his PhD from the University of Illinois at Urbana-Champaign, under the supervision of Professor ChengXiang Zhai. At Wayne State has been teaching graduate courses on Information Retrieval and NoSQL databases as well as undergraduate courses. This tutorial will cover his work on using semantic networks for query expansion and his recent work on entity retrieval from knowledge graphs.

Dr. Edgar Meij is a senior scientist at Bloomberg. Before this, he was a research scientist at Yahoo Labs and a postdoc at the University of Amsterdam, where he also obtained his Ph.D. He regularly teaches at the (post-)graduate level, including university courses and conference tutorials, e.g., at EACL 2009, SIGIR 2013, WWW 2013, and WSDM 2014. His research focuses on all applications and aspects of knowledge graphs, entity linking, and semantic search. This tutorial will cover his contributions on entity aspect mining and finding support passages for relations.

Acknowledgments

This work was in part funded by the Elitepostdoc program of the BW-Stiftung and the University of New Hampshire.

Collaborative Information Retrieval: Frameworks, Theoretical Models, and Emerging Topics

Lynda Tamine
Université de Toulouse UPS IRIT
118 Route de Narbonne
F-31062 Toulouse, France
tamine@irit.fr

Laure Soulier
Sorbonne Universités, UPMC Univ Paris 06,
CNRS, LIP6 UMR 7606
75005 Paris, France
laure.soulier@lip6.fr

ABSTRACT

A great amount of research in the IR domain mostly dealt with both the design of enhanced document ranking models allowing search improvement through user-to-system collaboration. However, in addition to user-to-system form of collaboration, user-to-user collaboration is increasingly acknowledged as an effective mean for gathering the complementary skills and/or knowledge of individual users in order to solve complex search tasks.This tutorial will first give an overview of the ways into collaboration has been implemented in IR models with the attempt of improving the search outcomes with respect to several tasks and related frameworks (ad-hoc search, group-based recommendation, social search, collaborative search). Second, as envisioned in collaborative IR domain (CIR), we will focus on the theoretical models that support and drive user-to-user collaboration in order to perform shared IR tasks. Third, we will develop a road map on emerging and relevant topics addressing issues related to collaboration design. Our goal is to provide participants with concepts and motivation allowing them to investigate this emerging IR domain as well as giving them some clues on how to tackle issues related to the optimization of collaborative tasks. More specifically, the tutorial aims to:

1. Give an overview of the key concept of collaboration in IR and related research topics;
2. Present state-of-the art CIR techniques and models;
3. Discuss about the emerging topics that deal with collaboration;
4. Point out some challenges ahead.

Keywords

Collaborative information retrieval; user behavior analysis

ICTIR '16, September 12–16, 2016, Newark, Delaware, USA.

© 2016 ACM. ISBN 978-1-4503-4497-5/16/09..

DOI: http://dx.doi.org/10.1145/2970398.2970442

1. TUTORIAL OUTLINE

Part 1: Collaboration in Information Seeking

We will present a large synthesis of the different forms of collaboration, whether user-to-system [24] or user-to-user [14, 11, 4]. Then, considering the particular scenario of collaborative search defined in [3, 4], we will introduce the different underlying paradigms.

1. The different forms of collaboration

- *User-to-system collaboration.*Yang et al. [24] defines dynamic IR as the process of exploiting and modeling users' feedback so as to anticipating future actions. This particular form of collaboration provides interesting insights in terms of users' actions leveraging which is essential in collaborative search. We will give a summary of the collaborative search models based particularly on the dynamic IR approach.
- *User-to-user collaboration.*We will present the fundamental principles of collaborative or group-based filtering, social IR, and collaborative IR. We will also point out the main differences between the underlying design of collaboration within those frameworks with respect to key dimensions of collaboration [4].

2. Collaboration Paradigms

Collaborative search is guided by three main paradigms avoiding redundancy between collaborators' actions and optimize the search effectiveness [2]: the division of labor, the sharing of knowledge, and the awareness.

Part 2: Models and Techniques for Collaborative Document Seeking and Retrieval

CIR models provide an algorithmic mediation that enables to leverage from collaborators' actions in order to enhance the effectiveness of the search process [19]. We distinguish two categories of models: system-mediated approaches [2, 9, 12, 16] and user-driven system-mediated approaches [18, 20]. To better understand these models, we will start by highlighting the challenges and issues of collaborative IR and presenting empirical studies surrounding collaborative search [15, 23, 21].

1. Challenges and Issues

Collaborative IR is a more complex setting than interactive IR and dynamic IR since it involves groups of users interacting with both the IR system and the other members of the group. We present here the different challenges and issues underlying this complex setting.

2. Empirical understanding of CIR

Several work has studied collaborative search in terms of behavioral process and search performance. We will present here interesting studies and their main results. We will end by a summary of learned lessons and design implications.

3. CIR models and techniques

- System-mediated Document Ranking models

The essence of these models is to leverage collaborators actions, namely relevance feedback, through algorithmic techniques by considering that users act according to particular predefined roles [4], whether collaborators act similarly [2, 9] or not [12, 16, 19].

- User-driven Document Ranking Models

While roles enable to structure the collaborative search session by setting collaborators' search strategies, an interesting perspective is to overpass the framework of predefined roles constraining users in search skills they might not really fit by rather focusing on latent roles of collaborators [18, 20].

Part 3: Emerging topics around collaboration

This tutorial part aims at motivating participants investigating emerging research topics relying on the key notion of collaboration. More particularly, we will focus on recent advances in social IR, community question-answering and crowd-sourcing.

1. Recommending users

Identifying and recommending experts or users in social-media platforms is a well-known challenge in IR. But, from the collaboration point of view, it leads to interesting perspectives since it would allow favoring interactions between the information provider and the recommended users. The most intuitive frameworks in which collaboration occurs are community question-answering [10] or social networks [7]. In this context, two approaches are emerging: (1) recommending users to mention in order to favor implicit collaboration [5], and (2) recommending users willing to answer based on explicit collaboration [6].

2. Building the right group of collaborators

A further step towards collaboration consists in recommending a cohesive and relevant group of users willing to collaborate to solve a task [17, 22]. One interesting challenge in this field is to build the collaborative group according to users' compatibility, availability, and expertise [1]. Regardless of the task goal, another emerging line of work focuses on collaborative task optimization in crowd-sourcing platforms [8, 13].

Part 4: Questions and Discussion

We will end with an open discussion with participants.

2. REFERENCES

[1] S. Chang and A. Pal. Routing questions for collaborative answering in community question answering. In *ASONAM '13*, pages 494–501. ACM, 2013.

[2] C. Foley and A. F. Smeaton. Synchronous Collaborative Information Retrieval: Techniques and Evaluation. In *ECIR '09*, pages 42–53. Springer, 2009.

[3] J. Foster. Collaborative information seeking and retrieval. *Annual Review of Information Science & Technology (ARIST)*, 40(1):329–356, 2006.

[4] G. Golovchinsky, P. Qvarfordt, and J. Pickens. Collaborative Information Seeking. *IEEE Computer*, 42(3):47–51, 2009.

[5] Y. Gong, Q. Zhang, X. Sun, and X. Huang. Who will you "@"? In *CIKM '15*, pages 533–542. ACM, 2015.

[6] B. Hecht, J. Teevan, M. R. Morris, and D. J. Liebling. Searchbuddies: Bringing search engines into the conversation. In *WSDM '14*, 2012.

[7] J.-W. Jeong, M. R. Morris, J. Teevan, and D. Liebling. A crowd-powered socially embedded search engine. In *ICWSM '13*. AAAI, 2013.

[8] H. Li, B. Zhao, and A. Fuxman. The wisdom of minority: Discovering and targeting the right group of workers for crowdsourcing. In *WWW '14*, pages 165–176. ACM, 2014.

[9] M. R. Morris, J. Teevan, and S. Bush. Collaborative Web Search with Personalization: Groupization, Smart Splitting, and Group Hit-highlighting. In *CSCW '08*, pages 481–484. ACM, 2008.

[10] B. Nushi, O. Alonso, M. Hentschel, and V. Kandylas. Crowdstar: A social task routing framework for online communities. In *ICWE '15*, pages 219–230, 2015.

[11] A. Pal and S. Counts. Identifying topical authorities in microblogs. In *WSDM '11*, pages 45–54. ACM, 2011.

[12] J. Pickens, G. Golovchinsky, C. Shah, P. Qvarfordt, and M. Back. Algorithmic Mediation for Collaborative Exploratory Search. In *SIGIR '08*, pages 315–322. ACM, 2008.

[13] H. Rahman, S. B. Roy, S. Thirumuruganathan, S. Amer-Yahia, and G. Das. "the whole is greater than the sum of its parts": Optimization in collaborative crowdsourcing. *CoRR*, abs/1502.05106, 2015.

[14] P. Resnick, N. Iacovou, M. Suchak, P. Bergstrom, and J. Riedl. GroupLens: An Open Architecture for Collaborative Filtering of Netnews. In *CSCW '94*, pages 175–186. ACM, 1994.

[15] C. Shah and R. González-Ibáñez. Evaluating the Synergic Effect of Collaboration in Information Seeking. In *SIGIR '11*, pages 913–922. ACM, 2011.

[16] C. Shah, J. Pickens, and G. Golovchinsky. Role-based results redistribution for collaborative information retrieval. *Information Processing & Management (IP&M)*, 46(6):773–781, 2010.

[17] C. Shah, M. L. Radford, and L. S. Connaway. Collaboration and synergy in hybrid q&a: Participatory design method and results. *Library & Information Science Research*, 37(2):92 – 99, 2015.

[18] L. Soulier, C. Shah, and L. Tamine. User-driven System-mediated Collaborative Information Retrieval. In *SIGIR '14*, pages 485–494. ACM, 2014.

[19] L. Soulier, L. Tamine, and W. Bahsoun. On domain expertise-based roles in collaborative information retrieval. *Information Processing & Management (IP&M)*, 50(5):752–774, 2014.

[20] L. Soulier, L. Tamine, and C. Shah. Minerank: Leveraging users' latent roles for unsupervised collaborative information retrieval. *Information Processing & Management(IP&M)*, page to appear, 2016.

[21] L. Tamine and L. Soulier. Understanding the impact of the role factor in collaborative information retrieval (regular paper). In *CIKM '15*. ACM, 2015.

[22] L. Tamine, L. Soulier, L. B. Jabeur, F. Amblard, C. Hanachi, G. Hubert, and C. Roth. Social media-based collaborative information access: Analysis of online crisis-related twitter conversations. In *HT '16*, 2016.

[23] Y. Tao and A. Tombros. An Exploratory Study of Sensemaking in Collaborative Information Seeking. In *ECIR '13*, pages 26–37. Springer, 2013.

[24] H. Yang and M. Sloan. Dynamic information retrieval modeling. In *WSDM '15*, 2015.

Topic Set Size Design and Power Analysis in Practice

Tetsuya Sakai
Waseda University, Japan.
tetsuyasakai@acm.org

ABSTRACT

Topic set size design methods provide principles and procedures for test collection builders to decide on the number of topics to create. These methods can then help us keep improving the test collection design based on accumulated data. Simple Excel tools are available for such purposes. Post-hoc power analysis tools, available as simple R scripts, can help IR researchers examine the achieved power of a reported experiment and determine future sample sizes for ensuring high power. Thus, for example, underpowered user experiments can be detected, and a larger sample size can be proposed. If used appropriately, these Excel and R tools should be able to provide the IR community with better experimentation practices. The main objective of this tutorial is to let IR researchers familiarise themselves with these tools and understand the basic ideas behind them.

Keywords

effect sizes; experimental design; statistical power; statistical significance; test collections; variances

1. MOTIVATION, RELEVANCE AND OBJECTIVES

Topic set size design methods provide principles and procedures for test collection builders to decide on the number of topics to create. These methods can then help us keep improving the test collection design based on accumulated data. Simple Excel tools are available for such purposes. Post-hoc power analysis tools, available as simple R scripts, can help IR researchers examine the achieved power of a reported experiment and determine future sample sizes for ensuring high power. Thus, for example, underpowered user experiments can be detected, and a larger sample size can be proposed. If used appropriately, these Excel and R tools should be able to provide the IR community with better experimentation practices. The main objective of this tutorial is to let IR researchers familiarise themselves with these tools and understand the basic ideas behind them.

ICTIR '16 September 12-16, 2016, Newark, DE, USA

© 2016 Copyright held by the owner/author(s).

ACM ISBN 978-1-4503-4497-5/16/09.

DOI: http://dx.doi.org/10.1145/2970398.2970443

2. AUDIENCE

Based on the reviewers' comments I received, I will start by explaining the basics of statistical significance testing. However, it is recommended that attendees read Ben Carterette's ICTIR 2015 tutorial on statistical significance testing in advance[1].

Attendees who would like a hands-on experience are expected to download the following on their laptops prior to the tutorial:

- Sample topic-by-run matrix[2]

- Excel topic set size design tools[3]

- (OPTIONAL: R needs to be installed first) R scripts for power analysis[4]

3. PROPOSER BIOGRAPHY

Tetsuya Sakai is a professor at the Department of Computer Science and Engineering, Waseda University, Japan. He is also an Associate Dean at the IT Strategies Division of Waseda, and a visiting professor at the National Institute of Informatics. He joined Toshiba in 1993. He obtained a Ph.D from Waseda in 2000. From 2000 to 2001, he was a visiting reseacher at the Computer Laboratory, University of Cambridge, where he was supervised by the late Karen Sparck Jones. In 2007, he joined a startup as the director of the Natural Language Processing Lab. In 2009, he joined Microsoft Research Asia. He joined the Waseda faculty in 2013. He is an editor-in-chief of the Information Retrieval Journal (Springer), an associate editor of ACM TOIS. He is a general co-chair of NTCIR. He is also a general co-chair of ACM SIGIR 2017.

4. TUTORIAL FORMAT AND OUTLINE

The tutorial consists of two 90-minute lectures, with a 30-minute coffee break in between. Attendees are encouraged to try my Excel tools (and if possible R tools as well) during the lectures.

Here is an outline of the tutorial.

1. Significance testing basics and limitations (50 minutes)

   1-1 Preliminaries

   1-2 How the t-test works

---

[1] http://ir.cis.udel.edu/ICTIR15tutorial/

[2] https://waseda.box.com/20topics3runs

[3] http://www.f.waseda.jp/tetsuya/CIKM2014/samplesizeTTEST.xlsx
http://www.f.waseda.jp/tetsuya/CIKM2014/samplesizeANOVA.xlsx
http://www.f.waseda.jp/tetsuya/FIT2014/samplesizeCI.xlsx

[4] https://waseda.box.com/SIGIR2016PACK

1-3 T-test with Excel and R (hands-on)

1-4 How ANOVA works

1-5 ANOVA with Excel and R (hands-on)

1-6 What's wrong with significance tests?

1-7 Significance tests in the IR literature, or lack thereof

2. Using the Excel topic set size design tools (80 minutes)

   2-1 Topic set sizes in IR

   2-2 Topic set size design

   2-3 With paired t-tests (hands-on)

   COFFEE BREAK

   2-4 With one-way ANOVA (hands-on)

   2-5 With confidence intervals (hands-on)

   2-6 Comparing the three methods

   2-7 How much pilot data do we need?

3. Using the R power analysis scripts (40 minutes)

   3-1 Power analysis

   3-2 With paired t-tests (hands-on)

   3-3 With unpaired t-tests (hands-on)

   3-4 With one-way ANOVA (hands-on)

   3-5 With two-way ANOVA without replication (hands-on)

   3-6 With two-way ANOVA (hands-on)

   3-7 Overpowered and underpowered experiments in IR

4. Summary, a few additional remarks, and Q&A (10 minutes)

5. MATERIALS

Figure 1 shows a screenshot of the t-test based Excel tool, which is one of the three topic set size design tools discussed in this tutorial. Figure 2 shows a screenshot of an R command line interface, in which two of the five power analysis tools discussed in this tutorial are used.

Besides the aforementioned Excel files for topic set size design and R scripts for power analysis, the tutorial slides can be downloaded from Slideshare[5].

6. ACKNOWLEDGEMENTS

This tutorial is largely based on the work of Sakai and his collaborators [2, 3, 4, 5, 6, 7], and the sample size design techniques of Nagata [1] and the power analysis tools of Toyoda [8]. I thank Professor Yasushi Nagata (Waseda Univeristy) for his valuable advice and Professor Hideki Toyoda for letting me modify his R code.

7. REFERENCES

[1] Y. Nagata. *How to Design the Sample Size (in Japanese)*. Asakura Shoten, 2003.

[2] T. Sakai. *Information Access Evaluation Methodology: For the Progress of Search Engines (in Japanese)*. Coronasha, 2015.

[5]http://www.slideshare.net/TetsuyaSakai/ICTIR2016tutorial

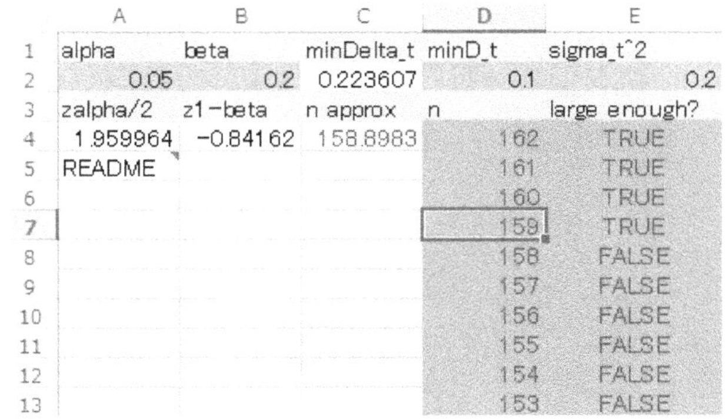

	A	B	C	D	E
1	alpha	beta	minDelta_t	minD_t	sigma_t^2
2	0.05	0.2	0.223607	0.1	0.2
3	zalpha/2	z1-beta	n approx	n	large enough?
4	1.959964	-0.84162	158.8983	162	TRUE
5	README			161	TRUE
6				160	TRUE
7				159	TRUE
8				158	FALSE
9				157	FALSE
10				156	FALSE
11				155	FALSE
12				154	FALSE
13				153	FALSE

Figure 1: Screenshot of the t-test based topic set size design tool. Just enter values in the orange cells (α: probability of Type I error; β: probability of Type II error; $minD_t$: minimum detectable difference between two systems for ensuring $100(1-\beta)$% power; and $\hat{\sigma}_t^2$: estimated variance of the difference between two systems. The required topic set size in this example is 159 topics.

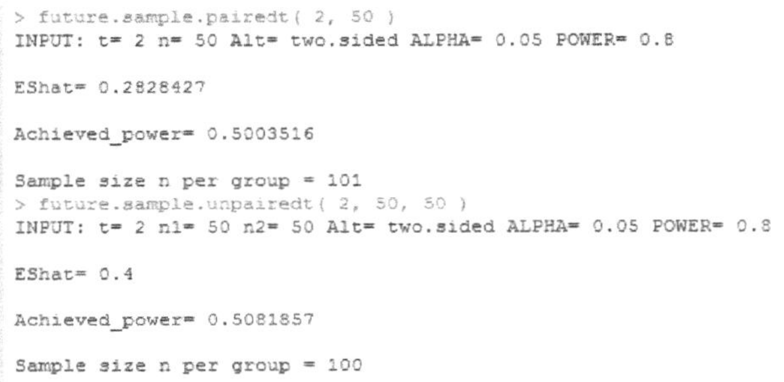
> future.sample.pairedt(2, 50)
INPUT: t= 2 n= 50 Alt= two.sided ALPHA= 0.05 POWER= 0.8
EShat= 0.2828427
Achieved_power= 0.5003516
Sample size n per group = 101
> future.sample.unpairedt(2, 50, 50)
INPUT: t= 2 n1= 50 n2= 50 Alt= two.sided ALPHA= 0.05 POWER= 0.8
EShat= 0.4
Achieved_power= 0.5081857
Sample size n per group = 100

Figure 2: Screenshot showing how power analysis can be done based on a paired and an unpaired t-test result. The first command computes the effect size, achieved power and a recommended future sample size, given a t-test result where the sample size is $n = 50$ and the t-statistic is 2. The second command does the same for an unpaired t-test result where the sample sizes are $n_1 = n_2 = 50$ and the t-statistic is 2.

[3] T. Sakai. Topic set size design. *Information Retrieval Journal*, 2015.

[4] T. Sakai. Statistical significance, power, and sample sizes: A systematic review of SIGIR and TOIS, 2006-2015. In *Proceedings of SIGIR 2016*, 2016.

[5] T. Sakai. Two sample t-tests for IR evaluation: Student or welch? In *Proceedings of SIGIR 2016*, 2016.

[6] T. Sakai and L. Shang. On estimating variances for topic set size design. In *Proceedings of EVIA 2016*, 2016.

[7] T. Sakai, L. Shang, Z. Lu, and H. Li. Topic set size design with the evaluation measures for short text conversation. In *Proceedings of AIRS 2015 (LNCS 9460)*, pages 319–331, 2015.

[8] H. Toyoda. *Introduction to Statistical Power Analysis: A Tutorial with R (in Japanese)*. Tokyo Tosyo, 2009.

Exploiting the Bipartite Structure of Entity Grids for Document Coherence and Retrieval

Christina Lioma
Department of Computer Science
University of Copenhagen, Denmark
c.lioma@di.ku.dk

Jakob Grue Simonsen and Casper Petersen
Department of Computer Science
University of Copenhagen, Denmark
{simonsen,cazz}@di.ku.dk

Fabien Tarissan
ISP, ENS Cachan & CNRS
University Paris-Saclay, France
firstname.lastname@cnrs.fr

Birger Larsen
Department of Communication
Aalborg University Copenhagen, Denmark
birger@hum.aau.dk

ABSTRACT

Document coherence describes how much sense text makes in terms of its logical organisation and discourse flow. Even though coherence is a relatively difficult notion to quantify precisely, it can be approximated automatically. This type of coherence modelling is not only interesting in itself, but also useful for a number of other text processing tasks, including Information Retrieval (IR), where adjusting the ranking of documents according to *both* their relevance *and* their coherence has been shown to increase retrieval effectiveness [34, 37].

The state of the art in unsupervised coherence modelling represents documents as bipartite graphs of sentences and discourse entities, and then projects these bipartite graphs into one–mode undirected graphs. However, one–mode projections may incur significant loss of the information present in the original bipartite structure. To address this we present three novel graph metrics that compute document coherence on the original bipartite graph of sentences and entities. Evaluation on standard settings shows that: (i) one of our coherence metrics beats the state of the art in terms of coherence accuracy; and (ii) all three of our coherence metrics improve retrieval effectiveness because, as closer analysis reveals, they capture aspects of document quality that go undetected by both keyword-based standard ranking and by spam filtering. This work contributes document coherence metrics that are theoretically principled, parameter-free, and useful to IR.

1. INTRODUCTION

Document coherence is the logical organisation and development of thematic content in a document. The more coherent a document is, the more understandable it tends to be. Automatically measuring document coherence is useful for several tasks, such as text summarisation [7, 33, 45], ma-

chine translation [23, 41, 42], and information retrieval (IR) [34, 37]. For IR in particular, document coherence is typically treated as a feature of document quality (similarly to e.g. readability [4], information-to-noise ratio [46], or comprehensibility [37]). Such document quality features have been found to improve retrieval performance when used to boost the ranking of documents which are more relevant *and* of better quality. We present three new ways of measuring document coherence, and we practically show their usefulness to IR.

The starting point of our work is the linguistic definition [11] of document coherence as the thematic unity that stems from the links among the underlying ideas of a document and from the logical organisation and development of its content. It is this *logical continuity of senses* that characterises coherent documents and makes them overall understandable. This continuity of senses is traditionally modelled as the transition of topics throughout sentences. Typically this topic transition is approximated by extracting salient discourse entities from a document (for instance, the subject and object of each sentence) and measuring their occurrence (and distance) through sentences in an *entity grid* [1] (see example in Table 1). Recently the elements of such an entity grid (i.e., the discourse entities and the sentences in which they occur) have been represented as a graph, the topology of which has been used to approximate document coherence, for instance as the average out-degree [14], pagerank, clustering coefficient, or betweenness [34] computed over the whole graph (each graph representing a single document). This type of graph-based coherence modelling, despite being completely unsupervised, performs comparably to equivalent supervised approaches, thus showing great promise. We posit that these existing graph-based computations of document coherence are suboptimal in capturing the transition of entities across sentences, and we present a principled solution for improving this. We explain this next.

Existing graph-based computations of text coherence [14, 34] represent each document as a *bipartite graph* of sentences and their discourse entities. A bipartite graph is a particular class of graph also known as *two-mode* graph. In the case of coherence, one type of vertices denotes discourse entities, and the other type denotes the sentences in which these entities appear. The edges in a bipartite graph in typical coherence modelling connect only vertices of unlike types, i.e. only entities and sentences. Current graph-based coherence

ICTIR '16, September 12-16, 2016, Newark, DE, USA
© 2016 ACM. ISBN 978-1-4503-4497-5/16/09...$15.00
DOI: http://dx.doi.org/10.1145/2970398.2970413

	Department	Trial	Microsoft	Evidence	Competitors	Markets	Products	Brands	Case	Netscape	Software	Tactics	Government	Suit	Earnings
1	s	o	s	x	o	-	-	-	-	-	-	-	-	-	-
2	-	-	o	-	-	x	s	o	-	-	-	-	-	-	-
3	-	-	s	o	-	-	-	-	s	o	o	-	-	-	-
4	-	-	s	-	-	-	-	-	-	-	-	s	-	-	-
5	-	-	-	-	-	-	-	-	-	-	-	-	s	o	-
6	-	x	s	-	-	-	-	-	-	-	-	-	-	-	o

1 [The Justice Department]$_s$ is conducting an [anti-trust trial]$_o$ against [Microsoft corp.]$_s$ with [evidence]$_x$ that [the company]$_s$ is increasingly attempting to crush [competitors]$_o$.

2 [Microsoft]$_o$ is accused of trying to forcefully buy into [markets]$_x$ where [its own products]$_s$ are not competitive enough to unseat [established brands]$_o$.

3 [The case]$_s$ revolves around [evidence]$_o$ of [Microsoft]$_s$ aggressively pressuring [Netscape]$_o$ into merging [browser software]$_o$.

4 [Microsoft]$_s$ claims [its tactics]$_s$ are commonplace and good economically.

5 [The government]$_s$ may file [a civil suit]$_o$ ruling that [conspiracy]$_s$ to curb [competition]$_o$ through [collusion]$_x$ is [a violation of the Sherman Act]$_o$.

6 [Microsoft]$_s$ continues to show [increased earnings]$_o$ despite [the trial]$_x$.

Table 1: Entity grid example from [1]. Discourse entities are inside square brackets, marked s, o, x for subject, object and other grammatical role, respectively.

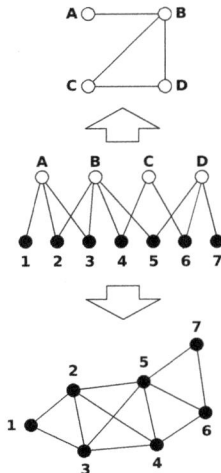

Figure 1: Bipartite graph (middle) and its two projections (top and bottom), from [30]. A–D and 1–7 denote two different types of vertices.

approaches project this bipartite graph of entities and their sentences onto a one-mode graph of only sentences that are connected if they contain at least one common entity. This projection is motivated by convenience: it is easier to work with direct connections between vertices of just one type. All current graph-based metrics of document coherence are computed solely on such one-mode projections of bipartite graphs.

Even though one-mode projections of two-mode graphs are widely employed, they are a less powerful representation of the data because they discard part of the information present in the structure of the original bipartite graph. This point is graphically illustrated in Figure 1, which shows a bipartite graph (middle) and its two one-mode projections (top and bottom). For entity bipartite graphs, the analogy would be that the sentences of a document are denoted by A-D and its entities are denoted by 1-7. As Figure 1 shows, part of the information captured by the bipartite graph about the entity transition throughout the document is lost or compressed with one-mode projections. We reason that this information loss is propagated to any coherence metric that is then computed on an one-mode projection of such a graph, resulting in potentially suboptimal approximations of document coherence.

We present three coherence metrics that are applied directly on the original bipartite graph, not on its one-mode projection (Section 3). Our metrics are new, constituting a contribution not only to coherence modelling but also to graph metrics. In addition, our bipartite metrics incur no additional efficiency cost over existing one–mode graph metrics. One of our metrics is shown to be a *much* more accurate approximation of document coherence than the state of the art computed from one-mode projections [14, 34] (Section 4). All three coherence metrics are shown to be useful to retrieval effectiveness (Section 5). To our knowledge, such two-mode graph-based coherence metrics have not been investigated before.

2. RELATED WORK

Several metrics using the entity grid (or extensions thereof) have been proposed for approximating the coherence of a document (see [34, 42, 43] for recent overviews). Broadly these methods compute probabilities of entity transitions on the grid, and use these probabilities to learn coherence in a supervised way. The particular line of research extending the entity grid that is relevant to our work transforms the entity grid into a bipartite graph of sentences and entities [14]. Coherence is then approximated in an unsupervised way as the average out-degree [14], pagerank, clustering coefficient, betweeness centrality, entity distance, or adjacent and non-adjacent topic flow [34] on one-mode projections on the sentence vertices of that graph (equivalent to the top projection in Figure 1). This process of reducing a two-mode "entity–and–sentence" graph into an one-mode "sentence–only" graph loses all information about *how many* and *which* entities two sentences share, as well as the *exact* entities occurring in a given sentence. Part of this information can be captured in one-mode projections by making the projection weighted. This has been done [14], by weighting each edge in the projection by the number of entities its two connecting vertices share. This type of weighted projection retains information about how many entities two sentences share, but still fails to capture the identity and the transition of those entities across sentences, thus removing the option of drawing entity-oriented insights from the graph. Another interesting weighted one-mode projection of such bipartite graphs has also been presented [14], which weights edges according to the grammatical roles of the entity vertices they share. This has been done by assigning arbitrary scores of 3, 2, 1 for the grammatical roles of subject, object or other, respectively, and then summing these scores over all shared entity vertices between two sentence vertices. This projection, despite being weighted, does not compensate for any information loss incurred by compressing a bipartite graph into an one-mode projection, but rather it attempts to enrich the graph with grammatical information. To our knowledge, our work is the first to propose coherence metrics computed directly on the bipartite graph and not on its one mode projections.

The document coherence metrics we present can be seen as estimating an aspect of *document quality*. A wide variety of document quality aspects have been used in IR, ranging from heuristics on document format (e.g., the fraction of anchor text on a hyperlinked document [31]), to hyperlinked-derived estimations of popularity (e.g., PageRank, HITS [31]). Another common type of document quality approximations are content-based. These are numerous and diverse, including for instance, ratios of information-to-noise, of stopwords per document, or of document words per stopword list [4, 46, 47]; average term length per document [17]; term part-of-speech [25, 26]; ratio of technical terminology per (scientific) document [20]; ratio of non-compositional phrases per document [29]; syllable, term and/or sentence statistics [37] as per standard readability indices [8, 15, 19, 27, 28]; discourse structure [24]; document entropy computed from terms [4] or discourse entities [34]. The lexical or syntactic features used in the above content-based document quality approximations are assumed to indicate syntactic or semantic difficulty. They are thus used to compute scores of document quality aspects such as readability, cohesiveness, comprehensibility or coherence, which are generally found to improve retrieval effectiveness when integrated into ranking, in particular with respect to precision at ranks 1–20 [4, 34, 37].

In addition to using document coherence for improving IR, the reverse has also been reported, namely using IR to improve coherence modelling [43]. The idea here is to link entities that have different lexical form but are semantically related (e.g. Gates and Microsoft), by retrieving mentions of those entities from multiple web sources and mining their relations. This approach gives good performance. Interestingly, when mining such relations between entities from web data, the task of characterising the type of these relations has also been addressed using graph representations and has been modelled as an IR, and specifically learning to rank, problem [40].

To our knowledge, the current state of the art in coherence modelling in terms of accuracy is the deep learning approach of [22], where a recursive neural network learns sentential compositionality and is then used to model document coherence. This approach is supervised and computationally much heavier than graph-based coherence modelling.

3. BIPARTITE GRAPH METRICS OF DOCUMENT COHERENCE WITHOUT PROJECTION

Our work builds on the early assumption [13] that a document is more coherent if its adjacent or near-adjacent sentences refer to the same entities. This *transition* of entities across sentences is typically represented as an *entity grid* [1]. The entity grid of a document is defined as a table whose rows represent (consecutive) sentences in that document, and whose columns represent discourse entities that occur in that document. Each cell (i, j) is either empty or contains infor-

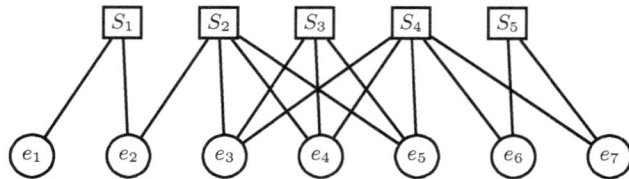

Figure 2: An example of a bipartite graph of an entity grid. Sentences are represented by squares, entities by circles. Syntactic roles are omitted for readability.

mation about the syntactic, discourse, or other grammatical role of entity j in sentence i. Table 1 displays an example of an entity grid borrowed from [1].

Following [14], we represent the entity grid as a bipartite graph $\mathbb{B} = (V_\top, V_\perp, E_\mathbb{B})$, where $V_\top$ is the set of *sentences* in the document, $V_\perp$ is the set of *entities* in the document, and $E_\mathbb{B} \subset \top \times \perp$ is the set of edges relating entities to the sentences in which the entities appear, each edge labelled with the value in cell (i, j). An example of such a bipartite graph $\mathbb{B}$ is given in Figure 2, where $\top$ vertices (sentences) are depicted by squares ($V_\top = \{S_1, S_2, S_3, S_4, S_5\}$) and $\perp$ vertices (entities) are depicted by circles ($V_\perp = \{e_1, e_2, e_3, e_4, e_5, e_6, e_7\}$). Every such bipartite graph can be *one–mode projected*, resulting for instance in a graph $G = (V, E)$ where $V = V_\top$ and $E = \{(u, v) \in V^2 \mid \exists w \in V_\perp, (u, w) \in E_\mathbb{B} \text{ and } (v, w) \in E_\mathbb{B}\}$ [1] (see example in Figure 1). This projection allows to re-use all metrics defined for one-mode graphs, but we claim that valuable information is discarded in the process.

In this paper, we extract information about coherence *from the bipartite structure itself*, without projecting the structure over entities nor sentences. We reason that principles from existing research on using (projected) graphs for coherence can be retained, and that bespoke metrics for bipartite graphs can be combined with these principles. We identify two primary such principles:

Length of paths: short paths between vertices representing entities generally imply rapid cognitive information processing [5], hence are good indicators of coherence.

Local density: locally dense documents tend to involve successive sentences that share similar concepts and entities, hence are good indicators of coherence.

In the remainder of this section, we propose coherence metrics that align with the above principles and are thus able to capture such short path or local density properties in the bipartite structure. It is worth noting that even though the notion of local density is well known for one-mode graphs, there exist no standard definitions for it for bipartite graphs. Indeed, the local density (usually captured by the *clustering coefficient* and the *transitive ratio*) consists in computing the number of triangles (three vertices, all connected) present in the graphs but, by definition, no such pattern can exist in a bipartite graph.

However, several extensions of the clustering coefficient have been proposed [6, 21, 32, 35, 44] to serve as proxy for this notion in bipartite graphs. These proxies have proven to be useful in many contexts, ranging from improving the modelling of the large-scale link structure of the Internet [39], to

---
[1] A dual projection can be defined for $\perp$ nodes.

analysing online social networks [36], or detecting landmark decisions in judicial decision networks [38].

Next, we show how to adapt those definitions to account for the specific context of local coherence estimation. We do so, reasoning on a bipartite graph, where $u \in V_\top$, and where we define $N_\top(u) = \{v \in \bot \mid (u, v) \in E_\mathbb{B}\}$ as the subset consisting of the vertices in $V_\bot$ that are linked to u.

3.1 Bipartite distance-based clustering coefficient (bipDCC)

We call our first coherence metric *bipartite distance-based clustering coefficient* (bipDCC). The *clustering coefficient* in standard graphs quantifies, roughly, how dense the graph is around its vertices. In our case, we are interested in estimating the extent to which successive sentences share similar or identical[2] entities (suggesting coherence). To do so, we propose the following adaptation of the bipartite clustering coefficient [21]. Given two sentences s_i and s_j that have at least one entity in common:

1. Compute the fraction of shared entities with respect to the number of total entities occurring in s_i and s_j (classic notion of bipartite clustering coefficient based on the Jaccard index [21]), and

2. Account for the relative position of the involved sentences by dividing the former quantity by the distance between s_i and s_j.

Formally, assuming that i and j denote the position of sentences s_i and s_j in the document:

$$\texttt{bipDCC}_\top(s_i, s_j) = \frac{1}{|j - i|} \cdot \frac{|N_\top(s_i) \cap N_\top(s_j)|}{|N_\top(s_i) \cup N_\top(s_j)|} \quad (1)$$

For instance, in Figure 2, $\texttt{bipDCC}_\top(s_i, s_j)$ would attain its highest values for vertices S_2 and S_3 ($\texttt{bipDCC}(S_2, S_3) = 0.75$).

Then, we define $\texttt{bipDCC}_\top(s_i)$ as the average value of $\texttt{bipDCC}_\top(s_i, s_j)$ for all s_j that share at least one entity with s_i. We compute the bipartite distance-based clustering coefficient, $\texttt{bipDCC}_\top(\mathbb{B})$, of the entire bipartite graph of the document as the average value of $\texttt{bipDCC}_\top(s_i)$ for all sentences s_i.

The intuition is that a coherent document will involve successive (or almost successive) sentences sharing similar or identical entities, thus increasing the value of the bipartite distance-based clustering coefficient.

Regarding the complexity of Equation 1, we note that by properly implementing the set operations (e.g., as bitwise operations on boolean strings) the worst-case complexity of computing the right-hand side of the formula is linear in the total number of bottom nodes.

3.2 Bipartite asymmetric clustering coefficient (bipACC)

The bipartite distance-based clustering coefficient proposed above gives a similar role to s_i and s_j. In particular, it does not account for the number of entities related to each of the sentences. This raises some issues for small (in terms of number of entities) sentences. In Figure 2 for instance, the reader might notice that $\texttt{bipDCC}_\top(s_5) = 0.4$, although the only two

entities involved in s_5 are both shared with another sentence, which turns out to be the closest in the document. As such, the coefficient should be the highest value (1.0).

In order to account for this, we propose the following *asymmetric* variant of bipDCC. Given two sentences s_i and s_j that share at least one common entity:

1. Compute the fraction of shared entities with respect to the number of entities that s_i *could have shared* with s_j, and

2. Use this fraction to discount the distance between s_i and s_j, as previously for the bipartite distance-based clustering coefficient.

Formally, we define the bipartite asymmetric clustering coefficient of s_i and s_j as:

$$\texttt{bipACC}_\top(s_i, s_j) = \frac{1}{|j - i|} \cdot \frac{|N_\top(s_i) \cap N_\top(s_j)|}{|N_\top(s_i)|} \quad (2)$$

Then, the bipartite asymmetric clustering coefficients of vertex s_i ($\texttt{bipACC}_\top(s_i)$) and of the whole document ($\texttt{bipACC}_\top(\mathbb{B})$) are respectively derived as averages, in the same way as for the distance-based clustering coefficient presented above. Note that while $\texttt{bipDCC}_\top(s_i, s_j) = \texttt{bipDCC}_\top(s_j, s_i)$, we have in general $\texttt{bipACC}_\top(s_i, s_j) \neq \texttt{bipACC}_\top(s_j, s_i)$ now.

By using this asymmetric variant of the bipartite distance-based clustering coefficient, we expect to highlight in particular short sentences that are well connected to each other. This might be particularly useful in domains where this type of writing is predominant (although we do not evaluate this potential domain adaptivity of this coherence metric in this work).

3.3 Bipartite Linkage Coefficient (bipLC)

The two coefficients proposed so far are straight-forward variants of the original bipartite clustering coefficient that attempt to capture local density in bipartite graphs. However, it has been shown in [21] that such coefficients might miss some important properties of the overlapping between $\top$ vertices (in our case sentence vertices) in the bipartite structures. This is why [21] suggested to use the *redundancy coefficient* $\texttt{rd}_\top(v)$ of a vertex. The redundancy coefficient focuses on the impact of removing v in regards to the $\bot$-projection.

To illustrate this impact on the example of Figure 2, consider sentences S_1 and S_5. Although they are both related to two entities, they have a very different way to relate to the rest of the sentences. One way to measure this consists in projecting the bipartite graph over the entities and comparing the resulting structure to the same projection if we remove S_1 or S_5. Removing vertex S_1 results in the loss of one edge (between e_1 and e_2). In contrast, if we look at the impact of removing vertex S_5, the projection is exactly the same with or without the vertex because the two entities it relates (e_6 and e_7) are also related by sentence S_4. In this respect, S_5 is said to be *redundant*. The above are two extreme cases; in practice a wide range of situations usually depict different levels of redundancy.

Following this principle of graph redundancy, and letting $v \in V_\top$, we define D_v as the set

$$D_v = |\{\{u, w\} \in N_\top(v)^2 \mid \exists v' \neq v, (v', u) \in E_\mathbb{B} \text{ and } (v', w) \in E_\mathbb{B}\}|$$

.

---

[2] The original definition of the entity grid allows to model the succession of only identical entities. This is the definition we adopt here. However, our coherence metrics also work for extensions of the entity grid that capture similar but not identical entities [43].

That is, D_v is the set of pairs of entities in sentence v such that there is (at least) another sentence containing both of them. The *redundancy* of a node $s \in V_\top$ is then formally defined as:

$$\mathtt{rd}_\top(v) = \frac{D}{\frac{|N_\top(v)|(|N_\top(v)|-1)}{2}} \quad (3)$$

Intuitively, a high value of the $\mathtt{rd}_\top(v)$ indicates that two entities that v relates are likely to be related by another sentence. In the example above, $\mathtt{rd}_\top(v)$ assumes its highest values for sentences S_3 and S_5. This is expected because all entities in these sentences occur in (perhaps several) other sentences.

As we wish to model coherence, and there is a natural order on sentences, we define a new variation of the redundancy that also captures closeness, which we call *bipartite linkage coefficient* (bipLC) as follows. Given a sentence s_i:

1. For each pair of entities (e_k, e_l) in s_i, compute the distance between s_i and the closest sentence that contains also e_k and e_l (∞ if there is no such other sentence), and

2. Compute the average of the inverse of the distances computed in step 1.

Formally, $\forall s_i$ and $\forall e_k, e_l \in N_\top(s_i)$, let $d_{ikl} = \min\{|j - i| \mid s_j \in N_\bot(e_k) \cap N_\bot(e_l) - \{s_i\}\}$. We define:

$$\mathtt{d}_{s_i}(e_k, e_l) = \begin{cases} \infty & \text{if } N_\bot(e_k) \cap N_\bot(e_l) = \{s\} \\ d_{ikl} & \text{otherwise} \end{cases}$$

Then, the *bipartite linkage coefficient* of a sentence s_i is:

$$\mathtt{bipLC}_\top(s_i) = \frac{\sum_{e_k, e_l \in N_\top(s_i)} \frac{1}{\mathtt{d}_{s_i}(e_k, e_l)}}{\frac{|N_\top(s_i)|(|N_\top(s_i)|-1)}{2}} \quad (4)$$

We then compute the linkage coefficient of the entire document $\mathtt{bipLC}_\top(\mathbb{B})$ as the average value of $\mathtt{bipLC}_\top(s_i)$ for all sentences s_i.

This coefficient is interesting because it explicitly relates the property of the bipartite structure to the one of the $\bot$-projection, i.e. to the projection of entities, which are central in modelling coherence.

4. COHERENCE EVALUATION

Before evaluating the effectiveness of our coherence metrics for IR, we perform a pre-study to assess how accurately our coherence metrics approximate actual coherence.

4.1 Experimental Setup

We use the standard dataset for coherence evaluation, *Earthquakes and Accidents*[3], which contains 200 newswire articles (henceforth documents) concerning earthquakes and accidents from the North American News Corpus and the National Transportation Safety Board. These documents are short (240 terms on average); we expect them to be coherent because they have been produced by human professionals aiming to inform the public. We parse these documents with the Stanford parser and consider as entities those words tagged by the parser as the subject(s) or object(s) of a sentence. We do not treat as entities words of other grammatical roles (marked x in Table 1) because we wish to consider only the most salient

---

[3] http://people.csail.mit.edu/regina/coherence/

entities (i.e. the closest approximation to topics) of a document, and not modifiers of those topics by e.g. prepositional or other peripheral phrases (such as with evidence, through collusion, into markets in Table 1). We use the extracted entities to build entity grids, represent them as bipartite graphs, and compute our three coherence metrics as described in Section 3. All three of our coherence metrics are unsupervised – they contain no parameters, hence no training is involved.

We compare our coherence metrics to four coherence modelling baselines:

1. Barzilay and Lapata's seminal entity grid model [1],

2. Barzilay and Lee's HMM-based model [2],

3. Guinaudeau and Strube's out-degree graph-based coherence metric [14], and

4. Petersen et al.'s entity distance graph-based coherence model (which is the best performing of all 11 coherence models presented in [34]).

Note that baselines (1) and (2) are not graph-based, and that baselines (3) and (4) use undirected one-mode projections; on the contrary, our bipDCC, bipACC, and bipLC coherence metrics are defined (and computed) directly on the bipartite graph of a document's entity grid, rather than on its one-mode projection.

We use the standard practice of evaluating coherence, which consists of re-ordering progressively larger numbers of sentences in actual, coherent documents. This has the effect of simulating grades of incoherence; hence, good coherence metrics would have *high* coherence scores for the original documents, but progressively *lower* coherence scores as more and more sentences are re-ordered.

For each document, we pick $n \in [1 .. 20]$ pairs of sentences at random and switch them (e.g., for $n = 20$, a total of 40 sentences switch places). We then compute our coherence metrics on both the original and each of the re-ordered documents. If the coherence score of the original document is not lower than the coherence score of the re-ordered document, then we reason that the coherence metric accurately predicts the re-ordered document to be less coherent that the original. The total number of accurate predictions is then averaged over all documents.

4.2 Coherence Accuracy Findings

Table 2 shows the accuracy of each coherence metric averaged over all re-ordered documents. We see that our bipLC metric is the most accurate, both on the individual subsets of the data, and on their overall average. Our two other metrics (bipDCC, bipACC) are less accurate than bipLC but also than the two graph-based baselines computed on one-mode projections (out-degree and entity distance) and the original entity grid, on average. A possible explanation is that bipDCC and bipACC focus primarily on local clusters of entities, whereas the other metrics focus more on entity linkages across sentences (in different ways for each metric). This emphasis on entity linkage as opposed to entity clustering is possibly better suited to approximating coherence, as all currently best performing graph-based models of coherence [14, 34] – which we use as baselines (3) and (4) – prioritise the (graph-based) distance between entities in a document. In particular, the best performing bipLC metric emphasises the likelihood that

	Earthquakes	Accidents	Average
Entity-grid (no graph)	69.7	67.0	68.4
HMM (no graph)	60.3	31.7	46.0
Out-degree (one-mode projection)	78.0	80.0	79.0
Entity distance (one-mode projection)	76.0	75.0	75.5
bipDCC (bipartite graph)	55.6	69.8	62.7
bipACC (bipartite graph)	55.5	70.1	62.8
bipLC (bipartite graph)	**80.9**	**94.0**	**87.5**

Table 2: Average coherence accuracy of baselines (top 4 rows) and our metrics (bottom 3 rows). The highest score in each column is shown in bold.

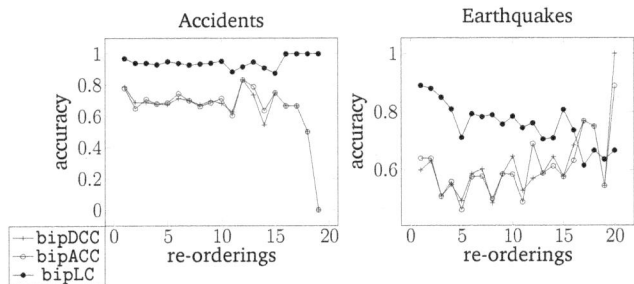

Figure 3: Coherence accuracy (vertical axis) vs. number of sentence re-orderings (horizontal axis) per document, for our bipDCC (+), bipACC (o) and bipLC (●) metrics, for *Accidents, Earthquakes*.

two entities that are linked by a sentence will be linked by another sentence too. This property is related to the theory of lexical chains [16], an early foundation in coherence modelling. To the best of our knowledge, of all existing coherence metrics, our bipLC metric models this idea of taking into account the trajectory of an entity across sentences the closest.

Figure 3 shows the average accuracy of the nth re-ordered document relative to the original document for each of the coherence metrics, separately for the Accidents and Earthquakes subsets. A perfect coherence metric would be a straight line with an accuracy of 1 as the coherence score of the original document would *always* be larger than a re-ordered version. Instead, we see fluctuations that diverge more (for bipDCC and bipACC) or less (bipLC) from that ideal straight line. Consistently with Table 2, bipLC has the most accurate and most robust performance. Of interest are the extreme peaks and drops as n increases: whereas for Accidents accuracy plummets for bipDCC and bipACC , for Earthquakes accuracy shoots up for bipDCC and bipACC but drops for bipLC. Closer inspection reveals that these more or less dramatic fluctuations are likely due to data sparsity: many documents are shorter than 40 sentences; thus, for high n values, there are fewer documents where it is possible to do n permutations, and consequently only a few documents determine the accuracy, making the overall findings less generalisable.

5. RETRIEVAL EVALUATION

We now test the usefulness of our coherence metrics to retrieval.

5.1 Integration of Coherence to Ranking

Our assumption is that more coherent documents are likely to be more relevant. To test this we rerank the top 1000[4] documents retrieved by a baseline model according to their coherence scores. In doing so, we treat document coherence as a type of query independent aspect of document quality that we combine with a query dependent baseline. The main idea is: (i) attach a static weight to each document based on its coherence; and (ii) combine this weight with the query dependent baseline score, to give a new score and ranking. For step (ii) we choose to use three types of linear combination which make it intuitively easy to interpret the impact of the coherence score on the final ranking. We present these next.

Let B be the baseline ranking score of a document. Let C be the coherence score of a document, computed according to each of our three coherence metrics presented in Section 3. Let R be the reranking score of a document, which should combine both B and C. We compute R as: $R = B + \widehat{C}$, where $\widehat{C}$ is a transformation of the document coherence score. We transform this document coherence score, in three different and increasingly parameterised ways, known to smooth out the integration of document quality features in general into ranking. Specifically we use the *log*, *satu* and *sigmoid* transformations [10], shown below:

$$\log(C, w) = w \log C \qquad (5)$$

where w is a smoothing parameter.

$$\text{satu}(C, w, k) = w \frac{C}{k + C} \qquad (6)$$

where w approaches the maximum as C increases, and k is a parameter controlling the value of C. The function *satu* can be reformulated as a *sigmoid* by introducing another parameter:

$$\text{sigmoid}(C, w, k, \alpha) = w \frac{C^{\alpha}}{k^{\alpha} + C^{\alpha}} \qquad (7)$$

where α is an extra parameter allowing for more fine smoothing. See [10] for a discussion of the rationale and behaviour of the *log*, *satu* and *sigmoid* transformations.

5.2 Experimental Setup

We compare retrieval performance between

1. a baseline ranking model (query likelihood language model with Dirichlet-smoothing, denoted LM) that does not use coherence, and

2. nine reranked versions of that baseline ranking that use document coherence (the three coherence metrics bipDCC, bipAcc, bipLC presented in Section 3 combined with the three integrations to ranking (*log* denoted ⊙, *satu* denoted ⊕, *sigmoid* denoted ⊗) presented in Section 5.1).

---

[4]Limiting the reranking to the top 1000 is more efficient than reranking all documents with a nonzero baseline score, without making a large difference to system effectiveness [10].

Method	MRR	P@10	ERR@20	NDCG@20	MAP@1000
LM (baseline)	46.08	31.19	15.78	15.68	09.67
LM ⊙ bipDCC	49.09	34.00	16.89	16.53	10.15
LM ⊕ bipDCC	48.62	34.00	18.63	16.61	10.07
LM ⊗ bipDCC	47.66	33.60	18.38	16.26	10.01
LM ⊙ bipACC	49.14	34.20	16.94	16.60	**10.18**
LM ⊕ bipACC	48.89	**34.40**	18.11	16.52	10.09
LM ⊗ bipACC	47.76	33.20	17.02	16.20	10.01
LM ⊙ bipLC	**52.82**	32.80	**18.69**	16.67	10.05
LM ⊕ bipLC	47.63	33.41	16.50	**16.76**	10.12
LM ⊗ bipLC	50.52	32.60	17.28	16.48	09.92

Table 3: Retrieval performance of coherence-based reranking. Improvements over the baseline are shaded and single best scores per evaluation measure are in bold.

We retrieve documents from the ClueWeb09 cat. B dataset using queries 150-200 from the Web AdHoc track of TREC 2012. We use the Indri IR system without stemming and without removing stopwords. Following [34], we remove spam from ClueWeb09 cat. B using the spam rankings of Cormack et al. [9] with a percentile-score < 90. This is a much higher threshold than the < 70 recommended in [9], practically meaning that we use much stricter spam filtering than recommended. We evaluate retrieval at different rank positions with MRR, Precision@10 (P@10), ERR@20, NDCG@20, and MAP@1000.

The baseline and our reranking methods include parameters μ (for Dirichlet smoothing), and w, k, α that we tune using 5-fold cross-validation. We report the average of the five test folds. We vary $\mu \in$ [100, 500, 800, 1000, 2000, 3000, 4000, 5000, 8000, 10000], $w \in$ [0.0, 2.0] in steps of 0.1, $k \in$ [0.0, 2.0] in steps of 0.1, and $\alpha \in$ [0.0, 1.0] in steps of 0.1.

5.3 Retrieval Findings

5.3.1 Retrieval Effectiveness

Table 3 displays the retrieval effectiveness of our coherence-based reranking experiments and the original ranking baseline. Coherence-based reranking improves over the baseline at all times. The best overall performance differs per evaluation measure: for MRR, ERR@20 and NDCG@20 our strongest coherence metric (as shown in the previous section), bipLC, is the best; for P@10 and MAP, bipACC is the best. All three MRR, ERR@20 and NDCG@20 are evaluation metrics of early precision: MRR measures the rank of the first relevant document, while ERR@20 and NDCG@20 focus in the top 20 ranks (they both consider the rank of a document, but they differ in that ERR conditions the usefulness of a document at rank i on the usefulness of the documents at ranks less than i, whereas NDCG assumes the usefulness of a document to be independent of the documents ranked above it). So it seems that bipLC is best for early precision measures. However, bipACC is best for P@10 (precision in the top 10 ranks), which is also an early precision measure. This could be due to the way P@10 computes precision, namely as the number of relevant documents in the top 10 but regardless of their ranking. In effect this transforms the top 10 into an unordered set of documents, whose measurement is not guaranteed to agree with rank order-oriented measures such as ERR and NDCG.

We also see that the bipDCC coherence metric is never the best. This could be because bipDCC does not account for the number of entities that are shared by sentences. As this is a major indication of coherence (topic transition across sen-

tences), it is likely that failing to account for this degrades coherence prediction (as we also saw in Table 2 on average and for the Accidents dataset). As a result, using for reranking a weaker coherence metric (bipDCC) improves retrieval less than when using our other two stronger coherence metrics. Note however that even though bipDCC is not the strongest coherence metric, it still benefits retrieval performance compared to the baseline.

Overall the difference in performance among the coherence runs in Table 3 is relatively small, except for MRR. The MRR exception is because the MRR score tends to change substantially for differences in even one rank position. For instance, when the first relevant document is at rank 1, MRR = 100; when at rank 2, MRR = 50.00; when at rank 3, MRR = 33.33, and so on. Considering this, even the largest difference in MRR among our coherence runs (from 52.82 to 47.63) is not indicative of considerable variation in rank position.

We also see in Table 3 that even though *sigmoid* (⊗) is more parameterised than the other two combinations, it is never the best. Instead, *log* (⊙) and *satu* (⊕) take turns at being best, indicating that the coherence-based reranking performance is not a byproduct of additional tuning parameters that smooth out retrieval regardless of coherence.

We further note that improvements over the baseline for MAP@1000 are smaller than improvements over the baseline for the other early precision measures. This is not surprising: typically as the depth of the measured precision increases, for instance from ranks 10–20 to rank positions >500, the actual precision score averaged over all retrieved documents up to that rank progressively deteriorates, because increasingly less relevant documents enter the ranking.

Finally, to contextualise the performance of our coherence metrics, we report that the retrieval performance of the two best *non-bipartite* coherence metrics in Table 2, out-degree and entity distance, never exceeds the scores of our best bipartite metrics[5].

5.3.2 Coherence and Query Difficulty

An aggregated overview of if and how much coherence-based reranking improves performance for queries of various levels of difficulty can be seen in Table 4. The percentages in Table 4 have been produced as follows. For each retrieval precision measure, we rank all queries decreasingly according to their baseline retrieval score. We then use these scores to sort queries into the four quantiles (Q1–Q4) shown in columns 2–

---

[5]The respective maximum scores of either out-degree or entity distance are MRR: 34.18, P@10: 22.40, ERR@20: 15.86, NDCG@20: 14.66, and MAP@1000: 07.22.

Method	Q1	Q2	Q3	Q4
LM ⊙ bipDCC	+4%	+12%	+2%	+9%
LM ⊕ bipDCC	+2%	+11%	+8%	+219%
LM ⊗ bipDCC	+3%	+12%	0%	+140%
LM ⊙ bipACC	+3%	+16%	+3%	+10%
LM ⊕ bipACC	+1%	+21%	+4%	+86%
LM ⊗ bipACC	+3%	+10%	+2%	+23%
LM ⊙ bipLC	0%	+45%	+19%	-2%
LM ⊕ bipLC	+3%	+18%	+30%	+3%
LM ⊗ bipLC	-2%	+24%	+28%	+7%
Average	+2%	+19%	+11%	+55%

Table 4: Average improvement in retrieval performance over the baseline. Darker cells mark higher improvements.

5. In effect these quantiles group queries according to their difficulty; Q1 contains those queries that have the highest baseline retrieval score (hence they are perceived as easier queries for the IR system to satisfy), whereas Q4 contains those queries with the lowest baseline retrieval score (which are perceived as the hardest for the IR system to satisfy). For the queries in each quantile, we compute their absolute difference in score between the baseline and each coherence-based reranking and turn this difference into a percentage. The percentages of each quantile correspond to the average improvement in retrieval performance over the baseline per quantile. This is the average over all queries in the quantile, and over all retrieval measures.

We see that Q4 gains the most, on average across all coherence runs. As Q4 corresponds to the hardest queries that an IR system has to process, this means that reranking by coherence can improve performance for those queries that standard ranking has the most trouble with. However, the percentages per coherence metric show that our strongest coherence metric, bipLC, benefits mostly Q2 – Q3, and very little or not at all Q4. This very small or no improvement in Q4 for bipLC is in fact an artefact of how we computed the percentages: because it is not possible to compute a percentage improvement over zero, we removed from Q4 those queries that had a zero baseline score. These were on average 10.5 queries per evaluation measure. Removing these highly difficult queries has the effect of underestimating the impact of coherence-based reranking in particular in Q4, and especially for bipLC.

Overall, the smallest improvement for all coherence-based reranking is in Q1, which corresponds to queries that baseline IR ranking can cope with satisfactorily. This indicates that the margin for improvement over the baseline may be smaller for those queries.

5.3.3 Error Analysis

To gain more insight into the type of contribution that coherence makes to retrieval, we look at those cases that benefit the most from coherence-based reranking. For query 174 (rock art), the documents ranked in the top two places by the baseline retrieval model receive a coherence score of 0.0 by all of our coherence metrics. These top two documents have no TREC relevance assessments (hence most IR evaluation metrics will treat them as non-relevant). Even though these documents have stayed in the dataset after we filtered out spam (using very strict spam thresholding, as discussed above), manual inspection reveals these documents to be largely non-informative. The first few lines of these documents are included below:

> [clueweb09-en0009-40-30672]: Music Democracy :: Unchain You Art username: Damn! I forgot my password password: The Music Democracy Team is attending MIDEM 09 in Cannes. If you're interested in a meeting, please contact us (link at the bottom of the page) Tests are underway and certain features could be unavailable punctually.We apologize for these inconveniences. HOME URBAN ROCK ELECTRO POP BLUES WORLD VARIOUS Registration as Musician * Username * Email * Retype email * Password (at least 6 characters) * Retype Password * Country (included province) Select Albania Algeria American Samoa Andorra Angola Anguilla Antarctica Antigua and Barbuda Argentina Armenia Aruba [···]

> [clueweb09-en0000-95-09794]: Outline of Art History - Ancient Art Search Art History Home Education Art History Email Art History Artists Styles Works of Art Filed In: Art History Outline of Art History - Ancient Art 30,000 BC - c. 400 AD Outline of Art History Part 1: Ancient Art Part 2: Medieval Art Part 3: Renaissance Art Part 4: Modern Art Part 5: Contemporary Art Related Resources Ancient Art Resources Prehistory Paleolithic (Old Stone Age) [···]

For documents like these, the baseline ranking function (which considers solely single term frequencies) has no way of detecting low document informativeness. The extremely frequent and uninformative (almost spam-like) repetition of the same terms, not only goes undetected in the baseline ranking, but can also result in the documents being ranked very high when they contain query terms (this is what happened for query 174). Our coherence metrics are particularly useful in these cases, because they can detect the low quality of these documents.

Of interest is also the document ranked by the baseline in position 4 for the same query 174. This document also has no TREC relevance assessments, and receives the following coherence scores: bipDCC=0.009, bipACC=0.022, bipLC=0.0. This document is a wikipedia listing of museums in Maryland:

> [clueweb09-enwp01-26-04667]: List of museums in Maryland [···] encompasses museums, defined for this context as institutions (including nonprofit organizations, government entities, and private businesses) that collect and care for objects of cultural, artistic, scientific, or historical interest and make their collections or related exhibits available for public viewing. Museums that exist only in cyberspace (i.e., virtual museums) are not included. Lists of Maryland institutions which are not museums are noted in the "See also" section, below. To use the sortable table, click on the icons at the top of each column to sort that column in alphabetical order; click again for reverse alphabetical order. Name Location Region Area of study Summary Aberdeen Room Archives & Museum Aberdeen Local history website Academy Art Museum Easton Art website, works on paper and contemporary works by American and European masters Adkins Historical Museum Mardela Springs Open air website, eight historical buildings and the gravestones of a Revolutionary War patriot and his wife, buildings open by appointment African-American Heritage Society Museum [···]

Both our clustering-based coherence metrics (bipDCC and bipACC) give to this document weights that concentrate on the dense clusters of entities. On the contrary, the bipLC metric emphasises more the transition of entities across sentences (which is extremely low in this document, as new entities (museum names and themes) keep on being introduced, mentioned in 1-2 sentences, and then quickly dropped). This is a specific discourse feature of text (to list or enumerate themes without linking them into the discourse), which goes undetected by clustering (bipDCC and bipACC), but not by bipLC. Note that this document was ranked as the fourth most relevant document for the query rock art. After manual inspection, we consider it neither very relevant, nor very coherent.

The above are examples of relatively low quality documents that are ranked (erroneously) high by the baseline but receive a very low coherence score (correctly) by our coherence metrics. Next we display examples of the opposite: high quality documents that are ranked (correctly) higher by coherence-based reranking than by the baseline.

> [clueweb09-enwp00-52-08632]: Rock art of the Chumash people. [· · ·] Chumash Rock Art is a type of artwork created by the Chumash people, mainly in caves or on cliffs in the mountains in areas of southern California. Contents: Chumash people, Rock Art Locations, Shamans and Visions, Shamans and Rock Art, Rock Art Characteristics, Meanings of Rock Art, Conclusion, References [· · ·] Chumash Rock Art is almost invariably found in caves or on cliffs in the mountains, although some small, portable painted rocks have been discovegray by Campbell Grant. The rock art sites are always found near streams, springs, or some other source of permanent water. In his research of southern California rock art, Grant recorded numerous sites from different areas that were all close to a water source. He found twelve painted sites in the highest parts of the mountainous Chumash territory, the Ventureno area [· · ·]

> [clueweb09-en0009-97-31173]: The Heilbrunn Timeline of Art History. The Metropolitan Museum of Art. African Rock Art. African Rock Art. Thematic Essay Categories. Recent Additions. All Thematic Essays. African Art. Central Africa. Eastern Africa. Southern Africa. Western Africa [· · ·] Africa's oldest continuously practiced art form. Depictions of elegant human figures, richly hued animals, and figures combining human and animal features called the rianthropes and associated with shamanism continue to inspire admiration for their sophistication, energy, and direct, powerful forms. The apparent universality of these images is deceptive; content and style range widely over the African continent. Nevertheless, African rock art can be divided into three broad geographical zones southern, central, and northern. The art of each of these zones is distinctive and easily recognizable, even to an untrained eye [· · ·]

The above documents are *both* coherent *and* relevant to query 174. Coherence-based reranking moves these documents three and two positions higher up in the ranking, respectively. Interestingly, for both of these documents `bipACC` gives the highest coherence score. This is because both these documents first list an index of subtopics that they contain and then discuss each of them under different specialised subheadings. This type of discourse, which is characterised by several local clusters that are however closely linked to each other by an underlying common theme (rock art in this case) is best modelled by `bipACC`, which focuses on local clusters (unlike `bipLC`) while also accounting for the number of entities that are shared by sentences (unlike `bipDCC`).

6. DISCUSSION

In Section 3 we present three bipartite metrics for approximating document coherence. Our metrics are not the only tailor-made metrics for bipartite graphs. There is substantial work in the field of network science aiming at defining metrics that highlight certain topological features of graphs, several of which may be related to coherence, but to the best of our knowledge this has not been done so far. For example, several techniques exist for community detection [12], which may potentially be used in combination with bipartite graph distance to afford more precise coherence scores. The rationale is that, if a document is coherent, sentences being identified as belonging to a particular community should be close in the document. Similarly, several techniques exist for detecting maximal bicliques [18] (i.e., maximal subsets of vertices where all ⊤ and ⊥-vertices are connected). Intuitively, maximal biclique detection could be used to detect document sentences and entities so related that there is no doubt they represent a coherent flow of discourse.

Regarding the integration of document coherence into ranking, we treat our document coherence metrics as a query-independent type of document quality score that we combine linearly with the retrieval status value of the baseline ranking to rerank retrieved documents. This is a straightforward reranking approach; more involved reranking functions [10] may be used to possibly improve retrieval effectiveness. For instance, studying the distribution of the document coherence scores as well as the distribution of the document relevance scores can inform functions that aim at fitting the former to the latter more closely. Another integration method that can be used is rank fusion. The idea here is to the turn the baseline and the coherence scores into two rankings, which are then fused, e.g. using CombMNZ, voting algorithms, or Bayesian inference [3]. This has the advantage of ignoring the coherence score distributions, so for example heavily skewed distributions of document coherence cannot be allowed to have too much impact upon the final ranking. Alternatively, document coherence can also be turned into a prior probability of relevance and combined with the language modelling baseline probability, which would produce a seamless "coherence-enhanced language model". All of the above directions are interesting to pursue in the future.

7. CONCLUSIONS

We presented three novel bipartite graph metrics of document coherence. Our metrics extend the state of the art in unsupervised coherence modelling by approximating coherence directly on bipartite graphs of discourse entities and sentences (unlike previous methods that use their one–mode projections). We experimentally evaluated the accuracy of our metrics in modelling coherence. Our bipartite metrics incurred no additional efficiency cost over existing one–mode graph metrics. One of our metrics was found to be *much* more accurate approximation of document coherence than the state of the art computed from one-mode projections [14, 34]. We also experimentally evaluated the usefulness of our document coherence metrics to IR, and found them overall successful, and in particular for early precision and "difficult" queries. Our results can be seen as another piece of evidence in a long string of results showing that algorithmic approximations of document *quality* can be exploited in IR to obtain better retrieval performance.

8. REFERENCES

[1] R. Barzilay and M. Lapata. Modeling local coherence: An entity-based approach. *ACL*, 34(1):1–34, 2008.

[2] R. Barzilay and L. Lee. Catching the drift: Probabilistic content models, with applications to generation and summarization. In *HLT-NAACL*, pages 113–120, 2004.

[3] S. M. Beitzel, O. Frieder, E. C. Jensen, D. Grossman, A. Chowdhury, and N. Goharian. Disproving the fusion hypothesis. In *SAC*, pages 823–827, 2003.

[4] M. Bendersky, W. B. Croft, and Y. Diao. Quality-biased ranking of web documents. In *WSDM*, pages 95–104, 2011.

[5] R. Blanco and C. Lioma. Graph-based term weighting for information retrieval. *Inf. Retr.*, 15(1):54–92, Feb. 2012.

[6] S. P. Borgatti and M. G. Everett. Network analysis of 2-mode data. *Social networks*, 19(3):243–269, 1997.

[7] A. Çelikyilmaz and D. Hakkani-Tür. Discovery of topically coherent sentences for extractive summarization. In *ACL*, pages 491–499, 2011.

[8] M. Coleman and T. L. Liau. A computer readability formula designed for machine scoring. *Journal of Applied Psychology*, (60):282–284, 1975.

[9] G. V. Cormack, M. D. Smucker, and C. L. Clarke. Efficient and effective spam filtering and re-ranking for large web datasets. *IR*, 14(5):441–465, 2011.

[10] N. Craswell, S. Robertson, H. Zaragoza, and M. Taylor. Relevance weighting for query independent evidence. In *SIGIR*, pages 416–423, 2005.

[11] R.-A. de Beaugrande and W. Dressler. *Introduction to Text Linguistics*. Longman London, New York, NY, USA, 1981.

[12] S. Fortunato. Community detection in graphs. *Physics Reports*, 486(3):75 – 174, 2010.

[13] B. J. Grosz, S. Weinstein, and A. K. Joshi. Centering: A framework for modeling the local coherence of discourse. *ACL*, pages 203–225, 1995.

[14] C. Guinaudeau and M. Strube. Graph-based local coherence modeling. In *ACL*, pages 93–103, 2013.

[15] R. Gunning. *The technique of clear writing*. McGraw-Hill, 1952.

[16] M. K. Halliday and R. Hasan. *Cohesion in English*. Longman, London, 1976.

[17] T. Kanungo and D. Orr. Predicting the readability of short web summaries. In *WSDM*, pages 202–211, 2009.

[18] E. Kayaaslan. On enumerating all maximal bicliques of bipartite graphs. In *Workshop on Graphs and Combinatorial Optimization*, pages 105–108, 2010.

[19] J. P. Kincaid, R. P. Fishburne, R. L. Rogers, and B. S. Chissom. Derivation of new readability formulas for navy enlisted personnel. Technical report, NTIS, 1975.

[20] B. Larsen, C. Lioma, I. Frommholz, and H. Schütze. Preliminary study of technical terminology for the retrieval of scientific book metadata records. In *SIGIR*, pages 1131–1132, 2012.

[21] M. Latapy, C. Magnien, and N. D. Vecchio. Basic notions for the analysis of large two-mode networks. *Social Networks*, 30(1):31–48, 2008.

[22] J. Li and E. H. Hovy. A model of coherence based on distributed sentence representation. In A. Moschitti, B. Pang, and W. Daelemans, editors, *EMNLP*, pages 2039–2048. ACL, 2014.

[23] Z. Lin, C. Liu, H. T. Ng, and M.-Y. Kan. Combining coherence models and machine translation evaluation metrics for summarization evaluation. In *ACL (1)*, pages 1006–1014. ACL, 2012.

[24] C. Lioma, B. Larsen, and W. Lu. Rhetorical relations for information retrieval. In *SIGIR*, pages 931–940, 2012.

[25] C. Lioma and I. Ounis. Extending weighting models with a term quality measure. In *SPIRE*, pages 205–216, 2007.

[26] C. Lioma and C. J. K. van Rijsbergen. Part of speech n-grams and information retrieval. *Revue française de linguistique appliquée*, XIII(1):9–11, 2008.

[27] G. McClure. Readability formulas: Useful or useless. *Trans. Prof. Comm.*, 30:12 – 15, 1987.

[28] G. H. McLaughlin. Smog grading – a new readability formula. *J. of Reading*, 12(8):639 – 646, 1969.

[29] L. Michelbacher, A. Kothari, M. Forst, C. Lioma, and H. Schütze. A cascaded classification approach to semantic head recognition. In *EMNLP*, pages 793–803, 2011.

[30] M. Newman. *Networks: An Introduction*. Oxford University Press, NY, USA, 2010.

[31] A. Ntoulas, M. Najork, M. Manasse, and D. Fetterly. Detecting spam web pages through content analysis. In *WWW*, pages 83–92, 2006.

[32] T. Opsahl. Triadic closure in two-mode networks: Redefining the global and local clustering coefficients. *Social Networks*, 35(2):159–167, 2013.

[33] D. Parveen and M. Strube. Integrating importance, non-redundancy and coherence in graph-based extractive summarization. In *IJCAI*, pages 1298–1304, 2015.

[34] C. Petersen, C. Lioma, J. G. Simonsen, and B. Larsen. Entropy and graph based modelling of document coherence using discourse entities: An application to IR. In *ICTIR*, pages 191–200, 2015.

[35] T. A. Snijders. The statistical evaluation of social network dynamics. *Sociological methodology*, 31(1):361–395, 2001.

[36] R. Tackx, J. Guillaume, and F. Tarissan. Revealing intricate properties of communities in the bipartite structure of online social networks. In *RCIS*, pages 321–326. IEEE, 2015.

[37] C. Tan, E. Gabrilovich, and B. Pang. To each his own: personalized content selection based on text comprehensibility. In *WSDM*, pages 233–242, 2012.

[38] F. Tarissan and R. Nollez-Goldbach. Analysing the first case of the international criminal court from a network-science perspective. *Journal of Complex Networks*, pages 1–19, 2016.

[39] F. Tarissan, B. Quoitin, P. Mérindol, B. Donnet, J.-J. Pansiot, and M. Latapy. Towards a bipartite graph modeling of the internet topology. *Computer Networks*, 57(11):2331–2347, 2013.

[40] N. Voskarides, E. Meij, M. Tsagkias, M. de Rijke, and W. Weerkamp. Learning to explain entity relationships in knowledge graphs. In *ACL*, pages 564–574, 2015.

[41] D. Xiong, Y. Ding, M. Zhang, and C. L. Tan. Lexical chain based cohesion models for document-level statistical machine translation. In *EMNLP*, pages 1563–1573, 2013.

[42] D. Xiong, M. Zhang, and X. Wang. Topic-based coherence modeling for statistical machine translation. *Trans. Audio, Speech and Lang. Proc.*, 23(3):483–493, Mar. 2015.

[43] M. Zhang, V. W. Feng, B. Qin, G. Hirst, T. Liu, and J. Huang. Encoding world knowledge in the evaluation of local coherence. In *NAACL HLT*, pages 1087–1096, 2015.

[44] P. Zhang, J. Wang, X. Li, M. Li, Z. Di, and Y. Fan. Clustering coefficient and community structure of bipartite networks. *Physica A: Statistical Mechanics and its Applications*, 387(27):6869–6875, 2008.

[45] R. Zhang. Sentence ordering driven by local and global coherence for summary generation. In *ACL*, pages 6–11, 2011.

[46] Y. Zhou and W. B. Croft. Document quality models for web adhoc retrieval. In *CIKM*, pages 331–332, 2005.

[47] X. Zhu and S. Gauch. Incorporating quality metrics in centralized/distributed information retrieval on the world wide web. In *SIGIR*, pages 288–295, 2000.

Efficient and Effective Higher Order Proximity Modeling

Xiaolu Lu
RMIT University
Melbourne, Australia
xiaolu.lu@rmit.edu.au

Alistair Moffat
The University of Melbourne
Melbourne, Australia
ammoffat@unimelb.edu.au

J. Shane Culpepper
RMIT University
Melbourne, Australia
shane.culpepper@rmit.edu.au

ABSTRACT

Bag-of-words retrieval models are widely used, and provide a robust trade-off between efficiency and effectiveness. These models often make simplifying assumptions about relations between query terms, and treat term statistics independently. However, query terms are rarely independent, and previous work has repeatedly shown that term dependencies can be critical to improving the effectiveness of ranked retrieval results. Among all term-dependency models, the Markov Random Field (MRF) [Metzler and Croft, SIGIR, 2005] model has received the most attention in recent years. Despite clear effectiveness improvements, these models are not deployed in performance-critical applications because of the potentially high computational costs. As a result, bigram models are generally considered to be the best compromise between full term dependence, and term-independent models such as BM25.

Here we provide further evidence that term-dependency features not captured by bag-of-words models can reliably improve retrieval effectiveness. We also present a variation on the highly-effective MRF model that relies on a BM25-derived potential. The benefit of this approach is that it is built from feature functions which require no higher-order global statistics. We empirically show that our new model reduces retrieval costs by up to 60%, with no loss in effectiveness compared to previous approaches.

Categories and Subject Descriptors

H.3.3 [**Information Storage and Retrieval**]: Information Search and Retrieval—*Retrieval models, search process*; H.3.4 [**Information Storage and Retrieval**]: Systems and Software—*Performance evaluation*

Keywords

Proximity; Experimentation; Measurement

1. INTRODUCTION

Bag-of-words models are widely used in information retrieval. Regardless of whether they are based on probabilistic ranking principles, such as BM25 [29], or drawn from a language modeling

family, such as the Query Likelihood model [25], those models assume either that the query terms are independent of each other, or are conditionally independent. To compute a document score, each term contributes according to its TF score and IDF weighting, with the sum across the terms taken as the score for the document as a whole. Bag-of-words models are widely used because they can be efficiently implemented, and in most applications also attain good retrieval effectiveness.

However, a range of sophisticated proximity models that allow terms to be dependent on each other have been proposed, and have shown a significant gain in retrieval effectiveness over bag-of-words models [12, 23, 32, 9, 14, 24]. Among term-dependency models, the Markov Random Field (MRF) [23] model has received considerable attention. Effectiveness is improved by considering all possible dependencies among query terms; the tradeoff cost arises in the form of higher computational costs. Bigram models can also be used as a compromise between full dependence, and fully independent models. However, the parameter tuning process for bigram models can be non-trivial, and may not obtain the expected effectiveness even if resources such as Google's N-grams are applied.

In order to achieve high effectiveness, current MRF term dependency models require global collection statistics, counting the frequency of each possible dependency. Such global statistics are expensive to obtain, except in the trivial case of single terms. Unless large amounts of storage and preprocessing time are used, global statistics describing two or more terms can only be computed at query time; the cost of doing that then becomes a significant bottleneck when evaluating term-dependency queries. In particular, two complete iterations over the postings lists of terms must be performed, meaning that long queries, or queries containing frequent words, may give rise to unacceptable query latencies.

In this paper, we first empirically reinforce the importance of proximity features in the retrieval process, and confirm that it is crucial to combine both term-independent and term-dependent score components in order to achieve maximum effectiveness. Then, to address the "global statistics" bottleneck associated with proximity models, we propose an alternative feature function that can be used in the MRF framework. We empirically test our new variant MRF model on three TREC collections, and show its effectiveness compared to other MRF models. Finally, having demonstrated the effectiveness of the approach, we turn our attention to execution cost, and show that our mechanisms reduce per-document retrieval costs by up to 60% compared to other methods.

2. BACKGROUND

Bag-of-Words Models Many different retrieval models have been proposed over the years. Most current approaches fall in to one of two categories: (i) BM25 scoring approaches; and (ii) language models. Other options include mechanisms based on divergence from randomness [1]. Here we focus on the unigram models associated with BM25 and with language models, because of their importance as components of proximity models. Although they have different theoretical explanations, both assume independence or conditional independence among query terms [27, 35].

Let $Q = \{q_0, q_1, \ldots, q_{k-1}\}$ be a query. Then the score of a document D relative to Q can be formulated as an accumulation of unigram scores:

$$Score(Q, D) = \sum_{q \in Q} Score(q, D) \qquad (1)$$

The BM25 model is based on the probabilistic ranking principle:

$$BM\text{-}Score(Q, D) = \sum_{q \in Q} w_q \cdot \frac{f_{q,D} \cdot (1 + k_1)}{f_{q,D} + K}$$
$$K = k_1 \cdot (1 - b + \frac{b \cdot |D|}{avg(|D|)}), \qquad (2)$$

where w_q is the IDF weighting, $f_{q,D}$ is the TF value of term q, and k_1 and b are tunable parameters. There are several variants of the BM25 model, with one categorization based on the IDF weighting, w_q. Either a Robertson-Spärck Jones parameter $w_q^{(1)}$ [28], or a Robertson-Walker parameter $w_q^{(2)}$ [17] can be applied, and calculated as:

$$w_q^{(1)} = \log \frac{N - N_q + 0.5}{N_q + 0.5} \text{ , and } w_q^{(2)} = \log \frac{N}{N_q}, \qquad (3)$$

where N is the total number of documents in the collection and N_q is the number containing term q. The $w_q^{(2)}$ version is implemented in ATIRE as recent work has shown it to be the most effective in practice. [33, 34].

Language models [25] score documents using a somewhat different approach. The widely used Language Model with Dirichlet Smoothing (LMDS) can be formulated as:

$$LM\text{-}Score(Q, D) = \sum_{q \in Q} \log \left(\frac{\mu \cdot f_{q,\mathcal{C}}/|\mathcal{C}| + f_{q,D}}{\mu + |D|} \right), \qquad (4)$$

where $|\mathcal{C}|$ is the size of the collection; $f_{q,\mathcal{C}}$ is the number of occurrences of term q in the collection; $f_{q,D}$ is the number of occurrences of q in document D (that is, the TF value), and μ is the Dirichlet smoothing parameter. As for the BM25 models, there are several variants in the LM family, using different smoothing methods, and/or based on a different assumption as to the underlying distribution of terms. We consider the LMDS approach of Equation 4 to be a good representative of language models for the purposes of our experiments, and the BM25 formulation of Equation 2 to be a representative probabilistic method. Both have been empirically shown to have reasonably good effectiveness on a wide variety of test collections, and can be efficiently implemented using a document-level inverted index [37].

In order to further improve retrieval effectiveness, the BM25 and LMDS models can be combined with information gleaned from other features, either query-independent or query-dependent, with the merging process often involving linear combinations. Query-independent features include static document scores such as PageRank and quality/spam scores; and one intuitively attractive query-dependent feature is to utilize term positions and the proximity of query terms in the document. This latter approach has received considerable attention in previous work [26, 9, 23, 6, 13, 32, 24]. While there have been empirical studies showing that the use of proximity statistics enhances the effectiveness of ranked retrieval

[12, 32], there are also several counterexamples that question the value of including proximity-based features in retrieval [35, 27], partly because of the expense of computing them.

In other related work, de Kretser and Moffat [10] combine localized term scores to allow terms to reinforce each other when they appear close together. Their approach makes use of a word-level inverted index so that term positions are known, but avoids the use of global statistics. The main strength of their approach is to locate more specific retrieval zones within long documents; it also can be used as an aid when preparing a document summary or caption.

Influence of Proximity Scores The question of whether proximity features boost bag-of-words scoring models arises because unigram models already incorporate some of the same influences. For example, if two query terms both appear in a document, then the document will almost certainly be scored more highly by a bag-of-words model than if only one of them appears, and it might be that the two occurrences are only rarely separated by a large span of terms anyway. In this case, using an auxiliary proximity model might not alter the underlying document ranking in any way. Part of our work here is to demonstrate the converse – that adding proximity features to the BM25 and LMDS unigram bag-of-words models unambiguously improves effectiveness, provided that the two parts are combined carefully. In particular, let $Score(Q, D)$ be the score of any bag-of-words model, $Score(\mathcal{I}, D)$ be the score derived solely from the model based on the proximity features in a document ($\mathcal{I}$ will be defined shortly as a set of *intervals*), and $\Pr(D = 1)$ be the probability of a document being a relevant one. Then if proximity features are a useful addition to the bag-of-words model, we would hope to demonstrate that if $Score(Q, D_1) = Score(Q, D_2) \wedge Score(\mathcal{I}, D_1) > Score(\mathcal{I}, D_2)$, then $\Pr(D_1 = 1) > \Pr(D_2 = 1)$. We present results supporting this hypothesis in Section 4.

Modeling Term Dependencies To model term dependencies, Metzler and Croft [23] propose a framework based on a Markov Random Field (MRF), an undirected graph model, in which potential functions applied over clique sets are defined according to a specific task. For IR applications, Metzler and Croft consider three generalized graph structures to represent different independence assumptions, namely Full Independence (FI), Sequential Dependence (SD) and Full Dependence (FD). There are three different types of clique sets in these structures [21]: (i) the query dependent clique set, which only contains query nodes matching subqueries $Q' \subseteq Q$; (ii) the query-document clique set, which contains query terms in Q' and a document; and (iii) the document clique set, in which only the document is considered. The first type of clique sets are query dependent features, and can be scored using IDF weightings. Any TF-IDF ranking functions can be used as feature functions of the second clique set; and the document clique set can be modeled using document-dependent features [21]. The potential function is then built from all of the feature functions.

Following the original definition of each clique set, let $T_{Q,D} = \{\{q_0, D\}, \{q_1, D\}, \ldots \{q_{k-1}, D\}\}$. Then the FI model only considers this type of clique set, and hence yields a bag-of-words model. Further, let n-$O_{Q,D}$ be a set of clique sets that matches phrases containing between two and n contiguous query terms, and let n-$U_{Q,D}$ be the set of clique sets matching subqueries formed containing between two and n query terms, without the requirement that the terms be adjacent in D. The SD model (SDM) only considers 2-$O_{Q,D}$ which are the bigrams in the query, while the FD model (FDM) considers $T_{Q,D}$ plus n-$O_{Q,D}$ plus n-$U_{Q,D}$. The LMDS feature function is applied over these clique sets based on a set of independence assumptions.

The INQUERY interface [8] provides operators that support these

MRF ranking options. Let $\mathcal{Q}$ be the set of all two-or-more term subsets of Q. Then the MRF model is formulated as:

$$
\begin{aligned}
\text{LM-M-Score}(Q,D) = & \lambda_t \cdot \text{LM-Score}(Q,D) + \\
& \lambda_o \cdot \sum_{Q' \in \mathcal{Q}} \text{LM-Score}(\#ow(Q'),D) + \\
& \lambda_u \cdot \sum_{Q' \in \mathcal{Q}} \text{LM-Score}(\#uwX(Q'),D),
\end{aligned}
\tag{5}
$$

in which λ_t, λ_o, and λ_u are weighting parameters for unigrams, ordered phrases and unordered phrases, respectively; where $\#ow(Q')$ denotes an exact match of Q' in D; and where $\#uwX(Q')$ denotes an unordered match of Q' within distance X. In FI, only the first term is considered (equivalent to $\lambda_o = \lambda_u = 0$); and SDM only considers bigram queries, in which Q' is formed from two adjacent terms in the query. All $Q' \in \mathcal{Q}$ are used in $n\text{-}U_{Q,D}$ and $n\text{-}O_{Q,D}$.

The MRF framework captures term-dependencies explicitly, and is readily adapted to make use of different potentials. Metzler [22] initially described BM25-derived potentials as well as LMDS-derived potentials, and subsequent work found that the differences in terms of effectiveness are not significant in most cases [11]. On the other hand, previous work has not explored the impact on efficiency when using different potentials.

Bigram Models as a Surrogate Both Zhai [35] and Robertson [27] note that higher-order proximity scoring is computationally intensive, and as a compromise suggest using bigrams only. One of the most widely used non-parametric bigram models, BCTP [6], is an extension of a BM25 model originally described by Rasolofo and Savoy [26]. BCTP takes the word distance between terms q_i and q_{i+1} in the document into consideration:

$$
\begin{aligned}
acc(q_i,D) &= acc(q_i,D) + w_j^{(2)} \cdot dist(q_i,q_j)^{-2} \\
acc(q_j,D) &= acc(q_j,D) + w_i^{(2)} \cdot dist(q_i,q_j)^{-2},
\end{aligned}
\tag{6}
$$

where $w_i^{(2)}$ and $w_j^{(2)}$ are the IDF weightings of q_i and q_j, and $dist(q_i,q_j)$ is the distance between the bigrams, leading to:

$$
\begin{aligned}
\text{TP-Score}(Q,D) = & \sum_{q \in Q} \text{BM-Score}(q,D) + \\
& \sum_{q \in Q} \min\{w_q^{(2)},1.0\} \cdot \frac{acc(q,D) \cdot (1+k_1)}{acc(q,D) + K}
\end{aligned}
\tag{7}
$$

in which the score $acc(q_i,D)$ for query term q_i is then combined with its bag-of-words BM25 score. In this model, BM25 uses the $w_q^{(2)}$ IDF weighting given in Equation 3, and k_1, K are the same parameters as in Equation 2, with each query term scored in the context of the intervals formed with other terms. Like the earlier method of de Kretser and Moffat [10], only unigram global statistics are required, together with term positions within documents. In both of these models the distance between occurrences of query terms plays a role in the scoring process. The BCTP model was also used in recent work by Broschart and Schenkel [5], who explore several hybrid indexing techniques capable of balancing query efficiency and index size.

As was noted above, SDM is obtained by considering only sequential dependencies of bigrams. Instead of using the default tuning parameters in each feature function as described by Metzler [22], it is also possible to use external resources to give each clique set a different weighting. The weighted SDM (WSDM) [14, 3, 4] yields superior performance compared to SDM, achieving similar effectiveness to FDM on some queries. BCTP tends to be less competitive when compared with a sequential dependency model (SDM) [23], especially when WSDM is used. Although a carefully tuned bigram model can be better than a high-order proximity model, Huston and Croft [14] also note a degradation in effectiveness on deep-pooled collections. If unweighted SDM is applied to the extents and compared to a higher proximity model such as FDM, the bigram model is less effective. Huston and Croft [14] also hypothesize that bigram models may be better than higher-order models for some queries, and that with the proper configuration, many-term dependency models can also be improved.

Higher-Order Proximity Consider the query "women ordained church of england" (Robust04, Query 621), and a section from a relevant document, with words annotated with their positions:

> ^{0}England ^{1}is ^{2}set ^{3}to ^{4}have ^{5}women ^{6}priests ^{7}within ^{8}two ^{9}years, ^{10}following ^{11}a ^{12}close ^{13}vote ^{14}in ^{15}the ^{16}Church ^{17}of ^{18}England's ^{19}general ^{20}synod ^{21}yesterday. $\ldots$ ^{50}if ^{51}women ^{52}were ^{53}ordained. ^{54}Mr ^{55}Gummer ^{56}had ^{57}suggested ^{58}that ^{59}he ^{60}might ^{61}leave ^{62}the ^{63}Church ^{64}of ^{65}England ^{66}over ^{67}women's ^{68}ordination.

In this query, "church of england" is clearly a phrase, and using the two bigrams it contains may yield a potential gain compared to a bag-of-words only query, since the phrase occurs twice in the example document. The other two terms, "woman" and "ordained", occur both as a phrase (words 67-68), and also as a proximity, separated by the word "were" (words 51-53); and all five query terms occur within a span of 6 (words 63-68), a higher-order proximity.

Multi-term dependency models assume that all terms may have informative interactions, and as a result may better capture a user's intent. These models can be roughly categorized into three different approaches, according to the proximity statistics used: (i) the statistics of a "span" [9, 30, 31] in a document; (ii) the statistics of all subqueries of the current query in a document [23]; and (iii) the statistics of term positional information [19, 36].

The use of span (or cover) statistics was proposed by Clarke et al. [9], and examined subsequently by Song et al. [30]. A span is a minimal interval formed by occurrences of two query terms. For example, consider the subquery $Q' = \{\text{england}, \text{women}\}$ when applied to the example document. The interval $[0\ldots5]$ is optimal, whereas the interval $[0\ldots51]$ is not, since the latter is a superset of the former. A more detailed definition is provided by Clarke et al. [9]. Span statistics are straightforward to use since the optimal intervals are naturally separated, even without specifying a distance constraint. Both Clarke et al. and Song et al. consider a chain of such intervals, the difference being: (i) Song et al. consider a non-overlapping version of "covers", and apply different weights using a function parameterized on both the number of query terms captured, and the distance of an interval; and (ii) Song et al. reformulate the BM25 model using redefined term contributions. The work of Song et al. [30] is based on a similar strategy as is used in the earlier BCTP model, and query terms are scored using different contexts, where "contexts" are spans containing the query term.

Unlike other models that have a separate bag-of-words component, these models integrate the proximity contributions for each query term directly into the BM25 computation. Let $I[p_\ell \ldots p_r]$ be a span, and the query terms bounded by the span be $I \cap Q$. Then $acc(q,D)$ is calculated for a query term contribution as:

$$
\begin{aligned}
\text{Span-Score}(Q,D) &= \sum_{q \in Q} w_q^{(1)} \cdot \frac{acc(q,D) \cdot (1+k_1)}{K + acc(q,D)} \\
acc(q,D) &= \sum_{q \in I} \frac{|I \cap Q|^\lambda}{(p_r - p_\ell)^\gamma},
\end{aligned}
\tag{8}
$$

where K is the same BM25 parameter as in Equation 2, and λ and γ are tuning parameters that are set on a per-collection basis. Song et al. show significant improvements relative to their baselines, and additional gains are made by Svore et al. [31] using features generated from external data sources.

The "window" statistics used in MRF [23] are a little different from these optimal intervals. The distance constraint must be specified, otherwise the computation degrades into a ranked Boolean query [8]. Consider a subquery $Q' = \{england, ordain\}$ for the same example document. If there is no distance constraint, the first match is $[0\ldots25]$, but if the default Indri settings are used, which is $4 \cdot |Q'|$ [23], the result will then be $[18\ldots25]$. As discussed above, a matched interval is an instance of a clique defined in the MRF.

The FDM approach considers all possible dependencies for all query terms. To make sure all of the clique sets are considered, the model scores $2^{|Q|} - |Q| - 1$ unordered window subqueries, and $|Q| \cdot (|Q| - 1)/2$ ordered window subqueries. Consider the feature function of an unordered window match as an example. If $\#uw(Q')$ is the set of matched intervals of a subquery Q', then the feature function is defined as:

$$LM\text{-}Score(\#uw(Q'), D) = \log \left(\frac{\mu \cdot f_{uw,\mathcal{C}}/|\mathcal{C}| + f_{uw,D}}{\mu + |D|} \right), \quad (9)$$

where $f_{uw,\mathcal{C}}$ is the number of matching unordered windows in the whole collection, and $f_{uw,D}$ is the within-document frequency of the unordered window. Other window statistics are calculated similarly, using the LMDS scoring regime as a feature function. Once all components have been computed, they are combined.

This model is still considered to be one of the best known higher-ordered proximity models, and the experimental results of Huston and Croft [14] on the TREC8 Robust04 Task and on GOV2 show that significant gains are possible compared to lower-order computations. Although a limited window size is applied in the scoring process, for simplicity this form of FDM actually omits the differences between cliques in the same clique set. Whilst effective, this model is also expensive to compute for two reasons: (i) a large number of subqueries must be enumerated (exponential in $|Q|$); and (ii) the need for global proximity statistics mandates a two-pass retrieval process. Macdonald et al. [20] observe that one way to avoid computing the global statistics is to use a constant, as is done in the Ivory System[1]. However, it is unclear how best to tune this value, and it may be sensitive to the collection being used. An alternative is to precompute and store the global statistics at indexing time, but enumerating all possible subqueries is still costly. Huston et al. [15] show that even considering only N-grams can be expensive. A possible trade-off is to consider an approximated scoring mechanism instead of an exact one, as is done by Elsayed et al. [11]. However, Elsayed et al. only consider the SDM model, in which only subqueries with adjacent term pairs are considered.

Positional Models The final class of models discussed here utilize the position information of terms in a document [19, 36]. These models focus on finding propagation functions to model position information of terms. For example, the Positional Language Model [19] generates all possible position propagations of the query terms; a computation that is costly, especially for long queries and large collections. Huston and Croft [14] give a detailed comparison of positional models; their results suggest that, although WSDM is best when averaged across all queries tested, the FDM model could still be improved with more time and effort.

Passage Retrieval Instead of applying the ranking mechanism at the document level, it is also possible to partition the document into

[1] http://lintool.github.io/Ivory/index.html

fixed-length overlapping or non-overlapping passages, and score these smaller pieces. Either an entire document, or a single passage can then be returned to the user [16]. Window-based methods can be implemented and represented using proximity operators [7], but differ from what we describe here. First, a fixed length passage can be generated dynamically by identifying a starting point based on one of the query terms, and computing a similarity score over the remainder of the extent, which does not necessarily contain all of the query terms; in contrast, the proximity features described in this work are extracted using a window capturing each subquery. And second, proximity-based models of the kind we consider here score at the document level, while passage retrieval uses passage-level statistics, including, for example, passage-level TF values.

3. A NEW APPROACH

We now describe a new form of high-order proximity computation that also does not require global statistics.

Intervals We use the definition of intervals originally proposed by Clarke et al. [9], but employ non-overlapping intervals as suggested by Song et al. [30]. That is, the next candidate interval of the current subquery must start at a position beyond the right end of the previous optimal interval. We also model term dependencies using the MRF framework, so that non-overlapping optimal intervals are still instances of the corresponding cliques. To determine the dependencies, we enumerate all possible matches for all subqueries, as is done for FDM, and the same span can be repeatedly used and scored differently according to the matching subquery, rather than just being included once.

Consider the sample document again, and the two subqueries: $Q_0 = \{woman, england\}$ and $Q_1 = \{woman, ordained, england\}$. According to the interval definition, the two sets of intervals are:

$$\mathcal{I}(Q_0) = \{[0\ldots5], [18\ldots51], [65\ldots67]\} \text{ and}$$
$$\mathcal{I}(Q_1) = \{[18\ldots53], [65\ldots68]\}.$$

The two sets may contain overlapping intervals. In the example, $[65\ldots67] \in \mathcal{I}(Q_0)$ is dominated by the interval $[65\ldots68] \in \mathcal{I}(Q_1)$. In the MRF framework, the smaller interval is not dropped, since it arises from a different subquery. The interval-finding process is iterated until the positions for all query terms are exhausted.

Scoring Intervals Each extracted interval is then scored using a feature function. In our case, we define the function in such a way that an interval will be scored more highly if it:

- captures more query terms over a shorter distance;
- captures more important terms; and
- is not bounded by common terms.

The first of these relationships is easiest to motivate, and has been widely applied in previous proximity ranking models. For example, in MRF models, only windows of up to some maximum length are considered. The second relationship is used to distinguish different subqueries. A complex weighting assignment process can be used to implement this effect, such as training with external resources, the approach used in WSDM. We prefer a more straightforward option, and use the IDF weightings of the terms. The third relationship relates to the interval instances that match a single subquery. In this case, we use the boundary term to determine whether the current matching is an imprecise representation of the current subquery, because when the LHS or RHS term is a common one, the interval is less representative than ones bounded by less-common terms. As a concrete example, consider the interval statistics for another subquery: $\mathcal{I}(woman, of, england) =$

$\{[0\ldots17],[18\ldots64]\}$. Both intervals are right bounded by the term "of", which is a common term. Although both of these intervals are valid candidates for this subquery, if the document also contained a valid interval such as "woman of england" that had the "of" in the middle, then all other things being equal, that third one should be favored. Indeed, intervals in $\mathcal{I}$(woman, of, england) have much the same effect as intervals in $\mathcal{I}$(woman, england) when "of" is one of the two endpoints.

To embody these three relationships, we suggest that candidate interval $I[p_\ell\ldots p_r]$ of a subquery Q' be scored as:

$$Score(I, D) = w_\ell^{(2)} \cdot w_r^{(2)} \cdot (p_r - p_\ell + 1)^{-2} \qquad (10)$$

where $w_\ell^{(2)}$ and $w_r^{(2)}$ are the IDF weights of the interval's two boundary terms, p_ℓ and p_r are the positions of those boundaries, and $w_q^{(2)}$ is the IDF weight of a term that is within the interval. The $w_r \cdot w_\ell$ component discounts intervals that are bounded by common terms (the third relationship), and borrowing from Büttcher et al. [6], we use $(p_r - p_\ell + 1)^{-2}$ to discount for distance. In addition, rather than count the number of query terms in the subquery, we use $\min\{w_q, 1.0\}$ to down-weight subqueries that consist of low weighted terms, thereby also incorporating the second relationship; an adjustment that is motivated at the level of intervals, but for convenience is included as a component of Equation 11. This factor is computed automatically during query processing, and does not require additional parameter tuning.

Combining Interval Scores Trotman et al. [34] observe that while there is no single ranking function that is consistently better than the others, the BM25 variants generally achieve good performance. Let $Score(Q', D)$ be the score of set of intervals $\mathcal{I}$ that match a subquery Q'. For our purposes the score for those intervals is defined in a BM25-like way as:

$$Score(Q', D) = \frac{\sum_{I \in \mathcal{I}} Score(I, D) \cdot (1 + k_1)}{\sum_{I \in \mathcal{I}} Score(I, D) + K'}$$
$$K' = K \cdot \left(\sum_{q \in Q'} \min\{w_q^{(2)}, 1.0\} \right)^2 , \qquad (11)$$

where K is the BM25 parameter used in Equation 2. As noted earlier, one of the reasons that FDM is expensive is because it uses collection-based frequencies, and hence two passes through the index. To avoid that cost, we refrain from any use of global higher-order counts in Equation 11.

We also include ordered phrase relationships in our overall formulation, even though phrases can sometimes degrade retrieval effectiveness. Let $\mathcal{Q}$ be the subquery set, and $\mathcal{Q}' \subset \mathcal{Q}$ be the set of sequentially dependent subqueries, that is, subsets of the query Q containing two or more terms in which term order is preserved relative to Q. We combine all of these features in the usual weighted manner, using the BM25 derived potentials in MRF, and obtain as a result our proposed method:

$$Score(Q, D) = (1 - \lambda) \cdot BM\text{-}Score(Q, D)$$
$$+ \lambda \cdot \sum_{Q' \in \mathcal{Q}'} Score(Q', D)$$
$$+ \lambda \cdot \sum_{Q' \in \mathcal{Q}} Score(Q', D) , \qquad (12)$$

that is, $(1 - \lambda)$ times the FI score, plus λ times the combined phrase score (over $Q' \in \mathcal{Q}'$) plus proximity score (also over $Q' \in \mathcal{Q}$).

Equation 12 makes it clear that Lkp – the name we give to this approach – captures both independent relationships as well as se-

Collection	N	$|\mathcal{C}|$	Queries	
			T-query	U-query
TREC8	0.5 M	253.4 M	250	1,933
GOV2	25.2 M	23,451.8 M	150	1,496
ClueWeb09B	50.1 M	40,416.4 M	3×50	–

Table 1: Test collections used, where N is the number of documents, and $|\mathcal{C}|$ is the total number of terms. The two "Queries" columns list the number of queries for each collection, with "T" denoting TREC title queries, and "U" denoting user queries [2].

quential and full dependencies among query terms, both of which may improve query effectiveness; and in doing so, echoes the factors employed in FDM. In this initial model the proximity statistics required will still grow rapidly relative to the query length, and lead to significant cost. However, global weightings are only required for unigram terms, which makes this model more amenable to further efficiency optimizations, since individual term weightings are stored in the inverted index. Moreover, our model benefits from optimal intervals, and, as described, does not require that a distance constraint be added as a further parameter to be tuned and set.

Variants Interval lengths can also be restricted if desired, with no impact on efficiency. Moreover, since our model is a variant of the original MRF model, if only bigram subqueries are considered, it reduces to a bigram model. Hence, three versions are proposed:

- Lkp: as described by Equations 10, 11, and 12;
- Lkfp: as for Lkp, but with intervals restricted to a maximum distance, set as $4 \cdot |Q'|$, as for FDM; and
- L2p: as for Lkp, but considering bigrams only, that is, pairs of words that are adjacent in the query.

4. EXPERIMENTS

We now describe the results of experiments on the effectiveness and efficiency of these three new similarity formulations.

Experimental Setup We use the TREC8, GOV2, and ClueWeb09-Category-B collections in our experiments, always in non-stopped forms, since proximity and phrase-based models can use combinations of stopwords to improve overall effectiveness for some queries (consider the query "the who" for example). Indexing is carried out using Indri[2], with a Krovetz stemmer. Two broad types of query sets are used. The primary resources are the title queries of the Robust Task 2004 (R04, with 250 queries in total), the Terabyte Task from 2004 to 2006 (TB04–TB06, with 150 queries in total), and the three ClueWeb Adhoc Tasks from 2010 to 2012 (C10–C12, with 50 queries each). As a secondary resource, we augment these with the user-generated query variants collected by Bailey et al. [2] in connection with the Robust03 and Terabyte04 Tasks, denoted here as R03-U and TB04-U. Table 1 summarizes the three document collections and seven query sets used; and Figure 1 summarizes the lengths of the five TREC-title query sets.

The top 1,000 documents are identified for each query in all effectiveness measurements. The TREC8 and GOV2 results are reported using two relatively deep metrics, average precision (AP) and rank-biased precision (RBP@0.95), in both cases based the full run and all available judgments. The three ClueWeb collections have shallow judgments, and hence are scored using expected reciprocal rank to depth 20 (ERR@20) and a more top-weighted

[2] http://www.lemurproject.org/indri/

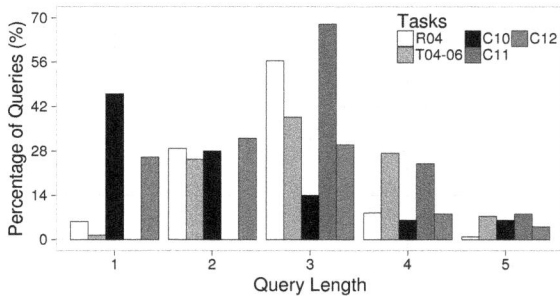

Figure 1: TREC title query lengths for five query sets: Robust04 (a subset of Topics 301–700), Terabyte04–06 (Topics 701–850), ClueWeb 2010 (Topics 51–100), ClueWeb 2011 (Topics 101–150), and ClueWeb 2012 (Topics 151–200).

Models	Type	Global lvl.	Params.
BM25$^{(1)}$	BM25	term	$k_1 = 0.9$, $b = 0.4$
BM25$^{(2)}$	BM25	term	$k_1 = 0.9$, $b = 0.3$
LMDS	LM	term	$\mu = 2500$
SDM	LM-B	bigram	$\lambda_o = 0.15$, $\lambda_u = 0.05$
FDM	LM-N	n-gram	$\lambda_o = 0.1$, $\lambda_u = 0.1$
BCTP	BM25-B	term	–
L2p	BM25-B	term	$\lambda = 0.4$
Lkp	BM25-N	term	$\lambda = 0.4$
L$k$fp	BM25-N	term	$\lambda = 0.4$

Table 2: Models used in experiments. "Type" indicates the family origin of the method, with suffix "B" denoting a bigram model, and "N" a higher-order proximity model. Column "Global lvl" indicates the highest level that global statistics are used; and "Params" lists the parameters, with bag-of-words parameters re-used in the proximity models and not listed a second time. For FDM and SDM we use the recommended configurations in the original paper, and for BM25 we use the settings recommended by Trotman et al. [34]. The parameters for the three new models were trained using the Robust04 query set and the TREC8 collection.

rank-biased precision (RBP@0.8), again based on the full run and all available judgments. Of these three metrics, ERR@20 is computed using graded relevance, with the maximum gain set according to the corresponding task; RBP and AP are both computed using binarized judgments. Experiments were performed on an Intel Xeon E5 CPU, 256 GB RAM, and RHEL-v6.3 Linux, implemented in C++, and compiled using GCC 4.8.1 with –O2 optimization.

Baselines The TREC title queries are used as effectiveness baselines. We use BM25 with Robertson-Walker $w^{(2)}$ IDF weighting as the baseline FI model, and also list the effectiveness scores for Indri's built-in version of Okapi BM25, which uses Robertson-Spärck Jones IDF weighting $w^{(1)}$. Methods from the language modeling family are also included; these results are generated using Indri and the default configurations. To validate the experiments of Huston and Croft [14], we also include the BCTP bigram model as a baseline. Parameters for these reference systems are listed in Table 2.

New Proximity Methods The Lkp method described in Equations 10, 11, and 12 is included in Table 2, as are the L$k$fp variant that employs a distance constraint (set to match the MRF models, that is, $4 \cdot |Q'|$), and the L2p method, which makes use of bigrams

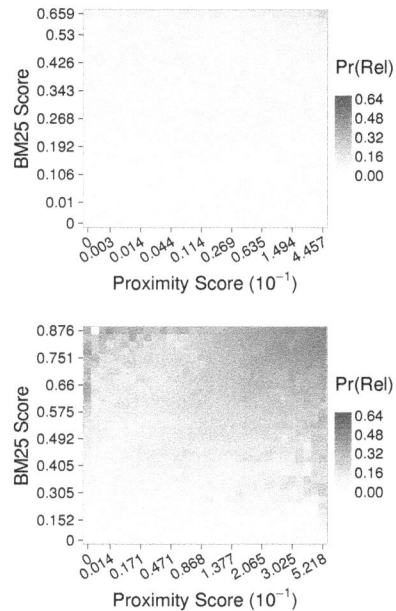

Figure 2: The relationship between BM25$^{(2)}$ scores and proximity scores. The top plot uses the R03 queries and the judged documents from the TREC8 collection; the lower plot the TB04 queries and the GOV2 collection. TREC title queries were used as well as the user queries. Measured document relevance in each of $1024 = 32^2$ bins is plotted, with blue cells having insufficient data to form estimates.

only. Parameters for the three new methods were trained using the Robust04 queries on TREC8 collection, and then applied to the other collections without further adjustment.

Evidence for Proximity Our first experiment tests the hypothesis stated in Section 2: that the additional proximity features included in Lkp and L$k$fp are not captured by the simpler bag-of-words models. Taking *P-Score*(Q, D) to be the measured proximity score, and *FI-Score*(Q, D) as the score of any bag-of-words model, we wish to know, for two documents D_0 and D_1 that have (approximately) equal scores according to *FI-Score*$()$, if there is a residual effect that reveals a correlation between their *P-Score*$()$ scores and the probability of being relevant.

We use the TREC title queries with more than one query term, together with R03-U and TB04-U in this experiment. Queries are treated as being independent even if derived from the same topic. On average, there are $1,512$ judged documents per topic for R03, of which an average of 78.15 are relevant. That is, across the judged documents the average probability of relevance is 5.04%. For the GOV2 TB04 task there are an average of $1,185$ judged documents per topic and 216.7 relevant, giving a background relevance probability of 18.73%. The experimental process carried out was:

(1) For each of the queries Q in the query set, and each judged document D, calculate *BM-Score*(Q, D) and *P-Score*(Q, D).

(2) Divide each of *P-Score*(Q, D) and *BM-Score*(Q, D) into 32 equal ranges after normalizing the score ranges to $[0, 1]$ on a per-query basis, giving 1024 bins in total.

(3) For each bin $B_{i,j}$, estimate $\Pr(D = 1 \mid D \in B_{i,j})$ using the relevance judgment associated with each document placed in to

	Robust04		GOV2 (TB04–06)	
	AP	RBP@0.95	AP	RBP@0.95
BM25[(1)]	0.254	0.318	0.293	0.489
BM25[(2)]	0.256	0.320	0.294	0.491
LMDS	0.248	0.308	0.290	0.474
SDM	0.262	0.322	0.319	0.506
FDM	0.264	0.322	**0.325**	0.512
BCTP	0.262	0.324	0.312	0.514
L2p	0.267	0.330[†]	0.320	**0.517**
Lkp	0.269	0.331[†]	0.321	0.515
L$k$fp	**0.270[†]**	**0.332[†]**	0.324	0.516
BestTrecRun	0.359	0.397	0.407	0.595

Table 3: Effectiveness of models on TREC8 and GOV2, using two metrics. Statistical tests were performed, with † indicating significance relative to FDM at $p = 0.05$. Note that while the TREC8/R04 combination was also used as training to set the parameter λ used in Lkp, L$k$fp, and L2p (Table 2), the generated scores are relatively insensitive to the value used.

that bin by any of the queries, possibly counting each document multiple times.

Results for the BM25[(2)] model are plotted in Figure 2, with blue cells indicating bins with fewer than 100 documents, for which it would be misleading to estimate relevance probabilities; and with dark cells indicating regions of high probability. Relevant documents receive zero scores if none of the query terms appear in them, making the first bin bigger than the others.

As expected, the higher the BM25[(2)] score, the higher the probability of relevance, and likewise for proximity scores. (These two claims can be confirmed by projecting the bin values to the vertical and horizontal axes respectively; in the interests of space we do not show these additional graphs.) If either of these factors were sufficient in their own right to predict relevance, with no influence from the other, the patterns of shade in the graphs would be parallel to the corresponding axis. In fact, the darkest area in both of the heatmaps is located in the upper-right corner, suggesting that a combination of BM25[(2)] and proximity score is a stronger indication of relevance than either of proximity alone. We also carried out the same process using LMDS as the bag-of-words model, with a similar pattern of results. Note that the lighter shades for R03 compared to TB04 are due to the overall lower background probability.

Effectiveness on TREC8 and GOV2 Table 3 gives effectiveness scores for the models listed in Table 2, using the TREC8 and GOV2 data, and queries R04 and TB04–TB06 respectively, with no stopping, and scoring based on runs of 1,000 returned documents. No RBP residuals (the score range allocated to unjudged documents) are shown in this table; but across the experiments listed, they were consistently around 0.03, because of the deep judgments available for these collections. The new L2p and Lkp methods are both better than the baseline BM25[(2)] model; the difference is significant at $p < 0.05$ when a two tailed t-test is performed, for both the AP and RBP@0.95 metrics. The higher-order proximity models also have a slight advantage compared to the bigram models, a relationship that echoes that between SDM and FDM. When adding the additional distance constraint on Lkp to compute L$k$fp, observed effectiveness again increases very slightly. No training was undertaken in this regard, and further exploration may lead to a heuristic that obtains additional improvement. Huston and Croft [14] report

an AP score of 0.329 on GOV2 for their WSDM-Int method, suggesting that applying additional resources to reweight subqueries may further improve performance.

Proximity improves performance on some queries and degrades it on others. The top row of graphs in Figure 3 plots the percentage change of score for Lkp compared to BM25[(2)], with queries grouped by the extent of the change in AP score measured on that query. All four of the methods plotted generate more queries with gains than there are queries with losses, and hence give rise to overall improved performance. The three graphs in the lower half of Figure 3 capture a similar comparison, but this time relative to the SDM scores. The situation with regard to improvement is less clear cut for BCTP in the first two panes, reflecting the overall rates listed in Table 3, but in the third pane, for the C10–12, all four of the methods plotted gain an advantage.

Despite the overall benefit of proximity-based methods, up to a third of queries give worse effectiveness using Lkp than they do using the BM25[(2)] bag-of-words approach. Table 4 lists the eight most degraded queries when BM25[(2)] is compared to Lkp, with degradation measured by percentage loss in AP. While there is no obvious common element to these queries, if one could be identified based on index-resident information (such as IDF values), then a hybrid system that "dialed down" the value of λ (Equation 12) for certain queries could, potentially, be better than both BM25[(2)] and Lkp. This is an area for future investigation.

Effectiveness on ClueWeb09B Table 5 lists retrieval effectiveness outcomes using the three ClueWeb query sets C10, C11, and C12; and the two rightmost plots in Figure 3 show the query improvement breakdown relative to BM25[(2)] and to SDM, aggregated across the three same three query sets. The BM25 baseline performs very well on the first of the three set of queries when measured using ERR, and BCTP works well on the other two sets when measured using RBP. Part of the explanation for the difference compared to the R04 and TB04–06 outcomes is that these queries contain more common words; the ClueWeb queries are also shorter overall, as is illustrated in Figure 1. Note also the relatively high RBP residuals observed for C12 in particular; that these are comparable in magnitude with the actual RBP scores is a warning that interpretation of these results needs to be undertaken with caution.

Table 6 lists the most badly affected queries when BM25[(2)] is compared to Lkp, now with "affected" determined by the percentage decrease in ERR. As with Table 4, there is no simple explanation as to why these queries suffer from the inclusion of proximity factors in the scoring regime. Note also – again, in common with Table 4 – that the FDM approach handles these queries just as poorly, and that the increased RBP residuals indicate that some of the loss of effectiveness may be a consequence of increased numbers of unjudged documents being retrieved compared to the BM25[(2)] runs. Were these documents to be judged, some of them might be relevant, lifting the Lkp scores.

Retrieval Cost of Proximity Models Table 7 lists per-document retrieval times. To compute these numbers, the time taken to compute the top 1,000 answers for a query was measured, and then divided by the number of documents scored in order to obtain a per-document cost. In all of these methods the number of documents scored is taken to be the union of the query terms' postings lists. Repeating that process across all of the queries in a collection allowed median, mean, and maximum values to be computed. Intervals for the L2p, Lkp, and L$k$fp methods were computed using the method described by Lu et al. [18].

The BM25 implementation is the fastest – it works solely with document-level statistics, and doesn't access term positional infor-

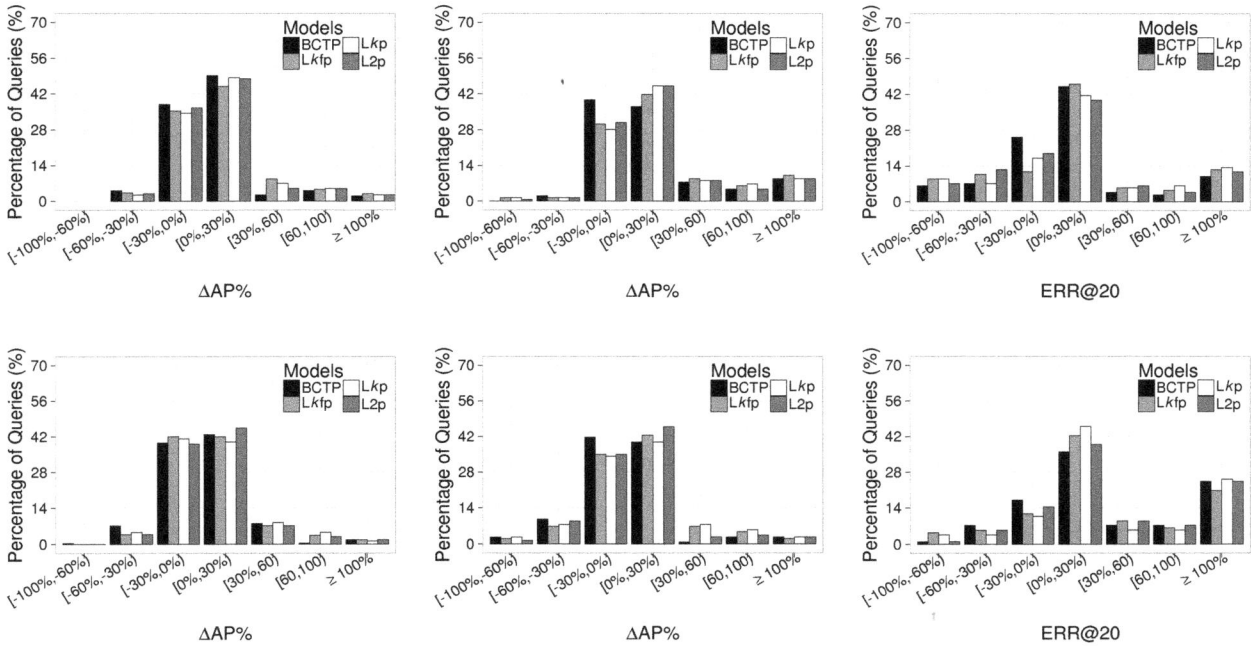

Figure 3: The first row shows the number of queries that fall into each of a set of percentage-difference buckets for each of Lkp, L$k$fp, L2p and BCTP, relative to the BM25 baseline run; and the second row shows the same computation carried out relative to SDM. The two leftmost plots are for R04 measured using AP; the two middle plots are for TB04 also measured using AP; and the two right-most plots are for C10-12 measured using ERR@20. On all three collections, we only consider queries with more than one term. The total number of queries used in the comparisons are 238, 147, and 112, respectively across the three columns.

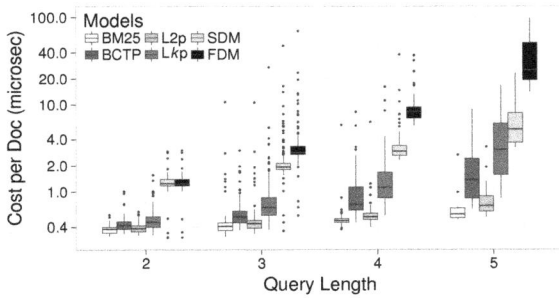

Figure 4: Per-document retrieval costs in microseconds, grouped by query length, with a logarithmic scale on the vertical axis. The measured query processing times are aggregated across all of the queries of lengths 2 to 5 in TREC title queries: R04, TB04–06, and C10–12. Unstopped indexes are used, and no query stopping.

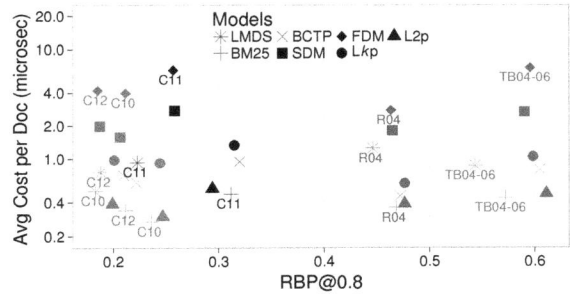

Figure 5: Trade-off graph for all retrieval models, across all collections, as indicated by the different colors. Time is measured as the mean cost per document scored in microseconds, and effectiveness using RBP@0.8.

mation. The L2p method is close behind, with times that are better than or the same as LMDS, and for the most part better than SDM. The Lkp approach is third overall in terms of speed, and it also executes more quickly than does SDM. As expected, FDM is slow – the cost of gathering the term statistics in a first pass is a substantial burden. The high cost of computing large numbers of dependencies on long queries shows in the very high maximum times associated with FDM, and to a lesser extent, Lkp. Note that the measurement methodology favors SDM and FDM, since every document in which any query term appears is assumed to be scored, amortizing the cost of the first processing pass over a large

number of evaluations. A more likely usage scenario would be to compute proximity statistics during a second phase, re-scoring a small subset of the documents that have been extracted using an efficient early stage candidate identification process. In this scenario the per-document costs shown in Table 7 remain accurate for the new methods, but are under-estimates for the SDM and FDM approaches. Dynamic pruning processes such as WAND, which reduce the number of documents scored, will have a similar effect.

Two further graphs conclude our presentation. Figure 4 plots per-document querying costs as a function of query length, and shows that SDM and FDM costs grow dramatically on long queries, and that L2p is only a little slower than BM25, at all query lengths.

Qid	Query	BM25$^{(2)}$		Lkp		Lkp	FDM
		AP	RBP@0.95	AP	RBP@0.95	ΔAP%	ΔAP%
TB04-749	puerto rico state	0.165	0.451 + 0.05	0.037	0.070 + 0.01	−78%	−54%
TB04-720	federal welfare reform	0.266	0.582 + 0.05	0.080	0.223 + 0.01	−70%	−46%
R04-628	us invasion of panama	0.249	0.277 + 0.00	0.109	0.124 + 0.00	−56%	−39%
R04-381	alternative medicine	0.058	0.102 + 0.00	0.027	0.083 + 0.00	−54%	−69%
TB06-832	labor union activity	0.159	0.581 + 0.02	0.084	0.431 + 0.19	−47%	−17%
R04-389	illegal technology transfer	0.026	0.209 + 0.00	0.014	0.156 + 0.02	−45%	−50%
R04-437	deregulation gas electric	0.003	0.018 + 0.02	0.002	0.002 + 0.06	−41%	−8%
TB05-799	animals in alzheimer s research	0.312	0.352 + 0.01	0.184	0.324 + 0.05	−41%	−68%

Table 4: The eight queries for which Lkp suffers the greatest degradation compared to BM25$^{(2)}$ on the R04 and TB04–06 query sets, measured using percentage difference in AP score. The final column shows the degradation of FDM relative to BM25$^{(2)}$.

	C10		C11		C12	
	ERR@20	RBP@0.8	ERR@20	RBP@0.8	ERR@20	RBP@0.8
BM25$^{(1)}$	0.112	0.230 + 0.10	0.130	0.241 + 0.13	0.125	0.200 + 0.18
BM25$^{(2)}$	**0.121**	0.236 + 0.02	0.166	0.312 + 0.02†	0.144	**0.212 + 0.12**
LMDS	0.096	0.183 + 0.03	0.109	0.223 + 0.05	0.128	0.188 + 0.14
SDM	0.093	0.207 + 0.02	0.145	0.258 + 0.03	0.113	0.188 + 0.12
FDM	0.096	0.212 + 0.03	0.147	0.257 + 0.03	0.130	0.188 + 0.12
BCTP	0.105	0.222 + 0.02	0.162	**0.320 + 0.02**†	0.155	0.210 + 0.10
L2p	0.117†	**0.247 + 0.03**†	0.150	0.294 + 0.02	0.157	0.199 + 0.12
Lkp	0.114†	0.244 + 0.04	**0.173**	0.315 + 0.04†	0.164	0.201 + 0.13
L$k$fp	0.114†	0.237 + 0.03	0.158	0.308 + 0.05†	**0.166**	0.200 + 0.13
BestTrecRun	0.226	0.415 + 0.00	0.223	0.361 + 0.00	0.290	0.362 + 0.00

Table 5: Evaluation results of different models on ClueWeb09B, using queries C10, C11, and C12, scored using ERR to depth 20 and RBP@0.8 using all available information. Statistical tests were performed, with $\dagger$ indicating significance relative to FDM at $p = 0.05$.

Finally, Figure 5 plots methods/collections in a trade-off graph in which the relationship between retrieval effectiveness and retrieval cost can be seen clearly. Each collection is colored differently, and each shape corresponds to a retrieval model. The benefits of our Lkp (the solid circles) and L2p (the solid triangles) methods then become apparent – they provide high levels of retrieval effectiveness at speeds comparable to those attained by the bag-of-words BM25 mechanism.

5. CONCLUSION

We have described a new way of incorporating proximity features into a BM25-like retrieval mechanism. The result compares favorably with FDM in terms of retrieval effectiveness, but executes substantially faster. In addition, it does not require global statistics, and hence can be applied in any pass of the retrieval process, without becoming proportionately more expensive. When the same scoring computation is restricted to query bigrams, speed is close to that of the simpler bag-of-words BM25 approach. It is worth noting that additional efficiency can be achieved by indexing some or all higher order term dependencies. This is an interesting problem in its own right, and several prior studies have proposed time-space trade-offs. Our current approach employs no additional space beyond the inclusion of positional information; how to strategically employ further index space is an area for future work.

Acknowledgment This work was supported by the Australian Research Council's *Discovery Projects* Scheme (DP140101587 and DP140103256). Shane Culpepper is the recipient of an Australian Research Council DECRA Research Fellowship (DE140100275).

References

[1] G. Amati. *Probability models for information retrieval based on divergence from randomness.* PhD thesis, University of Glasgow, 2003.

[2] P. Bailey, A. Moffat, F. Scholer, and P. Thomas. User variability and IR system evaluation. In *Proc. SIGIR*, pages 625–634, 2015.

[3] M. Bendersky and W. B. Croft. Modeling higher-order term dependencies in information retrieval using query hypergraphs. In *Proc. SIGIR*, pages 941–950, 2012.

[4] M. Bendersky, D. Metzler, and W. B. Croft. Parameterized concept weighting in verbose queries. In *Proc. SIGIR*, pages 605–614, 2011.

[5] A. Broschart and R. Schenkel. High-performance processing of text queries with tunable pruned term and term pair indexes. *ACM Trans. Inf. Sys.*, 30(1):1–32, 2012.

[6] S. Büttcher, C. L. A. Clarke, and B. Lushman. Term proximity scoring for ad-hoc retrieval on very large text collections. In *Proc. SIGIR*, pages 621–622, 2006.

[7] J. P. Callan. Passage-level evidence in document retrieval. In *Proc. SIGIR*, pages 302–310, 1994.

[8] J. P. Callan, W. B. Croft, and S. M. Harding. The INQUERY retrieval system. In *Proc. DEXA*, pages 78–83, 1992.

[9] C. L. A. Clarke, G. V. Cormack, and E. A. Tudhope. Relevance ranking for one to three term queries. *Inf. Proc. & Man.*, 36(2): 291–311, 2000.

[10] O. de Kretser and A. Moffat. Effective document presentation with a locality-based similarity heuristic. In *Proc. SIGIR*, pages 113–120, 1999.

[11] T. Elsayed, J. Lin, and D. Metzler. When close enough is good enough: Approximate positional indexes for efficient ranked retrieval. In *Proc. CIKM*, pages 1993–1996, 2011.

Qid	Query	BM25$^{(2)}$		Lkp		Lkp	FDM
		ERR@20	RBP@0.8	ERR@20	RBP@0.8	ΔERR@20%	ΔERR@20%
C11-150	tn highway patrol	0.034	0.022 + 0.00	0.000	0.000 + 0.00	−100%	−100%
C12-161	furniture for small spaces	0.003	0.004 + 0.06	0.000	0.000 + 0.26	−100%	−100%
C12-169	battles in the civil war	0.069	0.044 + 0.05	0.000	0.001 + 0.26	−100%	−86%
C11-120	tv on computer	0.032	0.076 + 0.31	0.000	0.000 + 0.62	−100%	−74%
C12-184	civil right movement	0.165	0.188 + 0.50	0.000	0.000 + 0.68	−100%	−25%
C11-115	pacific northwest laboratory	0.063	0.160 + 0.00	0.010	0.017 + 0.08	−83%	−80%
C11-106	universal animal cuts reviews	0.048	0.134 + 0.00	0.010	0.015 + 0.02	−80%	−68%
C11-145	vines for shade	0.239	0.405 + 0.00	0.052	0.078 + 0.02	−78%	−83%

Table 6: The eight queries for which Lkp suffers the greatest degradation compared to BM25$^{(2)}$ on the C10, C11, and C12 query sets, measured using percentage difference in ERR score. The final column shows the degradation of FDM relative to BM25$^{(2)}$.

	R04			TB04–TB06			C10			C11			C12		
	Med.	Avg.	Max.	Med.	Avg.	Max.	Med.	Avg.	Max.	Med.	Avg.	Max.	Med.	Avg.	Max.
BM25	**0.37**	**0.36**	**0.53**	**0.44**	**0.44**	**0.67**	**0.40**	**0.26**	**0.67**	**0.46**	**0.48**	**0.65**	**0.42**	**0.34**	**0.60**
LMDS	0.78	1.25	1.23	0.85	0.87	1.36	0.67	0.48	1.35	0.86	0.93	1.25	0.70	0.76	6.97
BCTP	0.43	0.46	1.42	0.60	0.80	6.90	0.43	0.61	8.89	0.66	0.95	8.27	0.48	0.71	7.24
SDM	1.81	1.81	9.63	2.37	2.68	9.12	1.17	1.58	16.65	2.24	2.76	14.69	1.39	1.99	14.16
FDM	2.67	2.77	15.48	3.76	6.84	74.84	1.18	3.98	73.28	3.43	6.50	32.59	1.42	4.21	59.60
L2p	0.39	0.39	0.63	0.47	0.48	0.95	0.43	0.30	1.32	0.50	0.54	1.24	0.45	0.39	1.17
Lkp	0.54	0.60	2.25	0.80	1.05	9.31	0.45	0.92	12.95	0.88	1.34	11.17	0.68	0.98	10.20

Table 7: Retrieval cost in microseconds per document scored, using non-stopped indexes. In the C10 results, Query 70 is dropped because of its extreme computation cost ("to be or not to be").

[12] D. Hawking and P. Thistlewaite. Proximity operators: So near and yet so far. In *Proc. TREC*, pages 131–143, 1995.

[13] B. He, J. X. Huang, and X. Zhou. Modeling term proximity for probabilistic information retrieval models. *J. of Information Sciences*, 181(14):3017–3031, 2011.

[14] S. Huston and W. B. Croft. A comparison of retrieval models using term dependencies. In *Proc. CIKM*, pages 111–120, 2014.

[15] S. Huston, J. S. Culpepper, and W. B. Croft. Indexing word sequences for ranked retrieval. *ACM Trans. Inf. Sys.*, 32(1):3, 2014.

[16] M. Kaszkiel and J. Zobel. Effective ranking with arbitrary passages. *J. Amer. Soc. Inf. Sc. Tech.*, 52(4):344–364, 2001.

[17] L. Lee. IDF revisited: A simple new derivation within the Robertson-Spärck Jones probabilistic model. In *Proc. SIGIR*, pages 751–752, 2007.

[18] X. Lu, A. Moffat, and J. S. Culpepper. On the cost of extracting proximity features for term-dependency models. In *Proc. CIKM*, pages 293–302, 2015.

[19] Y. Lv and C. Zhai. Positional language models for information retrieval. In *Proc. SIGIR*, pages 299–306, 2009.

[20] C. Macdonald, I. Ounis, and N. Tonellotto. Upper-bound approximations for dynamic pruning. *ACM Trans. Inf. Sys.*, 29(4):17, 2011.

[21] D. Metzler. *Beyond Bags of Words: Effectively Modeling Dependence and Features in Information Retrieval*. PhD thesis, University of Massachusetts, Amherst, 2007.

[22] D. Metzler. Automatic feature selection in the Markov random field model for information retrieval. In *Proc. CIKM*, pages 253–262, 2007.

[23] D. Metzler and W. B. Croft. A Markov random field model for term dependencies. In *Proc. SIGIR*, pages 472–479, 2005.

[24] J. Peng, C. Macdonald, B. He, V. Plachouras, and I. Ounis. Incorporating term dependency in the DFR framework. In *Proc. SIGIR*, pages 843–844, 2007.

[25] J. M. Ponte and W. B. Croft. A language modeling approach to information retrieval. In *Proc. SIGIR*, pages 275–281, 1998.

[26] Y. Rasolofo and J. Savoy. Term proximity scoring for keyword-based retrieval systems. In *Proc. ECIR*, pages 207–218, 2003.

[27] S. E. Robertson. The Probabilistic Relevance Framework: BM25 and Beyond. *Found. Trends in Inf. Ret.*, 3(4):333–389, 2009.

[28] S. E. Robertson and K. Spärck Jones. Relevance weighting of search terms. *J. Amer. Soc. Inf. Sc.*, 27(3):129–146, 1976.

[29] S. E. Robertson, S. Walker, S. Jones, M. Hancock-Beaulieu, and M. Gatford. Okapi at TREC-3. In *Proc. TREC*, 1994.

[30] R. Song, M. J. Taylor, J.-R. Wen, H.-W. Hon, and Y. Yu. Viewing term proximity from a different perspective. In *Proc. ECIR*, pages 346–357, 2008.

[31] K. M. Svore, P. H. Kanani, and N. Khan. How good is a span of terms? Exploiting proximity to improve web retrieval. In *Proc. SIGIR*, pages 154–161, 2010.

[32] T. Tao and C. Zhai. An exploration of proximity measures in information retrieval. In *Proc. SIGIR*, pages 295–302, 2007.

[33] A. Trotman, X. Jia, and M. Crane. Towards an efficient and effective search engine. In *Proc. SIGIR 2012 Wrkshp. Open Source Inf. Retr.*, pages 40–47, 2012.

[34] A. Trotman, A. Puurula, and B. Burgess. Improvements to BM25 and language models examined. In *Proc. Aust. Doc. Comp. Symp.*, pages 58–65, 2014.

[35] C. Zhai. *Statistical Language Models for Information Retrieval*. Synthesis Lectures on Human Language Technologies. Morgan & Claypool, 2008.

[36] J. Zhao, J. Huang, and B. He. CRTER: Using cross terms to enhance probabilistic information retrieval. In *Proc. SIGIR*, pages 155–164, 2011.

[37] J. Zobel and A. Moffat. Inverted files for text search engines. *ACM Comp. Surv.*, 38(2):6.1–6.56, 2006.

PDF: A Probabilistic Data Fusion Framework for Retrieval and Ranking

Ashraf Bah
Department of Computer Sciences
University of Delaware
Newark, Delaware, USA
ashraf@udel.edu

Ben Carterette
Department of Computer Sciences
University of Delaware
Newark, Delaware, USA
carteret@udel.edu

ABSTRACT

Data fusion has been shown to be a simple and effective way to improve retrieval results. Most existing data fusion methods combine ranked lists from different retrieval functions for a single given query. But in many real search settings, the diversity of retrieval functions required to achieve good fusion performance is not available. Researchers are typically limited to a few variants on a scoring function used by the engine of their choice, with these variants often producing similar results due to being based on the same underlying term statistics.

This paper presents a framework for data fusion based on combining ranked lists from different queries that users *could have* entered for their information need. If we can identify a set of "possible queries" for an information need, and estimate probability distributions concerning the probability of generating those queries, the probability of retrieving certain documents for those queries, and the probability of documents being relevant to that information need, we have the potential to dramatically improve results over a baseline system given a single user query. Our framework is based on several component models that can be mixed and matched. We present several simple estimation methods for components. In order to demonstrate effectiveness, we present experimental results on 5 different datasets covering tasks such as ad-hoc search, novelty and diversity search, and search in the presence of implicit user feedback. Our results show strong performances for our method; it is competitive with state-of-the-art methods on the same datasets, and in some cases outperforms them.

CCS Concepts

•Information systems → Information retrieval; **Probabilistic retrieval models; Combination, fusion and federated search;** *Information retrieval diversity;*

Keywords

Retrieval Models; Probabilistic Data Fusion; Search over Sessions; Diversified Ranking

ICTIR '16, September 12-16, 2016, Newark, DE, USA

© 2016 ACM. ISBN 978-1-4503-4497-5/16/09. . . $15.00

DOI: http://dx.doi.org/10.1145/2970398.2970419

1. INTRODUCTION

The idea that retrieval could be improved by simply combining results from multiple different retrieval systems—a sort of "wisdom of the crowd" for retrieval systems—has long been attractive to IR researchers and practitioners. This idea produced much work in *data fusion* methodologies, which use different ways of combining retrieval scores from different ranking functions or different rankings of documents to produce a final ranking based on input from all available systems.

Interestingly, ideas from data fusion have found their way into novelty and diversity ranking as well. Novelty retrieval aims at reducing redundancy in search results, while diversity retrieval aims to handle query ambiguity. Many methods for novelty and diversity retrieval attempt to identify possible *intents* or *subtopics* of a query, find documents relevant to those, then combine them into a single ranked list. The difference from traditional data fusion methodologies is that the combination procedure attempts to account for possible redundancy.

In practice, users sometimes solve the novelty/diversity problems themselves by simply reformulating their query several times over a session of interactions. In those cases the user is the fusion algorithm, mentally keeping track of the relevant documents they've seen over the course of the session. In such cases the user is fusing results from different query expressions of the same information need from the same retrieval engine, rather than fusing results from different retrieval engines for the same query.

What if instead the system was able to use the user's historical interactions with it to anticipate the user's needs and produce more relevant documents faster? After all, the user described in the previous paragraph may have a perfect understanding of their information need, but cannot possibly understand the extent of the full corpus as well as the system can. The system could use information from the user and other similar users to generate queries to produce results that can be literally fused for the user.

In this paper, we propose a theoretical probabilistic framework inspired by such a data fusion approach in order to tackle the problems of diversity and novelty ranking, search over session, as well as ad-hoc ranking. We argue that if we can obtain a collection of "possible queries" for an information need, and compute the probability of retrievability of documents with respect to that query as well as the probability of relevance of documents, we can achieve greater effectiveness by ranking documents in decreasing order of the product of the two probabilities. We can thus fuse the rankings over the possible queries, and obtain a strong final ranking. Using our framework, we were able to achieve significant results that are competitive with, and in some cases outperform the state-of-the-art methods known in the literature, using TREC Web 2013 and 2014 [9, 8], NTCIR IMine 2014 [24] and TREC Session track 2013 and 2014 datasets [17, 18].

This paper is organized as follows. Section 2 presents related work on data fusion, diversity and novelty ranking, and search over sessions. In Section 3 we describe the theoretical framework for our fusion model. Section 4 describes our experimental environment; Section 5 presents our results. We conclude in Section 6

2. RELATED WORK

Diversity and novelty retrieval systems aim to provide rankings that account for not only document relevance, but also differences in users' intents as well as different aspects of the information need. At the same time, many search topics that lead users to reformulate their queries at least once— that is, that are the subject of longer search sessions—are broad and/or ambiguous in nature. These commonalities between search over session and diversity ranking suggest that we could tackle both problems using the same method if the method is devised to exploit the commonalities. In this section, we present the diversity and novelty retrieval task and some existing approaches in the literature. Then we describe session search task and some existing approaches that tackle it. Finally, we present some work related to data fusion in IR.

2.1 Diversity and novelty ranking

Suppose a user submits the query "windows" to a search engine. The user could have meant "windows operating system" or "windows in a wall," and thus the query term "windows" could be subject to several possible interpretations. This is an example of ambiguous query that underscores the importance of building systems that account for many possible user intents. Since different users may have different intents, there is a need to diversify search results. Queries that may lead to different intents/interpretations are commonly referred to as ambiguous queries and a search task that involves such a query is referred to as an extrinsic diversity task. On the other hand the same query term could have been an underspecified query meant to fetch information about "windows OS courses" or "windows OS customer support" or "windows OS common issues" or "windows OS documentation." Intrinsic diversity tasks concern such queries that are broad and thus cover many aspects of the same topic, and necessitate the use of novelty ranking for better results.

Many of the diversity ranking approaches are inspired by the MMR algorithm introduced by Carbonnell and Goldstein [5]. The fundamental idea of MMR is to optimize for a set of retrieved documents that is both relevant and "diverse" in the sense that it does not contain documents that are similar to one another. Differences in implementations lie in how similarities are computed: Carbonnell and Goldstein suggest using any similarity function such as cosine similarity. Zhai et al. advocate for modifying the Language modeling framework to incorporate a model of relevance and redundanc [35]. Other researchers utilized the correlation between documents as a measure of their similarity in the

pursuit of diversification and risk minimization in document ranking [33]. Carterette and Chandar use a set-based probabilistic model to maximize the likelihood of covering all the aspects [6]. Radlinski and Dumais exploited a commercial search engine to obtain aspects of queries, and proceeded to diversify the ranking using query-query reformulations [27]]. Santos et al. utilize a query-driven approach wherein they explicitly account for aspects by using sub-queries to represent a query. They then estimate the relevance of each retrieved document to every identified sub-query, and the importance of each sub-query [30].

2.2 Search over sessions

In many cases, users tend to provide one or more reformulations of their original query in order to satisfy their information need. The TREC Session track was created to investigate such use cases. The main goal of that track is to improve the ranking of a current query given information about the previous interactions (document Id, title, URL, snippets, clicked URLs and dwell time of previous queries) [17, 18]. The track provides test collections that contain this data.

Several approaches have been proposed. Zhang et al. proposed to tackle the problem using a relevance feedback model that takes advantage of query changes in a session [36]. In Zhang's work, when computing the relevance score between a current query and a document, terms' weights are increased or decreased depending on whether the term was added, retained or removed from previous queries in the session. In a similar approach [14], Guan et al. proposed to model sessions as Markov Decision Processes wherein the user agent's actions correspond to query changes, and the search agent's actions correspond to increasing or decreasing or maintaining term weights.

Raman et al. used related queries to diversify results while maintaining cohesion with the current query in order to satisfy the current query as well as future queries [28]. They did so using a two-level dynamic ranking where the user's interaction in the first level is used to infer her intent in order to provide a better ranking that includes second level rankings.

Additionally, query aggregation has been used by Guan who identified text nuggets deemed interesting in each query and merges them to form a structured query [13]. Notable approaches used by TREC participants include the work of Jiang et al. [15] in which the authors combined Sequential Dependence Model features in both current queries and previous queries in the session for one system, and combined that method with pseudo-relevance feedback for other systems. Another notable approach is the use of anchor texts for query expansion proposed by Kruschwitz et al. [19] and adopted by others.

2.3 Data fusion

Most important to the present work, much previous research has shown that combining the evidence of multiple query representations [4], ranking functions [12], or document representations [16] helps improve results in information retrieval. Three very well-known methods are CombSUM, CombWSUM, and CombMNZ [22]. CombSUM reranks documents based on their cumulative standardized scores over all input ranked lists; CombWSUM is similar but weights each score by a function of the estimated effectiveness of the system that generated it. CombMNZ is a variant that promotes documents retrieved by many systems by multiplying the CombSUM value by the number of non-zero similarity values among all input ranked lists [22]. CombCAT is another recent variant that puts even more weight on the number of systems that retrieved the given document; it ranks documents first by that value, then breaks ties by the sum of their retrieval scores [2].

One difficulty with many traditional fusion methods is the fact that scores from different retrieval methods are usually not comparable, and thus cannot simply be added together. While some fusion techniques do use the scores of the documents across the ranked lists [3], others use their ranks instead [11, 21], and some others use their probability of occurring in a predefined segment of the lists [20, 23]. Aslam and Montague [1] avoid the problem by proposing models based on Borda Count, Bayesian Count and Condorcet voting [25], all of which are rank-based, and show that both usually outperform the best input system and are competitive with, and often outperform, existing metasearch strategies.

In most cases, using data fusion in IR helps obtain good results. However, that positive impact depends on the quality of the input result lists [11, 32, 26, 34]. Thus an essential part of our work is dedicated to finding appropriate sources of data to be used as various query representations.

3. MODEL

Our proposed model is a probabilistic framework inspired by both the Probability Ranking Principle (PRP) of Robertson [29] and the idea of data fusion. It is based on obtaining a collection of "possible queries" for an information need, obtaining ranked lists for each of those queries, then fusing ranked results in different ways.

The traditional PRP says that the optimal ranking of documents is in decreasing order of their relevance to the user's information need. For a given user need expressed as a query q and a particular document D, the probability that D is relevant is expressed as $P(rel|q, D)$. In most classical IR settings, the query q is the only available evidence about the user's need.

Language modeling approaches estimate $P(rel|q, D)$ as the probability of sampling the query q from a language model computed from the document D and other evidence, that is, $P(rel|q, D) \approx P(q|D)$. In our framework, we suppose instead that q has been sampled from larger space of possible queries that a user might have chosen for their original information need. Let us denote this space $\mathcal{Q}$. Then we could modify the PRP to rank documents in decreasing order of $P(rel|\mathcal{Q}, D)$. If q is still the only available evidence about the user's need, then $P(rel|\mathcal{Q}, D) = P(rel|q, D)$; the PRP is unaffected. But if there is more evidence about the space of possible queries a user might have chosen, we could expand the PRP by marginalizing over that space:

$$P(rel|\mathcal{Q}, D) = \sum_{q' \in \mathcal{Q}} P(rel|q', D)P(q'|\mathcal{Q}, D)$$

The efficacy of this model likely depends on our ability to identify the space $\mathcal{Q}$ and estimate probabilities of sampling queries from it. Note, however, its similarity to the data fusion scoring method CombWSUM: the probabilities $P(rel|q', D)$ can be seen as different retrieval scores being fused, while $P(q'|\mathcal{Q}, D)$ can be seen as a weight for that

score. If those weights are uniform, then the formulation is similar to CombSUM.

Now let us consider the probability that a document is *retrieved* rather than *relevant*. By analogy to the PRP, let us define $P(retr|q, D)$ as the probability that document D is retrieved given query q. Just as we can retrospectively take $P(rel|q, D)$ to be proportional to a score assigned by a retrieval system, we can retrospectively take $P(retr|q, D)$ to be proportional to the rank position of the document. Using the same expansion as above, we can say:

$$P(retr|\mathcal{Q}, D) = \sum_{q' \in \mathcal{Q}} P(retr|q', D)P(q'|\mathcal{Q}, D)$$

This allows us to use as evidence documents that have been ranked by some system for a query that is not q but that appears to be related to the same information need as q.

Note here that using uniform $P(q'|\mathcal{Q}, D)$ and a simple cutoff function for $P(retr|q', D)$ (that is, $P(retr|q', D) = 1$ if D is ranked above k for q' and 0 otherwise), the formulation is equivalent to the data fusion method CombCAT [2] described in Section 2.3 above.

Either of the probabilities $P(rel|\mathcal{Q}, D)$ or $P(retr|\mathcal{Q}, D)$ could be used as a scoring function by which to rank documents; their similarity to proven data fusion methods demonstrates their effectiveness. What we propose now is combining them into a single scoring function $P(retr\&rel|\mathcal{Q}, D)$. This model can be decomposed in two different ways. First, assuming that relevance and retrievability are conditionally independent given the full query sample space and a document, we obtain our first model:

$$M_1 = P(retr\&rel|\mathcal{Q}, D) = P(retr|\mathcal{Q}, D)P(rel|\mathcal{Q}, D) \quad (1)$$

Second, assuming that relevance and retrievability are conditionally independent given a single query and a document, we obtain our second model:

$$\begin{aligned} M_2 &= P(retr\&rel|\mathcal{Q}, D) \\ &= \sum_{q' \in Q} P(retr\&rel|q', D)P(q'|\mathcal{Q}, D) \\ &= \sum_{q' \in Q} P(retr|q', D)P(rel|q', D)P(q'|\mathcal{Q}, D) \quad (2) \end{aligned}$$

We additionally assume that q' is independent of D (that is, that the user did not have document D in mind when formulating query q', which may indeed be unrealistic), so $P(q'|\mathcal{Q}, D) = P(q'|\mathcal{Q})$.

Both models combine principles of the PRP and data fusion. Their effectiveness will rely on careful implementation of several components:

- the query sample space $\mathcal{Q}$
- the probability of sampling a query from that space $P(q'|\mathcal{Q})$
- the probability of relevance $P(rel|q', D)$
- the probability of retrieval $P(retr|q', D)$

In the following section we propose possible implementations of each of these.

3.1 Model components

Again, our model depends on our selection of implementations of several components. In this section we describe a few easy possibilities for each.

3.1.1 Query sample space $\mathcal{Q}$

One of the key components of this model is the space of possible queries for an information need. This is not information that is typically readily available. It may be possible to identify related queries in a large query log, but even that will be biased to how users tend to interact with that search engine (for example, large web search engines like Google would be biased towards very short keyword queries, while a e-discovery engine might be biased towards much longer, structured Boolean queries). Thus we must approximate such a space in some way.

We consider two primary sources of information: user search history over a session, and query suggestions provided by web search engines. For the former, when the last query a user inputs in a session is q, we look back over this history of the session and assemble $\mathcal{Q}$ from one of the following sources:

- Previous queries in the session. These could be seen as a sample of queries by the same user from the possible space.

- Titles of documents ranked for previous queries in the session. These could be seen as approximations of verbose queries, and could potentially identify new relevant documents that would not be found without longer queries.

- Snippets of documents ranked for previous queries in the session. Again, these could be seen as very verbose queries.

The TREC Session track provides data for these; we discuss this more in Section 4.1 below.

We can also obtain query suggestions from external sources (e.g. via commercial query generation services that provide an API through which we submit a query and obtain a list of query suggestions for that query). These give us "indirect" access to a large query log, assuming a query log was used to generate them. And similar to using snippets from a search session, we can also use snippets generated by a commercial search engine for the top 10 documents of a query. Specifically, we investigate the following:

- Query suggestions provided by the Bing API.

- Snippets of the top-10 documents retrieved from the Yahoo! BOSS API.

We treat these as "black boxes" for generating a query sample space, giving us something like an upper bound on the performance that could be expected.

3.1.2 Query sample probability $P(q'|\mathcal{Q})$

Once we have a query space $\mathcal{Q}$, we need a way to estimate the probability of sampling a particular query q' from that space. These probabilities become weights on the scores of documents retrieved for that query, or weights on whether that document was retrieved or not and at what rank.

For this work, we investigate a few simple heuristics:

- Uniform probabilities over unique queries. Each unique query has the same probability of being sampled.

- Uniform probabilities over all queries. Each non-unique query has the same probability of being sampled. This means that a query that appears twice in $\mathcal{Q}$ is twice as likely to be sampled as one that appeared only once.

- Proportional to the similarity between q' and the space $\mathcal{Q}$.

- Proportional to position in query suggestion rankings. The APIs we use to generate query suggestions provide them as a ranking, so we can weight them accordingly. For instance, we may assign twice as much sampling probability to query suggestions in the top half of the ranking as in the bottom half.

- Proportional to position in the session history. Queries that appear more recently may be given more weight than queries that appear further back. This can apply to titles and snippets taken from the session history as well.

The latter two are implemented by binning queries by position (either rank position or position in time). The similarity is implemented using cosine similarity. We provide more detail in Section 4.4 below.

3.1.3 Probability of relevance $P(rel|q', D)$

The probability of relevance is the score of the document for the sampled query q'. In general it can be any retrieval function. We have used the language model score computed by Indri, since the index of web pages that is available to us was built in Indri. Indri computes its retrieval score with a Dirichlet-smoothed language model as:

$$score(q', D) = \sum_{t \in q'} \log \frac{tf_{t,D} + \mu \frac{ctf_t}{|C|}}{|D| + \mu}$$

Here $tf_{t,D}$ is the frequency of term t in document D, ctf_t is the frequency of term t in the entire collection, $|D|$ is the length of document D in terms, $|C|$ is the length of the entire collection (the sum of the lengths of all documents in the collection), and μ is a smoothing parameter to guarantee no term has zero probability.

3.1.4 Probability of retrieval $P(retr|q', D)$

The probability of retrieval, in our work, is essentially proportional to whether a document has been ranked by a system for the query q' and at what position. We consider two possible methods to estimate this probability:

- A simple binary indicator function $I(rank_D \leq k)$. As mentioned above, we can decide that $P(retr|q', D) = 1$ if document D appears in the top-k ranking for q' and $P(retr|q', D) = 0$ otherwise.

- Discounting by rank. We use a simple linear discount by which the top-ranked document is assign probability proportional to 1, then each subsequent document is discounted by an additional $1/k$.

3.2 Connection to data fusion methods

We are proposing the models above as a framework from which new retrieval models can be produced. In this section we demonstrate how well-known fusion algorithms emerge from our framework.

One of the primary differences between our method and typical fusion methods is that we are issuing different *queries* to a single retrieval system, whereas fusion methods traditionally issue the same query to *different* retrieval systems.

Thus to connect to existing methods, we rewrite our framework so that it sums over different rankings rather than different queries. The modified version of M_2 (Eq. 2) looks like this:

$$M_2' = P(retr\&rel|\mathcal{R}, D)$$
$$= \sum_{R \in \mathcal{R}} P(retr\&rel|R, D)P(R|\mathcal{R}, D)$$
$$= \sum_{R \in \mathcal{R}} P(retr|R, D)P(rel|R, D)P(R|\mathcal{R}, D)$$

Note that we have essentially replaced q' and $\mathcal{Q}$, a query and a set of possible queries, with R and $\mathcal{R}$, a ranking and a set of possible rankings, respectively. The theoretical framework makes no substantive distinction between a query that produces a ranked list and a ranked list produced from a query, which means that different queries and different retrieval systems can be treated interchangeably. The only caveat is that the different queries should be related to the same information need, at least as closely as two different retrieval systems retrieved similar documents for the same query.

3.2.1 CombSUM

CombSUM simply sums the scores a document received from different retrieval algorithms, then ranks documents in decreasing order of score. Since different retrieval algorithms can produce scores on very different scales, typically some form of standardization is applied to scores before summing them.

In our model, CombSUM emerges when $P(R|\mathcal{R}, D) \propto 1$ (that is, all rankings are weighted equally), $P(retr|R, D) \propto 1$ for all documents D ranked above some cutoff k in ranking R, and $P(rel|R, Q, D)$ is the normalized score given by the system the ranking R corresponds to. Then:

$$P(retr\&rel|\mathcal{R}, D) = \sum_{R \in \mathcal{R}} score(R, D)$$
$$= CombSUM(\mathcal{R}, D)$$

3.2.2 CombWSUM

CombWSUM is very similar to CombSUM except that the scores are weighted, typically by some estimate of the average effectiveness of the system that produced the score. In our model, CombWSUM is obtained by using a non-uniform probability for $P(R|\mathcal{R}, D)$. Then, labeling that probability w_R, we have:

$$P(retr\&rel|\mathcal{R}, D) = \sum_{R \in \mathcal{R}} w_R \cdot score(R, D)$$
$$= CombWSUM(\mathcal{R}, D)$$

3.2.3 CombMNZ

CombMNZ also weights scores, but instead of weighting each individual system/document score by a system weight, it weights the sum of document scores across systems by the number of systems that gave that document a "non-zero" score (technically, the number of systems that ranked the document in the top-k retrieved). Let us refer to the number of non-zero scores as MNZ, and the sum of document scores as CombSUM as above. Then, using the first model

formulation Eq. 1 above:

$$P(retr\&rel|\mathcal{R}, D) = P(retr|\mathcal{R}, D)P(rel|\mathcal{R}, D)$$
$$= \sum_{R \in \mathcal{R}} I(rank_D(R) \leq k) \cdot \sum_{R \in \mathcal{R}} score(R, D)$$
$$= MNZ \cdot CombSUM(\mathcal{R}, D)$$
$$= CombMNZ(\mathcal{R}, D)$$

4. EXPERIMENTAL SETUP

4.1 Data

We performed experiments on five different datasets: the TREC 2013 and 2014 Web tracks, the TREC 2013 and 2014 Session tracks, and the NTCIR 2014 iMine track. All five use the full ClueWeb12 corpus, though the iMine track only used the ClueWeb12-B13 subset of it.

TREC Web tracks: Each of the 2013 and 2014 TREC Web track datasets contain 50 queries [9, 8] created after perusing candidate topics from query logs from commercial search engines. Some topics were faceted (with several possible subtopics), others were non-faceted with single intents, and a few others were ambiguous (queries with several intents). The task of TREC participants is to provide a diversified ranking of no more than 10000 documents per query for the 50 queries. Relevance judgments are provided at the level of topic as well as subtopic for computing diversity evaluation measures (see below).

TREC Session tracks: Like the Web track datasets, the Session track datasets contain queries. However, those queries are given in the context of user sessions consisting one or more interactions with a search engine [17, 18]. Each interaction includes a user-submitted query related to the topic, a ranked list of results from a search engine for that query, user clicks on those results, and the time spent by the user reading the clicked document. Finally, each session ends with a "current query", a query with no search engine results for which participants will provide ranked results, possibly using the session history to do so. The 2013 data includes 87 sessions, while the 2014 data include 1021 sessions, of which 100 were pooled for judging. The task is to leverage session history to rank documents for the last query (current query) in the session using the entire ClueWeb12 corpus for retrieval.

NTCIR IMine track: IMine is also a diversity-focused task. We use the English set, which consists of 50 queries for which the organizers provided query suggestions from Bing, Google and Yahoo as well as query "dimensions" generated using the method proposed by Dou et al. [10]. The task is to provide a diversified ranking of no more than 100 documents per query for the 50 queries, covering as many intents as possible [24].

4.2 Evaluation measures

Our primary evaluation measure is nDCG, the official measure of the TREC Session track and one of the measures for the TREC Web track. For Web track results, we also report α-nDCG, a modification of nDCG for measuring diversity of subtopics in ranked results. This measure works by penalizing redundancy in documents that appear in a ranked list [7].

4.3 Baselines

When we report a baseline, it is chosen from among the following: a standard Dirichlet-smoothed language model as implemented in Indri [31] and a set of runs obtained using Lavrenko & Croft's relevance models, varying the number of documents used for feedback. We choose the best-performing system from this set as the baseline.

4.4 System implementations

As discussed above, we can produce different system implementations from the framework by picking and choosing among different component methods. Given the large space produced just by the possibilities we have mentioned (which are only a subset of all possible choices), we cannot experiment and report on every combination. Here we list select combinations that we experimented with.

For the "possible queries" $\mathcal{Q}$, we mainly considered previous queries in a user session and titles of documents ranked for those queries (for the TREC Session track data) and query suggestions and snippets provided by two major search engines (for the TREC Session track data and the TREC Web track data). The NTCIR iMine track provided query suggestions from major search engines as well.

For the query sample probability $P(q'|\mathcal{Q}, D)$, we used all five of the methods described in Section 3.1.2 above. Cosine similarity is computed between a query q' and the full set of terms in $\mathcal{Q}$. However, because for many sources of $\mathcal{Q}$ the queries are quite short, we found that cosine similarity is not very useful in those cases. It is only useful when the queries in the set are relatively long, so we only report it in those cases.

To weight queries based on their distance in time, we use binning. We first decide on a number of bins m. Then, from a sequence of n queries making up a session, the most recent n/m are placed in the first bin, the next most recent n/m are placed in the second bin, and so on. The first bin is then given weight double that of the second bin, which receives weight double that of the third bin, and so on.

For the probability of relevance $P(rel|q', D)$, we only use Dirichlet-smoothed language models. This is because our index of ClueWeb12 was built using indri, and that is the default model indri uses.

For the probability of retrieval $P(retr|q', D)$, we use the rank-cutoff indicator function $I(rank_D \leq k)$ and the linear discounting function described in Section 3.1.3.

5. RESULTS

We present results organized by dataset below. Our primary results are those for the TREC Session track, since that is the dataset that provides access to session history data and thus the most direct additional information about the information need. We present results for the TREC Web track to show how our method can be adapted when session history is not directly available and to show results for novelty and diversity search. We present results for the NTCIR iMine track because that track provided suggestions from a commercial search engine (which gives precedent for our use of those queries). For each dataset, we break discussion of results out by model component.

5.1 Results for TREC Sessions

Table 1 summarizes all results for TREC Session track data. The baseline (line no. 1) is a simple Dirichlet-smoothed language model using only the query, ignoring session history and any other sources of possible information about the session or topic, though possibly using pseudo-relevance feedback as described above. The final line (no. 20) in the table is the reported best-performing system among all TREC submissions, taken from the respective TREC overview papers [17, 18]. The best TREC submission was 32% or 45% better than our baseline for 2013 and 2014 respectively, but we improve on our own weak baseline by up to 40% or 36% (respectively; both at line no. 17) for the "realistic" case of fusing results based on the user's history in the session.

5.1.1 Choice of possible queries $\mathcal{Q}$

Results are grouped by the selection of a source for the set of possible queries $\mathcal{Q}$. It is clear from 1 that this set has the biggest effect on performance, though how specifically it affects performance depends on the data: for the 2013 Session track data, using document titles as a source of possible queries (lines 8–14) tends to outperform the use of previous queries in the session (lines 2–7), while for 2014, using document titles performs much worse than the use of previous queries. In both cases, however, there is a clear difference between the two sets, with another tier of results achieved by drawing from a commercial search engine (the query suggestions on lines 18 and 19, and engine snippets on lines 15–17); in that tier, snippets clearly outperform query suggestions.

The differences in the effectiveness of previous queries and document titles between 2013 and 2014 may be explained by differences in the engine that generated search results, differences in the user population, and differences in the amount of data. On the first point, the 2014 engine would sometimes generate ranked lists that were much worse than the 2013 engine. When these poor results are used to generate new results for data fusion, it is not surprising that the end result would be worse. On the second and third points, the 2014 engine used Amazon Mechanical Turk to generate many more sessions and queries than were available in the 2013 data; it may be that the greater amount of data leads to greater effectiveness when using previous queries alone.

5.1.2 Choice of $P(retr|q', D)$

The next largest effect on performance is from the selection of "retrieval probability" $P(retr|q', D)$. Using the rank-based linear discount function (odd-numbered lines except lines 1 and 15) outperforms the simple rank-cutoff binary function in every case that they can be directly compared. This suggests that weighting documents by rank position *in addition to* retrieval sore can improve data fusion in general.

5.1.3 Choice of $P(q'|\mathcal{Q}, D)$

Finally, the method for weighting queries sampled from the space has a smaller, yet still clear in some cases, effect on effectiveness. In particular, using a uniform distribution over the *unique* queries (lines 4 & 5, 10 & 11) outperforms a uniform distribution over all queries (lines 2 & 3, 8 & 9), meaning that giving more weight to duplicates in the set typically results in worse performance.

For the cosine similarity and binning methods, we have few cases where we can directly compare effectiveness. Cosine similarity seems to be most useful when applied to snippets from a commercial search engine, where they unequivocally improve effectiveness over the baseline (by 28% or more

no.	sample space $\mathcal{Q}$	$P(q'|\mathcal{Q}, D)$	$P(retr|q', D)$	2013 Session		2014 Session	
				nDCG@10	%Δ	nDCG@10	%Δ
1	baseline	–	–	0.1474	–	0.1783	–
2	previous queries	uniform	$I(rank_D \leq k)$	0.1425	-3%	0.1849	4%
3	previous queries	uniform	linear discount	0.1574	7%	0.1999	12%
4	previous queries	unique	$I(rank_D \leq k)$	0.1457	-1%	0.1935	9%
5	previous queries	unique	linear discount	0.1574	7%	0.2057	15%
6	previous queries	bins by time	$I(rank_D \leq k)$	0.1463	-1%	0.1874	5%
7	previous queries	bins by time	linear discount	0.1648	12%	0.1920	8%
8	document titles	uniform	$I(rank_D \leq k)$	0.1570	7%	0.1521	-15%
9	document titles	uniform	linear discount	0.1609	9%	0.1587	-11%
10	document titles	unique	$I(rank_D \leq k)$	0.1599	8%	0.1603	-10%
11	document titles	unique	linear discount	0.1635	11%	0.1699	-5%
12	document titles	bins by time	$I(rank_D \leq k)$	0.1487	1%	0.1424	-20%
13	document titles	bins by time	linear discount	0.1562	6%	0.1484	-17%
14	document titles	cosine sim	$I(rank_D \leq k)$	0.1538	4%	0.1501	-16%
15	external snippets	uniform	$I(rank_D \leq k)$	0.1710	16%	0.2001	12%
16	external snippets	cosine	$I(rank_D \leq k)$	0.2000	*36%	0.2277	*28%
17	external snippets	uniform	linear discount	**0.2063**	*40%	**0.2427**	*36%
18	suggested queries	uniform	$I(rank_D \leq k)$	0.1589	8%	0.2261	*27%
19	suggested queries	uniform	linear discount	0.1595	8%	0.2059	15%
20	TREC best	–	–	0.1952	*32%	0.2580	*45%

Table 1: TREC Session track results for different combinations of model components. * indicates a statistically significant difference over the baseline by a paired t-test at the 0.05 level. The biggest improvement for each dataset is bolded.

at line no. 16). When applied to document titles, using cosine similarity to estimate query sampling probability does not provide any clear benefit (line 14).

For the binning method, we report the maximum effectiveness over number of bins. While this may be "cheating" (in the sense that we are optimizing on the testing data), we note that the binning methods nearly always give worse effectiveness than the uniform probability methods using the same retrieval probability. Thus it seems that binning based on session history is not worthwhile.

5.1.4 Additional analysis

The TREC Session track topics can be described by whether they are "factual", "intellectual", "specific", or "amorphous", referring to specific goals and products of the topic [18]. We investigated performance with different choices of $\mathcal{Q}$ when breaking topics out by these categories. Table 2 shows the results. Our methods seem to do the best job at improving results for "amorphous" and "factual" types, which represent, respectively, exploratory and fact-finding information needs. Moreover, they improve those types in both Session track datasets, suggesting that the improvement is independent of other differences between the datasets.

5.2 Results for TREC Web

Results from the previous section demonstrate that substantial effectiveness gains are possible when using information from the user's recent search history. In many retrieval contexts there *is* no such history; for example, the TREC Web track provides only a single query with no session history. Can we obtain similar effectiveness improvements with that limitation?

Table 3 summarizes all results when using Bing query suggestions and Yahoo! BOSS snippets. (Again, these were submitted as queries to our own LM index of ClueWeb12

to provide the input to our fusion methods.) Again we see substantial and consistent improvements over our baseline, with our best performance comparable to the best automatic TREC submissions despite the fact that our entire retrieval process is based on the weak LM baseline reported in the first line of the table.

We report both nDCG and the diversity measure α-nDCG to demonstrate the effectiveness of our methods for diversity retrieval. As Table 3 shows, we consistently obtain statistically significant gains for diversity as well as ad hoc retrieval.

5.2.1 Choice of possible queries $\mathcal{Q}$

Again, since we have no session history to draw from, we rely on query suggestions and snippets provided by external search engines. Both prove to be excellent sources for the set of possible queries, increasing effectiveness over our baseline for both 2013 and 2014 (with the 2013 results substantial and statistically significant). When used together (by taking the union of the two sets), effectiveness increases by up to 50% for the 2013 data, and 22% for the 2014 track.

We do not see as clear a difference between queries and snippets as we did between queries and titles in the Session track experiments above, though there is a clear gain from combining them.

5.2.2 Choice of $P(retr|q', D)$

For the Web track we were able to use the same methods as we did for the Session track. Again we see that using a linear discount function always improves over a simple rank cutoff in cases where they are directly comparable.

5.2.3 Choice of $P(q'|\mathcal{Q}, D)$

In most cases we were only able to test the uniform probability over the set. For the case of suggested queries, we could also try binning them by their rank position in the list. This did turn out to have a positive effect: when the

$\mathcal{Q}$		2013 Session				2014 Session		
	factual	intellectual	specific	amorphous	factual	intellectual	specific	amorphous
baseline	0.1402	0.1632	0.1608	0.1141	0.1598	0.1958	0.1773	0.1797
prev. q + titles	0.1912	0.1769	0.1769	0.1954	0.1719	0.1772	0.1537	0.1965
prev. q + snips	0.2739	0.1813	0.1541	0.2584	0.1307	0.1898	0.1362	0.1876
titles + snips	0.2069	0.1541	0.1750	0.2021	0.1689	0.1604	0.1369	0.1932
all	0.2119	0.1750	0.1750	0.2135	0.1762	0.1688	0.1427	0.2032

Table 2: TREC Session track results broken out by goal and product types.

$\mathcal{Q}$	$P(q'\|\mathcal{Q}, D)$	$P(retr\|q', D)$	2013 Web			
			nDCG@20	%Δ	α-nDCG	%Δ
baseline	–	–	0.1863	–	0.4664	–
suggested queries	uniform	$I(rank_D \le k)$	0.2298	*23%	0.5548	*19%
suggested queries	uniform	linear discount	0.2421	*30%	0.5695	22%
suggested queries	bins by rank	$I(rank_D \le k)$	0.2235	20%	0.5447	17%
external snips	uniform	$I(rank_D \le k)$	0.2443	*31%	0.5797	*24%
queries+snippets	uniform	$I(rank_D \le k)$	0.2758	*48%	**0.6359**	*36%
queries+snippets	uniform	linear discount	0.2815	*51%	0.6331	36%
TREC best	–	–	**0.3100**	66%	0.6280	35%
$\mathcal{Q}$	$P(q'\|\mathcal{Q}, D)$	$P(retr\|q', D)$	2014 Web			
			nDCG@20	%Δ	α-nDCG	%Δ
baseline	–	–	0.2562	–	0.5744	–
suggested queries	uniform	$I(rank_D \le k)$	0.2558	0%	0.6645	*16%
suggested queries	uniform	linear discount	0.2735	7%	0.6573	14%
suggested queries	bins by rank	$I(rank_D \le k)$	0.2782	9%	0.6847	19%
external snips	uniform	$I(rank_D \le k)$	0.2657	4%	0.6268	9%
queries+snippets	uniform	$I(rank_D \le k)$	0.2997	*17%	0.6677	*16%
queries+snippets	uniform	linear discount	**0.3134**	*22%	0.6788	18%
TREC best	–	–	0.2610	2%	**0.6940**	21%

Table 3: TREC Web track results for different sources of possible queries $\mathcal{Q}$. * indicates a statistically significant difference over the baseline by a paired t-test at the 0.05 level. The biggest improvement in each column is bolded. For the best reported TREC result, note that we report the highest value of the measure across all submissions; the system with the highest nDCG@20 is not necessarily the same as the system with the highest α-nDCG.

ranked list is split in half, with the top half receiving more weight than the bottom half, results improve over using no binning. However, the difference in effectiveness from the uniform distribution is negligible.

Note that using a uniform distribution over unique elements in the set does not have any effect for the Web track, since our suggested queries and external snippets never have any duplicates that could be removed.

5.3 Results for iMine 2014

The main difference between the iMine data and the other two sets is that the iMine organizers provided ready-made query suggestions that we can use in our method. We did not have much opportunity to explore other sources of queries or ways of combining them. Table 4 shows results, comparing the linear discount to the rank-cutoff function, again showing that linear discounting provides a benefit (though in this case very small and not significant).

6. CONCLUSION AND FUTURE WORK

In this paper, we propose a probabilistic data fusion framework, PDF, which makes a small amendment to the probability ranking function by suggesting to rank documents in decreasing order of their probability of relevance *and* retrieval by systems, as opposed to relevance only. We pro-

$\mathcal{Q}$	$P(q'\|\mathcal{Q}, D)$	$P(retr\|q', D)$	α-nDCG
query suggestions	uniform	$I(rank_D \le k)$	0.6962
query suggestions	uniform	linear discount	0.6968

Table 4: NTCIR iMine 2014 results using the query suggestions provided by the organizers of the task.

pose a way to estimate the probability that documents are retrieved by exploiting various sources of sample possible queries. We proceed to show the impacts of different choices for several model components by implementing different instances of our model and empirically show that, when used with very rich sources of sample possible queries, they are at least on-par with the best reported systems for different search scenarios including ad-hoc search, diversity search and search over sessions. Specifically, we show them to be at least competitive with the best reported systems for TREC Session track 2013 and 2014, TREC Web track 2013 and 2014 as well as NTCIR IMine 2014 dataset.

Future work will involve experimenting with different various values for each component. For instance, we will experiment with a query sampling probability that uses language model-style smoothed generation to allow the estimation for very short queries. We may try probabilities that account for training based on clicked documents, or that simply increase the voting rights of a possible query q' by the number of documents that were clicked when the ranking for q' was displayed to the user. We will also investigate the impact of using other discount functions for $P(retr|q', D)$, for instance a logarithmic discount (like nDCG) or a geometric discount (RBP).

Acknowledgements

This work was supported in part by the National Science Foundation (NSF) under grant number IIS-1350799. Any opinions, findings and conclusions or recommendations expressed in this material are the authors' and do not necessarily reflect those of the sponsor.

7. REFERENCES

[1] J. Aslam and M. Montague. Models for metasearch. In *Proc. SIGIR*, 2001.

[2] A. Bah and B. Carterette. Aggregating results from multiple related queries to improve web search over sessions. In *Proc. AIRS*, 2014.

[3] B. Bartell, G. Cottrell, and R. Belew. Automatic combination of multiple ranked retrieval systems. In *Proc. SIGIR*, 1995.

[4] N. J. Belkin, P. Kantor, E. Fox, and J. A. Shaw. Combining the evidence of multiple query representations for information retrieval. *IPM*, 31(3), 1995.

[5] J. Carbonell and J. Goldstein. The user of mmr, diversity-based reranking for reordering documents and producing summaries. In *Proc. SIGIR*, 1998.

[6] B. Carterette and P. Chandar. Probabilistic models of ranking novel documents for faceted topic retrieval. In *Proc. CIKM*, 2009.

[7] C. L. A. Clarke, M. Kolla, G. V. Cormack, O. Vechtomova, A. Ashkan, and S. Buttcher. Novelty and diversity in information retrieval evaluation. In *SIGIR*, 2008.

[8] K. Collins-Thompson, P. Bennett, and F. Diaz. TREC 2014 Web track overview. In *TREC*, 2014.

[9] K. Collins-Thompson, P. Bennett, F. Diaz, and C. L. A. Clarke. TREC 2013 Web track overview. In *TREC*, 2013.

[10] Z. Dou, S. Hu, Y. Luo, R. Song, and J. R. Wen. Finding dimensions for queries. In *Proc. CIKM*, 2011.

[11] E. A. Fox and J. A. Shaw. Combination of multiple searches. *NIST SP*, pages 243–243, 1994.

[12] J. Garofolo, C. Auzanne, and E. Voorhees. The trec spoken document retrieval track: A success story. In *TREC*, 2000.

[13] D. Guan. *Structured Query Formulation and Result Organization for Session Search*. PhD thesis, Georgetown University, 2013.

[14] D. Guan, S. Zhang, and H. Yang. Utilizing query change for session search. In *Proc. SIGIR*, 2013.

[15] J. Jiang, D. He, and S. Han. On duplicate results in a search session. In *Proc. TREC*, 2012.

[16] G. J. Jones, J. T. Foote, K. S. Jones, and S. J. Young. Retrieving spoken documents by combining multiple index sources. In *Proc. SIGIR*, 1996.

[17] E. Kanoulas, B. Carterette, P. D. Clough, and M. Sanderson. Overview of the TREC 2013 Session track. In *Proc. TREC*, 2013.

[18] E. Kanoulas, B. Carterette, P. D. Clough, and M. Sanderson. Overview of the TREC 2014 Session track. In *Proc. TREC*, 2014.

[19] U. Kruschwitz. University of essex at the trec 2012 session track. In *Proc. TREC*, 2012.

[20] G. Lebanon and J. Lafferty. Cranking: Combining rankings using conditional probability models on permutations. In *Proc. ICML*, 2002.

[21] J. Lee. Combining multiple evidence from different properties of weighting schemes. In *Proc. SIGIR*, 1995.

[22] J. H. Lee. Analyses of multiple evidence combination. In *Proc. SIGIR*, 1997.

[23] D. Lillis, F. Toolan, R. Collier, and J. Dunnion. Probfuse: a probabilistic approach to data fusion. In *Proc. SIGIR*, 2006.

[24] Y. Liu, R. Song, M. Zhang, Z. Dou, T. Yamamoto, M. Kato, and K. Zhou. Overview of the NTCIR-14 iMine task. In *Proc. NTCIR*, 2014.

[25] M. Montague and J. Aslam. Condorcet fusion for improved retrieval. In *Proc. CIKM*, 2002.

[26] K. B. Ng and P. B. Kantor. Predicting the effectiveness of naive data fusion on the basis of system characteristics. *Journal of the American Society for Information Science*, 51(13):1177–1189, 2000.

[27] F. Radlinski and S. Dumais. Improving personalized web search using result diversification. In *Proc. SIGIR*, 2006.

[28] K. Raman, P. N. Bennett, and K. Collins-Thompson. Toward whole-session relevance: exploring intrinsic diversity in web search. In *Proc. SIGIR*, 2013.

[29] S. E. Robertson. The probability ranking principle in ir. *Journal of Documentation*, 33(4):294–304, Dec. 1977.

[30] R. Santos, C. Macdonald, and I. Ounis. Exploiting query reformulations for web search result diversification. In *Proc. WWW*, 2010.

[31] T. Strohman, D. Metzler, H. Turtle, and W. B. Croft. Indri: A language model-based search engine for complex queries. In *Proceedings of the International Conference on Intelligent Analysis*, 2005.

[32] C. C. Vogt and G. W. Cottrell. Predicting the performance of linearly combined ir systems. In *Proc. SIGIR*, 1998.

[33] J. Wang and J. Zhu. Portfolio theory of information retrieval. In *Proc. SIGIR*, 2009.

[34] S. Wu and S. McClean. Performance prediction of data fusion for information retrieval. *Information processing & management*, 42(4):899–915, 2006.

[35] C. Zhai, W. Cohen, and J. Lafferty. Beyond independent relevance: methods and evaluation metrics for subtopic retrieval. In *Proc. SIGIR*, 2003.

[36] S. Zhang, D. Guan, and H. Yang. Query change as relevance feedback in session search. In *Proc. SIGIR*, 2013.

Learning to Rank with Labeled Features

Fernando Diaz
Microsoft
fdiaz@microsoft.com

ABSTRACT

Classic learning to rank algorithms are trained using a set of labeled documents, pairs of documents, or rankings of documents. Unfortunately, in many situations, gathering such labels requires significant overhead in terms of time and money. We present an algorithm for training a learning to rank model using a set of labeled features elicited from system designers or domain experts. Labeled features incorporate a system designer's belief about the correlation between certain features and relative relevance. We demonstrate the efficacy of our model on a public learning to rank dataset. Our results show that we outperform our baselines even when using as little as a single feature label.

CCS Concepts

●Information systems → Learning to rank;

Keywords

learning to rank

1. INTRODUCTION

Ranking is a fundamental subproblem of information retrieval research. Much of the early work in information retrieval studied text ranking in general and resulted in the development of several core retrieval functions. Ranking signals such as BM25 [16] have the advantage of portability to new domains, with little or no parametric tuning necessary for effective performance. Conversely, modern retrieval systems often employ machine learning to tune a large number of ranking function parameters by using a set of labeled query-document pairs [11].

Despite the success of machine learned ranking models, acquiring labeled data remains a pain point for system designers and researchers. Gathering editorially judged data requires nontrivial overhead in terms of time (e.g. drafting relevance guidelines, training assessors, waiting for judgments) and money (e.g. developing an annotation system,

ICTIR '16, September 12-16, 2016, Newark, DE, USA

© 2016 ACM. ISBN 978-1-4503-4497-5/16/09...$15.00

DOI: http://dx.doi.org/10.1145/2970398.2970435

paying assessors). By the same token, gathering user interaction data (e.g. clicks) requires an existing ranking system that already performs well, usually as a result of training from editorial data. This is not to mention the prerequisite of already having users. Enterprise search scenarios highlight the problems with traditional methods of learning to rank. Enterprise search providers must design systems with little or no knowledge about the target queries or corpus; often they default to a standard ranking signal such as BM25. Enterprise search customers, on the other hand, do not have the expertise or resources to gather or train models based on editorial or behavioral data. As a result, customers must either settle for a default ranking function or handtune elaborate ranking heuristics.

While existing solutions such as active sampling focus on reducing the cost of data acquisition [2, 3], these methods all require the development of an assessment infrastructure, including drafting relevance guidelines and training assessors.

In this paper, we contribute a new learning to rank paradigm where a system must estimate model parameters given a set of labeled ranking features. This problem, which we refer to as *learning to rank with labeled features*, offers an opportunity for saving money and time. In the context of enterprise search, systems that learning to rank with labeled features provide a means for customers to indicate which ranking signals they believe are important for their domain, without explicitly reasoning about the functional form of the final ranking function.

2. RELATED WORK

Much of the foundational work in information retrieval concentrated on understanding the fundamental principles involved in text ranking. These included notions of saturating term frequency, inverse document frequency, and term proximity. Fang *et al.* present many of these principles as information retrieval axioms common across several retrieval models [8]. As such, we have an understanding of, in general, what ranking signals are appropriate in different retrieval situations.

Initializing a model with prior knowledge has received attention in information retrieval. Mohan *et al.* present an algorithm for incorporating domain knowledge into the first stage of boosting [13]. Similarly, in some cases, knowledge from a related vertical or market can be exploited to warm start a ranking model [4, 12]. However, all of these techniques require editorially labeled queries and documents.

Our work is most similar to learning classifiers from labeled features. While Schapire *et al.* introduced the problem of learning from feature labels [17], others have extended this work to other modeling frameworks [15, 7]. Our work can be seen as extending this to thread of research from classification to learning to rank.

3. LEARNING TO RANK WITH LABELED FEATURES

Given a query q, each document in the corpus can be represented as a vector m feature values including factors such as the BM25 score, PageRank, and other ranking signals. The design matrix $\mathbf{\Phi}^q$ is the $n \times m$ matrix of feature values for all n documents in the corpus. The (unobserved) relevance of every document in the corpus to q is represented in the $n \times 1$ vector $\mathbf{y}^q$. For clarity, we will omit q from the notation.

Domain experts provide the system with direction through a set of feature labels. Each label encodes the confidence of i being ranked above j given a difference in the feature values of i and j. For example, the expert may believe, "if the value of the BM25 score of i is higher than that of j, then my confidence that $i \succ j$ scales linearly with the difference in the BM25 scores." More generally, a feature label is a) a ranking feature name and b) a scaling factor indicating the confidence in the judgment. In other words, if the candidate ranking feature is k, then for two documents i and j, we would like the expert to provide a scalar grade $\tilde{w}_k$ such that $\tilde{w}_k \times (\Phi_{ik} - \Phi_{jk})$ is proportional to the confidence that i is preferred to j. A positive score indicates a positive correlation between the feature difference and document ordering. A negative score indicates a negative correlation between the feature difference and document ordering. The magnitude reflects the confidence in the judgment (i.e. a score of zero indicates no preference). The set of feature labels is represented as a sparse $m \times 1$ vector $\tilde{\mathbf{w}}$.

As with most learning to rank problems, the goal is to learn a function $f : \Re^m \to \Re$ such that, when documents are sorted by the value of this function, some retrieval evaluation metric is maximized.

Whereas traditional learning to rank domains involve labeled documents (i.e. $\{\langle \mathbf{\Phi}^q, \mathbf{y}^q \rangle\}_{q \in \mathcal{Q}}$), we only provide the system with a set of unlabeled documents (i.e. $\{\mathbf{\Phi}^q\}_{q \in \mathcal{Q}}$) in addition to $\tilde{\mathbf{w}}$. An unlabeled dataset can be gathered offline with an indexed corpus and a set of queries.

4. AN ALGORITHM

Our approach to learning to rank with labeled features builds on existing work. Specifically, our functional form and training method follows LambdaRank [5]. We will begin with a review of this approach for labeled documents before extending it to labeled features.

4.1 Maximum Entropy Learning to Rank

Given a document i, we would like to learn a linear model, $\mathbf{w} \in \Re^m$, such that ranking documents by $f(\mathbf{\Phi}_i) = \mathbf{w}^\top \mathbf{\Phi}_i$ places relevant documents near the top. In learning to rank with labeled documents, we can train a linear function by using a pairwise ranking model. For example, we can estimate the probability of an ordering of two documents as a logistic

function of the individual document retrieval scores [5],

$$p(\mathbf{y}_i > \mathbf{y}_j | \mathbf{\Phi}_i, \mathbf{\Phi}_j) = \frac{1}{1 + \exp(-(f(\mathbf{\Phi}_i) - f(\mathbf{\Phi}_j)))} \quad (1)$$

$$= \frac{1}{1 + \exp(\sum_k w_k(\Phi_{jk} - \Phi_{ik}))} \quad (2)$$

Notice that Equation 2 highlights that such a model is learning a maximum entropy model based on the difference in feature values for pairs of instances. This allows us to train a model with observed preferences between documents instead of absolute document labels. The trained parameters, $\mathbf{w}$, for this model, then, can also be used to rank documents by $\mathbf{w}^\top \mathbf{\Phi}_i$. A similar intuition is used in the derivation of SVM^{rank}[10], although in this case we are optimizing for logistic loss. It is important to recognize that this framework optimizes the Kendall's τ between the model ranking and the ideal ranking [10, Section 3] instead of a core retrieval metric like NDCG.

When using labeled documents, we can infer a set of preference labels from the document labels (i.e. documents with high labels are preferred to those with low labels) and construct a new training set of the form, $\{\langle i \succ j, \mathbf{\Phi}_i, \mathbf{\Phi}_j \rangle\}$. With this preference data, we can learn the parameters $\mathbf{w}$ using stochastic gradient descent where the gradient magnitude is merely the prediction error,

$$\Delta_{ij} = \mathrm{I}(i \succ j) - p(\mathbf{y}_i > \mathbf{y}_j | \mathbf{\Phi}_i, \mathbf{\Phi}_j, \mathbf{w}) \quad (3)$$

This is the approach underlying RankNet [5].

The problem with the pairwise loss is that, although related, information retrieval evaluation metrics are often subtler than Kendall's τ. Metrics such as NDCG incorporate rank preference and graded relevance. Burges *et al.* introduce the notion of weighting the gradients in Equation 3 with the magitude of the rank loss [5]. In practice, we multiply the gradient by the change in the metric,

$$\alpha_{i,j} \equiv |\delta \mathcal{N}_{i,j}^{\mathbf{y}}| \times \Delta_{ij} \quad (4)$$

where we set $\delta \mathcal{N}_{i,j}^{\mathbf{y}}$ to be the change in NDCG from swapping documents in positions i and j.

As a result update rule for stochastic gradient descent over pairs of ordered instances is,

$$\mathbf{w}^t = \mathbf{w}^{t-1} + \gamma \alpha_{i,j} (\mathbf{\Phi}_i - \mathbf{\Phi}_j) \quad (5)$$

where γ is a learning rate.

4.2 Maximum Entropy with Labeled Features

Although we cannot infer preferences from document labels, we can estimate the preference with a simple model derived from $\tilde{\mathbf{w}}$. Specifically, we adopt a functional form consistent with Equation 2,

$$p(\mathbf{y}_i > \mathbf{y}_j | \mathbf{\Phi}_i, \mathbf{\Phi}_j, \tilde{\mathbf{w}}) = \frac{1}{1 + \exp(\sum_k \tilde{w}_k(\Phi_{jk} - \Phi_{ik}))} \quad (6)$$

where the score for document i is $f(\mathbf{\Phi}_i) = \tilde{\mathbf{w}}^\top \mathbf{\Phi}_i$. While there are many other methods for combining feature labels, we leave an exploration of this for future work.

If we replace the indicator function in Equation 3 with Equation 6, our gradient magnitude is,

$$\tilde{\Delta}_{ij} = p(\mathbf{y}_i > \mathbf{y}_j | \mathbf{\Phi}_i, \mathbf{\Phi}_j, \tilde{\mathbf{w}}) - p(\mathbf{y}_i > \mathbf{y}_j | \mathbf{\Phi}_i, \mathbf{\Phi}_j, \mathbf{w}) \quad (7)$$

As with labeled documents, we multiply the gradient by the change in the metric. Unfortunately, we cannot adopt a metric based on labeled documents. Instead, we adopt a preference-based version of NDCG [6] define as,[1]

$$\mathcal{N}^{\tilde{\mathbf{w}}}(\mathcal{O}_k) = \frac{1}{\mathcal{Z}} \sum_{\{(i,j):i \in \mathcal{O}_k\}} \frac{p(\mathbf{y}_i > \mathbf{y}_j | \mathbf{\Phi}_i, \mathbf{\Phi}_j, \tilde{\mathbf{w}})}{\log_2(\min\{\rho_i, \rho_j\} + 1)} \quad (8)$$

where the set $\mathcal{O}_k$ is defined as the top k set of documents ordered by the model, ρ_i is the rank of document i in the model ordering, and $\mathcal{Z}$ is a discounted preference gain of the optimal ordering. We can compute a $\delta \mathcal{N}_{i,j}^{\tilde{\mathbf{w}}}$, and as a result $\tilde{\alpha}_{i,j}$, in the same way as done with document-based NDCG.

Given a large pool of unlabeled documents, $\mathcal{U}$, we can use stochastic gradient descent to train the parameters with Equation 5, replacing $\alpha_{i,j}$ with $\tilde{\alpha}_{i,j}$.

4.3 Regularization

Readers may note that, unconstrained and with the right initialization of $\mathbf{w}$, following the gradient in Equation 7 will recover the original weights $\tilde{\mathbf{w}}$, rendering the whole process pointless. We can avoid this degenerate solution by introducing a regularization constraint that prevents the model from concentrating too much of $\mathbf{w}$ in a few features. We adopt an ℓ_2 penalty since it is of standard practice in gradient descent. This coverts our update rule into,

$$\mathbf{w}^t = (1 - \lambda\gamma)\mathbf{w}^{t-1} + \gamma\tilde{\alpha}_{i,j}(\mathbf{\Phi}_i - \mathbf{\Phi}_j) \quad (9)$$

where λ controls how much we penalize a model for having concentrated feature weights.

5. METHODS

We use the Microsoft Learning to Rank Dataset [14], consisting of 30,000 queries, with a standard training, validation, and testing splits. Documents are represented as 136-dimensional feature vectors, each rated on a five point relevance scale. We only use relevance labels for evaluation, never for training.[2]

We considered feature labels following a symmetric five point scale, $\sigma \in \{-2, -1, 0, 1, 2\}$. We then encode this feature level information into $\tilde{\mathbf{w}}$. We consider two feature label sets. The first consists of a single feature, the BM25 score of the title field, with a score of 2. In other words, this would represent an expert being very confident that a document with a higher BM25 score in the title should be preferred to another with a lower BM25 score in the title. The second feature label set consists of five features chosen by an information retrieval expert. The features include the BM25 score of the title, anchor text, and body as well as two query independent features, PageRank and a document quality score. Our expert has a PhD in information retrieval and is familiar with the various feature names but has never previously conducted research with the Microsoft dataset. We plan on study the sensitivity of our approach to expertise level in future work.

We use a γ of 10^{-5} and a regularization weight λ of 0.5. We leave as future work the automatic tuning of these parameters absent a labeled validation set. As a baseline, we

rank documents by $\tilde{\mathbf{w}}^\top \mathbf{\Phi}_i$, representing a naïve linear combination of labeled features. In all cases, including for baselines, we perform per-query feature normalization as is customary in the learning to rank literature.

We measure performance as a function of the number of *unlabeled* queries used for estimating the model parameters (Equation 9). For space reasons, we only present results for the mean NDCG.

6. RESULTS

We present the performance of our model as a function of unlabeled training set size in Figure 1. As we can see, our trained model are able to use $\tilde{\mathbf{w}}$ in order to learn a superior dense model $\mathbf{w}$. Interestingly, we are able to significantly outperform the straightforward baseline with as few as 100 queries for our single feature label condition and 500 queries for our multiple feature label condition. Recall that using handcrafted ranking function such as $\tilde{\mathbf{w}}^\top \mathbf{\Phi}_i$ remains the best approach for many domains. That said, we found performance to be roughly 65% of that when using the full set of labeled documents, suggesting that, if available, system designers should use these judgments.

In order to understand the model, we can inspect the feature weights $\mathbf{w}$ in Table 1. Both of our models demonstrate that highly weighted features tend to be correlated with the labeled features. For example, labeling the BM25 title results in a model which also highly weights other representations of the title field. Similarly, the model learned from expert feature labels heavily weights anchor text features, not only because these are correlated with the labeled anchor feature but also because they are correlated with the combination of other labeled features. The PageRank feature remains highly weighted because it is unlikely to be correlated with other features based mostly on the content. Interestingly, across both conditions we notice negative weights for features associated with document length and URL length. This suggests that very long documents or those deep in a website hierarchy are unlikely to be preferred by our labeled features.

7. CONCLUSION

Because unlabeled documents feature vectors can be easily gathered offline, we believe methods based on labeled features point to a compelling direction for low cost learning to rank model development.

Our preliminary algorithm outperforms a straightforward baseline but there are many opportunities for further research. From a modeling perspective, we believe that novel optimization objectives or functional forms can further improve performance. This may include the development of new preference-based evaluation metrics for training or setting hyperparameters. In addition to core modeling, there is opportunity to develop novel interfaces for eliciting feature labels such as those developed for text classification [1].

8. REFERENCES

[1] S. Amershi, M. Chickering, S. M. Drucker, B. Lee, P. Simard, and J. Suh. Modeltracker: Redesigning performance analysis tools for machine learning. In *Proceedings of the 33rd Annual ACM Conference on Human Factors in Computing Systems*, pages 337–346, 2015.

---

[1] We adjust the gain to use the probability of preference instead of an absolute label difference.

[2] We avoid using the LETOR 3.0 and 4.0 as they have methodological issues [9]. Other datasets such as those from Yahoo and Yandex only provide numeric feature indexes, not interpretable names required for feature assessment.

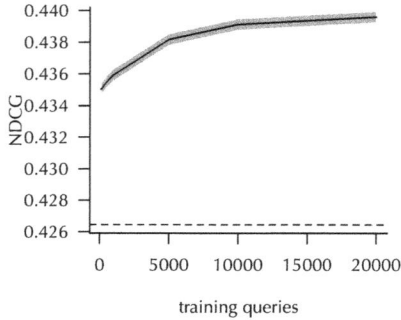

(a) BM25 title feature label

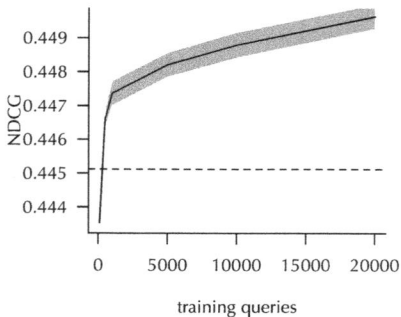

(b) Expert feature labels

Figure 1: Results for MSLR-30k dataset with simple and expert feature labels. The dashed line indicates the performance of our baseline $\tilde{\mathbf{w}}^\top \mathbf{\Phi}_i$. Shaded regions represent one standard error across twenty five random training samples of the given size. All improvements for training size great than or equal to 100 are statistically significant (t-test: $p < 0.001$).

Table 1: Sorted feature weights for our two feature label sets. Models shown for 5000 unlabeled instances and $\lambda = 1$. Labeled features are bolded.

BM25 title		expert	
feature$_k$	w_k	feature$_k$	w_k
BM25-title	**0.547**	**pageRank**	**0.817**
normTF-title	0.469	**BM25-anchor**	**0.392**
meanNormTF-title	0.469	VSM-anchor	0.382
LMABS-title	0.403	QTermRatio-anchor	0.330
LMJM-title	0.370	QTerm-anchor	0.330
maxNormTF-title	0.362	**BM25-title**	**0.319**
minNormTF-title	0.299	normTF-anchor	0.311
VSM-title	0.253	meanNormTF-anchor	0.311
QTerm-title	0.231	maxNormTF-anchor	0.270
QTermRatio-title	0.231	**quality**	**0.263**
$\vdots$			
bool-URL	-0.015	bool-URL	-0.001
DL-anchor	-0.016	siteRank	-0.006
DL-body	-0.016	minTFIDF-URL	-0.007
lengthURL	-0.018	minTF-URL	-0.008
DL-all	-0.018	DL-body	-0.039
DL-URL	-0.023	DL-all	-0.040
outLinks	-0.026	DL-title	-0.092
pageRank	-0.033	URL-length	-0.129
siteRank	-0.054	DL-URL	-0.131
DL-title	-0.164	URL-slashes	-0.134

[2] J. A. Aslam, E. Kanoulas, S. Pavlu, S. Savev, and E. Yilmaz. Document selection methodologies for efficient and effective learning-to-rank. In *SIGIR*, pages 468–475, 2009.

[3] J. A. Aslam, V. Pavlu, and E. Yilmaz. A statistical method for system evaluation using incomplete judgments. In *SIGIR*, pages 541–548, 2006.

[4] J. Bai, F. Diaz, Y. Chang, Z. Zheng, and K. Chen. Cross-market model adaptation with pairwise preference data for web search ranking. In *Proceedings of the 23rd International Conference on Computational Linguistics*, pages 18–26, 2010.

[5] C. J. Burges. From ranknet to lambdarank to lambdamart: An overview. Technical Report MSR-TR-2010-82, Microsoft Research, 2010.

[6] B. Carterette and P. N. Bennett. Evaluation measures for preference judgments. In *SIGIR*, pages 685–686, 2008.

[7] G. Druck, G. Mann, and A. McCallum. Learning from labeled features using generalized expectation criteria. In *SIGIR*, pages 595–602, 2008.

[8] H. Fang and C. Zhai. An exploration of axiomatic approaches to information retrieval. In *SIGIR*, pages 480–487, 2005.

[9] G. C. M. Gomes, V. C. Oliveira, J. M. Almeida, and M. A. Gonçalves. Is learning to rank worth it? a statistical analysis of learning to rank methods. *Journal of Information and Data Management*, 4(1):57–66, February 2013.

[10] T. Joachims. Optimizing search engines using clickthrough data. In *KDD*, pages 133–142, 2002.

[11] T.-Y. Liu. *Learning to Rank for Information Retrieval*. Springer, 2011.

[12] B. Long, Y. Chang, A. Dong, and J. He. Pairwise cross-domain factor model for heterogeneous transfer ranking. In *WSDM*, pages 113–122, 2012.

[13] A. Mohan, Z. Chen, and K. Q. Weinberger. Web-search ranking with initialized gradient boosted regression trees. *Journal of Machine Learning Research, Workshop and Conference Proceedings*, 14:77–89, 2011.

[14] T. Qin, T.-Y. Liu, W. Ding, J. Xu, and H. Li. Microsoft learning to rank datasets, May 2010.

[15] H. Raghavan, O. Madani, and R. Jones. Active learning with feedback on features and instances. *J. Mach. Learn. Res.*, 7:1655–1686, Dec. 2006.

[16] S. E. Robertson, S. Walker, S. Jones, M. Hancock-Beaulieu, and M. Gatford. Okapi at trec-3. In *Proceedings of the Third Text REtrieval Conference*, 1994.

[17] R. E. Schapire, M. Rochery, M. G. Rahim, and N. Gupta. Incorporating prior knowledge into boosting. In *ICML*, pages 538–545, 2002.

Total Recall: Blue Sky on Mars

Charles L. A. Clarke, Gordon V. Cormack, Jimmy Lin, and Adam Roegiest

David R. Cheriton School of Computer Science
University of Waterloo, Ontario, Canada

claclark@gmail.com, {gvcormac, jimmylin, aroegies}@uwaterloo.ca

ABSTRACT

There are presently plans to create permanent colonies on Mars so that humanity will have a second home. These colonists will need search, email, entertainment, and indeed most services provided on the modern web. The primary challenge is network latencies, since the two planets are anywhere from 4 to 24 light minutes apart. A recent article sketches out how we might develop search technologies for Mars based on physically transporting a cache of the web to Mars, to which updates are applied via predictive models. Within this general framework, we explore the problem of high-recall retrieval, such as conducting a scientific survey. We explore simple techniques for masking speed-of-light delays and find that "priming" the search process with a small Martian cache is sufficient to mask a moderate amount of network latency. Simulation experiments show that it is possible to engineer high-recall search from Mars to be quite similar to the experience on Earth.

1. INTRODUCTION

Mars needs search. And Mars needs recommendation, social media, streaming video, email, messaging, e-commerce, and indeed most services provided on the modern web. Unfortunately, providing these services for our permanent Martian colonists poses non-trivial challenges, most particularly due to network latencies associated with users who are 4 to 24 light minutes away. On Earth, a query to a commercial search engine takes under a second to return results. On Mars, without appropriate technology, the same query would take from hundreds to thousands of times longer.

Plans for permanent Martian colonies continue to move forward (see marstostay.com and mars-one.com), with public support from prominent figures such as Apollo astronaut Buzz Aldrin [1] and entrepreneur Elon Musk [7]. These plans call for colonists to move permanently to Mars, with no expectation of return. While some colonists may eventually return to Earth, as Martian resources and industry permit, some colonists may live their entire lives there. They will start families, grow old, and die there. In the short term the colonists would conduct scientific missions. In the longer term they may take on larger projects, including terraforming the planet. Humanity would have a second home.

Permanent Martian colonies are economically feasible with current science, requiring no new breakthroughs. However, making colonization a reality will require a substantial effort to create the individual technologies needed to support life on Mars, including technologies for information access. To conduct scientific work, but also to maintain important social and cultural connections to Earth, searching the web should be as easy from Mars as it is from Marseille.

In a recent article, Lin et al. [10] examined the requirements for searching from Mars. They envision the Martians of the future using the web much like the Earthlings of today: reading, watching, gaming, and interacting—even buying physical items as gifts for Earth-bound friends and family, or as precious cargo for themselves, delivered on the next supply freighter. These tasks must be accomplished despite round-trip latencies ranging from 8 to 48 minutes, depending on the relative positions of the two planets. With laser-based communication [11], reasonable bandwidth is possible, but physical laws prohibit latency improvements.

Lin et al. proposed a solution for searching on Mars that starts with a physical copy of the web shipped to Mars as cargo (i.e., the first interplanetary sneakernet), arriving either with or before the first colonists. Upon arriving on Mars, it becomes a cache for our Martian search engine. By the time it arrives, however, months or years later after liftoff from Earth, this cache will be stale, and so ongoing updates must be applied with live Earth data. Since bandwidth will remain precious for the foreseeable future, and we assume that all resources are to be used as parsimoniously as possible, these updates must be performed intelligently. In order to provide Earth-like response times, the Martian search engine must anticipate future searches and other interactions, prefetching data as needed using predictive models on Earth that act as proxies for the colonists on Mars. Lin et al. posed a challenge to information retrieval researchers to develop and validate these models.

In this paper, we take a small step towards our goal of searching on Mars. We focus on a single problem, that of high-recall retrieval, and examine the impact of high latency on this problem. We imagine a Martian conducting high-recall retrieval, such as an inquiry into the best mechanisms to achieve potato growth in recycled organic waste or a scientific survey of the flora and fauna of Barsoom. We assume the Martian cache contains some limited information on the retrieval topic, enough to initiate the search process. As the Martian searches, relevance information heads back to Earth, which responds with a stream of potentially relevant documents. We explore the impact of Mars-Earth latency and simple techniques for masking speed-of-light delays via simulations, by comparing against Earth-based search where latency is negligible. We find that "priming" the search process with a local (Martian) cache is sufficient to mask a moderate amount of network latency. Based on our simple techniques, the experience of searching from Mars can be engineered to be similar to searching from Earth.

The contribution of this paper is the first experimental study of searching from Mars, building on the proposals of Lin et al. [10] (who performed no actual experiments). Our work takes a rather (currently) fanciful problem, shows that there are substantive research questions worth exploring, demonstrates the inadequacies of naïvely applying current techniques, and evaluates simple solutions that address the relevant challenges. We hold this paper as an exemplar of how such research can be performed, with potential applications closer to home (e.g., searching from the Canadian Arctic or rural communities in India, both of which suffer from poor connectivity). Teevan et al. [15] proposed "slow search", which aims to relax latency requirements for a potentially higher-quality search experience; search from Mars was mentioned in passing as an illustrative example, but they did not propose any specific solutions.

2. TOTAL RECALL

Given that the focus of this paper is high-recall retrieval, our experiments are based on data from the TREC Total Recall Track [6], which evaluates high-recall retrieval systems using topics drawn from legal and other domains. The goal of the track is to develop and validate methods for identifying all relevant material on a given topic with as little user effort as possible, returning all relevant documents before all non-relevant documents. The track is focused around a task, similar to active learning, in which a (simulated) user judges documents proposed by the retrieval system. Starting with an initial query, the retrieval system aims to return a stream of relevant documents to the user.

2.1 AutoTAR

To facilitate system development for the TREC Total Recall Track [6], the coordinators released an implementation of Cormack and Grossman's AutoTAR [3, 5] protocol, which is itself an extension of their continuous active learning protocol [2, 4]. Since AutoTAR's effectiveness ranks among the best systems in the TREC evaluations, we use it as the basis of our experiments.

AutoTAR initially ranks the entire document collection by training on an initial query (treated as a pseudo-document) and 100 randomly selected documents, which are assumed to be non-relevant. AutoTAR requests that the user assesses the most relevant (i.e., highest scoring) document, and then trains on this new assessment along with the query and 100 new random (assumed non-relevant) documents. In an ideal situation, AutoTAR would repeat this process, selecting the top document for assessment and training on all available assessments. Since this is not computationally practical, AutoTAR requests assessments in exponentially increasing batches, starting with a batch size of one and increasing the batch size by $\text{MAX}(1, 0.1 \cdot \texttt{batch\_size})$ each iteration.

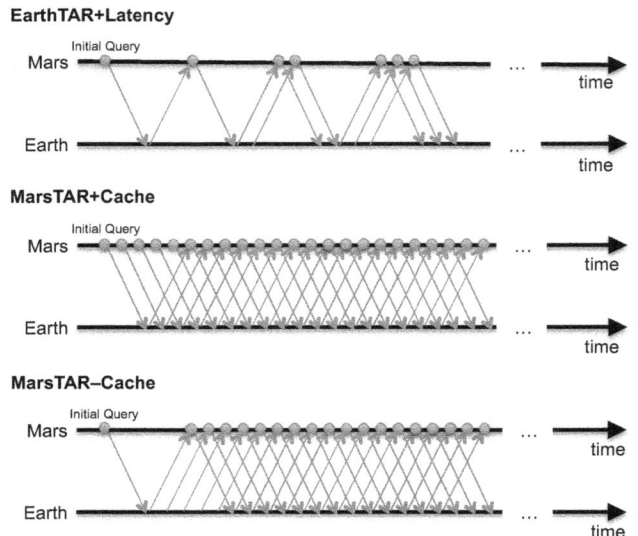

Figure 1: Illustration of various AutoTAR on Mars scenarios. Circles on the Mars timelines indicate relevance judgments.

It has been observed that for high-recall retrieval algorithms [12], assessor background and assessor experience can affect the judgments rendered [8, 17, 14]. Furthermore, changing the training and evaluative assessments can affect system performance in non-trivial ways [13, 16, 18]. In spite of these issues, we follow the Total Recall Track's premise and assume that the training and evaluative assessors are the same (i.e., the Martian researcher) and that the assessments would not change depending on the algorithm employed (i.e., that the Martian would always judge documents the same way, regardless of the order in which they are received).

2.2 AutoTAR on Mars

What would AutoTAR on Mars look like? We assume the same general setup of the Total Recall Track—the user provides binary relevance feedback on each document as it is judged, and the retrieval system uses this feedback to update its notion of relevance. The retrieval process continues back and forth, with the system proposing one or more documents, and the user providing judgments. Except that on Mars, each back-and-forth is subjected to speed-of-light latency constraints, a round trip time of 8 to 48 minutes. We consider the following three scenarios, with varying levels of latency awareness:

EarthTAR+Latency. As a naïve baseline, we could just run a replica of the Total Recall task with the added delay of communications latency, as if the Martian used the Earth-based software with no accommodations. Under this scenario, the Earth-based retrieval system waits for feedback from Mars before proposing new documents. While waiting for results, the Martian could perform other work, e.g., investigating crystalline structures in the Cydonia region of Mars, spreading pesticides to kill off Martian insects in algae fields, etc. This scenario is shown at the top of Figure 1.

MarsTAR+Cache. As an attempt to hide latency, we can stream documents to Mars at the rate they can be judged, with delayed relevance information modifying the stream as it is received. We assume that AutoTAR runs initially over the Martian cache, but once data begins arriving from Earth, this data is added to the cache. Under this approach, two versions of AutoTAR run concurrently: one on Mars with partial knowledge, and one on Earth with access to the complete document collection. The Earth-side AutoTAR sends documents to Mars for incorporation into the local Martian collection when it decides that it has received enough assessments to generate a new batch of documents (using exactly the AutoTAR algorithm described in Section 2.1).

Note that from the Martian perspective, although feedback is not reflected in the stream until after a round-trip communications delay, the searcher perceives no latency—she can continue judging documents in the Martian cache. In essence, we are using the Martian cache to hide latency. This scenario is shown in the middle of Figure 1.

MarsTAR−Cache. What if there are no cached documents on Mars? The Martian begins with the initial query that is sent to Earth, but needs to wait for one round-trip communications delay to have subsequent documents to judge. After that, the searcher can continuously assess documents with a (perceived) latency-free experience. Note that these documents are always the ones relayed from Earth. This scenario is shown at the bottom of Figure 1.

As an upper bound, we consider simply running AutoTAR on Earth, where the latency is negligible—this would be as if the Martian returned to Earth to perform the search, perhaps using Dr. Manhattan-like teleportation. We call this the **EarthTAR** condition, which of course, provides an upper bound on effectiveness. At the other end of the spectrum, EarthTAR+Latency serves as a lower bound. The question is, how good are our MarsTAR configurations in being able to replicate the search experience on Earth?

3. EXPERIMENTS AND RESULTS

To determine if high-recall retrieval is possible across intrasolar distances, we conducted a set of simulation experiments using the Reuters Corpus Volume 1 v2 (RCV1) [9], consisting of just over 800,000 newswire documents manually labeled with 103 topic codes. The benefit of using RCV1 is the presence of a time-delimited training and test split of the corpus, which facilitates the accurate simulation of the stale-cache scenario proposed by Lin et al. [10]. The "training" portion (i.e., the Mars cache) consists of the oldest 24,000 newswire documents, with the "test" portion comprising the remainder of the collection.

We used each of the 103 topic codes as information needs—i.e., the searcher's goal is to find all documents with a particular assigned code. Topic codes are hierarchically arranged in RCV1: each topic's pseudo-document (i.e., the initial query) is the topic code (string) label plus all parent labels concatenated together.

To simplify the simulations we assume that the time to send a document from Earth to Mars, a judgment from Mars to Earth, and the time required to judge a document all take one unit of Martian time, which we call a 'tal' (following Edgar Rice Burroughs). Since we anticipate that bandwidth to Mars will remain a precious resource, there is no sense to sending documents at a rate faster than the Martian can judge them—in this strategy, we conserve bandwidth for other purposes. Although this temporal coupling is not necessarily realistic, we believe that it is sufficient for the scenario we are trying to simulate.

Accordingly, we have chosen four levels of round-trip latencies between Earth and Mars: 30, 100, 300, and 1000 tals. We evaluate these variants of AutoTAR by measuring recall as a function of tals elapsed from the initial query time on Mars. To summarize the results of all 103 topics, we average recall across topics at fixed points of tals elapsed in simulation time (e.g., 100, 200, etc.) to generate a gain curve.

Results of our simulations are shown in Figure 2. Even with a latency of 30 tals, round-trip time has a clear impact on the EarthTAR+Latency scenario. With a latency of 1000 tals, recall for EarthTAR+Latency remains close to zero out to 5000 tals and beyond. Clearly, naïvely applying Earth-based technology for Mars is hopeless.

Under the MarsTAR+Cache scenario, the gain curves at low latencies approach that of Earth. With longer latencies, the impact of latency is noticeable, but gain begins to recover after the initial round trip. This means that we can replicate a high-recall search experience that is quite similar to search on Earth by masking the effects of latency with a local cache that is *only* 3% of the entire collection. While waiting for communications delay, the Martian can continue refining the system's model of relevance such that, under relatively short delays, the gain curve is practically indistinguishable from an Earth-based searcher.

Even without a local cache (i.e., MarsTAR−Cache), we find that the search experience degrades negligibly with low latencies. However, with large latencies, effectiveness suffers noticeably. By simply pipelining the relevance judgments, we can mask communications latencies to a large extent. The bottom line: high-recall retrieval from Mars? Totally doable. Pluto, on the other hand, might be a bit trickier.

4. CONCLUSION

I just had a terrible thought... what if this is a dream? — Douglas Quaid

Our line of research requires the acceptance of a fairly major assumption: searching from Mars. While this assumption might be viewed as unlikely in the short term, it is considerably more likely than the zombie apocalypse preparations advocated by the Centers for Disease Control.[1] Like that effort, theoretical considerations about unlikely scenarios can lead to insights with more immediate impact. For example, a better understanding of searching from Mars might lead to improved search from remote areas on Earth, such as Easter Island, where only satellite internet is available, the Canadian Arctic, where internet access remains prohibitively slow and expensive, and even rural villages in India.

Our experiments illustrate a methodology for developing search technologies for Mars. Starting with a defined task, we consider the impact of latency and develop methods to compensate for it. Effectiveness is measured by comparing the task without compensation as a baseline and the task on Earth as the "gold standard" target. We provide an exemplar of this approach in action, applied to high-recall retrieval on Mars, and demonstrate how we can come close to replicating the search experience on Earth.

Acknowledgments. This work was supported in part by the Natural Sciences and Engineering Research Council of Canada. Any opinions, findings, conclusions, or recommendations expressed are solely those of the authors.

---

[1] www.cdc.gov/phpr/zombies.htm

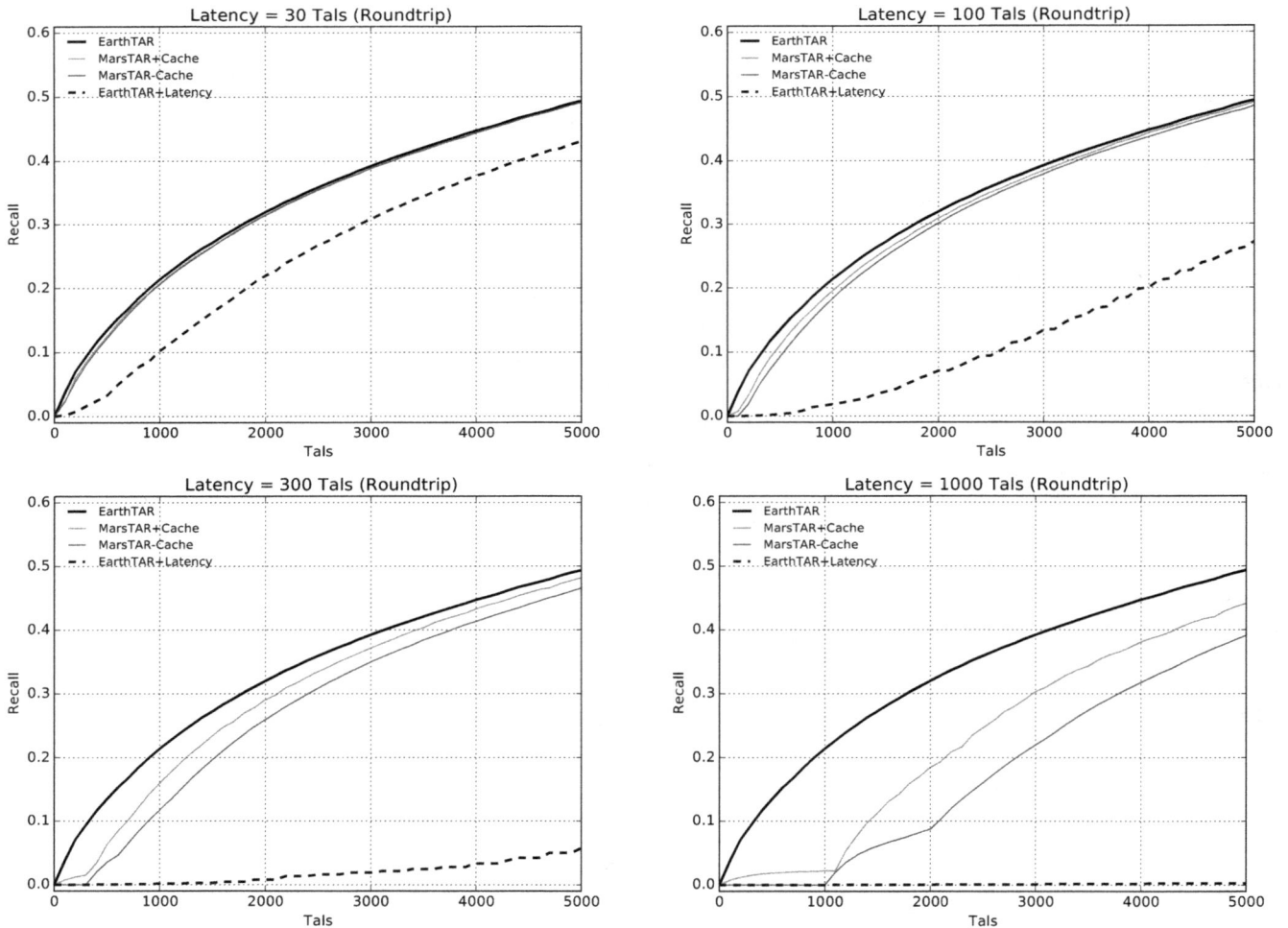

Figure 2: The effectiveness of our proposed strategies for high-recall retrieval from Mars under various round-trip latencies ('tals'). EarthTAR represents the "gold standard" of running AutoTAR on Earth; Earth-TAR+Latency represents a naïve baseline with no latency masking. MarsTAR conditions represent pipelining judgments, with and without a local Martian document cache.

5. REFERENCES

[1] B. Aldrin. The call of Mars. *New York Times*, June 2013.

[2] G. V. Cormack and M. R. Grossman. Evaluation of machine-learning protocols for technology-assisted review in electronic discovery. *SIGIR*, 2014.

[3] G. V. Cormack and M. R. Grossman. Autonomy and reliability of continuous active learning for technology-assisted review. *arXiv:1504.06868v1*, 2015.

[4] G. V. Cormack and M. R. Grossman. Multi-faceted recall of continuous active learning for technology-assisted review. *SIGIR*, 2015.

[5] G. V. Cormack and M. R. Grossman. Engineering quality and reliability in technology-assisted review. *SIGIR*, 2016.

[6] G. V. Cormack, M. R. Grossman, A. Roegiest, and C. L. A. Clarke. Overview of the TREC 2015 Total Recall Track. *TREC*, 2015.

[7] E. Howell. SpaceX's Elon Musk to reveal Mars colonization ideas this year. *Space.com*, January 2015.

[8] K. A. Kinney, S. B. Huffman, and J. Zhai. How evaluator domain expertise affects search result relevance judgments. *CIKM*, 2008.

[9] D. D. Lewis, Y. Yang, T. G. Rose, and F. Li. RCV1: A new benchmark collection for text categorization research. *Journal of Machine Learning Research*, 5, 2004.

[10] J. Lin, C. L. A. Clarke, and G. Baruah. Searching from Mars. *Internet Computing*, 20(1):77–82, 2016.

[11] B. S. Robinson, D. M. Boroson, D. A. Burianek, and D. V. Murphy. The Lunar Laser Communications Demonstration. *ICSOS*, 2011.

[12] A. Roegiest and G. V. Cormack. Impact of review set selection on human assessment for text classification. *SIGIR*, 2015.

[13] A. Roegiest, G. V. Cormack, C. L. Clarke, and M. R. Grossman. Impact of surrogate assessments on high-recall retrieval. *SIGIR*, 2015.

[14] F. Scholer, D. Kelly, W.-C. Wu, H. S. Lee, and W. Webber. The effect of threshold priming and need for cognition on relevance calibration and assessment. *SIGIR*, 2013.

[15] J. Teevan, K. Collins-Thompson, R. W. White, S. T. Dumais, and Y. Kim. Slow search: Information retrieval without time constraints. *HCIR*, 2013.

[16] E. M. Voorhees. Variations in relevance judgments and the measurement of retrieval effectiveness. *Information Processing & Management*, 36(5):697–716, 2000.

[17] J. Wang and D. Soergel. A user study of relevance judgments for e-discovery. *ASIST*, 2010.

[18] W. Webber and J. Pickens. Assessor disagreement and text classifier accuracy. *SIGIR*, 2013.

Classifying User Search Intents for Query Auto-Completion

Jyun-Yu Jiang
Department of Computer Science
University of California, Los Angeles
California 90095, USA
jyunyu.jiang@gmail.com

Pu-Jen Cheng
Department of Computer Science
National Taiwan University
Taipei 10617, Taiwan
pjcheng@csie.ntu.edu.tw

ABSTRACT

The function of query auto-completion[1] in modern search engines is to help users formulate queries fast and precisely. Conventional context-aware methods primarily rank candidate queries[2] according to term- and query- relationships to the context. However, most sessions are extremely short. How to capture search intents with such relationships becomes difficult when the context generally contains only few queries. In this paper, we investigate the feasibility of discovering search intents within short context for query auto-completion. The class distribution of the search session (i.e., issued queries and click behavior) is derived as search intents. Several distribution-based features are proposed to estimate the proximity between candidates and search intents. Finally, we apply learning-to-rank to predict the user's intended query according to these features. Moreover, we also design an ensemble model to combine the benefits of our proposed features and term-based conventional approaches. Extensive experiments have been conducted on the publicly available AOL search engine log. The experimental results demonstrate that our approach significantly outperforms six competitive baselines. The performance of keystrokes is also evaluated in experiments. Furthermore, an in-depth analysis is made to justify the usability of search intent classification for query auto-completion.

Keywords

query auto-completion; short context; search intent classification

1. INTRODUCTION

Query auto-completion is one of the most popular features implemented by modern search engines. The goal of query completion is to accurately predict the user's intended query with only few keystrokes (or even without any keystroke), thereby helping the user formulate a satisfactory query with less effort and less time. For instance, users can avoid misspelling and ambiguous queries with query completion services. Hence, how to capture user's search intents for precisely predicting the query one is typing is very important.

The context information, such as previous queries and click-through data in the same session[3], is usually utilized to capture user's search intents. It also has been extensively studied in both query completion [1, 21, 35] and suggestion [18, 25, 37]. Previous work primarily focused on calculating the relationship between candidates[2] and the context. Nevertheless, most of real query sessions are too short to identify such relations. In the AOL search engine log, more than 67% of multi-query sessions consist of only two queries; and only less than 13% of sessions have been constructed with more than three queries. The context consists of only single query if we would like to predict the last query of a 2-query session. Some works rank the candidates based on query similarity [1, 35] or user reformulation behavior [21] such as adding and reusing terms in the context. However, the number of terms in a query is very limited (average 2.3 terms in web search [10]), so the single-query context might be less likely to contain the identical terms to candidates. Moreover, queries might belong to similar topics, even though they utilize distinct and inconsistent terms. Other works [18, 25, 37] model query or term dependencies along whole search sessions, but such approaches will deteriorate to the naïve adjacent frequency one when there is only single query in the context. Consequently, short context might cause sparseness problems and ambiguous dependencies.

We then take a query session obtained from the AOL search engine logs to explain in more details: *"reverse address"* → *"white pages."* The query *"reverse address"* represents that the user would like to find a person's profile by an address, and it is also the purpose of the website *"white pages."* Suppose the last query, i.e., *"white pages,"* is the intended query, and the prefix is w. Its preceding one query serves as the context. The generated queries from conventional context-aware methods, such as *"www.google.com"* (from [1, 35]) and *"walmart"* (from [18, 21]), are not satisfactory in our experiments for the following reasons: (1) the actual query, i.e., "white pages," does not repeat any terms that appear in previous queries [1, 21]; (2) the query dependencies between "reverse address" and "white pages" do not

---

[1]For simplicity, *query auto-completion* is hereinafter referred to *query completion* in this paper.

[2]Candidate queries are those queries that start with the prefix entered by a user in a search box.

[3]A query session is a sequence of queries submitted in a short time period with the same information need.

ICTIR '16, September 12–16, 2016, Newark, Delaware, USA.

© 2016 ACM. ISBN 978-1-4503-4497-5/16/09...$15.00

DOI: http://dx.doi.org/10.1145/2970398.2970400

appear in the training data [18, 35]. That is, terms in the context might not provide enough information to predict accurately. One possible way to overcome the limitation and boost the performance is to discover the implication of the user's search intents in the query session. If the system can understand the high-level concepts of search intents, it would be better capable of recognizing the intended query.

Based on click-through data and external knowledge, classifying the whole search session, including queries and user click behavior, into a predefined set is a direct and effective way to discover the implication of user's search intents. It benefits not only query classification [24, 34] but also various applications such as relevance ranking [4]. If the search session and candidates are well classified and represented as search intents, the candidates can be ranked by their similarity to representative intents of the search session. For example, the search intents of *"white pages"* and *"reverse address"* are close to each other because they are all classified into the ODP[4] [14] category "Reference." It is reasonable because the website *"white pages"* is actually utilized to finding people, which is the purpose of *"reverse address."* However, mapping the search sessions into categories has been less investigated in query completion. Although some works on query suggestion [25, 37] have attempted to cluster or classify queries into several concepts with offline training click-through data, we further consider user's online click behavior so that the classification results can effectively reflect current search intents.

Moreover, search intent classification can be also effective in longer sessions because the user might change her mind. In other words, queries submitted earlier might be less likely to share similar search intents to latter queries. Take a session with 13 queries obtained from AOL logs as an example: *"shoes"* → *"timberland"* → *"adidas"* → · · · → *"cheetos"* → *"doritos."* The user originally searched for shoes and related manufacturers; however, she finally sought for snacks. If the system exploits earlier queries, it might obtain incorrect messages. To put it differently, if the latter queries can provide enough information and search intent classification can capture user's search intents more accurately based on the latter queries, the prediction may be more effective. Although some works [26, 39] attempt to discover the significant changes of search intents, none of them can directly predict the query most likely to be typed for completion.

In this paper, we focus on discovering users' search intents from search sessions by query classification. Given a prefix and its context together with a set of candidate queries that start with the prefix, the goal of this paper is learning to rank the candidate queries[5], so that the top-ranked queries are more likely to be the query the user is typing. The context includes previous queries and their click-through data in the same session. We first classify sessions and queries into a set of categories to form class distributions. Two kinds of class distributions including URL-class and query-class are considered here. Based on class distributions, we further derive the session-class distribution for the whole search session from three different aspects. For each candidate, eight distribution-based features are proposed to estimate its closeness to the context. Our method finally ranks the candidate queries based on a total of 22 distribution-

based features (1 query feature and 7 session/query-session features for three aspects of the session-class distribution). Furthermore, we propose to combine term-based conventional approaches and our proposed features into an ensemble model to obtain knowledge from different aspects and achieve better performance.

Extensive experiments have been conducted on the publicly available AOL search engine log. The experimental results reveal that prediction performance can be significantly improved based on our method, compared to six competitive baselines. Moreover, since the main purpose of query completion is to save users' keystrokes, we further examine whether our approach does effectively reduce the number of keystrokes, which is less verified in most of the previous work [1, 21, 35]. Finally, an in-depth analysis of search intent classification is also provided as evidence, which explains why our distribution-based features are effective.

In the rest of this paper, we make a brief review on related work in Section 2 and present our problem and framework for query completion in Section 3. The experimental results and analysis of search intent classification are presented in Sections 4 and 5, respectively. Finally, in Section 6, we give our discussions and conclusions.

2. RELATED WORK

In this section, we first give the background of query completion, and indicate the difference between our approach and previous work. Query suggestion, which is a task close to query completion, is then introduced and compared to our approach. Last but not least, we discuss query classification, which is relevant to search intent classification in this paper.

2.1 Query Auto-Completion

Before ranking queries for query completion, the sufficient candidate queries starting from the given prefix should be generated in advance. Most works on query completion extract candidates from query logs [21, 35] and document corpus [6]. Once candidates are generated, they can be ranked for various applications such as web search [1] and product search [12]. In this paper, the candidate queries are generated from query logs.

In the case of query completion in web search, the most common and intuitive approach is to rank candidates according to their past popularity. However, less popular query might be difficult to predict; on the other hand, the general popularity might not be favorable for every situation [36]. To achieve a better performance in prediction, the context information is usually utilized to rank candidates differently. Bar-Yossef and Kraus [1] and Shokouhi [35] measured the similarity to queries in the context. Jiang *et al.* [21] models users' reformulation behavior along the whole search session. Mitra [29] further automatically learns the distributed representation of query reformations by deep neural network models. Some other factors are also taken into account for improving performance. Shokouhi *et al.* [36] and Cai *et al.* [9] ranked candidates differently according to the temporal information. Whiting and Jose [38] predicted the query trends and distributions by a sliding window from the past few days. The personalization is also a possible solution considering users' personal information, such as demographics and search history [9, 35].

However, all of previous approaches in query completion

---

[4]Open Directory Project (ODP) uses a hierarchical ontology scheme for organizing site listings.

[5]In this paper, we focus on the ranking problem only.

utilized only query terms, but not class information of user's search intents along the whole search session. Our solution differs from these works in that we try to derive class distributions of sessions as users' search intents, thereby ranking candidate queries more effectively.

2.2 Query Suggestion

Query suggestion, which has been extensively studied in the field of IR, is closely related to query completion, but the goals of the two tasks are very distinct. Different from saving users' keystrokes by precise prediction in query completion, query suggestion concentrates on discovering relevant queries in relation to the context. However, the intended query that the user is typing might be in the list of suggested queries, so it could be applied in query completion and regarded as the related work.

The context information including query session and click-through data is also usually applied in query suggestion. Huang et al. [20] and Fonseca et al. [16] suggested queries with high frequency of co-occurrence with queries in the context. Moreover, Boldi et al. [7] and Song et al. [37] constructed transition graphs of queries and terms for mining the dependencies. Furthermore, some works [18,25] adopted sequential probabilistic models to model the transition probabilities. In addition to query terms, the click-through data is helpful to reveal queries with similar topics. Mei et al. [27] applied the random walk on click-through bipartite graphs to discover relevant queries. Liao et al. [25] also utilized such graphs to cluster queries into several concepts. To deal with the problems of data sparseness, some works [18,25] allowed the partial matching to the context. Liao et al. [25] clustered queries for flexibility. Furthermore, some works [31,33] applied machine learning frameworks with statistical features.

Compared to prior context-aware query suggestion methods, our approach can well exploit the context information and cope with the sparseness problems. Besides, none of the prevalent approaches to query suggestion attempts to classify user's search intents with the whole search session. Although some works [25,37] classified or clustered each query into a class or a group of relevant queries, they did not pay attention to the whole search sessions including preceding submitted queries and user click behavior, which represent users' actual search intents.

2.3 Query Classification

Query classification aims to classify a query into a predefined class or category. Gabrilovich et al. [17] identify queries and ad classes to improve the relevance of advertising. To classify queries, they make a weighted aggregation of the classes of URLs retrieved by search engines. Kang and Kim [22] utilized some IR and NLP measures as the features to classify queries and decide which algorithm for retrieval. With query logs from search engines, Beitzel et al. [3] made use of URLs information to pre-process queries into corresponding categories. The task of the 2005 KDD Cup [24] is also akin to query classification. The challenge of task is to classify queries with few training data. Most successful approaches [34] made use of external information such as ODP [14] or WordNet [28]. To enhance retrieval results, Bennett et al. [4] adopt ODP information and derive class distributions to improve ranked results. However, none of the previous work predicts users' intended queries with query classification. In our work, we attempt to derive class distributions with clicked URLs and ODP information for extracting distribution-based features of submitted queries and users' search intents.

3. QUERY AUTO-COMPLETION WITH SEARCH INTENT CLASSIFICATION

We first formally define the objective and the notations in this paper. A search context $\langle q_1, q_2, \cdots, q_{T-1} \rangle$ is defined as a sequence of $T-1$ queries issued by a user within a short period (i.e., the search session). Each query has the corresponding click information u_i, which is the set of clicked URLs in the search result page of q_i. Suppose a user intends to issue q_T and has already inputs p, i.e., the prefix of q_T in the search box, after the search context. We would like to predict q_T for query completion. Given a search context with $T-1$ preceding queries $\langle q_1, q_2, \cdots, q_{T-1} \rangle$ and a candidate set Q_T matched the prefix x, the goal is to give a ranking of candidates $q'_j \in Q_T$ so that queries in higher positions are more likely to be q_T.

In our work, we propose a supervised approach consisting of two components and leverage class information of users' search intents to query completion. First, we adopt click-through information and the predefined knowledge to derive URL-, query- and session-class distributions. Then several features are introduced to measure some important properties between class distributions of the session and candidates. With the training data collected from search engine logs, almost any learning-to-rank algorithm can be applied to obtain our ranking model. We finally choose *LambdaMART* [8], which is one of the state-of-the-art ranking models.

3.1 Query and Session Classification

During a search session, the user may have her own search intents. When the user determines her search intents, the class of information need may also be implicitly chosen by the user. Although some previous work [25] tried to cluster each query into a "concept" in advance, a query may belong to more than one concept or topic. This is also the reason why we calculate class distributions but classify a query or a session into a single class. In addition, they ignore that some predefined external information such as ODP categories [14] and reading levels [23] might be helpful for predicting user's intended query.

Different from previous work [4], we focus on deriving class distributions of not only queries but search sessions. Based on the URL-class and query-class distributions, we attempt to model session-class distributions from three views for discovering users' search intents. With the class distributions of the candidate query and the session, we can find relations between the candidate query and previous behaviors, including preceding submitted queries and click-through URLs in the session.

Classification Space. With some predefined knowledge, the queries and sessions can be classified into several categories such as topical categories, semantic categories and reading levels [23]. In this paper, ODP categories [14], which is a topical hierarchy structure, are adopted as the classification target. For conducting experiments, we used 16 topical categories from the top level of the ODP structure, which were crawled in December 2014. In our experiments, more than 53% of user clicks are covered by URLs in ODP. The remaining clicks are dealt by the smoothing techniques for computing a general distribution.

3.1.1 Query-class Distribution

Following the assumption mentioned in [4], we suppose that the query-class distribution is an aggregation over all relevant URLs. Moreover, here we assume that class distribution is only dependent to relevant URLs. Then we can calculate the query-class distributions with only query-URL relevance and URL-class distributions of all relevant URLs. More formally, the probability $P(c \mid q)$ is the query-class distribution for a query q and a class c. The probabilities $P(u \mid q)$ and $P(c \mid u)$ represents the query-URL relevance and the URL-class distribution. By marginalizing over all the relevant URL u of a query q and the above assumption, $P(c \mid q)$ can be re-written as follows:

$$P(c \mid q) = \sum_u P(c \mid u, q) \cdot P(u \mid q) \quad \text{(marginalization)}$$
$$= \sum_u P(c \mid u) \cdot P(u \mid q) \quad \text{(by assumption)},$$

then we can compute $P(u \mid q)$ and $P(c \mid u)$ separately for calculating the query-class distribution.

URL-class Distribution. With different targets of classification, there are various approaches for classifying URLs. Bennett et al. [4] and Kim et al. [23] built a classifier to estimate the class distribution $P(c \mid u)$ for each category. Baykan et al. [2] analyze characters of the URL to identify the category. However, building numerous and complex models for every category and all URLs is too inefficient for query completion, which aims to predict rapidly. In our approach, we assume that URLs which belong to the same host may have similar class distributions. Then we can pre-compute class distributions of plentiful URL hosts in advance and calculate a prior distribution $P(c)$ for URLs whose hosts are not in the pre-computed list with the smoothing technique.

The ODP data has been crawled and treated as the "gold-standard" classification results. Then we can derive class distributions for URLs by the smoothing computation as follows:

$$P(c \mid u) = \frac{Occurs(h(u), c) + m \cdot P(c)}{m + \sum_{c_i} Occurs(h(u), c_i)}.$$

Here m is a parameter for smoothing. The function $h(u)$ extracts the host of URL u. $Occurs(h(u), c)$ calculates how many websites with host $h(u)$ belong to category c in the contents of ODP. The prior distribution $P(c)$ can be computed by normalizing the number of websites in ODP for each category.

Query-URL Relevance. In order to estimate the relevance between queries and URLs, the click-through data is usually treated as a useful information and the relevance signal [11]. With such relevance signal, we attempt to derive the query-URL relevance from the large-scale search engine log. When a URL appearing in the search results of a query was clicked more times in search engine log, we trust that the URL is more relevant to the query than other URLs. However, some URLs are much rare in the log such that the estimated results may be dubious. To handle the sparseness problem, we keep following the assumption that URLs have similar distributions to their hosts. For remaining URLs whose hosts still do not appear in training data

with the query, we calculate a prior distribution for them. Then we can calculate query-URL relevance with smoothing technique as follows:

$$P(u \mid q) = \frac{C(h(u), q) + m \cdot P(h(u))}{m + \sum_{h(u)} C(h(u), q)}.$$

$C(h(u), q)$ counts the clicked times of the host $h(u)$ with query q in the log. The prior distribution $P(h(u))$ is calculated by normalizing the number of times URLs which belong to $h(u)$ are clicked in the log.

3.1.2 Session-class Distribution

The session-class distribution can be treated as the distribution of user's information need from the context, including preceding queries and clicked URLs. If we capture the user's search intents precisely, it can be matched to the class distributions of candidate queries. Formally, we extract the session-class distribution $P(c \mid \langle q_1, q_2, \cdots, q_{T-1} \rangle)$ to simulate user's search intents, given the context $\langle q_1, q_2, \cdots, q_{T-1} \rangle$. In our approach, we derive session-class distributions in three different views, including *All Preceding Queries*, *Last Query* and *Local-clicked URLs*.

All Preceding Queries (All). The user's search intents may be shown in the preference of submitted queries. Although queries are able to have various distributions, we try to obtain information from all preceding queries submitted by users. As we know how to estimate the query-class distributions in the above paragraph, we can perform the class distribution of the session as a linear weighted combination as follows:

$$P_{all}(c \mid \langle q_1, q_2, \cdots, q_{T-1} \rangle) = \frac{1}{\sum w_i} \sum w_i P(c \mid q_i).$$

Here w_i are the weight parameters. We assume that the more recent submitted query is more likely relevant to user's search intents, and the weights are monotonically decreasing. In our approach, we make weight function as a linear decay function $(w_i = 1/(T - i))$.

Last Query (Last). In a long session with many queries, the search intents of latter queries may be changed and different from the original ones. The last query (i.e., the most recent query in the context) could be treated as a sign of user's recent search intents. In this view, we assign the distribution of the last query in the context as the session-class distribution as follows:

$$P_{last}(c \mid \langle q_1, q_2, \cdots, q_{T-1} \rangle) = P(c \mid q_{T-1}).$$

Local-clicked URLs (Local). In addition to queries in the context, the clicked-through information is also a important information. As a relevance signal [11], a URL clicked in the session is more authentic than click-through data in the log. Also, a query may belong to more than one class or concept, the local click-through information helps us to identify the correct distribution of current session more precisely. To derive session-class distributions constructed by local-clicked URLs, we first define the local query-URL relevance. We treat whole context as a new "query" and a local log to calculate the relevance probability as follows:

$$P_{local}(u \mid \langle q_1, q_2, \cdots, q_{T-1} \rangle) = \frac{C_{local}(h(u)) + m \cdot P(h(u))}{m + \sum_{h(u)} C_{local}(h(u))},$$

where the function $C_{local}(h(u))$ counts the clicked times of the host $h(u)$ in the context. To avoid biasing to rare situations, we adopt the prior distribution to smooth the relevance score. Then we collect click-through URLs u_i in the session as a set of URLs $\boldsymbol{u}$, and calculate the session-class distribution as follows:

$$P_{local}(c \mid \langle q_1, q_2, \cdots, q_{T-1} \rangle)$$
$$= \sum_{u_i \in \boldsymbol{u}} P(c \mid u_i) P_{local}(u_i \mid \langle q_1, q_2, \cdots, q_{T-1} \rangle)$$

Three kinds of session-class distributions show different views to observe a search session and capture the user's search intents. We then use them to extract distribution-features with query-class distributions of candidate queries.

3.2 Distribution-based Features

Based on the class distributions of session and candidate queries, we then define various features and apply machine learning algorithms to discover and model interactions with other features. Features for learning to rank can be categorized into three classes, including query features, session features and query-session features. The query features and session features are extracted from only class distributions of candidate queries and the session. The query-session features consider both candidate queries and the session.

Query/Session Class Entropy (QCE/SCE). In our approach, class entropy measuring the entropy of the class distribution is the only feature of query feature and session feature. The class entropy is helpful to identify the ambiguity of a candidate query or the session information. Queries and sessions with lower entropy (i.e., belonging to fewer topics) might be submitted by users trying to narrow the search results to such topics.

Next, we model the query-session features aiming to measure how well a candidate query matches to the search session with the class distribution.

Class Match (CM). Among the class distribution, we can find the most likely class of a candidate query and the session. Users may submit queries in the identical class of the session and previous context. So we treat whether the most likely classes of the query and the session are matched as the *ClassMatch* feature.

ArgMaxOdds (AMO) & MaxOdds (MO). We then try to measure how well the session-class distribution matches the most likely class of the candidate query. Define the most likely class of the candidate query q as $c_q^* = \underset{c}{\arg\max} P(c \mid q)$, we calculate the *ArgMaxOdds* feature as follows:

$$P(c_q^* \mid q) \log \frac{P(c_u^* \mid \langle q_1, q_2, \cdots, q_{T-1} \rangle)}{P(c_q^*)}.$$

Here the prior $P(c_q^*)$ is adopted to weight the class distribution as the probability of observing that class. By relaxing the *ArgMaxOdds* feature, we calculate the *MaxOdds* over all classes and find the maximum measure as follows:

$$\max_c P(c \mid q) \log \frac{P(c \mid \langle q_1, q_2, \cdots, q_{T-1} \rangle)}{P(c)}.$$

KL Divergence (KL) & Cross Entropy (CE). The previous two features encode information of only one class, which is the most likely class or the class with maximum measure. We adopt *KL Divergence* to estimate how a candidate query matches the session upon the entire class dis-

Table 1: Eight distribution-based features and used information. Note that features related to sessions will be extracted three times for three aspects of session-class distribution (See Section 3.1.2), so there are totally 22 features in the model.

Feature	Query	Session	# in Model
Query Class Entropy (QCE)	√		1
Session Class Entropy (SCE)		√	3
Class Match (CM)	√	√	3
ArgMaxOdds (AMO)	√	√	3
MaxOdds (MO)	√	√	3
KL Divergence (KL)	√	√	3
Cross Entropy (CE)	√	√	3
Distribution Similarity (DS)	√	√	3

tribution, that is:

$$\sum_c P(c \mid q) \log \frac{P(c \mid q)}{P(c \mid \langle q_1, q_2, \cdots, q_{T-1} \rangle)},$$

and we handle the special cases $0 \log 0$ and zero denominator as 0. *Cross Entropy* is the other feature similar to *KL Divergence*. It measures how topics represented in a candidate query are covered by the session. The formula of *Cross Entropy* is shown as follows:

$$-\sum_c P(c \mid q) \log P(c \mid \langle q_1, q_2, \cdots, q_{T-1} \rangle).$$

Distribution Similarity (DS). Each distribution has probabilities in all classes. We treat such distribution of a query or a session as a n-dimensional vector, which n is the number of classes. With the vector representation, we calculate cosine similarity between two vectors and measure the relation of the candidate query and the session.

Table 1 gives the summary of proposed features and their used information. Note that we apply three aspects of session-class distribution as described in Section 3.1.2 to extract session-related features. Hence, there are finally 22 features in the model (one query feature and seven session/query-session features for each aspect).

3.3 Ensemble with Conventional Approaches

Our proposed approach mainly focus on utilizing click-though data and external knowledge to classify queries into certain categories. In other words, the similarity based on query terms, which is the principal idea of conventional approaches, does not be considered in our model. Hence, the performance may be further improved if there is an ensemble model to combine our approach and other conventional approaches. Moreover, traditional term-based methods may favor longer search sessions so that more information can be found in the context. Conversely, class distribution extracted from short context in our approach may be able to more precisely represent users' search intents. That is, an ensemble model of two solutions may simultaneously benefit short and longer search sessions.

As the first study, we simply adopt all 43 features proposed in [21] as the other side of the ensemble model because this is one of the state-of-the-art approaches based on query terms in the context. Here *LambdaMART* [8] is utilized again to train an ensemble model to incorporate features proposed in this paper and [21]. Note that the length of the search session is one of the utilized features, so theoretically the ranking model will learn the strength of each model and perform well with both long and short search sessions.

4. EXPERIMENTS

In this section, we conduct extensive experiments on the large-scale datasets to verify the performance of our approach predicting user's intended query in the session.

4.1 Datasets and Experimental Settings

We use the public AOL log [32] in our experiments. The data comprises sampled queries submitted to the AOL search engine from 1 March, 2006 to 31 May, 2006. The query log is first segmented into sessions with a 30-minute threshold as the session boundary. To remove misspelled and rare queries, queries appearing less than 10 times in the whole log are dropped. Sessions with only single query are discarded because there must be at least one preceding query as the context for context-aware methods. After removing rare queries and single-query sessions, there are 1,359,760 sessions and 141,975 unique queries in total. Here we notice that the number of unique queries is inconsistent with [35]. It might be caused by a different procedure, which is not mentioned in [35], to remove short sessions. For each session with T queries, we treat each query q_i from the second position (i.e., $i \geq 2$) as the ground truth, which is the intended query we want to predict. The context is composed of $i - 1$ preceding queries $\langle q_1, q_2, \cdots q_{i-1} \rangle$ and their click-through information. Note that the cleaning process in this paper is consistent with previous work [35, 36].

After cleaning, the data is then partitioned into two sets. The first 2-month data is used for training. The remaining 1-month data is for testing. Finally, we collect 891,145 sessions as our training set. We use query frequency to generate candidate set. After filtering out those queries not starting from the prefix, the top-10 queries ranked by frequency form our candidate queries. The prefix is set to be the first character of q_T. Note that most of our settings are consistent with previous work, including the removal of rare queries [35], the way to generate candidates [21, 35].

To evaluate performance on tasks with different lengths of context, the testing sessions are divided into three subsets, including "Short Context" (1 query), "Medium Context" (2 to 3 queries) and "Long Context" (4 or more queries). Besides, we tune our LambdaMART model with parameters of 1,000 decision trees across all experiments; and we set the smoothing parameter m as 0.04 after tuning.

4.2 Competitive Baselines

To compare our approach with others, the following conventional methods are adopted as the baselines:

Most Popular Completion (or MPC). MPC is a *Maximum Likelihood Estimation* approach. It simply ranks candidates by their frequencies.

Hybrid Completion (or Hyb.C). Hyb.C proposed in [1] is a context-sensitive query completion method, which considers both context information and the popularity. The ranking of a candidate is determined by linear combination of its popularity (i.e., MPC) and similarity to recent queries.

Personalized Completion (or Per.C). Per.C proposed in [35] is a personalized query completion method, which considers users' personal information including submitted queries and demographics information. In this paper, we implement this method with short-term history (i.e., queries in the session), long-term history (i.e., queries in the user's search history) and query frequency.

Query-based VMM (or QVMM). QVMM proposed in [18] is a context-aware query suggestion method. It learns the probability of query transition along the sessions with the variable memory Markov model, which is an extension of Markov chain model.

Concept-based VMM (or CACB). CACB proposed in [25] is a concept-based context-aware query suggestion method. It clusters queries into several concepts to overcome the sparseness problem. After mapping each query to its corresponding concept, CACB tries to model the concept transition, instead of query transition, with variable memory Markov model.

Reformulation-based Completion (or RC). RC proposed in [21] models users' reformulation behavior during search sessions. It considers three kinds of reformulation-related features, including term-level, query-level and session-level features. The features carefully capture how users change preceding queries along the query sessions. We use *LambdaMART* [8] to train the model with 43 reformulation-related features.

Note that we do not compare our approach with [38] and [9] because [38] does not apply context information, and the temporal information [9] is not the focus of this paper.

4.3 Evaluation Metrics

In our experiments, *mean reciprocal rank* (MRR) is applied to evaluate the quality of query completion. The *mean reciprocal rank* (MRR) takes account of the ranked position of the ground truth. Given the session context C and the ground truth q_T, the reciprocal rank (RR) of an algorithm A is defined as follows:

$$\mathrm{RR}(A) = \frac{1}{hitrank(A, C, q_T)},$$

where $hitrank(A, C, q_T)$ computes the position of the ground truth ranked by the algorithm A. Thus, MRR can be computed as the mean value of RR for all search sessions in the testing set.

4.4 Overall Performance

Table 2 shows the experimental results over different prefix lengths. Our approach is denoted as CC (Classification-based Completion), and the single context means that we use only one preceding query as the context. Note that although both CC and CC (Single Context) utilize only one query as the context in the short context set, results might be different because the latter exploits only a single query in the training stage. Besides, MRR shown in [35] is higher than our reports because they do not consider sessions whose ground truths are not in the candidate lists. In other words, our evaluation can more effectively reflect the real situations.

Based on the context information, all of context-based methods outperform MPC in most cases. The Hyb.C completion has similar performance to the MPC method for short context. This is because short sessions context too few terms for Hyb.C to match the query to the context. With personal history, the Per.C method has better performance than the Hyb.C method because it can capture personal characteristics. The QVMM and CACB methods outper-

Table 2: The MRR performance of seven methods in the overall testing set and three subsets over different lengths of typed prefixes #p. Our approach is denoted as CC (Classification-based Completion), and the single context denoted as SC consists of only one query for both training and testing. The ensemble model of the RC method [21] and our approach is denoted as RC + CC. All improvements of our methods against [21] are significant differences at 95% level in a paired t-test.

Dataset	#p	MPC	Hyb.C [1]	Per.C [35]	QVMM [18]	CACB [25]	RC [21]	CC	CC (SC)	RC + CC
Overall	1	0.1724	0.1796	0.1935	0.2028	0.1987	0.2049	0.2140	0.2159	0.2245
	2	0.2703	0.2733	0.2770	0.2868	0.2828	0.2841	0.2939	0.2965	0.3024
	3	0.4004	0.4025	0.4026	0.4066	0.4014	0.4122	0.4193	0.4230	0.4369
	4	0.5114	0.5137	0.5129	0.5179	0.5126	0.5244	0.5358	0.5406	0.5562
Short Context (1 Query)	1	0.1540	0.1538	0.1740	0.1858	0.1813	0.1842	0.1966	0.1975	0.2055
	2	0.2523	0.2524	0.2591	0.2704	0.2637	0.2635	0.2792	0.2804	0.2864
	3	0.3819	0.3805	0.3846	0.3912	0.3903	0.3934	0.4065	0.4083	0.4177
	4	0.4939	0.4923	0.4962	0.5042	0.4979	0.5072	0.5243	0.5266	0.5390
Medium Context (2 to 3 Queries)	1	0.2041	0.2233	0.2266	0.2317	0.2288	0.2399	0.2438	0.2449	0.2556
	2	0.3015	0.3094	0.3080	0.3153	0.3111	0.3196	0.3226	0.3241	0.3356
	3	0.4293	0.4320	0.4308	0.4356	0.4316	0.4419	0.4435	0.4455	0.4573
	4	0.5368	0.5392	0.5371	0.5398	0.5373	0.5498	0.5539	0.5565	0.5694
Long Context (4 or more Queries)	1	0.1922	0.2207	0.2155	0.2164	0.2146	0.2284	0.2247	0.2310	0.2439
	2	0.2892	0.3000	0.2953	0.3002	0.2987	0.3076	0.3036	0.3121	0.3182
	3	0.4291	0.4396	0.4303	0.4302	0.4304	0.4397	0.4328	0.4449	0.4592
	4	0.5443	0.5497	0.5439	0.5468	0.5449	0.5546	0.5473	0.5625	0.5801

form previous baseline methods since they model query transitions along the whole search session. The reformulation-based completion (RC) performs the best among all baseline methods because it comprises abundant and diverse user reformulation behavior in different levels.

For all testing datasets, our approach beats the entire six comparative baseline methods over all prefix lengths, and significantly outperforms the RC method at 95% level in a paired t-test. Our approach has the greatest improvement in short context, which are the majority in search logs. This is because our model derives high level information (i.e., class distribution of search intents) beyond the limitation of query terms. Hence, the relationships between candidates and search intents can be discovered with very short context. However, the improvements of our approach gradually decrease when the length of context increases. The performance in the long context is even worse than the RC method. The reason is that former queries or click-through information may represent different search intents from latter ones. In contrast, while considering only a single query in the context, the performance in longer context improves simultaneously. It shows that our features can precisely capture users' search intents in the very limited context and avoid the noises of premature queries. The results are also consistent with [5, 29], which have shown the importance of the immediate query in modelling query sessions.

After combining the RC method [21] and our approach, the ensemble model obviously outperforms each of single model. Compared to two single models, the performance with a character as the prefix achieves a 9.57% improvements against the RC method and a 3.98% improvement against the CC method. It is reasonable because two approaches utilize different information to solve the problem so that the ensemble model can obtain the knowledge from both methods. Moreover, the improvements in the dataset

of long context against the CC method are greater than the improvements in the datasets of shorter context. This is because the knowledge from the RC method mends the shortcoming of the CC method on long context and improves the performance. Hence, the ensemble model of term-based methods and classification-based completion methods can actually predict users' intended queries more precisely.

4.5 Feature Effectiveness Analysis

In order to analyze the importance of different features, we adopt the leave-one-out feature selection method to verify the feature effectiveness. Figure 1 shows the result of leave-one-out feature selection. For example, we calculate the performance loss of SCE by removing three features of SCE, and then re-training the model. Here we apply the first character as the prefix. Note that features with higher performance loss are more important to the model. It is worth noticing that QCE is the most effective single feature. The result is also consistent to the previous work [4]. This feature can be treated as a measure of query ambiguity [13], and it implicitly leads to different ranking functions for queries with many intents and only few intents. The features about most likely class, including CM, AMO and MO, have the least importance among query-session features in the model. The reason is that the most likely class only cannot well capture the relationship between candidate queries and user's search intents (i.e., session-class distributions). In contrast, KL and CE are the most important query-session features because they estimate how a candidate query matches the session upon the entire class distribution.

Recall that we derive the session-class distribution from three different views and extract distribution-based features for them separately. We also analyze the importance of these extraction methods. As shown in Fig. 1, the features extracted by local-clicked URLs are the most effective among

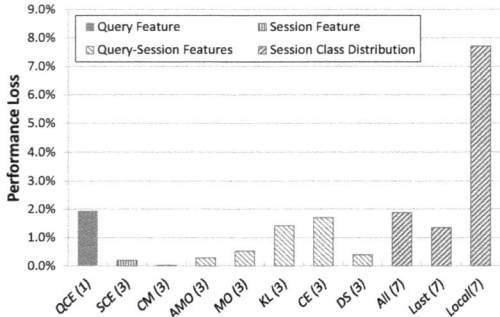

Figure 1: The performance loss of MRR for each individual feature category and each aspect of session-class distribution in leave-one-out feature selection. Note that the numbers in $(\cdot)$ represent the numbers of features in the model. All of abbreviations can be found in Section 3.

(a) Android Smartphone   (b) Google Maps

Figure 2: The illustrations of query completion systems on the Android smartphone and the Google Maps.

three views. It can be explained that the local-clicked URLs represent users' information needs correctly. Although we can derive general class distributions for queries in sessions, they may not fit the users' search intents well.

4.6 Keystroke Experiments

Although MRR is widely used as the evaluation measures for query completion, it might not reflect the user's actual demands. Both of two measures are sensitive to different positions of queries, but usually the user only hopes that the query appears in a high position. As shown in previous work [19, 30], the position biases generally exist in query completion and strongly affect its examination. Moreover, users usually can observe only few queries. For example, Figure 2 shows the illustrations of query completion systems on the Android smartphone and the Google Maps. Users can observe only five queries, so other queries ranked lower are meaningless for user experience and evaluation. Actually, users would like use *the least keystrokes* to make the desired query in a higher position. Although the query is ranked in a much low position (and out of the screen) with only one keystroke, the system may be still effective if it can rank the query in a very high position with two keystrokes.

Although this idea has already been proposed in previous work [15], few works utilized such measure to evaluate

Table 3: The keystroke performance of seven methods in the whole testing set. Our approach is denoted as CC (Classification-based Completion).

Measure	No Comp.	MPC	Hyb.C [1]	Per.C [35]
KS@1	11.0034	8.4294	6.8694	6.5761
KS@2	-	6.8625	5.6452	5.5078
KS@3	-	5.9830	4.9616	4.6965
KS@4	-	5.3038	4.5353	4.1793

Measure	QVMM [18]	CACB [25]	RC [21]	CC
KS@1	5.8704	6.1135	5.0129	**4.7479**
KS@2	4.1562	4.7813	3.9295	**3.6660**
KS@3	3.7044	4.0173	3.6523	**3.5880**
KS@4	3.6076	3.9138	3.5928	**3.5818**

the actual performance of query completion in a proper way. Here we evaluate our approach and baseline methods according to users' keystrokes. The *keystroke at top-k* (KS@k) is defined as the average keystrokes users spend so that the actual queries can be found in the top-k queries predicted for sessions.

Table 3 shows the keystroke performance of 5 methods in whole testing set. Because the average length of queries is about 11 characters, a user may spend 11 keystrokes averagely in a system without query completion. For query completion methods, it is obvious that all methods can save keystrokes. The results are also consistent to the performance shown in Table 2. Moreover, our approach still outperforms all comparative methods in the keystroke performance. For our approach, it can save 56.85% keystrokes for users. It represents that our approach is actually useful for user to save their time in typing queries.

5. ANALYSIS OF SEARCH INTENT CLASSIFICATION

In this section, we analyze the classes of users' search intents and further explain why our distribution-based features are effective to the query auto-completion.

5.1 Most Likely Class

Recall that the most likely class of the candidate query q is $c_q^* = \underset{c}{\mathrm{argmax}} P(c \mid q)$ and so is session's, we can compute the most likely class of a query or a session from derived class distribution. Figure 3 shows the percentage of sessions whose queries contain different number of topics. We can see that the queries in most sessions contain only a few classes for every length of sessions. That is, the candidates belonging to these few classes may have larger probability to be submitted as the next query. In other words, there are generally a small number of topics focused in a session. It is also the reason why our distribution-based features capturing the class distribution are effective in our experiments.

Next, we would like to know how the distribution-based features work in sessions within different length. Figure 4 shows the percentage of sessions whose most likely classes are identical to the last queries. Among three views of extracting session-class distribution, the view of local-clicked URLs has the highest percentages. It is consistent to the feature effectiveness analysis in Section 4.5. The percentages of shorter sessions are higher than longer ones in all

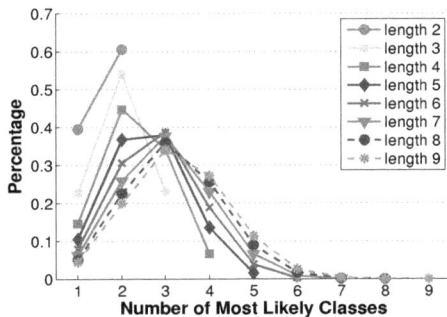

Figure 3: The percentage of sessions whose queries contain different number of most likely classes.

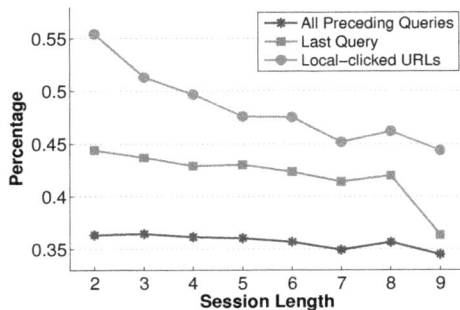

Figure 4: The percentage of sessions with the identical most likely classes to the last queries over different session length.

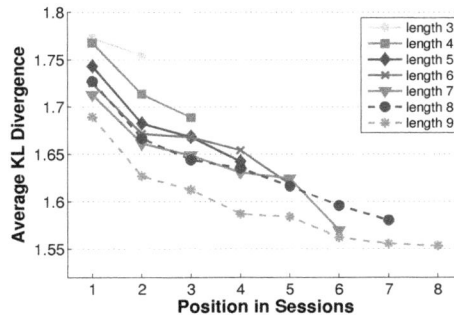

Figure 5: Average *KL Divergence* between local-clicked URLs and the last query over different position in sessions.

ground truths in *KL Divergence*. It is also consistent to the results in Section 4.5. The results show that the derived class distribution can well represent the characteristics of queries and sessions. Therefore, the distribution matching can advantageously identify the actual submitted query.

Table 4: Percentages of incorrect candidate queries whose features are larger than the ground truths of sessions over three views of the session distribution.

Feature	All Preceding Queries	Last Query	Local-clicked URLs
KL Divergence	0.6641	0.6406	0.8118
Cross Entropy	0.5994	0.5688	0.7072

three views. The reason might be that shorter context has fewer noises to be matched more precisely. It also explains why our approach has greater improvements with shorter context. However, there are more than 40% sessions whose the most likely classes are not identical to the last queries. This might be the reason why features of the most likely class are not so important in the model, as shown in Fig. 1.

5.2 Distribution Matching

Beyond the most likely class, this section discusses the matching between candidate queries and the search session. As the analysis in Section 4.5, *KL Divergence* and *Cross Entropy* are the most effective features among query-session features. That is, estimating how a candidate query matches the session upon entire class distributions is useful to identify the actual submitted query (or the ground truth) in the candidate query list. Table 4 shows the percentages of incorrect candidate queries whose *KL Divergence* and *Cross Entropy* are larger than the ground truths of sessions over three views of the session distribution. For a candidate query, lower feature values represent that the distribution of the query is more similar to the session. Both features can well distinguish the ground truths from other incorrect candidate queries. The *KL Divergence* values of submitted queries are less than at least 64% other incorrect candidates over each view of the session distribution. Among three views of the session distribution, features extracted by local-clicked URLs perform best on identifying the correct queries. More than 80% incorrect candidates are ranked lower than the

5.3 Local-clicked URLs

As the relevance signals in the search session, local-clicked URLs can provide copious information about users' search intents. The features extracted by such URLs are also effective in our model as shown in Section 4.5. This section discusses why local-clicked URLs are so useful.

The hosts of URLs are worth a thought because URLs under a same host might share similar search intents. For each session whose the last query has clicked URLs (i.e., $u_T \neq \emptyset$), there are 11.89% sessions which have URLs of the identical hosts within previous queries. Even though the space of URL hosts is very sparse and contains hundreds of thousands hosts, there are still numerous sessions with identical hosts. It shows that there will be more sessions with URLs of similar search intents, not only URLs with the identical hosts. It might also be the reason that the features of local-clicked URLs are so useful.

Next, we analyze the distribution matching between the last queries and local-clicked URLs in each position. Figure 5 shows the average *KL Divergence* between local-clicked URLs and the last query over different position in sessions. Note that the last queries are distinct in sessions of different session lengths, so *KL Divergence* values for different lengths are not comparable. From Fig. 5, it is worth noticing that the average *KL Divergence* decreases as the position increases. The class distribution of more recently clicked URLs are more similar to the query. It is also consistent to the results in Section 4. Shorter context might contain more clear information and obtain better improvements.

6. DISCUSSIONS AND CONCLUSIONS

In this paper, we proposed a novel approach for query completion aiming to predict users' next intended queries. Different from conventional context-aware methods discovering term- and query-level relationships between sessions and candidates, we classify users' search intents behind search sessions by deriving class distributions for predicting queries more precisely. We focus on discovering search intents with short context because most of search sessions are very short and limited. The results of extensive experiments demonstrate that our approach significantly outperforms several existing context-aware approaches. Such improvement is consistent across different context lengths. The reasons are as follows: (1) our classification-based model requires less training data. There are only few categories for classification. The sparseness problem can be solved; (2) class distributions of search sessions can well capture users' search intents. Several distribution-based features matching search sessions and candidate queries are considered for query completion. (3) with a high-level aspect, users' search intents can be well captured in the limited context. The results of analysis in Section 5 also support that our features are helpful and important. Moreover, the results of keystroke experiments in Section 4.6 show that our approach can effectively reduce users' keystrokes to complete queries.

As future work, users' reformulation behavior may further interact with search intent classification although we have proved their ensemble model has a excellent performance in Section 4. For example, some users' behavior may imply the change of search intents, then we can dynamically modify the classification-based model.

7. REFERENCES

[1] Z. Bar-Yossef and N. Kraus. Context-sensitive query auto-completion. In *WWW '11*, pages 107–116. ACM, 2011.

[2] E. Baykan, M. Henzinger, L. Marian, and I. Weber. Purely url-based topic classification. In *WWW '09*, pages 1109–1110. ACM, 2009.

[3] S. M. Beitzel, E. C. Jensen, D. D. Lewis, A. Chowdhury, and O. Frieder. Automatic classification of web queries using very large unlabeled query logs. *ACM TOIS*, 25(2):9, 2007.

[4] P. N. Bennett, K. Svore, and S. T. Dumais. Classification-enhanced ranking. In *WWW '10*, pages 111–120. ACM, 2010.

[5] P. N. Bennett, R. W. White, W. Chu, S. T. Dumais, P. Bailey, F. Borisyuk, and X. Cui. Modeling the impact of short-and long-term behavior on search personalization. In *SIGIR '12*, pages 185–194. ACM, 2012.

[6] S. Bhatia, D. Majumdar, and P. Mitra. Query suggestions in the absence of query logs. In *SIGIR '11*, pages 795–804. ACM, 2011.

[7] P. Boldi, F. Bonchi, C. Castillo, D. Donato, and S. Vigna. Query suggestions using query-flow graphs. In *WSCD '09*, pages 56–63. ACM, 2009.

[8] C. J. Burges, K. M. Svore, P. N. Bennett, A. Pastusiak, and Q. Wu. Learning to rank using an ensemble of lambda-gradient models. *JMLR*, 14:25–35, 2011.

[9] F. Cai, S. Liang, and M. de Rijke. Time-sensitive personalized query auto-completio. In *CIKM '14*, pages 1599–1608. ACM, 2014.

[10] C. Carpineto and G. Romano. A survey of automatic query expansion in information retrieval. *ACM Computing Surveys (CSUR)*, 44(1):1, 2012.

[11] O. Chapelle and Y. Zhang. A dynamic bayesian network click model for web search ranking. In *WWW '09*, pages 1–10. ACM, 2009.

[12] S. Chaudhuri and R. Kaushik. Extending autocompletion to tolerate errors. In *SIGMOD '09*, pages 707–718. ACM, 2009.

[13] K. Collins-Thompson and P. N. Bennett. Estimating query performance using class predictions. In *SIGIR '09*, pages 672–673. ACM, 2009.

[14] N. C. Corporation. Open directory project. http://www.dmoz.org, 2013.

[15] H. Duan and B.-J. P. Hsu. Online spelling correction for query completion. In *WWW '11*, pages 117–126. ACM, 2011.

[16] B. Fonseca, P. Golgher, B. Pôssas, B. Ribeiro-Neto, and N. Ziviani. Concept-based interactive query expansion. In *CIKM '05*, pages 696–703. ACM, 2005.

[17] E. Gabrilovich, A. Broder, M. Fontoura, A. Joshi, V. Josifovski, L. Riedel, and T. Zhang. Classifying search queries using the web as a source of knowledge. *ACM TWEB)*, 3(2):5, 2009.

[18] Q. He, D. Jiang, Z. Liao, S. C. H. Hoi, K. Chang, E.-P. Lim, and H. Li. Web query recommendation via sequential query prediction. In *ICDE '09*, pages 1443–1454, 2009.

[19] K. Hofmann, B. Mitra, F. Radlinski, and M. Shokouhi. An eye-tracking study of user interactions with query auto completion. In *CIKM '14*, pages 549–558. ACM, 2014.

[20] C.-K. Huang, L.-F. Chien, and Y.-J. Oyang. Relevant term suggestion in interactive web search based on contextual information in query session logs. *JASIST*, 54, 2003.

[21] J.-Y. Jiang, Y.-Y. Ke, P.-Y. Chien, and P.-J. Cheng. Learning user reformulation behavior for query auto-completion. In *SIGIR '14*. ACM, 2014.

[22] I.-H. Kang and G. Kim. Query type classification for web document retrieval. In *SIGIR '03*, pages 64–71. ACM, 2003.

[23] J. Y. Kim, K. Collins-Thompson, P. N. Bennett, and S. T. Dumais. Characterizing web content, user interests, and search behavior by reading level and topic. In *WSDM '12*, pages 213–222. ACM, 2012.

[24] Y. Li, Z. Zheng, and H. K. Dai. Kdd cup-2005 report: facing a great challenge. *SIGKDD Explor.*, 7(2):91–99, 2005.

[25] Z. Liao, D. Jiang, E. Chen, J. Pei, H. Cao, and H. Li. Mining concept sequences from large-scale search logs for context-aware query suggestion. *ACM Transactions on Intelligent Systems and Technology (TIST)*, 3(1):17, 2011.

[26] J. Luo, S. Zhang, X. Dong, and H. Yang. Designing states, actions, and rewards for using pomdp in session search. In *ECIR '15*, pages 526–537, 2015.

[27] Q. Mei, D. Zhou, and K. Church. Query suggestion using hitting time. In *CIKM '08*, pages 469–478. ACM, 2008.

[28] G. A. Miller. Wordnet: A lexical database for english. *CACM*, 38(11):39–41, 1995.

[29] B. Mitra. Exploring session context using distributed representations of queries and reformulations. In *SIGIR '15*, pages 3–12. ACM, 2015.

[30] B. Mitra, M. Shokouhi, F. Radlinski, and K. Hofmann. On user interactions with query auto-completion. In *SIGIR '14*, pages 1055–1058. ACM, 2014.

[31] U. Ozertem, O. Chapelle, P. Donmez, and E. Velipasaoglu. Learning to suggest: a machine learning framework for ranking query suggestions. In *SIGIR '12*, pages 25–34. ACM, 2012.

[32] G. Pass, A. Chowdhury, and C. Torgeson. A picture of search. In *InfoScale '06*, 2006.

[33] R. L. Santos, C. Macdonald, and I. Ounis. Learning to rank query suggestions for adhoc and diversity search. *Information Retrieval*, pages 1–23, 2012.

[34] D. Shen, J.-T. Sun, Q. Yang, and Z. Chen. Building bridges for web query classification. In *SIGIR '06*, pages 131–138. ACM, 2006.

[35] M. Shokouhi. Learning to personalize query auto-completion. In *SIGIR '13*, pages 103–112. ACM, 2013.

[36] M. Shokouhi and K. Radinsky. Time-sensitive query auto-completion. In *SIGIR '12*, pages 601–610. ACM, 2012.

[37] Y. Song, D. Zhou, and L. He. Query suggestion by constructing term-transition graphs. In *WSDM '12*, pages 353–362. ACM, 2012.

[38] S. Whiting and J. M. Jose. Recent and robust query auto-completion. In *WWW '14*, pages 971–982. ACM, 2014.

[39] H. Yang, D. Guan, and S. Zhang. The query change model: Modeling session search as a markov decision process. *ACM TOIS*, 33:20, 2015.

An Analysis of the Cost and Benefit of Search Interactions

Leif Azzopardi
University of Strathclyde
Glasgow, United Kingdom
leifos@acm.org

Guido Zuccon
Queensland University of Technology
Queensland, Australia
g.zuccon@qut.edu.au

ABSTRACT

Interactive Information Retrieval (IR) systems often provide various features and functions, such as query suggestions and relevance feedback, that a user may or may not decide to use. The decision to take such an option has associated costs and may lead to some benefit. Thus, a savvy user would take decisions that maximizes their net benefit. In this paper, we formally model the costs and benefits of various decisions that users, implicitly or explicitly, make when searching. We consider and analyse the following scenarios: *(i)* how long a user's query should be? *(ii)* should the user pose a specific or vague query? *(iii)* should the user take a suggestion or re-formulate? *(iv)* when should a user employ relevance feedback? and *(v)* when would the "find similar" functionality be worthwhile to the user? To this end, we build a series of cost-benefit models exploring a variety of parameters that affect the decisions at play. Through the analyses, we are able to draw a number of insights into different decisions, provide explanations for observed behaviours and generate numerous testable hypotheses. This work not only serves as a basis for future empirical work, but also as a template for developing other cost-benefit models involving human-computer interaction.

Keywords

Search Behaviour; User Models; Retrieval Strategies; Evaluation, Measures.

1. INTRODUCTION

Information Retrieval and Seeking activities take place in the context of a task (typically a work task) [29]. The evaluation of Information Retrieval has however largely focused on measuring and modeling the performance of a system based on an abstraction of the search process (e.g. the TREC/Cranfield paradigm [28, 56]). While it has been long recognised that such paradigms ignore many factors [28, 49], there has only recently been a drive to create new evaluation measures that go beyond precision and recall, incorporat-

ing: *(i)* more sophisticated user models that encode stopping and interaction behaviour [39, 42], *(ii)* the gain and usefulness of the documents encountered [13, 20, 30] *(iii)* the cost and effort of performing different interactions [2, 50, 62, 63] and *(iv)* the sequence of interactions within and across the sessions (as opposed to considering ranked lists in isolation) [4, 5, 31, 46]. Underpinning most measures is a user model [59]; so there has been a concerted effort to improve the current user models to develop more realistic and accurate measures [40]. While much of the research has focused on how users interact with a ranked list (resulting in numerous measures [17, 40]), less attention has been paid to modeling other interactions. Now with the drive towards task based evaluations and task completion engines [11, 13, 58], it is timely to consider modeling interactions outwith the ranked list, and to understand how the different choices users can make affect their overall session performance. Two common threads run through this recent work.

(i) The **cost** of interaction, through the inclusion of the effort or time involved in the search process within the evaluation measure. For example, measures like Time Biased Gain (TBG) [50] specifically incorporate the time to assess documents. While the effort involved in processing a document in terms of readability and understandability has been explicitly included in other measures (e.g., [2, 62, 63]).

(ii) The **benefit** of interaction, through the inclusion of a gain, graded relevance or the value of the information found. For example, the U-measure values shorter documents more than longer document [46]; while in RBP, DCG and variants of [18, 30, 39, 42], documents seen at a later point in the session are valued less.

A key assumption underpinning the modeling and measuring of user-system performance is that a system or search strategy results in greater net benefit (or utility)[1] is preferable than one that yields lower net benefit . Indeed, it has been posited that people will modify their search strategies in order to maximize their net benefit, and that systems and interfaces will evolve so as to maximize the net benefit for the user [43]. For example, an instantiation of the card playing model [61] shows how the interface can be adapted to maximize the information gain at each round of interaction. On the other hand, numerous attempts have been made to augment the standard search interface but have been met with limited success [33]. Taken together, this body of work

---

[1] Utility (or expected utility), expressed as the gain or gain over time.

ICTIR '16, September 12 - 16, 2016, Newark, DE, USA

© 2016 Copyright held by the owner/author(s). Publication rights licensed to ACM.
ISBN 978-1-4503-4497-5/16/09. . . $15.00

DOI: http://dx.doi.org/10.1145/2970398.2970412

motivates the development of user models that consider the costs and benefits of the decisions involved in searching and seeking so that we can better understand the process and support it appropriately through the interfaces and systems we develop. Consequently, in this work we begin building a series of cost-benefit models of various interactions from a user perspective. This allows us to: *(1)* reason about why users perform certain actions over others, *(2)* understand why certain features or interactions are preferable over others, and *(3)* develop core underlying user models for the development of task and session based measures. To this end, we consider different decisions the user faces when querying and interacting with the system/interface, where we consider questions such as:

- why is it so hard to get users to type longer queries?

- why are users reluctant to give relevance feedback?

- and why is the standard search interface preferable to "novel" search interfaces?

Through our analyses, we draw various insights regarding user behaviour and generate numerous testable hypotheses which can be explored in future work.

2. RELATED WORK

Early on in the history of IR, the notion of utility featured heavily and gave rise to the strong evaluation based traditions in the field [56]. In [22], Cooper put forward the proposition that utility forms the basis of measurement claiming that it would be the *ideal measure*. However the difficulty in obtaining judgements of utility meant that the field has resorted to relying upon the simple demarcations of non-relevant and relevant. Nonetheless, the idea of using the utility of a document has arisen in various guises (i.e. graded relevance, gain, benefit, usefulness and negative cost) and has formed the basis of much research. For example, in [44], Robertson examined the problem of ranking in terms of the costs and benefits. This led to the formulation of the Probability Ranking Principle (PRP) which essentially applies decision theory to the ranking problem [44]. The PRP makes a number of assumptions which are also implicit within most measures used, reflecting the user model, i.e. that documents are judged/valued independently, the costs/benefits of (non) relevant documents are the same, and that documents are judged in a linear fashion. Furthermore, most measures and models have focused on evaluating a ranked list. However, there is now impetus to go beyond the ranked list, and consider the whole session in the context of the task [4, 5, 11, 31, 46]. Thus, we need to revisit the idea of modeling the utility of the information found and the actions in the sessions that lead to ascertaining that utility. Here, we consider how much utility (or usefulness) one obtains in terms of the *costs* and *benefits* as suggested by Bates [12]. In [12], Bates describes one of the monitoring tactics people employ when searching is to *weigh* the costs and benefits of their decisions/interactions. While Bates did not elaborate on this tactic, a line of research has evolved from this notion which formally models the costs and benefits of interaction using different, but related, frameworks [45, 43, 6, 25]. For instance, in [45], they examine the cost structures associated with sense-making, and in [43] Pirolli adapts Foraging Theory to explore how searchers attempt to maximise the gain (benefit) over time.

A Note on Relevance, Cost & Benefit

In the literature, the *cost* and *benefit* of documents, information and interactions have been discussed and introduced in a variety ways. *Benefit*, or the value associated with a document, has been referred to as: *relevance, benefit, gain, utility, expected utility* and *usefulness* [7, 17, 20, 22, 25, 30, 44, 60]. For example, early on relevance was associated with utility [22] in the sense that one receives benefit or gain from a document that is relevant. Of course, what constitutes relevance is subject to much interpretation [38]. However, the point is that most researchers acknowledge that users are after some useful information to help them facilitate the completion of a task. How this usefulness, benefit, gain, etc. is measured is an open challenge. While in terms of *cost*, researchers have considered mental/cognitive, physical, financial and temporal costs [6, 26, 50]. Often time is considered as a proxy for cost, or as an independent variable to contextualize the rate of gain [43, 50]. Recently the cognitive costs and the effort in processing, reading and understanding a document have also been considered [2, 50, 62, 63]. However costs are difficult to define, quantify and measure, and this is also an open challenge in the field.

In this work we will develop and discuss the costs and benefits as abstract, but common, units. However, one can think about many of the models with respect to time or money as the cost and benefit [25], i.e., how much time do I have to spend, and how much time do I save? Or how much money do I have to spend, and how much money do I save or earn? In this paper we mainly use the terms cost and benefit, but may use some of the terms above interchangeably, where appropriate, and depending on the context.

Related Models

As previously mentioned, most measures are underpinned by a user model pertaining to how users interact with a ranked list of documents. For example, precision at k assumes that the user examines documents up until rank k and then stops. Furthermore, the measure implicitly assumes that the cost of processing each document is the same, and the value obtained from each document is also the same regardless. However, there has been a succession of innovations in modeling how the user interacts with a ranked list which has led to new measures (e.g. RBP [42], DCG [30], INST [39], etc.) and analyses of the relationship between measures and user stopping models [17, 40, 41]. Recently, other advances are being introduced into measures. For example in [48], Smucker empirically explores how changes in the cost of reading snippets and the quality of snippets affects the gain in terms of the number of documents. Later, Smucker and Clarke [50] extended this work by incorporating the time to process snippets and documents into TBG as a way to evaluate the gain over time. In [2], Arvola et al. also consider the effort required to read, creating measures of the expected reading effort. Other work shows that the effort (measured in time) to judge documents varies depending on the relevance [55, 60], again demonstrating that both cost and gain need to be considered. An excellent summary of such user models and how different measures employ them is provided in [41], while in [17] Carterette demonstrates that these IR evaluation measures can be interpreted as utility (or expected utility) when these user stopping models are used, thus bringing together cost, benefit and expectation resulting from the search interaction. Other researchers have focused on modeling the interaction with the ranked list by developing click models [19] such as the cascade model [23]. However, to model (and thus measure) the whole session and the task performance, it is necessary to consider the range of search interactions as well as other components of the search interface.

The focus of this paper is on other less considered aspects of the search process; rather than trying to measure, we focus on modeling the interactions to draw insights and reason about the behaviours and interactions of users. In this direction, previous research has modeled various aspects of the information seeking and search process. For example, in [21], Cooper models the costs and benefits of various searchers (the user and the librarian/system) to understand the trade-off between how much time each party should spend searching. In [54], Varian outlined how we could apply Stigler's theory of Optimal Search Behaviour to IR [53] and how to examine the economic value of information using consumer theory, "where a consumer is making a choice to maximize expected utility or minimise expected cost" [54]. This lead to various insights such as a document has little or no value if the information it contains is redundant. In [16], Birchler and Butler also explain how Stigler's theory can be applied to search in order to predict when a user should stop examining results in a ranked list, i.e., when the marginal benefit equals the marginal cost. While in [25], Fuhr generalizes the Probability Ranking Principle such that documents have different costs and benefits and that there is some uncertainty over accepting a decision.

Information Foraging Theory [43] (IFT) examines the profitability of items found by considering the net gain obtained given time spent (which is what TBG [50] attempts to measure). Under IFT, it is possible to model various situations, such as when the user should stop examining results and move to another patch. Interestingly, in [8] this was shown to make the same predictions as the iPRP and Search Economic Theory [5]. In [5], Azzopardi considers the economics (in terms of gain and cost) to examine the tradeoff and interplay between querying and assessing. This session-based model ascribes a cost and gain functions given the two different interactions. In follow up work this was extended to include inspecting snippets and paging [7]. The model enables various hypotheses to be generated depending on the changes in the performance (gain) from the interactions with the system and the cost of the various interactions [7].

In [32], Kashyap et al. define a cost model for browsing facets to minimize cost of interaction and thereby increasing the usefulness of the interface. In [9], Azzopardi and Zuccon model the browsing costs on the Search Engine Result Page (SERP), where they consider the size of the screen, the results viewable and the number of documents to browse through. While simple, their model is instructive in understanding the relationship between scrolling and paging. In [51], Smucker and Clarke model the switching behaviour of users engaging with ranked lists which provide different levels of gain. They show at what point it is optimal to switch. We continue in this line of research and

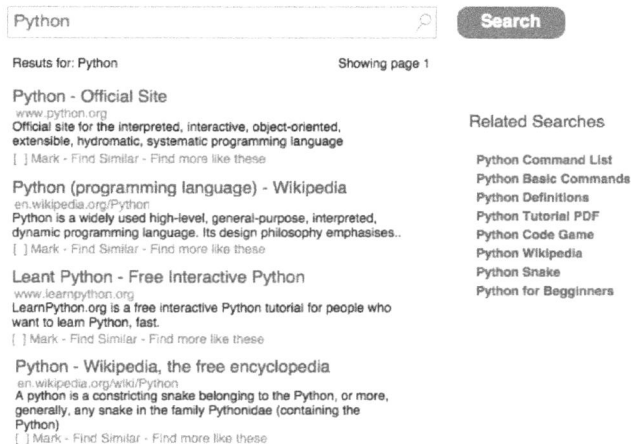

Figure 1: A search interface with related searches and the option to mark relevant documents, find similar and find more like the ones marked. For the query, "*Python*" the page displays results mostly about the Python programming language.

develop a number of simple models of various search interactions to add to the growing catalogue of user models for search interaction.

3. AIMS AND METHODOLOGY

The main aim of this paper is to build a number of models regarding different decisions, i.e. actions, interactions, choices that users can make when using a search system and interface under a common framework, a cost-benefit analysis. Under the cost-benefit analysis, costs and benefits are considered to be in the same units. A more general approach is a cost-utility analysis, where the cost and benefit are expressed in different units (i.e. benefit might be expressed as the number of relevant documents found and the cost expressed as time). However, as a starting point, for modeling these interactions, we will assume that the costs and benefits are in the same (albeit abstract) units, and thus use a cost-benefit framework. During the course of this paper we will consider the following scenarios: query length, query diversity, query suggestions, relevance feedback, and find similar. For each scenario, we will model salient aspects of the interaction in order to gain various insights.

Before we begin creating models of these different scenarios, we first ground our models based upon the search interface depicted in Figure 1. We then enumerate the different variables that we will use, followed by our approach.

3.1 Search Interface

For the purposes of modeling various interactions we base our analyses on the standard search interface which includes a query box, result snippets and navigational buttons (previous and next). Each snippet has a title (a blue link), a snippet from the document (black text), and url/domain (green text). However, we have also included a few extra features: *(i)* related searches / query suggestions, *(ii)* an option to find similar, and *(iii)* an option to mark documents as useful and then to find more like those marked. The later two features are different versions of explicit relevance feedback which we shall model[2]. In various works, researchers have

---

[2]We note that most interfaces don't provide such options or provide

$c(.)$	cost function
c_w	cost to enter a word
c_i	total cost of interaction
c_q	cost of issuing a query
c_s	cost of examining a snippet
c_a	cost of assessing a document
c_c	cost of a click
c_d	cost of deciding to mark and undertake relevance feedback
c_m	cost of judging and then marking a document as relevant (for relevance feedback)
c_{rq}	cost of remembering the issued query
c_{es}	cost of examining query suggestions

Table 1: Notation used for cost functions and associated variables.

$b(.)$	benefit function
b_{fp}	benefit provided by the first SERP
b_{np}	benefit provided by the next SERP
b_{nq}	benefit provided by the next query
b_{rf}	benefit provided by performing relevance feedback

Table 2: Notation used for benefit functions and associated variables.

π	profit (or net benefit)
W	number of query words
Z	number of aspects associated with a query
N	number of documents the user seeks
M	number of documents to be marked for relevance feedback
A	number of assessed documents
R	number of result in a SERP
S	number of snippets examined
Q_s	number of query suggestions

Table 3: Notation for other variables common across models.

experimented with different interfaces and techniques to increase the net benefit to the user. It is therefore of interest to explore the cost-benefit relationships formally. During the course of interaction, a user poses a query, waits for the page to load, examines the page, and a number of snippets, along with examining a number of documents. The user will decide at some point either to stop browsing the current page of results, and move onto the next page, reformulate their query, take a query suggestion, provide feedback or stop searching.

3.2 Notation and Preliminaries

Costs and benefits are associated to interactions. For example, users pay a cost when formulating a query (c_q) or assessing a document (c_a), but they may also extract some benefit when exposed to the information contained in a document. Table 1 provides the different costs for various interactions, while Table 2 provides an overview of the benefits from different interactions. Note that we have defined interactions at an action level (as opposed to a keystroke level) because different interactions can be implemented differently and so depend on the instantiation of the feature. In our analyses, we will loosely base the cost on the time it takes to perform such actions, where we ground the costs based on the values in [6, 50, 47]. Though the costs (and benefits) used in the examples (see Figures 2-5) are purely to illuminate the equations - estimating the costs and benefits is left for future work. During the discussion of the models, we will explain how the cost could change for different interactions depending on how it is implemented, and how this would affect the decision users take.

3.3 Methods of Analysis

To analyse each of the different scenarios, we will first define and enumerate the different costs and benefits associated with the different actions. Given these cost and benefit functions, we will then employ a number of related tech-

niques to determine: (a) how the net benefit π (or profit, i.e., benefit minus cost) changes as another variable of interest changes, or (b) whether one course of action leads to greater profit over another course of action. In our analysis we assume, like much of the previous work [5, 25, 43], that users will be rational in the sense that they will try to maximize their net benefit from interacting with the system.

The first method of analysis will be to examine the change in profit as the variable of interest (e.g., number of query words) changes. Here, we can determine when the profit is maximized by taking the derivative of the profit function, setting it to zero, and then solving.

The second method we employ is when we have two alternatives/decisions and we need to determine under what conditions one decision is preferable to the other. In this case, the profit resulting from each decision is compared using an inequality, to determine which decision is more profitable.

The third method we employ is similar to the second approach, except that we only consider the costs involved in the decision and assume the benefit is the same for both decisions.

4. QUERY INTERACTIONS

As argued in [4, 40], performance is determined by both the user and the system. How well a user can use the system will depend on what decisions they make. The initial decisions a user makes when starting a search session is what query to pose, how long, and how specific.

4.1 Querying Length

First, we consider the questions, why do user queries tend to be short, and how can we motivate users to type longer queries? In order to provide insights into these questions, we need to consider what factors affect the benefit of a query. While many factors are at play [29], one of the main drivers is query length. It has been shown on numerous occasions that longer queries tend to yield better performance [3, 14, 24]. Consequently, this has led to various attempts to try and elicit longer queries from users (e.g. [1, 34, 35]). However, these attempts have largely been ineffectual: we posit this is due to the costs and benefits at play. We further posit that inline autocomplete techniques are instead more effective in eliciting longer queries because they substantially lower the cost of entering a query while increasing the benefit.

We model the decision to issue a query of a particular length W to denote the number of words as follows: the benefit that a user receives is given by the benefit function $b(W)$ and the cost (or effort in querying) defined by the cost function $c(W)$. Now let's consider a benefit function

---

either the find similar or the find more like these options. We show them on the same interface for the purposes of illustration.

which denotes the situation where the user experiences diminishing returns such that as the query length increases they receive less and less benefit (as shown in [3, 14]). This can be modeled with the function:

$$b(W) = k.\log_a(W + 1) \tag{1}$$

where k represents a scaling factor, and a influences how quickly the user experiences diminishing returns. Let's assume then that the cost of entering a query is a linear function based on the number of words such that:

$$c(W) = W.c_w \tag{2}$$

where c_w represents how much effort must be spent to enter each word. This is, of course, a simple cost model and it is easy to imagine more complex cost functions. However the point is to provide a simple, but insightful, abstraction. Now given these two functions, we can compute the profit (net benefit) π that the user receives for a query of length W:

$$\pi = b(W) - c(W) = k.\log_a(W + 1) - W.c_w \tag{3}$$

To find the query length that maximizes the user's net benefit, we can differentiate and solve the equation:

$$\frac{\partial \pi}{\partial W} = \frac{k}{\log a} \times \frac{1}{W + 1} - c_w = 0 \tag{4}$$

This results in:

$$W^\star = \frac{k}{c_w.\log a} - 1 \tag{5}$$

Figure 2 illustrates the benefit (top) and profit (bottom) as query length increases. For the left plots $k = 10$, and for the right plots $k = 15$. Within each plot we show various levels of a. These plots show that as k increases (i.e. overall the performance of the system increases), then the model suggests that query length, on average, would increase, and if a increases (i.e. the performance of the system increases but at a faster rate), then queries decrease in length. Furthermore the model suggests that as the cost of entering a word, c_w, decreases users will tend to pose longer queries.

Summary

This simple model shows that to motivate longer queries either the cost of querying needs to decrease or the performance of the system needs to increase (via k and a). Ergo, reducing the cost of querying by providing inline autocomplete suggestions reduces the cost and increases the performance sufficiently that it motivates longer queries on average being issued. It further suggests that techniques to encourage the user to issue longer queries are insufficient on their own. They instead need to be backed up by increases in system performance or reductions in user interaction cost.

4.2 Specificity and Diversity

The next question we consider is whether it is better to pose a vague query or more specific query?[3]. This, of course, depends on how the system responds to such requests by returning diversified or non-diversified results.

---

[3]While specificity is related to length we wish to consider this separately for the time being, and leave considering the relationship between specificity and length for future work.

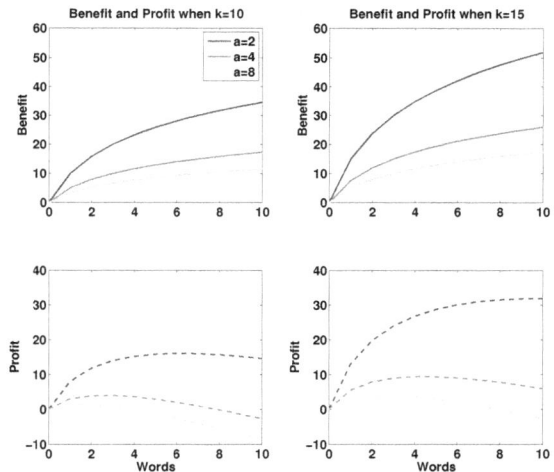

Figure 2: The top plots show the benefit while the bottom plots show the profit as the length of the query increases. Plots on the right show when the queries yield greater benefit. Each plot shows three levels of α which denotes how quickly diminishing returns sets in.

To provide the context, let's consider the following scenario. For simplicity we assume that the user is seeking N documents and their initial query is underspecified as it may refer to Z possible aspects/intents/interpretations. For example, if the user poses the query "*Python*" as shown in Figure 1, then there are several possible interpretations such as: the language, the snake, the movie, etc. We shall refer to these as *aspects* in the remainder of this paper.

Let's consider now how a system might respond. The system could take a diversified approach and provide some coverage of the Z aspects. Or it could take a non-diversified approach returning documents that correspond to the most popular or dominant aspect and thus return documents only from one aspect. Which approach would a user prefer? Or stated another way, under what circumstances would interacting with diversified results be less costly than interacting with non-diversified results? To answer this questions we consider how the user might interact with these different result lists, and then compare the costs and benefits.

When interacting with the diversified result list, the user pays a cost for issuing the query, c_{q_1}. For simplicity, we assume the diversified response blends the different aspects together uniformly so that approximately 1 in every Z results refers to a relevant aspect. This means the user would have to process $N.Z$ snippets to find the N results about that aspect in the best case. On average however, it is likely that only a proportion would be relevant, say p_r. Thus, on average they would have to inspect $\frac{N.Z}{p_r}$ snippets, but for simplicity we assume that $p_r = 1$.

With the cost of examining a snippet being c_s, the cost of interacting with the diversified results (c_i^D) is:

$$c_i^D = c_{q_1} + c_s.N.Z \tag{6}$$

On the other hand, the cost of interacting with the non-diversified results is slightly different. The user again pays the cost for issuing the first query, c_{q_1}. If the query retrieved documents for the correct aspect, the user only needs to examine N snippets, resulting in a cost of $c_s.N$ for examining all the snippets. For simplicity we further assume that the system returns the aspect the user had in mind with a uniform probability $1/Z$ [4].

If instead the query did not retrieve documents for the correct aspect, the user needs to issue a more specific query, paying an additional querying cost c_{q_2}. Since q_2 would typically mean adding one or more terms to the original query, then c_{q_2} is likely to be less than c_{q_1}. However, before they issue a new query, the user first examines k snippets, before realising that the response is inadequate. They then decide to re-formulate. For simplicity, we will assume that the more specific query means that the system will respond with the correct aspect (i.e., "python snake"). Of course, within this aspect, there could be sub-aspects, but again we will assume for simplicity that the re-formulated query is sufficient to retrieve documents that correspond to the user's intent. In this case, they reformulate with probability $1 - 1/Z$. Thus, the total cost of interaction with a non-diversified system ($c_{i,ND}$) is:

$$c_i^{ND} = c_{q_1} + \frac{1}{Z}c_s N + \left(1 - \frac{1}{Z}\right)\left(c_{q_2} + c_s(N+k)\right) \quad (7)$$

Given the two cost models, we can compare the two user-system interactions to determine if it is better to *(a)* pose an underspecified query and interact with the diversified result list, or *(b)* pose an underspecified query and interact with the non-diversified result list, then reformulate the query to retrieve the aspect of interest:

$$
\begin{aligned}
c_i^D &< c_i^{ND} \\
c_{q_1} + c_s N.Z &< c_{q_1} + \frac{1}{Z}c_s N \\
&\quad + \left(1 - \frac{1}{Z}\right)\left(c_{q_2} + c_s(N+k)\right) \\
c_{q_2} &> c_s(N.Z - k) \quad (8)
\end{aligned}
$$

Following Inequality 8 and as shown in Figure 3, in the presence of many aspects or when the user is seeking many documents for the intended aspect, it is best not to have to interact with a diversified list. Conversely, if the user has a navigational intent ($N = 1$) or is after a small number of documents, then it is better to interact with a diversified list. Alternatively if the ambiguity of the initial query (measured by the number of aspects Z) is low, then the user is also better off interacting with diversified results.

Summary

To derive the costs of interactions we made a number of simplifying assumptions; we revisit them next in light of Inequality 8. We assumed the diversified system would uniformly blend results from different aspects. However, more sophisticated strategies for blending results, e.g., by sampling with higher rate from popular aspects, may on average reduce the cost of interaction with the diversified system. When considering the non-diversified system, we also assumed that a user could issue a more specific query with cost c_{q_2} and this query would retrieve documents relevant to the desired aspect of interest. Often this may not be the case and it may take the user more than one query reformulation to obtain a more specific query to find the correct

---

[4]More complex weighted distributions are left for future work.

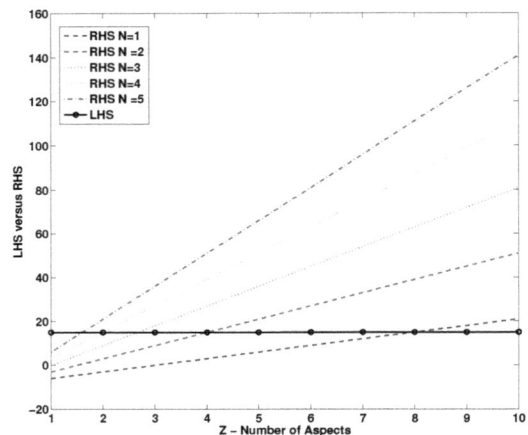

Figure 3: Plots of the left-hand side (LHS) and right-hand side (RHS) of inequality 8 where $k = 3$, showing that it is better to pose a more specific query as N and Z increase (i.e., when above the black dotted line denoting the LHS).

results. For example, consider the case where two query refinements are required to formulate a query that returns results for the correct aspect. In these circumstances, the cost of interaction becomes:

$$
\begin{aligned}
c_i^{ND} = c_{q_1} + \frac{1}{Z}c_s N + (1 - \frac{1}{Z})\Big[c_{q_2} + \\
(\frac{1}{Z-1})c_s(N+k) + (1 - \frac{1}{Z-1})(c_{q_3} + c_s(N+2k))\Big]
\end{aligned}
$$

When this is considered in Inequality 8, we find that diversifying search results is more attractive than before as, all other values being the same, the cost of interaction with the diversified system attracts one less cost than using the non-diversified system.

Admittedly, the above model is rather naive and there are numerous ways in which to improve it. For example, including the probability distribution over aspects, including a more sophisticated interaction with the ranked list and adding in further query refinements. Another refinement would be to link the length of the query (in terms of specificity) with the number of aspects. For example, consider the queries "*python*", "*python tutorial*", and "*python 3 tutorial*". Each are progressively longer and more specific - which also impact on how many aspects are returned. It would be interesting to consider how the user can control and manipulate the system and how worthwhile it is for them to do so.

4.3 Query Suggestions

Next, we consider whether a user should take a query suggestion or not. Observe the SERP in Figure 1 where the query "*python*" has been issued. Various query suggestions have been presented to the user that expose various aspects associated with "*python*", i.e., "*python commands*", "*python snake*", "*python tutorial*", etc.

Now let's consider the following scenario. A user enters a query to the system and the system does not retrieve any relevant document. Let's further assume that this is because the query is underspecified or impoverished in some way. The user now has the choice of reformulating the query: *(a)* by making it more specific, or *(b)* by taking a query suggestion. The cost of taking a suggestion involves examining the list of query suggestions provided, which we model as a function $c_{es}(.)$, where the cost is proportional to the number of suggestions, Q_s. If one of the suggestions is sufficiently specified, then the user will take the suggestion with some probability p_s. However, if the suggestions are not specific enough then the user resorts back to issuing a new query:

$$c_{q2} \quad < \quad c_{es}(Q_s) + p_s.c_c + (1 - p_s).c_{q2}$$
$$p_s.c_{q2} - p_s.c_c \quad < \quad c_{es}(Q_s)$$
$$c_{q2} - c_c \quad < \quad \frac{c_{es}(Q_s)}{p_s} \qquad (9)$$

While the cost of clicking on a suggestion is relatively cheap, the main factors influencing the selection of a suggestion is the cost of the subsequent query versus the cost of examining the suggestions and the probability of one of the suggestions being useful. In the best case scenario, the next query to be issued is within the suggestions i.e., $p_s = 1$, in which case the selection cost is not amplified. What is interesting in this case is that if there is some uncertainty as to whether the suggestions will contain a good next query, or if the cost of processing the suggestions is high, then re-formulating is preferable. In terms of processing the suggestions, more suggestions are likely to increase the cost, but also having similar alternatives is going to increase the cost because the user has to work out if they have different meanings (or not) and if they will result in different results (or not). On the other hand, if the user is finding it hard to think of a subsequent query, i.e. has run out of terms or ideas for querying, then it might be cheaper to process the suggestions. However, if the suggestions fail to provide an adequate query then the user must revert back to re-formulating (or some other action).

5. FEEDBACK

In this section we consider the question, is relevance feedback worth it? Let's consider an interface that allows users to mark which documents they think are relevant, and offers them the choice to find more documents like the ones selected (via the relevance feedback options on the SERP in Figure 1). An alternative interface would be one that provides a find similar button for each document instead. We will consider both options next.

5.1 Relevance Feedback

Let's assume that the user has issued a query to the system, and that the system has returned a set of results. The user has several options; among those we consider: *(1)* examining the results on the first page, then moving to the next page *(np)*, *(2)* examining the results on the first page, then issuing a new query *(nq)*, *(3)* examining the results on the first page, marking which documents are relevant, and then clicking the "find more like this" button *(rf)*.

Next, we consider the costs and benefits in each of these scenarios. Let b_{fp}, b_{np}, b_{nq}, b_{rf} be the gain of the first page, the gain from moving to the next page, the gain from the next query and the benefit from performing relevance feedback, respectively. The corresponding costs can be formulated as follows:

$$c_{np} = c_q + N.c_a + c_c + N.c_a \qquad (10)$$

$$c_{nq} = c_q + N.c_a + c_q + N.c_a \qquad (11)$$

$$c_{rf} = c_q + N.c_a + c_d + M.c_m + c_c + N.c_a \qquad (12)$$

where c_q is the cost of entering a query, c_a is the average cost to examine a document, c_c is the cost to click to the next page or click to find more, c_d is the cost of deciding to mark and undertake relevance feedback, c_m is the average cost of judging (explicitly) and then marking the document as relevant, where M documents are marked.

First, let's consider the case where the benefit from the next query is the same as the benefit from relevance feedback. In this case, the user should opt to re-querying when:

$$c_{nq} \quad < \quad c_{rf}$$
$$2.c_q + 2.N.c_a \quad < \quad c_q + 2.N.c_a + c_d + M.c_m + c_c$$
$$c_q \quad < \quad c_d + M.c_m + c_c \qquad (13)$$

Here we can see that if the cost of querying is less than the cost to decide, mark and find more, then querying is preferable. Further we can see that the number of documents to mark M is based upon the following inequality:

$$M > \frac{c_q - c_d - c_c}{c_m} \qquad (14)$$

In Figure 4, we have plotted Inequality 14, where we assume the costs for clicking and deciding are $c_c = 2$ and $c_d = 2$, respectively, and the cost of querying and assessing are $c_q = 15$ and $c_a = 20$, respectively. The figure shows the LHS for M from 1 to 5 versus the RHS where the cost of marking c_m increases from 1 to 5. From this plot, we can see that if the cost of marking is low, then the LHS is less than the RHS (i.e. the inequality does not hold) and so relevance feedback is preferable. As the cost of marking increases, then the option of relevance feedback becomes less desirable. Similarly, as the number of documents to be marked increases, then relevance feedback, again, becomes less desirable.

In the case of exploratory search, where the user wants to learn more about a domain, but is unsure of how to formulate a good query, then relevance feedback may become more attractive (assuming that they can do this at a low cost i.e. c_d). On the other hand, if the system provides support for querying, say by providing query suggestions, then the cost of querying could be lowered (though of course the user would have to pay the cost of shifting through the queries suggested[5]). Furthermore, since relevance feedback will typically find more of the same, if the user wants to explore other aspects of the topic, then it is likely that they will have to pose a new query in order to explore different aspects. Before we consider the case when querying and relevance feedback yield different amounts of benefit, we next consider the special case of finding similar.

5.2 Find Similar

Let's consider the find similar interface, where each document provides the option to find other similar documents. In this case, M always equals one, and the cost to find similar and mark becomes one and the same, i.e., the action to click the "find similar" button entails mentally marking the document (c_m) and then clicking the button c_c. Now the

---

[5] We leave this comparison between taking a query suggestion versus relevance feedback as an exercise for the reader.

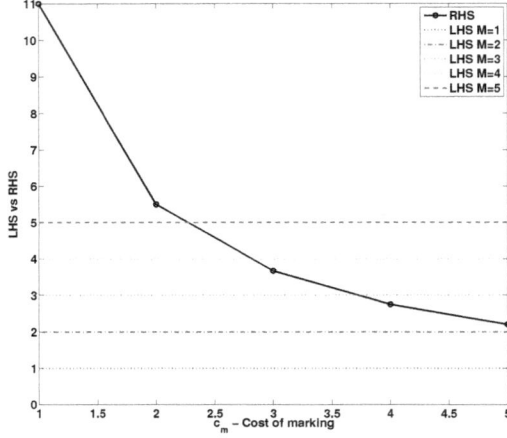

Figure 4: Inequality 14 showing that as the cost of marking increases (RHS), relevance feedback is less preferable as RHS < LHS which in turn violates the inequality.

decision to find similar is based on the inequality below:

$$c_q < c_d + c_m + c_c \qquad (15)$$

such that if the cost of querying is cheaper than deciding, marking and clicking, the user will query. In a study of Excite query logs, it was shown that the find similar option was taken 1 in 20 times [52]. Nevertheless, modern search engines have more or less abandoned the feature. However, given this expression, the find similar option is probably cheaper, so why has it been abandoned? Here we posit that this is because the benefit function from each option is different (where the more expensive query yields more benefit). However, in other domains, like academic search and recommender systems, related articles or "more like this" options are still provided, though we were not able to find statistics on their usage. We posit that in academic search finding related articles is likely to be of more benefit to the less experienced researcher, who knows less about the field, and may incur higher querying costs [57]. Whereas the seasoned researcher who is more knowledgeable of the field is likely to receive less net benefit because they can formulate queries for less. On the other hand, in the context of product or movie recommendations, the cost and benefits are quite different. For example, Netflix provides users with a "more like this" option for movies and TV shows. In the context of finding a movie to watch, posing a query is more difficult because expressing how you feel or what you want from a movie is rather amorphous and anomalous [15]. This is likely to make the querying rather costly, whereas taking the "more like this" option is relatively cheaper and cognitively less taxing. So in this context "find similar" is likely to be much more useful - and as a result used more often.

5.3 Different Benefit Functions

In the models above, we have assumed that the benefit between different options is the same. However, in this context the subsequent query and the relevance feedback are likely to yield different amounts of benefit. Here we consider the implications of this. The amount of benefit a user receives from traversing the ranked list has been showing to increase but at a diminishing rate, i.e. as a user goes down the ranked list they accrue more benefit but less and less at each rank [42, 30]. This can be modeled using the following form: $b(N) = k.N^\beta$ [6, 8], and, when considered in the context of multiple queries, subsequent queries are assumed to be discounted. Thus, the benefit function takes the form $b(Q, N) = k.Q^\alpha.N^\beta$ and follows a similar form as the gain functions in [5, 7, 30, 31].

Using this model of benefit we can associate different amounts of benefit to the two options. The benefit from examining the initial N documents is $b_q = k.N^\beta$ and the benefit from the next N documents on the subsequent page is $b_{np} = k.(2.N)^\beta - k.N^\beta$. Given the expression $b(Q, N)$ from above, the benefit of the next query is based on the N documents returned, and the discount of issuing the next query. The discount for for the Qth query is $d(Q) = Q^\alpha - (Q-1)^\alpha$, i.e. for first query, $d(Q = 1) = 1$, for the second query, $d(Q = 2) = 2^\alpha - 1$. So the benefit from the second query would be $b_{nq} = k.d(Q = 2).N^\beta$. And finally the benefit from the relevance feedback would be: $b_{rf} = k.d(Q = 2).N^\gamma$. Since the user has already examined N and extracted the benefit b_q, the pool of relevant material has been reduced, and so we can assume that the benefit from the next query and the relevance feedback is reduced. If we consider the profit associated with these options, we arrive at:

$$
\begin{aligned}
\pi_{np} &= b_q + b_{np} - (c_q + N.c_a + c_c + N.c_a) \\
&= k.(2.N)^\beta - (c_q + N.c_a + c_c + N.c_a)
\end{aligned}
$$

$$
\begin{aligned}
\pi_{nq} &= b_q + b_{nq} - (2.c_q + 2.N.c_a) \\
&= k.N^\beta + k.d(q).N^\beta - (2.c_q + 2.N.c_a)
\end{aligned}
$$

$$
\begin{aligned}
\pi_{rf} &= b_q + b_{rf} - (c_q + N.c_a + c_d \\
&\quad + M.c_m + c_c + N.c_a) \\
&= k.N^\beta + k.d(q).N^\gamma - (c_q + N.c_a + c_d + \\
&\quad + M.c_m + c_c + N.c_a)
\end{aligned}
$$

A user would issue a subsequent query over performing relevance feedback if the following holds:

$$
\begin{aligned}
\pi_{nq} &> \pi_{rf} \\
k.d(q).N^\beta - (c_q) &> +k.d(q).N^\gamma \\
&\quad -(c_d + M.c_m + c_c) \\
N^\beta - N^\gamma &> \frac{c_q - c_d - M.c_m - c_c}{k.d(q)} \qquad (16)
\end{aligned}
$$

This inequality shows that if the benefit that is received is greater from querying than relevance feedback, i.e. $\beta > \gamma$, then the Left Hand Side (LHS) will be positive. Unless the cost of relevance feedback is sufficiently low, such that the cost of querying is greater, then the user will re-query. However, note the impact of the discount $d(q)$, which is typically less than one because the user gets less benefit from subsequent interactions. Here it exaggerates the influence of the cost (positive or negative).

In Figure 5, we have plotted the LHS vs the RHS of Inequality 16, where we have assumed that the benefit function for the next query has β set to **0.5** (and the same costs as in the previous example shown in Figure 14). We have plotted varying levels of γ from **0.5** to **0.8**. The figure shows that

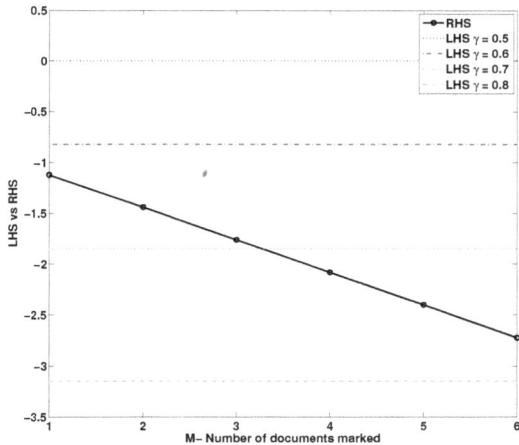

Figure 5: Inequality 16 where $c_c = 2$, $c_d = 2$, $k = 10$, $\alpha = 0.7$ and $\beta = 0.5$, showing that issuing a subsequent query is preferable when the LHS is above the black dotted line (RHS). The performance of the subsequent query would have to go up substantially before relevance feedback is worthwhile, i.e., $\gamma > 0.7\ 0.8$ vs. $\beta = 0.5$.

the benefit from relevance feedback needs to be substantially greater than the benefit of the next query for relevance feedback to be useful to the user.

Summary

We have considered a number of different aspects relating to relevance feedback and how the number of documents marked and the benefit are likely to shape the user interactions. However, we have not considered other aspects such as the relationship between the amount (and type) of relevance feedback given [27, 36, 37]. For instance in [36], Keskustalo et al. show that as the number of feedback documents increases, performance increases but at a diminishing rate. Furthermore, we have approximated many of the costs and perhaps underestimated some. For example in [10] they show that the cost of marking documents as relevant is cognitively taxing. Thus, further empirical work is needed to better estimate the costs and the benefits of these interactions. If this is achieved then it will be possible to determine whether relevance feedback is worthwhile, and specifically to determine how much better the performance of the relevance feedback needs to be before it is worthwhile.

6. DISCUSSION AND FUTURE WORK

In this paper, we have developed a series of cost-benefit models for various decisions that arise when interacting with a search system/interface. Although the models we have created are rather simple, they provide interesting insights into the drivers and forces that are at play during the information seeking and retrieval process. Of course, these are not the only factors at play, and we acknowledge that these abstractions are limited. For each of the models depicted, there are obvious avenues of refinement where more detail and sophistication can be added to improve their realism. The purpose of this paper is to provide an overview of how cost-benefit analysis can be applied to assess the choices that we as designers present to users, and to hypothesize about how user behaviour will change in response to the costs and benefits. There are many more scenarios and decisions which can be explored and modeled in the future using such a framework.

Empirically estimating the parameters of these models, evaluating how well they fit, and predicting actual behaviour are obvious next steps. As such, this work provides a number of directions to explore as well as providing the basis for modeling and developing other models regarding other decisions and interactions. Creating such models is beneficial because before any experiments are conducted one can reason about how the costs and benefits are likely to influence behaviour and attempt to manipulate them accordingly. However, a number of open challenges and research questions are surfaced through this work (though not necessarily explicitly discussed): *(i)* how do we measure the costs and benefits, *(ii)* how does risk and uncertainty affect the decisions and expectations, *(iii)* why do users learn to adopt certain behaviours or others, *(iv)* at what point do certain behaviours become habitual and what are the costs of overcoming such habits *(v)* how can we encourage users to adopt better information seeking practices (and how do we define such practices as better?), and, *(vi)* how do we deal with multiple objectives and multiple cost functions.

7. REFERENCES

[1] E. Agapie, G. Golovchinsky, and P. Qvarfordt. Leading people to longer queries. In *Proc. of the SIGCHI*, pages 3019–3022, 2013.

[2] P. Arvola, J. Kekäläinen, and M. Junkkari. Expected reading effort in focused retrieval evaluation. *Inf. Retr.*, 13(5):460–484, 2010.

[3] L. Azzopardi. Query side evaluation: an empirical analysis of effectiveness and effort. In *Proc. of SIGIR*, pages 556–563, 2009.

[4] L. Azzopardi. Usage based effectiveness measures: Monitoring application performance in information retrieval. In *Proc. of CIKM*, pages 631–640, 2009.

[5] L. Azzopardi. The economics in interactive information retrieval. In *Proc. of SIGIR*, pages 15–24, 2011.

[6] L. Azzopardi. Economic models of search. In *Proc of ADCS*, ADCS '13, page 1, 2013.

[7] L. Azzopardi. Modelling interaction with economic models of search. In *Proc. of SIGIR*, pages 3–12, 2014.

[8] L. Azzopardi and G. Zuccon. An analysis of theories of search and search behavior. In *Proc. of ICTIR*, pages 81–90, 2015.

[9] L. Azzopardi and G. Zuccon. Two scrolls or one click: A cost model for browsing search results. In *Proc. of ECIR*, pages 696–702, 2016.

[10] J. Back and C. Oppenheim. A model of cognitive load for IR: implications for user relevance feedback interaction. *Information Research*, 2001.

[11] K. Balog. Task-completion engines: A vision with a plan. *CEUR-WS*, 1338, 2015.

[12] M. J. Bates. Information search tactics. *JASIS*, 30(4):205–214, 1979.

[13] N. J. Belkin. Salton award lecture: People, interacting with information. In *Proc. of SIGIR*, pages 1–2, 2015.

[14] N. J. Belkin, D. Kelly, G. Kim, J.-Y. Kim, H.-J. Lee, G. Muresan, M.-C. Tang, X.-J. Yuan, and C. Cool. Query length in interactive information retrieval. In *Proc. of SIGIR*, pages 205–212, 2003.

[15] N. J. Belkin, R. N. Oddy, and H. M. Brooks. ASK for information retrieval: Part I. Background and theory. *J. Doc.*, 38(2):61–71, 1982.

[16] U. Birchler and M. Butler. *Information Economics*. Routledge, 1st edition, 2007.

[17] B. Carterette. System effectiveness, user models, and user utility: A conceptual framework for investigation. In *Proc. of SIGIR*, pages 903–912, 2011.

[18] O. Chapelle, D. Metlzer, Y. Zhang, and P. Grinspan. Expected reciprocal rank for graded relevance. In *Proc. of CIKM*, pages 621–630, 2009.

[19] A. Chuklin, I. Markov, and M. d. Rijke. Click models for web search. *Synthesis Lectures on Information Concepts, Retrieval, and Services*, 7(3):1–115, 2015.

[20] M. Cole, J. Liu, N. Belkin, R. Bierig, J. Gwizdka, C. Liu, J. Zhang, and X. Zhang. Usefulness as the criterion for evaluation of interactive information retrieval. In *Proc. of HCIR*, pages 1–4, 2009.

[21] M. D. Cooper. A cost model for evaluating information retrieval systems. *JASIS*, 23(5):306–312, 1972.

[22] W. S. Cooper. On selecting a measure of retrieval effectiveness. *JASIS*, 24(2):87–100, 1973.

[23] N. Craswell, O. Zoeter, M. Taylor, and B. Ramsey. An experimental comparison of click position-bias models. In *Proc. of WSDM*, pages 87–94, 2008.

[24] R. Cummins, M. Lalmas, and C. O'Riordan. The limits of retrieval effectiveness. In *Proc. of ECIR*, pages 277–282, 2011.

[25] N. Fuhr. A probability ranking principle for interactive information retrieval. *Inf. Retr.*, 11(3):251–265, June 2008.

[26] J. Gwizdka. Distribution of cognitive load in web search. *JASIST*, 61(11):2167–2187, 2010.

[27] D. Harman. Relevance feedback revisited. In *Proc. of SIGIR*, pages 1–10, 1992.

[28] D. Harman. Is the cranfield paradigm outdated? In *Proc. of SIGIR*, pages 1–1, 2010.

[29] P. Ingwersen and K. Järvelin. *The Turn: Integration of Information Seeking and Retrieval in Context*. Springer-Verlag New York, Inc., 2005.

[30] K. Järvelin and J. Kekäläinen. Cumulated gain-based evaluation of ir techniques. *ACM TOIS*, 20(4):422–446, 2002.

[31] K. Järvelin, S. L. Price, L. M. L. Delcambre, and M. L. Nielsen. Discounted cumulated gain based evaluation of multiple-query ir sessions. In *Proc. of ECIR*, pages 4–15, 2008.

[32] A. Kashyap, V. Hristidis, and M. Petropoulos. Facetor: cost-driven exploration of faceted query results. In *Proc. of CIKM*, pages 719–728, 2010.

[33] D. Kelly. Contours and Convergence: Past, Present and Future (interactive) IR Research Practice - KSJ Keynote at ECIR. In *Proc. of ECIR*, 2013.

[34] D. Kelly, V. D. Dollu, and X. Fu. The loquacious user: A document-independent source of terms for query expansion. In *Proc. of SIGIR*, pages 457–464, 2005.

[35] D. Kelly and X. Fu. Eliciting better information need descriptions from users of information search systems. *IP&M*, 43(1):30–46, 2007.

[36] H. Keskustalo, K. Järvelin, and A. Pirkola. The effects of relevance feedback quality and quantity in interactive relevance feedback: A simulation based on user modeling. In *Proc. of ECIR*, pages 191–204, 2006.

[37] H. Keskustalo, K. Järvelin, and A. Pirkola. Evaluating the effectiveness of relevance feedback based on a user simulation model: effects of a user scenario on cumulated gain value. *Inf. Retr.*, 11(3):209–228, 2008.

[38] S. Mizzaro. Relevance: The whole history. *JASIS*, 48(9):810–832, 1997.

[39] A. Moffat, P. Bailey, F. Scholer, and P. Thomas. INST: An Adaptive Metric for Information Retrieval Evaluation. In *Proc. of ADCS*, 2015.

[40] A. Moffat, F. Scholer, and P. Thomas. Models and Metrics: IR Evaluation As a User Process. In *Proc. of ADCS*, pages 47–54, 2012.

[41] A. Moffat, P. Thomas, and F. Scholer. Users versus models: What observation tells us about effectiveness metrics. In

[42] A. Moffat and J. Zobel. Rank-biased precision for measurement of retrieval effectiveness. *ACM TOIS*, 27(1):2, 2008.

[43] P. Pirolli. *Information Foraging Theory: Adaptive Interaction with Information*. Oxford University Press, Inc., 2009.

[44] S. E. Robertson. The probability ranking principle in ir. *J. Doc.*, 33(4):294–304, 1977.

[45] D. M. Russell, M. J. Stefik, P. Pirolli, and S. K. Card. The cost structure of sensemaking. In *Proc. of INTERACT/SIGCHI*, pages 269–276, 1993.

[46] T. Sakai and Z. Dou. Summaries, ranked retrieval and sessions: A unified framework for information access evaluation. In *Proc. of SIGIR*, pages 473–482, 2013.

[47] M. D. Smucker. A Plan for Making Information Retrieval Evaluation Synonymous with Human Performance Prediction. In *Proc. of SIGIR Workshop on Future of Evaluation*, 2009.

[48] M. D. Smucker. Towards timed predictions of human performance for interactive information retrieval evaluation. In *Proc. of HCIR*, page 3, 2009.

[49] M. D. Smucker and C. L. Clarke. The fault, dear researchers, is not in cranfield, but in our metrics, that they are unrealistic. In *Proc. of EuroHCIR*, pages 11–12, 2012.

[50] M. D. Smucker and C. L. Clarke. Time-based calibration of effectiveness measures. In *Proc. of SIGIR*, pages 95–104, 2012.

[51] M. D. Smucker and C. L. Clarke. Modeling Optimal Switching Behavior. In *Proc. of CHIIR*, pages 317–320, 2016.

[52] A. Spink, B. J. Jansen, and H. Cenk Ozmultu. Use of query reformulation and relevance feedback by excite users. *Internet Research*, 10(4):317–328, 2000.

[53] G. J. Stigler. The economics of information. *The Journal of Political Economy*, 69(3):213–225, 1961.

[54] H. R. Varian. Economics and search. *SIGIR Forum*, 33(1):1–5, 1999.

[55] R. Villa and M. Halvey. Is Relevance Hard Work? Evaluating the Effort of Making Relevant Assessments. In *Proc. of SIGIR*, pages 765–768, 2013.

[56] E. M. Voorhees, D. K. Harman, et al. *TREC: Experiment and evaluation in information retrieval*. MIT press Cambridge, 2005.

[57] R. W. White, S. T. Dumais, and J. Teevan. Characterizing the influence of domain expertise on web search behavior. In *Proc. of WSDM*, pages 132–141, 2009.

[58] E. Yilmaz, E. Kanoulas, M. Verma, B. Carterette, N. Craswell, and R. Mehrotra. Overview of the TREC 2015 Tasks Track. In *Proc. of TREC*, 2015.

[59] E. Yilmaz, M. Shokouhi, N. Craswell, and S. Robertson. Expected Browsing Utility for Web Search Evaluation. In *Proc. of CIKM*, pages 1561–1564, 2010.

[60] E. Yilmaz, M. Verma, N. Craswell, F. Radlinski, and P. Bailey. Relevance and effort: an analysis of document utility. In *Proc. of CIKM*, pages 91–100, 2014.

[61] Y. Zhang and C. Zhai. Information retrieval as card playing: A formal model for optimizing interactive retrieval interface. In *Proc. of SIGIR*, pages 685–694, 2015.

[62] Y. Zhang, J. Zhang, M. Lease, and J. Gwizdka. Multidimensional relevance modeling via psychometrics and crowdsourcing. In *Proc. of SIGIR*, pages 435–444, 2014.

[63] G. Zuccon. Understandability biased evaluation for information retrieval. In *Proc. of ECIR*, pages 280–292. Springer, 2016.

Lexical Query Modeling in Session Search

Christophe Van Gysel
cvangysel@uva.nl

Evangelos Kanoulas
e.kanoulas@uva.nl

Maarten de Rijke
derijke@uva.nl

University of Amsterdam, Amsterdam, The Netherlands

ABSTRACT

Lexical query modeling has been the leading paradigm for session search. In this paper, we analyze TREC session query logs and compare the performance of different lexical matching approaches for session search. Naive methods based on term frequency weighing perform on par with specialized session models. In addition, we investigate the viability of lexical query models in the setting of session search. We give important insights into the potential and limitations of lexical query modeling for session search and propose future directions for the field of session search.

1. INTRODUCTION

Many complex information seeking tasks, such as planning a trip or buying a car, cannot sufficiently be expressed in a single query [7]. These multi-faceted tasks are exploratory, comprehensive, survey-like or comparative in nature [14] and require multiple search iterations to be adequately answered [8]. Donato et al. [5] note that 10% of the user sessions (more than 25% of query volume) consists of such complex information needs.

The TREC Session Track [15] created an environment for researchers "to test whether systems can improve their performance for a given query by using previous queries and user interactions with the retrieval system." The track's existence led to an increasing number of methods aimed at improving session search. Yang et al. [16] introduce the Query Change Model (QCM), which uses lexical editing changes between consecutive queries in addition to query terms occurring in previously retrieved documents, to improve session search. They heuristically construct a lexicon-based query model for every query in a session. Query models are then linearly combined for every document, based on query recency [16] or document satisfaction [3, 10], into a session-wide lexical query model. However, there has been a clear trend towards the use of supervised learning [3, 12, 16] and external data sources [6, 11]. Guan et al. [6] perform lexical query expansion by adding higher-order n-grams to queries by mining document snippets. In addition, they expand query representations by including anchor texts to previously top-ranked documents in the session. Carterette et al. [3] expand document representations by including incoming anchor

texts. Luo et al. [12] introduce a linear point-wise learning-to-rank model that predicts relevance given a document and query change features. They incorporate document-independent session features in their ranker.

The use of machine-learned ranking and the expansion of query and document representations is meant to address a specific instance of a wider problem in information retrieval, namely the query document mismatch [9]. In this paper, we analyze the session query logs made available by TREC and compare the performance of different lexical query modeling approaches for session search, taking into account session length.[1] In addition, we investigate the viability of lexical query models in a session search setting.

The main purpose of this paper is to investigate the potential of lexical methods in session search and provide foundations for future research. We ask the following questions: (1) Increasingly complex methods for session search are being developed, but how do naive methods perform? (2) How well can lexical methods perform? (3) Can we solve the session search task using lexical matching only?

2. LEXICAL MATCHING FOR SESSIONS

We define a search session s as a sequence of n interactions (q_i, r_i) between user and search engine, where q_i denotes a user-issued query consisting of $|q_i|$ terms $t_{i,1}, \ldots, t_{i,|q_i|}$ and r_i denotes a result page consisting of $|r_i|$ documents $r_{i,1}, \ldots, r_{i,|r_i|}$ returned by the search engine (also referred to as SERP). The goal, then, is to return a SERP r_{n+1} given a query q_{n+1} and the session history that maximizes the user's utility function.

In this work, we formalize session search by modeling an observed session s as a query model parameterized by $\theta^s = \{\theta_1^s, \ldots, \theta_{|V|}^s\}$, where θ_i^s denotes the weight associated with term $t_i \in V$ (specified below). Documents d_j are then ranked in decreasing order of

$$\log P(d_j \mid s) = \sum_{k=1}^{|V|} \theta_k^s \log \theta_k^{d_j},$$

where θ^{d_j} is a lexical model of document d_j, which can be a language model (LM), a vector space model or a specialized model using hand-engineered features. Query model θ^s is a function of the query models of the interactions i in the session, θ^{s_i} (e.g., for a uniform aggregation scheme, $\theta^s = \sum_i \theta^{s_i}$). Existing session search methods [6, 16] can be expressed in this formalism as follows:

Term frequency (TF) Terms in a query are weighted according to their frequency in the query (i.e., $\theta_k^{s_i}$ becomes the frequency

---

[1] An open-source implementation of our testbed for evaluating session search is available at https://github.com/cvangysel/sesh.

of term t_k in q_i). Queries q_i that are part of the same session s are then aggregated uniformly for a subset of queries. In this work, we consider the following subsets: the *first query*, the *last query* and the *concatenation of all queries* in a session. Using the last query corresponds to the official baseline of the TREC Session track [3].

Nugget Nugget [6] is a method for effective structured query formulation for session search. Queries q_i, part of session s, are expanded using higher order n-grams occurring in both q_i and snippets of the top-k documents in the previous interaction, $r_{i-1,1}, \ldots, r_{i-1,k}$. This effectively expands the vocabulary by additionally considering n-grams next to unigram terms. The query models of individual queries in the session are then aggregated using one of the aggregation schemes. Nugget is primarily targeted at resolving the query-document mismatch by incorporating structure and external data and does not model query transitions. The method can be extended to include external evidence by expanding θ^s to include anchor texts pointing to (clicked) documents in previous SERPs.

Query Change Model (QCM) QCM [16] uses syntactic editing changes between consecutive queries in addition to query changes and previous SERPs to enhance session search. In QCM [16, Section 6.3], document model θ^d is provided by a language model with Dirichlet smoothing and the query model at interaction i, θ^{s_i}, in session s is given by

$$\theta_k^{s_i} = \begin{cases} 1 + \alpha(1 - P(t_k \mid r_{i-1,1})), & t_k \in q_{\text{theme}} \\ 1 - \beta P(t_k \mid r_{i-1,1}), & t_k \in +\Delta q \wedge t_k \in r_{i-1,1} \\ 1 + \epsilon \, \text{idf}(t_k), & t_k \in +\Delta q \wedge t_k \notin r_{i-1,1} \\ -\delta P(t_k \mid r_{i-1,1}), & t_k \in -\Delta q, \end{cases}$$

where q_{theme} are the session's theme terms, $+\Delta q$ ($-\Delta q$, resp.) are the added (removed) terms, $P(t_k \mid r_{i-1,1})$ denotes the probability of t_k occurring in SAT clicks, $\text{idf}(t_k)$ is the inverse document frequency of term t_k and α, β, ϵ, δ are parameters. The θ^{s_i} are then aggregated into θ^s using one of the aggregation schemes, such as the uniform aggregation scheme (i.e., the sum of the θ^{s_i}).

In §4, we analyze the methods listed above in terms of their ability to handle sessions of different lengths and contextual history.

3. EXPERIMENTS

3.1 Benchmarks

We evaluate the lexical query modeling methods listed in §2 on the session search task (G1) of the TREC Session track from 2011 to 2014 [15]. We report performance on each track edition independently and on the track aggregate. Given a query, the task is to improve retrieval performance by using previous queries and user interactions with the retrieval system. To accomplish this, we first retrieve the 2,000 most relevant documents for the given query and then re-rank these documents using the methods described in §2. We use the "Category B" subsets of ClueWeb09 (2011/2012) and ClueWeb12 (2013/2014) as document collections. Both collections consist of approximately 50 million documents. Spam documents are removed before indexing by filtering out documents with scores (GroupX and Fusion, respectively) below 70 [4]. Table 1 shows an overview of the benchmarks and document collections.

3.2 Evaluation measures

To measure retrieval effectiveness, we report Normalized Discounted Cumulative Gain at rank 10 (NDCG@10) in addition to

Mean Reciprocal Rank (MRR). The relevance judgments of the tracks were converted from topic-centric to session-centric according to the mappings provided by the track organizers.[2] Evaluation measures are then computed using TREC's official evaluation tool, `trec_eval`.[3]

3.3 Systems under comparison

We compare the lexical query model methods outlined in §2. All methods compute weights for lexical entities (e.g., unigram terms) on a per-session basis, construct a structured Indri query [13] and query the document collection using `pyndri`.[4] For fair comparison, we use Indri's default smoothing configuration (i.e., Dirichlet smoothing with $\mu = 2500$) and uniform query aggregation for all methods (different from the smoothing used for QCM in [16]). This allows us to separate query aggregation techniques from query modeling approaches in the case of session search.

For Nugget, we use the default parameter configuration ($k_{\text{snippet}} = 10$, $\theta = 0.97$, $k_{\text{anchor}} = 5$ and $\beta = 0.1$), using the strict expansion method. We report the performance of Nugget without the use of external resources (RL2), with anchor texts (RL3) and with click data (RL4). For QCM, we use the parameter configuration as described in [12, 16]: $\alpha = 2.2$, $\beta = 1.8$, $\epsilon = 0.07$ and $\delta = 0.4$.

In addition to the methods above, we report the performance of an oracle that always ranks in decreasing order of ground-truth relevance. This oracle will give us an upper-bound on the achievable ranking performance.

3.4 Ideal lexical term weighting

We investigate the maximally achievable performance by weighting query terms. Inspired by Bendersky et al. [1], we optimize NDCG@10 for every session using a grid search over the term weight space. We sweep the weight of every term between -1.0 and 1.0 (inclusive) with increments of 0.1, resulting in a total of 21 weight assignments per term. Due to the exponential time complexity of the grid search, we limit our analysis to the 230 sessions with 7 unique query terms or less (see Table 1). This experiment will tell us the maximally achievable retrieval performance in session search by the re-weighting lexical terms only.

4. RESULTS & DISCUSSION

In this section, we report and discuss our experimental results. Of special interest to us are the methods that perform lexical matching based on a user's queries in a single session: QCM, Nugget (RL2) and the three variants of TF. Table 2 shows the methods' performance on the TREC Session track editions from 2011 to 2014. No single method consistently outperforms the other methods. Interestingly enough, the methods based on term frequency (TF) perform quite competitively compared to the specialized session search methods (Nugget and QCM). In addition, the TF variant using all queries in a session even outperforms Nugget (RL2) on the 2011 and 2014 editions and QCM on nearly all editions. Using the concatenation of all queries in a session, while being an obvious baseline, has not received much attention in recent literature or by TREC [15]. In addition, note that the best-performing (unsupervised) TF method achieves better results than the supervised method of Luo et al. [12] on the 2012 and 2013 tracks. Fig. 1 depicts the boxplot of the NDCG@10 distribution over all track editions (2011–2014). The term frequency approach using all queries

[2]We take into account the mapping between judgments and actual relevance grades for the 2012 edition.

[3]https://github.com/usnistgov/trec_eval

[4]https://github.com/cvangysel/pyndri

Table 1: Overview of 2011, 2012, 2013 and 2014 TREC session tracks. For the 2014 track, we report the total number of sessions in addition to those sessions with judgments. We report the mean and standard deviation where appropriate; M denotes the median.

	2011	2012	2013	2014
Sessions				
Sessions	76	98	87	100 (1,021 total)
Queries per session	3.68 ± 1.79; M=3.00	3.03 ± 1.57; M=2.00	5.08 ± 3.60; M=4.00	4.34 ± 2.22; M=4.00
Unique terms per session	7.01 ± 3.28; M=6.50	5.76 ± 2.95; M=5.00	8.86 ± 4.38; M=8.00	7.79 ± 4.08; M=7.00
Topics				
Session per topic	1.23 ± 0.46; M= 1.00	2.04 ± 0.98; M= 2.00	2.18 ± 0.93; M= 2.00	20.95 ± 4.81; M= 21.00
Document judgments per topic	313.11 ± 114.63; M=292.00	372.10 ± 162.63; M=336.50	268.00 ± 116.86; M=247.00	332.33 ± 149.03; M=322.00
Collection				
Documents	21,258,800		15,702,181	
Document length	$1,096.18 \pm 1,502.45$		$649.07 \pm 1,635.29$	
Terms	3.40×10^7 (2.33×10^{10} total)		2.36×10^7 (1.02×10^{10} total)	
Spam scores	GroupX		Fusion	

Table 2: Overview of experimental results on 2011–2014 TREC Session tracks of the TF, Nugget and QCM methods (see §2). The ground-truth oracle shows the ideal performance (§3.3).

	2011		2012		2013		2014	
	NDCG@10	MRR	NDCG@10	MRR	NDCG@10	MRR	NDCG@10	MRR
Ground-truth oracle	0.777	0.868	0.695	0.865	0.517	0.920	0.410	0.800
TF (first query)	0.371	0.568	0.302	0.523	0.121	0.379	0.120	0.336
TF (last query)	0.358	0.598	0.316	0.586	0.133	0.358	0.156	0.458
TF (all queries)	**0.448**	**0.685**	0.348	0.604	0.162	0.477	**0.174**	**0.478**
Nugget (RL2)	0.437	0.677	0.352	0.609	**0.163**	0.488	0.173	0.476
Nugget (RL3)	0.442	0.678	**0.360**	**0.619**	0.162	**0.488**	0.172	0.477
Nugget (RL4)	0.437	0.677	0.352	0.609	0.163	0.488	0.173	0.476
QCM	0.440	0.661	0.342	0.575	0.160	0.484	0.162	0.450

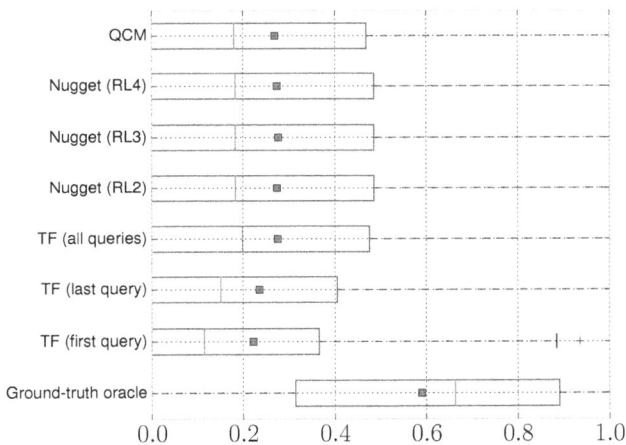

Figure 1: Box plot of NDCG@10 on all sessions of the TREC Session track (2011–2014). The box depicts the first, second (median) and third quartiles. The whiskers are located at 1.5 times the interquartile range on both sides of the box. The square and crosses depict the average and outliers respectively.

achieves the highest mean/median overall. Given this peculiar finding, where a generic retrieval model performs better than specialized session search models, we continue with an analysis of the TREC Session search logs.

In Fig. 2 we investigate the effect of varying session lengths in the session logs. The distribution of session lengths is shown in the top row of Fig. 2. For the 2011–2013 track editions, most sessions consisted of only two queries. The mode of the 2014 edition lies at 5 queries per session. If we examine the performance of the methods on a per-session length basis, we observe that the TF methods perform well for short sessions. This does not come as a surprise,

as for these sessions there is only a limited history that specialized methods can use. However, the TF method using the concatenation of all queries still performs competitively for longer sessions. This can be explained by the fact that as queries are aggregated over time, a better representation of the user's information need is created. This aggregated representation naturally emphasizes important *theme terms* of the session, which is a key component in the QCM [16].

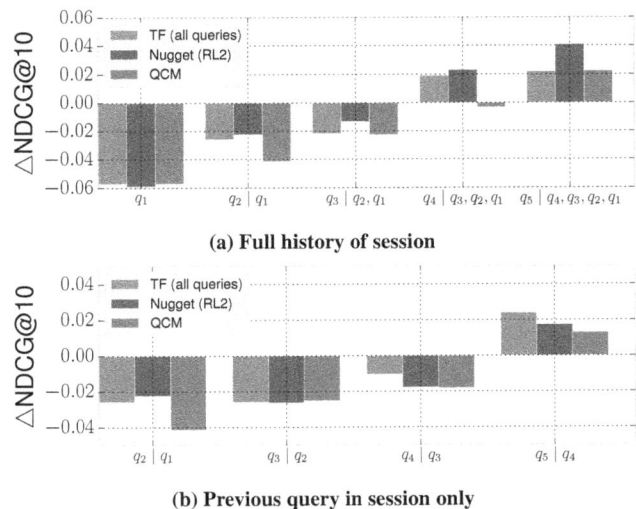

(a) Full history of session

(b) Previous query in session only

Figure 3: Difference in NDCG@10 with the official TREC baseline (TF using the last query only) of 5-query sessions (45 instances) with different history configurations for the 2011–2014 TREC Session tracks.

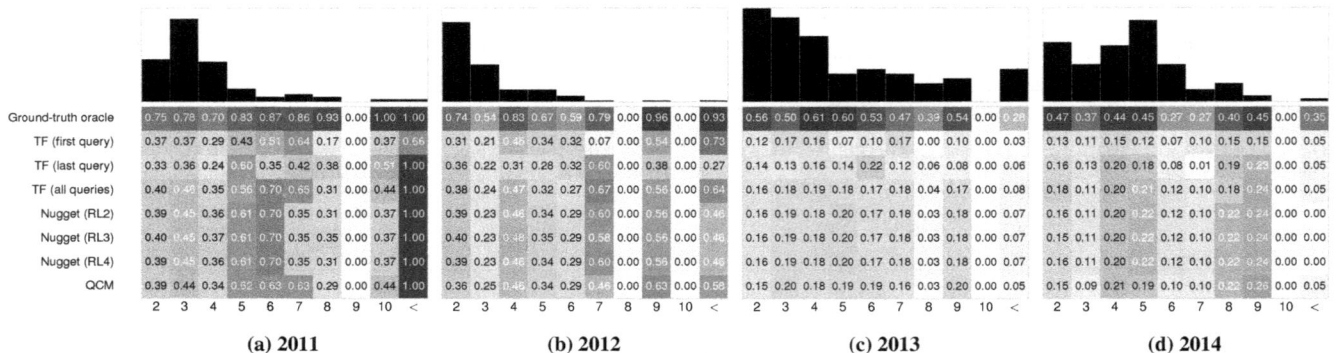

Figure 2: The top row depicts the distribution of session lengths for the 2011–2014 TREC Session tracks, while the bottom row shows the performance of the TF, Nugget and QCM models for different session lengths.

(a) 2011

	2	3	4	5	6	7	8	9	10	<
Ground-truth oracle	0.75	0.78	0.70	0.83	0.87	0.86	0.93	0.00	1.00	1.00
TF (first query)	0.37	0.37	0.29	0.43	0.51	0.64	0.17	0.00	0.37	0.66
TF (last query)	0.33	0.36	0.24	0.60	0.35	0.42	0.38	0.00	0.51	1.00
TF (all queries)	0.40	0.46	0.35	0.56	0.70	0.65	0.31	0.00	0.44	1.00
Nugget (RL2)	0.39	0.45	0.36	0.61	0.70	0.35	0.31	0.00	0.37	1.00
Nugget (RL3)	0.40	0.45	0.37	0.61	0.70	0.35	0.35	0.00	0.37	1.00
Nugget (RL4)	0.39	0.45	0.36	0.61	0.70	0.35	0.31	0.00	0.37	1.00
QCM	0.39	0.44	0.34	0.62	0.63	0.46	0.29	0.00	0.44	1.00

(b) 2012

	2	3	4	5	6	7	8	9	10	<
Ground-truth oracle	0.74	0.54	0.83	0.67	0.59	0.79	0.00	0.96	0.00	0.93
TF (first query)	0.31	0.21	0.46	0.34	0.32	0.07	0.00	0.54	0.00	0.73
TF (last query)	0.36	0.22	0.31	0.26	0.32	0.60	0.00	0.38	0.00	0.27
TF (all queries)	0.38	0.24	0.47	0.32	0.27	0.67	0.00	0.56	0.00	0.64
Nugget (RL2)	0.39	0.23	0.46	0.34	0.29	0.60	0.00	0.56	0.00	0.46
Nugget (RL3)	0.40	0.23	0.48	0.35	0.29	0.58	0.00	0.56	0.00	0.46
Nugget (RL4)	0.39	0.23	0.46	0.34	0.29	0.60	0.00	0.56	0.00	0.46
QCM	0.36	0.25	0.46	0.34	0.29	0.46	0.00	0.63	0.00	0.58

(c) 2013

	2	3	4	5	6	7	8	9	10	<
Ground-truth oracle	0.56	0.50	0.61	0.60	0.53	0.47	0.39	0.54	0.00	0.26
TF (first query)	0.12	0.17	0.16	0.07	0.10	0.17	0.00	0.10	0.00	0.03
TF (last query)	0.14	0.13	0.16	0.14	0.22	0.12	0.06	0.00	0.00	0.06
TF (all queries)	0.16	0.18	0.19	0.18	0.17	0.18	0.04	0.17	0.00	0.07
Nugget (RL2)	0.16	0.19	0.18	0.20	0.17	0.18	0.03	0.18	0.00	0.07
Nugget (RL3)	0.16	0.19	0.18	0.20	0.17	0.18	0.03	0.18	0.00	0.07
Nugget (RL4)	0.16	0.19	0.18	0.20	0.17	0.18	0.03	0.18	0.00	0.07
QCM	0.15	0.20	0.18	0.19	0.19	0.19	0.03	0.20	0.00	0.05

(d) 2014

	2	3	4	5	6	7	8	9	10	<
Ground-truth oracle	0.47	0.37	0.44	0.45	0.27	0.27	0.40	0.45	0.00	0.35
TF (first query)	0.13	0.11	0.15	0.12	0.07	0.10	0.15	0.15	0.00	0.05
TF (last query)	0.16	0.13	0.20	0.18	0.08	0.01	0.19	0.23	0.00	0.05
TF (all queries)	0.18	0.11	0.20	0.21	0.12	0.10	0.18	0.24	0.00	0.05
Nugget (RL2)	0.16	0.11	0.20	0.22	0.12	0.10	0.22	0.24	0.00	0.00
Nugget (RL3)	0.15	0.11	0.20	0.22	0.12	0.10	0.22	0.24	0.00	0.00
Nugget (RL4)	0.16	0.11	0.20	0.22	0.12	0.10	0.22	0.24	0.00	0.00
QCM	0.15	0.09	0.21	0.19	0.10	0.10	0.22	0.26	0.00	0.05

Table 3: NDCG@10 for TF weighting (§2), ideal term weighting (§3.4) and the ground-truth oracle (§3.3).

	2011	2012	2013	2014
TF (all queries)	0.391	0.333	0.179	0.183
Ideal term weighing	0.589	0.528	0.361	0.296
Ground-truth oracle	0.716	0.682	0.593	0.453

How do these methods perform as the search session progresses? Fig. 3 shows the performance of sessions of length five after every user interaction, when using all queries in a session (Fig. 3a) and when using only the previous query (Fig. 3b). We can see that NDCG@10 increases as the session progresses for all methods. Beyond half of the session, the session search methods outperform retrieving according to the last query in the session. We see that, for longer sessions, specialized methods (Nugget, QCM) outperform generic term frequency models. This comes as no surprise. Bennett et al. [2] note that users tend to reformulate and adapt their information needs based on observed results and this is essentially the observation upon which QCM builds.

Fig. 1 and Table 2 reveal a large NDCG@10 gap between the compared methods and the ground-truth oracle. How can we bridge this gap? Table 3 shows a comparison between frequency-based term weighting, the ideal term weighting (§3.4) and the ground-truth oracle (§3.3) for all sessions consisting of 7 unique terms or less (§3.4). Two important observations. There is still plenty of room for improvement using lexical query modeling only. Relatively speaking, around half of the gap between weighting according to term frequency and the ground-truth can be bridged by predicting better term weights. However, the other half of the performance gap cannot be bridged using lexical matching only, but instead requires a notion of semantic matching [9].

5. CONCLUSIONS

We have shown that naive frequency-based term weighting methods perform on par with specialized session search methods on the TREC Session track (2011–2014).[5] This is due to the fact that shorter sessions are more prominent in the session query logs. On longer sessions, specialized models are able to exploit session history more effectively. Future work should focus on creating benchmarks consisting of longer sessions with complex information needs. Perhaps more importantly, we have looked at the viability of lexical query matching in session search. There is still much room for improvement by re-weighting query terms. How-

ever, the query/document mismatch is prevalent in session search and methods restricted to lexical query modeling face a very strict performance ceiling. Future work should focus on better lexical query models for session search, in addition to semantic matching and tracking the dynamics of contextualized semantics in search.

Acknowledgments This work was supported by the Google Faculty Research Award and the Bloomberg Research Grant programs. Any opinions, findings and conclusions or recommendations expressed in this material are the authors' and do not necessarily reflect those of the sponsors. The authors would like to thank Daan Odijk, David Graus and the anonymous reviewers for their valuable comments and suggestions.

REFERENCES

[1] M. Bendersky, D. Metzler, and W. B. Croft. Effective query formulation with multiple information sources. In *SIGIR*, pages 443–452. ACM, 2012.
[2] P. N. Bennett, R. W. White, W. Chu, S. T. Dumais, P. Bailey, F. Borisyuk, and X. Cui. Modeling the impact of short- and long-term behavior on search personalization. In *SIGIR*, pages 185–194. ACM, 2012.
[3] B. Carterette, E. Kanoulas, M. M. Hall, and P. D. Clough. Overview of the trec 2014 session track. In *TREC*, 2014.
[4] G. V. Cormack, M. D. Smucker, and C. L. Clarke. Efficient and effective spam filtering and re-ranking for large web datasets. *Information retrieval*, 14(5):441–465, 2011.
[5] D. Donato, F. Bonchi, T. Chi, and Y. Maarek. Do you want to take notes?: identifying research missions in yahoo! search pad. In *WWW*, pages 321–330. ACM, 2010.
[6] D. Guan, H. Yang, and N. Goharian. Effective structured query formulation for session search. Techn. report, 2012.
[7] A. Hassan, R. W. White, S. T. Dumais, and Y.-M. Wang. Struggling or exploring?: disambiguating long search sessions. In *WSDM*, pages 53–62. ACM, 2014.
[8] A. Kotov, P. N. Bennett, R. W. White, S. T. Dumais, and J. Teevan. Modeling and analysis of cross-session search tasks. In *SIGIR*, pages 5–14. ACM, 2011.
[9] H. Li and J. Xu. Semantic matching in search. *Found. & Tr. in Information Retrieval*, 7(5):343–469, June 2014.
[10] J. Luo, X. Dong, and H. Yang. Modeling rich interactions in session search - georgetown university at trec 2014 session track. Techn. report, 2014.
[11] J. Luo, S. Zhang, and H. Yang. Win-win search: Dual-agent stochastic game in session search. In *SIGIR*, pages 587–596. ACM, 2014.
[12] J. Luo, X. Dong, and H. Yang. Session search by direct policy learning. In *ICTIR*, pages 261–270. ACM, 2015.
[13] D. Metzler and W. B. Croft. Combining the language model and inference network approaches to retrieval. *IPM*, 40(5):735–750, 2004.
[14] K. Raman, P. N. Bennett, and K. Collins-Thompson. Toward whole-session relevance: exploring intrinsic diversity in web search. In *SIGIR*, pages 463–472. ACM, 2013.
[15] TREC. Session Track, 2009–2014.
[16] H. Yang, D. Guan, and S. Zhang. The query change model: Modeling session search as a markov decision process. *TOIS*, 33(4): 20:1–20:33, May 2015.

---

[5]An open-source implementation of our testbed for evaluating session search is available at https://github.com/cvangysel/sesh.

The Effect of Document Order and Topic Difficulty on Assessor Agreement

Tadele T. Damessie
RMIT University
Melbourne, Australia
tadeletedla.damessie@rmit.edu.au

Falk Scholer
RMIT University
Melbourne, Australia
falk.scholer@rmit.edu.au

Kalervo Järvelin
University of Tampere
Tampere, Finland
kalvero.jarvelin@uta.fi

J. Shane Culpepper
RMIT University
Melbourne, Australia
shane.culpepper@rmit.edu.au

ABSTRACT

Human relevance judgments are a key component for measuring the effectiveness of information retrieval systems using test collections. Since relevance is not an absolute concept, human assessors can disagree on particular topic-document pairs for a variety of reasons. In this work we investigate the effect that document presentation order has on inter-rater agreement, comparing two presentation ordering approaches similar to those used in IR evaluation campaigns: decreasing relevance order and document identifier order. We make a further distinction between "easy" topics and "hard" topics in order to explore system effects on inter-rater agreement. The results of our pilot user study indicate that assessor agreement is higher when documents are judged in document identifier order. In addition, there is higher overall agreement on easy topics than on hard topics.

Keywords

Experimentation; measurement; relevance; assessor agreement; ordering effects

1. INTRODUCTION

Test collections are widely used for the evaluation of information retrieval system effectiveness. A key component of the approach is a set of relevance judgments, indicating which documents are considered to be appropriate answers in response to a topic. Differences in human judgments can potentially lead to alternative conclusions about system effectiveness, and so the question of judgment consistency is an important consideration for the generality of the conclusions that can be drawn from a test collection. Judgment consistency can be measured by calculating the *inter-rater agreement* between different human assessors who are asked to judge the relevance of common topic-document pairs in response to an information need. Given an information need, disagreement can exist

ICTIR'16, September 12–16, 2016, Newark, DE, USA
Copyright is held by the owner/author(s). Publication rights licensed to ACM.
ACM 978-1-4503-4497-5/16/09 ...$15.00.
http://dx.doi.org/10.1145/2970398.2970431.

between assessors as to which of the documents presented are relevant [4], and previous work has shown that topic familiarity [1], topic knowledge [11], document-specific factors [7], and the degree of relevance of documents that are presented early in the judging process [16], are all factors that can affect agreement.

In this work, we investigate the impact of presentation order on assessors when making relevance judgments, as measured by inter-rater agreement. We also analyze the stability of agreement in the context of topic difficulty, from both the system and user perspective. This issue has direct implications in information retrieval evaluation, and the design and construction of test collections [12]. Two document orderings are considered: decreasing relevance order, where documents are sorted from most to least relevant; and document identifier order, where documents are sorted by document identifier. We refer to these two orderings as *Rel order* and *DocID order* in the remainder of this paper. *Rel order* is similar to the approach used by the NTCIR evaluation campaign, where a pool of documents to be judged is sorted in decreasing *expected* relevance order, based on the number of participating systems that retrieved a document [13]. Here we use existing relevance judgments to ensure decreasing relevance order. *DocID order* is similar to that used by the TREC evaluation campaign, where the distribution of relevant documents can vary widely from topic to topic. Given these orderings, our main research questions are:

Research Quesiton (1): *Does the presentation order of documents for relevance judging affect inter-rater agreement?*

Research Quesiton (2): *Does topic difficulty influence inter-rater agreement with respect to the different presentation orderings?*

2. RELATED WORK

Several previous studies have investigated factors that influence assessor agreement. Bailey et al. [1] showed that agreement may be influenced by topic familiarity and topic origination. Their analysis demonstrated that assessors who are neither topic originators nor topic experts show more variation in their relevance judgments than those who are either topic originators or topic experts or both. Other studies have also shown a correlation between assessor experience and high agreement [3, 14].

Sormunen [17] compared the assessments of 5,271 documents from 38 topics chosen from TREC-7 and TREC-8 by a team of 9 master's students using a 4-point ordinal relevance scale with previous ratings from NIST assessors on a binary relevance scale. Of the TREC-relevant documents (2,772), 13% were re-assessed as highly relevant, 26% as relevant, 36% as marginally relevant and 25% as non-relevant. When the distribution of relevance agreement between TREC and the rejudged documents were compared, 25% of the documents rated relevant by TREC assessors were re-judged as non-relevant, 36% were judged to be marginally relevant, and 1% originally found to be non-relevant in the TREC assessment were judged relevant by the Sormunen assessors. These results clearly show the existence of disagreement between the two sets of assessors.

Huang and Wang [9] and Eisenberg and Barry [6] investigated the relationship between document order and relevance judgments. They found that document relevance is underestimated when documents are ordered from high relevance to low relevance, and document significance is overestimated if the order of documents is in reverse relevance order. Scholer et al. [16] studied the impact of the relevance of documents that are seen early in the judging process on the levels of relevance assigned to later documents, and concluded that presenting documents of varying relevance levels to assessors early on the judging process allowed assessors to calibrate their relevance thresholds.

Voorhees [19] studied the impact of assessor disagreement on retrieval system evaluation in terms of changes in system effectiveness rankings. Despite the existence of assessor disagreement, the study concluded that the relative effectiveness of systems is broadly stable. Though the study acknowledged the presence of disagreement between assessors, it did not investigate what causes the disagreement, or the implications on document ranking. In this work, we do not investigate how disagreement influences document ranking, but we do analyze the impact of document order on assessor agreement. Scholer et al. [15] studied assessment errors in relevance judgment files (or qrels) and demonstrated that inconsistencies in document assessments increase with time between judgments. However, they did not investigate how the ordering of documents affects assessor judgments.

Xu and Wang [20] examined cognitive aspects of relevance such as learning, subneed scheduling, and fatigue in a simulated retrieval task, and concluded that order effect on these cognitive aspects is weak at a document list length of 40. Xu and Wang suggested the need for further research on order effects and cognition.

In contrast to previous work, our current work focuses on a different aspect of inter-rater agreement – does document presentation ordering, or varying system topic difficulty, lead to a measurable impact on inter-rater agreement?

3. METHODOLOGY

To study the effect of document ordering on assessor agreement, we carried out a small scale user study using 120 documents, and 4 topics from the TREC-7 and TREC-8 collections that were judged both by NIST assessors on a binary scale, and later by Sormunen [17] using a 4-point scale. The graded relevance judgments from Sormunen are used as the ground truth in this experiment. The grades of the scale are: *Highly relevant (3)*, *Relevant (2)*, *Marginally relevant (1)*, and *Not relevant (0)*.

Query and Document Selection. For our study, we selected a mixture of hard and easy search topics, since we hypothesized that topic difficulty may have an effect on agreement. Following the approach of Carterette et al. [2] in the TREC Million Query track, we classified topic difficulty based on the per-topic *Average-Average-Precision* (AAP) scores (that is, average precision for each individual topic across a set of retrieval systems). We refer to this as *system topic difficulty* in the remainder of this paper. In our experiment, AAP was calculated for the topics of the 2004 Robust track

(which included the TREC-7 and TREC-8 topics with dual binary and ordinal relevance judgments) for the 110 runs that participated in the track. From this ordering, we selected the two highest and the two lowest AAP scoring topics: #365 *el nino* (0.723), #378 *euro opposition* (0.046), #410 *schengen agreement* (0.643), #448 *ship losses* (0.025).

For each of the chosen topics, 30 documents were selected for judging in our user study. The selection process was designed so that the distribution of documents at all four relevance levels in the sample was the same as the relevance distribution of the full set of documents available for each topic. For example, consider topic 365. There are a total of 198 documents, of which 33 are relevant, and the remaining 165 non-relevant. Out of the 33 relevant documents, 24 were judged as marginally relevant, 8 were judged relevant, and 1 was found to be highly relevant in the relevance judgement file (qrel) file. Given this distribution, the proportional selection was 25, 4, 1 and 0 for non-relevant, marginally relevant, relevant and highly relevant respectively. However, it is important to include at least one document of each relevance level whenever possible, in order to ensure that there is a clear distinction between relevant and non-relevant documents; therefore a minimum of 1 document at each relevance level was included in the final selection.

Assessment Interface. An online assessment system was developed to gather relevance assessments from participants. At the top of the screen, the system displayed a search topic, including the title, description and narrative of the official TREC topic statement. Below this, a single document was displayed. An assessor could enter a response by clicking on a radio button, to indicate their relevance assessment on the 4-point Sormunen scale. After selecting a relevance level, the user could click a button to record their judgment and move on to the next document. The system did not allow users to go back and change the ratings given to previous documents as presentation order is the key control variable in the study. Thus, a strict judging ordering was enforced by the assessment tool.

In addition to judging the 30 documents, we also required each assessor to rate their familiarity with the topics, the clarity of the topic description, and their confidence in identifying relevant documents, on a 5-point scale, both before and after the assessment exercise.

User study. A total of 16 participants were recruited from RMIT University to take part in the experiment, and were between the ages of 25 and 35. The study was approved by the RMIT University Ethics Board. All participants were computer science students, and all indicated familiarity with online searching in a pre-experiment questionnaire.

After arriving at the lab where the study was conducted, each participant was given an introduction to the experiment and a brief explanation of the online judging system. A hard copy of the definitions for each of the four relevance level was given to each judge at the start of the experiment, and was available for reference throughout the study. The main task required each participant to judge the relevance of documents for two topics. Participants were given up to one hour to judge each topic (one at the system easy and hard level), with a short break between the two topics. Topics and conditions were rotated when assigned to participants to control for possible ordering and learning effects [10]. The main factors being investigated in this study are document ordering – *Rel order* and *DocID order* – and topic difficulty – *easy* and *hard*. As participants judged documents for two topics, this led to eight combinations. The same process is repeated for the remaining two topics, giving

Table 1: Inter-rater agreement measured using Krippendorff's α for *Rel order* and *DocID order* presentation of documents, with ratings on a 4-level ordinal scale.

	Relevance	*DocID*	Assessors
All	0.570	0.700	16
Easy	0.668	0.746	8
Hard	0.473	0.655	8
Easy (`el nino`)	0.842	0.858	4
Easy (`schengen agreement`)	0.548	0.656	4
Hard (`euro opposition`)	0.428	0.612	4
Hard (`ship losses`)	0.417	0.672	4

a total number of 16 combinations (and assessors) for our experiment.

4. RESULTS AND DISCUSSION

Krippendorff's alpha(α) is a chance-corrected measure of rater agreement that takes into account the type of data (ordinal, nominal, interval or ratio) being measured, and adjusts to different sample and group sizes [5, 8]. The value of the α coefficient is bounded between -1 and 1, where zero indicates the absence of agreement (that is, observed agreement is equal to the level of agreement expected by chance), while 1 indicates perfect agreement between assessors. A negative value indicates that disagreement surpasses what is expected by random chance.

The agreement results from our user study as measured using Krippendorff's α are shown in Table 1. The overall level of agreement across all four topics is 0.57 for *Rel order* and 0.7 for *DocID order*: assessors in our study agreed more on relevance when they were shown documents in a *DocID order* based on a TREC document ID than when shown documents in decreasing relevance order. Splitting the topics into easy and hard groups (rows 2 and 3 of the table) shows that this effect is consistent: *DocID order* presentation leads to higher agreement in both cases. However, the difference in α is larger for the hard topics, suggesting that the choice of ordering plays a larger role when topics are difficult, and it would seem that documents for hard topics are harder to agree on than documents for the easy topics.

The results may appear surprising at first glance. Intuitively, when documents are shown in decreasing relevance order, one might expect that it is easier for assessors to recognize similar sources of evidence that are presented close together, and that they therefore give more similar ratings. However, an alternative interpretation is that variation plays an important role identifying relevant documents. For example, after seeing a number of non-relevant documents, a subsequent document that includes some relevant material may become easier to spot. This would lead to higher overall agreement between assessors.

To investigate this further, Figure 1 shows the presentation order and judging results for each of the 8 topic and ordering combinations. Each plot shows the 30 documents that were presented to assessors along the x-axis, and the corresponding relevance levels on the y-axis. The purple line shows the ground truth (Sormunen) relevance label, while the four colored bars show the judgments made by each of the four assessors for a particular topic-ordering combination. (Note since each experimental participant only judged two topics, the colors do not represent the same assessor in each graph.)

A particular feature that becomes apparent from the plots is that the *DocID order* for two topics, `el nino`; Figure 1(a) and Figure 1(b); and `ship losses`; Figure 1(g) and Figure 1(h), cluster relevant documents towards the end of the list, approaching a *reverse* relevance ordering. This is an artifact of following the TREC convention of ordering documents by the document ID string. A similar clustering effect is also present in the TREC judgments [15].

Vakkari and Sormunen [18] reported that test subjects are able to recognize highly relevant documents quite consistently, but tend to err on marginal and non-relevant ones. Sormunen [17] also found inconsistency of assessment between neighboring relevance levels. This concern motivates the need to assess user agreement on a binary scale in addition to a graded relevance scale. When using a binary relevance, the overall trends are similar to those shown for graded relevance, with *DocID order* leading to higher agreement than *Rel order* ($\alpha = 0.557$ for *Rel order*, and $\alpha = 0.673$ for *DocID order*).

Agreement between our study participants and the Sormunen judgments can be measured by computing Krippendorff's α between these two groups. The trend for this comparison is also consistent with the findings reported in this work (mean pairwise $\alpha = 0.668$ for *Rel order*, and $\alpha = 0.705$ for *DocID order*). We note that for some documents, the majority of our participants disagree with the Sormunen ratings, as can be seen in the plots in Figure 1; we plan to investigate the sources of this disagreement further in future work.

Finally, we briefly return to the problem of system versus user difficulty. Our study assumes the two are correlated; while this might not always be true, or post-hoc questionnaire provides some evidence that the two are aligned for the queries used in this study. Assessors were asked to answer the question "How easy was it to identify relevant documents for the search topic?" after completing assessments for each topic, with responses made on a five-point Likert scale, ranging from "Extremely easy (4)" to "Not easy at all (0)". The boxplot in Figure 2 shows the distribution of responses for all 16 assessors, aggregated by system difficulty. As can be seen in the plot, system and user topic difficulty align for the selected topics. We plan to investigate the distinction between system and user difficulty further in future work.

5. CONCLUSION

Relevance judgments are a key component of test collections, and the order in which documents are presented to assessors may influence the judging outcomes. In this work we investigated the influence of two common document orderings – *Rel order* and *DocID order* – on judgement consistency for easy and hard topics, using Krippendorff's α as a measure inter-rater agreement. We also consider the subtle distinction between system and user difficulty, as both can play an important role in the assessment process. The results of our pilot user study show that agreement tends to be higher when documents are presented in *DocID order*. A possible explanation for this effect is that a more mixed presentation of relevance ordering helps to create a "surprise" effect when items of more starkly different relevance levels follow each other, and this surprise effect, being relatively easier to spot, leads to greater overall rating consistency. Interestingly, topic difficulty can amplify this effect. We plan on using the lessons learned in this study to design a more comprehensive comparison of alternative document presentation orderings, and the effects of query difficulty on inter- and intra-rater agreement.

Acknowledgment. This work was supported by the Australian Research Council's *Discovery Projects* Scheme (DP140102655 and DP140103256). Shane Culpepper is the recipient of an Australian Research Council DECRA Research Fellowship (DE140100275).

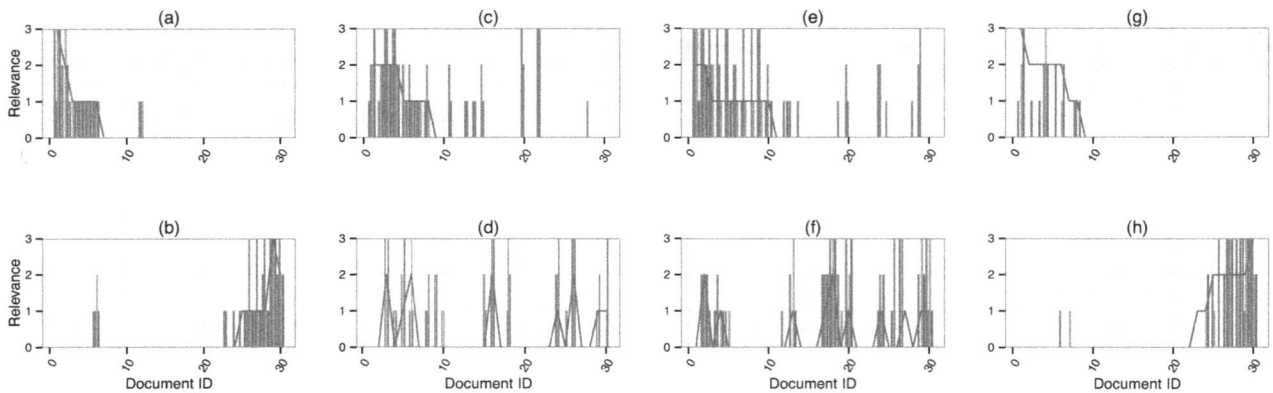

Figure 1: Document ordering and judgment results for the topic Easy (`el nino`) (a) & (b) and (`schengen agreement`) (c) & (d); Hard (`euro opposition`) (e) & (f) and (`ship losses`) (g) & (h) depicting *Rel order* (first row) and *DocID order* (second row).

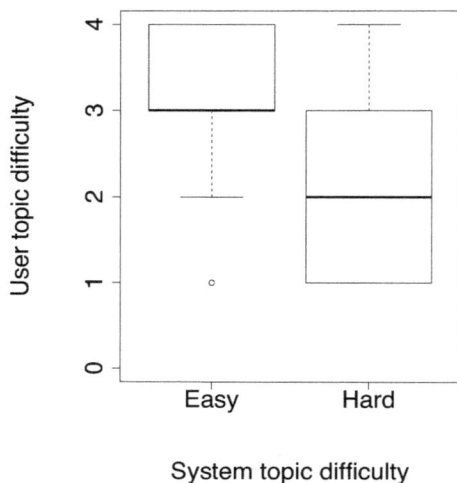

Figure 2: Relationship between system and user topic difficulty.

References

[1] P. Bailey, N. Craswell, I. Soboroff, P. Thomas, A. P. de Vries, and E. Yilmaz. Relevance assessment: are judges exchangeable and does it matter. In *Proc. SIGIR*, pages 667–674. ACM, 2008.

[2] B. Carterette, V. Pavlu, H. Fang, and E. Kanoulas. Million query track 2009 overview. In *TREC*, 2009.

[3] C. A. Cuadra, R. V. Katter, E. H. Holmes, and E. M. Wallace. *Experimental Studies of Relevance Judgments. Final Report. 3 Volumes.* System Development Corporation, 1967.

[4] D. Davidson. The effect of individual differences of cognitive style on judgments of document relevance. *J. Amer. Soc. Inf. Sc.*, 28(5):273–284, 1977.

[5] K. De Swert. Calculating inter-coder reliability in media content analysis using Krippendorff's alpha. *Center for Politics and Communication*, 2012.

[6] M. Eisenberg and C. Barry. Order effects: A study of the possible influence of presentation order on user judgments of document relevance. *J. Amer. Soc. Inf. Sc.*, 39(5):293–300, 1988.

[7] C. D. Gull. Seven years of work on the organization of materials in the special library. *American Documentation*, 7(4):320–329, 1956.

[8] A. F. Hayes and K. Krippendorff. Answering the call for a standard reliability measure for coding data. *Communication methods and measures*, 1(1):77–89, 2007.

[9] M.-H. Huang and H.-Y. Wang. The influence of document presentation order and number of documents judged on users' judgments of relevance. *J. Amer. Soc. Inf. Sc. Tech.*, 55(11):970–979, 2004.

[10] D. Kelly. Methods for evaluating interactive information retrieval systems with users. *Foundations and Trends in Information Retrieval*, 3(1–2):1–224, 2009.

[11] A. M. Rees and D. G. Schultz. A field experimental approach to the study of relevance assessments in relation to document searching. *Final Report to the National Science Foundation*, I, 1967.

[12] T. Sakai and N. Kando. Are popular documents more likely to be relevant? a dive into the ACLIA IR4QA pools. In *Proc. EVIA*, pages 8–9, 2008.

[13] T. Sakai and C. Lin. Ranking retrieval systems without relevance assessments: Revisited. In *Proc. EVIA*, pages 25–33, 2010.

[14] T. Saracevic. Effects of inconsistent relevance judgments on information retrieval test results: A historical perspective. *Library Trends*, 56(4):763–783, 2008.

[15] F. Scholer, A. Turpin, and M. Sanderson. Quantifying test collection quality based on the consistency of relevance judgements. In *Proc. SIGIR*, pages 1063–1072. ACM, 2011.

[16] F. Scholer, D. Kelly, W.-C. Wu, H. S. Lee, and W. Webber. The effect of threshold priming and need for cognition on relevance calibration and assessment. In *Proc. SIGIR*, pages 623–632. ACM, 2013.

[17] E. Sormunen. Liberal relevance criteria of TREC-Counting on negligible documents? In *Proc. SIGIR*, pages 324–330. ACM, 2002.

[18] P. Vakkari and E. Sormunen. The influence of relevance levels on the effectiveness of interactive information retrieval. *J. Amer. Soc. Inf. Sc. Tech.*, 55(11):963–969, 2004.

[19] E. M. Voorhees. Variations in relevance judgments and the measurement of retrieval effectiveness. *Information Processing & Management*, 36(5):697–716, 2000.

[20] Y. Xu and D. Wang. Order effect in relevance judgment. *J. Amer. Soc. Inf. Sc. Tech.*, 59(8):1264–1275, 2008.

A Reproducibility Study of Information Retrieval Models

Peilin Yang
University of Delaware
Newark, DE 19716
United States
franklyn@udel.edu

Hui Fang
University of Delaware
Newark, DE 19716
United States
hfang@udel.edu

ABSTRACT

Developing effective information retrieval models has been a long standing challenge in Information Retrieval (IR), and significant progresses have been made over the years. With the increasiqng number of developed retrieval functions and the release of new data collections, it becomes more difficult, if not impossible, to compare a new retrieval function with all existing retrieval functions over all available data collections. To tackle this problem, this paper describes our efforts on constructing a platform that aims to improve the reproducibility of IR research and facilitate the evaluation and comparison of retrieval functions. With the developed platform, more than 20 state of the art retrieval functions have been implemented and systematically evaluated over 16 standard TREC collections (including the newly released ClueWeb datasets). Our reproducibility study leads to several interesting observations. First, the performance difference between the reproduced results and those reported in the original papers is small for most retrieval functions. Second, the optimal performance of a few representative retrieval functions is still comparable over the new TREC ClueWeb collections. Finally, the developed platform (i.e., *RISE*) is made publicly available so that any IR researchers would be able to utilize it to evaluate other retrieval functions.

1. INTRODUCTION

One of the key challenges in Information Retrieval (IR) is to develop effective retrieval models. Since the beginning of the field, many retrieval models have been proposed and studied [5, 10, 26, 19, 23, 6, 20, 9, 7, 32, 25, 13, 1, 21, 27, 30, 31] and many data collections have been released [29]. The large number of developed retrieval functions and the increasing number of collections make it more challenging to conduct a comprehensive comparison in terms of the retrieval performance. The commonly used practice when evaluating a new retrieval function is to hand-pick a few existing retrieval functions as baseline methods and then com-

pare the performance of the new retrieval function with the baselines over several data collections. The choice of baseline methods and data collections varies based on the resources available for each researcher. As a result, there are many important IR basic research questions that remain unanswered. For example, given a standard TREC collection, which retrieval function is the most effective? How is the performance of function A compared with that of function B over collection C? We might be able to find the answers for some specific functions and collections from existing publications, but we are unable to answer the questions for any retrieval functions and collections. For example, it is difficult to find publications that report the performance comparison of traditional retrieval functions (e.g., Pivoted normalization method [27] and two stage language modeling method [30]) over newly released TREC ClueWeb collections. Moreover, it is also difficult to know which of two newly developed retrieval functions is more effective if such a comparison has not been reported in the paper. Thus, it is critical to conduct a comprehensive reproducibility study on information retrieval models to gain a better understanding on the performance of existing retrieval functions over a wide range of data collections.

In fact, there are quite a few recent studies that emphasized the importance of reproducibility in IR [2, 22, 28, 4, 3]. Armstrong et al. [3] evaluated the performances of five publicly available search systems over nine TREC collections and found no evidence that the retrieval models were improved from 1994 to 2005. Their follow-up study [4] further analyzed the retrieval results published at SIGIR and CIKM from 1998-2008, pointed out the baselines used in these publications were generally weak, and concluded that the ad hoc retrieval is not measurably improving. Both studies indicated the need of setting up a platform that can facilitate the reproducibility of existing retrieval functions and evaluation of new retrieval functions.

In this paper, we describe our efforts on conducting a reproducibility study for Information Retrieval models. First, we develop a web-based platform called *Reproducible Information retrieval System Evaluation* (**RISE**) for reproducing results for retrieval models. The RISE platform is designed to provide an easy yet controlled environment to facilitate the reproduce and fair comparison of different retrieval models. Second, we conduct a systematical comparison for a large number of representative retrieval functions over multiple data collections to see whether we can reproduce the reported performances and also generate benchmark results

ICTIR '16, September 12–16, 2016, Newark, Delaware, USA.

© 2016 ACM. ISBN 978-1-4503-4497-5/16/09. . . $15.00

DOI: http://dx.doi.org/10.1145/2970398.2970415

over the collections that have not been evaluated in the original papers.

Specifically, *RISE* can be regarded as an instantiation of Privacy Preserving Evaluation (PPE)[8] and Evaluation as a Service (EaaS)[17, 24]. When evaluating the retrieval performance of multiple retrieval functions over one collection, it provides the same underlying indexes of the collection and eliminates the impact of document pre-processing methods. Moreover, the format of queries is standardized and the evaluation measure can be comprehensive but yet flexible based on users need, e.g. choose title as the query of TREC query topic together with MAP reported as opposed to choose title and description as the query with P@10 reported. Thus, the *RISE* platform enables users to focus on the implementation of retrieval models themselves by automating other steps that are necessary for processing the document collections and evaluating retrieval models. Another important advantage of the *RISE* platform lies in its ability to evaluate retrieval models on the server side, which avoids the need of disseminating data collections.

With the developed *RISE* platform, we are able to conduct a more comprehensive reproducibility study for information retrieval models. In particular, we implement and evaluate more than 20 basic retrieval functions over 16 standard TREC collections. Experimental results allow us to make a few interesting observations. We first compare the evaluation results with those reported in the original papers, and find that the performance differences between the reproduced results and the original ones are small for majority of the retrieval functions. Among all the implemented functions, only one of them consistently generates worse performance than the one reported in the original paper. Moreover, we report the retrieval performance of all the implemented retrieval functions over all the 16 TREC collections including recently released ClueWeb sets. To the best of our knowledge, this is the first time of reporting such a large scale comparison of IR retrieval models. Such a comparison can be used as the performance references of the selected models.

The *RISE* platform is available at http://rires.info:8080/. Both source codes and evaluation results of the implemented retrieval functions can also be found on the website.

2. RELATED WORK

There have been significant efforts on developing various web services for IR evaluation. Lin et al. [16] proposed an open-source IR reproducibility challenge where they split the IR system into pieces of components such as two kinds of tokenization methods and four different IR toolkits. By easily configuring different combinations of these components, we can have a partially filled matrix indicating the performances of specific combinations of the components. Such transparent experiment set up makes it possible to have a better understanding about the impact of different components. Gollub et al. [11] described a reference implementation of their proposed IR evaluation web service which bears the important properties like web dissemination and peer-to-peer collaboration. Hanbury et al. [12] reviewed some of the existing automated IR evaluation approaches and proposed a framework for web service based component-level IR system evaluation. Lagun and Agichtein proposed a web service, which enables large scale studies of remote users[15]. Their system focused on providing a platform that repro-

duces and extends the previous findings on how users interact with the search engine especially the search results.

Our developed *RISE* system is closely related to the ideas of Privacy Preserved Evaluation (PPE)[8] and Evaluation as a Service (EaaS)[24, 17, 18]. The system is designed as a web service to provide a unified interface for the users to evaluate their models/algorithms. This design enables the system to host the data collections instead of shipping the data collections to researchers, which can ensure the privacy of the collections. VIRLab [8] provides similar Web service for users to implement retrieval functions, but it is mainly designed to facilitate teaching IR models. Thus, it does not support as many collection statistics as those provided in the *RISE* system, and the users can not see the functions implemented by other users. The uniqueness of *RISE* system is that it is specifically designed to facilitate the implementation and evaluation of retrieval functions.

The SIGIR 2015 Workshop on Reproducibility, Inexplicability, and Generalizability of Results (RIGOR) [14] is one of the venues that encourage the study of reproducibility. Their reproducibility challenge invited developers of 7 open-source search engines to provide baselines for TREC GOV2 collection. Trotman et. al. [28] and Muhleisen el. al. [22] have also tried to reproduce retrieval results for IR models, but the number of retrieval functions and the number of collections used in these studies (1 function 1 collection for [28] and 9 functions 10 collections for [22]) are not as large as what we studied in this paper.

Compared with the previous studies, our work is different in the following two aspects. First, the *RISE* system is specifically designed for the reproducibility study of retrieval models. It hides details about collection processing and evaluation, and enables users to focus on only the implementation of retrieval models. Due to its flexibility, we are able to implement and compare a wide range of retrieval functions that were not implemented in any other open-source toolkits. Second, our reproducibility study includes more retrieval functions and more data collections. The ultimate goal of the *RISE* system is to provide a complete set of benchmark results of IR models.

3. RISE - A REPRODUCIBILITY PLATFORM FOR RETRIEVAL MODELS

To reproduce the results of retrieval models, we implement a web-based Reproducible Information retrieval System Evaluation (*RISE*) platform. The platform is designed to provide a well-controlled environment for the users to implement and evaluate retrieval functions. Figure 1 shows the architecture of RISE. *RISE* is basically a web service built on top of a modified version of the Indri[1] toolkit. *RISE* hosts data collections on the server side, processes documents, and builds the indexes. Users need to upload their own implementations of retrieval functions based on the provided templates. After the code is uploaded, *RISE* automatically compiles it and evaluates it over the selected data collections. The evaluation results of the retrieval function will then be added to the score boards and thus be available for comparison.

Any registered users can contribute the implementation of a retrieval model to the system. Users are expected to be familiar with C++ but not necessarily familiar with In-

---

[1]http://sourceforge.net/projects/lemur/

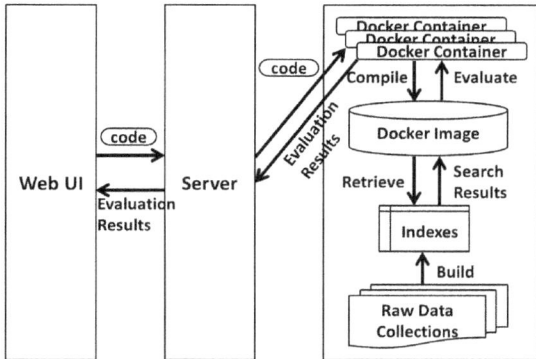

Figure 1: System Architecture

dri, as we provide detailed instructions with sample codes on how to access the statistics from the indexes and how to implement ranking models with the provided statistics. Moreover, *RISE* is an open system which allows any user to view any other users' implementations of the models. This functionality makes it possible for a user to easily try different variants of existing retrieval functions. The modified version of the Indri toolkit provides various statistics that are not available in the original version. These new statistics include query term frequency, average document term frequency, etc.

After the code is submitted to the server and successfully compiled, a Docker container is temporarily initiated on top of the static Docker image. (Docker container is like a sandbox which provides an isolated environment acting like an operating system. For more information please refer to https://www.docker.com/) The Docker image includes the indexes built from data collections and the modified Indri toolkit that will be used as the facility to run the model and generate the ranking list. A Docker image can be utilized by several Docker containers at the same time while keep the same underlying view of index and thus is the ideal choice for the system. Several Docker containers can be initiated in parallel so that multiple models can be compiled, run and evaluated at the same time. Moreover, by carefully setting the Docker container we can control the CPU and memory usage as well as security related settings (e.g. network, 3rd party libraries) so that the system is more robust against malicious/careless usage. The running Docker container compiles the codes, generate the ranking list, then evaluate the results. After that, the performance is rendered to the users and users can opt to choose other models to compare with.

There are several major benefits of the developed *RISE* platform. (1) The data collections are kept on the server side to preserve the data privacy. (2) The platform uses Docker to control the evaluation environment, which is more secure, faster and more reliable. (3) The platform provides a repository of the implementation of various retrieval functions. Registered users can upload their own codes, and these codes can be reused by other users. Such a repository could eliminate redundant efforts of implementing baseline methods among IR researchers. (4) The platform maintains the scores for each implemented retrieval function over all available data sets. The score boards could become a valu-

able reference when a new retrieval function needs to be evaluated and compared with the state of the art methods.

4. REPRODUCED RETRIEVAL FUNCTIONS

With the developed *RISE* platform, we conduct a reproducibility study of IR models with 21 representative retrieval functions. These retrieval functions include the representative ones from the vector space models [27, 23], the classic probabilistic models [25], the language modeling approaches [31, 30], the divergence from randomness models [1], the axiomatic models [9, 19], and the information theory based models [6].

Let us first explain the notations used in the paper.

- $|q|$: the number of terms in query q

- c_t^q: the number of occurrences of term t in query q

- c_t^d: the number of occurrences of term t in document d

- l_d: the length of document l

- c_d: the number of unique terms in document d

- F_t: the total number of term t in collection

- N_t: the number of documents containing term t

- $|C|$: the number of terms in collection

- N: the number of documents in collection

- L: the average document length in collection

We now provide more details about the retrieval functions that are included in the reproducibility study. All the implemented functions are summarized in Table 1 and Table 2.

4.1 Okapi BM25 and its variants

Okapi BM25 is one of the representative retrieval functions derived from the classical probabilistic retrieval model. It was first proposed at TREC-3 [25], and has become one of the most commonly used baseline retrieval functions. This function is denote as **BM25** in the paper.

Axiomatic approaches was first applied to Okapi BM25 to develop new retrieval functions [9] in 2005. The basic idea is to search for a retrieval function that can satisfy all reasonable retrieval constraints. Instead of blindly search for the function, one strategy is to start with an existing retrieval function, such as Okapi BM25, find its general form, and use the retrieval constraints to find different instantiations that can satisfy more retrieval constraints. The previous study derived two variants based on Okapi BM25, and they are referred to as **F2EXP** and **F2LOG** in the paper. Compared with the original BM25 function, these two variants have different implementations for both term frequency (TF) normalization part and the inverse document frequency (IDF) part.

Another variant of BM25 came from the study of Dirichlet Priors for term frequency normalization [13]. This variant, denoted as **BM3**, replaces the original TF normalization components in the BM25 function with the Dirichlet Priors TF normalization component.

Table 1: Retrieval functions that are reproduced in our study (Part 1)

Okapi BM25 and its variants	BM25	$\sum_{t \in q} \frac{(k_3+1) \cdot c_t^q}{k_3 + c_t^q} \cdot \frac{(k_1+1) \cdot c_t^d}{c_t^d + k_1 \cdot (1-b+b \cdot \frac{l_d}{l})} \cdot ln\left(\frac{N-N_t+0.5}{N_t+0.5}\right)$
	F2EXP	$\sum_{t \in q} \frac{c_t^d}{c_t^d + s + s \cdot \frac{l_d}{l}} \cdot \left(\frac{N+1}{N_t}\right)^k$
	F2LOG	$\sum_{t \in q} \frac{c_t^d}{c_t^d + s + s \cdot \frac{l_d}{l}} \cdot ln\left(\frac{N+1}{N_t}\right)$
	BM3	$\sum_{t \in q} \frac{(k_3+1) \cdot c_t^q}{k_3 + c_t^q} \cdot \frac{(k_1+1) \cdot tfn}{k_1 + tfn} \cdot ln\left(\frac{N-N_t+0.5}{N_t+0.5}\right)$ $tfn = \frac{c_t^d + \mu \cdot \frac{F_t}{|C|}}{l_d + \mu} \cdot \mu$
	BM25+	$\sum_{t \in q} \frac{(k_3+1) \cdot c_t^q}{k_3 + c_t^q} \cdot \left[\frac{(k_1+1) \cdot c_t^d}{c_t^d + k_1 \cdot (1-b+b \cdot \frac{l_d}{l})} + \delta\right] \cdot ln(\frac{N+1}{N_t})$
Pivoted and its variants	PIV	$\sum_{t \in q} \frac{1 + ln(1+ln(c_t^d))}{(1-s)+s \cdot \frac{l_d}{l}} \cdot ln\left(\frac{N+1}{N_t}\right)$
	F1EXP	$\sum_{t \in q} (1 + ln(1 + ln(c_t^d))) \cdot \frac{L+s}{L+s \cdot l_d} \cdot \left(\frac{N+1}{N_t}\right)^k$
	F1LOG	$\sum_{t \in q} (1 + ln(1 + ln(c_t^d))) \cdot \frac{L+s}{L+s \cdot l_d} \cdot ln\left(\frac{N+1}{N_t}\right)$
	PIV+	$\sum_{t \in q} \left[\frac{1 + ln(1+ln(c_t^d))}{(1-s)+s \cdot \frac{l_d}{l}} + \delta\right] \cdot ln\left(\frac{N+1}{N_t}\right)$
	NTFIDF	$\sum_{t \in q} \left[\left[\omega \cdot f\left(\frac{c_t^d}{l_d/c_d}\right) + (1-\omega) \cdot f\left(c_t^d \cdot log_2\left(1+\frac{L}{l_d}\right)\right)\right] \cdot \left[ln\left(\frac{N+1}{N_t}\right) \cdot f\left(\frac{F_t}{N_t}\right)\right]\right]$ $\omega = \frac{2}{1+log_2(1+|q|)}, f(x) = \frac{x}{1+x}$

Following the axiomatic methodology, Lv and Zhai [19] revealed a deficiency of the BM25 in its TF normalization component, i.e., the TF normalization component is not lower-bounded properly. To fix this problem, a variant of BM25, denoted as **BM25+**, was proposed. The main change is to add a lower bound to the TF normalization part.

4.2 Pivoted normalization function and its variants

Pivoted normalization method, denoted as **PIV**, is one of the most representative retrieval functions derived from the vector space model [27]. It can be regarded as one of the best-performing TF-IDF retrieval functions.

Axiomatic approaches were also applied to derive variants of the pivoted normalization method [9]. The two variants are denoted as **F1EXP** and **F1LOG**. Compared with the original function, the two variants are different in their implementations of IDF and TF normalization.

Similar to BM25, low-bounding term frequency normalization has also been applied to the pivoted function. The variant is denoted as **PIV+**, and it differs from the original function in having a lower bound added to the TF normalization component.

A novel TF-IDF term weighting scheme was proposed in 2013 to capture two different aspects of term saliency [23]. In particular, its TF component is a combination of two normalization strategies, in which one prefers short documents while the other prefers long documents. Its form is quite different from the pivoted normalization function. We include it as one of the variants for the pivoted normalization function because it uses a novel TF-IDF weighting strategy.

4.3 Language modeling approaches

Dirichlet prior method, denoted as **DIR**, is one of the representative retrieval functions derived using the language modeling approaches [31]. It uses the Dirichlet prior smoothing method to smooth a document language model and then

ranks the documents based on the likelihood of the query is generated by the estimated document language models.

Two-stage language models were proposed to explicitly capture the difference influences of the query and document collection on the optimal parameter setting [30]. Compared with the Dirichlet prior method, the two-stage smoothing method (denoted as **TSL**) interpolates the smoothed document language model with a query background language model.

Instead of assuming document models take the form of a multinomial distribution over words, Multiple-Bernoulli language models assume that the document is a sample from a Multiple-Bernoulli distribution [21]. The retrieval function is denoted as **BLM**.

Similar to BM25 and Pivoted, Dirichlet prior method has also been studied using axiomatic approaches. Two variants derived using the axiomatic approaches [9] are denoted as **F3EXP** and **F3LOG**. The variant derived based on the lower bound term frequency normalization [19] is denoted as **DIR+**.

4.4 Divergence from Randomness Models

The **PL2** model is a representative retrieval function of the divergence from randomness framework [1]. It measures the randomness of terms using Poisson distribution with Laplacian smoothing.

The first variant of the PL2 is to replace the original TF normalization component with the Dirichlet prior TF normalization [13]. This variant is denoted as **PL3**.

The second variant of the PL2 considered in this paper is to apply the lower bound term frequency normalization [19]. It is denoted as **PL2+**.

4.5 Information-based Models

A family of information-based models was proposed for ad hoc IR [6]. These models focused on modeling relevance based on how a word deviates from its average behavior. Two power law distributions (e.g., a smoothed power-law

Table 2: Retrieval functions that are reproduced in our study (Part 2)

Language modeling approaches	DIR	$\sum_{t\in q} ln\left(\dfrac{c_t^d + \mu\cdot\frac{F_t}{|C|}}{l_d+\mu}\right)$
	TSL	$\sum_{t\in q}\left((1-\lambda)\cdot\dfrac{c_t^d+\mu\cdot\frac{F_t}{|C|}}{l_d+\mu} + \lambda\cdot\dfrac{F_t}{|C|}\right)$
	BLM	$\sum_{t\in q}\dfrac{c_t^d+\mu\cdot\frac{F_t}{|C|}}{l_d+\frac{|C|}{F_t}+\mu-2}$
	F3EXP	$\sum_{t\in q}(1+ln(1+ln(c_t^d)))\cdot\left(\dfrac{N+1}{N_t}\right)^k - \dfrac{(l_d-|q|)\cdot|q|\cdot s}{L}$
	F3LOG	$\sum_{t\in q}(1+ln(1+ln(c_t^d)))\cdot ln\left(\dfrac{N+1}{N_t}\right) - \dfrac{(l_d-|q|)\cdot|q|\cdot s}{L}$
	DIR+	$\sum_{t\in q}\left[ln\left(1+\dfrac{c_t^d}{\mu\cdot\frac{F_t}{|C|}}\right)+ln\left(1+\dfrac{\delta}{\mu\cdot\frac{F_t}{|C|}}\right)\right]+|q|\cdot ln\dfrac{\mu}{l_d+\mu}$
Divergence from Randomness Models	PL2	$\sum_{t\in q}\dfrac{tfn\cdot log_2(tfn\cdot\lambda)+log_2 e\cdot(\frac{1}{\lambda}-tfn)+0.5\cdot log_2(2\pi\cdot tfn)}{tfn+1}$ $tfn=c_t^d\cdot log_2\left(1+c\cdot\dfrac{L}{l_d}\right)$
	PL3	$\sum_{t\in q}\dfrac{tfn\cdot log_2(tfn\cdot\lambda)+log_2 e\cdot(\frac{1}{\lambda}-tfn)+0.5\cdot log_2(2\pi\cdot tfn)}{tfn+1}$ $tfn=\dfrac{c_t^d+\mu\cdot\frac{F_t}{|C|}}{l_d+\mu}\cdot\mu$
	PL2+	$\sum_{t\in q,\lambda>1}\left[\dfrac{tfn\cdot log_2(tfn\cdot\lambda)+log_2 e\cdot(\frac{1}{\lambda}-tfn)+0.5\cdot log_2(2\pi\cdot tfn)}{tfn+1}+\dfrac{\delta\cdot log_2(\delta\cdot\lambda)+log_2 e\cdot(\frac{1}{\lambda}-\delta)+\frac{log_2(2\pi\delta)}{2}}{\delta+1}\right]$ $tfn=c_t^d\cdot log_2\left(1+c\cdot\dfrac{L}{l_d}\right)$
Information-based Models	SPL	$\sum_{t\in q}-ln\left(\dfrac{\lambda_t^{\frac{n_t^d}{n_t^d+1}}-\lambda_t}{1-\lambda_t}\right)$ $\lambda_t=\dfrac{F_t}{N}$ and $n_t^d=c_t^d+ln\left(1+c\cdot\dfrac{L}{l_d}\right)$
	LGD	$\sum_{t\in q}-ln\left(\dfrac{\lambda_t}{n_t^d+\lambda_t}\right)$ $\quad \lambda_t$ and n_t^d as shown above

distribution and log-logistic distribution) were used, and the corresponding functions are denoted as **SPL** and **LGD**.

5. EXPERIMENTS

We now describe the experiment design and results for our reproducibility study. The first set of experiments mainly focuses on whether we can reproduce the retrieval results that have been reported in the previous studies and whether the reproduced results are consistent with that have been reported. The second set of experiments aims to examine how well the retrieval functions perform on the newly released data sets and checks whether the conclusions are consistent with the previous findings. Finally, we also provide reference performance for all the reproduced retrieval functions over a wide range of TREC collections including the newly released ClueWeb collections.

5.1 Reproducibility study

5.1.1 Experiment Design

For the reproducibility experiments, we conduct experiments over 11 data sets that have been used in the ad hoc retrieval task at TREC-1, TREC-2, TREC-3, TREC-6, TREC-7, TREC-8; the small web track at TREC-8; the terabyte track at TREC 2004-2006; and the robust track at TREC 2004. The statistics of the data collections are summarized in Table 3.

All the collections are stemmed using Porter's stemmer. We mainly focus on the title part of the query topics. If the performance of title query is not reported by the original paper, then we use whatever query (e.g. description part or title+description+narrative) that was originally used. Please

note that for some papers the authors reported the performances on the combination of multiple query topic sets, e.g. TREC678 as one query set. For this kind of query we treat the three years' topics as one query set like what the original authors did.

We evaluate the retrieval functions over these data collections and compare our results with what have been reported in the previous studies. The results are evaluated with MAP@1000, and the evaluation results are computed using `trec_eval`[2].

5.1.2 Results

We evaluate the retrieval performance for each of the 21 retrieval functions described in the previous section over all the data collections mentioned in Table 3. We then compare our reproduced results of a retrieval function with the original results reported in the paper that proposed the function. Due to the space limit, we can not report all the reproduced results, so we summarize a few main findings here.

WT2G and **disk4&5** are the two commonly used document collections in the previous study. We summarize the performance comparison between the reproduced results and the original results on these two data sets in Table 4 and Table 5 respectively. Note that **disk4&5** refers to all the data sets that use disk 4 and 5 as document collections, and it includes TREC6, TREC7 and TREC8. Let us first explain the notations in the two tables. The `orig.` column lists the originally reported results. The `repd.` column are the reproduced results. Either positive or negative difference between `orig.` and `repd.` is shown as percentage w.r.t the `orig.` in column `diff.`. The free parameter(s) used by the original

[2]http://trec.nist.gov/trec_eval/

Table 3: Data collections used for the reproducibility study

	Topics	Doc. collection	#documents	avdl
ad hoc task at TREC-1	51-100			
ad hoc task at TREC-2	101-150	**disk1&2**	741,856	412.89
ad hoc task at TREC-3	151-200			
ad hoc task at TREC-6	301-350			
ad hoc task at TREC-7	351-400	**disk4&5**	528,155	467.553
ad hoc task at TREC-8	401-450			
robust track at TREC 2004	601-700			
small web task at TREC-8	401-450	**WT2G**	247,491	1057.59
terabyte track at TREC 2004	701-750			
terabyte track at TREC 2005	751-800	**GOV2**	25,205,179	937.252
terabyte track at TREC 2006	801-850			

Table 4: Performance comparison of reproduced and original results on **WT2G**

Models	orig.	repd.	diff.	para.
BM25 and its variants				
BM25	0.310	0.315	+1.61%	$b = 0.2$
F2EXP	0.289	0.297	+2.77%	$s = 0.2^*$
F2LOG	0.295	0.301	+2.03%	$s = 0.3^*$
BM3	0.316	0.295	-6.65%	$\mu = 2700$
BM25+	0.318	0.318	+0.00%	$b = 0.2$ $\delta = 1.0$
PIV and its variants				
PIV	0.292	0.295	+1.03%	$s = 0.1$
F1EXP	0.288	0.278	-3.47%	$s = 0.0^*$
F1LOG	0.288	0.277	-3.82%	$s = 0.0^*$
PIV+	0.295	0.299	+1.36%	$s = 0.01$ $\delta = 0.4$
Language modeling approaches				
DIR	0.294	0.310	+5.44%	$\mu = 3000$
TSL	0.278	0.312	+12.23%	$\mu = 3500^*$ $\lambda = 0.0^*$
F3EXP	0.288	0.290	+0.69%	$s = 0.05^*$
F3LOG	0.290	0.293	+1.03%	$s = 0.05^*$
DIR+	0.312	0.312	+0.00%	$\mu = 3000^*$ $\delta = 0.01$
Divergence from Randomness Models				
PL3	0.293	0.288	-1.71%	$\mu = 9700$
PL2+	0.326	0.327	+0.31%	$c = 23$ $\delta = 0.8$

Table 5: Performance comparison of reproduced and original results on **disk4&5**

RM	orig.	repd.	diff.	para.
BM25 and its variants				
BM25	0.254	0.247	-2.76%	$b = 0.4$
BM3	0.251	0.238	-5.18%	$\mu = 950$
BM25+	0.255	0.249	-2.35%	$b = 0.4$ $\delta = 1.0$
PIV and its variants				
PIV	0.241	0.221	-8.30%	$s = 0.05$
PIV+	0.246	0.238	-3.25%	$s = 0.5$ $\delta = 0.01$
Language modeling approaches				
DIR+	0.253	0.252	-0.40%	$\mu = 1000^*$ $\delta = 0.01$
Divergence from Randomness Models				
PL3	0.230	0.239	+3.91%	$\mu = 1600$
PL2+	0.254	0.255	+0.39%	$c = 9$ $\delta = 0.8$
Information-based Models				
LGD	0.250	0.251	+0.40%	$c = 2.0$
SPL	0.254	0.251	-1.18%	$c = 9.0$

paper are reported in column `para.` where * means the parameter is not explicitly reported in the original paper and we just pick the optimal one by grid search. The original paper of BM25 and PIV did not report the performances on the collections that we select. Instead, we use what were reported in [13, 19] for these two models as their `orig.` results. Note that some retrieval functions are missing from the table because their original papers did not report the performance on the corresponding collection.

The results show that the performance differences with respect to the original performance, i.e, `diff.`, are small. Most of them are in the range of $[-5\%, +5\%]$. This indicates that we are able to successfully reproduce the retrieval performance for these functions.

To gain a better understanding of the reproduced results for all retrieval function, we summarize the performance dif-

ference (both mean and standard deviation) between the original and reproduced results for each of the retrieval function. The results are shown in Table 6. Although the reproduced results are not exactly the same as what were reported, the differences are generally small. We do not have the results for BLM because the authors of that paper did not report the performances on any collection that we have selected.

Among all the retrieval functions, PL2 has the largest standard deviation for the performance differences, and NT-FIDF has the largest mean performance difference. We provide more detailed reproduced results for these two functions in Table 7. It is clear that the performance differences are consistent over almost all the collections. One possible explanation is that these two functions were originally implemented using the Terrier[3] retrieval system as opposed to Indri used in our paper. As pointed out in the previous study [22], using different toolkits could lead to different evaluation results.

---

[3]http://terrier.org/

Table 6: The mean and standard deviation of the performance difference between the reproduced and original results

Functions	Mean	Std.
BM25 and its variants		
BM25	-2.08%	4.11%
F2EXP	+0.68%	2.18%
F2LOG	+0.22%	1.63%
BM3	-5.92%	0.74%
BM25+	-0.67%	1.19%
PIV and its variants		
PIV	-3.64%	4.67%
F1EXP	-6.62%	2.23%
F1LOG	-7.76%	2.79%
PIV+	-0.94%	2.31%
NTFIDF	-17.08%	4.71%
Language modeling approaches		
DIR	+1.03%	3.26%
TSL	+4.09%	6.18%
F3EXP	-2.65%	2.72%
F3LOG	-4.11%	3.74%
DIR+	-0.20%	0.20%
Divergence from Randomness Models		
PL2	+5.54%	17.73%
PL3	+0.59%	2.41%
PL2+	+0.35%	0.04%
Information-based Models		
SPL	-4.60%	3.42%
LGD	-2.04%	2.45%

Table 7: Reproduced performance comparison for PL2 and NTFIDF

Functions	collections	orig.	repd.	diff.	para.
PL2	TREC1	0.207	0.257	+24.46%	$c = 1.0$
	TREC2	0.238	0.285	+19.60%	$c = 1.0$
	TREC3	0.271	0.327	+20.89%	$c = 1.0$
	TREC6	0.257	0.233	-9.30%	$c = 1.0$
	TREC7	0.221	0.196	-11.39%	$c = 1.0$
	TREC8	0.256	0.228	-11.01%	$c = 1.0$
NTFIDF	TREC678	0.234	0.209	-10.64%	
	ROBUST04	0.302	0.245	-18.84%	
	GOV2	0.317	0.248	-21.77%	

Table 9: Free Parameters used in Parameter Tuning

Model	Para. Range	Incr.
BM25	$b \in [0, 1]$	0.05
PIV, F1EXP, F1LOG, F2EXP, F2LOG, F3EXP, F3LOG	$s \in [0, 1]$	0.05
DIR, BLM,	$\mu \in [500, 5000]$	500
TSL	$\mu \in [500, 5000]$	500
	$\lambda \in [0, 1]$	0.1
PL2	$c \in [0.5] \cup [1, 25]$	1
BM3, PL3	$c \in [0.5] \cup [0.75] \cup [1, 9]$	1
	$\mu \in [500, 5000]$	500
BM25+	$b \in [0, 1]$	0.05
PIV+	$s \in [0, 1]$	0.05
DIR+	$\mu \in [500, 5000]$	500
PL2+	$c \in [0.5] \cup [1, 25]$	1
BM25+, PIV+, DIR+, PL2+	$\delta \in [0.0, 1.5]$	0.1

5.2 Performance Comparison on Web Search Collections

Not only can the *RISE* system provide a platform to reproduce the results of existing IR models, but also minimize the efforts when evaluating IR models over new collections. Whenever there is a new data collection available, the *RISE* system can easily run all the implemented retrieval functions on the new data collection and generate evaluate results for each function.

We conduct experiments to evaluate the performance of retrieval functions over 5 data sets used in the Web track from TREC 2010 to TREC 2014. The Web track at TREC 2010 to TREC 2012 used the ClueWeb09[4] as the document collection. Each year's Web track has 50 topics. Since the entire ClueWeb09 collection is too big to host on our server, we used the category B colleciton, which contains a subset of about 50 million English pages. The Web track at TREC 2013 to TREC 2014 used the ClueWeb12[5] as the document collection. Each data set has 50 topics developed by NIST. Again, due to the huge size of the original ClueWeb12 data set, we evaluate the retrieval functions over a subset of collection. The subset is generated by sampling documents from the raw collection. We use Indri default query likelihood baseline to retrieve top 10,000 documents for each query and make these documents as the sampled collection. Following the measured used at the TREC Web track,

---

[4]http://lemurproject.org/clueweb09/

[5]http://lemurproject.org/clueweb12.php/

ERR@20 is used to evaluate the performance for these data sets. Due to the space limit, instead of reporting the performance over each Web track data set, we report the performance based on the document collection used. For example, **CW09** corresponds to the data set combining data used in the Web track at TREC 2010-2012. Similarly, **CW12** corresponds to the data set combining data used in the Web track at TREC 2013-2014.

As discussed in the previous section, many variants have been proposed to improve the performance of representative retrieval functions such as BM25, PIV, DIR and PL2. All those studies were conducted over the traditional TREC collections. Thus, it would be interesting to see whether the improvement would still exist on the new Web collections.

Figure 2 shows the optimal performance comparison of the representative retrieval functions with their variants on the new Web collections. We can make a few interesting observations. First, it is interesting to see that most variants can outperform their original retrieval functions. For example, all the variants of BM25 performs better than BM25 on both collections. The only exception is the PIV function. PIV performs really well on the two new collections. Second, divergence from randomness models do not perform as well as other retrieval functions. Finally, the optimal performances of the BM25 variants, PIV variants and DIR variants are comparable.

Figure 2: Optimal Performances on ClueWeb Collections

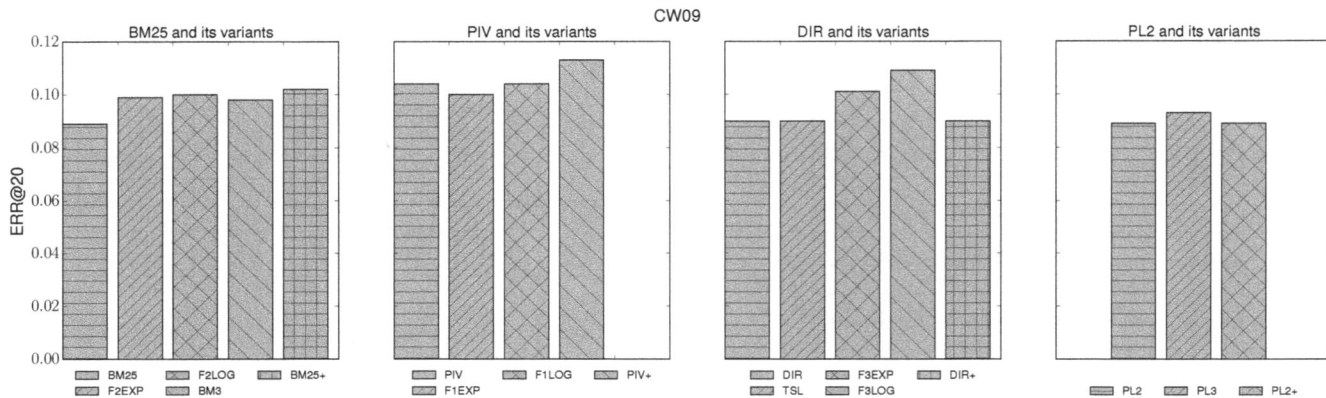

(a) Performances of selected models on CW09

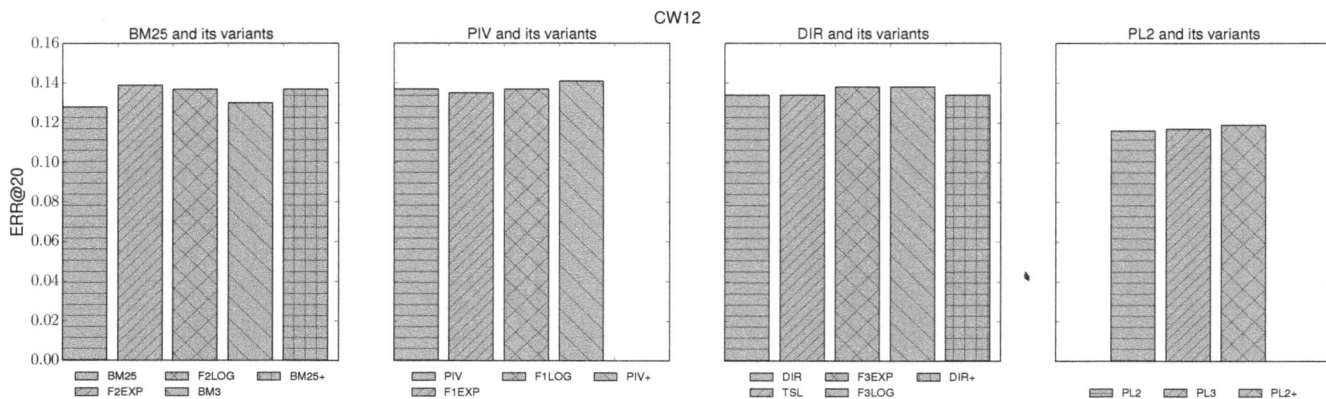

(b) Performances of selected models on CW12

5.3 Summary

To serve as a future reference, we summarize the optimal performance of all the retrieval functions over all the data sets in Table 8. Due to the space limit, the data sets are categorized based on the collections used, so data sets used in multiple tracks might be grouped into one because they used the same document collections. For each retrieval function, the free parameters are tuned via grid search and the parameter ranges are summarized in Table 9.

The optimal performances for the selected retrieval models on all collections are shown in Table 8. To the best of our knowledge this is the first time of reporting such large scale and comprehensive performances of retrieval models.

6. CONCLUSIONS AND FUTURE WORK

This paper describes our efforts on building the Reproducible Information retrieval System Evaluation (*RISE*) platform. *RISE* is a Web service that facilitates the implementation and evaluation of IR models. In particular, it can serve as an implementation repository of retrieval functions. Users can not only submit their own implementations but also view the implementations submitted by other users. With such an implementation repository, the *RISE* can also facilitate the evaluation of existing retrieval functions over new data collections. As demonstrated in the paper, we have imple-

mented 21 retrieval functions and evaluate them over 16 TREC data sets. All the implementations and the evaluation results are available at the *RISE* platform [6].

For the future work, we plan to provide continuous support to the *RISE* system so that other researchers from the community can contribute and leverage the system for their own research. Regarding the system design, we plan to provide more functionalities, such as training/testing data splitting, to facilitate the evaluation process.

7. ACKNOWLEDGMENT

This material is based upon work supported by the National Science Foundation under Grant Number IIS-1423002. We thank the reviewers for their useful comments.

8. REFERENCES

[1] G. Amati and C. J. Van Rijsbergen. Probabilistic models of information retrieval based on measuring the divergence from randomness. *ACM Trans. Inf. Syst.*, 20(4):357–389, 2002.

[2] J. Arguello, F. Diaz, J. Lin, and A. Trotman. Sigir 2015 workshop on reproducibility, inexplicability, and generalizability of results (rigor). In *Proceedings of the*

---

[6]http://rires.info:8080/

Table 8: Optimal MAP/ERR@20 for all collections. * indicates the model is significant better than the base model in its category (always the first one). † indicates the model is the best performed in its category. ‡ indicates the model is significant better than all other models in its category. All significant tests are at p = 0.05 by a paired one-tailed t-test.

RM	disk12	disk45	WT2G	GOV2	CW09	CW12
BM25 and its variants						
BM25	0.204	0.248	0.315	0.297	0.089	0.128
F2EXP	0.228*	0.251	0.297	0.284	0.099*	0.139†
F2LOG	0.231*	0.252†	0.302	0.297	0.100*	0.137
BM3	0.234*	0.241	0.296	0.283	0.098*	0.130
BM25+	0.235*†	0.249	0.318†	0.301†	0.102*†	0.137
PIV and its variants						
PIV	0.201	0.221	0.294	0.254	0.104	0.137
F1EXP	0.198	0.221	0.278	0.240	0.100	0.135
F1LOG	0.200	0.217	0.277	0.255	0.104	0.137
PIV+	0.207*†	0.239*‡	0.299*	0.265*	0.113†	0.141†
NTFIDF	0.205*	0.213	0.307*†	0.296*‡	0.097	0.129
Language Modeling Approaches						
DIR	0.227	0.252†	0.312	0.299	0.090	0.134
BLM	0.208	0.233	0.314†	0.222	0.072	0.113
TSL	0.228†	0.252	0.312	0.300†	0.090	0.134
F3EXP	0.205	0.234	0.290	0.250	0.101*	0.138
F3LOG	0.203	0.232	0.293	0.263	0.109*†	0.138†
DIR+	0.227	0.252	0.312	0.299	0.090	0.134
Divergence from Randomness Models						
PL2	0.228	0.252	0.325	0.303†	0.089	0.116
PL3	0.228†	0.241	0.290	0.269	0.093†	0.117
PL2+	0.214	0.255*‡	0.328*‡	0.301	0.089*	0.119*†
Information-based Models						
LGD	0.215†	0.251†	0.320†	0.300†	0.086	0.131†
SPL	0.213	0.251	0.313	0.299	0.093†	0.130

38th International ACM SIGIR Conference on Research and Development in Information Retrieval, SIGIR '15, pages 1147–1148, New York, NY, USA, 2015. ACM.

[3] T. G. Armstrong, A. Moffat, W. Webber, and J. Zobel. Has adhoc retrieval improved since 1994? In *Proceedings of the 32Nd International ACM SIGIR Conference on Research and Development in Information Retrieval,* SIGIR '09, pages 692–693, New York, NY, USA, 2009. ACM.

[4] T. G. Armstrong, A. Moffat, W. Webber, and J. Zobel. Improvements that don't add up: Ad-hoc retrieval results since 1998. In *Proceedings of the 18th ACM Conference on Information and Knowledge Management,* CIKM '09, pages 601–610, New York, NY, USA, 2009. ACM.

[5] C. Buckley, J. Allan, and G. Salton. Automatic routing and ad-hoc retrieval using smart : Trec 2. In *Proceedings of the Second Text REtrieval Conference (TREC-2), pages 45–56. NIST Special Publication,* pages 45–56, 1994.

[6] S. Clinchant and E. Gaussier. Information-based models for ad hoc ir. In *Proceedings of the 33rd International ACM SIGIR Conference on Research and Development in Information Retrieval,* SIGIR '10, pages 234–241, New York, NY, USA, 2010. ACM.

[7] A. P. de Vries and T. Roelleke. Relevance information: A loss of entropy but a gain for idf? In *Proceedings of the 28th Annual International ACM SIGIR Conference on Research and Development in Information Retrieval,* SIGIR '05, pages 282–289, New York, NY, USA, 2005. ACM.

[8] H. Fang, H. Wu, P. Yang, and C. Zhai. Virlab: A web-based virtual lab for learning and studying information retrieval models. In *Proceedings of the 37th International ACM SIGIR Conference on Research & Development in Information Retrieval,* SIGIR '14, pages 1249–1250, New York, NY, USA, 2014. ACM.

[9] H. Fang and C. Zhai. An exploration of axiomatic approaches to information retrieval. In *Proceedings of the 28th Annual International ACM SIGIR Conference on Research and Development in Information Retrieval,* SIGIR '05, pages 480–487, New York, NY, USA, 2005. ACM.

[10] M. Franz and J. S. McCarley. Word document density and relevance scoring (poster session). In *Proceedings of the 23rd Annual International ACM SIGIR Conference on Research and Development in Information Retrieval,* SIGIR '00, pages 345–347, New York, NY, USA, 2000. ACM.

[11] T. Gollub, B. Stein, and S. Burrows. Ousting ivory tower research: Towards a web framework for

providing experiments as a service. In *Proceedings of the 35th International ACM SIGIR Conference on Research and Development in Information Retrieval*, SIGIR '12, pages 1125–1126, New York, NY, USA, 2012. ACM.

[12] A. Hanbury and H. Müller. Automated component-level evaluation: Present and future. In *Proceedings of the 2010 International Conference on Multilingual and Multimodal Information Access Evaluation: Cross-language Evaluation Forum*, CLEF'10, pages 124–135, Berlin, Heidelberg, 2010. Springer-Verlag.

[13] B. He and I. Ounis. A study of the dirichlet priors for term frequency normalisation. In *Proceedings of the 28th Annual International ACM SIGIR Conference on Research and Development in Information Retrieval*, SIGIR '05, pages 465–471, New York, NY, USA, 2005. ACM.

[14] F. Hopfgartner, A. Hanbury, H. Müller, N. Kando, S. Mercer, J. Kalpathy-Cramer, M. Potthast, T. Gollub, A. Krithara, J. Lin, K. Balog, and I. Eggel. Report on the evaluation-as-a-service (eaas) expert workshop. *SIGIR Forum*, 49(1):57–65, June 2015.

[15] D. Lagun and E. Agichtein. Viewser: Enabling large-scale remote user studies of web search examination and interaction. In *Proceedings of the 34th International ACM SIGIR Conference on Research and Development in Information Retrieval*, SIGIR '11, pages 365–374, New York, NY, USA, 2011. ACM.

[16] J. Lin, M. Crane, A. Trotman, J. Callan, I. Chattopadhyaya, J. Foley, G. Ingersoll, C. MacDonald, and S. Vigna. Toward reproducible baselines: The open-source ir reproducibility challenge. In N. Ferro, F. Crestani, M.-F. Moens, J. Mothe, F. Silvestri, G. M. D. Nunzio, C. Hauff, and G. Silvello, editors, *ECIR*, volume 9626 of *Lecture Notes in Computer Science*, pages 408–420. Springer, 2016.

[17] J. Lin and M. Efron. Evaluation as a service for information retrieval. *SIGIR Forum*, 47(2):8–14, Jan. 2013.

[18] J. Lin and M. Efron. Infrastructure support for evaluation as a service. In *Proceedings of the 23rd International Conference on World Wide Web*, WWW '14 Companion, pages 79–82, New York, NY, USA, 2014. ACM.

[19] Y. Lv and C. Zhai. Lower-bounding term frequency normalization. In *Proceedings of the 20th ACM International Conference on Information and Knowledge Management*, CIKM '11, pages 7–16, New York, NY, USA, 2011. ACM.

[20] D. Metzler. Generalized inverse document frequency. In *Proceedings of the 17th ACM Conference on Information and Knowledge Management*, CIKM '08, pages 399–408, New York, NY, USA, 2008. ACM.

[21] D. Metzler, V. Lavrenko, and W. B. Croft. Formal multiple-bernoulli models for language modeling. In *Proceedings of the 27th Annual International ACM SIGIR Conference on Research and Development in Information Retrieval*, SIGIR '04, pages 540–541, New York, NY, USA, 2004. ACM.

[22] H. Mühleisen, T. Samar, J. Lin, and A. de Vries. Old dogs are great at new tricks: Column stores for ir prototyping. In *Proceedings of the 37th International ACM SIGIR Conference on Research & Development in Information Retrieval*, SIGIR '14, pages 863–866, New York, NY, USA, 2014. ACM.

[23] J. H. Paik. A novel tf-idf weighting scheme for effective ranking. In *Proceedings of the 36th International ACM SIGIR Conference on Research and Development in Information Retrieval*, SIGIR '13, pages 343–352, New York, NY, USA, 2013. ACM.

[24] J. Rao, J. Lin, and M. Efron. Reproducible experiments on lexical and temporal feedback for tweet search. In A. Hanbury, G. Kazai, A. Rauber, and N. Fuhr, editors, *Advances in Information Retrieval*, volume 9022 of *Lecture Notes in Computer Science*, pages 755–767. Springer International Publishing, 2015.

[25] S. Robertson, S. Walker, S. Jones, M. Hancock-Beaulieu, and M. Gatford. Okapi at trec-3. pages 109–126, 1996.

[26] S. E. Robertson, S. Walker, and M. M. Hancock-Beaulieu. Large test collection experiments on an operational, interactive system: Okapi at trec. In *Proceedings of the Second Conference on Text Retrieval Conference*, TREC-2, pages 345–360, Elmsford, NY, USA, 1995. Pergamon Press, Inc.

[27] A. Singhal, C. Buckley, and M. Mitra. Pivoted document length normalization. In *Proceedings of the 19th Annual International ACM SIGIR Conference on Research and Development in Information Retrieval*, SIGIR '96, pages 21–29, New York, NY, USA, 1996. ACM.

[28] A. Trotman, A. Puurula, and B. Burgess. Improvements to bm25 and language models examined. In *Proceedings of the 19th Australasian Document Computing Symposium*, ADCS '14, Melbourne, VIC, Australia, 2014. ACM.

[29] E. M. Voorhees and D. K. Harman. *TREC: Experiment and Evaluation in Information Retrieval (Digital Libraries and Electronic Publishing)*. The MIT Press, 2005.

[30] C. Zhai and J. Lafferty. Two-stage language models for information retrieval. In *Proceedings of the 25th Annual International ACM SIGIR Conference on Research and Development in Information Retrieval*, SIGIR '02, pages 49–56, New York, NY, USA, 2002. ACM.

[31] C. Zhai and J. Lafferty. A study of smoothing methods for language models applied to information retrieval. *ACM Trans. Inf. Syst.*, 22(2):179–214, Apr. 2004.

[32] J. Zhu, J. Wang, I. J. Cox, and M. J. Taylor. Risky business: Modeling and exploiting uncertainty in information retrieval. In *Proceedings of the 32Nd International ACM SIGIR Conference on Research and Development in Information Retrieval*, SIGIR '09, pages 99–106, New York, NY, USA, 2009. ACM.

Power Analysis for Interleaving Experiments by means of Offline Evaluation

Hosein Azarbonyad
University of Amsterdam, Amsterdam,
The Netherlands
h.azarbonyad@uva.nl

Evangelos Kanoulas
University of Amsterdam, Amsterdam,
The Netherlands
e.kanoulas@uva.nl

ABSTRACT

Evaluation in information retrieval takes one of two forms: collection-based offline evaluation, and in-situ online evaluation. Collections constructed by the former methodology are reusable, and hence able to test the effectiveness of any experimental algorithm, while the latter requires a different experiment for every new algorithm. Due to this a funnel approach is often being used, with experimental algorithms being compared to the baseline in an online experiment only if they outperform the baseline in an offline experiment. One of the key questions in the design of online and offline experiments concerns the number of measurements required to detect a statistically significant difference between two algorithms. Power analysis can provide an answer to this question, however, it requires an a-priori knowledge of the difference in effectiveness to be detected, and the variance in the measurements. The variance is typically estimated using historical data, but setting a detectable difference prior to the experiment can lead to suboptimal, upper-bound results. In this work we make use of the funnel approach in evaluation and test whether the difference in the effectiveness of two algorithms measured by the offline experiment can inform the required number of impression of an online interleaving experiment. Our analysis on simulated data shows that the number of impressions required are correlated with the difference in the offline experiment, but at the same time widely vary for any given difference.

Keywords

Information retrieval evaluation, Interleaving, Experimental design, Power Analysis

1. INTRODUCTION

Evaluation is key to building effective, efficient, and usable information retrieval (IR) systems as it enables their effectiveness to be quantified. For decades the primary approach to conduct IR evaluation was the Cranfield approach, that makes use of test collections, allowing systematic and repeatable evaluations to be carried out in a controlled manner. The Cranfield approach has often been criticized for not quantifying the actual user experience when served by the search algorithm under testing. Online evaluation on the other

ICTIR '16, September 12-16, 2016, Newark, DE, USA

© 2016 ACM. ISBN 978-1-4503-4497-5/16/09. . . $15.00

DOI: http://dx.doi.org/10.1145/2970398.2970432

hand – that is A/B testing [7] and Interleaving [6] – is performed on the basis of user interactions with the ranked list of results produced by the algorithms being tested.

Designing an experiment that enables the discovery of statistical significant effects is of paramount importance in both the online and the offline setting. Power analysis allows to determine the sample size (i.e. the number of measurements collected) required to detect an effect of a given size with a given degree of confidence. Conducting a power analysis however requires setting the effect size to be detected prior to the experiment [7, 12]. This often leads to suboptimal results: the actual effect size observed after having run the experiment is larger than the one specified, and therefore required fewer measurements than the ones dictated by the power analysis.

In this paper we make use of the *funnel approach* often used in information retrieval evaluation [7], according to which, an experimental algorithm is compared to a baseline/production algorithm in an online experiment only if it outperforms the production algorithm in an offline experiment. The question we answer in this work is whether the evaluation results of the offline experiment can inform the number of impressions required, and hence the duration, of an online interleaving experiment. In other words, given that two systems have $\Delta M = \alpha$, with M being any evaluation measure in an offline experiment, can we detect the number of impressions required for an interleaving experiment to conclude that the two systems are statistically significantly different? To study this question we first construct all the different pairs of relevance label rankings for which $\Delta M = \alpha$; then we interleave the rankings and simulate user clicks. We use the proportion of wins for the winning algorithm to calculate the number of impressions required for the experiment to consider that proportion statistically significant, and by repeating the experiment for different values of α try to establish a correlation between the number of required impressions and ΔM.

2. METHOD

Commercial search engines typically take a *funnel approach* in evaluating a new search algorithm [8]: first the experimental algorithm (E) is compared to the production algorithm (P) using an offline test collection; if E outperforms P with respect to the evaluation measure of their interest, the two algorithms are then compared online, e.g. through an interleaving experiment. In an interleaving experiment the ranked lists of results produced by P and E (for some user query) are interleaved in a single ranked list which is then presented to the user. The user interacts with the interleaved results by clicking on them, and the algorithm that receives most of the clicks wins the "dual". The experiment is repeated for a number of times (impressions) and the total wins for P are compared to those of E [10]. A Sign Test is then run to assess whether the difference in wins between the two algorithms is statistically significant. Alternatively a Binomial Proportion Test can be used for which one calculates the proportion of times E wins and tests whether this proportion, p, is greater than $p_0 = 0.5$. Prior to running an online experiment one would like to know what is an adequate sample size, i.e. what is the number of impressions required to detect a statistically significant difference between E and P. The proportion of time E winning is not known a priori, i.e. before actually running the experiment. If it was known one could perform a power analysis for the Binomial Proportion Test and find the necessary number of impressions. What is known is the margin by which E outperformed P in the offline experiments.

In this section we propose an experiment to test whether one can determine the sample size (i.e. the number of interleaved impressions) required for an interleaving experiment to identify statistical significant differences, given the margin, ΔM, by which E outperformed P in an offline experiment as measured by an evaluation measure M.

The experiment works as follows:

1. We generate pairs of ranked relevance labels, R_E and R_P for the experimental and production system respectively.

2. We measure the quality of the two rankings by some measure M, and compute the difference $\Delta M = M(R_E) - M(R_P)$.

3. We apply an interleaving algorithm to interleave the produced pairs of rankings.

4. We simulate user clicks over the interleaved ranking; for each of interleaved ranking we run k simulations of user interactions (clicking behaviour).

5. We measure the proportion p of wins for E against P.

6. We run a power analysis for the Binomial Proportion Test to determine the number of impressions required to find the observed proportion of win p statistically significant.

We use p to compute the sample size needed to detect such a proportion in a statistically significant manner. We allow a chance of falsely rejecting the null hypothesis (i.e. concluding that E is better than P, when it is not) of 5%, and a chance of falsely not rejecting the null hypothesis (i.e. not concluding that E is better than P, when it is) of 10%. We use the computed probability p for determining the number of required impressions using the proportion test. We assume that the sampling distribution for proportions can be approximated by a normal distribution [11], and therefore we can use the following equation for computing the minimum sample size [5]:

$$N' \geq (\frac{z_{1-\alpha}\sqrt{p_0(1-p_0)} + z_{1-\beta}\sqrt{p_1(1-p_1)}}{\delta})^2, \quad (1)$$

where we set $p_0 = 0.5$ to reflect that each system wins 50% of times. p_1 is the proportion of times E wins over P out of k simulations. α and β specify the level of significance. We set $\alpha = 0.05$ and $\beta = 0.1$. δ is $|p_1 - p_0|$ and z is the standard normal distribution. Finally, using the continuity correction the minimum sample size is determined as:

$$N = N' + 1/\delta \quad (2)$$

The procedure of determining the minimum number of impressions for an interleaved online experiment given ΔM is shown in Figure 1. Given the rankings produced by E and P and also the

```
1: procedure POWER ANALYSIS
      Input:
        R_E: ranking produced by E
        R_P: ranking produced by P
        ΔM: the delta of performance of E and P
      Output:
        N: number of impressions
2:    for i ← 1 to k do
3:        R = Interleave(R_E, R_P)
4:        Clicks = ClickModel(R)
5:        if Clicks_E > Clicks_P then
6:            wins_E ← wins_E + 1
7:        else
8:            wins_P ← wins_P + 1
9:        end if
10:   end for
11:   p_1 = wins_E/(wins_E + wins_P)
12:   N = determine sample size using Equation 2
13: end procedure
```

Figure 1: The procedure of determining number of required impressions in an online experiment given the performance of two systems in offline evaluation.

difference of their performance in offline evaluation, we simulate k experiments (line 2 to 10). In each simulation, we first interleave the rankings (line 3), then we produce clicks on the interleaved ranking using a click model (line 4). Then, in lines 6 to 9, we determine which system wins based on the number of clicks the documents corresponds to each system receive. Finally, based on the proportion of wins of E over P, we determine the number of required impressions in line 12.

A number of assumptions are being made by the above experiment:

1. *Accurate user behaviour*: We assume that the parametrized click models employed in the simulation are accurate, and representative of actual user bahviour.

2. *No query variability*: We assume that both the experimental and production system result in the exact same ranked list of relevance for all queries in the offline experiment, or in other words, there is a single query in the offline test collection, and hence no variability due to queries. In this way we integrate out any variance in the experiments due to the different nature of queries and only focus on variance due to the differences in user behaviour. We leave the integration of query variability as future work.

3. *Offline/Online query set alignment*: We assume that the queries (query) used in the online experiment is exactly the same as the one(s) used in the offline experiment. We leave the study of sampling online queries for the offline evaluation, and its impact on the power analysis of the online experiment as future work.

4. *Distinct documents*: We assume that the ranked list of documents produced by E and P are distinct, so that the analysis is not overly complicated by accounting for the de-duplication step of the interleaving algorithms.

The aforementioned assumptions essentially lead to a lower bound on the number of required impressions.

3. EXPERIMENTAL SETUP

In this paper we aim at answering two research questions:

RQ1 Are (simulated) interleaving and collection-based evaluation measures in agreement regarding the relative performance of two ranking algorithms?

RQ2 Can the retrieval performance in collection-based evaluation inform the sample size (i.e. inform the required number of impressions) of the interleaving experiment?

RQ1 concerns the correlation of the offline and (simulated) online effectiveness measures. To answer this question, we first generate pairs of rankings of relevance, for a production system P and an experimental system E, respectively. For that we assume a 5-graded relevance, i.e. $rel \in \{0, 1, 2, 3, 4\}$, and construct all possible P and E ranking pairs of length 5. We consider only those pairs for which E outperforms P in the offline evaluation. For each ranking pair we calculate $\Delta M = M(R_E) - M(R_P)$. We also calculate p_1, the chance that the experimental system E will outperform the production system P in the online experiment, by using the algorithm described in Figure 1 (line 11 of the algorithm). Finally we plot ΔM against p_1 to test the agreement between offline and online effectiveness measures. The results of experiments corresponding to RQ1 are described in §4.1.

RQ2 concerns the impact of ΔM on the required number of impressions in the online evaluation. To answer this question, again we generate pairs of rankings of relevance for P and E, and calculate the difference $\Delta M = M(R_E) - M(R_P)$. We still consider only those pairs for which E outperforms P and we group the differences in 10 bins/groups. For each bin/group, we calculate the average number of impressions that are required for the interleaving experiment to conclude that two systems are statistically significantly different. For that we use the algorithm described in Figure 1.The result of experiment regarding RQ1 are discussed in §4.2.

The collection-based evaluation measures used in our experiments are the Discounted Cumulative Gain (DCG), the Ranked Biased Precision (RBP), and the Expected Reciprocal Rank (ERR). Team-Draft interleaving [10] is used to interleave the rankings by P and E, and the Simplified Dependent Click Model (SDCM) [3], the User Browsing Model (UBM) [4], and the Dynamic Bayesian Network Model (DBN) [1] to simulate user clicks on the interleaved ranked list (line 4 of the algorithm). The click model parameters were estimated using the Yandex Relevance Prediction challenge click log. The number of simulations (k in Figure 1) was arbitrarily set to 50. The open-source implementation of our approach is available[1].

4. RESULTS

In this section, we analyze the correlation of ΔM in offline evaluation with the number of required impressions in the interleaved experiments.

4.1 Correlations of offline and online evaluation measures

Figure 2 shows the proportions of wins of E over P in the simulated interleaving experiments for different values of ΔM. We only considered cases for which $0 < \Delta M \le 0.1$. As illustrated in the figure, as ΔM increases p_1 also increases. However, it can also be observed that there is a high variance for p_1 for similar values of ΔM. This is inline with past results comparing in-situ interleaved and collection-based experiments [2, 9, 10].

[1]https://github.com/HoseinAzarbonyad/
Power-Analysis-for-Interleaving-Experiments

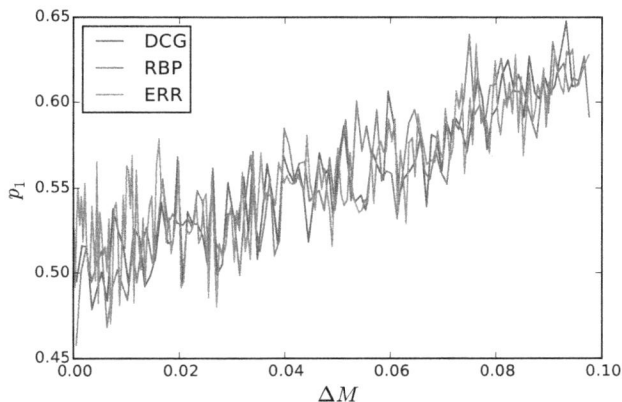

Figure 2: The proportions of wins of E over P for different values of ΔM. SDCM is used for simulating clicks over interleaved lists.

4.2 Analysis on the sample size in online evaluation

Figure 3 shows the number of impressions required by an interleaving experiment given that the difference in retrieval effectiveness as measured by a collection-based experiment is ΔM. The median and the 68% confidence interval (i.e. one standard deviation) is shown in the figure for each ΔM group. As it can be observed, as the value of ΔM increases, the number of required impression decreases, as expected.

The second observation is that the required number of impressions demonstrates a high variance, in particular for low values of ΔM. This result can be explained by the fact that $\Delta M = \alpha$ can happen in many different ways: relevance differences high in the ranking with small relevance gap, or low in the ranking with high relevance gap. Not not all of these cases however lead to an identical user behaviour. Consider two examples: 1) E returns the following ranked list of relevance labels, (4, 2, 2, 1, 0), while P returns (2, 2, 3, 1, 0), and 2) E returns (1, 1, 1, 3, 0) and P returns: (1, 2, 1, 0, 0). In both cases ΔDCG is about 0.2, however in the first example, if we simulate clicks using SDCM and estimate the number of required impressions using the algorithm described in Figure 1, we need 277 impressions, while the number for the second example is 381. In expectation interleaving will be able to identify that E outperforms P, however this will require less number of impressions for the former case than the latter.

5. CONCLUSION AND FUTURE WORK

In this work, we first posed the question of whether the performance difference between two ranking algorithms in an offline experiment can inform the required number of impressions for an online experiment to identify statistically significant results and proposed a simulation experiment to answer this question. Based on the proposed experiment, we (1) illustrated a strong correlation between the margin of the quality difference in offline evaluation and the required number of impressions in online evaluation – something expected – , but also (2) a large variability in the number of required expressions for the same margin. This indicates that the results of an offline experiment can inform the design of an online experiment, and in particular the power of the experiment to evaluate a new experimental system, it is beneficial to first conduct an offline evaluation and then based on the results achieved in offline evaluation, an estimate about the duration of the online experiment can be made.

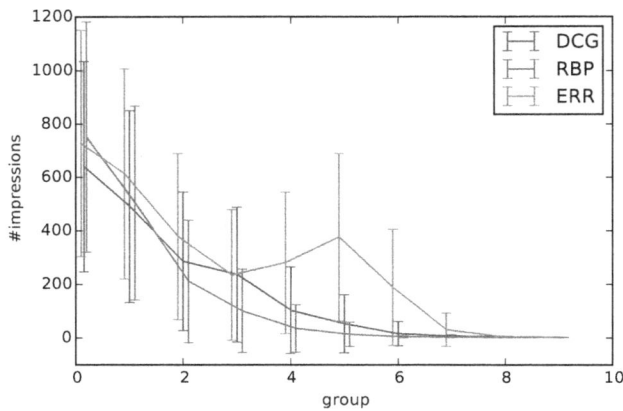

(a) SDCM

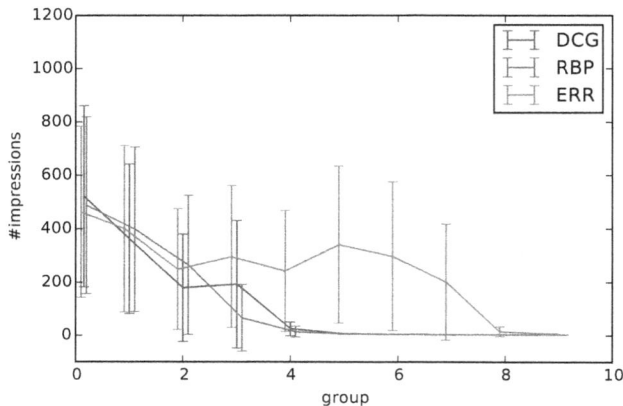

(b) UBM

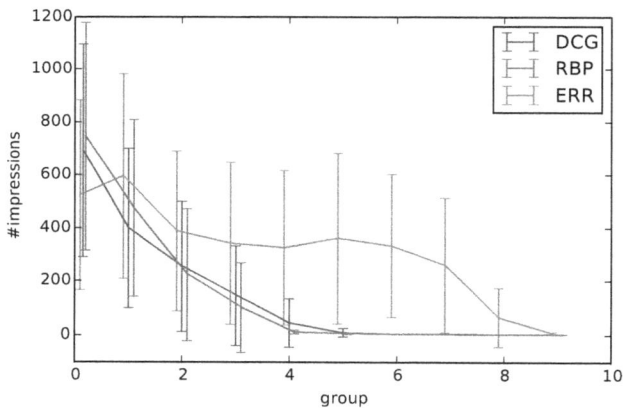

(c) DBN

Figure 3: Number of required impressions for online evaluation based on different groups of values of ΔM

The current work is simply a step forward towards better understanding the relation between offline collection-based evaluation, and online in-situ evaluation. In the future, we intent to extend the current work in a number of directions: (1) *Account for query variability*: The current work assumes that all offline/online queries are exactly the same. In other words, it integrates out any variability coming from queries, and only consider variability due to user interactions with the SERP; we intent to extend the experiment to account for query variability as well. (2) *Explore A/B Testing*: The

current work only focuses on interleaved experiments, integrating out between group variability. We intent to extend the experiment to account for this variability, present in A/B testing experiments. (3) *Closed-form solution*: The current work explores the power of an interleaved comparison between two ranking algorithms experimentally. We seek for a closed-form solution to the problem. (4) *Online experiments*: So far we have studied the problem using simulations; we intent to validate our findings using actual online experiments.

Acknowledgments

This work was supported in part by the Google Faculty Research Award scheme. Any opinions, findings and conclusions or recommendations expressed in this material are the authors' and do not necessarily reflect those of the sponsors.

REFERENCES

[1] O. Chapelle and Y. Zhang. A dynamic bayesian network click model for web search ranking. In *Proceedings of the 18th International Conference on World Wide Web*, WWW '09, 2009.

[2] O. Chapelle, T. Joachims, F. Radlinski, and Y. Yue. Large-scale validation and analysis of interleaved search evaluation. *ACM Trans. Inf. Syst.*, 30(1), 2012.

[3] A. Chuklin, I. Markov, and M. d. Rijke. Click models for web search. *Synthesis Lectures on Information Concepts, Retrieval, and Services*, 2015.

[4] G. E. Dupret and B. Piwowarski. A user browsing model to predict search engine click data from past observations. In *Proceedings of the 31st Annual International ACM SIGIR Conference on Research and Development in Information Retrieval*, SIGIR '08, 2008.

[5] J. L. Fleiss, B. Levin, and M. C. Paik. *Statistical methods for rates and proportions*. John Wiley & Sons, 2013.

[6] T. Joachims. Evaluating retrieval performance using clickthrough data. In *Text Mining*, pages 79–96. 2003.

[7] R. Kohavi, R. Longbotham, D. Sommerfield, and R. M. Henne. Controlled experiments on the web: survey and practical guide. *Data Mining and Knowledge Discovery*, 2008.

[8] R. Kohavi, A. Deng, B. Frasca, T. Walker, Y. Xu, and N. Pohlmann. Online controlled experiments at large scale. In *The 19th ACM SIGKDD International Conference on Knowledge Discovery and Data Mining, KDD 2013, Chicago, IL, USA, August 11-14, 2013*, pages 1168–1176, 2013.

[9] F. Radlinski and N. Craswell. Comparing the sensitivity of information retrieval metrics. In *Proceedings of the 33rd International ACM SIGIR Conference on Research and Development in Information Retrieval*, SIGIR '10, pages 667–674, New York, NY, USA, 2010. ACM.

[10] F. Radlinski, M. Kurup, and T. Joachims. How does clickthrough data reflect retrieval quality? In *Proceedings of the 17th ACM Conference on Information and Knowledge Management*, CIKM '08, 2008.

[11] D. Wackerly, W. Mendenhall, and R. L. Scheaffer. *Mathematical statistics with applications*. Nelson Education, 2007.

[12] W. Webber, A. Moffat, and J. Zobel. Statistical power in retrieval experimentation. In *Proceedings of the 17th ACM Conference on Information and Knowledge Management*, CIKM '08, 2008.

Retrievability in API-Based "Evaluation as a Service"

Jiaul H. Paik
Centre for Educational Technology
IIT Kharagpur
jia.paik@gmail.com

Jimmy Lin
Cheriton School of Computer Science
University of Waterloo
jimmylin@uwaterloo.ca

ABSTRACT

"Evaluation as a service" (EaaS) refers to a family of related evaluation methodologies that enables community-wide evaluations and the construction of test collections on documents that cannot be easily distributed. In the API-based approach, the basic idea is that evaluation organizers provide a service API through which the evaluation task can be completed, without providing access to the raw collection. One concern with this evaluation approach is that the API introduces biases and limits the diversity of techniques that can be brought to bear on the problem. In this paper, we tackle the question of API bias using the concept of retrievability. The raw data for our analyses come from a naturally-occurring experiment where we observed the same groups completing the same task with the API and also with access to the raw collection. We find that the retrievability bias of runs generated in both cases are comparable. Moreover, the fraction of relevant tweets retrieved through the API by the participating groups is at least as high as when they had access to the raw collection.

1. INTRODUCTION

The Cranfield Paradigm [2], especially operationalized in the Text Retrieval Conferences (TRECs) [7], provides the cornerstone of batch evaluation in information retrieval today. A fundamental assumption is that researchers can acquire the document collection under study—whether via physical CD-ROMs or DVDs (in the early days), hard drives, or directly downloadable "from the cloud". What if this were not possible? One example is a collection of tweets: Twitter's terms of service forbid redistribution of tweets, and thus it would not be permissible for an organization to host a collection of tweets for download. Although there are third-party resellers of Twitter data, the costs are too high to be a practical mechanism for distributing research collections. Other examples of data that make wide distribution difficult include electronic medical records, email, and enterprise data. Beyond sensitivity of the corpus, in many cases practical considerations—the sheer size of modern web collections—prevent researchers from acquiring the data to support experiments; this is especially true for researchers at institutions with fewer resources.

There have been a number of recent attempts at addressing these issues, collectively called "evaluation as a service" (EaaS) [3]. EaaS solutions are varied, but in this paper, we focus on a particular approach based on search APIs. The basic idea is that, instead of distributing the collection, the evaluation organizers provide an API through which the collection can be accessed for completing the evaluation task. The first large-scale deployment of this EaaS approach was the TREC 2013 Microblog track [5]. One concern that has previously been raised with this evaluation approach is that the API introduces biases and limits the diversity of techniques that can be brought to bear on the problem [4]. Voorhees et al. [8] tackled a related question concerning the diversity of the pools that are generated using API-based EaaS and revealed no obvious flaws with the approach.

In this paper, we build on previous studies and specifically tackle the question of API bias using the concept of retrievability [1]. We describe a naturally-occurring experiment that arose from the TREC Microblog evaluations in 2013, where we were able to observe system behavior with and without the API in a (roughly) paired setup. Thus, it is possible to study the potential biases introduced by the API. Analyses show that the retrievability bias of runs generated with access to the raw collection and runs generated using the API are comparable; the fraction of relevant tweets retrieved under both conditions are also comparable.

2. EVALUATION METHODOLOGY

Fortuitous circumstances in the TREC Microblog evaluation in 2013 created a naturally-occurring experiment that allowed us to examine the retrievability bias of a particular instance of API-based evaluation as a service. In TREC 2011 and 2012, the Microblog track evaluations used the Tweets2011 corpus: comprising of approximately 16 million tweets, it was small enough to be distributed via the "crawl-it-yourself" mechanism [6]. That is, participants obtained a list of tweet identifiers from the organizers that point to the tweets in the collection. Through a download mechanism (also developed by the organizers), each group essentially crawled a copy of the collection from twitter.com. The tweets were delivered to the participants directly by Twitter (and hence according to its terms of service). Participants could use the gathered tweet data locally for their experiments (but not to further redistribute).

ICTIR '16, September 12 - 16, 2016, Newark, DE, USA

© 2016 Copyright held by the owner/author(s). Publication rights licensed to ACM.
ISBN 978-1-4503-4497-5/16/09. . . $15.00

DOI: http://dx.doi.org/10.1145/2970398.2970427

Table 1: Statistics of Queries Submitted to the TREC Microblog Search API

Name	Topics	Runs	# Groups (official)	# Groups (API)	# Groups (common)	# API queries	# API queries (avg. per topic)	# rel. doc	# rel. doc (avg. per topic)
MB2011	49	184	59	12	6	17682	353	2965	59
MB2012	60	121	33	12	6	23050	384	6286	104

In TREC 2013, the Microblog track evaluation adopted a much larger collection, which was only accessible via a search API deployed by the organizers (since the crawling-based distribution mechanism had scalability limitations). That is, the official corpus of tweets used in the evaluation was not directly accessible to participants. The search API provided tweets ranked using Lucene's implementation of query-likelihood, based on arbitrary queries submitted by the participants. All participants were required to complete the evaluation task using this API (and whatever local resources they had also gathered).

To facilitate this shift in evaluation methodology, the track organizers concurrently deployed an API (the same implementation) on the Tweets2011 corpus for training purposes. As a result of this setup, we have logs of participants running their systems on old queries from TREC 2011 and 2012 (in 2013). We also have official runs that were submitted to TREC 2011 and 2012 based on access to the raw collection, and in a few cases, these are *the same groups*. Statistics for the API usage are summarized in Table 1.

In other words, we have a naturally-occurring experiment where we observed the same TREC groups (12 to be exact) running experiments on the raw collection and also using the API. Although an imperfect indicator, the same groups are likely to have used similar techniques in those experiments (particularly when training on old topics in preparation for a new corpus). This gives us sets of paired runs from which we can study the potential biases introduced by the API.

Our query logs from the API contain requests from TREC 2013 participants who were training their systems on topics from TREC 2011 and 2012. Each API request comprised the query, the id of the participating group, as well as a maximum tweet id that delimited the temporal range of the retrieved results. This maximum tweet id is unique for each topic, which means that it can be used to map from a submitted query to its intended topic. We filtered out duplicate queries from the same group, the results of which served as the starting point of our analyses.

2.1 Retrievability

In the API-based EaaS model, query modification is the only mechanism by which participants can access the documents in the collection. All queries submitted by the participants are created from the TREC topics, either by dropping some terms or by adding new terms to the query (both weighted and unweighted). Since traditional pool-based evaluations depend on the quality of the ranked lists produced by the participating groups in order to reliably evaluate unseen systems, it is important that the submitted runs contain as many relevant documents in the collection as possible. We ask: without changing the retrieval algorithm and only varying the queries, is it possible to retrieve the same quality of documents (compared to a setup where the groups had access to the raw collection)?

To answer this question, we compare the documents submitted by groups when they had access to the raw collection and the documents they retrieved through the search API. Specifically, we use the concept of retrievability, proposed by Azzopardi and Vinay [1], as well as the fraction of judged relevant documents that a particular group returns.

Informally, given a document collection, the retrievability of a document is a measure of how often the document is returned by a search system [1]. The retrievability of a document depends on two factors: The first factor is the number of queries that retrieves the document. The second factor takes into account the position of the document in a ranked list, which is motivated by how far a user is willing to examine the results. Given a universe Q of queries, the retrievability of a document d is formally defined as

$$R(d) = \sum_{q \in Q} w(q) \cdot f(d, q, c) \quad (1)$$

where the $w(q)$ is the weight of the query in the universe, $f(d, q, c)$ is a function that measures the utility of document d with respect to q, and c is the rank cutoff. In practice, $f(q, d, c)$ is considered a binary indicator function, which is set to one if the document d is returned within the top c position in the ranked list, otherwise it is set to zero.

The normalized $R(d)$ values measure the likelihood of a document being retrieved. However, in an operational setting, we need a method for approximating the retrievability of a document, since the "universe of queries" is not possible to gather in practice.

In our experimental setup, we have two sets of ranked lists: from the officially-submitted runs to TREC 2011 and TREC 2012 when the participants had access to the raw collection, and from queries submitted through the search API (we reissued those queries to gather results). In the first case, the retrievability of a document for a particular group is simply the fraction of submitted runs that contain the document within the specified rank cutoff. In the second case, it is the fraction of queries that retrieves the document.

2.2 Retrievability Bias

The retrievability bias of a system is its tendency to prefer a set of documents over others. For the EaaS model to enable the creation of reusable test collections, it is desirable to reduce the biases of the ranked lists generated by the participating systems. In our analyses, we compare the retrievability bias of the officially-submitted runs and the runs generated through the search API using the queries submitted by the participants. Following Azzopardi and Vinay [1], we use the Lorenz curve to visualize the retrievability bias of a system for a set of queries. In economics, the Lorenz curve shows the proportion of overall wealth possessed by the bottom $k\%$ of the population. For a population of size n, with their wealth, w_i, organized in non-decreasing order ($w_i \leq w_{i+1}$, $1 \leq i \leq n$), the Lorenz curve is a continuous piecewise linear function that connects $n + 1$ points

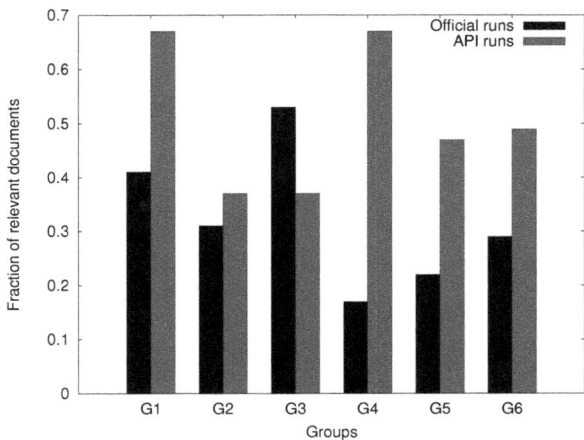

(a) TREC MB2011

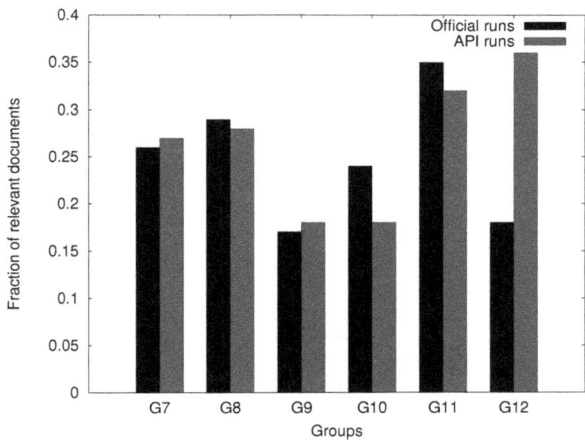

(b) TREC MB2012

Figure 1: Fraction of relevant tweets returned by the official runs and the API-based runs.

(x_i, y_i) $(0 \leq i \leq n)$, where $(x_0 = 0, y_0 = 0)$ and

$$(x_i = i/n, y_i = \sum_{j=1}^{i} w_j / \sum_{j=1}^{n} w_j).$$

For a perfectly equal wealth distribution, the Lorenz curve is depicted by the line $y = x$.

This same idea can be applied to a population of documents, where the retrievability scores are treated as wealth. We draw the Lorenz curve as follows: say, for a query, we have multiple ranked lists. We take the top c documents from each list, merge them, and then compute how many times a particular document appears in the merged list. We then normalize the scores, reorganize them in ascending order, and finally plot the cumulative distribution of the retrievability scores of the documents.

The Gini Coefficient G can be used to summarize the amount of bias in a Lorenz curve, and is defined as

$$G(R(\mathcal{D}, q)) = \frac{1}{\sum_{j=1}^{N} R(d_j)} \cdot \sum_{i=1}^{N} (2 \cdot i - N - 1) \cdot R(d_i). \quad (2)$$

where the retrievability values $R(d_i)$ are sorted in ascending order and N is the number of documents specific to the query. If $G = 0$, then all the documents that we have considered are equally retrievable, while $G = 1$ means only one document is retrievable. In the context of evaluation, higher G values are risky since the pools may not be adequately diverse. For a set of topics Q, we can define the Gini Coefficient as an average over all topics.

3. EVALUATION RESULTS

In our first set of experiments, we seek to gain an overall understanding of the reusability of relevance judgments created from the ranked lists generated by the API-based runs. We consider the TREC relevance judgments created by pooling tweets from the participants' runs (when they had access to the raw collection) as the reference gold standard. We compare the fraction of relevant tweets returned by a particular group that submitted a run (when they had access

to the raw collection) in either the TREC 2011 or TREC 2012 Microblog tracks and when the same group used the search API on the same queries. In both Microblog tracks, there are six such groups (not necessarily the same ones). For each group and for every topic, we take the top 100 tweets from their official runs and also from the API-based runs. Since we have multiple ranked lists for every topic in each of the cases, the final list is the union of tweets from each. We then compute the fraction of relevant tweets returned in each case. Note that none of the API-based runs contributed to the TREC judgment pools.

The fraction of relevant tweets returned by the official and the API-based runs from participating groups in MB2011 and MB2012 are shown in Figures 1a and 1b. Note that we have anonymized the identity of the groups and simply refer to them with numeric labels. On 2011 topics, except for G3, the API-based runs returned more relevant tweets in the top 100 than the official runs submitted by the same groups. Our analysis reveals that G3 used only the original topics as queries through the API, while all other groups issued at least 10 queries for each topic.

Analyses of the TREC 2012 topics paint a slightly different picture. For three of the six groups, the official runs performed slightly better than the API-based runs, with G12 being the notable exception. We reiterate that query modification is the only available operation through the API and therefore the quality of the runs generated by the API depends on the diversity of the issued queries. To dig deeper, we selected G10 and manually analyzed the queries submitted through the API. Our investigations suggest that the group issued a large number of single word queries, which consequently retrieved many non-relevant tweets within the top ranks. Since the API results of G12 were noticeably better than the group's official submissions, we also analyzed their queries. We notice that the API queries were very diverse, containing both weighted and unweighted expanded queries. This suggests, not surprisingly, that query modification (particularly, query expansion) is the key to extracting effective results from a fixed search API.

Next, we measured the retrievability bias of documents from the submitted runs and the API-based runs. In these

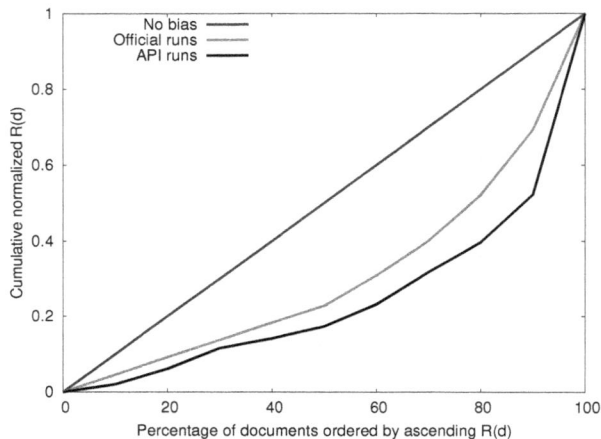

(a) TREC MB2011

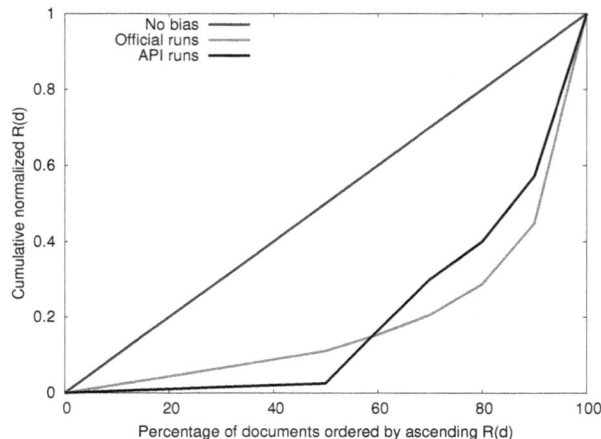

(b) TREC MB2012

Figure 2: Retrievability bias of the official runs and the API-based runs.

Table 2: Retrievability Bias Measured by Gini Coefficients.

Collection	Official	API-based
MB2011 (Figure 2a)	0.48	0.52
MB2012 (Figure 2b)	0.61	0.59

analyses, we treat all official submissions from a group as a single unit. This is created by taking the top 100 tweets from individual ranked lists, merging them together, and then counting the frequency of documents in the merged list to generate the retrievability scores. Similarly, we also considered the tweets returned by all API queries issued by a group as a single unit. Our main goal is to examine which of these contain more bias. We note that if a set of runs returns a particular set of documents more often than others, relevance judgments created from those runs may lack variability and may consequently produce lower quality pools, particularly for evaluating systems that did not originally contribute to the pools.

Figures 2a and 2b show the Lorenz curves characterizing retrievability bias from MB2011 and MB2012. On the 2011 topics, it is clear that the official runs exhibit less bias in retrieving documents, while on the 2012 topics the API-based runs and the official runs show comparable bias. The figures show that both runs are far from being perfectly unbiased, which in turn corroborates earlier findings [1] that there are substantial overlaps in top ranked documents returned by standard retrieval techniques. We also manually analyzed the queries submitted through the API created from the 2011 and the 2012 topics. We found that the average number of queries for each topic from 2012 is higher than from 2011, and the queries have higher variability in terms of structure (weighted vs. unweighted terms) and the average number of terms. This might explain why the retrievability bias of the API queries is smaller for the 2012 topics than for the 2011 topics, relative to the corresponding official runs. Table 2 compares the Gini Coefficients of the retrievability biases, based on the official runs and the API-based runs computed for Figure 2a and Figure 2b. Paired t-tests reveal that none of the differences in retrievability bias are significant (at $p < 0.05$).

4. CONCLUSION

Evaluation as a service represents a departure from the traditional Cranfield Paradigm, designed to address emerging challenges. In this paper, we tackle the question of API bias using the concept of retrievability and find that the bias introduced by a search API is no worse than the retrievability bias of various retrieval techniques when evaluation participants have access to the raw collection. Similar conclusions are reached when examining the fraction of relevant tweets retrieved. Our conclusions, however, are limited to a particular style of EaaS based on a search API. We recognize that EaaS encompasses diverse approaches, and that it is not possible to generalize to every alternative. Further meta-evaluations are necessary to properly validate a broader range of EaaS approaches.

Acknowledgments. This work was supported by the U.S. National Science Foundation (NSF) under IIS-1218043 and CNS-1405688 and the Natural Sciences and Engineering Research Council of Canada (NSERC). Any opinions, findings, conclusions, or recommendations expressed are solely those of the authors.

5. REFERENCES

[1] L. Azzopardi and V. Vinay. Retrievability: An evaluation measure for higher order information access tasks. *CIKM*, 2008.

[2] D. Harman. *Information Retrieval Evaluation*. Morgan & Claypool Publishers, 2011.

[3] F. Hopfgartner, A. Hanbury, H. Müller, N. Kando, S. Mercer, J. Kalpathy-Cramer, M. Potthast, T. Gollub, A. Krithara, J. Lin, K. Balog, and I. Eggel. Report on the Evaluation-as-a-Service (EaaS) Expert Workshop. *SIGIR Forum*, 49(1):57–65, 2015.

[4] J. Lin and M. Efron. Evaluation as a service for information retrieval. *SIGIR Forum*, 47(2):8–14, 2013.

[5] J. Lin and M. Efron. Overview of the TREC-2013 Microblog Track. *TREC*, 2013.

[6] I. Ounis, C. Macdonald, J. Lin, and I. Soboroff. Overview of the TREC-2011 Microblog track. *TREC*, 2011.

[7] E. M. Voorhees. The philosophy of information retrieval evaluation. *CLEF*, 2002.

[8] E. M. Voorhees, J. Lin, and M. Efron. On run diversity in evaluation as a service. *SIGIR*, 2014.

Simple and Effective Approach to Score Standardisation

Tetsuya Sakai
Waseda University, Japan.
tetsuyasakai@acm.org

ABSTRACT

Webber, Moffat and Zobel proposed score standardization for information retrieval evaluation with multiple test collections. Given a topic-by-run raw score matrix in terms of some evaluation measure, each score can be standardised using the topic's sample mean and sample standard deviation across a set of past runs so as to quantify how different a system is from the "average" system in standard deviation units. Using standardised scores, researchers can compare systems across different test collections without worrying about topic hardness or normalisation. While Webber *et al.* mapped the standardised scores to the $[0, 1]$ range using a standard normal cumulative density function, the present study demonstrates that linear transformation of the standardised scores, a method widely used in educational research, can be a simple and effective alternative. We use three TREC robust track data sets with graded relevance assessments and official runs to compare these methods by means of leave-one-out tests, discriminative power, swap rate tests, and topic set size design. In particular, we demonstrate that our method is superior to the method of Webber *et al.* in terms of swap rates and topic set size design: put simply, our method ensures pairwise system comparisons that are more consistent across different data sets, and is arguably more convenient for designing a new test collection from a statistical viewpoint.

Keywords

evaluation; measures; standardization; statistical power; statistical significance; test collections; topics; variances

1. INTRODUCTION

In Information Retrieval (IR) evaluation, researchers often use multiple test collections for the sake of generalisability. However, different test collections come with different topics with different levels of hardness. At SIGIR 2008, Webber, Moffat and Zobel [15] proposed *score standardization* for IR evaluation with multiple test collections. Given M runs and N topics, a topic-by-run raw score matrix $\{raw_{ij}\}$ $(i = 1, \ldots, M, j = 1, \ldots, N)$ is computed for a given evaluation measure. For each topic, let the *sample mean*

be $m_{\bullet j} = \frac{1}{M} \sum_i raw_{ij}$, and the *sample standard deviation* be $s_{\bullet j} = \sqrt{\frac{1}{M-1} \sum_i (raw_{ij} - m_{\bullet j})^2}$. The standardised score is then given by

$$std_{ij} = \frac{raw_{ij} - m_{\bullet j}}{s_{\bullet j}} , \qquad (1)$$

which quantifies how different a system is from the "average" system in standard deviation units. Using standardised scores, researchers can compare systems across different test collections without worrying about topic hardness (since, for every j, the mean $m_{\bullet j}$ across runs is subtracted from the raw score) or normalisation (since the standardised scores, which are in the $[-\infty, \infty]$ range, are later mapped to the $[0, 1]$ range as decribed below). In practice, runs that participated in the pooling process for relevance assessments (*pooled systems*) can also serve as the runs for computing the *standardisation factors* $(m_{\bullet j}, s_{\bullet j})$ for each topic (*standardising systems*) [15]. The same standardisation factors are then used also for evaluating new runs.

In order to map the standardised scores into the $[0, 1]$ range, Webber *et al.* chose to employ the cumulative density function (CDF) of the standard normal distribution. The main reasons appear to be that, after this transformation, a score of 0.5 means exactly "average" and that outlier data points are suppressed [15]. However, while the merits of standardisation (Eq. 1) itself is clear, whether it is appropriate to further apply the above *nonlinear* transformation is less so. In fact, in the present study, we demonstrate that there is a simpler alternative with a few advantages, namely, *linear transformation* after standardisation. This is a widely-used technique in educational research for comparing students' scores (Section 3). We use three TREC robust track data sets with graded relevance assessments and official runs to compare these two implementations of score standardisation by means of *leave-one-out* [16], *discriminative power* [8], *swap rate* tests [8, 14], and the recently-proposed *topic set size design* [10]. In particular, we demonstrate that our method is superior to the method of Webber *et al.* in terms of swap rates and topic set size design: put simply, our method ensures pairwise system comparisons that are more consistent across different data sets, and is arguably more convenient for designing a new test collection from a statistical viewpoint.

2. PRIOR ART

2.1 Webber/Moffat/Zobel: std-CDF

As was mentioned in Section 1, we follow Webber *et al.* [15] to explore the benefits and reliability of using standardised evaluation measure scores, but reconsider their approach of using the standard normal CDF function for the purpose of mapping the standardised scores into the $[0, 1]$ range while giving a score of 0.5 to the "aver-

ICTIR '16, September 12 - 16, 2016, Newark, DE, USA
© 2016 Copyright held by the owner/author(s). Publication rights licensed to ACM.
ISBN 978-1-4503-4497-5/16/09. . . $15.00
DOI: http://dx.doi.org/10.1145/2970398.2970399

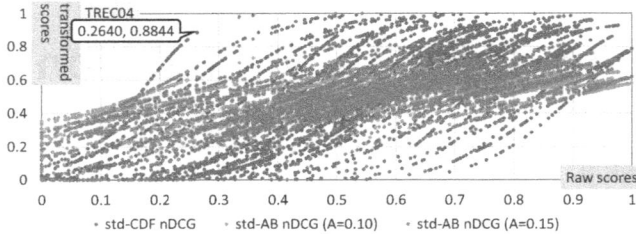

Figure 1: Raw scores vs. std-CDF and std-AB scores (TREC04: 49 topics times 110 runs for each scoring scheme).

age" system. Henceforth, we refer to their method as **std-CDF**. The blue dots in Figure 1 illustrate what **std-CDF** does: the x-axis represents 5,390 raw nDCG scores from the TREC 2004 robust track data (as we shall see in Section 4.1, we have 49 topics and 110 runs in this data set), while the y-axis represents the corresponding **std-CDF** scores[1]. Each curve represents the set of 110 runs for a particular topic. From the "S-shaped" curves, the property of **std-CDF** is clear: it supresses extremely high and extremely low standardised scores, while *emphasising moderately high and moderately low scores*. For example, the balloon in Figure 1 points to the fifth best run for Topic 666, whose raw nDCG score is 0.2640; whereas, its **std-CDF** score is as high as 0.8844. As we shall discuss in Section 3, our proposed method employs a linear transformation of the standardised scores instead, as indicated by the orange and red dots in the same figure.

Score standardisation relies on the per-topic standardisation factors $(m_{\bullet j}, s_{\bullet j})$ obtained from a set of standardising systems (See Eq. 1); these values are then used for evaluating new runs. To examine the longevity of the standardisation factors, Webber et al. [15] gradually reduced the number of standardisation systems to obtain new sets of standardisation factors, and showed that this has little effect on the system ranking, and concluded that only a small number of standardising systems is necessary for obtaining reliable standardisation factors. However, their experimental setting is not entirely satisfactory for demonstrating the robustness of standardised scores for the evaluation of *new* systems, as they did not remove the "new" systems' contributions from the original qrels (i.e., relevance assessments). In contrast, the present study employs a more practical setting, where both (a) standardisation factors are obtained from a small set of of known systems; *and* (b) qrels are also obtained from the *same* set of known systems.

Webber et al. [15] also conducted experiments on cross-collection comparisons by splitting the topic set in half and examining the score comparability and statistical significance across the two experiments. In the present study, we employ related but more standard techniques: *discriminative power* [8] and *swap rate* [14] tests. In addition, we use the recently-proposed *topic set size design* method of Sakai [10] that quantifies how within-system score variances translate to the number of topics required for conducting statistically reliable experiments.

Voorhees [13] applied **std-CDF** to *swap rate* experiments: a set of 100 topics (from the TREC 2004 robust track) was split in half many times, and in each trial, the number of discrepancies between the two sets (each containing 50 topics) was recorded, regarding whether one system is better than another. She concluded that **std-CDF** does not increase the reliability of system comparisons. Our results are in line with her finding, but furthermore demonstrate that our proposed method reduces swap rates substantially.

---

[1]We used Microsoft Excel's NORM.S.DIST function to implement **std-CDF**.

2.2 Other Related Work

As we have seen in Figure 1, **std-CDF** employs a nonlinear transformation that emphasises *moderately high and moderately low* scores. In the IR evaluation literature, a few other nonlinear transformations have been studied, albeit for different purposes. Robertson [7] advocate the use of *geometric* mean average precision (GMAP) for the purpose of studying hard topics. Essentially, GMAP is the arithmetic mean of the *logarithms* of average precisions; applying the log function means that the lower end of the average precision scale is magnified. Similarly, the logit function used in the TREC Spam Track stretches both the lower and upper ends [2]. Note that the objective of employing these nonlinear functions was specifically to emphasise what is happening near the *extreme* values of the raw measures. Other prior art related to the present study include the work of Mizzaro and Robertson [6] who considered only the numerator of Eq. 1: they did not take the standard deviation into account. Lee et al. [4] proposed a kind of weighted average across topics based on a view that topics for which runs show diverse performances should be weighted heavily; this is like emphasising "informative" topics, and is different from our (and Webber et al.'s) objective of removing topic hardness and thereby enabling cross-collection comparisons.

3. PROPOSED METHOD: STD-AB

Our proposal for score standardisation is simple. Instead of applying a standard normal CDF to Eq. 1 (i.e., **std-CDF**), we apply the following *linear* transformation:

$$lin_{ij} = A * std_{ij} + B = A * \frac{raw_{ij} - m_{\bullet j}}{s_{\bullet j}} + B , \qquad (2)$$

where A and B are constants. Hereafter, we shall refer to this proposed method as **std-AB**.

By construction, the sample mean and the standard deviation of std_{ij} over the known systems are 0 and 1, respectively ($j = 1, \ldots, N$). It then follows that the sample mean and the standard deviation of lin_{ij} are B and A, respectively ($j = 1, \ldots, N$). Regardless of what distribution raw_{ij} follows, Chebyshev's inequality guarantees that at least 89% of the transformed scores lin_{ij} fall within $[-3A, 3A]$. In the present study, we let $B = 0.5$ as we want to assign a score of 0.5 to "average" systems, and consider $A = 0.15$ and $A = 0.10$ to let the 89% score range be $[0.05, 0.95]$ and $[0.20, 0.80]$, respectively. Furthermore, to make sure that even outliers (which are in fact very rare) fall into the $[0, 1]$ range, we apply the following *clipping* step in our actual implementation:

    if $lin_{ij} > 1$ **then** $lin_{ij} = 1$
    else if $lin_{ij} < 0$ **then** $lin_{ij} = 0$;

This means that *extremely* good (bad) systems relative to others are all given a score of 1 (0). Note that if A is too small, the achieved range of the **std-AB** would be narrower than the desired $[0, 1]$; if it is too large, the above clipping would be applied to too many systems and we would not be able to distinguish among them. The above approach of using A and B with standardisation is quite common for comparing students' scores in educational research: for example, SAT (Scholastic Assessment Test) and GRE (Graduate Record Examinations) have used $A = 100, B = 500$ [5]; the Japanese *hensachi* ("standard score") uses $A = 10, B = 50$.

The orange and red dots in Figure 1 visualise how the raw nDCG scores (raw_{ij}) are mapped to **std-AB** scores. As for the aforementioned data point indicated with a baloon, the corresponding **std-AB** values are 0.6198 ($A = 0.10$) and 0.6796 ($A = 0.15$). Unlike **std-CDF**, **std-AB** does not emphasise moderately high (and moderately low) scores; on the contrary, it tries to preserve the property of the original evaluation measures.

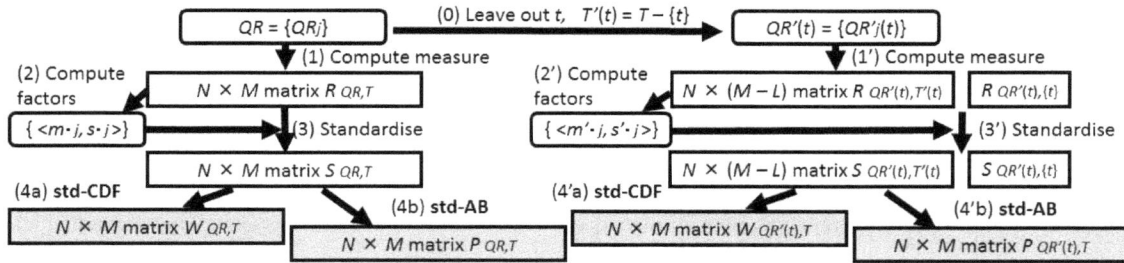

Figure 2: Data flow of the leave-one-out experiments.

AP and the sum of precisions will be equivalent; nDCG and DCG will be equivalent, and so on.

Table 2 compares the system rankings according to the three scoring schemes, i.e., raw, **std-CDF** and **std-AB** (with $A = 0.15$) scores, all based on the *original* qrels, in terms of Kendall's τ. The 95% confidence interval (CI) of a τ value for ranking r runs can be computed using a margin of error (MOE) given by $z_{0.025} \sqrt{(2(2r + 5))/(9r(r - 1))}$, where z_P is the one-sided critical z value for probability P. The MOE for each data set is given in the table caption; as indicated there, all of the τ values have a CI whose upper limit (given by $\tau + MOE$) is above 1, except for one cell with nERR. Even that cell has the CI upper limit of .999. In short, the system rankings according to the three scoring schemes are statistically indistinguishable if the same qrels file is used. That is, score standardisation (**std-CDF** and **std-AB**) enables cross-collection score comparisons without significantly affecting within-collection comparisons.

4.2 Handling New Systems: Leave One Out

Here, we report on our leave-one-out experiments to compare the reliability of **std-CDF** and **std-AB** in the context of handling new systems, under the premise that we already have a reasonable number of known systems. More specifically, with each of our TREC robust track data sets, we simulate a situation where one of the TREC teams was never involved in the test collection construction process, and see whether the runs from this "new" team can be evaluated fairly in comparison to the known systems. To this end, in *traditional* leave-one-out experiments, *unique contributions* from that one particular team (i.e., documents contributed to the pool by that particular team only, for a given pool depth) [9] is removed from the original relevance assessments. However, to evaluate the robustness of score standardisation to new systems, we need to examine the effect of removing one team not only for relevance assessments but also for obtaining the standardisation parameters for a given evaluation measure. As the experimental procedure is rather complex, we shall explain the steps using Figure 2.

The left half of Figure 2 is straightforward as it does not involve leave-one-out. Given qrels $QR = \{QR_j\}$ for N topics ($j = 1, \ldots, N$) and M runs contributed by a set of teams T, an $N \times M$ topic-by-run raw score matrix $R_{QR,T}$ is obtained for a particular evaluation measure (Step 1). From $R_{QR,T}$ (which relies on qrels QR to evaluate the runs from T), standardisation factors $(m_{\bullet j}, s_{\bullet j})$ are obtained for each j (Step 2), and then a standardised score matrix $S_{QR,T}$ is obtained using Eq. 1 (Step 3). Finally, either **std-CDF** or **std-AB** is employed to convert $S_{QR,T}$ into $W_{QR,T}$ or $P_{QR,T}$ (Steps 4a and 4b)[3].

The right half of Figure 2 depicts our leave-one-out procedure. First, from the original set of teams T, one particular team t is removed: $T'(t) = T - \{t\}$. For each topic, the unique contributions

Table 1: TREC robust track data used in this study.

	TREC03	TREC04	TREC05
Topics	50	49	50
Runs	78	110	74
Teams (with multiple runs)	16 (16)	14 (13)	17 (15)
Pool depth	125	100	55
Relevance levels	L0 (not relevant), L1 (relevant), L2 (highly relevant)		
Documents	528,155 (CD45 collection [12])	Approx. 1,033,000 (AQUAINT collection [12])	

Table 2: Kendall's τ between two different scoring schemes: raw vs. std-CDF vs. std-AB ($A = 0.15$). (a): 78 TREC03 runs ($MOE = .151$); (b): 110 TREC04 runs ($MOE = .127$); (c): 74 TREC05 runs ($MOE = .155$). The upper limit of the 95% CI for each cell exceeds 1, except for the cell indicated in bold: for this cell, the CI is $[.745, .999]$.

	raw vs. std-CDF	raw vs. std-AB	**std-CDF vs. std-AB**	raw vs std-CDF	raw vs. std-AB	**std-CDF vs. std-AB**
	(I) AP			(II) Q		
(a)	.924	.923	.970	.931	.935	.969
(b)	.907	.922	.960	.914	.931	.962
(c)	.926	.930	.960	.939	.947	.979
	(III) nDCG			(IV) nERR		
(a)	.946	.945	.971	.912	.906	.939
(b)	.944	.958	.968	**.872**	.879	.936
(c)	.956	.960	.966	.924	.942	.934

4. EXPERIMENTS

4.1 Data and Measures

For our experiments, we use the graded-relevance test collections and runs from the TREC 2003-2005 robust tracks; Table 1 summarises the key statistics. Note that we do not use the "old" topics from TREC 2003-2004 [12], because the relevance assessments for these topics were *not* obtained by pooling the "new" runs mentioned in the table. For our leave-one-out experiments, we need topics with runs that actually contributed to the pools. Also, the table shows that while there were 16, 14, 17 teams that participated in the three robust tracks, respectively, 16, 13, 15 teams submitted at least two runs. When leaving out a team, we consider these latter sets of teams only, as leaving out a team that contributed only one run is generally inconsequential. We considered four evaluation measures: *Average Precision* (AP), *Q-measure* (Q), the "Microsoft version" of *normalised Discounted Cumulative Gain* (nDCG), and *normalised Expected Reciprocal Rank* (nERR) [9]. They were computed using the `NTCIREVAL` tool[2]; for Q, nDCG and nERR, L2-relevant (i.e., highly relevant) documents were given a gain value of $(2^2 - 1 =)3$, while L1-relevant (i.e., relevant) documents were given a gain value of $(2^1 - 1) = 1$. Recall that normalisation is just redundant if the scores are to be standardised [15]:

---

[2]http://research.nii.ac.jp/ntcir/tools/ntcireval-en.html

[3]"W" and "P" stand for "Webber et al." and "Proposed".

Table 3: Kendall's τ between a run ranking based on the original qrels vs. that based on a leave-one-out data set. Based on the MOE's indicated in the leftmost column, the upper limit of the 95% CI for each cell is well above 1.

		(I) raw scores				(II) std-CDF				(III) std-AB ($A = 0.15$)			
		AP	Q	nDCG	nERR	AP	Q	nDCG	nERR	AP	Q	nDCG	nERR
(a) TREC03	lo-MU	.997	.994	.997	1	.998	.994	.995	.989	.993	.993	.995	.986
(MOE: .151)	lo-NLPR	.999	.999	.999	1	.991	.986	.969	.991	.987	.985	.966	.991
	lo-SABIR	.997	.998	.997	1	.995	.997	.997	.995	.993	.995	.996	.994
	lo-THUIR	.998	.995	.997	1	.995	.997	.995	.994	.993	.998	.997	.986
	lo-UAms	.997	.996	.996	1	.998	.996	.993	.994	.997	.995	.997	.995
	lo-UIUC	1	.998	.998	1	.995	.997	.998	.995	.994	.996	.998	.993
	lo-VT	.996	.999	.994	1	.990	.995	.992	.995	.989	.993	.995	.989
	lo-apl	.998	.995	.994	1	.993	.994	.991	.996	.987	.991	.995	.993
	lo-fub	1	.999	.999	1	.999	.996	.997	.989	.995	.997	.997	.997
	lo-hum	.999	.997	.997	1	.993	.993	.989	.989	.987	.989	.991	.991
	lo-oce	.998	.998	.999	1	.996	.999	.998	.994	.993	.994	.997	.995
	lo-pirc	.993	.997	.993	.999	.989	.990	.985	.995	.987	.989	.989	.991
	lo-rutcor	.997	.999	.999	1	.986	.985	.972	.966	.982	.987	.979	.959
	lo-uic	.997	.998	.996	1	.994	.992	.994	.990	.994	.997	.991	.988
	lo-uog	.999	.999	.999	1	.998	.997	.993	.999	.995	.997	.995	.994
	lo-uwmt	.995	.997	.991	1	.987	.989	.993	.989	.985	.984	.989	.990
	average	**.998**	**.997**	**.997**	**1**	**.994**	**.994**	**.991**	**.991**	**.991**	**.993**	**.992**	**.990**
(b) TREC04	lo-Juru	.998	.999	1	1	.996	.996	.994	.988	.998	.994	.992	.986
(MOE: .127)	lo-NLPR	.999	1	.999	1	.999	.995	.997	.992	.996	.995	.996	.994
	lo-SABIR	.989	.990	.992	1	.996	.993	.992	.991	.992	.990	.992	.993
	lo-apl	.999	.999	.998	1	.998	.996	.990	.997	.998	.997	.997	.997
	lo-fub	.998	.998	.997	1	.997	.995	.994	.991	.995	.996	.991	.992
	lo-hum	.998	.998	.997	1	.997	.994	.995	.992	.996	.994	.995	.986
	lo-icl	.998	.999	.997	1	.992	.995	.992	.981	.993	.990	.985	.978
	lo-mpi	.999	.999	.999	1	.987	.989	.979	.980	.990	.982	.977	.976
	lo-pirc	.998	.999	.999	1	.995	.994	.992	.992	.991	.993	.993	.992
	lo-polyu	.999	.999	.996	.999	.987	.990	.989	.978	.989	.982	.989	.977
	lo-uog	.998	.998	.995	1	.992	.991	.992	.994	.993	.991	.996	.995
	lo-vtum	.997	.999	.997	1	.994	.994	.996	.994	.997	.992	.994	.993
	lo-wdo	.999	.999	.999	1	.999	.995	.999	.996	.999	.996	.998	.996
	average	**.998**	**.998**	**.997**	**1**	**.995**	**.994**	**.992**	**.990**	**.994**	**.992**	**.992**	**.989**
(c) TREC05	lo-ASU	.996	.998	.998	1	.996	.993	.993	.990	.993	.997	.998	.979
(MOE: .155)	lo-CK	.995	.993	.995	1	.993	.996	.986	.970	.993	.993	.996	.978
	lo-HKPU	.992	.992	.991	.999	.993	.988	.990	.987	.993	.993	.995	.994
	lo-ICT	.999	.999	.998	1	.997	.995	.992	.996	.993	.996	.994	.996
	lo-Juru	.995	.993	.990	.999	.993	.993	.986	.995	.989	.992	.990	.994
	lo-QUT	.999	1	.997	1	.990	.994	.986	.976	.990	.993	.978	.981
	lo-RIM	.989	.990	.988	.996	.990	.987	.990	.990	.982	.987	.983	.990
	lo-UIUC	.999	.997	.996	1	.998	.999	.997	.994	.996	.997	.994	.993
	lo-apl	.996	.992	.990	1	.989	.993	.985	.990	.990	.992	.987	.985
	lo-hum	.999	.998	.996	1	.996	.999	.995	.993	.999	.996	.996	.995
	lo-indri	.996	.993	.994	1	.996	.993	.993	.991	.996	.993	.993	.991
	lo-pirc	.993	.991	.994	.997	.993	.994	.989	.991	.991	.991	.993	.986
	lo-rmit	.989	.993	.989	.999	.989	.992	.985	.987	.993	.985	.987	.990
	lo-sab	.964	.968	.964	.983	.971	.962	.963	.980	.944	.953	.964	.978
	lo-wdf	.993	.993	.993	.991	.993	.993	.990	.980	.987	.993	.994	.981
	average	**.993**	**.993**	**.992**	**.998**	**.992**	**.991**	**.988**	**.987**	**.989**	**.990**	**.989**	**.987**

from t to the document pool (with the pool depth as shown in Table 1) are removed from the original qrels; the resultant qrels file is denoted by $QR'(t) = \{QR'_j(t)\}$ (Step 0). Let L denote the number of runs from team t. The $(M - L)$ "known" runs from $T'(t)$ are evaluated using $QR'(t)$ to form an $N \times (M - L)$ matrix $R_{QR'(t),T'(t)}$; whereas, the L "new" runs from t are also evaluated using $QR'(t)$ to form an $N \times L$ matrix $R_{QR'(t),\{t\}}$ (Step 1'). The standardisation factors are then computed from $R_{QR'(t),T'(t)}$ (Step 2'). Note that $R_{QR'(t),\{t\}}$, which contains the raw scores of the runs from t, is not used for the computation of standardisation factors. Thus, our leave-one-out setting differs from the left half of the figure in two ways: firstly, $QR'(t)$ is used instead of QR; and secondly, standardsation factors are computed using the "known" runs (i.e., runs in $T'(t)$) only. As for Steps 3' and 4', they are basically the same as Steps 3 and 4 in the left half.

The robustness of the raw scores to new systems can be quantified in terms of Kendall's τ bewteen a system ranking based on mean scores from $R_{QR,T}$ and another ranking based on mean scores from $R_{QR'(t),T'(t)}$ (for "known" runs) and $R_{QR'(t),\{t\}}$ (for "new" runs). Similarly, the robustness of the **std-CDF** or **std-AB** scores to new systems can be quantified in terms of τ using $W_{QR,T}$ and

$W_{QR'(t),T}$, or using $P_{QR,T}$ and $P_{QR'(t),T}$. If the τ values are close to one, that means that the new systems are evaluated correctly relative to the known systems.

Table 3 shows the results of our leave-one-out experiments. For example, if we first rank the 78 TREC03 runs using **std-AB** nDCG with $A = 0.15$ (Section (a), Column (III)), and then rank the same set of runs using the leave-out-MU setting (recall that not only the qrels but also the standardisation factors are now different), the τ is .995. (The results for **std-AB** with $A = 0.10$ are very similar to those shown in Column (III) and are omitted for the sake of brevity.) It is clear that the upper limit of the 95% CI for each cell, which can be obtained by adding MOE to the point estimate in each cell, is well above 1. That is, *for all cells in the table, the original ranking and the leave-one-out ranking are statistically equivalent.* These results demonstrate that both **std-CDF** and **std-AB** can evaluate new systems fairly just as raw measures can, even though these new systems are not only outside the set of pooled systems but also outside the set of standardising systems, i.e., those used for obtaining the standardisation factors ($m_{\bullet j}, s_{\bullet j}$). Again, a premise here is that we already have a good number of pooled/standardising systems.

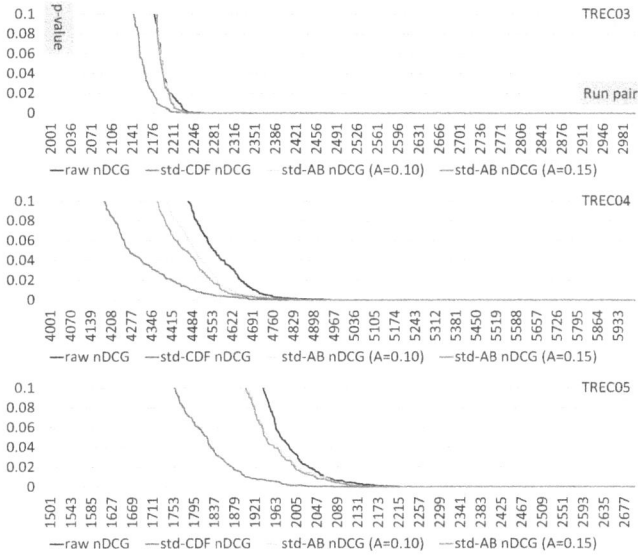

Figure 3: Discriminative power curves for nDCG.

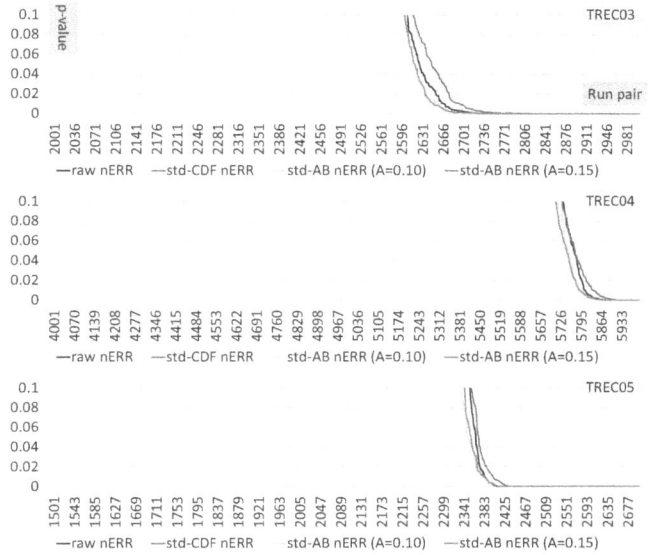

Figure 4: Discriminative power curves for nERR.

4.3 Discriminative Power

In this section, we compare **std-CDF**, **std-AB** and raw scores in terms of *discriminative power* [8], which is a popular method for comparing evaluation measures: a statistical significance test is conducted for every system pair, and the pairs are sorted by p-values. Curves that are closer to the origin represent measures that can report many significant differences ("highly discriminative" measures). Figure 3 shows the result of applying this test to our data with nDCG. We used the *randomised Tukey HSD test* [1, 9] with $B = 5000$ trials as the significance test to avoid the *familywise error rate* problem. This is a type of *multiple comparison procedure*[4] that ensures that the probability of having *at least one* Type I error is no greater than α. The trends for nDCG are clear and consistent across the data sets: **std-CDF** is substantially more discriminative than **std-AB** and the raw measure, while **std-AB** is similar to the raw measure or perhaps slightly more discriminative. The results for AP and Q, omitted due to lack of space, are very similar to Figure 3. However, Figure 4 shows that the superiority of **std-CDF** cannot be observed for nERR: in fact, **std-CDF** actually looks slightly less discriminative than others with the TREC03 data. This is possibly because while **std-CDF** tries to emphasise *moderately* high and low scores, there actually are few such scores for nERR: nERR values tend to be *very* high if there is just one highly relevant document near the top of the ranking.

In summary, while **std-CDF** achieves the highest discriminative power for nDCG, AP and Q, the same cannot be said for nERR. In the remainder of this paper, we show that, despite these results, **std-CDF** is not necessarily the best way to implement standardisation, through swap rate and topic set size design experiments.

4.4 Swap Rates

To quantify the consistency of experimental results across different topic sets, we also conducted *swap rate* [14] experiments with our data. We used the *bootstrap* version of the swap method [8], as this method can sample up to the original topic set size unlike the original method that uses sampling *without* replacement to split the

---

[4]If a significance test at α is conducted independently k times, the familywise error rate can amount to $1 - (1 - \alpha)^k$, where k is the number of individual tests.

> **foreach** system pair with a vector of per-topic differences **d**
>   **for** $b = 1$ **to** B
> $\bar{d}^{*b}$ = mean of the first bootstrap sample obtained from **d**;
> $\bar{d}'^{*b}$ = mean of the second bootstrap sample obtained from **d**;
> $count(BIN(\bar{d}^{*b})) + +$;
>   **if** ($\bar{d}^{*b} * \bar{d}'^{*b} \leq 0$) **then** $swapcount(BIN(\bar{d}^{*b})) + +$;
>   **end for**
> **foreach** bin i
> $swaprate(i) = swapcount(i)/count(i)$;

Figure 5: Bootstrap-based swap rate algorithm [8].

original set in half. Following previous work [8, 14], twenty-one bins are prepared: Bin 1 represents mean between-system differences ($\bar{d}$'s) such that $0 \leq \bar{d} < 0.01$; Bin 2 represents those such that $0.01 \leq \bar{d} < 0.02$; finally, Bin 21 represents those such that $0.20 \leq \bar{d}$. Let $BIN()$ denote a function that maps a given $\bar{d}$ to one of the above bins. Figure 5 shows the algorithm for computing the swap rate for each bin. We conducted $B = 1000$ iterations for each data set and for each measure.

Figure 6 shows our swap rate results for nDCG. It can be observed that, contrary to the discriminative power results, **std-CDF** is now the worst performer, which means that it often provides inconsistent results across different topic sets. Whereas, it can be observed that **std-AB** has the lowest swap rates for nDCG and that the $A = 0.10$ setting ensures fewer swaps than $A = 0.15$. Recall that $A = 0.10$ implies narrower score range (Section 3): it gives similar scores to different systems and therefore the chance of system swaps is reduced. For example, for Bin 6 ($0.05 \leq \bar{d} < 0.06$) with TREC03 (Figure 6 top graph), the swap rates with raw, **std-CDF**, **std-AB** ($A = 0.10$) and **std-AB** ($A = 0.15$) nDCG are 5.3%, 17.6%, 0.8% and 3.4%, respectively. The fact that the swap rates for **std-CDF** are substantially higher than those for raw measures suggests that it may be worth reconsidering.

Figure 7 shows our swap rate results for nERR: it shows that **std-AB** performs best even for this evaluation measure. Here, **std-CDF** nERR performs similarly to the raw nERR, probably for the reason mentioned earlier: **std-CDF** emphasises *moderately* high/low scores, but there are few such scores in the case of nERR. The graphs for AP and Q are very similar to Figure 6 (i.e., nDCG) and are omitted due to lack of space.

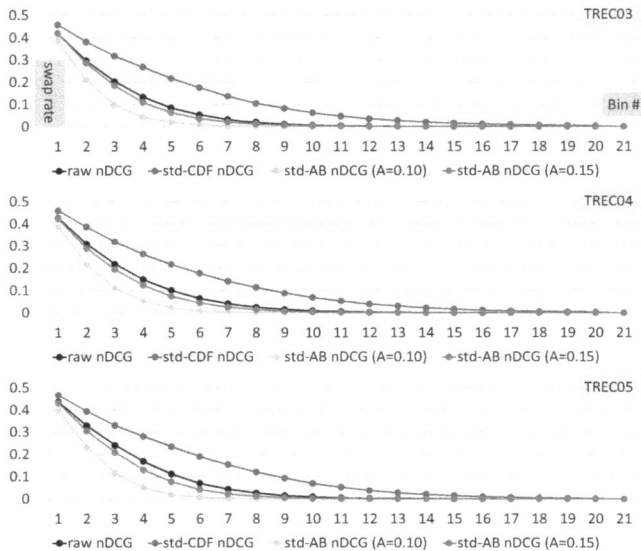

Figure 6: Swap rate curves for nDCG.

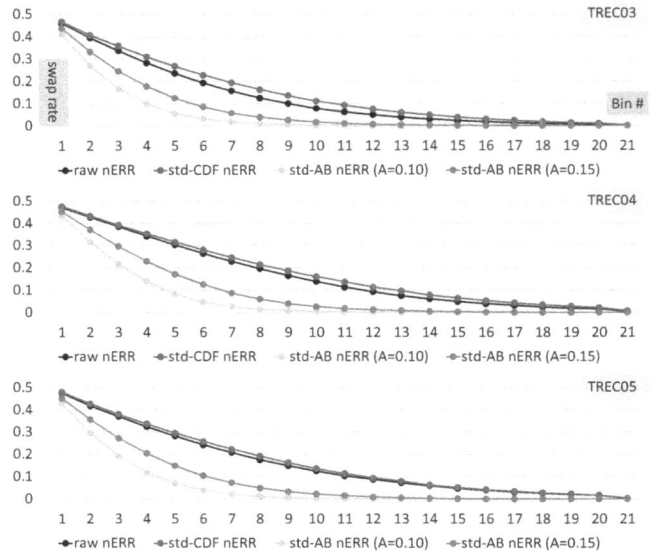

Figure 7: Swap rate curves for nERR.

Table 4: Significantly different run pairs according to the randomised Tukey HSD test ($\alpha = 0.05$) for (a) TREC03, (b) TREC04 and (c) TREC05. std-AB uses $A = 0.15$.

	Significantly different with (raw/**std-CDF/std-AB**):			
	(I) AP	(II) Q	(III) nDCG	(IV) nERR
(a)	767/822/791	836/890/851	810/844/812	378/357/386
(b)	1489/1710/1593	1656/1830/1734	1434/1723/1534	223/220/250
(c)	711/840/789	774/907/849	727/879/758	336/329/346

The above swap rate results considered *all* system pairs: $78 * 77/2 = 3,003$ pairs for TREC03; 5,995 pairs for TREC04; and 2,701 pairs for TREC05 (Table 1). However, do swaps really occur if two systems are statistically significantly different? To answer this question, we followed Sanderson and Zobel [11] and reran the swap experiments by feeding only statistically significantly different pairs to the algorithm shown in Figure 5. For this, we used the randomised Tukey HSD test results from Section 4.3, with $\alpha = 0.05$. Note that while Sanderson and Zobel applied the t-test, the Wilcoxon test and the sign test to each system pair individually, they did not consider the aforementioned familywise error rate problem; the same can be said for the t-test-based swap rate experiments of Voorhees [13]. By employing (randomised) Tukey HSD tests here, we ensure that the familywise error rate (i.e., the probability of obtaining at least one Type I error among the pairwise comparisons) is no greater than $\alpha = 0.05$.

Table 4 shows the number of significantly different pairs that we used in our additional swap rate experiments. Note that the numbers are substantially smaller than those for all system pairs, which means that $count(i)$ in Figure 3 (i.e., the denominator for the swap rate) are small in our additional experiments. Furthermore, we found that, after filtering out statistically insignificant pairs, the actual swaps (i.e., $swapcount(i)$ in Figure 3, the numerator for the swap rate) are extremely rare. For these reasons, here we use *six* bins intead of 21 bins for computing swap rates, where Bin $1'$ represents $0 \leq \bar{d} < 0.10$; Bin $2'$ represents $0.10 \leq \bar{d} < 0.20$ and so on; finally, Bin $6'$ represents $0.50 \leq \bar{d}$. Hence Bins 1-20 in Figures 6-7 correspond to Bins $1'$-$2'$. Table 5 shows the swap rate results for TREC03 through TREC05 with raw AP, Q, nDCG and nERR as well as the **std-CDF** and **std-AB** versions of these four

measures. Note that we cannot draw figures similar to Figures 6 and 7 as the swap rate is zero in most cases. For example, Table 5 Section (a) Column (I) shows that, out of the 767,000 comparisons (number of significantly different pairs shown in Table 4(I)(a) times 1,000 trials), only 19,208 fell into Bin $1'$ with the raw AP. Only one swap was observed for this bin, so its swap rate is 0.01%. No swaps were ever observed for Bins $4'$-$5'$ for any of the measures considered, so only Bins $1'$-$3'$ are shown in the table. It can be observed that the swap rates are below 1% in every cell. That is, after filtering run pairs with the randomised Tukey HSD test, swaps across different topic sets become negligible, regardless of the measure or the scoring scheme. These results suggest that, if IR researchers adopt an appropriate multiple comparison procedure such as the (randomised) Tukey HSD test, then the chance of obtaining a contradictory result in another experiment will actually be extremely small if they have around 50 topics (Table 1). Note that this is true not only for raw scores but also for standardised scores.

Although our first swap rate experiments with 21 bins (Figures 6 and 7) did not consider statistical significance, the fact that **std-CDF** had higher swap rates than the raw measure in that setting may be regarded as a disadvantage. The results imply that, even if System X outperforms Systems Y in terms of an **std-CDF** measure averaged across one topic set, there is a considerable chance that Y may outperform X on another topic set. Moreover, we may obtain more swaps with **std-CDF** than with raw scores (Figure 6). These results suggest that **std-AB** is a useful alternative to implementing score standardisation. While discriminative power and swap rate experiments are known to provide similar results for the purpose of comparing different *raw* evaluation measures [8], our results show that they can disagree when nonlinear transformation is involved. If the sole purpose of employing the standard normal CDF function is to map the standardised scores into the $[0, 1]$ range, the higher swap rates that it introduces may be an undesirable side effect.

4.5 Topic Set Size Design

Our fourth method for comparing raw measures, **std-CDF** and **std-AB** is Sakai's *topic set size design* [10]. More specifically, we

Table 5: Swap rates for run pairs with statistically significant differences (Bins 1' ($0 < \bar{d} \leq 0.10$), 2' ($0.10 < \bar{d} \leq 0.20$) and 3' ($0.20 < \bar{d} \leq 0.30$) only: there were no swaps for Bins 4'-6' ($0.30 < \bar{d}$), with (a) TREC03, (b) TREC04, and (c) TREC05. std-AB uses $A = 0.15$.

	Bin	(I) AP raw	std-CDF	std-AB	(II) Q raw	std-CDF	std-AB	(III) nDCG raw	std-CDF	std-AB	(IV) nERR raw	std-CDF	std-AB
(a)	1'	1/19208 =0.01%	1/256 =0.39%	0/10659 =0%	0/13544 =0%	1/55 =0.65%	0/7113 =0%	0/1938 =0%	0/60 =0%	0/2838 =0%	1/980 =0.10%	0/686 =0%	5/15400 =0.03%
	2'	0/357868 =0%	0/20092 =0%	0/314610 =0%	0/335159 =0%	0/15886 =0%	0/268022 =0%	0/135522 =0%	0/9840 =0%	0/145334 =0%	4/41522 =0.01%	1/27983 =0.00%	15/228177 =0.01%
	3'	0/336874 =0%	0/174069 =0%	0/376935 =0%	0/401198 =0%	0/150765 =0%	0/429505 =0%	0/363349 =0%	0/82705 =0%	0/421661 =0%	4/160153 =0.00%	4/143523 =0.00%	0/139427 =0%
(b)	1'	0/49300 =0%	0/507 =0%	1/24630 =0.00%	0/36980 =0%	1/415 =0.24%	1/25152 =0.00%	0/7532 =0%	0/337 =0%	0/16124 =0%	2/511 =0.39%	0/211 =0%	0/10901 =0%
	2'	0/1015665 =0%	0/41621 =0%	2/941334 =0.00%	0/1017520 =0%	0/36570 =0%	3/946042 =0.00%	0/471538 =0%	1/40841 =0.00%	1/635431 =0.00%	0/18654 =0%	0/11710 =0%	0/139610 =0%
	3'	0/383187 =0%	0/472556 =0%	1/549345 =0.00%	0/522940 =0%	0/457372 =0%	0/641132 =0%	0/619454 =0%	0/421278 =0%	0/646738 =0%	0/77048 =0%	2/76860 =0.00%	0/87622 =0%
(c)	1'	0/45287 =0%	0/334 =0%	0/20303 =0%	4/45156 =0.01%	1/335 =0.30%	0/18326 =0%	0/3275 =0%	0/261 =0%	0/13002 =0%	1/121 =0.09%	0/84 =0%	6/6773 =0.90%
	2'	2/480029 =0.00%	0/29878 =0%	0/486532 =0%	0/513537 =0%	0/29805 =0%	2/511904 =0.00%	0/277003 =0%	0/28638 =0%	1/393283 =0.00%	0/8159 =0%	0/9047 =0%	1/165448 =0.00%
	3'	0/171589 =0%	0/267406 =0%	0/220861 =0%	0/189791 =0%	0/270432 =0%	0/231289 =0%	0/189774 0%	0/260967 =0%	0/1489939 =0%	0/68192 =0%	0/80820 =0%	0/163101 =0%

use his ANOVA-based tool[5] for estimating the number of topics required for building a new test collection to compare M systems. The input to this tool are:

α Probability of Type I error, i.e., detecting a nonexistent difference;

β Probability of Type II error, i.e., missing a real difference;

M Number of systems to be compared;

$minD$ *Minimum detectable range*: we want to detect any real difference among the M systems with $(1-\beta)\%$ statistical power whenever the difference between the best and the worst system is $minD$ or higher;

$\hat{\sigma}^2$ An estimate of the population within-system variance, which is assumed to be common across all systems, as per ANOVA.

We follow *Cohen's five-eighty convention* [3] and let $(\alpha, \beta) = (0.05, 0.20)$ in this study. The interested reader may try other settings with our data and Sakai's tool. As for $\hat{\sigma}^2$, this can be obtained for a given evaluation measure as shown below.

For an existing test collection C with N_C topics and M_C runs, an $N_C \times M_C$ topic-by-run score matrix $\{x_{ij}\}$ ($i = 1, \ldots, M_C, j = 1, \ldots, N_C$) can be obtained for a particular evaluation measure. Given this matrix, the *residual variance* from one-way ANOVA provides a direct estimate of the population within-system variance [10]:

$$\hat{\sigma}_C^2 = \frac{\sum_{i=1}^{M_C} \sum_{j=1}^{N_C} (x_{ij} - \bar{x}_{i\bullet})^2}{M_C(N_C - 1)}, \quad (3)$$

where $\bar{x}_{i\bullet}$ is the sample mean for run i, given by:

$$\bar{x}_{i\bullet} = \frac{1}{N_C} \sum_{j=1}^{N_C} x_{ij}. \quad (4)$$

Furthermore, if multiple test collections with runs are available, the variances can be pooled to enhance the accuracy as follows:

$$\hat{\sigma}^2 = \frac{\sum_C (N_C - 1)\hat{\sigma}_C^2}{\sum_C (N_C - 1)}. \quad (5)$$

---

[5] http://www.f.waseda.jp/tetsuya/CIKM2014/samplesizeANOVA.xlsx

Eq. 3 has an interesting implication for **std-AB**. By replacing each x_{ij} in Eq. 4 with lin_{ij} as defined in Eq. 2 (Section 3), we can obtain the sample system mean for **std-AB** as:

$$\bar{lin}_{i\bullet} = \frac{1}{N_C} \sum_{j=1}^{N_C} (A\, std_{ij} + B) = B + \frac{A}{N_C} \sum_{j=1}^{N_C} std_{ij}. \quad (6)$$

That is, if we let $\bar{std}_{i\bullet} = \frac{1}{N_C} \sum_{j=1}^{N_C} std_{ij}$,

$$\bar{lin}_{i\bullet} = B + A\, \bar{std}_{i\bullet}. \quad (7)$$

Hence, to estimate the within-system variance from an **std-AB** matrix, we rewrite Eq. 3 by replacing x_{ij} with lin_{ij} and $\bar{x}_{i\bullet}$ with $\bar{lin}_{i\bullet}$ and obtain:

$$\hat{\sigma}_C^2 = \sum_{i=1}^{M_C} \sum_{j=1}^{N_C} (A\, std_{ij} + B - B - A\, \bar{std}_{i\bullet})^2/(M_C(N_C - 1))$$

$$= A^2 \sum_{i=1}^{M_C} \sum_{j=1}^{N_C} (std_{ij} - \bar{std}_{i\bullet})^2/(M_C(N_C - 1)). \quad (8)$$

That is, the magnitude of the variance estimate can be controlled by the parameter A.

Given $\alpha, \beta, m, minD$ and $\hat{\sigma}^2$, it is known that the required sample size can be estimated as [10]:

$$n = \frac{2\hat{\sigma}^2 \lambda}{minD^2}, \quad (9)$$

where λ is the *noncentrality parameter* of a *noncentral* χ^2 distribution[6]. Therefore, if A is set to a small value such as $A = 0.15$, the variance estimate for **std-AB** scores would be small (Eq. 8), and therefore the required sample size n would also be small (Eqs. 5 and 9) provided that $minD$ is held constant. This does not necessarily mean that **std-AB** is better than raw scores, because the meaning of $minD$ becomes different after standardisation and linear transformation: for example, a $minD$ of 0.10 in terms of raw nDCG scores may translate into a much smaller $minD$ in terms

---

[6] For $(\alpha, \beta) = (0.05, 0.20)$, λ can be approximated as $\lambda = 4.860 + 3.584\sqrt{M_C - 1}$. Details can be found elsewhere [10].

Table 6: Within-system variance estimates V_E for each data set, and the pooled estimates $\hat{\sigma}^2$ over TREC03-05.

	raw	std-CDF	std-AB	
(a) TREC03			($A = 0.10$)	($A = 0.15$)
AP	.0479	.0545	.0064	.0142
Q	.0471	.0495	.0057	.0128
nDCG	.0456	.0423	.0052	.0113
nERR	.1140	.0629	.0084	.0176
(b) TREC04			($A = 0.10$)	($A = 0.15$)
AP	.0481	.0565	.0069	.0151
Q	.0481	.0538	.0065	.0144
nDCG	.0472	.0494	.0061	.0132
nERR	.1155	.0789	.0090	.0198
(c) TREC05			($A = 0.10$)	($A = 0.15$)
AP	.0297	.0553	.0067	.0146
Q	.0289	.0534	.0064	.0140
nDCG	.0398	.0474	.0055	.0122
nERR	.1139	.0701	.0083	.0181
(d) pooled			($A = 0.10$)	($A = 0.15$)
AP	**.0419**	**.0554**	**.0067**	**.0146**
Q	**.0413**	**.0522**	**.0062**	**.0137**
nDCG	**.0442**	**.0463**	**.0056**	**.0122**
nERR	**.1145**	**.0706**	**.0086**	**.0185**

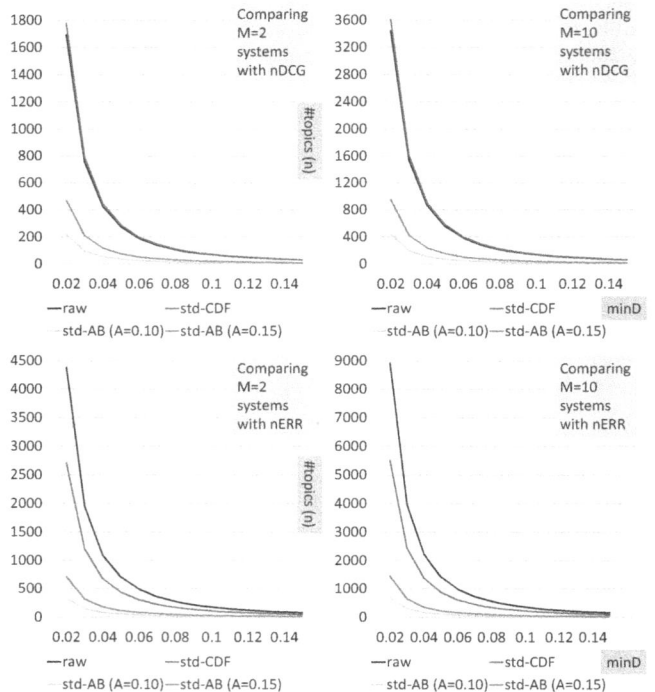

Figure 8: Topic set size n vs. the minimum detectable range $minD$ for nDCG and nERR, based on the pooled variances shown in Table 6 ($(\alpha, \beta) = (0.05, 0.20)$, $m = 2, 10$).

of **std-AB** nDCG scores[7]. Nevertheless, being able to control the magnitude of $\hat{\sigma}^2$ may be a convenient feature, as discussed below.

Table 6 shows the actual variance estimates obtained for each data set using Eq. 3 for all raw, **std-CDF** and **std-AB** matrices, as well as the pooled variances obtained over the three data sets using Eq. 5. It can indeed be observed that the variance estimates based on the **std-AB** matrices are substantially smaller than those obtained based on the raw and **std-CDF** matrices, and that the variance estimates for the $A = 0.10$ setting is smaller than those for the $A = 0.15$ setting due to the reason discussed above. Also, note that the variances for the **std-CDF** scores are often larger than those for the raw scores, but not always. Using the pooled variances shown in Table 6(d) with the aforementioned tool of Sakai, Figure 8 shows the relationship between the sample size n and the minimum detectable range $minD$ for nDCG and nERR, with $M = 2, 10$. The graphs for AP and Q are similar to those for nDCG and are omitted due to lack of space. For example, the top-left graph shows that if raw or **std-CDF** nDCG is to be used for comparing $M = 2$ systems under $(\alpha, \beta) = (0.05, 0.20)$, and if we have about 200 topics in the test collection, then the $minD$ would be about 0.06; whereas, if **std-AB** ($A = 0.15$) is to be used with 200 topics, then the $minD$ would be about 0.03. That is, whenever the difference between the two systems in terms of **std-AB** nDCG is at least 0.03 with 200 topics, we can guarantee 80% statistical power. It is clear from the curves that while the required topic set sizes become unrealistically large with raw and **std-CDF** scores as smaller $minD$ values are considered, the required topic set sizes for **std-AB** grow substantially more slowly. While it deserves to be stressed again that $minD$ values are not comparable across scoring schemes (i.e., raw vs. **std-CDF** vs. **std-AB**), having manageable topic set sizes even for small $minD$ values is probably a convenient feature: test collection builders who employ topic set size design will not have to consider unrealistically large topic set sizes.

---

[7]Consider a case where the raw scores are transformed directly using A and B, without going through standardisation. In this case, the variance estimate will be A^2 times the estimate for raw scores (*cf.* Eq. 8); whereas, a value of $minD$ in terms of raw scores would be exactly $A * minD$ in terms of the transformed scores. Hence, the A's will cancel out in Eq. 9, and the transformation would not affect the required sample size at all.

4.6 Relying on Fewer Teams for Standardisation and Topic Set Size Design

Our leave-one-out experiments have demonstrated that both **std-CDF** and **std-AB** can evaluate new systems just as fairly as raw scores do, provided that we already have a reasonable number of pooled and standardising systems. While **std-CDF** may achieve higher discriminative power than **std-AB** and raw scores for some evaluation measures, our swap rate experiments showed that **std-AB** provides experimental results that are substantially more consistent across different topic sets than **std-CDF** and raw scores. Furthermore, our topic set size design experiments have demonstrated that **std-AB** require more realistic topic set sizes even for small values of minimum detectable ranges than **std-CDF** and raw scores, as the within-system variance estimates for **std-AB** are small due to the A parameter. It is probably fair to conclude from these results that **std-AB** is a useful alternative to **std-CDF**.

In this section, we focus on **std-AB** only and report on an additional set of experiments to examine the robustness of both standardisation parameters $(m_{\bullet j}, s_{\bullet j})$ and within-system variance estimates $\hat{\sigma}^2$ to rigorous reduction in the number of teams that contributes to the topic-by-run matrix. If reasonably accurate estimates of $(m_{\bullet j}, s_{\bullet j})$ can be obtained from a small number of standardising teams, that would mean that the standardisation step is highly practical. Furthermore, if reasonably accurate estimates of $\hat{\sigma}^2$ can be obtained from a small number of teams, that would mean that topic set size design using **std-AB** is highly practical.

We consider using only a few teams for estimating $(m_{\bullet j}, s_{\bullet j})$ and $\hat{\sigma}^2$, by removing more and more teams from the original data (rather than just one team in each experiment as we did in Section 4.2). For this purpose, the TREC05 data is not ideal because the pools for this test collection relies not only on the robust track runs but also on the HARD track runs [12]. Hence, we use only the TREC03 and TREC04 data. Recall that the TREC03 data has 16 teams that each contributed multiple runs (Table 1). In the first step of our additional experiments, one team was selected at random and a leave-one-out qrels file was created; runs from the other 15 teams were evaluated with the modified qrels, and $(m_{\bullet j}, s_{\bullet j})$ and $\hat{\sigma}^2$ were obtained from the leave-one-out topic-by-run matrix for each evaluation measure. This was repeated 10 times. In the second step, two teams were selected at random and a leave-*two*-out qrels file was created; runs from the other 14 teams were evaluated, and again, $(m_{\bullet j}, s_{\bullet j})$ and $\hat{\sigma}^2$ were obtained. This was repeated 10 times. Finally, in the 14-th step, 14 teams were seleceted at random and a leave-14-out qrels files (that rely on only two teams) was created, and so on. Thus, from the TREC03 data, $14 * 10 = 140$ different versions of qrels were created. Similarly, from the TREC04 data, $11 * 10 = 110$ qrels files were created: the 11-th step relied only on two teams with multiple runs plus one team with a single run (Table 1). For each step, we report the averages of $(m_{\bullet j}, s_{\bullet j})$ and of $\hat{\sigma}^2$ over the 10 trials.

Figure 9 shows the average $m_{\bullet j}$ and $s_{\bullet j}$ values for every topic and for every team reduction step, where the x axis represents the number of teams (K) that have been removed. As indicated by the baloons in the figure, the leftmost values are the original values of $m_{\bullet j}$ and $s_{\bullet j}$ based on the full set of teams, while the rightmost values are the corresponding values based on only two teams (plus one run, for TREC04), averaged over 10 trials[8]. It can be observed that, even removing (say) 10 teams from the TREC03 data (or 8 teams from the TREC04 data) and therefore relying on (say) 6 teams does not substantially affect the values of $m_{\bullet j}$ and $s_{\bullet j}$. These results are in line with those of Webber *et al.* ("*A small set of systems, therefore, is sufficient to provide standardization factors that give reliable system rankings, far smaller than is needed to provide the relevance judgments.*" [15]), but recall that they used the *original* qrels throughout their experiments: in their setting, the teams that were removed from the set of standardising systems still contributed to the qrels. In this respect, our experimental setting is more realistic and stringent. It remains to be seen, however, how often the standardisation factors will have to be revised for *future* systems: the robustness of standardisation parameters to substantial technological advances is an open question, as our experiments rely only on "present" systems, i.e., those from the same round of TREC.

Figure 10 shows the effect of removing K teams on the within-system variance estimate of **std-AB** nDCG/nERR. As each removal step had 10 trials, 95% CIs are shown as error bars. Again, the leftmost values are those obtained using the original data, and they are the same as the values shown in Table 6; whereas, the rightmost values represent the variances estimated from only two teams (plus one run, for TREC04). It can be observed that the estimates are quite stable. These results show that it is not difficult to obtain reasonably accurate variance estimates from a small number of teams, in order to conduct reliable topic set size design with **std-AB** scores. Note that, even if systems with substantially high mean effectiveness scores emerge in the future, that does not necessarily imply that the within-system variance σ^2 will change: the basic assumption behind ANOVA (and hence ANOVA-based topic set size design) is that σ^2 is the same for all systems[9].

---

[8]Confidence intervals are omitted for the sake of brevity.

[9]This *homoscedasticity* assumption can of course be violated: see Carterette [1]. Nevertheless, we consider topic set size design to be a useful method, as it provides a simple justification for the choice of a particular topic set size for a new test collection [10].

5. CONCLUSIONS

Using standardised scores, researchers can compare systems across different test collections without worrying about topic hardness or normalisation. In this study, we demonstrated a few advantages of **std-AB** over the nonlinear **std-CDF** of Webber *et al.*[15]. **std-AB** employs a simple linear transformation just like the SAT, GRE and the Japanese *hensachi* scores in educational research [5]. We demonstrated that, due to the parameter A, **std-AB** achieves substantially lower swap rates than raw and **std-CDF** scores, and that it requires more manageable topic set sizes for practical values of the minimum detectable range (i.e., the difference between the best and worst systems that we want to detect with $(1 - \beta)\%$ power) compared to raw and **std-CDF**. Hence, the use of nonlinear transformation in **std-CDF** to emphasise moderately high/low scores as visualised in Figure 1 may not be the best idea for the purpose of mapping standardised scores into the $[0, 1]$ range; we have demonstrated through extensive experiments that **std-AB** is a good alternative. In practice, we recommend the use of **std-AB** with $A = 0.15, B = 0.50$, which ensures that at least 89% of the transformed scores will lie within $[0.05, 9.95]$ (Section 3).

A useful by-product of our swap rate experiments is the observation that system swaps across topic sets rarely occur if a proper multiple comparison procedure (a randomised Tukey HSD test in our case) is applied. Recall that prior art that examined pairwise system swaps applied a significance test for every system pair independently [11, 13], and did not consider the familywise error rate problem; these studies observed considerable number of swaps even for system pairs that were statistically significantly different. In contrast, our swap rate experiments, which fed only statistically significantly different pairs according to the randomised Tukey HSD test to the swap rate algorithm (Figure 5), showed that the swap rate is well below 1% even for Bin 1' $(0 < \bar{d} \leq 0.10)$. Hence we recommend the use of a multiple comparison procedure such as the randomised Tukey HSD test when the IR researcher is interested in the difference between every system pair in his/her experiment.

While we demonstrated that reliable estimates of the standardisation factors $(m_{\bullet j}, s_{\bullet j})$ and the within-system variances $\hat{\sigma}^2$ can be obtained from a small number of teams, one limitation is that all of the teams used in our experiments come from the same rounds of TREC. In order to investigate the longevity of these estimates across years, we have launched a new web search task at NTCIR[10], which will be run as follows. In Year 1, we run a standard ad hoc IR task and form a Year-1 version of qrels. We release the evaluation scores but not the qrels at this point, to avoid tuning. In the following years, we collect new runs for the same ("frozen") topic set, and augment the qrels internally. We release all X versions of qrels only after Year X, and compare the absolute values of $(m_{\bullet j}, s_{\bullet j})$ and $\hat{\sigma}^2$ obtained using runs from Years 1-X with the Year-X qrels ("Version X values") against those obtained from Year-1 runs with the Year-1 qrels ("Version 1 values"). We also compare the ranking of the Year-X runs based on the Year-X qrels against that based on the Year-1 qrels. In practice, a "fresh" topic set will be introduced every year alongside the "frozen" set, so that participants will gain access to some new topics with relevance assessments every year.

All of the topic-by-run matrices created in our experiments are available at https://waseda.box.com/ICTIR2016PACK.

Acknowledgement

I would like to thank Professor Yasushi Nagata of Waseda University for helpful discussions.

---

[10]http://www.thuir.cn/ntcirwww/

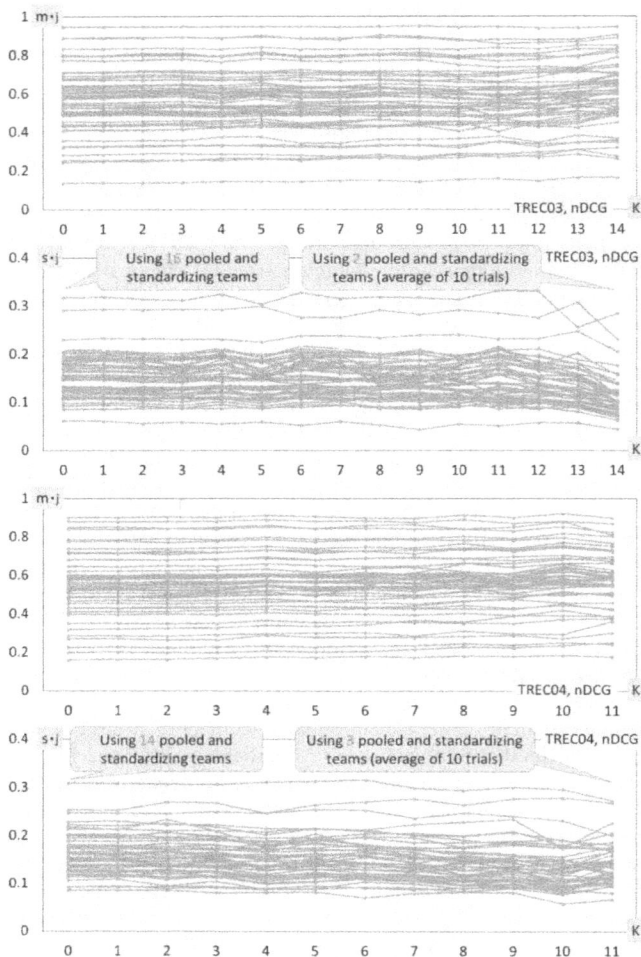

Figure 9: Effect of leave-K-out on $m_{\bullet j}, s_{\bullet j}$ for nDCG. Each curve represents a topic.

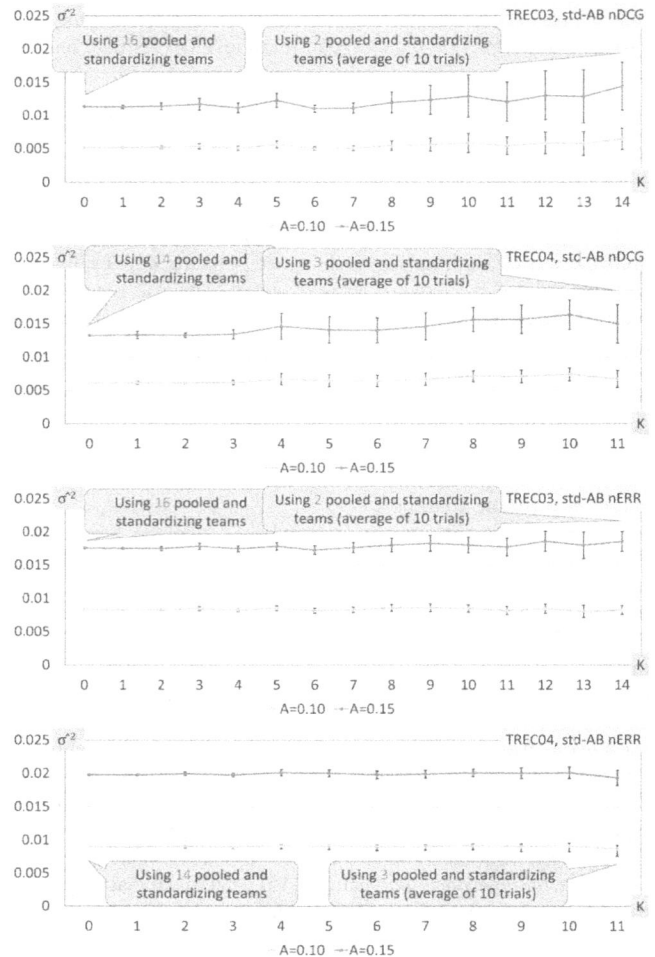

Figure 10: Effect of leave-K-out on $\hat{\sigma}^2$ for std-AB nDCG/nERR.

6. REFERENCES

[1] B. Carterette. Multiple testing in statistical analysis of systems-based information retrieval experiments. *ACM TOIS*, 30(1), 2012.

[2] G. Cormack and T. Lynam. TREC 2005 spam track overview. In *Proceedings of TREC 2005*, 2006.

[3] P. D. Ellis. *The Essential Guide to Effect Sizes*. Cambridge University Press, 2010.

[4] C. T. Lee, V. Vinay, E. M. Rodrigues, G. Kazai, N. Milić-Frayling, and A. Ignjatović. Measuring system performance and topic discernment using generalized adaptive-weight mean. pages 2033–2036, 2009.

[5] M. G. Lodico, D. T. Spaulding, and K. H. Voegtle. *Methods in Educational Research (Second Edition)*. Jossey-Bass, 2010.

[6] S. Mizzaro and S. Robertson. HITS hits TREC – exploring IR evaluation results with network analysis. In *Proceedings of ACM SIGIR 2007*, pages 479–486, 2007.

[7] S. Robertson. On GMAP – and other transformations. In *Proceedings of ACM CIKM 2006*, pages 78–83, 2006.

[8] T. Sakai. Evaluating evaluation metrics based on the bootstrap. In *Proceedings of ACM SIGIR 2006*, pages 525–532, 2006.

[9] T. Sakai. Metrics, statistics, tests. In *PROMISE Winter School 2013: Bridging between Information Retrieval and Databases (LNCS 8173)*, pages 116–163, 2014.

[10] T. Sakai. Topic set size design. *Information Retrieval*, 19(3):256–283, 2016.

[11] M. Sanderson and J. Zobel. Information retrieval system evaluation: Effort, sensitivity, and reliability. In *Proceedings of ACM SIGIR 2005*, pages 162–169, 2005.

[12] E. M. Voorhees. Overview of the TREC 2005 robust retrieval track. Technical report, NIST SP 500-266, 2006.

[13] E. M. Voorhees. Topic set size redux. In *Proceedings of ACM SIGIR 2009*, pages 806–807, 2009.

[14] E. M. Voorhees and C. Buckley. The effect of topic set size on retrieval experiment error. In *Proceedings of ACM SIGIR 2002*, pages 316–323, 2002.

[15] W. Webber, A. Moffat, and J. Zobel. Score standardization for inter-collection comparison of retrieval systems. In *Proceedings of ACM SIGIR 2008*, pages 51–58, 2008.

[16] J. Zobel. How reliable are the results of large-scale information retrieval experiments? In *Proceedings of ACM SIGIR 1998*, pages 307–314, 1998.

The Impact of Fixed-Cost Pooling Strategies
on Test Collection Bias

Aldo Lipani[1]   Guido Zuccon[2]   Mihai Lupu[1]   Bevan Koopman[3]   Allan Hanbury[1]

[1]Inst. of Software Technology & Interactive Systems, Vienna University of Technology, Vienna, Austria
{lipani, lupu, hanbury}@ifs.tuwien.ac.at

[2]Faculty of Science & Technology, Queensland University of Technology, Brisbane, Australia
g.zuccon@qut.edu.au

[3]Australian e-Health Research Centre, CSIRO, Brisbane, Australia
bevan.koopman@csiro.au

ABSTRACT

In Information Retrieval, test collections are usually built using the pooling method. Many pooling strategies have been developed for the pooling method. Herein, we address the question of identifying the best pooling strategy when evaluating systems using precision-oriented measures in presence of budget constraints on the number of documents to be evaluated. As a quality measurement we use the bias introduced by the pooling strategy, measured both in terms of Mean Absolute Error of the scores and in terms of ranking errors. Based on experiments on 15 test collections, we conclude that, for precision-oriented measures, the best strategies are based on Rank-Biased Precision (RBP). These results can inform collection builders because they suggest that, under fixed assessment budget constraints, RBP-based sampling produces less biased pools than other alternatives.

Keywords

Pooling Method, Pooling Strategies, Pool Bias

1. INTRODUCTION

Traditional evaluation of information retrieval systems relies on the idea of a controlled test collection, comprising of documents, information need statements synthesized into queries, and relevance assessments that capture the relevance relations between documents and information needs. Due to the large scale of modern test collections, it is infeasible to assess every document in the collection for relevance to a query. Instead, documents for which relevance assessments are required are selected from document rankings generated by systems for the queries in the test collection [6]. This method of selection of documents for relevance assessment is called *pooling*. The assumption behind pooling is that if a large enough variety of (good) systems contribute results for pooling and pools are sampled at large enough depths, then the pool should contain the almost totality of relevant documents and thus provide reliable evaluations.

ICTIR '16, September 12 - 16, 2016, Newark, DE, USA

© 2016 Copyright held by the owner/author(s). Publication rights licensed to ACM.
ISBN 978-1-4503-4497-5/16/09. . . $15.00

DOI: http://dx.doi.org/10.1145/2970398.2970429

Different pooling strategies exist that influence the number of documents that are required to be assessed, the type of measures that can be used to evaluate the systems, the bias of the collection towards specific systems or retrieval techniques and features and thus the reusability of the test collection to evaluate systems that did not contribute to the pool. A standard pooling strategy, called fixed-depth pooling, consists of using all documents retrieved by systems up to a cut-off depth k. Alternative pooling strategies extend the fixed-depth strategy by sampling documents from this pool to create smaller pools, or by combining sampled portions of document rankings (strata) to form stratified pools. Finally, more sophisticated pooling strategies have also been proposed. For example, in this paper we consider the strategies proposed by Moffat et al. [5], aimed at reducing the volume of required relevance assessments and based on RBP.

Pool size affects assessment budget, with larger pools involving larger costs. Under budget constraints, it is vital to limit the size of pools, without compromising the quality of the evaluation and the reusability of the collection. In fact, small pools may be affected by large bias and may render the collection unsuited to evaluate systems that did not participate in the pool. Previous work has investigated the influence of pooling bias on inferred measures and precision at fixed cut-off ($P@n$) when pooling with fixed-depth, uniform sampling, and stratified pooling strategies [7, 4]. Other work has examined alternative pooling methods and how to correct bias towards unpooled systems [1, 2, 3, 5, 8].

In this paper, we focus on controlling the balance between the cost of relevance assessments required by specific pooling strategies (and thus the pool size) and the bias introduced by different pooling strategies (and thus the reliability and reusability of the test collection). Specifically, we consider the setting where a fixed budget for relevance assessments has been given. We then empirically investigate which strategy among (a) a standard constrained pooling strategy and (b) Moffat et al.'s pooling strategies [5], would manifest a lower bias.

The results of our empirical investigation demonstrate that the least bias is obtained when we use information generated in the assessment process itself. This result is of interest for researchers building new test collections because it suggests that, under fixed budget constraint for relevance assessment, they should prefer RBP-based sampling over the alternatives investigated in this work because it returns pools with less bias towards specific systems.

2. BACKGROUND

In this section we introduce the pooling strategies analyzed in this paper. The first two are variations of the most common fixed-depth at k ($Depth@k$), already described in the introduction. The remaining three pooling strategies were developed by Moffat et al. [5]. First, let us fix the notations and the shared elements required among all of the following strategies, R_p is the set of runs to be pooled and N is the maximum number of documents to be judged.

We start with the variants of $Depth@k$. Despite its common use in practice, $Depth@k$ does not allow to impose a fixed number of documents to be judged. For this reason, we explore two possible variants, $Take@N$ and $Take+@K\&N$ that allows to fix such a constraint:

Take@N (strategy T): This strategy is the most commonly adopted in practice if a fixed pool size is required (e.g., due to budget constraints) and is based on the rank at which documents have been retrieved. It starts assigning to every retrieved document d the highest rank ρ to which d has been retrieved by R_p, then it continues taking the first N documents with the highest ρ and pools them. The main drawback of this strategy with respect to $Depth@k$ is that it does not guarantee fairness among all the pooled runs. In $Depth@k$ all the runs contribute equally to the pool with their first k documents, here some runs can get more judged documents than others.

Take+@K&N (strategy $T+$): This strategy aims to address the lack of fairness of the previous strategy by introducing a non-deterministic selection of the documents to be judged. It may be thought of as an application of the *Stratified* pooling strategy [9]. The *Stratified* strategy defines multiple strata, each characterized by a depth and a sample rate. Each document is assigned to a stratum based on the rank at which it has been retrieved first, then sampled based on the sample rate of the stratum. By definition, this strategy guarantees fairness because it forces a constant number of pooled documents per run. The $Take+@K\&N$ strategy defines a stratification of two strata, where K is its maximum depth. For the first stratum we fix a sample rate $r_1 = 1.0$ and depth k_1 as deep as the number of documents to be judged does not overcome the imposed limit of N judgments. If we call N^{k_1} and N^K the estimated pooled documents for a $Depth@k$ strategy at depth k_1 and K, the second stratum is characterized by $k_2 = K - k_1$ and sample rate $r_2 = (N - N^{k_1})/(N^K - N^{k_1})$, which makes the stratification able to reach, in expectation, N, the number of documents to be judged.

In the above strategies, documents that have been retrieved on top by at least one run are more likely to be pooled, but no distinction is made if a document has been retrieved by multiple runs or just by one. If we were to apply this last distinction as a mere pooling strategy we would count how many runs have retrieved a certain document, and pool the most retrieved ones. Such a strategy would have the effect of over-emphasizing the importance of highly retrieved documents with respect to the uniquely retrieved ones, thereby rewarding conformity and creating collections with the strongest pool bias possible due to the systematic avoidance of documents that have been uniquely retrieved by a single run. But if this distinction is combined with information about the rank at which the documents were retrieved, as pointed out by Moffat et al. [5], it may lead to pooling strategies that are more effective in selecting documents to pool, because it would select documents that provide more benefit to the final result.

Before describing the three variants of this strategy, let us review some terminology. Moffat et al. [5] defined *base* RBP as the RBP calculated on the assumption that unjudged documents are non-relevant. It is a lower threshold to the real RBP value which would have been obtained had all documents been judged. For instance, if RBP is defined as:

$$RBP = (1 - p) \sum_{i=1} u_i \cdot p^{i-1} \qquad (1)$$

where $u_i \in [0,1] \cup \{?\}$ denotes the relevance judgment of the document at position i (taking values between 0 and 1 if judged and ? if unjudged) and $p \in\,]0, 1[$ is a constant, then the *base* RBP is:

$$b_r = (1 - p) \sum_{i:u_i \neq ?} u_i \cdot p^{i-1} \qquad (2)$$

As a complement, the paper also defined *residual* RBP as:

$$e_r = (1 - p) \sum_{i:u_i = ?} p^{i-1} \qquad (3)$$

For a run r, $b_r + e_r$ is therefore the maximum RBP value that could be obtained by that run (i.e., if all unjudged documents are actually relevant). Given these definitions, the following pooling strategies can be formalized:

RBPBasedA@N&p (strategy A): To every retrieved d in every pooled run $r \in R_p$ is associated a score equal to the RBP residual, in Eq. (4), which is a function of the rank ρ to which d has been retrieved in r and a parameter p, fixed in advance:

$$c_{r,d} = (1 - p)p^{\rho(r,d)-1} \qquad (4)$$

Then, a weight is assigned to every retrieved d, which is calculated by summing up all the scores obtained in the pooled runs R_p, as follows:

$$w_d = \sum_{r \in R_p} c_{r,d} \qquad (5)$$

Finally, the first N documents with highest weight are included in the pool. This strategy rewards documents that have been retrieved by multiple runs at high ranks, but it has the drawback of leaving runs' residuals free (unconstrained), which may be undesirable.

RBPBasedB@N&p (strategy B): Like strategy A, but the weighting function is calculated by multiplying the RBP gain-based score with the current residual of r from which d comes:

$$w_d = \sum_{r \in R_p} c_{r,d} \cdot e_r \qquad (6)$$

This pooling strategy, with respect to the others, adapts the weights w_d at every pooled document, due to the inclusion in the weighing schema of the residuals, which are in function of the current set of judged documents. This strategy is characterized by N sequential re-weighting stages in which at each stage the document with the highest w_d is pooled. It is worth mentioning that the re-weighting is independent of the actual judgment of the document.

RBPBasedC@N&p (strategy C): Like strategy B, but the weighting function is calculated taking into account also the current RBP score of the run r:

$$w_d = \sum_{r \in R_p} c_{r,d} \cdot e_r \cdot (b_r + e_r/2)^3 \qquad (7)$$

This strategy rewards the runs that have retrieved more relevant documents.

Note that pooling strategies B and C are adaptive, in that they select the next document to pool according to the relevance assessments done up to that point.

3. EXPERIMENTS & RESULTS

To determine which of the examined pooling strategies produces a test collection with lower bias we use a set of 15 test collections selected from TREC: 7 test collections from the Ad-Hoc track, 3 from the Web track, and 5 from more domain specific IR tracks: Genomics, Robust, Legal, Medical and Microblog. Each collection was created using a *Depth@k* pooling strategy; this allows us to create synthetic pools with the pooling strategies examined here. In particular this is done for the only pooled runs $R_p \subseteq R$ of the test collections, for which the pooling strategy guarantees the complete judgment of the first k documents. To measure the bias that a new run would have observed if it had not been part of the construction of the pool, we simulate its absence performing a leave-one-organization-out approach for which at each iteration a new synthetic pool is generated excluding all the runs submitted by the organization for which the selected run belongs to. The bias measures used, as in a previous study [3, 4], are: 1) Mean Absolute Error (MAE), 2) System Rank Error (SRE), and 3) System Rank Error with Statistical Significance (SRE*). MAE is the mean, over all the runs, of the absolute difference between the score of a run when it is and is not part of the pool. SRE is the sum, over all the runs, of the difference in ranks between the run when it is and is not part of the pool. SRE* is like SRE, but the difference is counted only if the runs in between are statistically different (Tukey's test, $p < 0.05$).

Herein, we experiment with a real case study where we have a budget that allows the collection builder to judge a maximum of 10,000 documents (N). We also assume that the measures targeted by the evaluation task are $P@10$ and RBP with $p = 0.80$ (this is a common setting for p). We test all the pooling strategies with fixed $N = 10,000$. For strategy $T+$, we fixed K to 20. For strategies A, B and C, two instantiations of p have been tested, $p = 0.80$ (in line with the setting for the RBP evaluation measure), indicated by A^{80}, B^{80} and C^{80} in Tab. 1 and $p = 0.73$, indicated by A^{73}, B^{73} and C^{73} in Tab. 1 (this value was found to correlate best with observed user behavior, see Zhang et al. [10]).

4. DISCUSSION & CONCLUSION

In Tab. 1 we observe that the best performing pooling strategy is $RBPBasedC@N\&p$ with $p = 0.80$ (C^{80}), which sometimes matches the performance of the same strategy but with $p = 0.73$ (C^{73}). This is an expected result since this strategy uses the most information. However, although this is the best performing strategy, it presents several limitations when used for building test collections in practice:

1. If the test collection builders require that relevance labels for a document are aggregated across judgements from

multiple assessors, then the use of this pooling strategy puts an additional burden on the collection builders. This is because the strategy requires information about the relevance of documents already assessed to decide which documents to pool next (i.e., the strategy is adaptive). This in turns requires that the assessment process is co-ordinated such that the selection and assessment of the next document to assess cannot start until all assessors have judged the current document: this may happen at different times due to different assessor cognitive abilities, workload, and work scheduling.

2. A per-topic parallelization of the assessment exercise is not possible (i.e., the practice of distributing documents that are retrieved for the same topic across multiple assessors to speed up assessment). However, this limitation could be potentially mitigated, to a certain extent, by parallelizing the process across topics (i.e., exclusively assign each topic to an assessor, but assigning different topics to different assessors).

3. The third limitation is introduced by the impossibility of randomizing the pooled documents in order to mitigate assessment bias coming from the judgment of documents in order of their predicted relevance. This bias is usually overcome by the standard pooling strategies by randomizing the pooled documents before presenting them to the assessors.

These limitations make the $RBPBasedC@N\&p$ strategy of difficult practical application.

The second best strategy is $RBPBasedA@N\&p$ (A^{80}) with $p = 0.80$. This strategy does not present the previous limitations since all the documents to be assessed are pooled with no required human intervention. The peculiarity of this strategy is that it rewards documents that have been retrieved by multiple runs at high ranks, yet it does minimize pool bias.

In summary, this paper examined a number of strategies aimed at selecting documents for relevance assessment under fixed budget constraints while minimizing pool bias. The empirical results demonstrate that variants A and C of Moffat et al.'s strategies [5], a static and an adaptive strategy based on RBP, should be preferred over traditional fixed-depth or stratified pooling when deciding upon the pooling strategy to be used to form a new test collection under fixed assessment budget constraints. However, due to the limitations introduced by the strategy C, we recommend in practice the strategy A.

The software used to create and analyze the pooling strategies examined in this paper are made available on the website of the first author.

Acknowledgments

This research was partly supported by the Austrian Science Fund (FWF) project number P25905-N23 (ADmIRE).

5. REFERENCES

[1] B. Carterette, J. Allan, and R. Sitaraman. Minimal test collections for retrieval evaluation. In *Proc. of SIGIR*, 2006.

[2] G. V. Cormack, C. R. Palmer, and C. L. Clarke. Efficient construction of large test collections. In *Proc. of SIGIR*, 1998.

Table 1: Results obtained using only the pooled runs (R_p) of each test collection (C). Pool bias measures, MAE, SRE and SRE* (the lower the values, the better; bold values are the best for the test collection), computed on five pooling strategies (S) via leave-one-organization-out. $|R|$ total number of run of the test collection; $|O|$ number of organizations; k depth of the original pool; $|T|$ number of topics; Q number of judged documents; $|Q^r|$ number of documents judged relevant; $|Q_n^r|$ number of documents judged relevant for the synthetic pool, and; $|Q_n^?|$ number of documents non-judged for the synthetic pool.

C	Stats	S	$|Q_n^r|$	$|Q_n^?|$	P@10 MAE	SRE	SRE*	RBP ($p=0.80$) MAE	SRE	SRE*
Ad Hoc 2	$|R|{:}38$ $|O|{:}22$ $|R_p|{:}30$ $k{:}100$ $|T|{:}50$ $|Q^r|{:}11645$ $|Q|{:}62620$	T	3627	0	0.0422	106	9	0.0441	113	5
		T+	3523	0	0.0436	104	10	0.0447	99	7
		A^{80}	3651	0	0.0398	103	8	0.0410	105	5
		B^{80}	3626	0	0.0418	106	9	0.0436	113	5
		C^{80}	**3818**	0	**0.0392**	**100**	**8**	**0.0401**	**97**	**4**
		A^{73}	3641	0	0.0407	106	9	0.0424	108	5
		B^{73}	3628	0	0.0422	106	9	0.0441	115	5
		C^{73}	3788	0	0.0398	103	8	0.0415	109	4
Ad Hoc 3	$|R|{:}40$ $|O|{:}22$ $|R_p|{:}21$ $k{:}200$ $|T|{:}50$ $|Q^r|{:}9805$ $|Q|{:}97319$	T	2946	0	0.0234	20	0	0.0258	22	0
		T+	2520	0	0.0301	25	1	0.0331	26	0
		A^{80}	2971	0	0.0226	19	0	0.0250	21	0
		B^{80}	2931	0	0.0229	20	0	0.0254	21	0
		C^{80}	**3143**	0	**0.0199**	**15**	0	**0.0225**	**17**	0
		A^{73}	2963	0	0.0228	19	0	0.0251	21	0
		B^{73}	2939	0	0.0232	21	0	0.0258	22	0
		C^{73}	3128	0	0.0206	17	0	0.0230	17	0
Ad Hoc 4	$|R|{:}33$ $|O|{:}19$ $|R_p|{:}24$ $k{:}60$ $|T|{:}50$ $|Q^r|{:}6503$ $|Q|{:}87069$	T	1954	0	0.0361	68	2	0.0373	68	3
		T+	1921	0	0.0355	62	1	0.0371	60	3
		A^{80}	1979	0	0.0342	65	2	0.0354	62	2
		B^{80}	1946	0	0.0357	66	2	0.0369	66	3
		C^{80}	**2224**	0	**0.0287**	**54**	**0**	**0.0293**	**52**	**0**
		A^{73}	1970	0	0.0347	66	2	0.0359	64	3
		B^{73}	1946	0	0.0357	67	2	0.0371	66	3
		C^{73}	2199	0	0.0289	54	0	0.0298	52	0
Ad Hoc 5	$|R|{:}61$ $|O|{:}21$ $|R_p|{:}53$ $k{:}100$ $|T|{:}50$ $|Q^r|{:}5524$ $|Q|{:}133681$	T	1482	0	0.0234	154	21	0.0242	167	21
		T+	1495	0	0.0239	161	20	0.0248	175	23
		A^{80}	1532	0	0.0217	148	14	0.0224	154	16
		B^{80}	1468	0	0.0231	156	16	0.0235	157	17
		C^{80}	**1762**	0	**0.0189**	**122**	**3**	**0.0198**	**132**	**6**
		A^{73}	1506	0	0.0220	146	15	0.0227	154	16
		B^{73}	1479	0	0.0236	158	16	0.0241	165	19
		C^{73}	1736	0	0.0192	124	4	0.0200	137	7
Ad Hoc 6	$|R|{:}74$ $|O|{:}29$ $|R_p|{:}25$ $k{:}100$ $|T|{:}50$ $|Q^r|{:}4611$ $|Q|{:}72270$	T	1544	0	0.0304	35	2	0.0312	37	2
		T+	1605	0	0.0289	35	2	0.0290	30	0
		A^{80}	1561	0	0.0294	34	1	0.0302	35	0
		B^{80}	1532	0	0.0301	35	2	0.0309	37	2
		C^{80}	**1762**	0	**0.0254**	**29**	1	**0.0258**	**23**	0
		A^{73}	1553	0	0.0296	35	2	0.0305	35	0
		B^{73}	1538	0	0.0306	35	2	0.0315	38	2
		C^{73}	1739	0	0.0258	29	1	0.0264	25	0
Ad Hoc 7	$|R|{:}103$ $|O|{:}42$ $|R_p|{:}63$ $k{:}100$ $|T|{:}50$ $|Q^r|{:}4674$ $|Q|{:}80344$	T	1697	0	0.0149	132	25	0.0160	114	15
		T+	1694	0	0.0141	129	25	0.0149	104	15
		A^{80}	1728	0	0.0133	105	12	0.0142	86	10
		B^{80}	1682	0	0.0151	132	25	0.0162	115	15
		C^{80}	**1921**	0	**0.0116**	**92**	12	**0.0123**	**74**	**7**
		A^{73}	1719	0	0.0136	107	13	0.0147	88	10
		B^{73}	1682	0	0.0149	131	25	0.0160	111	15
		C^{73}	1900	0	0.0123	94	12	0.0129	81	7
Ad Hoc 8	$|R|{:}129$ $|O|{:}41$ $|R_p|{:}66$ $k{:}100$ $|T|{:}50$ $|Q^r|{:}4728$ $|Q|{:}86830$	T	1566	0	0.0199	130	20	0.0201	142	15
		T+	1611	0	0.0191	117	19	0.0190	125	11
		A^{80}	1653	0	0.0168	101	15	0.0168	106	12
		B^{80}	1559	0	0.0193	121	17	0.0194	135	15
		C^{80}	**1874**	0	**0.0148**	**80**	**8**	**0.0146**	**80**	**6**
		A^{73}	1619	0	0.0178	107	17	0.0178	122	14
		B^{73}	1559	0	0.0200	131	19	0.0202	142	15
		C^{73}	1850	0	0.0152	79	8	0.0152	84	6
Web 9	$|R|{:}104$ $|O|{:}23$ $|R_p|{:}39$ $k{:}100$ $|T|{:}50$ $|Q^r|{:}2617$ $|Q|{:}70070$	T	912	0	0.0136	74	0	0.0145	78	0
		T+	953	0	0.0127	71	0	0.0135	79	0
		A^{80}	942	0	0.0134	75	0	0.0141	80	0
		B^{80}	916	0	0.0137	74	0	0.0146	80	0
		C^{80}	**1062**	0	**0.0105**	**54**	0	**0.0112**	**67**	0
		A^{73}	932	0	0.0132	73	0	0.0139	77	0
		B^{73}	919	0	0.0136	75	0	0.0147	80	0
		C^{73}	1048	0	0.0106	55	0	0.0115	69	0

C	Stats	S	$|Q_n^r|$	$|Q_n^?|$	P@10 MAE	SRE	SRE*	RBP ($p=0.80$) MAE	SRE	SRE*
Web 2001	$|R|{:}97$ $|O|{:}29$ $|R_p|{:}35$ $k{:}100$ $|T|{:}50$ $|Q^r|{:}3363$ $|Q|{:}70400$	T	1272	0	0.0111	43	0	0.0125	67	0
		T+	1221	0	0.0105	43	0	0.0118	63	0
		A^{80}	1286	0	0.0100	40	0	0.0112	55	0
		B^{80}	1260	0	0.0109	42	0	0.0121	62	0
		C^{80}	**1383**	0	**0.0087**	**33**	0	**0.0097**	**49**	0
		A^{73}	1280	0	0.0100	39	0	0.0114	59	0
		B^{73}	1260	0	0.0112	43	0	0.0125	65	0
		C^{73}	1370	0	0.0088	35	0	0.0099	52	0
Web 2002	$|R|{:}69$ $|O|{:}16$ $|R_p|{:}60$ $k{:}50$ $|T|{:}50$ $|Q^r|{:}1574$ $|Q|{:}56650$	T	588	0	0.0185	296	0	0.0195	330	0
		T+	580	0	0.0184	297	0	0.0196	326	0
		A^{80}	626	0	0.0170	264	0	0.0179	297	0
		B^{80}	600	0	0.0184	292	0	0.0194	326	0
		C^{80}	645	0	**0.0159**	**253**	0	**0.0165**	**279**	0
		A^{73}	618	0	0.0179	284	0	0.0188	314	0
		B^{73}	595	0	0.0185	292	0	0.0195	329	0
		C^{73}	**649**	0	0.0161	255	0	0.0169	288	0
Genomics 2005	$|R|{:}62$ $|O|{:}32$ $|R_p|{:}46$ $k{:}60$ $|T|{:}49$ $|Q^r|{:}4584$ $|Q|{:}39958$	T	1905	0	0.0218	265	0	0.0236	326	2
		T+	1919	0	0.0193	**230**	0	0.0215	308	3
		A^{80}	1924	0	0.0203	244	0	0.0219	304	2
		B^{80}	1894	0	0.0215	260	0	0.0229	314	2
		C^{80}	**2046**	0	0.0193	239	0	**0.0206**	298	2
		A^{73}	1912	0	0.0209	254	0	0.0225	309	2
		B^{73}	1898	0	0.0217	264	0	0.0232	321	2
		C^{73}	2029	0	**0.0192**	239	0	0.0208	300	2
Robust 2005	$|R|{:}74$ $|O|{:}21$ $|R_p|{:}18$ $k{:}55$ $|T|{:}50$ $|Q^r|{:}6561$ $|Q|{:}37798$	T	2624	0	0.0422	35	11	0.0446	35	10
		T+	2325	0	0.0488	43	13	0.0511	43	13
		A^{80}	2644	0	0.0408	32	11	0.0430	34	10
		B^{80}	2607	0	0.0423	35	11	0.0446	37	10
		C^{80}	**3033**	0	**0.0358**	**28**	10	**0.0374**	31	10
		A^{73}	2639	0	0.0418	35	11	0.0440	35	10
		B^{73}	2611	0	0.0424	35	11	0.0448	36	10
		C^{73}	3002	0	0.0360	29	10	0.0376	**31**	10
Legal 2006	$|R|{:}34$ $|O|{:}8$ $|R_p|{:}11$ $k{:}10$ $|T|{:}39$ $|Q^r|{:}4323$ $|Q|{:}31739$	T	539	7181	0.0794	53	6	0.0947	59	8
		T+	539	2650	0.1032	63	13	0.1227	77	26
		A^{80}	539	7181	0.0789	51	5	0.0936	59	8
		B^{80}	539	7181	0.0792	52	6	0.0945	59	8
		C^{80}	539	7181	**0.0742**	**47**	**3**	**0.0876**	**55**	**6**
		A^{73}	539	7181	0.0792	51	5	0.0944	59	8
		B^{73}	539	7181	0.0792	52	6	0.0945	59	8
		C^{73}	539	7181	0.0744	47	3	0.0879	55	6
Medical 2011	$|R|{:}127$ $|O|{:}29$ $|R_p|{:}46$ $k{:}10$ $|T|{:}34$ $|Q^r|{:}1765$ $|Q|{:}8865$	T	**1443**	4909	0.0193	100	0	0.0258	126	**0**
		T+	**1443**	4019	0.0219	107	0	0.0293	137	2
		A^{80}	**1443**	4909	0.0186	97	0	0.0248	116	**0**
		B^{80}	**1443**	4909	0.0194	101	0	0.0258	126	**0**
		C^{80}	1442	4942	**0.0157**	**86**	0	**0.0202**	**92**	**0**
		A^{73}	**1443**	4909	0.0190	99	0	0.0251	118	**0**
		B^{73}	**1443**	4909	0.0197	102	0	0.0262	129	**0**
		C^{73}	1441	4941	0.0163	90	0	0.0214	97	**0**
Microblog 2011	$|R|{:}184$ $|O|{:}58$ $|R_p|{:}49$ $k{:}30$ $|T|{:}49$ $|Q^r|{:}2965$ $|Q|{:}60129$	T	1760	42	0.0179	100	0	0.0181	109	29
		T+	1707	15	0.0174	91	0	0.0179	100	26
		A^{80}	1790	47	0.0159	89	0	0.0164	96	26
		B^{80}	1767	44	0.0179	102	0	0.0184	109	29
		C^{80}	**1912**	114	**0.0132**	**68**	0	**0.0137**	**75**	**18**
		A^{73}	1788	44	0.0168	94	0	0.0171	106	29
		B^{73}	1756	42	0.0181	102	0	0.0184	109	29
		C^{73}	1887	95	0.0138	71	0	0.0142	77	20

[3] A. Lipani, M. Lupu, and A. Hanbury. Splitting water: Precision and anti-precision to reduce pool bias. In *Proc. of SIGIR*, 2015.

[4] A. Lipani, M. Lupu, and A. Hanbury. The curious incidence of bias corrections in the pool. In *Proc. of ECIR*, 2016.

[5] A. Moffat, W. Webber, and J. Zobel. Strategic system comparisons via targeted relevance judgments. In *Proc. of SIGIR*, 2007.

[6] K. Spärck Jones and C. J. van Rijsbergen. Report on the need for and provision of an "ideal" information retrieval test collection. *British Library Research and Development Report No. 5266*, 1975.

[7] E. M. Voorhees. The effect of sampling strategy on inferred measures. In *Proc. of SIGIR*, 2014.

[8] W. Webber and L. A. Park. Score adjustment for correction of pooling bias. In *Proc. of SIGIR*, 2009.

[9] E. Yilmaz, E. Kanoulas, and J. A. Aslam. A simple and efficient sampling method for estimating AP and NDCG. In *Proc. of SIGIR*, 2008.

[10] Y. Zhang, L. A. F. Park, and A. Moffat. Click-based evidence for decaying weight distributions in search effectiveness metrics. *Information Retrieval*, 2009.

Unbiased Comparative Evaluation of Ranking Functions

Tobias Schnabel
Cornell University, Ithaca, NY
tbs49@cornell.edu

Adith Swaminathan
Cornell University, Ithaca, NY
adith@cs.cornell.edu

Peter I. Frazier
Cornell University, Ithaca, NY
pf98@cornell.edu

Thorsten Joachims
Cornell University, Ithaca, NY
tj@cs.cornell.edu

ABSTRACT

Eliciting relevance judgments for ranking evaluation is labor-intensive and costly, motivating careful selection of which documents to judge. Unlike traditional approaches that make this selection deterministically, probabilistic sampling enables the design of estimators that are provably unbiased even when reusing data with missing judgments. In this paper, we first unify and extend these sampling approaches by viewing the evaluation problem as a Monte Carlo estimation task that applies to a large number of common IR metrics. Drawing on the theoretical clarity that this view offers, we tackle three practical evaluation scenarios: comparing two systems, comparing k systems against a baseline, and ranking k systems. For each scenario, we derive an estimator and a variance-optimizing sampling distribution while retaining the strengths of sampling-based evaluation, including unbiasedness, reusability despite missing data, and ease of use in practice. In addition to the theoretical contribution, we empirically evaluate our methods against previously used sampling heuristics and find that they often cut the number of required relevance judgments at least in half.

CCS Concepts

•Information systems → Test collections; Relevance assessment;

Keywords

Importance Sampling, Evaluation, Crowd Sourcing, Pooling

1. INTRODUCTION

Offline evaluation of retrieval systems requires annotated test collections that take substantial effort and cost to amass. The most significant cost lies in eliciting relevance judgments for query-document pairs, and the size of realistic test collections makes it infeasible to annotate every query-document pair in the corpus. This has spurred research on intelligently choosing the subset of pairs to judge. Analogous annotation

ICTIR '16, September 12 - 16, 2016, Newark, DE, USA

© 2016 Copyright held by the owner/author(s). Publication rights licensed to ACM.
ISBN 978-1-4503-4497-5/16/09. . . $15.00

DOI: http://dx.doi.org/10.1145/2970398.2970410

problems also exist in other domains, like machine translation or sequence tagging in natural language processing. Moreover, with the advent of crowd-sourced annotations for applications like image recognition and protein sequencing, the problem of judgment elicitation has become even more relevant.

Unfortunately, if not the whole corpus is judged, the missing judgments may bias the performance estimates. There are two broad approaches to addressing this problem. The first develops new evaluation measures that are robust to incompletely judged test collections [21]. For such measures, heuristics like pooling can then be employed effectively, but the evaluation measure may not precisely capture the notion of quality one requires. The other approach is to leave the design of the evaluation measure as unrestricted as possible, but instead design general evaluation methodologies and estimators that guarantee unbiased estimates even under missing data [2, 27, 18, 28]. We follow this second approach, specifically focusing on sampling approaches that possess the following desirable properties:

1. Unbiasedness. On average, estimates have no systematic error, and behave like we had judged all query-document pairs.

2. Reusability. Collecting judgments is labor-intensive and costly, and sampling-based approaches allow reuse of past data without introducing bias.

3. Statelessness. We often need to collect tens of thousands of judgments. Sampling is embarrassingly parallel and can be done in a single batch.

4. Sample Efficiency. Sampling distributions can be designed to optimize the number of judgments needed to confidently and accurately estimate a metric.

In this paper, we focus on three comparative evaluation scenarios that frequently arise in practice, and derive new estimators and principled sampling strategies that substantially improve sample efficiency while retaining the other desirable properties of sampling-based evaluation. In particular, we investigate the problem of estimating the performance difference between two systems, the problem of estimating k systems' performance relative to a baseline, and the problem of estimating a ranking of k systems. For all three scenarios, we propose importance-weighted estimators and their variance-optimizing sampling distributions, enabling the estimators to elicit relative performance differences much more efficiently than previous sampling approaches. We show that these estimators apply to any linearly decomposable performance metric (e.g., DCG, Precision@k), and that they are unbiased even with missing judgments. In addition to these theoretical arguments, empirical results show that our estimators and samplers can substantially reduce the number of required judgments compared to previously used sampling heuristics, making them a practical and effective alternative to pooling and heuristic sampling methods. Beyond these specific contributions, the paper more generally contributes a unified treatment of all prior sampling approaches in terms of Monte Carlo estimation and its theory, providing a rigorous basis for future research.

2. RELATED WORK

The Cranfield methodology [7] using pooling [24] is the most established approach to IR evaluation. Pooling aims to be fair to all submitted systems by exhaustively judging the top-ranked document from all systems, hoping for good coverage of all relevant documents for a query (implicitly through diversity in the submitted runs). However, pooling bias is a well known problem when re-using these pooled collections to evaluate novel systems that retrieve relevant but unjudged documents [31] – see [22] and the references therein for a detailed overview. Attempts have been made to correct this pooling bias, either using a small set of exhaustively judged queries [26] or using sample corrections that apply for MAE and Precision@k [4, 13].

Generally, however, the size of today's corpora has prevented complete judging of test collections, and this has driven research on evaluation strategies that are robust to missing judgments [6]. One approach to handling incomplete judgments is to define an IR metric that is robust to missing judgments, like Bpref [3], RankEff [1] and Rank-Biased Precision [16]. Sakai and Kando [21] provide an excellent review of these approaches. Another approach, and the one we build on in this paper, uses random sampling of ranked documents to construct a collection of judgments [8, 2, 27, 18, 28]. We unify all these sampling approaches by viewing them as Monte Carlo estimates of IR metrics and extend them to relative comparisons.

The idea of relative comparisons rather than absolute evaluation of IR measures has been studied before. Deterministic elicitation schemes have been proposed for differentiating two systems based on AP [5], and to rank multiple systems according to Rank-Biased Precision [15]. More recently, multi-armed bandit approaches have been studied to construct judgment pools [14]. These schemes suffer from the same bias that plagues pooling when comparing new systems. We extend the provably unbiased sampling approaches to these comparative scenarios, inheriting the improved sample efficiency of relative comparisons while yielding re-usable test collections. We anticipate future work that combines the simplicity of batch sampling with the sample efficiency of active learning and bandit algorithms to adaptively elicit judgments.

We note that the sampling approach we take here naturally incorporates noisy judgments, making it suitable for many tasks involving crowd-sourcing. Existing works have heuristically resolved noisy judgments as a pre-processing step before constructing the test collection [10, 19].

Ideas from Monte Carlo estimation and importance sampling [17] have been successfully applied in closely related problems like unbiased recommender evaluation [23, 12], although in those applications, the sampling distribution is typically not under the experimenter's control. Finally, a related problem to the judgment elicitation problem we study here is that of picking the most informative set of queries [9]. Our Monte Carlo formulation can offer a reasonable starting point to answer this question as well.

3. SAMPLING BASED EVALUATION

To support our novel sampling approaches to comparative evaluation, described in the following three sections, we first lay out a unified framework of Monte Carlo estimation for sampling-based evaluation of a single system, unifying existing IR work [2, 27, 18, 28] with the extensive literature and theory in Monte Carlo estimation.

3.1 Illustrative Example

Consider a retrieval system S that maps each input query x to a ranking $S(x)$. Given a set of $|X|$ queries X, we would like to estimate the average Discounted Cumulative Gain (DCG) with depth cut-off 100 of S on X,

$$
\begin{aligned}
DCG@100(S) &= \frac{1}{|X|} \sum_{x \in \mathcal{X}} \sum_{r=1}^{100} \frac{\text{rel}(x, S(x)_r)}{\log(1+r)} \\
&= \sum_{(x,r)} \frac{\text{rel}(x, S(x)_r)}{|X| \cdot \log(1+r)} \\
&= \sum_{(x,r)} V(x, r).
\end{aligned}
$$

$S(x)_r$ is the document at rank r in the ranking of S for query x, and $\text{rel}(\cdot)$ denotes its assessed relevance. The key insight behind sampling-based evaluation is the following: we do not need to know all summands $V(x, r)$ in this large sum to get a good estimate of $DCG@100(S)$. In particular, even if we just uniformly at random sample n query-document pairs $D = ((x_1, r_1), ..., (x_n, r_n))$ and elicit the value of $V(x, r)$ for those, the following average is a reasonable estimate of $DCG@100(S)$ even when $n < 100 \cdot |X|$.

$$
DCG@100(S) \approx \frac{100 \cdot |X|}{n} \sum_{(x_i, r_i) \in D} V(x_i, r_i).
$$

But what are the quality guarantees we can give for such estimates? Is uniform sampling the best we can do? What about other performance measures? And what about statistical testing and comparisons of multiple systems? To address these questions, we now formalize sampling-based evaluation in the framework of Monte Carlo estimation.

3.2 Formalizing Evaluation

A ranking system $S(x)$ (e.g. search engine, recommendation system) maps an input $x \in \mathcal{X}$ (e.g. query, user context) to a ranking y. Each predicted ranking $y = S(x)$ has a certain utility $U(x, y)$ for a given x which quantifies the quality of ranking y for x. To aggregate quality over multiple (x, y) pairs, virtually all evaluation approaches use the expected utility over the distribution $P(x)$ as a summary of the overall quality of a system.

$$
U(S) = \mathbb{E}_{P(x)}[U(x, y)] = \int U(x, y) d\, P(x),
$$

Most often though, we wish to evaluate *multiple* systems, i.e., we have a number of systems $\mathcal{S} = \{S_1, \ldots S_k\}$ which

Metric	$u(\boldsymbol{x}, y)$	$\lambda(y \mid \boldsymbol{y})$
Prec@k	$\mathrm{rel}(\boldsymbol{x}, y) \in \{0, 1\}$	$\mathbf{1}_{\mathrm{rank}(y) \leq k}/k$
DCG	$\mathrm{rel}(\boldsymbol{x}, y) \in [0, M]$	$1/\log(1 + \mathrm{rank}(y))$
Gain@k	$\mathrm{rel}(\boldsymbol{x}, y) \in [0, M]$	$\mathbf{1}_{\mathrm{rank}(y) \leq k}/k$
MAE	$\|\mathrm{error}(\boldsymbol{x}, y)\| \in [0, M]$	$1/\|\boldsymbol{y}\|$
MSE	$(\mathrm{error}(\boldsymbol{x}, y))^2 \in [0, M]$	$1/\|\boldsymbol{y}\|$
RBP-p [16]	$\mathrm{rel}(\boldsymbol{x}, y) \in \{0, 1\}$	$(1 - p)/p^{\mathrm{rank}(y)}$
#ofSwaps	$\mathrm{swapped}(\boldsymbol{x}, y) \in \{0, 1\}$	$1/\|\boldsymbol{y}\|$
wSwaps	$\mathrm{swapped}(\boldsymbol{x}, y) \in \{0, 1\}$	$1/(\|\boldsymbol{y}\| \cdot \mathrm{rank}(\tilde{y}_1)$ $\cdot \mathrm{rank}(\tilde{y}_2))$
AP	$\mathrm{rel}(\boldsymbol{x}, \tilde{y}_1) \cdot \mathrm{rel}(\boldsymbol{x}, \tilde{y}_2)$ $\in \{0, 1\}$	$\mathbf{1}_{\mathrm{rank}(\tilde{y}_2) \leq \mathrm{rank}(\tilde{y}_1)}$ $/(R \cdot \mathrm{rank}(\tilde{y}_1))$

Table 1: **A selection of popular metrics that can be written as expectations over single item judgments (top) or pairwise judgments (bottom).** $R = \sum_{\tilde{y}} \mathrm{rel}(x, \tilde{y})$.

we wish to evaluate on a distribution of inputs $\mathrm{P}(\boldsymbol{x})$. Taking web-search as an example, $\mathcal{S}$ would be a collection of retrieval systems, $\mathrm{P}(\boldsymbol{x})$ the distribution of queries, and the utility of a ranking $U(\boldsymbol{x}, \boldsymbol{y})$ would be measured by some IR metric like Precision@10. We will now discuss how to obtain values of $U(\boldsymbol{x}, \boldsymbol{y})$.

3.3 Linearly Decomposable Metrics

Since assessing the utility $U(\boldsymbol{x}, \boldsymbol{y})$ of an entire ranking $\boldsymbol{y}$ is difficult for human assessors, it is typically aggregated from the utilities of the individual documents it contains. Formally, we assume U decomposes as a sum of the utilities of the parts

$$U(\boldsymbol{x}, \boldsymbol{y}) = \sum_{y \in \boldsymbol{y}} \lambda(y \mid \boldsymbol{y}) \, u(\boldsymbol{x}, y). \tag{1}$$

The weights $\lambda(y \mid \boldsymbol{y}) \geq 0$ with which the utility of each document y of ranking $\boldsymbol{y}$ enters the overall utility is defined by the particular performance measure. The utilities $u(\boldsymbol{x}, y) \in \mathbb{R}^+$ refer to the individual utilities of each part y in $\boldsymbol{y}$. Taking Precision@k as an example, $u(\boldsymbol{x}, y) = \mathrm{rel}(\boldsymbol{x}, y) \in \{0, 1\}$ denotes binary relevance of document $\boldsymbol{y}$ for query $\boldsymbol{x}$, and the weights $\lambda(y \mid \boldsymbol{y})$ are $1/k$ if y appears among the top k documents in the ranking $\boldsymbol{y}$, and zero otherwise.

The top half of Table 1 shows more examples of performance measures that are linear functions of the individual parts y of $\boldsymbol{y}$. The bottom half of Table 1 presents examples of performance measures whose natural decomposition of $\boldsymbol{y}$ is into pairs of variables, i.e., $y = (\tilde{y}_1, \tilde{y}_2)$. These examples demonstrate the wide applicability of the decomposition in Eq. (1). Furthermore, one can estimate normalized measures (e.g. AP, NDCG) by taking ratios of estimated U at the expense of a typically small bias [2, 28]. Other structured prediction tasks, like sequence labeling, parsing, and network prediction, use similar part-based performance measures, and much of what we discuss can be extended to evaluation problems where $\boldsymbol{y}$ is a more general structured object (e.g. sequence, parse tree).

3.4 Evaluation as Monte Carlo Estimation

Previous work has realized that one can use sampling over the documents y in the rankings $\boldsymbol{y} = S(\boldsymbol{x})$ to estimate Average Precision and NDCG [2, 27, 18]. However, the idea of sampling over the components y applies not only to these

performance measures, but to any linearly decomposable performance measure that can be written in the form of Eq. (1). Making the connection to Monte Carlo methods, we start by defining the following distribution over the documents y of a ranking $\boldsymbol{y} = S(\boldsymbol{x})$,

$$\mathrm{Pr}(y \mid \boldsymbol{x}; S) = \frac{\lambda(y \mid S(\boldsymbol{x}))}{\sum_{y'} \lambda(y' \mid S(\boldsymbol{x}))}.$$

To simplify the exposition, we assume that the weights are scaled to sum to 1 (i.e., $\sum_{y'} \lambda(y' \mid S(\boldsymbol{x})) = 1$) for all systems S and inputs $\boldsymbol{x}$. We can now replace the sum over the components with its expectation,

$$
\begin{aligned}
U(S) &= \mathbb{E}_{\mathrm{P}(\boldsymbol{x})} \sum_{y \in S(\boldsymbol{x})} \lambda(y \mid S(\boldsymbol{x})) \, u(\boldsymbol{x}, y) \\
&= \mathbb{E}_{\mathrm{P}(\boldsymbol{x})} \mathbb{E}_{\mathrm{Pr}(y \mid \boldsymbol{x}; S)} [u(\boldsymbol{x}, y)]. \tag{2}
\end{aligned}
$$

This expectation can now be estimated via Monte Carlo, since we can sample from both $\mathrm{P}(\boldsymbol{x})$ and $\mathrm{Pr}(y|\boldsymbol{x}, S)$ without expensive utility assessments.

3.5 Importance Sampling Estimators

To obtain an unbiased sampling-based estimate of $U(S)$ in Eq. (2), one could simply sample queries and documents from $\mathrm{P}(\boldsymbol{x}) \cdot \mathrm{Pr}(y|\boldsymbol{x}, S)$ and average the results. However, this naive strategy has two drawbacks. First, to evaluate each new system S, it would sample documents from a new distribution, requiring additional expensive utility assessments. Second, there may be other sampling distributions that are statistically more efficient.

In principle, we can use any unbiased Monte Carlo technique to overcome these two drawbacks of naive sampling, and [28] have used stratified sampling. We deviate from their choice and focus on importance sampling for four reasons. First, importance sampling makes it straightforward to incorporate prior knowledge into the sampling distribution. This could be knowledge about the utility values $u(x, y)$ or about the systems being evaluated. Second, we can obtain confidence intervals with little additional overhead. Third, importance sampling offers a natural and simple way to re-use previously collected judgments for evaluating new systems. Finally, as we will show in this paper, the importance sampling framework extends naturally to scenarios involving concurrent evaluation of multiple systems, providing closed-form solutions that are easy to use in practice.

Central to importance sampling is the idea of defining a sampling distribution $Q(\boldsymbol{x}, y)$ that focuses on the regions of the space that are most important for accurate estimates. We consider the family of sampling distributions that first draws a sample $\boldsymbol{X}$ of $|\boldsymbol{X}|$ queries from $\mathrm{P}(\boldsymbol{x})$[1], and then samples query-document pairs with replacement from this set. This two-step sampling via $\boldsymbol{X}$ has the advantage that the assessment overhead of understanding a query can now be amortized over multiple judgments per query. Note that we may repeatedly sample the same query-document pair. See Section 3.7 for a discussion on whether to actually judge the same query-document pair more than once.

For a sample of n observations $\{(\boldsymbol{x}_i, y_i)\}_{i=1}^n$ drawn i.i.d. from a sampling distribution $Q(\boldsymbol{x}, y)$ and a target distribu-

---

[1] One may also consider sampling queries $\boldsymbol{x}$ from some other distribution than $\mathrm{P}(\boldsymbol{x})$, which may be beneficial if different types of queries contribute with different variability to the overall estimate [9, 20].

111

tion $\Pr(\boldsymbol{x}, y | S) = \Pr(y | \boldsymbol{x}, S) / |\boldsymbol{X}|$ for a given $\boldsymbol{X}$, the importance sampling estimator for Eq. (2) on $\boldsymbol{X}$ is

$$\hat{U}_n(S) = \frac{1}{n} \sum_{i=1}^{n} u(\boldsymbol{x}_i, y_i) \frac{\mathrm{P}(\boldsymbol{x}_i, y_i \mid S)}{Q(\boldsymbol{x}_i, y_i)}. \qquad (3)$$

Given any sampling distribution $Q(\boldsymbol{x}, y)$ and a budget of n samples, applying this importance sampling estimator results in the following simple procedure:

1. Draw a sample $\boldsymbol{X}$ of $|\boldsymbol{X}|$ queries from $\mathrm{P}(\boldsymbol{x})$. For $i = 1, \ldots, n$:
   - draw query/document pair $(\boldsymbol{x}_i, y_i)$ from $Q(\boldsymbol{x}, y)$,
   - collect assessment $u(\boldsymbol{x}_i, y_i)$ and record $Q(\boldsymbol{x}_i, y_i)$.

   The result is a test collection

   $$\mathcal{D} = ((\boldsymbol{x}_i, y_i, u(\boldsymbol{x}_i, y_i), Q(\boldsymbol{x}_i, y_i))_{i=1}^{n}.$$

2. For systems $\mathcal{S} = \{S_1, \ldots S_k\}$, compute $\hat{U}_n(S_j)$ according to Eq. (3) using $\mathcal{D}$.

The following shows that this provides an unbiased estimate of $U(S)$ [17], if one ensures that $Q(\boldsymbol{x}, y)$ has sufficient support, i.e. $u(\boldsymbol{x}, y) \mathrm{P}(\boldsymbol{x}, y | S) \neq 0 \Rightarrow Q(\boldsymbol{x}, y) > 0$.

$$
\begin{aligned}
\mathbb{E}[\hat{U}_n(S)] &= \mathbb{E}_{\mathrm{P}(\boldsymbol{X})} \mathbb{E}_{Q(\boldsymbol{x}_i, y_i)} \left[\frac{1}{n} \sum_{i=1}^{n} u(\boldsymbol{x}_i, y_i) \frac{\mathrm{P}(\boldsymbol{x}_i, y_i \mid S)}{Q(\boldsymbol{x}_i, y_i)} \right] \\
&= \mathbb{E}_{\mathrm{P}(\boldsymbol{X})} \mathbb{E}_{Q(\boldsymbol{x}, y)} \left[u(\boldsymbol{x}, y) \frac{\mathrm{P}(\boldsymbol{x}, y \mid S)}{Q(\boldsymbol{x}, y)} \right] \\
&= \mathbb{E}_{\mathrm{P}(\boldsymbol{X})} \left[\sum_{\boldsymbol{x}, y} u(\boldsymbol{x}, y) \frac{\mathrm{P}(\boldsymbol{x}, y \mid S)}{Q(\boldsymbol{x}, y)} Q(\boldsymbol{x}, y) \right] \\
&= \mathbb{E}_{\mathrm{P}(\boldsymbol{X})} \left[\frac{1}{|\boldsymbol{X}|} \sum_{\boldsymbol{x} \in \boldsymbol{X}} \sum_{y} u(\boldsymbol{x}, y) \Pr(y \mid \boldsymbol{x}, S) \right] \\
&= \mathbb{E}_{\mathrm{P}(\boldsymbol{x})} \left[\sum_{y} u(\boldsymbol{x}, y) \Pr(y \mid \boldsymbol{x}, S) \right] \\
&= \mathbb{E}_{\mathrm{P}(\boldsymbol{x})} \mathbb{E}_{\Pr(y | \boldsymbol{x}; S)} [u(\boldsymbol{x}, y)] = U(S).
\end{aligned}
$$

Note that we used the fact that the pairs $(\boldsymbol{x}_i, y_i)$ were drawn i.i.d. to arrive at the second line.

3.6 Designing the Sampling Distribution Q

What remains to be addressed is the question of which sampling distribution $Q(\boldsymbol{x}, y)$ to use for sampling the documents to be assessed for each query in $\boldsymbol{X}$. Since every $Q(\boldsymbol{x}, y)$ with full support ensures unbiasedness, the key criterion for choosing $Q(\boldsymbol{x}, y)$ is statistical efficiency [2]. Concretely, the variance $\boldsymbol{Var}_Q[\hat{U}_n(S)]$ of the estimator $\hat{U}_n(S)$ governs efficiency and is our measure of estimation quality,

$$\Sigma(Q) = \boldsymbol{Var}_Q \left[\hat{U}_n(S) \right].$$

We therefore wish to pick a distribution Q that minimizes $\Sigma(Q)$. Let z_Q be short-hand for $u(\boldsymbol{x}, y) \frac{\mathrm{P}(\boldsymbol{x}, y | S)}{Q(\boldsymbol{x}, y)}$, then

$$\Sigma(Q) = \frac{1}{n} \boldsymbol{Var}_Q [z_Q] = \frac{1}{n} \left(\mathbb{E}_Q[z_Q^2] - (\mathbb{E}_Q[z_Q])^2 \right).$$

The first equality follows since $(\boldsymbol{x}_i, y_i)$ are i.i.d. and $\hat{U}_n(S)$ is a sample mean, and the second expands the definition of variance. Notice that our earlier proof of unbiasedness implies that $\mu = \mathbb{E}_Q[z_Q] = \sum_{\boldsymbol{x}, y} u(\boldsymbol{x}, y) \mathrm{P}(\boldsymbol{x}, y | S)$ is a constant independent of Q.

A key result for importance sampling is that the following Q^* is optimal for minimizing $\Sigma(Q)$ [11, 2]:

$$Q^*(\boldsymbol{x}, y) = u(\boldsymbol{x}, y) \cdot \mathrm{P}(\boldsymbol{x}, y \mid S) / \mu. \qquad (4)$$

To see this, observe that for any other sampling distribution Q different from Q^*,

$$
\begin{aligned}
\boldsymbol{Var}_{Q^*}[z_{Q^*}] + \mu^2 &= \sum_{\boldsymbol{x}, y} \frac{(u(\boldsymbol{x}, y) \mathrm{P}(\boldsymbol{x}, y \mid S))^2}{u(\boldsymbol{x}, y) \cdot \mathrm{P}(\boldsymbol{x}, y \mid S) / \mu} \\
&= \mu \sum_{\boldsymbol{x}, y} u(\boldsymbol{x}, y) \mathrm{P}(\boldsymbol{x}, y \mid S) \\
&= (\mathbb{E}_Q[z_Q])^2 \\
&\leq \mathbb{E}_Q[z_Q^2] = \boldsymbol{Var}_Q[z_Q] + \mu^2.
\end{aligned}
$$

The first line is the definition of $\boldsymbol{Var}_{Q^*}[z_{Q^*}^2]$, and the last line follows from Jensen's inequality.

Since we do not have access to the true $u(\boldsymbol{x}, y)$ in practice, one usually substitutes approximate utilities $\tilde{u}(\boldsymbol{x}, y)$ based on prior side information (e.g. the Okapi BM25 score of document y for query x) into Equation (4). Any $\tilde{u}(\boldsymbol{x}, y) > 0$ retains unbiasedness, and the better the estimates $\tilde{u}(\boldsymbol{x}, y)$, the better the efficiency of the estimator.

3.7 Practical Concerns

Using the importance sampling framework outlined above offers straightforward solutions to a number of matters of practical interest.

Noisy Utility Assessments. In practice, there is often no consensus on what the true utility $u(\boldsymbol{x}, y)$ is, and different assessors (and users) will have different opinions. An example is crowd-sourcing, where labels get consolidated from multiple noisy judges. Note that our framework naturally lends itself to these noisy settings, if we think of individual assessments $u(\boldsymbol{x}, y | a)$ as conditioned on the assessor a that is drawn from a distribution $\mathrm{P}(a)$ and define

$$v(\boldsymbol{x}, y) = \mathbb{E}_{\mathrm{P}(a)}[u(\boldsymbol{x}, y \mid a)].$$

Our estimator (3) stays the same, and remains unbiased by linearity of expectation. Also, the theoretical results for picking the optimal Q^* remain essentially unaltered. The only thing that changes is that we replace the true $u(\boldsymbol{x}, y)$ with the true expected utility $v(\boldsymbol{x}, y)$.

Reusing Existing Data. Given that any sampling distribution $Q(\boldsymbol{x}, y)$ with full support provides unbiased estimates, reusing old data $\mathcal{D} = ((\boldsymbol{x}_i, y_i, u(\boldsymbol{x}_i, y_i), Q(\boldsymbol{x}_i, y_i))_{i=1}^{n}$ is straightforward. To guarantee full support over all query-document pairs, we can use a mixture sampling distribution such as

$$Q(\boldsymbol{x}, y) \propto \tilde{u}(\boldsymbol{x}, y) \cdot P(\boldsymbol{x}, y \mid S) + \epsilon,$$

where ϵ is a small constant added to ensure Q has sufficiently heavy tails [29]. A larger ϵ will make the collected samples more reusable for any new system, but sacrifices statistical efficiency for evaluating the current S.

In addition, it is easy to see that not all data used in the estimator from Eq. (3) has to be collected using the same $Q(\boldsymbol{x}, y)$ or the same sample of queries $\boldsymbol{X}$, and that we can combine datasets that accumulate over time. As long as we keep track of Q for every $(\boldsymbol{x}_i, y_i)$ that was sampled, each sample may be drawn from a different $Q_i(\boldsymbol{x}_i, y_i)$, and we can use the mixture

$$Q(\boldsymbol{x}, y) = \frac{1}{n} \sum_{i=1}^{n} Q_i(\boldsymbol{x}, y), \qquad (5)$$

in the denominator of our estimator. This is a direct application of the balance heuristic for Multiple Importance Sampling [17]. Furthermore, Equation (5) provides guidance on how to draw new samples given the distributions $Q_i(\boldsymbol{x}, y)$ of the existing $\mathcal{D}$, if we eventually want the overall data to be close to a particularly efficient distribution $Q^*(\boldsymbol{x}, y)$ for a new evaluation task.

Quantifying Evaluation Accuracy. An advantage of the sampling approach to evaluation is that it allows us to easily quantify the accuracy of the estimates on $\boldsymbol{X}$. For large sample sizes n, our estimate $\hat{U}_n(S)$ converges in distribution to a normal distribution. From the central limit theorem, we then obtain

$$\left[\hat{U}_n(S) - t_{\alpha/2} \frac{\hat{\sigma}_n(S)}{\sqrt{n}}, \hat{U}_n(S) + t_{\alpha/2} \frac{\hat{\sigma}_n(S)}{\sqrt{n}} \right] \qquad (6)$$

as the approximate $1 - \alpha$ confidence interval. For example, a 95% confidence interval would be $\hat{U}_n(S) \pm 1.96 \frac{\hat{\sigma}_n(S)}{\sqrt{n}}$. We can estimate $\hat{\sigma}_n(S)$ from the same samples $\{(\boldsymbol{x}_i, y_i)\}_{i=1}^{n}$ that we used to compute $\hat{U}_n(S)$ as follows:

$$\hat{\sigma}_n(S) = \sqrt{\frac{1}{n-1} \sum_{i=1}^{n} \left(\frac{u(\boldsymbol{x}_i, y_i) \operatorname{P}(\boldsymbol{x}_i, y_i \mid S)}{Q(\boldsymbol{x}_i, y_i)} - \hat{U}_n(S) \right)^2}.$$

Note that the rate of convergence of $\hat{U}_n(S)$ to its true value depends on the skewness of the distribution of z_Q, and we will empirically evaluate the quality of the confidence intervals in Section 7.2.

4. COMPARING TWO SYSTEMS

Up until now this paper has only considered the problem of estimating the performance of one system in isolation. In practice, however, we are typically much more interested in the relative performance of multiple systems. In the case of two systems S and S', we may be interested in measuring how much they differ in performance $\Delta(S, S') = U(S) - U(S')$. To this effect, we consider the estimator

$$\hat{\Delta}_n(S, S') = \frac{1}{n} \sum_{i=1}^{n} u(\boldsymbol{x}_i, y_i) \frac{\operatorname{P}(\boldsymbol{x}_i, y_i \mid S) - \operatorname{P}(\boldsymbol{x}_i, y_i \mid S')}{Q(\boldsymbol{x}_i, y_i)}. \quad (7)$$

Again, this estimator is unbiased, and it can be computed using data $\mathcal{D} = ((\boldsymbol{x}_i, y_i, u(\boldsymbol{x}_i, y_i), Q(\boldsymbol{x}_i, y_i))_{i=1}^{n}$ sampled from any Q with sufficient support. But what does the most efficient sampling distribution Q^* look like? Like in the single system case, the sample efficiency of the estimator is governed by its variance,

$$\Sigma(Q) = \boldsymbol{Var}_Q \left[\hat{\Delta}_n(S, S') \right]. \qquad (8)$$

Analogous to $\hat{U}_n(S)$, $\hat{\Delta}_n(S, S')$ is the average of n i.i.d. random variables $z_Q = u(\boldsymbol{x}, y) \frac{\operatorname{P}(\boldsymbol{x}, y \mid S) - \operatorname{P}(\boldsymbol{x}, y \mid S')}{Q(\boldsymbol{x}, y)}$. So, $\Sigma(Q)$ is proportional to $\boldsymbol{Var}_Q[z_Q]$ and the only term that depends on Q is $\mathbb{E}_Q[(z_Q)^2]$. Following a similar argument as before,

the optimal sampling distribution is

$$Q^*(\boldsymbol{x}, y) \propto u(\boldsymbol{x}, y) \cdot \left| \operatorname{P}(\boldsymbol{x}, y \mid S) - \operatorname{P}(\boldsymbol{x}, y \mid S') \right|. \quad (9)$$

$\mathbb{E}_{Q^*}[(z_{Q^*})^2] = \mathbb{E}_Q[|z_Q|]^2 \leq \mathbb{E}_Q[(z_Q)^2]$ by Jensen's inequality, so Q^* from Equation (9) minimizes $\Sigma(Q)$.

Note that this Q^* is very intuitive – items that have similar weights $\operatorname{P}(\boldsymbol{x}, y | \cdot)$ in both systems will get sampled with a low probability, since they have negligible effect on the performance difference. This Q^* is different from the heuristic Q previously used in multi-system evaluation [28], where Q is simply the average of $\operatorname{P}(\boldsymbol{x}, y | S)$ and $\operatorname{P}(\boldsymbol{x}, y | S')$. In particular, this heuristic Q fails to recognize that documents at identical positions in both rankings contribute no information about the performance difference. In Section 7.3 we empirically compare against this heuristic Q.

5. COMPARING MULTIPLE SYSTEMS TO A BASELINE

We now consider another evaluation use case that is frequently encountered in practice. We have a current production system S' and several new candidate systems $\mathcal{S} = \{S_1, \ldots S_k\}$. The goal of evaluation is to estimate by how much each candidate improves (or not) over the baseline S'.

We can formulate this goal in terms of k comparative evaluation problems $\Delta(S_i, S') = U(S_j) - U(S')$, and we want reliable estimates for all performance differences $\Delta(S_1, S')$, ..., $\Delta(S_k, S')$. We can use the estimator $\hat{\Delta}_n(S_j, S')$ from Equation (7) for each $\Delta(S_j, S')$, and the procedure for computing it is identical to Section 4. This is one of the strengths of the sampling approach: once a sampling distribution Q is designed, multiple systems and multiple differences can be concurrently evaluated from one batch of judgments using a unified, unbiased procedure.

But what is the optimal Q^* for this new use case? Since we are now considering k estimates in parallel, we consider the sum of estimator variances as our measure of estimation quality to optimize:

$$\Sigma(Q) = \sum_{j=1}^{k} \boldsymbol{Var}_Q \left[\hat{\Delta}_n(S_j, S') \right]. \qquad (10)$$

We will show that the distribution minimizing $\Sigma(Q)$ is

$$Q^*(\boldsymbol{x}, y) \propto u(\boldsymbol{x}, y) \cdot \sqrt{\sum_{j=1}^{k} (\operatorname{P}(\boldsymbol{x}, y \mid S_j) - \operatorname{P}(\boldsymbol{x}, y \mid S'))^2}. \tag{11}$$

To see this, collect the terms of $\Sigma(Q)$ that depend on Q (up to a scaling constant n) and denote them as,

$$T(Q) = \mathbb{E}_Q \left[\left(\frac{u(\boldsymbol{x}, y)}{Q(\boldsymbol{x}, y)} \right)^2 \sum_{j=1}^{k} (\operatorname{P}(\boldsymbol{x}, y \mid S_j) - \operatorname{P}(\boldsymbol{x}, y \mid S'))^2 \right].$$

We can then show that

$$T(Q^*) = \left[\sum_{\boldsymbol{x}, y} u(\boldsymbol{x}, y) \sqrt{\sum_{j=1}^{k} (\operatorname{P}(\boldsymbol{x}, y \mid S_j) - \operatorname{P}(\boldsymbol{x}, y \mid S'))^2} \right]^2$$

$$= \mathbb{E}_Q \left[\frac{u(\boldsymbol{x}, y)}{Q(\boldsymbol{x}, y)} \sqrt{\sum_{j=1}^{k} (\operatorname{P}(\boldsymbol{x}, y \mid S_j) - \operatorname{P}(\boldsymbol{x}, y \mid S'))^2} \right]^2$$

113

$$\leq \mathbb{E}_Q\left[\left(\frac{u(\boldsymbol{x},y)}{Q(\boldsymbol{x},y)}\right)^2 \sum_{j=1}^k (P(\boldsymbol{x},y \mid S_j) - P(\boldsymbol{x},y \mid S'))^2\right]$$
$$= T(Q).$$

Our results here complement recent work in multidimensional importance sampling [30] which studies multidimensional $u(\boldsymbol{x},y)$ and a single target distribution $P(\boldsymbol{x},y|S)$. The choice of sum-of-variances as the $\Sigma(Q)$ objective yields a simple closed-form optimal sampling distribution Q^* for this evaluation scenario. Several other $\Sigma(Q)$ are possible (for instance, the maximum variance $\max_j \boldsymbol{Var}_Q[\hat{\Delta}_n(S_j, S')]$), however closed form Q^* that optimize these may not exist. We defer further study of different objectives characterizing estimation quality in these scenarios to future work.

6. RANKING MULTIPLE SYSTEMS

Finally, we consider the use-case of ranking a collection of systems $\mathcal{S} = \{S_1, \ldots S_k\}$ in order of their performance $\{U(S_1), \ldots, U(S_k)\}$. A first thought may be to estimate each $U(S_j)$ directly, which we call the absolute evaluation strategy. However, we can often do much better using comparative evaluations, since accurate ranking merely requires that we can estimate $\{U(S_1) + \delta, \ldots, U(S_k) + \delta\}$ up to some arbitrary constant δ.

Why should this comparative problem be more accurate than absolute evaluation? Imagine three systems, two of which are poor ($U(S_1), U(S_2) \simeq 0$) while the third is good ($U(S_3) \gg 0$). Consider the case where there are a lot of "easy" documents that all three system rank correctly, and that the large difference between S_3 and systems S_1/S_2 is due to a few "hard" documents where S_3 is superior. Furthermore, S_1 and S_2 may be small variants of the same system that produce almost identical rankings. Designing Q^* to optimize for the sum of absolute variances $\sum_{j=1}^3 \boldsymbol{Var}_Q[\hat{U}_n(S_j)]$ would be ignorant to all this structure.

To design a more informed estimator and sampler for ranking, we propose to merely estimate each system's performance relative to some baseline system τ,

$$\Delta(S_1, \tau), \ldots \Delta(S_k, \tau), \tag{12}$$

and then rank the systems using the estimator $\hat{\Delta}(S_i, \tau)$ from Equation (7). We could then use the optimal sampling distribution Q^* from Section 5 to sample query-document pairs and collect judgments.

What remains to be shown is how to construct the optimal baseline system τ. Using

$$\Sigma(\tau) = \sum_{j=1}^k \boldsymbol{Var}_{Q^*}\left[\hat{\Delta}_n(S_j, \tau)\right]$$

as our measure of estimator quality analogous to the previous sections, we prove that the optimal τ corresponds to

$$P(\boldsymbol{x}, y|\tau) = \frac{1}{k}\sum_{j=1}^k P(\boldsymbol{x}, y \mid S_j)$$

for each query-document pair $(\boldsymbol{x}, y)$.

PROOF. From the results of Section 5, we know that for any system τ, the optimal sampling distribution $Q^*(x,y) \propto u(\boldsymbol{x},y) \cdot \sqrt{\sum_{j=1}^k (P(\boldsymbol{x},y|S_j) - P(\boldsymbol{x},y|\tau))^2}$. If we plug in this Q^* into $\Sigma(\tau)$ and simplify (note that all terms of the variance

	True $U(S)$	Shallow Pool	Deep Pool	Sampling $\hat{U}(S)$
OPT	284.40	16.98	284.48 ± 1.69	284.54 ± 1.22
REV-75	277.63	10.00	277.79 ± 1.75	277.58 ± 1.07
REV-150	271.32	8.51	271.21 ± 1.59	271.18 ± 0.97
SHIFT-5	274.94	4.72	275.03 ± 1.69	274.73 ± 1.10
SHIFT-7	269.87	0.00	269.90 ± 1.75	269.98 ± 1.12
mds08a3	6.96	1.93	7.32 ± 5.05	6.86 ± 0.76
nttd8ale	9.01	2.41	8.79 ± 5.30	8.97 ± 0.87
weaver2	7.48	1.94	8.40 ± 6.59	7.53 ± 0.83

Table 2: Mean and standard deviation of DCG estimates across 100 trials for all systems in SYNTH (top) and three randomly chosen systems in TREC (bottom). The first column shows the true $U(S)$ that ShallowPool, DeepPool, and $\hat{U}(S)$ from Equation (3) (with approximate Q^* sampling) aim to estimate.

depend on τ),

$$\Sigma(\tau) = \left[\sum_{\boldsymbol{x},y} u(x,y)\sqrt{\sum_{j=1}^k (P(\boldsymbol{x},y \mid S_j) - P(\boldsymbol{x},y \mid \tau))^2}\right]^2$$
$$- \sum_{j=1}^k \left[\sum_{\boldsymbol{x},y} u(x,y)\{P(\boldsymbol{x},y \mid S_j) - P(\boldsymbol{x},y \mid \tau)\}\right]^2.$$

Let each $P(\boldsymbol{x}, y|\tau)$ be a variable $\tau_{\boldsymbol{x},y}$ which we minimize over. $\Sigma(\tau)$ is convex in each $\tau_{\boldsymbol{x},y}$. A minimum requires that $\partial \Sigma(\tau)/\partial \tau_{\boldsymbol{x},y} = 0$, subject to $\tau_{\boldsymbol{x},y} \geq 0$ for all $(\boldsymbol{x},y)$ and $\sum_{\boldsymbol{x},y} \tau_{\boldsymbol{x},y} = 1$. To begin, $\partial \Sigma(\tau)/\partial \tau_{\boldsymbol{x}_i,y_i} = 0$ yields that $\forall(\boldsymbol{x}_i, y_i)$:

$$\sum_{\boldsymbol{x},y} u(\boldsymbol{x},y)\left[\sum_{j=1}^k P(\boldsymbol{x},y|S_j) - \tau_{\boldsymbol{x},y}\right] + \alpha \sum_{j=1}^k P(\boldsymbol{x}_i, y_i|S_j) - \tau_{\boldsymbol{x}_i, y_i} = 0$$

where $\alpha = \dfrac{\sum_{\boldsymbol{x},y} u(\boldsymbol{x},y)\sqrt{\sum_{j=1}^k (P(\boldsymbol{x},y \mid S_j) - \tau_{\boldsymbol{x},y})^2}}{\sqrt{\sum_{j=1}^k (P(\boldsymbol{x}_i, y_i \mid S_j) - \tau_{\boldsymbol{x}_i, y_i})^2}}.$

Observe that $\tau_{\boldsymbol{x}_i, y_i} = \frac{1}{k}\sum_{j=1}^k P(\boldsymbol{x}_i, y_i|S_j)$ satisfies all the equations simultaneously, which completes the proof. $\square$

Putting everything together, the optimal sampling distribution is

$$Q^*(\boldsymbol{x}, y) \propto u(\boldsymbol{x},y)\sqrt{\sum_{j=1}^k \left(P(\boldsymbol{x},y|S_j) - \frac{1}{k}\sum_{i=1}^k P(\boldsymbol{x},y|S_i)\right)^2}. \tag{13}$$

7. EXPERIMENTS

The following experiments evaluate to what extent the theoretical contributions developed in this paper impact evaluation accuracy empirically. We compare sampling-based approaches only in this section, recognizing that deterministic approaches do not deliver the same guarantees as laid out in the introduction. To study effects in isolation, we first explore our estimator and sampling distribution design principles on the problem of single-system evaluation. We then in turn consider the three comparative multi-system evaluation problems.

7.1 Datasets and Experiment Setup

We use two datasets for our experiments, *SYNTH* and *TREC*, which give us different levels of experimental control and different application scenarios. The SYNTH dataset is designed to resemble judgments as they occur in a recommender system. To create SYNTH, we generated a sample $\boldsymbol{X}$ of 6000 users (i.e. queries) and 2000 items (i.e. documents). The ground truth judgments $u(x, y) \in \{0, ...4\}$ for each user/item pair were drawn from a categorical distribution whose parameters were drawn from a Dirichlet distribution with hyper-parameters $\alpha = (.54, .25, .175, .03, .005)$, so as to give high ratings a low probability. Based on this data, we created ranking systems S_j of different quality in the following way. S_{OPT} denotes the perfect ranking system where each user ranking $\boldsymbol{y}$ is sorted according to the true relevances $u(x, y)$. The $S_{SHIFT-m}$ ranking system shifts all rankings of S_{OPT} down by m entries; elements that get shifted beyond the last position get reintroduced at the first. S_{REV-m} reverses the order of the top m elements in S_{OPT}. The collection of systems was $\mathcal{S} = \{S_{OPT}, S_{REV-75}, S_{REV-150}, S_{SHIFT-5}, S_{SHIFT-7}\}$. As evaluation measure, we use DCG@2000.

The TREC dataset contains binary relevance judgments and mimics a typical information retrieval scenario. To generate the dataset, we start with the TREC-8 ad hoc track [25], which comprises 149 systems that submitted rankings $\boldsymbol{y}$ of size 1000 as response to 50 queries $\boldsymbol{X}$. To eliminate unwanted biases due to unjudged documents which could confound our empirical evaluation, we only consider a random subset of 20 systems for which we ensured that all the top 100 documents of each of the 50 queries were fully judged. Correspondingly, we truncated all rankings to length 100 and evaluate in terms of DCG@100.

Approximate Utilities. If not noted otherwise, we use approximate utilities $\tilde{u}_S(\boldsymbol{x}, y)$ when designing the sampling distribution in all of our experiments. We use the following simple heuristic to define $\tilde{u}_S(\boldsymbol{x}, y)$ and we will evaluate empirically to what degree this can be improved. For SYNTH and any given system S, we use $\tilde{u}_S(\boldsymbol{x}, y) = 4 \cdot (1 - \frac{\text{rank}(S(\boldsymbol{x}), y)}{2000})$ – reflecting the fact that relevances ranged between 0 and 4. We have an analogously rank-decreasing function $\tilde{u}_S(\boldsymbol{x}, y) = \frac{16}{\text{rank}(S(\boldsymbol{x}), y) + 34}$ for TREC. To define approximate utilities for a set of systems $\mathcal{S} = \{S_1, ..., S_k\}$, we simply average the $\tilde{u}_{S_j}(\boldsymbol{x}, y)$.

Comparing systems. When performing comparative evaluations in Sections 7.3 to 7.5, we focus on the most difficult comparisons in the following way. We rank all systems by their true performance $U(S)$ on our ground truth set, and then compare adjacent systems in Section 7.3 and a sliding window of five systems in Sections 7.4 and 7.5. In Section 7.4, the middle system is used as the baseline S'. Each experiment is replicated 100 times.

7.2 Empirical Verification of Design Principles

We first evaluate how the design of the sampling distribution $Q(x, y)$ affects the efficiency of the $\hat{U}(x, y)$ estimator in Equation (3). To study the effect in isolation and in comparison to conventional pooling methods, we first focus on the single-system evaluation problem.

Comparison to Deterministic Pooling. To ground our experiments with respect to conventional practice, we start by comparing the sampling approach to deterministic pooling [24] historically used in TREC. The depth of the

	Q^*	Q^P	Q^{unif}
OPT	1.22	1.98	3.05
REV-75	1.07	1.45	2.64
REV-150	0.97	1.33	2.20
SHIFT-5	1.10	1.67	2.63
SHIFT-7	1.12	1.45	2.45
mds08a3	0.76	0.84	0.97
nttd8ale	0.87	0.98	1.18
weaver2	0.83	0.92	1.05

Table 3: Standard deviation of $\hat{U}(S)$ for DCG@k estimates under different sampling methods across 100 trials for all systems in SYNTH (top) and three randomly chosen systems in TREC (bottom).

pool b, i.e., the number of top-b documents being judged, vs the number of queries $|\boldsymbol{X}|$ is the key design choice when pooling under a judgment budget. We use two pooling methods that choose this trade-off differently. Given a budget of n assessments, the *ShallowPool* methods gets judgments for the top $b' = \frac{n}{|\boldsymbol{X}|}$ items of each query and computes the average performance based on these judgments. The *DeepPool* method randomly selects $l' = \frac{n}{b}$ queries and judges all pooled documents for those queries.

Table 2 compares estimated DCG@k for the deterministic baselines ShallowPool and DeepPool with the sampling estimates $\hat{U}(S)$ from Eq. (4) with a total budget of $n = 5 \cdot |\boldsymbol{X}|$ assessments. We repeated each experiment 100 times, and average the estimates across all 100 runs. The error intervals correspond to the empirical standard deviations of the estimates. Note that ShallowPool has standard deviation of zero, since it is deterministic given $\boldsymbol{X}$.

Unsurprisingly, Table 2 shows that ShallowPool is heavily biased by the missing judgments and systematically underestimates the true $U(S)$ given in the first column. The bias of ShallowPool is so strong that even its average estimates do not reflect the correct ordering of the ranking functions on SYNTH.

Table 2 shows that our $\hat{U}(S)$ estimator is indeed unbiased. DeepPool is also unbiased, since it has a non-zero probability of eliciting judgments for any returned document. However, $\hat{U}(S)$ has substantially lower standard deviation especially on TREC. This is not surprising, since DeepPool suffers from between-query variability when sampling only a few queries from $\boldsymbol{X}$. In fact, the standard deviations of DeepPool are much larger than the estimated differences on TREC, indicating that DeepPool cannot reliably distinguish the ranking performance of the systems.

Impact of Prior Knowledge. We now study the impact of the sampling distribution on sampling efficiency. Table 3 compares three sampling approaches: Q^* with approximate utilities as in the previous experiment, Q^P with $\tilde{u}(x, y) = 1$, and uniform sampling Q^{unif}.

We see in Table 3 that the standard deviation increases as we transition from Q^* to Q^P, and it increases even further if we sample uniformly in Q^{unif}. Note that an estimator with half the standard deviation requires only roughly half the sample size to reach the same level of estimation accuracy. We conclude that the choice of Q is of great practical significance. This is in line with importance sampling theory that indicates that good estimates of $\tilde{u}$ can substantially improve

	$\hat{U}(S)$	ConfInt	$\hat{P}_{\text{cov}}$
OPT	284.54 ± 1.22	± 2.21	0.92
REV-75	277.58 ± 1.07	± 2.10	0.96
REV-150	271.18 ± 0.97	± 2.05	0.95
SHIFT-5	274.73 ± 1.10	± 2.18	0.93
SHIFT-7	269.98 ± 1.12	± 2.18	0.94
mds08a3	6.86 ± 0.76	± 1.50	0.95
nttd8ale	8.97 ± 0.87	± 1.65	0.94
weaver2	7.53 ± 0.83	± 1.58	0.95

Table 4: Average confidence intervals and coverage probabilities for the $\hat{U}(S)$ estimator using Q^*.

estimation quality. Given these findings, all following experiments will be based on the Q^* sampler with approximate utilities.

Confidence Intervals. Another feature of the sampling-based approach is that one can quantify its accuracy using confidence intervals. But are the approximate confidence intervals proposed in Section 3.7 accurate in practice? For each of the 100 runs from Table 2, we computed 95% confidence intervals according to Equation (6). We also computed the coverage probability $\hat{P}_{\text{cov}}$ of the confidence intervals, defined as the number of times the true value was within the confidence interval. As we can see from Table 4, the coverage probabilities of the approximate intervals are usually very close to 95% as desired. We can also verify that the empirical standard deviation of $\hat{U}(S)$ is roughly $1/1.96$ of the average confidence intervals.

7.3 Is pairwise comparative evaluation more efficient than individual evaluation?

We now evaluate how much comparative estimation can improve upon individual system evaluation. Prior work [28] uses $Q(\boldsymbol{x}, y) \propto \tilde{u}(\boldsymbol{x}, y)(\text{P}(\boldsymbol{x}, y|S) + \text{P}(\boldsymbol{x}, y|S'))/2$ which we compare to the pairwise $Q^*(\boldsymbol{x}, y)$ with approximate utilites from Equation (9).

Table 5 shows the estimator variance $\Sigma(Q)$ as defined in Equation (8) for both sampling methods (up to scaling by the sample size n). On both datasets, the pairwise Q^* substantially improves estimator accuracy over Naive sampling. Note that reducing estimator variance by a quarter corresponds to halving the sample size needed to get a particular level of estimation accuracy. The table also contains the variance $\Sigma(Q)$ when using the true utilities $u^*(\boldsymbol{x}, y)$ for the design of the sampling distribution instead of the approximate utilities $\tilde{u}(\boldsymbol{x}, y)$. Comparing the variance gains between Naive and Q^* to the gains we could get by moving from $\tilde{u}(\boldsymbol{x}, y)$ to $u^*(\boldsymbol{x}, y)$, we see that the pairwise Q^* has improved sample efficiency far more than we could still hope to improve by finding a better $\tilde{u}(\boldsymbol{x}, y)$ for these datasets. Note that all numbers in Table 5 were computed analytically, so there are no errorbars.

While Table 5 measures estimator accuracy in terms of mean-squared-error, we are often merely interested in the binary decision of which system is better, i.e. $\text{sign}(\Delta(S, S'))$. Figure 1 compares the accuracy with which the sign of our estimate $\text{sign}(\hat{\Delta}(S, S'))$ predicts the true order of the systems on our query sample $\boldsymbol{X}$ correctly, $Acc = \mathbb{I}[\Delta(S, S') \cdot \hat{\Delta}(S, S') > 0]$. On both datasets, the pairwise Q^* sampling outperforms Naive. The magnitude of the gain is largest on

	SYNTH		TREC	
	$\tilde{u}(x,y)$	$u^*(x,y)$	$\tilde{u}(x,y)$	$u^*(x,y)$
Naive	2.15	1.13	6.60	4.65
pair Q^*	0.24	0.21	1.45	0.77

Table 5: Variance $\Sigma(Q) \cdot n$ defined in Equation (8) for the pairwise comparison problem. The table compares naive averaging with our optimal Q^* from Equation (9) under perfect and approximate knowledge of utilities.

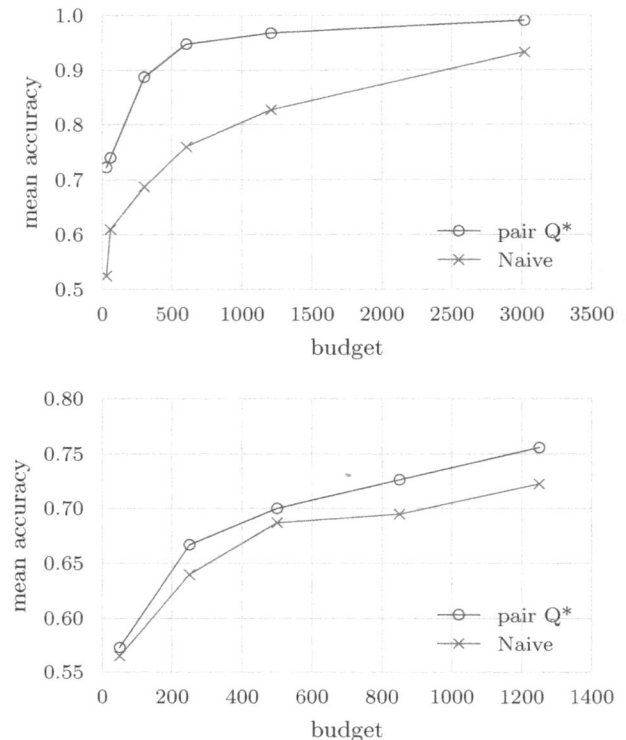

Figure 1: Mean pairwise accuracy on the SYNTH dataset (top) and the TREC dataset (bottom).

the SYNTH dataset, where the rankings produced by different systems are more similar to each other than for the TREC systems.

7.4 Is comparative evaluation against a baseline better than individual evaluation?

We now evaluate the statistical efficiency of our method for the problem of comparing multiple systems against a baseline. Table 2 shows the aggregate variance $\Sigma(Q)$ according to Eq. (10) computed analytically for both the SYNTH and the TREC datasets. The table shows that our Q^* for comparative evaluation as defined in Eq. (11) substantially outperforms the naive heuristic of sampling according to $Q(\boldsymbol{x}, y) \propto \tilde{u}(\boldsymbol{x}, y) \sum_j \text{P}(\boldsymbol{x}, y|S_j)$ (which originates from Multiple Importance Sampling and Mixture Importance Sampling [17]). The gain is particularly large for the realistic case of approximate utilities.

Figure 2 evaluates the accuracy with which the estimated $\mathbb{I}[\hat{\Delta}(S_j, S') \geq 0]$ predicts the true $\mathbb{I}[\Delta(S_j, S') \geq 0]$. Mean

	SYNTH		TREC	
	$\tilde{u}(x,y)$	$u^*(x,y)$	$\tilde{u}(x,y)$	$u^*(x,y)$
Naive	1.31	0.70	15.08	1.77
comp Q^*	0.18	0.15	6.82	1.28

Table 6: **Aggregate variance $\Sigma(Q)\cdot n$ defined in Equation (10) for the problem of comparing against a baseline. The table compares naive averaging with our optimal Q^* from Equation (11) under perfect and approximate knowledge of utilities.**

	SYNTH		TREC	
	$\tilde{u}(x,y)$	$u^*(x,y)$	$\tilde{u}(x,y)$	$u^*(x,y)$
Naive	0.86	0.46	38.64	1.79
rank Q^*	0.11	0.09	12.40	1.12

Table 7: **Aggregate variance $\Sigma(Q)\cdot n$ defined in Equation (10) for the ranking problem. The table compares naive averaging with our optimal Q^* from Equation (13) under perfect and approximate knowledge of utilities.**

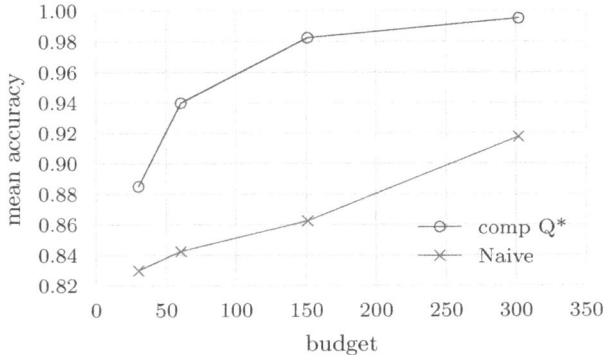

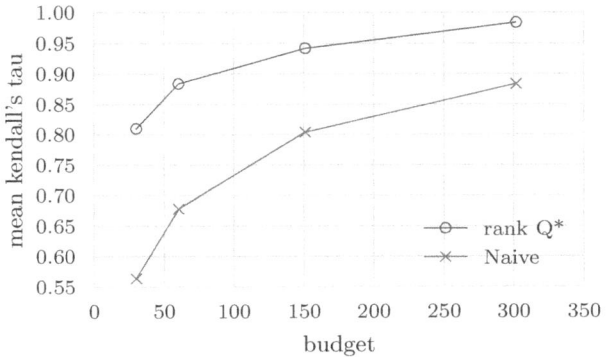

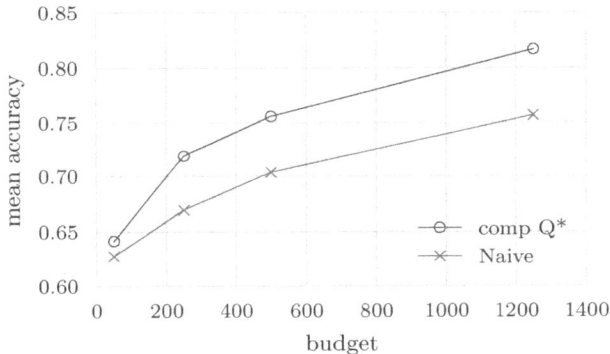

Figure 2: **Average accuracy when comparing four new systems against a baseline system on the SYNTH dataset (top) and the TREC dataset (bottom).**

Figure 3: **Kendall's tau for one set of 5 systems on SYNTH (top) and 16 sets of 5 systems on TREC (bottom).**

accuracy is defined as $Acc = \mathbb{I}[\Delta(S_j, S') \cdot \hat{\Delta}(S_j, S') > 0]$ over all comparisons using the sliding window approach described in Section 7.1. Again, we see large gains in efficiency from using our Q^* over naive averaging – both samplers using approximate utilites – reducing the required sample size for a desired accuracy by a half or more on both datasets.

7.5 Is comparative ranking more efficient than individual evaluation?

Finally, we turn to the problem of estimating the relative performance of k systems. Following the pattern from the previous two subsections, we first compare our Q^* from Eq. (13) with the naive averaging sampler in terms of their aggregate variance $\Sigma(Q)$ as defined in Eq. (10). Sets of systems to compare were chosen using the sliding-window approach described in Section 7.1. Again, the gains in statistical efficiency are especially large for the practical case,

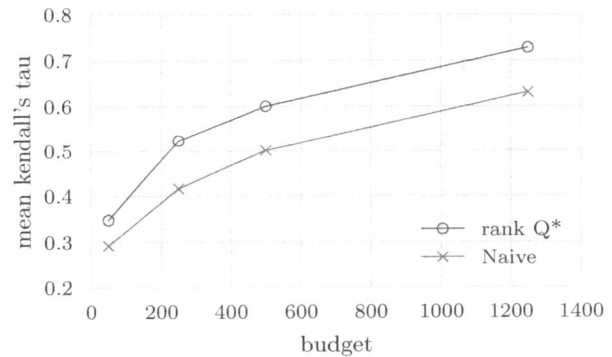

where the utilities are approximated.

Figure 3 evaluates to what extent this gain in mean squared estimation error translates into an improved accuracy for system ranking. In particular, we measure Kendall's tau when ranking by $\hat{\Delta}(S_j, \tau)$, which is identical to ranking by $\hat{U}(S_j)$. Analogous to the previous experiments, we see that our Q^* sampler for ranking is again substantially more accurate than naive sampling.

8. CONCLUSIONS AND FUTURE WORK

We developed a general and practical framework for evaluating ranking systems, making explicit the tight connections to Monte-Carlo estimation. This formal framework brings improved clarity and generality to the problem of sampling-based evaluation, including the design of estimators for new performance measures, conditions for unbiasedness, the reuse of data, and the design of sampling distributions. In particular, we focused on the question of how to design estimators and sampling distributions for comparative system evaluations, deriving variance-optimizing strategies for pairwise evaluation, comparing k-systems against a baseline, and ranking k systems. Empirical results show that these evaluation strategies lead to substantial improvements over previously used heuristics.

There are many directions for future work. First, much of the methodology should be applicable in other complex evaluation tasks as well, e.g., in NLP. Second, it would be interesting to see how to better approximate $u(x, y)$ by learning from previously collected judgments. This could potentially also be done in an adaptive fashion – similar to adaptive importance sampling. Third, there are other evaluation questions involving k systems, e.g., sampling so as to maximize the probability of finding the best out of k systems.

9. ACKNOWLEDGMENTS

This work was supported in part through NSF Awards IIS-1247637, IIS-1217686, IIS-1513692, also through a gift from Bloomberg. Peter Frazier was partially supported by NSF CMMI-1254298, NSF CMMI-1536895, NSF IIS-1247696, AFOSR FA9550-15-1-0038, AFOSR FA9550-16-1-0046, and DMR-1120296.

10. REFERENCES

[1] P. Ahlgren and L. Grönqvist. Retrieval evaluation with incomplete relevance data: A comparative study of three measures. In *CIKM*, pages 872–873, 2006.

[2] J. A. Aslam, V. Pavlu, and E. Yilmaz. A statistical method for system evaluation using incomplete judgments. In *SIGIR*, pages 541–548, 2006.

[3] C. Buckley and E. M. Voorhees. Retrieval evaluation with incomplete information. In *SIGIR*, pages 25–32, 2004.

[4] S. Büttcher, C. L. A. Clarke, P. C. K. Yeung, and I. Soboroff. Reliable information retrieval evaluation with incomplete and biased judgements. In *SIGIR*, pages 63–70, 2007.

[5] B. Carterette, J. Allan, and R. Sitaraman. Minimal test collections for retrieval evaluation. In *SIGIR*, pages 268–275, 2006.

[6] B. Carterette, V. Pavlu, E. Kanoulas, J. A. Aslam, and J. Allan. If I had a million queries. In *ECIR*, pages 288–300, 2009.

[7] C. W. Cleverdon. The significance of the cranfield tests on index languages. In *SIGIR*, pages 3–12, 1991.

[8] G. V. Cormack and T. R. Lynam. Statistical precision of information retrieval evaluation. In *SIGIR*, pages 533–540, 2006.

[9] J. Guiver, S. Mizzaro, and S. Robertson. A few good topics: Experiments in topic set reduction for retrieval evaluation. *TOIS*, 27(4):21:1–21:26, 2009.

[10] M. Hosseini, I. J. Cox, N. Milic-Frayling, G. Kazai, and V. Vinay. On aggregating labels from multiple crowd workers to infer relevance of documents. In *ECIR*, pages 182–194, 2012.

[11] H. Kahn and A. W. Marshall. Methods of reducing sample size in monte carlo computations. *Journal of the Operations Research Society of America*, 1(5):263–278, 1953.

[12] L. Li, W. Chu, J. Langford, and X. Wang. Unbiased offline evaluation of contextual-bandit-based news article recommendation algorithms. In *WSDM*, pages 297–306, 2011.

[13] A. Lipani, M. Lupu, and A. Hanbury. The curious incidence of bias corrections in the pool. In *ECIR*, pages 267–279, 2016.

[14] D. E. Losada, J. Parapar, and A. Barreiro. Feeling lucky? Multi-armed bandits for ordering judgements in pooling-based evaluation. In *SAC*, 2016.

[15] A. Moffat, W. Webber, and J. Zobel. Strategic system comparisons via targeted relevance judgments. In *SIGIR*, pages 375–382, 2007.

[16] A. Moffat and J. Zobel. Rank-biased precision for measurement of retrieval effectiveness. *TOIS*, 27(1):2:1–2:27, 2008.

[17] A. B. Owen. *Monte Carlo theory, methods and examples*. Draft, 2013.

[18] V. Pavlu and J. Aslam. A practical sampling strategy for efficient retrieval evaluation. Technical report, Northeastern University, 2007.

[19] D. D. Peng Ye. Combining preference and absolute judgements in a crowd-sourced setting. In *ICML Workshop: Machine Learning Meets Crowdsourcing*, 2013.

[20] S. E. Robertson and E. Kanoulas. On per-topic variance in IR evaluation. In *SIGIR*, pages 891–900, 2012.

[21] T. Sakai and N. Kando. On information retrieval metrics designed for evaluation with incomplete relevance assessments. *Information Retrieval*, 11(5):447–470, 2008.

[22] M. Sanderson. Test collection based evaluation of information retrieval systems. *Foundations and Trends in Information Retrieval*, 4(4):247–375, 2010.

[23] T. Schnabel, A. Swaminathan, A. Singh, N. Chandak, and T. Joachims. Recommendations as treatments: Debiasing learning and evaluation. *CoRR*, abs/1602.05352, 2016.

[24] K. Sparck-Jones and C. J. V. Rijsbergen. Report on the need for and provision of an "ideal" information retrieval test collection. Technical report, University of Cambridge, 1975.

[25] E. M. Voorhees and D. Harman. Overview of the ninth text retrieval conference (TREC-8). In *NIST Special Publication 500-246*, 1999.

[26] W. Webber and L. A. F. Park. Score adjustment for correction of pooling bias. In *SIGIR*, pages 444–451, 2009.

[27] E. Yilmaz and J. A. Aslam. Estimating average precision with incomplete and imperfect judgments. In *CIKM*, pages 102–111, 2006.

[28] E. Yilmaz, E. Kanoulas, and J. A. Aslam. A simple and efficient sampling method for estimating AP and NDCG. In *SIGIR*, pages 603–610, 2008.

[29] C. Yuan and M. J. Druzdzel. How heavy should the tails be? In *FLAIRS*, pages 799–805, 2005.

[30] P. Zhao and T. Zhang. Stochastic optimization with importance sampling for regularized loss minimization. In *ICML*, pages 1–9, 2015.

[31] J. Zobel. How reliable are the results of large-scale information retrieval experiments? In *SIGIR*, pages 307–314, 1998.

A Topical Approach to Retrievability Bias Estimation

Colin Wilkie
School of Computing Science,
University of Glasgow
Glasgow, United Kingdom
c.wilkie.3@research.gla.ac.uk

Leif Azzopardi
University of Strathclyde
Glasgow, United Kingdom
leifos@acm.org

ABSTRACT

Retrievability is an independent evaluation measure that offers insights to an aspect of retrieval systems that performance and efficiency measures do not. Retrievability is often used to calculate the retrievability bias, an indication of how accessible a system makes all the documents in a collection. Generally, computing the retrievability bias of a system requires a colossal number of queries to be issued for the system to gain an accurate estimate of the bias. However, it is often the case that the accuracy of the estimate is not of importance, but the relationship between the estimate of bias and performance when tuning a systems parameters. As such, reaching a stable estimation of bias for the system is more important than getting very accurate retrievability scores for individual documents. This work explores the idea of using topical subsets of the collection for query generation and bias estimation to form a local estimate of bias which correlates with the global estimate of retrievability bias. By using topical subsets, it would be possible to reduce the volume of queries required to reach an accurate estimate of retrievability bias, reducing the time and resources required to perform a retrievability analysis. Findings suggest that this is a viable approach to estimating retrievability bias and that the number of queries required can be reduced to less than a quarter of what was previously thought necessary.

1. INTRODUCTION

Retrievability is an estimate of how easily documents in a collection can be found using a particular retrieval system [2]. Retrievability offers an alternative view of a retrieval system by investigating the influence the system exerts on the collection by which documents it provides access to. Performing a retrievability analysis is primarily done to evaluate whether a system is biased towards a particular set of documents for inappropriate reasons, such as a system favouring documents that are incredibly long. This is particularly useful when assessing new systems for any unknown biases which may influence performance. Retriev-

ability can also be used to identify individual documents that are hard to find which can help identify problem areas where important documents are difficult to access in enterprise settings. Retrievability has also been shown to correlate with some performance measures and so, researchers have suggested that it could be used to tune a system depending on what aspect of performance is most important to the user [14]. Doing so would avoid recourse to relevancy judgements when the standard method of computing retrievability is performed. These aspects of retrievability make it a valuable tool in the evaluation of systems, however, retrievability has not yet seen widespread use due to some limitations in how it is computed.

The biggest limitation when performing a retrievability analysis concerns the resources required, especially in terms of time as the current method of computing retrievability requires a brute force approach, launching large sets of queries to cover a range of potential queries that could be issued to the system. Typically, these large query sets are generated automatically, often by extracting very large numbers of bigrams from the whole collection to attempt to cover all the documents in the collection. This means that a retrievability analysis simply cannot be performed on large data sets as the compute time would be huge. This analysis also cannot be performed on continually streaming data sets as each new document would require the retrievability to be recomputed for the full collection. This is a huge problem as it limits the usefulness of retrievability in its current state. This work provides an investigation into providing an alternate, more efficient, method of computing the overall retrievability bias of a system. This method, however, will not allow for an accurate retrievability score to be generated for every document in the collection. This novel method of computing retrievability is based on the idea that there are particular topics within a collection that can be deemed important and as such should be the focus of such an analysis. In focussing on these documents, the space is reduced in such a way that important documents are assessed in a much more efficient way.

The remainder of this paper will introduce the relevant background material covering both retrievability and its place in research literature so far. Following this, the method used to garner results for this analysis is described before an analysis of these results is performed, detailing the key findings of this study. Finally, future work is listed to confirm the generalisability of these findings as well as how to expand on these findings and further applications of this work.

2. BACKGROUND

Retrievability is a document centric evaluation method [2], that provides an alternate view on how a retrieval system interacts with a collection. Retrievability measures how *likely* a document is to be retrieved by a particular configuration of an IR system. The retrievability $\mathbf{r}$ of a document $\mathbf{d}$ with respect to the configuration of an IR system is defines as:

$$\mathbf{r(d)} \propto \sum_{\mathbf{q} \in \mathbf{Q}} \mathbf{f(k_{dq}, c)}$$

where $\mathbf{q}$ is a query from the large query set $\mathbf{Q}$. $\mathbf{k_{dq}}$ is the rank at which $\mathbf{d}$ is retrieved given $\mathbf{q}$, therefore the utility function $\mathbf{f(k_{dq}, c)}$ determines the score that document $\mathbf{d}$ attains for query $\mathbf{q}$ given the rank cutoff $\mathbf{c}$. $\mathbf{r(d)}$ is calculated by summing over all queries $\mathbf{q}$ in query set $\mathbf{Q}$. Theoretically, $\mathbf{Q}$ represents the universe of all possible queries, but in practice $\mathbf{Q}$ is very large set of queries [1, 2, 5, 7, 12]. The standard measure of retrievability used employs the utility function $\mathbf{f(k_{dq}, c)}$, such that if a document, $\mathbf{d}$, is retrieved in the top $\mathbf{c}$ documents given $\mathbf{q}$, then $\mathbf{f(k_{dq}, c) = 1}$, otherwise $\mathbf{f(k_{dq}, c) = 0}$. This measure provides an intuitive value for each document as it is simply the number of times that the document is retrieved in the top $\mathbf{c}$ documents. Documents falling outside the the top $\mathbf{c}$ attain no scores.

The typical approach to compute retrievability has been to extract a large query set from the collection in the form of either bigrams, unigrams, n-grams or a combination of all. This set is often very large and so authors have put in artificial limits that dictate how many times a query must appear in the collection before it will be added to the set [11]. Once the query set has been created, all the queries are issued to the system in question and the top 100 (dependant on the $\mathbf{c}$ selected) results are recorded. Once all queries have been issued, each result is taken in turn and the scores for each document are applied (based on the chosen utility function.) From all the results, a list of the $\mathbf{r(d)}$ for every document in the collection will be generated. This allows the user to investigate individual document scores and see which documents are particularly difficult or easy to find.

To convert the $\mathbf{r(d)}$ for each document into a single value describing bias, an inequality metric is used to assess the distribution of wealth in a population. However, the retrievability of a document in a collection fits this paradigm as the retrievability can be considered the documents wealth and the collection is the population that retrievability is distributed amongst. The Gini Coefficient can be used to calculate the level of inequality in a population by comparing the distribution to the Lorenz Curve. This estimate indicates the retrievability bias, with a score near 1 indicating total inequality while a score approaching 0 denotes total equality.

Research by a number of authors has began to address the issue of resources required to compute effective estimates of retrievability. The most naive approach, by Wilkie and Azzopardi [13] investigated the impact of simply reducing the number of bigrams issued to the collection. In this work, the authors followed their previous methodology of extracting bigrams from the whole collection and issuing them to a system and estimating retrievability however, they created multiple sets of bigrams for each collection which were all subsets of the original bigram extraction. The authors ordered the bigrams by their log likelihood scores and then removed percentages of the lowest scoring bigrams to create new sets. This way, they created 10 sets of bigrams rang-

ing from 10% of the highest scoring bigrams up to all of the bigrams extracted in intervals of %10 (i.e. 10%, 20%, 30%... etc). The findings of this work revealed that, on very biased systems (i.e. systems that have very high Gini Coefficients, like TF.IDF) large amounts of the bigrams can be removed, using sets as small as 40% of all bigrams, still produced a very reasonable estimate of the Gini Coefficient for the collection. On the other hand, systems that were know to be less biased, such as BM25 and PL2, had very little leeway in the number of bigrams necessary and that removing as few as 10% on a well tuned system lead to statistically significant differences in the estimation of the Gini Coefficient. Therefore, this work demonstrated that reducing the number of bigrams was not a viable method of reducing the required resources to compute retrievability bias accurately. More recent work by Lipani and Lupu [8] laid the groundwork for the creation of an analytical method of computing retrievability bias. This work, essentially, creates an upper bound to how retrievable a document can be by employing a boolean model. The work can be broken down to two main findings, when using bigrams with an *AND* between terms, the document containing both terms accumulate retrievability while all other documents receive no retrievability. When using an *OR*, any document that contains either term will receive a share of retrievability. The disadvantage of this technique is that there is no document ranking in place, therefore every document must be considered equally retrievable, thus cumulative and gravity scoring models have no place here. The method, in its current state, is therefore too naive to effectively compute an accurate estimate of retrievability but is useful for defining this upper bound. Finally, work by Bashir [4] also attempted to take an alternate, analytical approach to calculating retrievability bias. In this work, Bashir employed features of the documents in the collection (such as length, unique vocabulary, etc) to estimate retrievability. The key findings of the work were that this method could actually be used to estimate the Gini Coefficient reasonably well but, like the other work mentioned here, was unable to efficiently and accurately estimate the individual retrievability score of the documents in the collection. Therefore, further work is still required to find a method of efficient estimation that can accurately determine both the Gini Coefficient of the system as a whole and the individual retrievability scores of the documents in the collection.

Another important aspect of research regarding retrievability focuses on the relationship between retrievability bias and retrieval performance [2, 3, 5, 6, 11, 12, 14]. Work by Wilkie and Azzopardi has investigated this relationship in a variety of ways including the relationship between performance and bias when selecting which system to employ [12] as well as the relationship when tuning a particular systems length normalisation settings [11, 14]. The authors found the relationship between performance and bias to be nonlinear when TREC performance measures are used. However, when the authors investigated system tuning using metrics like Time Biased Gain [10] and U-Measure [9], the parameter setting that minimised bias also maximised performance. This was a very important finding as it suggested that it could be possible to tune a system well using the results of a retrievability analysis, thus removing the need for resorting to relevancy judgments.

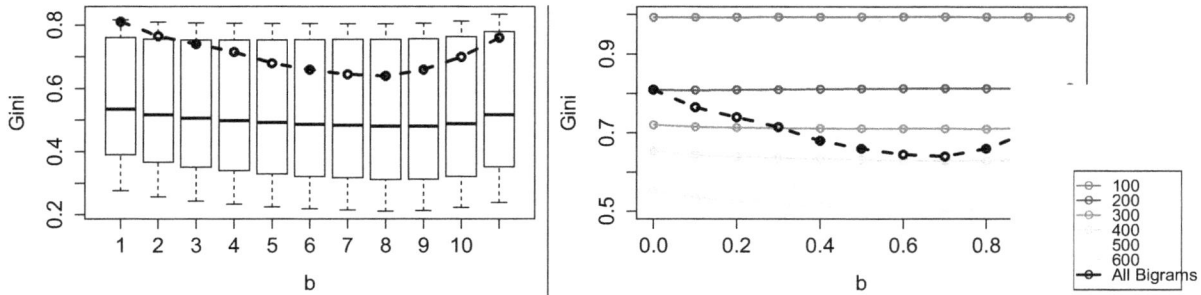

Figure 1: (Left) Box plot showing the max, min and mean Gini score across the 50 topics issued. The dashed line represents the Gini computed when using bigrams from the whole collection. (Right) Line plot showing the mean Gini Coefficient for each query set used. The lines are ordered from top to bottom by increasing volume of queries in each set.

3. METHOD

The focus of this work is to analyse whether or not retrievability bias can be accurately estimated by using a novel topic centric approach. This approach focusses on the topic pools of the TREC collections. Given that this approach is viable, the next step of the investigation will assess how few queries are needed, per topic, to arrive at a reasonable estimation of retrievability bias, that agrees with the estimate of the more traditional, high volume approach.

The new method is performed by first identifying the pool of documents that were judged for a topic. Bigrams are then extracted from these pooled documents only, thus creating a small bigram set which is, theoretically, topic centric. This is repeated for each topic, thus giving several small bigram query sets. The query sets generated were trimmed down to 600 queries as this was near the average number of queries extracted for each topic. Doing so prevented a small set of topics being overly dominant in the study as some topics were providing in excess of 20,000 queries on their own. The sets were trimmed down to the 600 queries with the highest log likelihood scores thus creating a set of 600 'realistic' bigrams. Following this, the bigrams are issued to the system and the top 100 results recorded, this is repeated for several parameter settings of the retrieval system. Next, the retrievability of each document is calculated by counting how many times each document occurs in the top 100 results for each query issued. However, unlike previous studies, retrievability is only calculated for documents that are retrieved at least once from any of the queries issued. Essentially, all documents that are never retrieved are ignored, thus removing the large set of documents with 0 score. Finally, retrievability bias is computed as normal, using the Gini Coefficient. This produces an estimate of retrievability for a set of bigrams extracted from a single topic, therefore the process is repeated for each topic in the collection. Once the process has been done for every topic, the Gini Coefficients from each topic are averaged across to give a single estimate of Gini.

The experiment detailed above was performed on the Associated Press (AP) collection as this study is an initial investigation of the viability of the ideas presented. With AP, topics numbered 151 to 200 were used as were their respective relevancy judgements. The system used was BM25 and the b parameter space was investigated. b was set to values ranging from 0.0 to 1.0 in intervals of 0.1.

4. RESULTS AND ANALYSIS

Analysing the results the method used created, a number of interesting observations are apparent. To begin with, the left plot of Figure 1 presents information regarding the Gini coefficient calculated from each of the 50 topics, using their respective (600 query) query sets. The plot presents the mean, quartiles, maximum and minimum Gini coefficients found as the b parameter of BM25 is adjusted. The plot demonstrates that the topics have a very broad range of estimations for Gini, generally covering a range of roughly 0.8 to 0.2. This obviously suggests that the Gini Coefficient of the system cannot be accurately estimated when using a random set of topics and as the range is so broad (as indicated by the quartiles) it would be difficult to effectively select a subset of topics to create an estimate with. It is also worth noting that the mean Gini at each b value follows a similar trend to the Gini found when the traditional approach was used. Upon further investigation, it was found that a very strong, significant correlation of 0.982 between the traditional approach and this new approach exists. This suggests that, for this collection and system, a user can predict the b setting at which the minimum Gini coefficient will be found as well as the consequences of either increasing or decreasing b. The benefit of this approach is the large reduction in queries that must be issued to accurately predict the b setting for minimum Gini. The traditional approach requires 81,000 queries to be issued to the system, the new method only requires 30,000 queries issued. This is a huge saving in terms of resources however, it must be noted that although it is possible to predict the setting for minimum Gini, this method gives a very different estimate of Gini due to the fact that it is only performed on a subset of the documents in the collection (i.e. only documents that were retrieved for at least 1 of the 30,000 queries).

Finding that the b parameter can be estimated using this new approach, the next step in the investigation was to find how few queries were needed from the 50 topics to gain a reasonable estimate of Gini. The right plot of Figure 1 presents the results of the retrievability analysis when query sets containing various amounts of queries (between 100 and 600 queries) are issued to the system. It is immediately evident that lower volumes of queries (100 - 300) are not producing

No. Queries	100	200	300	400	500	600	All
Min. Gini	0.99	0.81	0.71	0.63	0.56	0.50	0.64
b	0.0	0.1	0.8	0.7	0.7	0.7	0.7
Corr. w/ All	*-0.96	-0.41	*0.83	*0.95	*0.97	* 0.98	1

Table 1: Table presenting the actual minimum Gini values, along with the b parameter setting it was found at, and the correlation with the traditional method of calculating Gini. * denotes statistical significance at p<0.05.

any notable differences when the b parameter is adjusted. However, we see that the Gini estimates for the traditional method (dashed black line) sits in the region between the estimates produced from 200 to 400 queries being issued. However, as noted before, this traditional method is calculating Gini based on the retrievability of all the documents in the collection, while this new method only computes Gini based on documents retrieved. Therefore, the Gini estimate for the traditional method is expected to remain high as not all documents have the chance to be retrieved. From the plot it can be established that the lowest Gini estimate in the traditional method appears when b is set to 0.7. This plot also shows that the point of minimum Gini for 400, 500 and 600 query set is also $b = 0.7$ however, launching less than 400 queries results in different minimum settings being found, also demonstrated in Table 1. This table also shows that with as few as 400 queries issued for the 50 topics, a strong, significant correlation with the traditional method is still found. This suggests that as few as 20,000 queries can be issued to the system and still produce an accurate estimation of Gini, less than a quarter of the queries originally needed.

5. CONCLUSIONS AND FUTURE WORK

The investigation performed in this work was an initial exploration of an alternative, cheaper way to calculate retrievability by extracting the queries from the topic pools, rather than the full collection, and computing the Gini coefficient across documents which were retrieved for at least one query, instead of all documents. The key findings were, for this collection and configuration of the system, a very strong significant correlation is observed between the traditional estimate of Gini and the estimate produced by the method introduced in this paper. Further to this, this work expanded on the efficiency aspect by finding that a user can further reduce the number of queries extracted from each topic pool an still reach a reasonable estimate of Gini for identifying the b parameter setting which minimises Gini. These findings suggest that this is a viable method for computing retrievability bias cheaper than the existing approaches by utilising less than a quarter of the volume of queries originally required. However, as this is an initial study, performed on only one small collection, it is vital that these findings are explored on a wide range of both test collections and retrieval models before any wider conclusions can be drawn. It would also be pertinent to investigate how the Gini estimates relate to performance on a topic level to find if particular topics suggest that minimising Gini also maximises performance.

6. REFERENCES

[1] Azzopardi, L., Bache, R.: On the relationship between effectiveness and accessibility. In: Proc. of the 33rd ACM SIGIR. pp. 889–890 (2010)

[2] Azzopardi, L., Vinay, V.: Retrievability: An evaluation measure for higher order information access tasks. In: Proc. of the 17th ACM CIKM. pp. 561–570 (2008)

[3] Bache, R.: Measuring and improving access to the corpus. In: Current Challenges in Patent Information Retrieval, The Information Retrieval Series, vol. 29, pp. 147–165 (2011)

[4] Bashir, S.: Estimating retrievability ranks of documents using document features. Neurocomput. 123, 216–232 (Jan 2014), http://dx.doi.org/10.1016/j.neucom.2013.07.011

[5] Bashir, S., Rauber, A.: Improving retrievability of patents with cluster-based pseudo-relevance feedback documents selection. In: Proc. of the 18th ACM CIKM. pp. 1863–1866 (2009)

[6] Bashir, S., Rauber, A.: Improving retrievability & recall by automatic corpus partitioning. In: Trans. on large-scale data & knowledge-centered sys. II, pp. 122–140 (2010)

[7] Bashir, S., Rauber, A.: Improving retrievability of patents in prior-art search. In: Proc. of the 32nd ECIR. pp. 457–470 (2010)

[8] Lipani, A., Lupu, M., Aizawa, A., Hanbury, A.: An initial analytical exploration of retrievability. In: Proc. of the 2015 ICTIR. pp. 329–332. ICTIR '15, ACM (2015)

[9] Sakai, T., Dou, Z.: Summaries, ranked retrieval and sessions: a unified framework for information access evaluation. In: Proc. of the 36th ACM SIGIR. pp. 473–482. SIGIR '13 (2013)

[10] Smucker, M.D., Clarke, C.L.: Time-based calibration of effectiveness measures. In: Proc. of the 35th ACM SIGIR. pp. 95–104 (2012)

[11] Wilkie, C., Azzopardi, L.: Relating retrievability, performance and length. In: Proc. of the 36th ACM SIGIR conference. pp. 937–940 (2013)

[12] Wilkie, C., Azzopardi, L.: Best and fairest: An empirical analysis of retrieval system bias. Advances in Information Retrieval pp. 13–25 (2014)

[13] Wilkie, C., Azzopardi, L.: Efficiently estimating retrievability bias. In: Advances in Information Retrieval. pp. 720–726 (2014)

[14] Wilkie, C., Azzopardi, L.: A retrievability analysis: Exploring the relationship between retrieval bias and retrieval performance. In: Proc. of the 23rd ACM CIKM. pp. 81–90 (2014)

Estimating Embedding Vectors for Queries

Hamed Zamani
Center for Intelligent Information Retrieval
College of Information and Computer Sciences
University of Massachusetts Amherst
Amherst, MA 01003
zamani@cs.umass.edu

W. Bruce Croft
Center for Intelligent Information Retrieval
College of Information and Computer Sciences
University of Massachusetts Amherst
Amherst, MA 01003
croft@cs.umass.edu

ABSTRACT

The dense vector representation of vocabulary terms, also known as word embeddings, have been shown to be highly effective in many natural language processing tasks. Word embeddings have recently begun to be studied in a number of information retrieval (IR) tasks. One of the main steps in leveraging word embeddings for IR tasks is to estimate the embedding vectors of queries. This is a challenging task, since queries are not always available during the training phase of word embedding vectors. Previous work has considered the average or sum of embedding vectors of all query terms (AWE) to model the query embedding vectors, but no theoretical justification has been presented for such a model. In this paper, we propose a theoretical framework for estimating query embedding vectors based on the individual embedding vectors of vocabulary terms. We then provide a number of different implementations of this framework and show that the AWE method is a special case of the proposed framework. We also introduce pseudo query vectors, the query embedding vectors estimated using pseudo-relevant documents. We further extrinsically evaluate the proposed methods using two well-known IR tasks: query expansion and query classification. The estimated query embedding vectors are evaluated via query expansion experiments over three newswire and web TREC collections as well as query classification experiments over the KDD Cup 2005 test set. The experiments show that the introduced pseudo query vectors significantly outperform the AWE method.

CCS Concepts

•Information systems → Query representation; Query reformulation;

Keywords

Word embedding; query embedding vector; pseudo query vector; query expansion; query classification

ICTIR '16, September 12-16, 2016, Newark, DE, USA
© 2016 ACM. ISBN 978-1-4503-4497-5/16/09...$15.00
DOI: http://dx.doi.org/10.1145/2970398.2970403

1. INTRODUCTION

Computing semantic similarity between vocabulary terms has been an important issue in natural language processing (NLP) and information retrieval (IR) for many years. Many approaches, such as latent semantic indexing [10] and the information content-based method [31], have been proposed to capture semantically similar terms. Recent developments in distributed semantic representations based on dense vectors, also called word embeddings, have been proven to be highly effective in many NLP tasks, such as word analogy [27] and named-entity recognition [11]. Word embedding techniques are unsupervised learning algorithms that assign each term a low-dimensional (compared to the vocabulary size) vector in a "semantic vector space". In this space, the embedding vectors of semantically or syntactically similar terms are designed to be close to each other. Word2vec [27] and GloVe [29] are examples of successful implementations of word embedding vectors. Word2vec and GloVe learn the word embedding vectors using neural network-based language model and matrix factorization technique, respectively.

Following the impressive results achieved by word embedding techniques in NLP tasks, these techniques have begun to be studied in IR tasks [28, 35, 39, 40]. However, there are still several issues that need to be addressed in order to effectively use word embeddings in many IR tasks. In this paper, we address one of the main problems in this area: how to compute the embedding vectors of search queries? This is a challenging problem, since (1) search queries are not always available during the training time of embedding vectors, and (2) queries may contain several keywords that do not co-occur with each other frequently in the corpus, which makes training the embedding vectors for such queries problematic. Therefore, previous studies, such as [21, 24, 28, 35, 39], have decided to average or sum the word embedding vectors of all query terms to generate the query embedding vector. However, to the best of our knowledge, there has been no theoretical justification for such a decision.

In this paper, we propose a theoretical framework based on maximum likelihood estimation to estimate query embedding vectors using the individual embedding vectors of vocabulary terms. This framework which is independent of the embedding learning algorithms, maximizes the likelihood of a query language model and the probabilistic distribution over vocabulary terms computed based on the query embedding vector. The proposed framework consists of two main components. The first component is the similarity function that computes the similarity of two given embedding vectors.

The second component is the query language model. We develop our framework based on two different and effective similarity functions: the softmax and the sigmoid transformations of the cosine similarity. For the softmax function, we derive a closed-form formula to estimate query embedding vectors. For the sigmoid function which has recently been introduced to transform embedding similarity scores [37], a gradient-based approach is proposed to maximize the defined objective function. Furthermore, we estimate the query language models (the second component) using maximum likelihood estimation and a pseudo-relevance feedback technique.

An interesting outcome of our framework is that when the similarities of embedding vectors are computed using the softmax function and the query language model is estimated using maximum likelihood estimation, the computed query embedding vector is equivalent to the average or sum of the embedding vectors for all query terms. Therefore, a theoretical justification is introduced for the heuristic method that has been used in previous work [21, 24, 28, 35, 39] to estimate query embedding vectors.

We extrinsically evaluate the estimated query embedding vectors based on different implementations of the proposed framework using two well-known IR tasks: query expansion and query classification. In the query expansion experiments, we consider three standard TREC collections: Associated Press (AP), the TREC Robust Track 2004 collection, and the TREC Terabyte Track 2004-2006 collection (GOV2). In the query classification experiments, we consider the KDD Cup 2005 test set that contains web queries from real users. Our experiments show that the proposed pseudo query vectors (estimating query embedding vector based on pseudo-relevant documents) in general outperform the methods based on maximum likelihood estimation of query language models, significantly.

To summarize, the contributions of this paper include proposing a theoretical framework for estimating query embedding vectors, providing a theoretical justification for a widely used approach to estimate query embedding vectors (i.e., AWE), introducing pseudo query vectors that outperform the existing AWE method, and evaluating different query embedding vectors in two IR tasks.

2. RELATED WORK

In this section, we first review previous studies on word embeddings applied to IR tasks. We further briefly introduce related work on the query expansion and the query classification tasks.

2.1 Word Embedding for IR

Unlike NLP, where word embeddings have been successfully employed in several tasks, word embedding techniques in IR have only recently begun to be studied. The Fisher Vector (FV) [8] is a document representation framework based on continuous word embeddings, that aggregates a non-linear mapping of word embedding vectors into a document-level representation. Although FV was shown to perform better than latent semantic indexing (LSI) [10] in ad-hoc retrieval, it does not outperform popular IR frameworks, such as the TF-IDF and the divergence from randomness retrieval models. A number of approaches based on word embedding vectors have been proposed to improve retrieval performance. Zheng and Callan [39] proposed a supervised

embedding-based term re-weighting technique applied to the language modeling and BM25 retrieval models. BWESG [35], a bilingual word embedding method, has recently been developed and applied to information retrieval. This model learns bilingual embedding vectors from document-aligned comparable corpora. Ganguly et al. [15] considered the semantic similarities between vocabulary terms to smooth document language models. Zuccon et al. [40] proposed to employ word embeddings within the well-known translation model for IR. Sordoni et al. [33] employed word embedding techniques for expanding queries in a supervised manner. They used click-through and task-specific data.

Computing the semantic similarity between documents has been studied for a number of IR-related tasks. Paragraph vector [24] is a popular method that trains embedding vectors for phrases, paragraphs, and even documents. Word mover's distance (WMD) [22] is an interesting approach that measures the minimum traveling distance from the embedded words of one document to another one. This approach was shown to be effective in document classification. Kenter and de Rijke [20] proposed a supervised approach to compute semantic similarity between short texts. Training word embedding vectors based on additional data, like query logs and click-through data, was also studied in [16, 17, 18], which are out of the scope of this paper. More recently, Diaz et al. [12] proposed to train word embedding vectors on topically-constrained corpora, instead of large topically-unconstrained corpora. These locally-trained embedding vectors were shown to perform well for the query expansion task.

While query embedding vectors play a key role in a number of the aforementioned methods, such as [35, 39], they only considered the average or sum of word embedding vectors of all query terms as the query vector. Therefore, estimating accurate query embedding vectors can improve the performance of many of the embedding-based methods that need to compute query vectors. It should be noted that in a realistic case, queries are not available during the training time of embedding vectors. This makes training of query embedding vectors problematic. In this paper, we focus on estimating embedding vectors for queries based on the embedding vectors of individual terms.

2.2 Query Expansion

Query expansion is the process of adding relevant terms to a query to improve the retrieval performance. There are a number of query expansion methods based on linguistic resources such as WordNet, but they have not substantially improved the retrieval performance [34]. Although a number of data-driven query expansion methods, such as [1], can improve the average retrieval performance, they can be unstable across queries [9]. Therefore, although query expansion is not a new technique for improving retrieval effectiveness, it is still a challenging task [7]. As suggested by Xu and Croft [36], query expansion techniques can use global or local document analysis. Global analysis often relies on external resources or document collections, such as a similarity thesaurus [30] and Wikipedia [13]. On the other hand, local analysis expands queries using the documents that are related to them, such as the top-retrieved documents. This kind of query expansion is called pseudo-relevance feedback (PRF). PRF has been proven to be highly effective in improving retrieval performance [23, 36, 38].

2.3 Query Classification

Query classification, also known as query categorization, has the goal of classifying search queries into a number of pre-defined categories. Two types of classification have been studied. In the first, the labels are query types, such as navigational queries, informational queries, and transactional queries, e.g., [4, 25]. The other task is classifying queries based on their topics. Early work only considered local information about queries, i.e., the terms of queries [2, 3]. More recently, a number of methods were proposed to enrich queries using external information, such as the top-retrieved documents [14, 32] and query context [6]. Given the importance of the query classification task in web search, the 2005 ACM Knowledge Discovery and Data Mining competition (called, KDD Cup 2005) [26] focused on this task: classifying the queries issued by real web users based on query topics. Successful submissions in this competition used search engines to retrieve relevant documents for enriching initial queries [26]. The usefulness of the query classification task for web search has been shown in the literature, e.g., [19].

3. QUERY EMBEDDING VECTORS

Estimating accurate query models is a crucial component in every retrieval framework. It has been extensively studied in existing retrieval models and several approaches have been proposed for estimating query models, especially in the language modeling framework. On the other hand, while word embedding techniques have been shown to be highly effective in capturing semantic similarities in many NLP tasks, their usefulness in IR tasks is still relatively unstudied. In this paper, we focus on query representation in the embedding semantic space: how to estimate accurate embedding vectors for queries? More formally, let E denote a set of d-dimensional embedding vectors for each vocabulary term w. Given a query $q = \{w_1, w_2, \cdots, w_k\}$ with the length of k, the problem is to estimate a d-dimensional vector $\vec{q}$, henceforth called *query embedding vector*, for the query q.

In this section, we propose a probabilistic framework to estimate query embedding vectors based on maximum likelihood estimation. The main idea behind our approach is to maximize the likelihood of an accurate query language model and a probabilistic distribution that can be calculated using the embedding semantic space for each query vector. To do so, let $\delta(\cdot, \cdot)$ denote a similarity function that computes the similarity between two embedding vectors. Hence, the probability of each term w given a query vector $\vec{q}$, henceforth called *query embedding distribution*, can be calculated as:

$$p(w|\vec{q}) = \frac{\delta(\vec{w}, \vec{q})}{Z} \qquad (1)$$

where $\vec{w} \in E$ denotes the embedding vector of the given term w. The normalization factor Z can be calculated as follows:

$$Z = \sum_{w' \in V} \delta(\vec{w'}, \vec{q}) \qquad (2)$$

where V denotes the set of all vocabulary terms.[1] On the other hand, assume that there is a query language model θ_q for the query q, that shows how much each word contributes to the query. Our claim is that a query embedding

---

[1] In this paper, we assume that the embedding vectors of all query terms are available.

vector $\vec{q^*}$ is a proper query embedding vector, if the query embedding distribution (see Equation (1)) is "close to" the query language model θ_q. In other words, our purpose is to find a query embedding vector that maximizes the following log-likelihood function:

$$\vec{q^*} = \arg\max_{\vec{q}} \sum_{w \in V} p(w|\theta_q) \log p(w|\vec{q}) \qquad (3)$$

The high computational complexity of the normalization factor in calculating the query embedding distribution (see Equation (2)) makes optimizing the log-likelihood function expensive. Note that since the normalization factor Z depends on the query embedding vector, it cannot be computed offline. Therefore, similar to many other optimization problems, we need to relax our objective function. To this end, we assume that the normalization factor Z in Equation (1) is equal for all query vectors. Although this simplifying assumption is not true, our observations indicate that this is not a harmful assumption. To give an intuition about the validity of this assumption, we consider many ($> 200,000$) random query vectors and calculate the normalization factor Z for all of these query vectors. The mean and standard deviation for all Z values are $(1.7 \pm 0.15)^{*10^4}$. The mean value is an order of magnitude larger than the the standard deviation, and this shows that most of the Z values are close to the mean value, which indicates that our assumption is reasonable. It is worth noting that all the following calculations can be done without this assumption, but with high computational cost.

Therefore, based on this relaxation, we can re-write our objective function as follows:

$$\arg\max_{\vec{q}} \sum_{w \in V} p(w|\theta_q) \log \delta(\vec{w}, \vec{q}) \qquad (4)$$

As shown in Equation (4), our framework consists of two main components: the query language model θ_q and the similarity function δ. Since the output of $\delta(\vec{w}, \vec{q})$ is dependent on the query vector $\vec{q}$, the function δ can affect the way that we can optimize the objective function. In the following subsection, we solve this optimization problem for two effective similarity functions. We further discuss how we calculate the query language models.

3.1 Similarity Functions

There are several similarity metrics for word embedding vectors, including the cosine similarity, which have been considered for NLP tasks, e.g., [11, 27]. In the following, we describe two different functions to compute the similarity between embedding vectors. We also explain how our objective function can be optimized based on these functions.[2]

3.1.1 Softmax Function

The similarity function δ for computing the similarity between two embedding vectors can be calculated using the softmax function as follows:

$$\delta(\vec{w}, \vec{w'}) = \exp\left(\frac{\sum_{i=1}^{d} \vec{w}_i \vec{w'}_i}{\|\vec{w}\| \|\vec{w'}\|}\right) \qquad (5)$$

---

[2] These similarity functions are transformations of the cosine similarity. Since the results obtained by the cosine similarity (without transformation) are substantially lower than those achieved by these transformations, for the sake of space, we do not consider the cosine similarity itself.

where d denotes the dimension of embedding vectors. Without loss of generality, assume that the embedding vectors of all vocabulary terms are unit vectors, and thus their norms are equal to 1. Therefore, our objective function (see Equation (4)) can be re-written as follows:

$$\arg\max_{\vec{q}} \sum_{w \in V} p(w|\theta_q).\frac{\sum_{i=1}^{d} \vec{w}_i \vec{q}_i}{\|\vec{q}\|} \quad (6)$$

To make this objective function even simpler, we add a constraint to force the query vector be a unit vector. In other words, we consider the following constraint: $\|q\| = 1$. Based on this constraint, we obtain the Lagrange function as follows:

$$\mathcal{L}(\vec{q}, \lambda) = \sum_{w \in V} \left(p(w|\theta_q) \sum_{i=1}^{d} \vec{w}_i \vec{q}_i \right) + \lambda \left(1 - \sum_{i=1}^{d} (\vec{q}_i)^2 \right) \quad (7)$$

where λ denotes the Lagrange multiplier. Using the mathematical optimization method of Lagrange multipliers, we compute the first derivatives of the Lagrange function as follows:

$$\begin{cases} \frac{\partial \mathcal{L}}{\partial \vec{q}_i} = \sum_{w \in V} \vec{w}_i p(w|\theta_Q) - 2\lambda \vec{q}_i \\ \frac{\partial \mathcal{L}}{\partial \lambda} = 1 - \sum_{i=1}^{d} (\vec{q}_i)^2 \end{cases} \quad (8)$$

where $\vec{q}_i$ denotes the ith element of the query vector $\vec{q}$. By setting the above partial derivatives to zero, we can find the stationary point of our objective function as below:

$$\vec{q}_i = \frac{\sum_{w \in V} \vec{w}_i p(w|\theta_Q)}{\sqrt{\sum_{j=1}^{d} (\sum_{w \in V} \vec{w}_i p(w|\theta_Q))^2}} \quad (9)$$

Therefore, the query embedding vector can be calculated using the above closed-form formula.

3.1.2 Sigmoid Function

In this subsection, we consider the sigmoid function as another mapping function for transforming the cosine similarity scores, which was proposed by Zamani and Croft [37]. The similarity function δ can be computed based on the sigmoid function as follows:

$$\delta(\vec{w}, \vec{w'}) = \frac{1}{1 + \exp\left(-a \left(\frac{\sum_{i=1}^{d} \vec{w}_i \vec{w'}_i}{\|\vec{w}\| \|\vec{w'}\|} - c \right) \right)} \quad (10)$$

where a and c are two free parameters. Similar to the previous subsection, without loss of generality, we can assume that embedding vectors of all vocabulary terms are unit vectors. Therefore, the objective function in this case is calculated as below:

$$\arg\max_{\vec{q}} \sum_{w \in V} -p(w|\theta_q) \log \left(1 + \exp\left(-a \left(\frac{\sum_{i=1}^{d} \vec{w}_i \vec{q}_i}{\|\vec{q}\|} - c \right) \right) \right) \quad (11)$$

The partial derivative of the above objective function (called $\mathcal{F}$) with respect to each element of the query embedding vector is computed as:

$$\frac{\partial \mathcal{F}}{\partial \vec{q}_i} = \sum_{w \in V} p(w|\theta_q) \left(a \left(\frac{\vec{w}_i}{\|\vec{q}\|} - \frac{\vec{q}_i \sum_{j=1}^{d} \vec{w}_j \vec{q}_j}{\|\vec{q}\|^3} \right) (1 - \delta(\vec{w}, \vec{q})) \right) \quad (12)$$

where δ is the sigmoid-based similarity function as shown in Equation (10). Query embedding vectors can be now

estimated using gradient-based optimization methods. Note that this objective function is not convex, and thus the initial value of the query embedding vectors can affect the results.

3.2 Estimating Query Language Model

As described earlier, the query language model is the other component in our framework to compute the query embedding vectors. Several approaches have been proposed to estimate query language models. In this subsection, we introduce two of these methods that have been widely explored in the language modeling literature.

3.2.1 Maximum Likelihood Estimation

Maximum likelihood estimation (MLE) is a simple yet effective approach for estimating query language models. MLE for a given query q can be calculated by relative counts:

$$p(w|\theta_q) = \frac{\text{count}(w, q)}{|q|} \quad (13)$$

where θ_q, $\text{count}(w, q)$, and $|q|$ denote the unigram query language model, the count of term w in the query q, and the query length, respectively.

3.2.2 Pseudo-Relevance Feedback

Pseudo-relevance feedback (PRF) has been shown to be highly effective at improving retrieval effectiveness. PRF in the language modeling framework estimates a query language model from a small set of top-retrieved documents. In PRF, in addition to updating the weights of query terms, a number of new terms will be added to the query. In this paper, we consider the relevance model (with the i.i.d. sampling assumption) [23], a state-of-the-art PRF method, to estimate the query language model as follows:

$$p(w|\theta_q) \propto \sum_{d \in F} p(w|d) \prod_{w' \in q} p(w'|d) \quad (14)$$

where F denotes the set of feedback documents. The probability of each term in the document (e.g., $p(w|d)$) can be computed by smoothing the maximum likelihood estimation probability. The top m terms with highest probabilities are usually selected in the feedback language models. We call the query embedding vectors estimated using the PRF distributions, *pseudo query vectors* (PQV).

4. DISCUSSION

Average word embedding (AWE) is a popular method to estimate query embedding vectors. Although AWE has been shown to be effective in previous studies, this method of embedding vector construction was ad-hoc. In this section, we first show that AWE is a special case of the proposed framework, and thus there is a theoretical justification for this very simple approach. We further compare the two ways of optimizing the defined objective function based on the softmax and the sigmoid functions, respectively.

4.1 Special Case: Average Word Embedding

AWE, averaging or summing the embedding vectors of all query terms, has been previously used to construct embedding vectors of queries [21, 24, 28, 35, 39]. In this subsection, we show that AWE is a special case of the proposed theoretical framework.

Table 1: Statistics of the collections employed in the query expansion experiments.

ID	collection	queries (title only)	#docs	doc length	#qrels
AP	Associated Press 88-89	TREC 1-3 Ad-Hoc Track, topics 51-200	165k	287	15,838
Robust	TREC Disks 4 & 5 minus Congressional Record	TREC 2004 Robust Track, topics 301-450 & 601-700	528k	254	17,412
GOV2	2004 crawl of .gov domains	TREC 2004-2006 Terabyte Track, topics 701-850	25,205k	648	26,917

Assume that we consider the softmax function as the similarity function to compute the similarity between two embedding vectors. As shown in Subsection 3.1.1, each element of the query embedding vector can be calculated using Equation (9). In this equation, the denominator is just a normalization factor to force the embedding vector be a unit vector. Now, assume that the query language model θ_q is estimated using maximum likelihood estimation, as explained in Subsection 3.2.1. Therefore, the query embedding vector is calculated as:

$$\vec{q}_i \propto \sum_{w \in q} \frac{\text{count}(w, q)}{|q|} . \vec{w}_i \quad (15)$$

where $\vec{q}_i$ denotes the ith element of the query vector. In the above equation, the summation is just over the query terms, since the count of other terms is equal to zero, and thus they will not affect the result. The above equation is equivalent to AWE. To summarize, when the similarity of embedding vectors is calculated using the softmax function and the query language model is estimated using maximum likelihood estimation, the proposed framework will produce the AWE method.

4.2 Softmax vs. Sigmoid

In this subsection, we discuss the differences between using the softmax and the sigmoid functions in estimating query vectors. As calculated above, we come up with a closed-form formula for query embedding vectors when using the softmax function. This formula is easy to compute and very efficient, especially when only a limited number of terms have non-zero probability in the query language model θ_q. In addition, the calculated query vector is the global optimum solution for the defined objective function. The method based on the sigmoid function is an iterative gradient-based method. Since the objective function in this case is not convex, achieving the global optimum solution is not guaranteed. It should be noted that the objective function depends on the similarity function (see Equation (4)) and the local optimum solution of the objective function based on the sigmoid function might produce a better query vector compared to the global optimum of the one with the softmax function.

Furthermore, there are two free parameters involved in the sigmoid function, which make it more flexible than the softmax function. We expect that this flexibility leads to better performance for near-optimal parameter settings.

5. EXPERIMENTS

In this section, we extrinsically evaluate the proposed query embedding vectors in two well-known IR tasks: query expansion and query classification. In all experiments, we employed the word embedding vectors computed using the GloVe method [29]. The word embedding vectors were extracted from a 6 billion token collection (Wikipedia 2014

plus Gigawords 5), unless otherwise stated.[3] The dimension of embedding vectors are set to 300 in all experiments, except those related to studying the sensitivity of methods to the embedding dimension. In the experiments related to the pseudo query vector (PQV) methods (estimating query embedding vectors using pseudo-relevance feedback language models), the number of feedback documents is set to 10. For optimization of the sigmoid-based query embedding vector estimation, we employed the MALLET[4] implementation of the limited-memory BFGS algorithm (LBFGS) [5]. We used the MLE+Softmax method (AWE) as the initial query vector for the sigmoid-based methods.

In the following, we first employ query word embeddings for query expansion. We further consider the constructed query embedding vectors for the query classification task.

5.1 Evaluation via Query Expansion

In the first set of extrinsic evaluations, we consider query word embeddings for expanding query models in the language modeling framework. In the following, we first briefly explain how we expand query language models using the query word embeddings and then introduce our experimental setup. We afterward report and discuss the results.

5.1.1 Query Expansion Using Query Vectors

In these experiments, we use the language modeling framework. To expand the query language models, we first calculate the probability of each term given the query vector using Equation 1. We then linearly interpolate this probability with the maximum likelihood estimation of the original query, as follows:

$$p(w|\theta_q^*) = \alpha \, p_{mle}(w|\theta_q) + (1 - \alpha) \, p(\vec{w}|\vec{q}) \quad (16)$$

where α denotes the interpolation coefficient and controls the weight of the original query language model. We consider the top m terms with highest probabilities in θ_q^* as the expanded query language model.

5.1.2 Experimental Setup

To evaluate the proposed query embedding vectors in the query expansion task, we used three standard TREC collections: AP (Associated Press 1988-1989), Robust (TREC Robust Track 2004 collection), and GOV2 (TREC Terabyte Track 2004-2006 collection). The first two collections contain high-quality news articles and the last one is a large web collection. We report the statistics of these collections in Table 1. The titles of topics are considered as queries. In the experiments, we only considered the queries where the embedding vectors of all terms are available. Therefore, 146 out of 150, 241 out of 250, and 147 out of 150 queries were considered for AP, Robust, and GOV2, respectively.

---

[3]We consider this corpus, since it is a relatively large corpus containing formal texts with a diverse vocabulary set.
[4]http://mallet.cs.umass.edu/

127

Table 2: Comparing the proposed query embedding vectors via query expansion. The superscripts 0/1/2 denote that the improvements over QL/MLE+Softmax/MLE+Sigmoid are statistically significant.

Collection	Metric	QL	MLE+Softmax (AWE)	MLE+Sigmoid	PQV+Softmax	PQV+Sigmoid
AP	MAP	0.2236	0.2470[0]	0.2486[0]	0.2695[012]	**0.2717[012]**
	P@5	0.4260	0.4452[0]	0.4507[0]	0.4493[0]	**0.4548[01]**
	P@10	0.4014	0.4260[0]	**0.4274[0]**	0.4226[0]	0.4233[0]
Robust	MAP	0.2190	0.2299[0]	0.2303[0]	0.2355[012]	**0.2364[012]**
	P@5	0.4606	**0.4730[0]**	0.4714[0]	0.4564	0.4591
	P@10	0.3979	0.4237[0]	**0.4245[0]**	0.4083[0]	0.4141[0]
GOV2	MAP	0.2696	0.2719	0.2727	0.2771[012]	**0.2798[012]**
	P@5	0.5592	0.5837[0]	**0.5864[0]**	0.5755[0]	**0.5864[0]**
	P@10	0.5531	0.5653[0]	**0.5721[01]**	0.5694[0]	**0.5721[01]**

The standard INQUERY stopword list was employed in all experiments, and no stemming was performed.

We considered the KL-divergence retrieval model with the Dirichlet prior smoothing method. All experiments were carried out using the Galago toolkit[5].

Parameters Setting. In all the experiments, the Dirichlet prior smoothing parameter μ was set to Galago's default value of 1500. In all the experiments (unless otherwise stated), the parameters α (the linear interpolation coefficient), m (the number of terms added to each query), and n (the number of feedback terms considered in the PQV methods) were set using 2-fold cross-validation over the queries in each collection. We swept the parameter α between $\{0.1, \ldots, 0.9\}$. The values of parameters m and n were also selected from $\{10, 20, ..., 100\}$. The sigmoid parameters (i.e., a and c in Equation 10) were also set using the same procedure from the $[0, 50]$ and $[0.8, 0.9]$ intervals, respectively.

Evaluation Metrics. Mean Average Precision (MAP) of the top-ranked 1000 documents and the precision of the top 5 and 10 retrieved documents (P@5 and P@10) are used to evaluate the retrieval effectiveness. Statistically significant differences of performances are determined using the two-tailed paired t-test computed at a 95% confidence level.

5.1.3 Results and Discussion

In this subsection, we first evaluate the proposed query embedding vectors. We further study the parameters sensitivity of the methods. Finally, we study the sensitivity of the methods to different word embedding vectors. In our experiments, we evaluate all combinations of using softmax vs. sigmoid as similarity function and MLE vs. PRF (PQV) as the query language model. We compare our results with those obtained by the standard maximum likelihood estimation of query language models without query expansion (QL). As explained in Subsection 4.1, the MLE+Softmax method is equivalent to the AWE method, previously used in [21, 24, 35]. Since the contribution of this paper is to estimate accurate query embedding vectors, not proposing the most effective query expansion technique, we do not compare our methods with a large number of state-of-the-art query expansion methods. It should be also noted that queries are not accessible during the training time of word embedding vectors, which makes training of query embedding vectors problematic.

The results of the proposed methods are reported in Table 2. According to this table, the results achieved by the embedding-based query expansion methods outperforms QL

[5]http://www.lemurproject.org/galago.php

in all collections, in terms of MAP. These improvements are often statistically significant, especially in the newswire collections (AP and Robust). In GOV2, expanding query language models using both PQV methods significantly outperforms the QL baseline, in terms of MAP. The relative and absolute MAP improvements in the newswire collections are higher than those in the GOV2 collection. The reason could be related to the word embedding vectors that we used in our experiments. As explained in the beginning of Section 5, the embedding vectors were extracted from the Wikipedia and the Gigawords corpora that contain formal texts. At the end of this subsection, we report the results achieved by word embedding vectors extracted from other corpora. The proposed query expansion methods also outperform QL, in terms of P@5 and P@10, in most cases.

The results achieved by the MLE methods (i.e., MLE+Softmax (AWE) and MLE+Sigmoid) show that MLE+Sigmoid always outperforms MLE+Softmax in terms of the considered evaluation metrics (except in terms of P@5 in Robust). Similar behaviour can be observed by comparing the results achieved by PQV+Softmax and PQV+Sigmoid, i.e., PQV+Sigmoid always outperforms PQV+Softmax in terms of MAP, P@5 and P@10. It is notable that although the improvements of the sigmoid function over the softmax function are not statistically significant, the sigmoid-based methods consistently outperform the softmax-based methods, in terms of all evaluation metrics.

Comparing the results achieved by the PQV methods with those obtained by the MLE methods highlights substantial and statistically significant improvements between employing the aforementioned query language model distributions (i.e., MLE and PRF) in estimating the query embedding vectors. In other words, the PQV methods significantly outperform the MLE methods in all the collections, in terms of MAP. However, this is not the case for precision at top-retrieved documents. The MLE methods are better than the PQV methods in some cases, in terms of P@5 and/or P@10. In particular in the Robust collection, the MLE methods perform well, in terms of P@5 and P@10. These results indicate that using PRF distributions to estimate query embedding vectors can successfully improve the overall retrieval performance, but sometimes it harms the precision of the top-ranked documents.

Parameters Sensitivity. To study the sensitivity of the proposed methods to the free parameters, we set the parameters m (the number of expansion terms), α (the interpolation coefficient in Equation (16)), and n (the number of feedback terms considered to estimate PQVs) to 50, 0.5, and 10, respectively. In each set of experiments, we sweep one

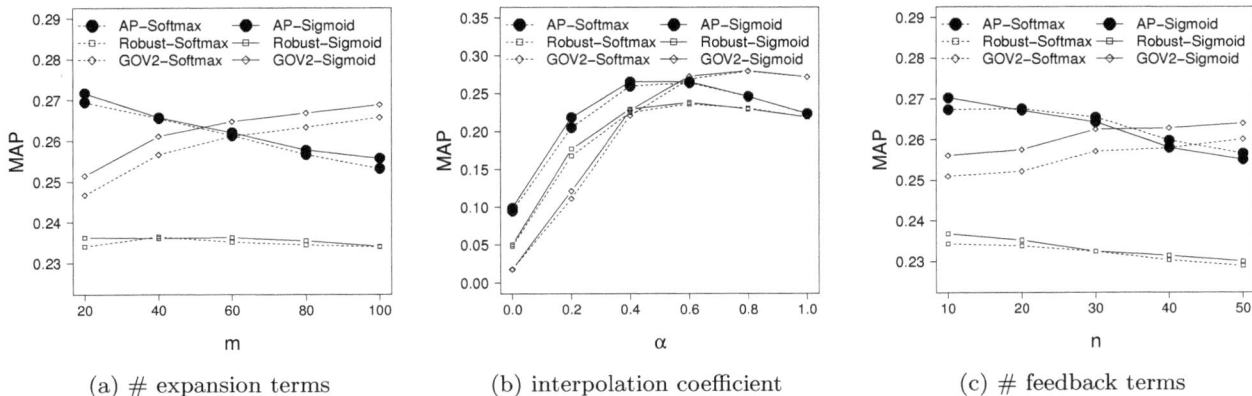

| (a) # expansion terms | (b) interpolation coefficient | (c) # feedback terms |

Figure 1: Sensitivity of PQV+Softmax and PQV+Sigmoid to the number of expansion terms (m), the interpolation coefficient (α), and the feedback term count used to estimate query embedding vectors (n), in terms of MAP.

of these parameters and plot the performance of methods, in terms of MAP. The results are plotted in Figure 1. For the sake of visualization, we only plot the results of PQV methods, but MLE methods also behave similarly.

According to Figure 1a, the behaviour of performance changes with respect to the number of expansion terms (m) completely depends on the retrieval collection. For instance, by increasing the number of expansion terms in GOV2, the performance significantly increases; while in AP, the performance drops. In Robust, the performance in general slightly decreases by increasing the number of expansion terms, but the performance changes are not significant. The results indicate that in the newswire collections (AP and Robust), a few top expansion terms are highly relevant to the query; while in the web collection (GOV2) there are a number of good expansion terms that are not very close to the estimated query embedding vector, and thus more expansion terms are needed.

Figure 1b plots the sensitivity of the methods to the parameter α. According to this plot, the PQV methods behave similarly in the newswire collections: they achieve their best performance when α is set to 0.6. This means that the weight of the generated language model using the estimated query embedding vectors should be close to the weight of the original query language model. In contrast, in the GOV2 collection, the PQV methods achieve their best results when α is equal to 0.8. This means that more weights should be given to the original query language model. Therefore, quality of the generated language model using query embedding vectors in AP and Robust might be higher than in GOV2.

According to Figure 1c, the number of feedback terms needed to estimate query embedding vectors in the newswire collections is much lower than those needed in the web collection. This plot again shows that the methods behave similarly in the newswire collections. All plots in Figure 1 show that the results achieved by the PQV method based on the sigmoid function in most cases are higher than those obtained based on the softmax function. These differences are higher in the GOV2 collection. This shows that while there is no guarantee to find global optimum solution for the sigmoid-based methods, they generally outperform the softmax-based methods.

Sensitivity to the Embedding Vectors. In this set of experiments, we study the sensitivity of PQV+Sigmoid (the method with highest MAP values) to the employed embed-

Table 3: Sensitivity of PQV+Sigmoid to the dimension of embedding vectors in query expansion, in terms of MAP. The superscripts 1/2/3 denote that the MAP improvements over the dimensions of 50/100/200 are significant.

Collection	Dimension			
	50	100	200	300
AP	0.2455	0.2604[1]	0.2648[1]	**0.2717**[123]
Robust	0.2305	0.2321	0.2351[12]	**0.2364**[12]
GOV2	0.2751	0.2762	0.2786[12]	**0.2798**[12]

Table 4: The corpora used for training the embedding vectors.

ID	Corpus	#tokens	#vocab.
Wiki	Wikipedia 2004 & Gigawords 5	6b	400k
Web 42b	Web crawl	42b	1.9m
Web 840b	Web crawl	840b	2.2m

ding vectors. We first train embedding vectors with different dimensions on the same corpus (Wikipedia 2004 & Gigawords 5). The achieved MAP values are reported in Table 3. According to this table, increasing the dimension of embedding vectors improves the retrieval performance. The MAP differences are statistically significant in many cases. This shows that the embedding vectors with very dense representations cannot be optimal for capturing semantic similarities in the proposed PQV+Sigmoid method.

To analyze the robustness of the proposed methods to the choices made in training the word embedding vectors, we consider three different corpora: Wiki, Web 42b, and Web 840b. The statistics of these corpora are reported in Table 4.[6] The dimension of embedding vectors is set to 300. The MAP values achieved by employing each of the embedding vectors trained on different corpora are reported in Table 5. Note that to have fair comparisons, we only consider the queries that the embedding vectors of all their query terms are available in all the embedding vector sets. The number of queries that are used for evaluation is mentioned in Table 5. Interestingly, although both web crawl corpora are much larger than the Wiki corpus, the PQV+Sigmoid method achieves its best performance in the newswire collections when the embedding vectors are extracted from the

---

[6]The embedding vectors are freely available at http://nlp.stanford.edu/projects/glove/.

Table 5: Sensitivity of PQV+Sigmoid to the embedding corpus in query expansion, in terms of MAP. The superscripts 1/2/3 denote that the MAP improvements over Wiki/Web 42b/Web 840b are statistically significant.

Collection	Wiki	Web 42b	Web 840b
AP (146 queries)	**0.2717^3**	0.2644	0.2602
Robust (240 queries)	**0.2365^2**	0.2329	0.2347
GOV2 (146 queries)	0.2788	0.2765	**0.2795**

Wiki corpus. Conversely, for the GOV2 collection, employing the embedding vectors trained on the Web 840b corpus leads to the best performance. The reason is that the content of documents in the Wiki corpus is more similar to the news articles, compared to web corpora. Therefore, the type of documents used for training embedding vectors is an important factor which should be taken into account.

5.2 Evaluation via Query Classification

In this subsection, we extrinsically evaluate the estimated query embedding vectors in the query classification task. The task is to assign each query a number of labels (categories). Labels are pre-defined and some training data are available for each label.

To classify each query, we consider a very simple approach based on query embedding vectors. We first compute the probability of each category/label given each query q and then select the top t categories with highest probabilities. In fact, this method is based on k-nearest neighbors classification. The probability $p(C_i|q)$ can be easily computed using the following formula:

$$p(C_i|q) = \frac{\delta(\vec{C}_i, \vec{q})}{\sum_j \delta(\vec{C}_j, \vec{q})} \propto \delta(\vec{C}_i, \vec{q}) \qquad (17)$$

where C_i denotes the ith category. $\vec{C}_i$ is the centroid vector of all query embedding vectors with the label of C_i. In the above equation, we drop the normalization factor, since it is the same for all categories. For PQV methods, we linearly interpolate the above probability with those computed using the MLE methods with the interpolation of α.

5.2.1 Experimental Setup

We consider the dataset that was previously employed to evaluate the query classification approaches submitted to the KDD Cup 2005: Internet user search query categorization [26]. This evaluation set contains 800 web queries that were issued by real users. These queries were randomly selected and do not contain junk and non-English words/phrases. The queries were tagged by three individual human editors. The KDD Cup 2005 organizers pre-defined 67 categories (labels) and each editor selected up to 5 labels among them for each query. The embedding vectors of all query terms of 700 out of 800 queries are available in our embedding collection. We only consider these 700 queries in our evaluations. The spelling errors in queries are corrected in a pre-processing phase.

In our evaluations, we consider 5-fold cross-validation over the queries and the reported results are the average of all results obtained over the test folds. In each step we have 560 and 140 training and test queries, respectively.

In the experiments related to PQV, we use the Robust collection (see Table 1 for details) to retrieve pseudo-relevant documents. The retrieval details are exactly similar to what

Table 6: Comparing query embedding vectors via query classification. The superscripts 1/2 denote that the improvements over MLE+Softmax/MLE+Sigmoid are significant. The best result for each evaluation metric is marked by *.

t	Metric	MLE+ Softmax (AWE)	MLE+ Sigmoid	PQV+ Softmax	PQV+ Sigmoid
1	F1	0.2675	0.2657	**0.2802^{12}**	0.2784^{12}
	Prec.	0.5738	0.5700	**0.6009^{12*}**	0.5971^{12}
2	F1	0.3617	0.3590	0.3741^{12}	**0.3752^{12}**
	Prec.	0.4783	0.4747	0.4947^{12}	**0.4961^{12}**
3	F1	0.3916	0.3859	0.4069^{12}	**0.4073^{12}**
	Prec.	0.4106	0.4046	0.4266^{12}	**0.4271^{12}**
4	F1	0.3938	0.3930	0.4142^{12}	**0.4144^{12*}**
	Prec.	0.3589	0.3582	0.3774^{12}	**0.3777^{12}**
5	F1	0.3904	0.3892	**0.4095^{12}**	0.4082^{12}
	Prec.	0.3237	0.3227	**0.3395^{12}**	0.3384^{12}

were considered in the query expansion experiments (see Subsection 5.1.2). In all experiments, stopwords are removed from queries and no stemming was performed. We employed the INQUERY stopword list.

Parameters Setting. In all experiments unless explicitly mentioned, the parameters α (the linear interpolation coefficient), and n (the number of feedback terms considered in the PQV methods) were tuned on the training data. We swept the parameter α between $\{0.1, \ldots, 0.9\}$. The values of parameter n were also selected from $\{10, 20, ..., 100\}$.

Evaluation Metrics. We consider two widely used evaluation metrics that were also used in KDD Cup 2005 [26]: precision and F1-measure. Since the labels assigned by the three human editors differ in some cases, all the label sets should be taken into account. We compute these two metrics in the same way as was used to evaluate the KDD Cup 2005 submissions [26]. Statistically significant differences are determined using the two-tailed paired t-test computed at a 95% confidence level.

5.2.2 Results and Discussion

In this subsection, we first evaluate the proposed query embedding vectors. We further study the parameters sensitivity of the proposed methods. Finally, we discuss the results obtained by a number of different word embeddings. Similar to the query expansion experiments, we consider all combinations of softmax vs. sigmoid and MLE vs. PQV for the query classification experiments. As explained earlier, the purpose of this paper is to propose a theoretical framework for estimating query embedding vectors. Thus, we want to extrinsically evaluate different query embedding vectors. Therefore, we do not consider any other baselines.

The results achieved by the proposed methods are reported in Table 6. According to this table, by increasing the number of labels assigned to each query (i.e., t), the precision values decrease in all the methods, which is expected. In other words, assigning only one tag with highest probability achieves the best precision value. Therefore, as shown in Table 6, the best precision is achieved by PQV+Softmax when $t = 1$. Furthermore, the results indicate that PQV methods outperform MLE methods in all cases, in terms of both precision and F1-measure. The F1-measure improvements are always statistically significant. It is an interesting observation that while the PRF distributions in PQV meth-

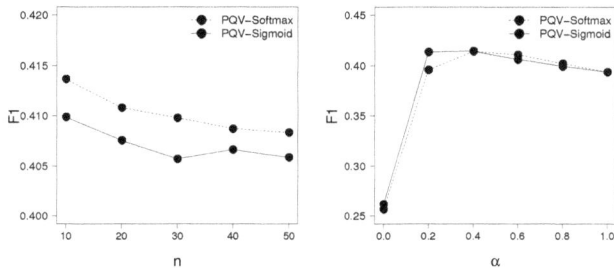

(a) # feedback terms   (b) interpolation coefficient

Figure 2: Sensitivity of PQV methods to the feedback term count used to estimate query embedding vectors (n) and the interpolation coefficient (α), in terms of F1-measure.

ods are estimated using the Robust collection (a newswire collection) and the queries in the KDD Cup 2005 dataset contains general web queries, the pseudo query vectors perform better than the MLE estimations.

In all the proposed methods, the best F1-measure value is achieved when t is equal to 4. The highest F1-measure is obtained by the PQV+Sigmoid method. Although our experimental setup differs from those considered by the KDD Cup 2005 submissions and it is not fair to compare our results with theirs, the best precision and F1-measure values achieved by the proposed method are relatively high and this is a good evidence of the effectiveness of employing word embedding vectors for the query classification task.

Parameters Sensitivity. To study the parameters sensitivity of the proposed PQV methods, we set the number of categories assigned to each query (i.e., t) to 4, where the methods achieve their best F1-measure. In this set of experiments, we set n (the number of feedback terms considered to estimate PQVs) and α (the interpolation coefficient introduced earlier) to 10 and 0.5, respectively. We sweep each parameter and plot the performance of the PQV methods, in terms of F1-measure (the MLE methods do not have these parameters). The results are plotted in Figure 2.

As shown in Figure 2a, by increasing the number of feedback terms for estimating query embedding vectors using PQV, the performance of methods generally decreases. In other words, the best F1-measure is achieved when n is equal to 10. Figure 2b demonstrates that the best performance is achieved when the parameter α is set to 0.4. In fact, when $\alpha = 0$ (the probability of each category is just computed based on the PQV method and it is not interpolated with the one computed based on MLE), the performance is relatively low. The reason could be related to the characteristics of the documents that are used to estimate the PRF distributions (because queries are general web queries, while documents are news articles). However, when this probability is linearly interpolated with the probability obtained based on MLE, the performance increases and the best performance is significantly higher than those obtained by the MLE methods.

Sensitivity to the Embedding Vectors. In this set of experiments, we study the sensitivity of PQV+Sigmoid to the embedding vectors.[7] Similar to the query expansion experiments, we first consider embedding vectors with different dimensions trained on the same corpus (Wikipedia

---

[7]For the sake of space, we only consider the method with the best F1-measure (see Table 6).

Table 7: Sensitivity of PQV+Sigmoid to the dimension of embedding vectors in query classification. The superscripts 1/2/3 denote that the improvements over the dimension of 50/100/200 are statistically significant.

Method	Metric	Dimension			
		50	100	200	300
PQV+	F1	0.3541	0.3886^1	0.4123^{12}	$\mathbf{0.4144^{12}}$
Sigmoid	Prec.	0.3227	0.3541^1	0.3757^{12}	$\mathbf{0.3777^{12}}$

Table 8: Sensitivity of PQV+Sigmoid to the embedding corpus in query classification. The superscripts 1/2 denote that the improvements over Wiki/Web 42b are significant.

Method	Metric	Wiki	Web 42b	Web 840b
PQV+	F1	0.4144	0.4284^1	$\mathbf{0.4359^{12}}$
Sigmoid	Prec.	0.3777	0.3846^1	$\mathbf{0.3972^{12}}$

2004 & Gigawords 5). We set the number of categories per query (t) to 4, where the methods achieve their best F1-measure. The achieved F1-measure values are reported in Table 7. According to this table, increasing the dimension of embedding vectors improves the query classification performance. Similar behaviour can be observed in the query expansion experiments (see Table 3).

We further evaluate the proposed methods using the embedding vectors trained on different corpora. The details of these corpora are reported in the query expansion experiments (see Table 4). The results are reported in Table 8. According to this table, the results achieved by the embedding vectors trained on the largest web corpus are higher than those achieved by other embedding vectors. The reason is that the queries were issued by web users and the vectors trained on web collections could provide better semantic representations for this type of queries.

6. CONCLUSIONS AND FUTURE WORK

In this paper, we addressed the problem of estimating dense vector representations for search queries in the embedding semantic space. To this end, we proposed a probabilistic framework to estimate query embedding vectors based on the individual embedding vectors of vocabulary terms. This framework consists of two major components: the similarity function and the query language model. We further developed our framework using two different similarity functions (the softmax and the sigmoid transformations of the cosine similarity) and two well-known query language models (the maximum likelihood estimation and the pseudo-relevance feedback). The proposed framework also provides a theoretical justification for the method that has been heuristically used in previous work: averaging the embedding vectors of all query terms. We extrinsically evaluated the proposed query vectors using two well-known IR tasks: query expansion and query classification. Our extensive query expansion experiments on three newswire and web collections indicate that employing the sigmoid function can consistently outperform the softmax function, although these improvements are not statistically significant. In addition, the embedding vectors estimated using a pseudo-relevance feedback model (called pseudo query vectors) in general improve the other embedding estimations, significantly. This finding was also verified by the query classification experiments over the KDD Cup 2005 test set.

Estimating query embedding vectors can open up many future directions. In this paper, we show that these vectors

can be simply applied in two well-known IR tasks. Employing query vectors in other IR tasks can be studied in future. In addition, we only considered basic query expansion and query classification methods to compare different query embedding vectors. Developing more complex embedding-based approaches to improve the state-of-the-art query expansion and query classification methods is also left for future work. Furthermore, different developments for the components of the proposed framework can be studied in future. For instance, estimating query language models based on mutual-information and more complex language models (bigram, trigram, etc.) can be considered in future studies.

7. ACKNOWLEDGEMENTS

This work was supported in part by the Center for Intelligent Information Retrieval and in part by NSF grant #CNS-0934322. Any opinions, findings and conclusions or recommendations expressed in this material are those of the authors and do not necessarily reflect those of the sponsor.

8. REFERENCES

[1] J. Bai, J.-Y. Nie, G. Cao, and H. Bouchard. Using Query Contexts in Information Retrieval. In *SIGIR '07*, pages 15–22, 2007.

[2] S. M. Beitzel, E. C. Jensen, O. Frieder, D. Grossman, D. D. Lewis, A. Chowdhury, and A. Kolcz. Automatic Web Query Classification Using Labeled and Unlabeled Training Data. In *SIGIR '05*, pages 581–582, 2005.

[3] S. M. Beitzel, E. C. Jensen, O. Frieder, D. D. Lewis, A. Chowdhury, and A. Kolcz. Improving Automatic Query Classification via Semi-Supervised Learning. In *ICDM '05*, pages 42–49, 2005.

[4] A. Broder. A Taxonomy of Web Search. *SIGIR Forum*, 36(2):3–10, 2002.

[5] J. Byrd, Richard H.and Nocedal and R. B. Schnabel. Representations of Quasi-Newton Matrices and Their Use in Limited Memory Methods. *Math. Program.*, 63(1):129–156, 1994.

[6] H. Cao, D. H. Hu, D. Shen, D. Jiang, J.-T. Sun, E. Chen, and Q. Yang. Context-aware Query Classification. In *SIGIR '09*, pages 3–10, 2009.

[7] C. Carpineto and G. Romano. A Survey of Automatic Query Expansion in Information Retrieval. *ACM Comput. Surv.*, 44(1):1:1–1:50, 2012.

[8] S. Clinchant and F. Perronnin. Aggregating Continuous Word Embeddings for Information Retrieval. In *CVSC@ACL '13*, pages 100–109, 2013.

[9] K. Collins-Thompson. Reducing the Risk of Query Expansion via Robust Constrained Optimization. In *CIKM '09*, pages 837–846, 2009.

[10] S. Deerwester, S. T. Dumais, G. W. Furnas, T. K. Landauer, and R. Harshman. Indexing by latent semantic analysis. *Journal of the American Society for Information Science*, 41(6):391–407, 1990.

[11] P. Dhillon, D. P. Foster, and L. H. Ungar. Multi-View Learning of Word Embeddings via CCA. In *NIPS '11*, pages 199–207, 2011.

[12] F. Diaz, B. Mitra, and N. Craswell. Query Expansion with Locally-Trained Word Embeddings. In *ACL '16*, 2016.

[13] H. Fang. A Re-examination of Query Expansion Using Lexical Resources. In *ACL '08*, pages 139–147, 2008.

[14] E. Gabrilovich, A. Broder, M. Fontoura, A. Joshi, V. Josifovski, L. Riedel, and T. Zhang. Classifying Search Queries Using the Web As a Source of Knowledge. *ACM Trans. Web*, 3(2):5:1–5:28, 2009.

[15] D. Ganguly, D. Roy, M. Mitra, and G. J. Jones. Word Embedding Based Generalized Language Model for Information Retrieval. In *SIGIR '15*, pages 795–798, 2015.

[16] M. Grbovic, N. Djuric, V. Radosavljevic, and N. Bhamidipati. Search Retargeting Using Directed Query Embeddings. In *WWW '15*, pages 37–38, 2015.

[17] P.-S. Huang, X. He, J. Gao, L. Deng, A. Acero, and L. Heck. Learning Deep Structured Semantic Models for Web Search Using Clickthrough Data. In *CIKM '13*, pages 2333–2338, 2013.

[18] D. Kang. Query2Vec: Learning Deep Intentions from Heterogeneous Search Logs. Technical report, Carnegie Mellon University, 2015.

[19] I.-H. Kang and G. Kim. Query Type Classification for Web Document Retrieval. In *SIGIR '03*, pages 64–71, 2003.

[20] T. Kenter and M. de Rijke. Short Text Similarity with Word Embeddings. In *CIKM '15*, pages 1411–1420, 2015.

[21] R. Kiros, R. S. Zemel, and R. R. Salakhutdinov. A Multiplicative Model for Learning Distributed Text-Based Attribute Representations. In *NIPS '14*, pages 2348–2356, 2014.

[22] M. J. Kusner, Y. Sun, N. I. Kolkin, and K. Q. Weinberger. From Word Embeddings to Document Distances. In *ICML '15*, pages 957–966, 2015.

[23] V. Lavrenko and W. B. Croft. Relevance Based Language Models. In *SIGIR '01*, pages 120–127, 2001.

[24] Q. V. Le and T. Mikolov. Distributed Representations of Sentences and Documents. In *ICML '14*, pages 1188–1196, 2014.

[25] U. Lee, Z. Liu, and J. Cho. Automatic Identification of User Goals in Web Search. In *WWW '05*, pages 391–400, 2005.

[26] Y. Li, Z. Zheng, and H. K. Dai. Kdd cup-2005 report: Facing a great challenge. *SIGKDD Explor. Newsl.*, 7(2):91–99, 2005.

[27] T. Mikolov, I. Sutskever, K. Chen, G. S. Corrado, and J. Dean. Distributed Representations of Words and Phrases and their Compositionality. In *NIPS '13*, pages 3111–3119, 2013.

[28] E. Nalisnick, B. Mitra, N. Craswell, and R. Caruana. Improving Document Ranking with Dual Word Embeddings. In *WWW '16*, pages 83–84, 2016.

[29] J. Pennington, R. Socher, and C. Manning. GloVe: Global Vectors for Word Representation. In *EMNLP '14*, pages 1532–1543, 2014.

[30] Y. Qiu and H.-P. Frei. Concept Based Query Expansion. In *SIGIR '93*, pages 160–169, 1993.

[31] P. Resnik. Using Information Content to Evaluate Semantic Similarity in a Taxonomy. In *IJCAI '95*, pages 448–453, 1995.

[32] D. Shen, R. Pan, J.-T. Sun, J. J. Pan, K. Wu, J. Yin, and Q. Yang. Query Enrichment for Web-query Classification. *ACM Trans. Inf. Syst.*, 24(3):320–352, 2006.

[33] A. Sordoni, Y. Bengio, and J.-Y. Nie. Learning Concept Embeddings for Query Expansion by Quantum Entropy Minimization. In *AAAI '14*, pages 1586–1592, 2014.

[34] E. M. Voorhees. Query Expansion Using Lexical-semantic Relations. In *SIGIR '94*, pages 61–69, 1994.

[35] I. Vulić and M.-F. Moens. Monolingual and Cross-Lingual Information Retrieval Models Based on (Bilingual) Word Embeddings. In *SIGIR '15*, pages 363–372, 2015.

[36] J. Xu and W. B. Croft. Query Expansion Using Local and Global Document Analysis. In *SIGIR '96*, pages 4–11, 1996.

[37] H. Zamani and W. B. Croft. Embedding-based Query Language Models. In *ICTIR '16*, 2016.

[38] C. Zhai and J. Lafferty. Model-based Feedback in the Language Modeling Approach to Information Retrieval. In *CIKM '01*, pages 403–410, 2001.

[39] G. Zheng and J. Callan. Learning to Reweight Terms with Distributed Representations. In *SIGIR '15*, pages 575–584, 2015.

[40] G. Zuccon, B. Koopman, P. Bruza, and L. Azzopardi. Integrating and Evaluating Neural Word Embeddings in Information Retrieval. In *ADCS '15*, pages 12:1–12:8, 2015.

Analysis of the Paragraph Vector Model for Information Retrieval

Qingyao Ai[1], Liu Yang[1], Jiafeng Guo[2], W. Bruce Croft[1]
[1]College of Information and Computer Sciences,
University of Massachusetts Amherst, Amherst, MA, USA
{aiqy, lyang, croft}@cs.umass.edu
[2]CAS Key Lab of Network Data Science and Technology, Institute of Computing Technology,
Chinese Academy of Sciences, China
guojiafeng@ict.ac.cn

ABSTRACT

Previous studies have shown that semantically meaningful representations of words and text can be acquired through neural embedding models. In particular, paragraph vector (PV) models have shown impressive performance in some natural language processing tasks by estimating a document (topic) level language model. Integrating the PV models with traditional language model approaches to retrieval, however, produces unstable performance and limited improvements. In this paper, we formally discuss three intrinsic problems of the original PV model that restrict its performance in retrieval tasks. We also describe modifications to the model that make it more suitable for the IR task, and show their impact through experiments and case studies. The three issues we address are (1) the unregulated training process of PV is vulnerable to short document overfitting that produces length bias in the final retrieval model; (2) the corpus-based negative sampling of PV leads to a weighting scheme for words that overly suppresses the importance of frequent words; and (3) the lack of word-context information makes PV unable to capture word substitution relationships.

CCS Concepts

•Information systems → Language models; *Document representation;*

Keywords

Paragraph Vector; Language Model

1. INTRODUCTION

Most tasks in information retrieval (IR) benefit from representations that do not treat individual words and documents as unique symbols but reflect their semantic relationships. A common paradigm is to project both words and documents to a latent semantic space and perform matching or language estimation accordingly. This has led to a range of research that incorporates topic models into ad-hoc retrieval tasks. For example, the cluster-based retrieval model [15] and the LDA-based retrieval model [24] have been used to smooth the probability estimation in language modeling approaches with a cluster-based topic model and a Latent Dirichlet Allocation model, respectively. Both methods obtained consistent improvement over the original language models [19].

Recent advances in neural embedding models potentially provide new methods to acquire semantically meaningful representations for words and documents. In particular, Le et al. [13] propose a paragraph vector (PV) model that can jointly learn word and document embeddings through estimating a document level language model. In contrast to topic models, PV does not define a fixed number of topics as a priori. Documents and words are flexibly clustered through the learning of embedding vectors. Meanwhile, PV can be trained with stochastic gradient decent algorithm (SGD), which is simple yet efficient for large-scale learning problems. Previous studies showed that PV has superior performance on several linguistic tasks [5] and great potential for IR [13].

Since PV estimates a document language model, a natural idea is to incorporate it into the language model framework for IR tasks. However, according to our initial experiments, directly combining the original PV with language modeling approaches produces unstable performance and limited improvement. Recently, Ai et al. [1] proposed a retrieval model based on a modified version of PV-DBOW – the paragraph vector model with distributed bags of words assumption. Specifically, they introduced three modifications on the original PV-DBOW: document-frequency based negative sampling, L2 regularization and a joint learning objective. Although they reported positive results on standard ad-hoc retrieval tasks, they did not give detailed analysis on how their modifications affect the language estimation of PV and why they are beneficial for IR.

In this paper, we conduct both a theoretic and empirical analysis on PV-DBOW to define its limitation as a language model for IR. Specifically, we notice three problems when incorporating the original PV-DBOW into language modeling approaches. First, the unregulated learning objective makes PV-DBOW vulnerable to over-fitting. This version of the model tends to retrieve more short documents as

ICTIR '16, September 12-16, 2016, Newark, DE, USA

© 2016 ACM. ISBN 978-1-4503-4497-5/16/09. . . $15.00

DOI: http://dx.doi.org/10.1145/2970398.2970409

training iterations increase. Second, the corpus-frequency based negative sampling strategy of PV-DBOW leads to a ICF-like weighting scheme for words in documents, which overly suppresses frequent words. Third, PV-DBOW does not capture word-context information, which makes it unable to model word substitution. By not capturing the substitution relations between words, PV-DBOW produces suboptimal vectors for words and documents which leads to inferior language estimation. In addition to the detailed analysis of these problems, we also provide clear explanations of how they are addressed by L2 regularization, document-frequency based negative sampling, and a joint learning objective. Results on TREC collections indicate that the proposed modifications improve both the effectiveness and robustness of PV-based retrieval models.

The rest of the paper is structured as follows. Section 2 describes the related work and Section 3 introduces the basic structure of PV-based retrieval models. Analysis of the problems and modifications for PV-based retrieval models is presented in Section 4. The proposed modifications are validated with experiments in Section 5. Finally, we conclude our work in Section 6.

2. RELATED WORK

In this section, we briefly review the previous studies in two research fields related to our work, including language smoothing with topic models for IR and neural embedding models.

2.1 Language Smoothing with Topic Models

Language model based retrieval models have been proven to be highly effective for ad hoc retrieval[19, 9]. These models rank documents according to the likelihood of observing a query given the document's language model. The simple language modeling approach estimates language models based on the bag-of-words assumption. This method, however, fails when the query words are not observed in documents. A common solution to this problem is applying smoothing techniques by incorporating a corpus language model for unobserved words. Example approaches include Jelinek-Mercer method, Absolute discounting, and Bayesian smoothing with Dirichlet priors [25].

One issue of language smoothing with the corpus language model is the lack of discrimination. Corpus-based smoothing techniques assume that all documents have similar background probability distributions for unseen words, which makes it difficult to differentiate semantic differences between documents. To overcome this problem, topic models were proposed to produce document specific language estimation by projecting both documents and queries to a same latent semantic space. For example, Deerwester et al. [6] proposed the Latent Semantic Indexing (LSI) technique to extract latent representations for words and documents through the SVD analysis of term frequency matrix. Hoffman [10] introduced the probability Latent Semantic Indexing (pLSI) that models words and documents as mixtures of topics. Blei et al. [3] further extend pLSI by drawing topic mixtures from a conjugate Dirichlet priori. Although these topic models do not work well in retrieval tasks on themselves [2], their combination with the original language models produces positive results. For example, Liu and Croft [15] showed that document clustering can significantly improve the effectiveness of language modeling approaches. Further-more, Wei and Croft [24] introduced a LDA-based retrieval model that consistently outperforms cluster-based retrieval model and produces state-of-the-art performance for topic models in ad-hoc retrieval.

2.2 Neural Embedding Models

Neural embedding models have received considerable attention in the natural language processing (NLP) community[17, 16, 13, 22]. Mikelov et al. [16] proposed a skip-gram model for learning high-quality word embeddings from large amounts of unstructured text data. These representations capture word similarities at a semantic level and have good compositionality. Le et al. [13] introduced paragraph vector models that project both words and documents into a single semantic space and estimate word probabilities accordingly. Experiments show that paragraph vector models outperform LDA in many NLP tasks such as sentiment analysis and document clustering [5, 13].

Recently, researchers in IR community have applied neural embedding models for retrieval tasks. Vulić et al. [23] and Mitra et al. [18] represented both queries and documents with a composition of word vectors and performed ranking based on the cosine similarity between them. The compositional model with word embedding performs poorly by itself, but it can improve the overall performance of word-based models through rank fusions. Ganguly et al. [7] and Zuccon et al. [27] applied word embeddings in the translation language model framework. They defined translation probabilities based on the cosine similarity between word vectors. More recently, Ai et al. [1] introduced a new method to incorporate neural embedding representations for IR models. Instead of computing cosine similarity, they focused on the probabilistic framework of PV models and its application in language smoothing. They proposed three modifications to adapt PV for retrieval tasks and reported that the enhanced PV can significantly outperform the original PV and existing LDA-based retrieval models. In this paper, we provide a formal analysis and further modifications of this approach.

3. PARAGRAPH VECTOR MODEL FOR IR

In this section, we describe the details of how to apply the original PV model for information retrieval. In this paper, we focus on a specific type of PV model with distributed bag-of-words assumption (PV-DBOW) due to its direct connection with language models of documents.

3.1 PV-DBOW

The original PV-DBOW was proposed by Le et al. [13]. The concept of "paragraph" stands for texts with varied lengths, which can be sentences, paragraphs and, in our case, the whole documents. PV-DBOW assumes the independence between words in a document and uses the document to predict each observed word in it. In this way, PV-DBOW learns both document and word embeddings by estimating a document level language model. Specifically, each document d is first projected into a semantic space and then trained to predict its words w. With the bag-of-words assumption, the generative probability of word w in document d is obtained through a softmax function over vocabulary V_w:

$$P(w|d) = \frac{exp(\vec{w} \cdot \vec{d})}{\sum_{w' \in V_w} exp(\vec{w'} \cdot \vec{d})} \qquad (1)$$

where $P(w|d)$ denotes the probability of word w given document d, $\vec{w}$ and $\vec{d}$ denote the vector representations for w and d. To reduce the cost of gradient computation for Equation (1) given a large vocabulary, Mikolov et al. [17] proposed a negative sampling strategy. Negative sampling randomly samples several words according to a predefined noise distribution and uses these words to approximate the denominator of Equation (1). With negative sampling, the global objective of PV-DBOW that sums over all possible word-document pairs is:

$$
\begin{aligned}
\ell = & \sum_{w \in V_w} \sum_{d \in V_d} \#(w,d) \log(\sigma(\vec{w} \cdot \vec{d})) \\
& + \sum_{w \in V_w} \sum_{d \in V_d} \#(w,d)(k \cdot E_{w_N \sim P_V}[\log \sigma(-\vec{w_N} \cdot \vec{d})])
\end{aligned}
\tag{2}
$$

where $\#(w,d)$ is the frequency of observed word-document pairs, V_d represents the corpus of documents, k is the number of negative samples, $\sigma(x)$ is the sigmoid function $\sigma(x) = \frac{1}{1+e^{-x}}$ and $E_{w_N \sim P_V}[\log \sigma(-\vec{w_N} \cdot \vec{d})]$ is the expected value of $\log \sigma(-\vec{w_N} \cdot \vec{d})$ given the noise distribution P_V.

The embedding process of PV-DBOW captures high level semantic information and conveys two major advantages over traditional topic models such as LDA. First, PV-DBOW does not have a fixed number of topics. Documents and words are automatically clustered through the training process without any prior assumptions. Second, PV-DBOW can be efficiently trained through SGD, which is more scalable to a large corpus than traditional probabilistic topic models. According to our experience, training PV-DBOW on a million documents is ten times faster than training LDA with Gibbs sampling on the same collection.

3.2 PV-based Retrieval Model

For each document, PV-DBOW builds a language model that directly estimates the probability of word given a certain document ($P(w|d)$). Therefore, a natural way to use PV-DBOW in the IR scenario is to combine its language estimation with traditional language modeling approaches. Inspired by the idea of the LDA-based retrieval model [24], we use PV-DBOW for language model smoothing in the query likelihood model (QL). Suppose that the word probability estimated with QL (with Dirichlet smoothing) and PV-DBOW are $P_{QL}(w|d)$ and $P_{PV}(w|d)$, the final word probability $P(w|d)$ is obtained through Jelinek-Mercer smoothing:

$$
P(w|d) = (1-\lambda)P_{QL}(w|d) + \lambda P_{PV}(w|d)
\tag{3}
$$

where λ is the parameter that controls smoothing strength. In our experiments, we tried other smoothing methods such as Dirichlet smoothing, but we observed no significant difference between them in retrieval performance.

3.3 Stability of the Model

Our initial experiment show that the PV-based retrieval model indeed outperforms QL model, but its improvement is unstable throughout the training process. On Robust04, we trained PV-DBOW with 300 dimensions and evaluated QL and the PV-based retrieval model with a 5-fold cross validation on title queries (detailed settings are described in Section 5.2 and 5.3). The best mean average precision (MAP) of the PV-based retrieval model with the original PV-DBOW is 0.259, while that for QL model is 0.253. The difference between the PV-based retrieval model and QL is

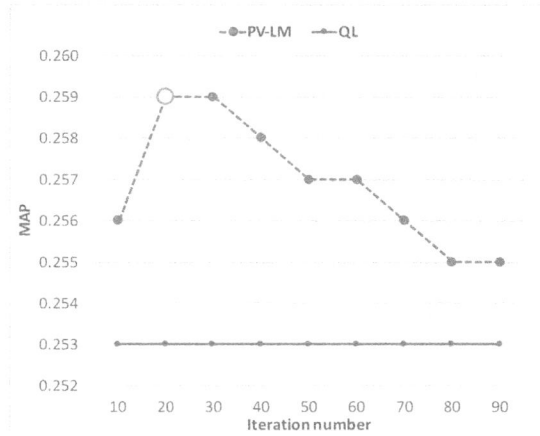

Figure 1: The MAP of QL and the PV-based retrieval model with the original PV-DBOW on Robust04 with title queries in respect of different training iteration. The point with an open circle is the result from Ai et al. [1].

significant ($p < 0.05$), which demonstrates the effectiveness of language smoothing with PV-DBOW. However, we noticed that the performance of PV-based retrieval model is highly sensitive to the training iterations of PV-DBOW. As shown in Figure 1, the MAP of the PV-based retrieval model increases in the beginning, but starts to decrease after 20 iterations. The final performance in the 80 iterations is only slightly better than QL. In the worst cases, the performance improvement from PV-DBOW is inconsistent and marginal, which motivates us to further analyze the limitations of PV-DBOW in language estimation.

4. PROBLEMS AND MODIFICATIONS

In this section, we conduct an analysis of the reasons for the unstable performance and marginal improvements of the original PV-based retrieval model. Based on this analysis, we talk about the corresponding modifications and show how these modifications affect the language estimation of the PV model.

4.1 Over-fitting on Short Documents

As shown in Section 3.3, one interesting phenomenon is that the performance of the PV-based retrieval model does not converge along with the training iterations. To analyze the possible reasons, we conducted experiments over the top retrieved results of the PV models. Figure 2 shows the distribution of documents with respect to document length in the top 50 documents retrieved by the PV-based retrieval model on Robust04 with title queries. We equally split the domain of document length (0 to 2500) into 50 bins and ignore documents longer than 2500 words (which accounts for less than 4% of the top 50 documents). To avoid confusion, all the models depicted in Figure 2 only use the probability produced by PV-DBOW in language estimation (namely $\lambda = 1$ in Equation (3)). As shown in Figure 2, the distribution of documents with respect to document length gradually moves to the left as training iterations increase for PV-DBOW. The median document length for PV-DBOW is 750-800 under 5 iterations, 600-650 under 20 iterations, and 550-600 under

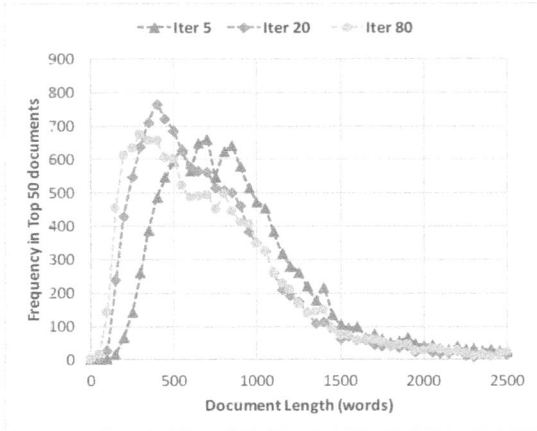

Figure 2: The distribution of documents in respect of document length for top 50 documents retrieved by PV-based retrieval model on Robust04 (title queries). Documents with more than 2500 words are ignored.

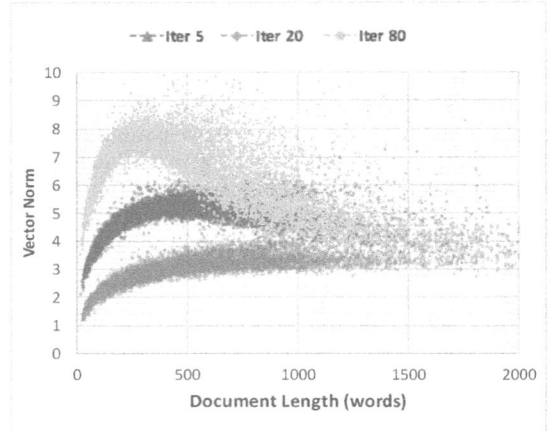

Figure 3: The distribution of vector norms in respect of document length for 10,000 documents randomly sampled from Robust04.

80 iterations. The results indicate that the training process of PV-DBOW introduces increasingly stronger bias toward short documents in the final retrieval model.

To understand the fundamental reason for this length bias, let us look back at the learning process of the PV-DBOW model. As shown in Equation (1), the prediction task of PV-DBOW requires the model to assign higher probability to words that occur in a document than others. In other words, the model will try to align the document vector to the word vectors that appear in the document. This alignment is much easier for short documents since on average the word vectors in short documents would be more concentrated than that in long documents. In practice, concentrated word vectors lead to concentrated gradient directions for document vectors. The partial derivative of the global objective with respect to a certain document d is computed as follows:

$$\frac{\partial \ell}{\partial d} = \sum_{w \in V_w} \#(w, d) \log(\sigma(-\vec{w} \cdot \vec{d}))\vec{w} \\ - \sum_{w \in V_w} \#(w, d)(k \cdot E_{w_N \sim P_V}[\log \sigma(\vec{w_N} \cdot \vec{d})]\vec{w_N}) \quad (4)$$

Despite the part with w_N (which is randomly sampled according to a global noise distribution), we can see that the gradient of d is a weighted sum of its word vectors. Because short documents have less words, their gradients could easily converge to a direction that is not far from all the word vectors. This would result in more rapid increase of norms for short document vectors. Therefore, given an observed word, the probability produced by short documents will become higher and higher, leading to a potential over-fitting.

To verify this, we further plot the variation of the learned document vectors with respect to the document length under different learning iterations. Figure 3 shows the distribution of vector norms for 10,000 documents randomly sampled from Robust04. For documents with more than 1,000 words, vector norms in PV-DBOW with 5, 20 and 80 iterations show no significant difference. However, for doc-

uments with less than 1,000 words, the norms of document vectors increases rapidly as iteration number increases.

This analysis shows that the original PV-DBOW suffers from the over-fitting problem along with the training process, and this over-fitting problem is more severe for short documents. A direct method to solve the over fitting problems is to regularize the learning objective of PV-DBOW. Because the over-fitting problem is mainly caused by the unrestricted document vectors, we add an L2 regularizer over the document vectors. More formally, the local objective function for each (w, d) pair with regularization is now as follows:

$$\ell'(w, d) = \ell(w, d) - \frac{\gamma}{|d|}||\vec{d}||^2 \quad (5)$$

where $\ell(w, d)$ represents the local objective function for PV-DBOW, $||\vec{d}||$ denotes the norm of vector $\vec{d}$ and γ denotes a hyper-parameter that control the strength of regularization. Because each iteration of PV-DBOW goes through each word once, a length factor $\frac{1}{|d|}$ where $|d|$ denotes the number of words in document d (namely the length of d) is used to guarantee the same regularization term for all the documents in the training corpus.

The effect of L2 regularization on the language model of PV-DBOW is twofold. First, with L2 regularization, the vector norms for both short documents and long documents are roughly the same along with training iterations. Severe over-fitting on short documents no longer exists in long term training. Second, the restriction on vector norms makes the probability distribution in Equation (1) smoother, which potentially benefits the language smoothing of PV-based retrieval models.

4.2 Improper Noise Distribution

To analyze the reason for the limited performance improvement of the PV-based retrieval model, we first look at the learning objective of PV-DBOW. Inspired by the analysis of the skip-gram model in Levy et al. [14], we derive the local objective for a specific word-document pair from

Equation (2) as:

$$\ell(w,d) = \#(w,d)\log\sigma(\vec{w}\cdot\vec{d}) + k\#(d)P_V(w)\log\sigma(-\vec{w}\cdot\vec{d}) \quad (6)$$

where $\#(d)$ represents the length of d. Define $x = \vec{w}\cdot\vec{d}$, then the objective's partial derivative on x would be:

$$\frac{\partial\ell(w,d)}{\partial x} = \#(w,d)\cdot\sigma(-x) - k\cdot\#(d)\cdot P_V(w)\cdot\sigma(x) \quad (7)$$

Let the partial derivative equal to zero, then the only valid solution for Equation (7) is

$$\vec{w}\cdot\vec{d} = \log(\frac{\#(w,d)}{\#(d)}\cdot\frac{1}{P_V(w)}) - \log k \quad (8)$$

We can see that the original PV-DBOW model conducts implicit factorization over the term-document co-occurrence matrix. The noise distribution of negative sampling actually decides how we weight the terms in a document. The original negative sampling [17] adopts empirical word distribution in the whole corpus as the noise distribution P_V, which is defined as:

$$P_V(w_N) = \frac{\#w_N}{|C|} \quad (9)$$

where $\#(w_N)$ is the corpus frequency of w_N and $|C|$ is the size of the corpus. In Equation (8), $\frac{\#(w,d)}{\#(d)}$ is the normalized TF of w in d, and $\frac{1}{P_V(w)}$ (namely $\frac{|C|}{\#w}$) is the ICF value of w. Therefore, the original PV-DBOW with negative sampling is optimizing for a variation of TF-ICF weighting scheme.

However, TF-ICF is not a popular weighting scheme in IR. One direct reason is that ICF-based term weighting computes the discriminative ability of words only according to their frequency in the corpus and does not consider any form of document structure information. Empirically, a word with high corpus frequency could still be discriminative if it only appears in a small group of documents. This partially explains why PV-DBOW performs well on NLP tasks but not on IR tasks.

Based on these above ideas, one approach to address the problem of PV-DBOW is applying a document-frequency (DF) based negative sampling strategy. More formally, we replace P_V in the original negative sampling with a new noise distribution P_D as follows:

$$P_D(w_N) = \frac{\#D(w_N)}{|N|} \quad (10)$$

where $\#D(w_N)$ denotes the document frequency of w_N and $|N| = \sum_{w'\in V_w}\#D(w')$. After substituting P_V with P_D in Equation (8), we get the new optimal solution as

$$\vec{w}\cdot\vec{d} = \log(\frac{\#(w,d)}{\#(d)}\cdot\frac{|N|}{\#D(w)}) - \log(k) \quad (11)$$

Because $\frac{|N|}{\#D(w)}$ is a variant of the inverse document frequency (IDF) of w, PV-DBOW with DF-based negative sampling is factorizing a shifted matrix of TF-IDF, which is usually considered to be a better scheme for term weighting than TF-ICF [20].

We further plot both the corpus-frequency and document-frequency based distributions in Figure 4 (P_V and P_D respectively). Similar to Church and Gale [4], we observe considerable difference between these sampling distributions, especially on frequent words. As we can see from Fig-

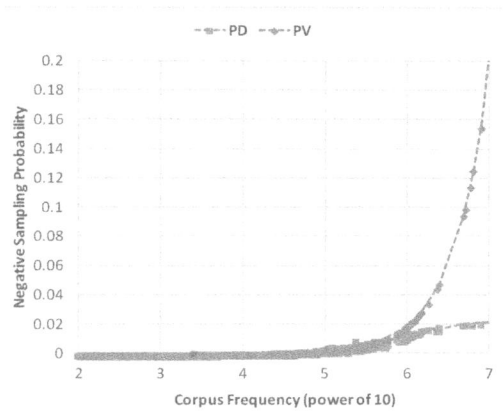

Figure 4: The distribution of the original negative sampling (P_V) and the document-frequency based negative sampling (P_D). The horizontal axis represents log value of word frequency (base 10).

ure 4, P_V grows in an exponential way and assigns much higher sample probability to frequent words compared to P_D, which may over-penalize frequent words in the learning of language model. For example, in Robust04 query 339 ("alzheimers drug treatment"), the probability estimated by PV-DBOW with corpus-frequency based negative sampling for "alzheimers" (0.042) is higher than "drug" (0.002) in document FT933-3956, even when "drug" appears two times more than "alzheimers". This suppression makes "drug" less important for the final ranking and consequentially hurts the performance of this query. With document-frequency based negative sampling, the term weighting is moderated and produces more reasonable language estimation (0.056 for "alzheimers" and 0.069 for "drugs" in FT933-3956).

In practice, negative sampling with a very skew distribution is suboptimal for the approximation of softmax function in the learning objective of PV-DBOW. This is the reason why Mikolov et al. [17] applied a unigram distribution raised to the power of 0.75. Similarly, we adopt a power version of document frequency that uses $\#D(w)^\eta(0\le\eta\le1)$ to replace $\#D(w)$ in Equation (10).

4.3 Insufficient Modeling for Word Substitution

From the analysis in the prior section, we find that the optimal solution of PV-DBOW's objective function (Equation (6)) is actually an implicit factorization over the term-document matrix. As shown in [22], models that leverage distributed information over the term-document matrix mainly capture words' syntagmatic relations but ignore paradigmatic relations. Syntagmatic relations relate words that co-occur in the same text region. For example, "NBA" is related to "basketball" because they often co-occur in same documents. Paradigmatic relations, namely substitution relations, relate words that often share similar context but may not co-occur in documents. For example, "subway" and "underground" are synonyms and often occur in similar contexts, but American people usually use "subway" while British people tend to use "underground". The original PV-DBOW aligns word vectors to document vectors so that words with high co-occurrence tend to have similar represen-

Table 1: The cosine similarities between *clothing, garment* and four relevant documents in Robust04 query 361 ("clothing sweatshops"). EPV-DR represents the PV-based retrieval model with document-frequency based negative sampling and L2 regularization. EPV-DRJ is EPV-DR with a joint objective.

	EPV-DR		EPV-DRJ	
	clothing	*garment*	*clothing*	*garment*
clothing	1.000	0.632	1.000	0.638
LA112689-0194 ($TF_{clothing} = 2, TF_{garment} = 26$)	0.044	0.134	0.107	0.169
LA112889-0108 ($TF_{clothing} = 0, TF_{garment} = 10$)	-0.003	0.100	0.126	0.155
LA021090-0137 ($TF_{clothing} = 7, TF_{garment} = 9$)	0.052	0.092	0.147	0.119
LA022890-0105 ($TF_{clothing} = 6, TF_{garment} = 6$)	0.066	0.079	0.107	0.107

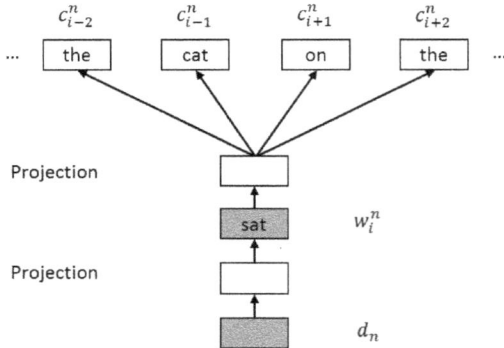

Figure 5: The structure of two-layer PV-DBOW. The document is trained to predict the observed word and then the observed word is trained to predict its context.

tations. However, it cannot model the semantic similarity between words that occur with similar context but not in the same document.

Word paradigmatic information, or word substitution relation is important for IR because it directly alleviates the problem of term mismatch. Term mismatch is common in IR tasks because a query term mismatches 40% to 50% of relevant documents on average [26]. A language model that cannot capture word substitution relation would be vulnerable to the mismatch problem and have limited smoothing ability. Here we take Robust04 query 361 ("clothing sweatshops") as an example. In this query, "garment" is frequent in relevant documents while "clothing" is not. Table 1 lists the cosine similarities between "clothing", "garment" and four relevant documents in the enhanced PV-based retrieval model with document-frequency based negative sampling and L2 regularization (EPV-DR). Intuitively, "clothing" should receive a similar probability to "garment" because they are synonyms. However, EPV-DR assigns much lower cosine similarities for "clothing" than "garment", which consequentially decreases the probability of "clothing" in these relevant documents and lowers their final ranks.

To model word substitution relations, we apply a joint learning objective for PV-DBOW as suggested in [5, 22]. As shown in Figure 5, the first layer of the model uses the document vector to predict the observed word. Then, the second layer of the model uses the observed word to predict its context. More formally, the local objective of the PV-DBOW with the joint objective function can be expressed

Table 2: Statistics of experimental data sets.

Collection	#Docs	#Words	Size	TREC Topics
Robust-04	528K	253M	1.9G	351-450, 601-700
Gov2	25,205K	24,007M	426G	701-850

as

$$\ell = \log(\sigma(\vec{w_i} \cdot \vec{d})) + k \cdot E_{w_N \sim P_D}[\log \sigma(-\vec{w_N} \cdot \vec{d})]$$
$$+ \sum_{\substack{j=i-L \\ j \neq i}}^{i+L} \log(\sigma(\vec{w_i} \cdot \vec{c_j})) + k \cdot E_{c_N \sim P_D}[\log \sigma(-\vec{w_i} \cdot \vec{c_N})] \quad (12)$$

where $\vec{c_j}$ is the context vector for word w_j, c_N denotes the sampled context and L represents the context window size.

From a learning perspective, adding the prediction objective between words and context actually regularizes the learning objective of PV-DBOW. This regularization usually results in better representations for words and documents according to previous studies [5, 22]. In Table 1, after incorporating EPV-DR with the joint objective (EPV-DRJ), the cos similarities between "clothing" and those four relevant documents increase considerably. Even LA112889-0108 (the document in which "clothing" never appears) now has similar cosine similarities for "clothing" and "garment". Therefore, the language estimation of EPV-DRJ based retrieval model gives higher probabilities for "clothing" in those documents and increases the final retrieval performance.

5. EXPERIMENTS

In this section, we conduct empirical experiments to verify the effectiveness of different modifications on PV-DBOW for IR.

5.1 Data Set and Baselines

Two TREC collections (Robust04 and GOV2) have been used to evaluate the retrieval performance of PV-based retrieval models and proposed modifications. The statistics of Robust04 and GOV2 are provided in Table 2. We use the Galago search engine[1] to index the corpus and stemmed terms with the Krovetz stemmer [12]. Stop words in queries are removed in advance as suggested in [11]. To better understand the effectiveness of paragraph vector models in information retrieval, we include results from two baselines, i.e. the query likelihood model [19] and the LDA-based retrieval model [24].

Query likelihood (QL) [19] is a basic language modeling

---

[1]http://www.lemurproject.org/galago.php

approach for information retrieval. It constructs document models with bag-of-words representation and ranks documents according to the log likelihood of query words given the document models. Standard query likelihood model with Dirichlet smoothing [25] can be formulated as Equation (13):

$$P_{QL}(Q|D) = \sum_{w \in Q} tf_{w,Q} log \frac{tf_{w,D} + \mu P(w|C)}{|D| + \mu} \quad (13)$$

where $tf_{w,Q}$ is the number of times that w occurs in the query, $tf_{w,D}$ is the number of times that w occurs in the document, $|D|$ is the length of the document, μ is a parameter for Dirichlet smoothing and $P(w|C)$ is a background language model that is computed as the number of w in the whole corpus divided by the corpus size. To simplify the parameter tuning for both baselines and PV-based retrieval models, we do not tune μ in our experiments and use the average value of the 5-fold validation on Robust04 and GOV2 from Huston and Croft [11]. Specifically, for Robust04 collection, we set $\mu = 934$ for title queries and $\mu = 2166$ for description queries. For GOV2 collection, we set $\mu = 1481$ for title queries and $\mu = 2107$ for description queries.

LDA-based retrieval model (LDA-LM) [3]: LDA is a popular topic model based on a formal generative model of documents. It draws the document-topic distribution $\hat{\theta}$ and topic-word distribution $\hat{\phi}$ from two conjugate Dirichlet priors and models the posterior estimation of word w in document d as:

$$P_{Lda}(w|d) = \sum_{z=1}^{K} P(w|z, \hat{\phi}) P(z|d, \hat{\theta}) \quad (14)$$

where K is the number of topics in LDA model. Proposed by Wei and Croft [24], LDA-based retrieval models combines the original document model from QL with LDA model as:

$$P(w|d) = (1 - \lambda)P_{QL}(w|d) + \lambda P_{Lda}(w|d) \quad (15)$$

where $P_{QL}(w|d)$ is the maximum likelihood estimation of word w in document d with the query likelihood model and $P_{lda}(w|d)$ is the posterior estimation of w given d in the LDA model. In experiments, we use Gibbs sampling to estimate the parameters of LDA and empirically set topic number as $K = 800$. Following previous study [8], the symmetric Dirichlet priors in LDA are set as $\alpha = \frac{50}{K}$ and $\beta = 0.01$.

5.2 Evaluation Framework

We employ four standard retrieval metrics for evaluation: mean average precision (MAP), normlized discounted cumulative gain at 20 (nDCG@20) and precision at 20 (P@20). We list Ai et al. [1]'s results on Robust04 and our own experiments on GOV2 to show the overall retrieval performance of PV-based retrieval model.

Due to the limited number of annotated queries in our experiment collections, we conduct 5-fold cross-validation. We follow the same settings as Huston and Croft[11] and split the query topics for each collections randomly into 5 folds. We tune λ (the combination weight for the LDA-based retrieval model and PV-based retrieval models) with 4 of the 5 folds and test on the remaining 1 fold. The reported numbers are the average value over all test folds. As suggested by Smucker et al.[21], statistical significance is computed with Fisher randomization test with threshold 0.05.

For efficient computation, we adopt a re-ranking strategy. The initial retrieval is performed with query likeli-

Table 3: Results from Ai et al. [1] on Robust04 collection measured by MAP. *, + means significant difference over QL, LDA-LM respectively at 0.05 significance level measured by Fisher randomization test.

Method	Robust04 collection	
	Titles	Descriptions
QL	0.253	0.246
LDA-LM	0.259*	0.251*
PV-LM	0.259*	0.247
EPV-R-LM	0.259*	0.247
EPV-DR-LM	0.262*	0.252*
EPV-DRJ-LM	**0.267*+**	**0.253***

hood model to obtain 2,000 candidate documents. Then re-ranking is performed with different models. The final evaluation is carried out on the top 1,000 results.

We trained LDA and paragraph vector models with documents in Robust04 and GOV2 separately. However, handling large scale dataset like GOV2 is computational expensive for LDA. For fair comparison, we randomly sampled 500k documents (including the candidates retrieved by QL) from GOV2 and trained LDA and paragraph vector models on the sampled subset.

5.3 Settings for Paragraph Vector Models

We tested four types of PV-based retrieval models:

- PV-LM: the PV-based retrieval model with PV-DBOW proposed by Le et al. [13].

- EPV-R-LM: the PV-LM model with L2 regularization.

- EPV-DR-LM: the EPV-R-LM model with document-frequency based negative sampling.

- EPV-DRJ-LM: the EPV-DR-LM model with a joint learning objective.

The tuning of all hyper-parameters in PV-DBOW requires considerable effort and is not the core of this paper, so we set most parameters same with the default settings from skip-gram word embedding model proposed in [17][2] except for iteration number. The iteration number is tuned offline with PV-LM from 10 to 80 (10 per step) on Robust04 titles. We observed the best performance under 20 iterations and fix this number for all PV-based retrieval models.

Modification-specific hyper-parameters are tuned separately for EPV-R-LM, EPV-DR-LM and EPV-DRJ-LM. For models with document-frequency based negative sampling, we tuned η from 0.0 to 1.0 (0.1 per step). The best performance for EPV-DR-LM and EPV-DRJ is 0.4 and 0.1. For models with L2 regularization, we tested γ from 0.1, 1, 10 and 100. The best performance is consistently obtained with 10 in EPV-R-LM, EPV-DR-LM and EPV-DRJ-LM.

5.4 Results and Discussion

Ai et al. [1] showed that the proposed modifications for PV-DBOW improve the performance of PV-based retrieval model on Robust04. However, they only reported the best retrieval scores of each model and did not illustrate how

[2]https://code.google.com/p/word2vec/

Table 4: Comparison of different models over GOV2 collection. $*$, $+$ means significant difference over QL, LDA-LM respectively at 0.05 significance level measured by Fisher randomization test. The best performance is highlighted in boldface.

	GOV2 collection					
	Titles			Descriptions		
Method	MAP	nDCG@20	P@20	MAP	nDCG@20	P@20
QL	0.295^+	0.409	0.510^+	0.249^+	0.371	0.470
LDA-LM	0.290	0.406	0.505	0.245	**0.376**	0.468
PV-LM	0.294	0.409	0.510^+	0.246	0.364	0.463
EPV-R-LM	0.295^+	0.410	0.511^+	0.250^+	0.368	0.467
EPV-DR-LM	0.296^+	0.412	0.512	0.250^+	0.371	0.470
EPV-DRJ-LM	$\mathbf{0.297^+}$	$\mathbf{0.415^{*+}}$	$\mathbf{0.519^{*+}}$	$\mathbf{0.252^{*+}}$	0.371	**0.472**

those models behave in different parameter settings. We extend their work with analysis on PV-based retrieval models with different training iterations and vector dimensions. Our experiments show that the proposed modifications improve both the effectiveness and robustness of PV-based retrieval models.

5.4.1 Overall Performance

We refer the results on Robust04 from Ai et al. [1] in Table 3 and further extend the evaluation of baselines and PV-based retrieval models on GOV2 in Table 4. As observed by previous studies [24, 15, 1], topic level estimation is beneficial for language modeling approach. Both LDA-LM and PV-LM outperform QL on Robust04 titles and descriptions. The relative improvements in respect of MAP for LDA-LM are 2.4% on titles and 2.0% on descriptions; for PV-LM are 2.4% on titles and 0.4% on descriptions. The performance of LDA-LM and PV-LM show no significant difference. After adding L2 regularization, document-frequency based negative sampling and a joint objective, the performance of PV-LM increases and finally outperforms all baselines in both Robust04 and GOV2. On Robust04, the relative improvements of MAP for EPV-R-LM, EPV-DR-LM and EPV-DRJ-LM over PV-LM are 0.0%, 1.2% and 3.1% on titles, 0.0%, 2.0% and 2.4% on descriptions; on GOV2, the relative improvements of MAP for EPV-R-LM, EPV-DR-LM and EPV-DRJ-LM over PV-LM are 0.3%, 0.7% and 1.0% on titles, 1.6%, 1.6% and 2.4% on descriptions.

We notice that topic level smoothing tends to be more effective on short queries than long queries. Both LDA-LM and PV-based retrieval models achieve better improvement over QL in title queries than in description queries. For example, the best PV-based retrieval model, EPV-DRJ-LM, outperforms QL with 5.5% on Robust04 titles but 2.5% on Robust04 descriptions in respect of MAP. An explanation for this phenomenon is that vocabulary mismatch is more severe in short queries. With less words in short queries, the missing of one word could hurt the maximum likelihood estimation of QL. In contrast, long queries like descriptions usually have sufficient terms to express their query intents and are more robust to mismatch problems. The introduction of semantic matching to long queries could bring less benefits but more noise. We will give more examples in Section 5.4.4.

In our experiments, GOV2 receives less benefits from semantic smoothing (comparing to Robust04). The incorporation of LDA even damages the performance of language modeling approach in most metrics. One potential reason

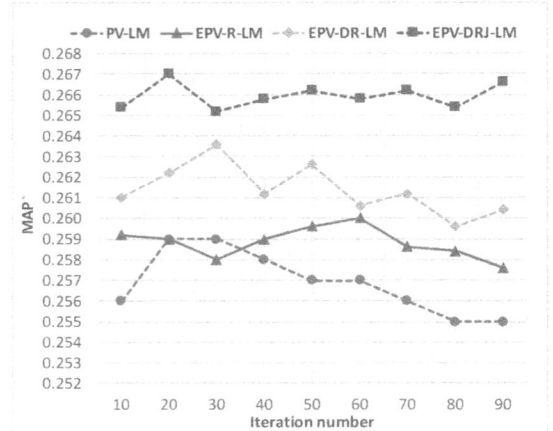

Figure 6: MAP variation of PV-based retrieval models with respect to iteration number. The horizontal axis represents the number of training iterations, and the vertical axis represents MAP on Robust04 title queries.

is that GOV2 consists of web pages, which have a complex and noisy topic distribution comparing to news articles in Robust04. Because our experiments restrict the number of topic in LDA to 800 (due to efficiency), the topics learned by LDA may be too vague and coarse for language estimation. In comparison, although the dimension of the vectors is 300, the number of topics in paragraph vector models is not limited. Because documents are automatically clustered without prior assumptions about topic distribution, PV-DBOW could capture finer semantic relations in a noisy environment. In our experiments, the EPV-DRJ-LM outperforms both QL and LDA-LM in most metrics.

5.4.2 Iteration Number

Our analysis shows that the number of training iterations in PV-DBOW have a considerable effect on the language estimation of PV-based retrieval models. To study the effect of training iterations, we depict the MAP value of PV-based retrieval models under different iteration numbers on Robust04 titles in Figure 6.

As shown in Figure 6, the over-fitting problem of PV-LM without L2 regularization is evident as iteration number increases. The best performance of PV-LM (0.259) is observed at 20 iterations, but it drops to 0.255 at 90 iterations. In contrast, the results of PV-based retrieval models with L2 regularization (EPV-R-LM, EPV-DR-LM and EPV-DRJ-LM) are steady across different iteration numbers. The MAP of EPV-R-LM slightly wave around 0.259 and consistently outperforms PV-LM after 30 iterations.

Although the L2 regularization can effectively solve the over fitting problem of PV-based retrieval models, it does not significantly improve retrieval performance. By incorporating document-frequency based negative sampling strategy and the join objective, we observed improvement in the MAP scores on Robust04. These results indicate that those modifications together can significantly improve the robustness and effectiveness of PV-based retrieval models.

5.4.3 Vector Dimensionality

Previous studies find that higher dimensional vector representation can improve the performance of neural embedding models in NLP tasks [16]. To understand the effect of vector dimensionality, we test PV-based retrieval models with different vector sizes on Robust04 titles and show the results in Figure 7.

In Figure 7, the vector size in PV-DBOW shows a minor correlation with the performance of PV-based retrieval models. Although the MAP value of EPV-DRJ-LM increases slowly from 0.263 to 0.268 when vector dimensionality changes from 50 to 500, the performance of PV-LM fluctuates between 0.256 and 0.259. The improvement caused by increasing vector dimensionality is not consistent in different PV-based retrieval models. Zuccon et al. [27] find that vector dimensionality in word embedding has a minor effect on model performance in ad-hoc retrieval. Similarly, we notice that the setting of dimensionality for PV-based retrieval models is not as important as it is for LDA-LM [24] in language estimation. A potential explanation is that the dimensionality of document vectors is not explicitly linked with the topic number in paragraph vector models. Even with low-dimensional vectors, paragraph vector models can still model a complex topic structure. In our experiments, the EPV-DRJ-LM with 50 dimensions still outperforms the LDA-LM with 800 topics on Robust04 (MAP 0.263 v.s. 0.259).

5.4.4 Case Studies

To further illustrate how paragraph vector models work for information retrieval, we conduct case studies to show the advantages and disadvantages of PV-based retrieval models.

The advantages of PV-based retrieval models mostly come from its semantic matching process. We use Robust04 title query 317 ("unsolicited faxes") as an example. In Robust04, only three documents have "unsolicited" and "faxes" simultaneously and two of them contain each word exactly once. QL failed in this case (MAP 0.186) because it cannot reasonably differentiate the relevance of documents that do not have "unsolicited" or "faxes". By projecting documents into semantic concepts, paragraph vector models and LDA provide finer information for the query words and the mismatched documents. As a result, the MAP for EPV-DRJ-LM and LDA-LM in query 317 outperform QL by 75.3% (0.186 to 0.326) and 19.4% (0.186 to 0.222). The results show that both the PV-based and LDA-based retrieval models can improve retrieval performance by involving semantic matching information in language modeling approaches, while PV models can provide even better estimation than LDA model.

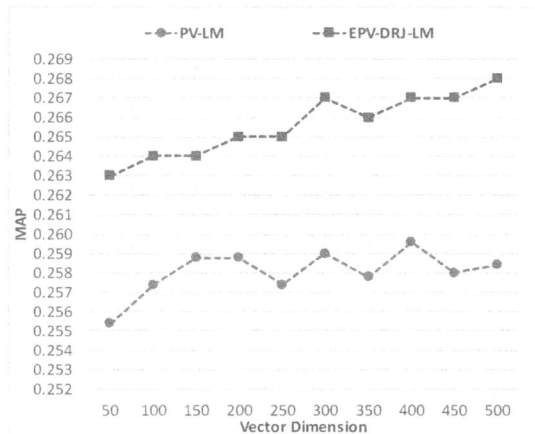

Figure 7: MAP variation of PV-based retrieval models with respect to vector dimensions. The horizontal axis represents vector dimensions, and the vertical axis represents MAP on Robust04 title queries.

However, the semantic matching in PV-based retrieval models may sometimes not work well on long queries. One representative example in our experiments is Robust04 query 614: *flavr savr tomato* (the title), *find information about the first genetically modified food product to go on the market flavr savr also flavor saver tomato developed by calgene* (the description with stopwords removed). With the query title, EPV-DRJ-LM performs better than QL (MAP 0.522 v.s. 0.174) because most of the documents in Robust04 do not contain the exact matching of these query words (only four documents contain "flavr" or "savr"). However, the situation changes when replacing the query title with the query description. One reason is that the query description expands the query title with high quality words that can significantly boost the performance of exact matching model (such as "genetical", "food" and "calgene"). In our experiments, the MAP value of QL is increased by 336.8% (0.174 to 0.76), but the gain for EPV-DRJ-LM is only 44.1% (from 0.522 to 0.752 in MAP). Generally, long queries describe query intents with sufficient information. In this case, semantic matching may bring less benefits but more noise to retrieval models.

6. CONCLUSION

In this paper, we study PV-DBOW with both theoretic and empirical analysis to understand its limitation as a language model for IR. We discuss three problems that restrict the effectiveness of PV-DBOW in IR scenario: over-fitting on short documents, improper negative sampling strategy and lack of word substitution modeling. To address these problems, three modifications for the original PV-DBOW have been proposed. We analyze how these modifications affect the language estimation in PV-DBOW and how they improve the performance of PV-based retrieval models. Experiments and case studies on standard TREC collections are presented to better illustrate and backup our analysis.

Although the discussions of this paper mainly focuses on PV-DBOW for IR, some results are also instructive for future work on other neural embedding models. First, the noise distribution of negative sampling can significantly affect the performance of PV-based retrieval models. With formal inductions, we show that different noise distributions lead PV-DBOW to optimize a different weighting scheme. In this way, one may easily adapt neural embedding models to incorporate different information for different tasks. Second, the norms of embedding vectors contain important information for IR. Previous work mainly focuses on the cosine similarities between embedding vectors, but our analysis show that the norms of embedding vectors also influence the language estimation of PV models. Vector norms in neural embedding models are related to both word frequency and document structures, which could be potentially useful for future studies.

7. ACKNOWLEDGMENTS

This work was supported in part by the Center for Intelligent Information Retrieval, in part by NSF IIS-1160894, and in part by NSF grant IIS-1419693. Any opinions, findings and conclusions or recommendations expressed in this material are those of the authors and do not necessarily reflect those of the sponsor.

8. REFERENCES

[1] Q. Ai, L. Yang, J. Guo, and W. B. Croft. Improving language estimation with the paragraph vector model for ad-hoc retrieval. In *Proceedings of the 39th annual international ACM SIGIR conference on Research and development in information retrieval*. ACM, 2016.

[2] A. Atreya and C. Elkan. Latent semantic indexing (lsi) fails for trec collections. *ACM SIGKDD Explorations Newsletter*, 12(2):5–10, 2011.

[3] D. M. Blei, A. Y. Ng, and M. I. Jordan. Latent dirichlet allocation. *J. Mach. Learn. Res.*, 3:993–1022, Mar. 2003.

[4] K. W. Church and W. A. Gale. Poisson mixtures. *Natural Language Engineering*, 1(02):163–190, 1995.

[5] A. M. Dai, C. Olah, Q. V. Le, and G. S. Corrado. Document embedding with paragraph vectors. In *NIPS Deep Learning Workshop*, 2014.

[6] S. C. Deerwester, S. T. Dumais, T. K. Landauer, G. W. Furnas, and R. A. Harshman. Indexing by latent semantic analysis. *JAsIs*, 41(6):391–407, 1990.

[7] D. Ganguly, D. Roy, M. Mitra, and G. J. Jones. Word embedding based generalized language model for information retrieval. In *Proceedings of the 38th International ACM SIGIR Conference on Research and Development in Information Retrieval*, pages 795–798. ACM, 2015.

[8] T. L. Griffiths and M. Steyvers. Finding scientific topics. *PNAS*, 101(suppl. 1):5228–5235, 2004.

[9] D. Hiemstra and W. Kraaij. Twenty-one at trec-7: Ad-hoc and cross-language track. 1999.

[10] T. Hofmann. Probabilistic latent semantic indexing. In *Proceedings of the 22nd annual international ACM SIGIR conference on Research and development in information retrieval*, pages 50–57. ACM, 1999.

[11] S. Huston and W. B. Croft. A comparison of retrieval models using term dependencies. In *Proceedings of the 23rd ACM International Conference on Conference on Information and Knowledge Management*, pages 111–120. ACM, 2014.

[12] R. Krovetz. Viewing morphology as an inference process. In *Proceedings of the 16th annual international ACM SIGIR conference on Research and development in information retrieval*, pages 191–202. ACM, 1993.

[13] Q. Le and T. Mikolov. Distributed representations of sentences and documents. In *Proceedings of the 31st International Conference on Machine Learning (ICML-14)*, pages 1188–1196, 2014.

[14] O. Levy and Y. Goldberg. Neural word embedding as implicit matrix factorization. In *Advances in Neural Information Processing Systems*, pages 2177–2185, 2014.

[15] X. Liu and W. B. Croft. Cluster-based retrieval using language models. In *Proceedings of the 27th annual international ACM SIGIR conference on Research and development in information retrieval*, pages 186–193. ACM, 2004.

[16] T. Mikolov, K. Chen, G. Corrado, and J. Dean. Efficient estimation of word representations in vector space. *arXiv preprint arXiv:1301.3781*, 2013.

[17] T. Mikolov, I. Sutskever, K. Chen, G. S. CJorrado, and M. I. Dean, Jeffdan. Distributed representations of words and phrases and their compositionality. In *Advances in neural information processing systems*, pages 3111–3119, 2013.

[18] E. Nalisnick, B. Mitra, N. Craswell, and R. Caruana. Improving document ranking with dual word embeddings. In *Proceedings of the 25th International Conference Companion on World Wide Web*, pages 83–84. International World Wide Web Conferences Steering Committee, 2016.

[19] J. M. Ponte and W. B. Croft. A language modeling approach to information retrieval. In *Proceedings of the 21st annual international ACM SIGIR conference on Research and development in information retrieval*, pages 275–281. ACM, 1998.

[20] S. Robertson. Understanding inverse document frequency: on theoretical arguments for idf. *Journal of documentation*, 60(5):503–520, 2004.

[21] M. D. Smucker, J. Allan, and B. Carterette. A comparison of statistical significance tests for information retrieval evaluation. In *Proceedings of the sixteenth ACM conference on Conference on information and knowledge management*, pages 623–632. ACM, 2007.

[22] F. Sun, J. Guo, Y. Lan, J. Xu, and X. Cheng. Learning word representations by jointly modeling syntagmatic and paradigmatic relations. In *Proceedings of the 53rd Annual Annual Meeting of the Association for Computational Linguistics*, 2015.

[23] I. Vulić and M.-F. Moens. Monolingual and cross-lingual information retrieval models based on (bilingual) word embeddings. In *Proceedings of the 38th International ACM SIGIR Conference on Research and Development in Information Retrieval*, pages 363–372. ACM, 2015.

[24] X. Wei and W. B. Croft. Lda-based document models for ad-hoc retrieval. In *Proceedings of the 29th Annual International ACM SIGIR Conference on Research and Development in Information Retrieval*, SIGIR '06, pages 178–185, New York, NY, USA, 2006. ACM.

[25] C. Zhai and J. Lafferty. A study of smoothing methods for language models applied to ad hoc information retrieval. In *Proceedings of the 24th annual international ACM SIGIR conference on Research and development in information retrieval*, pages 334–342. ACM, 2001.

[26] L. Zhao and J. Callan. Term necessity prediction. In *Proceedings of the 19th ACM international conference on Information and knowledge management*, pages 259–268. ACM, 2010.

[27] G. Zuccon, B. Koopman, P. Bruza, and L. Azzopardi. Integrating and evaluating neural word embeddings in information retrieval. In *Proceedings of the 20th Australasian Document Computing Symposium*, pages Article–No. ACM, 2015.

End to End Long Short Term Memory Networks for Non-Factoid Question Answering

Daniel Cohen
Center for Intelligent Information Retrieval
University of Massachusetts Amherst
Amherst, MA
dcohen@cs.umass.edu

W. Bruce Croft
Center for Intelligent Information Retrieval
University of Massachusetts Amherst
Amherst, MA
croft@cs.umass.edu

ABSTRACT

Retrieving correct answers for non-factoid queries poses significant challenges for current answer retrieval methods. Methods either involve the laborious task of extracting numerous features or are ineffective for longer answers. We approach the task of non-factoid question answering using deep learning methods without the need of feature extraction. Neural networks are capable of learning complex relations based on relatively simple features which make them a prime candidate for relating non-factoid questions to their answers. In this paper, we show that end to end training with a Bidirectional Long Short Term Memory (BLSTM) network with a rank sensitive loss function results in significant performance improvements over previous approaches without the need for combining additional models.

Keywords: deep learning; question answering; non-factoid

1. INTRODUCTION

Traditional information retrieval (IR) methods focus on the relevance of documents to queries. In query based IR, documents are deemed relevant if they address the topic implied by the query. Collections often have more than one relevant document, and term overlap can be an effective measure of potential relevance. For the task of factoid question answering (QA), the relevant document becomes a single sentence or entity that answers the specific information request of the question. As these factoid questions are specific, a small window of text surrounding an answer can be used in a retrieval method. An example of this is seen in a sample factoid question from the TREC QA task:

Question: What is crips' gang color?

Answer: Prosecutors said the "rampage of murder and mayhem" was carried out with bullets that had been painted blue, the crips' signature color.

ICTIR '16, September 12-16, 2016, Newark, DE, USA
© 2016 ACM. ISBN 978-1-4503-4497-5/16/09...$15.00
DOI: http://dx.doi.org/10.1145/2970398.2970438

These two tasks contrast with the more recent task of *non-factoid QA* [11], where there is typically a range of possible answers due to the open ended nature of the question, but correctness is determined by more than topical relevance. Non-factoid answers can span multiple sentences with the majority of the text having little term overlap with the question. A typical question demonstrating these issues from the dataset used in this paper is shown below:

Question: How do male penguins survive without eating for four months?

Top Answer: Male penguins don't eat for 60 days. The female comes back after 2 months, and the male goes to feed again. During the incubation period, the male's one and only job is to keep the egg warm. So he conserves energy by not moving at all. They just huddle. During this time he can lose up to 1/3 to 1/2 of his body weight.

Here, the answer is correct, but large amounts of the text in the answer have little direct overlap with the question beyond the first sentence. While present in all QA applications, this disconnect causes significant issues for retrieving non-factoid answers. Additionally, there is often only one correct answer provided in the standard testbeds making the task even more difficult.

Deep learning, specifically recurrent neural networks (RNN), are able to learn representations of text across positions in a sequence, bridging the lexical gap between the question and its corresponding answer by receiving updates from previous information in the sequence. LSTMs expand on this by storing an internal cell state even if that cell does not activate, allowing for semantic relations that span across sentences to be learned. This is encouraging as other methods rely on a complex empirical process of determining which features to extract, and modeling semantic and syntactic dependencies is often computationally intensive [10]. LSTM networks are capable of learning representations based on their loss function [2] without the need for feature extraction [8]. This is particularly useful in the realm of non-factoid QA as conventional features often fail to significantly boost performance [11].

2. RELATED WORK

Surdeanu et al. [11] previously investigated IR methods in the Webscope L4 dataset. However, their implementation involved reranking the top N results retrieved by a standard IR system. They used a large number of features for the reranking process, and the FG2 group of features focusing on translation dependencies offered the greatest increase in performance over all other features extracted.

Deep learning in the realm of IR is not new. Severyn and Moschitti [10] have shown the efficacy of using a deep convolutional neural network (CNN) to learn pooled representations of question and answer sentences for the factoid QA task. The network they implemented involved multiple convolutional layers which evaluated the question and answer as separate inputs. A subsequent matrix computes the similarity between the two representations and is concatenated with individually pooled representations of the sentences and externally computed term frequency statistics prior to a dense layer. While this network was only applied to factoid QA pairs where the answer was no longer than a sentence, it demonstrates that deep networks succeed in learning distributional relations between the queries and relevant answers.

Iyyer et al. [3] have demonstrated the application of RNNs to the task of quiz bowl questions by modeling textual compositionality over a standard RNN with a specific ranking loss function. However, their application involves long queries with single word answers with multiple questions having the same answer.

Wang et al. [16, 15] expand on this work by investigating the performance of a BLSTM on the TREC QA task and the non-factoid task. They implemented a BLSTM, but used pretrained embeddings independent of the network and a non rank specific loss function. Their implementation fails to outperform the previous CNN network [10] on the TREC QA task, but achieves mean average precision and precision at 1 metrics within 3% and 1% of the CNN. Additionally, the final model's output is boosted using a gradient boosted regression tree with each answer's BM25 score as the BLSTM is unable to capture that information.

All of the previous work mentioned has been trained on data passed through an embedding matrix [10, 3, 16]. The most commonly used is Mikolov's skip-gram word2vec [7], though there exists continuous bag-of-words (CBOW) and GloVe [9] implementations. These methods all capture distributional representations, and Arora et al. [1] have shown that these representations are noisy factorized pairwise mutual information (PMI) matrices. Levy et al. [5] have shown that different implementations all perform at a similar level.

3. A NEURAL NETWORK FOR NON FACTOID RETRIEVAL

In this paper, we use a variant of a LSTM network structure implemented in [16] and [2]. The standard RNN architecture described in [2] is used such that each layer not only receives input from the layer below it, but also its own output from the previous time step. LSTM units replace the standard neuron of a RNN with additional internal structures to manage vanishing and exploding gradients. These structures consist of input, forget, and output gates that manage the information flow of the cell's internal state.

We utilize a bidirectional neural network as in [2, 16], which can be viewed as inputting the sequence in reverse order to a second layer at the same level of the graph, and then merged either through concatenation or element-wise summation. The bidirectional layers for this paper were implemented via concatenation. A simplified representation

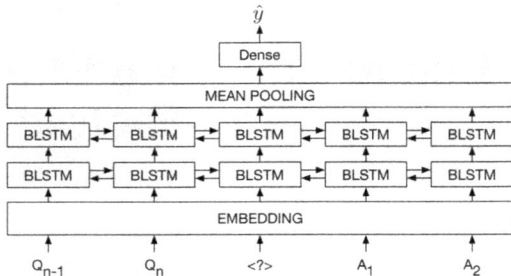

Figure 1: A simplified representation of the BLSTM network with an n length question

of the network is shown in Figure 1 with the output of the network represented as $\hat{y}$.

Previous work [3, 10, 16] involved training word2vec embeddings externally of the neural network, which resulted in representations learned independently from the network. In the network implemented in this paper, we create an embedding layer below the BLSTM network, such that the performance during training would backpropagate to the word embedding layer which learns dense representations. In addition, we train with a rank sensitive loss function rather than treating the learning stage as a pure classification task.

4. EXPERIMENTS

4.1 Data

Tokens	Webscope L4	nfL6
Min	6	10
Max	350	79
μ	77.4	39.0
σ	62.0	13.2

Table 1: Statistical description of tokens per question-answer pair in nfL6 and Webscope L4 after preprocessing

The datasets used for our experiments were Yahoo's Webscope L4 and a filtered, lower quality non-factoid set created from Yahoo's general Webscope L6, named nfL6. The L4 set has been used previously [11] for non-factoid QA and is sometimes referred to as the "manner" collection. It consists of 142,627 questions, of which we select 138,340 questions that satisfy the condition of being under 351 words when combined with their corresponding answer and do not contain websites. The word limit was used as LSTM networks are not capable of capturing dependencies on arbitrary length sequences and would not be able to learn representations of greater length answers. All questions are of the manner "how {to|do|did|does|can|would|could|should}..." and are high quality. Each question contains a noun and verb, and each answer is well formed. All answers that were not the highest voted answer were removed for each question as multiple answers for a question could be correct. This was done so the network would learn to better differentiate between correct and incorrect answers and not try to learn which answers would receive the highest votes.

The nfL6 dataset, after processing, consists of 87,361 questions. Unlike L4, the questions in this dataset are more generic and contains questions such as "Why is the sky blue?" and "Why do people steal?". Furthermore, answers are not as high quality. As there does not exist any equivalent dataset of generic non-factoid questions, this set was created using a linear kernel with a support vector machine. Initial training data is from UIUC's question dataset [6]. Fine grained classes of *description, manner,* and *reason* within the coarse grained class DESC were used as positive examples, with all others as negative examples. 3,500 additional training examples were attained from active training based on their distances to the hyperplane [14]. Additionally, to reduce noise, negative classifiers were trained on ENTITY, ABB, LOCATION, NUMERIC, and HUMAN classes to further reduce factoid questions in the collection.

Training, validation, and testing sets[1] for the BLSTM implementation were created in a similar fashion to [3]. A small pool of candidate answers were collected for each question based on top results in a BM25 search.

4.2 Network Configuration

For input to the network, each question is concatenated with its answer and a `<?>` character is inserted between the two strings as shown in Figure 1. Incorrect answers were concatenated the same way with the question string to create negative training examples. The `<?>` character was used similar to the `<EOS>` and `<S>` mark in [12] and [16, 15] respectively. This mark signifies the transition between source and target sentences and is depicted in Figure 1.

The specific network configuration consisted of a 256 dimension embedding matrix initialized uniformly, which feeds directly into two 512 length BLSTM layers with concatenated outputs. The cell activation function for the LSTM nodes is the sigmoid function, with internal gates using the *tanh* function. The output of the last BLSTM layer is mean pooled across time steps and fed into a single dense node with a sigmoid activation function. As mentioned previously, the embedding layer is part of the network during training, and thus will change word representations to best fit the loss function.

Optimization was done using the Adam algorithm [4] and trained to minimize the binary cross entropy weighted by how well the answers are separated with respect to the non-relevant training examples for each query as shown below.

$$L = \sum_{q \in Q} (1 - (q_r - \mu_{q_{nr}})) BCE_q$$

With Q as all questions, BCE_q as standard binary cross entropy for the question, q_r as the relevant answer score and $\mu_{q_{nr}}$ as the mean of all non relevant candidate answer scores for q. As the task cares about relative ranking over binary classifications, this scales the loss relative to the distance in scores such that weights will change based on the questions with the hardest to differentiate answers.

4.3 Evaluation

The evaluation metrics used are mean reciprocal rank (MRR) and precision at 1 (P@1) which are both common in IR and QA evaluations. Precision at 1 is a binary metric that is 1 if the correct answer is ranked highest, and 0 otherwise. The mean is then taken to evaluate performance over a collection of questions. The reciprocal rank is the

---

[1]Available at https://people.cs.umass.edu/dcohen

Q: How do I get a auto loan?

LSTM: Develop a relationship with a credit union. Start building a savings and get to know the loan officer. Make an appointment with a loan officer and ask them what it would take to get a loan with them. They will tell you.

BM25: with a flywheel puller. get a cheap one at any auto parts. Some will rent or loan. DONT BEAT ON IT this usually doesn't work and your asking for trouble. the stator and crankshaft have several bearings and seals that weren't meant to be beat on.

Figure 2: Example of a question in which the BLSTM implementation successfully returns the correct answer while BM25 does not.

multiplicative inverse of the highest ranking correct answer retrieved for a question. Thus the mean is $\frac{1}{|Q|} \sum_{i=1}^{|Q|} \frac{1}{rank_i}$ with Q being the set of questions.

The test collection was created from pooling the top 10 results from a BM25 search for each question, and including the correct answer as the 10th answer if it is not included in the list. These were then processed into sequences described in Section 4.2.

5. RESULTS AND DISCUSSION

The work done in [11] examined the L4 dataset using hand crafted features for reranking. However, they only selected the subset of queries which their initial IR system returned correct answers for the top N retrieved. This is not a realistic measure as it only takes into account 3.1% of all queries in the case of the BM25 benchmark for the top 10 retrieved. Additionally, performance gain is biased towards queries that behave favourably with the BM25 algorithm.

The end to end BLSTM network is instead compared against previous deep learning implementations and the BM25 baseline in Table 3. BM25 was chosen for the baseline as Yih et al. [13] have shown that *tf.idf* models are a competitive benchmark. While the CNN in [10] fails to capture any dependency between questions and answers in the L4 data, the BLSTM implementations are successful in learning a relation between them. Furthermore, end to end training significantly improves results over using an independently trained word embedding matrix without the need of an additional model to incorporate term frequency information and BLSTM layer as used in [16, 15]. This performance difference becomes more apparent when the language gap between training and testing of the embedding matrix grows. The nfL6 dataset contains slang and abbreviations not present in typical training text, which causes a hyperparameter tuned BLSTM implemented in [16, 15] to perform well below the modifications used in this paper.

The effect of the rank sensitive loss function results in significant improvement as well, referenced as BLSTM-Loss in Table 3. In training and evaluation, the network's range for $\hat{y}$ is dependent on the question rather than consistently centered around one point in [0,1]. As the task focuses on the relative rankings of candidate answers, weights are updated based on the difference of non-relevant and relevant answers instead of solely based on their respective entropy.

An interesting characteristic for these datasets is the poor performance of BM25 on both non-factoid collections. It cannot differentiate between relevant and non-relevant when

Table 2: Results on Webscope L4 and nfL6

Implementation	L4		nfL6	
	P@1	**MRR**	**P@1**	**MRR**
Okapi BM25	0.0783	0.1412	0.1312	0.2660
Severyn and Moschitti	0.0989	0.2434	0.1438	0.2842
Wang and Nyberg	0.4414	0.6152	0.1232	0.3271
BLSTM	0.4752*	0.6377*	0.2002*	0.4043*
BLSTM-Loss	0.5157*†	0.6642*†	0.2375*†	0.4219*

Table 3: Significant differences relative to Wang and Nyberg denoted by *, † denotes relative to BLSTM (using two tailed t-test with $p < 0.05$)

the answers no longer echo terms used in the query. Figure 2 provides an example in the L4 dataset where the BLSTM correctly identifies the answer, and BM25 fails. BM25 retrieves an answer that has more query terms than the BLSTM retrieved answer; however, it does not answer the question. The BLSTM is able to learn a representation of "loan" to "credit" and "union" in addition to leveraging the query term "loan". This reflects in the results of the Severyn and Moschitti [10] as the use of term overlap features appended to the output of a hidden layer does not improve results over the sequence based approach of the LSTM.

6. CONCLUSIONS AND FUTURE WORK

Implementing an end to end BLSTM with a rank sensitive loss function results in significant improvement over previous deep learning implementations without the need of term overlap information.

As the results indicate that the non-factoid RNN networks are sensitive to the training of the embedding layer, a possible character level embedding might negate the need to learn an embedding for each corpus and allow the network to update weights to represent the combination of character vectors as words.

In addition, using a convolutional layer as input to the BLSTM network can potentially result in better abstractions for the LSTM layers to process, as CNNs have been able to capture factoid level information comparable to recurrent networks for the TREC QA task [10].

7. ACKNOWLEDGMENT

This work was supported in part by the Center for Intelligent Information Retrieval, in part by NSF grant #CNS-0934322, and in part by NSF grant #IIS-1419693. Any opinions, findings and conclusions or recommendations expressed in this material are those of the authors and do not necessarily reflect those of the sponsor.

8. REFERENCES

[1] S. Arora, Y. Li, Y. Liang, T. Ma, and A. Risteski. Random walks on context spaces: Towards an explanation of the mysteries of semantic word embeddings. *CoRR*, abs/1502.03520, 2015.

[2] A. Graves, N. Jaitly, and A.-R. Mohamed. Hybrid speech recognition with deep bidirectional lstm. In *ASRU, 2013*, pages 273–278, Dec 2013.

[3] M. Iyyer, J. Boyd-Graber, L. Claudino, R. Socher, and H. Daumé III. A neural network for factoid question answering over paragraphs. In *EMNLP*, 2014.

[4] D. P. Kingma and J. Ba. Adam: A method for stochastic optimization. *CoRR*, abs/1412.6980, 2014.

[5] O. Levy, Y. Goldberg, and I. Dagan. Improving distributional similarity with lessons learned from word embeddings. *TACL*, 3:211–225, 2015.

[6] X. Li and D. Roth. Learning question classifiers. In *COLING - Volume 1*, COLING '02, pages 1–7, Stroudsburg, PA, USA, 2002. ACL.

[7] T. Mikolov, K. Chen, G. Corrado, and J. Dean. Efficient estimation of word representations in vector space. *CoRR*, abs/1301.3781, 2013.

[8] H. Palangi, L. Deng, Y. Shen, J. Gao, X. He, J. Chen, X. Song, and R. K. Ward. Deep sentence embedding using the long short term memory network: Analysis and application to information retrieval. *CoRR*, abs/1502.06922, 2015.

[9] J. Pennington, R. Socher, and C. D. Manning. Glove: Global vectors for word representation. In *EMNLP*, pages 1532–1543, 2014.

[10] A. Severyn and A. Moschitti. Learning to rank short text pairs with convolutional deep neural networks. In *SIGIR*, SIGIR '15, pages 373–382, New York, NY, USA, 2015. ACM.

[11] M. Surdeanu, M. Ciaramita, and H. Zaragoza. Learning to rank answers on large online qa collections. In *ACL:HLT*, pages 719–727, 2008.

[12] I. Sutskever, O. Vinyals, and Q. V. Le. Sequence to sequence learning with neural networks. *CoRR*, abs/1409.3215, 2014.

[13] W. tau Yih, M.-W. Chang, C. Meek, and A. Pastusiak. Question answering using enhanced lexical semantic models. In *ACL*. ACL, August 2013.

[14] S. Tong and D. Koller. Support vector machine active learning with applications to text classification. *J. Mach. Learn. Res.*, 2:45–66, Mar. 2002.

[15] D. Wang and E. Nyberg. A recurrent neural network based answer ranking model for web question answering. In *WebQA Workshop, SIGIR '15, Santiago, Chile*.

[16] D. Wang and E. Nyberg. A long short-term memory model for answer sentence selection in question answering. In *ACL-IJCNLP, ACL 2015, July 26-31, 2015, Beijing, China, Volume 2: Short Papers*, pages 707–712, 2015.

Embedding-based Query Language Models

Hamed Zamani
Center for Intelligent Information Retrieval
College of Information and Computer Sciences
University of Massachusetts Amherst
Amherst, MA 01003
zamani@cs.umass.edu

W. Bruce Croft
Center for Intelligent Information Retrieval
College of Information and Computer Sciences
University of Massachusetts Amherst
Amherst, MA 01003
croft@cs.umass.edu

ABSTRACT

Word embeddings, which are low-dimensional vector representations of vocabulary terms that capture the semantic similarity between them, have recently been shown to achieve impressive performance in many natural language processing tasks. The use of word embeddings in information retrieval, however, has only begun to be studied. In this paper, we explore the use of word embeddings to enhance the accuracy of query language models in the ad-hoc retrieval task. To this end, we propose to use word embeddings to incorporate and weight terms that do not occur in the query, but are semantically related to the query terms. We describe two embedding-based query expansion models with different assumptions. Since pseudo-relevance feedback methods that use the top retrieved documents to update the original query model are well-known to be effective, we also develop an embedding-based relevance model, an extension of the effective and robust relevance model approach. In these models, we transform the similarity values obtained by the widely-used cosine similarity with a sigmoid function to have more discriminative semantic similarity values. We evaluate our proposed methods using three TREC newswire and web collections. The experimental results demonstrate that the embedding-based methods significantly outperform competitive baselines in most cases. The embedding-based methods are also shown to be more robust than the baselines.

CCS Concepts

•Information systems → Query representation; Query reformulation; Language models;

Keywords

Word embedding; language models; pseudo-relevance feedback; query expansion

ICTIR '16, September 12-16, 2016, Newark, DE, USA
© 2016 ACM. ISBN 978-1-4503-4497-5/16/09...$15.00
DOI: http://dx.doi.org/10.1145/2970398.2970405

1. INTRODUCTION

Capturing the semantic similarities between vocabulary terms have been an interesting and challenging issue in natural language processing (NLP) and information retrieval (IR) for some time. Many approaches have been proposed for finding semantically similar words, such as latent semantic indexing [7] and the information content-based method [23]. Recent developments in distributed semantic representations, also called word embedding, have been shown to be highly effective in many NLP tasks, such as word analogy [19] and named-entity recognition [8]. Word embedding techniques assign each term a low-dimensional (compared to the vocabulary size) vector in a "semantic vector space". In this space, close vectors are supposed to demonstrate high semantic or syntactic similarity between the corresponding words. Word2vec [19] and GloVe [21] are examples of successful implementations of word embeddings that respectively use neural networks and matrix factorization to learn embedding vectors.

Although word embeddings have shown significant improvements in many NLP tasks, there is less known about the use of word embedding vectors to improve retrieval performance. In this paper, we focus on the vocabulary mismatch problem, i.e., the mismatch of different vocabulary terms with the same concept. This is a fundamental IR problem, since users often use different words to describe a concept in the queries than those that authors of documents use to describe the same concept [28]. Therefore, it will cause poor retrieval performance. We address the vocabulary mismatch problem in the language modeling framework for ad-hoc information retrieval by focusing on the semantic similarity between terms. Recently, the word embedding techniques have been employed to improve the accuracy of document language models in [10, 32]. In contrast, in this paper, we focus on estimating accurate language models for queries based on word embedding vectors, which leads to more efficient and effective methods. In addition to the terms that appear in the query, we incorporate and weight the words that do not occur in the query, but are semantically similar to the query terms. To do so, we propose two query expansion models with different simplifying assumptions. The first model assumes that given each term w, all query terms are conditionally independent. The second model assumes that the semantic similarity between each pair of vocabulary terms is independent of the queries.

A well-known and effective technique in ad-hoc information retrieval to address the vocabulary mismatch problem is pseudo-relevance feedback (PRF) [15, 18, 24, 28, 29]. PRF assumes that a small set of top-retrieved documents is relevant to the query, and thus a number of relevant terms can be selected from this set of feedback documents (also called pseudo-relevant documents) to be added to the query model. In this paper, we extend the relevance model approach [15], one of the most effective and robust PRF methods, by considering the semantic similarity between the terms, in addition to the term matching similarity.

Furthermore, we observe that the semantic similarity scores of the vocabulary terms in the embedding semantic space are not sufficiently discriminative for our task, and potentially for many other IR tasks. Previous work on word embedding considers typical similarity functions, e.g., the cosine similarity or the Euclidean distance functions, that are shown to be very effective in detecting nearest words in terms of their semantic similarity [12, 17]. In fact, these metrics are sufficient when the order of words in terms of their semantic similarity to a given word is needed. In contrast, the similarity values are not sufficiently discriminative to be used in IR models. Thus, we propose transforming the similarity values using the well-known sigmoid function.

We evaluate the proposed methods using three standard TREC collections: Associated Press (AP), the TREC Robust Track 2004 collection, and the TREC Terabyte Track 2004-2006 collection (GOV2). The first two collections contain high-quality news articles, while the last one is a large web collection. The results indicate that the proposed methods outperform competitive baselines, in all collections. The MAP improvements in most cases are statistically significant. The proposed methods also perform quite well in improving the precision of top retrieved documents. We also show that the proposed methods are more robust than the baselines. In addition, the experimental results suggest that the sigmoid transformation of embedding similarities can significantly improve the performance.

2. RELATED WORK

In this section, we first briefly review previous work on query expansion and pseudo-relevance feedback. Then, we introduce the applications of word embeddings in information retrieval.

2.1 Query Expansion

Query expansion is the process of adding relevant terms to a query to improve the retrieval effectiveness. There are a number of query expansion methods based on linguistic resources, such as WordNet, but they have not substantially improved the retrieval performance [26]. Although a number of data-driven query expansion methods, such as [3], can improve the average retrieval performance, they are shown to be unstable across queries [4, 6]. According to Xu and Croft [28], the aforementioned query expansion techniques are based on global analysis. Global analysis often relies on external resources or document collections. On the other hand, local analysis expands queries using the documents that are related to them, like top-retrieved documents. Query expansion via pseudo-relevance feedback is a common technique used to improve retrieval effectiveness in many retrieval models [15, 18, 24, 29]. Relevance models [15], mixture model, and divergence minimization model [29] are the first PRF methods proposed for the language modeling framework. Since then, several other methods have been proposed, but relevance models are shown to

be still among the state-of-the-art PRF methods and perform more robustly than many other methods [18]. Recently, Montazeralghaem et al. [20] stated that PRF models can be improved by taking the semantic similarity between feedback terms and the query into account. There are also a number of learning-based PRF methods. Although some of these methods have promising performance, they are not related to our work and are not considered in this paper. In this paper, the first two proposed query expansion models are based on global analysis, while the third model is a combination of local and global analysis.

2.2 Word Embeddings for IR

Unlike NLP, where word embeddings have been successfully employed in several tasks, word embedding techniques in IR are still relatively unstudied. Recently, Zheng and Callan [30] proposed a supervised embedding-based technique to reweight terms for the IR models, e.g., BM25. They learned term weights using the distributed semantic representations. Clinchant and Perronnin [5] proposed Fisher Vector (FV), a document representation framework based on continuous word embeddings, which aggregates the nonlinear mapping of word vectors into a document-level representation. Although FV outperforms latent semantic indexing (LSI) [7] in ad-hoc retrieval, it does not perform better than popular IR frameworks, such as TF-IDF and the divergence from randomness retrieval model.

A number of methods have focused on computing the semantic similarity between two documents. Le and Mikolov [16] proposed Paragraph Vector (PV), a method to compute an embedding vector for each sentence, paragraph, or document. Since queries are not available during the training time of embedding vectors, PV cannot always be employed for computing the embedding vectors of queries. Kusner et al. [13] recently proposed word mover's distance (WMD), a distance function between two documents, which measures the minimum traveling distance from the embedded words of one document to another one. WMD achieved good performance in the document classification task. A supervised method for computing the semantic similarities between short texts was also proposed by Kenter and de Rijke [12]. Zhou et al. [31] recently proposed an embedding-based method for question retrieval in the community question answering systems.

BWESG [27], a bilingual word embedding method, has recently been developed and applied to information retrieval. This model learns bilingual embedding vectors from document-aligned comparable corpora. Regarding the well-defined structure of language modeling framework in information retrieval, a number of methods have been proposed to improve the performance of language models using the word embedding vectors. For instance, Ganguly et al. [10] considered the semantic similarities between vocabulary terms to smooth document language models. Recently, Zuccon et al. [32] proposed to employ word embeddings within the well-known translation model for IR. Their proposed method achieves comparable performance to the mutual information-based translation language models [11]. The main idea behind the methods proposed in [10] and [32] is similar. Both methods consider semantic similarity in computing the probability of terms in the documents. Recently, ALMasri et al. [2] proposed a heuristic query expansion method based on word embedding similarities. Their method is a term-by-term ex-

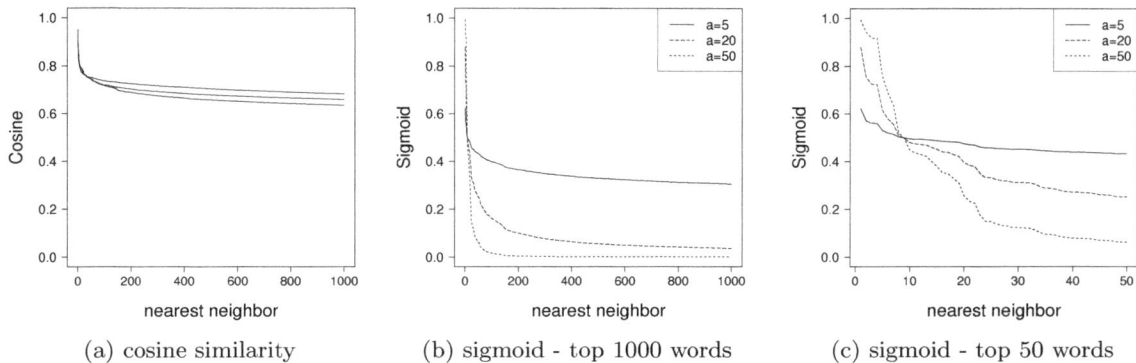

| (a) cosine similarity | (b) sigmoid - top 1000 words | (c) sigmoid - top 50 words |

Figure 1: The cosine similarity function (the left plot) and its sigmoid transformation (the two right plots) of nearest neighbors (in descending order in terms of their similarity value). For the sigmoid function, the parameter c is set to 0.8.

pansion instead of expanding the whole query. Sordoni et al. [25] also proposed a query expansion method based on concept embedding. Their method is a supervised learning approach with the quantum entropy loss function that uses click-through data. More recently, Diaz et al. [9] proposed locally-trained word embeddings for query expansion.

The main difference between this paper and the existing work is that we focus on estimating accurate query language models which efficiently outperforms the embedding-based document language models [10].

3. EMBEDDING-BASED QUERY MODELS

In the language modeling framework [22], estimating accurate query language models plays a key role in achieving high retrieval accuracy. Maximum Likelihood Estimation (MLE) is a simple yet effective method for estimating query language models. Several techniques, such as pseudo-relevance feedback (PRF), have been proposed to estimate more accurate query language models. The goal of this paper is to estimate accurate query language models by employing word embedding vectors to address the vocabulary mismatch problem in information retrieval. In this section, we first introduce the idea behind the word embedding techniques whose purpose is to capture the semantic similarity between vocabulary terms. We propose to use the sigmoid function over the well-known similarity metrics to achieve more discriminative similarity values between terms. We further propose to employ word embedding vectors to estimate query language models via query expansion in a weighted manner. We afterward extend the idea of relevance models [15], one of the most effective and robust PRF methods [18], by leveraging word embedding vectors.

3.1 Word Embedding

Word embedding techniques learn a low-dimensional vector (compared to the vocabulary size) for each vocabulary term in which the similarity between the word vectors can show the semantic as well as the syntactic similarities between the corresponding words. This is why word embeddings are also called distributed semantic representations. Note that the word embedding methods are categorized as unsupervised learning algorithms, since they only need a large amount of raw textual data in their training phase. A popular method to compute these word embedding vectors is neural network-based language models. For instance,

Mikolov et al. [19] introduced word2vec, an embedding method that learns word vectors via a neural network with a single hidden layer. Another successful trend in learning semantic word representations is employing global matrix factorization over the word-word matrices. GloVe [21] is an example of such methods.

Word embeddings have been shown to be extremely useful in many NLP tasks, such as word analogy [19] and named-entity recognition [8]. In these tasks, the semantic similarity between terms are often computed using the cosine similarity of the word embedding vectors. Figure 1a plots the cosine similarity[1] of the top 1000 similar words to three random words.[2] As shown in this figure, these three curves have similar behaviours. An interesting observation in this figure is that there are no substantial differences (e.g., two times more) between the similarity of the most similar term and the 1000th similar term to a given term w, while the 1000th word is unlikely to have any semantic similarity with w. In other words, the similarity values are not discriminative enough. On the other hand, as extensively explored in various NLP tasks, the order of words in terms of their semantic similarity to a given term is accurate, especially for the very close terms. Therefore, we need a monotone mapping function to transform the similarity scores achieved by the popular similarity metrics, such as the cosine similarity.

Intuitively, there will be a small number of words that are semantically similar to a given word w. Hence, the similarity of most of words with w should have a value close to zero. Therefore, we propose using the well-known sigmoid function to transform the similarity scores coming from the cosine similarity function. The sigmoid function is a non-linear mapping function that maps values in $[-\infty, +\infty]$ to the $[0, 1]$ interval. This function, which has been used in many machine learning algorithms, such as the logistic regression and neural networks, can be calculated as:

$$S(x) = \frac{1}{1 + e^{-a(x-c)}} \qquad (1)$$

where x denotes the input of the sigmoid function with two free parameters a and c. Figure 1b plots the cosine similar-

---

[1] In this paper, we linearly transform the cosine similarity values to the $[0, 1]$ interval.
[2] In Figure 1, we plot the cosine similarity over the vectors learned by the GloVe method. The other popular similarity metrics, such as the Euclidean distance and the KL-divergence, also suffer from the same problem.

ity values of the top 1000 similar words to a random word that are transformed using the sigmoid function with different values of a. By increasing the value of a, the similarity scores drop more quickly. To have a better understanding of the sigmoid behaviour, we also plot the same curves for only the top 50 words in Figure 1c. As shown in this figure, when a is set to a large number, the similarity scores drop quickly and more close values are assigned to the top terms (e.g., top 10 terms). The parameters a and c make the sigmoid function a flexible transformation for similarity scores, that can be employed in different scenarios. For instance, when there are a few semantically similar words to a word w, but there is not much distinction between them, in terms of their similarity to w, the sigmoid transformation can give close weights to the very similar terms, in addition to dropping very fast. Another advantage of transforming the similarity scores using the sigmoid function is that the results are always in the $[0, 1]$ interval, and thus all distance functions with unbounded values can be used for computing the similarity between embedding vectors. These behaviours of the sigmoid function make it suitable for our task.[3]

3.2 Embedding-based Query Expansion

Similar to most language modeling-based methods, we focus on unigram language models. Therefore, for each vocabulary term w, we should estimate $p(w|\theta_Q)$ where θ_Q denotes the language model of the query Q. In this subsection, we propose two novel estimations for the query language models by making use of semantic similarity between the terms coming from the similarity between the word embedding vectors. These two estimations have different simplifying assumptions. The first method considers that there is a conditional independence assumption between the query terms; while the second method assumes that the semantic similarity between two given terms is independent of the query. Interestingly, as we will see in the following, the first assumption leads to an expansion method based on multiplicative similarity, i.e., the expanded terms should be similar to all query terms. On the other hand, the second assumption leads to an additive similarity (a mixture model).

3.2.1 Conditional Independence of Query Terms

To estimate $p(w|\theta_Q)$, we first consider the Bayes rule as follows:

$$p(w|\theta_Q) = \frac{p(\theta_Q|w)p(w)}{p(Q)} \propto p(\theta_Q|w)p(w) \quad (2)$$

In the above equation, we ignore $p(Q)$ since it is independent of the term w. We assume that query terms are independent of each other, but we keep their dependence on w. Therefore, we can estimate the query language model as follows:

$$p(w|\theta_Q) \propto p(q_1, q_2, \ldots, q_k|w)p(w) = p(w) \prod_{i=1}^{k} p(q_i|w) \quad (3)$$

where $q_1, q_2, \ldots, q_k$ are the query terms and k is the query length. To compute $p(q_i|w)$, we consider the word embed-

ding similarities which can capture the semantic similarity between vocabulary terms. To do so, we compute this probability as follows:

$$p(q_i|w) = \frac{\delta(q_i, w)}{\sum_{w' \in V} \delta(w', w)} \quad (4)$$

where δ and V denote the similarity function (e.g., the sigmoid function over the cosine similarity) and the vocabulary set, respectively. Considering the law of total probability, we compute $p(w)$ using the following equation:[4]

$$p(w) = \sum_{w' \in V} p(w, w') \propto \sum_{w' \in V} \delta(w, w') \quad (5)$$

The generated language model θ_Q can be linearly interpolated with the maximum likelihood estimation of the query language model with the coefficient of α.

3.2.2 Query-Independent Term Similarities

To estimate the query language model θ_Q, we first use the law of total probability as follows:

$$p(w|\theta_Q) = \sum_{w' \in V} p(w, w'|\theta_Q) = \sum_{w' \in V} p(w|w', \theta_Q)p(w'|\theta_Q) \quad (6)$$

In the above calculations, we use the Bayes rule. We assume that the semantic similarity between the terms is independent of the query language model. Therefore, $p(w|w', \theta_Q)$ can be computed as follows:

$$p(w|w', \theta_Q) = p(w|w') = \frac{\delta(w, w')}{\sum_{w'' \in V} \delta(w'', w')} \quad (7)$$

where δ denotes the semantic similarity between two given terms and can be calculated by transforming the cosine similarity values using the sigmoid function.

Considering the maximum likelihood estimation, we can rewrite Equation 6 as follows:

$$p(w|\theta_Q) \propto \sum_{w' \in Q} \frac{\delta(w, w')}{\sum_{w'' \in V} \delta(w'', w')} \times \frac{c(w', Q)}{|Q|} \quad (8)$$

where $c(w', Q)$ and $|Q|$ denote the count of term w' in the query and the query length, respectively.

Similar to the previous embedding-based estimation of query models, the generated query language model can be linearly interpolated with the maximum likelihood estimation of the query language model with a coefficient of α.

3.3 Embedding-based Relevance Model

Pseudo-relevance feedback has been shown to be highly effective in improving the retrieval performance [15, 18, 29]. In PRF, it is assumed that the top-retrieved documents are relevant to the query, and thus they can be used to improve the query language model accuracy. In this subsection, we propose an embedding-based relevance model, a method inspired by the relevance model approach proposed by Lavrenko and Croft [15], which has been shown to be one of the most effective and robust PRF methods [18].

---

[3]We have examined other transformation functions, such as the softmax and the power functions, but the sigmoid transformation provides more reasonable similarity scores, which leads to better performance. For the sake of space, we only introduce the best transformation function that we found.

[4]Intuitively, a word with higher semantic similarity with all the other words will achieve higher probability. In other words, general terms are supposed to have high probabilities according to this definition, which is also consistent with the other definitions for $p(w)$, such as the the frequency ratio of the word w in a large corpus.

Table 1: Collections statistics.

ID	collection	queries (title only)	#docs	doc length	#qrels
AP	Associated Press 88-89	TREC 1-3 Ad-Hoc Track, topics 51-200	165k	287	15,838
Robust	TREC Disks 4 & 5 minus Congressional Record	TREC 2004 Robust Track, topics 301-450 & 601-700	528k	254	17,412
GOV2	2004 crawl of .gov domains	TREC 2004-2006 Terabyte Track, topics 701-850	25,205k	648	26,917

We compute the feedback language model as follows:

$$p(w|\theta_F) \propto \sum_{D \in F} p(w, Q, D) = \sum_{D \in F} p(Q|w, D)p(w|D)p(D) \quad (9)$$

where θ_F and F respectively denote the feedback language model and the set of feedback documents, i.e., the top-retrieved documents. To compute $p(Q|w, D)$, we consider both term matching and semantic similarities. This probability can be computed via a linear interpolation with the coefficient of β:

$$p(Q|w, D) = \beta \, p_{tm}(Q|w, D) + (1 - \beta) \, p_{sem}(Q|w, D) \quad (10)$$

where p_{tm} and p_{sem} denote the probabilities coming from the term matching similarities and the semantic similarities, respectively. Similar to RM3 [1, 15], $p_{tm}(Q|w, D)$ can be estimated by considering the independence assumption of terms (query terms and w) as follows:

$$p_{tm}(Q|w, D) = \prod_{i=1}^{k} p(q_i|D) \quad (11)$$

where q_i denotes the ith term of the query Q with the length of k. To compute $p_{sem}(Q|w, D)$, we assume that query terms are independent of each other, but we keep their dependence to the term w and document D. Therefore, we can calculate this probability as follows:

$$p_{sem}(Q|w, D) = \prod_{i=1}^{k} p_{sem}(q_i|w, D) \triangleq \prod_{i=1}^{k} \frac{\delta(q_i, w)c(q_i, D)}{Z} \quad (12)$$

where δ computes the semantic similarity between two given terms and $c(q_i, D)$ is the count of term q_i in the document D. Z is a normalization factor, which is only needed to be a summation over the terms appeared in the document D (instead of all vocabulary terms), and thus it is not computationally expensive.

Similar to RM3, we compute $p(w|D)$ (see Equation (9)) using the maximum likelihood estimation (MLE) smoothed by a reference language model.[5] We assume that there is no prior knowledge available about the relevance score of pseudo-relevant documents, and thus we calculate $p(D)$ using a uniform distribution. It is notable that the proposed embedding-based relevance model satisfies the "semantic effect" constraint recently proposed by Montazeralghaem et al. [20]. The updated query language model can be calculated using the linear interpolation of the original query language model with the computed feedback language model:

$$p(w|\theta_Q^*) = \alpha \, p(w|\theta_Q) + (1 - \alpha) \, p(w|\theta_F) \quad (13)$$

---

[5]We also considered embedding-based semantic similarities in computing this probability using the law of total probability $(p(w|D) = \sum_{w' \in V} p(w, w'|D))$, but there is no significant improvement over the MLE estimation in our experiments. Therefore, we keep it as simple as possible.

Note that the original query language model can be computed using either the maximum likelihood estimation, or one of the embedding based query language models proposed in Section 3.2.

It should be noted that since the retrieval models, such as the KL-divergence retrieval model, compute the similarity between the query and documents with respect to the terms that appeared in the query, it is reasonable that the updated query model has limited number of terms with non-zero weights. Hence, in the proposed embedding-based relevance model as well as in the two proposed query expansion models (see Section 3.2), we select the top m terms in the updated language model with highest probabilities to be added to the query.

4. EXPERIMENTS

4.1 Experimental Setup

To evaluate the proposed methods, we used three standard TREC collections: AP (Associated Press 1988-1989), Robust (TREC Robust Track 2004 collection), and GOV2 (TREC Terabyte Track 2004-2006 collection). The first two collections contain high-quality news articles and the last one is a large web collection. The statistics of these collections are reported in Table 1. We considered the title of topics as queries in our experiments. The standard INQUERY stopword list was used in all experiments, and no stemming was performed.

We employed the KL-divergence retrieval model [14] with the Dirichlet prior smoothing method. All experiments were carried out using the Galago toolkit[6]. In all the experiments, we used the word embeddings extracted using the GloVe method [21]. The word embeddings were extracted from a 6 billion token collection (the Wikipedia dump 2014 plus the Gigawords 5).[7] Note that we considered only the queries where the embedding vectors of all query terms are available. The employed embedding vectors contain all query terms for 146 (out of 150), 241 (out of 250), and 147 (out of 150) queries in AP, Robust, and GOV2, respectively. Note that to have a fair evaluation, we also used these queries for the baselines methods.

4.1.1 Parameters Setting

In all the experiments, the Dirichlet prior smoothing parameter μ was set to Galago's default value of 1500. In the experiments related to the pseudo-relevance feedback, the number of feedback documents was set to the typical value of 10. In all the experiments (except in those that explicitly mentioned), the parameters α (the linear interpolation coefficient), m (the number of terms added to the queries), and β (see Section 3.3) were set using 2-fold cross-validation to optimize MAP over the queries of each collection. We swept the parameters α and β between $\{0.1, \ldots, 0.9\}$.

---

[6]http://www.lemurproject.org/galago.php
[7]Statistics of this collection is reported in Table 4.

Table 2: Comparing the proposed embedding-based query expansion methods with the baselines. The superscript 1/2/3/4 denotes that the MAP improvements over MLE/GLM/VEXP/AWE are statistically significant. The highest value in each row is marked in bold.

Dataset	Metric	MLE	GLM	VEXP	AWE	EQE1	EQE2
AP	MAP	0.2236	0.2254	0.2338	0.2304	0.2388^{1234}	$\mathbf{0.2391}^{1234}$
	P@5	0.4260	0.4369	0.4412	0.4356	0.4397	**0.4466**
	P@10	0.4014	0.4051	0.4038	0.4058	**0.4075**	0.4014
	RI	–	0.10	0.18	0.14	**0.32**	**0.32**
Robust	MAP	0.2190	0.2244	0.2253	0.2224	$\mathbf{0.2292}^{124}$	0.2257^{1}
	P@5	0.4606	0.4523	0.4722	0.4680	**0.4739**	0.4622
	P@10	0.3979	0.3929	0.4133	0.4066	0.4162	**0.4183**
	RI	–	0.22	0.17	0.14	**0.30**	0.22
GOV2	MAP	0.2696	0.2684	0.2687	0.2657	$\mathbf{0.2745}^{1234}$	0.2727^{4}
	P@5	0.5592	0.5537	0.5932	0.5537	**0.5959**	0.5810
	P@10	0.5531	0.5483	0.5537	0.5503	**0.5660**	0.5517
	RI	–	-0.14	0.10	-0.18	**0.20**	0.08

The value of the parameter m and the number of feedback documents (for PRF experiments) were also selected from $\{10, 20, ..., 100\}$. The sigmoid parameters (a and c in Equation (1)) were chosen using cross-validation from $\{5, 10, ..., 50\}$ and $\{0.7, 0.75, ..., 0.9\}$, respectively. The free hyper-parameters of the baselines were also set using the same procedure. In all experiments unless explicitly mentioned, the dimension of embedding vectors was set to 200.

4.1.2 Evaluation Metrics

Mean Average Precision (MAP) of the top-ranked 1000 documents is selected as the main evaluation metric to evaluate the retrieval effectiveness. Furthermore, we also consider the precision of the top 5 and 10 retrieved documents (P@5 and P@10). Statistically significant differences of performances are determined using the two-tailed paired t-test computed at a 95% confidence level based on the average precision per query.

To evaluate the robustness of methods, we consider the robustness index (RI) [6] which is defined as $\frac{N_+ - N_-}{|Q|}$, where $|Q|$ denotes the number of queries, and N_+/N_- shows the number of queries improved/decreased by each method compared to the maximum likelihood estimation baseline.[8] The RI value is in the $[-1, 1]$ interval and the higher RI values determine more robust methods.

4.2 Results and Discussion

In this subsection, we first evaluate the two proposed embedding-based query expansion models. We further evaluate the proposed methods in the PRF scenario. Then, we experiment the sensitivity of the proposed methods to the word embedding vectors. At the end, we briefly analyze the behaviour of the sigmoid function in our task.

4.2.1 Embedding-based Query Expansion Models

To evaluate the two proposed embedding-based query expansion models (EQE1 and EQE2), we consider four baselines: (1) the standard maximum likelihood estimation of the query model (MLE), (2) the embedding-based document language model smoothing method (GLM)[9] [10] (which is

also similar to [32]), (3) a heuristic-based query expansion method based on word embeddings (VEXP) [2], and (4) a query expansion method based on the similarity of vocabulary term vectors and the average embedding vector of all query terms (AWE). Although the AWE baseline was not previously used for the query expansion purpose, the idea of averaging vectors of query/sentence terms has been previously used in a number of previous work [16, 27, 30]. Note that we do not use supervised approaches, such as [30, 25], as well as the methods that use external resources, such as knowledge graphs, as baseline.

The results achieved by the proposed methods (EQE1 and EQE2) and the baselines are reported in Table 2. According to this table, both proposed methods outperform all the baselines in all collections, in terms of MAP, P@5, P@10, and RI. The t-test shows that the MAP improvements of EQE1 compared to all the baselines are always significant, except compared to VEXP in the Robust collection. Although in some cases EQE2 outperforms EQE1, we can generally claim that in most cases EQE1 has superior performance. Note that EQE1 is based on multiplicative similarity, while EQE2 is based on additive similarity. Multiplicative similarity means that the expanded terms should be close to all query terms.

As shown in Table 2, the improvements over the MLE baseline in AP and Robust are higher than those in the GOV2 collection. The reason could be related to the corpus used for extracting the embedding vectors. This corpus mostly contains formal texts. Therefore, the context of the employed word embedding vectors is more similar to the context of the newswire collections rather than the GOV2 collection.[10] It should be noted that the results achieved by EQE1 and EQE2 can be further improved. For instance, we show in Section 4.2.3 that by increasing the dimension of word embedding vectors, the results will be improved.

In the next set of experiments, we study the sensitivity of the proposed methods (EQE1 and EQE2) to the two parameters α and m (see Section 3.2), in terms of MAP. We set α and m to 0.5 and 50, respectively. In each step, we sweep one of these parameters and fix the other one. Figures 2a and 2b respectively plot the sensitivity of EQE1 and EQE2 to the parameter α, the coefficient of interpolating the original query language model with the generated embedding-based

---

[8]To avoid the influence of very small average precision differences in the RI values, we only consider the improvements/losses higher than 10% (relatively).

[9]Note that all other methods use Dirichlet prior smoothing, but GLM is a linear interpolation smoothing method with constant coefficients.

[10]The results achieved by the embedding vectors trained on other corpora are reported in Section 4.2.3.

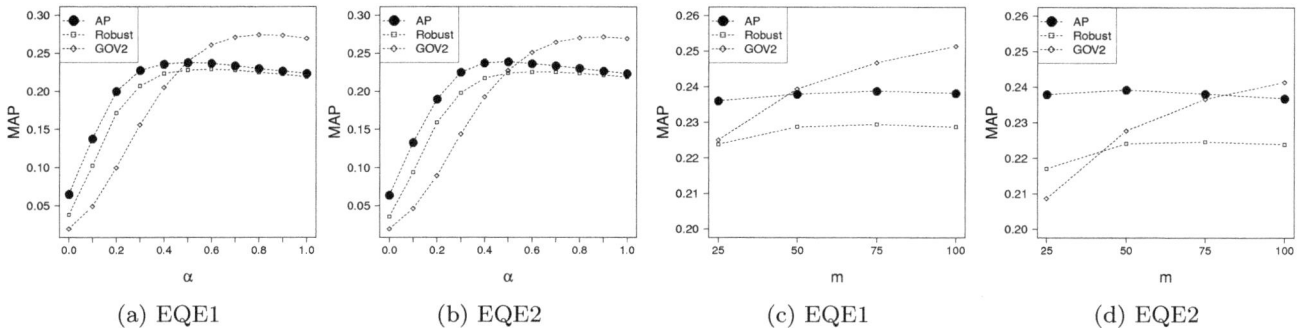

| (a) EQE1 | (b) EQE2 | (c) EQE1 | (d) EQE2 |

Figure 2: Sensitivity of EQE1 and EQE2 to the interpolation coefficient (α) and the term count (m), in terms of MAP.

Table 3: Evaluating the proposed methods in the pseudo-relevance feedback scenario. The superscript 1/2 denotes that the MAP improvements over MLE/RM3 are statistically significant. The highest value in each row is marked in bold.

Dataset	Metric	MLE	MLE+RM1 (RM3)	EQE1+RM1	EQE2+RM1	MLE+ERM	EQE1+ERM	EQE2+ERM
AP	MAP	0.2236	0.3051	0.3118[12]	0.3115[12]	0.3102[12]	**0.3178[12]**	0.3140[12]
	P@5	0.4260	0.4644	0.4808	0.4795	0.4699	**0.4822**	0.4644
	P@10	0.4014	0.4500	0.4500	0.4452	0.4521	**0.4568**	0.4479
	RI	–	0.47	0.45	0.41	**0.52**	0.47	**0.52**
Robust	MAP	0.2190	0.2677	0.2712[12]	0.2710[12]	0.2711[12]	0.2731[12]	**0.2750[12]**
	P@5	0.4606	0.4581	0.4747	0.4722	0.4639	**0.4797**	0.4730
	P@10	0.3979	0.4191	0.4241	0.4295	0.4241	0.4307	**0.4369**
	RI	–	0.31	**0.39**	0.35	0.31	0.32	0.36
GOV2	MAP	0.2696	0.2938	0.2987[12]	0.2922[1]	0.3005[12]	**0.3012[12]**	0.2957[1]
	P@5	0.5592	0.5592	0.5687	0.5673	0.5823	**0.5850**	0.5782
	P@10	0.5531	0.5599	0.5816	0.5714	0.5830	**0.5844**	0.5782
	RI	–	0.15	**0.22**	0.14	**0.22**	0.20	0.20

query language model. According to these figures, the performance of both methods when the original query language model is not considered (i.e., $\alpha = 0$) is quite low. This indicates that the generated embedding-based language model needs to be interpolated with the original language model. The reason is that we do not consider the query terms in the generated language model and these terms play key roles in the retrieval effectiveness. According to these two figures, the behaviours of both methods are similar to each other. Interestingly, the curves corresponding to AP and Robust (the two newswire collections) have similar behaviours. The results show that the best value for the parameter α in these two collections is 0.5. In contrast, in the GOV2 collection, the original language model needs to get higher weight in the linear interpolation. The best α values for EQE1 and EQE2 in GOV2 are 0.8 and 0.9, respectively.

Figures 2c and 2d respectively show the sensitivity of EQE1 and EQE2 to the parameter m (term count). According to these figures, by varying the term count parameter, the retrieval performance in AP and Robust does not change dramatically, compared to GOV2. In the GOV2 collection, by increasing the number of terms, the performance is improved. While in AP and Robust, 50 or 75 are the best values for the parameter m.

To summarize, Figure 2 shows that α and m are collection-dependent parameters, and thus proper values should be chosen for them with respect to the test collection. In addition, the similar behaviours of curves corresponding to AP and Robust show that the retrieval performances in similar collections behave similarly. Thus, these parameters can be tuned in one collection and be set for another similar one.

4.2.2 Embedding-based Pseudo-Relevance Feedback

In this subsection, we evaluate the proposed embedding-based query language models in the pseudo-relevance feedback scenario. In these experiments, we consider two baselines: (1) the maximum likelihood estimation without feedback (MLE), and (2) the relevance model with the i.i.d. sampling assumption (i.e., RM3) [1, 15], a state-of-the-art PRF method that has been shown to perform well in various collections [18]. There are several other PRF methods that also perform well. Since the proposed ERM model is an extension of the RM3 model, we only consider it as the baseline, which is the most similar method to the proposed one.

The results are reported in Table 3. According to this table, RM3 significantly outperforms MLE in all collections in terms of MAP. This shows the effectiveness of pseudo-relevance feedback in information retrieval. As known, RM3 is the linear interpolation of MLE with RM1 [1]. More details about the RM1 feedback model can be found in [15]. In the first set of experiments, we employ EQE1 and EQE2 instead of MLE in the RM3 calculations. In other words, we linearly interpolate EQE1/EQE2 with RM1. As reported in Table 3, EQE1+RM1 outperforms RM3 in all collections, in terms of MAP, P@5, and P@10 (both methods achieve the same P@10 value in the AP collection). Except in two cases (MAP in GOV2 and P@10 in AP), EQE2+RM1 also outperforms RM3 in all collections, in terms of MAP, P@5, and P@10. In GOV2, RM3 performs better than EQE2+RM1, in terms of MAP. The reason is that EQE2 achieves lower P@10 compared to MLE in this collection (see Table 2) and since the feedback terms are extracted from the top retrieved documents, it leads to more accurate feedback models in

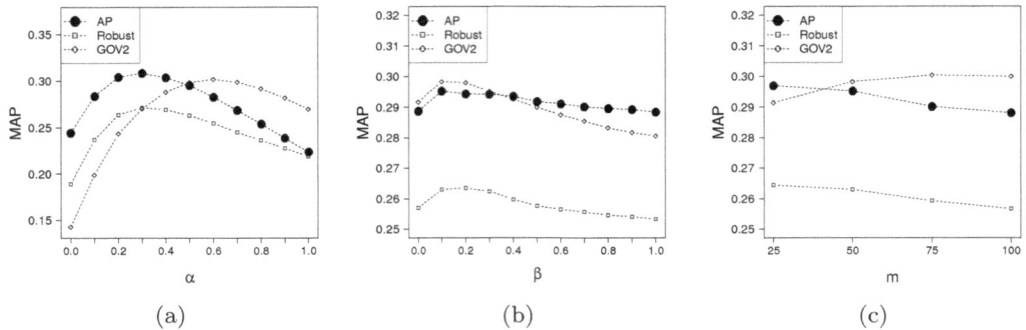

Figure 3: Sensitivity of MLE+ERM to the parameters α, β, and m (term count), in terms of MAP.

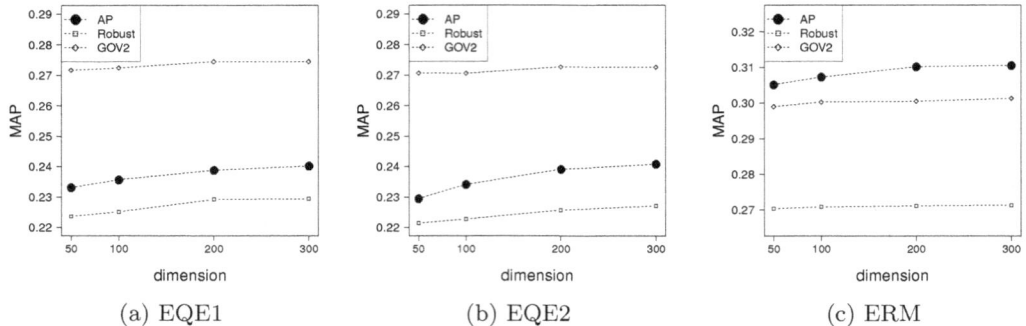

Figure 4: Sensitivity of EQE1, EQE2, and ERM (MLE+ERM) to the dimension size of embedding vectors, in terms of MAP.

RM3. It is worth noting that RM3 does not perform well in terms of improving the precision of the top-retrieved documents in the GOV2 collection. In contrast, by employing EQE1/EQE2 instead of MLE in RM3, P@5 and P@10 values are substantially improved. The robustness index metric demonstrates that EQE1+RM1 is more robust than RM3 in the Robust and GOV2 collections. In AP, RM3 is slightly more robust than EQE1+RM1.

To evaluate the proposed ERM feedback method, we linearly interpolate it with MLE, EQE1, and EQE2. According to Table 3, MLE+ERM outperforms RM3 (MLE+RM1), in terms of MAP, P@5, P@10, and RI, in all collections (the same RI value achieved in the Robust collection). The MAP improvements of MLE+ERM over RM3 are always statistically significant. Similar to EQE1+RM1 and EQE2+RM1, MLE+ERM also achieves high P@5 and P@10 values compared to RM3, especially in GOV2. This shows the importance of capturing semantic similarities for the PRF task. Among all the considered feedback methods, EQE1+ERM outperforms all the other methods in AP and GOV2, in terms of MAP, P@5, and P@10. In Robust, EQE2+ERM performs well, in terms of MAP and P@10. This shows the effectiveness of the proposed embedding-based models for query reformulation. Note that as reported in [18], the RM3 method is a very robust PRF method, and the experiments show that RM3 is less robust than MLE+ERM, EQE1+ERM, and EQE2+ERM. This indicates the robustness of the proposed ERM method.

The next set of experiments focuses on studying the sensitivity of the proposed ERM (MLE+ERM) method to the three hyper-parameters α, β, and m. In all these experiments, we set α, β, and m to 0.5, 0.1, and 50. Then, in each step, we sweep one of these parameters. The results are shown in Figure 3. According to the plots in this figure, the behaviour of MLE+ERM in AP and Robust are simi-

lar to each other since they are both newswire collections with similar characteristics. Figure 3a plots the MAP values achieved by MLE+ERM with different α values. This parameter controls the influence of the original query model (MLE) in the final query language model. Based on this figure, the best value for the parameter α in both AP and Robust collections is 0.3. This means that higher weight should be given to the feedback language model generated by ERM, compared to MLE. In contrast, the best α value in GOV2 is 0.6. The reason is that although the P@10 values achieved by MLE in GOV2 are higher than those achieved in AP and Robust, the feedback language models in AP and Robust are more accurate than those in the GOV2 collection. An interesting observation in this figure is that the MAP values achieved in the Robust and GOV2 collections when $\alpha = 1$ are higher than those when $\alpha = 0$. In other words, the generated language model by ERM itself (without interpolating with MLE) is a better representation for the query than the original query language model.

Figure 3b plots the sensitivity of the proposed MLE+ERM method to the parameter β. According to this figure, the performance does not change drastically, when we sweep the value of the parameter β. The best MAP values are achieved when β is set to 0.1 (in AP and GOV2) or 0.2 (in Robust). As mentioned in Section 3.3, the parameter β controls the influence of term matching similarity vs. semantic similarity. Therefore, the results show that the term matching similarities are still more important than the semantic similarities in the relevance feedback.

According to Figure 3c, in newswire collections, we can have a very good query representation with a small number of words added to the query. In fact, by increasing the number of feedback terms, the performance slightly decreases. In the GOV2 collection, more feedback terms are needed to be added to the query, which is also similar to the query expan-

Table 4: The corpora used for training the embedding vectors.

ID	corpus	#tokens	#vocab.
Wiki	Wikipedia 2004 & Gigawords 5	6b	400k
Web 42b	Web crawl	42b	1.9m
Web 840b	Web crawl	840b	2.2m

Table 5: The MAP values achieved by EQE1, EQE2, and ERM (MLE+ERM) with different corpora for training the embedding vectors (dimension = 300).

Dataset	Method	Wiki	Web 42b	Web 840b
AP (146 queries)	EQE1	0.2402	0.2356	0.2362
	EQE2	0.2408	0.2352	0.2400
	ERM	0.3106	0.3094	0.3081
Robust (240 queries)	EQE1	0.2294	0.2255	0.2273
	EQE2	0.2271	0.2237	0.2266
	ERM	0.2713	0.2705	0.2683
GOV2 (146 queries)	EQE1	0.2745	0.2729	0.2767
	EQE2	0.2726	0.2713	0.2743
	ERM	0.3013	0.2989	0.3021

sion experiments (see Figure 2). The reason could be related to the characteristics of these collections and the amount of noise terms that the documents of each collection contain.

4.2.3 Sensitivity to the Embedding Vectors

In this section, we study the sensitivity of the proposed methods to the employed embedding vectors. We first analyze how sensitive the proposed methods are to the dimension of embedding vectors. Then, we study the performance of the proposed methods when the corpus that embedding vectors are trained on changes.

The plots in Figure 4 demonstrate the performance of EQE1, EQE2 and ERM (MLE+ERM) with respect to changes in the dimension of embedding vectors. All vectors are extracted from the same corpus (Wikipedia 2004 + Gigawords 5), with the same configuration. As shown in this figure, by increasing the dimension of embedding vectors, the performance of both EQE1 and EQE2 methods are increased in the AP and Robust collections. In contrast, the performance of these methods is not stable in the GOV2 collection. Note that these performance changes are minor (non-significant). According to Figure 4, the performance of ERM is not highly sensitive to the dimension of embedding vectors, especially in the Robust and GOV2 collections. In AP, by increasing the dimension of embedding vectors, the ERM performance is slightly improved, but these improvements are not statistically significant.

To analyze the robustness of the proposed methods to the choices made in training the word embedding vectors, we consider three external corpora: Wiki, Web 42b, and Web 840b. The Wiki corpus mostly contains articles with formal language; while the other two corpora are two web collections containing 42 and 840 billion tokens. The statistics of these corpora are reported in Table 4.[11] The dimension of embedding vectors extracted from these corpora is 300. We report the MAP of queries that all the embedding vector sets contain all of the query terms. The results are reported

Table 6: The MAP values achieved by EQE1, EQE2, and ERM (MLE+ERM) with and without the sigmoid transformation for computing the similarity of embedding vectors. The superscript * indicates significant differences.

Dataset	Method	EQE1	EQE2	ERM
AP	Cosine	0.2293	0.2366	0.3038
	Sigmoid	**0.2388***	**0.2391**	**0.3102***
Robust	Cosine	0.2247	0.2233	0.2677
	Sigmoid	**0.2292***	**0.2257**	**0.2711***
GOV2	Cosine	0.2709	0.2654	0.2971
	Sigmoid	**0.2745***	**0.2727***	**0.3005**

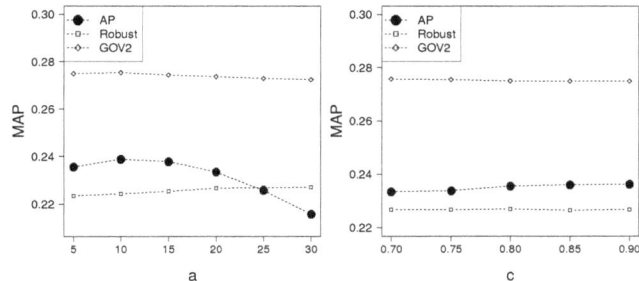

Figure 5: Performance of EQE1 with respect to the changes in the sigmoid parameter values.

in Table 5. According to this table, the results are robust to the corpus that is used for training the word embedding vectors. There is no significant differences between the values obtained by employing different corpora for learning the embedding vectors. In the GOV2 collection, the Web 840b corpus seems to be slightly better than the other ones. Despite the large gap between the size of Wiki and the other two corpora, the results achieved by Wiki are higher than those obtained by the other ones, in the newswire collections.

4.2.4 Analysis of the Sigmoid Function

In this subsection, we study the behaviour of the proposed sigmoid transformation of the cosine similarity scores. To do this, we compare the proposed methods with two different similarity functions: the cosine similarity and its sigmoid transformation. The results are reported in Table 6.[12] According to this table, the results achieved by employing the sigmoid function are always higher than those obtained by the cosine similarity function. These improvements are statistically significant, in most cases.

To analyze the behaviour of the proposed EQE1 method[13] to the changes in the values of the sigmoid parameters (see Equation (1)), we fix one of these parameters ($a = 10$ and $c = 0.8$) and sweep the other one. The results are shown in Figure 5. According to these plots, the performance of EQE1 is sensitive to the value of parameter a. Therefore, a proper value for this parameter should be selected based on the retrieval collection. The best values for the parameter a are 10 for AP and GOV2, and 30 for Robust. Conversely, the performance is not very sensitive to the value of c. Note that we varied the value of c between $[0.7, 0.9]$. Based on our observations in Figure 1a, the selected interval is reasonable.

---

[11]Embedding data is available at http://nlp.stanford.edu/projects/glove/.

[12]For the sake of space, we just report the MAP values.
[13]The other proposed methods also behave similarly.

5. CONCLUSIONS AND FUTURE WORK

In this paper, we first proposed two novel query expansion methods to estimate accurate query language models based on word embeddings. We further proposed the embedding-based relevance model, a pseudo-relevance feedback method based on word embeddings. The proposed methods use the semantic similarity of terms computed based on the similarity between the embedding vectors corresponding to the given terms. To obtain discriminative similarity scores that can be used in our methods, we transformed the cosine similarity scores by the sigmoid function.

We evaluated the proposed methods using three standard TREC newswire and web collections. The results indicated not only that the proposed methods significantly outperform the baselines in nearly all cases, but also they were shown to be more robust than the baselines. Studying the sensitivity of the proposed methods to the hyper-parameters showed that, in most cases, each proposed method behaves similarly in both newswire collections. The results also suggest that the sigmoid transformation of embedding similarities can significantly outperform the cosine similarity function.

Instead of employing the sigmoid function, an interesting future direction would be modifying the learning process of embedding vectors to produce discriminative similarity values that can be employed in many IR tasks. In addition, the theoretical analysis of employing sigmoid function for this purpose could be a possible future work. We also intend to study the use of word embeddings in other aspects of IR.

6. ACKNOWLEDGEMENTS

The authors thank Jiafeng Guo and Faegheh Hasibi for their invaluable comments. This work was supported in part by the Center for Intelligent Information Retrieval and in part by NSF grant #CNS-0934322. Any opinions, findings and conclusions or recommendations expressed in this material are those of the authors and do not necessarily reflect those of the sponsor.

7. REFERENCES

[1] N. Abdul-jaleel, J. Allan, W. B. Croft, F. Diaz, L. Larkey, X. Li, D. Metzler, M. D. Smucker, T. Strohman, H. Turtle, and C. Wade. UMass at TREC 2004: Novelty and HARD. In *TREC '04*, 2004.

[2] M. ALMasri, C. Berrut, and J.-P. Chevallet. A Comparison of Deep Learning Based Query Expansion with Pseudo-Relevance Feedback and Mutual Information. In *ECIR '16*, pages 709–715, 2016.

[3] J. Bai, J.-Y. Nie, G. Cao, and H. Bouchard. Using Query Contexts in Information Retrieval. In *SIGIR '07*, pages 15–22, 2007.

[4] C. Carpineto and G. Romano. A Survey of Automatic Query Expansion in Information Retrieval. *ACM Comput. Surv.*, 44(1):1:1–1:50, 2012.

[5] S. Clinchant and F. Perronnin. Aggregating Continuous Word Embeddings for Information Retrieval. In *CVSC@ACL '13*, pages 100–109, 2013.

[6] K. Collins-Thompson. Reducing the Risk of Query Expansion via Robust Constrained Optimization. In *CIKM '09*, pages 837–846, 2009.

[7] S. Deerwester, S. T. Dumais, G. W. Furnas, T. K. Landauer, and R. Harshman. Indexing by latent semantic analysis. *Journal of the American Society for Information Science*, 41(6):391–407, 1990.

[8] P. Dhillon, D. P. Foster, and L. H. Ungar. Multi-View Learning of Word Embeddings via CCA. In *NIPS '11*, pages 199–207, 2011.

[9] F. Diaz, B. Mitra, and N. Craswell. Query Expansion with Locally-Trained Word Embeddings. In *ACL '16*, 2016.

[10] D. Ganguly, D. Roy, M. Mitra, and G. J. Jones. Word Embedding Based Generalized Language Model for Information Retrieval. In *SIGIR '15*, pages 795–798, 2015.

[11] M. Karimzadehgan and C. Zhai. Estimation of Statistical Translation Models Based on Mutual Information for Ad Hoc Information Retrieval. In *SIGIR '10*, pages 323–330, 2010.

[12] T. Kenter and M. de Rijke. Short Text Similarity with Word Embeddings. In *CIKM '15*, pages 1411–1420, 2015.

[13] M. J. Kusner, Y. Sun, N. I. Kolkin, and K. Q. Weinberger. From Word Embeddings to Document Distances. In *ICML '15*, pages 957–966, 2015.

[14] J. Lafferty and C. Zhai. Document Language Models, Query Models, and Risk Minimization for Information Retrieval. In *SIGIR '01*, pages 111–119, 2001.

[15] V. Lavrenko and W. B. Croft. Relevance Based Language Models. In *SIGIR '01*, pages 120–127, 2001.

[16] Q. V. Le and T. Mikolov. Distributed Representations of Sentences and Documents. In *ICML '14*, pages 1188–1196, 2014.

[17] O. Levy, Y. Goldberg, and I. Dagan. Improving Distributional Similarity with Lessons Learned from Word Embeddings. *TACL*, 3:211–225, 2015.

[18] Y. Lv and C. Zhai. A Comparative Study of Methods for Estimating Query Language Models with Pseudo Feedback. In *CIKM '09*, pages 1895–1898, 2009.

[19] T. Mikolov, I. Sutskever, K. Chen, G. S. Corrado, and J. Dean. Distributed Representations of Words and Phrases and their Compositionality. In *NIPS '13*, pages 3111–3119, 2013.

[20] A. Montazeralghaem, H. Zamani, and A. Shakery. Axiomatic Analysis for Improving the Log-Logistic Feedback Model. In *SIGIR '16*, pages 765–768, 2016.

[21] J. Pennington, R. Socher, and C. Manning. GloVe: Global Vectors for Word Representation. In *EMNLP '14*, pages 1532–1543, 2014.

[22] J. M. Ponte and W. B. Croft. A Language Modeling Approach to Information Retrieval. In *SIGIR '98*, pages 275–281, 1998.

[23] P. Resnik. Using Information Content to Evaluate Semantic Similarity in a Taxonomy. In *IJCAI '95*, pages 448–453, 1995.

[24] J. J. Rocchio. Relevance Feedback in Information Retrieval. In *The SMART Retrieval System: Experiments in Automatic Document Processing*, pages 313–323. 1971.

[25] A. Sordoni, Y. Bengio, and J.-Y. Nie. Learning Concept Embeddings for Query Expansion by Quantum Entropy Minimization. In *AAAI '14*, pages 1586–1592, 2014.

[26] E. M. Voorhees. Query Expansion Using Lexical-semantic Relations. In *SIGIR '94*, pages 61–69, 1994.

[27] I. Vulić and M.-F. Moens. Monolingual and Cross-Lingual Information Retrieval Models Based on (Bilingual) Word Embeddings. In *SIGIR '15*, pages 363–372, 2015.

[28] J. Xu and W. B. Croft. Query Expansion Using Local and Global Document Analysis. In *SIGIR '96*, pages 4–11, 1996.

[29] C. Zhai and J. Lafferty. Model-based Feedback in the Language Modeling Approach to Information Retrieval. In *CIKM '01*, pages 403–410, 2001.

[30] G. Zheng and J. Callan. Learning to Reweight Terms with Distributed Representations. In *SIGIR '15*, pages 575–584, 2015.

[31] G. Zhou, T. He, J. Zhao, and P. Hu. Learning Continuous Word Embedding with Metadata for Question Retrieval in Community Question Answering. In *ACL '15*, pages 250–259, 2015.

[32] G. Zuccon, B. Koopman, P. Bruza, and L. Azzopardi. Integrating and Evaluating Neural Word Embeddings in Information Retrieval. In *ADCS '15*, pages 12:1–12:8, 2015.

Learning to Rank User Queries to Detect Search Tasks

Claudio Lucchese
ISTI–CNR, Pisa, Italy
claudio.lucchese@isti.cnr.it

Franco Maria Nardini
ISTI–CNR, Pisa, Italy
francomaria.nardini@isti.cnr.it

Salvatore Orlando
Università Ca' Foscari
Venezia, Italy
orlando@unive.it

Gabriele Tolomei
Yahoo, London, UK
gtolomei@yahoo-inc.com

ABSTRACT

We present a framework for discovering sets of web queries having similar latent needs, called *search tasks*, from user queries stored in a search engine log. The framework is made of two main modules: *Query Similarity Learning* (QSL) and *Graph-based Query Clustering* (GQC). The former is devoted to learning a query similarity function from a ground truth of manually-labeled search tasks. The latter represents each user search log as a graph whose nodes are queries, and uses the learned similarity function to weight edges between query pairs. Finally, search tasks are detected by clustering those queries in the graph which are connected by the strongest links, in fact by detecting the strongest *connected components* of the graph. To discriminate between "strong" and "weak" links also the GQC module entails a learning phase whose goal is to estimate the best threshold for pruning the edges of the graph. We discuss how the QSL module can be effectively implemented using *Learning to Rank* (L2R) techniques. Experiments on a real-world search engine log show that query similarity functions learned using L2R lead to better performing GQC implementations when compared to similarity functions induced by other state-of-the-art machine learning solutions, such as logistic regression and decision trees.

1. INTRODUCTION

In the early era of web search, users were accustomed to interact with search engines by issuing simple and isolated keyword queries. However, user *search sessions*[1] have been becoming more and more complex. In fact, users interact with search engines to perform sophisticated *search tasks*, which typically require multiple, and sometimes intertwined, queries with a common latent need.

---

[1] A *search session* is generally considered as a sequence of queries where the elapsed time between two consecutive queries is not larger than Δ: common values of Δ range from 30 [8, 21] to 90 minutes [7].

ICTIR '16, September 12-16, 2016, Newark, DE, USA

© 2016 ACM. ISBN 978-1-4503-4497-5/16/09. . . $15.00

DOI: http://dx.doi.org/10.1145/2970398.2970407

Table 1 shows an example of real-world search engine log, where a user performs multiple complex tasks, also spanning across several search sessions (e.g., **Car-** and **Travel-**related tasks). Moreover, we may notice that queries appearing within the same session, here represented with the same color, may be part of different tasks (e.g., chrysler performance minnesota and flamingo hotel las vegas).

Query	Timestamp	Task
mopar electronic ingnition	2006-03-01 17:35:25	Car
mopar minneapolis	2006-03-01 18:08:55	
chrysler performance minnesota	2006-03-01 18:42:59	
. . .	. . .	. . .
flamingo hotel las vegas	2006-03-01 19:08:19	Travel
las vegas	2006-03-01 19:13:02	
. . .	. . .	. . .
performance hugo mn mopar	2006-03-10 18:14:07	Car
1966 chrysler new yorker	2006-03-10 18:20:07	
. . .	. . .	. . .
las vegas journal	2006-03-14 19:23:33	Travel
el cortez	2006-03-14 19:49:06	

Table 1: Complex tasks in a real user search log [7].

Modern web search engines still satisfy user needs on a *query-by-query* fashion by retrieving web pages that are supposed to be the most relevant results to each individual query [24, 2, 1]. We argue that a crucial challenge for modern search engines is to understand, thereby answer, complex requests by early recognizing the emerging *task-by-task* behavior of users. This may help search engines to find more relevant results to each task as a whole; design novel user interfaces which go beyond search result pages rendered as "ten blue links"; positively affect user engagement with the service (e.g., by implementing task-based recommendations [17]); increase their revenue (e.g., by designing task-based advertising) just to name a few.

Unfortunately, detecting search tasks from a flat sequence of past observed queries is inherently hard. On the one hand, users formulate the same need using different queries (*task ambiguity*) while, on the other hand, the same query may refer to several needs (*query ambiguity*). Moreover, user behaviors are characterized by *multi-tasking* during web searches [25]: users typically "search-and-switch" between several topics, even within a single search session. Therefore, any task detection method should consider not only query's issuing time (i.e., the query order), but also lexical and semantic similarities to capture common underlying needs between queries.

In this paper, we propose the *Search Task Discovery* (STD) framework. This is a framework to discover user search tasks that may span across multiple user sessions. It is made of two components: a *Query Similarity Learning* (QSL) module, and a *Graph-based Query Clustering* (GQC) module. The former is devoted to learning a query similarity function from a ground truth of manually-labeled search tasks. The latter represents each user search log as a graph (*user query graph*) whose nodes are queries, and uses the learned similarity function to weight edges between query pairs. The weight on an edge can be interpreted as the probability of the two queries being part of the same task.

In order to induce the query similarity function we exploit state-of-the-art *Learning to Rank* (L2R) techniques. Specifically, we reduce the problem of learning a query similarity function to an instance of the L2R problem. For example, given a query q, we consider all the other queries that are part of the whole user search log as "documents" to be ranked according to their relevance to q. Therefore, we aim at learning a *ranking function* such that only those queries included in the same task of q are relevant to q, and thereby scored (ranked) higher than the others.

Finally, the GQC module extracts search tasks by clustering those queries in the user query graph which are connected by the strongest links, in fact by detecting the strongest *connected components* of the graph. To discriminate between "strong" and "weak" edges, thereby to determine the final connected components, also the GQC module entails a learning phase whose goal is to globally estimate the best threshold for pruning the edges of the graph. It is worth remarking that while QSL only looks at individual query pairs to estimate their similarities, GQC inspects the entire user search log as a whole, and predicts the task membership for all the queries simultaneously by choosing the best query clustering.

The main contributions of this work are the following:

(i) We propose the STD framework, a two-module pipeline for discovering search tasks from search engine logs: *Query Similarity Learning* (QSL) and *Graph-based Query Clustering* (GQC);

(ii) We show how we can profitably exploit *Learning to Rank* (L2R) techniques in QSL to estimate query similarity from ranking queries of user search logs;

(iii) We adopt an unprecedented set of features extracted from query pairs and exploited by both L2R methods and other state-of-the-art machine learning approaches. We also assess the relative importance of the features proposed in terms of the quality of the L2R model extracted;

(iv) In GQC we adopt a graph-based representation of all the queries issued by a user, which makes use of the learned query similarity but also of a suitable edge-pruning threshold, in turn globally estimated from the ground truth of tasks. Detecting search tasks consists in discovering the strongest connected components of the above graph;

(v) We present a comprehensive evaluation of each solution on a real-world dataset of manually-annotated search tasks performed by multiple users. Experimental results show that implementing QSL with L2R-based approaches outperforms the quality of tasks detected by other methods.

2. RELATED WORK

Jones and Klinkner [9] present the first *high-level* task-by-task analysis of user search behavior, by introducing the concept of *hierarchical search*. They argue that within a user query stream it is possible to recognize complex *search missions* (i.e., a set of topically-related information needs), which are in turn composed of simpler *search goals*. The authors discuss a supervised binary classifier which detects whether query pairs belong to the same goal.

Mei *et al.* [19] present a framework to analyze sequences of user search activities. This framework adopts the same hierarchical model introduced by Jones and Klinkner [9], and is able to capture sequences of user behavior at multiple levels of granularity. Donato *et al.* [4] develop *SearchPad*, a novel *Yahoo* application. This is still built on the top of the hierarchical structure of searches proposed in [9], and is able to automatically identify search missions "on-the-fly", as the user interacts with the search engine. Guo *et al.* [6] introduce the concept of *intent-aware* query similarity, namely a novel approach for computing query pair similarity, which takes into account the potential search intents behind user queries, and then measures query similarity under different intents using intent-aware representations. The authors show the validity of their approach by applying it to query recommendation, thereby suggesting related queries in a structured way to the users.

Kotov *et al.* [10] propose a classification framework for modeling and analyzing user search behavior spanning over multiple search sessions. The authors focus on two problems: *(i)* given a user query, identify all related queries from previous sessions that the user has issued, and *(ii)* given a multi-query task for a user, predict whether the user will return to *this* current task in the future. Lucchese *et al.* [15, 16] introduce the search task discovery problem *within* user search sessions, and propose solutions based on a graph-based representation of queries (similar to the *query flow graph* proposed by Boldi *et al.* [1]).

Hagen *et al.* [7] discuss a new algorithm for the detection of tasks spanning multiple user session, based on the state-of-the-art cascading heuristic which combines effectiveness with efficiency. Raman *et al.* [22] approach the problem of detecting when the user is engaged in complex search patterns by distinguishing between *intrinsic* and *extrinsic* diversity (in search results). Li *et al.* [12] propose a probabilistic method that relies on the following observation: queries that are issued temporally close are likely to belong to the same search task, while different users having the same information need tend to submit topically coherent search queries. The authors use *Hawkes processes* to model query temporal patterns.

Very recently, Li *et al.* [13] propose an unsupervised approach to identify search tasks via topic membership along with topic transition probabilities. They introduce a novel hidden semi-Markov model to represent topic transitions by considering not only the semantic information of queries but also the latent search factors that are assumed to be originated from user search behaviors. From observed query sequences and search behaviors, the authors propose a variational inference algorithm to simultaneously estimate the topic membership of each query as well as those search factors and the corresponding topic transition matrices.

Wang *et al.* [26] also discuss the problem of detecting search tasks across users sessions. The paper defines the "prototype" of search task as a particular connected component within the query similarity graph. Each query in a search task can be linked to only one past query of the task ("best-link" or "most-similar query"), so that a task is eventually modeled as a tree. The authors propose an SVM-based method aiming to identify the best hidden embedded trees within a similarity graph, whose links connect pairs of queries belonging to the same search task. The idea of modeling a task as a tree, by looking for the most-similar query in the past only, can lead the method by Wang *et al.* to split a search tasks into multiple query clusters. For this reason, in this paper we relax the best-link concept: according to [16], a search task is a sparse connected component in the similarity graph, where *at least* one link exists between one query and the others which belong to the same task. Specifically, we improve over the QC-HTC method [15, 16], by generalizing it from *within-session* to *cross-session* search task discovery: we still detect connected components of the graph, but we refer to the graph derived from the whole user search log instead of individual user session graphs. In addition, the STD framework employs a second learning step, whose goal is to globally estimate the best threshold for pruning the weak edges of the user query graph, thus improving over the previous heuristic proposed by QC-HTC.

3. THE STD FRAMEWORK

The high-level architecture of our proposed STD framework is depicted in Figure 1. This is a mixture of supervised learning and clustering approaches consisting of three steps.

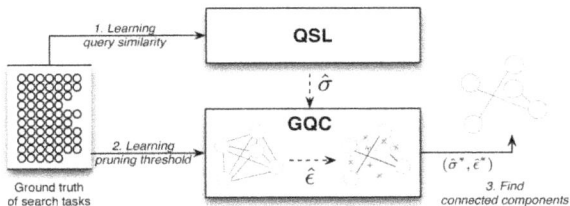

Figure 1: High-level architecture of the STD framework.

We assume there exists a *target* query similarity function σ. In the first step, the QSL module is responsible for finding an *estimate* $\hat{\sigma} \approx \sigma$ using a ground truth of search tasks, which are manually extracted from a search engine log. The learned similarity function is then used by the GQC module to weight the edges of the user query graph $G_{\hat{\sigma}}^u$. The GQC module also estimates the edge-pruning threshold ($\hat{\epsilon}$) which is used to remove "weak" edges and sparsify the complete graph $G_{\hat{\sigma}}^u$, thus obtaining the final graph $G_{\hat{\sigma},\hat{\epsilon}}^u$. Note that different optimization criteria may lead to different $\hat{\sigma}$ and $\hat{\epsilon}$. In the last step, GQC outputs the clusters of queries (i.e., search tasks) corresponding to the *connected components* of the graph which is generated using the overall best estimates of query similarity ($\hat{\sigma}^*$) and edge-pruning threshold ($\hat{\epsilon}^*$).

Notation. Let U be a set of users of a search engine, and $\mathcal{Q}$ be a query log defined as $\mathcal{Q} = \{Q^u \mid Q^u \subset \mathcal{Q}, \ u \in U\}$, where Q^u is the search log of user u. We denote by $T_j^u \subseteq Q^u$ a *task* of u characterized by queries with the same latent intent. Moreover, given Q^u, we assume that the set of *tasks* T^u conducted by user u forms a proper *partition* of Q^u. In fact, Q^u and every T_j^u are temporally ordered sequences of queries. Let $Q^u = \langle q_1^u, \ldots, q_l^u \rangle$, where $\forall i \in [1, \ldots l] \ \tau(q_i^u) < \tau(q_{i+1}^u)$ and $\tau(q_i^u)$ is the timestamp of query submission.

3.1 Query Similarity Learning (QSL)

The QSL module aims at finding an estimate of a target query similarity function σ from a ground truth of manually-labeled search tasks. Given two queries $q_i^u, q_j^u \in Q^u$, we let $\sigma(q_i^u, q_j^u) = 1$ if they belong to the same *task* T_k^u, and 0 otherwise.

Each query pair is associated with a binary class label: same-task (*positive*) or not-same-task (*negative*). Therefore, estimating σ naturally reduces to a binary classification problem.

Assuming the existence of a *loss function* L, which measures the quality of any query similarity estimate s, the output of QSL will be the estimate $\hat{\sigma}$ which optimizes for L as follows:

$$\hat{\sigma} = \underset{s}{\arg\min} \frac{1}{|U|} \sum_{u \in U} L(\sigma(q_i^u, q_j^u), s(q_i^u, q_j^u)).$$

In the traditional classification setting, the loss function L is designed so as to minimize the the empirical classification error rate over a given training set (or equivalently to maximize the classification accuracy).

In this work, however, we reduce the problem of approximating the true query similarity function σ to an instance of the *Learning to Rank* (L2R) problem rather than that of a simpler binary classification problem. That is, instead of predicting if two queries are part of the same task, we aim to learn a *ranking function* $\hat{\sigma}$ that, given a query $q \in Q^u$, sorts all the other queries of Q^u such that same-task queries are ranked highest.

It is worth noting that same-task does not necessarily imply "similar query pair", even if the goal of our learning task is to approximate a function that guesses query similarities. Moreover, supervised learning is not the only approach to devise a suitable query similarity function. Other work propose cascading heuristics to effectively capture the lexical and semantic similarity of queries [15, 7]. However, results presented in [16] prove that the supervised learning solutions perform better.

Since we have argued that the prototype of a search task is a connected component of the user query graph, we are aware that the same-task pairs are a biased estimate of (i.e., they tend to overestimate) the true similar pairs. Unfortunately, information about the actual similar query pairs is generally not available from the ground truth. However, approaches employing looser embedded graph structures, such as trees [26] or chains [9], drastically reduce the already relatively small set of same-task examples in the training set. Conversely, the solution we propose which relies on extracting connected components using L2R, is able to fully exploit same-task and not-same-task relationships between queries in the same user session.

3.2 Graph-based Query Clustering (GQC)

The GQC module first transforms each user search log Q^u into a *weighted query graph* $G_{\hat{\sigma}}^u$, where nodes are queries and edges are labeled using the query similarity function $\hat{\sigma}$ estimated by the QSL module. Note also that $\hat{\sigma}$ can be either *symmetric* or *asymmetric*, resulting in a *directed* or *undirected* graph respectively. In the latter case, we transform

$G^u_{\hat{\sigma}}$ into a directed graph by taking the *maximum* weight of edges with opposite direction.

If the QSL module was able to find the optimal $\hat{\sigma} = \sigma$, then the user *tasks* would correspond to the connected components of the graph $G^u_{\hat{\sigma}}$. In order to overcome the error introduced by $\hat{\sigma}$, we remove "weak" edges from $G^u_{\hat{\sigma}}$ with the goal of keeping only its *strongest connected components*. Note that the extraction of connected components allows us to enforce a very selective pruning as only one path should be preserved between any pair of queries in the same task. This makes the algorithm quite tolerant to the errors introduced by $\hat{\sigma}$ and it fits well with the objective of the L2R approach, which provides high accuracy between very similar (top ranked) queries.

GQC uses an ϵ-neighborhood technique to select the set of edges to include in the final pruned graph $G^u_{\hat{\sigma},\epsilon}$: an edge will be retained in this graph only if its weight is larger than ϵ. It follows that different similarity thresholds ϵ lead to different graphs, and therefore to different clusterings into connected components. The goal of the GQC is to find the best estimate $\hat{\epsilon}$ that optimize some given external measure of clustering quality.

DEFINITION 1 (SEARCH TASK DISCOVERY PROBLEM). *Given a user session Q^u, a clustering algorithm $\mathcal{C}$ that extracts the connected components of the graph, and a quality function γ measuring the quality of a clustering, the* Search Task Discovery Problem *requires to find the best similarity function $\hat{\sigma}$ and similarity threshold $\hat{\epsilon}$ that maximize the average quality of the clusters $\mathcal{C}(G^u_{\hat{\sigma},\hat{\epsilon}})$ for all $u \in U$. More formally:*

$$(\hat{\sigma}^*, \hat{\epsilon}^*) = \operatorname*{argmax}_{\hat{\sigma},\hat{\epsilon}} \frac{1}{|U|} \sum_{u \in U} \gamma(\mathcal{C}(G^u_{\hat{\sigma},\hat{\epsilon}})).$$

4. REDUCING QSL TO LEARNING TO RANK

We now introduce a L2R-based implementation of the QSL module to find an estimate $\hat{\sigma}$ of a target query similarity measure σ. L2R has been widely adopted by the biggest search companies to automatically learn a *ranking model*, which allows sorting web documents according to their relevance to user queries [11].

Without loss of generality, L2R provides a set of supervised techniques for learning a *ranking function* given a collection of *training examples*. Specifically, in the field of document retrieval a typical training set consists of n queries $\{q_1, \ldots, q_n\}$, where each q_i is associated with a set of candidate documents $\mathcal{D}^{(i)} = \{d_1^{(i)}, d_2^{(i)}, \ldots\}$. Each document $d_j^{(i)}$ is associated with a *relevance judgement* $y_j^{(i)} \in \mathbf{y}^{(i)}$, which states how relevant document $d_j^{(i)}$ is to query q_i. It turns out that each $\mathbf{y}^{(i)}$ is a $|\mathcal{D}^{(i)}|$-dimensional vector. The vector of relevance judgements $\mathbf{y}^{(i)}$ induces a partial order, which defines the *ideal ranking* of the documents $\mathcal{D}^{(i)}$ for the query q_i. L2R methods aim to discover a document scoring function that matches the ranking order induced by $\mathbf{y}^{(i)}$.

A ground truth for L2R is a set of n tuples:

$$\langle q_i, \quad \langle \mathcal{D}^{(i)}, \quad \mathbf{y}^{(i)} \rangle \rangle_{i=1,\ldots,n}$$

L2R algorithms [14] can be broadly grouped into three classes: *point-wise*, *pair-wise*, and *list-wise*. While pointwise attempts to predict the relevance label for each document, pair-wise methods aim to rank relevant documents

higher than non-relevant ones. Finally, list-wise techniques take the entire list of documents to rank and try to directly optimize for retrieval measures defined upon this list. In this paper, we consider two state-of-the-art L2R methods: a point-wise one, called Gradient-Boosted Regression Trees (GBRT) [5] (a.k.a. MART), and a list-wise one named LambdaMART [27]. In fact, LambdaMART is an extension of a pair-wise method called LambdaRank [27], which uses MART as a regressor, and maximizes popular measures of ranking quality in information retrieval, such as *normalized Discounted Cumulative Gain* (*nDCG*).

In the following, we show that learning a query similarity function may reduce to a ranking problem, and how the L2R framework can in turn be adapted to approximate such a function. We propose two approaches in order to prepare a suitable ground truth for this purpose: *query-centric* and *user-centric*.

Query-centric. We are interested in discovering a query similarity function that scores higher those queries that appear in the same task and lower those queries belonging to different tasks. We can frame this criterion into the L2R framework by using the query similarity function to rank, given a query q_i^u, all the other queries in the same user search log Q^u. For any given $q_i^u \in T_k^u$, we say that q_j^u is relevant to q_i^u if $q_j^u \in T_k^u$, and irrelevant otherwise. We can thus define the L2R ground truth as follows:

$$\mathcal{L}' = \langle q_i^u, \quad \langle Q^u, \quad \mathbf{y}^{(u,i)} \rangle \rangle_{q_i^u \in Q^u, Q^u \subset \mathcal{Q}}$$

where $y_j^{(u,i)} = 1$, $y_j^{(u,i)} \in \mathbf{y}^{(u,i)}$, if q_i^u and q_j^u belong to the same task, and 0 otherwise.

We define the size of the ground truth as the number of relevance labels $y_j^{(u,i)}$ it contains. We thus have $|\mathcal{L}'| = \sum_u |Q^u|^2$.

The similarity function $\hat{\sigma}$ learned from $\mathcal{L}'$ is *asymmetric*, i.e., there is no constraint forcing $\hat{\sigma}(q_i^u, q_j^u)$ to be equal to $\hat{\sigma}(q_j^u, q_i^u)$.

User-centric. According to this approach, the symmetric query similarity function we expect to learn should promote every pair of objects in the same cluster, and conversely demote pairs belonging to different clusters. To obtain such a function, we provide the given machine learning tool with a view of the *whole* set of objects to be clustered. Therefore, given any pair of queries (q_i^u, q_j^u) in the user search log Q^u we require their similarity to be large *iff* they belong to the same task. We can thus define a new ground truth as follows:

$$\mathcal{L}'' = \langle u, \quad \langle \{(q_i^u, q_j^u) \mid (q_i^u, q_j^u) \in Q^u \times Q^u, i \leq j\}, \quad \mathbf{y}^{(u)} \rangle \rangle_{u \in U}$$

where the relevance score of the query pair (q_i^u, q_j^u) is denoted by $y_{\{i,j\}}^{(u)} \in \mathbf{y}^{(u)}$, and $y_{\{i,j\}}^{(u)} = 1$ if q_i^u and q_j^u belong to the same task, and 0 otherwise.

Note that the queries q_i^u and q_j^u occur *together* twice in $\mathcal{L}'$, i.e., (q_i^u, q_j^u) and (q_j^u, q_i^u), the former with the tuple related to q_i^u and the latter with the tuple related to q_j^u, generating the aforementioned asymmetry. This is not the case for $\mathcal{L}''$, since we have a single *ordered* pair (q_i^u, q_j^u), where $i \leq j$, associated with the tuple for user u. The binary relation "$\leq$" between queries is given by the order of their issuing times. Still we can compute the size of the ground truth as the number of relevance labels $y_{\{i,j\}}^{(u)}$ it contains, which results to be $|\mathcal{L}''| = \sum_u \binom{Q^u}{2}$.

Interestingly, L2R methods applied to a user-centric ground truth can learn functions that exploit a global knowledge about all the pair-wise query relationships of a (long-term) user search log Q^u.

Feature Extraction. Typically, in L2R the representation of the instances includes both the query q_i and the document $d_j^{(i)}$, since the relevance of a document depends on the query. A vector $\mathbf{x} \in \mathbb{R}^m$ of m numerical features is extracted, containing query-dependent and document-dependent features, as well as features related to both. In our query-centric and user-centric ground truth datasets, namely $\mathcal{L}'$ and $\mathcal{L}''$, we require a feature vector $\mathbf{x}_{\{i,j\}}^{(u)} \in \mathbb{R}^m$ representing the relation between any two queries $q_i^u, q_j^u \in Q^u$. In addition to that, since both queries are issued by the same user u, the vector can also include some "global" features, referring to the whole user query log $Q^u \in \mathcal{Q}$.

We assume the feature vector to include two classes of features: *symmetric* and *asymmetric*. The former refers to features that evaluate the same when computed either on the (q_i^u, q_j^u) pair, or on the corresponding swapped one (q_j^u, q_i^u). The latter, instead, comprised those features that might differ if computed on (q_i^u, q_j^u) and (q_j^u, q_i^u).

Concerning $\mathcal{L}'$, each pair (q_i^u, q_j^u) is naturally represented by the vector of asymmetric features associated with it. However, this representation includes some symmetric features as well (i.e., the same we also add to the vector for the swapped pair (q_j^u, q_i^u)). Conversely, regarding $\mathcal{L}''$ each *ordered* pair (q_i^u, q_j^u) is well represented by the vector of symmetric features. Nevertheless, its representation includes also the corresponding asymmetric features. Here, the feature vector is obtained by appending the features as computed on both the pairs (q_i^u, q_j^u) and (q_j^u, q_i^u), $i \leq j$, in this specific order.

The features we use are described in three tables. Table 2 reports symmetric features concerning a set of statistics on all the queries in Q^u. Table 3 describes all the symmetric features we extract from each pair of queries. Note that all of them are included in the vectors associated with q_i^u and q_j^u for both $\mathcal{L}'$ and $\mathcal{L}''$, except for *Is_Proper_Subset_Any*, which is not used in $\mathcal{L}'$. In fact, there exists a corresponding asymmetric feature in $\mathcal{L}'$ that captures the concept of proper subsetting. Table 4 illustrates all the asymmetric features. Many of those are only used in $\mathcal{L}'$, except for the two concerning the conditional probabilities of co-occurrence. Note that Table 2 and Table 4 are divided into sections to distinguish among several kinds of query features. Specifically, there are lexical content features, time/ordering clues, query frequency, conditional and joint probability, and finally semantic content features (i.e., *Wikipedia_Cosine*).

5. IMPLEMENTING THE STD

In this section we describe each module of the STD framework we have been discussing. We start from the QSL module and how we implement it using traditional machine learning methods for classification, specifically logistic regression and decision trees, as well as our newly introduced L2R-based solution. Then, we present the GQC module and the measures of clustering quality which we optimize for.

Since our framework is a mixture of supervised and clustering strategies, to prevent the risk of overfitting we follow a standard *k-fold cross validation* approach. At each of the k stages, the ground truth of search tasks has been partitioned by users into *training*, *validation*, and *test* sets. Each training set portion is exploited by the QSL module to learn the best similarity function $\hat{\sigma}$ (see Section 5.1), and later into the GQC module to choose the best similarity threshold $\hat{\epsilon}$ (see Section 5.2).

The learning algorithms adopted have some hyperparameters which lead to different pairs $(\hat{\sigma}, \hat{\epsilon})$. We used the validation sets to fine-tune those hyperparameters and to chose the corresponding best $(\hat{\sigma}, \hat{\epsilon})$. The model that performs best on average on the validation sets is denoted with the pair $(\hat{\sigma}^*, \hat{\epsilon}^*)$ and evaluated on the test sets.

5.1 Query Similarity Learning Module

Binary Classification. As stated in Section 3.1, a traditional approach treats query similarity learning as a binary classification problem. In this respect, we implemented QSL using two state-of-the-art classifiers already introduced by Jones and Klinkner [9] and Lucchese *et al.* [16]: logistic regression (LogReg) and decision trees (DT). The former aims to minimize the *logistic loss* whereas the latter is a CART that exploits *information gain* (entropy) to recursively best-splitting the dataset [23]. LogReg includes a regularization factor, which was fine-tuned on the validation data in the range $[10^{-3}, 10^4]$. Similarly, we tuned the minimum leaf support of DT classifier by validating thresholds in the interval $[10, 200]$ with step size 10. Both implementations come from the Python scikit-learn toolkit[2].

Learning to Rank (L2R). We are interested in showing that when QSL is deployed using L2R it leads to better search task discovery. In Section 4, we have shown how to build two different ground truths ($\mathcal{L}'$ and $\mathcal{L}''$) for fitting a L2R framework. We adopted two state-of-the-art L2R algorithms, i.e., Gradient-Boosted Regression Trees [5] and LambdaMart [27], as implemented in QuickRank [3]. We denote the models learned from those algorithms by GBRT and λMART, respectively. Note that the two models differ significantly in the loss function L they minimize. The GBRT model minimizes the Root Mean Squared Error (RMSE) in predicting the relevance label, while λMART optimizes *nDCG* [18].

We generated four different query similarity estimates: $\hat{\sigma}_{\text{LogReg}}$, $\hat{\sigma}_{\text{DT}}$, $\hat{\sigma}_{\text{GBRT}}$ and $\hat{\sigma}_{\lambda\text{MART}}$, namely one for every QSL implementation.

5.2 Graph-based Query Clustering Module

Through the QSL module, we generated four different query similarity graphs: $G^u_{\hat{\sigma}_{\text{LogReg}}}$, $G^u_{\hat{\sigma}_{\text{DT}}}$, $G^u_{\hat{\sigma}_{\text{GBRT}}}$ and $G^u_{\hat{\sigma}_{\lambda\text{MART}}}$. Before applying any clustering algorithm to a user graph, GQC prunes those edges whose weight is below a given threshold ϵ. The ideal threshold is the one that leads to the best clustering, i.e., to the best matching between connected components and the search tasks of the ground truth. Therefore, GQC should optimize for a measure of clustering validity and pick the estimate $\hat{\epsilon}$ that maximizes such indicator.

Optimizing for Clustering Quality. We used *external* measures to evaluate the quality of clustering. This can be done because we know from the ground truth the *true* clusters for each Q^u, i.e., those corresponding to the tasks T_j^u of Q^u.

Two popular measures of clustering quality are *Rand* and *Jaccard* indices [20]. Note that the *Rand* index takes also

---

[2]http://scikit-learn.org

Table 2: Symmetric "global" features based on the specific user log Q^u ("[$\diamond$]" symbol indicates newly introduced features).

Symmetric "global" features based on Q^u extracted from the query pair (q_i^u, q_j^u) for $\mathcal{L}'$ and $\mathcal{L}''$			
Feature name	$\mathcal{L}'$	$\mathcal{L}''$	**Description**
Session_Num_Queries	✓	✓	This is the number of queries of the whole user search log, i.e., $|Q^u|$.
Session_Time_Span	✓	✓	This is equal to $|end - init|$, where $init$ (end) is the absolute timestamp when the first (last) query of Q^u was issued.
Avg_Session_Query_Len [$\diamond$]	✓	✓	This is the average length $\mathrm{Avg}(|q^u|)$ of all the queries in Q^u.
Var_Session_Query_Len [$\diamond$]	✓	✓	This is the variance of the length $\mathrm{Var}(|q^u|)$ of all the queries in Q^u.
Session_Num_Clicks [$\diamond$]	✓	✓	This is the total number of clicks on all the search result pages returned by all the queries $q_i^u \in Q^u$.

Table 3: Symmetric features ("[$\diamond$]" symbol indicates newly introduced features).

Symmetric features extracted from the query pair (q_i^u, q_j^u) for $\mathcal{L}'$ and $\mathcal{L}''$			
Feature name	$\mathcal{L}'$	$\mathcal{L}''$	**Description**
Hamming	✓	✓	The Hamming similarity between the two query strings is computed in terms of the number of positions where a character mismatch occurs.
Levenshtein	✓	✓	The Levenshtein similarity (also called *edit-distance*) is computed by determining the least number of edit operations (i.e., deletion, insertion, and substitution) that are necessary to transform one query string into the other.
Jaro_Winkler	✓	✓	The Jaro-Winkler similarity between two strings is a type of edit similarity.
Sorensen_Dice	✓	✓	This similarity measure considers a *character-based* set representation of the two query strings, and is maximum when the two sets are the same.
Sorensen_Dice (3-grams)	✓	✓	The same as Sorensen-Dice, but the character set representation regards all the possible 3-grams (subsequences of characters) occurring in a string.
Jaccard	✓	✓	This similarity measure considers a *character-based* set representation of the two strings, and it is the ratio between the set-intersection and the set-union of the two sets.
Jaccard (3-grams)	✓	✓	The same as Jaccard, but the character set representation regards all the possible 3-grams (subsequences of 3 characters) occurring in a string.
Longest_Common_Substring	✓	✓	Once detected the substring s common to both the queries.
Longest_Common_Subsequence	✓	✓	Once detected the subsequence s common to both the queries.
Are_Equal (term-set)	✓	✓	This is a binary feature that considers the *term-based* set representations s_i^u and s_j^u of the two queries.
Is_Proper_Subset_Any (term-set)		✓	This is a binary feature that considers the *term-based* set representations s_i^u and s_j^u of the two queries.
Δ_*Time_From_Init* [$\diamond$]	✓	✓	If t is the earliest issuing time of one of the two queries, and $init$ is the time of the first issued query of Q^u, this measure is $|t - init|$.
Δ_*Time_From_End* [$\diamond$]	✓	✓	If t is the latest issuing time of one of the two queries, and end is the time of the last issued query of Q^u, this measure is $|end - t|$.
Δ_*Time*	✓	✓	The absolute difference between the issuing times of the two queries in Q^u, expressed in seconds.
*Normalized*_Δ_*Time*	✓	✓	This measure is equal to $\frac{\Delta\_Time}{|end-init|}$, where $init$ (end) is the timestamp of the first (last) issued query of Q^u.
Δ_*Pos_From_Init* [$\diamond$]	✓	✓	If p is the position of the first issued query between q_i^u and q_j^u, this measure is simply p.
Δ_*Pos_From_End* [$\diamond$]	✓	✓	If p is the position of the last issued query between q_i^u and q_j^u, this measure is simply $|Q^u| - p$.
Δ_*Pos* [$\diamond$]	✓	✓	The absolute difference between the positions of the two queries q_i^u and q_j^u, as they appear in Q^u.
*Normalized*_Δ_*Pos* [$\diamond$]	✓	✓	This measure is equal to $\frac{\Delta\_Pos}{|Q^u|}$.
Num_Clicks_Query_Pair [$\diamond$]	✓	✓	The total number of clicks on the search result pages returned by the two queries q_i^u and q_j^u.
Freq$_{former}$ [$\diamond$]	✓	✓	The number of times the first issued query between q_i^u and q_j^u appears, normalized by $|Q^u|$.
Freq$_{latter}$ [$\diamond$]	✓	✓	The number of times the second issued query between q_i^u and q_j^u appears, normalized by $|Q^u|$.
Freq$_{avg}$ [$\diamond$]	✓	✓	This is the average of the two frequencies: $\frac{Freq_{latter} + Freq_{latter}}{2}$.
Global_Joint_Prob (queries) [$\diamond$]	✓	✓	The probability of finding the query pair (q_i^u, q_j^u) in the whole query log $\mathcal{Q}$.
Global_Joint_Prob (terms) [$\diamond$]	✓	✓	The probability of finding a pair of terms appearing in q_i^u and q_j^u in the whole query log $\mathcal{Q}$.
Wikipedia_Cosine [$\diamond$] [16]	✓	✓	This measure is the *cosine similarity* of the two vectors representing the two queries in the Wikipedia space, i.e., $\vec{v}(q_i^u)$ and $\vec{v}(q_j^u)$.

Table 4: Asymmetric features ("[◇]" symbol indicates newly introduced features).

Asymmetric features extracted from the query pair (q_i^u, q_j^u) for $\mathcal{L}'$ and $\mathcal{L}''$			
Feature name	$\mathcal{L}'$	$\mathcal{L}''$	Description
Is_Next	✓		This is a binary feature, which is 1 if q_i^u and q_j^u occur consecutively in Q^u and q_j^u occurs *after* q_i^u, 0 otherwise.
Is_Prev	✓		This is a binary feature, which is 1 if q_i^u and q_j^u occur consecutively in Q^u and q_j^u occurs *before* q_i^u, 0 otherwise.
Is_After	✓		This is a binary feature, which is 1 if q_j^u occurs *after* q_i^u, 0 otherwise.
Is_Proper_Subset (term-set)	✓		This is a binary feature that considers the *term-based* set representations s_i^u and s_j^u of the two queries: the feature is 1 if $s_i^u \subset s_j^u$, 0 otherwise.
Is_Proper_Superset (term-set)	✓		This is a binary feature that considers the *term-based* set representations s_i^u and s_j^u of the two queries: the feature is 1 if $s_i^u \supset s_j^u$, 0 otherwise.
Global_Conditional_Prob (queries) [◇]	✓	✓	The probability of finding q_j^u in *any* user query log Q^u, given that q_i^u occurs in the same log.
Global_Conditional_Prob (terms) [◇]	✓	✓	The probability of finding a term of q_j^u in *any* user query log Q^u, given that another term of q_i^u occurs in the same log.

into account the number of times the algorithm correctly assigns two unrelated queries to different clusters. As we measured that nearly 84% of the query pairs are indeed labeled as not-same-task, we conclude that the *Rand* index may score well models that are not effective in predicting same-task query pairs. The *Jaccard* index instead considers only the accuracy in predicting same-task query pairs.

We also proposed two ways to evaluate the F-measure. The first, denoted by F_1, computes the F-measure by considering as relevant the same-task query pairs and by retrieved all the query pairs in the extracted clusters. We then used a fine-grained average weighted F-measure, denoted with $F_{1\text{avg}}$. We can measure the F_1 of a cluster w.r.t. to a ground-truth task T_j^u by considering as relevant the query pairs in T_j^u only. The overall F_1 of a task T_j^u, i.e., $F_1(T_j^u)$, is the best F_1 achieved by any cluster of Q^u. Finally, $F_{1\text{avg}}$ is the average of $F_1(T_j^u)$ over the tasks $T_j^u \in Q^u$ and weighted by task sizes.

A family of quality measures considers the pairwise relationships between the objects to be clustered, i.e., the queries in Q^u. Specifically, these measures are higher if any two queries of Q^u that result to be in the same cluster C_i^u are also in the same task T_j^u, and vice versa. In practice, we need to compare two binary matrices for each Q^u:

- The *cluster matrix*, where the generic (h,k)-th entry is 1 if the two queries q_h^u and q_k^u are in the same cluster C_i^u, 0 otherwise;

- The *task matrix*, where the generic (h,k)-th entry is 1 if the two queries q_h^u and q_k^u are in the same task T_j^u, 0 otherwise.

Note that the 1's and 0's in the task matrix correspond to the *positive* and *negative* class labels to guess, i.e., same-task and not-same-task, respectively. Therefore, we consider the entries of the cluster matrix as *predictions* of the correct class labels, either positive or negative, to associate with each pair (h,k). We thus build a 2×2 confusion matrix including the number of correct predictions, i.e., the number of *true positives* (tp) and *true negatives* (tn), and the number of wrong predictions, i.e., *false positives* (fp) and *false negatives* (fn), where $tp + tn + fp + fn = \binom{|Q^u|}{2}$. On the basis of this confusion matrix, we determine the following measures of clustering validity. The first one is the *Rand* index, which is a measure of the percentage of correct decisions made by the algorithm: $Rand = \frac{tp+tn}{tp+tn+fp+fn}$.

It is worth noting that the *Rand* index can be misleading in our case, since the binary values in the task matrices[3] are *asymmetric*. Specifically, negative values (0's) are the most common in the task matrices due to the skewness of the real class label distribution, i.e., nearly 84% of all the query pairs are labeled with the not-same-task class. Therefore, it should be easier for any algorithm to guess the negative pairwise relationships than the positive ones. The *Jaccard* index takes explicitly into account this unbalance of class labels, and does not consider the tn count in the confusion matrix. In fact, *Jaccard* deems the agreement of two 1's (a present-present match, or a positive match) much more relevant than the agreement of two 0's (an absent-absent match, or a negative match): $Jaccard = \frac{tp}{tp+fp+fn}$.

From the confusion matrix, we in turn compute the *precision* ($p = \frac{tp}{tp+fp}$) and the *recall* ($r = \frac{tp}{tp+fn}$), and finally the F_1 score, which is the harmonic mean of p and r: $F_1 = \frac{2 \cdot p \cdot r}{p+r}$.

Other external indicators of clustering validity compute the degree to which the tasks of Q^u, i.e., the true clusters, actually correspond to the clusters detected by the clustering algorithm. Unlike previous scores, these measures do not consider the pairwise links between queries induced by the clustering. Indeed, the index we use is a variant of F_1, denoted by $F_{1\text{avg}}$ and computed as follows. Given a true cluster T_j^u (task), we measure precision and recall with respect to all clusters C_i^u. Specifically, $p(i,j)$ is the *precision*, i.e., the fraction of a cluster C_i^u that consists of objects (queries) of a specified true cluster T_j^u. The measure $r(i,j)$ is the *recall*, i.e., the extent to which a cluster C_i^u contains all objects (queries) of a true cluster T_j^u (task). Finally, $F_1(i,j)$ corresponds to the harmonic mean of $p(i,j)$ and $r(i,j)$:

$$F_1(i,j) = \frac{2 \cdot p(i,j) \cdot r(i,j)}{p(i,j) + r(i,j)}$$

To compute a global F_1 of the whole clustering of a single user, for each true cluster T_j^u we take the *maximum* F_1, i.e., $F_{1\max}(j)$ of T_j^u with respect to the best matching cluster C_i^u, as follows: $F_{1\max}(j) = \max_i F_1(i,j)$.

The final $F_{1\text{avg}}$ is the weighted average of $F_{1\max}(j)$ for all j: $F_{1\text{avg}} = \sum_j \frac{m_j}{m} F_{1\max}(j)$ where $m_j = |T_j^u|$ and $m = |Q^u|$.

Note that all the cluster validity measures above are discussed considering the queries of a single user Q^u. In fact, each measure is averaged across all users in U, both in the learning and in the evaluation processes.

---

[3]There is one matrix associated with each user search log $Q^u \in \mathcal{Q}$.

Extracting Search Tasks. So far we have estimated both the set of query similarity functions and the corresponding best edge-pruning thresholds from the training set of users. Similarly to the former, we denote the latter by $\hat{\epsilon}_{\mathsf{LogReg}}$, $\hat{\epsilon}_{\mathsf{DT}}$, $\hat{\epsilon}_{\mathsf{GBRT}}$ and $\hat{\epsilon}_{\lambda\mathsf{MART}}$, respectively. Then, pruned graphs are generated for every user u in the validation set: $G^u_{\hat{\sigma}_{\mathsf{LogReg}},\hat{\epsilon}_{\mathsf{LogReg}}}$, $G^u_{\hat{\sigma}_{\mathsf{DT}},\hat{\epsilon}_{\mathsf{DT}}}$, $G^u_{\hat{\sigma}_{\mathsf{GBRT}},\hat{\epsilon}_{\mathsf{GBRT}}}$ and $G^u_{\hat{\sigma}_{\lambda\mathsf{MART}},\hat{\epsilon}_{\lambda\mathsf{MART}}}$. We extracted connected components from all those graphs, and we performed parameter sweeping over both $\hat{\sigma}$ and $\hat{\epsilon}$ by optimizing one of the measures of clustering quality for all the users in the validation set. Overall, the best *search task discovery* method is that provided by one of the models among LogReg, DT, GBRT and λMART, parametrized by the $(\hat{\sigma}, \hat{\epsilon})$, which led to the maximum average clustering quality on the validation sets. Eventually, such model is used to cluster the queries of the test sets into *search task*, and the performance of the model is evaluated with the aforementioned measures of clustering quality.

6. EXPERIMENTS

This section discusses the experimental results we obtain. We briefly describe the dataset used to evaluate our proposed techniques and some important statistics about the task composing each user search log Q^u. Then, we detail the L2R algorithms adopted for implementing the QSL module, as well as the baseline solutions. Finally, we assess our L2R-based techniques and we show their superiority over two state-of-the-art competitors (i.e., logistic regression [9, 16] and decision trees [16]) when used to implement the GQC module for detecting search tasks.

Analysis of the Dataset. We conducted our experiments on the dataset[4] presented by Hagen *et al.* in [7]. This is a three-month sample of queries from the 2006 AOL query log. It is made of 8,840 queries issued by 127 users and labeled by two human assessors into 1,378 user search tasks (in fact, called *missions* in the original paper). Firstly, we performed some preprocessing to remove stopwords, noisy characters, to normalize query strings to lowercase, and we removed the longest and shortest user search logs. After preprocessing, we obtained a total of 6,381 queries from 125 users.

Figure 2 shows four plots regarding different *cumulative distribution functions* (CDFs) extracted from the dataset. Specifically, in Figure 2a, the x-axis reports the number $X = x$ of queries per-task while the y-axis the probability of finding a task whose number of queries is not greater than x. The plot shows that about 41% of the tasks in the dataset is composed of only one query: we call them *singleton tasks*. Moreover, tasks composed of three (or less) queries accounts for about 70% of all the tasks in dataset. The majority of the tasks are in fact small.

Concerning Figure 2b, the x-axis reports the number $X = x$ of queries per-task while the y-axis reports the probability of finding a user that performed *at least* a task whose number of queries is not greater than x. The plot shows that about 20% of the users perform at least a singleton task, and that more than 80% of the users performed at least one task composed of 10 or less queries.

In Figure 2c, the x-axis reports the number $X = x$ of per-user tasks while the y-axis reports the probability of discovering a user query log containing no more than x tasks.

---

[4]http://www.webis.de/research/corpora/corpus-webis-smc-12/data-oair13-paper.zip

We observe that about 70% of the users perform no more than 10 tasks. This means that there are a few "topics" users are interested in the long-term (i.e., three months) and, consequently, some tasks are repeated periodically.

Finally, as regards Figure 2d the x-axis reports the number $X = x$ of singleton tasks, and the y-axis the probability of a user performing at most x singleton tasks. The plot shows that there is a small fraction of users, namely 12%, who do not perform any singleton task at all. Moreover, about 15% (27% - 12%) of the users perform just one singleton task in their history. The same number increases to 31% if we consider two or less singleton tasks, and raises up to 43% for three or less singleton tasks, thus proving that singleton tasks are appearing across all the users in the dataset without being related to any particular "noisy" behavior.

Evaluating Search Task Discovery. To assess the ability of our framework in effectively discovering search tasks, we provide different implementations of the QSL and GQC modules. All the implementations are evaluated on the same datasets and using the same experimental methodology as described in Section 5, applying standard *k-fold cross validation* $(k = 5)$. Each method is validated by computing the external measures of clustering quality discussed in Section 5.2, i.e., *Rand*, *Jaccard*, F_1, and $F_{1\,\mathrm{avg}}$.

We compared the following machine learning solutions to implement QSL, namely to estimate query similarity: both L2R methods GBRT and λMART, and two binary classifiers, i.e., LogReg and DT. The latter two can be seen as variants of two state-of-the-art competitors exploiting logistic regression [9, 16] and decision trees [16], boosted by the clustering optimization achieved by the GQC module. We also present the results of a baseline, called Singleton: this is a binary classifier that, for each pair of queries, always predicts the majority class label (i.e., not-same-task). Intuitively, this means that Singleton is able to correctly detect *all and only* the singleton tasks.

Results averaged across 5 cross-validation folds are reported in Table 5(a) for the query-centric $\mathcal{L}'$ dataset, and Table 5(b) for the user-centric $\mathcal{L}''$ dataset.

We measure the statistical significance of results using *paired t-test*. More specifically, for each quality metrics we test against the null hypothesis that there is no difference between our proposed solutions (i.e., GBRT and λMART) and other baseline approaches. The symbol (*) indicates when we are able to reject the null hypothesis at the significance level $\alpha = .05$ (i.e., *p*-value $< .05$). We can confirm that all the results obtained by our methods are statistically significant different from those generated by the baselines, except for *Rand* index as measured on $\mathcal{L}'$.

Note that the Singleton baseline is not able to achieve interesting results, not even considering *Rand* index. LogReg and DT have similar performance, but LogReg seems to achieve higher quality on average. Remarkably, GBRT and λMART improve over other methods on both $\mathcal{L}'$ and $\mathcal{L}''$. In particular, λMART enhances *Jaccard* and F_1 scores by about 7.5% and 5.6%, respectively. However, this is not the case of *Rand* score, for which LogReg works better. This depends on the ability of logistic regression of correctly predicting the negative labels. To some extent, anyway, guessing the negative labels may be considered "easy", due to the skewness of class labels distribution in our dataset. Therefore, even though it is a widely used measure, *Rand* index is not completely able to provide insights about the quality

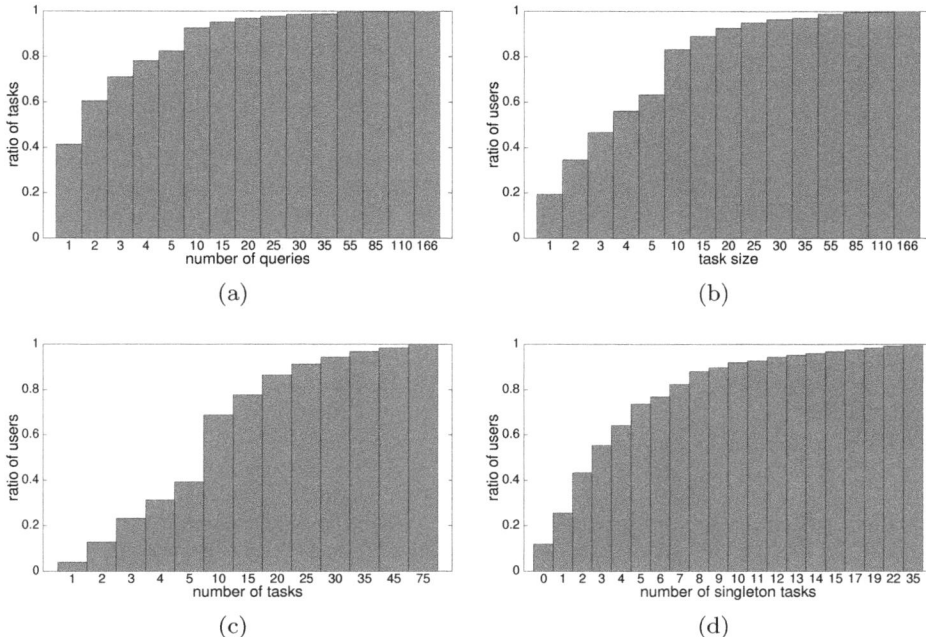

Figure 2: Properties of the dataset.

Table 5: Comparison of L2R techniques and baselines in terms of *Rand*, $F_{1\text{avg}}$, *Jaccard*, and F_1 averaged across 5 cross-validation folds. Best results are shown in **boldface**, and there is a (*) next to those which are statistically significant at $\alpha = .05$.

(a) *Query-centric* dataset $\mathcal{L}'$

Method	Metric			
	Rand	$F_{1\text{avg}}$	*Jaccard*	F_1
Singleton	0.738	0.458	0	0
DT	0.898	0.853	0.620	0.714
LogReg	**0.919**	0.868	0.639	0.737
GBRT	0.915	**0.889**(*)	0.670	0.763
λMART	**0.919**	0.879	**0.687**(*)	**0.778**(*)

(b) *User-centric* dataset $\mathcal{L}''$

Method	Metric			
	Rand	$F_{1\text{avg}}$	*Jaccard*	F_1
Singleton	0.738	0.458	0	0
DT	0.880	0.843	0.604	0.706
LogReg	**0.921**(*)	0.868	0.639	0.738
GBRT	0.913	**0.875**(*)	0.682	0.771
λMART	0.914	0.873	**0.684**(*)	**0.778**(*)

of our clustering. We conclude that the presented framework, thanks to the exploitation of a L2R approach is able to improve over the state of the art.

6.1 Feature Ranking

We now discuss the importance of the various features used by the best performing task discovery solution, i.e., the L2R-based method λMART. Several approaches have been proposed to assess how relevant a feature is to a ranking model. Since λMART rankers are based on GBRT, we borrow a method for feature evaluation from the original work by Friedman [5]. During the construction of each tree, we compute for each feature i its associated *gain* g_i by considering the various splitting nodes in the trees and their related gains. We measure for each feature a cumulative gain, which is then used to rank the features. Figure 3 reports the top-17 features for the λMART-based model, learned on the Fold-1 of $\mathcal{L}'$. Specifically, the x-axis reports the logarithm of the feature importance. We can observe that the most discriminative features are those regarding the relative issuing times and positions of a given pair of queries. This is reasonable, since the chance of two close queries to be part of the same task is generally higher. Besides, two queries that

are far away from each other will less likely end up in same task. The second most important feature regards a global statistic about the user search log. The first lexical content signal occurs only at the fifth position, while the semantic feature (i.e., *Wikipedia_Cosine*) appears as the last one in this ranking.

7. CONCLUSION

We discussed the problem of discovering user *search tasks*, i.e., clusters of web queries with the same latent need, from a real-world search engine log, and proposed the Search Task Discovery (**STD**) framework. The *Query Similarity Learning* (**QSL**) module of **STD** learns a query similarity function from a ground truth of manually-labeled search tasks. The other module of **STD**, namely the *Graph-based Query Clustering* (**GQC**) one, models the user search log as a graph whose nodes are queries, where the learned similarity function is exploited to weight edges between query pairs. We described how the **QSL** module can be effectively implemented using *Learning to Rank* (**L2R**) techniques. We tested our approach using a large ground truth of tasks from a sample of a real-world query log. Experiments showed that query similarity

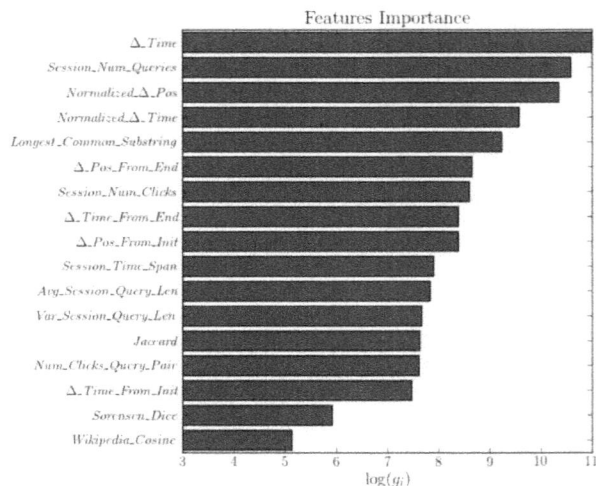

Figure 3: Ranking of features by their "importance".

functions learned using L2R led to better performing GQC implementations when compared to similarity functions induced by other existing state-of-the-art solutions, such as logistic regression and decision trees. As future work we plan to employ STD "online" to detect tasks in (pseudo) real-time, using partial information available from the latest queries issued by users.

Acknowledgements

This work was partially supported by the EC H2020 Program INFRAIA-1-2014-2015 "SoBigData: Social Mining & Big Data Ecosystem" (654024), and by the MIUR national projects PON ADAPT (SCN00447).

8. REFERENCES

[1] P. Boldi, F. Bonchi, C. Castillo, D. Donato, A. Gionis, and S. Vigna. The query-flow graph: model and applications. In *CIKM'08*, pages 609–618. ACM, 2008.

[2] A. Broder. A taxonomy of web search. *SIGIR Forum*, 36:3–10, September 2002.

[3] G. Capannini, C. Lucchese, F. M. Nardini, S. Orlando, R. Perego, and N. Tonellotto. Quality versus efficiency in document scoring with learning-to-rank models. *Information Processing & Management*, 2016.

[4] D. Donato, F. Bonchi, T. Chi, and Y. Maarek. Do you want to take notes? identifying research missions in yahoo! search pad. In *WWW '10*, pages 321–330. ACM, 2010.

[5] J. H. Friedman. Greedy function approximation: a gradient boosting machine. *Annals of Statistics*, pages 1189–1232, 2001.

[6] J. Guo, X. Cheng, G. Xu, and X. Zhu. Intent-aware query similarity. In *CIKM '11*, pages 259–268. ACM, 2011.

[7] M. Hagen, J. Gomoll, A. Beyer, and B. Stein. From search session detection to search mission detection. In *OAIR'13*, pages 85–92, 2013.

[8] D. He, A. Göker, and D. J. Harper. Combining evidence for automatic web session identification. *IP&M*, 38:727–742, September 2002.

[9] R. Jones and K. L. Klinkner. Beyond the session timeout: automatic hierarchical segmentation of search topics in query logs. In *CIKM'08*. ACM, 2008.

[10] A. Kotov, P. N. Bennett, R. W. White, S. T. Dumais, and J. Teevan. Modeling and analysis of cross-session search tasks. In *SIGIR'11*, pages 5–14. ACM, 2011.

[11] H. Li. A short introduction to learning to rank. *IEICE Transactions*, 94-D(10):1854–1862, 2011.

[12] L. Li, H. Deng, A. Dong, Y. Chang, and H. Zha. Identifying and labeling search tasks via query-based hawkes processes. In *KDD'14*, pages 731–740. ACM, 2014.

[13] L. Li, H. Deng, Y. He, A. Dong, Y. Chang, and H. Zha. Behavior driven topic transition for search task identification. In *WWW '16*, pages 555–565. ACM, 2016.

[14] T.-Y. Liu. Learning to rank for information retrieval. *Foundations and Trends in Information Retrieval*, 3(3):225–331, March 2009.

[15] C. Lucchese, S. Orlando, R. Perego, F. Silvestri, and G. Tolomei. Identifying task-based sessions in search engine query logs. In *WSDM'11*, pages 277–286. ACM.

[16] C. Lucchese, S. Orlando, R. Perego, F. Silvestri, and G. Tolomei. Discovering user tasks in long-term web search engine logs. *ACM TOIS*, 31(3):1–43, July 2013.

[17] C. Lucchese, S. Orlando, R. Perego, F. Silvestri, and G. Tolomei. Modeling and predicting the task-by-task behavior of search engine users. In *OAIR'13*, 2013.

[18] C. Manning, P. Raghavan, and H. Schütze. *Introduction to Information Retrieval*. Cambridge University Press, New York City, NY, USA, 2008.

[19] Q. Mei, K. Klinkner, R. Kumar, and A. Tomkins. An analysis framework for search sequences. In *CIKM '09*, pages 1991–1994, New York City, NY, USA, 2009. ACM.

[20] T. Pang-Ning, M. Steinbach, V. Kumar, et al. Introduction to data mining. In *Library of Congress*, page 74, 2006.

[21] F. Radlinski and T. Joachims. Query chains: learning to rank from implicit feedback. In *KDD '05*, pages 239–248. ACM, 2005.

[22] K. Raman, P. N. Bennett, and K. Collins-Thompson. Toward whole-session relevance: exploring intrinsic diversity in web search. In *SIGIR'13*. ACM, 2013.

[23] L. Rokach and O. Maimon. Top-down induction of decision trees classifiers - a survey. *IEEE Transactions on Systems, Man, and Cybernetics (Part C)*, 35(4):476–487, November 2005.

[24] F. Silvestri. Mining query logs: Turning search usage data into knowledge. *Foundations and Trends in Information Retrieval*, 1(1-2):1–174, January 2010.

[25] A. Spink, M. Park, B. J. Jansen, and J. Pedersen. Multitasking during web search sessions. *IP&M*, 42(1):264–275, January 2006.

[26] H. Wang, Y. Song, M.-W. Chang, X. He, R. W. White, and W. Chu. Learning to extract cross-session search tasks. In *WWW'13*, pages 1353–1364. ACM, 2013.

[27] Q. Wu, C. Burges, K. Svore, and J. Gao. Adapting boosting for information retrieval measures. *Information Retrieval*, 2010.

Fast Feature Selection for Learning to Rank

Andrea Gigli
Department of Computer Science,
University of Pisa, Italy
andrgig@gmail.com

Claudio Lucchese,
Franco Maria Nardini,
Raffaele Perego
ISTI–CNR, Italy and Istella Srl
{name.surname}@isti.cnr.it

ABSTRACT

An emerging research area named Learning-to-Rank (LtR) has shown that effective solutions to the ranking problem can leverage machine learning techniques applied to a large set of features capturing the relevance of a candidate document for the user query. Large-scale search systems must however answer user queries very fast, and the computation of the features for candidate documents must comply with strict back-end latency constraints. The number of features cannot thus grow beyond a given limit, and Feature Selection (FS) techniques have to be exploited to find a subset of features that both meets latency requirements and leads to high effectiveness of the trained models.

In this paper, we propose three new algorithms for FS specifically designed for the LtR context where hundreds of continuous or categorical features can be involved. We present a comprehensive experimental analysis conducted on publicly available LtR datasets and we show that the proposed strategies outperform a well-known state-of-the-art competitor.

Keywords

Feature Selection, Learning to Rank

1. INTRODUCTION

Feature Selection (FS) is the complex process of identifying in a training dataset a subset of relevant features that can be used to learn an effective model for the task addressed. In this paper we investigate FS techniques in the context of Learning-to-Rank (LtR) [12].

The problem of ranking documents on the basis of their relevance to user queries is nowadays addressed by leveraging machine learning techniques. A LtR-based ranking function is learned from a large *ground-truth* composed of training examples. The examples consist of a collection of queries $\mathcal{Q}$, where each query $q \in \mathcal{Q}$ is associated with a set of assessed documents $\mathcal{D} = \{d_0, d_1, \dots\}$. Each pair (q, d_i) is thus labeled with a *relevance judgment* y_i, usually a positive

integer in a fixed range, stating the degree of relevance of the document to the query. These labels induce a partial ordering over the assessed documents and define the *ideal ranking* [9]. Using LtR methods we can learn high-quality ranking functions by exploiting a large number of features. Since the number of features cannot grow beyond a given limit due to the costs incurred for their computation, FS techniques have to be exploited to find a subset of features that both meets latency requirements of the back-end and lead to high effectiveness of the trained models. FS provides a number of advantages. Filtering out the irrelevant features leads in fact to enhance the generalization performance of the learned model. Identifying key features also helps to reverse engineer the predictive model and to interpret the results obtained. More importantly, working with a reduced set of highly discriminative and non redundant features results in a reduced feature extraction cost and in faster learning and classification. FS techniques typically fall into three categories: *filter*, *wrapper*, and *embedded methods* [7]. With filter methods, FS is performed as a preprocessing step before learning. A filter method computes a score for each feature independently of the learning algorithm and selects those with the largest score. Wrappers use instead a search algorithm to explore the space of possible features subsets. The quality of each subset is estimated by the performance of a model trained by exploiting only those features in the subset. Finally, in embedded methods the FS technique is integrated within the learning process.

Despite its importance, FS for LtR has not been deeply investigated as it deserves. Geng *et al.* highlight the need for FS techniques explicitly tailored to the ranking problem and propose the Greedy Search Algorithm (GAS) [5]. GAS performs feature selection iteratively by choosing at each step the feature that maximizes relevance and minimizes similarity with the ones previously chosen. Hua *et al.* propose a FS method based on clustering [8]: k-means is first used to aggregate similar features, then the most relevant feature in each cluster is chosen. Pan *et al.* [14] use boosted regression trees to investigate greedy and randomized wrapper methods selecting features by discounting the relative relevance by similarity. Lai *et al.* [10] and Laporte *et al.* [11] use embedded methods for selecting features and building the ranking model at the same step, by solving a convex optimization problem. Naini and Altingovde use greedy diversification methods to the feature selection problem [13]. Dang and Croft propose a wrapper-based method that uses best first search and coordinate ascent to greedily partition a set of features into subsets to select [4].

ICTIR '16, September 12 - 16, 2016, Newark, DE, USA

© 2016 Copyright held by the owner/author(s). Publication rights licensed to ACM.
ISBN 978-1-4503-4497-5/16/09. . . $15.00

DOI: http://dx.doi.org/10.1145/2970398.2970433

In this paper we propose three novel FS filter methods for LtR providing flexible and model-free feature selection. We focus on filter methods because their computational efficiency and independence from the learning algorithm used are particularly useful characteristics of a FS method for LtR. Wrapper or embedded methods usually have an higher computational cost which make them not suitable to LtR scenarios involving hundreds of continuous or categorical features. Moreover, the methods we are going to propose are general and can be applied to many other learning application. In order to assess the performance of our algorithms we applied them to LambdaMART [18] models trained on publicly available LtR datasets using the GAS method as state-of-the-art competitor. Experimental results show that our strategies are effective and in some cases can discard up to 80% of the input features without affecting the ranker quality.

2. FAST FEATURE SELECTION

Let $\mathcal{F} = \{f_1, f_2, \ldots, f_N\}$ be a set of N features, $r(f_i)$ the relevance of feature f_i, and $s(f_i, f_j)$ a symmetric measure of similarity between features f_i and f_j in $\mathcal{F}$. In the following we propose three new *filter* algorithms for feature selection exploiting the above generic measures of feature relevance and similarity.

NGAS. The first FS algorithm is called Naïve Greedy search Algorithm for feature Selection (NGAS), and its pseudocode is reported in Algorithm 1. NGAS computes iteratively a set $\mathcal{S}$ of $n, n < N$ features. First the most relevant feature of $\mathcal{F}$ is added to empty set $\mathcal{S}$. Then, NGAS enters a loop executed $(n-1)$ times where it adds to $\mathcal{S}$ the feature minimizing similarity and maximizing relevance. Being $\mathcal{C} = \mathcal{F} \setminus \mathcal{S}$ the set of candidate features not yet selected, similarity is minimized by selecting the feature $v_l \in \mathcal{C}$ which is less similar to the one added last to $\mathcal{S}$. Relevance is maximized by first considering the feature $v_h \in \mathcal{C}$ that is most similar to v_l, and then selecting the one with the largest relevance score between v_l and v_h. The selected feature is added to $\mathcal{S}$ and removed from $\mathcal{C}$ before staring a new iteration.

XGAS. The second FS algorithm is XGAS (eXtended naïve Greedy search Algorithm for feature Selection). XGAS encompasses an higher degree of freedom in the selection process. At each step, rather than pivoting the selection on the feature v_l, XGAS retrieves the fraction p of features being less similar to the last one added to $\mathcal{S}$. The next feature is

then selected within such pool of $\lceil p \cdot |\mathcal{C}| \rceil$ features by ranking them according to their relevance score and taking the top one. When $p = 1$, the XGAS algorithm selects the best n features according to their relevance score, disregarding any notion of similarity. On the opposite side, for $p = 0$ XGAS selection is driven by similarity considerations only, and the relevance score is considered only in the selection of the first feature. The hyper-parameter p can be fine-tuned on a validation set. It is worth mentioning that the choice of introducing an hyper-parameter to make the selection process more flexible is also made in GAS [5].

HCAS. Hierarchical agglomerative Clustering Algorithm for feature Selection (HCAS) brings forward a redundancy minimization principle. It performs a hierarchical agglomerative clustering phase that partitions the feature set $\mathcal{F}$ into n groups. To minimize redundancy, only one feature per group, i.e., the one with the largest relevance score, is selected and added to $\mathcal{S}$.

We investigated two variants of HCAS exploiting two different algorithms for hierarchical clustering: Single Linkage [6] and the Ward's method [17]. The first one combines pairwise clusters that contain the closest pair of elements not yet belonging to the same cluster, while the second one at each step merges clusters that minimize the global within-cluster variance. In both the implementations the feature distance is defined as a function of the feature similarity. i.e., $d(f_i, f_j)^2 = (1 - |s(f_i, f_j)|)$.

3. EXPERIMENTS

In the following we describe how we applied NGAS, XGAS and HCAS to the LtR context and the results of our preliminary experimental analysis.

3.1 Datasets and Experimental Protocol

Experiments are conducted by using publicly available LtR datasets: the MSN[1] and the Yahoo! LETOR[2] challenge datasets. The first one is split into five folds, consisting of vectors of 136 features extracted from query-document pairs, while the second one consists of two distinct datasets (Y!S1 and Y!S2), made up of vectors of 700 features. In this work, we focus on MSN-1, the first MSN fold, and Y!S1 datasets. The features vectors of the two selected datasets are labeled with relevance judgments ranging from 0 (irrelevant) to 4 (perfectly relevant). Each dataset is split in training, validation and test sets. The MSN-1 dataset consists of 18,919, 6,306, and 6,306 queries for training, validation and testing respectively. The Y!S1 dataset consists of 19,944 training queries, 2,994 validation queries and 6,983 test queries.

We compare the performance of our algorithms w.r.t. the state-of-the-art GAS solution that in [5] is shown to outperform traditional feature selection methods on the LtR task. The experimental protocol adopted is the following:

1. we measure the relevance $r(f_i)$ of each feature, and the similarity $s(f_i, f_j)$ of each pair of features on the train data;

2. we evaluate the FS algorithms by comparing the quality achived on the test set by the models learned on the *projected* training set.

Algorithm 1: The NGAS Algorithm

$NGAS(\mathcal{F}, n)$:
1    $f^+ \leftarrow \underset{f_k \in \mathcal{F}}{\operatorname{argmax}}\ r(f_k)$
2    $\mathcal{C} \leftarrow \mathcal{F} \setminus \{f^+\}$
3    $\mathcal{S} \leftarrow \{f^+\}$
4   **for** $i \leftarrow 1$ **to** $n - 1$ **do**
5      $v_l \leftarrow \underset{f_k \in \mathcal{C}}{\operatorname{argmin}}\ s(f_k, f^+)$
6      $v_h \leftarrow \underset{f_k \in \mathcal{C}}{\operatorname{argmax}}\ s(f_k, v_l)$
7      $f^+ \leftarrow \underset{v \in \{v_l, v_h\}}{\operatorname{argmax}}\ r(v)$
8      $\mathcal{C} \leftarrow \mathcal{C} \setminus \{f^+\}$
9      $\mathcal{S} \leftarrow \mathcal{S} \cup \{f^+\}$
10   **return** $\mathcal{S}$

---

[1] http://research.microsoft.com/en-us/projects/mslr/
[2] http://learningtorankchallenge.yahoo.com

As LtR algorithm we employed the QuickRank [3] implementation of LambdaMART [18]. In particular, we trained and tested LambdaMART models consisting of 100 trees trained using a learning rate equal to 0.01 and a maximum tree depth of 4 levels. The training was driven by the optimization of the average Normalized Discounted Cumulative Gain (NDCG) [9] with cutoff at 10 results. The same measure was used for the evaluation of the FS algorithms on the test set. We report the results of the models learned on the subsets of 5%, 10%, 20%, 30%, 40% of the total number of features available. We also performed a randomization test [15] to assess if the differences in performance are statistically significant. We both check i) the statistical significance of the difference in the performance (average NDCG@10) of each candidate w.r.t. GAS, and ii) the null hypothesys that the model produced by using the subset computed by one of our proposal is better than the one induced by GAS, at significance levels of 5% and 10%.

3.2 Relevance Measures

Our FS algorithms require the definition of functions $r(f_i)$ and $s(f_i, f_j)$. Our objective for choosing relevance function $r(f_i)$ is to find a robust correlation measure between f_i and documents' relevance labels in the training data. We took into consideration Normalized Mutual Information (NMI), Spearman's Rank (S), Kendall's τ (K) and Average Group Variance (AGV) [16, 1, 2]. Finally, we measured the relevance of a feature f_i by the average NDCG@10 achieved by a LambdaMART model trained on the single feature f_i. We name this strategy LM-1. The higher the values of NMI, S, K, LM-1 the higher the relevance of the feature analyzed, and conversely for AGV.

We assess all the above feature relevance measures by considering the ranking quality (i.e., measured in terms of NDCG@10 on the test set) achieved by LambdaMART models learned on the subsets of top-ranked features selected by the different measures.

Results reported in Table 1 show that LM-1 is the relevance measure globally providing the best performance in terms of NDCG@10 on both MSN-1 and Y!S1 datasets. Geng et al. report a similar result on different datasets [5]. On

MSN-1 data, LM-1 is a good relevance predictor in particular when the subset of the selected features is small. On the same dataset, results show that AGV, S, and K are not competitive as feature relevance estimators with significant differences w.r.t. LM-1. In the rest of the analysis we thus use LM-1 as the relevance measure $r(f_i)$ employed by all the FS algorithms.

Regarding feature similarity $s(f_i, f_j)$, Geng et al. exploit the Kendall's τ computed between lists of results produced by two LtR models trained on two different features, i.e., f_i and f_j [5]. Differently from them, we exploit the Spearman's rank correlation coefficient as feature similarity function $s(f_i, f_j)$. This measure fits well a ranking scenario and it is much more efficient to be computed than other measures such as Kendall's τ and Normalized Mutual Information while producing similar results. For lack of space we do not report the results confirming this behavior.

3.3 Effectiveness Evaluation

We evaluated the effectiveness of our proposed FS algorithms against GAS by measuring the quality of ranking models trained after feature selection. The best FS algorithm for a given size of the subset of features is the one causing the smallest quality loss w.r.t. to the model built on the full feature set $\mathcal{F}$.

XGAS and GAS algorithms require the tuning of the hyperparameter p and c, respectively. We tune these parameters by applying a bisection method in the range $[0, 1]$. During each search step, the selected features are evaluated by training a new LtR model with those features and measuring its performance on the validation set. Bisection process continues until no significant improvement is observed on the resulting model.

Table 2: Performance of FS algorithms in terms of NDCG@10 of the induced model. Statistically significant differences against GAS are highligthed with $\triangle\triangledown$ (increment/decrement) at 10% significance level and ▲▼ (increment/decrement) at 5% significance level.

Y!S1					
Subset %	NGAS	XGAS p = 0.8	HCAS "single"	HCAS "ward"	GAS c = 0.01
5%	0.7430▼	**0.7655**	0.7349▼	0.7571▽	0.7628
10%	0.7601	**0.7666**	0.7635	0.7626	0.7649
20%	0.7672	**0.7723**	0.7666	0.7704	0.7671
30%	0.7717	0.7742	0.7738	**0.7743**	0.7730
40%	0.7724	0.7751	0.7742	**0.7755**	0.7737
Full	0.7753	0.7753	0.7753	0.7753	0.7753

MSN-1					
Subset %	NGAS	XGAS p = 0.05	HCAS "single"	HCAS "ward"	GAS c = 0.01
5%	0.4011▼	0.4376▲	**0.4423▲**	0.4289	0.4294
10%	0.4459	0.4528	**0.4643▲**	0.4434▼	0.4515
20%	0.4710	0.4577▼	**0.4870▲**	0.4820	0.4758
30%	0.4739▼	0.4825	0.4854	**0.4879**	0.4848
40%	0.4813	0.4834	0.4848	0.4853	**0.4863**
Full	0.4863	0.4863	0.4863	0.4863	0.4863

Table 1: Quality induced by different feature relevance functions measured in terms of NDCG@10.

Y!S1					
Subset	NMI	AGV	S	K	LM-1
5%	0.7549	**0.7552**	0.7523	0.7541	0.7545
10%	0.7582	0.7578	0.7575	0.7560	**0.7622**
20%	0.7641	0.7664	0.7652	0.7663	**0.7717**
30%	0.7654	0.7717	0.7722	0.7688	**0.7734**
40%	0.7686	0.7720	0.7719	0.7705	**0.7748**
Full	0.7753	0.7753	0.7753	0.7753	0.7753

MSN-1					
Subset	NMI	AGV	S	K	LM-1
5%	0.3548	0.3340	0.3280	0.3313	**0.4304**
10%	0.3742	0.3416	0.3401	0.3439	**0.4310**
20%	0.4240	0.3776	0.3526	0.3533	**0.4330**
30%	**0.4625**	0.3798	0.4312	0.3556	0.4386
40%	**0.4627**	0.3850	0.4330	0.3788	0.4513
Full	0.4863	0.4863	0.4863	0.4863	0.4863

Results in Table 2 show that the best performance in selecting features is obtained by XGAS and HCAS "ward" on the Y!S1 test set and by HCAS and GAS on the MSN-1 test set. In details, on the Y!S1 test set XGAS significantly outperforms GAS in selecting features for small subset sizes, i.e., (5%, 10%, 20%). When increasing the subset size (30%, 40%), our HCAS exploiting Ward's method obtains the best NDCG@10 values. Interestingly, when selecting 40% of the original set of features with HCAS "ward", the learned model achieves a higher effectiveness than the one learned by employing all the feature set (Full). Even if the difference is not statistically significant, GAS never achieves the same result.

Regarding the MSN-1 test set, the best performance on small subset sizes, i.e., (5%, 10%, 20%), is obtained by HCAS exploiting the Single Linkage clustering algorithm and the differences w.r.t GAS are statistically significant at 5%. XGAS also shows a statistically significant gain of NDCG@10 when 5% of the original set of features are selected. Moreover, HCAS "ward" wins when selecting 30% of the original set, while GAS obtains the best NDCG@10 scores for subsets of 40% of the original set. As for Y!S1, HCAS allows to train models that score better than the one produced with the entire set of features (100%) for subsets of 20%, and 30%. Even if the differences are not statistically significant, this result does not hold for GAS. GAS in fact obtains the best performance for subsets of 40% of the original set but is never able to outperform the model trained by using all the features.

3.4 Efficiency Considerations

From an efficiency point of view it is worth mentioning that, differently from NGAS and HCAS, XGAS and GAS require to optimize the hyper-parameters p and c, respectively. This optimization step is computationally expensive as each iteration of the bisection algorithm produces a new set of features to be evaluated by training a LtR model and by measuring its performance on the validation set. Formally, let c_{FS} be the execution time of the FS algorithm, c_{LtR} be the time needed for training the LtR algorithm, and N_{steps} be the number of steps performed by the optimization process. The total time for selecting features by using NGAS and HCAS is c_{FS} while it is $(c_{FS} + c_{LtR}) \cdot N_{steps}$ for both XGAS and GAS.

NGAS and HCAS are instead very efficient in performing the feature selection task. Experiments show that both NGAS and HCAS employs seconds to perform the whole FS process, while GAS and XGAS need hours for tuning and completing the same task.

4. CONCLUSIONS AND FUTURE WORK

We proposed three new algorithms for FS in the LtR scenario: NGAS, XGAS, and HCAS. NGAS employs a greedy selection of candidate features given theur relevance and pair similarity. XGAS extends NGAS by considering a larger number of candidates at each iteration. HCAS exploits hierarchical clustering to aggregate group of features in order to extract the most relevant ones. Experiments show that HCAS outperforms the state-of-the-art competitor, GAS, on both MSN-1 and Y!S1 datasets for subset sizes equal or bigger than 10% of the full feature set. Moreover, results confirm that NGAS and XGAS shows comparable results w.r.t. GAS in most cases. The experimental assessment also show that NGAS and HCAS require orders of magnitude less time than GAS and XGAS to perform feature selection.

As future work we intend to continue our study by investigating three different dimensions. We intend to test both the effectiveness and the efficiency of our proposals on other LtR datasets, using different relevance and similarity measures. Moreover, we want to extend our analysis to other classes of learning algorithms, e.g., binary classification. Finally, we are interested in defining combinations of NGAS with XGAS for increasing the efficiency of the optimization process.

Acknowledgements. This work was partially supported by the EC H2020 Program INFRAIA-1-2014-2015 SoBig-Data: Social Mining & Big Data Ecosystem (654024).

5. REFERENCES

[1] A. Agresti. *Analysis of Ordinal Categorical Data (Second ed.)*. 2010.
[2] S. Baccianella, A. Esuli, and F. Sebastiani. Feature selection for ordinal text classification. *Neural computation*, 26(3):557–591, 2014.
[3] G. Capannini, C. Lucchese, F. M. Nardini, S. Orlando, R. Perego, and N. Tonelotto. Quality versus efficiency in document scoring with learning-to-rank models. *Information Processing & Management*, 2016.
[4] V. Dang and B. Croft. Feature selection for document ranking using best first search and coordinate ascent. In *ACM SIGIR workshop on feature generation and selection for information retrieval*, 2010.
[5] X. Geng, T.-Y. Liu, T. Qin, and H. Li. Feature selection for ranking. In *Proc. SIGIR'07*. ACM, 2007.
[6] J. C. Gower and G. Ross. Minimum spanning trees and single linkage cluster analysis. *Applied statistics*, pages 54–64, 1969.
[7] I. Guyon and A. Elisseeff. An introduction to variable and feature selection. *The Journal of Machine Learning Research*, 3:1157–1182, 2003.
[8] G. Hua, M. Zhang, Y. Liu, S. Ma, and L. Ru. Hierarchical feature selection for ranking. 2010.
[9] K. Järvelin and J. Kekäläinen. Cumulated gain-based evaluation of ir techniques. *ACM TOIS*, 20(4):422–446, 2002.
[10] H. Lai, Y. Pan, Y. Tang, and R. Yu. Fsmrank: Feature selection algorithm for learning to rank. *Transactions on Neural Networks and Learning Systems*, 24(6), 2013.
[11] L. Laporte, R. Flamary, S. Canu, S. Déjean, and J. Mothe. Non-convex regularizations for feature selection in ranking with sparse svm. *Transactions on Neural Networks and Learning Systems*, 10(10), 2012.
[12] T.-Y. Liu. Learning to rank for information retrieval. *Foundations and Trends in Information Retrieval*, 3(3):225–331, 2009.
[13] K. D. Naini and I. S. Altingovde. Exploiting result diversification methods for feature selection in learning to rank. In *Proc. ECIR*, pages 455–461. Springer, 2014.
[14] F. Pan, T. Converse, D. Ahn, F. Salvetti, and G. Donato. Feature selection for ranking using boosted trees. In *Proc. CIKM'09*. ACM, 2009.
[15] M. D. Smucker, J. Allan, and B. Carterette. A comparison of statistical significance tests for information retrieval evaluation. In *Proc. CIKM '07*. ACM, 2007.
[16] J. A. T. Thomas M. Cover. *Elements of Information Theory*. 2006.
[17] J. H. Ward Jr. Hierarchical grouping to optimize an objective function. *Journal of the American statistical association*, 58(301):236–244, 1963.
[18] Q. Wu, C. J. Burges, K. M. Svore, and J. Gao. Ranking, boosting, and model adaptation. Technical report, Microsoft Research, 2008.

A Unified Energy-based Framework for Learning to Rank

Yi Fang
Department of Computer Engineering
Santa Clara University
Santa Clara 95053, CA, USA
yfang@scu.edu

Mengwen Liu
College of Computing and Informatics
Drexel University
Philadelphia 19104, PA, USA
ml943@drexel.edu

ABSTRACT

Learning to Rank (L2R) has emerged as one of the core machine learning techniques for IR. On the other hand, Energy-Based Models (EBMs) capture dependencies between variables by associating a scalar energy to each configuration of the variables. They have produced impressive results in many computer vision and speech recognition tasks. In this paper, we introduce a unified view of Learning to Rank that integrates various L2R approaches in an energy-based ranking framework. In this framework, an energy function associates low energies to desired documents and high energies to undesired results. Learning is essentially the process of shaping the energy surface so that desired documents have lower energies. The proposed framework yields new insights into learning to rank. First, we show how various existing L2R models (pointwise, pairwise, and listwise) can be cast in the energy-based framework. Second, new L2R models can be constructed based on existing EBMs. Furthermore, inspired by the intuitive learning process of EBMs, we can devise novel energy-based models for ranking tasks. We introduce several new energy-based ranking models based on the proposed framework. The experiments are conducted on the public LETOR 4.0 benchmarks and demonstrate the effectiveness of the proposed models.

Keywords

Learning to Rank; Energy-based Models

1. INTRODUCTION

Ranking is the central problem in many IR tasks including document retrieval, entity search, question answering, meta-search, collaborative filtering, online advertisement, and so on. These tasks usually work with high dimensional feature vector representations of the items to be ranked. The typical features range from query independent ones to information measuring the match between user or query and retrieved item. The dimensionality of feature vectors and the complexity of statistical relationships involved are such that accurate results cannot be achieved by designing the relevant ranking functions manually. Therefore, learning to rank (L2R) from

examples has become the dominant approach for designing and optimizing ranking systems. Recent years have witnessed significant efforts on research and development of learning to rank technologies. L2R models can be classified into three broad families: pointwise, pairwise, and listwise methods [16, 15]. Benchmark datasets like LETOR [17] have been released to facilitate the research on learning to rank. It has become a key technology in the industry. Several major search engine companies are using L2R techniques to train their ranking models [16].

On the other hand, energy-based models (EBMs) [13, 12] are a family of learning models that capture dependencies between variables by associating a scalar energy to each configuration of the variables. Making a decision (an inference) with an EBM consists of comparing the energies associated with various configurations of the variable to be predicted, and choosing the one with the lowest energy. Such systems are trained to associate low energies to the desired configurations and higher energies to undesired ones. Unlike probabilistic models that associate a probability to those configurations, energy-based models eliminate the need for proper normalization of probability distributions. The main question in EBMs is how to design a loss function so that minimizing this loss function with respect to the parameter vector will have the effect of "digging holes and building hills" at the required places on the energy surface. Energy-based models have been widely applied to computer vision and speech recognition tasks, and demonstrated their effectiveness and efficiency [20, 18]. Some recent successes of deep learning architectures are largely due to energy-based learning [25].

In this paper, we attempt to shed new light on learning to rank by formulating it in an energy-based framework. To the best of our knowledge, no prior work has investigated the link between learning to rank and energy-based learning. We present a unified energy-based framework for learning to rank. We demonstrate how various existing learning to rank models (pointwise, pairwise, and listwise) can be cast in this framework. Moreover, we propose new learning to rank techniques based on the energy-based framework. The advantages of the energy-based framework for learning to rank are multi-fold. First of all, it can demonstrate the similarity and difference between various L2R methods from the energy-based perspective, which may help us gain further insights into the strengths and weaknesses of each ranking algorithm. Moreover, there exists an extensive research on energy-based models in machine learning and computer vision communities. We can explore and apply them to learning to rank problems. Last but not the least, the energy-based framework can provide sensible guidelines to design and propose new learning to rank models. The energy-based learning aims to reshape the energy functions so that the desired outcomes have

ICTIR '16, September 12-16, 2016, Newark, DE, USA

© 2016 ACM. ISBN 978-1-4503-4497-5/16/09... $15.00

DOI: http://dx.doi.org/10.1145/2970398.2970416

lower energies. The loss and energy functions can be intuitively designed to achieve this effect.

2. RELATED WORK

2.1 Learning to Rank

Learning to rank models can be classified into three broad families: pointwise, pairwise, and listwise methods [16]. Pointwise approaches postulate a scoring function and attempt to estimate the relevance score of every item. The relevance score is typically the rank of the item in the list or a transformed version of it. At prediction time, the items returned for a query are sorted according to their estimated scores. Linear and logistic regression are examples of scoring functions used in pointwise approaches. Pairwise methods score ordered pairs of items instead of individual items. The goal is now to learn the order of such pairs correctly. In other words, the task is to score more relevant items higher than less relevant ones. In general, this approach is preferable to the pointwise approach, because it does not require to learn absolute relevance scores. RankSVM [10] is one of the most popular pairwise approaches. It formalizes ranking as a binary classification problem of item pairs and uses support vector machines as the underlying binary classifier. RankBoost [8] is another pairwise ranking model, where boosting is used to learn the ranking. The idea is to construct a sequence of weak rankers over iteratively reweighted training data, and then to make rank predictions using a linear combination of the weak learners. While the predictive power of RankBoost is greater in theory, it only marginally improves the quality of ranking in practice. Burges et al. [3] propose the RankNet algorithm, which is also based on pairwise classification like RankSVM and RankBoost. The major difference lies in that it employs Neural Network as ranking model and uses cross entropy as loss function. Finally, listwise approaches assume that the training examples are lists of ranked items. They attempt to minimize a loss function defined over the whole list instead of ordered pairs extracted from the list. ListMLE [29] and ListNet [4] are two representative listwise models. The loss functions are defined using the probability distribution on permutations. AdaRank [30] is another listwise approach, based instead on boosting. There exist an abundance of learning to rank techniques in the literature. Liu [16] and Li [15] provide two comprehensive surveys.

2.2 Energy-based Learning

The energy-based framework was first proposed by LeCun and Huang [13, 11] as a deterministic alternative to probabilistic graphical models. It provides a very general framework for dealing with learning systems, and immediately puts machine learning to the scope of mathematical optimization. Zhang [31] proves that probably approximately correct (PAC) learning is guaranteed for the energy-based learning. Energy-based models were successfully applied to various machine learning tasks including computer vision [20], speech recognition [18], unsupervised learning [23], reinforcement learning [9], relational learning [1], missing value imputation [2]. BoltzRank [27] is the only explicit energy-based L2R model in the literature, based on an energy function that depends on a scoring function composed of individual and pairwise potentials. To the best of our knowledge, no prior work has systematically studied the relationship between learning to rank and energy-based learning.

Recently, energy-based models are used to learn deep, distributed representations of high-dimensional data (such as images) and model high-order dependencies. An important class of energy-based models are Restricted Boltzmann Machines [28]. Energy-based deep

Table 1: Some commonly used energy functions in Energy-Based Models [11].

$\frac{1}{2}\lVert f_\theta(x) - y \rVert^2$
$\lVert f_\theta(x) - y \rVert_1$
$-y f_\theta(x)$
$\frac{1}{2}\lVert f_{\theta_x}(x) - g_{\theta_y}(y) \rVert^2$
$\sum_{k=1}^{K} \delta(y-k)\lVert U^k - f_\theta(x) \rVert^2$

Table 2: A list of commonly used loss functions in Energy-Based Models [11].

Energy loss	$E_\theta(x, y)$
Perceptron	$E_\theta(x, y) - \min_{y \in Y} E_\theta(x, y)$
Hinge	$\max(0, m + E_\theta(x, y) - E_\theta(x, \bar{y}))$
Log	$\log(1 + e^{E_\theta(x,y) - E_\theta(x,\bar{y})})$
MCE	$(1 + e^{-(E_\theta(x,y) - E_\theta(x,\bar{y}))})^{-1}$
LVQ2	$\min(M, \max(0, E_\theta(x, y) - E_\theta(x, \bar{y})))$
square-square	$E_\theta(x, y)^2 - (\max(0, m - E_\theta(x, \bar{y})))^2$
square-exp	$E_\theta(x, y)^2 + \beta e^{-E_\theta(x,\bar{y})}$
NLL	$E_\theta(x, y) + \frac{1}{\beta}\log\sum_{y \in Y} e^{-\beta E_\theta(x,y)}$
MEE	$1 - \frac{e^{-\beta E_\theta(x,y)}}{\sum_{y \in Y} e^{-\beta E_\theta(x,y)}}$

learning models have been applied to a range of challenging tasks including motion capture modeling [26], modeling of transformations in natural images [19], and visual tracking [14]. Establishing the link between L2R and EBMs may facilitate applications of deep learning to information retrieval.

3. BACKGROUND

3.1 Energy-based Models

The entire framework of energy-based models, by its name, is centered around the concept of *energy*. It captures dependencies by associating a scalar energy (a measure of compatibility) $E(x, y)$ to each configuration of the input variable x and output y. In inference, i.e., making prediction or decision, the model produces the answer $y \in Y$ that is most compatible with the observed x, for which $E(x, y)$ is the smallest:

$$y^* = \operatorname*{argmin}_{y \in Y} E(x, y) \qquad (1)$$

As a result, model learning consists in finding an energy function that associates low energies to correct values of the variables, and higher energies to incorrect values. The energy function is often assumed within a family of energy functions E_θ indexed by parameter θ. The energy function could be as simple as a linear combination of basis functions or a set of neural network architectures with weight values. One advantage of the energy-based framework is that it puts very little restrictions on the nature of the architecture of the energy function. Table 1 contains some common energy functions.

A *loss functional* (function of function) is defined over energy functions. It is minimized during learning and used to measure the quality of the available energy functions. Within this common inference/learning framework, the wide choices of energy functions and loss functionals allow for the design of many types of learning models, both probabilistic and non-probabilistic. Table 2 shows a list of commonly used loss functions in EBMs. In the table, $\bar{y}$ denotes the most offending incorrect answers, i.e., the answer that has the lowest energy among all the incorrect answers.

EBMs have several advantages over maximum likelihood learning. By trying to model the whole joint distribution of a data set, a large part of the flexibility of probabilistic models is used to capture relationships that might not be necessary for the task of interest. An energy model with a deterministic inference method can make predictions that are directly optimized for the task of interest itself. Moreover, since the normalization constant of many generative models is intractable, inference needs to be done with methods like sampling or variational inference. Deterministic energy-based models circumvent this problem. LeCun et al. [11] provides a survey on energy-based models.

3.2 Notations

Learning to rank is comprised of training and testing as a supervised learning task. The training data contains queries, documents, and relevance judgments. Each query is associated with a number of documents. The relevance of the documents with respect to the query is represented by a label which is at multiple grades. The higher grade a document has, the more relevant the document is. Suppose that Q is the query set, D is the document set, and $R = \{1, 2, ..., l\}$ is the label set. There exists a total order between the grades $l \succ l - 1... \succ 1$, where $\succ$ denotes the order relation. Further suppose that $\{q_1, q_2, ..., q_m\}$ is the set of queries for training and q_i is the i-th query. $D_i = \{d_{i,1}, d_{i,2}, ..., d_{i,n_i}\}$ is the set of documents associated with query q_i and $r_i = \{r_{i,1}, r_{i,2}, ..., r_{i,n_i}\}$ denotes the corresponding labels of those documents, where n_i denotes the sizes of D_i; $d_{i,j}$ denotes the j-th document in D_i; and $r_{i,j} \in R$ represents the relevance degree of $d_{i,j}$ with respect to q_i. A feature vector $\mathbf{x_{i,j}}$ is created from each query-document pair $(q_i, d_{i,j})$.

4. AN ENERGY-BASED RANKING FRAMEWORK

The main goal of learning to rank is to learn the relationship between document d and its relevance r given query q. We propose an energy-based ranking framework to encode dependencies among them, by associating a scalar energy $E_\theta(q, d, r)$ to each configuration of d and r given q. The family of possible energy functions is parameterized by a parameter vector θ, which is to be learned from the training data. Similar to other EBMs, this energy function can be viewed as a measure of "compatibility" between d and r given q. In the following sections, we use the convention that small energy values correspond to highly compatible configurations of the variables, while large energy values correspond to highly incompatible configurations of the variables. There are three key components in the energy-based ranking framework.

- *Loss functional* is used to measure the quality of the available energy functions. Unlike the traditional loss functions in machine learning, the loss function in energy-based learning is defined on energy functions and thus is a *functional*. Similar to the other loss functions, it is minimized during the training process.

- *Learning* consists in finding an energy function that associates low energies with the desired documents, and higher energies with the undesired documents. It is worth noting that the existing EBMs only adjusts the energies on the same instance, but for different output values (correct vs. incorrect). For ranking problems, we attempt to adjust the energies on different instances (i.e., documents), especially for pairwise and listwise learning. This is one of the major differences between the existing EBMs and the proposed ranking framework.

- *Ranking* generates a list of documents that are ranked based on their energies in the ascending order.

Mathematically, to train an energy-based ranking model, we minimize the loss functional with respect to θ as follows

$$\theta^* = \min_\theta \left(\frac{1}{m} \sum_{i=1}^m L_q\big(E_\theta(q_i, d, r)\big) + R(\theta) \right) \quad (2)$$

where $L_q\big(E_\theta(q_i, d, r)\big)$ is the per-query loss functional defined on the energy function $E_\theta(q_i, d, r)$. $R(\theta)$ is the regularizer and can be used to embed our prior knowledge about which energy functions in our family are preferable to others.

The ranking process consists of two steps in general. The first step is to find the relevance degree r that is most compatible with the document d given query q_i and model parameter θ (learned from training), which is to minimize the energy function with respect to r:

$$E_\theta(q_i, d) = \min_{r \in R} E_\theta(q_i, d, r) \quad (3)$$

The documents can then be ranked based on $E_\theta(q_i, d)$ in ascending order. In other words, the most relevant document given query q_i is

$$d^* = \operatorname*{argmin}_{d \in D_i} E_\theta(q_i, d) = \operatorname*{argmin}_{d \in D_i} \min_{r \in R} E_\theta(q_i, d, r) \quad (4)$$

In the cases where the energy function does not depend on r, we can just rank the documents based on $E_\theta(q_i, d)$. It is worth noting that the energy function is minimized during the ranking process while the loss functional is minimized during the learning process.

Besides the advantages of EBMs pointed out in Section 3.1, the key characteristic of energy-based learning is the process of reshaping the energy function based on training data so that the desired results would have lower energies. It can be viewed that the loss function is operated on energy functions instead of parameters. This functional point of view can shed new light on learning to rank. With a properly designed loss function, the energy-based ranking process should have the effect of "pushing down" on the energies of the desired documents and "pulling up" on the undesired ones. The following subsections will cast several existing learning to rank models in the energy-based ranking framework. In Section 5, we derive novel learning to rank models based on this framework.

4.1 Pointwise

In the pointwise approach, the ranking problem is transformed to classification or regression. The existing methods for classification or regression are applied. The loss function in learning is pointwise in the sense that it is defined on a single object (feature vector). The energy-based models have been studied extensively for traditional classification and regression models. For completeness, we just briefly show how some widely used classification models including support vector machine (SVM), logistic regression, and linear regression can be cast in the energy-based ranking framework.

For simplicity, assuming the relevance is binary: $r_{ij} \in \{1, -1\}$, the energy function can be defined as:

$$E_\theta(q_i, d_{ij}, r_{ij}) = -r_{ij} f(q_i, d_{ij}; \theta) = -r_{ij} \theta^{\mathrm{T}} \mathbf{x_{i,j}} \quad (5)$$

where $f(q_i, d_{ij}; \theta)$ is a discriminant function parameterized by θ and assumed a linear model here. By plugging this energy function into the hinge loss in Table 2, we obtain the per-query loss function as follows

$$L_q = \sum_{j=1}^{D_i} \max(0, M + 2r_{ij} \theta^{\mathrm{T}} \mathbf{x_{i,j}}) \quad (6)$$

where M is the margin parameter. If the regularizer takes the form $||\theta||_2^2$, the loss will result in the linear SVM.

If we plug the energy function in Eqn.(5) into the Log loss in Table 2, the per-query loss function becomes:

$$L_q = \sum_{j=1}^{D_i} \log \left(1 + \exp(-2r_{ij}\theta^{\mathrm{T}}\mathbf{x_{i,j}}) \right) \qquad (7)$$

which gives the logistic regression model. The loss functions in Eqn.(6) and Eqn.(7) are slightly different from the standard ones for SVM and logistic regression, but they are equivalent since the multiplier of 2 can be absorbed into the parameter θ.

If an energy function is defined as the squared error between $\theta^{\mathrm{T}}\mathbf{x_{i,j}}$ and r_{ij} as follows:

$$E_\theta(q_i, d_{ij}, r_{ij}) = (\theta^{\mathrm{T}}\mathbf{x_{i,j}} - r_{ij})^2 \qquad (8)$$

then the Energy loss, Perceptron loss, and negative log-likelihood (NLL) loss in Table 2 are all equivalent and lead to the regression loss function in the pointwise model called Subset Ranking with Regression [6]. The reason is the contrastive term of the NLL loss becomes constant since it is a Gaussian integral with a constant variance, and that of the Perceptron loss is zero.

4.2 Pairwise

The pairwise approach does not focus on accurately predicting the relevance degree of each document; instead, it cares about the relative order between two documents. In this sense, it is closer to the concept of "ranking" than the pointwise approach. In this section, we cast two representative pairwise L2R models, RankSVM and RankNet, in the energy-based ranking framework.

4.2.1 RankSVM

RankSVM [10] is one of the first learning to rank methods. It is based on the pairwise comparison between two documents. The RankSVM model can be formulated in the energy-based framework by assuming the following energy function:

$$E_\theta(q_i, d_{ij}, r_{ij}) = -f(q_i, d_{ij}; \theta) \qquad (9)$$

with a linear feature model

$$f(q_i, d_{ij}; \theta) = \theta^{\mathrm{T}}\mathbf{x_{i,j}} \qquad (10)$$

The loss function L_p for a pair of documents d_{ij} and d_{ik} given query q_i is defined as

$$L_p = \max \left(0, 1 + y_{jk} \big(E_\theta(q_i, d_{ij}, r_{ij}) - E_\theta(q_i, d_{ik}, r_{ik}) \big) \right) \qquad (11)$$

where y_{jk} is an indicator variable. If document d_{ij} is preferred over d_{ik} (i.e., $r_{ij} > r_{ik}$) given query q_i, $y_{jk} = 1$; otherwise, $y_{jk} = -1$. The combination of the energy and loss with the L_2 regularizer leads to the following loss function for all the pairwise instances:

$$\min_\theta \sum_{i,(j,k)} \max \left(0, 1 - y_{jk}\theta^{\mathrm{T}}(\mathbf{x_{i,j}} - \mathbf{x_{i,k}}) \right) + \lambda||\theta||_2^2 \qquad (12)$$

This unconstrained optimization problem is equivalent to the following constrained optimization problem [15]:

$$\min_{\theta,\xi} \tfrac{1}{2}||\theta||_2^2 + C\sum_{i,(j,k)} \xi_{i,(j,k)} \qquad (13)$$

$$s.t. \qquad y_{jk}\theta^{\mathrm{T}}(\mathbf{x_{i,j}} - \mathbf{x_{i,k}}) \geq 1 - \xi_{i,(j,k)} \qquad (14)$$

$$\xi_{i,(j,k)} \geq 0 \qquad (15)$$

where $C = \frac{1}{2\lambda}$. This is the objective function of the RankSVM model [10].

It is worth noting that the loss in Eqn.(11) is different from the hinge loss used in EBMs shown in Table 2. As discussed in the beginning of Section 4, in the energy-based ranking framework, we aim to reshape the energy function over different instances (i.e., documents) while the existing EBMs usually focus on the energy function of a single instance but with different output values.

4.2.2 RankNet

RankNet [3] is one of the learning-to-rank algorithms used by commercial search engines [16]. It is also based on the comparison of a pair of documents. Let us define a loss functional of the energy functions as follows:

$$L_p = \log \left(1 + \exp \big(E_\theta(q_i, d_{ij}, r_{ij}) - E_\theta(q_i, d_{ik}, r_{ik}) \big) \right) \qquad (16)$$

where d_{ij} is preferred over d_{ik} for query q_i. The following energy function can be used:

$$E_\theta(q_i, d_{ij}, r_{ij}) = -f(q_i, d_{ij}; w) \qquad (17)$$

$$= -f(\sum_s w_s f_s(\sum_t w_{st}x_{(t)} + b_s) + b) \qquad (18)$$

where f is a three layer neural network with a single output node. $x_{(t)}$ denotes the t-th element of input $\mathbf{x_{i,j}}$, w_{st}, and b_s, and f_s denote the weight, bias, and activation function of the first layer, respectively, w_s, b, and f denote the weight, bias, and activation function of the second layer, respectively. The activation functions are usually sigmoid functions. By plugging the energy function in Eqn.(17) into the loss in Eqn.(16), we obtain the following optimization problem:

$$\min_w \sum_{i,(j,k)} \log \left(1 + \exp \big(f(q_i, d_{ik}; w) - f(q_i, d_{ij}; w) \big) \right) \qquad (19)$$

which is equivalent to the objective function in RankNet. In fact, this objective is also equivalent to the Bayesian Personalized Ranking (BPR) optimization criterion [24] (if f is factorized as the product of user and item latent factors), which is widely used in recommender systems for dealing with implicit feedback.

4.3 Listwise

The listwise approach addresses the ranking problem in a more natural way. Specifically, it takes ranked lists as instances in the learning process. The group structure of ranking is maintained. In this section, we study a representative listwise L2R model: ListMLE [29], which exploits the Plackett-Luce (PL) model studied in statistics. PL model defines a probability distribution over permutations of objects, referred to as permutation probability. Let π denote a permutation (ranked list) of the objects and $\pi^{-1}(i)$ denote the object in the ith rank (position) in π. Further suppose that there are non-negative scores assigned to the objects. Let $s = \{s_1, s_2, ..., s_n\}$ denotes the scores of the objects. The PL model defines the probability of permutation π based on scores s as follows.

$$P_s(\pi) = \prod_{i=1}^{n} \frac{s_{\pi^{-1}(i)}}{\sum_{j=i}^{n} s_{\pi^{-1}(j)}} \qquad (20)$$

The probabilities of permutations naturally form a probability distribution. In document ranking, given feature vectors $\mathbf{z_1}, \mathbf{z_2}, ..., \mathbf{z_n}$, the top k probability of subgroup $g[\mathbf{z_1}, \mathbf{z_2}, ..., \mathbf{z_n}]$ is calculated as

$$P_s(g[\mathbf{z_1}, \mathbf{z_2}, ..., \mathbf{z_n}]) = \prod_{j=1}^{k} \frac{\exp \big(s(\mathbf{z_j}; \theta) \big)}{\sum_{t=j}^{n} \exp \big(s(\mathbf{z_t}; \theta) \big)} \qquad (21)$$

ListMLE maximizes the likelihood of the ground truth ranked lists, which is equivalent to minimizing the following energy-based loss function:

$$L = -\sum_{i=1}^{m} \log \prod_{j=1}^{k} \frac{\exp\left(-E(x_{i,\pi_i^{-1}(j)};\theta)\right)}{\sum_{t=j}^{n_i} \exp\left(-E(x_{j,\pi_i^{-1}(t)};\theta)\right)} \quad (22)$$

where $E(x_{i,\pi_i^{-1}(j)};\theta) = -f(x_{i,\pi_i^{-1}(j)};\theta)$ and f is a neural network model with parameter θ. π_i is the ranking according to the ground truth ranked list for query q_i.

Let us investigate the loss function L_q for query q_i as follow:

$$L_q = -\log \prod_{j=1}^{k} \frac{\exp\left(-E(x_{i,\pi_i^{-1}(j)};\theta)\right)}{\sum_{t=j}^{n_i} \exp\left(-E(x_{i,\pi_i^{-1}(t)};\theta)\right)}$$

$$= \sum_{j=1}^{k} E(x_{i,\pi_i^{-1}(j)};\theta) + F(\pi,E;\theta) \quad (23)$$

where $F(\pi,E;\theta)$ is the contrastive term defined as

$$F(\pi,E;\theta) = \sum_{j=1}^{k} \log \sum_{t=j}^{n_i} \exp\left(-E(x_{i,\pi_i^{-1}(t)};\theta)\right) \quad (24)$$

Based on Eqn.(23), we can explain ListMLE in the energy-based ranking framework as follows. To minimize the loss function in Eqn.(23), we need to "push down" the energies of the top k documents while "pull up" all the energies of the contrastive term (since it is the decreasing function of the energies). For the top i^{th} position, the energies of all the documents below i and including i are pulled up due to the contrastive term, but the energy at the i-th position is pushed down harder by the first term. This can be seen in the expression of the gradient:

$$\frac{\partial L_q}{\partial \theta} = \sum_{j=1}^{k} \frac{\partial E(x_{i,\pi_i^{-1}(j)};\theta)}{\partial \theta}$$

$$- \sum_{j=1}^{k} \sum_{t=j}^{n_i} \frac{\partial E(x_{i,\pi_i^{-1}(t)};\theta)}{\partial \theta} P(x_{i,\pi_i^{-1}(t)};\theta) \quad (25)$$

where

$$P(x_{i,\pi_i^{-1}(t)};\theta) = \frac{\exp\left(-E(x_{i,\pi_i^{-1}(t)};\theta)\right)}{\sum_{t=j}^{n_i} \exp\left(-E(x_{i,\pi_i^{-1}(t)};\theta)\right)} \quad (26)$$

Thus, for each top position i, the contrastive term pulls up on the energy of each document (below or including i) with a force proportional to the negative energy of that document under the model.

5. NEW ENERGY-BASED RANKING MODELS

The energy-based ranking framework establishes the link between learning to rank and EBMs. The existing research in EBMs (e.g., various loss and energy functions) can be readily utilized to solve ranking problems. Furthermore, the energy-based perspective may provide new insights and sensible intuitions to devise novel ranking models. The training of EBMs is essentially the process of reshaping the energy surface. In the pointwise approaches, the energies of correct relevance labels should be decreased, and the energies of incorrect labels should be increased, particularly if they are lower than that of the correct labels. In the pairwise and listwise approaches, we look at the energies of more than a single document. The energies of desired documents are decreased, and

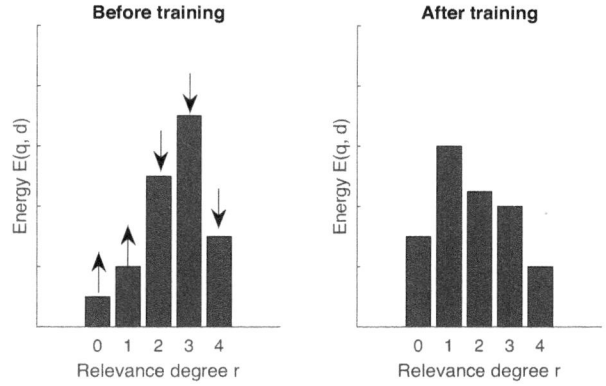

Figure 1: The effect of training on the energy surface in the pointwise case. The energy of the correct relevance label is decreased, and the energies of incorrect labels are increased.

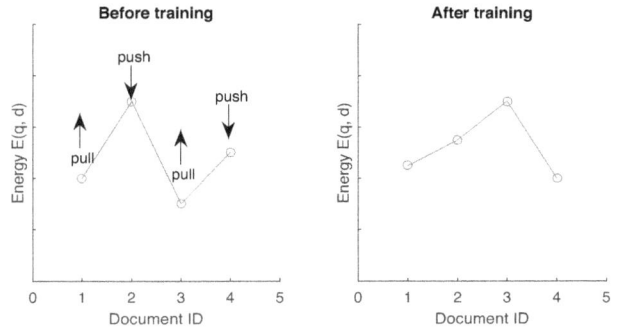

Figure 2: The effect of training on the energy surface in the pairwise and listwise cases. The energies of the desired documents are decreased, and the energies of the undesired documents are increased.

the energies of undesired documents are increased. Figure 1 and Figure 2 illustrate the training processes in energy-based ranking. In this section, we present one new model for each of the three representative L2R approaches: pointwise, pairwise, and listwise, respectively.

5.1 Pointwise

While many traditional classification and regression models were applied to learning to rank, some energy-based loss functions have not been explored for ranking problems. In this section, we utilize the square-exponential loss (in Table 2) which has demonstrated impressive effectiveness in computer vision applications [13, 5, 20]. The per-query loss functional is defined as follows

$$L_{\text{sq\_exp}} = \sum_{j=1}^{D_i} \left(E_\theta(q_i,d_{ij},r_{ij})\right)^2 + \gamma \exp\left(-E_\theta(q_i,d_{ij},\bar{r}_{ij})\right)$$

where $\bar{r}_{ij}$ is the most offending label for d_{ij} given q_i (i.e., the label that has the lowest energy among all incorrect labels). This loss function aims to push down the energy of correct predictions towards zero while push up the energy of incorrect predictions. To the best of our knowledge, no prior work has applied the square-exponential loss to ranking problems.

The energy function can be defined as the absolute value of the difference between the predicted relevance label and ground truth label of the document as follows:

$$E_\theta(q_i, d_{ij}, r_{ij}) = ||f(q_i, d_{ij}; \theta) - r_{ij}||_1 \quad (27)$$

where f is a discriminant function as defined in Section 4.1. In the experiments, we assume a simple linear model $f(q_i, d_{ij}; \theta) = \theta^T x_{i,j}$. We can use the stochastic gradient descent (SGD) algorithm to update the parameters θ as follows

$$\theta := \theta - \eta \frac{\partial E_\theta(q_i, d_{ij}, r_{ij})}{\partial \theta} \Big(E_\theta(q_i, d_{ij}, r_{ij}) - \gamma \exp \big(- E_\theta(q_i, d_{ij}, \bar{r}_{ij}) \big) \Big)$$

where η is a positive learning rate.

5.2 Pairwise

For the pairwise model, we propose to adapt the learning vector quantization (LVQ2) loss functional (in Table 2), which has achieved excellent results in discriminatively training sequence labeling systems, particularly speech recognition systems [7, 18, 11]. The loss functional L_p for a pair of documents d_{ij} and d_{ik} given query q_i is defined as

$$L_{lvq2} = \min \Big(M, \max \big(0, E_\theta(q_i, d_{ij}, r_{ij}) - E_\theta(q_i, d_{ik}, r_{ik}) \big) \Big)$$

where d_{ij} is preferred over d_{ik} for query q_i. Such a loss functional encourages the energy $E_\theta(q_i, d_{ij}, r_{ij})$ of the desired document to be lower than the energy $E_\theta(q_i, d_{ik}, r_{ik})$ of the other document with a margin of zero.

We can use the same energy function with that for RankSVM and RankNet, as defined in Eqn.(9) and Eqn.(17) in Section 4.2. To estimate the parameters θ, we apply the stochastic gradient descent (SGD) update rule as follows given each pair of documents:

$$\theta := \theta - \eta \Big(\frac{\partial E_\theta(q_i, d_{ij}, r_{ij})}{\partial \theta} - \frac{\partial E_\theta(q_i, d_{ik}, r_{ik})}{\partial \theta} \Big) \quad (28)$$
$$\text{if} \quad 0 \leq E_\theta(q_i, d_{ij}, r_{ij}) - E_\theta(q_i, d_{ik}, r_{ik}) \leq M$$

where η is the learning rate. Such gradient descent essentially takes steps proportional to the negative of the difference between the gradients of the energies of the document pair.

5.3 Listwise

Section 4.3 illustrates the ListMLE model from the energy-based point of view. It essentially pushes down the energies of the top k documents while pulls up the energies of ALL the documents given a query. Inspired by this observation and Eqn.(25), we devise a new listwise approach by defining the following energy function for a ranked list π_i:

$$E_{list}(\pi_i; \theta) = \sum_{j=1}^{k} E(x_{i, \pi_i^{-1}(j)}; \theta) \quad (29)$$
$$- \sum_{j=1}^{k} \sum_{t=j}^{n_i} E(x_{i, \pi_i^{-1}(t)}; \theta) P(x_{i, \pi_i^{-1}(t)}; \theta) \quad (30)$$

where $E(x_{i, \pi_i^{-1}(j)}; \theta)$ is the energy of the individual document $x_{i, \pi_i^{-1}(j)}$ as defined in Section 4.3 for ListMLE. The listwise energy function $E_{list}(\pi_i; \theta)$ has two parts. The first part (i.e., Eqn.(29)) is the sum of the energies of the top k documents. The second part (i.e., Eqn.(30), the contrastive term) is the sum of the expected energies of the k ranked sublists. These sublists include the documents from the jth position to the end, where $j \in [1, k]$, respectively. In

other words, $E_{list}(\pi_i; \theta)$ is the sum of top-k discrepancy between the energy of the document in the top j^{th} position and the expectation of energy of documents that are ranked from the jth position to the bottom. If we want to minimize the energy $E_{list}(\pi_i; \theta)$ of the whole list, we need to lower the energy of the first part and raise the energy of the second part. As a result, this will make the top k documents more distinguishable from the rest of the documents in the ranked list.

Different from ListMLE, we define $P(x_{i, \pi_i^{-1}(t)}; \theta)$ only based on the rank position t:

$$P(x_{i, \pi_i^{-1}(t)}; \theta) = \begin{cases} \frac{1}{1 + \sum_{t=2}^{n_i} 1/\log(t)}, & t = 1 \\ \frac{1/\log(t)}{1 + \sum_{t=2}^{n_i} 1/\log(t)}, & t > 1 \end{cases} \quad (31)$$

This is motivated by the discounting factor in Normalized Discounted Cumulative Gain (NDCG). The rank position based probability does not depend on the features of individual documents or parameters and thus it is more efficient than that defined in Eqn.(26)) for ListMLE.

Given the energy function $E_{list}(\pi_i; \theta)$ defined over the list π_i, we can use various loss functionals of the energy-based models, e.g., the LVQ2 loss as follows:

$$\mathcal{L}_{lvq2\text{-}list} = \frac{1}{m} \sum_{i=1}^{m} \min \Big(M, \max \big(0, E_{list}(\pi_i; \theta) \big) \Big) \quad (32)$$

where m is the total number of queries/ranked lists. This loss aims to minimize $E_{list}(\pi_i; \theta)$ by some margin M. We can use the stochastic gradient descent to update the parameters as follows:

$$\theta := \theta - \eta \sum_{j=1}^{k} \Big(\frac{\partial E(x_{i, \pi_i^{-1}(j)}; \theta)}{\partial \theta} - \sum_{t=j}^{n_i} \frac{\partial E(x_{i, \pi_i^{-1}(t)}; \theta)}{\partial \theta} P(x_{i, \pi_i^{-1}(t)}; \theta) \Big)$$
$$\text{if} \quad 0 \leq E_{list}(\pi_i; \theta) \leq M$$

It is worth noting that the above model is just one example of listwise approaches based on the energy oriented perspective of ListMLE. In the future work, we will explore to cast other existing listwise L2R models into the energy-based ranking framework, which may offer further insights into devising new listwise techniques.

6. EXPERIMENTS

6.1 Testbeds

We use the benchmark datasets from the LETOR 4.0 learning to rank testbeds[1]. The datasets includes two tasks, MQ2007 and MQ2008, which are drawn from the data in TREC 2007 and 2008 collection. Table 3 provides the statistics about the two corpora. The size of the MQ2007 dataset is larger than that of MQ2008 in terms of the number of queries (1,692 vs. 784) and query-document pairs (69,623 vs. 15,211). The average number of documents per query in the MQ2007 dataset is two times larger than that in the MQ2008 dataset, while the number of documents per query in the MQ2008 dataset is more varied (22.074 vs. 6.684). Each example in the dataset stands for a query-document pair, which is represented by 46 features related to information retrieval such as TF-IDF similarity measures between query and document, PageRank,

---

[1] http://research.microsoft.com/en-us/um/beijing/projects/letor//letor4dataset.aspx

Table 3: Statistics of the LETOR 4.0 datasets

	MQ2007	MQ2008
#queries	1,692	784
#query-document pairs	69,623	15,211
#Min. documents per query	6	5
#Max. documents per query	147	121
#Avg. documents per query	41.148	19.402
#Std. documents per query	6.684	22.074

and BM25 [22]. The relevance between a query and document is judged on three levels $\{0, 1, 2\}$ with 2 being most relevant.

Each task is partitioned for five-fold cross validation, including training (60%), validation (20%), and test (20%) data sets. All the proposed energy-based approaches as well as the baselines are trained using the entire training data, and their performance is evaluated on the test data. The parameters are determined on the validation data. We use coarse grid search to tune model parameters (see Section 7.1) and report the mean test values and perform statistical significance tests across 30 runs of 5-fold cross validation (see Section 7.3).

6.2 Baselines

We compare the three proposed energy-based learning to rank models against the following state-of-the-art pointwise, pairwise, and listwise learning to rank methods [16]. For pointwise approaches, we choose L_2-regularized linear regression, L_2-regularized logistic regression, and support vector machine (SVM). We rely on the Scikit-learn package [21] to train and test those models with multiple regularization parameters. For pairwise approaches, we use RankNet [3] and RankSVM [10]. RankLib[2] is used to train and test RankNet models with default parameters; and we use SVM^{rank}[3] to train and test RankSVM[4]. For listwise approaches, we use ListMLE [29] with linear neural network as ranking function. All these baselines are also formulated as energy-based ranking models in Section 4. We will make our source code publicly available.

6.3 Evaluation Metrics

In the experiments, we use the following metrics for evaluation: (1) Precision at position k (P@k) where k is set to 5, 10, 15, and 20, respectively; (2) Mean Average Precision (MAP), which measures the averaged P@k of all queries; (3) Normalized Discount Cumulative Gain at position k (NDCG@k), which measures the ranking quality for each query at position k. We choose k as 5, 10, 15, and 20; (4) Mean Reciprocal Rank (MRR), which measures the averaged rank position of the first relevant document for each query; and (5) Mean Squared Error (MSE), which measures the differences between predicted relevance labels and ground truth labels. This metric is only applicable to evaluate pointwise approaches. We rely on the TREC evaluation script[5] to calculate these metrics.

7. RESULTS

7.1 Parameter Analysis

We first examine the impact of parameters γ, M, and k on our proposed energy-based pointwise, pairwise, and listwise learning

---

[2]https://sourceforge.net/p/lemur/wiki/RankLib/

[3]https://www.cs.cornell.edu/people/tj/svm_light/svm_rank.html

[4]http://research.microsoft.com/en-us/um/beijing/projects/letor/LETOR4.0/Baselines/RankSVM-Struct.html

[5]http://trec.nist.gov/trec_eval/

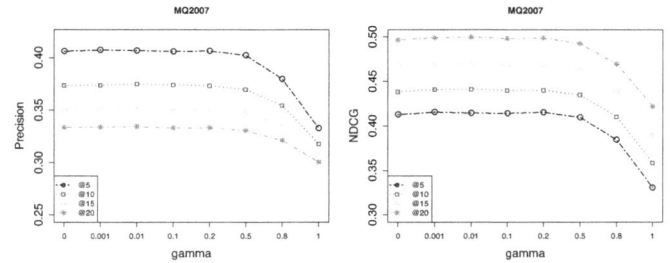

Figure 3: Average metrics in 5 runs of energy-based pointwise approach with different γ on MQ2007 dataset

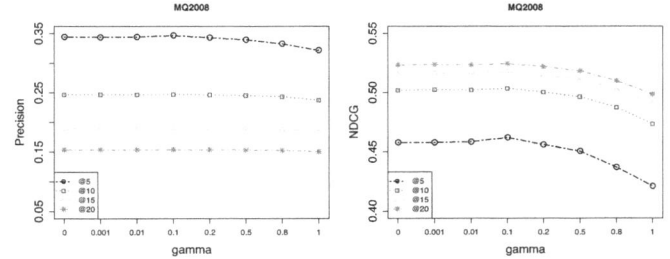

Figure 4: Average metrics in 5 runs of energy-based pointwise approach with different γ on MQ2008 dataset

to rank approaches introduced in section 5, respectively and thus determine the parameter settings. Figure 3 to 8 show the average Precision and NDCG values at different levels achieved by different parameters across 5 runs of 5 fold cross validation on the MQ2007 and MQ2008 tasks.

For pointwise approaches, Figure 3 and 4 show that when γ is set between 0 and 0.2 on the MQ2007 dataset and 0 and 0.1 on the MQ2008 dataset, the precision and NDCG values remain stable, indicating that the exponential component in the square-exponential loss function plays a less important role than the square component does. Those γ values are good choices. When γ becomes larger, the metrics start to decrease quickly except the precision values on the MQ2008 dataset. We select $\gamma = 0.001$ for the MQ2007 dataset and $\gamma = 0.1$ for the MQ2008 dataset based on the performance on the validation set. For pairwise approaches (see Figure 5 and Figure 6), as M increases from 0.001 to 10.0, the precision and NDCG scores at all levels decrease on both datasets. Thus, we set $M = 0.001$. For listwise approaches (see Figure 7 and 8), we have two parameters for tuning, M and k. For MQ2007 dataset, the precision and NDCG values are increasing when k increases from 1 to 5, and they start to decrease when $k = 10$. Therefore, we set $k = 5$. While M is growing until $M = 1.0$, both precision and

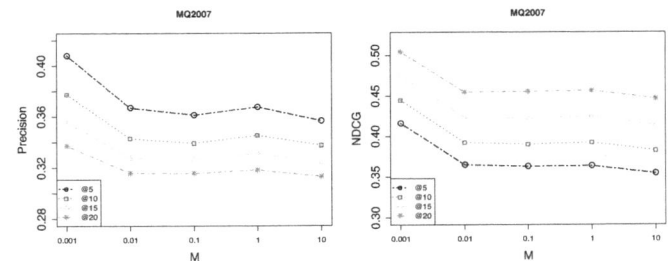

Figure 5: Average metrics in 5 runs of energy-based pairwise approach with different M on MQ2007 dataset

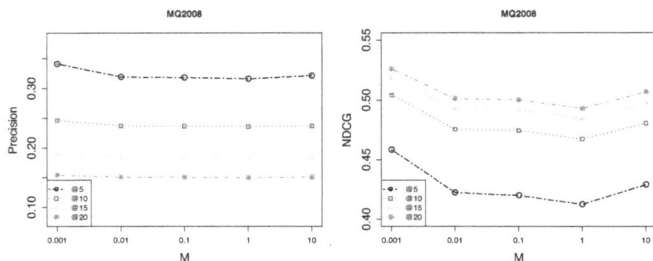

Figure 6: Average metrics in 5 runs of energy-based pairwise approach with different M on MQ2008 dataset

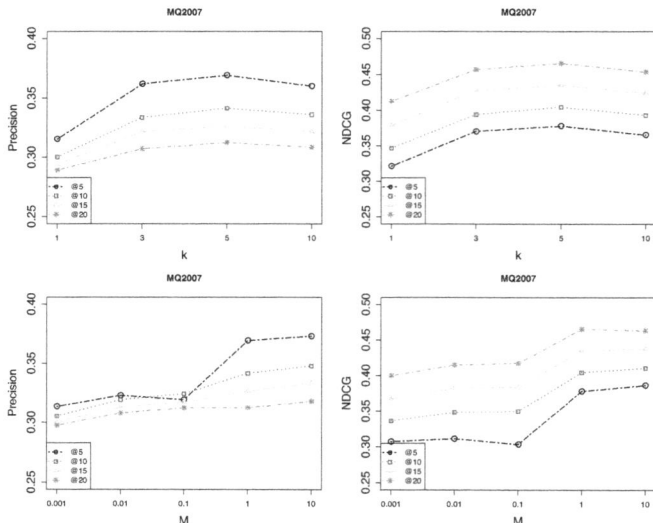

Figure 7: Average metrics in 5 runs of energy-based listwise approach with different M and k on MQ2007 dataset

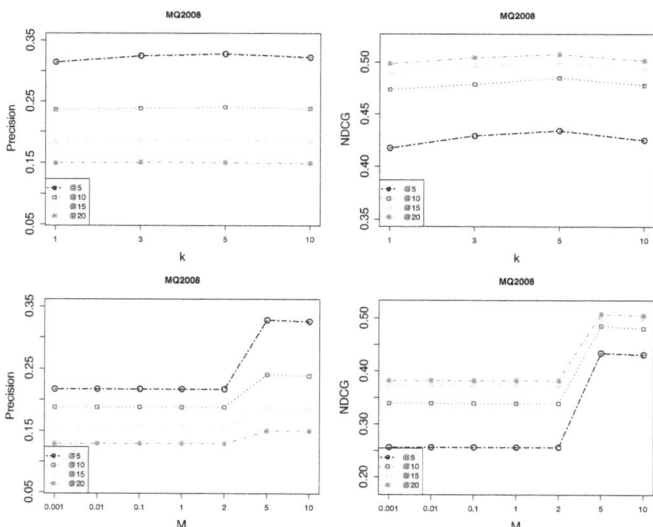

Figure 8: Average metrics in 5 runs of energy-based listwise approach with different M and k on MQ2008 dataset

Table 4: Parameters for Energy-based Approaches

Model	Parameter	MQ2007	MQ2008
Pointwise	# of iterations	20	20
	L_2-Regularizer	0.1	0.1
	Learning rate	5e-4	5e-4
	γ	0.001	0.001
Pairwise	# of iterations	10	10
	L_2-Regularizer	0.1	0.1
	Learning rate	1e-4	1e-4
	M	1.0	0.1
	k	5	1
Listwise	# of iterations	10	10
	L_2-Regularizer	0.1	0.1
	Learning rate	1e-4	1e-5
	M	1.0	5.0
	k	5	5

NDCG scores are increasing and they slighly decrease when M is getting larger. Thus, we choose $M = 1.0$. For MQ2008 dataset, the NDCG values decrease and precision values remain relatively stable when k is growing, but they reach the peak when k is set to 5, so we set $k = 5$. Regarding M, both precision and NDCG values remain unchanged when M is increasing from 0.001 to 2.0. The metrics start to increase when M is set to 5.0 and decrease slightly afterwards. Thus, $M = 5.0$ seems a good choice.

We also experiment with different settings of other parameters, e.g., L_2-regularizer, learning rate, and number of SGD iterations, but leave out their analysis. The parameter settings obtained for our proposed methods are shown in Table 4.

7.2 Analysis of Shaping Energy Surface

Recall that training an energy-based learning to rank model aims to shape an energy function that produces the best ranking results given a set of documents retrieved by a query. The best ranking list is expected to have the lowest energy than all other permutations. We demonstrate the changes of energy function that is defined on the listwise approach introduced in Section 5.3. Figure 9 plots the curve of decreasing rate of energy of sum of documents ranked in top-5 positions (Eqn.(29)) and that of contrastive documents that are ranked from the 5-th position to the bottom (Eqn.(30)) over 30 rounds of SGD on the MQ2008 dataset. As we can see, at the beginning of the SGD algorithm, the energy of desired documents are decreasing sharply (over 100%), and the energy of undesired documents are also decreasing but with a very tiny rate (around 1%), which is hardly seen in the figure. After 10 rounds of SGD, the decreasing rate of the energy of desired documents reduces to 10%, while the decreasing rate of energy of undesired documents remains consistently low. The SGD algorithm ends up with the energy of desired documents decreased to just 3% of the energy obtained at the beginning, and energy of undesired documents decreased to only 70% compared with the original energy. Hence, the energy function defined over all ranked lists are decreasing during the training phase, due to that the energy of all documents are pushed down, but not as hard as it is pushed down by the first term.

7.3 Baseline Comparison

The results for the two tasks achieved by different learning to rank methods obtained using the parameter settings in Section 7.1 are shown in Table 5 and Table 6. Boldface stands for best performance with respect to each evaluation metric for pointwise, pairwise, and listwise learning to rank methods, respectively. As pair-

Table 5: Average performance on MQ2007 dataset

Method	MAP	MRR	P@5	P@10	P@15	P@20	N@5	N@10	N@15	N@20	MSE
Linear Regression	0.4257	0.5393	0.3797	0.3546	0.3378	0.3238	0.3803	0.4087	0.4399	0.4712	0.3094
Logistic Regression	0.3393	0.4388	0.2915	0.2825	0.2749	0.2684	0.2746	0.2985	0.3249	0.3540	0.4196
SVM	0.3308	0.4129	0.2805	0.2764	0.2708	0.2659	0.2570	0.2835	0.3113	0.3414	0.4241
Energy-based Pointwise	**0.4520**	**0.5622**	**0.4074**	**0.3737**	**0.3509**	**0.3335**	**0.4153**	**0.4402**	**0.4695**	**0.4989**	**0.3060**
RankNet	0.4279	0.5316	0.3727	0.3480	0.3337	0.3206	0.3755	0.4042	0.4372	0.4695	-
RankSVM	**0.4637**	**0.5762**	**0.4133**	**0.3810**	**0.3587**	**0.3380**	**0.4246**	**0.4517**	**0.4825**	**0.5091**	-
Energy-based Pairwise	0.4583	0.5672	0.4078	0.3773	0.3556	0.3371	0.4162	0.4445	0.475	0.5043	-
ListMLE	0.3967	0.5048	0.3412	0.3218	0.3116	0.3023	0.3457	0.3748	0.4074	0.4395	-
Energy-based Listwise	**0.4212**	**0.5306**	**0.3692**	**0.3416**	**0.3266**	**0.3125**	**0.3779**	**0.4043**	**0.4351**	**0.4653**	-

Table 6: Average performance on MQ2008 dataset

Method	MAP	MRR	P@5	P@10	P@15	P@20	N@5	N@10	N@15	N@20	MSE
Linear Regression	0.4332	0.4958	0.3214	0.2367	0.1845	0.1508	0.4231	0.4733	0.4917	0.5002	0.2878
Logistic Regression	0.3290	0.4023	0.2306	0.1916	0.1584	0.1299	0.2919	0.3666	0.3975	0.4069	0.3725
SVM	0.3124	0.3670	0.2194	0.1885	0.1569	0.1293	0.2645	0.3463	0.3787	0.3885	0.3769
Energy-based Pointwise	**0.4651**	**0.5250**	**0.3464**	**0.2469**	**0.1887**	**0.1534**	**0.4618**	**0.5034**	**0.5173**	**0.5244**	**0.2764**
RankNet	0.4360	0.4893	0.3168	0.2329	0.1816	0.1481	0.4181	0.4694	0.4875	0.4960	-
RankSVM	**0.4707**	0.5266	**0.3477**	**0.2487**	**0.1894**	0.1536	**0.4630**	**0.5080**	**0.5214**	**0.5286**	-
Energy-based Pairwise	0.4677	**0.5279**	0.3412	0.2464	0.1892	**0.1541**	0.4585	0.5043	0.5184	0.5262	-
ListMLE	0.4308	0.4877	0.3128	0.2353	0.1821	0.1491	0.4159	0.4723	0.4889	0.4980	-
Energy-based Listwise	**0.4445**	**0.5046**	**0.3278**	**0.2402**	**0.1843**	**0.1497**	**0.4337**	**0.4849**	**0.4995**	**0.5073**	-

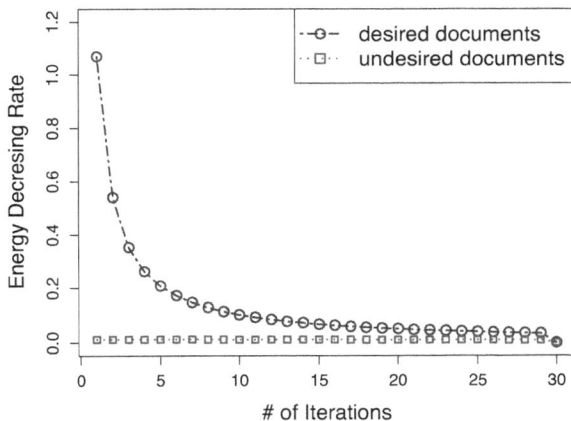

Figure 9: The effect of training on the energy surface in the listwise case on MQ2008 dataset

wise and listwise L2R approaches are not designed to predict relevance for documents, we do not report the MSEs obtained in these two cases.

In comparison with the results achieved on the two tasks, the precision scores (MAP and P@N) obtained on the MQ2007 dataset are consistently higher than that obtained on the MQ2008 dataset for all L2R approaches. This may be due to the fact that the number of query-document pairs of the MQ2007 dataset is four times larger than that of the MQ2008 dataset. Therefore, more training instances contribute to the better performance of identifying relevant documents. On the contrary, the scores (MRR and NDCG@N) achieved on the MQ2007 dataset is lower than that achieved on the MQ2008 dataset, which may be caused by the larger number of averaged documents per query in the MQ2007 dataset (see Table 3).

For pointwise approaches, linear regression yields better results in terms of all the evaluation metrics on both tasks than the other two pointwise baselines, logistic regression and SVM do. Our proposed energy-based pointwise method achieves the best performance over all the pointwise baselines with statistically significant improvement ($p < 0.001$) for all precision and ranking evaluation metrics. On the MQ2007 dataset, the energy based pointwise approach achieves more than 20% of precision values than logistic regression and SVM do, and 3% than linear regression does. In terms of NDCG values, the proposed model can obtain more than 40% of improvement compared with logistic regression and SVM, and 5% of improvement over linear regression. On the MQ2008 dataset, the improvement on the precision values are over 15% compared with logistic regression and SVM, and over 1% compared with linear regression. The model also yields significant MSEs on both datasets with $p = 0.05$ and $p < 0.001$. It outperforms linear regression by 1.1% on the MQ2007 dataset and 3.96% on the MQ2008 dataset.

For pairwise approaches, RankSVM shows better results than RankNet does for all evaluation metrics on both tasks. Our proposed energy-based pairwise method outperforms RankNet significantly ($p < 0.001$) on all evaluation metrics on both datasets. The model outperforms RankNet in terms of precision values by at least 5% and NDCG values by 7% on the MQ2007 dataset; and it achieves more than 4% of precision values and 6% of NDCG values on the MQ2008 dataset. The energy-based pairwise approach yields competitive results with RankSVM does with slightly lower precision and ranking scores on both datasets (except MRR and P@20 obtained on the MQ2008 dataset) without significant difference. The difference of all evaluation metrics achieved by RankSVM and our proposed model is just around 1% for both tasks. The best performance obtained by pairwise approach is higher or competitive with the best performance obtained by pointwise L2R approaches.

For listwise approaches, the results obtained by ListMLE and our proposed models are slightly inferior to that obtained by pointwise and pairwise approaches for both tasks. Our proposed energy-based listwise approach yields significant results over ListMLE ($p = 0.01$) on both datasets in terms of all precision and NDCG scores. On the MQ2007 dataset, the proposed model outperforms ListMLE by 3% for precision values and 5% for NDCG values. On the MQ2008 dataset, the improvement on the precision values is over 1% except P@20 and that on the NDCG values is over 1%.

In summary, our proposed energy-based pointwise and listwise methods surpass the corresponding learning to rank baselines with significant improvement. For the pairwise approach, the proposed model outperforms RankNet with a significant margin and achieves competitive results with RankSVM. Our results differ from the previous ones on LETOR in the following way. The energy-based pairwise method achieves the best performance consistently across the two tasks, despite the fact that the previous studies favored listwise approaches [29, 4]. This may be due to the fact that the tasks used for experiments are different. The dataset used for their study is LETOR 3.0, while we use LETOR 4.0 for experiments. Another possible reason is that we only use linear models to construct our energy functions in the experiments. We leave experimenting with nonlinear models and larger testbeds in our future work.

8. CONCLUSION AND FUTURE WORK

In this paper, we establish the link between learning to rank and energy-based learning. We cast various existing L2R models in a unified energy-based ranking framework. Moreover, we present several new energy-based ranking models based on the established link. The experiments are conducted on the LETOR 4.0 benchmark datasets and demonstrate the effectiveness of the proposed models.

This work is an initial step towards a promising research direction. In the future work, we will cast more sophisticated L2R models in the energy-based framework and propose new ranking algorithms accordingly. Furthermore, we plan to investigate latent variable architectures where energy functions depend on a set of hidden variables whose correct values are unobserved. The use of latent variables in ranking may be able to model the hidden characteristics of queries, documents, and relevance. We will also explore deep architectures based on the energy-based models with hierarchical latent variables. Last but not the least, the existing energy-based learning theories may not be directly applied to ranking. We will conduct theoretical analysis for energy-based ranking such as necessary or sufficient conditions for energy and loss functions and generalization ability and statistical consistency of energy-based ranking models. The new theories may utilize the energy-based perspective to help explain and justify the choices of loss functions in L2R.

9. REFERENCES

[1] A. Bordes, X. Glorot, J. Weston, and Y. Bengio. A semantic matching energy function for learning with multi-relational data. *Machine Learning*, 94(2):233–259, 2014.

[2] P. Brakel, D. Stroobandt, and B. Schrauwen. Training energy-based models for time-series imputation. *JMLR*, 14(1):2771–2797, 2013.

[3] C. Burges, T. Shaked, E. Renshaw, A. Lazier, M. Deeds, N. Hamilton, and G. Hullender. Learning to rank using gradient descent. In *ICML*, pages 89–96. ACM, 2005.

[4] Z. Cao, T. Qin, T.-Y. Liu, M.-F. Tsai, and H. Li. Learning to rank: from pairwise approach to listwise approach. In *ICML*, pages 129–136. ACM, 2007.

[5] S. Chopra, R. Hadsell, and Y. LeCun. Learning a similarity metric discriminatively, with application to face verification. In *CVPR*, volume 1, pages 539–546. IEEE, 2005.

[6] D. Cossock and T. Zhang. Subset ranking using regression. In *Learning theory*, pages 605–619. Springer, 2006.

[7] X. Driancourt, L. Bottou, and P. Gallinari. Learning vector quantization, multi layer perceptron and dynamic programming: comparison and cooperation. In *IJCNN*, volume 2, pages 815–819. IEEE, 1991.

[8] Y. Freund, R. Iyer, R. E. Schapire, and Y. Singer. An efficient boosting algorithm for combining preferences. *JMLR*, 4:933–969, 2003.

[9] N. Heess, D. Silver, and Y. W. Teh. Actor-critic reinforcement learning with energy-based policies. In *EWRL*, pages 43–58, 2012.

[10] T. Joachims. Optimizing search engines using clickthrough data. In *SIGKDD*, pages 133–142, 2002.

[11] Y. LeCun, S. Chopra, R. Hadsell, M. Ranzato, and F. Huang. A tutorial on energy-based learning. *Predicting structured data*, 1:0, 2006.

[12] Y. LeCun, S. Chopra, M. Ranzato, and F. J. Huang. Energy-based models in document recognition and computer vision. In *ICDAR*, volume 7, pages 337–341, 2007.

[13] Y. LeCun and F. J. Huang. Loss functions for discriminative training of energy-based models. In *AISTATS*, 2005.

[14] J. Lei, G. Li, D. Tu, and Q. Guo. Convolutional restricted boltzmann machines learning for robust visual tracking. *Neural Computing and Applications*, 25(6):1383–1391, 2014.

[15] H. Li. Learning to rank for information retrieval and natural language processing. *Synthesis Lectures on Human Language Technologies*, 7(3):1–121, 2014.

[16] T.-Y. Liu. Learning to rank for information retrieval. *Foundations and Trends in Information Retrieval*, 3(3):225–331, 2009.

[17] T.-Y. Liu, J. Xu, T. Qin, W. Xiong, and H. Li. Letor: Benchmark dataset for research on learning to rank for information retrieval. In *SIGIR Workshop on Learning to Rank for Information Retrieval*, pages 3–10, 2007.

[18] E. McDermott. *Discriminative training for speech recognition*. PhD thesis, Waseda University, 1997.

[19] R. Memisevic and G. E. Hinton. Learning to represent spatial transformations with factored higher-order boltzmann machines. *Neural Computation*, 22(6):1473–1492, 2010.

[20] M. Osadchy, Y. L. Cun, and M. L. Miller. Synergistic face detection and pose estimation with energy-based models. *JMLR*, 8:1197–1215, 2007.

[21] F. Pedregosa, G. Varoquaux, A. Gramfort, V. Michel, B. Thirion, O. Grisel, M. Blondel, P. Prettenhofer, R. Weiss, V. Dubourg, et al. Scikit-learn: Machine learning in python. *JMLR*, 12:2825–2830, 2011.

[22] T. Qin and T.-Y. Liu. Introducing letor 4.0 datasets. *arXiv preprint arXiv:1306.2597*, 2013.

[23] M. Ranzato, Y.-L. Boureau, S. Chopra, and L. Yann. A unified energy-based framework for unsupervised learning. In *AISTATS*, 2007.

[24] S. Rendle, C. Freudenthaler, Z. Gantner, and L. Schmidt-Thieme. Bpr: Bayesian personalized ranking from implicit feedback. In *UAI*, pages 452–461. AUAI Press, 2009.

[25] A. R. Sankar and V. N. Balasubramanian. Similarity-based contrastive divergence methods for energy-based deep learning models. In *ACML*, pages 391–406, 2015.

[26] G. W. Taylor and G. E. Hinton. Factored conditional restricted boltzmann machines for modeling motion style. In *ICML*, pages 1025–1032. ACM, 2009.

[27] M. N. Volkovs and R. S. Zemel. Boltzrank: learning to maximize expected ranking gain. In *ICML*, pages 1089–1096. ACM, 2009.

[28] M. Welling, M. Rosen-Zvi, and G. E. Hinton. Exponential family harmoniums with an application to information retrieval. In *NIPS*, pages 1481–1488, 2004.

[29] F. Xia, T.-Y. Liu, J. Wang, W. Zhang, and H. Li. Listwise approach to learning to rank: theory and algorithm. In *ICML*, pages 1192–1199. ACM, 2008.

[30] J. Xu and H. Li. Adarank: a boosting algorithm for information retrieval. In *SIGIR*, pages 391–398. ACM, 2007.

[31] X. Zhang. *PAC-Learning for Energy-based Models*. PhD thesis, Courant Institute of Mathematical Sciences New York, 2013.

Bag-of-Entities Representation for Ranking

Chenyan Xiong
Language Technologies Institute
Carnegie Mellon University
Pittsburgh, PA 15213, USA
cx@cs.cmu.edu

Jamie Callan
Language Technologies Institute
Carnegie Mellon University
Pittsburgh, PA 15213, USA
callan@cs.cmu.edu

Tie-Yan Liu
Microsoft Research
Beijing, 100080, P. R. China
tie-yan.liu@microsoft.com

ABSTRACT

This paper presents a new bag-of-entities representation for document ranking, with the help of modern knowledge bases and automatic entity linking. Our system represents query and documents by bag-of-entities vectors constructed from their entity annotations, and ranks documents by their matches with the query in the entity space. Our experiments with Freebase on TREC Web Track datasets demonstrate that current entity linking systems can provide sufficient coverage of the general domain search task, and that bag-of-entities representations outperform bag-of-words by as much as 18% in standard document ranking tasks.

Keywords

Text Representation, Document Representation, Knowledge Base, Bag-of-Entities

1. INTRODUCTION

In the earliest information retrieval systems, query and documents were represented by terms manually picked from predefined controlled vocabularies [6]. The controlled vocabulary representation conveys clean and distilled information, and can be ranked accurately by simple methods. However, it also requires manual annotations and suffers from the small size of controlled vocabularies, thus is mainly used for specific search domains. As full-text search became popular, query and documents are mainly represented by their bag-of-words vectors, and more sophisticated ranking models are used to rank documents in the word space.

Recently, knowledge bases, as the modern version of controlled vocabularies but at larger scale, have provided a new opportunity to improve ranking. The rich semantic information in knowledge bases has been successfully used by ranking systems to better understand general domain queries, for example, to generate better expansion terms [8], richer learning to rank features [1], and additional connections between query and documents [5, 7]. Also, automatic entity annotation is made possible by entity linking research, and is

ICTIR '16, September 12-16, 2016, Newark, DE, USA

© 2016 ACM. ISBN 978-1-4503-4497-5/16/09. . . $15.00

DOI: http://dx.doi.org/10.1145/2970398.2970423

becoming increasingly efficient and effective for both query and documents.

This paper presents a new bag-of-entities based representation for document ranking, as a heritage of the classic controlled vocabulary based representation, but with the aid of modern large scale knowledge bases and automatic entity linking systems. We represent query and documents by their bag-of-entities constructed from the annotations provided by three entity linking systems: Google's `FACC1` [3] with high precision, `CMNS` [4] with high recall, and `TagMe` [2] with balanced precision and recall. With the deeper text understanding provided by entity linking, documents can be ranked by their overlap with the query in the entity's explicit semantic space.

To investigate the effectiveness of bag-of-entities representations, we conducted experiments with a state-of-the-art knowledge base, Freebase, and two large scale web corpora, ClueWeb09-B and ClueWeb12-B13, together with their queries from the TREC Web Track. Our evaluation results first confirm that current entity linking systems can provide sufficient coverage over general domain queries and documents. Then we compare bag-of-entities with bag-of-words in standard document ranking tasks and demonstrate that although the accuracy of entity linking is not perfect (about $50\% - 60\%$ on TREC Web Track queries), the ranking performance can be improved by as much as 18% with bag-of-entities representations.

2. BAG-OF-ENTITIES REPRESENTATION

We construct bag-of-entities representations for queries and documents using several entity linking systems. When annotating texts, an entity linking system does not just match the n-grams with entity names, but makes the decision jointly by also considering external evidences such as the entity's descriptions and relationships in the knowledge base, and corpus statistics like commonness, linked probability and contexts of entities. As a result, representing texts by entities naturally incorporates deeper text understanding from the linking process: Entity synonyms are aligned, polysemy in entity mentions is disambiguated, and global coherence between entities is incorporated.

The choice of knowledge base in this paper is Freebase, one of the largest public knowledge bases frequently used in recent IR research [1, 5, 7, 8]. Several entity linking systems have been developed for it. This work explore the following three popular ones to annotate queries and documents with Freebase entities.

FACC1 is the Freebase annotation of TREC queries and ClueWeb corpora provided by Google [3]. It aims to achieve high precision, which is believed to be around 80-85% based on a small-scale human evaluation[1].

TagMe is an entity linking system [2] widely used in prior research [4, 7]. It balances precision and recall, both at about 60% in various evaluations.

CMNS is an entity linking system that spots texts using surface forms from FACC1 annotation, and links all of them to their most frequently linked entities [4]. It can achieve almost 100% recall on some query entity linking datasets, but the precision may be lower [4].

Given the annotations of a query or document, we construct its bag-of-entities vector $\vec{E}_q$ or $\vec{E}_d$, in which each dimension ($\vec{E}_q(e)$ or $\vec{E}_d(e)$) refers to an entity e in Freebase, and its weight is the frequency of that entity appears in the annotation of the query or the document.

The bag-of-entities representation uses entities as its basic information unit. As with controlled vocabulary terms, entities are more informative than words. However, whereas controlled vocabulary terms are often assigned manually, entity linking is done automatically, which is more efficient but also more uncertain. With controlled vocabularies, simple ranking methods such as Boolean retrieval work well, because the representation is clean and distilled [6], while with bag-of-words more sophisticated ranking models are more effective. Given the heritage to the classic controlled vocabulary based search systems, we start simple and use the following two basic ranking models to study the power of bag-of-entities representations.

Coordinate Match (COOR) ranks a document by the number of query entities it contains:

$$f_{\text{COOR}}(q,d) = \sum_{e:\vec{E}_q(e)>0} \mathbb{1}(\vec{E}_d(e) > 0) \qquad (1)$$

Entity Frequency (EF) ranks document by the frequency of query entities in it:

$$f_{\text{EF}}(q,d) = \sum_{e:\vec{E}_q(e)>0} \vec{E}_q(e) \log(\vec{E}_d(e)) \qquad (2)$$

$f_{\text{COOR}}(q,d)$ and $f_{\text{EF}}(q,d)$ are the ranking scores of document d for query q using coordinate match (**COOR**) and entity frequency (**EF**) respectively. $\mathbb{1}(\cdot)$ is the indicator function.

COOR performs Boolean retrieval, which is the most basic ranking method and often works well with controlled vocabularies. **EF** studies the value of term frequency information, another basis for document ranking. These simple models investigate basic properties of ranking with bag-of-entities, and provide understanding and intuition for the future development of more advanced ranking models.

3. EXPERIMENT METHODOLOGY

Dataset: Our experiments are conducted on TREC Web Track datasets. TREC Web Tracks use two large web corpora: ClueWeb09 and ClueWeb12. We use the ClueWeb09-B and ClueWeb12-B13 subsets. There are 200 queries with relevance judgments from TREC 2009-2012 for ClueWeb09, and 100 queries in 2013-2014 for ClueWeb12. Manual annotations provided by Dalton et al. [1] and Liu et al. [5] are used as query annotation labels.

[1]http://lemurproject.org/clueweb09/FACC1/

Table 1: Entity linking performance on ClueWeb queries. All methods are evaluated by **Prec**ison, **Rec**all and **F1**.

	CW09 Query			CW12 Query		
	Prec	**Rec**	**F1**	**Prec**	**Rec**	**F1**
FACC1	0.274	0.236	0.254	NA	NA	NA
TagMe	0.581	0.597	0.589	0.460	0.555	0.503
CMNS	0.577	0.596	0.587	0.485	0.575	0.526

Indexing: We indexed both corpora with Indri, using their bag-of-words. Default stemming and stopword removal were used. Spam in ClueWeb09 was filtered using the default threshold (70%) of Waterloo spam scores. Spam filtering was not used for ClueWeb12 because its effectiveness is unclear. The evaluation of entity linking, and the re-ranking using bag-of-entities are performed on the top 100 documents per query retrieved by Indri's language model with default Dirichlet smoothing ($\mu = 2500$).

Entity Linking Systems: We used **TagMe** software provided by Ferragina et al. [2] to annotate queries and documents with Wikipedia entities, which are then aligned to Freebase entities using the Wikipedia ID field in Freebase. **CMNS** is implemented by ourselves, following Hasibi et al. [4]. The boundary overlaps of surface forms are resolved by only linking the earliest and then the longest one [4]. **FACC1** entity annotations for ClueWeb documents are provided by Google [3]. They also annotated ClueWeb09 queries' intent descriptions, but not the queries. We used the descriptions' annotations as approximations of queries' annotations, and manually filtered out entities that did not appear in the original queries to reduce disturbance. ClueWeb12's queries are not annotated by Google so we are only able to study **FACC1** annotations on ClueWeb09.

Baselines: We used two standard unsupervised bag-of-words ranking models as baselines: Indri's unstructured language model (**Lm**) and sequential dependency model (**SDM**), both with default parameters: $\mu = 2500$ for **Lm**, and query weights $(0.8, 0.1, 0.1)$ for **SDM**. Typically these baselines do well in competitive evaluations such as TREC. There are better rankers, for example learning to rank methods. However, methods that combine many sources of evidence usually outperform methods that use a single source of evidence, thus such comparison would not reveal much about the value of the bag-of-entities representation.

There were three representations for ClueWeb09 (**FACC1**, **TagMe** and **CMNS**), and two for ClueWeb12 (**TagMe** and **CMNS**). All annotations are done automatically. All annotated entities are used, since filtering using the annotation score lowers the annotation accuracy in our experiments. **COOR** and **EF** were used to *re-rank* the top 100 documents per query retrieved by **Lm**. Ties were broken by **Lm**'s score.

Evaluation Metrics: The entity annotations were evaluated by the lean evaluation metric from Hasibi et al. [4]. It averages the annotation performances (precision or recall) of at the whole query level, e.g. whether all entities in a query are correctly annotated or not, and on the individual entity level. The ranking performances were evaluated by the TREC Web Track Ad-hoc Task's official evaluation metrics: ERR@20 and NDCG@20. Statistical significance was tested by the Fisher randomization test (permutation test) with $p < 0.05$.

Table 2: Coverage of annotations. `Freq` and `Dens` are the average number of entities linked per query/document and per word respectively. `Missed` is the percentage of queries or documents that have no annotation at all. ClueWeb12 queries do not have `FACC1` annotations as they are published later than `FACC1`.

	ClueWeb09						ClueWeb12					
	Query			Document			Query			Document		
	Freq	Dens	Missed	Freq	Dens	Missed	Freq	Dens	Missed	Freq	Dens	Missed
FACC1	0.42	0.20	62%	15.95	0.13	30%	NA	NA	NA	24.52	0.06	26%
TagMe	1.54	0.70	1%	92.31	0.20	2%	1.77	0.57	0%	246.76	0.37	0%
CMNS	1.50	0.69	1%	252.41	0.55	0%	1.75	0.55	0%	324.37	0.48	0%

4. EVALUATION RESULTS

This section evaluates the accuracy and coverage of entity annotations, and bag-of-entities' performance in ranking.

4.1 Annotation Accuracy and Coverage

Table 1 shows the precision, recall, and F1 of `FACC1`, `TagMe` and `CMNS` on ClueWeb queries. `TagMe` performs the best on ClueWeb09 queries with higher precision, while `CMNS` performs better on ClueWeb12 queries. The ClueWeb09 queries are more ambiguous because they needed to support the TREC Web Track's Diversity task; `TagMe`'s disambiguation was more useful on this set. ClueWeb12 queries needed to support risk minimization research, and have been shown to be harder; both systems perform worse on them. `FACC1` query annotation does not perform well as its goal was to annotate the query's description, not the query itself.

There is no gold standard entity annotation for ClueWeb documents. Nevertheless, our manual examination confirms that `FACC1` has high precision; `TagMe` performs a little better on documents with more contexts; and `CMNS` performs worse than `TagMe` on documents as it only uses the surface forms.

One concern of controlled vocabulary based search systems is the low coverage on general domain queries, restricting their usage mainly to specific domains. With the much larger scale of current knowledge bases, it is interesting to study whether they can influence the majority of general domain queries. Table 2 shows the coverage results of our entity annotations on ClueWeb queries and their top 100 retrieved documents. `Freq` and `Dens` are the average number of entities linked per query/document, and per word respectively. `Missed` is the percentage of queries/documents that have no linked entity. The results show that `TagMe` and `CMNS` have good coverage on ClueWeb queries and documents. Almost all queries and documents have at least one linked entity. The annotations are no longer sparse. There can be up to 324 entities linked per documents on average. However, precision and coverage have not been achieved together yet. `FACC1` has the highest precision but provides very few entities per document and misses many documents.

These results show that the entity linking is still an open research problem. Precision and coverage can not yet be achieved at the same time. Thus, the ranking method must be robust and able to accommodate a noisy representation.

4.2 Ranking Performance

The performances of bag-of-entities in ranking are shown in Table 3a. `EF` and `COOR` rerank top retrieved documents using the bag-of-entities from `FACC1`, `TagMe` and `CMNS`. The percentages are relative performances over `SDM`. W/T/L refer to the number of queries improved (Win), unchanged (Tie) and hurt (Loss) comparing with `SDM`.

On ClueWeb09, both `TagMe` and `CMNS` work well with `EF` and `COOR`, and outperform all baselines on all evaluation metrics. The best method, `TagMe-EF`, outperforms `SDM` as much as 18% on ERR@20. On ClueWeb12, `COOR` outperforms all baselines on all evaluation metrics by about 12%. These results demonstrate that even with current imperfect entity linking systems, bag-of-entities is a valuable representation on which very basic ranking models can significantly outperform standard bag-of-words based ranking.

Bag-of-entities' representation power correlates with the entity linking system's accuracy. ClueWeb09 queries are more ambiguous, favoring `TagMe` in annotation accuracy, and `TagMe` provides the most improvements when ranking for ClueWeb09 queries. ClueWeb12 queries have lower annotation quality, and bag-of-entities based ranking is not as powerful as on ClueWeb09 queries. `FACC1`'s coverage is too low and can not well represent the documents. This also explains why prior research mainly uses it as a pool to select query entities [1, 7, 8].

Entity linking is a rapidly developing area; improvement in the future is likely. To study how the bag-of-entities can benefit from improvements in annotation accuracy, we used the manual query annotations [1, 5] to divide queries into two groups: *Correctly Annotated*, whose ground truth entities are all correctly linked, and *Mistakenly Annotated*, whose entities are not all correctly linked. Table 3b shows the ranking performances of `TagMe` and `CMNS` on the two groups in ClueWeb09. We omit `FACC1` as it always hurts, and ClueWeb12 queries as there are not enough queries in either group to provide reliable observations. The relative performance, W/T/L and statistical significance over `SDM` are calculated on the same group of queries for each method. The results are as expected: On Correctly Annotated queries, bag-of-entities provides more accurate ranking; on Mistakenly Annotated queries, the improvements are smaller, and sometimes bag-of-entities reduces accuracy.

Our experiments show that intuitions developed for bag-of-words representations do not necessarily apply directly to bag-of-entitites representations. A long line of research shows that frequency based (e.g., tf.idf) ranking models are superior to Boolean ranking models. Thus, one might expect `EF` to provide consistently more accurate ranking than `COOR`, however that is not the case in our experiments. We found that the majority of annotation errors are missed annotations, which makes entity frequency counts less reliable. However, it is rare for the entity linker to miss every mention of an important entity in a document, thus the Boolean model is robust to this majority type of errors.

We also examined the effectiveness of other ranking intuitions, such as inverse document frequency (idf) and document length normalization. In our bag-of-entities represen-

Table 3: Ranking accuracy of bag-of-entities based ranking models. FACC1, TagMe and CMNS refer to the bag-of-entities representation constructed from each type of annotation. COOR and EF refer to the coordinate match and entity frequency ranking models. Percentages show the relative changes compared to SDM. **W/T/L** are the number of queries improved (**W**in), unchanged (**T**ie) and hurt (**L**oss) compared to SDM. † and ‡ indicate statistic significance ($p < 0.05$ in permutation test) over Lm and SDM. The best method for each metric is marked **bold**.

(a) Overall Accuracy

	ClueWeb09						ClueWeb12					
	NDCG@20		ERR@20		W/T/L		NDCG@20		ERR@20		W/T/L	
Lm	0.176	-12.92%	0.119	-5.23%	39/88/71		0.106	-2.10%	0.086	-4.69%	28/29/43	
SDM	$0.202^{\dagger}$	–	$0.126^{\dagger}$	–	–		0.108	–	0.090	–	–	
FACC1-COOR	0.173	-14.16%	0.126	-0.21%	64/56/78		NA	NA	NA	NA	NA	
FACC1-EF	0.167	-17.32%	0.116	-8.14%	63/51/84		NA	NA	NA	NA	NA	
TagMe-COOR	$0.211^{\dagger}$	4.55%	$0.133^{\dagger}$	5.55%	108/35/55		$0.117^{\dagger,\ddagger}$	8.35%	$0.095^{\dagger}$	5.02%	42/20/38	
TagMe-EF	$\mathbf{0.229^{\dagger,\ddagger}}$	**13.71%**	$0.149^{\dagger}$	**18.04%**	96/24/78		0.107	-0.90%	0.091	1.08%	42/18/40	
CMNS-COOR	$0.210^{\dagger}$	4.08%	$0.131^{\dagger}$	4.21%	105/37/56		$\mathbf{0.120^{\dagger,\ddagger}}$	**11.03%**	$0.101^{\dagger}$	11.20%	43/22/35	
CMNS-EF	$0.216^{\dagger}$	6.97%	0.136	7.52%	97/22/79		0.110	2.03%	**0.102**	**12.71%**	36/20/44	

(b) Accuracy on queries whose entities are all correctly annotated and those whose are not all correctly annotated. The relative performance, **W/T/L** and statistical significance are calculated by comparing with SDM on the same query set for each method.

	Correctly Annotated Queries						Mistakenly Annotated Queries					
	NDCG@20		ERR@20		W/T/L		NDCG@20		ERR@20		W/T/L	
TagMe-COOR	$0.214^{\dagger,\ddagger}$	14.56%	$0.153^{\dagger,\ddagger}$	12.71%	59/16/17		$0.200^{\dagger}$	−3.28%	0.111	−1.93%	49/21/38	
TagMe-EF	$\mathbf{0.243^{\dagger,\ddagger}}$	**30.43%**	$\mathbf{0.178^{\dagger,\ddagger}}$	**31.19%**	53/10/29		0.209	0.65%	0.118	4.30%	43/16/49	
CMNS-COOR	$0.211^{\dagger}$	4.28%	$0.146^{\dagger}$	4.89%	53/22/20		$\mathbf{0.201^{\dagger}}$	**3.90%**	**0.112**	**3.40%**	52/17/36	
CMNS-EF	$0.240^{\dagger,\ddagger}$	18.44%	0.168	20.74%	52/11/32		0.185	−4.09%	0.100	−8.12%	45/13/47	

tations they did not provide improvements when used individually or in language modeling and BM25 rankers. We speculate that idf had less impact because most queries contained just one or two entities, thus most of the queries were 'short' in the entity space; idf is known to be less important for short queries. We also speculate that the lack of improvement from document length normalization is related to the lack of improvement from frequency based weighting (EF), as discussed above. Our work suggests that better ranking will require thinking carefully about models designed for the unique characteristics of entities, rather than simply assuming that entities behave like words.

5. CONCLUSIONS AND FUTURE WORK

This paper presents a new bag-of-entities representation for ranking documents. Query and documents are represented by bag-of-entities representations developed from entity annotations, and ranking is performed by matching them in the entity space. Experiments on TREC Web Track datasets demonstrate that the coverage of bag-of-entities representations is sufficient and bag-of-entities representations can outperform bag-of-words representations by as much as 18% in standard document ranking tasks.

Entity linking is a rapidly-developing research area; its further improvements is likely to improve ranking accuracy, for example by providing more reliable entity frequencies. The bag-of-entities provides new evidence from knowledge bases, but also introduces new types of errors and uncertainties. How to better utilize bag-of-entities' strength and handle its noises is an important future research direction.

Prior research on using knowledge bases for search was mainly query-based, for example, selecting a few entities for the query and using them to enhance the bag-of-words

based ranking [1, 5, 7, 8]. This work focuses more on the document representation and operates directly in the entity space. How to combine the earlier work with the work described in this paper is another open problem.

6. ACKNOWLEDGMENTS

This research was supported by National Science Foundation (NSF) grant IIS-1422676. Any opinions, findings, and conclusions expressed in this paper are the authors' and do not necessarily reflect those of the sponsors.

7. REFERENCES

[1] J. Dalton, L. Dietz, and J. Allan. Entity query feature expansion using knowledge base links. In *Proceedings of the 37th Annual International ACM SIGIR Conference on Research and Development in Information Retrieval (SIGIR 2014)*, pages 365–374. ACM, 2014.

[2] P. Ferragina and U. Scaiella. Fast and accurate annotation of short texts with Wikipedia pages. *arXiv preprint arXiv:1006.3498*, 2010.

[3] E. Gabrilovich, M. Ringgaard, and A. Subramanya. FACC1: Freebase annotation of ClueWeb corpora, Version 1 (Release date 2013-06-26, Format version 1, Correction level 0), June 2013.

[4] F. Hasibi, K. Balog, and S. E. Bratsberg. Entity linking in queries: Tasks and evaluation. In *Proceedings of the first ACM International Conference on The Theory of Information Retrieval (ICTIR 2015)*, pages 171–180. ACM, 2015.

[5] X. Liu and H. Fang. Latent entity space: A novel retrieval approach for entity-bearing queries. *Information Retrieval Journal*, 18(6):473–503, 2015.

[6] G. Salton and M. J. McGill. Introduction to modern information retrieval. 1986.

[7] C. Xiong and J. Callan. EsdRank: Connecting query and documents through external semi-structured data. In *Proceedings of the 24th ACM International Conference on Information and Knowledge Management (CIKM 2015)*, pages 951–960. ACM, 2015.

[8] C. Xiong and J. Callan. Query expansion with Freebase. In *Proceedings of the first ACM International Conference on the Theory of Information Retrieval (ICTIR 2015)*, pages 111–120. ACM, 2015.

On Horizontal and Vertical Separation
in Hierarchical Text Classification

Mostafa Dehghani[1] Hosein Azarbonyad[2] Jaap Kamps[1] Maarten Marx[2]

[1]Institute for Logic, Language and Computation, University of Amsterdam, The Netherlands
[2]Informatics Institute, University of Amsterdam, The Netherlands
{dehghani,h.azarbonyad,kamps,maartenmarx}@uva.nl

ABSTRACT

Hierarchy is a common and effective way of organizing data and representing their relationships at different levels of abstraction. However, hierarchical data dependencies cause difficulties in the estimation of "separable" models that can distinguish between the entities in the hierarchy. Extracting separable models of hierarchical entities requires us to take their relative position into account and to consider the different types of dependencies in the hierarchy. In this paper, we present an investigation of the effect of separability in text-based entity classification and argue that in hierarchical classification, a separation property should be established between entities not only in the same layer, but also in different layers.

Our main findings are the followings. First, we analyse the importance of separability on the data representation in the task of classification and based on that, we introduce a "Strong Separation Principle" for optimizing expected effectiveness of classifiers decision based on separation property. Second, we present Hierarchical Significant Words Language Models (HSWLM) which capture all, and only, the essential features of hierarchical entities according to their relative position in the hierarchy resulting in horizontally and vertically separable models. Third, we validate our claims on real world data and demonstrate that how HSWLM improves the accuracy of classification and how it provides transferable models over time. Although discussions in this paper focus on the classification problem, the models are applicable to any information access tasks on data that has, or can be mapped to, a hierarchical structure.

Keywords
Separation, Hierarchical Significant Words Language Models, Hierarchical Text Classification

1. INTRODUCTION

Hierarchy is an effective and common way of representing information and many real-world textual data can be organized in this way. Organizing data in a hierarchical structure is valuable since it determines relationships in the data at different levels of resolution and picks out different categories relevant to each of the different layers of memberships. In a hierarchical structure, a node at any layer could be an indicator of a document, a person, an organization, a category, an ideology, and so on, which we refer to them as "hierarchical entities". Taking advantage of the structure in the hierarchy requires a proper way for modeling and representing entities, taking their relation in the hierarchy into consideration.

There are two types of dependencies in the hierarchies: i) *Horizontal dependency*, which refers to the relations of entities in the same layer. A simple example would be the dependency between siblings which have some commonalities in terms of being descendants of the same entity. ii) *Vertical dependency*, which addresses the relations between ancestors and descendants in the hierarchy. For example the relation between root and other entities. Due to the existence of two-dimensional dependencies between entities in the hierarchy, modeling them regardless of their relationships might result in overlapping models that are not capable of making different entities distinguishable. Overlap in the models is harmful because when the data representations are not well-separated, classification and retrieval systems are less likely to work well [22]. Thus, *two-dimensional separability*, i.e. *horizontal and vertical separability*, is one of the key requirements of hierarchical classification.

As a concrete example, consider a simple hierarchy of a multi-party parliament as shown in Figure 1, which determines different categories relevant to the different layers of membership in the parliament. We can classify these entities based on text, in particular the transcripts of all speeches in parliament as recorded in the parliamentary proceedings. That is, we can characterize an individual member of parliament by her speeches, a political party by their member's speeches, the opposition by the speeches of members of opposition parties, etc. However, in this way, all classifiers are based on speeches of (set of) individual members, making it important to take relations between different layers of the hierarchy explicitly taken into account. That is, in order to represent a party in this hierarchy, a proper model would show common characteristics of its members—not members of other parties (*horizontal* separation), and capture the party's generic characteristics—not unique aspects of the current members captured in the individual member's layer or aspects of whether the party is in government or opposition captured in the status layer (*vertical* separation).

The concept of separability is of crucial importance in information retrieval, especially when the task is not just ranking of items based on their probability of being relevant, but also making a boolean decision on whether or not an item is relevant, like in information filtering. Regarding this concern, Lewis [23] has presented the Probability Threshold Principle (PTP), as a stronger version of the Probability Ranking Principle [27], for binary classification, which discusses optimizing a threshold for separating items regarding their probability of class membership. PTP is a principle based on the separability in the score space. In this paper, we discuss separability

ICTIR '16, September 12 - 16, 2016, Newark, DE, USA

ⓒ 2016 Copyright held by the owner/author(s). Publication rights licensed to ACM.
ISBN 978-1-4503-4497-5/16/09. . . $15.00

DOI: http://dx.doi.org/10.1145/2970398.2970408

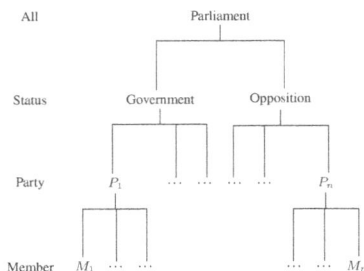

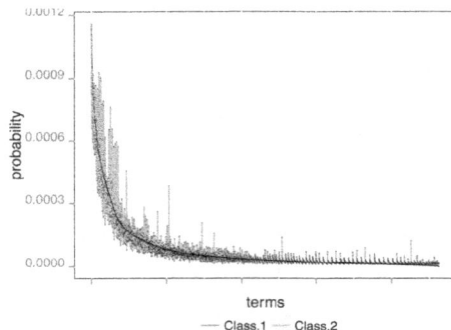

(a) A non-separable representation of data   **(b)** A well-separable representation of data

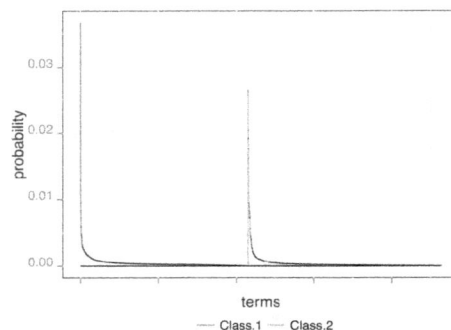

Figure 1: Hierarchical relations in the parliament   **Figure 2:** Probability distribution over terms for data in two different classes, (entities in the statues layer of the parliament), sorted based on the term weights in one of the classes.

in the data representation and define a *Strong Separation Principle* as the counterpart of PTP in the feature space.

Separation in the data or feature space is a favorable property that not only helps to improve for ranking or classification algorithms, but also brings out characteristic features for human inspection. Figures 2a and 2b illustrate two different ways of modeling two entities in the status layer of the parliamentary hierarchy, i.e., government and opposition. Each model is a probability distribution over terms (language model) based on the speeches given by all the members in the corresponding status. In each figure, we sort the terms based on their weights in one of the models, and plot the other in the same order. As can be seen, although distributions over terms in Figure 2a for two classes are different, they do not suggest highly separable representations for classes. However, estimated language models in Figure 2b provide highly separable distributions over terms for two classes, identifying the characteristic terms that uniquely represent each class, and can be directly interpreted. Moreover, the language models in Figure 2b select a small set of characteristic features, making it easy to learn effective classifiers for classes of interest.

The main aim of this paper is *to understand and validate the effect of the separation property on hierarchical classification and discuss how to provide horizontally and vertically separable language models for text-based hierarchical entities.* We break this down into three concrete research questions:

RQ1 *What makes separability a desirable property for classifiers?*

We demonstrate that based on the ranking and classification principles, *separation property* in the data representation theoretically follows separation in the scores and consequently improves the accuracy of classifiers' decisions. We state this as the "Strong Separation Principle" for optimizing expected effectiveness of classifiers. Furthermore, we define two-dimensional separation in the hierarchical data and discuss its necessity for hierarchical classification

RQ2 *How can we estimate horizontally and vertically separable language models for the hierarchical entities?*

We show that to estimate horizontally and vertically separable language models, they should capture *all*, and *only*, the essential terms of the entities taking their positions in the hierarchy into consideration. Based on this, extending [11], we introduce Hierarchical Significant Words Language Models (HSWLM) and evaluate them on the real-world data to demonstrate that they provide models for hierarchical entities that possess both horizontal and vertical separability.

RQ3 *How separability improves transferability?*

We investigate the effectiveness of language models of hierarchical entities possessing two-dimensional separation across time and show that separability makes the models capture essential characteristics of a class, which consequently improves transferability over time.

The rest of the paper is structured as follows. Next, in Section 2, we discuss some related work. In Section 3, we argue how separability theoretically improves the accuracy of classification results and discuss horizontal and vertical separation in hierarchical structure. Then, we discuss how to estimate HSWLM as two-dimensionally separable models for hierarchical entities in Section 4. In Section 5, we analyse separability of HSWLM and provide some experiments to assess the transferability of models using HSWLM. Finally, Section 6 concludes the paper and suggests some extensions to this research as the future work.

2. RELATED WORK

This section discusses briefly the separation property in the related domains and review principles in information retrieval and text classification, which are associated with the concept of separability. In addition, some research on classification and topic modeling of hierarchical texts are discussed.

Separability is a property which makes the data representation sufficient to distinguish instances and consequently enables autonomous systems to easily interpreter the data [22]. For instance in the classification task, classifiers learn more accurate data boundaries when they are provided with separable representations of data from different classes [23]. The importance of separability in classifiers has led to the fact that making data separable becomes part of classification. As the most familiar instances, SVM by adding extra dimensions implicitly transform the data into a new space where they are linearly separable [6].

Separation is also a pivoting concept in the information retrieval. Separating relevant from non-relevant documents is a fundamental issue in this domain [21, 27, 28]. In IR, separation plays more important role when instead of giving a rank list, a decision should be made about relevancy of documents, for example in the information filtering task [22]. As another instance, in the task of relevance feedback, there are some efforts on estimating a distinctive model for relevant documents so that it reflects not only their similarity, but also their difference from whole collection, i.e., what makes them stand out or separated [17, 32, 40].

In this paper, we address the separation property in the textual data that are organizable in a hierarchical structure. In a hierarchy, due to the existence of dependencies between entities, estimating separated models is a complex task. There is a range of work on the problem of hierarchical text classification [29, 33], which tried to model hierarchical text-based entities. McCallum et al. [24] proposed a method for modeling an entity in the hierarchy which tackles the problem of data sparseness in lower layer entities. They used a shrinkage estimator to smooth the model of each leaf entity with the model of its ancestors to make the models more reliable. There is also similar research on XML data processing, as hierarchically structured data, which try to incorporate evidence from other layers as the context through mixing each element language models by its parent's models [25, 30].

Recently, Song and Roth [31] tackled the problem of representing hierarchical entities with a lack of training data for the task of hierarchical classification. In their work, given a collection of instances and a set of hierarchical labels, they tried to embed all entities in a semantic space, then they construct a semantic representation for them to be able to compute meaningful semantic similarity between them.

Zhou et al. [41] proposed a method that directly tackles the difficulty of modeling similar entities at lower levels of the hierarchy. They used regularization so that the model of lower level entities have the same general properties as their ancestors, in addition to some more specific properties. Although these methods tried to model hierarchical texts, but their concerns were not making the models separable. Instead, they mostly addressed the problem of *training data sparseness* [16, 24, 31] or presenting techniques for *handling large scale data* [15, 16, 26, 36].

In terms of modeling hierarchical entities, Kim et al. [20] used Hierarchical Dirichlet Process [HDP, 34] to construct models for entities in the hierarchies using their own models as well as the models of their ancestors. Also, Zavitsanos et al. [39] used HDP to construct the model of entities in a hierarchy employing the models of its descendants. This research tries to bring out precise topic models using structure of the hierarchy, but they do not aim to estimate separable models.

As we will discuss in Section 5, our proposed approach can be employed as a feature selection method for text classification. Prior research on feature selection for textual information [1, 14] tried to improve classification accuracy or computational efficiency, while our method aims to provide a separable representation of data that helps train a transferable model. Apart from considering the hierarchical structure, our goals also differ from prior research on transferability of models. For instance, research on constructing dynamic models for data streams [4, 37] first discovered the topics from data and then tried to efficiently update the models as data changes over the time, while our method aims to identify tiny precise models that are more robust and remain valid over time. Research on domain adaptation [7, 35] also tried to tackle the problem of missing features when very different vocabulary are used in test and training data. This differs from our approach considering the hierarchical relations, as we aim to estimate separable models that are robust against changes in the structure of entities relations, rather than changes in the corpus vocabulary.

3. SEPARABILITY IN THE HIERARCHIES

In this section, we address our first research question: "What makes separability a desirable property for classifiers?"

In addition to the investigation of the separation property in general foundational property of classification and defining a *Strong Separation Principle*, we discuss a two-dimensional separation property of hierarchical classification.

3.1 Separation Property

Separability is a highly desirable property for constructing and operating autonomous information systems [23], and especially

classifiers. Here, we present a step by step argument which shows that based on the classification principles, having better separability in the feature space leads to better accuracy in the classification results.

Based on the *Probability Ranking Principle (PRP)* presented by Robertson [27], Lewis [23] has formulated a variant of PRP for binary classification:

> *For a given set of items presented to a binary classification system, there exists a classification of the items such that the probability of class membership for all items assigned to the class is greater than or equal to the probability of class membership for all items not assigned to the class, and the classification has optimal expected effectiveness.*

Since in many applications, autonomous systems need to decide how to classify an individual item in the absence of entire items set, Lewis has extended the PRP to the *Probability Threshold Principle (PTP)*:

> *For a given effectiveness measure, there exists a threshold p, $0 < p < 1$, such that for any set of items, if all and only those items with probability of class membership greater than p are assigned to the class, the expected effectiveness of the classification will be the best possible for that set of items.*

PTP in fact discusses optimizing the effectiveness of classifiers by making items separable regarding their probability of class membership, which is a discussion on "separability in the score space". Based on PTP, optimizing a threshold for separating items is a theoretically trivial task, however, there are practical difficulties. The main difficulty refers to the fact that retrieval models are not necessarily capable of measuring actual probabilities of relevance for documents [2], so they do not guarantee to generate a set of scores from which the optimum cutoff can be inferred. In this regard, a great deal of work has been done on analysing the score distribution over relevant and non-relevant documents to utilize this information for finding the appropriate threshold between relevant and non-relevant documents [2, 3, 19]. It is a clear fact that the more the score distributions of relevant and non-relevant documents are separable, the easier it is to determine the optimum threshold. So, obtaining the *separation property* in the scores distributions of relevant and non-relevant documents is one of the key focus areas for retrieval models.

There are two ways to obtain separability in the scores distributions. We could address the complex underlying process of score generation and investigate ranking functions that yield a separable score distribution, as in the score distributional approaches [e.g. 2]. Alternatively, we can investigate ways to provide existing scoring functions with a highly separable representation of the data. That is, the "term distribution" directly provides information about the "probability of relevance" [8] and if there are separable distributions over *terms* of relevant and non-relevant documents, a scoring function satisfying PRP will generate scores that separate the classes of relevant and non-relevant documents. Thus, a *separation property* on feature distribution for representing the data is a favorable property, which follows better accuracy of classifiers' decisions.

This paper is a first investigation in the role of separation in the term or feature spaces, in which we introduce a formal definition for separability and formulate a principle on the effectiveness of classification based on separation property and leave a more formal treatment to future work. As a formal and general definition, we can refer to the model separability as follows:

DEFINITION 1. *The model of an entity is epistemologically "separable" if, and only if, it has unique, non-overlapping features that distinguish it from other models.*

We argued that how separability in feature space leads to the separability in score space. Based on this and the given definition of the separability, we present *Strong Separation Principle (SSP)*, which is a counterpart of the PTP [23] in the feature space:

For a given set of items presented to a classification system, for each class there exists at least one feature δ in the representation of items, and a threshold τ, such that for any set of items, if all and only those items with $\delta > \tau$ are assigned to the class, the classification will have the optimal possible performance for that set of items in terms of a given effectiveness measure.

SSP in general is a stronger version of PTP. In strict binary classification, if you have PTP, which holds on the whole feature space, SSP will be satisfied, however in the multi-class case, SSP is stronger and it implies PTP, but not the other way around. Based on PTP, there is always an underlying probabilistic scoring function on the set of *whole* features, which generates membership probabilities as the scores of items and these scores make items separable with regards to a threshold. So, the scoring function can be deemed as a mapping function which maps items to a new feature space in which the score of each item is a single feature representation of that item (membership probabilities (or scores) in PTP would be equivalent to δ in SSP). Thus, when the SSP holds, the PTP and PRP will also hold. One could envision a stronger version of the SSP in which "all" the features in the representations need to be non-overlapping, but the SSP is sufficient for optimizing the effectiveness of the classifier. The separation principle can be formally extended to hierarchical classification in a straightforward way. In the rest of this section, we will discuss the separation property in the hierarchical classification and explain how to estimate separable representations with the aim of satisfying SSP in order to improve the classification effectiveness.

3.2 Horizontal and Vertical Separability

In hierarchical text classification, there are two types of boundaries existing in the data, horizontal boundaries, and vertical boundaries. Hence, a separation property should be established in two dimensions. It means, not only separation between entities' representation in one layer is required, but also separation between the distribution of terms in different layers is needed.

Separation between entities in the same layer is a related concept to the fundamental goal of all classifiers on the data with flat structure, which is making the data in different classes distinguishable [29]. However, separation between entities in different layers is a concept related to difference of abstraction level and modeling data in different layers in a separable way can help the scoring procedures to figure out the meaning behind the layers and make their decisions less affected by the concepts of other unrelated layers, thus leading to conceptually cleaner and theoretically more accurate models.

Based on Definition 1, we formally define horizontal and vertical separability in the hierarchy as follows:

DEFINITION 2. *The model of an entity in the hierarchy is "horizontally separable" if, and only if, it is separable compared to other entities in the same layer, with the same abstraction level.*

DEFINITION 3. *The model of an entity in the hierarchy is "vertically separable" if, and only if, it is separable compared to other entities in the other layers, with different abstraction levels.*

To formalize these concepts, consider we have a simple three layers hierarchy of text documents with "IsA" relations, where the individual documents take place in the lowest layer, and each node in the middle layer determines a category, representing a group of documents, i.e. its children, and the super node on the top of the hierarchy deemed to represent all the documents in all the groups in the hierarchy. There is a key point in this hierarchy to which we will refer for estimating models for the hierarchical entities: "each node in the hierarchy is a general representation of its descendants".

First assume that the goal is to estimate a language model representing category c, as one of the entities in the middle layer of the hierarchy, and we need the estimated model possessing *horizontal separability*. To estimate a horizontally separable model of a category, which represents the category in a way that it is distinguishable from other categories in the middle layer, the key strategy is to eliminate terms that are common across all the categories (overlapping features) and preserve only the discriminating ones.

To do so, we consider there is a general model that captures all the *common* terms of all the categories in the middle layer, θ_c^g. Also we assume that the standard language model of c, i.e the model estimated from concatenation of all the documents in c using MLE, θ_c, is drawn from the mixture of the *latent horizontally separable model*, θ_c^{hs}, and general model that represents shared terms of all categories, i.e. θ_c^g:

$$p(t|\theta_c) = \lambda p(t|\theta_c^{hs}) + (1 - \lambda)p(t|\theta_c^g), \qquad (1)$$

where λ is the mixture coefficient. Regarding the meaning of the relations between nodes in the hierarchy, top node in the hierarchy is supposed to be a general representation of all categories. On the other hand θ_c^g supposed to be a model capturing general features of all the categories in the middle layer. Thus, we can approximate θ_c^g with the estimated model of the top node in the hierarchy, θ_{all}:

$$p(t|\theta_c) \approx \lambda p(t|\theta_c^{hs}) + (1 - \lambda)p(t|\theta_{all}). \qquad (2)$$

We estimate θ_{all} using MLE as follows:

$$p(t|\theta_{all}) = \frac{tf(t, all)}{\sum_{t'} tf(t', all)} = \frac{\sum_{c \in all} \sum_{d \in c} tf(t, d)}{\sum_{c \in all} \sum_{d \in c} \sum_{t' \in d} tf(t', d)}, \quad (3)$$

where $tf(t, d)$ indicates the frequency of term t in document d and θ_{all} is in fact collection language model.

Now, the goal is to extract θ_c^{hs}. With regard to the generative models, when a term t is generated using the mixture model in Equation 2, first a model is chosen based on λ and then the term is sampled using the chosen model. The log-likelihood function for generating the whole category c is:

$$\log p(t|\theta_c^{hs}) = \sum_{t \in c} tf(t, c) \log \left(\lambda p(t|\theta_c^{hs}) + (1 - \lambda)p(t|\theta_{all}) \right),$$
$$(4)$$

where $tf(t, c)$ is the frequency of occurrence of term t in category c. With the goal of maximizing this likelihood function, the maximum likelihood estimation of $p(c|\theta_c^{hs})$ can be computed using the Expectation-Maximization (EM) algorithm by iterating over the following steps:

E-step:

$$e_t = tf(t|c).\frac{\lambda p(t|\theta_c^{hs})}{\lambda p(x|\theta_c^{hs}) + (1 - \lambda)p(x|\theta_{all})}, \qquad (5)$$

M-step:

$$p(x|\theta_c^{hs}) = \frac{e_t}{\sum_{t' \in \mathcal{V}} e_t'}, \text{ i.e. normalizing the model,} \qquad (6)$$

where $\mathcal{V}$ is the set of all terms with non-zero probability in θ_c. In Equation 5, θ_c is the maximum likelihood estimation of category

---
Algorithm Modified Model Parsimonization

1: **procedure** PARSIMONIZE(e,B)
2:     **for all** term t in the vocabulary **do**
3:         $P(t|\theta_B) \xleftarrow{normalized} \Sigma_{b_i \in B} \left(P(t|\theta_{b_i}) \prod_{\substack{b_j \in B \\ j \neq i}} (1 - P(t|\theta_{b_j})) \right)$
4:         **repeat**
5:         E-Step: $P[t \in \mathcal{V}] \leftarrow P(t|\theta_e) \cdot \frac{\alpha P(t|\tilde{\theta}_e)}{\alpha P(t|\tilde{\theta}_e) + (1-\alpha)P(t|\theta_B)}$
6:         M-Step: $P(t|\tilde{\theta}_e) \leftarrow \frac{P[t \in \mathcal{V}]}{\Sigma_{t' \in \mathcal{V}} P[t' \in \mathcal{V}]}$
7:         **until** $\tilde{\theta}_t$ becomes stable
8:     **end for**
9: **end procedure**

Figure 3: Pseudo-code for procedure of modified model parsimonization.

Algorithm Estimating Hierarchical Significant Words Language Models
---
1: **procedure** ESTIMATEHSWLMS
    Initialization:
2:     **for all** entity e in the hierarchy **do**
3:         $\theta_e \leftarrow$ standard estimation for e using MLE
4:     **end for**
5:     **repeat**
6:         SPECIFICATION
7:         GENERALIZATION
8:     **until** models do not change significantly anymore
9: **end procedure**

Figure 4: Pseudo-code for the overall procedure of estimating HSWLM.

c: $p(t|\theta_c) = \Sigma_{d \in c} c(t,d)/\Sigma_{d \in c} \Sigma_{t' \in d} c(t',d)$ and θ_c^{hs} represents the horizontally separable model, which in the first iteration it is initialized by the maximum likelihood estimation, similar to θ_c.

Considering the above process, a horizontally separable model is a model which is **specified** by taking out general features that have high probability in "all" categories, or lets say collection language model, which is similar to the concept of the parsimonious language model, introduced by Hiemstra et al. [17].

Now assume that we want to extract a language model possessing *vertical separability* for the category c, i.e. a model that makes this category distinguishable from entities both in the lower layer (each individual document) and the top layer (collection of all documents). In the procedure of making the model horizontally separable, we argued that we can reduce the problem to removing terms representing the top node, which results in a model that is separable from the top node in the upper layer. This means that we are already half-way towards making a model vertically separable, thus, the model only requires to be separable from its descendant entities in the lower layer. Back to the meaning of the "IsA" relations in the hierarchy, the model of each node is a general representation of all its descendants. So making the model of a category separable from its descendant documents means to remove terms that describe each individual documents, but not all of them. We call these terms, document specific terms. For each category c, we assume there is a model, θ_d^s, that captures document specific terms, i.e. terms from documents in that category that are good indicators for individual documents but not supported by all of them. Also we assume that the standard language model of c, θ_c, is drawn from the mixture of the *latent vertically separable model*, θ_c^{vs}, and θ_d^s:

$$p(t|\theta_c) = \lambda p(t|\theta_c^{vs}) + (1-\lambda)p(t|\theta_d^s) \quad (7)$$

where λ is the mixing coefficient. We estimate θ_d^s using the following equation:

$$p(t|\theta_d^s) \xleftarrow{normalized} \sum_{d_i \in c} \left(p(t|\theta_{d_i}) \prod_{\substack{d_j \in c \\ j \neq i}} (1 - p(t|\theta_{d_j})) \right), \quad (8)$$

where $p(t|\theta_{d_i}) = c(t,d_i)/\Sigma_{t' \in d_i} c(t',d_i)$. This equation assigns a high probability to a term if it has high probability in one of the document models, but not others, marginalizing over all the document models. This way, the higher the probability is, the more specific the term will be. Now, the goal is to extract the θ_c^{vs}. An EM algorithm, similar to Equations 5 and 6 can be applied for estimating θ_c^{vs} by removing the effect of θ_d^s from θ_c.

Considering the above process, a vertically separable model is a model which is **generalized** by taking out specific terms that have high probability in one of the descendant documents, but not others.

3.3 Two-Dimensional Separability

In order to have fully separable models in hierarchical classification, they should own two-dimensional separation property. We define two-dimensional separability as follows:

DEFINITION 4. *The model of an entity in the hierarchy is "two-dimensionally separable" if, and only if, it is both horizontally and vertically separable at the same time.*

Intuitively, if a model of an entity is two-dimensionally separable, it should capture *all*, and *only*, the essential features of the entity taking its relative position in the hierarchy in to consideration. In the next section, we will discuss how to estimate two-dimensional separable models for entities in the hierarchies with more than three layers.

In summary, based on the discussions on this section, we can say that the separation property is a desirable foundational property for classifiers. We see that based on PRP, separation in the feature space follows by separation in the score space, which leads to improvement in classification accuracy. We also notice that separation property in hierarchies is defined in two dimensions, thus, fully separable hierarchical models would possess both horizontal and vertical separation.

4. Hierarchical Significant Words Language Models

In this section, we address our second research question: "How can we estimate horizontally and vertically separable language models for the hierarchical entities?" We introduce Hierarchical Significant Words Language Models (HSWLM) which is an extension of Significant Words Language Model proposed by Dehghani et al. [11] to be applicable for hierarchical data. HSWLM is in fact a particular arrangement of multiple passes of the procedures of making hierarchical entities' models vertically and horizontally separable, as they are explained in Section 3.2. Generally speaking, hierarchical significant words language models are an extension of parsimonious language models [17] tailored to text-based hierarchical entities. In parsimonious language model, given a raw probabilistic estimation, the goal is to re-estimate the model so that non-essential parameters of the raw estimation are eliminated with regard to the background estimation. The proposed approach for estimating hierarchical significant words language model iteratively reestimates the standard language models of entities to minimize their overlap by discarding non-essential terms from them.

In the original parsimonious language model [17], background model is explained by the estimation of the *collection model*, i.e. the

Specification Stage
1: **procedure** SPECIFICATION
2:     Queue ← all entities in breadth first order
3:     **while** Queue is not empty **do**
4:         e ← Queue.pop()
5:         l ← e.Depth()
6:         **while** $l > 0$ **do**
7:             A ← e.GETANCESTOR(l)
8:             PARSIMONIZE(e,A)
9:             $l ← l - 1$
10:         **end while**
11:     **end while**
12: **end procedure**

(a) Procedure of Specification. e.GETANCESTOR(l) gives the ancestor of entity e with l edges distance from it.

Generalization Stage
1: **procedure** GENERALIZATION
2:     Stack ← all entities in breadth first order
3:     **while** Stack is not empty **do**
4:         e ← Stack.pop()
5:         l ← e.Height()
6:         **while** $l > 0$ **do**
7:             D ← e.GETDECEDENTS(l)
8:             PARSIMONIZE(e,D)
9:             $l ← l - 1$
10:         **end while**
11:     **end while**
12: **end procedure**

(b) Procedure of Generalization. e.GETDECEDENTS(l) gives all the decedents of entity e with l edges distance from it.

Figure 5: Pseudo-code for stages of estimating HSWLM. Function PARSIMONIZE(e,B) parsimonizes θ_e toward background models in B

model representing all the entities, similar to Equation 3. However, with respect to the hierarchical structure, and our goal in HSWLM for making the entities' models separable from each other, we need to use parsimonization technique in different situations: 1) toward ancestors of an entity, and 2) toward its descendants. Hence, beside parsimonizing toward a single parent entity in the upper layers, as the background model, we need to be able to do parsimonization toward multiple descendants in the lower layers. Figure 3 presents pseudo-code of Expectation-Maximization algorithm which is employed in the modified model parsimonization procedure. In the equation in line 3 of the pseudo-code in Figure 3, B is the set of background entities—either one or multiple, and θ_{b_i} demonstrates the model of each background entity, b_i, which is estimated using MLE. As can be seen, in case of having a single ancestor node as the background model, this equation will be equal to Equation 3 and in case of having multiple descendants as the background models, it results same as Equation 8. In this procedure, in general, in the E-step, the probabilities of terms are adjusted repeatedly and in the M-step, adjusted probability of terms are normalized to form a distribution. Another change in the modified version of model parsimonization, which practically makes no difference in the final estimation, is that in the E-step, instead of using $tf(t,e)$, we employ $p(t|\theta_e)$, where θ_e is the model represents entity e and initially it is estimated using MLE. This is because in the multi-layer hierarchies, there are more than one parsimonization pass for a particular entity and after the first round, we need to use the probability of terms estimated from the previous pass, not the raw information of their frequency.

Model parsimonization is an almost parameter free process. The only parameter is the standard smoothing parameter λ, which controls the level of parsimonization, so that the lower values of λ result in more parsimonious models. The iteration is repeated a fixed number of times or until the estimates do not change significantly anymore.

The pseudo-code of overall procedure of estimating HSWLM is presented in Figure 4. Before the first round of the procedure, a standard estimation like maximum likelihood estimation is used to construct the initial model for each entity in the hierarchy. Then, models will be updated in an iterative process until all the estimated models of entities become stable. In each iteration, there are two main stages: a *Specification stage* and a *Generalization stage*. In these stages, language models of entities in the hierarchy are iteratively made "specific," by taking out terms explained at higher levels, and "general," by eliminating specific terms of lower layers,

which results in models that are both *horizontally* and *vertically* separable as it is described in Section 3.2.

In the specification stage, the goal is to eliminate the general terms of the language model of each entity so that the resulted language model demonstrates entity's specific properties. To do so, the parsimonization method is used to parsimonize the language model of an entity towards its ancestors, from the root of the hierarchy to its direct parent, as the background estimations. The order in the hierarchy is of crucial importance here. When a language model of an ancestor is considered as the background language model, it should demonstrate the "specific" properties of that ancestor. Due to this fact, it is important that before considering the language model of an entity as background estimation, it has already passed the specification stage, and we have to move top-down. Pseudo-code of the recursive procedure of specification of entities' models in the hierarchy is depicted in Figure 5a.

In the generalization stage, the goal is to refine language models by removing terms which do not address the concepts in the level of abstraction of the entity's layer. To do so, again parsimonization is exploited but towards descendants, which leads to elimination of specific terms. Here also, before considering the model of an entity as the background estimation, it should be already passed the generalization stage, so generalization moves bottom up. Figure 5b presents the pseudo-code for the recursive procedure of generalization of entities' language models in the hierarchy. In the generalization step, the background models of descendants are supposed to be specific enough to show their extremely specific properties. Hence, generalization stages must be applied on the output models of specification stages: specification should precede generalization, as shown in Figure 4 before.

In this section, we explained the procedure of estimating hierarchical significant words language model, which terminates in the language models that capture *all*, and *only* the essential terms regarding the hierarchical positions of entities. We will investigate the effectiveness of HSWLM on the real data in the next section.

5. EXPERIMENTS

In order to evaluate the separability of Hierarchical Significant Words Language Models, we use parliamentary data as one of the interesting collections with hierarchically structured data, using the hierarchical entities as shown in Figure 1. First we introduce the collection we have used and then we analyse the quality of HSWLM on providing horizontal and vertical separability over the hierarchy.

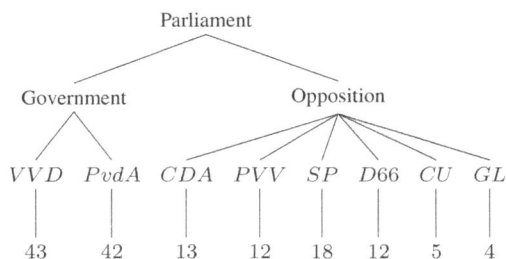

Figure 6: Composition of house of representatives of Dutch parliament, 2012-2014. *VVD*:People's Party for Freedom and democracy, *PvdA*:Labour Party, *CDA*:Christian Democratic Appeal, *PVV*:Party for Freedom, *SP*:The Socialist Party, *D66*:Democrats 66, *GL*:Green-Left, *CU*:Christian-Union

5.1 Experimental Dataset

We have made use of the Dutch parliamentary data to do a number of experiments. As a brief background, the Dutch parliament is a bicameral parliament which consists of the senate and the house of representatives. The house of representatives is the main chamber of parliament, where discussion of proposed legislation and review of the government's actions takes place. The Dutch parliamentary system is a multi-party system, requiring a coalition of parties to form the government [9]. For the experiments and analysis, we have used the data from the House of Representatives of Netherlands, consisting of literal transcripts of all speeches in parliament with rich annotation of the speaker and debate structure. We have chosen the last periods of parliament where eight main parties have about 95 percent of the 150 seats in the parliament. This data collected from March 2012 to April 2014 and consist of 62,206 debates containing 3.7M words. Figure 6 shows the hierarchical structure of house of representatives in this period. For each member, all speeches are collected from the discussions in the parliament and members for which the length of all their given speeches is less than 100 words are removed from the data instances. No stemming and no lemmatization is done on the data and also stop words and common words are not removed in data preprocessing.

5.2 Two-Dimensional Separability of HSWLM

In this section we investigate the ability of HSWLM on providing language models for hierarchical entities that are two-dimensionally separable. Based on the explained procedure of estimating HSWLM, the language models of entities in the hierarchy is repeatedly updated, so that the resulting models are both *horizontally* and *vertically* separable in the hierarchy. In order to assess this fact, we estimate HSWLM on the parliamentary data and look into the separability between entities in the same layer or in different layers.

Figures 7a and 7b illustrate the probability distribution over terms based on the estimated HSWLM in the status and party layer respectively. We sort the probability distribution on the term weight of the first model, and plot the other models in this exact order. As can be seen in the status layer, Figures 7a, the distributions over terms for government and opposition cover almost separated set of terms. Since in this layer these two entities are supposed to be against each other, a high level of separability can be expected. On the other hand, in the party layer, Figures 7b, it is possible that two parties share some ideological issues and consequently share some terms. So, in this layer a complete separability of terms would not be practically possible for all the parties. Nevertheless, HSWLM provides an acceptable horizontal separability in this layer.

In addition, we illustrate the horizontal separability of HSWLM of some pairs of parties. Figures 8a, 8b, and 8c show the separability of models of two parties in three cases, respectively: 1) different

statuses, 2) both in the status of opposition, 3) both in the status of government. It can be seen that in all cases of being in the same status or different status, estimated hierarchical significant words language models are separable. The interesting point is in Figure 8c that presents the models of two government parties that are strongly separable. This rooted in the fact that in this period there was an unusual coalition government consisting of a right-wing and a left-wing party. So, although they have agreement in the status layer, their model is highly separable in terms of having opposite spectrum in party layer.

In order to illustrate the vertical separability of HSWLM, we choose two different branches in the hierarchy: one from leader of one of the opposition parties to the root, and the other from leader of one of the government parties to the root. Figures 9a and 9b show probability distributions over words based on HSWLM of all entities in these two branches. They demonstrate that using HSWLM, we can decompose distribution over all terms to the highly separable distributions, each one representing the language usage related to the meaning behind the layer of the entity in the hierarchy.

Two-dimensional separation property of HSWLM in the hierarchy is essentially due to the parsimonization effect in two directions. Intuitively, the horizontal separability is mainly the result of specification stage. For example, when an entity is parsimonized toward its direct parent, since the data in its parent is formed by pooling the data from the entity and its siblings, parsimonization makes the model of the entity separable from its siblings, which provide *horizontal separation* in the resulting language models. On the other hand, vertical separability is mainly due to generalization stage (and implicitly specification). For example, when an entity is parsimonized towards its children, since they are specified already, parsimonization gets rid of the specific terms of the lower layer from the entity's model.

5.3 Separability for Transferability

Here, we address our third research question: "How separability improves transferability?"

To address this question, we investigate the effectiveness of the models in the cross period classification task in the parliamentary dataset, which is to predict the party that a member of the parliament belongs to, having all the speeches given by that member in a period, as well as all the speeches given by the members of all parties in a different period of parliament. In the parliament, the status of the parties may change over different periods. Since the speeches given by the members are considerably affected by the status of their party, a dramatic change may happen in the parties' language usage. Due to this fact, learning a transferable model for party classification over periods is a very challenging task [18, 38].

To evaluate the transferability of the models, besides the debates from the last period of Dutch parliament, we have used debates from October 2010 to March 2012 where VVD and CDA were pro-government parties and others were oppositions. We use SVM as the base classifier to predict party that each member belongs to, give the speaches of the members. We have done classification using the SVM itself as well as using SVM by considering probabilities of terms in HSWLM as the weights of features in order to evaluate the effectiveness of HSWLM as the separable representation of data. This way, we make use of HSWLM like a feature selection approach that filters out features that are not essential in accordance to the hierarchical position of entities and make the data representation more robust by taking out non-stable terms. We have also tried SVM along with other feature selection methods [5, 14] as the baselines, here we report the results of using Information Gain (IG) as the best feature selection method in our task in the parliament

191

(a) HSWLM in the status layer

(b) HSWLM in the party layer

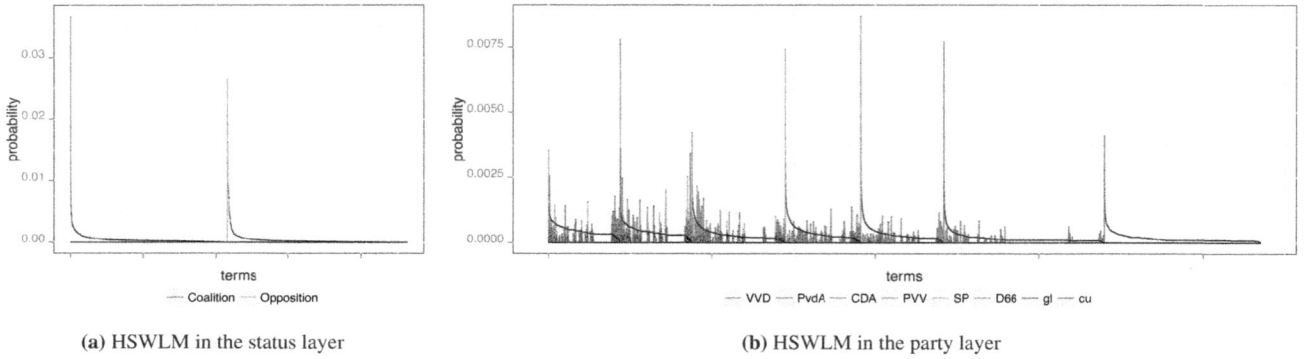

Figure 7: *Horizontal Separability*: probability distribution over terms based on hierarchical significant words language models in status layer and party layer.

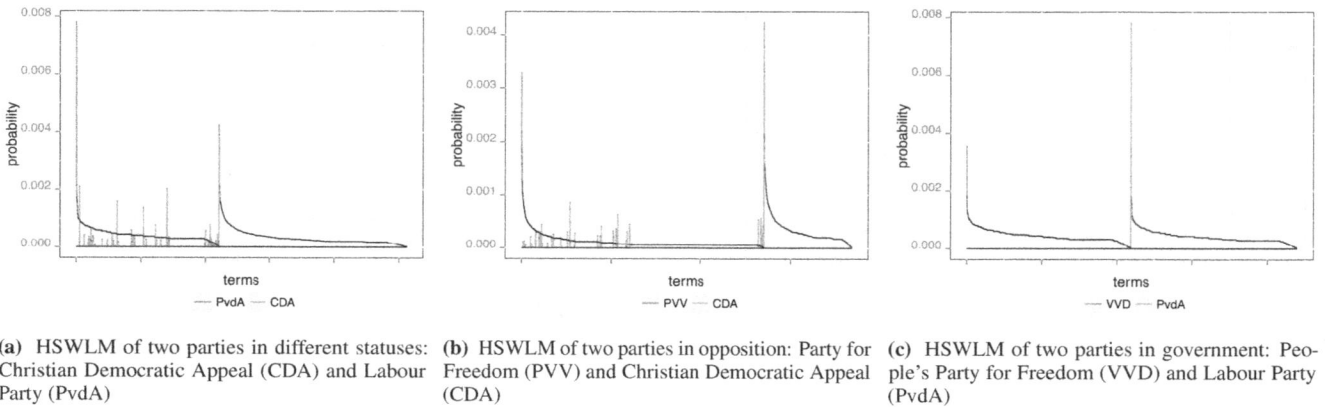

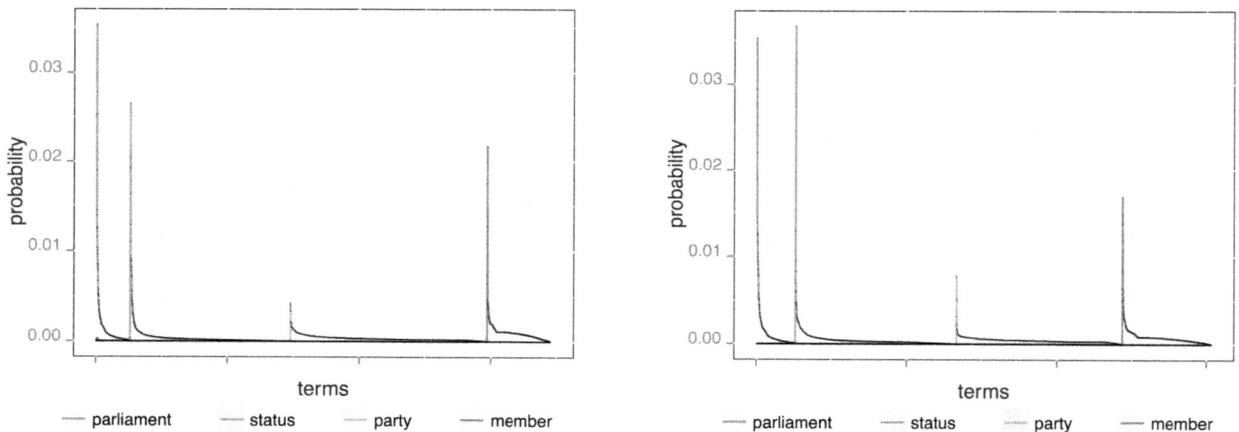

(a) HSWLM of two parties in different statuses: Christian Democratic Appeal (CDA) and Labour Party (PvdA)

(b) HSWLM of two parties in opposition: Party for Freedom (PVV) and Christian Democratic Appeal (CDA)

(c) HSWLM of two parties in government: People's Party for Freedom (VVD) and Labour Party (PvdA)

Figure 8: *Horizontal Separability*: probability distribution over terms based on hierarchical significant words language models in party layer

(a) HSWLM of S. van Haersma Buma (as the member of parliament - Leader of CDA), Christian Democratic Appeal (as the party), Opposition (as the status), and the Parliament

(b) HSWLM of D. Samson (as the member of parliament - Leader of PvdA), Labour Party (as the party), Government (as the status), and the Parliament

Figure 9: *Vertical Separability*: probability distribution over terms in different layers based on hierarchical significant words language models in complete paths from the root to the terminal entities in the hierarchy

Table 1: Results of party classification task in terms of macro-average accuracy. We have conducted paired t-test to investigate statistical significance of the improvements of the best method over the second best method, in the corresponding experiments. Improvements that are annotated with ⁀ are statistically significant with p-value < 0.005.

		Test					
		SVM		SVM_{IG}		SVM_{HSWLM}	
	Period	2010-2012	2012-2014	2010-2012	2012-2014	2010-2012	2012-2014
Train	2010-2012	40.90	35.57	**43.11** ⁀	34.12	41.83	**40.02**⁀
	2012-2014	30.51	44.96	30.38	47.18	**39.11**⁀	**47.28**

dataset. We have employed conventional 5-fold cross validation for training and testing and to maintain comparability, we have used the same split for folding in all the experiments. Tables 1 shows the performance of SVM, SVM_{IG}, and SVM_{HSWLM} on party classification over two periods in terms of macro-average accuracy. Comparing the results, it can be seen that SVM_{HSWLM} improves the performance of classification over SVM in all the experiments.

Although SVM_{IG} performs very well in terms of accuracy in within period experiments, it fails to learn a transferable model in cross period experiments and even it performs a little bit worse than the SVM itself. We looked into the confusion matrices of cross-period experiments and observed that most of the errors in both SVM and SVM_{IG} are because of misclassified members of CDA to PvdA and vice versa. These are the two parties that their statuses have been changed in these periods.

We investigate models of these two parties to understand how separation in the feature representation affects the performance of cross period classification. To do so, for each of these two classes, in each period, we extract three probability distributions on terms indicating their importance based on different weighting approaches: 1) Term Frequency (used as feature weights in SVM), 2) Information Gain (used as feature weights in SVM_{IG}), and 3) probability of terms in HSWLM (used as feature weights in SVM_{HSWLM}). Then, as a metric to measure separability of features, we use the Jensen-Shannon divergence to calculate diversity of probability distributions in three cases: 1) Different Parties in the Same Period, 2) Same Party in Different Periods 3) Different Parties in Different Periods. To avoid the effect of the number of features on the value of divergence, we take the top 500 high scored terms of each of weighting methods as the fixed length representatives of them. Figure 10 shows the average diversity of distributions in each of the three cases for each of the three weighting methods.

As expected, the diversity of features for different parties in a same period is high for all the methods and IG provides the more separable representation in this case, which results in its high accuracies in within period experiments. However, when we calculate the diversity of features for a same party in different periods, feature representations are different in both TF and IG, which causes false negative errors in the classification of these two parties. An interesting observation is in the case of having different parties in different periods, while we have two different parties their feature representations are similar in both TF and IG, which leads to false positive errors in the classification.

Considering these observations together reveals that SVM and SVM_{IG} learn models on the basis of features that are indicators of issues related to the status of parties, since they are the most discriminating terms considering one period and in within period experiments, the performance of SVM_{IG} and SVM is indebted to the separability of parties based on their statuses. Hence, after changing the status in the cross period experiments the trained model of the previous period generated by SVM and SVM_{IG} fails

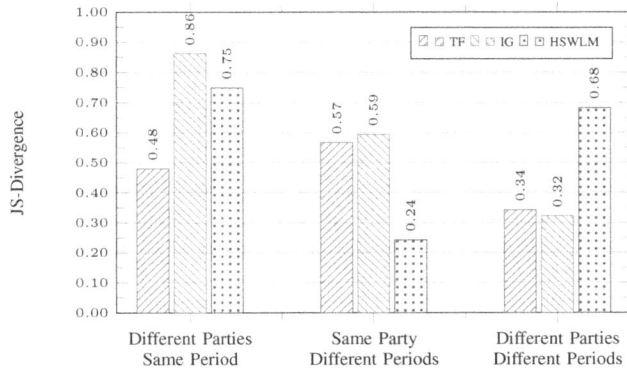

Figure 10: Average diversity of the representation of features of CDA and PvdA in different situations

to predict the accurate party. In the same way, the status classifier is affected by different parties forming a government in different periods, leading to lower accuracies.

This is exactly the point which the strengths of HSWLM kicks in. In fact, two-dimensional separability in the feature representation, enables SVM to tackle the problem of having non-stable features in the model when the status of a party changes over time. In other words, eliminating the effect of the status layer in the party model, which is the result of the horizontal separation, ensures that the party model captures the terms related to the party ideology, not its status. Thereby, not only SVM_{HSWLM} learns an effective model with acceptable accuracy in within period experiments, but also its learned models remain valid when the statuses of parties change.

We furthermore looked into the size of estimated HSWLMs by the number of terms with non-zero probability and, on average, the size of the models are about 100 times smaller than the number of features selected by IG in the corresponding models. So, although HSWLM takes considerable risk of loosing accuracy in within period experiments by aggressively pruning the overlapping terms, it provides small and precise models that are not only effective over time, but also efficient when the size of data is large.

In summary, we demonstrated that HSWLM indeed exhibit the two-dimensional separation property for the parliamentary data, as predicted by our theoretical analysis in the earlier sections. In addition, we empirically validated the transferability of models using HSWLM which is the result of its two-dimensional separability.

6. CONCLUSIONS

In this paper, we investigated the separation property in hierarchical data focusing on hierarchical text classification.

Our first research question was: "*What makes separability a desirable property for classifiers?*" We demonstrated that based on the ranking and classification principles, the *separation property* in the data representation is a desirable foundational property which leads to separability of scores and consequently improves the accuracy

193

of classifiers' decisions. We stated this as the "Strong Separation Principle" for optimizing expected effectiveness of classifiers.

Our second research question was: *"How can we estimate horizontally and vertically separable language models for the hierarchical entities?"* We showed that in order to have horizontally and vertically separable models, they should capture all, and only, the essential terms of the entities taking their position in the hierarchy into account. Based on this, we introduced Hierarchical Significant Words Language Models for estimating separable models for hierarchical entities. We investigated HSWLM and demonstrated that it offers separable distributions over terms for different entities both in case of being in the same layer or in different layers.

Our third research question was: *"How separability improves transferability?"* We evaluated the performance of classification over time using separable representation of data and showed that separability makes the model more robust and transferable over time by filtering out non-essential non-stable terms.

The models we proposed in this paper are IR models which are applicable to a range of information access tasks [10–13], not just hierarchical classification, as many complex ranking models combine different layers of information. There are number of extensions we are working on in future work. First, in this research we focused on text-dominant environment and considered all terms in the text as features. However, this can be done considering terms with a specific part of speech, or even on non-textual models with completely different types of features. Second, it would be beneficial to construct mixture models for terminal entities using HSWLM in a way that constructed mixture models are capable of reflecting local interactions of terminal entities in different layers.

Acknowledgments This research is funded in part by Netherlands Organization for Scientific Research through the *Exploratory Political Search* project (ExPoSe, NWO CI # 314.99.108), and by the Digging into Data Challenge through the *Digging Into Linked Parliamentary Data* project (DiLiPaD, NWO Digging into Data # 600.006.014).

References

[1] Feature generation and selection for information retrieval. Workshop of SIGIR, 2010.

[2] A. Arampatzis and A. van Hameran. The score-distributional threshold optimization for adaptive binary classification tasks. In *SIGIR '01*, pages 285–293, 2001.

[3] A. Arampatzis, J. Kamps, and S. Robertson. Where to stop reading a ranked list?: Threshold optimization using truncated score distributions. In *SIGIR '09*, pages 524–531, 2009.

[4] D. M. Blei and J. D. Lafferty. Dynamic topic models. In *ICML*, pages 113–120, 2006.

[5] J. Brank, M. Grobelnik, N. Milic-Frayling, and D. Mladenic. Feature selection using linear support vector machines. Technical Report MSR-TR-2002-63, Microsoft Research, 2002.

[6] C. J. Burges. A tutorial on support vector machines for pattern recognition. *Data mining and knowledge discovery*, 2(2):121–167, 1998.

[7] M. Chen, K. Q. Weinberger, and J. Blitzer. Co-training for domain adaptation. In *NIPS '24*, pages 2456–2464. 2011.

[8] F. Crestani, M. Lalmas, C. J. Van Rijsbergen, and I. Campbell. "is this document relevant?... probably...": A survey of probabilistic models in information retrieval. *ACM Comput. Surv.*, 30(4):528–552, Dec. 1998.

[9] A. de Swaan. *Coalition Theories and Cabinet Formations: A Study of Formal Theories of Coalition Formation Applied to Nine European Parliaments after 1918*, volume 4 of *Progress in Mathematical Social Sciences*. Elsevier, New York, 1973.

[10] M. Dehghani. Significant words representations of entities. In *SIGIR '16*, pages 1183–1183, 2016.

[11] M. Dehghani, H. Azarbonyad, J. Kamps, D. Hiemstra, and M. Marx. Luhn revisited: Significant words language models. In *CIKM '16*, 2016.

[12] M. Dehghani, H. Azarbonyad, J. Kamps, and M. Marx. Generalized

[13] M. Dehghani, H. Azarbonyad, J. Kamps, and M. Marx. Two-way parsimonious classification models for evolving hierarchies. In *CLEF '16*, 2016.

[14] G. Forman. An extensive empirical study of feature selection metrics for text classification. *J. Mach. Learn. Res.*, 3:1289–1305, 2003.

[15] S. Gopal and Y. Yang. Recursive regularization for large-scale classification with hierarchical and graphical dependencies. In *SIGKDD*, pages 257–265, 2013.

[16] V. Ha-Thuc and J.-M. Renders. Large-scale hierarchical text classification without labelled data. In *WSDM*, pages 685–694, 2011.

[17] D. Hiemstra, S. Robertson, and H. Zaragoza. Parsimonious language models for information retrieval. In *SIGIR*, pages 178–185, 2004.

[18] G. Hirst, Y. Riabinin, J. Graham, and M. Boizot-Roche. Text to ideology or text to party status? *From Text to Political Positions: Text analysis across disciplines*, 55:93–15, 2014.

[19] E. Kanoulas, V. Pavlu, K. Dai, and J. Aslam. Modeling the score distributions of relevant and non-relevant documents. In *ICTIR'09*, volume 5766, pages 152–163. Springer Berlin Heidelberg, 2009.

[20] D.-k. Kim, G. Voelker, and L. K. Saul. A variational approximation for topic modeling of hierarchical corpora. In *ICML*, pages 55–63, 2013.

[21] V. Lavrenko and W. B. Croft. Relevance based language models. In *SIGIR '01*, pages 120–127, 2001.

[22] D. D. Lewis. *Representation and Learning in Information Retrieval*. PhD thesis, Amherst, MA, USA, 1992.

[23] D. D. Lewis. Evaluating and optimizing autonomous text classification systems. In *SIGIR '95*, pages 246–254, 1995.

[24] A. McCallum, R. Rosenfeld, T. M. Mitchell, and A. Y. Ng. Improving text classification by shrinkage in a hierarchy of classes. In *ICML*, pages 359–367, 1998.

[25] P. Ogilvie and J. Callan. Hierarchical language models for xml component retrieval. In *INEX*, pages 224–237, 2004.

[26] H.-S. Oh, Y. Choi, and S.-H. Myaeng. Text classification for a large-scale taxonomy using dynamically mixed local and global models for a node. In *ECIR*, pages 7–18, 2011.

[27] S. Robertson. The probability ranking principle in ir. *Journal of Documentation*, 33(4):294–304, 1977.

[28] T. Saracevic. Relevance: A review of the literature and a framework for thinking on the notion in information science. *JASIST*, 26:321–343, 1975.

[29] F. Sebastiani. Machine learning in automated text categorization. *ACM Comput. Surv.*, 34(1):1–47, Mar. 2002.

[30] B. Sigurbjörnsson, J. Kamps, and M. de Rijke. An element-based approach to xml retrieval. In *INEX*, pages 19–26, 2004.

[31] Y. Song and D. Roth. On dataless hierarchical text classification. In *AAAI*, pages 1579–1585, 2014.

[32] K. Sparck Jones, H. D. Robertson, Stephen, and Z. Hugo. Language modeling and relevance. In *Language Modeling for Information Retrieval*, pages 57–71. 2003.

[33] A. Sun and E.-P. Lim. Hierarchical text classification and evaluation. In *ICDM*, pages 521–528, 2001.

[34] Y. W. Teh, M. I. Jordan, M. J. Beal, and D. M. Blei. Hierarchical dirichlet processes. *Journal of the American Statistical Association*, 101(476):1566–1581, 2006.

[35] G.-R. Xue, W. Dai, Q. Yang, and Y. Yu. Topic-bridged plsa for cross-domain text classification. In *SIGIR '08*, pages 627–634, 2008.

[36] G.-R. Xue, D. Xing, Q. Yang, and Y. Yu. Deep classification in large-scale text hierarchies. In *SIGIR*, pages 619–626, 2008.

[37] L. Yao, D. Mimno, and A. McCallum. Efficient methods for topic model inference on streaming document collections. In *SIGKDD*, pages 937–946, 2009.

[38] B. Yu, S. Kaufmann, and D. Diermeier. Classifying party affiliation from political speech. *Journal of Information Technology & Politics*, 5 (1):33–48, 2008.

[39] E. Zavitsanos, G. Paliouras, and G. A. Vouros. Non-parametric estimation of topic hierarchies from texts with hierarchical dirichlet processes. *J. Mach. Learn. Res.*, 12:2749–2775, 2011.

[40] C. Zhai and J. Lafferty. Model-based feedback in the language modeling approach to information retrieval. In *CIKM '01*, pages 403–410, 2001.

[41] D. Zhou, L. Xiao, and M. Wu. Hierarchical classification via orthogonal transfer. In *ICML*, pages 801–808, 2011.

From "More Like This" to "Better Than This"

Haggai Roitman
IBM Research - Haifa
Mount Carmel, Haifa 31905
haggai@il.ibm.com

Doron Cohen
IBM Research - Haifa
Mount Carmel, Haifa 31905
doronc@il.ibm.com

Shay Hummel
IBM Research - Haifa
Mount Carmel, Haifa 31905
shayh@il.ibm.com

ABSTRACT

In this paper we address a novel retrieval problem we term the *"Better Than This"* problem. For a given pair of a user query to be answered by some search engine and a single example answer provided by the user that may or may not be a correct answer to the query, we determine whether or not there exists some better answer within the search engine. The approach we take is to test whether the user's provided answer can be used for relevance feedback in order to improve the ability of the search engine to better answer the user's query. If this is indeed the case, then we determine that the original answer provided by the user is good enough and there is no need to consider a better alternative. Otherwise, we decide that the best alternative that the search engine can provide should be considered as a better answer. Using a simulation based evaluation, we demonstrate that, our approach provides a better decision making solution to this problem, compared to several other alternatives.

1. INTRODUCTION

In this paper we study the following retrieval problem: *"given some answer, obtained by a given user query in some way, can we find a single better alternative answer to suggest the user?"*. We term this problem the *"Better Than This"* problem. This is in contrast to previous *"More Like This"* retrieval tasks[1], whose goal is to provide answers that are similar to a given example answer.

As a motivating example to this problem, let's consider a case with an ordinary user who wish to resolve some technical problem that goes beyond that user's expertise (e.g., an installation of a new computer hardware). The user may decide to turn for the help of some technical related forum, hoping to find there a resolution to the problem. Lets further assume that, while browsing the forum for answers, the user encounters some suggested resolution (answer) proposed by

some member of the forum to some problem description that seems to resemble the one faced by the user. Yet, being a "novice" in this technical domain, the user finds it hard to determine whether this answer really resolves the problem or is actually completely irrelevant. In the later case, the user may need to continue searching for an alternative resolution. In such a situation, the user may benefit from a search service that may help with such a complex decision.

In this paper, we suggest a general solution to this problem as follows. For a given (user) query and an answer, which was obtained for that query in some way (e.g., from another search engine, forums, social media, etc.), we use a search engine to determine whether or not there exists some alternative answer that can better cover the information need expressed in the (user's) query. In case we predict that the search engine can better serve the query with an alternative answer, we provide that answer to the user; otherwise, we inform the user that the answer she has obtained is the best one she could get, compared to what the search engine has to offer.

The approach we take is to test whether the user's provided answer can be used for relevance feedback in order to improve the ability of the search engine to better answer the user's query. If this is indeed the case, then we determine that the original answer provided by the user is good enough and there is no need to consider a better alternative. Otherwise, we decide that the best alternative that the search engine can provide should be considered as a better answer. Using a simulation based evaluation, we demonstrate that, our approach provides a better decision making solution to this problem, compared to several other alternatives.

The rest of this paper is organized as follows. In Section 2 we shortly discuss related work. Then, in Section 3 we present our proposed decision making approach to the problem, which is then evaluated in Section 4. Finally, we conclude in Section 5.

2. RELATED WORK

Our work has some relationship with several previous works that have also tried to select among several retrieval strategies [1, 2, 4, 7, 8, 9]. Within these works, Balasubramanian and Allan [1] have chosen the best ranker among several candidate rankers using query performance prediction. To this end, each ranker was judged based on the predicted quality of its top-k retrieved answers [1]. Sheldon et al. [7] have used several QPP methods as gating features for learning to rank, used for choosing the best strategy for query blending (fusion) of result lists that were retrieved for several

---

[1]Such an option is available today by many state-of-the-art search engines, e.g., Elasticsearch: https://www.elastic.co/guide/en/elasticsearch/reference/current/query-dsl-mlt-query.html.

ICTIR '16, September 12-16, 2016, Newark, DE, USA

© 2016 ACM. ISBN 978-1-4503-4497-5/16/09. . . $15.00

DOI: http://dx.doi.org/10.1145/2970398.2970421

different query reformulations of the same original query. Balasubramanian et al. [2] have explored the usage of QPP methods for learning an optimal query reduction strategy for long queries. Wang et al. [9] have suggested a cascade-based retrieval approach, aiming at solving the effectiveness vs. efficiency retrieval tradeoff. Soskin et al. [8] have combined the rankings induce by several pseudo relevance models. Various relevance models were weighed according to their estimated ability to correctly represent the original information need [8]. Finally, Izsak et al. [4] have studied a related search diversification problem termed by the authors the *"The Search Duel"*. Given two rankers, one strong and one weak, the authors have explored several strategies for improving the search quality of the weak ranker using the results retrieved by the strong ranker. Such improvement was measured in the ability of the weak ranker to retrieve new relevant answers that were not suggested so far by the strong ranker.

This work differs from such previous works in several aspects. First, compared to previous works, we have **no access to the full retrieved top-k list of all rankers** but only to a single ranker we use in order to determine whether we can find a better alternative answer or not. Given such a restricted setting, applying most methods that were proposed by previous works on rankers selection into our problem is quite unpractical. Similar to Soskin et al. [8], we evaluate the ability of a given relevance model to correctly capture the information need. Yet, the motivation in [8] is completely different. Finally, an imminent difference of our work from that of Izsak et al. [4] is that, compared to [4], **we make no prior assumptions on which ranker is strong and which is weak** (actually the source that retrieved the "competitor" answer is assumed to be unknown).

3. DECISION STRATEGIES

Let q denote a given (user) query, and let d_q denote a single answer obtained for q form some **unknown** source. Let C denote a given corpus of documents which can be used to retrieve alternative answers $d \in C$ by employing some retrieval method $\mathcal{M}$ for evaluating q over C. Let $score_{\mathcal{M}}(d; q)$ further denote the retrieval score assigned by method $\mathcal{M}$ to answer $d \in C$ given query q. For a given pair (q, d'), with $d' \in C \cup \{d_q\}$, let $P(R = 1; q, d') \in [0, 1]$ denote the odds that d' is a relevant (correct) answer to query q.

Our decision making problem can be now formalized as follows: *for a given pair* (q, d_q), *determine whether* $P(R = 1; q, d_q) \geq P(R = 1; q, d^*)$, *where* $d^* = \underset{d \in C}{\operatorname{argmax}}\, score_{\mathcal{M}}(d; q)$ *is the best answer retrieved by retrieval method* $\mathcal{M}$ *in response to query* q *over corpus* C. In case we can confirm that this is true, then we determine that, compared to the alternative answers in corpus C, d_q is a "better" answer. Otherwise, we conclude that d^* is a better alternative (which can be suggested to the user).

3.1 Basic Strategies

At a first glance, it seems that such a decision can be trivially made as follow (termed **Direct** decision strategy): *given* (q, d_q), *treat answer* d_q *as yet another potential answer within corpus* C, *and therefore, simply return as an answer:* $d_{direct} = \underset{d' \in C \cup \{d_q\}}{\operatorname{argmax}}\, score_{\mathcal{M}}(d'; q)$. While the **Direct** strategy to the problem seems quite reasonable, in this paper

we shall show that much better decision strategies can be implemented.

Inspired by Izsak et al. [4] and other previous works on relevance feedback and query expansion [5, 3, 10], we next derive an alternative basic strategy as follows. A relevance model is induced from the (single) answer d_q and an expanded query q_e based on such feedback is evaluated over C using method $\mathcal{M}$. The highest scored answer: $d_e^* = \underset{d \in C}{\operatorname{argmax}}\, score_{\mathcal{M}}(d; q_e)$ is then considered as another single alternative answer. Assuming that answer d_q is indeed a true answer to query q, we can only hope that answer d_e^* will be also correct. This decision strategy is now termed **Feedback** and always returns answer d_e^* as the alternative answer.

3.2 Risk Aware Strategies

More educated decision strategies to be presented herein are based on the following hypothesis: *if the underlying retrieval method* $\mathcal{M}$ *improves its ability to provide an answer to* q *given* q_e, *then that only implies that the user's provided answer* d_q *is already a better answer compared to the best answer in* C *that method* $\mathcal{M}$ *may provide.*

In case we can confirm this hypothesis, then we determine that the original answer d_q is good enough and there is no need to consider a better alternative. Otherwise, we decide that the best alternative in C according to $\mathcal{M}$ (i.e., d^*) should be considered as a better answer. We next suggest two alternative strategies based on our hypothesis. Both strategies consider potential risks that may be incurred by using query q_e as a reference query for an educated decision making.

3.2.1 Query Ambiguity-Aware Strategy

We now consider both available pairs of a query and an alternative answer, i.e., (q, d^*) and (q_e, d_e^*). Assuming that answer d_q is a correct answer, and the underlying retrieval method $\mathcal{M}$ can better answer the expanded query q_e than the original one q, then we simply decide that neither d^* nor d_e^* should be considered as alternative answers. Our guiding principle here is that, since an expanded query q_e may be better answered than the original one q, then it implies that q has some **ambiguity issues** we would like to avoid dealing with. Moreover, using q_e to generate an alternative answer d_e^* instead of d^* also incurs a risk we wish to avoid. In accordance, a more "educated" decision strategy (termed *Query Ambiguity-Aware*) is now suggested as follows: *if* $P(R = 1; q_e, d_e^*) \geq P(R = 1; q, d^*)$, *then declare that both answers are inferior to answer* d_q; *otherwise, suggest answer* d^* *as the alternative.*

Obviously, we cannot really know which of the two answers d^* or d_e^* is better, since $P(R = 1; q_e, \cdot)$ for both answers is unknown. Instead, following [6], we simply estimate the quality of each answer based on the ratio between its score and the score of the k-*th* best answer returned by $\mathcal{M}$ over C for each query $q' \in \{q, q_e\}$. Here, the rational is that, the higher the ratio is, the better is the ability of method $\mathcal{M}$ to locate the best answer and hence, the more confident we can be that this is a correct answer. Let $\hat{P}(d')$ now denote the estimate quality of a given answer $d' \in \{d^*, d_e^*\}$. Let $\triangle(d^*, d_e^*) = \max\{0, \hat{P}(d^*) - \hat{P}(d_e^*)\}$ be the rectified difference in predicted quality between the two answers and let τ be a threshold parameter. The *Query Ambiguity-Aware* (**QAA** for short) decision strategy is now given by the following modified rule: *if $\sigma(\triangle(d^*, d_e^*)) \geq \tau$, then return d^* as an alternative answer; otherwise, stick with d_q.* $\sigma(x) = 1/(1 + \exp^{-x})$ is the *sigmoid* function, used to represent the quality difference in a probabilistic term.

3.2.2 Query Ambiguity and Drift Aware Strategy

We now make a final observation that, answer d_q by itself may be completely irrelevant to the information need expressed in q. Hence, using d_q for deriving a relevance model (now denoted θ_{d_q}), we may actually face the risk of **query drift** [5]. Therefore, our decision may be based on a false assumption on d_q's relevance. To mitigate such potential risk, we further try to evaluate to what extent the relevance model induced from d_q correctly models the information need expressed in q. To this end, following previous works on selective query expansion [3, 10] we estimate such query drift risk by measuring the similarity between the query q's model (denoted θ_q) and the relevance model θ_{d_q} as follows: $sim(q; \theta_{d_q}) = \exp^{-D_{KL}(\theta_q \| \theta_{d_q})}$; where $D_{KL}(\theta_q \| \theta_{d_q}) = \sum_{w \in q} p(w; \theta_q) \log \frac{p(w; \theta_q)}{p(w; \theta_{d_q})}$ is the *Kullback-Leibler divergence* between the query (language) model θ_q and θ_{d_q}. Hence, the similar the two models are, the better the relevance model captures the information need of query q (also termed *Faithfulness of Relevance Model* in [8]).

Using such an estimate we now derive an extended decision strategy (further termed *Query Ambiguity and Drift Aware* or **QADA** for short) which combines both risk-aware features as follows:
if $\sigma(\alpha \cdot \triangle(d^*, d_e^*) + \beta \cdot sim(q; \theta_{d_q})) \geq \tau$, then return d^* as an alternative answer; otherwise, stick with d_q. Here α and β are two additional learning parameters that control the relative importance of each quality (risk) feature. Please note, **QAA** is simply an instance of **QADA** with $\alpha = 1$ and $\beta = 0$.

4. EVALUATION

4.1 Datasets and Setup

Corpus	# of documents	Queries	Disks
GOV2	25,205,179	701-850	GOV2
WT10G	1,692,096	451-550	WT10g
ROBUST	528,155	301-450, 601-700	4&5-{CR}
AP	242,918	51-150	1-3
WSJ	173,252	151-200	1-2

Table 1: TREC data used for experiments.

We evaluate the various decision strategies that were presented in Section 3 (and few more) using a simulated environment that mimics our usecase of interest. On each simulation, for a given query, we first retrieve the best (single) answer over a given TREC corpus, using some (relatively strong) baseline retrieval method. Both the query and that answer are then provided as a "challenge" for decision making. Given a different retrieval method that should be used to retrieve alternative answers, we determine whether to use the best answer of that method or stick with the initial answer retrieved by the first baseline method.

The TREC corpora and queries used for the evaluation are specified in Table 1. Titles of TREC topics were used as queries and retrieved documents as answers. The Apache

Lucene[2] open source search library (version 5.2.1) was used for indexing and searching documents. Documents and queries were processed using Lucene's English text analysis (i.e., tokenization, stemming, stopwords, etc). Two baseline retrieval methods that are implemented within Lucene were chosen as the baseline retrieval methods for our simulation. These methods are the query-likelihood (**QL**) with Dirichlet smoothing[3] and Okapi-BM25[4] (**BM25**). Free parameters[5] of both methods were tuned so as to *optimize* MAP.

The RM3 pseudo relevance feedback model [5] was used for deriving the relevance model θ_{d_q} as follows. Answer d_q was assumed to be relevant (i.e., serving as a feedback answer). Let w denote a term in the vocabulary and let $p_x^{[\mu]}(\cdot)$ denote text x's Dirichlet smoothed language model with smoothing parameter μ [5, 11]. The likelihood of a given term w according to the RM3 relevance model in our case is simply calculated as follows:

$$p_{RM3}(w; \theta_{d_q}) \stackrel{def}{=} \lambda \cdot p_q^{[0]}(w) + (1 - \lambda) \cdot p_{d_q}^{[1000]}(w),$$

with $\lambda = 0.9$, following [5]. The top-10 terms with the highest $p_{RM3}(w; \theta_{d_q})$ were further chosen to construct the expended query q_e. For a given expanded query q_e, we further obtained the top-$k = 100$ documents from corpus C using method $\mathcal{M}$.

For each corpus, among the two retrieval methods that we used (i.e., either **QL** or **BM25**), the better performing retrieval method (according to MAP) was chosen to simulate the "unknown" source of the user's provided answer, and the second one served as the instantiation of method $\mathcal{M}$. Using such a setting, the **Direct** strategy is simply implemented by considering the best answer returned for query q using the weaker retrieval method (which represents method $\mathcal{M}$) for scoring documents. This further allows us to directly compare with the *WeakReRank* strategy of Izsak et al. [4], which in this setting is actually the same as the **Feedback** strategy. We further evaluated two other "trivial" strategies. The first, denoted **SingleBest**, always chooses d_q as the answer. Hence, **SingleBest** strategy represents the best choice based on the best single retrieval method (i.e., either **QL** or **BM25**) used to generate d_q in our simulation. The second, denoted **Random**, randomly selects between d_q and d^*.

Finally, we compared our proposed decision strategies (i.e., **QAA** and **QADA**) that were described in Section 3 with the other strategies using accuracy (i.e., Precision@1) as the target measure. To this end, using 5-fold cross validation, for each TREC corpus, the various learning parameters (i.e., α, β and τ) were optimized using 80% of the queries, while the rest 20% were used for evaluation. We report the average accuracy obtained over all folds. Statistical significant differences in performance were further measured using the paired two-tailed Student's t-test for 95% of confidence.

4.2 Results

---

[2] http://lucene.apache.org
[3] https://lucene.apache.org/core/5_2_1/core/index.html?org/apache/lucene/search/similarities/LMDirichletSimilarity.html
[4] https://lucene.apache.org/core/5_2_1/core/index.html?org/apache/lucene/search/similarities/BM25Similarity.html
[5] For QL: (Dirichlet-smoothing parameter) $\mu \in \{100, 200, \ldots, 5000\}$. For BM25: $k1 \in \{0, 0.1, \ldots, 3.0\}$ and $b \in \{0, 0.1, \ldots, 2.0\}$.

	ROBUST	WT10g	GOV2	AP	WSJ
SingleBest	57.6^{rd}	38.8^{rd}	70.0^{rd}	53.1^{rd}	58.2^{rd}
Random	56.9	36.7	68.0^{d}	49.21^{d}	57.1
Direct	56.8	37.8^{r}	61.3	47.2	56.4
Feedback	57.6^{rd}	38.8^{rd}	68.7^{d}	56.1^{rd}	58.2^{rd}
QAA	58.4^{rd}_{sf}	40.2^{rd}_{sf}	71.0^{rd}_{sf}	57.0^{rd}_{s}	62.3^{rd}_{sf}
QADA	$\mathbf{58.8}^{rd}_{sf}$	$\mathbf{40.8}^{rd}_{sfq}$	$\mathbf{72.1}^{rd}_{sf}$	$\mathbf{58.1}^{rd}_{sf}$	$\mathbf{64.1}^{rd}_{sf}$

Table 2: Relative accuracy (i.e., Precision@1) of the various alternative decision strategies for various corpora. The letters s, r, d, f, q and t denote a statistically better performance compared to the SingleBest, Random, Direct, Feedback, QAA and QADA methods, respectively.

The results of our evaluation are reported in Table 2. As we would have expected, the **SingleBest** strategy, from which we obtained the initial answer for each query, is significantly better than the **Direct** strategy that provides the answer based on the underlying method $\mathcal{M}$ used for retrieving an alternative answer from the corpus. The former, is further better than making a random choice (i.e., **Random** strategy). Compared to the **Direct** approach, having a random (uneducated) choice may incur a risk, where a mixed performance trend between both **Direct** and **Random** strategies was observed.

Examining the **Feedback** strategy, we observe that, in most cases, it is always a better strategy than the **Random** and **Direct** strategies. This implies that, in many cases, an educated decision should avoid returning the direct answer d_{direct}, but rather stick with the original answer that was proposed. Yet, as we can observe by further comparing this strategy to the **QAA** and **QADA** strategies, having a more educated decision can even further improve performance. We next observe that, in three out of the five corpora, the **Feedback** and **SingleBest** strategies had the same performance. This may imply that, in these corpora, the **Feedback** strategy, when using the **SingleBest** answer as a query, returns an answer that is the same one or very similar to it. Hence, in these cases, the **Feedback** strategy provides an answer to the "*More Like This*" task. Interestingly enough, we further observed a mixed outcome in the two other corpora (GOV2 and AP), where the **Feedback** and **SingleBest** strategies behaved differently.

Finally, we observe that, overall, the **QAA** and **QADA** decision strategies, which aim at reducing the risk of answer misselection, provide the best decision making. Among the two, **QADA** was the overall best choice, further providing a significant improvement to the **SingleBest** and **Direct** strategies that are based on the two baseline retrieval methods that were used for the simulation (between 2%-10% better accuracy compared to the best one among the two). This demonstrates that, using an educated decision based on our proposed strategies provides a much better selection among the two alternative retrieval methods.

5. CONCLUSIONS

In this work we provided several solutions to a novel "*Better Than This*" problem. In addition to several basic decision making strategies, we suggested a couple of strategies (**QAA** and **QADA**) that test whether the user's provided answer can be used for relevance feedback in order to improve the ability of the search engine to better answer the user's query. These strategies allowed to make more educated decisions by considering the possibilities of query ambiguity or query drift that may accompany our assumption about the base example query answer used for decision making.

As future work, we plan devise an extended strategy that make decisions based on answers that come from several hidden sources. One possible direction would be to follow a cascade decision approach, similar in fashion to [9].

6. REFERENCES

[1] Niranjan Balasubramanian and James Allan. Learning to select rankers. In *Proceedings of the 33rd International ACM SIGIR Conference on Research and Development in Information Retrieval*, SIGIR '10, pages 855–856, New York, NY, USA, 2010. ACM.

[2] Niranjan Balasubramanian, Giridhar Kumaran, and Vitor R. Carvalho. Exploring reductions for long web queries. In *Proceedings of the 33rd International ACM SIGIR Conference on Research and Development in Information Retrieval*, SIGIR '10, pages 571–578, New York, NY, USA, 2010. ACM.

[3] Steve Cronen-Townsend, Yun Zhou, and W. Bruce Croft. A framework for selective query expansion. In *Proceedings of CIKM '04*.

[4] Peter Izsak, Fiana Raiber, Oren Kurland, and Moshe Tennenholtz. The search duel: A response to a strong ranker. In *Proceedings of the 37th International ACM SIGIR Conference on Research & Development in Information Retrieval*, SIGIR '14, pages 919–922, New York, NY, USA, 2014. ACM.

[5] Victor Lavrenko and W. Bruce Croft. Relevance based language models. In *Proceedings of SIGIR '01*.

[6] Ahmet Murat Ozdemiray and Ismail Sengor Altingovde. Query performance prediction for aspect weighting in search result diversification. In *Proceedings of CIKM '14*.

[7] Daniel Sheldon, Milad Shokouhi, Martin Szummer, and Nick Craswell. Lambdamerge: Merging the results of query reformulations. In *Proceedings of the Fourth ACM International Conference on Web Search and Data Mining*, WSDM '11, pages 795–804, New York, NY, USA, 2011. ACM.

[8] Natali Soskin, Oren Kurland, and Carmel Domshlak. Navigating in the dark: Modeling uncertainty in ad hoc retrieval using multiple relevance models. In *Proceedings of the 2Nd International Conference on Theory of Information Retrieval: Advances in Information Retrieval Theory*, ICTIR '09, pages 79–91, Berlin, Heidelberg, 2009. Springer-Verlag.

[9] Lidan Wang, Jimmy Lin, and Donald Metzler. A cascade ranking model for efficient ranked retrieval. In *Proceedings of SIGIR '11*.

[10] Mattan Winaver, Oren Kurland, and Carmel Domshlak. Towards robust query expansion: Model selection in the language modeling framework. In *Proceedings of SIGIR '07*.

[11] ChengXiang Zhai and John Lafferty. A risk minimization framework for information retrieval. *Inf. Process. Manage.*, 42(1):31–55, January 2006.

Understanding the Message of Images with Knowledge Base Traversals

Lydia Weiland, Ioana Hulpuş, Simone Paolo Ponzetto, and Laura Dietz
Data and Web Science Group
University of Mannheim
68131 Mannheim, Germany
{lydia, ioana, simone, dietz}@informatik.uni-mannheim.de

ABSTRACT

The message of news articles is often supported by the pointed use of iconic images. These images together with their captions encourage emotional involvement of the reader. Current algorithms for understanding the semantics of news articles focus on its text, often ignoring the image. On the other side, works that target the semantics of images, mostly focus on recognizing and enumerating the objects that appear in the image. In this work, we explore the problem from another perspective: Can we devise algorithms to understand the *message* encoded by images and their captions? To answer this question, we study how well algorithms can describe an image-caption pair in terms of Wikipedia entities, thereby casting the problem as an entity-ranking task with an image-caption pair as query. Our proposed algorithm brings together aspects of entity linking, subgraph selection, entity clustering, relatedness measures, and learning-to-rank. In our experiments, we focus on media-iconic image-caption pairs which often reflect complex subjects such as sustainable energy and endangered species. Our test collection includes a gold standard of over 300 image-caption pairs about topics at different levels of abstraction. We show that with a MAP of 0.69, the best results are obtained when aggregating content-based and graph-based features in a Wikipedia-derived knowledge base.

Keywords

Image understanding;media-iconic images;entity ranking

1. INTRODUCTION

Newspaper articles and blog posts are accompanied by figures which consist of an image and a caption. While in some cases figures are used as mere decoration, more often figures support the message of the article in stimulating emotions and transmitting intentions. This is especially the case on matters of controversial topics, such as *global warming*, where emotions are conveyed through so-called **media-icons** [29, 9]: images with high suggestive power that illustrate the topic. A picture of a polar bear on melting shelf ice is a famous example cited by advocates stopping carbon emissions [27, 26]. As such, many images are able to broadcast abstract concepts and emotions [25], beyond the physical objects they illustrate.

ICTIR '16, September 12 - 16, 2016, Newark, DE, USA

© 2016 Copyright held by the owner/author(s). Publication rights licensed to ACM.
ISBN 978-1-4503-4497-5/16/09. . . $15.00

DOI: http://dx.doi.org/10.1145/2970398.2970414

Previous research has focused on the identification and labeling of tangible objects that are *visible* in the image (e.g., PascalVOC [11], MS COCO [20], Im2Text [28]). While this is an important prerequisite towards image understanding, in this paper, we take a step further and study how to identify the abstract (*invisible*) concepts or themes that an image conveys. CaptionBot [38] aims at generating captions for a given image. However these also only focus on the literal aspects. For the example in Figure 1b, the generated caption states: "I think it's a sign in front of a forest."

This paper is concerned particularly with the identification and ranking of these overarching concepts, that capture the message of the image, hereafter called **gist**. Thus, we cast the problem of gist detection as an entity ranking task with the following twist:

Task (Gist detection): Given an image-caption pair as *query*, rank entities from Wikipedia according to how relevant they describe the gist expressed in the image.

To address this task, we study the combination between (1) content-based features, extracted from the analysis of Wikipedia text, and (2) graph-based features obtained by analyzing Wikipedia's underlying article-category graph. By using the knowledge base as a graph, we represent the entities therein as nodes. For consistency, in the following we use the term **node** to refer to Wikipedia entities. Consequently, a node that corresponds to the gist of an image is referred to as **gist node**.

We approach the problem of detecting the gist that represents the message conveyed by an image and its caption with the following pipeline: First, detected **objects** in the image and detected entity **mentions** in the caption are projected onto nodes of the knowledge base (called *seed nodes*). Next, the node neighborhood of the seeds in the knowledge graph is inspected as a possible set for gist candidates. Finally, several graph and text measures are combined into a node ranking.

Of course, this is only a simple representation of a much bigger problem of interpreting images. Nevertheless, we see this study as a starting point for following research on gist-based image search and classification, detection of themes in images, and recommending images from the web when writing new articles for news, blogs, and Wikipedia. But even in the simple form of casting image understanding as an *entity ranking problem*, we see immediate utility: Being able to tag and annotate images with Wikipedia concepts provides a new way of traversing large image collections, such as Wikimedia commons (more than 30 million images). It also enables the detection of fake photographic evidence on social media, or whenever pictures are taken out of context and presented with a political spin.

The underlying idea of the knowledge base expansion is based on the following hypothesis: Especially for images and captions that express an abstract meaning, such as media-icons, we assume that

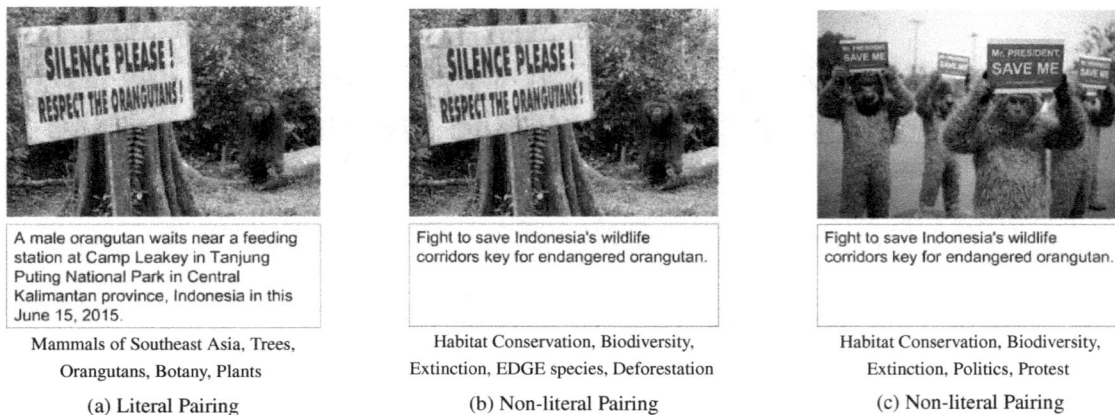

A male orangutan waits near a feeding station at Camp Leakey in Tanjung Puting National Park in Central Kalimantan province, Indonesia in this June 15, 2015.	Fight to save Indonesia's wildlife corridors key for endangered orangutan.	Fight to save Indonesia's wildlife corridors key for endangered orangutan.
Mammals of Southeast Asia, Trees, Orangutans, Botany, Plants	Habitat Conservation, Biodiversity, Extinction, EDGE species, Deforestation	Habitat Conservation, Biodiversity, Extinction, Politics, Protest
(a) Literal Pairing	(b) Non-literal Pairing	(c) Non-literal Pairing

Figure 1: Example image-caption pairs sharing either images or captions with their respective gist nodes[1].

the concepts that describe the gist of the pair best, are neither visible on the image, nor explicitly mentioned in the caption. Example of such entities transmitting the message referred to as gist are *global warming*, *endangered species*, *biodiversity*, or *sustainable energy*. Despite not being visible and consequently identifiable by image recognition, the gist nodes will likely be in close proximity to the objects in the image that are visible as well as to the entities mentioned in the captions. If this hypothesis is true, the node neighborhood of the seed nodes will not only contain the true gist nodes, but entity relatedness measures will help to pinpoint them.

We show through an extensive evaluation that the graph properties of nodes in the background knowledge base indicate that local and global measures are required to select correct gist nodes. This correlates with the overall working assumption that the gist of an image-caption pair is a product of common knowledge (e.g., a polar bear is an endangered animal), while being at the same time topic-specific (e.g., the polar bear is endangered through loss of its arctic habitat, partly caused by an increase in carbon emissions).

In this paper, we study the utility of our pipeline on a gold standard of 8200 true gist annotations (using relevance levels from 0 to 5), on more than 300 image-caption pairs about the discussed topic, global warming. To study the effectiveness of different measures, we use learning-to-rank as an experimentation environment.

Outline. We detail the problem statement and definitions in Section 2 and the related work in Section 3. In Section 4, we detail well-established methods that are used by our approach which is described in Section 5. We report findings from our experimental evaluation in Section 6 before concluding the paper.

2. PROBLEM STATEMENT AND GOLD STANDARD

In this work, we call an image instance and its associated textual caption an **image-caption pair**. Depending on the intention of the image-caption pair, we distinguish two types of pairs as follows. **Literal** pairs are those in which the caption describes or enumerates the objects depicted in the image. Figure 1a exemplifies a literal image-caption pair. **Non-literal** pairs, where the media-iconic pairs are a subclass of, are those which convey an abstract message, complemented and/or controlled by the image. As a running

[1]http://www.reuters.com/article/us-environment-orangutan-idUSKCN0Q50HN20150801, http://www.thehindu.com/opinion/op-ed/how-oil-palm-could-kill-orangutans/article5777819.ece, last accessed: 07/18/2016.

example, we use a topic on how deforestation affects endangered species. Figure 1 depicts three image-caption pairs, where two of them are on that topic and one (cf. Figure 1a) is a literal pair. When used to enrich text, images form a union with their captions. To understand the gist of an image-caption pair, both the image and the caption are needed. The image by itself might be given a different message by changing the caption, while the same caption will change semantics if accompanied by a different image.

For example, the pair in Figure 1a, presents an orangutan in what seems to be a national park. The gist of this figure is "Mammals of Southeast Asia". By exchanging the caption it becomes apparent that the gist is to stop deforestation to save an endangered animal (cf. Figure 1b). Considering the corresponding caption thus allows for disambiguation of the gist.

On the other hand, captions alone are often brief and when taken out from the context of the image, they fail to convey the entire message. For instance, by inspecting only the caption "Fight to save Indonesia's jungle corridors key for endangered orangutan.", it is not clear whether the focus is on the negative effects of deforestation as depicted in Figure 1b, or on people who fight against the causes of these negative effects, as depicted in Figure 1c. Only an image can disambiguate the gist. We consequently consider image-caption pairs as the targeted *queries* for which gist entities are ranked.

Furthermore, without a basic familiarity with the topic or domain of the intended message, it is very hard even for humans to grasp its gist from just looking at it. Media-icons nearly always play with prior knowledge of the user and might be differently understood in different cultural circles. (Our assessors are European.)

2.1 Research Questions

In this paper we are studying the following research questions according to our task of **gist detection** (cf. Section 1).

RQ1: How to link objects and mentions to seed nodes? We hypothesize that a simple string-match for linking image objects and entity mentions of the captions onto seed nodes without direct disambiguation, best represents the initial image-caption pair as query. The graph traversal and the re-ranking will serve as indirect disambiguation strategy.

RQ2: How close are gist nodes to seed nodes? We further hypothesize that good gist nodes are found in close proximity to the seed nodes. We study proximity in three layers: seed nodes, nodes in between seed nodes (**intermediate nodes**), and nodes two hops away from intermediate nodes (**border nodes**). In RQ2 we study the distribution of highly relevant gist nodes in these different layers and with respect to non-literal, literal, and both types of pairs.

RQ3: What is the benefit of the node neighborhood? We hypothesize that graph features, such as clusters and centrality measures, derived from the subgraph that includes border nodes, provide useful indicators for the true gist nodes. In RQ3 we separately study features involving border nodes from other features based on text as well as global graph properties.

2.2 Gold Standard

To the best of our knowledge there is yet no dataset covering the topic of non-literal image-caption detection, especially not including both, literal *and* non-literal pairs. To arrive at a challenging and realistic dataset, we collect images and captions for six topics related to global warming from the newspaper The Guardian, Our World magazine, and the website of the organization Union of Concerned Scientists. We confirm that all of them fall in the class of non-literal image-caption pairs.

To obtain equivalent literal image-caption pairs, we create an alternative descriptive caption for each image. The result is a balanced collection of 328 image-caption pairs (164 unique images).

Our aim is to evaluate the gist candidate selection and ranking approach without the complications from imperfect image processing (which is a research question for a different audience). Instead, we assign objects in images with bounding boxes and textual labels from a list of 43 object labels (e.g., Windmill, Solar panel, Orangutan), which are visible on the images.

To study the gist detection task, for each pair (both literal and non-literal) experts assess which of the nodes from the knowledge base represent the gist expressed in the image-caption pair. Gist nodes assessments are graded by relevance levels 0 to 5, from 0 (non-relevant), to 4 (relevant), reserving grade 5 for the six original non-literal topics such as *Biodiversity* and six corresponding literal topics such as *Orangutan*. Of the 8191 non-zero gist node annotations in total ($\approx$25 per pair), 3100 obtain a grade of 4 or higher.

To evaluate RQ1, annotators separately assess links between entity mentions from the caption and objects of the image to nodes in the knowledge base.

Compared to other test collections in computer vision, this dataset of 328 "queries" is rather a small collection. However, this is the first test collection for literal and non-literal image-caption pairs with gold standard gist annotations and simulated object tags[2].

3. RELATED WORK

This work touches on different research communities evolving around the fields object detection from images, entity linking and retrieval, and using graph structure and content of knowledge bases.

Object detection from images. Triggered through benchmark collections, for image retrieval [37] and benchmarking tasks [33], a large body of works focuses on how to detect objects in images (e.g., PascalVOC [11], MS COCO [20], Im2Text [28]). These either train object detectors from images with bounding box annotations or use captions to guide the training or generate captions for images, based on an unsupervised model from the spatial relationship of such bounding boxes [10].

Since many images are accompanied by captions, approaches have been devised that use text in such captions to aid the detection

of objects and actions depicted in the image. This idea is exploited using supervised ranking [16], using entity linking and WordNet distances [39], and using deep neural networks [35]. One application is image question answering [32]. Research to this end has thus far focused on literal image-caption pairs, where the caption enumerates the objects visible in the image. In contrast, the emphasis of this work is on non-literal image-caption pairs with media-iconic messages, which allude to an abstract gist concept that is not directly visible.

Even though datasets such as ImageNet, provide over 14 Mio. images, only 8% have bounding boxes, which are crucial for training object detectors. The lack of such training material is the only barrier for application in our domain. For this reason and to facilitate reproducibility of our research, we only simulate object detection in this work.

Entity linking. Detecting entity mentions in text and linking them to nodes in a knowledge base is a task well studied in the TAC KBP venue [24]. Most approaches include two stages: The first stage identifies candidate mentions of entities in the text with a dictionary of names. These candidates are disambiguated in the following stage using structural features from the knowledge graph, such as entity relatedness measures [5] and other graph walk features [36]. A prominent entity linking tool is the TagMe! system [12]. A simpler approach, taken by DBpedia spotlight [22], focuses on unambiguous entities and breaks ties by popularity. We evaluate both approaches in Section 6.

Entity retrieval. We cast our gist detection task as an entity retrieval task, with an image-caption pair as the query. Entity retrieval tasks have been studied widely in the IR community in INEX and TREC venues [8, 1]. The most common approach is to represent entities through textual and structural information in a combination of text-based retrieval models and graph measures [41].

Different definitions of entities have been explored. Recently, the definition of an entity as "anything that has an entry on Wikipedia" has become increasingly popular. Using entities from a knowledge base that are (latently) relevant for a query for ad hoc document retrieval has lead to performance improvements [6, 31]. Moreover, using text together with graphs from article links and category membership for entity ranking has been demonstrated to be effective on freetext entity queries such as "ferris and observation wheels" [7]. In contrast to this previous work, our paper focuses on a graph expansion and clustering approach.

In order to facilitate robust ranking behaviour, clustering is often combined into a back-off or smoothing framework. This has been successfully applied for document ranking by Raiber et al. [30], and our approach adopts it for the case of entity ranking.

Topic and document cluster labeling. Other research directions that are closely related to ours are concerned with labeling pre-computed topic models [21, 18] and with labeling document clusters [4]. Topic model labeling is the task of finding the gist of a topic resulted from probabilistic topic modeling. Solutions to these related problems make implicit or explicit use of knowledge about words and concepts harvested from a document corpus. Such knowledge is not available for our problem rendering most of these approaches inapplicable.

Entity relatedness. The purpose of entity relatedness is to score the strength of the semantic association between pairs of concepts or entities. The research on this topic dates back several decades [40], and a multitude of approaches have been researched. Among them, we place particular emphasis on measures that use a knowledge base for computing relatedness. We distinguish two main direc-

---

[2]https://github.com/lweiland/GistDataset

tions: (i) works that use the textual content of the knowledge base [14, 17], particularly Wikipedia, and (ii) works that exploit the graph structure behind the knowledge base, particularly Wikipedia or Freebase hyperlinks [23], DBpedia [34, 19].

4. PRELIMINARIES

The main idea behind our approach is that a general-purpose knowledge base such as Wikipedia can aid the algorithmic understanding of the message conveyed by image and caption. We hypothesize that the way articles and categories are connected in Wikipedia can be exploited to identify nodes that capture the gist of the image-caption pair.

4.1 Knowledge Graphs

Given a knowledge base, we define a **knowledge graph** as the directed or undirected graph $KG(V, E, T, \tau)$ such that the set of nodes V contains all nodes representing entities in the knowledge base, every edge $e_{ij} \in E$ corresponds to one relation in the knowledge base between two nodes v_i and v_j, the set T contains the relation types in the knowledge base, and the function $\tau : E \rightarrow T$ assigns each edge in E exactly one type in T. In this paper, we mostly consider the knowledge graph undirected, unless specified otherwise. In the following, we shortly explain preliminaries that are applied within our pipeline, but that are not part of our contribution.

Node properties. One of the most commonly used properties of nodes is their *degree* [15]. The degree of a node is the count of all edges that are adjacent to it. Another property of nodes is their tendency of being part of triangles called *local clustering coefficient* [15]. It is computed as the probability that any two random neighbors of a node are connected themselves.

Our intuition is that, these measures help to find a balance between specific and trivial nodes, and thus, the correct gist nodes. The degree and clustering coefficient of nodes are local measures that describe the nodes only in their closest vicinity.

Graph centrality measures. In the domain of network analysis, a wide range of graph centrality measures have been used with the purpose of locating the most important or influential nodes in the network. The PageRank [3] scores nodes based on their stationary probability that a random surfer will visit them. Betweeness centrality [13] defines a node as the more important the more often it lies on the shortest path between any two nodes in the graph.

Given a knowledge graph KG, as we detail later, our approach makes use of a distance metric $\sigma^{(-1)} : V \times V \rightarrow \Re^+$ between two nodes. This metric captures the inverse of a similarity, relatedness, or semantic association measure between the concepts that are represented by the nodes. There are two of the main classes of measures: (i) those based on textual content associated with nodes and (ii) those based on a graph measure. In this work we are interested in using both content and graph structure.

4.2 Entity Relatedness

Content-based relatedness. Additionally we incorporate a content-based measure of relatedness. As each node in the DBpedia knowledge graph has a corresponding article in Wikipedia, we leverage a retrieval index on Wikipedia articles.

For a given entity mention, an object tag, or textual representation of the whole image-caption pair, we can use a retrieval model, which uses a query likelihood, to associate a measure of relevance with each node.

Graph-based relatedness. A great variety of semantic relatedness measures have been studied [40]. We follow Hulpus et al. [19] who introduce the exclusivity-based measure, which we use as a node metric $\sigma^{(-1)}$. The authors found that it works particularly well on knowledge graphs of categories and article membership (which we use also) for modeling concept relatedness. It was shown to outperform simpler measures that only consider the length of the shortest path, or the length of top-k shortest paths, as well as the measure proposed in [34].

The exclusivity-based measure assigns a *cost* for any edge $s \xrightarrow{r} t$ of type r between source node s and target node t. The cost function is the sum between the number of alternative edges of type r starting from s and the number of alternative edges of type r ending in t, as shown in Formula 1.

$$\text{cost}(s \xrightarrow{r} t) = |\{s \xrightarrow{r} *\}| + |\{* \xrightarrow{r} t\}| - 1, \quad (1)$$

where 1 is subtracted to count $s \xrightarrow{r} t$ only once.

The more neighbors connected through the type of a particular edge, the less informative that edge is, and consequently the less evidence it bears towards the relatedness of its adjacent concepts. By summing up the costs of all edges of a path p, one can compute the cost of that path, denoted $\text{cost}(p)$. The higher the cost of a path, the lower its support for relatedness between the nodes at its ends. Thus, given two nodes, s and t, their relatedness is computed as the inverse of the weighted sum of the costs of the top-k shortest paths between them (ties are broken by cost function). Each path's contribution to the sum is weighted with a length based discounting factor α:

$$\sigma(s, t) = \sum_{i=1}^{k} \alpha^{\text{length}(sp_i)} \times \frac{1}{\text{cost}(sp_i)} \quad (2)$$

where sp_i denotes the i'th shortest path between s and t. $\alpha \in (0, 1]$ is the length decay parameter and k is a number of shortest paths to consider.

5. APPROACH: GIST DETECTION

As previously stated, the main idea behind our approach is that given a knowledge graph that covers the subject of the image-caption pair, the gist nodes lie in the proximity of the concepts mentioned in the caption or illustrated in the image. Furthermore, we define features of candidate gist nodes based on their graph relations. These come from different pipeline steps where we introduce them and are used in a final supervised reranking (Step 5). We present these steps as a pipeline that is illustrated in Figure 2. To further transmit the intuition of the approach, we make use of a running example (Figure 1) that shows each step according to the pipeline in Figure 2. The running example will be the media-iconic pair of Figure 1b. As explained in the gold standard (cf. Section 2), objects are given, e.g., "orangutan" and "sign". From the caption we extract mentions, e.g.,"wildlife corridor", "Indonesia", and "orangutan". Those objects and mentions serve as input data for Step 1, where we continue with our running example.

5.1 The Knowledge Graph

Wikipedia provides a large general-purpose knowledge base about objects, concepts, and topics. Furthermore, and even more importantly for our approach, the link structure of Wikipedia can be exploited to identify topically associative nodes. DBpedia is a structured version of Wikipedia. All DBpedia concepts have their source in Wikipedia pages. In this work, our knowledge graph contains as nodes all the Wikipedia articles and Wikipedia Categories. As for

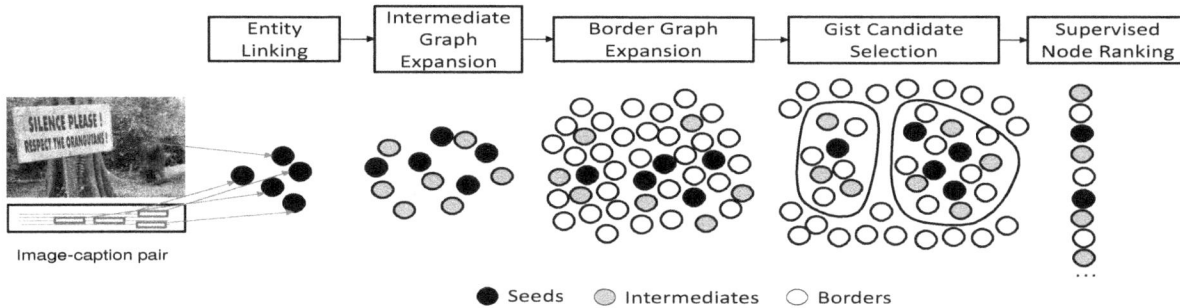

Figure 2: Gist extraction and ranking pipeline for a given image-caption pair. For simplicity, in this figure we omit the edges between nodes.

edges, we consider the following types of relations T, named by their DBpedia link property:

- **dcterms:subject** The category membership relations that link an article to the categories it belongs to, e.g., Wildlife corridor dcterms:subject Wildlife conservation.

- **skos:broader** Relationship between a category and its parent category in a hierarchical structure, e.g., Wildlife conservation skos:broader Conservation.

- **skos:narrower** Relationship between a category and its subcategories, e.g., Conservation skos:narrower EDGE species.

5.2 Step 1: Image and Caption Node Linking

The first step is to project objects depicted in the image and entities mentioned in the caption onto nodes in the knowledge base.

To identify and create entity links for concepts mentioned in the caption to Wikipedia, we identify nouns and noun phrases in the caption as candidates for entity mentions. These candidate mentions are linked to the knowledge base nodes, which we call **caption nodes** in the following.

Where entity linking for text is a well established field, methods for linking objects in images to knowledge base nodes is still an open research question. As a consequence, out-of-the-box object detectors only provide limited object vocabulary trained on a dataset with bounding box information, i.e., bicycles, people, fruits, and houses. For the purpose of this work, we simulate an object recognizer and provide manual tags for a variety of theoretically recognizable object classes such as "grass", "orangutan", "vegetation", or "sign". Linking these object class labels to knowledge base nodes yields a set of **image nodes**. The mapped caption and image nodes are called **seed nodes** in the following.

We use a simple entity linking strategy that is both applicable to caption nodes and image nodes which are linked to nodes in the knowledge graph that represent articles as follows: First, we attempt to link noun phrases and image labels with exact matches to the article title. Whenever we would link to a title of a disambiguation page, we include all redirected articles that are within 2-hop distance to already-linked nodes. (Using unambiguous links for disambiguation is a standard entity linking strategy.)

In the experimental evaluation in Section 6, we demonstrate that this approach is as successful as using the TagMe [12] entity linking system for the domain at hand.

Example. As shown in the pipeline (Figure 2) objects in the image (orangutan, sign, trunk, tree, ground, and vegetation) and the entity mentions of the caption (fight, Indonesia, jungle, corridor, key, and orangutan) are linked to seed nodes, e.g., *Wildlife corridor* and *Orangutan* (Figure 3, depicted in grey).

5.3 Step 2: Intermediate Graph Expansion

Especially for media-iconic pairs, the gist refers to an abstract non-depictable concept, such as *Endangered Species*. Therefore, Step 1 may not be sufficient to identify such a gist by simple entity linking. However, one of our hypotheses is that gist nodes will be found in the knowledge base on paths between seed nodes.

In order to extract the nodes that enable the connection between the seed nodes, we extract all the paths with length shorter than 4, i.e., 2-hop, that connect all pairs of seeds. We call the nodes on these paths, except the seed nodes, **intermediate nodes**. The graph resulted from combining all the nodes on these paths (including the seeds) as well as the edges of the paths, is what we call the **intermediate graph**.

Example. Figure 3 shows the paths shorter than 4 edges that connect the three concepts: *Orangutan*, *Indonesia* and *Wildlife corridor*. Note that there is no path shorter than 4 directly connecting *Indonesia* to *Wildlife corridor*.

5.4 Step 3: Border graph & Metric

In order to further assess the graph properties of the seeds and intermediates, we expand the graph that contains all their 2-hop neighbors and the edges between them. We name this graph the **border graph**. The nodes that are added to the graph as a consequence of the expansion are called **border nodes**, as they lie between the seeds, intermediates, and the rest of the knowledge graph. Figure 4 shows a part of the border graph obtained from expanding the intermediate graph shown in Figure 3.

For all the nodes in the border graph, we compute a distance metric σ between all nodes in the border graph. Actually, it suffices to compute $\sigma(x, y)$ for $x \in S \cup I$ and $y \in S \cup I \cup B$.

between each seed and intermediate node as well as all border nodes and seed/intermediate nodes. This metric is used in two ways when extracting the top gist candidates:

- Step 4a) clustering the seed and intermediate nodes;

- Step 4b) selecting border nodes close to clusters.

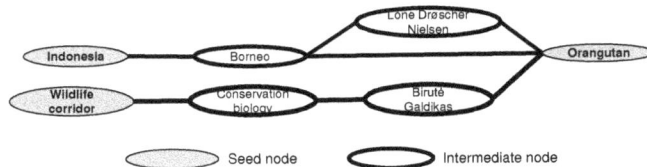

Figure 3: Example of intermediate graph for the image-caption pair in Figure 1 b.

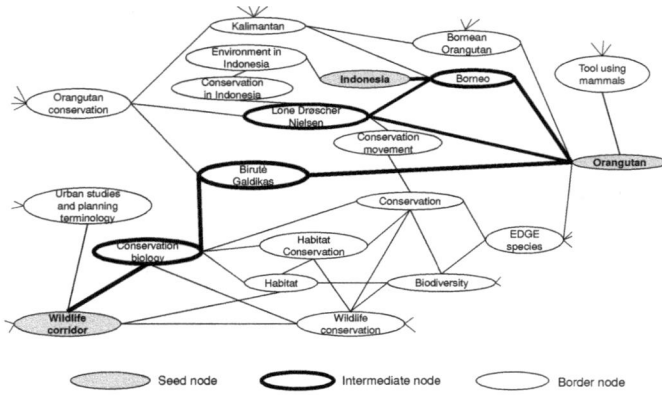

Figure 4: Border graph example for image-caption pair in Figure 1 b. For simplicity, the image does not make the distinction between article nodes and category nodes, and it also omits edge directions and edge costs.

As metric choices for the metric σ, we focus on the semantic relatedness measure defined in Equation 2, Section 4. This measure ingests information from the border nodes into the metric for two nodes from the joint seed/intermediate set (which is one way in which we exploit the border nodes). For this and many other graph-based measures it is sufficient to only consider the border graph. As the border graph is expected to be much smaller than the complete knowledge graph, this provides an upper bound on the computational complexity of this approach.

Example. According to Figure 4, with this step we include many border nodes such as, *Habitat, Biodiversity*, and *EDGE species*. Some of these constitute good candidates for gist nodes. But more importantly they affect the pairwise metric distance between the seed nodes. From the sparse information in the intermediate graph (Figure 3), it seems that *Indonesia* and *Wildlife Corridor* are equally far apart from *Orangutan*. However, metric uses information from the border graph to identify that *Indonesia* and *Orangutan* are much closer than *Wildlife Corridor* and *Orangutan*. An illustration of the distances is given in Figure 5.

5.5 Step 4a: Cluster Seed and Intermediates

After the previous step, we obtain a graph that contains all the concepts from the image and its caption, as well as multiple other concepts from the knowledge graph that lie in close proximity. As previously stated, our assumption is that the gist nodes are part of this graph, and that their graph properties will make them identifiable. However, a challenge is that often, an image-caption pair covers multiple sub-topics. Directly using the border graph between in the presence of multiple topics, will most often result in semantic drift and low-quality results.

To overcome this issue, we propose to identify weakly related sub-topics of an image-caption pair by clustering the joint set of seed and intermediate nodes based on their pairwise metric σ. We therefore anchor the set of gist candidate nodes to concepts that only arise in the context of the particular image-caption pair. To this end, we use the metric σ between all pairs of the joint seed and intermediate set, and apply Louvain clustering [2], a non-parametric modularity optimization network clustering algorithm. This clustering results in groups of seeds and intermediates that broadly correspond to different sub-topics of the image-caption pair.

Example. For the example in Figure 4, this step identifies several

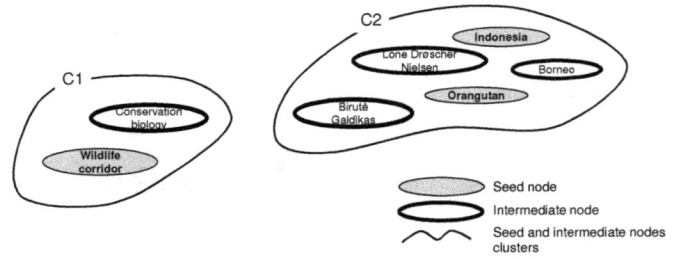

Figure 5: Example of seeds and intermediates, clustered based on their pairwise metric.

clusters, of which two are illustrated in Figure 5: Cluster C_1 is about wildlife conservation, containing the seed node *Wildlife Corridor*, and cluster C_2 represents topics about Indonesia, including both *Orangutan* and *Indonesia*.

5.6 Step 4b: Selecting Top Border Nodes

In this step, we identify a subset of suitable border nodes that would make good gist candidates. We hypothesize that these border nodes are close to any of the clusters according to the metric σ. We therefore compute for every border node x, its average metric distance $\bar{\sigma}$ for every cluster C as shown in Formula 3.

$$\bar{\sigma}(x, G^C) = \frac{1}{|S^C \cup I^C|} \sum_{y \in S^C \cup I^C} \sigma(x, y) \qquad (3)$$

In order to keep the number of gist candidates reasonable, for each cluster we select the top-k closest borders as well as all seeds and all intermediates. These nodes constitute the candidate node set which is ranked in the following step.

Example. The association of top border nodes with the two example clusters is illustrated in Figure 6. For instance, the wildlife cluster C_1 includes *Habitat* and *Biodiversity*, where both *Orangutan Conservation* and the the geographic region *Kalimantan* are associated with cluster C_2. The border node *Conservation* is associated with both clusters. These border nodes are included in the candidate set, in contrast to borders with a high distance such as *Urban studies and planning terminology* which are left out.

5.7 Step 5: Supervised Node Ranking

For each of the candidate nodes, a feature vector is created and ranked for relevance with supervised learning-to-rank. The feature vector consists of features listed in Table 1 collected from the various steps of the pipeline:

Seed and intermediate features (Step 1–2). Seed and intermediate nodes are distinguished by two binary features. For all the nodes in the intermediate graph, we compute and retain their betweenness centrality and their PageRank score as features.

Border features (Step 3–4). After the expansion into the border graph, we introduce a feature indicating the border nodes.

We leverage information from the clustering step by associating each node with its proximity $\bar{\sigma}(n, c)$ (inverse metric) to the nearest cluster c. This feature is also used as an unsupervised baseline in the experimental evaluation.

As border nodes can be associated with more than one cluster (cf. *Conservation* in Figure 6) we additionally add features capturing the sum (and average) proximity to all clusters $\sum_c \bar{\sigma}(n, c)$.

We assume that the more seed nodes are member of a cluster, the more relevant this cluster is for expressing the gist of the image-caption pair. This assumption is expressed in two features: a binary

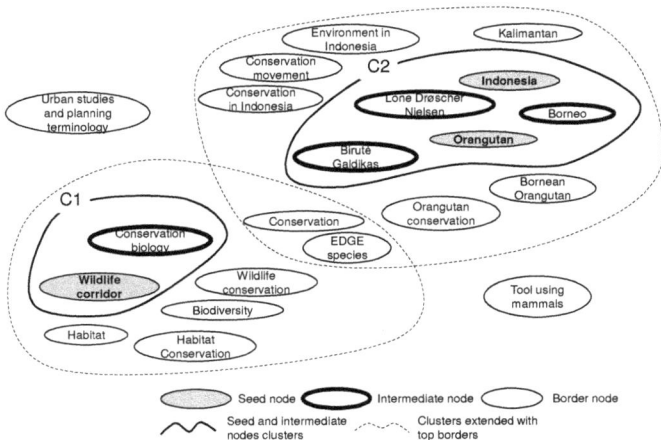

Figure 6: Example of clusters of seeds and intermediates, extended with their most highly related border nodes (top borders). The border nodes that have only weak semantic associations to the clusters are filtered out (e.g., *Tool using mammals* and *Urban studies and planning terminology*).

Table 1: Features for supervised re-ranking. Border features marked with X; baselines marked with †.

Description	Step	feat. set	
is seed node?	1		
is intermediate node?	2		
is border node?	3	X	
Page Rank on intermediate graph	2		
Betweenness Centrality on intermediate graph	2		
max node-cluster relatedness	4	X	†
avg node-cluster relatedness	4	X	
sum node-cluster relatedness	4	X	
is member of cluster with most seed nodes	4	X	
is member of cluster with most seed/intermediate nodes	4	X	
fraction of seeds in cluster	4	X	
fraction of seeds and intermediates in cluster	4	X	
query likelihood on KB text	cont.		†
indegree of node	glob.		
clustering coefficient	glob.		

feature indicating nodes which are members of the cluster that contains the highest number of seed nodes; and a fraction of all seed nodes that this node is sharing a cluster with (summing fractions for nodes with multiple cluster memberships).

Exploiting potential benefit of the joint set of seed and intermediate nodes, we further indicate membership of the cluster with highest number of nodes that are seed or intermediate nodes, as well as the fraction of all seed or intermediate nodes in shared clusters.

Content features. We include a content-based similarity measure for image-caption pairs. For this we concatenate all (distinct) entity mentions from the caption and all object annotations from the image as a keyword query. We use the query to retrieve textual content associated with article and category nodes using the query likelihood model with Dirichlet smoothing. We use this retrieval model to only rank nodes in the candidate set relative to each other.

We use this ranking as a baseline for the experimental evaluation and include the reciprocal rank as a node feature.

Global features. Finally we also include global node features that are independent of the image-caption pair. These include the indegree of a node in the graph as well as the clustering coefficient.

These generated feature vectors serves as an input for a listwise

Table 2: Number of image and caption nodes after entity linking.

	Non-Literal		Literal		Overall
	Image	Caption	Image	Caption	
Unique nodes	43	684	43	306	806
Total occurrences	640	1412	640	843	3535

Table 3: Correctness of different entity linking methods for image and caption nodes. ("No answer" counted as mistake.)

Linking Method	P	R
String2Article	0.9	0.97
String2Category	1.0	0.27
TagMe	0.7	0.83
Wikipedia index	0.81	0.98

learning-to-rank model, trained with respect to the target metric Mean-average precision (MAP). The model is evaluated with five-fold cross validation based on MAP, NDCG, and Precision@k.

6. EXPERIMENTAL EVALUATION

The utility of our pipeline is evaluated on gold standard annotations on 328 image-caption pairs from the wide topical domain of global warming. The evaluation is presented according to the research questions (**RQ**) of Section 2.1. In the gold standard gist nodes are assessed with a grade, ranging from 0-5, where 0 is non-relevant and 5 represents maximally relevant. Unless noted otherwise, we binarize the assessments and call a node relevant if and only if it is rated with a grade of 4 or 5. Among all relevant nodes in this study: 54,6 % of all gist nodes are entities and 45,4% are categories.

Experimental setup. We use a combined knowledge base aligning Wikipedia (WEX dump from 2012), Freebase (from 2012), and DBpedia (from 2014). This knowledge base is used to entity linking, deriving edges for the graph, and the content-based retrieval methods. The knowledge base is indexed with Galago.[3] With respect to the relatedness measure we use for metric $\sigma^{(-1)}$, we follow Hulpus et al. [19], Formula 2. We use their settings for hyperparameters $\alpha = 0.25$ and take the $k = 3$ shortest paths.

6.1 RQ 1: Seed node linking

We first evaluate the entity linking performance of the simple string-match method used in Step 1 to produce a set of image nodes and caption nodes. These together form the set of seed nodes. We use a separate gold standard to evaluate the correctness of the established links (i.e., not the gold standard in Section 2, which is used in RQ2 and RQ3). We verify all links for correctness, especially those with multiple meanings. In our application domain of global warming, most entities and objects denote general concepts as common nouns – people and organizations are an exception.

Image and caption nodes. We find that a total of 806 different nodes are reached from image or caption across all pairs. These result in 3535 links from image objects or caption mentions across the dataset. In total, only 5 noun phrases in captions are not linkable to the knowledge base (e.g., underwater view).

Table 2 presents the total number of different image nodes and caption nodes, where we distinguish between literal and non-literal image-caption pairs. We see that all images make use of an object vocabulary that can be disambiguated to 43 different nodes (different senses are counted multiple times) with a total frequency of

---

[3]http://lemurproject.org/galago.php

Table 4: Quality of gist candidate selection method. Significance is indicated by * (paired t-test, p-value $\leq$ 0.05).

	Avg cands.	P	R	F1	ΔF1%
Seeds	8.6	0.18	0.16	0.17	0.0
Intermediates	11.4	0.19	0.22	0.21	+19.0%*
Top Borders	31	0.09	0.30	0.14	-21.4%*

Table 5: Statistics about proportion of highly ranked gists (grade > 3 and grade > 4), with respect to the found gist nodes in Table 4).

	Grade 4 or 5			Grade 5	
	All	Non-Lit.	Literal	Non-Lit.	Literal
Seeds	53.79%	53.46%	53.96%	57.89%	70.75%
Intermediates	21.05%	21.70%	20.73%	07.89%	17.92%
Borders	25.16%	24.84%	25.32%	34.21%	11.32%

640 linkable objects across all images. As each image gives rise to a literal and non-literal pair, there is no difference between these columns. We observe a much wider range of nodes when linking entity mentions in the caption. In particular we notice a smaller vocabulary for literal image-caption pairs (306 unique nodes) compared to non-literal pairs (684 unique nodes), where each node is mentioned about three times on average. However, we find that the caption nodes set from literal versus non-literal pairs have nearly no overlap.

Entity linking. The set of seed nodes is formed by the union of image and caption nodes. In Step 1 we link objects/mentions to article nodes. However, the same procedure could have been applied to category names as well. We first compare these two methods in comparison to entity links produced by the TagMe system. Furthermore, we use the retrieval index of texts associated with nodes and output the top ranked node (Wikipedia index).

Table 3 presents precision and recall achieved by these four methods on the set of all 806 unique image/caption nodes. We find that all methods perform reasonably well, where the category-based linking strategy cannot associate a vast majority of 581 objects / mentions. In particular, we find that our heuristics in Step 1 outperforms TagMe and is better in precision than retrieving from the Wikipedia index.

Discussion Step 1. The TagMe system is a strong state-of-the-art entity linking system. How can it be outperformed by such simple heuristics? TagMe is particularly strong whenever interpretation and association is required, for instance to disambiguate ambiguous people names, organizations, and abbreviations. In contrast, the concepts we are linking in this domain are mostly common nouns, for which Wikipedia editors have done the work for us already. In the remaining cases that need disambiguation, our heuristic is likely to encounter a disambiguation page. At this point, we are using a well known disambiguation heuristic by using graph connections to unambiguous contextual mentions/objects.

We conclude that our simple entity linking method on articles works much better than on categories and as well as TagMe, thus its use is justified in our pipeline.

6.2   RQ2: Distribution of Relevant Gist Nodes

The research question is, whether good gist nodes are found in close proximity neighborhood to the directly depicted and mentioned seed nodes. We distinguish proximity in the three expansion layers of seed nodes, intermediate nodes, and top border nodes and evaluate the benefits of each graph expansion step.

Benefits of expansions. Taking nodes with gist grades of 4 and 5 as relevant, we study how precision and recall changes with the different expansion/filtering steps along the pipeline (Step 1, 2, 4b). The results are presented in Table 4, where we give precision, recall, and F1 together with the number of average candidates per image-caption pair. In order to judge the significance of improvement for F1 we evaluate with the relative increase in precision, on a per-image-caption-pair basis, and report the average (denoted Δ). Significance is verified with a paired-t-test with level 0.05.

We find that especially the expansion into the intermediate graph increases both recall and precision. While the increase in F1 is relatively small, it is statistically significant across the image-caption pairs, where it yields an average increase of 19%.

The expansion into the border graph of Step 3 and its contraction to the closest border nodes in Step 4b yields the new set of top border nodes. While it increases recall quite drastically, the loss in precision leads to a significant loss in F1 (over the seed set).

Visible versus invisible gists. We subdivide the set of true gists (grade 4 or 5) into visible gists and invisible gists. Visible gists can be depicted, such as *Orangutan* or *Plants*. In contrast, invisible gists are non-tangible concepts such as *Biodiversity*. Confirming our intuition, we find a much higher fraction of non-visible gists in the candidate set of non-literal image-caption pairs (34%) than in literal image-caption pairs (10%). This trend is even more pronounced when we look at the seed sets associated with image-caption pairs, where 99% of relevant seeds for literal image-caption pairs are visible.

Distribution of high quality gists. We change perspective and ask in which expansion set the majority of high-quality gists are to be found. Initially, we hypothesized that especially for non-literal caption pairs, fewer good gists will be found in the seed set, which motivated the graph expansion approach. Accordingly we separately report findings on literal and non-literal subsets.

We study two relevance thresholds in Table 5, for relevant gists (grade 4 or 5) as well as a stricter threshold including grade 5 only. Gists graded with 5 are limited to the one major gist of the image-caption pair, which in almost all non-literal cases refers to an abstract topic such as *Biodiversity*.

Focusing on the distribution relevant gists (grade 4 or 5) in Table 5, left, we notice that more than half of the gists are already contained in the seed set and about 20% are found in the intermediate set. The much larger border set still contains a significant portion of relevant gists. Focusing on the differences between literal and non-literal pairs, we verify that there are no significant differences between the distributions. Where gists with grade 4 or 5 are highly relevant, they still include the most important visible concepts for non-literal image-caption pairs.

However, if we focus only on the distribution of gists with grade 5 in Table 5, right, we notice that 71% of high-quality gists in literal pairs are found in the seed set which is in stark contrast to only 58% for non-literal pairs. Also, for non-literal image-caption pairs we found the most useful gists in the set of border nodes with high cluster proximity.

Discussion of Steps 2–4. We confirm that many relevant (grade 4) and high-quality (grade 5) gists are found in the seed set and the node neighborhood. The large fraction of nodes available in the border set (compared to the intermediate set) suggests that limiting the intermediate graph expansion in Step 2, to be between seed nodes is too restrictive. We see our initial assumptions confirmed in that literal image-caption pairs, which is where most of the related work is focusing on, contain more visible gists, and those are directly visible/mentioned. For non-literal pairs, the high-quality

Table 6: Entity ranking results (grade 4 or 5) of supervised learning-to-rank. Significance is indicated by * (paired t-test, p-value ≤ 0.05).

	Both				Non-Literal				Literal			
	MAP	Δ%	NDCG @10	P @10	MAP	Δ%	NDCG @10	P @10	MAP	Δ%	NDCG @10	P @10
All Features	0.69	0.0	0.73	0.7	0.56	0.0	0.6	0.56	0.82	0.0	0.87	0.84
All But Borders	0.66	-4.35%*	0.7	0.67	0.54	-3.5%	0.57	0.55	0.78	-4.88%*	0.83	0.8
Only Borders	0.63	-8.70%*	0.64	0.64	0.52	-7.14%*	0.54	0.52	0.73	-10.98%*	0.74	0.76
Wikipedia ranking	0.43	-37.68%*	0.48	0.37								
max node-cluster relatedness	0.29	-57.97%*	0.57	0.40								

gists are not only invisible, but also more often only implicitly given. Nevertheless, the graph-based relatedness measures are able to identify a reasonable candidate set.

6.3 RQ3: Value of Border Features

The last research question assesses the quality of our supervised node ranking. We further inspect the question whether features generated by global and local graph centrality measures, especially those derived from border graph expansions enhances the overall gist node ranking.

For this study we use a supervised learning-to-rank approach to evaluate the benefit of the feature sets. Here we use the RankLib[4] package using all features, in comparison to the subset of border features only (cf. Step 5), and all but the border features. We train RankLib using the ground truths of gist nodes (grade 4 or 5 as relevant) optimizing for the metric mean-average precision. We use coordinate ascent with a linear kernel and perform 5-fold cross validation using each image-caption pair as one "query". This way we predict 328 node rankings for all image-caption pairs, while keeping training and testing data separate.

To assess the different aspects of content and semantic relatedness, we compare the results of Step 5 with the three feature sets and two baselines (marked with † in Table 1): One retrieves Wikipedia text using the query likelihood model on all entity mentions and object annotations concatenated, the other is based on an unsupervised ranking according to the maximal node-cluster relatedness measure, as described in Step 4. We use a learning-to-rank a model to study the value of border features (marked with b in Table 1). The results in Table 6 are tested for significance (p-value ≤ 0.05).

We study the research question with respect to both, non-literal, and literal pairs in Table 6, where we report ranking quality in terms of mean-average precision (MAP), NDCG@10, and precision (P@10) of the top ten ranks.

Overall entity ranking results. On the whole, our approach achieves relative high ranking performance of 0.69 MAP across all image-caption pairs. As expected, ranking non-literal image-caption pairs is much harder (MAP:0.56) than for literal pairs (MAP:0.82). Yet, even in the non-literal case, more than half of the nodes in the top 10 are relevant.

In contrast, both baselines are much worse. The baseline which ranks nodes by the query likelihood model on all entity mentions and objects achieves a MAP of 0.43 (being 38% worse). The baseline which just includes the max node-cluster relatedness obtains an even worse performance of 0.29 MAP, even though both achieve the same P@10 performance).

Value of border features. One research question was to study whether the border features, which include the metric (relatedness), clustering, and membership of largest cluster provide value. We

---
[4]http://lemurproject.org/ranklib.php

therefore compare the performance changes of the learning-to-rank approach, when we vary the feature set from full, to border features (and also an ablation study of all but border features). In both cases, the ranking quality drops significantly by 4–11%, where the literal pairs seem to benefit slightly more from border features.

Discussion of Step 4–5. The fact that our full re-ranking pipeline improves so drastically over both a retrieval baseline and a cluster-relatedness baseline demonstrates the benefit of our approach. Here, both baselines are incorporated with further information such as centrality, degree, and expansion zone. Regarding research question RQ3, we can verify that measures that are derived from border nodes (Step 4) are contributing a significant performance benefit.

7. CONCLUSION

Given an image-caption pair, our aim is to automatically understand the message it conveys. To this end, we focus on non-literal image-caption pairs with media-iconic elements as found in news articles.

Using a test collection of 328 image-caption pairs as "queries", we cast the problem of message understanding as an entity ranking task. First, objects in the image and entities in the caption are linked to nodes in a knowledge base. Then graph expansions and clustering are used to select a candidate set of knowledge base entities that represent the message. Candidates are ranked based on graph-based and content-based features, which outperform baselines using either as well as feature subsets.

We find that easy heuristics are sufficient to link objects to the knowledge base (RQ1). Furthermore, while for literal pairs, good gist nodes are often directly linked and often visible on the image, we find that for non-literal pairs about 40% of very important entities are only found in the expanded graph (RQ2). Simple graph expansion will introduce too much noise, but by using a supervised learning-to-rank approach which is capable of exploiting even far away nodes (RQ3) achieving a MAP 0.56 for image-caption pairs with a message.

Acknowledgements

This work is funded by the Research Seed Capital (RiSC) programme of the Ministry of Science, Research and the Arts Baden-Württemberg, and used computational resources offered from the bwUni-Cluster within the framework program bwHPC. Furthermore, this work was in part funded through the Elitepostdoc program of the BW-Stiftung and the University of New Hampshire.

8. REFERENCES

[1] K. Balog, P. Serdyukov, and A. P. d. Vries. Overview of the TREC 2010 entity track. Technical report, DTIC Document, 2010.

[2] V. D. Blondel, J.-L. Guillaume, R. Lambiotte, and E. Lefebvre. Fast unfolding of communities in large networks. *Journal of Statistical Mechanics: Theory and Experiment*, P10008:1–12, Oct. 2008.

[3] S. Brin and L. Page. The anatomy of a large-scale hypertextual web search engine. In *WWW*, pages 107–117, 1998.

[4] D. Carmel, H. Roitman, and N. Zwerdling. Enhancing cluster labeling using wikipedia. In *SIGIR*, pages 139–146, 2009.

[5] D. Ceccarelli, C. Lucchese, S. Orlando, R. Perego, and S. Trani. Learning relatedness measures for entity linking. In *CIKM*, pages 139–148, 2013.

[6] J. Dalton, L. Dietz, and J. Allan. Entity query feature expansion using knowledge base links. In *SIGIR*, pages 365–374, 2014.

[7] G. Demartini, C. S. Firan, T. Iofciu, and W. Nejdl. *WISE 2008*, chapter Semantically Enhanced Entity Ranking, pages 176–188. Springer, Berlin, Heidelberg, 2008.

[8] G. Demartini, T. Iofciu, and A. P. De Vries. Overview of the inex 2009 entity ranking track. In *Focused Retrieval and Evaluation*, pages 254–264. Springer, 2009.

[9] B. Drechsel. The berlin wall from a visual perspective: comments on the construction of a political media icon. *Visual Communication*, 9(1):3–24, 2010.

[10] D. Elliott and A. de Vries. Describing images using inferred visual dependency representations. In *ACL*, pages 42–52, 2015.

[11] M. Everingham, L. Gool, C. K. Williams, J. Winn, and A. Zisserman. The pascal visual object classes (VOC) challenge. *Int. J. Comput. Vision*, 88(2):303–338, 2010.

[12] P. Ferragina and U. Scaiella. Tagme: on-the-fly annotation of short text fragments (by wikipedia entities). In *CIKM*, pages 1625–1628. ACM, 2010.

[13] L. C. Freeman. Centrality in social networks conceptual clarification. *Social Networks*, page 215, 1978.

[14] E. Gabrilovich and S. Markovitch. Computing semantic relatedness using wikipedia-based explicit semantic analysis. In *IJCAI*, pages 1606–1611, 2007.

[15] T. L. Griffiths, J. B. Tenenbaum, and M. Steyvers. Topics in semantic representation. *Psychological Review*, 114:2007, 2007.

[16] M. Hodosh, P. Young, and J. Hockenmaier. Framing image description as a ranking task: Data, models and evaluation metrics. *Journal of Artificial Intelligence Research*, pages 853–899, 2013.

[17] J. Hoffart, S. Seufert, D. B. Nguyen, M. Theobald, and G. Weikum. Kore: Keyphrase overlap relatedness for entity disambiguation. In *CIKM*, pages 545–554, 2012.

[18] I. Hulpus, C. Hayes, M. Karnstedt, and D. Greene. Unsupervised graph-based topic labelling using DBpedia. In *WSDM*, pages 465–474, 2013.

[19] I. Hulpuş, N. Prangnawarat, and C. Hayes. Path-based semantic relatedness on linked data and its use to word and entity disambiguation. In *ISWC*, pages 442–457, 2015.

[20] T.-Y. Lin, M. Maire, S. Belongie, J. Hays, P. Perona, D. Ramanan, P. Dollár, and C. L. Zitnick. Microsoft COCO: Common objects in context. In *ECCV*, 2014.

[21] Q. Mei, X. Shen, and C. Zhai. Automatic labeling of multinomial topic models. In *SIGKDD*, pages 490–499, 2007.

[22] P. N. Mendes, M. Jakob, A. García-Silva, and C. Bizer. Dbpedia spotlight: Shedding light on the web of documents. In *I-Semantics*, pages 1–8, 2011.

[23] D. Milne and I. H. Witten. Learning to link with wikipedia. In *CIKM*, pages 509–518, 2008.

[24] NIST. *Proceedings of the Sixth Text Analysis Conference, TAC 2013, Gaithersburg, Maryland, USA, November 18-19, 2013*, 2013.

[25] S. O'Neill and S. Nicholson-Cole. Fear won't do it: promoting positive engagement with climate change through imagery and icons. *Science Communication*, 30(3):355–379, 2009.

[26] S. O'Neill and N. Smith. Climate change and visual imagery. *Wiley Interdisciplinary Reviews: Climate Change*, 5(1):73–87, 2014.

[27] S. J. O'Neill and M. Hulme. An iconic approach for respresenting climate change. *Global Environmental Change*, 19(4), 2009.

[28] V. Ordonez, G. Kulkarni, and T. L. Berg. Im2text: Describing images using 1 million captioned photographs. In *NIPS*, 2011.

[29] D. D. Perlmutter and G. L. Wagner. The anatomy of a photojournalistic icon: Marginalization of dissent in the selection and framing of 'a death in Genoa'. *Visual Communication*, 3(1), Feb. 2004.

[30] F. Raiber and O. Kurland. Ranking document clusters using markov random fields. In *SIGIR*, pages 333–342, 2013.

[31] H. Raviv, O. Kurland, and D. Carmel. Document retrieval using entity-based language models. In *SIGIR*, 2016.

[32] M. Ren, R. Kiros, and R. Zemel. Exploring models and data for image question answering. In *NIPS*, pages 2935–2943, 2015.

[33] O. Russakovsky, J. Deng, H. Su, J. Krause, S. Satheesh, S. Ma, Z. Huang, A. Karpathy, A. Khosla, M. Bernstein, et al. ImageNet large scale visual recognition challenge. *International Journal of Computer Vision*, pages 1–42, 2014.

[34] M. Schuhmacher and S. P. Ponzetto. Knowledge-based graph document modeling. In *WSDM*, pages 543–552, 2014.

[35] R. Socher, A. Karpathy, Q. V. Le, C. D. Manning, and A. Y. Ng. Grounded compositional semantics for finding and describing images with sentences. *ACL*, 2:207–218, 2014.

[36] P. P. Talukdar, J. Reisinger, M. Paşca, D. Ravichandran, R. Bhagat, and F. Pereira. Weakly-supervised acquisition of labeled class instances using graph random walks. In *EMNLP*, pages 582–590, 2008.

[37] B. Thomee and A. Popescu. Overview of the ImageCLEF 2012 Flickr photo annotation and retrieval task. In *CLEF*, 2012.

[38] K. Tran, X. He, L. Zhang, J. Sun, C. Carapcea, C. Thrasher, C. Buehler, and C. Sienkiewicz. Rich image captioning in the wild. *arXiv preprint arXiv:1603.09016*, 2016.

[39] R. Weegar, L. Hammarlund, A. Tegen, M. Oskarsson, K. Åström, and P. Nugues. Visual entity linking: A preliminary study. In *AAAI-14 Workshop on Computing for Augmented Human Intelligence*, 2014.

[40] Z. Zhang, A. L. Gentile, and F. Ciravegna. Recent advances in methods of lexical semantic relatedness - a survey. *Natural Language Engineering*, 19:411–479, 10 2013.

[41] N. Zhiltsov, A. Kotov, and F. Nikolaev. Fielded sequential dependence model for ad-hoc entity retrieval in the web of data. In *SIGIR*, pages 253–262, 2015.

Exploiting Entity Linking in Queries for Entity Retrieval

Faegheh Hasibi
Norwegian University of
Science and Technology
faegheh.hasibi@idi.ntnu.no

Krisztian Balog
University of Stavanger
krisztian.balog@uis.no

Svein Erik Bratsberg
Norwegian University of
Science and Technology
sveinbra@idi.ntnu.no

ABSTRACT

The premise of entity retrieval is to better answer search queries by returning specific entities instead of documents. Many queries mention particular entities; recognizing and linking them to the corresponding entry in a knowledge base is known as the task of entity linking in queries. In this paper we make a first attempt at bringing together these two, i.e., leveraging entity annotations of queries in the entity retrieval model. We introduce a new probabilistic component and show how it can be applied on top of any term-based entity retrieval model that can be emulated in the Markov Random Field framework, including language models, sequential dependence models, as well as their fielded variations. Using a standard entity retrieval test collection, we show that our extension brings consistent improvements over all baseline methods, including the current state-of-the-art. We further show that our extension is robust against parameter settings.

CCS Concepts

•Information systems → Retrieval models and ranking;

Keywords

Entity retrieval; entity linking; semistructured retrieval

1. INTRODUCTION

The past decade has witnessed an emergence of entity-oriented information access technology [30]. Among these are two main tasks that have been extensively addressed: (i) answering information needs with specific entities, a problem referred to as *entity retrieval* [7, 25, 35, 36, 38, 46], and (ii) identifying and disambiguating entities in text, a process known as *entity linking* [8, 19, 22]. Both these tasks represent key building blocks for semantic search [30] and are typically backed by a large-scale knowledge base. Despite this common ground, the two tasks have so far been studied mostly on their own, as standalone problems. We say mostly, as entity ranking, to a limited extent, has already met entity linking: most entity linking approaches involve an entity retrieval component for collecting candidate entities for a given text

ICTIR '16, September 12–16, 2016, Newark, Delaware, USA.

© 2016 ACM. ISBN 978-1-4503-4497-5/16/09. . . $15.00

DOI: http://dx.doi.org/10.1145/2970398.2970406

segment, see, e.g., [8, 19, 22]. The other direction, utilizing entity linking for entity retrieval, to the best of our knowledge, has not been explored yet. This study is a first attempt at bridging this gap by performing entity linking on search queries and using the resulting annotations to improve entity retrieval.

It has been shown in prior work that entity retrieval can be improved by leveraging semantic annotations of the query, such as target entity types or related entities, see, e.g., [4, 10, 24, 39]. These studies, using the TREC Entity [3] and INEX-XER [17] benchmarking platforms, assume that semantic annotations are provided as part of the definition of the information need, i.e., complement the keyword query. Further, these test suites comprise a homogeneous set of queries, where all queries are of the same general type or even follow some predefined template (e.g., input entity, target type, and required relation for the related entity finding task at TREC [3]). In this work, we use a heterogeneous query set, ranging from short keyword queries to natural language questions, and obtain entity annotations automatically. It is further worth pointing out that virtually all existing work is limited to term-based representation of entities. A few studies stand as exceptions, but those address the entity ranking task in some specific flavor, such as list completion [11], or focus on a particular property of entities, like types [4]. Our approach, on the other hand, considers both term- and entity-based representations of entities for general-purpose entity retrieval; see Figure 1.

It is worth relating our efforts to the large body of prior work that has shown that leveraging information about entity annotations of queries can improve document retrieval performance [9, 16, 27, 28, 43, 44]. Importantly, this task is very different from ours: we search for entities in a (manually curated) knowledge base where entities are first-class citizens. This stands in contrast with document retrieval, where the entity annotations are a result of some automated process, which always involves a degree of uncertainty. Not only the task, but the techniques used for utilizing entity annotations are also different; in document retrieval entities are typically used for query expansion or as simple features in a learning-to-rank framework (see §2.3). We, on the other hand, represent and match entities directly as a separate component in the retrieval model.

Against this background, the main research question driving our work is this: *What is a theoretically sound way of extending term-based entity retrieval models with the capability of leveraging linked entities in the query?* To address this question, we introduce (i) a new component for matching entity annotations of the query with entity relationships recorded in a knowledge base and (ii) a general framework for leveraging this component into the term-based models. Our framework is based on the Markov Random Field (MRF) model [31]. There are several reasons for this particular choice of framework, including its solid theoretical foundations, good empirical performance, the fact that it can encompass a number of

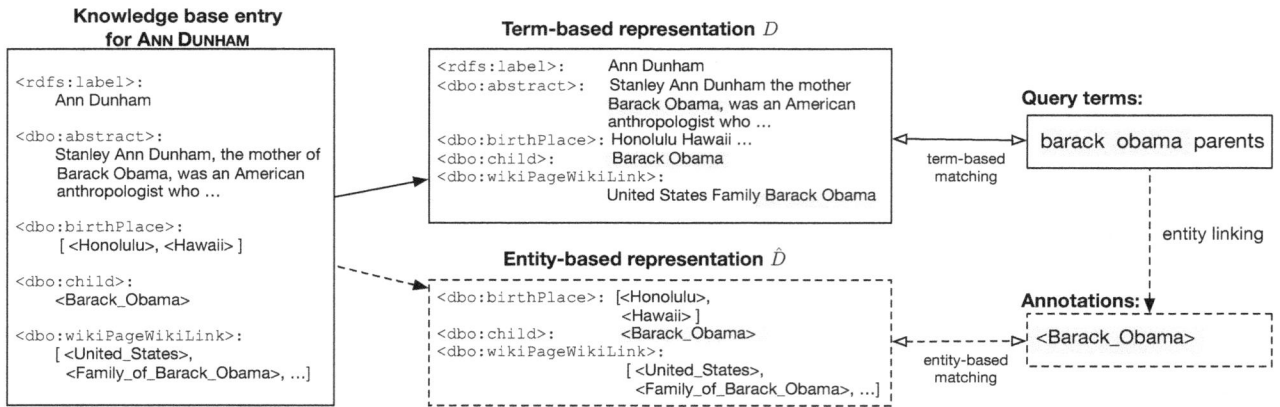

Figure 1: Demonstration of term- and entity-based representation of entities. The query terms match against the term-based representation of entity ANN DUNHAM, while the entity annotations of the queries match against the entity-based representation. The dashed parts indicate the novel elements of our work.

existing retrieval models, and last but not least, the current state-of-the-art in ad-hoc entity retrieval is also based on MRF [46]. Within this framework, we introduce a new component for matching the linked entities from the query. This component, termed ELR (for "Entity Linking incorporated Retrieval"), may be seen as an extension that can be applied on top of any text-based retrieval model that can be instantiated in the MRF framework. Entity matches are facilitated by an additional entity-based representation that preserves entity relationships as recorded in the knowledge base; see the block denoted with $\hat{D}$ in Figure 1. We address a number of technical and modeling issues that stem from the differences between terms and entities, including the spareness of entity-based representations compared to term-based ones, varying number of entity annotations per query, dealing with uncertainties involved with entity linking, and mapping of entities to fields. We conduct experiments on a test collection consisting of close to 500 heterogeneous queries and show that our model can consistently and significantly improve upon standard language models [45], semi-structured [25], and term-dependence models [31, 46], and outperforms the current state-of-the-art on ad-hoc entity retrieval by over 6% in terms of MAP. In addition, we demonstrate its robustness against parameter setting and entity linking configuration.

The resources developed within this paper are made publicly available at http://bit.ly/ictir2016-elr.

2. RELATED WORK

Our work falls in the intersection of entity retrieval, entity linking, and exploiting query annotation in retrieval.

2.1 Entity retrieval

One main theme in entity retrieval research concerns the representation of entities; once a term-based representation is created, entities can be ranked using traditional retrieval models, much like documents. Early work, especially in the context of expert search, obtains such representations by considering mentions of the given entity across the document collection [2, 4]. The INEX 2007-2009 Entity Retrieval track (INEX-XER) [17, 18] studies entity retrieval in Wikipedia, while the INEX 2012 Linked Data track goes one step further and considers Wikipedia articles together with RDF properties from the DBpedia and YAGO2 knowledge bases [42]. Much of the recent work represents entities as fielded documents, extracted from a knowledge base [1, 7, 46] or from multiple information sources [20]. In this work, we introduce a new representation layer, referred to as entity-based representation, based on entity relationships stored in the knowledge base.

Entity retrieval models can be categorized into two main groups: semistructured retrieval models [1, 36, 46] and learning-to-rank approaches [20, 41] . Our focus in this paper is on the first category, where fielded representations of entities are ranked using fielded variations of standard document retrieval models, e.g., BM25F [40] or the mixture of language models [37]. This is indeed the predominant approach for ad-hoc entity retrieval [1, 7, 36]. In a recent effort, Zhiltsov et al. [46] extend the Sequential Dependence Model [31] to multi-field representation of entities. Within this context, the choice of fields and estimation of field weights remain a challenge. Our work also addresses these challenges by using a principled and parameter-free estimation method [25].

Entity retrieval has also been explored in the context of specific tasks, such as list completion at INEX-XER [17, 18, 39] or related entity finding at the TREC Entity track [3, 5]. In both these cases, types or entities are provided as part of the topic definition. Our approach obtains the entity annotations for queries automatically.

2.2 Entity linking

Early work on entity linking has focused on long texts, based on contextual and semantic similarities between a document and candidate entities [13, 15, 26, 33, 34]. More recently, the focus has slightly shifted towards annotating short texts such as tweets and queries [8, 19, 21, 29]. Entity linking for short texts is challenging, mainly because of the lack of context. In case of queries, there are additional efficiency considerations, as entity linking needs to be performed on-the-fly. TAGME is one of the early systems that addresses entity linking in short texts and has received due attention since [23]. It is one of the best performing systems, both in terms of efficiency and effectiveness [12, 14], and also offers a public API.

The problem of entity linking in queries has recently been identified as a separate task, different from conventional entity linking for short/long texts [12, 22]. The difference lies in the number of entities that can be assigned to a mention: for short/long texts a single entity is ought to be returned for each mention, while entity linking in queries can associate multiple entities with a single mention, if the ambiguity cannot be resolved. Hasibi et al. [22] discuss that entity linking in queries should be presented as a set of entity linking interpretations, where each interpretation consists of semantically related entities. For our approach, we are interested in the annotation of individual entities and are not concerned with entity linking interpretations. Therefore, any type of entity linking systems can be used with our approach. Due to reproducibility considerations [23], we employ the TAGME API as a black-box entity linker and incorporate the resulting annotations into the entity retrieval system.

2.3 Exploiting query annotations in retrieval

Exploiting semantic annotations of queries for various retrieval tasks has attracted due attention over the recent years. Examples include the INEX and TREC entity benchmarking efforts as already discussed in §2.1. Much of the recent work has focused on incorporating entity-related information to improve document retrieval [9, 16, 27, 28, 43, 44]. There are three major differences between this line of work and ours. First and foremost, the task is different; the referred approaches address ad-hoc document retrieval, while we search for entities in a knowledge base. Second, the way entity annotations are utilized is different; we aim to directly incorporate entity annotations into the retrieval model, while existing approaches either employ query expansion techniques [9, 16, 27, 44] or operate in a latent entity space [28, 43]. Finally, our approach requires only the identifiers of the linked entities, thereby making it a generic and effective model (also in terms of implementation), while others rely on additional entity-related information from the knowledge base.

Schuhmacher et al. [41] address a variant of the ad-hoc entity ranking task for informational queries, which is "close in spirit to ad-hoc document search" [41]. Even though this task is different from ours, there are some similarities. They also leverage entity annotations of queries, but they do so in a learning-to-rank framework by introducing two binary features: whether the query entity (i) contains or (ii) is related to the candidate entity or not. The findings on the merits of these features are somewhat inconclusive; while they are shown to be influential on the Robust04 dataset, they were less helpful on ClueWeb12 dataset. The conclusiveness of these results might be further limited by the low number of queries (25 and 22 for Robust and ClueWeb12, respectively).

3. BACKGROUND

In this section, we describe the Markov Random Field (MRF) model [31], which is the basis of our proposed approach (following in §4). We further discuss two specific variations of the MRF model: the Sequential Dependence Model [31] in §3.2 and the Fielded Sequential Dependence Model [46] in §3.3.

3.1 The Markov Random Field model

Markov Random Field models for information retrieval were first introduced by Metzler and Croft [31] to model the dependencies between query terms. Given a document D and a query Q, the goal of these models is to compute the joint probability $P(Q, D)$:

$$P(D|Q) = \frac{P(Q, D)}{P(Q)} \overset{rank}{=} P(Q, D) \qquad (1)$$

This probability is estimated based on a Markov Random Field, which is a common practice to compute the joint probabilities of random variables. For document retrieval, a MRF is defined by a graph G with nodes consisting of query terms q_i and the document D, and edges representing the dependence between the nodes. The joint probability over variables of the graph G is computed as:

$$P_\Lambda(Q, D) = \frac{1}{Z_\Lambda} \prod_{c \in C(G)} \psi(c; \Lambda),$$

where $C(G)$ is the set of cliques in G and $\psi(c; \Lambda) = \exp[\lambda_c f(c)]$ is a non-negative *potential function*, parametrized by the weight λ_c

and the *feature function* $f(c)$. The parameter Z_Λ serves as a normalization factor, which is generally ignored due to computational infeasibility. Substituting all these elements into Eq. (1), the final ranking function becomes:

$$P(D|Q) \overset{rank}{=} \sum_{c \in C(G)} \lambda_c f(c). \qquad (2)$$

This ranking function provides a solid theoretical basis for a wide spectrum of retrieval models: from traditional unigram-based models to more sophisticated ones involving n-grams as well as additional task- or domain-specific features [6, 39]. To build a ranking function, all one needs to do is to define the graph structure and the potential functions over the graph cliques.

3.2 Sequential Dependence Model

The Sequential Dependence Model (SDM) is a popular MRF-based retrieval model, which provides a good balance between retrieval effectiveness and efficiency [31]. In the underlying graph of this model, only adjacent query terms are connected to each other, meaning that query terms are sequentially dependent on each other; i.e., the white nodes in Figure 2. Under this assumption, the potential functions are defined for two types of cliques: (i) 2-cliques involving a query term and the document, (ii) cliques containing two contiguous terms and the document. The potential function for the first type of cliques is:

$$\psi(q_i, D; \Lambda) = \exp[\lambda_T f_T(q_i, D)], \qquad (3)$$

where $f_T(q_i, D)$ is the feature function for the query term q_i and the document D. There are two possibilities for the second type of cliques (two terms): either the terms occur contiguously in the query or they do not. These two cases make up the potential functions for *ordered* and *unordered* matches, and are denoted by the O and U subscripts, respectively:

$$\psi(q_i, q_{i+1}, D; \Lambda) = \exp[\lambda_O f_O(q_i, q_{i+1}, D) + \\ \lambda_U f_U(q_i, q_{i+1}, D)]. \qquad (4)$$

By substituting the two potential functions $\psi(q_i, D; \Lambda)$ in Eq. (3) and $\psi(q_i, q_{i+1}, D; \Lambda)$ in Eq. (4) into Eq. (2), and factoring out the λ parameters, the SDM ranking function becomes:

$$P(D|Q) \overset{rank}{=} \lambda_T \sum_{q_i \in Q} f_T(q_i, D) + \\ \lambda_O \sum_{q_i, q_{i+1} \in Q} f_O(q_i, q_{i+1}, D) + \\ \lambda_U \sum_{q_i, q_{i+1} \in Q} f_U(q_i, q_{i+1}, D), \qquad (5)$$

where the parameters should meet the constraint of $\lambda_T + \lambda_O + \lambda_U = 1$. The specific feature functions are set as follows:

$$f_T(q_i, D) = \log[\frac{tf_{q_i, D} + \mu \frac{cf_{q_i}}{|C|}}{|D| + \mu}] \qquad (6)$$

$$f_O(q_i, q_{i+1}, D) = \log[\frac{tf_{\#1(q_i, q_{i+1}), D} + \mu \frac{cf_{\#1(q_i, q_{i+1})}}{|C|}}{|D| + \mu}] \qquad (7)$$

$$f_U(q_i, q_{i+1}, D) = \log[\frac{tf_{\#uwN(q_i, q_{i+1}), D} + \mu \frac{cf_{\#uwN(q_i, q_{i+1})}}{|C|}}{|D| + \mu}], \qquad (8)$$

where tf_D is the frequency of the term(s) in the document D and cf denotes the total number of occurrences of the term(s) in the entire collection. The function $\#1(q_i, q_{i+1})$ searches for the exact

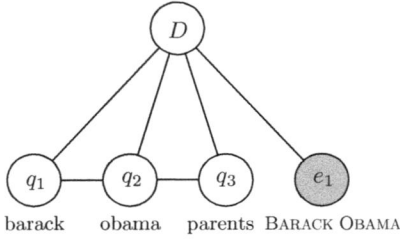

Figure 2: Graphical representation of the ELR model for the query "barack obama parents". Here, all the terms are sequentially dependent and the phase "barack obama" is linked to the entity BARACK OBAMA.

match of the phrase q_i, q_{i+1}, while $\#uwN(q_i, q_{i+1})$ counts the co-occurrence of terms within a window of N words (where N is set to 8 based on [31]). The parameter μ is the Dirichlet prior, which is taken to be the average document length in the collection.

Putting all these together, SDM is basically the weighted sum of language model scores obtained from three sources: (i) query terms, (ii) exact match of query bigrams, and (iii) unordered match of query bigrams. Our approach in §4 employs the same sequential dependence assumption that SDM does.

3.3 Fielded Sequential Dependence Model

The Fielded Sequential Dependence Model (FSDM) [46] extends the SDM model to support structured document retrieval. In essence, FSDM replaces the document language model of feature functions (Eqs. (6), (7), and (8)) with those of the Mixture of Language Models (MLM) [37]. Given a fielded representation of a document (e.g., title, body, anchors, metadata, etc. in the context of web document retrieval), MLM computes a language model probability for each field and then takes a linear combination of these field-level models. Hence, FSDM assumes that a separate language model is built for each document field and then computes the feature functions based on fields $f \in \mathcal{F}$, with $\mathcal{F}$ being the universe of fields. For individual terms, the feature function becomes:

$$f_T(q_i, D) = \log \sum_f w_f^T \frac{tf_{q_i, D_f} + \mu_f \frac{cf_{q_i, f}}{|C_f|}}{|D_f| + \mu_f}, \qquad (9)$$

while ordered and unordered bigrams are estimated as:

$$f_O(q_i, q_{i+1}, D) =$$
$$\log \sum_f w_f^O \frac{tf_{\#1(q_i, q_{i+1}), D_f} + \mu_f \frac{cf_{\#1(q_i, q_{i+1}), f}}{|C_f|}}{|D_f| + \mu_f} \qquad (10)$$

$$f_U(q_i, q_{i+1}, D) =$$
$$\log \sum_f w_f^U \frac{tf_{\#uwN(q_i, q_{i+1}), D_f} + \mu_f \frac{cf_{\#uwN(q_i, q_{i+1}), f}}{|C_f|}}{|D_f| + \mu_f}. \qquad (11)$$

The parameters w_f are the weights for each field, which are set to be non-negative with the constraint $\sum_f w_f = 1$. Zhiltsov et al. [46] trained both the field weights (w_f) and the feature function weights ($\lambda_T, \lambda_O, \lambda_U$ in Eq. (5)) in two stages using the Coordinate Ascent algorithm [32].

4. THE ELR APPROACH

This section presents our approach for incorporating entity linking into entity retrieval. We start by introducing our general MRF-based framework in §4.1, and continue with describing the feature functions in §4.2 and fielded representation of entities in §4.3.

4.1 Model

Our *Entity Linking incorporated Retrieval* (ELR) approach is an extension of the MRF framework for incorporating entity annotations into the retrieval model. We note, without detailed elaboration, that ELR is applicable to a wide range of retrieval problems where documents, or document-based representations of objects, are to be ranked, and entity annotations are available to be leveraged in the matching of documents and queries. Our main focus in this paper, however, is limited to entity retrieval; entity annotations are an integral part of the representation here, cf. Figure 1. (This is unlike to traditional document retrieval, where documents would need to be annotated by an automated process that is prone to errors). To show the generic nature of our approach, and also for the sake of notational consistency with the previous section, we shall refer to documents throughout this section. We detail how these documents are constructed for our particular task, entity retrieval, in §4.3.

Our interest in this work lies in incorporating entity annotations and not in creating them. Therefore, entity annotations of the query are assumed to have been generated by an external entity linking process, which we treat like a black box. Formally, given an input query $Q = q_1...q_n$, the set of linked entities is denoted by $E(Q) = \{e_1, ..., e_m\}$. We do not impose any restrictions on these annotations, i.e., they may be overlapping and a given query span might be linked to multiple entities. It might also be that $E(Q)$ is an empty set. Further, we assume that annotations have confidence scores associated with them. For each entity $e \in E(Q)$, let $s(e)$ denote the confidence score of e, with the constraint of $\sum_{e \in E(Q)} s(e) = 1$.

The graph underlying our model consists of document, term, and entity nodes. As shown in Figure 2, we assume that the query terms are sequentially dependent on each other, while the annotated entities are independent of each other and of the query terms. Based on this assumption, the potential functions are computed for three types of cliques: (i) 2-cliques consisting of edges between the document and a term node, (ii) 3-cliques consisting of the document and two term nodes, and (iii) 2-cliques consisting of edges between the document and an entity node. The potential functions for the first two types are identical to the SDM model (Eqs. (3) and (4)). We define the potential function for the third clique type as:

$$\psi_E(e, D; \Lambda) = \exp[\lambda_E f_E(e, D)],$$

where λ_E is a free parameter and $f_E(e, D)$ is the feature function for the entity e and document D (to be defined in §4.2). By substituting all feature functions into Eq. (2), the MRF ranking function becomes:

$$P(D|Q) \overset{rank}{=} \sum_{q_i \in Q} \lambda_T f_T(q_i, D)+$$
$$\sum_{q_i, q_{i+1} \in Q} \lambda_O f_O(q_i, q_{i+1}, D)+$$
$$\sum_{q_i, q_{i+1} \in Q} \lambda_U f_U(q_i, q_{i+1}, D)+$$
$$\sum_{e \in E(Q)} \lambda_E f_E(e, D).$$

This model introduces an additional parameter for weighing the importance of entity annotations, λ_E, on top of the three parameters ($\lambda_{\{T,O,U\}}$) from the SDM model (cf. §3.2). There is a crucial difference between entity-based and term-based matches with regards to the λ parameters. The number of cliques for term-based matches is proportional to the length of the query ($|Q|$ for unigrams and $|Q| - 1$ for ordered and unordered bigrams), which makes them compatible (directly comparable) with each other, irrespective of the length of the query. Therefore, in SDM, $\lambda_{\{T,O,U\}}$ are taken out of the summations (cf. Eq. (5)) and can be trained without having to worry about query length normalization. The parameter λ_E, however, cannot be treated the same manner for two reasons. Firstly, the number of annotated entities for each query varies and it is independent of the length of the query. For example, a long natural language query might be annotated with a single entity, while shorter queries are often linked to several entities, due to their ambiguity. Secondly, we need to deal with varying levels of uncertainty that is involved with entity annotations of the query. The confidence scores associated with the annotations, which are generated by the entity linking process, should be integrated into the retrieval model.

To address the above issues, we re-write the λ parameters as a parameterized function over each clique and define them as:

$$\lambda_T(q_i) = \lambda_T \frac{1}{|Q|},$$

$$\lambda_O(q_i, q_{i+1}) = \lambda_O \frac{1}{|Q| - 1},$$

$$\lambda_U(q_i, q_{i+1}) = \lambda_U \frac{1}{|Q| - 1},$$

$$\lambda_E(e) = \lambda_E s(e),$$

where $|Q|$ is the query length and $s(e)$ is the confidence score of entity e obtained from the entity linking step. Considering this parametric form of the λ parameters, our final ranking function takes the following form:

$$
P(D|Q) \overset{rank}{=} \lambda_T \sum_{q_i \in Q} \frac{1}{|Q|} f_T(q_i, D) +
$$
$$
\lambda_O \sum_{q_i, q_{i+1} \in Q} \frac{1}{|Q| - 1} f_O(q_i, q_{i+1}, D) +
$$
$$
\lambda_U \sum_{q_i, q_{i+1} \in Q} \frac{1}{|Q| - 1} f_U(q_i, q_{i+1}, D) +
$$
$$
\lambda_E \sum_{e \in E(Q)} s(e) f_E(e, D), \qquad (12)
$$

where the free parameters λ are placed under the constraint of $\lambda_T + \lambda_O + \lambda_U + \lambda_E = 1$. This model ensures that the scores for the different type of matches (i.e., term, ordered window, unordered window, and entities) are normalized and the λ parameters, which are to be trained, are not influenced by the length of the query or by the number of linked entities. In addition, it provides us with a general ranking framework that can encompass various retrieval models. If the λ_O and λ_U parameters are set to zero, the model is an extension of unigram based models, such as LM and MLM. Otherwise, it extends SDM and FSDM. We also note that due to the normalizations applied to the different set of matches, the *full dependence* variant of MRF model [31] could also be instantiated in our framework; this, however, is outside the scope of this study.

4.2 Feature functions

Feature functions form an essential part of MRF-based models. We now discuss the estimation of these for the ELR model. For all feature functions, we use a fielded document representation of entities, as it is a common and effective approach for entity retrieval, see, e.g., [1, 7, 20, 35, 46]. The first three feature functions in Eq. (12), f_T, f_O, and f_U, are computed as defined in Eqs. (9), (10), and (11), respectively.

Let us then turn to defining the function $f_E(e, D)$ in Eq. (12), which is a novel feature introduced by our ELR model. This function measures the goodness of the match between an entity e linked in the query and a document D. These matches are facilitated by an entity-based representation of documents. For each document D an entity-based representation $\hat{D}$ is obtained by ignoring document terms and considering only entities. In the context of our work, the entity represented by document D stands in typed relationships with a number of other entities, as specified in the knowledge base. The various relationships are modeled as fields in the document. Consider the example in Figure 1, where the document represents the entity Ann Dunham, who is being linked to the entity Barack Obama (via the relationship <dbo:child>). This entity-based representation differs from the traditional term-based representation in at least two important ways. Firstly, each entity appears at most once in each document field. Secondly, if an entity appears in a field, then it should be considered a match, irrespective of what other entities may appear in that field. Consider again the example in Figure 1, where the field <dbo:birthplace> has multiple values, Honolulu and Hawaii. Then, if either of these entities is linked in the query, that should account for a perfect match against this particular field, irrespective of how many other locations are present in that field. Motivated by these observations, we define the feature function f_E as:

$$
f_E(e, D) = \log \sum_{f \in \mathcal{F}} w_f^E \left[(1 - \alpha) t f_{\{0,1\}}(e, \hat{D}_f) + \alpha \frac{df_{e,f}}{df_f} \right], \quad (13)
$$

where the linear interpolation implements the Jelinek-Mercer smoothing method, with α set to 0.1, and $tf_{\{0,1\}}(e, \hat{D}_f)$ indicates whether the entity e is present in the document field $\hat{D}_f$ or not. For the background model, we employ the notion of document frequency as follows: $df_{e,f} = |\{\hat{D}|e \in \hat{D}_f\}|$ is the total number of documents that contain the entity e in field f and $df(f) = |\{\hat{D}|\hat{D}_f \neq \emptyset\}|$ is the number of documents with a non-empty field f.

All of the feature functions f_T, f_O, f_U, and f_E involve free parameters w_f, which control the field weights. Zhiltsov et al. [46] set these type of parameters using a learning algorithm, which leads to a large number of parameters to be trained (the number of feature functions times the number of fields). Instead, we employ a parameter-free estimation of field weights, using field mapping probabilities, introduced in the Probabilistic Retrieval Model for Semistructured Data (PRMS) [25]. This probability infers the importance of each field, with respect to a given query term, based on collection statistics of that term. Specifically, the probability of a field f, from the universe of fields $\mathcal{F}$, is computed with respect to a given term t as follows:

$$
P(f|t) = \frac{P(t|f)P(f)}{\sum_{f' \in \mathcal{F}} P(t|f')P(f')}. \quad (14)
$$

Here, $P(f)$ is the prior probability of field f, which is set proportional to the frequency of the field (across all documents in the collection), and $P(t|f)$ is estimated by dividing the number of occurrences of term t in field f by the sum of term counts in f across the whole collection. We compute the probability $P(f|t)$ for all query terms, ordered and unordered bigrams, and use the resulting values for the weights w_f^T, w_f^O, and w_f^U (used in Eqs. (9)-(11)), respectively. The weights w_f^E (used in Eq. (13)) are also estimated using Eq. (14), but this time we compute this probability for entities instead of terms (i.e., t is replaced with e).

Employing the mapping probability $P(f|.)$ instead of free parameters w_f [46] has three advantages. First, the field mapping probability specifies field importance for each query term (or bigram) individually, while the w_f parameters are the same for all

"finland"		FINLAND	
Field name	Mapping prob.	Field name	Mapping prob.
`<dcterms:subject>`	0.210	`<dbo:country>`	0.223
`<dbo:wikiPageWikiLink>`	0.178	`<dbo:wikiPageWikiLink>`	0.201
`types`	0.168	`contents`	0.189
`contents`	0.113	`<dbo:birthPlace>`	0.170
`<rdfs:comment>`	0.089	`<dbo:hometown>`	0.053
`<dbo:abstract>`	0.070	`<dbo:location>`	0.047
`<rdfs:label>`	0.069	`<dbo:nationality>`	0.041
`names`	0.059	`<dbo:deathPlace>`	0.034
`<foaf:isPrimaryTopicOf>`	0.040	`<dbo:locationCountry>`	0.028
`yago:<rdf:type>`	0.001	`<dbo:ground>`	0.0129

Table 1: Selected fields with the corresponding mapping probabilities for the term "finland" and the entity FINLAND.

query terms (or bigrams). Second, the number of free parameters in the feature functions f_T, f_O, f_U, and f_E reduces from $4 * |\mathcal{F}|$ to zero. Hence, the final model is more robust and can be employed in various settings, without risking overfitting. Lastly and most importantly, estimating the field weights this way allows us to have a query-specific selection of fields, depending on the linked entity, as opposed to having pre-trained (fixed) field weights.

4.3 Fielded representation of entities

We now detail how the term-based and entity-based representation are obtained for entities, from the knowledge base entry (i.e., subject-predicate-object triples) describing the entity. One of the challenges of working with a fielded document-based representation of entities is the appropriate selection of fields. While grouping SPO triples by predicates and mapping each predicate to a separate document field is straightforward, retrieval can become highly inefficient because of the large number of fields [35]. Previous work has suggested a number of solutions to alleviate this problem by reducing the number of fields, which can be summarized under two main categories: (i) selecting a subset of fields that are considered and (ii) grouping fields together into a handful of predefined categories. When using the first approach, predicates are commonly ordered by frequency and a rank-based cutoff is applied, e.g., top 1000 in [1]. There are two choices for assigning the field weights in this setting: to simply use uniform values for all fields or to employ some estimation technique (such as the field mapping probabilities in the PRMS model) as training is generally infeasible due to the large number of fields. Examples of the second technique, referred to as "predicate folding" in [35], include grouping fields into a handful of predetermined categories based on type [35, 46] or manually determined importance [7]. It has been shown in [36] that it is possible to achieve solid performance even with as few as two fields, "title" and "content." One main advantage of predicate folding is that the estimation of field weights becomes tractable. The disadvantage is that a large part of the semantics associated with the individual predicates is discarded.

In this work we combine these two strategies to get the best of both approaches. We employ predicate folding for three designated fields: names, types, and content (see §5.1). In addition, we consider all fields, which are not included in names or types, on their own. From this combined set, we then select the top-N most frequent fields across the whole knowledge base and use them for the term-based entity representation.

The entity-based representation requires a different field selection procedure from the above, as entities (SPO triples with an URI value as object) occur less often and follow an entirely different pattern than terms. For instance, the entity FINLAND mostly occurs in the `<dbo:country>` and `<dbo: birthPlace>` fields, while the entity ANCIENT ROMAN ARCHITECTURE often appears in the `<dbo:architecturalStyle>` field. This illustrates that it is not desirable to have the same (and fixed) set of fields for all entities, but field selection should be performed on an entity-specific manner. Therefore, for each entity, we select the top-N fields, from the entity-based representations, that the entity occurs in. As this computation can be performed offline, it does not negatively impact on the efficiency of retrieval. Table 1 shows an excerpt of the mapping probability distribution for a given term and entity.

5. EXPERIMENTAL SETUP

This section presents our experimental setup, including the data set (§5.1), field selection (§5.2), parameter settings (§5.3), and how entity linking is performed (§5.4).

5.1 Data

We use DBpedia version 3.9 as our knowledge base along with the DBpedia-entity test collection [1].

Indices. For our experiments, we created two fielded indices from subject-predicate-object triples: a *term-based index*, where all entities (URI objects) are resolved to terms, and an *entity-based index*, where only URI objects are kept. The former index is used to compute the unigram and bigram term probabilities (Eqs. (9)-(11)), while the latter is employed for the entity probability computations (Eq. (13)). We built the indices using Lucene and made use of SpanNearQuery to get the statistics for ordered and unordered phrases. Our indices are confined to entities having a name and a short abstract (i.e. fields `<rdfs:label>` and `<rdfs:comment>`), resulting in a total of 3,984,580 entities. They contain the top-1000 most frequent DBpedia predicates as fields, together with three other fields: (i) the `names` field, which is the constitution of entity predicates `<rdfs:label>`, `<foaf:name>`, and redirected entities; (ii) the `types` field, which contains `<rdf:type>` and attribute names ending in "subject"; (iii) the `contents` field, which holds the contents of all entity fields except entity links in other languages (`<owl:sameAs>`). In the term-based index, terms are lowercased and stopped using the default Lucene stopwords list, and all URIs are replaced with the name of the corresponding entity. In the entity-based index, only URIs are indexed and all literal objects are ignored. In addition, the URI of each entity itself is also added to the `contents` field in the entity-based index.

Queries. We evaluate the effectiveness of our models using the DBpedia-entity collection [1], which comprises 485 queries from a number of entity retrieval benchmarking campaigns. Following [6], queries are stopped using a handful of stop patterns ("which", "who",

Query subset	#queries	Avg. len	#rel
SemSearch ES	130	2.7	1115
ListSearch	115	5.6	2390
INEX_LD	100	4.8	3680
QALD-2	140	7.9	5773
Total	485	5.3	12958

Table 2: Query subsets of the DBpedia-entity test collection.

"what", "where", "give me", "show me") to improve entity linking and initial retrieval performance. We perform stopwords removal after the entity linking step, using the default Lucene stopwords list. We break down retrieval results according to the four categories suggested by Zhiltsov et al. [46]:

- **SemSearch ES**: Keyword queries targeting specific entities, which are often ambiguous (e.g., "madrid," "hugh downs").

- **ListSearch**: Combination of INEX-XER, SemSearch LS, and TREC Entity queries, targeting a list of entities that match a certain criteria (e.g., "Airports in Germany," "the first 13 american states").

- **INEX_LD**: General keyword queries, involving a mixture of names, types, relations, and attributes (e.g., "Eiffel," "vietnam war movie," "gallo roman architecture in paris").

- **QALD-2**: Natural language queries (e.g., "which country does the creator of miffy come from," "give me all female russian astronauts").

Table 2 provides descriptive statistics on these query subsets.

5.2 Field selection

The number of fields used in the term-based representation is a parameter shared by all but two of the evaluated models (single-field LM and SDM). We examined retrieval performance against a varying number of fields ($n = 10^i, i = 0, 1, 2, 3$), see Figure 3. Note that fields are ordered by frequency. It is clear from the figure that the best results are obtained when the top 10 most frequent fields are used. We used this setting in all our experiments, unless stated otherwise. For consistency, we also used the same setting, i.e., top 10 fields, for the entity-based representation.

5.3 Parameter setting

This section describes the parameter settings used in our experiments. The Dirichlet prior μ in language models is set to the average document/field length across the collection. The unordered window size N in Eqs. (8) and (11) is chosen to be 8, as suggested in [31, 46]. To estimate the λ parameters involved in SDM, FSDM, and our approach, we employ the Coordinate Ascent (CA) algorithm [32] and directly optimize Mean Average Precision (MAP). CA is a commonly used optimization technique, which iteratively optimizes a single parameter while holding all other parameters fixed. We make use of the CA implementation provided in the RankLib framework and set the number of random restarts to 3. Following [46], we estimate the λ parameters of SDM, FSDM*, and ELR-based approaches using 5-fold cross validation for each of the 4 query subsets separately. We note that Zhiltsov et al. [46] train both the λ and w parameters (Eq. (5)-(11)) for the FSDM model. As we use different entity representation from [46] (with 10 as opposed to 5 fields), training parameters in this manner would result in cross-validation of 33 parameters for each query subset, which would be prone to overfitting. We avoid this issue by employing the PRMS field mapping probability for field weights w

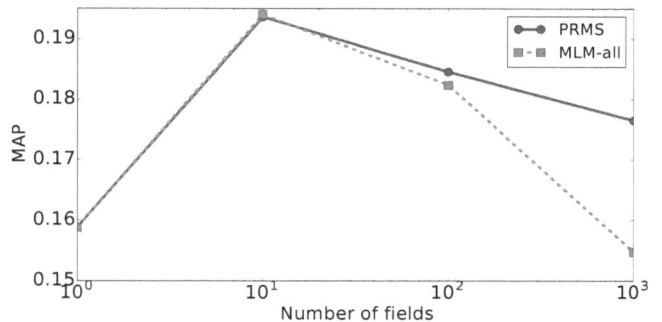

Figure 3: Effect of varying number of fields on MAP.

(i.e., Eq. (14)). Therefore, our implementation of FSDM slightly deviates from the original paper [46]; in acknowledgement of this distinction, we will refer to our implementation as FSDM*.

For all experiments, we employ a two stage retrieval method: first an initial set of top 1000 results is retrieved using Lucene's default search settings, then this set is re-ranked with the specific retrieval model (using an in-house implementation). Evaluation scores are reported on the top 100 results. To perform cross-validation, we randomly create train and test folds from the initial result set, and use the same folds throughout all the experiments. To measure statistical significance we employ a two-tailed paired t-test and denote differences at the 0.01 and 0.05 levels using the ▲ and △ symbols, respectively.

5.4 Entity linking

Entity linking is a key component of the ELR approach. For the purpose of reproducibility, all the entity annotations in this work are obtained using an open source entity linker, TAGME [19], accessed through its RESTful API.[1] TAGME is one of the best performing entity linkers for short queries [12, 14]. As suggested in the API documentation, we use the default threshold 0.1 in our experiments; we analyze the effect of the threshold parameter in §6.5.

6. RESULTS AND ANALYSIS

We begin by enumerating our research questions, then present a series of experiments conducted to answer them.

6.1 Research questions

We address the following research questions:

- **RQ1**: Can entity retrieval performance be improved by incorporating entity annotations of the query? (§6.2)

- **RQ2**: How are the different query subsets impacted by ELR? (§6.3)

- **RQ3**: How robust is our method with respect to parameter settings? (§6.4)

- **RQ4**: What is the impact of the entity linking component on end-to-end performance? (§6.5)

6.2 Overall performance

To find out whether entity linking in queries can improve entity retrieval performance (RQ1), we compare a number of entity retrieval approaches proposed in the literature. The first four (LM,

---

[1]http://tagme.di.unipi.it/

Model	SemSearch ES		ListSearch		INEX-LD		QALD-2	
	MAP	**P@10**	**MAP**	**P@10**	**MAP**	**P@10**	**MAP**	**P@10**
LM	.2485	.2008	.1529	.1939	.1129	.2210	.1132	.0729
LM + ELR	.2531$^\triangle$ (+1.8%)	.2008	.1688▲ (+10.4%)	.2096	.1244▲ (+10.2%)	.2330	.1241▲ (+9.6%)	.0836▲
PRMS	.3517	.2685	.1722	.2270	.1184	.2240	.1180	.0893
PRMS + ELR	.3573 (+1.6%)	.2700	.1956▲ (+14.1%)	.2417	.1303▲ (+10%)	.2330	.1343▲ (+13.8%)	.1064▲
SDM	.2669	.2108	.1553	.1948	.1167	.2250	.1369	.0750
SDM + ELR	.2641 (-1%)	.2115	.1689$^\triangle$ (+8.8%)	.2174▲	.1264▲ (+8.3%)	.2340	.1472$^\triangle$ (+7.5%)	.0857
FSDM*	.3563	.2692	.1777	.2165	.1261	.2290	.1364	.0921
FSDM* + ELR	.3581 (+.5%)	.2677	.1973$^\triangle$ (+11%)	.2391▲	.1332 (+5.6%)	.2330	.1583$^\triangle$ (+16%)	.1086▲

Table 4: Results of ELR approach on different query types. Significance is tested against the line above; the numbers in parentheses show the relative improvements, in terms of MAP.

Model	MAP	P@10
LM	0.1588	0.1664
MLM-tc	0.1821	0.1786
MLM-all	0.1940	0.1965
PRMS	0.1936	**0.1977**
SDM	0.1719	0.1707
FSDM*	**0.2030**	0.1973
LM + ELR	0.1693▲ (+6.6%)	0.1757▲ (+5.6%)
MLM-tc + ELR	0.1937▲ (+6.4%)	0.1895▲ (+6.1%)
MLM-all + ELR	0.2082▲ (+7.3%)	0.2054$^\triangle$ (+4.5%)
PRMS + ELR	0.2078▲ (+7.3%)	0.2085▲ (+5.5%)
SDM + ELR	0.1794▲ (+4.4%)	0.1812▲ (+6.1%)
FSDM* + ELR	**0.2159**▲ (+6.3%)	**0.2078**▲ (+5.3%)

Table 3: Retrieval results for baseline models (top) and with ELR applied on top of them (bottom). Significance is tested against the corresponding baseline model. Best scores are in boldface.

MLM-tc, MLM-all, and PRMS) are language modeling-based methods that were introduced as standard baselines for the DBpedia-entity test collection [1]. The other two (SDM and FSDM) are taken from [46], the work that reported the best results on this collection so far. Specifically, the baseline models considered are:

- **LM**: The standard language modeling approach [45], against the `contents` field.

- **MLM-tc**: The Mixture of Language Models [37] with two fields, `names` and `contents`, with weights 0.2 and 0.8, respectively, as suggested in [36].

- **MLM-all**: The Mixture of Language Models using the top 10 fields with equal weights.

- **PRMS**: The Probabilistic Retrieval Model for Semistructured Data [25], using the top 10 fields.

- **SDM**: The Sequential Dependence Model [31], against the `contents` field.

- **FSDM***: The Fielded Sequential Dependence Model [46] on the top 10 fields, with field weights estimated using PRMS.

The top section of Table 3 displays the results of these baselines, all implemented from scratch.[2] The bottom part of Table 3

[2]We note the slight differences compared to the numbers reported in [1] and [46]. One major source of the differences is that we use a different DBpedia version, v3.9 with the updated DBpedia-entity

shows the results we get by applying ELR on top of these baselines. We observe consistent improvements over all baselines; the relative ranking of models remains the same (LM < SDM < MLM-tc < MLM-all < PRMS < FSDM*), but their performance is improved by 4.4–7.3% in terms of MAP, and by 4.5–6.1% in terms of P@10. All improvements are statistically significant. Based on these results, we answer our first research question positively: entity annotations of the query can indeed improve entity retrieval performance.

For the analysis that follows later in this section we retain four of these models: LM, PRMS, SDM, and FSDM*. This selection enables us to make a meaningful and consistent comparison across two dimensions: (i) single vs. multiple fields (LM and SDM vs. PRMS and FSDM*), and (ii) term independence vs. dependence (LM and PRMS vs. SDM and FSDM*).

6.3 Breakdown by query subsets

How are the different query subsets impacted by ELR (RQ2)? Intuitively, we expect ELR to improve the effectiveness of queries that mention entities plus contain some additional terms (e.g., specifying an attribute or relation). Queries that mention a single entity, without any modifiers, are less likely to benefit from our approach.

Table 4 provides a breakdown of results by query type. We find that the biggest improvements are obtained for the ListSearch and QALD-2 queries (+7.5–16% in terms of MAP and +6.5–19.1% in terms of P@10). The queries in these sets often seek entities related to other entities; a lot can be gained here from entity linking. The INEX-LD queries are also significantly improved by ELR (with the exception for FSDM*), but the relative improvements are smaller than for ListSearch and QALD-2 (here, it is +5.6–10.2% for MAP and +1.7–5.4% for P@10), but still significant in all but one case. This set is more diverse than the other two and comprises a mixture of short entity queries, type queries, and long natural language style queries. Finally, on the SemSearch ES subset, ELR could make a significant difference only for the weakest baseline, LM. These are short keyword queries, which are already handled effectively by a fielded representation (cf. PRMS and FSDM*; also note that adding term dependence does not improve performance).

To understand how much importance is attributed to entity-based matches, we plot the values of the $\lambda_{\{T,O,U,E\}}$ parameters for each

test collection, as opposed to v3.7 (used both in [1] and [46]). Our MLM-all and PRMS results are better than [1] because we use the top 10 fields, while top 1000 fields are used in [1] (cf. Figure 3). Compared to [46], we got higher scores for PRMS and lower ones for FSDM. The main reason behind this is the different choice of fields. Furthermore, as explained in §5.3, field weights are trained for each query subset in [46], while we employ a parameter-free estimation of field weights based on PRMS.

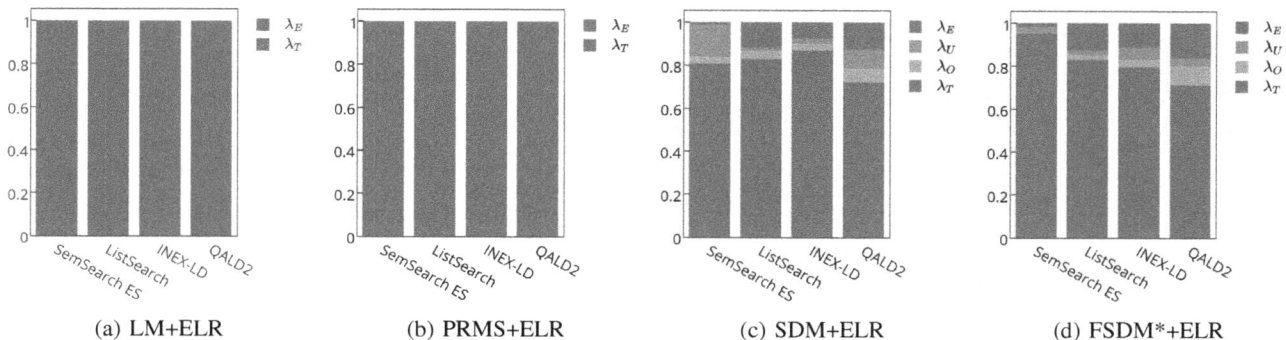

| (a) LM+ELR | (b) PRMS+ELR | (c) SDM+ELR | (d) FSDM*+ELR |

Figure 4: Values of the λ parameters (λ_T: unigrams, λ_O: ordered bigrams, λ_U: unordered bigrams, λ_E: entities) in our experiments, by the different query subsets (trained using Coordinate Ascent).

query subset in Figure 4. The values are obtained by averaging the trained parameter values across all folds of the cross-validation process. We can observe a similar trend across all retrieval methods: ListSearch and QALD-2 queries are assigned the highest λ_E values, INEX-LD gets a somewhat lower but still sizable portion of the distribution, while for SemSearch ES it bears little importance.

Based on Table 4 and Figure 4, we conclude that different query types are impacted differently by the ELR method. The results confirm our hypothesis that ELR can improve complex (ListSearch and QALD-2) as well as heterogeneous (INEX-LD) query sets, which involve entity relationships. On the other hand, short keyword queries, referring to a single, albeit often ambiguous, entity (SemSearch ES) are mostly unaffected.

6.4 Parameter settings

How sensitive is ELR to the choice of λ parameters (RQ3)? To answer this question, we compare two configurations: (i) default parameter settings, and (ii) parameters trained using the CA algorithm. The default parameters are set as follows. For SDM and FSDM, we follow [31, 32] and set $\lambda_T = 0.8$, $\lambda_O = 0.1$, and $\lambda_U = 0.1$. For the other models with ELR applied, we set λ_E to the single best performing value across the entire query set; that is, we do not train it separately for the different query subsets, like before. The resulting configurations are: (i) $\lambda_T = 0.9$ and $\lambda_E = 0.1$ for LM + ELR and PRMS + ELR, and (ii) $\lambda_T = 0.8$, $\lambda_O = 0.05$, $\lambda_U = 0.05$, and $\lambda_E = 0.1$ for SDM + ELR and FSDM* + ELR.

Table 5 compares retrieval results using default and trained parameters. Note that LM and PRMS do not involve any parameters, hence the empty cells. We find that the results are robust, i.e., ELR can improve the performance of term-based models, even with default parameter values. MAP differences are significant for all methods, except SDM + ELR. (For that model, the default λ_E value is higher than it would be optimal for SemSearch ES queries, thereby reducing overall retrieval effectiveness.) This experiment also confirms that our improvements are not a result of overfitting.

6.5 Impact of entity linking

What is the impact of the entity linking component on end-to-end entity retrieval performance (RQ4)? Entity linking systems typically involve a threshold parameter that defines the required degree of certainty for linking entities. This threshold for TAGME ranges between 0 and 1, where 0 returns the maximum number of entities and 1 returns no entity. To answer the above research question, we measure retrieval performance while varying the entity linking threshold value. Figure 5 reports the results for the best performing model, FSDM* + ELR, for both trained and default λ parameters.

Model	Default params.		Trained params.	
	MAP	P@10	MAP	P@10
LM	0.1588	0.1664		
LM + ELR	0.1668△	0.1724	0.1693▲	0.1757▲
PRMS	0.1936	0.1977		
PRMS + ELR	0.2028▲	0.2035	0.2078▲	0.2085▲
SDM	0.1672	0.1685	0.1719	0.1707
SDM + ELR	0.1721	0.1722	0.1794▲	0.1812▲
FSDM	0.1969	0.1973	0.2030	0.1973
FSDM + ELR	0.2043▲	0.1996	0.2159▲	0.2078▲

Table 5: Comparison of default vs. trained λ parameters over all queries. Significance is tested against the line above.

Apart from the small fluctuations in the 0.4–0.6 range, retrieval performance is shown to improve as the entity linking threshold is lowered. This observation implies that ELR is robust with respect to entity linking; considering more entity annotations, even those with low confidence, improves retrieval performance. The entity linker currently used allows for the annotation of overlapping entity mentions, but it returns a single entity for each mention. In future work it might be worth experimenting with multiple entities per mention, especially in highly ambiguous situations, as our framework seems to be able to benefit from having more annotations.

7. CONCLUSION

This paper represents a first attempt at incorporating entity linking into entity retrieval. We have presented a novel retrieval approach that complements term-based retrieval models with entity-based matches, using automatic means to annotate queries with entities. Our model is based on Random Markov Fields and is presented as a general framework, in which the entity-based matching component can be applied to a wide range of entity retrieval models, including standard language models, term dependence models, and their fielded variations. We have applied our approach as an extension to various state-of-the-art entity retrieval models and have shown significant and consistent improvements over all of them. The results have also shown that our model especially benefits complex and heterogeneous queries (natural language, type and relation queries), which are considered difficult queries in the context of entity retrieval. We have further demonstrated the robustness of our approach against parameter setting and entity linker configuration.

There are several directions for future work. First is to explore the effectiveness of our model using the entity linking systems specif-

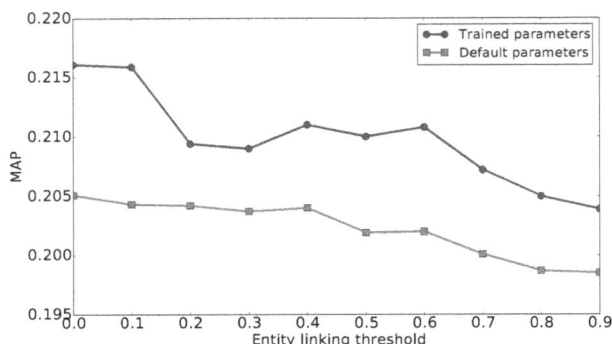

Figure 5: Effect of changing entity linking threshold (TAGME) on the performance of FSDM* + ELR model.

ically designed for queries, where a mention may be linked to multiple entities [12, 22]. Additional avenues for future work include applying our model to other retrieval problems and considering different flavors of semantic annotations, e.g., entity types.

Acknowledgments. We thank Hamed Zamani for his helpful comments during the preparation of the final version of this paper.

References

[1] K. Balog and R. Neumayer. A test collection for entity search in DBpedia. In *Proc. of SIGIR*, pages 737–740, 2013.

[2] K. Balog, L. Azzopardi, and M. de Rijke. Formal models for expert finding in enterprise corpora. In *Proc. of SIGIR*, pages 43–50, 2006.

[3] K. Balog, A. P. de Vries, P. Serdyukov, P. Thomas, and T. Westerveld. Overview of the TREC 2009 entity track. In *Proc. of TREC*, 2010.

[4] K. Balog, M. Bron, and M. De Rijke. Query modeling for entity search based on terms, categories, and examples. *ACM Trans. Inf. Syst.*, 29:22:1–22:31, 2011.

[5] K. Balog, P. Serdyukov, and A. P. de Vries. Overview of the TREC 2011 entity track. In *Proc. of TREC*, 2012.

[6] M. Bendersky, D. Metzler, and W. B. Croft. Learning concept importance using a weighted dependence model. In *Proc. of WSDM*, pages 31–40, 2010.

[7] R. Blanco, P. Mika, and S. Vigna. Effective and efficient entity search in RDF data. In *Proc. of ISWC*, pages 83–97, 2011.

[8] R. Blanco, G. Ottaviano, and E. Meij. Fast and space-efficient entity linking in queries. In *Proc. of WSDM*, pages 179–188, 2015.

[9] W. C. Brandão, R. L. T. Santos, N. Ziviani, E. S. de Moura, and A. S. da Silva. Learning to expand queries using entities. *JASIST*, 65(9): 1870–1883, 2014.

[10] M. Bron, K. Balog, and M. de Rijke. Ranking related entities: Components and analyses. In *Proc. of CIKM*, pages 1079–1088, 2010.

[11] M. Bron, K. Balog, and M. de Rijke. Example based entity search in the web of data. In *Proc. of ECIR*, pages 392–403, Berlin, Heidelberg, 2013.

[12] D. Carmel, M.-W. Chang, E. Gabrilovich, B.-j. P. P. Hsu, and K. Wang. ERD' 14: Entity recognition and disambiguation challenge. *SIGIR Forum*, 48:63–77, 2014.

[13] D. Ceccarelli, C. Lucchese, S. Orlando, R. Perego, and S. Trani. Learning relatedness measures for entity linking. In *Proc. of CIKM*, pages 139–148, 2013.

[14] M. Cornolti, P. Ferragina, and M. Ciaramita. A framework for benchmarking entity-annotation systems. In *Proc. of WWW*, pages 249–260, 2013.

[15] S. Cucerzan. Large-scale named entity disambiguation based on Wikipedia data. In *Proc. of EMNLP-CoNLL*, pages 708–716, 2007.

[16] J. Dalton, L. Dietz, and J. Allan. Entity query feature expansion using knowledge base links. In *Proc. of SIGIR*, pages 365–374, 2014.

[17] A. de Vries, A.-M. Vercoustre, J. Thom, N. Craswell, and M. Lalmas. Overview of the INEX 2007 entity ranking track. *Focused Access to XML Documents*, 4862:245–251, 2008.

[18] G. Demartini, T. Iofciu, and A. de Vries. Overview of the INEX 2009 entity ranking track. *Focused Retrieval and Evaluation*, 6203: 254–264, 2010.

[19] P. Ferragina and U. Scaiella. TAGME: On-the-fly annotation of short text fragments (by Wikipedia entities). In *Proc. of CIKM*, pages 1625–1628, 2010.

[20] D. Graus, M. Tsagkias, W. Weerkamp, E. Meij, and M. de Rijke. Dynamic collective entity representations for entity ranking. In *Proc. of WSDM*, 2016.

[21] S. Guo, M.-W. Chang, and E. Kiciman. To link or not to link? a study on end-to-end tweet entity linking. In *Proc. of HLT-NAACL*, pages 1020–1030, 2013.

[22] F. Hasibi, K. Balog, and S. E. Bratsberg. Entity linking in queries: Tasks and evaluation. In *Proc. of ICTIR*, pages 171–180, 2015.

[23] F. Hasibi, K. Balog, and S. E. Bratsberg. On the reproducibility of the TAGME entity linking system. In *Proc. of ECIR*, pages 436–449, 2016.

[24] R. Kaptein, P. Serdyukov, A. De Vries, and J. Kamps. Entity ranking using Wikipedia as a pivot. In *Proc. of CIKM*, pages 69–78, 2010.

[25] J. Kim, X. Xue, and W. B. Croft. A probabilistic retrieval model for semistructured data. In *Proc. of ECIR*, pages 228–239, 2009.

[26] S. Kulkarni, A. Singh, G. Ramakrishnan, and S. Chakrabarti. Collective annotation of Wikipedia entities in Web text. In *Proc. of KDD*, pages 457–466, 2009.

[27] R. Li, L. Hao, X. Zhao, P. Zhang, D. Song, and Y. Hou. A query expansion approach using entity distribution based on Markov Random Fields. In *Proc. of AIRS*, pages 387–393, 2015.

[28] X. Liu and H. Fang. Latent entity space: A novel retrieval approach for entity-bearing queries. *Inf. Retr.*, 18(6):473–503, 2015.

[29] E. Meij, W. Weerkamp, and M. de Rijke. Adding semantics to microblog posts. In *Proc. of WSDM*, pages 563–572, 2012.

[30] E. Meij, K. Balog, and D. Odijk. Entity linking and retrieval for semantic search. In *Proc. of WSDM*, pages 683–684, 2014.

[31] D. Metzler and W. B. Croft. A Markov Random Field model for term dependencies. In *Proc. of SIGIR*, pages 472–479, 2005.

[32] D. Metzler and W. B. Croft. Linear feature-based models for information retrieval. *Inf. Retr.*, 10(3):257–274, 2007.

[33] R. Mihalcea and A. Csomai. Wikify!: Linking documents to encyclopedic knowledge. In *Proc. of CIKM*, pages 233–242, 2007.

[34] D. Milne and I. H. Witten. Learning to link with Wikipedia. In *Proc. of CIKM*, pages 509–518, 2008.

[35] R. Neumayer, K. Balog, and K. Nørvåg. On the modeling of entities for ad-hoc entity search in the Web of Data. In *Proc. of ECIR*, pages 133–145, 2012.

[36] R. Neumayer, K. Balog, and K. Nørvåg. When simple is (more than) good enough: Effective semantic search with (almost) no semantics. In *Proc. of ECIR*, pages 540–543, 2012.

[37] P. Ogilvie and J. Callan. Combining document representations for known-item search. *Proc. of SIGIR*, pages 143–150, 2003.

[38] J. Pound, P. Mika, and H. Zaragoza. Ad-hoc object retrieval in the Web of Data. In *Proc. of WWW*, pages 771–780, 2010.

[39] H. Raviv, D. Carmel, and O. Kurland. A ranking framework for entity oriented search using Markov Random Fields. In *Proc. of International Workshop on Entity-Oriented and Semantic Search*, JIWES, 2012.

[40] S. Robertson, H. Zaragoza, and M. Taylor. Simple BM25 extension to multiple weighted fields. In *Proc. of CIKM*, pages 42–49, 2004.

[41] M. Schuhmacher, L. Dietz, and S. Paolo Ponzetto. Ranking entities for Web queries through text and knowledge. In *Proc. of CIKM*, pages 1461–1470, 2015.

[42] Q. Wang, J. Kamps, G. R. Camps, M. Marx, A. Schuth, M. Theobald, S. Gurajada, and A. Mishra. Overview of the INEX 2012 linked data track. In *CLEF 2012 Evaluation Labs and Workshop, Online Working Notes*, 2012.

[43] C. Xiong and J. Callan. EsdRank: Connecting query and documents through external semi-structured data. In *Proc. of CIKM*, pages 951–960, 2015.

[44] C. Xiong and J. Callan. Query expansion with Freebase. In *Proc. of ICTIR*, pages 111–120, New York, NY, USA, 2015.

[45] C. Zhai. Statistical language models for information retrieval a critical review. *Found. Trends Inf. Retr.*, 2:137–213, 2008.

[46] N. Zhiltsov, A. Kotov, and F. Nikolaev. Fielded sequential dependence model for ad-hoc entity retrieval in the Web of Data. In *Proc. of SIGIR*, pages 253–262, 2015.

Query Anchoring Using Discriminative Query Models

Saar Kuzi
saarkuzi@campus.technion.ac.il

Anna Shtok
annabel@tx.technion.ac.il

Oren Kurland
kurland@ie.technion.ac.il

Technion — Israel Institute of Technology

ABSTRACT

Pseudo-feedback-based query models are induced from a result list of the documents most highly ranked by initial search performed for the query. Since the result list often contains much non-relevant information, query models are anchored to the query using various techniques. We present a novel *unsupervised* discriminative query model that can be used, by several methods proposed herein, for query anchoring of existing query models. The model is induced from the result list using a learning-to-rank approach, and constitutes a discriminative term-based representation of the initial ranking. We show that applying our methods to generative query models can improve retrieval performance.

1. INTRODUCTION

There is a large body of work on devising pseudo-feedback-based query models (e.g., expanded query forms) [5]. The models are created using information induced from a result list of the documents most highly ranked by some initial search performed in response to the query. The goal is to create a more effective representation of the presumed information need than the query which is often very short. A case in point, query models can help to bridge the vocabulary mismatch between the query and relevant documents.

Documents in the result list (a.k.a. the pseudo feedback list) could be non relevant, and relevant documents can contain non query-pertaining information [11, 13, 20]. Thus, a query model induced from these documents can drift away from the information need [22]. Hence, several techniques, often referred to as *query anchoring*, have been proposed for mitigating the risk in relying on pseudo feedback. These techniques essentially use the original query as an anchor when utilizing pseudo feedback. For example, interpolating the query model with a model of the original query is a commonly used direct query anchoring technique (e.g., [23, 4, 1, 33, 21, 6]). Using the original query model as a prior for the pseudo-feedback-based query model is another example of direct anchoring [27, 28].

Indirect query anchoring techniques are based on various assumptions with regard to the pseudo feedback and its connection to the information need. For instance, clipping the query model by using only the terms to which it assigns the highest importance weights is common practice (e.g., [2, 30, 33, 1, 31]). The assumption is that these terms are the most likely to represent the information need as they represent the result list. Another indirect technique is attributing more importance to term occurrence in documents highly ranked in the result list than to that in low ranked documents [17, 1, 27, 25]. The premise is that the higher the document is ranked, the higher its relevance likelihood by the virtue of the way the result list was created; that is, in response to the query.

We present a novel indirect query anchoring approach that can be applied to existing query models. The approach utilizes a novel *unsupervised* discriminative pseudo-feedback-based query model induced from the result list. The model serves as an accurate discriminative term-based representation of the *initial ranking* of the result list. As such, the model can be used, by several methods proposed herein, for query anchoring.

More specifically, the proposed query model is produced by training a pairwise learning-to-rank method using the initial result list ranking. The resultant model is composed of terms whose presence in documents is either positively or negatively correlated with the initial result list ranking. Accordingly, these terms can be used for query anchoring.

We demonstrate the merits of applying several methods, which use our new query model, on two highly effective generative query models: the relevance model [17, 1] and the mixture model [32]. Although these models employ several query anchoring approaches, applying our methods results in performance improvements.

2. RELATED WORK

As already noted, a few query anchoring approaches have been proposed in past work. We show that using our methods in addition to several of these most commonly used and effective approaches — interpolation with the original query model [23, 4, 1, 33, 21][1], term clipping [2, 30, 33, 1, 31], and differential weighting of documents in the result list [17, 1, 27, 25] — helps to further improve retrieval performance.

Fusing the initial ranking with the ranking produced by using the pseudo-feedback-based query model was suggested

ICTIR '16, September 12-16, 2016, Newark, DE, USA

© 2016 ACM. ISBN 978-1-4503-4497-5/16/09. . . $15.00

DOI: http://dx.doi.org/10.1145/2970398.2970402

---

[1]There has been work on tuning the interpolation on a per query basis when constructing the query model from *true*, rather than pseudo, relevant documents [21].

for indirect query anchoring [34]. In contrast, our methods operate on the query model by integrating it, at the model level, with a representation of the initial ranking (i.e., the proposed discriminative query model). Our methods are shown to substantially outperform this fusion approach [34].

There are various methods for improving the quality of the pseudo feedback result list used for inducing a query model (e.g., [22, 24, 18, 12, 15]). The discriminative query model used by our methods can be applied to any ranked list. Thus, our methods are complementary to these past approaches, and more generally, to methods that improve an initial pseudo-feedback-based query model (e.g., [3, 8]).

It was shown that among the terms attributed the highest importance by a pseudo-feedback-based query model, some are highly effective for retrieval while others can be detrimental [3, 29]. Accordingly, a supervised term classification approach was applied using various term features, the most effective of which were based on proximity to query terms in documents in the result list [3]. In contrast, our approach is unsupervised and applies a learning-to-rank method on documents in the result list. Furthermore, we focus on unigram query models and leave the treatment of term-proximity-based query models for future work.

Formal analysis of methods for inducing pseudo-feedback-based query models, and the properties of terms that should be assigned high importance by query models, was presented [21, 7]. Our findings provide additional novel characterization: the importance weight of terms whose presence in documents is positively correlated with the *initial ranking* should be increased while that of terms whose presence is negatively correlated should be decreased.

3. QUERY MODELS

Let $\mathcal{D}_{init}^{[k]}$ (henceforth $\mathcal{D}_{init}$) be a result list of the k documents most highly ranked by initial retrieval performed over the document corpus D in response to query q.

Information induced from $\mathcal{D}_{init}$, often referred to as the pseudo feedback result list, can be used to create a *query model* (e.g., an expanded query form). For example, the model can attribute high importance to terms frequent in documents in $\mathcal{D}_{init}$ but not in the corpus [2, 30, 4, 17, 32, 21, 5]. The goal is to create a query model that represents the underlying information need more effectively than a model based only on the terms in q which is often very short.

As noted above, pseudo-feedback-based query models are often anchored to the query (e.g., via interpolation with the original query model) so as to mitigate the "risk" in relying on pseudo feedback; that is, documents in $\mathcal{D}_{init}$ can be non-relevant and relevant documents can contain much non query-pertaining information [11, 13, 20].

We present a novel query anchoring approach. The approach utilizes a newly proposed discriminative query model induced from the result list, $\mathcal{D}_{init}$. The model constitutes a term-based representation of $\mathcal{D}_{init}$'s *initial ranking*. Thus, the model can be used to query anchor existing pseudo-feedback-based query models as shown below.

Although our query model induction approach is not committed to a specific retrieval paradigm, it is convenient to present it in the language modeling framework given the large body of work on language-model-based query models [21]. We therefore start by describing the language model notation that will be used throughout this paper. In Section 3.1 we survey two highly effective methods of induc-

ing generative query models. In doing so, we will refer to the query anchoring techniques that these methods employ. Then, in Section 3.2 we describe our novel discriminative query model, and in Section 3.3 present a few methods of applying it on an existing language-model-based query model so as to improve retrieval performance.

Language model notation. We use unigram language models. $p_{MLE}(t|x) \stackrel{def}{=} \frac{tf(t \in x)}{|x|}$ is the maximum likelihood estimate (MLE) of term t with respect to the text (or text collection) x; $tf(t \in x)$ is the number of occurrences of t in x; $|x| \stackrel{def}{=} \sum_{t' \in x} tf(t' \in x)$ is x's length. The MLE can be smoothed, for example, using a Dirichlet prior: $p_{Dir}(t|x) \stackrel{def}{=} \frac{tf(t \in x) + \mu p_{MLE}(t|D)}{|x| + \mu}$; μ is a free parameter [33]. We compare two language models, θ_1 and θ_2, using cross entropy [16]:

$$CE\left(p(\cdot|\theta_1) \,\middle\|\, p(\cdot|\theta_2)\right) \stackrel{def}{=} -\sum_t p(t|\theta_1) \log p(t|\theta_2); \quad (1)$$

lower values correspond to increased similarity.

3.1 Generative query models

3.1.1 Relevance model

The relevance model is based on the assumption that the query and documents relevant to the query are generated by a latent relevance language model [17]. Assuming that $\mathcal{D}_{init}$ was retrieved using the query likelihood approach [26], which ranks document d by $p(q|d) \stackrel{def}{=} \prod_{t \in q} p_{Dir}(t|d)$, the relevance model RM1 is defined as:

$$p(t|RM1) \stackrel{def}{=} \sum_{d \in \mathcal{D}_{init}} p_{Dir}(t|d)p(d|q); \quad (2)$$

$p(d|q) \stackrel{def}{=} \frac{p(q|d)}{\sum_{d' \in \mathcal{D}_{init}} p(q|d')}$ is the normalized query likelihood of d. RM1 is a linear mixture of the language models of documents in $\mathcal{D}_{init}$. The effect of high ranked documents on RM1 is greater than that of low ranked documents because the query likelihood values of documents serve as mixture weights. This differential effect was mentioned in Section 1 as an indirect query anchoring approach. Term clipping applied to RM1, which yields $RM1^{clipped}$, is an additional indirect query anchoring technique: assigning zero probability to all but the ν terms to which RM1 assigns the highest probability; ν is a free parameter; the probabilities of the ν terms are sum-normalized to produce a probability distribution. A third, direct query anchoring approach is applied by the RM3 relevance model [1]; namely, interpolating $RM1^{clipped}$ with the original query model (MLE) using a parameter λ:

$$p(t|RM3) \stackrel{def}{=} \lambda p_{MLE}(t|q) + (1 - \lambda)p(t|RM1^{clipped}). \quad (3)$$

3.1.2 Mixture model

The mixture model [32] is based on the assumption that the terms in documents in $\mathcal{D}_{init}$ are generated by a mixture of two language models: a topic model, θ_T, and the corpus language model. To estimate θ_T, the log likelihood of the documents in $\mathcal{D}_{init}$,

$$\sum_{d \in \mathcal{D}_{init}} \sum_{t \in d} tf(t \in d) \log\left((1 - \gamma)p(t|\theta_T) + \gamma p_{MLE}(t|D)\right),$$

is maximized using the EM algorithm; γ is a free parameter. In contrast to RM1, the relative ranking of documents in $\mathcal{D}_{\text{init}}$ does not affect the estimation of θ_T.[2]

As is the case for the relevance model, θ_T is clipped, yielding $\theta_T^{clipped}$; a non-zero probability is assigned only to the ν terms to which θ_T assigns the highest probability and these probabilities are sum normalized. Direct query anchoring is performed via interpolation with the original query model, yielding the mixture model, MM:

$$p(t|MM) \stackrel{def}{=} \lambda p_{MLE}(t|q) + (1 - \lambda)p(t|\theta_T^{clipped}). \quad (4)$$

Thus, while RM3 is based on three techniques for query anchoring: (i) differential impact of documents on the query model based on their query likelihood, (ii) term clipping, and (iii) interpolation with the original query model, the mixture model MM applies only the latter two. To use a query model θ (relevance model or mixture model) for ranking document d, the cross entropy (Equation 1) between the model and d's language model is used.

3.2 A discriminative query model

Term clipping (applied by RM3 and MM) and differential impact of documents in $\mathcal{D}_{\text{init}}$ (applied by RM3) are indirect query anchoring techniques. That is, the underlying assumptions are that (i) the terms most representative of $\mathcal{D}_{\text{init}}$ are likely to represent the information need; and (ii) the higher a document is ranked in $\mathcal{D}_{\text{init}}$, the higher its relevance likelihood. The latter is essentially the pseudo feedback assumption.

We leverage the pseudo feedback assumption in a different, novel way. Specifically, we directly utilize the premise that for *any* two documents d_1 and d_2 in $\mathcal{D}_{\text{init}}$, if d_1 is ranked higher than d_2, then d_1 is more likely to be relevant than d_2. Using the resultant pairwise document preferences in a pairwise learning-to-rank method [19], namely SVMrank [14], yields a discriminative query model. The model constitutes a discriminative term-based representation of $\mathcal{D}_{\text{init}}$'s *ranking*. As such, the model is used as a (indirect) query anchor for the generative query models by a few methods we present in Section 3.3.

There are a few important differences between using SVMrank — or any other learning-to-rank method — in our work and in a standard learning-to-rank setting [19]. In a standard setting, the goal is to learn a ranking function using feature vectors that represent document-query pairs. Here, the goal is to create a term-based representation of a single given ranking. A feature vector is a query independent term-based representation of a document. Thus, the query model induction approach we present does not explicitly account for the query used to create $\mathcal{D}_{\text{init}}$.

The different goals in applying learning-to-rank in the standard setting and in our setting entail differences in the way the models are trained. In supervised models, different techniques are applied to avoid overfitting and to improve generalization from training data to unseen data. In contrast, we use SVMrank to produce for a given query an accurate representation of $\mathcal{D}_{\text{init}}$'s ranking. This representation is used for anchoring with respect to the given query,

rather than for generalization to unseen queries. Finally, our approach is unsupervised in that it utilizes pairwise preferences that are based on pseudo feedback, while learning-to-rank methods are usually used in supervised settings and utilize either relevance labels or implicit feedback (e.g., click-through information) [19].

Let $r(d)$ be the rank of document d in $\mathcal{D}_{\text{init}}$. The rank of the highest ranked document is 1. We use V to denote the vocabulary used in $\mathcal{D}_{\text{init}}$; i.e., the set of terms that appear in documents in $\mathcal{D}_{\text{init}}$. Document d ($\in \mathcal{D}_{\text{init}}$) is represented by the $|V|$ dimensional feature vector $\Phi(d)$ defined over V; the i'th component of $\Phi(d)$ is $\log p_{Dir}(t_i|d)$ where t_i is the i'th term in V and $p_{Dir}(t_i|d)$ is the probability assigned to t_i by d's Dirichlet smoothed language model[3]. We apply SVMrank to find a weight vector $\vec{w}$ defined over V that is the solution for:

$$minimize \qquad \frac{1}{2}\vec{w} \cdot \vec{w} + C\sum_{i,j}\xi_{i,j}$$

$$(5)$$

$$subject\ to:$$

$$\forall i \forall j. \ r(d_i) < r(d_j): \qquad \vec{w}\Phi(d_i) \geq \vec{w}\Phi(d_j) + 1 - \xi_{i,j}$$

$$\forall i \forall j. \ r(d_i) < r(d_j): \qquad \xi_{i,j} \geq 0$$

Equation 5 defines a soft margin SVM where $\xi_{i,j}$ are the slack variables and C is the regularization parameter. Higher values of C result in stricter adherence to the given pseudo-relevance-based pairwise preferences. As our goal is to fit the model as closely as possible to the ranking of $\mathcal{D}_{\text{init}}$, we will use in the experiments a very high value of C.[4]

There are at most $\frac{1}{2}k(k-1)$ constraints of the form $\vec{w}\Phi(d_i) \geq \vec{w}\Phi(d_j) + 1 - \xi_{i,j}$ in Equation 5 where k is the number of documents in $\mathcal{D}_{\text{init}}$; these constraints correspond to all[5] pairs of documents d_i and d_j in $\mathcal{D}_{\text{init}}$ where d_i is ranked *higher* than d_j (i.e., $r(d_i) < r(d_j)$). The vector $\vec{w}$ can be thought of as a query model that contains positive and negative values that correspond to terms in V. The inner product $\vec{w}\Phi(d)$ serves for scoring documents. Given the definition of document feature vectors, we arrive to the following implication of using the pairwise constraints from Equation 5.

Let $\vec{w}_+$ be the vector obtained from $\vec{w}$ by setting to zero negative components. Let $\vec{w}_-$ be the vector obtained from $\vec{w}$ by setting to zero positive components, and taking the absolute value of negative components. Then, the pairwise constraint from Equation 5 amounts, in spirit[6], to:

$$-CE(p(\cdot|\theta_{\vec{w}_+}) \parallel p_{Dir}(\cdot|d_i)) + CE(p(\cdot|\theta_{\vec{w}_-}) \parallel p_{Dir}(\cdot|d_i)) \geq$$
$$-CE(p(\cdot|\theta_{\vec{w}_+}) \parallel p_{Dir}(\cdot|d_j)) + CE(p(\cdot|\theta_{\vec{w}_-}) \parallel p_{Dir}(\cdot|d_j)) +$$
$$1 - \xi_{i,j}; \qquad (6)$$

---

[2]A regularized mixture model [28] uses the original query model, $p_{MLE}(t|q)$, as a Bayesian prior. This is yet another direct query anchoring technique. However, the retrieval performance is similar to that of using the original mixture model we discuss here [21].

[3]Using $\log p_{Dir}(t_i|d)$ results in cross entropy semantics for the constraints presented in Equation 5.

[4]An alternative hard-margin SVM formulation is not guaranteed to have a solution.

[5]For pairs of documents with exactly the same initial retrieval score in $\mathcal{D}_{\text{init}}$ we do not use a constraint.

[6]We write "in spirit" as the weight vectors $\vec{w}_+$ and $\vec{w}_-$ that are parts of the solution to Equation 5 have to be normalized so as to yield valid probability distributions. Therefore, the values compared in the constraints in Equation 5 are not valid CE values. Yet, the observations made with respect to Equation 6, and consequently to Equation 5, still hold. We use the CE expressions to simplify the discussion.

$\theta_{\vec{x}}$ is a language model over V attained by applying L_1 normalization to $\vec{x}$. Since larger CE values correspond to decreased similarity, we get that the inequality holds to a larger extent (specifically, with lower values of $\xi_{i,j}$) when: (i) $p_{Dir}(\cdot|d_i)$ is high for terms with a (high) positive value in $\vec{w}$ and low for terms with a (low) negative value in $\vec{w}$; and, (ii) $p_{Dir}(\cdot|d_j)$ is low for terms with a (high) positive value in $\vec{w}$ and high for terms with a (high) negative value in $\vec{w}$.

As d_i is ranked above d_j, we attain the following result. Terms with a positive value in $\vec{w}$ are positively correlated with $\mathcal{D}_{init}$'s ranking — i.e., for a pair of documents in $\mathcal{D}_{init}$ they will tend to have more substantial presence in the document ranked higher. We refer to these terms as *positive anchors*. Accordingly, terms with negative values in $\vec{w}$ are negatively correlated with $\mathcal{D}_{init}$'s ranking, and are hence referred to as *negative anchors*.

It is important to highlight the difference between the discriminative query model, $(p(\cdot|\theta_{\vec{w}_+}), p(\cdot|\theta_{\vec{w}_-}))$, and the generative query models described in Section 3.1. A generative query model assigns high probability to terms that are presumably related to the underlying information need by the virtue of having substantial presence in $\mathcal{D}_{init}$. In contrast, the goal of the discriminative model is to represent the *ranking* of $\mathcal{D}_{init}$. Indeed, it attributes high positive importance to terms (positive anchors) whose presence in a document corresponds to higher ranking in $\mathcal{D}_{init}$, and high negative importance to terms (negative anchors) whose presence corresponds to lower ranking. We empirically demonstrate the difference between the two types of language models in Section 4.3. As a result, the generative query models and the discriminative model are of complementary nature. We leverage this fact in Section 3.3 by designing methods that use the discriminative query model to query anchor the generative query models.

3.3 Using the discriminative query model

Let θ be a generative query model. The positive anchor model, $\theta_{\vec{w}_+}$, assigns non-zero probability to positive anchor terms which are positively correlated with $\mathcal{D}_{init}$'s ranking. Boosting the probabilities of these terms in a generative query model can serve for query anchoring.

The **AnchorPos** method (named for anchoring using the positive anchor terms) integrates θ with $\theta_{\vec{w}_+}$ as follows. Let λ_1, λ_2 and λ_3 be free parameters of non-negative values used below to weigh different components of the proposed model; $\lambda_1 + \lambda_2 + \lambda_3 = 1$. We define the score $s(t)$ for term t:

$$s(t) \stackrel{def}{=} \lambda_2 p(t|\theta) + \lambda_3 p(t|\theta_{\vec{w}_+}).$$

Term clipping is applied by setting to non-zero the probability of only the ν terms t with the highest $s(t)$; this term set is denoted S; ν is a free parameter. The scores of the terms in S are sum-normalized to yield a valid language model ϑ_+ over the corpus vocabulary. That is, $p(t|\vartheta_+) \stackrel{def}{=} 0$ for $t \notin S$; for $t \in S$: $p(t|\vartheta_+) \stackrel{def}{=} \frac{s(t)}{\sum_{t' \in S} s(t')}$. In addition, direct query anchoring is applied to yield the AnchorPos model:

$$p(t|\theta_{AnchorPos}) \stackrel{def}{=} \lambda_1 p_{MLE}(t|q) + (1 - \lambda_1)p(t|\vartheta_+). \quad (7)$$

If θ is RM1 or θ_T, described in Section 3.1, we will refer to AnchorPos as operating on RM3 and MM, respectively. The reason is that for $\lambda_3 = 0$, Equation 7 amounts to RM3 and MM, respectively. In comparison to RM3 and MM which

apply term clipping and direct query anchoring (RM3 applies in addition differential weighting of documents in $\mathcal{D}_{init}$) AnchorPos also applies anchoring using $\theta_{\vec{w}_+}$.

Our next order of business is devising a method that uses the negative anchor model, $\theta_{\vec{w}_-}$, to query anchor a generative query model θ.

Let S_e be the e percent of terms assigned the highest $p(t|\theta_{\vec{w}_-})$ and which are not in the query q; e is a free parameter. These terms are the most negatively correlated with $\mathcal{D}_{init}$'s ranking. We select the ν terms to which θ assigns the highest probability and which are not in S_e. We sum-normalize the probabilities assigned to these terms by θ which yields the ϑ_- model. All other terms in the vocabulary are assigned a zero probability. Additional direct query anchoring, using a parameter λ, yields the **ClipNeg** model:

$$p(t|\theta_{ClipNeg}) \stackrel{def}{=} \lambda p_{MLE}(t|q) + (1 - \lambda)p(t|\vartheta_-). \quad (8)$$

Thus, in comparison to the RM3 and MM generative models, which apply several previously proposed query anchoring techniques, the ClipNeg method also applies clipping of negative anchor terms. If θ is RM1 or θ_T we will refer to ClipNeg as operating on RM3 and MM, respectively. Specifically, for $e = 0$, i.e. when the negative anchor query model is not used, Equation 8 becomes RM3 and MM, respectively.

To leverage both the positive anchor and negative anchor query models, we devise the **AnchorClip** method which boosts the probability of positive anchor terms and sets to zero the probability of negative anchor terms. As was the case for AnchorPos, we use the parameters λ_1, λ_2 and λ_3 ($\lambda_1 + \lambda_2 + \lambda_3 = 1$) and define the score of term t as: $\lambda_2 p(t|\theta) + \lambda_3 p(t|\theta_{\vec{w}_+})$. The ν terms with the highest scores, and which are not in S_e (the e percent of terms with the highest $p(t|\theta_{\vec{w}_-})$ and which are not in q) are selected to have a non-zero probability; the probability for all other terms is set to zero. Specifically, the scores of these terms are sum-normalized to yield the language model ϑ which is then interpolated with the original query model:

$$p(t|\theta_{AnchorClip}) \stackrel{def}{=} \lambda_1 p_{MLE}(t|q) + (1 - \lambda_1)p(t|\vartheta). \quad (9)$$

For $e = 0$ and for $\lambda_3 = 0$, AnchorClip amounts to AnchorPos and ClipNeg, respectively.

All query models are used to rank the corpus by comparing them with Dirichlet smoothed document language models using the cross entropy (Equation 1).

4. EVALUATION

We present an evaluation of the methods from Section 3.3 that use the discriminative query model. The methods are applied to the relevance model, RM3 [1], and to the mixture model [32], MM, described in Section 3.1. These two generative query models were the most effective in a study of unigram language-model-based query models [21].

4.1 Experimental setup

The datasets specified in Table 1 were used for experiments. TREC123 and ROBUST are (mainly) newswire document collections, and WT10G is a Web collection. Titles of TREC topics serve for queries. Krovetz stemming and stopword removal (using the INQUERY list) were applied to documents and queries. We used for experiments the Indri toolkit (www.lemurproject.org).

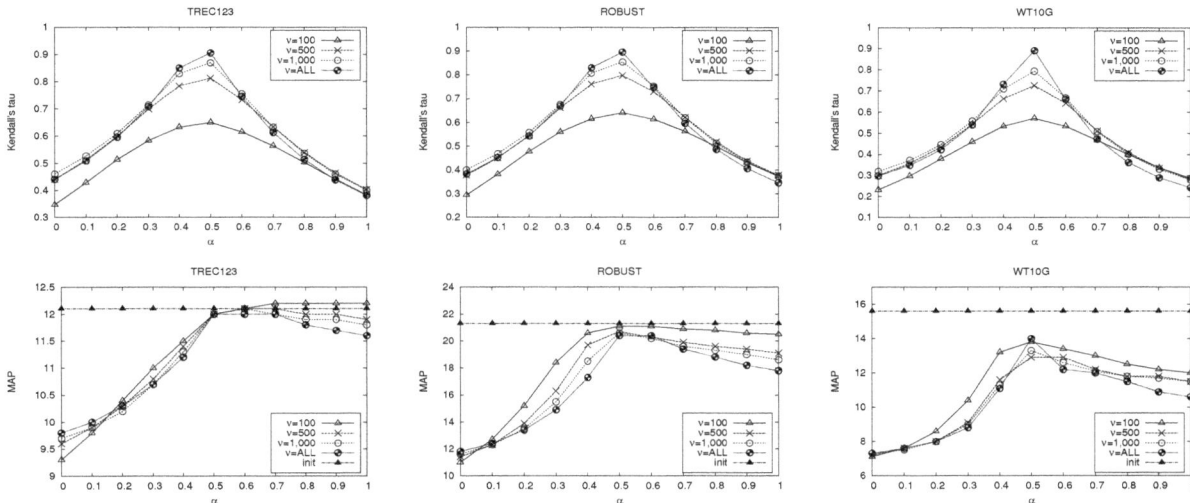

Figure 1: Using the discriminative query model to re-rank an initial list of 100 documents from which it is induced. The Kendall-τ between the initial ranking (init) and the re-ranking, and their MAP(@100), are reported. The positive and negative anchor models are clipped to use ν terms; ν =ALL means no clipping. Note: figures are not to the same scale.

Table 1: TREC datasets used for experiments.

Collection	TREC disks	# of Docs	Topics
TREC123	Disks 1&2	741,856	51-200
ROBUST	Disks 4,5-{CR}	528,155	301-450, 601-700
WT10G	WT10g	1,692,096	451-550

The initial result list $\mathcal{D}_{init}$, which serves for pseudo feedback, is retrieved using a standard language model method [16] which uses cross entropy (see Equation 1): document d is scored by $-CE\left(p_{MLE}(\cdot|q) \,\|\, p_{Dir}(\cdot|d)\right)$. The ranking is equivalent to that produced by the query likelihood model [26] used in the relevance model. Here and after, the Dirichlet smoothing parameter, μ, is set to 1000 [33].

We use Mean Average Precision (MAP@1000) and the precision of the top-5 documents (p@5) for evaluation measures. Statistically significant differences of performance are determined using the two-tailed paired t-test at a 95% confidence level. We also report the reliability of improvement (RI) [24] for the query models: $100 \cdot \frac{|Q_+|-|Q_-|}{|Q|}$; Q is the set of queries; Q_+ and Q_- are the sets of queries for which the average precision (AP) is higher and lower, respectively, than that of the initial ranking. The RI measure quantifies the performance robustness of using a pseudo-feedback-based query model with respect to using only the query. In Section 4.2.3 we extend the robustness analysis by using risk-reward graphs [8].

As mentioned in Section 3.2, we use SVMrank [14] to construct the discriminative query model; the regularization parameter C is set to 100, 000. All other parameters of SVM-rank are set to default values[7]. The resultant model is nearly a hard margin SVM fitted to $\mathcal{D}_{init}$'s ranking. Recall that our goal is to create an accurate representation of this ranking. Indeed, lower values of C resulted in less effective anchor-

ing models. Actual numbers are omitted as they convey no additional insight.

Our methods apply the discriminative query model, which represents $\mathcal{D}_{init}$'s ranking, to query anchor the generative query models. Thus, they could be viewed as fusing a representation of the initial ranking with the generative query model at the language model level. Hence, we use a reference comparison, **Fusion**, that fuses the initial ranking with the generative query models at the retrieval score level [34]. Specifically, the top-1000 documents in the initial ranking are fused, using CombMNZ [10], with the top-1000 documents in a ranking produced by using the generative query model [34][8]. The idea is to reward documents highly similar both to the pseudo-feedback-based query model and to the query. The implementation details are as in [34].

Free-parameter values. All the methods we consider: the generative query models RM3 and MM, our methods (AnchorPos, ClipNeg and AnchorClip) and the reference comparison Fusion incorporate free parameters. We set the values of all free parameters of each method using leave-one-out (LOO) cross validation performed over the queries in a dataset[9]. That is, the free parameters of a method for a query are set to values that optimize average performance over all other queries in the dataset. To avoid metric divergence issues, following previous recommendations in work on query expansion [9] we use the same evaluation metric (MAP or p@5) to train free-parameter values and to report the resultant performance. The following free-parameter value ranges were used. The number of documents, k, in the initial list $\mathcal{D}_{init}$ is in $\{25, 50, 100\}$. The number of terms used in

---

[7] http://www.cs.cornell.edu/people/tj/svm_light/svm_rank.html

[8] CombMNZ was more effective in our setting than the alternative interpolation-based fusion method [34].

[9] The performance of *all* methods when using 10-fold cross validation was sometimes slightly lower than that of using LOO; but, most differences were statistically indistinguishable, and the relative performance patterns were the same.

Table 2: Main result. Boldface: best result in a column in a generative model block. Statistically significant differences with the initial ranking (init), generative model (RM3 or MM), Fusion and ClipNeg are marked with 'i', 'g', 'f' and 'c', respectively.

	TREC123			ROBUST			WT10G		
	MAP	p@5	RI	MAP	p@5	RI	MAP	p@5	RI
init	23.0	52.7	–	24.9	47.6	–	19.8	35.5	–
	Relevance Model								
RM3	28.4^i	$\mathbf{57.7}^i$	48.0	28.2^i	48.6	30.9	$\mathbf{21.9}^{i,g}$	37.7	5.2
Fusion	$27.0^{i,g}$	54.1^g	46.7	27.7^i	48.9^i	39.0	$20.8^{i,g}$	37.9	7.2
ClipNeg	$28.8^{i,g}_f$	$\mathbf{57.7}^i_f$	52.0	$28.9^{i,g}_f$	$50.0^{i,g}_f$	36.5	21.6^i	$\mathbf{38.1}$	8.2
AnchorPos	$\mathbf{29.2}^{i,g}_{f,c}$	$\mathbf{57.7}^i_f$	53.3	$\mathbf{29.6}^{i,g}_f$	$50.1^{i,g}$	31.3	21.8^i	37.7	−2.1
	Mixture Model								
MM	28.1^i	55.1	38.7	27.6^i	48.8	25.3	20.8^i	$\mathbf{36.3}$	12.4
Fusion	$27.7^{i,g}$	53.6^g	39.3	27.8^i	48.4	29.7	20.2^g	35.1	−3.1
ClipNeg	28.3^i	53.3	38.7	27.6^i	46.1^g_f	18.9	21.0^i_f	33.2^g	$\mathbf{16.5}$
AnchorPos	$\mathbf{29.1}^{i,g}_{f,c}$	$\mathbf{55.9}$	40.0	$\mathbf{29.2}^{i,g}_{f,c}$	50.0^i_c	30.9	21.3^i_f	34.0	9.3

the query models, ν, is in $\{25, 50, 75\}$. The mixture model parameter, γ, is in $\{0.1, 0.5, 0.9\}$. The percentage of negative anchor terms, e, clipped in ClipNeg and AnchorClip is in $\{0, 5, 10, 25, 50, 75, 100\}$ for ClipNeg and in $\{75, 100\}$ for AnchorClip[10]. We show in Section 4.2.3 that clipping a low percentage of negative anchor terms yields worse performance than clipping a high percentage. The parameters λ, λ_1, λ_2 and λ_3 are set to values in $\{0, 0.2, \ldots, 1\}$.

4.2 Experimental results

4.2.1 The discriminative model

We first study the extent to which the discriminative query model represents the initial ranking of the list, $\mathcal{D}_{\text{init}}$, from which it is constructed. To that end, we re-rank $\mathcal{D}_{\text{init}}$ using the model. The score of d ($\in \mathcal{D}_{\text{init}}$) is the interpolation of d's similarity with the positive anchor model and dissimilarity with the negative anchor model: $-\alpha CE(p(\cdot|\theta_{\vec{w}_+}) \| p_{Dir}(\cdot|d)) + (1-\alpha) CE(p(\cdot|\theta_{\vec{w}_-}) \| p_{Dir}(\cdot|d))$; α ($\in \{0, 0.1, \ldots, 1\}$) is a free parameter; $\theta_{\vec{w}_+}$ and $\theta_{\vec{w}_-}$ are clipped to use the ν terms to which they assign the highest probabilities. We report the Kendall-τ between the re-ranking of $\mathcal{D}_{\text{init}}$ and its initial ranking as a function of α and ν. The correlation takes values in $[-1, 1]$ where -1 and 1 represent perfect negative and positive correlation, respectively. The analysis, presented in Figure 1, is applied to $\mathcal{D}_{\text{init}}$ of $k = 100$ documents. We also report MAP(@100) for the rankings[11].

We see in Figure 1 that the highest correlation is always attained for $\alpha = 0.5$; increasing the number of terms, ν, results in higher correlation. Specifically, using all terms in documents in $\mathcal{D}_{\text{init}}$ with $\alpha = 0.5$ yields a correlation of around 0.9 which is very high. Thus, we see that by attributing the same importance to the positive and negative anchor models (i.e., $\alpha = 0.5$) the discriminative model ($\theta_{\vec{w}_+}, \theta_{\vec{w}_-}$) becomes quite an accurate representation of $\mathcal{D}_{\text{init}}$'s ranking.

We also see in Figure 1 that for $\alpha = 0.5$, and regardless of the number of terms used, re-ranking performance can be quite close, or identical, to that of the initial ranking. This finding resonates with the high correlation between the rankings. Furthermore, low values of α (< 0.5) are more detrimental for performance than high values (> 0.5). This

implies that using the positive anchor model is somewhat more effective in improving performance than the negative anchor model. We further support this finding below.

We see in Figure 1 that for $\alpha \neq 0.5$ a low number of terms often yields better performance than a high number. This finding implies that the terms assigned with the highest probability by the positive and negative anchor models are the most positively and negatively correlated, respectively, with the initial ranking. Indeed, terms with a high absolute value in $\vec{w}$ in SVMrank are the most influential in establishing the decision boundary.

4.2.2 Main result

Table 2 presents the performance comparison of our Clip-Neg and AnchorPos methods with the initial ranking, the generative model on which they are applied (RM3 and MM) and the Fusion reference comparison. The performance of the AnchorClip method, which integrates ClipNeg and AnchorPos, is studied below. We see in Table 2 that all methods outperform in most cases — often to a statistically significant degree — the initial ranking.

Our AnchorPos and ClipNeg methods improve over the generative query model on which they are applied (RM3 or MM) in terms of MAP and p@5 in most relevant comparisons (3 corpora $\times$ 2 evaluation measures $\times$ 2 generative models); the majority of MAP improvements for Anchor-Pos are statistically significant[12]. Furthermore, the RI of ClipNeg and AnchorPos is in most cases higher than that of the generative model. These findings attest to the merits of using our discriminative query model to query anchor generative query models which already apply a few query anchoring techniques. We also see in Table 2 that using positive anchor terms (AnchorPos) is almost always more effective in terms of retrieval effectiveness (MAP and p@5) than using negative anchor terms (ClipNeg). More gener-

---

[10]Since $e \neq 0$ for AnchorClip, we enforce clipping.

[11]This is the only case where MAP@100 rather than MAP@1000 is used, since we focus here on re-ranking a list of 100 documents.

[12]The relative p@5 performance patterns reflect those for p@20 which was the focus of some work on query expansion [8]. For example, RM3 attained p@20 of 51.8, 36.8 and 26.4 over TREC123, ROBUST and WT10G, respectively. Applying AnchorPos to RM3 yields 52.7, 38.0, and 26.3, respectively, and applying ClipNeg yields 52.4, 37.8, and 25.5, respectively. MM attained p@20 of 50.3, 36.8 and 25.8 for the three corpora; applying AnchorPos on MM yields 51.5, 38.2, and 26.3; applying ClipNeg yields 50.8, 37.0 and 26.3. For ROBUST, the improvements of ClipNeg over RM3 and of AnchorPos over MM are statistically significant.

Table 3: Comparison of AnchorClip with ClipNeg and AnchorPos. Boldface: best result in a column in a generative model block. Statistically significant differences with ClipNeg are marked with 'c'. There are no statistically significant differences between AnchorClip and AnchorPos.

	TREC123			ROBUST			WT10G		
	MAP	p@5	RI	MAP	p@5	RI	MAP	p@5	RI
Relevance Model									
ClipNeg	28.8	**57.7**	52.0	28.9	50.0	**36.5**	21.6	**38.1**	**8.2**
AnchorPos	29.2^c	**57.7**	53.3	**29.6**	50.1	31.3	**21.8**	37.7	−2.1
AnchorClip	$\mathbf{29.4}^c$	56.7	52.0	29.5	**51.1**	34.1	21.1	37.3	2.1
Mixture Model									
ClipNeg	28.3	53.3	38.7	27.6	46.1	18.9	21.0	33.2	**16.5**
AnchorPos	29.1^c	55.9	**40.0**	$\mathbf{29.2}^c$	$\mathbf{50.0}^c$	30.9	21.3	**34.0**	9.3
AnchorClip	$\mathbf{29.4}^c$	$\mathbf{56.4}^c$	38.7	29.1^c	$\mathbf{50.4}^c$	28.1	**21.5**	32.6	8.2

ally, in most cases, AnchorPos is the most effective method in Table 2 in terms of MAP and p@5. In terms of RI, neither AnchorPos nor ClipNeg dominates the other.

The ClipNeg and AnchorPos methods outperform the Fusion reference comparison, in terms of MAP and p@5, in a vast majority of the cases; many of the improvements posted by AnchorPos are statistically significant. In most cases, Fusion is outperformed (MAP and p@5) by the generative query model on which it is applied (RM3 and MM), while it often improves RI. Indeed, the goal of Fusion is to improve performance robustness even at the expense of hurting average retrieval effectiveness [34]. Yet, the RI of Fusion is in most cases inferior to that of AnchorPos.

Table 2 shows that the effectiveness of the initial ranking, which is used to induce the generative models and our discriminative model that is applied to the generative models, is much lower for WT10G than for TREC123 and ROBUST. Consequently, the improvements posted by the generative models over the initial ranking, and those posted by our ClipNeg and AnchorPos methods over the generative models, are much smaller for WT10G than for those for TREC123 and ROBUST. In some cases for WT10G, ClipNeg and AnchorPos are outperformed by the generative model although the difference is statistically significant only in a single case (for ClipNeg). Still, ClipNeg and AnchorPos are more effective in terms of MAP, and to a statistically significant degree, than the initial ranking for WT10G. For reference comparison, the Fusion method is almost always outperformed by the generative models for WT10G — statistically significantly so in two cases. Another related finding about the differences between WT10G and the other two corpora is that the RI values of all pseudo-feedback-based methods are much smaller for WT10G. Indeed, we found that the (learned) value of the query-anchoring parameter (i.e., the weight of the original query model) in all pseudo-feedback-based models is consistently higher for WT10G than for the other two corpora. This further attests to the overall limited effectiveness of using pseudo feedback for WT10G.

AnchorClip. The AnchorClip method, presented in Section 3.3, integrates the ClipNeg and AnchorPos methods by boosting the probabilities of positive anchor terms as in AnchorPos and clipping negative anchor terms as in ClipNeg. Table 3 presents a performance comparison of AnchorClip with ClipNeg and AnchorPos.

We see that AnchorClip outperforms (in terms of MAP and p@5) ClipNeg in most cases; several of the improvements are statistically significant. However, neither of An-

chorClip and AnchorPos dominates the other; specifically, the performance differences between these methods are never statistically significant. This finding implies that that there is no clear merit in clipping negative anchor terms in addition to boosting the probabilities of positive anchor terms. We hasten to point out, however, that this finding could potentially be attributed to the fact that AnchorClip incorporates more free parameters than AnchorPos (specifically, the percentage of negative anchor terms to clip). Setting the values of all these parameters using cross validation with the relatively small query sets at hand can fall short. Indeed, experiments — actual numbers omitted as they convey no additional insight — show that if free-parameter values are set to optimize average performance over all queries in a dataset, then AnchorClip yields consistent improvements over AnchorPos, albeit not statistically significant.

4.2.3 Further analysis

We next turn to further explore the utilization of positive anchor terms (the AnchorPos method) and negative anchor terms (the ClipNeg method).

AnchorPos. Setting $\lambda_2 = 0$ in AnchorPos yields a query model, **Q+Pos**, that interpolates the original query model with the clipped positive anchor model; the generative query model is not used. Setting $\lambda_1 = 0$ results in the **M+Pos** method which integrates the positive anchor model with the generative query model; term clipping is applied but not interpolation with the original query model. Table 4 presents the performance of these specific cases of AnchorPos.

In most cases, Q+Pos statistically significantly outperforms (MAP and p@5) the initial ranking and is outperformed (often, statistically significantly so) by the generative query model (RM3 and MM). The latter finding comes as no surprise as the goal of the discriminative query model is to accurately represent the ranking of the initial result list rather than the information need. Yet, the superiority of Q+Pos to the initial ranking provides further support to the merits of using positive anchor terms for retrieval.

The MAP performance of M+Pos is often in-between that of the initial ranking and the generative query model except for WT10G; yet, the p@5 performance of M+Pos is almost always below that of the initial ranking. These findings show that direct anchoring using the original query, which is not applied in M+Pos, is highly important. More generally, the superiority of AnchorPos to Q+Pos and M+Pos attests to the merits of applying both the discriminative model and direct query anchoring to a generative model.

Table 4: AnchorPos and its two specific cases: Q+Pos and M+Pos. The performance of Q+Pos is identical for RM3 and MM as it does not incorporate the generative query model. The best result in a column in a generative model block is boldfaced. Statistically significant differences with the initial ranking, the generative query model (RM3 or MM), AnchorPos and Q+Pos are marked with 'i', 'g', 'a' and 'p', respectively.

	TREC123			ROBUST			WT10G		
	MAP	p@5	RI	MAP	p@5	RI	MAP	p@5	RI
init	23.0	52.7	–	24.9	47.6	–	19.8	35.5	–
Relevance Model									
RM3	28.4^i	57.7^i	48.0	28.2^i	48.6	30.9	$\mathbf{21.9}^i$	37.7	5.2
AnchorPos	$\mathbf{29.2}^{i,g}$	57.7^i	53.3	$\mathbf{29.6}^{i,g}$	$\mathbf{50.1}^{i,g}$	31.3	21.8^i	37.7	−2.1
Q+Pos	$25.3^{i,g}_a$	55.3^i	28.7	$26.6^{i,g}_a$	49.7^i	4.8	20.4^g_a	36.3	10.3
M+Pos	$27.4^i_{a,p}$	56.8^i	17.3	27.0^i_a	$43.9^{i,g}_{a,p}$	3.6	$15.5^{i,g}_{a,p}$	34.6	−50.5
Mixture Model									
MM	28.1^i	55.1	38.7	27.6^i	48.8	25.3	20.8^i	$\mathbf{36.3}$	12.4
AnchorPos	$\mathbf{29.1}^{i,g}$	$\mathbf{55.9}$	40.0	$\mathbf{29.2}^{i,g}$	50.0^i	30.9	$\mathbf{21.3}^i$	34.0	9.3
Q+Pos	$25.3^{i,g}_a$	55.3^i	28.7	26.6^i_a	49.7^i	4.8	20.4	$\mathbf{36.3}$	10.3
M+Pos	$26.8^{i,g}_a$	$48.4^{i,g}_{a,p}$	2.7	25.9^g_a	$45.9^g_{a,p}$	−1.2	$14.7^{i,g}_{a,p}$	$30.3^{i,g}_a$	−45.4

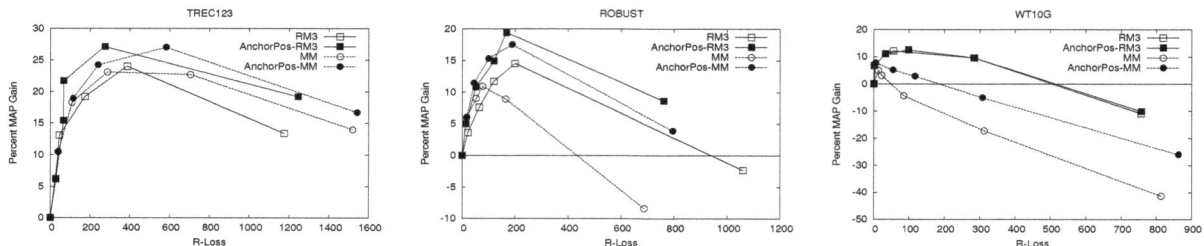

Figure 2: MAP risk-reward curves [8]. Note: figures are not to the same scale.

To further study the performance robustness of Anchor-Pos, in Figure 2 we present its MAP risk-reward curves [8] when applied to RM3 and MM and those of the generative models themselves. A curve is created by varying the value of the query anchoring parameter (λ for RM3 and MM, and λ_1 for AnchorPos) from 1 (using only the original query) to 0 (no direct query anchoring) with .2 decrement[13]; all other free parameters are set here to optimize MAP over all queries so as to study the potential risk-reward tradeoffs of the models. The x-axis (R-loss) is the resultant difference, over all queries for which the difference is non negative, between the number of relevant documents retrieved using only the original query and using the pseudo-feedback-based query model; the y-axis (reward) is the percentage of MAP improvement over all queries of applying the query model with respect to using only the original query.

Figure 2 shows that in most cases the curves for Anchor-Pos dominate those for the generative models; i.e., for the same value of query anchoring parameter, the point on the curve of AnchorPos would be to the left of, and higher than, that for the generative model. In the other cases, Anchor-Pos posts higher reward at the expense of higher risk for the same value of query anchoring parameter. These findings further support the merits of using positive anchor terms.

ClipNeg. In the ClipNeg method, the e percent of negative anchor terms that are assigned the highest probability

by the negative anchor model are clipped from the given query model. Additional standard clipping is applied by the original probabilities assigned to terms by the query model.

Figure 3 contrasts the performance of ClipNeg with that of **ClipRand**;[14] ClipRand clips randomly selected, rather than negative anchor, terms using the exact same approach applied by ClipNeg. The number of terms, ν, assigned with a non-zero probability in the final model is one of the parameters tuned to optimize average retrieval performance. Thus, the performance for $e = 0$ corresponds to optimal standard term clipping — i.e., according to the probabilities they are assigned by the generative query model — while that for $e > 0$ corresponds to optimal combined negative anchor term clipping and standard term clipping. The results are presented for an initial list, $\mathcal{D}_{init}$, of size $k = 100$.

Figure 3 shows that in most cases the performance of ClipNeg increases monotonically with increasing percentage of clipped negative anchor terms. ClipNeg often substantially outperforms ClipRand; the improvements for RO-BUST are statistically significant for almost all values of e; the improvements for TREC123 and WT10G are statistically significant for very high values of e except for those for MM over WT10G. Evidently, the performance differences between ClipNeg and ClipRand are smaller for MM

---

[13]The only case where the loss did not increase with decreasing the value of the anchoring parameter was for applying AnchorPos to MM in WT10G: the second and third points on the curve correspond to 0.6 and 0.8, respectively.

[14]In contrast to the evaluation results presented in Tables 2, 3 and 4, where leave-one-out cross validation was used to set free-parameter values, the values of the parameters of all methods considered here are set to optimize MAP over all queries as was the case in the risk-reward analysis above: the goal is to study the potential of clipping negative anchor terms while ameliorating the effects of the generalization, or lack thereof, of effective free-parameter values across queries.

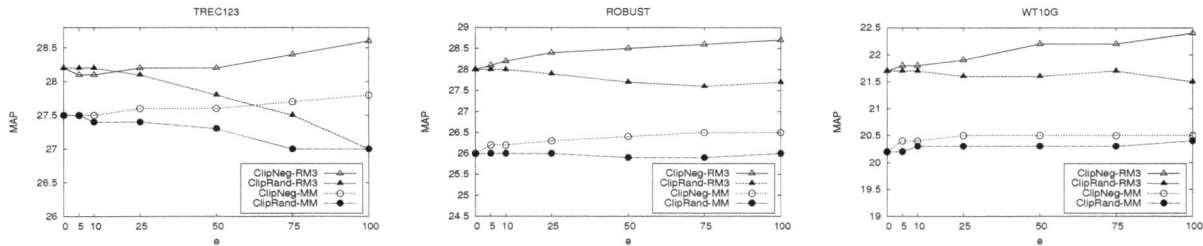

Figure 3: The MAP performance of ClipNeg and ClipRand as a function of the percentage of clipped negative anchor terms (e). ClipRand clips randomly selected terms. ClipNeg and ClipRand are applied on RM3 and MM. Initial list, $\mathcal{D}_{\mathrm{init}}$, of 100 documents is used. Note: figures are not to the same scale.

than for RM3 as the latter is more effective than the former. A case in point, ClipRand does not improve over standard term clipping ($e = 0$) for RM3, but it does so for MM over WT10G; yet, these improvements are never statistically significant. In contrast, the performance of ClipNeg for $e > 0$ is consistently better than that for $e = 0$; for ROBUST, all improvements are statistically significant; for WT10G many are, while for TREC123 they are not.

All in all, the findings from above further support the merits of clipping negative anchor terms from a query model.

4.3 The discriminative vs. the generative query models

To illustrate the differences between the discriminative and generative query models, we provide in Figure 4 examples of the query models induced for two queries from the ROBUST dataset. All query models are constructed from a result list, $\mathcal{D}_{\mathrm{init}}$, of 100 documents; the query models were clipped to use 25 terms. The retrieval performance reported is that attained by an optimized interpolation, with a parameter λ or λ_1, of each of the three query models with the original query model (as in Equations 3, 4 and 7). The models resulting from the interpolation are RM3 (based on RM1), MM (based on θ_T) and Q+Pos (based on $\theta_{\vec{w}_+}$; see Section 4.2.3 for details) which interpolates the positive anchor model ($\theta_{\vec{w}_+}$) with the original query model.

Figure 4 shows that for both queries, the generative models assign high probabilities to the original query terms or their variants. Indeed, generative query models, as most pseudo-feedback-based query models, reward terms with substantial presence in $\mathcal{D}_{\mathrm{init}}$. In contrast, the positive anchor model, $\theta_{\vec{w}_+}$, rewards terms that distinguish high ranked documents from low ranked ones. A case in point, the original query terms are not necessarily positive anchors as can be seen in Figure 4. Indeed, if $\mathcal{D}_{\mathrm{init}}$'s ranking is dominated by one of the query terms, the presence of others might have little, or even negative, correlation with the ranking.

We also see in Figure 4 that for query #341, the positive anchor model assigns high probability to query related terms (e.g., "terrorist", "baggage" and "passenger") to a more substantial extent than the generative models; and, its retrieval performance is superior. The fact that the optimal value of λ for interpolating the generative query models with the original query model is 1 attests to the fact that these two are completely ineffective for query #341, in contrast to the positive anchor model.

For query #308, using all three models improves over the initial ranking, although the positive anchor model is the

least effective. However, as noted above, the positive query anchor model is not intended to be a stand-alone query model, but rather used to query anchor the generative query models using the methods presented in Section 3.3.

Next, we provide some statistics (across the three corpora and corresponding query sets) that shed light on the commonalities and differences between the query models. We found that the positive anchor model assigns high probability to terms with a much higher IDF (inverse document frequency) value than that of terms assigned a high probability by the generative query models. For example, we see in Figure 4 that the relevance model can reward low IDF terms such as "new" and "make" for query #341. On the other hand, the discriminative query model seeks to differentiate high ranked from low ranked documents in $\mathcal{D}_{\mathrm{init}}$ and is therefore likely to reward high IDF terms. (The importance of using high IDF terms for query expansion has been noted in past work [21, 5, 7].)

Additional finding is that the average number of shared terms among the 25 assigned the highest probability by RM1 and θ_T is 2.33 and 3.5 times higher than that shared by the positive anchor model with RM1 and θ_T, respectively. In other words, the generative models are much more similar to each other, with respect to the terms they promote, than they are to the positive anchor model. This finding provides further support to the complementary nature of the generative models and the discriminative model.

We do not provide visualization of the negative anchor model ($\theta_{\vec{w}_-}$) as it conveys no additional insight. We found that terms assigned high probability by the negative anchor model often have high IDF values. These terms can help to differentiate a low ranked document from a high ranked one, as is the case for terms assigned high probability by the positive anchor model. In addition, around 40% of the 25 terms assigned the highest probability by the two generative query models are negative anchor terms; i.e., they are assigned a non-zero probability by $\theta_{\vec{w}_-}$. Clipping negative anchor terms promoted by the generative models is a method (ClipNeg) we presented in Section 3.3 and whose effectiveness was demonstrated above.

5. CONCLUSIONS AND FUTURE WORK

We presented a novel unsupervised pseudo-feedback-based discriminative query model. The model is induced from an initially retrieved list using a learning-to-rank-approach by considering pairwise document preferences induced from the list. The resultant query model constitutes a term-based representation of the list ranking.

#341: "airport security"	#308: "implant dentistry"
init (AP=24.8)	init (AP=44.8)
RM1 (AP=24.8; $\lambda = 1$)	RM1 (AP= 60.8; $\lambda = 0.4$)
airport 2 3 company 1 cent new make time govern 5 two information number work state area air force secure 000 part operate agent S	market tmj manufacture implant state dental patient new dentist class year fda comment device effect panel prosthesis recommend say
θ_T (AP=24.8; $\lambda = 1$)	θ_T (AP=54.5; $\lambda = 0.4$)
airport air border secure	university dentist dental dentistry com chiropractic medicine device women breast fda health medical dow silicone
$\theta_{\vec{w}_+}$ (AP=49.3; $\lambda_1 = 0.4$)	$\theta_{\vec{w}_+}$ (AP=51.6; $\lambda_1 = 0.6$)
screen balpa secure hijack misroute transport jetliner bag heathrow luggage deterrent unchallenged operational terrorist detector baggage checkpoint shum impractical lapse passenger ardbrecknish mortar incendiary busiest	surgery health patient 408 shadow faculty green bioplasty labour blunkett squibb attack mcghan scheme ryles free traineeship dentistry hrsa jul 6837 dental cosmetic

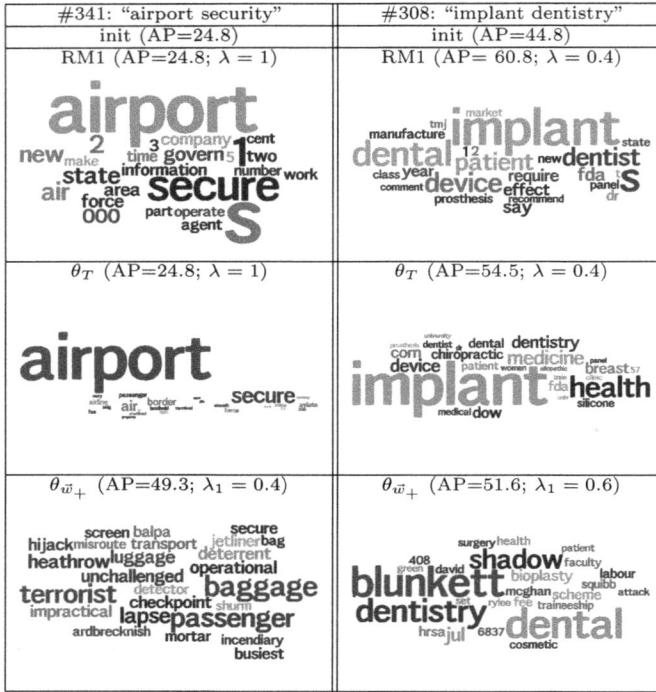

Figure 4: Examples of the generative query models (RM1 and θ_T from the mixture model) and the positive anchor model ($\theta_{\vec{w}_+}$). The size of a visualized term is proportional to the probability it is assigned by the query model. The average precision (AP) is the optimal attained by interpolating the query model with the original query model and tuning the interpolation parameter λ (for RM1 and θ_T) and λ_1 (for $\theta_{\vec{w}_+}$). Note: models are not to the same scale.

We demonstrated the empirical merits of methods using the discriminative model to query anchor existing query models: emphasizing (clipping) terms that are positively (negatively) correlated with the initial ranking.

We intend to apply the discriminative query model on additional pseudo-feedback-based query models, and study the utilization of additional learning-to-rank methods to induce a term-based representation from a retrieved list.

Acknowledgments. We thank the reviewers for their comments. This work was supported in part by the Israel Science Foundation (grant no. 433/12), the Technion-Microsoft Electronic Commerce Research Center and by the Irwin and Joan Jacobs Fellowship for graduate students.

6. REFERENCES

[1] N. Abdul-Jaleel, J. Allan, W. B. Croft, F. Diaz, L. Larkey, X. Li, M. D. Smucker, and C. Wade. UMASS at TREC 2004 — novelty and hard. In *Proc. of TREC-13*, 2004.

[2] C. Buckley, G. Salton, J. Allan, and A. Singhal. Automatic query expansion using SMART: TREC3. In *Proc. of TREC-3*, pages 69–80, 1994.

[3] G. Cao, J.-Y. Nie, J. Gao, and S. Robertson. Selecting good expansion terms for pseudo-relevance feedback. In *Proc. of SIGIR*, pages 243–250, 2008.

[4] C. Carpineto, R. de Mori, G. Romano, and B. Bigi. An information-theoretic approach to automatic query expansion. *ACM Transactions on Information Systems*, 19(1):1–27, 2001.

[5] C. Carpineto and G. Romano. A survey of automatic query expansion in information retrieval. *ACM Computing Surveys*, 44(1):1, 2012.

[6] S. Clinchant and É. Gaussier. Information-based models for ad hoc IR. In *Proc. of SIGIR*, pages 234–241, 2010.

[7] S. Clinchant and É. Gaussier. A theoretical analysis of pseudo-relevance feedback models. In *Proc. of ICTIR*, 2013.

[8] K. Collins-Thompson. Reducing the risk of query expansion via robust constrained optimization. In *Proc. of CIKM*, pages 837–846, 2009.

[9] F. Diaz and D. Metzler. Improving the estimation of relevance models using large external corpora. In *Proc. of SIGIR*, pages 154–161, 2006.

[10] E. A. Fox and J. A. Shaw. Combination of multiple searches. In *Proc. of TREC-2*, 1994.

[11] D. Harman. Relevance feedback revisited. In *Proc. of SIGIR*, pages 1–10, 1992.

[12] B. He and I. Ounis. Finding good feedback documents. In *Proc. of CIKM*, pages 2011–2014, 2009.

[13] B. He and I. Ounis. Studying query expansion effectiveness. In *Proc. of ECIR*, pages 611–619, 2009.

[14] T. Joachims. Optimizing search engines using clickthrough data. In *Proc. of SIGKDD*, pages 133–142, 2002.

[15] M. Keikha, J. Seo, W. B. Croft, and F. Crestani. Predicting document effectiveness in pseudo relevance feedback. In *Proc. of CIKM*, pages 2061–2064, 2011.

[16] J. D. Lafferty and C. Zhai. Document language models, query models, and risk minimization for information retrieval. In *Proc. of SIGIR*, pages 111–119, 2001.

[17] V. Lavrenko and W. B. Croft. Relevance-based language models. In *Proc. of SIGIR*, pages 120–127, 2001.

[18] K.-S. Lee, W. B. Croft, and J. Allan. A cluster-based resampling method for pseudo-relevance feedback. In *Proc. of SIGIR*, pages 235–242, 2008.

[19] T.-Y. Liu. Learning to rank for information retrieval. *Foundations and Trends in Information Retrieval*, 3(3), 2009.

[20] Y. Lv and C. Zhai. Adaptive relevance feedback in information retrieval. In *Proc. of CIKM*, pages 255–264, 2009.

[21] Y. Lv and C. Zhai. A comparative study of methods for estimating query language models with pseudo feedback. In *Proc. of CIKM*, pages 1895–1898, 2009.

[22] M. Mitra, A. Singhal, and C. Buckley. Improving automatic query expansion. In *Proc. of SIGIR*, pages 206–214, 1998.

[23] J. J. Rocchio. Relevance feedback in information retrieval. In G. Salton, editor, *The SMART Retrieval System: Experiments in Automatic Document Processing*, pages 313–323. Prentice Hall, 1971.

[24] T. Sakai, T. Manabe, and M. Koyama. Flexible pseudo-relevance feedback via selective sampling. *ACM Transactions on Asian Language Information Processing (TALIP)*, 4(2):111–135, 2005.

[25] J. Seo and W. B. Croft. Geometric representations for multiple documents. In *Proc. of SIGIR*, pages 251–258, 2010.

[26] F. Song and W. B. Croft. A general language model for information retrieval. In *Proc. of SIGIR*, pages 279–280, 1999.

[27] T. Tao and C. Zhai. A mixture clustering model for pseudo feedback in information retrieval. In *Proc. of IFCS*, pages 541–552, 2004. Invited paper.

[28] T. Tao and C. Zhai. Regularized estimation of mixture models for robust pseudo-relevance feedback. In *Proc. of SIGIR*, pages 162–169, 2006.

[29] R. Udupa, A. Bhole, and P. Bhattacharyya. "A term is known by the company it keeps": On selecting a good expansion set in pseudo-relevance feedback. In *Proc. of ICTIR*, pages 104–115, 2009.

[30] J. Xu and W. B. Croft. Query expansion using local and global document analysis. In *Proc. of SIGIR*, pages 4–11, 1996.

[31] Z. Ye, B. He, X. Huang, and H. Lin. Revisiting Rocchio's relevance feedback algorithm for probabilistic models. In *Proc. of AIRS*, pages 151–161, 2010.

[32] C. Zhai and J. D. Lafferty. Model-based feedback in the language modeling approach to information retrieval. In *Proc. of CIKM*, pages 403–410, 2001.

[33] C. Zhai and J. D. Lafferty. A study of smoothing methods for language models applied to ad hoc information retrieval. In *Proc. of SIGIR*, pages 334–342, 2001.

[34] L. Zighelnic and O. Kurland. Query-drift prevention for robust query expansion. In *Proc. of SIGIR*, pages 825–826, 2008.

Rank-at-a-Time Query Processing

Ahmed Elbagoury, Matt Crane, and Jimmy Lin

David R. Cheriton School of Computer Science
University of Waterloo, Ontario, Canada

{ahmed.elbagoury,matt.crane,jimmylin}@uwaterloo.ca

ABSTRACT

Query processing strategies for ranked retrieval have been studied for decades. In this paper we propose a new strategy, which we call rank-at-a-time query processing, that evaluates documents in descending order of quantized scores and is able to directly compute the final document ranking via a sequence of boolean intersections. We show that such a strategy is equivalent to a second-order restricted composition of per-term scores. Rank-at-a-time query processing has the advantage that it is anytime score-safe, which means that the retrieval algorithm can self-adapt to produce an *exact* ranking given an arbitrary latency constraint. Due to the combinatorial nature of compositions, however, a naïve implementation is too slow to be of practical use. To address this issue, we introduce a hybrid variant that is able to reduce query latency to a point that is on par with state-of-the-art retrieval engines.

1. INTRODUCTION

The information retrieval literature discusses three classes of query processing strategies for ranked retrieval: document-at-a-time (DAAT), term-at-a-time (TAAT), and score-at-a-time (SAAT). Each of these strategies has advantages and disadvantages, and are inherently tied to the layout of the inverted index. For example, in DAAT processing, postings are usually sorted in order of document id, whereas for TAAT and SAAT processing, postings are usually sorted in decreasing frequency or score order. Regardless of the technique, query processing involves traversing postings, computing document/score combinations that are held in some intermediate data structure, which is then manipulated to extract the final results.

We describe a novel query processing strategy called rank-at-a-time (RAAT) processing. The core insight is that if we pre-compute and quantize per-term scores, ranked retrieval can be decomposed into a sequence of boolean intersections. More precisely, we show that such a query processing strategy is equivalent to a second-order restricted composition

of per-term scores. Due to the combinatorial nature of this problem, a naïve implementation is too slow to be of practical use. However, we introduce a hybrid variant that is able to reduce query latency to a point that is on par with state-of-the-art retrieval engines.

2. RELATED WORK

The DAAT, TAAT, and SAAT processing strategies have been well studied in the literature (see discussion below). Research largely focuses on techniques to improve efficiency (i.e., reduce query processing time) without negatively impacting retrieval quality.

For DAAT processing, most research focuses on methods for skipping documents in the postings lists that cannot appear in the top k results. The most common strategy revolves around WAND [4], where the skipping decision is based on the upper bounds of query term scores. The introduction of term weighting parameters and a threshold θ determines whether the query is interpreted as an AND or an OR query, or a hybrid. An enhancement to WAND-style processing is to group postings into fixed-size blocks and to process the groups block-wise using the BM-WAND algorithm [7, 8].

The TAAT strategy has attracted research into reducing the overhead of accumulators to store partial document scores. Moffat et al. [12] proposed a method in which the processing of the query switches from OR to AND in order to limit the number of accumulators that need to be created. Moffat and Zobel [11] extended this method to allow for heuristics on when such a switch should occur.

Frequency-ordered indexes were first proposed by Persin et al. [14]. Anh et al. [1] observed that term weights could be stored in such an index instead of the term frequencies. To facilitate compression, they quantized these weights into integer values (called impact scores); cf. Moffat et al. [12]. The SAAT strategy processes blocks of postings in decreasing impact score, potentially hopping from term to term. Lin and Trotman [10] showed that a specific instance of such a strategy called JASS supports anytime ranking, in which the retrieval algorithm can self-adapt to produce a document ranking given an arbitrary latency constraint. However, JASS achieves anytime ranking by introducing approximations (and hence is not score-safe). One variant of JASS was the fastest in a recent reproducibility evaluation comparing several open-source search engines [9], and thus JASS forms a strong baseline for this paper.

Also of note from the same evaluation is the "model B" two-pass retrieval approach of Boldi and Vigna [3], whose MG4J system was the second fastest. Their approach first

Term	(Quantized) Impact-Ordered Postings			
a	$10:[\ldots]$	$9:[\ldots]$	$6:[\ldots]$	$2:[\ldots]$
b	$15:[\ldots]$	$12:[\ldots]$	$3:[\ldots]$	
c	$11:[\ldots]$	$9:[\ldots]$	$6:[\ldots]$	

Table 1: Example terms with (quantized) impact-ordered postings. Each $[\ldots]$ indicates a group of document ids with the same impact score.

employs pure boolean retrieval to generate a candidate set, which is then scored using BM25 and sorted to produce the final document ranking. We show that their technique represents a special case of our grouped rank-at-a-time query processing variant (see Section 5).

3. RANK-AT-A-TIME EVALUATION

We make the key observation that using a quantized index with pre-computed per-term scores (i.e., impact scores) allows us to generate document rankings directly in descending order of rank via decomposition into boolean intersection queries. Consider the example terms and associated impact-ordered postings shown in Table 1. In this example, the highest score that any document can achieve is 36, obtained when a document has a score contribution of 10 from term a, 15 from b, and 11 from c. We denote these blocks of postings by their term and score contribution $\{a:10\}$, $\{b:15\}$, and $\{c:11\}$, respectively.

In rank-at-a-time query processing, for each document score descending from the highest possible, we enumerate all combinations of score contributions, which correspond to intersection queries that are then executed. The results of these intersection queries are directly added to the final output, since they are by design sorted by score. In this manner, we compute documents that appear in rank one, rank two, etc. (hence the name RAAT), but allowing for score ties in cases where the intersection queries produce multiple documents. In this example, there are unique combinations that yield scores 36, 35, and 34, and two that produce a score of 33, namely $\{a:10\} \cap \{b:12\} \cap \{c:11\}$ and $\{a:9\} \cap \{b:15\} \cap \{c:9\}$.

The set of possible combinations that yield a given score is exactly the set of integer compositions for that score. In a so-called A-restricted composition, each term must draw from the same set of values. For example, one A-restricted composition of 36 might be $(12, 12, 12)$, which is not a valid combination given the postings in our running example. To eliminate invalid combinations, we require what Page [13] calls a second-order restricted composition, which allows the set of possible values for each term to be different (drawn from the actual impact scores). Page describes an algorithm for generating second-order restricted compositions, which we refer to simply as compositions for the remainder of the paper. Note that in our current implementation, we generate compositions that require all terms to be present, which corresponds to conjunctive query processing (i.e., an AND query). In future work we discuss extending our approach to so-called *weak* compositions, which do not require the presence of all query terms.

For a given query q and a score s, there are a total of $\binom{s-1}{|q|-1}$ integer compositions. This calculation, however, does not take into account the range of impact scores for each postings list. We empirically compute and plot the number

of compositions that are generated for test queries in the experimental section.

Rank-at-a-time query processing is an anytime ranking method (as discussed in Section 2). Since each intersection is independent, we can simply perform as many intersections as time allows. RAAT is simultaneously score-safe, in that it computes exact document scores (unlike JASS [10]). Because results are generated in rank order, processing lower ranks has no impact on higher ranks.

4. INITIAL EXPERIMENTS

To evaluate RAAT query processing, we follow the approach of Lin and Trotman [10] for JASS: we consume indexes that have been produced by the ATIRE system [15] and construct our own internal representation. This allows direct comparison against JASS, while removing all confounding issues related to index construction. We follow the method of Crane et al. [5] for computing a quantization range (1–255 for .GOV2) that does not reduce effectiveness.

The internal representation we chose uses Elias-Fano codes to store the document ids for each impact score. This was selected because it has been reported in information retrieval contexts as being efficient, particularly for intersection queries [16]. We use Facebook's implementation of Elias-Fano encoding in their open-source Folly library.[1] Intersections were performed using the holistic method presented by Culpepper and Moffat [6].

To evaluate the efficiency of our method we use the .GOV2 collection with TREC queries 701–850. These were selected so that our experiments could be directly compared to results from the RIGOR Reproducibility Challenge [9]. To that end, we ran our experiments on the same EC2 instance type (r3.4xlarge instance) to maximize comparability. To further support reproducibility, our software is open source and available on Github.[2]

Table 2 compares RAAT and JASS in terms of effectiveness (nDCG@10 and AP) and efficiency (mean and median query processing time) for different values of k in top k retrieval. We show two configurations of JASS: exhaustive processing and approximate processing with $\rho = 2.5M$. Although the later condition is not score safe, it was the fastest algorithm at the RIGOR Reproducibility Challenge [9], so this is a strong baseline. In terms of effectiveness, the differences between JASS (exhaustive) and RAAT can be attributed to the difference between disjunctive query processing in JASS and conjunctive query processing in RAAT (since we only generate compositions that include all terms), as well as idiosyncrasies of how scoring ties are broken. JASS ($\rho = 2.5M$) introduces approximations, although the degradation in effectiveness from JASS (exhaustive) is negligible.

As we can see, a direct implementation of RAAT is too slow to be of practical use. Analyses in Fig. 1 show why. On the left we plot the relationship between the maximum possible score in a query and the number of compositions generated at $k = 1000$ for all 150 .GOV2 queries. The scatterplot is broken down by query length, and note that the y-axis is in log scale. Longer queries and queries with higher maximum possible scores clearly generate more compositions. On the right, we plot the relationship between the number of compositions generated and query processing time across all

[1] https://github.com/facebook/folly
[2] https://github.com/lintool/efir

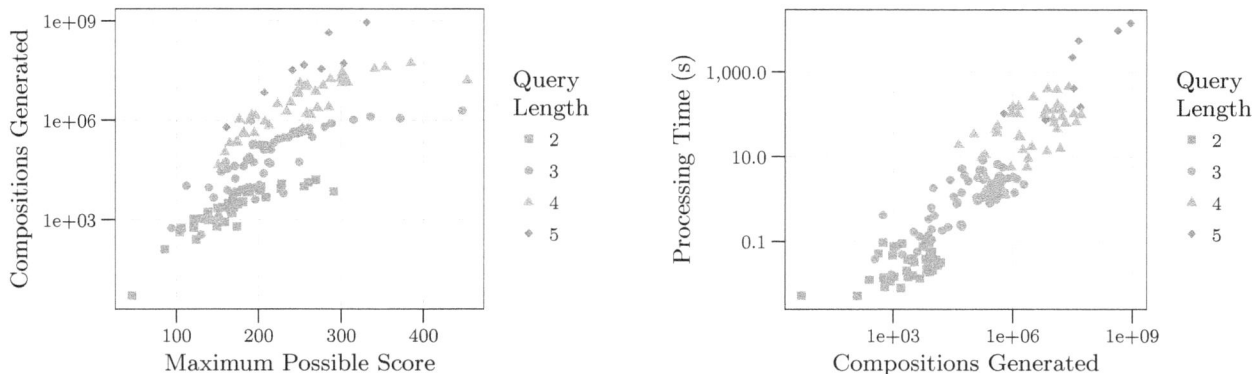

Figure 1: On the left, the number of compositions generated vs. maximum possible score (note y-axis in log scale). On the right, the relationship between the number of compositions generated and query processing time (note axes in log scale). Both plots show queries 701–850 for .GOV2 with $k = 1000$.

System	k	nDCG@10	AP	ms mean	median
JASS (exhaustive)	1000	0.4395	0.2897	47	33
JASS (exhaustive)	100	0.4395	0.1672	47	33
JASS (exhaustive)	50	0.4395	0.1169	47	33
JASS (exhaustive)	10	0.4429	0.0441	47	33
JASS ($\rho = 2.5$M)	1000	0.4372	0.2866	26	29
JASS ($\rho = 2.5$M)	100	0.4372	0.1662	26	29
JASS ($\rho = 2.5$M)	50	0.4372	0.1168	26	29
JASS ($\rho = 2.5$M)	10	0.4402	0.0440	26	29
RAAT	1000	0.4409	0.2646	243,977	1,440
RAAT	100	0.4409	0.1676	63,808	252
RAAT	50	0.4409	0.1191	30,376	118
RAAT	10	0.4412	0.0443	6,447	33
gRAAT	1000	0.4406	0.2570	171	22
gRAAT	100	0.4404	0.1610	58	9
gRAAT	50	0.4334	0.1146	34	6
gRAAT	10	0.4258	0.0439	19	5

Table 2: The effectiveness and efficiency of JASS variants, RAAT, and gRAAT on queries 701–850 for .GOV2 with different k values.

150 queries at $k = 1000$. The plot also breaks down queries into different lengths. Note that both axes are in log scale. As expected, we see that query processing time is directly related to the number of intersections that are generated and evaluated, which in turn is dependent on query length. These effects are expected due to the combinatorial nature of the compositions. However, for all queries of length less than three, results are returned in less than 110 milliseconds, indicating that overall efficiency is particularly impeded by the large number of compositions for longer queries.

5. HYBRID RANK-AT-A-TIME

Initial experiments show that a straightforward implementation of RAAT is impractically slow due to the enormous number of intersections queries that are generated, particularly for long queries.

To address this issue, we introduce a hybrid variant of RAAT that dramatically reduces the number of intersection queries that are generated. We call this *grouped* RAAT, or gRAAT, and it begins by dividing each postings list into three equal groups based on their impact scores—for convenience, we refer to these groups as {high, medium, low}

scores. We can then apply RAAT at the level of these groups, starting with $\{a : high\} \cap \{b : high\} \cap \{c : high\}$, backing off to $\{a : high\} \cap \{b : high\} \cap \{c : med\}$, $\{a : high\} \cap \{b : high\} \cap \{c : low\}$, etc., repeatedly dropping "score levels" across terms in a depth-first manner until k documents have been retrieved.

Note that these intersections do not produce documents in strictly descending score order, and therefore we need to keep track of document scores in a heap. Also, gRAAT is not score-safe because of its termination condition—the algorithm stops as soon as k documents have been retrieved—and the way the backoffs are sequenced. It is possible that results from subsequent intersection queries yield documents with scores higher than current scores.

This technique can be viewed as a generalization of Boldi and Vigna's model B [3]. In their approach, a sequence of boolean queries is generated with drop-one backoff until k documents have been returned. These candidates are then scored with BM25 and sorted. For example, with three query terms, model B performs $\{a\} \cap \{b\} \cap \{c\}$, backing off to $\{a\} \cap \{b\}$, $\{a\} \cap \{c\}$, $\{b\} \cap \{c\}$, etc. Thus, model B can be viewed as a special case of gRAAT in which each postings list consists of only a single group.

Experimental results with gRAAT are shown in Table 2, organized in the same manner as JASS and RAAT. We see that grouping postings to reduce the number of intersection queries is successful in reducing query processing time. For small values of k, gRAAT is competitive with JASS, and at $k = 10$, gRAAT is actually faster. The tradeoff is a marginal, but not statistically significant, decrease in effectiveness.

A more detailed analysis in Fig. 2 breaks query processing time down by query length in box-and-whiskers plots for $k = 10$. The horizontal lines in the boxes show the medians, and the diamonds show the means (note log scale). We see that for single term queries, RAAT and gRAAT are both substantially faster than both variants of JASS. For queries of length two, RAAT is the fastest: there are relatively few compositions generated, and RAAT does not have the additional scoring overhead introduced by groupings in gRAAT. Both are faster than the JASS variants. The performance of RAAT substantially degrades for longer queries but the postings grouping technique in gRAAT cuts down on the number of intersections and thus keeps query processing time low, remaining competitive with the JASS variants.

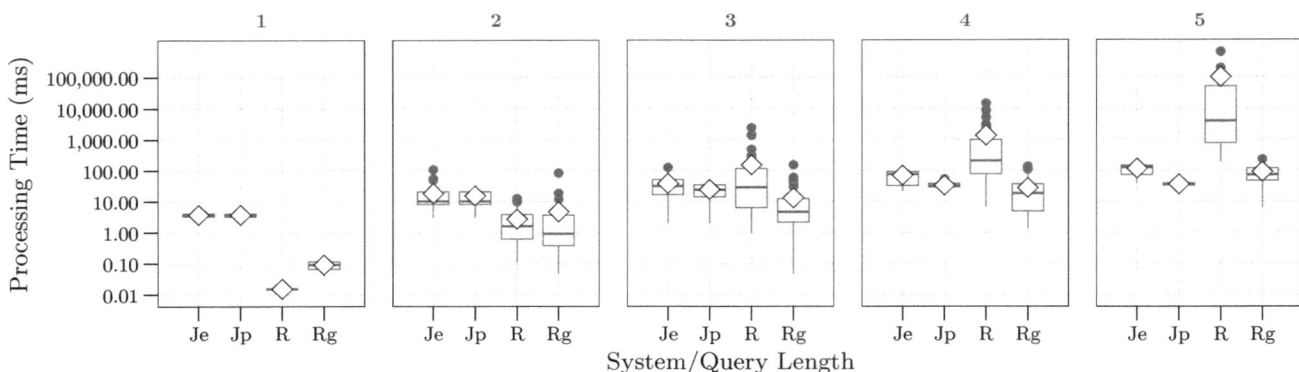

Figure 2: Comparison of query processing time in box-and-whiskers plots (means as diamonds) for JASS exhaustive (Je), JASS $\rho = 2.5M$ (Jp), RaaT (R), and gRaaT (Rg), broken down by query length for $k = 10$.

6. FUTURE WORK AND CONCLUSIONS

This paper presents a novel rank-at-a-time query processing strategy that takes advantage of the equivalence between compositions and boolean intersection queries in quantized indexes to directly compute document scores in rank order. Although a naïve implementation is impractically slow, a hybrid variant achieves query processing time on par with state-of-the-art techniques. This promising result can be improved upon in a number of ways.

Our current RAAT implementation generates compositions in which all query terms must be present. It is straightforward to extend this algorithm to generate *weak* compositions in which terms can be absent. Translated into query processing, a non-weak composition corresponds to conjunctive query processing (i.e., AND), whereas a weak composition corresponds to standard "bag of words" ranking.

Experiments show that controlling the number of compositions, particularly for longer queries, is the key to achieving good performance. Our approach of grouping postings into {high, medium, low} scores appears to be effective in accomplishing this, but is rather crude. Obvious extensions include parameterizing the number of groupings, allowing us to tune the tradeoff between the number of compositions generated and the additional work involved in storing disparate document scores. We currently create a fixed number of groups within each postings list, but alternatively, groupings can be based on absolute scores.

The number of compositions can be reduced in other ways. The generation algorithm can be modified to discard compositions that cannot possibly yield results: for instance, if the first two terms of a composition yield no results, then all other compositions that contain the same two terms can be discarded. Alternatively, caching sub-intersections across score compositions can help eliminate unnecessary work.

Finally, there are other ways of extending RAAT. We do not presently support static document scores, which is important for many applications. There are additionally many opportunities for exploring approximate (i.e., not rank-safe) query processing, trading off effectiveness for efficiency, particularly in the context of multi-stage ranking [2].

Information retrieval researchers have extensively studied three classes of query processing strategies for ranked retrieval to date: DAAT, TAAT, SAAT. To this list we contribute RAAT. We have only begun to explore the properties

of this approach, and anticipate further advances building on future work outlined above.

Acknowledgments. This work was supported in part by the Natural Sciences and Engineering Research Council of Canada. Any opinions, findings, conclusions, or recommendations expressed are those of the authors and do not necessarily reflect the views of the sponsors.

7. REFERENCES

[1] V. N. Anh, O. de Kretser, and A. Moffat. Vector-space ranking with effective early termination. *SIGIR*, 2001.

[2] N. Asadi and J. Lin. Effectiveness/efficiency tradeoffs for candidate generation in multi-stage retrieval architectures. *SIGIR*, 2013.

[3] P. Boldi and S. Vigna. MG4J at TREC 2006. *TREC*, 2006.

[4] A. Z. Broder, D. Carmel, M. Herscovici, A. Soffer, and J. Zien. Efficient query evaluation using a two-level retrieval process. *CIKM*, 2003.

[5] M. Crane, A. Trotman, and R. O'Keefe. Maintaining discriminatory power in quantized indexes. *CIKM*, 2013.

[6] J. S. Culpepper and A. Moffat. Efficient set intersection for inverted indexing. *TOIS*, 29(1), 2010.

[7] C. Dimopoulos, S. Nepomnyachiy, and T. Suel. Optimizing top-k document retrieval strategies for block-max indexes. *WSDM*, 2013.

[8] S. Ding and T. Suel. Faster top-k document retrieval using block-max indexes. *SIGIR*, 2011.

[9] J. Lin, M. Crane, A. Trotman, J. Callan, I. Chattopadhyaya, J. Foley, G. Ingersoll, C. Macdonald, and S. Vigna. Toward reproducible baselines: The Open-Source IR Reproducibility Challenge. *ECIR*, 2016.

[10] J. Lin and A. Trotman. Anytime ranking for impact-ordered indexes. *ICTIR*, 2015.

[11] A. Moffat and J. Zobel. Self-indexing inverted files for fast text retrieval. *TOIS*, 14(4):349–379, 1996.

[12] A. Moffat, J. Zobel, and R. Sacks-Davis. Memory efficient ranking. *IP&M*, 30(6):733–744, 1994.

[13] D. R. Page. Generalized algorithm for restricted weak composition generation. *Journal of Mathematical Modelling and Algorithms in Operations Research*, 12(4):345–372, 2013.

[14] M. Persin, J. Zobel, and R. Sacks-Davis. Filtered document retrieval with frequency-sorted indexes. *JASIS*, 47(10):749–764, 1996.

[15] A. Trotman, X. Jia, and M. Crane. Towards an efficient and effective search engine. *OSIR Workshop*, 2012.

[16] S. Vigna. Quasi-succinct indices. *WSDM*, 2013.

A Study of Document Expansion using Translation Models and Dimensionality Reduction Methods

Saeid Balaneshin-kordan
Department of Computer Science
Wayne State University
Detroit, Michigan 48202
saeid.balaneshinkordan@wayne.edu

Alexander Kotov
Department of Computer Science
Wayne State University
Detroit, Michigan 48202
kotov@wayne.edu

ABSTRACT

Over a decade of research on document expansion methods resulted in several independent avenues, including smoothing methods, translation models, and dimensionality reduction techniques, such as matrix decompositions and topic models. Although these research avenues have been individually explored in many previous studies, there is still a lack of understanding of how state-of-the-art methods for each of these directions compare with each other in terms of retrieval accuracy. This paper attempts to fill in this void by reporting the results of an empirical comparison of document expansion methods using translation models estimated based on word co-occurrence and cosine similarity between low-dimensional word embeddings, Latent Dirichlet Allocation (LDA) and Non-negative Matrix Factorization (NMF), on standard TREC collections. Experimental results indicate that LDA-based document expansion consistently outperforms both types of translation models and NMF according to all evaluation metrics for all and difficult queries, which is closely followed by translation model using word embeddings.

CCS Concepts

•Information systems → Document collection models;

Keywords

Document Expansion; Translation Models; Latent Dirichlet Allocation; Non-negative Matrix Factorization; Word Embeddings

1. INTRODUCTION

Vocabulary mismatch is one of the fundamental problems in Information Retrieval (IR), which in the context of language modeling approaches, has been traditionally addressed through expansion of document or query language models (LM) with semantically related terms. However,

finding such terms for a particular document or query is a challenging task. While query expansion methods are applied on-line and typically identify such terms in external resources or top-retrieved documents (i.e. using local analysis [19]), document expansion can be done off-line and attempts to identify semantic structure in a collection (i.e. using global analysis [19]).

Depending on their theoretical foundation, the proposed approaches to identifying such structure resulted in several independent research avenues. Statistical translation models [1] quantify the strength of semantic relationship between pairs of words. Translation models estimated using mutual information [7] or term co-occurrence [8] have been shown to improve the performance of language modeling based retrieval models. In addition to these methods, the utility of word embeddings [16] has also been evaluated for estimation of translation models [22].

Dimensionality reduction techniques, such as Latent Dirichlet Allocation (LDA) [2], Probabilistic Latent Semantic Indexing (pLSI) [6], and Non-Negative Matrix Factorization (NMF) [13, 20], approximate document collection using its lower dimensional representations. In particular, topic models (LDA and pLSI) estimate the parameters of a probabilistic generative process, while NMF approximates sparse high-dimensional document-term space with dense low-dimensional subspaces. Although LDA has been shown to be effective for ad hoc IR by several previous studies [18, 21], NMF has been primarily studied in the context of text mining [11], and its application to IR requires further investigation.

Although these research avenues have been individually explored in previous studies, there is a lack of understanding of how state-of-the-art methods for them compare with each other in terms of retrieval accuracy. This paper attempts to fill this void by reporting the results of an empirical comparison of document expansion methods using LDA, NMF, and translation models estimated based on word co-occurrence and cosine similarity between word embeddings on newswire and Web TREC collections.

2. RELATED WORK

Translation models [1] have been extensively studied in the context of IR. Karimzadehgan and Zhai [8] have shown that the translation model derived using axiomatic framework and estimated based on term co-occurrences outperforms the translation model estimated based on mutual information [7]. In [22, 4], word embeddings were integrated into language modeling based retrieval models. Zuccon et al. [22] have compared estimation of translation model using word embeddings and mutual information [8]. The translation model proposed in [4] is a generalized version of the model in [22], which also accounts for the fitness of query terms in the context of a document.

Topic models (LDA and pLSI) consider documents as finite mixtures over an underlying set of latent topics inferred from correlations between words. LDA has been proposed as an improvement of pLSI, in which the mixtures of topics for documents are assumed to be drawn from the same Dirichlet prior. This modification makes LDA more robust to overfitting than pLSI and other more restrictive models, such as the mixture of unigrams. Nevertheless, Lu et al. [14] found out that document expansion methods based on pLSI and LDA have comparable retrieval accuracy on different collections. They also observed that topic models can hurt retrieval performance of document expansion if they are not properly applied and optimized. Masada et al. [15] compared pLSI and LDA for classification tasks in terms of computation time and found out that LDA does not offer any significant improvement over pLSI in terms of F-measure, while training LDA requires more time. Ding et al. [3] found out that NMF with I-divergence objective function and pLSI both have very close accuracy, entropy, purity, Rand index when used for document clustering, while Gaussier and Goutte [5] have shown that NMF and pLSI are equivalent in the sense that both optimize the same objective function.

3. METHODS

We used the query likelihood retrieval model [17] with Dirichlet prior smoothing [12] (QL-DIR) in conjunction with all document expansion methods. Given query q, this model calculates the retrieval score of each document d as:

$$p(d|q) = \prod_{w \in q} \left(\frac{c(w;d) + \mu p(w|C)}{|d| + \mu} \right) \tag{1}$$

where $c(w;d)$ is the count of word w in document d, $p(w|C)$ is the collection language model, $|d|$ is the length of document d and μ is the Dirichlet prior. Basic language modeling approaches, such as QL-DIR, are based on exact matching of query terms. Since queries are typically short and relevant documents may use different vocabulary, such models often suffer from vocabulary mismatch. Incorporating document expansion language model (LM) constructed using the methods discussed below into the original document LM can potentially address this problem. In this case, (1) can be rewritten as:

$$p(d|q) = \prod_{w \in q} \left((1-\lambda) \frac{c(w;d) + \mu p(w|C)}{|d| + \mu} + \lambda p_{\exp}(w|d) \right) \tag{2}$$

where $p_{\exp}(w|d)$ is the document expansion LM and λ is the interpolation coefficient.

3.1 Translation Models

Translation models [1] estimate document expansion LMs on a term-by-term basis by "translating" each original document term u according to the translation probabilities $p_{\mathrm{tr}}(w|u)$. Each "translation" constitutes addition of one or several semantically related terms to the original document LM. Therefore, a document expansion LM is constructed using trans-

lation model as follows:

$$p_t(w|d) = \sum_{u \in \mathbb{V}} p_{\mathrm{tr}}(w|u) p_{\mathrm{ml}}(u|d) \tag{3}$$

In (3), $p_{\mathrm{ml}}(u|d) = c(u;d)/|d|$ is the original document LM, where $c(u;d)$ is the number of occurrences of word u in document d. $p_{\mathrm{tr}}(w|u)$ in the above equation can be obtained from the number of co-occurrences of word w with word u (i.e., $c(w,u)$) and the number of co-occurrences of word w with other words in the collection vocabulary as follows (TM-CX) [8]:

$$p_{\mathrm{tr}}(w|u) = \frac{c(w,u)}{\sum_{v \in \mathbb{V}} c(v,u) + |V|} \tag{4}$$

where $|V|$ is the size of collection vocabulary V.

Another way to approximate the translation model is to utilize word embeddings that are pre-trained for the document collection [16]. In this method, which is denoted by TM-WE, semantic similarity between the words in the word embeddings space is calculated based on the cosine similarity of their corresponding word vectors [22]. The translation probability is obtained by normalizing this cosine similarity.

3.2 Latent Dirichlet Allocation

Topic models, such as LDA and its extensions, can also be used to construct document expansion LMs [9, 10, 18] based on the assumption that the words belonging to the same topic are semantically related. LDA considers each document d in the collection as a mixture of multinomials (topics) z drawn from a symmetric Dirichlet prior $\mathrm{Dir}(\alpha)$ with parameter α and models it according to the following generative process:

- for each document d, draw a distribution over topics (i.e., $p_\theta(z|d)$) from $\mathrm{Dir}(\alpha)$

    - for each word position in d, draw a topic z from the distribution $p_\theta(z|d)$
    - draw a word w from the distribution $p_\phi(w|z)$.

where $p_\theta(z|d)$ and $p_\phi(w|z)$ represent the probability distributions of topics in document d and words in topic z, respectively. The vocabulary gap can be eliminated by including the terms in the topics that have a high probability in the topic distribution of a document into the expansion LM for that document. Document expansion LM can be constructed based on the output of topic models as follows:

$$p_{\mathrm{lda}}(w|d) = \sum_{z \in Z} p_\phi(w|z) p_\theta(z|d) , \tag{5}$$

where Z is the number of topics.

3.3 Non-negative Matrix Factorization

Similar to LDA, NMF can also be used to discover topics in word-document matrix, $\mathbf{P}$. If the probability of word w given topic z is denoted by $p_{\mathrm{b}}(w|z)$ and the likelihood of topic z given document d is denoted by $p_{\mathrm{e}}(z|d)$, then:

$$p_{\mathrm{nmf}}(w|d) = \sum_{z \in Z} p_{\mathrm{b}}(w|z) p_{\mathrm{e}}(z|d) \tag{6}$$

This equation can be written in matrix form as $\mathbf{P} = \mathbf{P_b P_e}$, where $\mathbf{P_b}$ and $\mathbf{P_e}$ are non-negative matrices of size $K \times R$ and $R \times M$, respectively, the inner dimension (R) of which can be considered as the number of "topics". It is assumed that $R < \min(K, M)$, therefore the matrices $\mathbf{P}_{\mathrm{b}}$ and $\mathbf{P}_{\mathrm{e}}$ are lower-dimensional factors, the product of which approximates $\mathbf{P}$. The matrices $\mathbf{P}_{\mathrm{b}}$ and $\mathbf{P}_{\mathrm{e}}$ are obtained by solving the following optimization problem:

$$\min_{\mathbf{P}_{\mathrm{b}}, \mathbf{P}_{\mathrm{e}}} \frac{1}{2} \sum_i \sum_j [\mathbf{P}_{i,j} - (\mathbf{P}_{\mathrm{b}}\mathbf{P}_{\mathrm{e}})_{i,j}]^2 \qquad (7)$$

In the above problem, $\mathbf{P}_{i,j}$ is the (i, j)-th element of the TF-IDF document-term matrix $\mathbf{P}$ and $(\mathbf{P}_{\mathrm{b}}\mathbf{P}_{\mathrm{e}})_{i,j}$ is the (i, j)-th element of the matrix $(\mathbf{P}_{\mathrm{b}}\mathbf{P}_{\mathrm{e}})$. Although all the elements of $\mathbf{P}_{\mathrm{b}}$ and $\mathbf{P}_{\mathrm{e}}$ are non-negative, they should be normalized to represent probabilities.

4. EXPERIMENTS

Experimental evaluation of document expansion methods using the translation models and dimensionality reduction techniques presented in the previous section was performed using standard TREC collections (TREC7-8, ROBUST04, and GOV) and query sets (100 topics from TREC 2007-2008 Ad Hoc track, 250 topics from TREC 2004 ROBUST track, 225 topics from TREC 2004 Web track).

All retrieval methods were implemented using Indri 5.9 IR toolkit[1]. Experimental collections were pre-processed using INQUERY stoplist and Porter stemmer. Very frequent terms (that occur in more than 15% of documents) and very rare terms (that occur in less than 5 documents) were ignored for estimation of translation models, LDA and NMF. We used the implementation of NMF from scikit-learn 17.1[2]. We used Double Singular Value Decomposition for non-random initialization of factors and Coordinate Descent solver for optimization. The values of LDA hyperparameters α and β for the Dirichlet priors in LDA were set to $1/Z$ (where Z is the number of topics) and 0.01, respectively. Gibbs sampler for posterior inference of LDA parameters was run for 200 iterations, and the convergence threshold for NMF was set to 10^{-5}. Word embeddings were obtained by using word2vec (version 0.1c) tool[3] (by using Skip-gram architecture for its training). The following values for the parameters of the word2vec were used: size of word vectors was set to 100, max skip length between words, threshold for word occurrence and the number of negative examples were set to 5, and the starting learning rate was set to 0.025.

Parameters of translation models (# of translated words) and dimensionality reduction techniques (# of topics for LDA and the inner dimension for NMF), as well as the interpolation coefficient of the original document LM and document expansion LM for all methods were empirically optimized based on the Mean Average Precision (MAP) for each of the datasets separately. These parameters are determined at each step of a three-fold cross-validation by using grid search with step size 0.1 for continuous parameters between 0 and 1 and step size 200 for discrete parameters, like the number of topics.

Figure 1 illustrates how the retrieval accuracy of document expansion based on LDA and NMF changes depending on the number of topics (inner components). As follows from Figure 1, document expansion based on LDA clearly outperforms document expansion based on NMF. Retrieval accuracy of LDA-based document expansion has a pronounced peak at around 1000 topics for TREC7-8 and around 1500 for ROBUST04 and GOV, after which it saturates and slowly decreases. It is evident that NMF, on the other hand, peaks early, when the number of inner components is around 100 for GOV, around 300 for TREC7-8 and around 400 for ROBUST04 and then its effectiveness remarkably deteriorates. We attribute this to an empirical observation that a large number of popular words, which are not useful for retrieval, appear in many NMF topics.

Table 1 summarizes retrieval accuracy of `QL-DIR` and document expansion methods using different types of translation models, LDA and NMF across different collection for both all and difficult queries macro-averaged based on 3-fold cross validation. Difficult queries are defined as the ones for which the average precision of `QL-DIR` is less than 0.05. Several important conclusions can be made based on the results in this table. First, the LDA-based document expansion (`LDA`) achieves the best performance according to all metrics, outperforming both types of translation models and `NMF`. Particularly significant improvement of `LDA` over `TM-CX` ($\sim$9% for all queries and 162% for difficult queries) is achieved on the TREC7-8 dataset. Using the translation model based on word embeddings (`TM-WE`) generally results in smaller yet comparable improvement to `LDA`. `TM-WE` is however much less computationally expensive document expansion method than `LDA`. Second, while `NMF` generally outperformed `TM-CX` in terms of all metrics, it had lower MAP than `TM-WE` on all collections for all queries and on TREC7-8 and GOV for difficult queries. `TM-WE` was particularly more effective than `NMF` for all and difficult queries on TREC7-8. Third, estimating translation model based on cosine similarity between word embedding vectors (`TM-WE`) is consistently more effective than using Conditional Context (`TM-CX`) for all queries, and particularly for difficult ones.

5. CONCLUSION

In this paper, we attempted to fill in the void in theoretical IR literature by performing a comparative study of retrieval effectiveness of document expansion methods based on different types of translation models with the ones based on dimensionality reduction techniques, such as topic models and matrix decomposition, on publicly available collections of different size and type. We found out that, although LDA-based document expansion generally outperforms document expansion methods based on NMF and translation models, its performance is comparable to document expansion using translation model estimated based on word embeddings.

6. REFERENCES

[1] A. Berger and J. Lafferty. Information retrieval as statistical translation. In *Proceedings of the 22nd ACM SIGIR*, pages 222–229, 1999.

[2] D. M. Blei, A. Y. Ng, and M. I. Jordan. Latent Dirichlet allocation. *Journal of Machine Learning Research*, 3:993–1022, 2003.

[3] C. Ding, T. Li, and W. Peng. On the equivalence between non-negative matrix factorization and probabilistic latent semantic indexing. *Computational Statistics & Data Analysis*, 52(8):3913–3927, 2008.

[4] D. Ganguly, D. Roy, M. Mitra, and G. J. Jones. Word embedding based generalized language model for information retrieval. In *Proceedings of the 38th ACM SIGIR*, pages 795–798, 2015.

[5] E. Gaussier and C. Goutte. Relation between pLSA and NMF and implications. In *Proceedings of the 28th ACM SIGIR*, pages 601–602, 2005.

---

[1] http://www.lemurproject.org/indri.php
[2] http://scikit-learn.org/
[3] http://code.google.com/archive/p/word2vec/

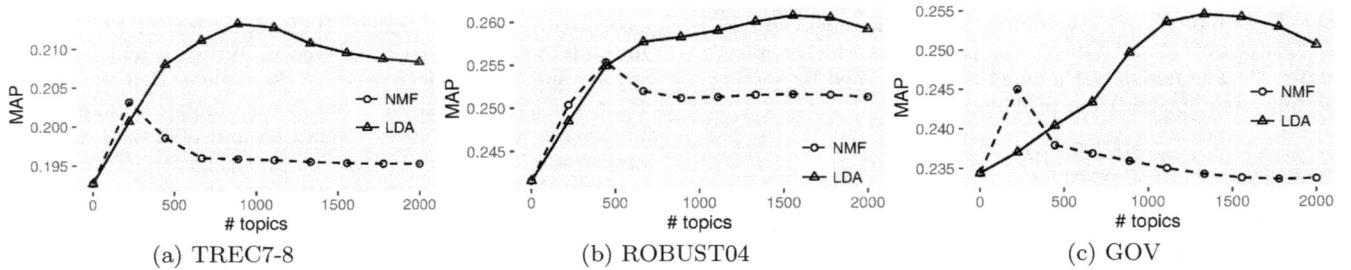

| | (a) TREC7-8 | (b) ROBUST04 | (c) GOV |

Figure 1: **MAP of NMF and LDA-based document expansion methods for different number of topics.**

Table 1: **Retrieval performance of document expansion methods for all and difficult queries.** * and † indicate statistically significant improvement in terms of MAP ($p < 0.05$) using Wilcoxon signed rank test over the QL-DIR and TM-CX, respectively. Relative improvement over QL-DIR and TM-CX is shown in parenthesis.

Col.	Method	All Queries			Difficult Queries		
		MAP	NDCG@20	P@20	MAP	NDCG@20	P@20
TREC7-8	QL-DIR	0.1927	0.4142	0.339	0.0205	0.1303	0.1326
	TM-CX	0.1963	0.4149	0.3603	0.0216	0.1346	0.1165
	TM-WE	0.2084 *† (+8.1%/+6.2%)	0.4155 (+0.3%/+0.1%)	0.3678 (+8.5%/+2.1%)	0.0434 *† (+111.7%/+100.9%)	0.1431 (+9.8%/+6.3%)	0.151 (+13.9%/+29.6%)
	NMF	0.2035 *† (+5.6%/+3.7%)	0.4143 (+0.0%/-0.1%)	0.3655 (+7.8%/+1.4%)	0.0229 * (+11.7%/+6.0%)	0.1317 (+1.1%/-2.2%)	0.1174 (-11.5%/+0.8%)
	LDA	**0.2138 *†** (+10.9%/+8.9%)	**0.4312** (+4.1%/+3.9%)	**0.3745** (+10.5%/+3.9%)	**0.0565 *†** (+175.6%/+161.6%)	**0.1605** (+23.2%/+19.2%)	**0.1652** (+24.6%/+41.8%)
ROBUST04	QL-DIR	0.2416	0.4065	0.3504	0.023	0.0997	0.0962
	TM-CX	0.2543	0.4104	0.3607	0.0353	0.1004	0.0972
	TM-WE	0.2582 *† (+6.9%/+1.5%)	0.4191 (+3.1%/+2.1%)	0.3634 (+3.7%/+0.7%)	0.0345 * (+50.0%/-2.3%)	0.1026 (+2.9%/+2.2%)	0.0979 (+1.8%/+0.7%)
	NMF	0.2557 *† (+5.8%/+0.6%)	0.4188 (+3.0%/+2.0%)	0.3641 (+3.9%/+0.9%)	0.0348 * (+51.3%/-1.4%)	0.1012 (+1.5%/+0.8%)	0.0983 (+2.2%/+1.1%)
	LDA	**0.2608 *†** (+7.9%/+2.6%)	**0.4197** (+3.2%/+2.3%)	**0.3629** (+3.6%/+0.6%)	**0.0353 *** (+53.5%/+0.0%)	**0.1052** (+5.5%/+4.8%)	**0.101** (+5.0%/+3.9%)
GOV	QL-DIR	0.2344	0.3942	0.5141	0.0183	0.1214	0.0353
	TM-CX	0.2449	0.4021	0.5191	0.0216	0.1225	0.0371
	TM-WE	0.2515 *† (+7.3%/+2.7%)	0.4101 (+4.0%/+2.0%)	0.5329 (+3.7%/+2.6%)	0.0276 * (+50.8%/+27.8%)	0.1278 (+5.2%/+4.3%)	0.0383 (+8.9%/+3.2%)
	NMF	0.2467 * (+5.2%/+0.7%)	0.4082 (+3.6%/+1.5%)	0.5289 (+2.9%/+1.9%)	0.0232 * (+26.8%/+7.4%)	0.1227 (+1.0%/+0.1%)	0.0379 (+7.4%/+2.2%)
	LDA	**0.2539*†** (+8.3%/+3.7%)	**0.4131** (+4.8%/+2.7%)	**0.5365** (+4.4%/+3.3%)	**0.0296 *†** (+61.7%/+37.0%)	**0.1327** (+9.3%/+8.3%)	**0.0394** (+11.6%/+6.2%)

[6] T. Hofmann. Probabilistic latent semantic indexing. In *Proceedings of the 22nd ACM SIGIR*, pages 50–57, 1999.

[7] M. Karimzadehgan and C. Zhai. Estimation of statistical translation models based on mutual information for ad hoc information retrieval. In *Proceedings of the 33rd ACM SIGIR*, pages 323–330, 2010.

[8] M. Karimzadehgan and C. Zhai. Axiomatic analysis of translation language model for information retrieval. In *Proceedings of the 34th ECIR*, pages 268–280. 2012.

[9] A. Kotov, V. Rakesh, E. Agichtein, and C. K. Reddy. Geographical latent variable models for microblog retrieval. In *Proceedings of the 38th ECIR*, pages 635–647, 2015.

[10] A. Kotov, Y. Wang, and E. Agichtein. Leveraging geographical metadata to improve search over social media. In *Proceedings of the 22nd WWW*, pages 151–152, 2013.

[11] D. Kuang, J. Choo, and H. Park. Nonnegative matrix factorization for interactive topic modeling and document clustering. In *Partitional Clustering Algorithms*, pages 215–243. 2015.

[12] J. Lafferty and C. Zhai. Document language models, query models, and risk minimization for information retrieval. In *Proceedings of the 24th ACM SIGIR*, pages 111–119, 2001.

[13] D. D. Lee and H. S. Seung. Algorithms for non-negative matrix factorization. In *Proceedings of NIPS*, pages 556–562, 2001.

[14] Y. Lu, Q. Mei, and C. Zhai. Investigating task performance of probabilistic topic models: an empirical study of pLSA and LDA. *Information Retrieval*, 14(2):178–203, 2011.

[15] T. Masada, S. Kiyasu, and S. Miyahara. Comparing lda with plsi as a dimensionality reduction method in document clustering. In *Proceedings of the 3rd LKR*, pages 13–26, 2008.

[16] T. Mikolov, I. Sutskever, K. Chen, G. S. Corrado, and J. Dean. Distributed representations of words and phrases and their compositionality. In *Proceedings of NIPS*, pages 3111–3119, 2013.

[17] J. M. Ponte and W. B. Croft. A language modeling approach to information retrieval. In *Proceedings of the 21st ACM SIGIR*, pages 275–281, 1998.

[18] X. Wei and W. B. Croft. LDA-based document models for ad-hoc retrieval. In *Proceedings of the 29th ACM SIGIR*, pages 178–185, 2006.

[19] J. Xu and W. B. Croft. Query expansion using local and global document analysis. In *Proceedings of the 19th ACM SIGIR*, pages 4–11, 1996.

[20] W. Xu, X. Liu, and Y. Gong. Document clustering based on non-negative matrix factorization. In *Proceedings of the 26th ACM SIGIR*, pages 267–273, 2003.

[21] X. Yi and J. Allan. A comparative study of utilizing topic models for information retrieval. In *Proceedings of the 31st ECIR*, pages 29–41. 2009.

[22] G. Zuccon, B. Koopman, P. Bruza, and L. Azzopardi. Integrating and evaluating neural word embeddings in information retrieval. In *Proceedings of the 20th ADCS*, pages 1–8, 2015.

Estimating Retrieval Performance Bound
for Single Term Queries

Peilin Yang
University of Delaware
Newark, DE 19716
United States
franklyn@udel.edu

Hui Fang
University of Delaware
Newark, DE 19716
United States
hfang@udel.edu

ABSTRACT

Various information retrieval models have been studied for decades. Most traditional retrieval models are based on bag-of-term representations, and they model the relevance based on various collection statistics. Despite these efforts, it seems that the performance of "bag-of-term" based retrieval functions has reached plateau, and it becomes increasingly difficult to further improve the retrieval performance. Thus, one important research question is whether we can provide any theoretical justifications on the empirical performance bound of basic retrieval functions.

In this paper, we start with single term queries, and aim to estimate the performance bound of retrieval functions that leverage only basic ranking signals such as document term frequency, inverse document frequency and document length normalization. Specifically, we demonstrate that, when only single-term queries are considered, there is a general function that can cover many basic retrieval functions. We then propose to estimate the upper bound performance of this function by applying a cost/gain analysis to search for the optimal value of the function.

1. INTRODUCTION

Developing effective retrieval models has been one of the most important and well-studied topics in Information Retrieval (IR). Various retrieval models have been proposed and studied [9, 10, 14]. Many of them are based on "bag-of-term" representation and leverage only basic ranking signals such as TF, IDF and document length normalization [4]. Although more advanced ranking signals, such as term proximity [11] and term semantic similarity [4, 7], have been integrated into the retrieval functions to improve the retrieval performance, it remains unclear whether we have reached the performance upper bound for retrieval functions using only basic ranking signals. If so, what is the upper bound performance? If not, how can we do better?

To find the performance upper bound is quite challenging: although most of the IR ranking models deal with basic sig-

nals, how they combine the signals to compute the relevance scores are quite diverse due to different implementations of IR heuristics [4]. This kind of variants makes it difficult to generalize the analysis. Moreover, typically there are one or more free parameters in the ranking models which can be tuned via the training collections. These free parameters make the analysis more complicated.

This paper aims to tackle the challenge through the simplest problem setup. In particular, we focus on single-term queries and study how to estimate the performance bound for retrieval functions utilizing only basic ranking signals. With only one term in a query, many retrieval functions can be greatly simplified. For example, Okapi BM25 and Pivoted normalization functions have different implementations for the IDF part, but this part can be omitted in the functions for single-term queries because it would not affect the ranking of search results. All the simplified functions can then be generalized to a general function form for single-term queries. As a result, the problem of finding the upper bound of retrieval function utilizing basic ranking signals becomes that of finding the optimal performance of the generalized retrieval function. We propose to use cost/gain analysis to solve the problem [1, 3, 2]. As the estimated performance upper bound of simplified/generalized model is in general better than the existing ranking models, our finding provides the practical foundation of the potentially more effective ranking models for single term queries.

2. PERFORMANCE BOUND ANALYSIS

2.1 A General Form of Retrieval Functions for Single-Term Queries

The implementations of retrieval functions are quite diverse, and it is often difficult to develop a general function form that can cover many retrieval functions. However, if we consider only single-term queries (i.e,. those with only one query term), the problem can be greatly simplified.

Let us start with a specific example. Dirichlet prior function is one of the representative functions derived using language modeling approaches [14], and is shown as follows:

$$f(Q, d) = \sum_{t \in Q} \ln \left(\frac{c(t, d) + \mu \cdot p(t|C)}{|d| + \mu} \right), \quad (1)$$

where $c(t, d)$ is the frequency of term t in document d, $|d|$ is the document length; $p(t|C)$ is the maximum-likelihood of the term frequency in the collection and μ is the model parameter. When a query contains only a term t, the retrieval

Table 1: Instantiations of the general retrieval form

Retrieval Functions	$g(\cdot)$	α	c_1	γ	β	c_2
DIR	1	1	$\mu \cdot p(t\|C)$	0	1	μ
BM25 & BM25+	1	$k_1 + 1$	0	1	$\frac{k_1 \cdot b}{avdl}$	$k_1 \cdot (1-b)$
PIV & PIV+	$1 + ln(1 + ln(\cdot))$	1	0	0	$\frac{s}{avdl}$	$1 - s$
F1EXP & F1LOG	$1 + ln(1 + ln(\cdot))$	$avdl + s$	0	0	s	$avdl$
F2EXP & F2LOG	1	1	0	1	$\frac{s}{avdl}$	s
BM3	1	1	$\mu \cdot p(t\|C)$	μ	k_1	$k_1 \cdot \mu + \mu^2 \cdot p(t\|C)$
DIR+	1	$\mu \cdot p(t\|C) + \delta$	$\mu^2 \cdot p^2(t\|C) + \delta \cdot \mu \cdot p(t\|C)$	0	$\mu \cdot p(t\|C)$	$\mu^2 \cdot p(t\|C)$

function can be simplified to:

$$f(\{t\}, d) = \frac{c(t,d) + \mu \cdot p(t|C)}{|d| + \mu} \qquad (2)$$

Note the natural logarithm function in Equation (1) is omitted since it is a monotonically increasing function and would not affect the ranking results. Since $p(t|C)$ is a collection-dependent constant, the function can be further simplified as:

$$f(t, d) = \frac{c(t,d) + c_1}{|d| + c_2}. \qquad (3)$$

Similarly, Okapi BM25 [9] can be simplified to:

$$\begin{aligned} f(t, d) &= \frac{(k_1 + 1) \cdot c(t,d)}{c(t,d) + k_1 \cdot (1 - b + b \cdot |d|/avdl)} \\ &= \frac{\alpha \cdot c(t,d)}{c(t,d) + \beta \cdot |d| + c_2}, \end{aligned} \qquad (4)$$

where α absorbs $k_1 + 1$, and $\beta = k_1 \cdot b/avdl$ is a collection-dependent variable and $c_2 = k_1 \cdot (1 - b)$ is a parameter.

Furthermore, the pivoted normalization function (PIV) [10] can also be simplified to:

$$\begin{aligned} f(t, d) &= \frac{1 + ln(1 + ln(c(t,d)))}{(1 - s + s \cdot |d|/avdl)} \\ &= \frac{g(c(t,d))}{(\beta \cdot |d| + c_2)}, \end{aligned} \qquad (5)$$

where $g(\cdot) = 1 + ln(1 + ln(\cdot))$ and can be further generalized as an arbitrary non-linear function. $\beta = s/avdl$ is a collection related variable and $c_2 = 1 - s$ is a parameter.

All of the above three simplified functions (i.e., Eq. (3), Eq. (4) and Eq. (5)) can be generalized as the following form:

$$F(c(t,d), |d|) = \frac{\alpha \cdot g(c(t,d)) + c_1}{\gamma \cdot c(t,d) + \beta \cdot |d| + c_2}, \qquad (6)$$

where $g(\cdot)$ is an arbitrary non-linear function and $\alpha, \beta, \gamma, c_1, c_2$ are free parameters. This generalized function form is essentially a linear transformation of a non-linear transformation of term frequency divided by a linear transformation of document length. The denominator optionally adds adjusted term frequency as a method to dampen the impact of increasing term frequency. Note that IDF is not part of the function because it would not affect the document ranking for single-term queries.

In fact, we find that the generalized retrieval function as shown in Eq. (6) can cover at least 11 retrieval functions. In addition to the above three retrieval functions, the following functions can also be generalized: (1) F1EXP, F1LOG, F2EXP and F2LOG from the axiomatic retrieval models [5],

(2) BM3 derived from the Dirichlet Priors for term frequency normalization model [6], and (3) BM25+, DIR+, PIV+ derived from the lower bounding term frequency normalization models [8]. Table 1 summarizes the instantiations for each of the retrieval functions.

2.2 Upper Bound Estimation for MAP

Given the general form as shown in Equation (6), one straightforward solution to estimate the performance bound for single-term queries would be to simply try all possible values/instantiations for the parameters and functions and then report the best performance. Thus, the problem of estimating performance bound boils down to the problem of searching for optimal parameter settings in terms of the retrieval performance. More specifically, given Eq. (6), we need to find parameter settings for $\alpha, \beta, \gamma, c_1, c_2$ that can optimize the retrieval performance measured (i.e., MAP in this paper). We do not consider the instantiation of $g(\cdot)$ here, and leave it as our future work.

Since it is infeasible to try all possible parameter values and find the optimal setting, we propose to apply the cost/gain analysis to find the optimal parameter setting.

Let us explain the notations first. d_i and d_j are a pair of documents. Given a query, $s_i = f(\{t\}, d_i)$ and $s_j = f(\{t\}, d_j)$ denote the relevance score of these two documents computed using a retrieval function.

For a given query, each pair of documents d_i and d_j with different relevance labels (currently we only consider the binary case, i.e. whether the document is relevant or non-relevant) a ranking model computes the scores $s_i = f(d_i)$ and $s_j = f(d_j)$. Follow the previous studies about RankNet [1, 2], we define the cost function as the pairwise cross-entropy cost applied to the logistic of the difference of the relevance scores:

$$C_{ij} = \frac{1}{2}(1 - S_{ij})\sigma(s_i - s_j) + \log(1 + e^{-\sigma(s_i - s_j)}) \qquad (7)$$

where $S_{ij} \in \{0, \pm 1\}$ denotes the ground-truth ranking relationship of document pair d_i and d_j: 1 if d_i is relevant and d_j is non-relevant, -1 if d_i is non-relevant and d_j is relevant, 0 if they have the same label. The gradient of the cost function is then:

$$\frac{\partial C_{ij}}{\partial s_i} = \sigma\left(\frac{1}{2}(1 - S_{ij}) - \frac{1}{1 + e^{\sigma(s_i - s_j)}}\right) = -\frac{\partial C_{ij}}{\partial s_j} \qquad (8)$$

If we only consider the total cost of ranking non-relevant documents before the relevant documents, S_{ij} is always 1. We will always consider that d_i is relevant and d_j is non-

Table 2: collections and queries

	disk12	Robust04	WT2G	GOV2
#queries	4	11	3	2
qid	57,75, 77,78	312,348,349, 364,367,379, 392,395,403, 417,424	403,417, 424	757,840

Table 3: Upper Bound of MAP

		disk12	Robust04	WT2G	GOV2
Models with Basic Signals	DIR	0.4009	0.3823	0.3660	0.2083
	BM25	**0.4016**	**0.3824**	**0.4038**	0.2896
	PIV	0.3987	0.3812	**0.4038**	**0.3079**
	F2EXP	0.4000	0.3682	0.3183	0.1950
	BM3	0.4015	0.3823	0.3792	0.2554
	DIR+	0.4009	0.3823	0.3794	0.2083
Upper Bounds	DIR^U	0.4244†	0.4136†	0.4055	0.2724
	TFDL1^U	0.4273†	0.4209†	0.4095	0.3193†
	TFDL2^U	**0.4273†**	**0.4209†**	**0.4095**	**0.3255†**

relevant from now on. The Eq. (8) is then simplified as:

$$\frac{\partial C_{ij}}{\partial s_i} = \frac{-\sigma}{1 + e^{\sigma(s_i - s_j)}} \quad (9)$$

The upper bound of the performance is then obtained when the cost is minimized by parameters optimization. The parameters $p_k \in \mathbb{R}$ used in the ranking model could be updated so as to reduce the cost via stochastic gradient descent:

$$p_k \to p_k - \eta \frac{\partial C}{\partial p_k} = p_k - \eta \left(\frac{\partial C}{\partial s_i} \frac{\partial s_i}{\partial p_k} + \frac{\partial C}{\partial s_j} \frac{\partial s_j}{\partial p_k} \right) \quad (10)$$

Unfortunately, the cost defined in Eq. (9) is actually the "optimization" cost instead of the target cost (the actual cost) [1] and thus minimizing the cost may not necessarily lead to the optimal MAP. However, MAP is either flat or non-differentiable everywhere which makes the direct optimization toward it difficult [13]. To overcome this we modify Eq. (9) by multiplying the derivative of the cost by the size of the change in MAP gain from swapping a pair of differently labeled documents for a given query q. The pairwise λ (we change cost C to λ and λ is the gain instead of cost) can be written as:

$$\lambda_{ij} = \frac{\sigma}{1 + e^{\sigma(s_i - s_j)}} \frac{1}{|R|} \left(\left| \frac{n}{r_j} - \frac{m}{r_i} \right| + \sum_{k=r_j+1}^{r_i-1} \frac{I(k)}{k} \right) \quad (11)$$

where r_i and r_j are the ranking positions of d_i and d_j; m and n are the number of relevant documents before position r_i and r_j; $I(k) = 1$ if the document at kth position of the ranking list is relevant and 0 otherwise; $|R|$ is the number of relevant document for the query. The model parameters are adjusted based on the aggregated λ for all pairs of documents for the query using a small (stochastic gradient) step.

The optima are local optima with 99% of the confidence by following the Monte-Carlo method with model parameters chosen from 459 random directions [3].

3. EXPERIMENTS

3.1 Testing Collections

We use four TREC collections: disk12, Robust04, WT2G and Terabyte (GOV2) to conduct the experiments. For the queries, only the title fields of the query topics with only one query term are used (20 in total). We use Dirichlet language model with default $\mu = 2500$ to retrieve at most top 10,000 documents as the documents pool for the pairwise comparison for each query. For relevance labels that less or equal to zero is treated as non-relevant and labels greater than zero are treated as relevant. An overview of the involved collections and queries are listed in Table 2.

3.2 Experiment Setup

We tested both using the cost function only and using the cost function together with λ component of MAP. The

results are very close and the cost with λ seems to be a little bit superior so we just report that part of the results. We basically tried several different models based on Eq. (6):

- **DIR^U**: Dirichlet Language Model, denoted as $\frac{c(t,d)+\mu \cdot p(t|C)}{|d|+\mu}$

- **TFDL1^U**: which only contains c_1 and c_2 as model parameters, denoted as $\frac{c(t,d)+c_1}{|d|+c_2}$

- **TFDL2^U**: which takes α, β, c_1, c_2 as parameters, denoted as $\frac{\alpha \cdot c(t,d)+c_1}{\beta \cdot |d|+c_2}$

For other possible format of Eq. (6) they are essentially covered by TFDL2^U so we do not report the results for them [1].

For all of our experiments, we varied the learning rate η between 10^0 to 10^{10} with step size 10 times to previous value. We have found that optimal learning rate brings marginal gain in terms of overall performance. So we just report the performance on the optimal learning rate. For the starting point, we choose α, β, c_1, c_2 from $[0.1, 10000]$ with step size 10 times to previous value. We set the learning iteration at most 500 epochs and it stops if the gain was constant over 20 epochs.

3.3 Results

Table 3 lists both the optimal performances of previously proposed ranking models with optimal parameters chosen from a wide range (e.g. for DIR and DIR+ $\mu \in [0, 5000]$ with step size 500; for BM25, BM3, PIV, F2EXP b or $s \in [0, 1]$ with step size 0.1) and optima of proposed models. The values listed in the table are the MAPs of single term queries only (not the whole set of the queries). It is shown that the generalized models are better than classic ranking models for the most cases (indicated by the † which means the two-tailed paired t-test at p value of 0.05 comparing with the optimal performances of selected models which are boldfaced). Furthermore, different collections have different gains. Robust04 has the largest gain between the two results which indicating that possibly the previously proposed ranking models do not capture the critical ranking signals well or the statistics they use contradicts with the actual properties of relevant documents. Also, for WT2G we get very little gain by applying our analysis (the performances are even not significant better than the selected models). This probably

---

[1] Actually they are possibly covered by Eq. (6). But if we choose wide spectrum of the starting points then they are covered by large chance.

Table 4: Parameters

Model	Paras	disk12	Robust04	WT2G	GOV2
DIR^U	μ	4.66e3	3.54e7	1.43e6	0
TFDL1^U	$\frac{c_1}{c_2}$	2.49e-3	1.0	6.87e-5	6.0e-1
TFDL2^U	$\frac{c_1}{c_2}$	1.55e-2	5.86e-2	1.08e1	1.39e-1
	$\frac{\alpha}{\beta}$	1.37e-4	1.43e-2	1.01e-2	1.13e-2

means that if we would like to further improve the performance on WT2G we need to find other forms of the ranking models which may look different than Eq. (6).

3.4 Parameters

Next, we would like to investigate the parameters that lead to the optima for the proposed models. The parameters are worthy to look at since they might inspire or provide intuition of better performing models in the future. Table 4 lists those parameters. As we can see, for DIR^U the optimal parameters μ obtained for Robust04 and WT2G are much larger than 10^3 which is suggested value by the original authors of DIR [14]. For TFDL1^U we choose to report the ratio $\frac{c_1}{c_2}$. The values vary between collections. For example, the optimal values for Robust04 is 1.0 which indicates that the better performed models would have larger dampen factor for document length than other collections. For TFDL2^U both $\frac{c_1}{c_2}$ and $\frac{\alpha}{\beta}$ are reported. We find that α is in several magnitude levels smaller than β. But this is not always the truth for $\frac{c_1}{c_2}$. We would expect more impact on $\frac{\alpha}{\beta}$ than $\frac{c_1}{c_2}$ and the values of $\frac{\alpha}{\beta}$ could be better incorporated by better performing models in the future.

4. RELATED WORK

Although there are lots of effective ranking models proposed by researchers, there are fewer studies dedicated to the theoretical analysis of their performances upper bound. One related domain is the constraint analysis [4] which proposes formal constraints that a reasonable ranking model should bear. Examples of the constraints including how should a ranking model incorporate TF, how to regulate the interaction of TF and DL, how to penalize long document in the collection, etc. The constraint analysis provides a general guide of how a reasonable ranking model should be designed. Our work further explores this direction by providing the practical performance upper bound as well as the optimal parameters which helps to fine tune the constraint theory.

Our estimation method is mostly inspired by the RankNet [1, 2] and the LambdaRank [2, 3] which are successful in the learning to rank domain. In their works they apply the pair-wise documents comparison for a specific query which is also adopted by our work. However, we did two different things in our work: (1) the aforementioned techniques apply neural network as the underlying model while we follow the rationale proposed by some classic ranking model, i.e. the ranking score should be positively correlated with TF and inversely correlated with DL, to find the local optimum of the generalized ranking models. (2) we aim to optimize MAP instead of NDCG and we proposed a simplified equation for calculating the difference of MAP if two documents are swapped in the ranking list which can make the analysis more efficiency. There is another work which indeed directly optimizes MAP called SVMMAP [13]. SVMMAP is actu-

ally another learning to ranking algorithm based on support vector machine. It performs optimization only on a working set of constraints which is extended with the most violated constraint at each optimization step. Taylor et al. [12] used the cost analysis to predicate a family of BM25 ranking models. They however did not apply the gain analysis which has shown to be superior in our experiments.

5. CONCLUSIONS AND FUTURE WORK

In this paper we have applied cost/gain analysis to the performance upper bound of single term queries for TREC collections. The found upper bounds of MAP provide sound foundation of potentially better performed ranking models in the future. Moreover, the parameters that lead to the local optimums provide more insight about how the future models could better incorporate proper statistics/signals.

Future work may include expanding the analysis to multiple terms queries and finding more mathematically restricted way to prove the performance upper bounds.

6. ACKNOWLEDGMENT

This material is based upon work supported by the National Science Foundation under Grant Number IIS-1423002. We thank the reviewers for their useful comments.

7. REFERENCES

[1] C. Burges, R. Ragno, and Q. Le. Learning to rank with non-smooth cost functions. In *Advances in Neural Information Processing Systems 19*. MIT Press, Cambridge, MA, January 2007.

[2] C. J. Burges. From ranknet to lambdarank to lambdamart: An overview. Technical Report MSR-TR-2010-82, June 2010.

[3] P. Donmez, K. M. Svore, and C. J. Burges. On the local optimality of lambdarank. In *SIGIR*. Association for Computing Machinery, Inc., July 2009.

[4] H. Fang, T. Tao, and C. Zhai. A formal study of information retrieval heuristics. In *Proceedings of the 27th Annual International ACM SIGIR Conference on Research and Development in Information Retrieval*, SIGIR '04, pages 49–56, New York, NY, USA, 2004. ACM.

[5] H. Fang and C. Zhai. An exploration of axiomatic approaches to information retrieval. SIGIR '05, pages 480–487, New York, NY, USA, 2005. ACM.

[6] B. He and I. Ounis. A study of the dirichlet priors for term frequency normalisation. SIGIR '05, pages 465–471, New York, NY, USA, 2005. ACM.

[7] X. Liu and H. Fang. Latent entity space: a novel retrieval approach for entity-bearing queries. *Information Retrieval Journal*, 2015.

[8] Y. Lv and C. Zhai. Lower-bounding term frequency normalization. In *Proceedings of the 20th ACM International Conference on Information and Knowledge Management*, CIKM '11, pages 7–16, New York, NY, USA, 2011. ACM.

[9] S. Robertson, S. Walker, S. Jones, M. Hancock-Beaulieu, and M. Gatford. Okapi at trec-3. pages 109–126, 1996.

[10] A. Singhal, C. Buckley, and M. Mitra. Pivoted document length normalization. SIGIR '96, pages 21–29, New York, NY, USA, 1996. ACM.

[11] T. Tao and C. Zhai. Regularized estimation of mixture models for robust pseudo-relevance feedback. SIGIR '06, pages 162–169, New York, NY, USA, 2006. ACM.

[12] M. Taylor, H. Zaragoza, N. Craswell, S. Robertson, and C. Burges. Optimisation methods for ranking functions with multiple parameters. CIKM '06, pages 585–593, New York, NY, USA, 2006. ACM.

[13] Y. Yue, T. Finley, F. Radlinski, and T. Joachims. A support vector method for optimizing average precision. SIGIR '07, pages 271–278, New York, NY, USA, 2007. ACM.

[14] C. Zhai and J. Lafferty. A study of smoothing methods for language models applied to information retrieval. *ACM Trans. Inf. Syst.*, 22(2):179–214, Apr. 2004.

Optimization Method for Weighting Explicit and Latent Concepts in Clinical Decision Support Queries

Saeid Balaneshin-kordan
Department of Computer Science
Wayne State University
Detroit, Michigan 48202
saeid.balaneshinkordan@wayne.edu

Alexander Kotov
Department of Computer Science
Wayne State University
Detroit, Michigan 48202
kotov@wayne.edu

ABSTRACT

Accurately answering verbose queries that describe a clinical case and aim at finding articles in a collection of medical literature requires capturing many explicit and latent aspects of complex information needs underlying such queries. Proper representation of these aspects often requires query analysis to identify the most important query concepts as well as query transformation by adding new concepts to a query, which can be extracted from the top retrieved documents or medical knowledge bases. Traditionally, query analysis and expansion have been done separately. In this paper, we propose a method for representing verbose domain-specific queries based on weighted unigram, bigram, and multi-term concepts in the query itself, as well as extracted from the top retrieved documents and external knowledge bases. We also propose a graduated non-convexity optimization framework, which allows to unify query analysis and expansion by jointly determining the importance weights for the query and expansion concepts depending on their type and source. Experiments using a collection of PubMed articles and TREC Clinical Decision Support (CDS) track queries indicate that applying our proposed method results in significant improvement of retrieval accuracy over state-of-the-art methods for ad hoc and medical IR.

CCS Concepts

•Information systems → Query reformulation;

Keywords

Medical Literature Retrieval; Clinical Decision Support; Feature-based Retrieval Models; Optimization Methods

1. INTRODUCTION

Given descriptive summary of a medical case as a query, the goal of information retrieval systems for clinical decision support (CDS) is to return articles from a collection of medical literature that are relevant to the query and can assist a clinician in making decisions regarding the case, such as prescribing a medication, procedure or treatment. A fundamental challenge faced by those systems is that although CDS queries are typically verbose and may consist of several sentences (e.g. *"33-year-old male presents with severe abdominal pain one week after a bike accident, in which he sustained abdominal trauma. He is hypotensive and tachycardic, and imaging reveals a ruptured spleen and intraperitoneal hemorrhage"*), only a small subset of query terms (henceforth referred to as explicit concepts) correspond to the key query concepts, such as *"bike accident"*, *"abdominal trauma"*, *"tachycardia"*, *"splenic rupture"*, *"intraperitoneal hemorrhage"*, which represent the information need behind this query, while many other important concepts that are relevant to this information need (e.g. *"spontaneous spleen rupture"*, *"splenic trauma"*, etc.) are not directly mentioned in the query (henceforth referred to as latent concepts). Providing complete and accurate retrieval results for CDS queries requires both correct identification of the key explicit concepts and addition of important latent concepts to the query, as well as precise weighting of explicit and latent concepts in the modified query.

While previous work on general and domain-specific IR has focused on identification of the key statistical concepts in verbose queries [3, 4, 5], latent query concepts in external resources ([14, 30, 37, 38]) and the top-retrieved (PRF) documents [5, 17] individually, to the best of our knowledge, no query transformation method that uses both explicit concepts from the query and latent concepts from diverse sources, such as external resources and PRF documents, has been previously proposed. For example, Latent Concept Expansion (LCE) [17] and Parameterized Query Expansion (PQE) [5] methods use only unigrams from the top-retrieved documents as latent concepts, while [11] uses only unigrams from structured knowledge bases as latent concepts for query expansion.

In this work, we propose a novel method to represent verbose clinical decision support queries using unigram, bigram and multi-term concepts from the query itself, as well as from the PRF documents and external knowledge bases (such as the Unified Medical Language System). Our method is based on linear feature-based learning-to-rank retrieval framework [18], in which the relative importance weight is determined for each matching query concept individually as a linear combination of features. We also propose a set of features for each concept type, which is determined based on whether a concept is a unigram, bigram or multi-term phrase

ICTIR '16, September 12-16, 2016, Newark, DE, USA

© 2016 ACM. ISBN 978-1-4503-4497-5/16/09. . . $15.00

DOI: http://dx.doi.org/10.1145/2970398.2970418

and whether it occurs in the query itself or is extracted from a top retrieved document or a knowledge base.

Since the parameter spaces of linear feature-based retrieval models can be reduced to a multinomial manifold, their parameters can be estimated by direct maximization of the target rank-based retrieval metric (e.g. NDCG) over this manifold using derivative-free unconstrained multi-dimensional optimization methods, such as coordinate ascent [19] or hill-climbing [21]. These methods are based on the Powell's method, which divides a complex multi-dimensional optimization problem into several simple one-dimensional ones. After that, it iteratively optimizes a multivariate objective function by optimizing each parameter individually, while holding all other parameters fixed. Since line search is a local optimization method, the efficiency and accuracy of both the coordinate ascent and hill-climbing rely on the assumption of smoothness and convexity of objective function when a free parameter is optimized, which is often violated in practice. Figure 1, which shows the behavior of the target retrieval metric by varying the value of a parameter that corresponds to the weight of a feature, illustrates this case. It can be seen that the objective function shown in this figure has several local maxima.

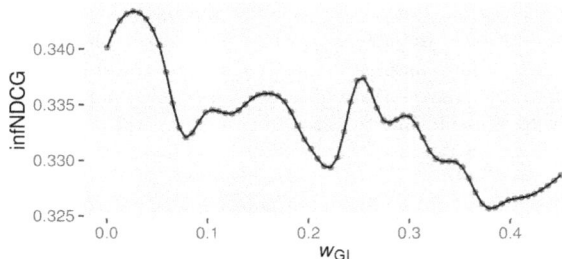

Figure 1: The values of objective function corresponding to infNDCG retrieval metric by varying the weight of one of the features (GI presented in Section 3.3), which determines the importance of concept matches of certain type.

The optimization method for learning the weights of concept importance features in feature-based retrieval models proposed in this paper leverages the Graduated Non-Convexity (GNC) (or continuation) optimization method [6] to address the issue of non-smooth and non-convex objective functions, when individual parameters are optimized using the Powell's method. GNC is a derivative-free method specifically designed for global optimization of non-smooth and non-convex objective functions. Graduated Non-Convexity (GNC) is an iterative method, which applies different degrees of smoothing to the original objective function to generate smoother and more convex objective functions, which have their global maximum close to the one of the original objective function. The method starts by applying the highest degree of smoothing and then gradually decreases the rate of smoothing at each subsequent iteration using the result obtained at the previous iteration as the starting point for the next iteration until the global maximum for the original non-smoothed objective function is found. Although the quality of the solution attained by this approach heavily depends on the choice of the smoothing method, it was recently shown that Gaussian smoothing of a non-convex function is optimal in a sense that it evolves any function into its convex envelope [20].

The remainder of this paper is organized as follows. After a brief summary of related work in Section 2, we discuss the details of the ranking function, the features and the optimization method to estimate the concept importance weights in Section 3. Section 4 provides the results of an experimental evaluation of retrieval accuracy of the proposed method with respect to the state-of-the-art baselines, while Section 5 concludes the paper.

2. RELATED-WORK

Depending on the type of concepts used for query expansion, general-purpose and domain-specific retrieval methods can be categorized into the ones that are based on statistical concepts (i.e. determined based on term popularity and co-occurrence in a given collection) [3, 5, 16, 17, 31], the ones that are based on semantic concepts (i.e. that are extracted from a knowledge repository) [13, 29, 30, 37], and those that combine semantic and statistical concepts [7, 25, 34, 9]. Below we provide an overview of the previously proposed methods in each of these 3 categories.

Retrieval methods using statistical concepts. In the simplest case, these retrieval models utilize only unigrams from the top retrieved documents for query expansion [31]. More recent retrieval methods utilizing statistical concepts are based on the Markov Random Field (MRF) framework introduced by Metzler and Croft [16]. It assigns the same importance weight to all matching statistical query concepts of the same type (unigrams and sequential bigrams), when the retrieval score of a document is calculated. Latent Concept Expansion (LCE) extends MRF by also using unigrams from the PRF documents as latent concepts for query expansion. The requirement of having fixed weights for unigrams and bigram concepts in the MRF-based retrieval model was relaxed by the Weighted Sequential Dependence (WSD) model [4], which estimates the importance of each concept individually. A similar relaxation of LCE weights was implemented in the Parameterized Query Expansion (PQE) [5] model. Overall, query representation methods based on statistical concepts typically consider unigrams and bigrams in the query and/or unigrams in PRF documents.

Retrieval methods using semantic concepts. Semantic concepts for query expansion are typically extracted from domain-specific, such as the Unified Medical Language System (UMLS) [13], Medical Subject Headings (MeSH) [15] and Systematized Nomenclature of Medicine-Clinical Terms (SNOMED-CT) [10], or general-purpose knowledge repositories, such as Wikipedia [29, 35]. The utility of this type of concepts has been studied for a variety of medical IR tasks including medical literature retrieval [27, 38]. UMLS concepts are typically extracted from queries and top-retrieved documents using MetaMap [1, 8, 13, 28, 29, 32, 33].

Soldaini et al. [29] proposed two methods for medical literature retrieval that use Wikipedia-based heuristics to filter out non-medical concepts from the original query and top retrieved documents. The first method (referred to as `HT` in [29] and `Wiki-Orig` in this work) is a query reduction method, which retains only those bigram concepts in the original query that are determined to be health-related according to a heuristic. On the other hand, the second method (referred to as `HT-PRF` in [29] and `Wiki-TD` in this work) expands the original query with a number of health-related concepts that are extracted from the top-retrieved documents and filtered out using the same heuristic.

Accounting for semantic types of concepts[1] can also significantly improve the accuracy of query expansion, as they can be used to filter out the candidate expansion concepts. The method proposed in [13] (referred to as UMLS-TD in this work), expands medical queries only with the UMLS concepts extracted from the top retrieved documents that have pre-selected semantic types. A semantic type is pre-selected if the concepts of this type improve the accuracy of retrieval results when added to the queries in the training set. For example, the semantic type "signs and symptoms" is pre-selected for a query about the diagnosis of a disease. [32] proposed another approach to using semantic types in the query, in which the semantic types of concepts are used to weight the concepts (concepts that are more likely to be effective, get higher weight).

Retrieval models using both semantic and statistical concepts. The benefit of integrating semantic and statistical concepts was shown in [7, 9, 25, 34]. The methods in [7, 25, 34] focused only on explicit concepts (query unigrams and bigrams along with UMLS concepts extracted from the query using MetaMap). A medical IR system that integrates a graph-based representation of the corpus, structured knowledge sources and a retrieval model combining statistical IR methods with an inference mechanism implemented as graph traversal has been proposed in [9].

The key difference of the proposed method from existing methods for medical literature and ad hoc document retrieval is that it uses both statistical and semantic concepts extracted from diverse sources (query itself, knowledge bases and top retrieved documents) for query representation. The proposed method also leverages an efficient optimization technique to learn the relative importance weight of different types of query concepts on the same scale.

3. METHOD

In this section, we present the details of the proposed query reformulation method, a set of features used with it and a method to optimize the weights of those features with respect to the target retrieval metric. The proposed query reformulation method combines explicit and latent query concepts from diverse sources and determines the weight of each individual concept as a linear combination of features, which depend on a concept type. The type of a query concept is determined by its source and whether the concept is represented by a unigram, bigram or multi-word phase. The set of concept sources considered in our method includes the query itself, top retrieved documents for the original query, and external knowledge repositories.

3.1 Retrieval model

To account for term dependencies, the proposed method adopts a Markov Random Field (MRF) retrieval framework [16], in which the retrieval score of a document is determined as a weighted linear combination of the matching scores of different concept types in a given query. In particular, our method extends the parametrized concept retrieval model in [5], according to which the retrieval score of document D

[1] http://metamap.nlm.nih.gov/SemanticTypesAndGroups.shtml

with respect to query Q is calculated as:

$$sc(Q, D) = \sum_{T \in \mathcal{T}_Q} \sum_{c \in \mathcal{C}_T} \lambda_T(c) f_T(c, D) \quad (1)$$

where $\mathcal{C}_T$ is a set of concepts belonging to concept type T, and $\lambda_T(c)$ is defined as the importance weight of concept c, which depends on its type. In the above equation, $f_T(c, D)$ is the matching score function of concept c in document D, which is defined as:

$$f_T(c, D) = \log((1-\lambda) \frac{n(c, D) + \mu \frac{n(c, Col)}{|Col|}}{|D| + \mu} + \lambda \frac{n(c, Col)}{|Col|}) \quad (2)$$

where $n(c, D)$ ($n(c, Col)$) and $|D|$ ($|Col|$) are the counts of concept c in document D (entire collection) and the size of document D (entire collection), respectively. The above matching function utilizes a two-stage smoothing method from [36], where λ and μ are Jelinek-Mercer and Dirichlet smoothing coefficients, respectively. Since only unigrams as well as ordered and unordered bigrams are considered in the MRF retrieval framework, concepts that are represented by multi-word phrases are broken down into unigrams and sequential bigrams. The set of concept types considered for a query Q is designated by $\mathcal{T}_Q$ and is shown in Table 2. This table also provides information about the concept extraction methods and a set of features corresponding to each concept type, which will be explained in detail below.

The importance weight of concept c is parameterized using a set of importance features $\Phi_T(c)$. Each concept type T is associated with its own set of importance features, summarized in Table 1. Thus, the weight of concept c with type T is determined as a weighted linear combination of importance features:

$$\lambda_T(c) = \sum_{n=1}^{N} w_\phi^n \phi_n , \quad (3)$$

where $\{\phi_1, \dots, \phi_N\}$ is a set of features for concepts with type T (i.e., $\Phi_T(c) = \{\phi_1, \dots, \phi_N\}$), and w_ϕ^n is the importance weight of the n-th feature (i.e., ϕ_n). The intuition behind this concept weighting scheme is that different concept types have different importance and should be weighted accordingly. Intuitively, knowledge-based concepts (such as the UMLS concepts) that are linked from the concepts in the original query should have a different importance weight than the concepts that are extracted from the top retrieved documents. Similarly, bigrams corresponding to UMLS concepts identified in the original query should be weighted differently than other bigrams in the original query. On the other hand, features determining the importance of a concept from a graph structured knowledge repository (e.g. UMLS), like the degree of the node corresponding to this concept, are different from the features that determine the importance of a unigram concept in top retrieved documents.

3.2 Optimization Method

Learning the feature weights that maximize the target retrieval metric on a training data can be considered as a multivariate optimization problem and is typically addressed by decomposing it into a set of one-dimensional optimization problems. Instead of performing a line search along every single dimension in optimizing a set of feature weights with respect to the target retrieval metric, we propose to use graduated optimization [6], an efficient global optimization technique.

3.2.1 Graduated optimization

Graduated optimization is an iterative optimization method that gradually finds the global optimum of a given objective function by finding the optima for a series of simplified objective functions. Each of these simplified objective functions is obtained from the original objective function by applying different degree of smoothing to make the original function more convex. It starts from the solution to the most simplified optimization problem (i.e., when the maximum degree of smoothing is applied to the original objective function) and considers this solution as the starting point for the second less simplified problem (i.e. less smoothed original objective function). This process continues until the global optimum for the original objective function is found. This procedure is based on the assumption that the global optimum of a given objective function at the current iteration is close enough to its global optimum at the next iteration. Therefore, at the next iteration, the region of the parameter space that is far enough from the optimum point at the current iteration is ignored. As a result, a smaller region that is close to the optimum point at the current iteration is searched for the optimal parameter setting at the next iteration.

3.2.2 Smoothing method

In case of a univariate optimization problem with a single parameter w_ϕ, the smoothed objective function, $\tilde{E}(w_\phi)$, can be obtained by taking sample values from $E(w_\phi)$, the original objective function. To compute $\tilde{E}(w_\phi)$ at a specific region around the starting point $w_{\phi,0}$, samples are taken from $\tilde{E}(w_\phi)$ for the following values of w_ϕ:

$$\mathbf{w}_{s,\phi} = [w_{\phi,-M}, \ldots, w_{\phi,0}, \ldots, w_{\phi,M}] \quad (4)$$

where

$$w_{\phi,m} = w_{\phi,0} + m\Delta w_\phi, \quad m \in [-M, \ldots, M] \quad (5)$$

and Δw_ϕ is the sampling interval.

When a polynomial of degree K is used for the smoothed objective function at point $w_{\phi,m}$:

$$\tilde{E}(w_{\phi,m}) = \sum_{k=0}^{K} a_k m^k, \quad m \in [-M, \ldots, M] \quad (6)$$

The weight a_k is determined so that the following Mean Square Error (MSE) is minimized:

$$\varepsilon_\phi = \frac{1}{2M+1} \sum_{m=-M}^{M} (\tilde{E}(w_{\phi,m}) - E(w_{\phi,m}))^2 \quad (7)$$

As shown in [24], optimal $\mathbf{a} = [a_1, \ldots, a_M]$ is found as:

$$\mathbf{a} = (\mathbf{J}^T\mathbf{J})^{-1}\mathbf{J}^T\mathbf{w}_{s,\phi}, \quad (8)$$

where $\mathbf{J}$ is a Jacobian of the vector $[\tilde{E}(w_{\phi,-M}), \ldots, \tilde{E}(w_{\phi,M})]$, and its (m,k)-th element is obtained as

$$[\mathbf{J}]_{m,k} = (m - M)^k, \quad m \in [0, 2M], \ k \in [0, K]. \quad (9)$$

where M, Δw_ϕ and K control the smoothing rate of the objective function.

Figure 2 illustrates three iterations of the smoothing procedure to find the optimal weight for one of the features

(w_{GI}). Points in Figure 2 indicate the samples taken from the objective function at each iteration, while the solid lines indicate the smoothed curves (i.e. estimated polynomials). The maximum of the smoothed curve is found and used as the starting point for the next iteration. At each subsequent iteration, the degree of smoothing is reduced by lowering Δw from 2.5×10^{-2} to 2.5×10^{-3} and then to 2.5×10^{-4}, while increasing K from 4 to 5 and 6, while keeping M constant ($M = 18$). As follows from Figure 2, the smoothing standard deviation (σ) is decreasing at each iteration of the optimization process, which indicates less smoothing and hence closer representation to the original objective function.

3.2.3 Multi-variate optimization

The multivariate optimization method to train the weights of all features with respect to the target retrieval metric is summarized in Algorithm 1. We denote the vector of feature weights by $\mathbf{w}_\phi = [w_\phi^n]_{n=1}^N$. As mentioned earlier, the weight w_ϕ^n is estimated by using $n - 1$ previously estimated weights at iteration j (i.e., $\hat{w}_\phi^1, \ldots, \hat{w}_\phi^{n-1}$) and the $N - n$ estimated weights at the iteration $j-1$ (i.e., $\hat{w}_\phi^{n+1}, \ldots, \hat{w}_\phi^N$). Therefore, the univariate objective function to estimate the weight w_ϕ^n can be written as:

$$E^{n,j}(w_\phi^n) = E([\hat{w}_\phi^1, \ldots, \hat{w}_\phi^{n-1}, w_\phi^n, \hat{w}_\phi^{n+1}, \ldots, \hat{w}_\phi^N]) \quad (10)$$

where $E^{n,j}(w_\phi^n)$ is a univariate objective function for the weight of the n-th feature at the j-th iteration.

As can be seen from Algorithm 1, first explicit and latent concepts of training queries are extracted from different sources (line 1) and then $\mathbf{w}_\phi$ is randomly initialized (line 2). At each iteration of the proposed optimization method (line 3), $\mathbf{w}_\phi$ is randomly shuffled (line 4). After that for each element of $\mathbf{w}_\phi$ (line 5) and for each sampling policy (line 6), the objective function (i.e., $E^{n,j}(w_\phi^n)$) is sampled at the points $\mathbf{w}_{s,\phi}^n = [w_{\phi,m}^n]_{m=-M}^M$ (line 7). The sampling policy determines the values of M, K, and Δw at each iteration of the optimization approach. The smoothed objective function $\tilde{E}^{n,j}(w_{\phi,m}^n)$ is obtained using the samples from $E^{n,j}(w_\phi^n)$ (line 7). Then, the optimum point of $\tilde{E}^{n,j}(w_{\phi,m}^n)$ (i.e., $\hat{w}_{\phi,m}^n$) is estimated (line 9). Next, the n-th element of $\mathbf{w}_\phi$ is replaced by its estimated value (i.e., $\hat{w}_{\phi,m}^n$) (line 10). These iterations continue until the number of iterations (i.e., j) goes beyond $j_{\max}$ (line 3) or convergence (lines 13-15).

3.3 Features

Table 1 summarizes all distinct features that are used to calculate the importance weight of each query concept c depending on its type. The list of concept types, which are determined by concept source, term representation and identification method, along with a set of features that are used to calculate the importance weight of query concepts of each type are shown in Table 2. Concepts belonging to some concept types come from only one source, while other concept types assume two sources. For example, since the concepts of type TUU are UMLS concepts that are represented by unigrams and extracted from the top retrieved documents, this concept type is associated with two concept sources (top retrieved documents and UMLS).

As can be seen from Table 2, there are four different methods for identifying explicit and latent concepts in a query. The first and simplest method is to consider all unigrams and bigrams in a query or top retrieved documents as query

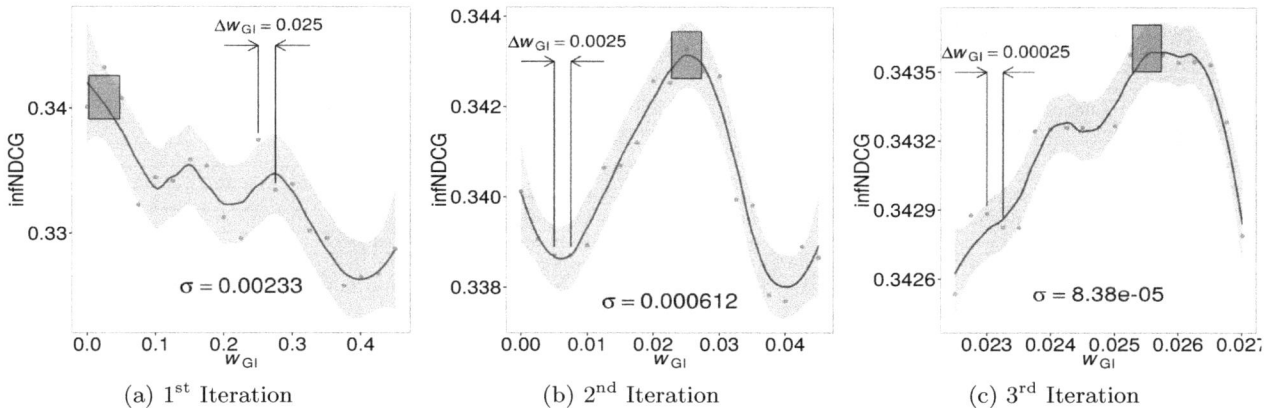

| (a) 1st Iteration | (b) 2nd Iteration | (c) 3rd Iteration |

Figure 2: Application of graduated optimization to estimate the weight of the feature GI using TREC 2014 CDS track queries as the training set. Red boxes indicate the range of w_{GI} considered at the next iteration. σ is defined as the smoothing standard deviation.

Algorithm 1 Algorithm to optimize the feature weights with respect to the target retrieval metric using graduated optimization.

1: Identify explicit and latent concepts
2: Randomly initialize the feature weights vector ($\mathbf{w}_\phi$)
3: **for** $j = 1 : j_{max}$ **do**
4:     Randomly shuffle $\mathbf{w}_\phi$
5:     **for** $n = 1 : N$ **do**
6:         **for** each sampling policy **do**
7:             Sample $E^{n,j}(w_\phi^n)$
8:             Obtain $\tilde{E}^{n,j}(w_{\phi,m}^n)$
9:             Obtain the optimum point $\hat{w}_\phi^n$
10:            Update n-th element of $\mathbf{w}_\phi$ by $\hat{w}_\phi^n$
11:         **end for**
12:     **end for**
13:     **if** Convergence **then**
14:         Break
15:     **end if**
16: **end for**

---

concepts. The second approach uses MetaMap [1] to identify UMLS concepts in a query or top-retrieved documents. The third approach uses the Wikipedia-based health relatedness measure defined in [29] as:

$$hrm(c) = \frac{P(p \text{ is health-related}|c \in p)}{1 - P(p \text{ is health-related}|c \in p)} \quad (11)$$

where $P(p \text{ is health-related}|c \in p)$ is the probability that a Wikipedia page p is health-related given that c occurs in p. Concepts for which this probability exceeds a pre-defined threshold are assumed to be health-related. The fourth approach uses the UMLS relationships table (MRREL.RRF table[2], which we further also refer to as the UMLS concept graph) to select the concepts related to the UMLS concepts identified in a query as latent concepts.

All features in Table 1, except Semantic Direction (SD), Semantic Popularity (SP) and Type Effectiveness (TE), are relatively simple and do not require a detailed explanation. Semantic direction is defined as follows. If S_c is the seman-

tic type of concept c, S_o is the semantic type of the query concept o, to which concept c is related and $d(S_r, S)$ is the distance (i.e. the number of edges) from the root node (S_r) to node S in the UMLS semantic network, then the expansion concept c is defined to have an inward direction relative to the original concept o in the UMLS semantic network (i.e. the expansion concept is more general than the original query concept), if $d(S_r, S_c) < d(S_r, S_o)$. This feature is defined only for the UMLS expansion concepts that are related to the UMLS concepts in the original query.

Semantic popularity of concept c is defined as the number of concepts that are related to concept c in the UMLS concept graph (it can also be viewed as a node degree of concept c in the UMLS concept graph). A large value of this feature indicates popularity and generality of concept c. Type effectiveness is a binary feature that indicates whether the UMLS semantic type of concept c is effective for query expansion. As defined earlier, a semantic type is effective if its corresponding concepts can increase the precision of retrieval results when added to a query. The concept of effective semantic types for medical query expansion was first proposed in [13]. Using the training queries and relevance judgments, we fine tuned the set of effective semantic types from [13] to the collection and query sets used in this work. This will be explained in detail later.

4. EXPERIMENTS

4.1 Experimental Setup

The experimental results reported in this work were obtained using the corpus, which includes around 730,000 documents from PubMed Central (PMC), and queries from the Clinical Decision Support (CDS) track at TREC 2014 [26] and 2015 [23]. 3-fold cross-validation was used to evaluate the performance of the proposed method (INTGR) and the baselines, which were first trained using the query set and relevance judgments from the CDS track of TREC 2014 to maximize infNDCG, the official retrieval metric of the CDS track [26]. The proposed method and the baselines were implemented using Indri retrieval toolkit[3]. The optimal val-

---

[2]http://www.ncbi.nlm.nih.gov/books/NBK9685/

[3]http://www.lemurproject.org/indri/

Table 1: Brief description of features used to estimate the importance weight of concept c.

Feature	Description
TI	TF-IDF of concept c in the collection
CA	Average collection co-occurrence of concept c with other concepts in the query
CM	Maximum collection co-occurrence of concept c with other concepts in the query
NT	Number of top retrieved documents containing concept c
RS	Sum of retrieval scores of top-ranked documents containing concept c
TM	Maximum co-occurrence of concept c with other query concepts in top retrieved documents
TA	Average co-occurrence of concept c with other query concepts in top retrieved documents
GI	Do infoboxes of Wikipedia articles corresponding to concept c contain any health-related keywords?
IS	Does any of the terms of concept c exist in the title of any Wikipedia health-related articles?
CD	Average distance between concept c in the UMLS concept graph and other query, top document and related UMLS concepts identified for a query
SP	Popularity (node degree) of concept c in the UMLS concept graph
SD	Direction of concept c with respect to query concepts in the UMLS semantic network
TE	Does concept c have a UMLS semantic type that is effective for medical query expansion?

Table 2: List of types for explicit and latent query concepts along with a set of features to estimate the importance of concepts of each type (Top-docs stands for top retrieved documents for the original query).

Concept Type	Concept Source(s)	Concept Representation	Concept Extraction	Features
QU	Query	unigrams	all query unigrams	TI, NT, RS, CA, CM, TA, TM
QOB	Query	ordered bigrams	all query bigrams	TI, NT, RS, CA, CM, TA, TM
QUB	Query	unordered bigrams	all query bigrams	TI, NT, RS, CA, CM, TA, TM
QUU	Query, UMLS	unigrams	MetaMap	TI, NT, RS, CA, CM, TA, TM, TE, SP, CD
QUOB	Query, UMLS	ordered bigrams	MetaMap	TI, NT, RS, CA, CM, TA, TM, TE, SP, CD
QUUB	Query, UMLS	unordered bigrams	MetaMap	TI, NT, RS, CA, CM, TA, TM, TE, SP, CD
QDU	Query, Wikipedia	unigrams	health-relatedness measure	TI, NT, RS, CA, CM, TA, TM, GI, IS
QDOB	Query, Wikipedia	ordered bigrams	health-relatedness measure	TI, NT, RS, CA, CM, TA, TM, GI, IS
QDUB	Query, Wikipedia	unordered bigrams	health-relatedness measure	TI, NT, RS, CA, CM, TA, TM, GI, IS
TU	Top-docs	unigrams	direct identification	TI, NT, RS, CA, CM, TA, TM
TOB	Top-docs	ordered bigrams	direct identification	TI, NT, RS, CA, CM, TA, TM
TUB	Top-docs	unordered bigrams	direct identification	TI, NT, RS, CA, CM, TA, TM
TUU	Top-docs, UMLS	unigrams	MetaMap	TI, NT, RS, CA, CM, TA, TM, TE, SP, CD
TUOB	Top-docs, UMLS	ordered bigrams	MetaMap	TI, NT, RS, CA, CM, TA, TM, TE, SP, CD
TUUB	Top-docs, UMLS	unordered bigrams	MetaMap	TI, NT, RS, CA, CM, TA, TM, TE, SP, CD
TDU	Top-docs, Wikipedia	unigrams	health-relatedness measure	TI, NT, RS, CA, CM, TA, TM, GI, IS
TDOB	Top-docs, Wikipedia	ordered bigrams	health-relatedness measure	TI, NT, RS, CA, CM, TA, TM, GI, IS
TDUB	Top-docs, Wikipedia	unordered bigrams	health-relatedness measure	TI, NT, RS, CA, CM, TA, TM, GI, IS
UU	UMLS	unigrams	UMLS relationships	TI, NT, RS, CA, CM, TA, TM, TE, SP, SD, CD
UOB	UMLS	ordered bigrams	UMLS relationships	TI, NT, RS, CA, CM, TA, TM, TE, SP, SD, CD
UUB	UMLS	unordered bigrams	UMLS relationships	TI, NT, RS, CA, CM, TA, TM, TE, SP, SD, CD

ues of Dirichlet prior, Jelinek-Mercer interpolation coefficient, the sizes of ordered and unordered bigram windows in the Indri query language were empirically determined to be 2500, 0.4, 4 and 17, respectively. Figure 3 illustrates how infNDCG changes by varying the number of PRF documents (used to extract concepts) and the number of concepts extracted from PRF documents. The values of these parameters that maximize infNCDG were used in experiments using TREC 2015 CDS track queries.

Besides the proposed graduated optimization approach, we used exhaustive line search to optimize individual feature weights as another baseline (INTGR-LS). This method examines the parameter space in uniform increments and chooses the setting that results in the highest infNDCG. For both INTGR and INTGR-LS methods, the convergence threshold for the change in infNDCG was set to 0.001 and the number of iterations was limited to 20.

4.2 Baselines

The first baseline that was used in experiments is two-stage smoothing [36] (Two-Stage). Two-stage smoothing was also used as the smoothing method in implementing all other baselines and the proposed method. The other baselines used in experiments are Relevance Model (RM) [12],

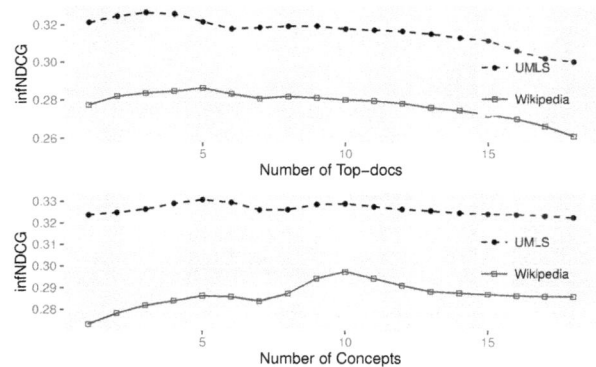

Figure 3: Average infNDCG on TREC 2014 CDS track queries by varying the number of top retrieved documents used to extract the concepts and the number of UMLS and Wikipedia concepts extracted from the top retrieved documents.

Parameterized Query Expansion (PQE) [5], Wiki-Orig and Wiki-TD [29], which use a Wikipedia-based health relatedness measure defined in (11). Other baselines that use only semantic concepts are UMLS-orig [25] and UMLS-TD [13]. UMLS-orig extracts UMLS concepts only from the query itself and breaks the phrases designating UMLS concepts into bigrams in order to incorporate them into the SDM retrieval model [17]. UMLS-TD extracts UMLS concepts from the top retrieved documents according to their semantic types. Since the original implementations of UMLS-TD and Wiki-TD are based on bag-of-words retrieval models, UMLS-TD* and Wiki-TD* are the modifications of UMLS-TD and Wiki-TD that use the SDM retrieval model to account for term dependencies when a concept is designated by a phrase.

We also compare the performance of the proposed method to the best performing methods (which used topic summaries as queries) in the CDS track of TREC in 2014 [22] and 2015 [2] (designated as TREC best). [22] used an ensemble of state-of-art unsupervised knowledge-based query expansion, re-ranking and relevance feedback methods. In [2], queries are expanded with unigrams and UMLS concepts identified in the query itself and the top retrieved documents.

4.3 Results

An initial list of 16 semantic types known to be effective for query expansion in medical records search was taken "as is" from [13]. We observed from the preliminary experiments that not all of these semantic types are effective for expansion of CDS queries. Therefore, we fine-tuned this initial list of semantic types by excluding those semantic types, for which the corresponding concepts did not improve infNDCG of retrieval results on training queries. The 5 semantic types retained from the initial list proposed in [13] are "Clinical Drug", "Disease or Syndrome", "Injury or Poisoning", "Sign or Symptom" and "Therapeutic or Preventive Procedure".

Tables 3 and 4 provide a summary of retrieval accuracy in terms of different retrieval metrics of the proposed method (INTGR) and the baselines on the query sets from the CDS track of TREC 2014 and 2015. As can be seen from Table 3, Wiki-TD* is the best performing baseline (since the best performing TREC methods are different for different query sets, they are not considered as the best performing baselines). Furthermore, the proposed algorithm outperforms INTGR-LS and the best methods in TREC 2014 and 2015.

Table 4 shows the degree of improvement and its statistical significance of the proposed method over the three best performing baselines (i.e., PQE, Wiki-TD, Wiki-TD*) and INTGR-LS. As follows from Table 4, INTGR significantly outperforms all of the best performing baselines in terms of all retrieval metrics. Using graduated non-convexity as a univariate optimization method results in 5-9% improvement of retrieval accuracy in terms of infNDCG, 10-23% improvement in terms of infAP and 8% improvement in terms of P@5 on different query sets.

Table 5 illustrates the effect of using different knowledge bases in conjunction with INTGR on its performance in terms of different evaluation metrics. As follows from Table 5, using INTGR only with Wikipedia results in the smallest improvement of retrieval accuracy across all retrieval metrics (and even a decrease of P@5). It also follows from this table that using INTGR with UMLS results in significantly greater improvement of all retrieval metrics, while the biggest improvement is achieved when explicit and latent concepts of a query are extracted from both UMLS and Wikipedia.

Figure 4 provides performance comparison of INTGR with all of the baselines in terms of P@k for k from 1 to 10 (with a step size of 1). As can be seen from this figure, for all values of k except $k = 1$ in case of TREC 2014 CDS track queries, INTGR significantly outperforms all other baselines. It also follows from Figure 4 that for most of the values of k, the methods that expand the queries with the concepts extracted from the top-ranked documents (RM, UMLS-TD, UMLS-TD*, PQE, Wiki-TD, Wiki-TD* and INTGR) outperform the methods that represent the queries with the concepts extracted from them (Wiki-Orig and UMLS-orig). The average improvements of INTGR in terms of P@k for different values of k over the weakest and strongest baselines are 0.1560 and 0.0380, respectively, on the query set from TREC 2014 CDS track, while on the query set from TREC 2015 CDS track the improvements are 0.0988 and 0.0481, respectively.

Figure 5 illustrates topic level differences between the retrieval accuracy of INTGR in terms of infNDCG with the best performing baselines (Wiki-TD* for the CDS track of TREC 2014 and PQE for the CDS track of TREC 2015) on both query sets. From Figure 5(a), it follows that infNDCG of INTGR is greater than that of Wiki-TD* on 67% of the queries in the CDS track of TREC 2014, while from Figure 5(b) it follows that infNDCG of INTGR is greater than that of PQE on 73% of the queries in the CDS track of TREC 2015. The average improvement of INTGR over Wiki-TD* in terms of infNDCG on TREC 2014 CDS track queries is 0.0518 with standard deviation 0.12, while the average improvement of INTGR over PQE in terms of infNDCG on TREC 2015 CDS track queries is 0.0345 with standard deviation 0.0734. The topics, on which INTGR has the greatest improvement and decline relative to Wiki-TD* in terms of infNDCG among those used in TREC 2014 CDS track are 16 (with 0.4593 improvement) and 14 (with 0.1462 decline). We can also observe that on the query set of TREC 2015 CDS track INTGR has the greatest improvement of 0.3026 and the greatest decline of 0.0512 in terms of infNDCG on topics 6 and 8, respectively. Figure 6 also provides a detailed comparison of retrieval accuracy of INTGR in terms of infNDCG with the best performing baselines (Wiki-TD* for TREC 2014 CDS track and PQE for TREC 2015 CDS track) at the level of each individual topic in the CDS track of TREC 2014 and 2015.

We continued empirical evaluation of INTGR by analysis of its performance on difficult queries. We define a query as *difficult* if infNDCG of Two-Stage on this query is less than 0.1 and as *very difficult* if infNDCG of Two-Stage is less than 0.05. We observed that INTGR outperformed Wiki-TD* on 59% of difficult queries and on 86% of very difficult queries in the CDS track of TREC 2014. We also observed that INTGR outperformed PQE on 56% of difficult queries and on 77% of very difficult queries in CDS track of TREC 2014.

4.4 Discussion

Based on experimental analysis of INTGR presented in the previous section, we can conclude that the subset of UMLS semantic types that are effective for expansion of CDS queries is fairly small (includes less than 4% of UMLS semantic types). These semantic types can be grouped into three categories: "Disorders", "Chemical & Drugs" and "Procedures". These three categories in turn can be conceptually mapped

Table 3: Summary of retrieval accuracy of the proposed method and the baselines on the query sets from the CDS track of TREC 2014 and 2015.

Query set	TREC 2014 CDS track			TREC 2015 CDS track		
Method	infNDCG	infAP	P@5	infNDCG	infAP	P@5
Two-Stage [36]	0.1945	0.0493	0.3533	0.2110	0.0449	0.4200
Wiki-Orig [29]	0.2069	0.0550	0.3533	0.2193	0.0457	0.4133
UMLS-Orig [25]	0.2074	0.0569	0.3867	0.2206	0.0478	0.4400
RM [12]	0.2662	0.0836	0.4400	0.2765	0.0740	0.4600
UMLS-TD [13]	0.2577	0.1523	0.4067	0.2429	0.0748	0.4600
UMLS-TD*	0.2724	0.0810	0.4133	0.2503	0.0614	0.4667
PQE [5]	0.2796	0.0873	0.4733	0.2792	0.0762	0.4400
Wiki-TD [29]	0.2764	0.0881	0.4467	0.2418	0.0597	0.4267
Wiki-TD*	0.2883	0.0944	0.4600	0.2519	0.0633	0.4600
TREC best [22, 2]	0.2631	0.0757	0.4067	0.2928	0.0777	0.4467
INTGR-LS	0.3114	0.0993	0.4867	0.2987	0.0792	0.4800
INTGR	**0.3401**	**0.1229**	**0.5267**	**0.3135**	**0.0873**	**0.5200**

Table 4: Statistical significance and improvement in retrieval accuracy of the proposed method (INTGR) relative to its modification (INTGR-LS) and three best performing baselines (Wiki-TD, PQE and Wiki-TD*) on the query sets from the CDS track of TREC 2014 and 2015. $\star$ and † indicate statistically significant improvement with $p < 0.05$ and $p < 0.1$, respectively.

Query set	TREC 2014 CDS track			TREC 2015 CDS track		
Method	infNDCG	infAP	P@5	infNDCG	infAP	P@5
Wiki-TD	23.05%$\star$†	39.50%$\star$†	17.91%$\star$†	29.65%$\star$†	46.23%$\star$†	23.81%†
PQE	21.64%$\star$†	40.78%$\star$†	11.28%†	12.28%†	14.56%$\star$	18.18%$\star$†
Wiki-TD*	17.97%$\star$†	30.19%$\star$†	14.50%$\star$†	24.45%$\star$†	37.91%$\star$†	13.04%$\star$†
INTGR-LS	9.22%$\star$†	23.77%$\star$†	8.22%$\star$†	4.95%$\star$†	10.22%$\star$	8.33%$\star$†

Table 5: Comparison of effectiveness of different knowledge bases on the query sets from the CDS track of TREC 2014 and 2015.

Query set	TREC 2014 CDS track			TREC 2015 CDS track		
Method	infNDCG	infAP	P@5	infNDCG	infAP	P@5
INTGR using no knowledge bases	0.2673	0.0875	0.4601	0.2771	0.0758	0.4633
INTGR using only Wikipedia	0.2975 (11.30%)	0.0936 (6.97%)	0.4533 (-1.47%)	0.2954 (6.60%)	0.0779 (2.77%)	0.4667 (0.09%)
INTGR using only UMLS	0.3309 (23.79%)	0.1170 (33.71%)	0.5200 (13.02%)	0.3012 (8.67%)	0.0786 (3.93%)	0.5033 (7.93%)
INTGR using UMLS and Wikipedia	0.3401 (27.23%)	0.1229 (40.46%)	0.5267 (14.47%)	0.3135 (13.14%)	0.0873 (15.17%)	0.5200 (11.52%)

to the three main types of CDS queries: "Diagnosis", "Treatment" and "Test".

From tables 3 and 4, it follows that the proposed query representation method significantly outperforms all baselines in terms of all evaluation metrics and on both training and evaluation query sets. Furthermore, although INTGR was trained on the CDS track queries of TREC 2014 with the goal of maximizing infNDCG, INTGR also achieved significant (and, in many cases, even greater) improvement over the baselines in terms of other evaluation metrics (i.e., infAP and P@5) on both training and testing query sets. Also, as can be seen from Tables 3 and 4, the proposed method has significantly better performance when it is used in conjunction with graduated optimization method (INTGR) than when it is used with exhaustive line search (INTGR-LS), which we attribute to the ability of graduated optimization to efficiently find global optima of non-smooth and non-convex objective functions. Line search, on the other

hand, may miss global optima, if the step size is not sufficiently small. In general, choosing the appropriate step-size is non-trivial and can dramatically affect the performance of line search.

As follows from Table 3, methods that utilize semantic (Wiki-TD/Wiki-TD* and UMLS-TD/UMLS-TD*) and statistical (RM and PQE) concepts for query representation and expansion behave differently on training and evaluation query sets. In particular, methods using semantic concepts show better results than the methods based on statistical concepts on the training query set, while the methods based on statistical concepts show better results on evaluation query set. However, the proposed method (INTGR) provides excellent results on both query sets, which indicates the utility of accounting for both types of concepts in a retrieval method for CDS queries. On the other hand, Table 5 demonstrates that for the methods based on semantic concepts, UMLS is a better choice than Wikipedia with respect to all metrics, if only

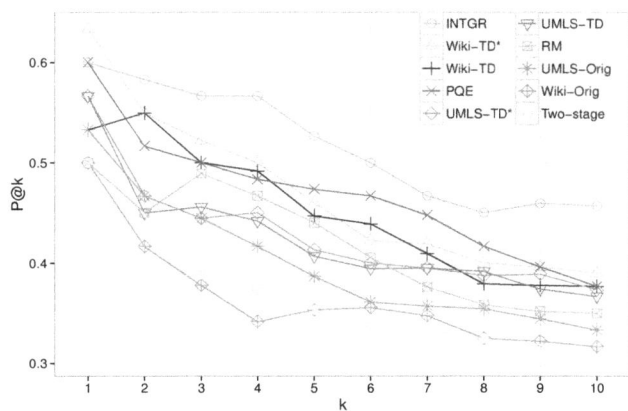

(a) TREC 2014 CDS track topics

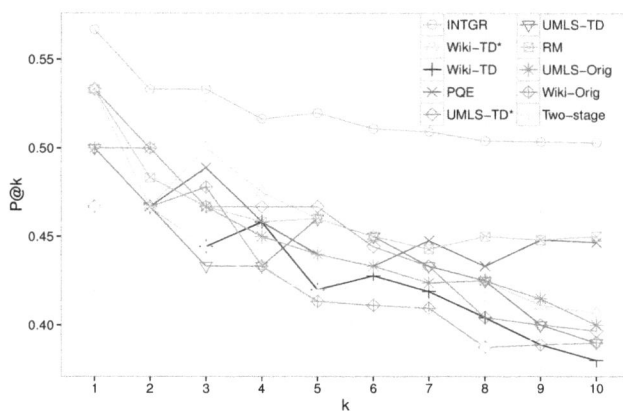

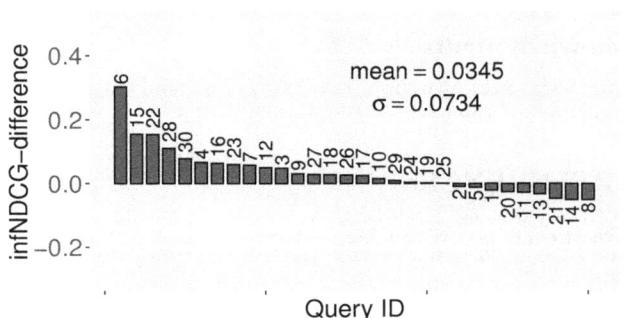

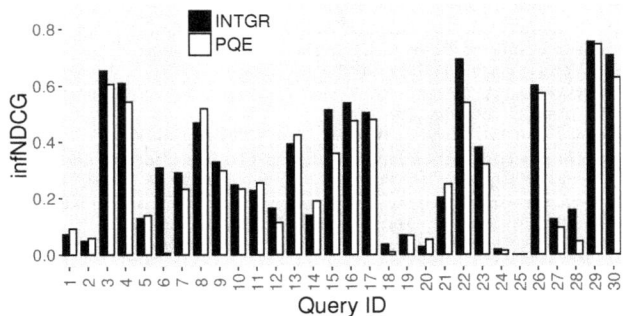

(b) TREC 2015 CDS track topics

Figure 4: Comparison of INTGR with the baselines in terms of P@k for $k \leq 10$ on the query sets from the CDS track of TREC 2014 and 2015.

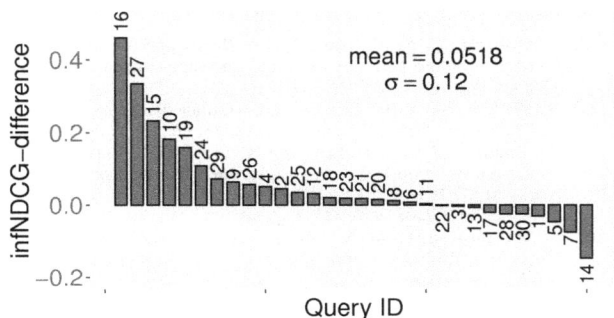

(a) TREC 2014 CDS track topics

(b) TREC 2015 CDS track topics

Figure 5: Topic-level differences of the infNDCG values for INTGR and the best-performing baselines (Wiki-TD* for TREC 2014 CDS track and PQE for TREC 2015 CDS track).

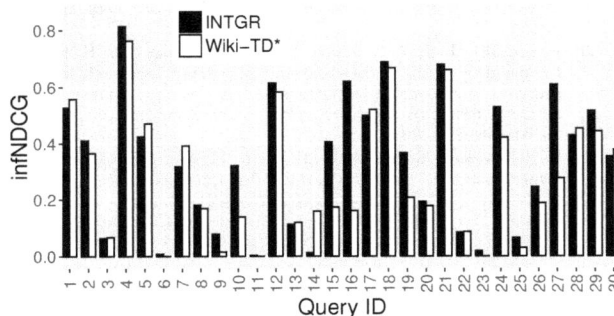

(a) TREC 2014 CDS track

(b) TREC 2015 CDS track

Figure 6: Topic-level comparison of the infNDCG values for INTGR, the best performing baselines (Wiki-TD* for TREC 2014 CDS track and PQE for TREC 2015 CDS track).

one knowledge repository is used. However, as follows from Table 5, combining both knowledge bases results in better retrieval accuracy than using any one of them individually.

Although from Figures 4 and 5 as well as Tables 3 and 4 it follows that INTGR has slightly lower accuracy improve-

ment over its best-performing baseline and Two-Stage on the testing query set than on the training query set, the improvement that INTGR achieves over Two-Stage is much higher than the improvement of the best performing baseline over Two-Stage. However, as follows from Figures 6 and

249

5, there is a greater number of topics on which `INTGR` has better retrieval accuracy than the best performing baseline on both training and testing query sets. Therefore, based on these observations, we can conclude that `INTGR` is robust to overfitting, due to its use of multiple and diverse relevance signals and concept sources.

5. CONCLUSION

In this paper, we proposed a method to represent CDS queries using statistical and semantic concepts from the query, top retrieved documents and knowledge bases. Our work logically extends previous research, which focused only on studying the utility of statistical query concepts [4], semantic query concepts [3], statistical and semantic query concepts [7], statistical [17, 5] and semantic [29] concepts from the query and top retrieved documents for query expansion. Experiments using a collection of PubMed articles and TREC Clinical Decision Support (CDS) track queries indicate that the proposed method significantly outperforms state-of-the-art baselines for ad hoc and medical IR.

Acknowledgments

This work was partially supported by the National Institutes of Health under the grant R21 DK108071-01A1.

6. REFERENCES

[1] A. R. Aronson and F.-M. Lang. An overview of MetaMap: historical perspective and recent advances. *Journal of the American Medical Informatics Association*, 17(3):229–236, 2010.

[2] S. Balaneshin-kordan, A. Kotov, and R. Xisto. WSU-IR at TREC 2015 clinical decision support track: Joint weighting of explicit and latent medical query concepts from diverse sources. In *Proceedings of TREC'15*, 2015.

[3] M. Bendersky and W. B. Croft. Discovering key concepts in verbose queries. In *Proceedings of SIGIR'08*, pages 491–498, 2008.

[4] M. Bendersky, D. Metzler, and W. B. Croft. Learning concept importance using a weighted dependence model. In *Proceedings of WSDM'10*, pages 31–40, 2010.

[5] M. Bendersky, D. Metzler, and W. B. Croft. Parameterized concept weighting in verbose queries. In *Proceedings of SIGIR'14*, pages 605–614, 2011.

[6] A. Blake and A. Zisserman. *Visual reconstruction*, volume 2. MIT press Cambridge, 1987.

[7] S. Choi, J. Choi, S. Yoo, H. Kim, and Y. Lee. Semantic concept-enriched dependence model for medical information retrieval. *Journal of Biomedical Informatics*, 47:18–27, 2014.

[8] J. I. Garcia-Gathright, F. Meng, and W. Hsu. UCLA at TREC 2014 clinical decision support track: Exploring language models, query expansion, and boosting. *Proceedings of TREC'14*, 2014.

[9] B. Koopman, G. Zuccon, P. Bruza, L. Sitbon, and M. Lawley. Information retrieval as semantic inference: a graph inference model applied to medical search. *Information Retrieval Journal*, 19(1-2):6–37, 2016.

[10] B. Koopman, G. Zuccon, A. Nguyen, D. Vickers, L. Butt, and P. Bruza. Exploiting SNOMED CT concepts & relationships for clinical information retrieval: Australian e-Health Research Centre and Queensland University of Technology at the TREC 2012 medical track. *Proceedings of TREC'12*, 2012.

[11] A. Kotov and C. Zhai. Tapping into knowledge base for concept feedback: leveraging conceptnet to improve search results for difficult queries. In *Proceedings of WSDM'12*, pages 403–412, 2012.

[12] V. Lavrenko and W. B. Croft. Relevance based language models. In *Proceedings of SIGIR'01*, pages 120–127, 2001.

[13] N. Limsopatham, C. Macdonald, and I. Ounis. Inferring conceptual relationships to improve medical records search. In *Proceedings of OAIR'13*, pages 1–8, 2013.

[14] J. Lin and D. Demner-Fushman. The role of knowledge in conceptual retrieval: a study in the domain of clinical medicine. In *Proceedings of SIGIR'06*, pages 99–106, 2006.

[15] Z. Lu, W. Kim, and W. J. Wilbur. Evaluation of query expansion using mesh in PubMed. *Information retrieval*, 12(1):69–80, 2009.

[16] D. Metzler and W. B. Croft. A Markov random field model for term dependencies. In *Proceedings of SIGIR'05*, pages 472–479, 2005.

[17] D. Metzler and W. B. Croft. Latent concept expansion using Markov random fields. In *Proceedings of SIGIR'07*, pages 311–318, 2007.

[18] D. Metzler and W. B. Croft. Linear feature-based models for information retrieval. *Information Retrieval*, 10(3):257–274, 2007.

[19] D. A. Metzler, W. B. Croft, and A. McCallum. Direct maximization of rank-based metrics for information retrieval. Technical report, CIIR, 2005.

[20] H. Mobahi and J. W. Fisher III. On the link between gaussian homotopy continuation and convex envelopes. In *EMMCVPR'15*, pages 43–56, 2015.

[21] W. Morgan, W. Greiff, and J. Henderson. Direct maximization of average precision by hill-climbing, with a comparison to a maximum entropy approach. In *Proceedings of NAACL-HLT'04*, pages 93–96, 2004.

[22] A. Mourao, F. Martins, and J. Magalhaes. NovaSearch at TREC 2014 clinical decision support track. *Proceedings of TREC'14*, 2014.

[23] K. Roberts, M. S. Simpson, E. Voorhees, and W. R. Hersh. Overview of the trec 2015 clinical decision support track. *Proceedings of TREC'15*, 2015.

[24] R. W. Schafer. What is a Savitzky-Golay filter?[lecture notes]. *IEEE Signal Processing Magazine*, 28(4):111–117, 2011.

[25] W. Shen, J.-Y. Nie, X. Liu, and X. Liui. An investigation of the effectiveness of concept-based approach in medical information retrieval GRIUM@ CLEF2014eHealthTask 3. *Proceedings of the ShARe/CLEF eHealth Evaluation Lab*, 2014.

[26] M. S. Simpson, E. M. Voorhees, and W. Hersh. Overview of the trec 2014 clinical decision support track. *Proceedings of TREC'14*, 2014.

[27] C. A. Sneiderman, D. Demner-Fushman, M. Fiszman, N. C. Ide, and T. C. Rindflesch. Knowledge-based methods to help clinicians find answers in MEDLINE. *Journal of the American Medical Informatics Association*, 14(6):772–780, 2007.

[28] L. Soldaini, A. Cohan, A. Yates, N. Goharian, and O. Frieder. Query reformulation for clinical decision support search. *Proceedings of TREC'14*, 2014.

[29] L. Soldaini, A. Cohan, A. Yates, N. Goharian, and O. Frieder. Retrieving medical literature for clinical decision support. In *Advances in Information Retrieval*, pages 538–549. Springer, 2015.

[30] P. Sondhi, J. Sun, C. Zhai, R. Sorrentino, and M. S. Kohn. Leveraging medical thesauri and physician feedback for improving medical literature retrieval for case queries. *Journal of the American Medical Informatics Association*, 19(5):851–858, 2012.

[31] P. Srinivasan. Retrieval feedback in MEDLINE. *Journal of the American Medical Informatics Association*, 3:157–167, 1996.

[32] C. Wang and R. Akella. Concept-based relevance models for medical and semantic information retrieval. In *Proceedings of CIKM'15*, pages 173–182, 2015.

[33] Y. Wang and H. Fang. Exploring the query expansion methods for concept based representation. *Proceedings of TREC'14*, 2014.

[34] Z. Xie, Y. Xia, and Q. Zhou. Incorporating semantic knowledge with MRF term dependency model in medical document retrieval. In *NLPCC'15*, pages 219–228. Springer, 2015.

[35] Y. Xu, G. J. Jones, and B. Wang. Query dependent pseudo-relevance feedback based on wikipedia. In *Proceedings of SIGIR'02*, pages 59–66, 2009.

[36] C. Zhai and J. Lafferty. Two-stage language models for information retrieval. In *Proceedings of SIGIR'02*, pages 49–56, 2002.

[37] M. Zhong and X. Huang. Concept-based biomedical text retrieval. In *Proceedings of SIGIR'06*, pages 723–724, 2006.

[38] W. Zhou, C. Yu, N. Smalheiser, V. Torvik, and J. Hong. Knowledge-intensive conceptual retrieval and passage extraction of biomedical literature. In *Proceedings of SIGIR'07*, pages 655–662, 2007.

Exploring Urban Lifestyles Using a Nonparametric Temporal Graphical Model*

Shoaib Jameel[1], Yi Liao[2], Wai Lam[2], Steven Schockaert[1], Xing Xie[3]
[1]School of Computer Science and Informatics, Cardiff University
[2]Dept. of Systems Engineering and Engineering Management, The Chinese University of Hong Kong
[3]Microsoft Research
{jameels1,schockaerts1}@cardiff.ac.uk   {yliao, wlam}@se.cuhk.edu.hk
xingx@microsoft.com

ABSTRACT

We propose a new unsupervised nonparametric temporal topic model to discover lifestyle patterns from location-based social networks. By relating the textual content, time stamps, and venue categories associated to user check-ins, our framework detects the predominant lifestyle patterns in a given geographic region. The temporal component of our model allows us to analyse the evolution of lifestyle patterns throughout the year. We provide examples of interesting patterns that have been discovered by our model, and we show that our model compares favourably to existing approaches in terms of lifestyle pattern quality and computation time. We also quantitatively show that our model outperforms existing methods in a time stamp prediction task.

Keywords

Graphical models, location-based social networks, text mining, lifestyle patterns, urban computing

1. INTRODUCTION

A city is more than a place in space, it is a drama in time. – Patrick Geddes

The lifestyles of different groups of people can differ considerably, and this is reflected in the types of places they visit. For example, an office worker may go to the office in the morning, visit a sandwich shop at midday, and go home in the evening. Moreover, these lifestyle patterns are not fixed, as people constantly adapt to changes in their environment [15, 9, 36], e.g., the changing weather across different seasons. Our aim in this paper is to characterize the predominant lifestyle patterns in a given geographic region, and to analyse how they evolve throughout the year.

In this paper, we will characterize lifestyle patterns from information that is shared publicly on location-based social networks (LBSNs) such as Facebook Places and Foursquare, which enable people to share information about the places they visit. A check-in or digital footprint, in this context, is a record of the venue which a user has visited along with a time stamp of that visit. Several authors have proposed models for analysing check-in data to get insights into human mobility patterns [35, 32]. For example, [35] proposed a hybrid model, based on a combination of two existing topic models, that combines check-in information with a friendship graph. While their method was able to discover some interesting results, it is computationally demanding and cannot discover interpretable patterns from small datasets. Most importantly, the model lacks a temporal component, which makes it harder to distinguish between some lifestyle patterns (e.g., office workers who go to the pub just after work, compared to students who go to the pub late in the evening) and means that it cannot be used to analyse changes over time.

In this paper, we present a new statistical model for discovering interpretable lifestyle patterns from check-in data in which we address the aforementioned issues. By relating the textual content, time stamps and venue categories associated with user check-ins, our framework detects the predominant lifestyle patterns for a given geographic region, where a lifestyle pattern is characterised by the kinds of places that are frequented by a given group of people at different times in the day and different days of the week. To tackle the pattern discovery problem, we develop an unsupervised nonparametric temporal topic model. The temporal component of our model allows us to analyse the evolution of lifestyle patterns throughout the year. To deal with sparsity issues in small datasets, we abstract away from raw check-in data, and instead consider latent venue types and discrete temporal units. This allows us, among others, to study lifestyle patterns at a finer spatial granularity or in areas of the world where the uptake of LBSNs is relatively limited.

*The work described in this paper is substantially supported by grants from the Research Grant Council of the Hong Kong Special Administrative Region, China (Project Codes: 14203414) and the Direct Grant of the Faculty of Engineering, CUHK (Project Code: 4055034). This work is also supported by ERC Starting Grant 637277. We thank Dr. Zhiyuan Cheng, Google for providing the raw check-in dataset and Prasanta Bhattacharya of the National University of Singapore for giving us valuable information about crawling data. This work was done when the first author was a Postdoctoral Fellow at the Chinese University of Hong Kong.

As we illustrate in Section 4, our method can be used to gain insight into the lifestyles of different groups of people in a given region. Among others, the obtained lifestyle patterns could provide valuable information for advertising, by informing marketers about when and where they can most effectively reach a particular target audience [22, 9]. The temporal component of the lifestyle patterns would also be useful for developing time-sensitive recommendation systems (e.g., not recommending sandwich shops to office workers during the weekend). Developing models of people's lifestyles could furthermore be useful for the field of medical science [1], although the fact that LBSNs only cover particular demographics would constitute an important drawback for such applications. While this could be alleviated by applying our model to data sources that have a wider coverage, such as credit card transaction data or mobile phone traces [35], a lack of access to such data sources means that we have not considered this in our experiments. It is important to note that the use of check-in data is mostly a matter of convenience. We indeed expect that other sources of data, such as credit card transactions and mobile phone logs would enable more detailed predictions. However, we believe that the model we propose could be straightforwardly applied to such data sources. The advantage of using check-in data is that this information is publicly available, which we believe makes it a suitable information source for developing and evaluating the model.

2. RELATED WORK

The most closely related work is [35], where the authors propose an approach that combines the relational topic model (RTM) [7] with the hierarchical latent Dirichlet allocation (hLDA) model [4] to discover so-called urban lifestyle patterns from LBSNs. Specifically, the output of this method is a hierarchical topical pattern, which closely resembles the tree structure generated by the hLDA model. Each node of this tree corresponds to a topic, where the further down the tree we go, the more specific these topics become. The topics are called living patterns in [35] and intuitively correspond to soft clusters of related venues, encoded as probability distributions over footprints. Each branch of the tree represents a lifestyle pattern. In other words, a lifestyle pattern corresponds to a set of living patterns, some of which are shared with many other lifestyle patterns (viz. those corresponding to nodes close to the root) while others may be more specific. The RTM component of the model is used to take into account a social friendship graph, capturing the intuition that friends tend to have similar lifestyles. As mentioned in the introduction, the main limitations of the approach from [35], which we address in our model, are the fact that it is computationally demanding, cannot discover interpretable patterns from small datasets and does not have a temporal component. In contrast to the approach from [35], our model generates flat patterns. The main reason why a tree structure is used in [35] is to capture correlations between different lifestyle patterns. However, this tree structure makes the model computationally too demanding, and as we will explain in the next section, in our model we can still capture correlations between lifestyles patterns, by using a two-level topic structure. Another important difference is that our model has a temporal component, which requires a considerably different posterior inference scheme than the one that was proposed in [35].

Some authors have already studied topic models with a temporal component. For example, [5] proposes a Markovian temporal topic model, which generates topics based on the change in co-occurrence information over time. A non-Markovian temporal topic model has been proposed in [31], based on the assumption that document time stamps are generated from a Beta distribution. Several temporal topic models that are specifically aimed at social network data have recently been proposed. Yin et al. [34] proposed topic models to capture user behaviour in social media. Their underlying assumption is that users' intrinsic interests depend on the temporal context. Some nonparametric temporal topic models have been proposed as well [10]. Temporal features have also been used in [28], which focuses on linking Twitter posts to external documents to improve the quality of topic models. However, to the best of our knowledge, temporal topic models have not yet been considered for studying lifestyle patterns. The reason why we need a new model to capture lifestyle patterns is that existing temporal topic models are aimed at modelling documents (which are associated with single time stamps) whereas we need to model user behaviour (which is associated with sequences of time stamps), and because lifestyles are best modelled using two levels of topics, as we will discuss below.

Some works have extended topic models with both temporal and spatial features. For example, Zhou et al. [38] proposed a location-time constrained topic model to capture Twitter events. In [16], the authors study urban dynamics using the LDA model [6], analysing the temporal and spatial nature of topics in a post-hoc step. Bauer et al. [2] proposed a topic model that considers both spatial and temporal features to model the topics discussed by Foursquare users, aiming to provide insights into the cultural idiosyncrasies of different cities. Temporal and spatial features are also prominent in approaches that study human mobility patterns. For example, [23] studies the structural and temporal changes in the spatial network formed by human movement patterns. Kim et al. [14] used the LDA model to discover topic-based place semantics without using any predefined semantic categories. In addition, the authors studied the temporal dynamics of the place semantics.

The idea of two-level topic models is also used in the Pachinko Allocation Model (PAM) [20], which generates super and sub-topics that can be represented as a directed acyclic graph. A nonparametric extension to the PAM model has been proposed in [19]. A nonparametric extension of PAM for short texts has been proposed in [26]. In [25] and [12], graphical models have been proposed that generate a hierarchy of topics, aimed respectively at document co-clustering and topic segmentation. In [37], a hierarchical topic structure is proposed consisting of different levels of the Hierarchical Dirichlet Processes (HDP) [27] model. Our model is significantly different from the above graphical models, which do not consider the change of topics over time. Moreover, in contrast to the PAM model, our model does not impose any arbitrary relationships on the hierarchy.

3. OUR FRAMEWORK

A lifestyle pattern in our model corresponds to a probability distribution over lifestyle topics, which are in turn probability distributions over abstract footprints (see below). Lifestyle topics play a similar role as the living patterns in [35], but they are based on latent venue categories rather than individual venues and they incorporate a temporal component. Intuitively, a lifestyle topic models one aspect of a given lifestyle. By describing lifestyles in terms of such topics, we allow the model to make explicit the commonalities between different lifestyles. This high-level view makes lifestyle patterns easier to interpret and enables us to more clearly describe how two lifestyle patterns differ or how a given lifestyle pattern changes over time. Moreover, the fact that lifestyle patterns can share lifestyle topics means that fewer parameters have to be learned, leading to more robust results.

An important issue in dealing with check-in data is sparsity, as we may only have limited information about some venues. This problem is exacerbated by our use of a temporal component, which requires sufficient numbers of check-ins for different times of the day, days of the week and months of the year. To deal with this issue, we abstract away from specific venues and specific time stamps, as we explain in Section 3.1. This design makes our model more reliable, essentially avoiding overfitting by estimating topics from the abstract check-in behaviour of many users. In Section 3.2, we then introduce the graphical model which relates the resulting abstract footprints to lifestyle patterns. Section 3.3 explains how we can do posterior inference in this model to discover these lifestyle patterns.

3.1 Dealing with Sparsity

The input to our method consists of a set of check-ins for each user, along with the user comments associated with the check-ins and the tags and categories associated with each venue. Rather than estimating lifestyles from the check-in data directly, we first convert each check-in to an abstract footprint, in which the specific name of the venue is replaced by a venue category. While we could use the categories provided by Foursquare and similar services, the taxonomies which are used by these LBSNs are not always sufficiently fine-grained. Moreover, these taxonomies are LBSN-specific, which causes problems when we want to integrate check-in data from different LBSNs.

To obtain a suitable category structure, we first represent each venue as a bag of words, consisting of (i) the tags associated with each venue, (ii) the names of the categories assigned to the venue, and (iii) the nouns and adjectives occurring in the user comments associated with the venue. To generate the venue categories that will be used in the abstract footprints, we then use the Hierarchical Dirichlet Process (HDP) model, a nonparametric counterpart of the well-known Latent Dirichlet Allocation (LDA) method in which the appropriate number of topics is chosen automatically based on the characteristics of the data. The output of the HDP method consists of a number of latent topics, which we will interpret as venue categories. Note that each venue category is thus represented as a probability distribution over words. Finally, we assign a label to each of the discovered venue categories. To this end, we select the most representative word from each probability distribution using the PMI based technique from [18]. In cases where there is more than one category with the same label, the second most representative word is added to the label. While this method is simpler than some other existing label selection methods [17, 21, 18], we found it to yield good results in this context.

The time stamp associated with check-in records will be used in two ways. First we will use it to analyse how lifestyle

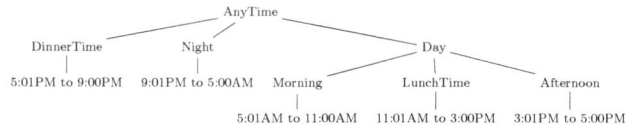

Figure 1: Intra-day temporal concept ontology

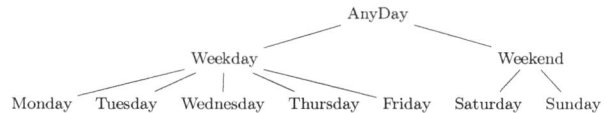

Figure 2: Intra-week temporal concept ontology

topics evolve throughout the year. Second, the lifestyle topics themselves will have a temporal component, which relates venues to times of the day and days of the week. For example, we may want to express that a given group of people tends to go to the pub in the evening on weekdays. For the latter purpose, we consider the discrete temporal units shown in Figures 1 and 2. Note that the boundaries of units such as Morning are necessarily somewhat arbitrary. Although we could learn appropriate boundaries from data (e.g., making the boundaries dependent on the geographic region), the definitions in Figures 1 and 2 will be sufficient to explain the main principles. The aim of these temporal units is to allow us to express information about the context of typical visits. This idea could be extended to capture weather information (e.g., allowing us to express that some group of people tends to go to the beach on sunny days) or particular types of recurring events (e.g., train strikes, bank holidays, school holidays, sales periods). Including such additional context factors offers scope for making the proposed model more useful in practice, but it does not affect any of the technical details.

In summary, we represent each check-in record as an abstract footprint, which is composed of a venue category, an intra-day time unit and an intra-week time unit. An example of an abstract footprint is [Restaurant:(LunchTime, Weekday)].

3.2 Lifestyle Pattern Discovery

For each user, we construct a user activity document, consisting of the abstract footprints that correspond to the user's check-ins. In this section, we propose a novel Bayesian nonparametric graphical model for discovering lifestyle patterns from a given set of such user activity documents. Specifically, the model will discover lifestyle topics, which intuitively correspond to soft clusters of abstract footprints, and lifestyle patterns, which intuitively correspond to soft clusters of lifestyle topics. At the same time, lifestyle patterns will correspond to hard clusters of users. An example of a lifestyle topic is:

{[Office:(Weekday,Morning) 0.5],
[Restaurant:(Weekday,LunchTime) 0.2],
[Gym:(Weekday,DinnerTime) 0.1],...}

where the probabilities reflect the proportions of check-ins that correspond to each abstract footprint. Note that lifestyle topics are similar to the topics that are considered in LDA, but instead of considering distributions over unigrams, we consider distributions over abstract footprints. Lifestyle patterns capture the intuition that there will typically be several lifestyle topics that apply to a given user. For example, an office worker who enjoys going for a hike in the weekend may be modelled as a mixture of an "office-worker" topic and an "outdoor" topic. In the model, each user will be assigned to one of the lifestyle patterns. The output can thus be interpreted as a clustering of users, where each cluster corresponds to a lifestyle pattern.

Each user activity document corresponds to a single lifestyle pattern, but is associated with a mixture of different lifestyle topics. Therefore, the lifestyle topics are sampled from a Dirichlet process whereas hierarchical Dirichlet processes are used to generate samples from the lifestyle topics. To generate the abstract footprints of a user activity document, we first sample a lifestyle pattern. Given that lifestyle pattern, we then sample a sequence of lifestyle topics for the document, each time also sampling an abstract footprint from the lifestyle topic.

Figure 3 depicts the model in plate notation, where plates signify repetition of variables and latent variables are represented in unshaded circles. Note that our model captures various interactions of the user with respect to the location, time, activity, and comments all in a unified model. In addition, interactions between topic hierarchies are also modelled in the same graphical model, which makes our task more challenging. The number of repetitions for the inner larger plate corresponds to the number $|C|$ of abstract footprints in a given user's activity document, while the number of repetitions for the outer plate corresponds to the number of users $|U|$. The observed variables correspond to the abstract footprints f_i and their time stamp t_i.

The variable ω is the parameter or hyperparameter of the Dirichlet process associated with the lifestyle patterns. The variable α represents the distribution over lifestyle patterns. Each user corresponds to a specific lifestyle pattern l, which is drawn from the distribution α. The lifestyle pattern l is used to determine a probability distribution θ over lifestyle topics for the user. Specifically, θ is obtained from a Dirichlet process mixture, based on a corpus-wide distribution of lifestyle topics π and a vector τ_l of hyperparameters that is dependent on the chosen lifestyle pattern l. These hyperparameters are encoded for each lifestyle pattern l in the matrix τ. Note that because of the two-level topic structure, a matrix of hyperparameters is needed, as opposed to a vector in traditional HDP models. The variable γ is the hyperparameter of π. The distribution θ is subsequently used to assign a lifestyle topic z_i to each abstract footprint in the corresponding user activity document. The matrix Ψ defines each of the lifestyle topics as a probability distribution over abstract footprints. It depends on the vector ρ, whose dimension is equal to the number of footprints in the vocabulary. In particular, ρ determines a Dirichlet distribution, so a sample from ρ is a distribution over footprints.

The remaining variables of our model aim to capture how the prevalence of lifestyle topics evolves throughout the year. The observed variable t_i in Figure 3 corresponds to the time stamp associated with abstract footprint f_i, at a given level of granularity, e.g., t_i could be the month or season in which the check-in occurred. While we will only consider discrete time units in the analysis of the lifestyle pattern, assuming a continuous distribution in the underlying model allows for a more faithful analysis [10, 31, 29]. The discrete time com-

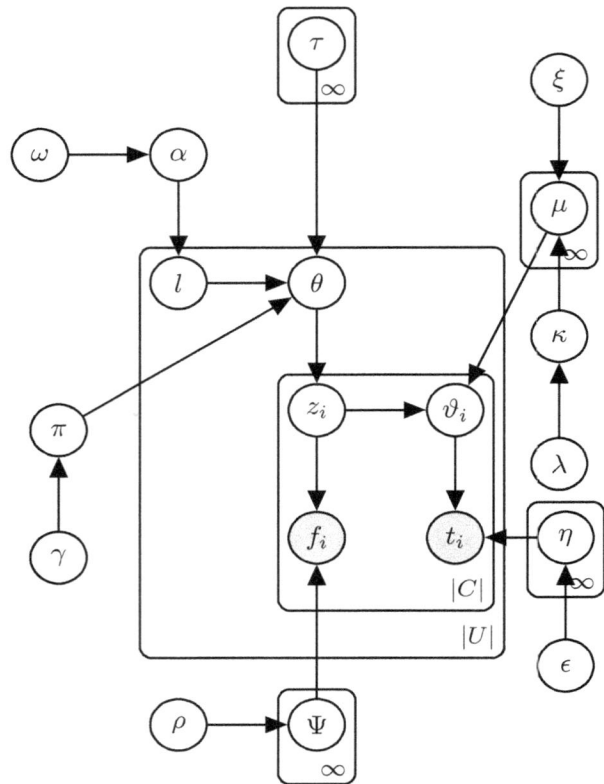

Figure 3: Graphical representation of our model.

ponent t_i of footprint f_i is modelled using a hierarchical Dirichlet process mixture of Gaussians, which is a distribution suitable to model multimodal variation on an unbounded timeframe. In addition, it can maintain tractable inference. To allow a flexible distribution over time, we use a Dirichlet process as the mixing measure. In particular, for each lifestyle topic z_i, a distribution μ_{z_i} of temporal components is obtained from a Dirichlet process with parameters ξ and κ, where κ depends on the hyperparameter λ. Each of these temporal components μ_{z_i} is associated with a Gaussian η_{z_i}, which has been sampled from a Normal-Inverse Gamma distribution (whose four parameters are denoted by ϵ in the graphical model for simplicity). Note that the components of the mixtures of Gaussians are thus shared among different lifestyle topics, which allows us to model correlations between the evolution of different topics.

The hyperparameters ω, γ, and τ are estimated from the data. To this end, we place hyper-hyperpriors or hyper-hyperparameters on these hyperparameters (not shown in Figure 3). The idea of using hyper-hyperpriors has already been adopted in some topic models such as [4, 27], where the aim is to find the posterior of the hyperparameters based on the data characteristics rather than explicitly specifying the hyperparameter values. However, we manually set weak hyperparameter values for the priors ρ, ξ, λ, and ϵ, as we found that automatically inferring the values of these parameters did not affect the results much in this case, while setting these values manually makes inference more efficient. The complete generative process of our model is as follows:

1. Draw a global base distribution over latent lifestyle patterns $\alpha|\omega \sim \mathbf{GEM}(\omega)^1$.

2. Draw a global base distribution over time component distributions $\kappa|\lambda \sim \mathbf{GEM}(\lambda)$

3. For each lifestyle topic $z = 1, 2, \cdots$

   (a) Draw a distribution over abstract footprints $\Psi_z|\rho \sim \mathbf{Dirichlet}(\rho)$

   (b) Draw a distribution over time components $\mu_z|\xi, \kappa \sim \mathbf{DP}(\xi, \kappa)$

4. For each time component $t = 1, 2, \cdots$

   (a) Draw a distribution over time $\eta_t|\epsilon \sim \mathbf{Normal\text{-}inverse}$ $\mathbf{Gamma}(\epsilon)$

5. For each user document $u = 1, 2, \cdots, |U|$

   (a) Draw the lifestyle pattern $l|\omega \sim \omega$

   (b) Draw a distribution over lifestyle topics $\theta|l, \pi, \tau \sim \mathbf{DP}(\pi, \tau_l)$

   (c) For each abstract footprint $f_i, i = 1, 2, \cdots, |C|$ in the user activity document

      i. Draw the lifestyle topic $z_i|\theta \sim \theta$

      ii. Draw the abstract footprint $f_i|\Psi_{z_i} \sim \mathbf{Multinomial}(\Psi_{z_i})$

      iii. Draw a time component indicator $\vartheta_i|\mu_{z_i} \sim \mu_{z_i}$

      iv. Draw a time-stamp $t_i|\eta \sim \eta_{\vartheta_i}$

3.3 Posterior Inference

We use Gibbs sampling to perform posterior inference. As in some existing nonparametric topic models [10], we adopt a marginalization technique to speed up posterior inference, where we marginalize over the temporal distributions in order to sample lifestyle topics, and then sample the temporal distribution conditioned on the lifestyle topics. Note that this only has a minimal impact on the quality of the desired posterior [10]. In order to compute the posterior of the hyper-hyperpriors, we interleave the Metropolis Hastings (MH) steps between iterations of the Gibbs sampler to obtain new values of the hyper-hyperpriors. After some iterations of the sampler, these values are computed and updated and the sampler moves forward with the updated values. Computing the posterior of the hyper-hyperpriors using Gamma distributions has been discussed in [27].

In our model, there is an unbounded number of lifestyle patterns and an unbounded number of lifestyle topics. Note that because of the two-level topic structure, existing posterior inference methods such as those used in the HDP model or in [10] cannot be directly applied. In our model, the Dirichlet process which is responsible for generating the lifestyle patterns generates an infinite number of HDPs. Each of these HDPs is comprised of a time HDP and a lifestyle topic HDP, which are responsible for generating temporal assignments and lifestyle topics assignments respectively. The Gibbs sampling algorithm also has to take into account that topic distributions might change over time. Although the sampling mechanism which we propose is similar to sampling in

other temporal topic models [29, 31, 10], an important difference is that each of the abstract footprints have their own time stamp. Therefore, our Gibbs sampler needs to sample lifestyle topics in the usual way, but in addition, it has to compute the change in the lifestyle topic patterns over time. This sampling model is also different from [35], which borrows the Gibbs sampling procedure of the hLDA model [4], where the sampler determines the topic hierarchies.

To enable Gibbs sampling, we need to derive the sampling equations to generate the lifestyle patterns and topics. For sampling the lifestyle patterns, we can use the Gibbs sampling method of the stick breaking construction of the Dirichlet process mixture model. Specifically, the method to find out the lifestyle patterns follows the Chinese Restaurant Process (CRP) scheme of the Dirichlet process mixture models. We refer to [11] for a detailed explanation of this standard sampling procedure. Note that we can only give a brief overview of the sampling equations of our model in this section. Some of the derivations are not shown here, as they can easily be derived from the derivations of the existing HDP model, as both models make an exchangeability assumption. For example, sampling the abstract footprint in a lifestyle topic, conditioned on time, closely resembles the HDP based sampling mechanism. The only difference is that the vector of hyperparameters τ_l depends on the lifestyle pattern l assigned to that document.

To generate the lifestyle topics given a lifestyle pattern l, we use a sampling mechanism with two types of HDPs, one for the abstract footprints and another for the temporal component, the latter being associated with a Gaussian distribution over time. Accordingly, each abstract footprint will have two assignments: a lifestyle topic assignment and a temporal assignment. In each iteration, both assignments need to be sampled.

For abstract footprints, we denote the global pool of lifestyle topics associated with lifestyle pattern l as $\mathbf{k}_l$. This global pool is reminiscent of the set of available dishes in the Chinese restaurant Franchise (CRF) analogy for the HDP model. In addition to the global pool of lifestyle topics, we have a pool of local lifestyle topic assignments $\mathbf{z}_l$, specifying a lifestyle topic z_{il}^u for each abstract footprint f_i^u in each user activity document u. This pool of assignments is reminiscent of the tables in the Chinese restaurant analogy. The mechanism is that we first sample a topic k_l from the global pool of lifestyle topics, and then k_l is added to one of the local assignments in the pool $\mathbf{z}_l$, which corresponds to assigning a lifestyle topic to one of the abstract footprints in the corresponding user activity document. Each local assignment can involve several topics k_l, as a user activity document is considered to be a mixture of different lifestyle topics.

Let $h_{k_l}^{\neg f_i^u}$ denote the conditional density associated with the abstract footprint f_i^u in a lifestyle pattern l, given the mixture component k_l and all lifestyle topic assignments except f_i^u. In other words, $h_{k_l}^{\neg f_i^u}(f_i^u)$ is the probability that f_i^u belongs to the topic k_l. Throughout this section, whenever we place the $\neg$ symbol, it means that we are ignoring that variable in the counts. Marginal counts are represented with dots. Let h denote the probability density function of H, where H is a base measure. Let g denote one of the components from $G(\Psi)$, which is the emission distribution. As in the usual topic modeling approach, H can be assumed to be a Dirichlet distribution over the vocabulary and G

---

[1]Recall that $\mathbf{GEM}$ is a one-parameter stochastic process obtained from the $\mathbf{Beta}(a, b)$ distribution where $a = 1$ [24].

is a topic-word multinomial distribution. We estimate the probability $h_{k_l}^{\neg f_i^u}(f_i^u)$ as follows:

$$\frac{\int h_l(f_i^u|\Psi_{k_l}) \prod_{k_l'} \prod_{(u',i')\neq(u,i),z_{i'l}^{u'}=k_l'} h_l(f_{i'}^{u'}|\Psi_{k_l'})g(\Psi_{k_l'})\mathrm{d}\Psi_{k_l'}}{\int \prod_{k_l'} \prod_{(u',i')\neq(u,i),z_{i'l}^{u'}=k_l'} h_l(f_{i'}^{u'}|\Psi_{k_l'})g(\Psi_{k_l'})\mathrm{d}\Psi_{k_l'}} \tag{1}$$

where z_i^u is the lifestyle topic that has been assigned to the abstract footprint f_i^u for a lifestyle pattern l. It can be shown that:

$$h_{k_l}^{\neg f_i^u}(f_i^u) = \frac{\rho + n_{lzv}^{\neg ui}}{V\rho + n_{lz.}^{\neg ui}} \tag{2}$$

where n_{lzv} is the number of times an abstract footprint v has been sampled in a topic $z = k_l$ and $n_{lz.}$ denotes the number of abstract footprints belonging to the topic $z = k_l$. The form of $g(\Psi_{k_l})$ is as follows:

$$g(\Psi_{k_l}) = \mathrm{Dirichlet}(\rho) = \frac{\Gamma(\sum_{v=1}^V \rho_v)}{\prod_{v=1}^V \Gamma(\rho_v)} \prod_{v=1}^V \Psi_{lzv}^{\rho_v - 1} \tag{3}$$

where Γ denotes the Gamma function. We also need to derive the link between the pool of local lifestyle topic assignments $\mathbf{z}_l$ and the global pool of lifestyle topics $\mathbf{k}_l$. Let $\mathbf{f}_u^z$ be the set of all abstract footprints assigned with lifestyle topic z in the user activity document u. Changing the topic assignment of all abstract footprints in $\mathbf{f}_u^z$ changes the component membership of all data items associated with that topic. Let us write $h_{k_l}^{\neg \mathbf{f}_u^z}(\mathbf{f}_u^z)$ for the likelihood of the assignment of $\mathbf{f}_u^z$ to topic z, given all data items associated with mixture component k_l leaving out $\mathbf{f}_u^z$. It is evaluated as follows:

$$\frac{\int \prod_{k_l} \prod_{f_i^u \in \mathbf{f}_u^z} h_l(f_i^u|\Psi_{k_l}) \prod_{f_{i'}^{u'} \notin \mathbf{f}_u^z, z_{i'l}^{u'}=k_l} h_l(f_{i'}^{u'}|\Psi_{k_l})g(\Psi_{k_l})\mathrm{d}\Psi_{k_l}}{\prod_{f_{i'}^{u'} \notin \mathbf{f}_u^z, z_{i'l}^{u'}=k_l} h_l(f_{i'}^{u'}|\Psi_{k_l})g(\Psi_{k_l})\mathrm{d}\Psi_{k_l}} \tag{4}$$

It can be shown that the above equation can be written as:

$$\frac{\prod_{v=1}^V \Gamma(\rho + n_{lzv})}{\Gamma(V\rho + n_{lz.})} \cdot \frac{\Gamma(V\rho + n_{lz.}^{\neg f_i^u})}{\prod_v \Gamma(\rho + n_{lzv}^{\neg f_i^u})} \tag{5}$$

where n_{lzv} is the number of times an abstract footprint v has been sampled in a topic $z = k_l$, where z is one of the topics from the global pool of lifestyle topics $\mathbf{k}_l$ associated with lifestyle pattern l; $n_{lzv}^{\neg f_i^u}$ denotes the number of times an abstract footprint v has been sampled excluding the current abstract footprint for user u from the count, V denotes the number of unique abstract footprints in the entire dataset and $n_{lk.}$ denotes the number of abstract footprints associated with lifestyle topic $z = k_l$. Let $n_{lzv}^{\neg uz}$ denote the number of abstract footprints with $z = k_l$ as one of the topics from the global pool of lifestyle topics $\mathbf{k}_l$ associated with lifestyle pattern l excluding the current topic assignment.

In order to sample the temporal dynamics of the lifestyle topics, we define the conditional distribution of the lifestyle topics given the temporal information. This definition is as follows:

$$P(z_i^u|\mathbf{z}^{\neg ui},\mathbf{k},\mathbf{t},l)P(f_i^u,t_i^u|z_i^u,\mathbf{f}^{\neg ui},\mathbf{t}^{\neg ui},\mathbf{z}^{\neg ui},\boldsymbol{\vartheta}^{\neg ui},l) \tag{6}$$

Let m_{luk} denote the number of lifestyle topics associated with k_l in the user activity document u. Let n_{luk} denote the number of abstract footprints associated with the global topic k_l in u. Let $m_{l..}$ denote the total number of lifestyle topics associated with k_l in all user activity documents. Let $\mathbf{r}$ denote the global pool of time components. Let R denote the number of time related components which can increase or decrease. Let $c_{lk\vartheta}$ denote the number of abstract footprints associated with lifestyle topic k_l drawn from the global pool and time component ϑ. Let e_r denote the total number of time components associated with r. Then (6) can be written as:

$$\begin{cases} n_{luk}^{\neg ui} \frac{\rho+n_{lzv}^{\neg ui}}{V\rho+n_{lz.}^{\neg ui}} \sum_{\vartheta_i} \frac{c_{lk\vartheta}^{\neg ui}}{c_{lk.}^{\neg ui}+\xi} S_r^{\mathbf{t}}(t_i^u) + \\ \frac{\xi}{c_{lk.}^{\neg ui}+\xi}\left(\sum_{r=1}^R \frac{e_r}{e.+\lambda}S_r^{\mathbf{t}^{\neg ui}}(t_i^u) + \frac{\lambda}{e.+\lambda}S_{r_{\mathrm{new}}}(t_i^u)\right) \\ \quad \text{if it is an existing lifestyle topic} \\ \tau l \left(\sum_{k_l=1}^K \frac{m_{luk}}{m_{l..}+\gamma}\frac{\rho+n_{lzv}^{\neg ui}}{V\rho+n_{lz.}^{\neg ui}} + \frac{\gamma}{m_{l..}+\gamma}\frac{\Gamma(V\rho)}{\prod_v \Gamma(\rho)}\frac{\Gamma(\rho+1)\prod_{w\neq v}\Gamma(\rho)}{\Gamma(V\rho+1)} \right) \\ \sum_{\vartheta_i} \frac{c_{lk\vartheta}^{\neg ui}}{c_{lk.}^{\neg ui}+\xi} S_r^{\mathbf{t}}(t_i^u) + \frac{\xi}{c_{lk.}^{\neg ui}+\xi}\left(\sum_{r=1}^R \frac{e_r}{e.+\lambda}S_r^{\mathbf{t}^{\neg ui}}(t_i^u) + \right. \\ \left. \frac{\lambda}{e.+\lambda}S_{r_{\mathrm{new}}}(t_i^u)\right) \quad \text{if a new lifestyle topic is drawn} \end{cases}$$

Finally, $S_r^{\mathbf{t}^{\neg ui}}(t_i^u)$ is the posterior predictive time distribution, defined as follows:

$$\int_0^\infty \frac{1}{\overline{\sigma}}\exp(-\frac{1}{2\overline{\sigma}^2}n(\overline{\mu}-\overline{x})^2)\overline{\sigma}^{-\nu-2}\exp(-\frac{\nu s^2}{2\overline{\sigma}^2})\mathrm{d}\overline{\sigma}^2 \tag{7}$$

where $\overline{\mu}$ is the uninformative location mean prior, $\overline{\sigma}$ is the uninformative scale prior, $\overline{x}$ is the sample mean, n is the total number of sample points, ν is the number of degrees of freedom and s is the sample variance.

In order to resample the component memberships of all the data items associated with the lifestyle topic z, we marginalize over the time assignments of all the abstract footprints, as the sampler will otherwise be too slow to converge. In order to speed up this process, we adopt a selective block based procedure where we conduct approximation only for a subset of the abstract footprints associated with that lifestyle topic. We write the estimates as $P_{\mathrm{est}}(\mathbf{t})$, which will be used to estimate the true Gibbs sampling probabilities. The process can be written as:

$$P(k_{luz=\mathrm{new}}|z_i^u,\mathbf{f}^{\neg uk},\mathbf{t}^{\neg uk},\mathbf{z}^{\neg uk},\boldsymbol{\vartheta}^{\neg uk},l) \propto$$

$$\begin{cases} m_{l.k}^{\neg uz=k_l} \frac{\prod_{v=1}^V \Gamma(\rho+n_{lkv}^{\neg uz=k_l})}{\Gamma(V\rho+n_{lk.}^{\neg uz=k_l})} \cdot \frac{\Gamma(V\rho+n_{lk.}^{\neg uz=k_l})}{\prod_v \Gamma(\rho+n_{lkv}^{\neg uz=k_l})} P_{\mathrm{est}}(\mathbf{t}) & k_l \text{ is existing} \\ \gamma \frac{\Gamma(V\rho)\prod_v \Gamma(\rho+n_{l.v}^{\neg uz=k_{\mathrm{new}}})}{\Gamma(V\rho+n_{l..}^{\neg uz=k_{\mathrm{new}}})\prod_v \Gamma(\rho)} P_{\mathrm{est}}(\mathbf{t}) & k_l = k_{\mathrm{new}} \end{cases} \tag{8}$$

4. EXPERIMENTAL RESULTS

In this section we present a number of qualitative and quantitative results. In particular, we provide several examples of lifestyle patterns that have been discovered by our method (Section 4.1), and we illustrate how the model can be used to analyse the temporal variation in the importance of lifestyle topics. We present quantitative results related to lifestyle pattern quality discovery (Section 4.2). We then present an analysis of the required running time (Section

4.3). We also quantitatively compare our method against state-of-the-art comparative models on a time stamp prediction task (Section 4.4).

The raw dataset used in the experiments has been obtained from the lead author of [8], who initially obtained it from Foursquare check-ins reported on Twitter over a period of five months. This dataset contains check-in data, including any associated user comments, but only contains the IDs of the venues. Using these IDs, we have crawled additional venue description data from Foursquare using its public API, collecting the tags, categories, name and location of each venue. We refer interested readers to find the statistics and additional details about the dataset from [8]. We have considered the following countries in our experiments: USA (approximately 8 million check-ins, 93,501 users and 879,476 venues), India (approximately 800,000 check-ins, 2220 users and 12,277 venues), Singapore (approximately 500,000 check-ins, 1207 users and 18,082 venues), Hong Kong (approximately 400,000 check-ins, 3788 users and 5282 venues), Australia (approximately 1 million check-ins, 1000 users and 30,880 venues) and Indonesia (approximately 6 million check-ins, 69,805 users and 302,725 venues). Note that the friendship graph that was used in [35] is no longer publicly available, due to a change in the sharing policies adopted by the content providers.

In all experiments, the Gibbs sampler for our model is run for 1000 iterations, which we empirically found was sufficient for the parameters of the model to converge. We have set $\rho = 0.01$, $\xi = 0.02$, $\epsilon = 0.01$, and $\lambda = 0.05$ which represent weak prior values as we have found experimentally that selecting different weak prior values did not have much impact on the results. The following Gamma priors have been placed on the hyperparameter values: $\omega = \text{Gamma}(1.0, 1.0)$, $\tau = \text{Gamma}(1.0, 10.0)$ and $\gamma = \text{Gamma}(1.0, 1.0)$. While these priors have parameters, such hyper-hyperparameters have a much weaker impact on the inference results than fixing the original hyperparameters for these distributions [4, 3].

4.1 Illustrative Example

Figure 4 displays some of the lifestyle patterns that have been discovered from the USA check-in data by our approach. In the figures, each dot corresponds to a lifestyle pattern while each text box shows the most prominent abstract footprints of a given lifestyle topic. Arrows in the diagram indicate which lifestyle topics are associated with which lifestyle patterns. Since different lifestyle patterns can share the same lifestyle topics, overlap between lifestyle patterns is made clear. To generate these diagrams from the graphical model, we have adopted the following procedure. For each lifestyle pattern x, we rank the lifestyle topics y according to the corresponding Dirichlet parameter τ_{xy}. After the model is trained, it outputs the change in topic distributions over time. We can use this information to present results based on any desired temporal granularity level, such as seasons, by doing a post-hoc analysis. For example, some lifestyle topics will have a high probability in some seasons and a much lower probability in other seasons. Figure 4 highlights some topics which are specific to summer and some topics which are specific to winter.

The lifestyle patterns in Figure 4 intuitively correspond to students, researchers and office workers. The figure makes explicit the common aspects of their lifestyles, e.g., every

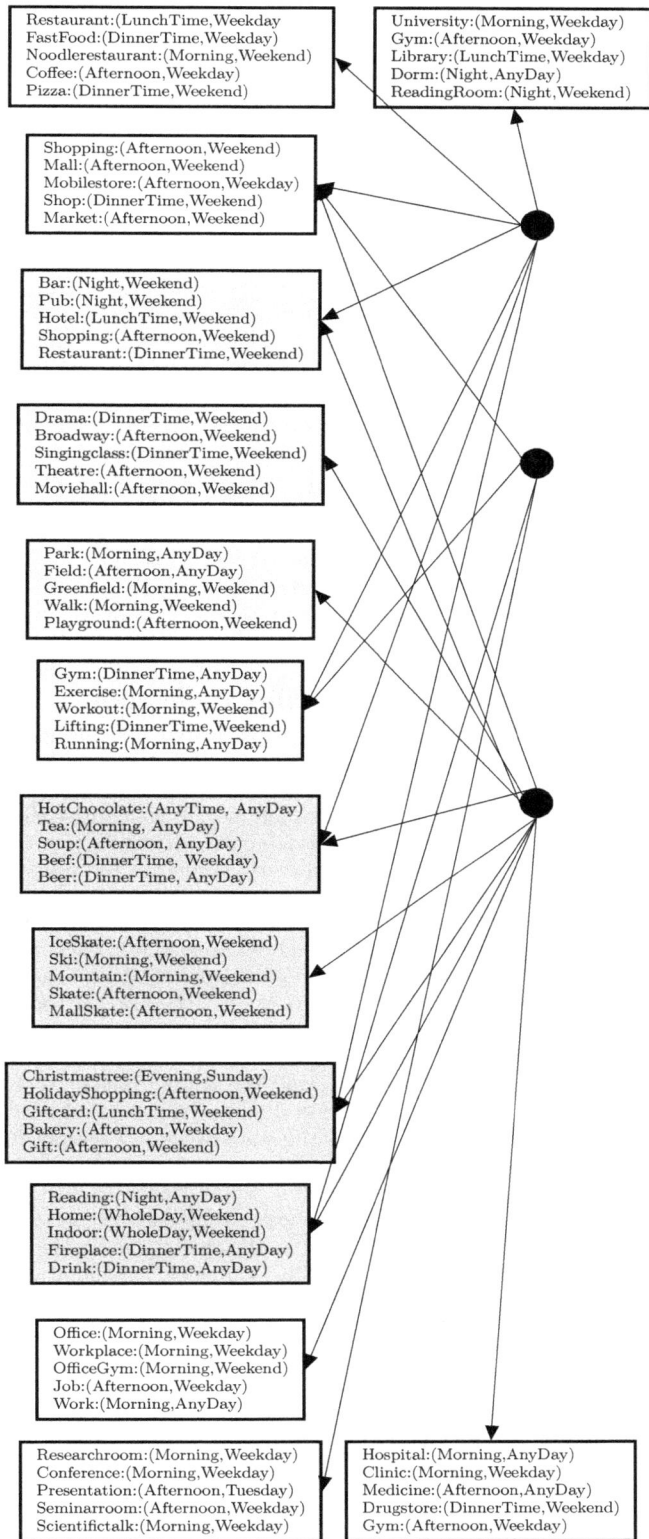

Figure 4: **Combined lifestyle patterns of some people in the USA. In the figure, the coloured light green rectangles represent the living patterns in summer and coloured light red rectangles represent the living patterns during the winter season.**

257

group is associated with a shopping related lifestyle topic. Furthermore, the summer and winter specific topics clearly show how people's lifestyles change based on the seasons, e.g., researchers and office workers go to the park in summer while rather staying at home and reading a book in winter. Other winter specific topics are related to hot drinks, winter sports and Christmas shopping.

In [35], lifestyle patterns are modelled as branches of a tree, where common topics appear towards the top of the tree, while topics that are specific to particular groups appear further down. While this tree representation captures commonalities between different lifestyles in a natural way, it relies on the rather restrictive assumption that a single hierarchical clustering of individuals can be found that explains all commonalities between people's lifestyle patterns. In contrast, in our model commonalities are modelled by having topics that are connected to many lifestyle patterns. This allows us to model various forms of overlap between groups of users. For example, a university related topic may apply to both students and professors (but not office workers), while an office environment related topic may apply to both professors and office workers (but not students). A single tree representation would not be able to capture both types of commonality.

4.2 Lifestyle Pattern Quality Evaluation

We evaluate the quality of the discovered lifestyle patterns by comparing our model with temporal as well as non-temporal topic models. One recent work that can discover lifestyle patterns is the one described in [35], which uses the hLDA model to generate a lifestyle spectrum (i.e. a tree of lifestyle patterns). We cannot directly apply the full model from [35] because we do not have access to the friendship connections it is based on. However, we can compare the lifestyle pattern quality of our model with the hLDA component of their model. As comparative models, we use Latent Dirichlet Allocation (LDA) [6], the Biterm topic model (BTM), which is a topic model suited for short texts [33], PAM model [20], nPAM model [19], the topics over time model (TOT), described in [31], and the nonparametric topics over time model (npTOT), described in [10]. These latter two models can be regarded as the state-of-the-art temporal topic models. Note that using these comparative models for our task required us to make some adaptations. In particular, the original TOT model assumes that each document has a unique time stamp, which applies to all the words in that document. Our user activity documents, on the other hand, contain different footprints, each with their own time stamp, i.e., the time stamp associated with words is not constant for all words of the document. We modified the Gibbs samplers for the TOT and npTOT models to allow each word to be associated with a different time stamp. To analyse the usefulness of using a mixture of Gaussians, we also consider a variant of our model where the mixture of Gaussians is replaced by a single Gaussian distribution. We call this model Variant in our experimental results. Publicly shared implementations have been used for all comparative models, except for npTOT and nPAM.

We use the perplexity metric to quantify the lifestyle pattern quality. In order to compute the perplexity for our model we followed the technical details from [30]. Lower perplexity results represent better generalization ability of the model. In this experiment, the original data was randomly

Table 1: Perplexity results for the raw dataset.

	LDA	BTM	PAM	nPAM	TOT	npTOT	hLDA	Variant	Our
US	32374	49832	23450	31245	23982	18934	45938	21758	**13029**
Ind	198	215	212	254	173	154	213	153	**132**
Sin	213	324	255	301	243	199	243	176	**154**
HK	156	214	201	205	143	140	197	134	**121**
Aus	5483	6847	5223	5558	5321	4382	6785	5201	**4219**
Indo	15032	20543	18503	21504	18914	13754	24543	20101	**12433**

Table 2: Perplexity results for the abstract footprint dataset.

	LDA	BTM	PAM	nPAM	TOT	npTOT	hLDA	Variant	Our
US	31832	54321	22251	20432	21514	15983	42874	21203	**12908**
Ind	143	178	155	163	154	143	175	**119**	121
Sin	209	301	201	167	198	154	214	216	**122**
HK	123	212	175	134	127	132	154	123	**109**
Aus	4322	5487	5111	4858	4274	4132	5187	4154	**4091**
Indo	13493	18732	17233	20876	15786	11876	21435	21492	**11234**

split into training and testing sets. We learn the parameters of the model using the training data (75%), and report the perplexity results on the held-out data (25%). For the parametric topic models, we use a tuning set to determine the number of topics following the tuning procedure described in [13]. Our objective is to compare how well our model has learned all parameters and how it performs in terms of its generalization ability.

Tables 1 and 2 report the perplexity results for the raw and abstract footprint data respectively. The non-temporal topic models do not use the timestamps in the user activity document during parameter estimation. We apply them in a traditional setting where the entire user document is the input to the model.

From the results in Tables 1 and 2, we can see that our model has the lowest perplexity on the held-out data in most of the datasets. It consistently performs better in the raw dataset showing its robustness in handling noisy data. For the abstract footprint data in Table 2, our model also performs best overall, although the Variant model is slightly better in the India dataset. We also observe that using abstract footprints improves the perplexity of most models, with the Variant model on the Singapore and Indonesia datasets being an exception. This clearly shows the usefulness of the abstract footprints for dealing with sparsity, regardless of the specific model being used.

4.3 Running Time Comparison

In this section, we compare the running time of our method with a number of existing methods. We present results in terms of the number of CPU hours spent on generating the topic model (based on the abstract footprints). We used a single-threaded implementation in the C programming language for all models. The models were run on an Intel Core i7-3820 3.6GHz machine with 64GB of primary memory. The number of iterations of the Gibbs sampler was set to 1000 in all cases.

As the results in Table 3 show, the latent topic representations of our model can be found considerably faster than those of the hLDA model. In this comparison, we applied hLDA with three levels, which we consider an absolute minimum for describing lifestyle patterns. The running time of the hLDA model, however, depends crucially on the number of levels, and the model quickly becomes intractable as this number is increased. The reason why our model generates latent representations faster than hLDA is that we have a

Table 3: Running time performance in CPU hours.

	US	Ind	Sin	HK	Aus	Indo
hLDA	5.50	0.55	1.02	0.23	3.45	4.32
nPAM	6.02	1.03	0.55	0.31	2.33	4.11
npTOT	3.24	0.54	0.56	0.20	1.45	2.23
Variant	2.25	0.29	0.35	0.14	1.33	2.11
Our	2.29	0.28	0.35	0.14	1.32	2.11

much simpler CRF representation, which speeds up the posterior inference computation. The hierarchical tree generation, which arranges topics based on their commonalities also takes up computational resources, whereas similar commonalities can easily be obtained as a post-hoc analysis.

Table 3 also shows the running time of npTOT, which is again slower than that of our model. In particular, the npTOT model took a considerable amount of time to estimate the temporal distribution of every abstract footprint in the document, as it was not designed with this kind of information in mind. The Variant model, which is a simpler version derived from our model, matches the running speed of our model and is in some cases slightly better.

4.4 Time stamp Prediction

In this experiment we consider time stamp prediction, where the objective is to predict the month of a given check-in, given its abstract footprint. We quantitatively compare our model with TOT and npTOT. Existing non-temporal topic models such as LDA and its proposed extensions cannot solve this task because they are not designed to handle different time stamps in the same document and they do not incorporate time stamp related meta data in their graphical model. We have split the collection of user activity documents for each country into a training set (approximately 75% of the data) and a test set. The model is learned using the training set, where the time stamps are visible. In the test set, we hide the time stamps and try to predict the correct month. We did not randomly split this data, but the testing set has later timestamps, where we intend to predict the future events given the past.

To select the number of topics for the TOT model, we used 25% of the training set as a tuning set and trained the model on the remaining 75% of the training set. We then selected the number of topics that led to the highest accuracy. Using the learned model we can predict the time stamp of an abstract footprint by choosing the time stamp the maximizes the posterior.

We measure the performance of the models using three metrics described in [31]. Specifically, we use the L1 error measure, denoted as L1 in our results, and its expected value, denoted as E(L1). We also compute accuracy. The L1 and E(L1) error measures are to be minimized while accuracy is to be maximized. Table 4 shows the micro-average results for two different configurations: one configuration in which the abstract footprints were used (as elsewhere throughout this paper) and one configuration where the actual venue was used instead of the latent venue category. In this way, we can see to what extent the use of abstract venue categories helps each of the models. The results clearly show that our model outperforms the comparative models. The results again show the usefulness of the abstract footprints as a mechanism for addressing sparsity. The better performance of our model can be explained by the fact that it has

more parameters, which helps it fit the data better. Note that the issues of overfitting and underfitting are avoided because the nonparametric nature of our model means that it automatically chooses the complexity of the model based on the data characteristics. It can outperform npTOT, which is also a nonparametric model, because our model generates two levels of topics, which enables it to better exploit the correlations between different topics.

The considered time stamp prediction task is a very hard task, which we believe cannot be adequately solved by simple methods. Even for humans, for most check-in records we can only guess in which month they have taken place, but there are some check-ins where reasonable estimates can be made (e.g., check-ins at a beach are more likely to be in summer). We certainly don't claim that our method can solve this task. However, we do believe that it allows us to quantitatively show that our model captures temporal trends in a better way than the baselines. The fact that the accuracy scores are only marginally better than random guessing is simply a consequence of the fact that for many venue types, the distribution over months is fairly uniform.

The aim of the perplexity and time stamp tasks is simply to quantitatively show that our model is capturing certain aspects of lifestyle patterns better than existing methods. The fact that we have to use these tasks, rather than tasks which would directly evaluate the quality of the lifestyle patterns, is because this notion of quality is so subjective, and because testing the effectiveness of deploying such a model in real-world applications (e.g. advertising campaigns) would be extremely challenging for which labeled data sets are difficult to obtain.

5. CONCLUSIONS

We have proposed a text mining framework for analysing the lifestyles of users of location-based social networks such as Foursquare. In particular, our framework is based on a novel topic modelling approach, in which we explicitly address the sparsity of check-in data and incorporate a temporal component for analysing how lifestyle patterns change throughout the year. The output of our method consists of a set of lifestyle patterns, each of which corresponds to a probability distribution over lifestyle topics, the latter intuitively corresponding to soft clusters of related venues. The nonparametric nature of our model means that we do not have to specify the number of lifestyle patterns and topics a priori. Our experimental results show that useful lifestyle patterns can indeed be obtained in this way, and that the model can capture the dynamics of lifestyle topics more faithfully than existing topic models.

6. REFERENCES

[1] A. Agarwal, N. R. Desai, R. Ruffoli, and A. Carpi. Lifestyle and testicular dysfunction: a brief update. *Biomedicine & Pharmacotherapy*, 62(8):550–553, 2008.

[2] S. Bauer, A. Noulas, D. O. Séaghdha, S. Clark, and C. Mascolo. Talking places: Modelling and analysing linguistic content in Foursquare. In *SocialCom*, pages 348–357, 2012.

[3] J. M. Bernardo and A. F. M. Smith. *Bayesian Theory*. John Wiley & Sons, 1994 (ISBN: 0-471-92416-4).

[4] D. M. Blei, T. L. Griffiths, and M. I. Jordan. The nested Chinese restaurant process and Bayesian

Table 4: Time stamp prediction performance.

	Raw Footprints												Abstract Footprints											
	TOT			npTOT			Variant			Our			TOT			npTOT			Variant			Our		
	L1	E(L1)	ACC.	L1	E(L1)	ACC.	L1	E(L1)	ACC.	L1	E(L1)	ACC.	L1	E(L1)	ACC.	L1	E(L1)	ACC.	L1	E(L1)	ACC.	L1	E(L1)	ACC.
US	3.12	3.42	0.23	2.87	3.01	0.26	2.65	2.83	0.29	2.54	2.59	0.24	2.98	3.01	0.29	2.85	2.92	0.28	2.58	2.89	0.25	2.43	2.39	0.39
Ind	2.28	2.31	0.24	2.13	2.34	0.26	2.09	2.29	0.29	1.89	2.04	0.24	2.11	2.15	0.26	2.14	2.33	0.28	2.14	2.16	0.29	1.77	1.89	0.39
Sin	3.45	3.54	0.24	3.21	3.25	0.28	2.61	2.62	0.29	2.55	2.54	0.21	3.44	3.45	0.28	3.09	3.19	0.29	2.88	2.91	0.34	2.31	2.45	0.34
HK	1.99	2.33	0.23	1.98	2.11	0.31	1.72	1.67	0.31	1.54	1.59	0.21	1.87	1.92	0.31	1.78	2.19	0.33	1.58	1.65	0.31	1.49	1.59	0.31
Aus	3.12	3.45	0.25	2.91	2.95	0.26	2.92	2.96	0.34	2.86	2.92	0.24	3.1	3.15	0.31	2.87	3.01	0.31	2.89	3.01	0.33	2.85	3.01	0.36
Indo	2.11	2.31	0.29	2.15	2.21	0.32	2.11	2.19	0.36	2.01	2.11	0.26	2.02	2.19	0.31	2.01	2.19	0.33	2.00	2.21	0.34	1.99	2.06	0.39

nonparametric inference of topic hierarchies. *JACM*, 57(2):7, 2010.

[5] D. M. Blei and J. D. Lafferty. Dynamic topic models. In *ICML*, pages 113–120, 2006.

[6] D. M. Blei, A. Y. Ng, and M. I. Jordan. Latent Dirichlet allocation. *JMLR*, 3:993–1022, 2003.

[7] J. Chang and D. M. Blei. Relational topic models for document networks. In *AISTATS*, pages 81–88, 2009.

[8] Z. Cheng, J. Caverlee, K. Lee, and D. Z. Sui. Exploring millions of footprints in location sharing services. *ICWSM*, 2011:81–88, 2011.

[9] Y. Dingqi. *Understanding Human Dynamics from Large-Scale Location-Centric Social Media Data: Analysis and Applications.* PhD thesis, 2015.

[10] A. Dubey, A. Hefny, S. Williamson, and E. P. Xing. A nonparametric mixture model for topic modeling over time. In *SDM*, pages 530–538, 2013.

[11] H. Ishwaran and L. F. James. Gibbs sampling methods for stick-breaking priors. *JASA*, 96(453), 2001.

[12] S. Jameel and W. Lam. An unsupervised topic segmentation model incorporating word order. In *SIGIR*, pages 203–212, 2013.

[13] S. Jameel, W. Lam, and L. Bing. Supervised topic models with word order structure for document classification and retrieval learning. *Information Retrieval Journal*, 18(4):283–330, 2015.

[14] E. Kim, H. Ihm, and S.-H. Myaeng. Topic-based place semantics discovered from microblogging text messages. In *WWW*, pages 561–562, 2014.

[15] K. B. Kirk and J. J. Thomas. The lifestyle project. *Journal of Geoscience Education*, 51(5):496–499, 2003.

[16] F. Kling and A. Pozdnoukhov. When a city tells a story: Urban topic analysis. In *SIGSPATIAL*, pages 482–485, 2012.

[17] J. H. Lau, K. Grieser, D. Newman, and T. Baldwin. Automatic labelling of topic models. In *ACL-HLT*, pages 1536–1545, 2011.

[18] J. H. Lau, D. Newman, S. Karimi, and T. Baldwin. Best topic word selection for topic labelling. In *ACL*, pages 605–613, 2010.

[19] W. Li, D. Blei, and A. McCallum. Nonparametric Bayes Pachinko allocation. 2007.

[20] W. Li and A. McCallum. Pachinko allocation: DAG-structured mixture models of topic correlations. In *ICML*, pages 577–584, 2006.

[21] Q. Mei, X. Shen, and C. Zhai. Automatic labeling of multinomial topic models. In *KDD*, pages 490–499, 2007.

[22] R. D. Michman, E. M. Mazze, and A. J. Greco. *Lifestyle marketing: reaching the new American consumer.* Greenwood Publishing Group, 2003.

[23] A. Noulas, B. Shaw, R. Lambiotte, and C. Mascolo.

Topological properties and temporal dynamics of place networks in urban environments. In *WWW*, pages 431–441, 2015.

[24] J. Pitman. Poisson–Dirichlet and GEM invariant distributions for split-and-merge transformations of an interval partition. *CPC*, 11(05):501–514, 2002.

[25] M. M. Shafiei and E. E. Milios. Latent Dirichlet co-clustering. In *ICDM*, pages 542–551, 2006.

[26] D. Shepard. Nonparametric Bayes Pachinko allocation for super-event detection in Twitter. In *TENCON*, pages 1–5, 2014.

[27] Y. W. Teh, M. I. Jordan, M. J. Beal, and D. M. Blei. Hierarchical Dirichlet processes. *JASA*, 101(476), 2006.

[28] J. Vosecky, D. Jiang, K. W.-T. Leung, K. Xing, and W. Ng. Integrating social and auxiliary semantics for multifaceted topic modeling in Twitter. *ACM TOIT*, 14(4):27:1–27:24, 2014.

[29] D. D. Walker, K. Seppi, and E. K. Ringger. Topics over nonparametric time: A supervised topic model using Bayesian nonparametric density estimation. In *UAI*, 2012.

[30] H. M. Wallach, I. Murray, R. Salakhutdinov, and D. Mimno. Evaluation methods for topic models. In *ICML*, pages 1105–1112, 2009.

[31] X. Wang and A. McCallum. Topics over time: A non-Markov continuous-time model of topical trends. In *KDD*, pages 424–433, 2006.

[32] L. Wu, Z. S. Ye Zhi, and Y. Liu. Intra-urban human mobility and activity transition: Evidence from social media check-in data. *PLoS ONE*, 9(5):e97010:993–1022, 2014.

[33] X. Yan, J. Guo, Y. Lan, and X. Cheng. A biterm topic model for short texts. In *WWW*, pages 1445–1456, 2013.

[34] H. Yin, B. Cui, L. Chen, Z. Hu, and X. Zhou. Dynamic user modeling in social media systems. *ACM TOIS*, 33(3):10:1–10:44, 2015.

[35] N. J. Yuan, F. Zhang, D. Lian, K. Zheng, S. Yu, and X. Xie. We know how you live: exploring the spectrum of urban lifestyles. In *OSN*, pages 3–14, 2013.

[36] Q. Yuan, G. Cong, K. Zhao, Z. Ma, and A. Sun. Who, Where, When, and What: A nonparametric Bayesian approach to context-aware recommendation and search for Twitter users. *TOIS*, 33(1):2:1–2:33, 2015.

[37] E. Zavitsanos, G. Paliouras, and G. A. Vouros. Non-parametric estimation of topic hierarchies from texts with hierarchical Dirichlet processes. *JMLR*, 12:2749–2775, 2011.

[38] X. Zhou and L. Chen. Event detection over Twitter social media streams. *VLDBJ*, 23(3):381–400, 2014.

EventMiner: Mining Events from Annotated Documents

Dhruv Gupta[*†]   Jannik Strötgen[*]   Klaus Berberich[‡*]

[*]Max Planck Institute for Informatics   [†]Saarbrücken Graduate School for Computer Science   [‡]htw saar
Saarbrücken, Germany

dhgupta@mpi-inf.mpg.de, jstroetge@mpi-inf.mpg.de, kberberi@mpi-inf.mpg.de

ABSTRACT

Events are central in human history and thus also in Web queries, in particular if they relate to history or news. However, ambiguity issues arise as queries may refer to ambiguous events differing in time, geography, or participating entities. Thus, users would greatly benefit if search results were presented along different events. In this paper, we present EVENTMINER, an algorithm that mines events from top-k pseudo-relevant documents for a given query. It is a probabilistic framework that leverages semantic annotations in the form of temporal expressions, geographic locations, and named entities to analyze natural language text and determine important events. Using a large news corpus, we show that using semantic annotations, EVENTMINER detects important events and presents documents covering the identified events in the order of their importance.

Keywords

Information Retrieval; Text Mining; Semantic Annotations.

1. INTRODUCTION

Typically, events happen during particular time intervals at multiple locations. In previous works, it was shown that these two dimensions of events are also very frequent in web queries. In particular, 13.8% and 17.1% of web queries are explicitly and implicitly time-sensitive in nature, respectively [38]. Similarly, 12.7% of queries in *Yahoo!* query logs were reported to contain a geographic location [40]. Thus, we claim that events could be an important feature to navigate the Web. We show that events can be used as user intents to improve retrieval effectiveness. For this, we define that an event involves multiple named entities, at multiple locations, during multiple time intervals. An example of a textually realized event, which will be explained in detail in the next section, is presented in Figure 1. Due to marked accuracy and scalability of tools that provide semantic annotations in the form of temporal expressions, geographic locations, and named entities, the large-scale detection of events has become possible in the last years.

ICTIR '16, September 12-16, 2016, Newark, DE, USA

© 2016 ACM. ISBN 978-1-4503-4497-5/16/09... $15.00

DOI: http://dx.doi.org/10.1145/2970398.2970411

Cold war was a conflict involving Soviet Union$^{\langle GEO:Soviet\_Union \rangle}$ and the US$^{\langle GEO:USA \rangle}$ under the presidency of Mikhail Gorbachev$^{\langle WIKI:Mikhail\_Gorbachev \rangle}$ and Ronald Reagan$^{\langle WIKI:Ronald\_Reagan \rangle}$ respectively, during late 1980s$^{\langle 01-01-1985, 31-12-1989 \rangle}$.

Figure 1: Sample text with semantic annotations.

The understanding of time and space is essential to detect events. Temporal expressions can be highly uncertain (e.g., `late 1980s`) and ambiguous (e.g., `last spring`). Mentions of locations in text can also be highly uncertain and thus difficult to anchor on a map (e.g., `Springfield`). A document may talk about a single event in entirety or may shift its focus between different events. Considering these issues in addition to named entities increases the challenges manifold to mine and determine the importance of events from text. Prior approaches [3, 17, 24, 26] have tried to solve somewhat similar tasks albeit disregarding many of the issues outlined above when modeling an event.

In this paper, we describe EVENTMINER, a probabilistic framework which leverages text and multiple kinds of semantic annotations to mine important events. EVENTMINER is based on the family of *Dirichlet process mixture* models to cluster *semantically* similar text to mine events. The notion of *importance* in our algorithm is measured by statistical frequency. In order to analyze these annotations, we present simple mathematical models for complex notions of time and space that can aid in computing these similarities efficiently and effectively. Our model of time takes into account temporal uncertainty as well as temporal proximity in order to identify events that might occur very close to each other on a timeline (e.g., `1990` is close to `1991`). We additionally model geographic locations so that events happening at locations that neighbor each other are also captured (e.g., `USA` neighbors `Canada`). We additionally take into account similarity behind named entities (e.g., `Ronald Reagan` is related to `Nancy Reagan`) when identifying the important events. We evaluate our methods by comparing the summary of events computed for *history-oriented* queries [11] with their *Wikipedia*[1] page.

Applications. In many scenarios, e.g., in the context of *digital humanities*, there is a need for tools to analyze large text collections. Given keyword-only queries related to (historical) entities or events, EVENTMINER is able to mine these important events which can be further used to explore the retrieved documents.

---

[1]https://en.wikipedia.org/

Contributions. Our major contribution, EVENTMINER, is an algorithm that mines important events from semantically annotated text. In doing so, we present a novel time model that incorporates *proximity* between uncertain temporal expressions.

Outline. We first formally define the problem setting in Section 2. We describe computational models for annotations in Section 3 and EVENTMINER in Section 4. Our evaluation setup and experimental findings are given in Section 5. Related work is surveyed in Section 6. Conclusions drawn from the study are summarized in Section 7.

2. PRELIMINARIES

In this section, we describe and formally define the various semantic annotations of text that we use, how we preprocess, and index the data. We also formally put forward the hypothesis and the problems we solve in this article.

2.1 Semantic Annotations

Consider the piece of text with semantic annotations in Figure 1 as an illustrative example.

Temporal Expressions, as natural language in general, are highly ambiguous in nature. They can be categorized as *explicit, implicit, relative,* and *underspecified* [7, 12, 27]. An explicit expression in Figure 1 is `late 1980s`. As all temporal expressions, explicit expressions can be of different granularities, e.g., `May 5, 2001` or `1992`. Implicit expressions may not be immediately identifiable as they are characterized by words that carry a latent temporal meaning, e.g., `Christmas`. Words whose temporal meaning can only be resolved with respect to some other time point (e.g., the publication date) are known as relative (e.g., `yesterday`) or underspecified if the relation to the reference time has to be determined additionally (e.g., `April`). Tools that perform the complex task of extracting and normalizing such types of temporal expressions are HeidelTime [27] and SUTime [8], which we used in this work to resolve temporal expressions.

Geographic Locations and Other Named Entities. Detection and disambiguation of named entities is a nontrivial task. We use AIDA [14] to identify, disambiguate and link named entities in text to an external ontology. AIDA performs *named entity recognition and disambiguation* by leveraging statistical popularity of named entities and a contextual similarity algorithm to disambiguate them. Examples of named entities in Figure 1 are `Mikhail Gorbachev` and `Ronald Reagan` which have been disambiguated and linked to the *Wikipedia* identifier in the YAGO ontology [29]. Geographic locations mentioned in text are called *toponyms* [25]. The process of resolving these toponyms to a specific location is known as *toponym resolution*. We use the geographical locations obtained as part of the detected and disambiguated named entities by AIDA. Examples of disambiguated locations in Figure 1 are `Soviet Union` and `US`.

Document Collection. We used The New York Times Annotated corpus[2] which consists of around two million news articles published between 1987 and 2007. We utilized a news archive for evaluating our methods since it has been shown in prior work [11, 19] that they cover historic events very well. All the annotations along with text are preprocessed using the HADOOP map-reduce framework and subsequently indexed using the ELASTICSEARCH[3] software.

[2]https://catalog.ldc.upenn.edu/LDC2008T19
[3]https://www.elastic.co/

2.2 Problem Statement

Consider a document collection D consisting of N documents d:

$$D = \{d_1, d_2, \ldots d_N\}$$

further each document $d \in D$ consists of sentences s:

$$d = \langle s_1, s_2, \ldots s_n \rangle$$

Each sentence s then contains a multiset of temporal expressions $s_\mathcal{T}$, geographic locations $s_\mathcal{G}$, named entities $s_\mathcal{E}$, and words $s_\mathcal{W}$ from a vocabulary $\mathcal{V}$:

$$s = \langle s_\mathcal{T}, s_\mathcal{G}, s_\mathcal{E}, s_\mathcal{W} \rangle.$$

The cardinalities of these multisets are given by $|s_\mathcal{T}|$, $|s_\mathcal{G}|$, $|s_\mathcal{E}|$, and $|s_\mathcal{W}|$. The aim is to design an algorithm:

$$\text{EVENTMINER}(S, Q, \Lambda),$$

where, S is a set of input sentences, Q is a keyword query, and Λ consists of a set of parameters $\Lambda \in \mathbb{R}^m$. The input set of sentences S is obtained from the pseudo-relevant set of documents R obtained via an information retrieval engine using the keyword query Q:

$$R = \text{IR}(D, Q, K, \Theta),$$

where Θ is set of parameters and K specifies the number of documents to be returned by the retrieval method. The algorithm should output a totally ordered set of events:

$$\mathcal{C} = \langle c_1, c_2, \ldots c_k \rangle,$$

where c_i is an event. The ordering of events in $\mathcal{C}$ is done by using the scores obtained for each cluster given by the EVENTMINER algorithm. Using $\mathcal{C}$ we re-rank R to obtain a set of documents $\hat{R}$ so that the user sees at least one document from each event $c \in \mathcal{C}$.

An *event* that can be detected in text, is defined to involve multiple named entities $c_\mathcal{E}$, occurring during a time interval $[b, e] \in c_\mathcal{T}$ at locations $g \in c_\mathcal{G}$, and described by words $c_\mathcal{W}$. Thus each event $c \in \mathcal{C}$:

$$c = \langle c_\mathcal{T}, c_\mathcal{G}, c_\mathcal{E}, c_\mathcal{W} \rangle.$$

We hypothesize that using events as proxies for user intents we can increase the retrieval effectiveness of traditional information retrieval methods, which have largely relied on term statistics [11].

2.3 Assumptions

We make the following assumptions:

- Each semantic annotation occurs independent of each other. Hence, we can consider a sentence to contain a multiset of temporal expressions $s_\mathcal{T}$, geographic locations $s_\mathcal{G}$, and named entities $s_\mathcal{E}$.

- A multiset of geographic locations $s_\mathcal{G}$ or named entities $s_\mathcal{E}$ can be empty. However, they cannot be empty *simultaneously* in a sentence. A multiset of temporal expressions $s_\mathcal{T}$ in a sentence *cannot* be empty. In case no temporal expression occurs in a sentence we utilize the document publication date.

- Geographic annotations are a subset of named entity annotations, that is $s_\mathcal{G} \subseteq s_\mathcal{E}$.

3. COMPUTATIONAL MODELS

Here we describe the computational models used to represent and compute similarities between annotations for time, space, and named entities.

3.1 Time Model

We next explain two time models that we use in the EVENTMINER algorithm. Figure 2 illustrates these models.

Uncertainty-aware Time Model (UTM). UTM is a time model for uncertain temporal expressions [5], for instance **1990s**, where begin and end of the time interval $[b, e]$ cannot be clearly identified. UTM models this uncertainty by allowing for a *lower* and *upper* bound in the start (end) of the interval. Formally, a temporal expressions is modeled as a four-tuple:

$$t = \langle b_\ell, b_u, e_\ell, e_u \rangle,$$

where $b \leq e$, $b_\ell \leq b \leq b_u$ and $e_\ell \leq e \leq e_u$. The elements of t are obtained from a time domain $\mathbb{T}$. Thus, $[b, e] \in \mathbb{T} \times \mathbb{T}$. Hence, **1990s** is represented as $\langle 1990, 1999, 1990, 1999 \rangle$. The number of time intervals that can be generated from a temporal expression is denoted by $|t|$. The probability of generating a time interval $[b, e]$ from temporal expression t is estimated as [5]:

$$P([b, e] | t) = \frac{\mathbb{1}([b, e] \in t)}{|t|}.$$

Thus the likelihood of generating t' from t is:

$$P(t' | t) = \frac{1}{|t'|} \sum_{[b, e] \in t'} P([b, e] | t). \tag{1}$$

Following, UTM, we can for example, generate the time interval $[1995, 1998]$ from the temporal expression $\langle 1990, 1999, 1990, 1999 \rangle$. However, a time interval $[2000, 2001]$ will receive zero probability given the same temporal expression.

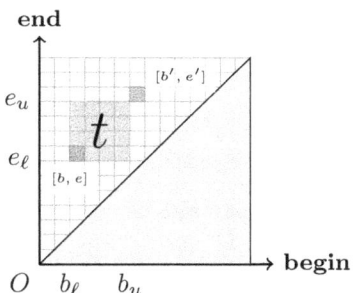

Figure 2: Graphical representation illustrating how a time interval $[b, e]$ is generated from t using UTM. It also represents graphically how the time interval $[b', e']$ obtains zero probability from UTM but a non-zero probability using PTM.

Proximity-aware Time Model (PTM). In UTM a time interval $[b, e] \notin t$ obtains zero probability. However, time intervals that are *temporally close* to time intervals in t should obtain non-zero probability [28]. This is required for computing similarity between events that have close but non-overlapping time intervals of occurrence (e.g., **1990** and **1991**). We compute the *proximity* by multivariate kernel density estimates. Concretely,

$$P([b, e] | t) = \frac{1}{|t|} \sum_{[b', e'] \in t} \mathcal{K}_A([b, e] - [b', e']),$$

where, $\mathcal{K}_A$ is a multivariate kernel estimator with bandwidth matrix A. The difference between time intervals is carried

out element-wise, i.e., $[b - b', e - e'] = [b, e] - [b', e']$. The kernel density estimator $\mathcal{K}_A$ is defined as [13]:

$$\mathcal{K}_A(\bullet) = \frac{1}{|A|} \mathcal{K}\left(A^{-1} \bullet\right),$$

where, the bandwidth matrix A is:

$$A_{2 \times 2} = k \cdot I_{2 \times 2} = \begin{bmatrix} k & 0 \\ 0 & k \end{bmatrix},$$

where, $|A|$ represents the matrix determinant and A^{-1} its inverse. Proximity between t' and t can be estimated by:

$$P(t' | t) = \frac{1}{|t'|} \sum_{[b, e] \in t'} \frac{1}{|t|} \sum_{[b', e'] \in t} \mathcal{K}_A([b, e] - [b', e']). \tag{2}$$

For $\mathcal{K}_A(\bullet)$, we utilized the Epanechnikov kernel, since its support is $[-1, 1]$ and density at a point is computed using the values lying in the cube surrounding it [13]. It can be written as [13]:

$$\mathcal{K}_A(v) = \frac{3}{4}(1 - v^T v) \mathbb{1}(|\sqrt{v^T v}| \leq 1),$$

where $v = [b, e]$ is a time interval and the indicator function $\mathbb{1}(\bullet)$ evaluates to one iff the argument is true. The proximity between two temporal expressions can be varied by scaling k in the bandwidth matrix A.

The proximity model thus allows us to associate a non-zero probability with non-overlapping temporal expressions. Thus, the time interval $[2000, 2001]$ can now be generated from the temporal expression $\langle 1990, 1999, 1990, 1999 \rangle$.

3.2 Space Model

Each geographic location g in our model is represented as a *minimum bounding rectangle* (MBR) with coordinates for its lowermost coordinate ℓ and uppermost coordinate u: $g = \langle \ell, u \rangle$.

Each coordinate lies in a two dimensional geodesic space, that is $\ell = (x_\ell, y_\ell)$ and $u = (x_u, y_u)$. For any two geographic locations described by their MBRs we can find similarity by computing the *area overlap* in the geodesic space. Similarly proximity can be found by their closeness in the geodesic space. Using the geodesic system to represent MBRs helps in avoiding distortion along the poles. Figure 3 shows how a MBR for **UK** is obtained from its set of coordinates.

(a) Plot of coordinates of UK.   *(b) Plot of the MBRs of UK.*

Figure 3: Depiction of how MBRs are obtained from a set of geographic coordinates. For each dense region of coordinates we compute a MBR.

For an efficient indexing and querying of geographic locations, we utilize an R-TREE [36]. Each location's MBRs are indexed in an R-TREE. We can subsequently query the R-TREE for containment or proximity queries.

3.3 Entity Model

Each entity that is disambiguated by AIDA [14] is linked to the YAGO [29] ontology. Each YAGO entity is in turn linked to its Wikipedia entry. To compute the similarity between two entities e and e' we thus look at the *relatedness* in terms of Wikipedia links. This similarity is known as *Milne-Witten* entity-entity relatedness — MWSIM(e, e') [34]. Formally, with W_e and $W_{e'}$ being the sets of articles that are linked to the Wikipedia articles corresponding to the entities e and e', respectively. Let W represent all articles in Wikipedia; the similarity is computed as [34]:

$$\text{MWSIM}(e, e') = \frac{log(max(|W_e|, |W_{e'}|)) - log(|W_e \cap W_{e'}|)}{log(|W|) - log(min(|W_e, W_{e'}|))}$$

4. EVENTMINER ALGORITHM

The EVENTMINER algorithm is a probabilistic model that takes into account the similarity between the semantic annotations in order to mine important events. It is based on the family of *Dirichlet process mixture* (DPM) models [4, 23, 37]. The rationale behind using DPM models is two-fold. First, they allow to *jointly* model the marginal distributions underlying the different dimensions for the events. Second, they allow to model an *infinite* number of clusters without knowing their number apriori. Each cluster identified by EVENTMINER is treated as an important event for the given keyword query. We next describe how the various semantic similarities are considered together, and how to perform inference over the probabilistic model.

Generating Sentences. Let $\mathcal{V}$ be the vocabulary associated with the document collection. Further, let the event clusters that are identified by EVENTMINER be described by a multinomial θ_c distributed over $\mathcal{V}$. We describe the probability of generating the sentence s_i given θ_c as [23, 37]:

$$P(s_i | \theta_c) = \prod_{v \in \mathcal{V}} \theta_c(v)^{tf(v, s_i)},$$

where the probability of obtaining the term v from cluster c is denoted by $\theta_c(v)$ and the term frequency of v in sentence s_i is denoted by $tf(v, s_i)$.

Given a term distribution over sentences, we now consider the similarity between the various semantic annotations.

Temporal Similarity. Let us consider an existing event cluster c, for a sentence containing a multiset of temporal expressions $s_\mathcal{T}$ to be similar in the temporal domain to c, we need to compute the temporal similarity. This is done by considering the temporal similarity of $t \in s_\mathcal{T}$ with all temporal expressions $t' \in c_\mathcal{T}$ in the event cluster c as:

$$w_t(s, c) = \frac{1}{|c_\mathcal{T}|} \sum_{t' \in c_\mathcal{T}} \frac{1}{|s_\mathcal{T}|} \sum_{t \in s_\mathcal{T}} \mathbb{1}(t \in t'),$$

where the function $\mathbb{1}(t \in t')$ indicates likelihood of generating the temporal expression t from t' by Eq. (1) or (2).

Geographic Similarity. Similarly, given an event cluster c, to consider the similarity of a sentence along the spatial dimension we compute it as:

$$w_g(s, c) = \frac{1}{|c_\mathcal{G}|} \sum_{g' \in c_\mathcal{G}} \frac{1}{|s_\mathcal{G}|} \sum_{g \in s_\mathcal{G}} \mathbb{1}(g \in g'),$$

where the function $\mathbb{1}(g \in g')$ indicates the likelihood of generating the geographic location g from the geographic location g'.

Entity Similarity. On similar lines, we can compute the similarity between named entities in a sentence with an event cluster c as follows:

$$w_e(s, c) = \frac{1}{|c_\mathcal{E}|} \sum_{e' \in c_\mathcal{E}} \frac{1}{|s_\mathcal{E}|} \sum_{e \in s_\mathcal{E}} \mathbb{1}(e \sim e'),$$

where the function $\mathbb{1}(e \sim e')$ computes the relatedness between the entities e and e' using MWSIM($\bullet$). The motivation for computing the average entity-entity relatedness (as compared to maximum entity-entity relatedness) between sentence s and cluster c is to maintain the cluster coherence.

Joint Similarity. We combine all the semantic similarities in a weighted average. This can be written as:

$$w(s, c) = \frac{\rho_1 \cdot w_t(s, c) + \rho_2 \cdot w_g(s, c) + \rho_3 \cdot w_e(s, c)}{\rho_1 + \rho_2 + \rho_3}.$$

Chinese Restaurant Process. To incorporate the different semantic similarities in the Dirichlet process mixture model framework, we need to consider the *clustering* behavior of Dirichlet processes [31]. We briefly explain the framework next, following its description in [31, 33].

Consider a Dirichlet process (DP), $G_0 \sim DP(\alpha, H_0)$, with a prior (base) distribution H_0 [31, 37]. Further let the prior follow a Dirichlet distribution, $H_0 \sim Dir(\beta m)$; where, m is the normalized term frequency vector over $\mathcal{V}$ and β is a hyperparameter [18, 31, 37, 39]. Let, the sample multinomial distributions be drawn *iid* from G_0 be $\theta_1, \theta_2, \ldots, \theta_i$. For the predictive distribution θ_{i+1} it has been shown in [6, 31, 33] that:

$$\theta_{i+1} | \theta_1, \ldots, \theta_i, \alpha, H_0 \sim \sum_{\ell=1}^{i} \frac{1}{i+\alpha} \delta_{\theta_\ell} + \frac{\alpha}{i+\alpha} H_0,$$

where, δ_{θ_ℓ} is a Dirac delta at θ_ℓ. We can clearly see that if a sample is drawn more than once, it shall have a higher probability of being drawn again leading to a "positive reinforcement effect" or equivalently "rich gets richer effect" from the above equation [31, 33, 39]. This phenomenon is more often described in the literature as the *Chinese Restaurant Process*. The analogy is described as follows, consider unlimited tables to sit at a Chinese restaurant [31]. A new customer will sit at a table in the restaurant with probability that is dependent on the count of customers already occupying that table [31]. It can also be proven that the number of clusters in a Dirichlet process grows logarithmically [31].

Following this framework, we can incorporate the probability of assigning sentence s_i to cluster c, given all the other event cluster assignments as follows:

$$P(z_i = c | z_{-i}) = \begin{cases} \frac{w(s_i, c)}{\sum_{c'} w(s_i, c') + \alpha}, & \text{if } c \text{ is in cluster set} \\ \frac{\alpha}{\sum_{c'} w(s_i, c') + \alpha}, & \text{if } c \text{ is a new cluster} \end{cases}$$

where α is the concentration parameter.

Inference. To infer the cluster label z given the semantically annotated text, we can use the following inference:

$$P(z_i = c | z_{-c}, S) \propto P(z_i = c | z_{-i}) P(s_i | s_{-i} \in z_i = c),$$

where z_{-c} is used to denote all the cluster assignments except z_c, and $s_{-i} \in z_i = c$ denotes all the sentences in cluster c except s_{-i} [23, 37]. Since each type of expression is associated with a multiset, the order, in which semantic annotations are observed, can safely be ignored. Thus the first term, $P(z_i | z_{-i})$, can be computed by taking z_i as last in the order [23, 31].

The second term, $P(s_i|s_{-i} \in z_i = c)$, can be computed with the help of the Dirichlet process described earlier. It has been shown to be equal to [18, 23, 37]:

$$P(s_i|s_{-i} \in z_i = c) = \int p(s_i|\theta)p(\theta|s_{-i} \in z_i = c)d\theta$$

$$= \left(\frac{\Gamma(\sum_v tf(v, s_{-i} \in z_i = c) + \beta)}{\prod_v \Gamma(tf(v, s_{-i} \in z_i = c) + \beta m_v)} \right)$$

$$\left(\frac{\prod_v \Gamma(tf(v, s_i) + tf(v, s_{-i} \in z_i = c) + \beta m_v)}{\Gamma(\sum_v tf(v, s_i) + \sum_v tf(v, s_{-i} \in z_i = c) + \beta)} \right)$$

where the Gamma function is denoted by $\Gamma(\bullet)$, the term frequency of v in the set of sentences (excluding s_i) in cluster c is given by $tf(v, s_{-i} \in z_i = c)$, and the term frequency of v in sentence s_i is given by $tf(v, s_i)$.

The graphical model corresponding to our EVENTMINER algorithm, is illustrated in Figure 4. We utilized a modified Gibbs Sampler based on [37] for a single machine implementation. Similar to their implementation, our modified Gibbs Sampler also has time complexity of $\mathcal{O}(|S|^2)$.

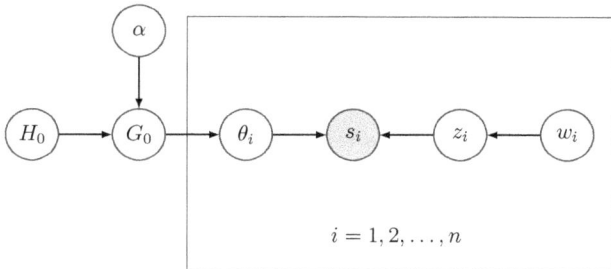

Figure 4: Graphical representation of the EVENTMINER algorithm based on [37]. It shows a Dirichlet process G with concentration parameter α and its base measure H_0. Where, a sentence is denoted by s, its cluster label is denoted by z, and the joint similarity incorporating time, geographic location, and named entities is denoted by w. The duplicated random variables are represented in the box; with i denoting the multiplicity. Observed node is shaded in gray.

Exploring Search Results with Event-Clusters. For each event-cluster c we can associate the documents from which the sentences were derived. This can thus be used to explore the search results in an event-centric manner.

5. EVALUATION

In this section we first describe the experimental setup and then discuss the results of the experiments.

5.1 Experimental Setup

We describe the experimental setup of our evaluation next.

History-Oriented Queries. In order to test the effectiveness of our method, we utilize history-oriented queries that have multiple important events associated with them. Specifically, we considered three types of query categories, namely: events [9], entities[4], and wars [20]. The keywords corresponding to these queries are shown in Table 1. This dataset of history-oriented queries and corresponding *Wikipedia* articles has been made publicly available as part of the research work carried out by Gupta and Berberich [11].

---

[4]http://usatoday30.usatoday.com/news/top25-influential.htm

Americas	american civil war | american revolution | mexican revolution
Europe	world war II | world war I | french revolution | punic wars | spanish civil war | russo-polish war
Africa	french algreian war | biafran nigerian civil war
Asia	vietnam war | korean war | iraq war | persian wars | chinese civil war | iran iraq war | russian civil war | french indochina war | russo-japanese car

(a) Wars.

Sports	commonwealth games | asian games | summer olympics | winter olympics | super bowl winners
Music	u2 album | nirvana album | beatles album | red hot chilli peppers album | michael jackson album
Movies	harry potter movie | oscar academy awards | lord of the rings movie
Politics	german federal elections | us presidential elections | australia federal elections

(b) Events.

Business	bill gates | sergey brin | larry page | howard schultz | sam walton
Science	stephen hawking | francis collins | craig venter
Politics	ronald reagan | mikhail gorbachev | george w. bush | deng xiaoping | nelson mandela | bill clinton | hillary clinton
Arts	j. k. rowling | oprah winfrey | russell simmons | bono
Religion	pope john paul II
Sports	lance armstrong | michael jordan
Other	ryan white | homer simpson | osama bin laden

(c) Entities.

Table 1: History-oriented queries [11].

Metrics. For each history-oriented query, our aim is to detect as many important events as possible. This task can be considered equivalent to producing a *summary* for a given topic. However, in our setting we disregard grammatical structure or temporal ordering. Rather our focus is specifically on *recall* and *precision* of information. We consider the frequent words in each event cluster $\mathcal{W}$ as a sentence and concatenate them from some top-ranked clusters to form a *system-generated summary*. In order to test this objectively, we utilized the ROUGE-N measure [35] for evaluating the quality of summaries produced by our methods. We used the *Wikipedia* entry corresponding to the history-oriented query as the gold standard summary. ROUGE-N then computes the overlap of n-grams between the gold standard summary and the summary produced by the system under test. We report the ROUGE-N recall, precision and F_1.

Systems. We compare three systems. For them, we consider the EVENTMINER algorithm incorporating semantic similarity with increasing sophistication. As a naïve baseline, EVENTMINER computes similarities of various semantics by only considering *surface-level* equivalence. That is two semantic annotations are considered to be similar iff their tokens match. For example, 1995 and 1990s are *not* similar to each other. We call this system EMBASELINE. For the second system, we compute the temporal similarity using uncertainty-aware time model UTM; the geographic similarity by computing area overlap in MBRs; and entity-entity similarity with MWSIM. Therefore, in this system, 1995 and 1990s are similar; as are New York and USA; and also Ronald Reagan and Nancy Reagan. We call this system EMSIMILAR. For the final system we compute the similarity between temporal expressions using proximity-aware time model PTM; the geographic similarity by computing closeness between MBRs; and entity-entity similarity with MWSIM. Therefore, this system considers 1999 and 2000 proximate; also Canada and USA are considered to be proximate. We call this system EMPROXIMITY.

5.2 Experiments

In this section, we describe the results obtained for the evaluation setup presented earlier.

Parameter Tuning. We performed the experiments by retrieving top-25 pseudo-relevant documents, i.e., $K = 25$ for every keyword query in the testbed. We choose this as a conservative estimate for the number of highly relevant documents given the keyword query. For retrieving these documents, we used the state-of-the-art *Okapi BM25* method with standard parameter settings $k_1 = 1.2$ and $b = 0.75$. These documents are subsequently split at sentence-level granularity.

The different EVENTMINER systems are next executed with these sentences as input. Weights for different similarities are: $\rho_1 = 0.50$, $\rho_2 = 0.25$, and $\rho_3 = 0.25$, giving more importance to temporal similarity as compared to the other two similarities. This was due to the observation that annotations for time were more accurate as compared to named entity annotations. Hence, temporal similarity was given a higher weight in computing joint similarity to obtain coherent clusters. Further, the concentration parameter was set to $\alpha = 0.1$ and the strength of prior for text similarity $\beta = 0.1$. The concentration parameter is directly proportional to the probability of creating a new event cluster. Both these values were set by observing their effect on three sample queries, namely: summer olympics, us presidential elections, and george w bush. We perform Gibbs Sampling for a total of 50 iterations, with early termination of the algorithm if cluster assignments do not change between subsequent iterations. We limited ourselves to a moderate number of iterations keeping in mind the quadratic complexity of the EVENTMINER algorithm. For each system, we picked top-5 clusters ranked by their scores.

After obtaining the top-most clusters, we next take the most frequent keywords in each cluster and concatenate them into one sentence and then each of the sentences is concatenated into a *system-generated* summary. We compare this *system* summary with the *model* or ground truth summary from the corresponding *Wikipedia* entry of the issued keyword query. For comparing the summaries, we use the ROUGE-1 score which tests the overlap of uni-grams between the two summaries and provides us with *precision, recall* and F_1 scores *averaged* over all the queries in that category. Note that the order of the words appearing in each summary has no consequence on the scores. The ROUGE software package[5] was utilized for this purpose. We computed these scores by stemming all the words and by removing all stopwords in all the summaries. Further, 1000 samples were considered for its bootstrap re-sampling. The results reported are within 95% confidence intervals.

Results for the three different categories of the history-oriented queries are shown in Table 2. The results for the history-oriented queries concerning events show that consid-

---

[5]http://www.berouge.com/Pages/default.aspx

Category	System	ROUGE-1		
		Recall	*Precision*	F_1
Event	EMBASELINE	0.31	0.24	0.17
	EMSIMILAR	0.29	0.26	0.17
	EMPROXIMITY	0.25	0.28	0.18
War	EMBASELINE	0.15	0.31	0.17
	EMSIMILAR	0.15	0.32	0.17
	EMPROXIMITY	0.11	0.36	0.15
Entity	EMBASELINE	0.13	0.49	0.16
	EMSIMILAR	0.12	0.50	0.15
	EMPROXIMITY	0.10	0.52	0.15

Table 2: ROUGE-1 *scores for various systems which are grouped by different categories of history-oriented queries. Precision, recall and F_1 scores are averaged for all queries in that category for each system. Across query categories, we can clearly see an increase in the values of precision as we consider more advanced models for time and space that incorporate proximity.*

ering EVENTMINER algorithm with similarity-based models for semantic annotations increases precision as compared to the baseline method considering only surface level similarity. This, however, comes at marginal cost of decrease in recall. Taking into account time and geographical model that considers proximity increases the precision of the events identified by the EVENTMINER algorithm again at small decrease in recall. This trend is replicated in other history-oriented queries concerning wars and entities.

We additionally describe some anecdotal results produced by EVENTMINER in the Appendix.

5.3 Discussion

In conducting this research, we faced several pitfalls which we aim to tackle in future.

Quality of Annotations. We noticed that empirically the quality of annotations for temporal expressions or for geographic locations is of significantly better quality than for named entities. Thus, there is a need of restricting the analysis to only high precision annotations.

Cluster Coherence. Considering a joint similarity between time and geographic locations can cause cluster coherence to decrease. This might arise due to the fact that some keyword queries may have large temporal ambiguity but little or no geographic ambiguity and vice-versa.

Dependencies between Annotations. Clearly assuming an independence assumption between the annotations has not helped us in recalling more events. Our model thus needs to incorporate this aspect.

Scalability. Worst-case time complexity of the EVENTMINER algorithm is quadratic; this is not desirable if analysis is required for large number of documents. To tackle this, one potential solution is to use hierarchical Dirichlet process mixture models [32, 33].

Evaluation Metrics. Our evaluation metric was highly objective and based on overlap of n-grams computed from text. However, ROUGE metric can additionally be modified to take into account similarity between summaries in terms of time, geography and named entities in an ontology. Another avenue to explore will be to have subjective *crowd-sourced* based evaluation for the identified events.

6. RELATED WORK

In this section, we describe prior models and work with respect to our problem setting.

Related Models. Prior work [23, 37] are examples of clustering algorithms that compute document similarity based on text and contextual temporal expressions. Both have leveraged the framework of Dirichlet process mixture (DPM) models. Zhu et al. [37] present a time-sensitive Dirichlet process mixture model. The authors consider the use case of organizing an email inbox by using the arrival time of these emails. For computing similarity between different instances, they utilize an exponential decay function which gives more weight to recent emails. Building on this work, Qamra et al. [23] develop a *content-community-time* model that tries to identify similar blogs in a community of blogosphere. While utilizing the framework of DPM models, we expand on the notion of temporal similarity by taking into account uncertainty and proximity. Additionally, we incorporate similarity along the geographic dimension and also similarity between named entities in an ontology.

Temporal Information Retrieval is a sub-field of IR with special emphasis on temporal information present in documents in forms of *metadata*, e.g., publication dates or *temporal expressions* [7]. Anchoring documents or queries in time is an integral part of a time-sensitive search engine. Jatowt et al. [15] address the problem of estimating the time period which the document focuses on. They do this by constructing a weighted undirected graph which captures the associations between terms and time. Gupta and Berberich [9] address the problem of providing interesting time intervals to a keyword query by using temporal expressions in pseudo-relevant document set. Building on this they can also classify keyword queries to determine if its: *i.* (a)temporal *ii.* temporally unambiguous *iii.* temporal ambiguity at different granularities (e.g., year, month, or day) *iv.* temporally (a)periodic [10].

Timeline Generation. One of the initial works for *automatically generating timelines* was by Swan and Allan [30]. For this their model utilized the *relative frequency* of important features such as named entities and noun phrases. The method involved calculating the frequency of the features at different time points and capturing the significance of its frequency by computing χ^2 statistic. One of the more recent works involves exploring documents via timelines [3]. In their approach the authors specifically pay attention to the temporal expressions in the documents. Temporal expressions are used for constructing *temporal document profiles*. These profiles are subsequently used for clustering and re-ranking of documents.

Event Detection. A large body of work exists in analyzing different kinds of semantic annotations in isolation. However, we have tried to address the interplay between different kinds of semantic annotations, which in the past has received markedly little attention.

The *Topic Detection and Tracking* (TDT) [2] was the first initiative in the direction of modeling and detecting events. The task focused on organizing an incoming stream of text first into a broad category of *topic*, built from *stories* which comprised of *events*. However, the approaches published in [2] at that time did not have access to scalable and accurate semantic annotators. In light of these new technologies, several works have leveraged these semantic annotations to find events [1, 17] and also predict future events [16, 24].

Kuzey et al. [17] most recently addressed the task of deriving events from a news corpus to use them for ontology population. This is done by constructing a *multi-view attribute* graph that incorporates features such as: textual content of document, publication date of documents, named entities (e.g., people, organization, and location) in documents with their semantic types (e.g., protest, hurricane etc.). They then present algorithms that *distill* events from this graph. Another recent publication by Abujabal and Berberich [1] mines events from semantically annotated corpora by utilizing frequent itemset mining. Both approaches disregard any special treatment for time and geographic location; which has been adequately addressed in our work.

Focusing specifically on predicting the future, Radinsky et al. [24] developed the *Pundit* algorithm. Events are modeled as a tuple of state, actor, objects, instrument, location, and time. It predicts future events by performing *hierarchical agglomerative clustering* on events. The similarity between events is computed by using distances in a semantic network. The aim is to derive future events via causality in events that have already occurred. Utilizing only temporal data, Jatowt and Yeung [16] also present a model-based clustering algorithm for predicting future events. They capture the inherent uncertainty in temporal expressions by modeling them as probability distributions. The model-based clustering subsequently derives the similarity between these distributions using the Kullback-Leibler (KL) divergence.

Paying special attention to how events are covered in historical document collections, Yeung and Jatowt [19] study topics as they change with time. They utilize the *Google News Archive* for the time period from 1990 to 2010 for thirty two different countries. For analysis, they extract temporal expressions and also topics by using topic models such as *Latent Dirichlet Allocation*. They study the distributions of various kinds of temporal expressions that specifically refer to the past. Furthermore, they then look at how topics change over time, what *triggered* the re-collection of past events, how the events were forgotten over time, and how countries are similar when comparing their topic distribution over time.

Event-Centric Search. Using semantic annotations for clustering documents and consequently using them as means for document exploration has been addressed in works [25, 26, 28]. All the approaches however do not incorporate ontological named entities in form of person or organization. Strötgen and Gertz [26] present a method for deriving events by using time and geographic locations in text to identify events. An event in their model is a co-occurrence of a temporal and geographic expression. Building on this notion of event they provide a unique framework for querying by developing a multi-dimensional query language based on the extended Backus-Norm-Form (EBNF) language. Another work by Strötgen and Gertz [28] tries to re-rank documents for a given query by computing similarity and proximity with respect to text, time, and geography. Samet et al. [25] discuss *NewsStand*, a system which allows users to find news anchored by its location on a map. *NewsStand* does this by detecting and resolving toponyms. The method predominantly involves the use of a streaming clustering algorithm. Some of the features used for ranking the clusters are the size of the clusters, number of news sources, cluster's rate of propagation, and its timestamp.

7. CONCLUSION

In this article we presented EVENTMINER, an algorithm that clusters sentences in a semantically annotated corpus to identify important events. Our proposed method is based on the framework of Dirichlet process mixture models. We adapted this framework to incorporate similarity along time that leverages uncertainty and proximity in temporal expressions. It also considers similarity and proximity between geographic expressions. Finally, it also accounts for similarity between named entities in an ontology. We tested our method on a collection of history-oriented queries and their corresponding Wikipedia pages to show that considering proximity between temporal and geographic dimension as well as similarity between named entities in an ontology can recall accurate events.

8. REFERENCES

[1] A. Abujabal and K. Berberich. Important events in the past, present, and future. *WWW 2015-Companion Volume*.

[2] J. Allan, editor. *Topic Detection and Tracking: Event-based Information Organization*. Kluwer Academic Publishers, Norwell, MA, USA, 2002.

[3] O. Alonso et al. Clustering and exploring search results using timeline constructions. *CIKM 2009*.

[4] C. E. Antoniak. Mixtures of dirichlet processes with applications to bayesian nonparametric problems. *Ann. Statist.*, 2(6):1152–1174, 11 1974.

[5] K. Berberich et al. A language modeling approach for temporal information needs. *ECIR 2010*.

[6] D. Blackwell and J. B. MacQueen. Ferguson distributions via polya urn schemes. *Ann. Statist.*, 1(2):353–355, 03 1973.

[7] R. Campos et al. Survey of temporal information retrieval and related applications. *ACM Computing Survey*, 47(2):15:1–15:41, 2014.

[8] A. X. Chang and C. D. Manning. SUTIME: A library for recognizing and normalizing time expressions. *LREC 2012*.

[9] D. Gupta and K. Berberich. Identifying time intervals of interest to queries. *CIKM 2014*.

[10] D. Gupta and K. Berberich. Temporal query classification at different granularities. *SPIRE 2015*.

[11] D. Gupta and K. Berberich. Diversifying search results using time. Research Report MPI-I-2016-5-001, 2016.

[12] D. Gupta and K. Berberich. A probabilistic framework for time-sensitive search. *NTCIR-12 2016*.

[13] W. Härdle et al. *Nonparametric and semiparametric models*. Springer Series in Statistics. Springer-Verlag, New York, 2004.

[14] J. Hoffart et al. Robust disambiguation of named entities in text. *EMNLP 2011*.

[15] A. Jatowt et al. Estimating document focus time. *CIKM 2013*.

[16] A. Jatowt and C. Man Au Yeung. Extracting collective expectations about the future from large text collections. *CIKM 2011*.

[17] E. Kuzey et al. A fresh look on knowledge bases: Distilling named events from news. *CIKM 2014*.

[18] D. J. C. MacKay and L. C. B. Peto. A hierarchical dirichlet language model. *Natural Language Engineering*, 1:289–308, 9 1995.

[19] C. Man Au Yeung and A. Jatowt. Studying how the past is remembered: towards computational history through large scale text mining. *CIKM 2011*.

[20] P. P. Mazur and R. Dale. Wikiwars: A new corpus for research on temporal expressions. *EMNLP 2010*.

[21] D. Metzler et al. Improving search relevance for implicitly temporal queries. *SIGIR 2009*.

[22] S. Nunes, et al. Use of temporal expressions in web search. *ECIR 2008*.

[23] A. Qamra, et al. Mining blog stories using community based and temporal clustering. *CIKM 2006*.

[24] K. Radinsky et al. Learning causality for news events prediction. *WWW 2012*.

[25] H. Samet et al. Reading news with maps by exploiting spatial synonyms. *Commun. ACM*, 57(10):64–77, 2014.

[26] J. Strötgen and M. Gertz. Event-centric search and exploration in document collections. *JCDL 2012*.

[27] J. Strötgen and M. Gertz. Multilingual and cross-domain temporal tagging. *Language Resources and Evaluation*, 47(2):269–298, 2013.

[28] J. Strötgen and M. Gertz. Proximity2-aware ranking for textual, temporal, and geographic queries. *CIKM 2013*.

[29] F. M. Suchanek et al. Yago: A large ontology from wikipedia and wordnet. *Web Semantics*, 6(3):203–217, 2008.

[30] R. C. Swan and J. Allan. Automatic generation of overview timelines. *SIGIR 2000*.

[31] Y. W. Teh. Dirichlet processes. *Encyclopedia of Machine Learning*. Springer, 2010.

[32] Y. W. Teh et al. Sharing clusters among related groups: Hierarchical Dirichlet processes. *Advances in Neural Information Processing Systems*, volume 17, 2005.

[33] Y. W. Teh et al. Hierarchical Dirichlet processes. *Journal of the American Statistical Association*, 101(476):1566–1581, 2006.

[34] I. Witten and D. Milne. An effective, low-cost measure of semantic relatedness obtained from Wikipedia links. In *AAAI Workshop on Wikipedia and AI*, 2008.

[35] C. Y. Lin. Rouge: a package for automatic evaluation of summaries. *ACL 2004*.

[36] A. Guttman. R-Trees: A Dynamic index structure for spatial searching. *SIGMOD 1984*.

[37] X. Zhu et al. Time-sensitive dirichlet process mixture models. Technical report, DTIC Document, 2005.

[38] N. Kanhabua, et al. Temporal information retrieval. *Foundations and Trends in Information Retrieval*, 9(2):91–208, 2015.

[39] L. Hu et al. TSDPMM: Incorporating Prior Topic Knowledge into Dirichlet Process Mixture Models for Text Clustering. *EMNLP 2015*.

[40] V. Zhang et al. Geomodification in query rewriting. *GIR 2006*.

APPENDIX

A. ANECDOTAL RESULTS

Next we discuss some anecdotal results for a few history-oriented queries, namely: george w bush, bill clinton, ronald reagan, ryan white, deng xiaoping, pope john paul ii, stephen hawking, us presidential elections, soviet afghanistan war, lord of the rings movie, iraq war, and iraq iran war.

Each result shows the most coherent and representative cluster with its ten most frequent keywords, geographic locations and time intervals that appear in that cluster. The results were obtained by executing the EMPROXIMITY system with 150 iterations of Gibbs Sampling and rest settings same as used for the experimental setup. The captions accompanying the figures elaborate on the event depicted.

---

[6] https://en.wikipedia.org/wiki/George_W._Bush
[7] https://en.wikipedia.org/wiki/Bill_Clinton
[8] https://en.wikipedia.org/wiki/Ronald_Reagan
[9] https://en.wikipedia.org/wiki/Ryan_White
[10] https://en.wikipedia.org/wiki/Deng_Xiaoping
[11] https://en.wikipedia.org/wiki/Pope_John_Paul_II
[12] https://en.wikipedia.org/wiki/A_Brief_History_of_Time
[13] https://en.wikipedia.org/wiki/Soviet-Afghan_War
[14] https://en.wikipedia.org/wiki/The_Lord_of_the_Rings_(film_series)
[15] https://en.wikipedia.org/wiki/Iraq_War
[16] https://en.wikipedia.org/wiki/Iran-Iraq_War

Keywords	[bush] [wife] [campaign] [george] [washington] [marvin] [gore] [al] [st] [louis]
Time	[12-Apr-2000 , 12-Apr-2000] [04-Aug-2000 , 04-Aug-2000] [01-Jan-2000 , 31-Dec-2000]
Locations	none
Entities	[YAGO:George_W._Bush] [YAGO:Republican_Party_(United_States)] [YAGO:Republican_National_Convention]

*Table 3: An event cluster for query **george w. bush**. The event identified is that of the inaugural presidential campaign of George W. Bush, whose political affiliation was to the Republican Party.[6]*

Keywords	[clinton] [bill] [top] [address] [news] [page] [africa] [front] [african] [home] [hillary]
Time	[01-Jan-1999 , 01-Jan-1999] [23-Aug-1998 , 23-Aug-1998] [03-Apr-1998 , 03-Apr-1998] [01-Jan-1999 , 31-Dec-1999]
Locations	[YAGO:Africa] [YAGO:White_House] [YAGO:United_States]
Entities	[YAGO:Bill_Clinton] [YAGO:Monica_Lewinsky] [YAGO:Hillary_Rodham_Clinton] [YAGO:White_House] [YAGO:Africa] [YAGO:United_States]

*Table 4: An event cluster for query **bill clinton**. The event identified Bill Clinton's impeachment from presidency due to the affair with Monica Lewinsky in 1999.[7]*

Keywords	[reagan] [ronald] [legacy] [opinion] [top] [government] [social] [politics] [corrections] [wilson] [attack]
Time	[27-Jun-2004 , 27-Jun-2004] [01-Jan-2004 , 01-Jan-2004] [07-Jun-2004 , 07-Jun-2004] [01-Jan-1911 , 01-Jan-1911] [11-Jun-2004 , 11-Jun-2004] [14-Jan-1993 , 14-Jan-1993]
Locations	[YAGO:Palo_Alto,_California] [YAGO:California] [YAGO:United_States]
Entities	[YAGO:Ronald_Reagan] [YAGO:California] [YAGO:Nancy_Reagan] [YAGO:United_States] [YAGO:Palo_Alto,_California] [YAGO:Culture_of_the_United_States] [YAGO:Dick_Cheney] [YAGO:Ron_Reagan]

*Table 5: An event cluster for query **ronald reagan**. Ronald Reagan passed away on June 5, 2004 in California.[8] The cluster reports his funeral which took place on June 11, 2004.[8]*

Keywords	[ryan] [school] [white] [senior] [friends] [mother] [kokomo] [edward] [president] [riley] [attendance] [family]
Time	[01-Jan-1984 , 01-Jan-1984] [01-Jan-1199 , 31-Dec-1199]
Locations	[YAGO:New_York] [YAGO:Kingston,_New_York] [YAGO:Cicero,_Illinois] [YAGO:Indianapolis] [YAGO:Kokomo,_Indiana]
Entities	[YAGO:Megan] [YAGO:Saint_Joseph] [YAGO:Edward_VI_of_England] [YAGO:New_York] [YAGO:Matt_Ryan] [YAGO:Ronald_Reagan] [YAGO:Nancy_Reagan] [YAGO:Hamilton_Heights_School_Corporation] [YAGO:Cicero,_Illinois] [YAGO:Indianapolis] [YAGO:Kokomo,_Indiana] [YAGO:Taco_Bell] [YAGO:Kelly_Ryan] [YAGO:Ryan_White] [YAGO:Kingston,_New_York] [YAGO:Kelly_Osbourne]

*Table 6: An event cluster for query **ryan white**. It depicts the event when Ryan White was not allowed to attend school due to health concerns related to his HIV/AIDS infection.[9] The time interval [01-Jan-1199, 31-Dec-1199] is mined due to erroneous annotation by the temporal annotator.*

Keywords	[top] [china] [deng] [lee] [news] [li] [asia] [world] [government] [nicholas]
Time	[17-Jun-1989 , 17-Jun-1989] [03-Jan-1996 , 03-Jan-1996] [01-Jan-1970 , 31-Dec-1970] [23-Jul-1989 , 23-Jul-1989]
Locations	[YAGO:China] [YAGO:Australia] [YAGO:New_York_City] [YAGO:Ithaca,_New_York]
Entities	[YAGO:China] [YAGO:Australia] [YAGO:Fang_Lizhi] [YAGO:New_York_City] [YAGO:Tiananmen_Square_protests_of_1989] [YAGO:Deng_Xiaoping] [YAGO:Overseas_Chinese] [YAGO:Ithaca,_New_York]

*Table 7: An event cluster for query **deng xiaoping**. It reports the Tiananmen Square protests of 1989; in which Fang Lizhi and Deng Xiaoping were key named entities.[10]*

Keywords	[pope] [opinion] [savior] [cahill] [thomas] [paul] [john] [ii] [editor] [top] [catholic] [april] [saddened]
Time	[08-Apr-2005 , 08-Apr-2005] [02-Apr-2005 , 02-Apr-2005] [05-Apr-2005 , 05-Apr-2005] [03-Apr-2005 , 03-Apr-2005]
Locations	[YAGO:Florida] [YAGO:West_Palm_Beach,_Florida]
Entities	[YAGO:Pope_John_Paul_II] [YAGO:Thomas_Cahill] [YAGO:Kingdom_of_Italy] [YAGO:Camillo_Ruini] [YAGO:Catholic_Church] [YAGO:Judaism] [YAGO:Florida] [YAGO:West_Palm_Beach,_Florida]

*Table 8: An event cluster for query **pope john paul ii**. The event described is that of his death on April 2, 2005.[11]*

Keywords	[dr] [black] [hawking] [hole] [gilliam] [physicist] [time] [york] [caltech] [mr]
Time	[01-Nov-1998 , 30-Nov-1998] [01-Jan-1999 , 31-Dec-1999] [01-Jan-1900 , 01-Jan-1900] [03-Apr-1988 , 03-Apr-1988] [01-Jan-1988 , 31-Dec-1988]
Locations	[YAGO:University_of_Cambridge] [YAGO:Wildwood,_New_Jersey] [YAGO:Arizona]
Entities	[YAGO:Larry_Doyle_(writer)] [YAGO:University_of_Cambridge] [YAGO:Leonard_Susskind] [YAGO:Robert_Redford] [YAGO:William_Morris] [YAGO:A_Brief_History_of_Time] [YAGO:Wildwood,_New_Jersey] [YAGO:Arizona] [YAGO:Associated_Press] [YAGO:Random_House] [YAGO:Lou_Gehrig]

Table 9: An event cluster for query **stephen hawking**. The cluster shows the dates on which first edition of his book "A Brief History of Time" was released — 1988 and tenth anniversary edition of the book was released — 1998.[12]

Keywords	[presidential] [elections] [2000] [election] [government] [quest] [gore] [al] [pres] [vice] [politics] [campaign]
Time	[01-Jan-2000 , 01-Jan-2000] [01-Jan-2000 , 31-Dec-2000]
Locations	[YAGO:United_States]
Entities	[YAGO:United_States] [YAGO:Al_Gore]

Table 10: An event cluster for query **us presidential elections**. The cluster points to the US Presidential Elections in 2000 for which Al Gore ran as vice president.

Keywords	[soviet] [afghanistan] [war] [military] [beginning] [party] [forces] [union] [exhibition] [mixed]
Time	[01-Jan-1938 , 01-Jan-1938] [01-Jan-1980 , 01-Jan-1980] [29-Apr-1988 , 29-Apr-1988] [01-Jan-1979 , 01-Jan-1979] [01-Apr-1988 , 01-Apr-1988] [29-Jul-1987 , 29-Jul-1987] [01-Jan-1950 , 01-Jan-1950]
Locations	[YAGO:Soviet_Union] [YAGO:Afghanistan] [YAGO:Moscow] [YAGO:Kabul] [YAGO:United_States]
Entities	[YAGO:Soviet_Union] [YAGO:Afghanistan] [YAGO:Mohammad_Najibullah] [YAGO:Moscow] [YAGO:Bosniaks] [YAGO:Kabul] [YAGO:United_States]

Table 11: An event cluster for query **soviet afghanistan war**. It depicts the Soviet-Afghanistan conflict that lasted from 1979 to 1989.[13]

Keywords	[lord] [rings] [top] [movie] [motion] [opinion] [pictures] [article] [elvis] [jackson] [trilogy] [movies]
Time	[15-Dec-2002 , 15-Dec-2002] [01-Jan-1987 , 01-Jan-1987] [25-Jan-2004 , 25-Jan-2004] [12-Nov-2002 , 12-Nov-2002] [01-Jan-2003 , 31-Dec-2003] [01-Jan-1982 , 01-Jan-1982] [11-Jan-2004 , 11-Jan-2004] [28-Dec-2002 , 29-Dec-2002] [07-Sep-2003 , 07-Sep-2003] [01-Dec-2003 , 31-Dec-2003]
Locations	[YAGO:Weldon,_Northamptonshire] [YAGO:Wellington]
Entities	[YAGO:J._R._R._Tolkien] [YAGO:Weldon,_Northamptonshire] [YAGO:Wellington] [YAGO:Carol_Ann_Lee] [YAGO:Peter_Jackson]

Table 12: An event cluster for query **lord of the rings movie**. It captures the location where the movie was shot — Wellington and the author of the book on which the movie is based on — J. R. R. Tolkien.[14]

Keywords	[iraq] [states] [united] [war] [opinion] [top] [international] [relations] [defense] [armament] [president] [time] [fearful] [david]
Time	[13-Apr-2006 , 13-Apr-2006] [15-Jun-2005 , 15-Jun-2005] [16-Jul-2003 , 16-Jul-2003] [16-Oct-2003 , 16-Oct-2003] [30-Jun-2005 , 30-Jun-2005]
Locations	[YAGO:New_York_City] [YAGO:Port_Washington,_Wisconsin] [YAGO:Radcliff,_Kentucky] [YAGO:Iraq] [YAGO:United_States]
Entities	[YAGO:Iraq] [YAGO:United_States_Army] [YAGO:Donald_Rumsfeld] [YAGO:United_States_Department_of_Defense] [YAGO:George_W._Bush] [YAGO:Jim_Folsom] [YAGO:New_York_City] [YAGO:Port_Washington,_Wisconsin] [YAGO:Radcliff,_Kentucky] [YAGO:United_States]

Table 13: An event cluster for query **iraq war**. The cluster shows the start of Iraq War in 2003.[15]

Keywords	[iraq] [iran] [war] [oil] [international] [top] [faw] [port] [east] [world] [delegate] [rafsanjani]
Time	[01-Mar-1986 , 31-Mar-1986] [01-Sep-1980 , 01-Sep-1980] [01-Sep-1980 , 30-Sep-1980] [01-Jan-1970 , 31-Dec-1970] [01-Jan-1980 , 01-Jan-1980] [23-Sep-2003 , 23-Sep-2003] [25-Jan-1991 , 25-Jan-1991] [01-Aug-1988 , 31-Aug-1988] [17-Mar-2006 , 17-Mar-2006] [01-Jan-1000 , 01-Jan-1000] [01-Jan-1988 , 31-Dec-1988] [02-Oct-2003 , 02-Oct-2003]
Locations	[YAGO:Iran] [YAGO:Iraq] [YAGO:Geneva]
Entities	[YAGO:Iran] [YAGO:Iraq] [YAGO:United_Nations] [YAGO:Akbar_Hashemi_Rafsanjani] [YAGO:Iranian_peoples] [YAGO:Gulf_War] [YAGO:Geneva] [YAGO:United_Nations_Security_Council] [YAGO:Fao_Landing] [YAGO:Western_world] [YAGO:Persian_people] [YAGO:Iran-Iraq_War] [YAGO:National_Iraqi_News_Agency]

Table 14: An event cluster for query **iraq iran war**. It describes the conflict between Iran and Iraq that lasted from 1980 to 1988.[16]

Who Wants to Join Me? Companion Recommendation in Location Based Social Networks*

Yi Liao[1], Wai Lam[1], Shoaib Jameel[2], Steven Schockaert[2], Xing Xie[3]

[1]Dept. of Systems Engineering and Engineering Management, The Chinese University of Hong Kong
[2]School of Computer Science and Informatics, Cardiff University
[3]Microsoft Research

{yliao, wlam}@se.cuhk.edu.hk
{jameels1,schockaerts1}@cardiff.ac.uk   xingx@microsoft.com

ABSTRACT

We consider the problem of identifying possible companions for a user who is planning to visit a given venue. Specifically, we study the task of predicting which of the user's current friends, in a location based social network (LBSN), are most likely to be interested in joining the visit. An important underlying assumption of our model is that friendship relations can be clustered based on the kinds of interests that are shared by the friends. To identify these friendship types, we use a latent topic model, which moreover takes into account the geographic proximity of the user to the location of the proposed venue. To the best of our knowledge, our model is the first that addresses the task of recommending companions for a proposed activity. While a number of existing topic models can be adapted to make such predictions, we experimentally show that such methods are significantly outperformed by our model.

1. INTRODUCTION

Fuelled by the popularity of mobile devices, location based social networks (LBSNs) such as Foursquare have started to flourish in recent years. Users on such social networks use an app to report the venues they are visiting, typically in real time. LBSN providers thus obtain valuable data about their users in the form of lists of so-called check-in records, i.e. records of the time and venue of each reported visit. These lists can then be used to recommend venues that might be of interest to the user, and to target advertising, among others. For example, a large number of authors have looked at the problem of place-of-interest (POI) recommendation, i.e. the problem of recommending new venues based on a user's past check-in behavior [23, 22, 50, 20, 24, 51, 8, 19].

In this paper, we study a new task for LBSNs which we call companion recommendation. In particular, we consider the scenario of a user who is planning a visit (e.g. going to the movies, going to the park for a picnic, going to a concert) and who is looking for

*We thank Dr. Zhiyuan Cheng, Google for providing the raw check-in dataset and Prasanta Bhattacharya of the National University of Singapore for giving us valuable information about crawling data.

ICTIR '16, September 12-16, 2016, Newark, DE, USA

© 2016 ACM. ISBN 978-1-4503-4497-5/16/09. . . $15.00

DOI: http://dx.doi.org/10.1145/2970398.2970420

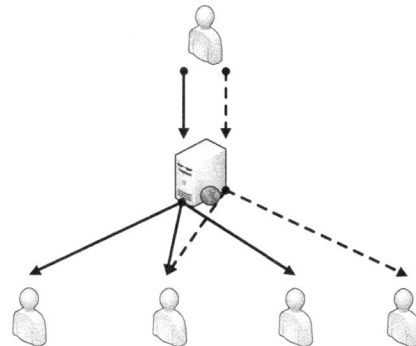

Figure 1: The solid line represents the message "I'm going to the beach on Saturday. Who wants to join me?"; The dashed line represents the message "Tonight at the movie. Who wants to come along?"

friends who would like to join. In such a case, the user may post a message such as "I'm going to the beach on Saturday. Who wants to join me?". The task we address in this paper is to predict who among a given user's friends is most likely to be interested in joining the proposed activity. The core idea is that we can cluster each user's friends based on the interests they share with the user. For example, a user may have colleagues with whom they have lunch on weekdays, friends with whom they go to concerts, other friends who share a passion for hiking, and yet other friends with whom they go out on Saturday evenings. Our proposed model will automatically induce the different kinds of friendship types that are found in a given LBSN from the past check-in behaviour of the users, and will allow us to predict which of these friendship types is most closely related to the proposed visit. This model can be used in various ways by an LBSN. For example, when a user is posting a message announcing a planned visit, the system can automatically recommend groups of friends with whom this message could be shared, as depicted in Figure 1. Along similar lines, the predictions made by the model could feed into the ranking algorithm that is used to display news feeds, i.e. the message could be given more prominence in the news feeds of friends who are more likely to be interested in joining. Finally, the model could also directly recommend companions to the user, which could be useful in some cases as users are not always aware of all interests of their online friends, given that many friendship ties on social networks are weak ties [6, 11].

Several authors have looked at the friend recommendation task

[13, 41, 44, 34], where the aim is to predict missing friendship relations, based on information collected from social networks. While this task also involves friendship relations, it is clearly different from companion recommendation, as it does not take into account the characteristics of a specific venue, which is a key element in our proposed setting. Another related task is predicting the strength of existing friendship relations [43, 37, 16]. The framework proposed by Xiang et al. [43], for instance, makes use of the users' check-in history and previous interactions to predict friendship strength. However, such models cannot solve the companion recommendation tasks in a satisfactory way, as again they do not take into account what exactly are the shared interests between two friends. For example, two users may be close friends but enjoy very different types of music, in which case they should not be recommended to each other when planning to attend a concert. Companion recommendation is furthermore different from the task of group recommendation [35, 45, 29, 3, 33], which also involves multiple users, but where the aim is to recommend the most satisfactory venue to a group of users. Finally, the proposed companion recommendation tasks is also clearly different from POI recommendation. To the best of our knowledge, no previous works have investigated the task of recommending companions to a user planning to visit a given venue.

To tackle the companion recommendation task, we propose a probabilistic graphical model which captures the inter-relationships among the essential elements of this problem: venues, users and friendship relations. Our framework uses a first set of latent variables to model user interests and a second set of latent variables to model friendship types. User interests are modelled as distributions over venue categories, whereas friendship types are modelled as distributions over users that share particular interests. The latent variables are estimated based on the categories of the venues that have previously been visited by all users, and, for each pair of users, the list of venues which they have both visited in the past. An important underlying assumption is that the categories of the venues which two friends have both visited semantically characterizes their friendship type. Furthermore, our model also takes into account the distance between the location of the proposed venue and the location of each candidate companion (estimated from the locations of the venues which they have visited in the past). This is important, as users are clearly more likely to visit places in their vicinity. This observation, which is known as geographical mobility, has been utilized in various LBSN-based approaches [23, 55, 49, 5, 17, 42, 15, 31, 12, 54, 26].

The remainder of this paper is structured as follows. In the next section, we discuss in more detail how our model is related to existing methods. Section 3 then introduces our model, and explains how its parameters can be estimated and how it can be used to make predictions. Finally, in Section 4 we evaluate our model by comparing it to a number of baselines. While there are no existing method for the task of companion recommendation that against which we can compare directly, our evaluation will demonstrate that straightforward modifications to existing models cannot offer a competitive solution.

2. RELATED WORK

As mentioned in the introduction, we are not aware of any existing approaches that solve the task of companion recommendation. In this section, we discuss existing models for the three most closely related tasks: friendship prediction, POI recommendation and group recommendation.

2.1 Friendship Prediction

The problem of modelling how social networks evolve has attracted a lot of attention in recent years. Among others, several models have been proposed to predict which friendship relations are likely to be formed. A common approach is to treat friendship prediction as a classical link prediction problem and rely on proximity measures in the social network graph. An early example of such an approach, in the context of co-authorship networks, is presented in [25], where a model that takes into account network topology was shown to perform substantially better than random guessing. Other methods for measuring the proximity between two users include the common neighbors, Jaccard coefficient, and Admic/Adar methods, as surveyed by [25]. While the aforementioned methods look at the local neighbourhood structure, methods such as random walk approaches [2, 21] can be regarded as global proximity methods [48]. For example, Backstrom et al., [1] propose a supervised random walk algorithm for friendship prediction, incorporating users' attributes. Some studies have also found interesting patterns in existing friendship networks. For example, triadic closure is a typical structural pattern in friendship networks and has been investigated by [37, 32, 30]. Some models also focus on semantic features. In [36], for instance, the authors present a model that predicts friendship relations based the similarity between user profiles. Recent work such as [38] studies the top-k link prediction problem in social networks, which emphasizes the precision of top-k users in the recommended ranking list. Some other works such as [47, 49] study the link prediction problem by transferring information from aligned multi-networks, where multiple social networks are partially aligned at the same time. Subbian et al., [39] build a robust and effective classifier for link prediction using multiple auxiliary networks. In multi-networks, users can be extensively correlated with each other by various connections.

The aforementioned works only deal with binary friendship. However, some authors have also considered the problem of predicting the strength of existing friendship relations [16, 43]. For example, Xiang et al., [43] propose a framework to infer latent friendship strength from the similarity of the users' profiles and the frequency of their interactions. In contrast with all the existing work on friendship prediction, our model takes into account different types of friendship links to tailor companion recommendations to the characteristics of the specific venue being visited.

2.2 POI Recommendation

POI or venue recommendation is a widely studied problem in the context of LBSNs. In most models, spatial information plays a prominent role, since the probability for a user to visit a venue is closely related to the distance the user needs to travel to reach the venue (as suggested by Tobler's First Law of Geography). In [20, 53, 18, 17] the authors study GPS records, encoded as a series of time points with associated geo-coordinates, to capture patterns of user movement. Lian et al., [24] propose a framework based on matrix factorization, augmenting latent factors with vector representations, to capture the so-called activity areas of users and the influence areas of POIs. Temporal aspects of venue recommendation are studied in [9, 46], which take account of the fact that people's activities and movements vary over time.

With online social networks increasingly storing users' present and past movements, content-based venue recommendation has recently attracted much attention. In [15] the authors explore a spatial topic modeling approach to predict future venues of interest based on the textual content of a user's posts. Liu et al., [27] exploit various aspects of venue profiles and develop a joint model for venue recommendation. More recently, Gao et al., [10] propose

Symbol	Description
u, U	user and user set respectively
$|M|$	size of check-in records for a particular user
v, V	venue and venue set respectively
l, L	category label and category label set respectively
c, C_u	companion and companion candidates for user u
$f, |F|$	friendship type and number of friendship types
g	geographical location of a venue
H	historical check-in data for a companion
θ	user-specific distribution on topics
$z, |Z|$	topic associated with each visit and number of topics respectively
Φ^f	topic-specific distribution over friendship type
Φ^v	topic-specific distribution over venues
Φ^l	distribution over category labels specific to friendship type
$\Phi^c_{u,f}$	preference on companions specific to pairs of user u and friendship type f

Table 1: Some basic notations

a POI recommendation framework by relating three types of content information to different aspects of users' check-in behavior. Lian et al. [23] propose an Implicit-feedback based Content-aware Collaborative Filtering (ICCF) framework to incorporate semantic content and steer clear of negative sampling.

2.3 Group Recommendation

Group recommendation methods [45, 29, 3, 33, 52] aggregate the preferences of a group of users and seek to recommend venues that are most suitable for the group as a whole. For example, Yuan et al., [45] propose a generative model that studies different influences for users in a group. Cheng et al., [3] investigate multiple user behaviors in group recommendation. Salehi-Abari and Boutilier [35] have developed probabilistic inference methods for predicting individual preferences and exploit these predictions to make group decisions or recommendations based on techniques from the field of social choice theory. Given that the group recommendation task is about recommending venues, it is clear that this task is different from the problem we discuss in this paper.

3. OUR FRAMEWORK

We assume that the following data is available to support the task of companion recommendation: a list of previous check-ins for each user, a profile document for each venue, and the (generic) friendship relation between the users. We assume that each check-in record consists of (i) the venue which the user has visited, and (ii) a list of friends from the user who have also visited that venue. Furthermore, the venue profile document consists of a set of categories and a location (in the form of geo-coordinates). The set of categories in a venue profile document can contain up to three labels that describe the nature of the venue (e.g. Indian restaurant, hotel, primary school). Given the aforementioned information, and a given input user u and venue v, the task is to predict which of u's friends are most likely to be interested in joining the visit to v.

Our proposed framework is a probabilistic graphical model capturing the inter-relationships between user interests, friendship types and check-in records. In particular, we consider a generative process, in which a user u has a specific interest in mind, which is encoded as the latent topic z. We can think of z as representing the purpose of the planned visit, e.g. going to a restaurant with an Asian cuisine. The interests of a given user are sampled from a

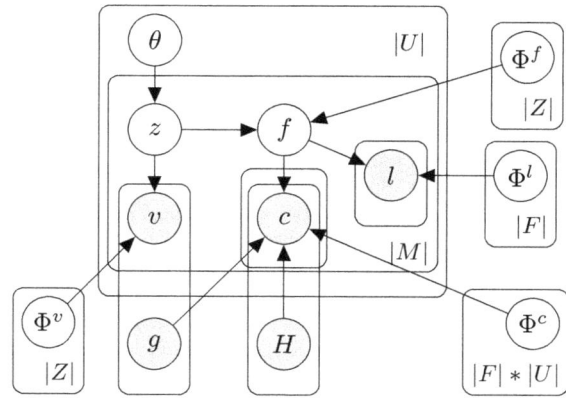

Figure 2: Graphical model for companion recommendation

multinomial distribution, which models the overall interests of that user. Each topic z is viewed as a soft cluster of venues v, which are intuitively the venues that the user might choose to visit to satisfy z. For example, if z represents the purpose of going to a restaurant with Asian cuisine, the the associated cluster of venues will, among others, include specific Thai restaurants.

To identify candidate companions, we introduce the notion of a friendship type. Our model uses latent variables to encode these friendship types. Furthermore, each friendship type f is related to the latent topics that are used for modelling user interests. For example, there might be a friendship type for *Asian Food*, a friendship type for *Hiking*, etc. This captures the intuition that the suitable companions for a given visit depend on the characteristics of the place being visited. For example, some friends who often join the user to the gym, might not be interested in joining a visit to a Thai restaurant. Different friendship types may be compatible with a given topic to some degree. Consequently, we assign to each topic z a multinomial distribution over friendship types, capturing the suitability of different friendship types for a proposed visit.

After a suitable friendship type f is determined, we further relate the friendship type f to the list of friends from the user who have also visited that venue, denoted as companions c. Though they may not have visited the venue together with the user so far, they are potential companions when the user visits a venue next time. Friendship relations between the user and his friends, encoded as friendship type, are learned by our model, which is further used in companion recommendation in the future. For example, next time the user plans to visit a restaurant with an Asian cuisine, friends whose friendship relation with the user is identified as friendship type for *Asian Food*, is recommended as companion for this visit.

Different types of evidence are taken into account to learn the latent representations. First, we use the category information of the venues visited by each user to estimate the topics in which they are interested. Given that friendship types are related to these topics, the category information thus indirectly also serves to assign meaning to these friendship types. Second, to recommend companions for a given visit, the model takes into account the geographic location of each candidate companion, in addition to a preference score derived from the latent friendship model.

3.1 Description of the model

Figure 2 shows the graphical model, while some basic notations are explained in Table 1. Note that for clarity we do not show the hyper-priors of the parameters in the graphical model, focusing instead on the main elements of the model only. The outer rectangle is a plate representing a set of users and the inner rectangle is a plate representing the set of check-ins of a particular user. A latent topic assignment z for the check-in record is first sampled from a user-specific multinomial distribution θ, representing the user's interest. The selected topic is then used to generate both a venue and a friendship type. Specifically, the topic z is associated with a multinomial distribution Φ_z^v from which a specific venue is sampled, as well as a multinomial distribution Φ_z^f from which a specific friendship type is sampled.

To ensure that the friendship types can be characterized in terms of venue categories, we assume that for each friendship type f we have a multinomial distribution Φ_f^l from which venue categories are sampled. Note that a venue may belong to several categories. Thus a category label is sampled several times. Note that in this way, the categories of the venue being visited act as a soft constraint on the kinds of friendship types that might be selected.

To sample a companion c, we take into account both the selected friendship type and the geographic location of the user and proposed venue. The friendship type is taken into account by associating a preference vector $\Phi_{u,f}^c$ with each user and each friendship type. Note that the vector $\Phi_{u,f}^c$ is not a multinomial distribution, since the companion c is sampled with a different type of distribution in contrast with the other nodes, which will be described later. This vector captures which friends are most likely to be companions given the specific user u and the specific friendship type f. Note that we only consider companion candidates from the user's friend list, as we assume that users are only interested in visiting the venue with people they already know.

In addition to the friendship type, geographical information also plays an important role. For example, it does not seem useful to recommend a user who lives in New York as a companion when the target venue is a gym located in California. To take into account geographical mobility, for each candidate companion c, we take into account the set $\mathbf{H}_c$ containing the locations of all c's previous check-ins. Specifically, the geographical compatibility between companion c and venue v is computed by averaging the negative exponential value of the distance between the location of venue v and the venues in $\mathbf{H}_c$, as expressed by the following equation:

$$G(c, v) = \frac{1}{|\mathbf{H}_c|} \cdot \sum_{v' \in \mathbf{H}_c} exp(-||g_{v'} - g_v||^2) \qquad (1)$$

Note that, intuitively, a venue that is near the venues in $\mathbf{H}_c$ will get high compatibility score. Let $P(c|f, \mathbf{H}_c, g_v, \Phi^c)$ denote the probability that friend c is chosen as companion given the friendship type f and venue location g_v. The estimation of this probability is inspired by the Sparse Additive Generative Model (SAGE) [7, 42]. When a variable is affected by multiple facets, a common approach is to design a weighted addition of the multiple facets. In our case, the addition would be $P(c|f, \mathbf{H}_c, g_v, \Phi^c) \propto \lambda + (1 - \lambda)G(c, v)$, where λ is a parameter that needs to get estimated. However, the estimation of λ could make the inference procedure complicated and sometimes may even result in overfitting. The idea of SAGE is to combine multiple facets through simple addition in log space, avoiding the inference of switching parameter. Eisenstein et al., [7] has demonstrated its applicability in many complex multifaceted generative models. Following the idea, $P(c|f, \mathbf{H}_c, g_v, \Phi^c)$ is designed as follows:

$$P(c|f, \mathbf{H}_c, g_v, \Phi^c) = \frac{exp(\Phi_{u,f,c}^c + G(c, v))}{\sum_{c' \in C_u} exp(\Phi_{u,f,c'}^c + G(c', v))} \qquad (2)$$

We can now summarize the generative process as follows.

1. For each user u, draw a distribution $\theta_u \sim Dirichlet(\alpha)$ on topics, where α is a hyper-prior.

2. For each friendship type f, draw a distribution on category labels $\Phi_f^l \sim Dirichlet(\kappa)$, where κ is a hyper-prior.

3. For each topic

   (a) Draw a distribution on venues, $\Phi_z^v \sim Dirichlet(\xi)$, where ξ is a hyper-prior.

   (b) Draw a distribution on friendship type, $\Phi_z^f \sim Dirichlet(\psi)$, where ψ is a hyper-prior.

4. For each check-in record of the user u:

   (a) Draw a topic $z \sim Multinomial(\theta_u)$

   (b) Draw the friendship type and companion as follows:

      i. Draw a friendship type $f \sim Multinomial(\Phi_z^f)$

      ii. For each companion, i.e. friend of the user who have also visited the venue, draw c according to (2).

      iii. For each category label of the venue, draw $l \sim Multinomial(\Phi_f^l)$

   (c) Draw a check-in venue $v \sim Multinomial(\Phi_z^v)$

3.2 Parameter Estimation

The complete likelihood of the model is as follows:

$$P(z, f, v, \boldsymbol{l}, \boldsymbol{c}|\alpha, \psi, \xi, \beta, \kappa, g_v, \mathbf{H}_c) \qquad (3)$$
$$= \int p(z|\theta)p(\theta|\alpha)d\theta \cdot \int p(f|z, \Phi_{z,f}^f)p(\Phi_{z,f}^f)d\Phi_{z,f}^f \cdot$$
$$\int p(v|z, \Phi_{z,v}^v)p(\Phi_{z,v}^v|\xi)d\Phi_{z,v}^v \cdot$$
$$\prod_l^l \int p(l|f, \Phi_{f,l}^l)p(\Phi_{f,l}^l|\kappa)d\Phi_{f,l}^l \cdot \prod_c^c P(c|f, \mathbf{H}_c, g_v, \Phi^c)$$

where $\boldsymbol{l}$ is the set of category labels l of the venue and $\boldsymbol{c}$ is the set of companions c. Note that the last factor $P(c|f, \mathbf{H}_c, g_v, \Phi^c)$ refers to (2). In contrast to the other factors, it does not integrate over Φ^c, as the companion c is not sampled from a multinomial distribution. Furthermore, due to the specific way in which we have defined $P(c|f, \mathbf{H}_c, g_v, \Phi^c)$, Gibbs Sampling [14], which has been widely used for the inference of many probabilistic graphical models, cannot to be directly applied to our proposed model. To cope with this, we apply the Gibbs EM algorithm [40] for parameter estimation.

E-step: The latent topic assignment and friendship type assignment are sampled by fixing all the parameters. To sample the topic, the standard Gibbs Sampling method for Latent Dirichlet Allocation is employed. Let $n_{u,z}$ denote the number of times the topic z is assigned to the user u. Let $n_{z,f}$ denote the number of times the friendship type f is assigned to the topic z. Let $n_{z,v}$ denote the number of times the venue v is assigned to the topic z. Let $n_{f,l}$ denote the number of the instances of the category label l that is assigned to the friendship type f. Let $|L|_v$ denote the total number of category labels of the venue and let $|C|_i$ be the number of companions for this check-in record. As usual, when we place the $\neg$ symbol, it means that the counts exclude the current case; when we place the $\cdot$ symbol, it means that the counts for all possible values of the missing index are added up. For example, $n_{f,\cdot}$ is the total number of category labels that are assigned to the friendship type

f. Topics are sampled as follows:

$$P(z_i = j|z_{\neg i}, f, v)$$

$$\propto \quad (n_{u,j}^{\neg i} + \alpha) \cdot \left(\frac{n_{j,f_i}^{\neg i} + \psi_{f_i}}{n_{j,\cdot}^{\neg i} + \psi} \right) \cdot \left(\frac{n_{j,v_i}^{\neg i} + \xi_{v_i}}{n_{j,\cdot}^{\neg i} + \xi} \right) \quad (4)$$

Friendship types are sampled, given the fixed parameter Φ^c, as follows:

$$P(f_i = j|f_{\neg i}, z, u, c, l) \propto (n_{z_i,j}^{\neg i} + \psi_j) \cdot$$

$$\left(\prod_{\varsigma=1}^{|L|_v} \frac{n_{j,l_\varsigma}^{\neg i} + \kappa_{l_\varsigma}}{n_{j,\cdot}^{\neg i} + \kappa} \right) \cdot \left(\prod_{\varsigma=1}^{|C_u|_i} P(c_\varsigma|f, \mathbf{H}_{c_\varsigma}, g_v, \Phi^c) \right) \quad (5)$$

M-step: We optimize the parameter Φ^c to maximize the logarithm of the complete likelihood denoted in Equation 3. We employ the quasi-Newton method [28] to solve the problem. This is an iterative algorithm to find local maxima or minima, which has a higher computational efficiency than the standard Newton method. The gradients of the log-likelihood regarding parameter Φ^c are calculated as follows:

$$\frac{\partial L}{\partial \Phi_{u,f,c}^c} = n_{u,f,c} - \sum_{i \in M_{u,f}} \frac{exp(\Phi_{u,f,c}^c + G(c,v_i))}{\sum_{c' \in C_u} exp(\Phi_{u,f,c'}^c + G(c',v_i))} \quad (6)$$

where $n_{u,f,c}$ denotes the number of times the companion c is assigned to the pair (u, f). $M_{u,f}$ denotes the the set of check-in records that have been assigned to the friendship type f for the user u.

The remaining parameters can be estimated by using standard Gibbs sampling [14] for topic modeling. After a sufficient number of iteration, the other parameters are calculated as follows:

$$\theta_{u,z} = \frac{n_{u,z} + \alpha_z}{\sum_z^Z (n_{u,z} + \alpha_z)} \quad (7)$$

$$\Phi_{z,f}^f = \frac{n_{z,f} + \psi_f}{\sum_f^F (n_{z,f} + \psi_f)} \quad (8)$$

$$\Phi_{z,v}^v = \frac{n_{z,v} + \xi_v}{\sum_v^V (n_{z,v} + \xi_v)} \quad (9)$$

$$\Phi_{f,l}^l = \frac{n_{f,l} + \kappa_l}{\sum_l^L (n_{f,l} + \kappa_l)} \quad (10)$$

3.3 Companion Recommendation

Given a user u who wants to visit a venue v, the output of the considered task is a ranked list of recommended companions. Consider a user u who plans to visit a venue v. To generate suitable recommendations, we make use of the category information l of the venue for the inference of friendship types. The friendship type f is chosen with the following probability:

$$P(f|u, v, l) = \sum_{z=1}^{|Z|} P(f|z, l)P(z|u, v) \quad (11)$$

where $P(z|u, v)$ denotes the probability of drawing the topic z given the user u and the venue v and $P(f|z, l)$ denotes the probability of drawing the friendship type f given the topic z and the category labels l. They can be derived using Bayes' theorem as follows:

$$P(z|u, v) \propto P(z|u)P(v|z) = \theta_{u,z}\Phi_{z,v}^v \quad (12)$$

$$P(f|z, l) \propto P(f|z)P(l|f) = \Phi_{z,f}^f \prod_{i=1}^{|L|_v} \Phi_{f,l_i}^l \quad (13)$$

Number of	NYC	CA	USA
Users	2219	2692	16872
Venues	5588	7828	58205
Check-in Records	54247	67689	470074
Avg. Records/User	24.45	25.14	27.86
Avg. Friends/User	26.89	29.51	40.51
Avg. Companion/Record	2.11	3.25	2.18
Avg. Category Labels/Venue	1.72	1.55	1.31

Table 2: Statistics of datasets

where $|L|_v$ is the total number of category labels of the venue.

The overall probability that the companion c is selected can then be computed as follows:

$$P(c|u, v, l, \mathbf{H}_c, g_v, \Phi^c) = \sum_{f=1}^{|F|} P(c|f, \mathbf{H}_c, g_v, \Phi^c)P(f|u, v, l)$$

where $P(c|f, \mathbf{H}_c, g_v, \Phi^c)$ is evaluated as in (2) and $P(f|u, v, l)$ is evaluated as in (11).

4. EXPERIMENTS AND RESULTS

4.1 Experimental Setup

We conduct experiments on real-world check-in data obtained from Foursquare, a location based social network. We obtained a raw dataset[1] from the first author of [4]. It contains a tuple (UserID, VenueID, Location) for each check-in record, which was collected from Twitter Stream. Note that the UserID refers to ID of a user in Twitter while VenueID refers to ID of a venue in Foursquare. Indeed when such a tuple occurs, it means the user has linked his/her Foursquare account to Twitter account. We have aggregated all the tuples with the same UserID as the historical check-in records of the particular user. We have enriched the dataset by crawling the venue profile information for the venues occurring in the dataset via the public Foursquare Application Programming Interface (API) with VenueID. We have furthermore obtained friendship information among the users via the public Twitter API with UserID.

From the overall collection, we have selected three datasets, which we will refer to as the New York City (NYC) dataset, the California (CA) dataset, and the United States of America (USA) dataset. These datasets were chosen because they allow us to evaluate our method at different geographic scales. Note that we have excluded the New York and California data from the USA dataset, to ensure that all three datasets are disjoint. The check-in records in NYC dataset are located in NYC, which can be regarded as a city-wise dataset; Check-in records in the CA dataset are distributed across several major cities in CA, and thus we can regard this as a state-wise dataset. The USA dataset contains check-in records across the whole country, and thus this can be regarded as a country-wise dataset.

The same processing strategy was adopted for all three datasets. For each user, we first allocated 60% of his/her check-in records to the training set, 20% to the validation set, and 20% to the testing set. The splits between these datasets are chronological. After splitting each dataset, check-in records were enriched by adding companion information and venue profiles. For a particular check-in record associated with a venue, we define companions as friends of the user who have also checked-in at this venue. Although they may not have visited the venue together with the user, they are treated

---

[1]http://infolab.tamu.edu/data/

Dataset	USA			CA			NYC		
Metric	Acc@1	Pre@5	Rec@5	Acc@1	Pre@5	Rec@5	Acc@1	Pre@5	Rec@5
Core	0.532	0.220	0.719	0.567	0.241	0.732	0.483	0.212	0.689
Core-NoG	0.493	0.184	0.698	0.516	0.213	0.709	0.431	0.172	0.603
VP	0.454	0.183	0.647	0.462	0.207	0.668	0.312	0.154	0.538
RSM	0.382	0.161	0.593	0.426	0.191	0.626	0.249	0.121	0.432
LDA	0.364	0.150	0.607	0.403	0.179	0.655	0.270	0.139	0.471

Table 3: Performance of companion recommendation

as companions so that they can be potentially recommended in the future. Note that companions are generated separately within each split. Moreover, we have extracted category labels of all venues and added them to the check-in records associated with the venues. We then removed those check-in records that have no companions. We also removed users who have less than five check-in records. The statistics of the datasets, after these preprocessing steps is shown in Table 2.

Following previous works on recommendation [45, 27, 17], we evaluate the recommendation performance of our framework using three metrics: Pre@5(Precision at five), Rec@5 (Recall at five), and the average accuracy of the one-companion recommendation task.

The parameters of our model include the number of latent friendship types and the number of latent topics. We make use of the validation dataset to select suitable values for these parameters. In this way, for the NYC, CA and USA datasets, the number of friendship types was selected as 70, 100, and 100, respectively, and the number of latent topics was selected as 100, 150, and 150.

Our full framework is denoted as *CORE* (for Companion Recommender). We also investigate one variant of our framework that does not consider geographical information, denoted as *CORE-NoG*. Specifically, the value of $G(c, v)$ is set to zero for all companions and venues in this variant.

4.2 Comparative Methods

Since companion recommendation is a new task, there are no existing models that directly solve it. Therefore, we have instead adapted some related models to tackle the task of performance comparison, as described below. Specifically, we employ three comparative methods. The first comparative method is treated as a representative of friendship-strength based methods. By comparing with this method, we can investigate the importance of considering the target venue in handling our proposed task. The second method is based on Latent Dirichlet Allocation (LDA). A major difference between our proposed model and LDA is that we model friendship relations between users. This comparison will enable us to analyse the effectiveness of using friendship types. The third method is an intuitive approach that is based on user's preference on venue. Friends that have high preference score on the target venue is recommended as companions. These three comparative methods are described next.

Relationship-Strength Method (RSM): Xiang et al. [43] proposed a model to predict the strength of relationship between two friends, which can be adopted to solve the companion recommendation task. This comparative model infers the friendship strength between two users on LinkedIn and Facebook. For each user pair, it considers two kinds of features: the similarity between the two users and a binary interaction vector. Each entry of the latter vector indicates whether the corresponding interaction exists between the user pair. The interactions include one user views the profile of the other user, recommends the other user, and so on. We adapt their algorithm with features derived from check-in records. In particular, we cal-

culate the similarity value by counting how many times they have checked in at the same venue. Furthermore, interactions are captured by checking whether they ever checked-in at venues with the same category, where each entry in the interaction vector is associated with a particular category. Companion recommendations for each user can be obtained by ranking the user's friends according to their friendship strength. Note that in contrast with our model, this model will generate the same set of recommended companions for each venue.

LDA-Based Method (LDA). This comparison method makes use of LDA to learn the topic relations between users, companions and venues. Given the user u and the venue v, candidate companions c are ranked according to the following score: $\sum_z \theta_{u,z} * \theta_{c,z} * p_v(z)$, where $\theta_{u,z}$ and $\theta_{c,z}$ are the posterior distributions over topics z for u and c, representing the interest of the user u and the user c respectively, and $p_v(z)$ is the posterior distribution of venues for the topic z, representing the topics of the venue.

Venue-Preference Method (VP). A score evaluating the preference is calculated for each pair of user and venue. To tackle the companion recommendation problem, where a query user and a target venue are given, companions are ranked by the preference score to the target venue. We adapt a state-of-the-art POI recommendation model [17] to compute the user's preference on venues.

4.3 Quantitative Results

The performance of our framework and the comparative methods on the testing dataset is shown in Table 3. The results show that the performance of our framework is consistently and substantially better than the comparative methods across all the datasets. The differences between our model, on the one hand, and the Relationship-Strength method, LDA-based method, and Venue-Preference method, on the other hand, are statistically significant for all datasets and all evaluation metrics, based on the paired t-test with $p < 0.01$.

The Relationship-Strength method performs substantially worse than our framework. The main underlying reason is that it recommends companions based on the strength of the relationship between two users, regardless of the given input venue. Although this method can infer stronger ties between users who have more check-ins at the same venue and more similarity in profiles, it cannot exploit information about the target venue when making companion recommendations. We observe from the results that the incorporation of geographical information would generally improves the performance, which is consistent with what is found in most LBSN-based tasks. When removing the geographical information from our framework, it still performs better than the LDA-based method. The major difference between these two methods is again that our framework makes companion recommendations with suitable friendship types that match the characteristics of the target venue. This confirms our hypothesis that incorporating friendship types results in better companion recommendations. Our frame-

Friendship Type	Category Labels
1	College Stadium, Convenience Store, College Hockey Rink, Rock Climbing Spot, Climbing Gym, Yoga Studio, College Basketball Court, College Gym, College Auditorium, Synagogue
2	Art Gallery, Art Museum, Museum, Park, Music Venue, Hotel, History Museum, Non-Profit, Concert Hall, Opera House
3	Asian Restaurant, Japanese Restaurant, Sushi Restaurant, Ramen/Noodle House, Thai Restaurant, Chinese Restaurant, Korean Restaurant, Sandwich Place, American Restaurant, Vietnamese Restaurant
4	Gym, Gym/Fitness Center, Athletics & Sports, Event Space, Community Center, Yoga Studio, Pool, College Gym, College Rec Center, Tanning Salon
5	Office, Coworking Space, Event Space, Tech Startup, Building, Advertising Agency, Professional & Other Places, Conference Room, General Entertainment, Design Studio
6	Event Space, Conference Room, Office, Wine Bar, Winery, General Entertainment, Convention Center, Performing Arts Venue, Vineyard, Cafeteria

Table 4: Semantic representation of friendship types

Friendship Type	Names of Venues Visited
1	Hoover Tower, STAPLES Center, Rose Bowl Stadium, Clancey's Market & Deli, 7-Eleven
2	Last Rites Tattoo Theatre and Art Gallery, Japan Society, Art Directors Club
3	Mingalaba Restaurant, Carnitas' Snack Shack, CUCINA urbana, Sol Food Puerto Rican Cuisine
4	Fit Athletic Club, Chuze Fitness, Equinox, UCSF Bakar Fitness & Rec Center
5	Tesla Motors HQ, Foursquare SF, Festival Pavilion, Yahoo!
6	Yahoo!, Zero Zero, The Strand

Table 5: Venues that pairs of users with corresponding friendship types both visited

work is also better than the method based on venue preference, which is adapted from a POI recommendation system.

4.4 Qualitative Analysis

4.4.1 Friendship Type Analysis

Because the category labels of venues are taken into account when modeling friendship types, we can use our framework to produce a semantic description of the latent friendship types. In particular, the parameter Φ^l inferred from our model encodes the relevance of friendship types to categories. To illustrate this, we present some friendship types and their most relevant categories in Table 4. From the category labels describing the corresponding friendship types, we can clearly understand the nature of these friendship types. Intuitively, the friendship types 1 to 5 in Table 4 correspond, respectively, to schoolmates, friends interested in art, friends interested in Asian food, friends interested in sports, co-workers. Friendship type 6, which is slightly different with friendship types 1 to 5, corresponds to co-workers who are also interested in entertainment after work.

Our framework can also characterize the latent friendship types via the inferred parameter Φ^c. To illustrate this, we have selected some user pairs whose friendship types match the ones listed in Table 4. For these user pairs, we then analyze which venues they have most frequently visited. Several of these top venues are listed in Table 5, where the friendship types match those from 4 line by line. We can observe from Table 5 that the venues which the user pairs have ever visited are indeed tightly related to the friendship types described in Table 4. This further illustrates the effectiveness of our framework in characterizing the friendship types between users.

4.5 Sensitivity Analysis

4.5.1 Effect of Parameters

We evaluate the performance of our framework under different settings of the number of friendship types and the number of topics as depicted in Figure 3. When we vary the number of friendship types, we keep the number of topics fixed at 100. Similarly, when we vary the number of topics, we keep the number friendship types fixed at 20. The results show that the performance of our framework is rather robust to changes in the number of friendship types and the number of topics, for the three considered datasets. The performance generally increases as the corresponding parameters increase and becomes stable after a certain point.

4.5.2 Convergence Analysis

We employ the Gibbs EM method for the inference of parameters. The convergence behavior is shown in Figure 5. It shows that the performance of our framework generally gets stable after 700 iterations for the NYC and CA datasets. For USA dataset, it takes about 1000 iterations for the performance to converge.

5. CONCLUSION

We have proposed a framework to solve the problem of recommending companions to users, given a particular venue that the user is interested in visiting. Companion recommendations are made by learning the relationship between latent venue topics and latent friendship types, between latent venue topics and the previous check-in behaviour of users, and between latent friendship types and the categories of previously visited venues. Experimental results show that our framework can solve this task effectively.

6. ACKNOWLEDGMENTS

The work described in this paper is supported by a grant from the Research Grant Council of the Hong Kong Special Administrative Region, China (Project Code: 14203414). This work is also supported by ERC Starting Grant 637277. Another support is from Microsoft Research Asia Urban Informatics Grant FY14-RES-Sponsor-057.

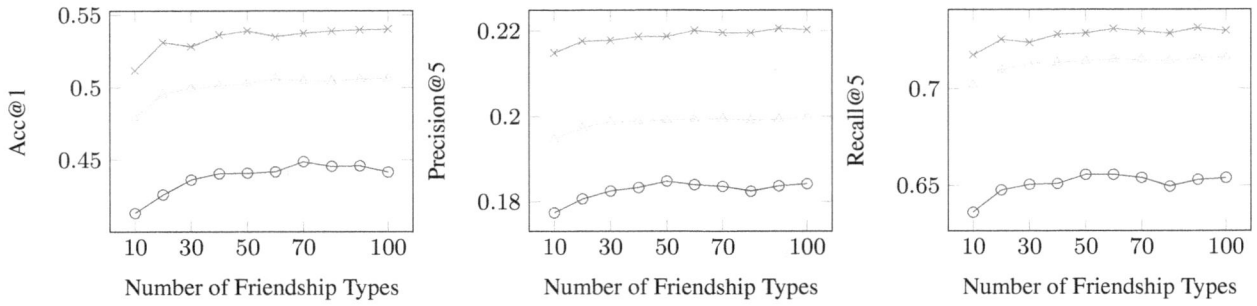

Figure 3: Effect of varying the number of friendship types in our model. ⸺ denotes results for USA, ⸺×⸺ denotes for CA, and ⸺○⸺ denotes for NYC.

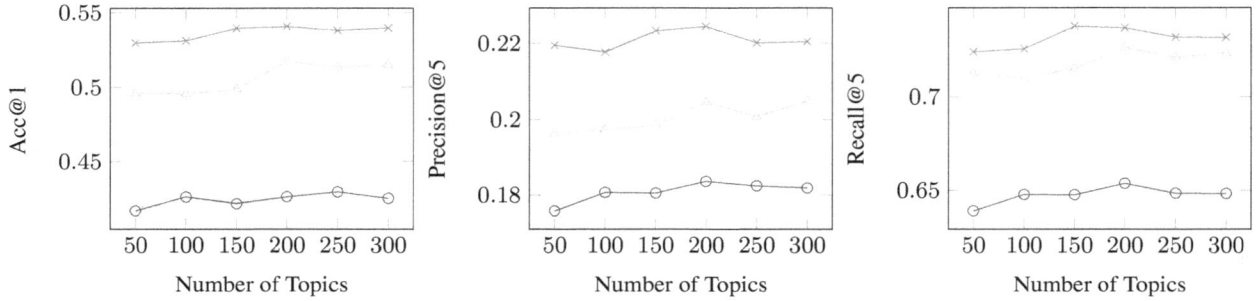

Figure 4: Effect of varying the number of topics in our model. ⸺ denotes results for USA, ⸺×⸺ denotes for CA, and ⸺○⸺ denotes for NYC.

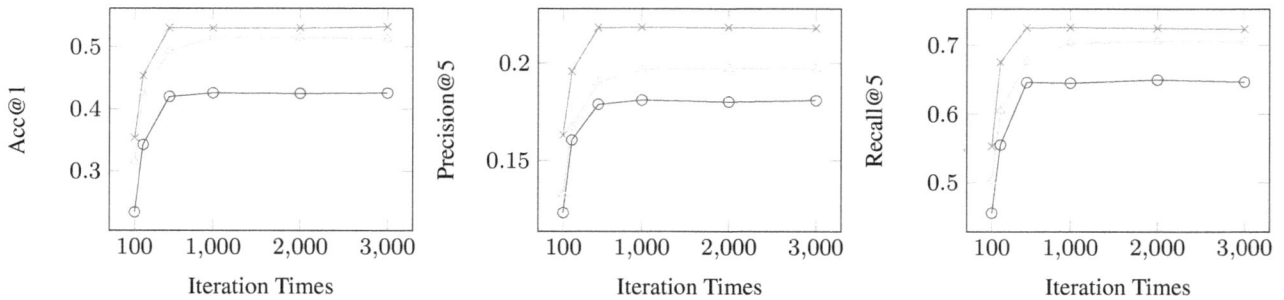

Figure 5: Effect of iteration times in our model. ⸺ denotes results for USA, ⸺×⸺ denotes for CA, and ⸺○⸺ denotes for NYC.

7. REFERENCES

[1] L. Backstrom and J. Leskovec. Supervised random walks: predicting and recommending links in social networks. In *WSDM*, pages 635–644, 2011.

[2] Z. Burda, J. Duda, J. Luck, and B. Waclaw. Localization of the maximal entropy random walk. *Physical Review Letters*, 102(16):160602, 2009.

[3] J. Cheng, T. Yuan, J. Wang, and H. Lu. Group latent factor model for recommendation with multiple user behaviors. In *SIGIR*, pages 995–998, 2014.

[4] Z. Cheng, J. Caverlee, K. Lee, and D. Z. Sui. Exploring millions of footprints in location sharing services. *ICWSM*, 2011:81–88, 2011.

[5] E. Cho, S. A. Myers, and J. Leskovec. Friendship and mobility: User movement in location-based social networks. In *KDD*, pages 1082–1090, 2011.

[6] P. De Meo, E. Ferrara, G. Fiumara, and A. Provetti. On facebook, most ties are weak. *Communications of the ACM*, 57(11):78–84, 2014.

[7] J. Eisenstein, A. Ahmed, and E. P. Xing. Sparse additive generative models of text. In *ICML*, 2011.

[8] S.-S. Feng, X.-T. Li, Y.-F. Zeng, C. Gao, Y.-M. Chee, and Q. Yuan. Personalized ranking metric embedding for next new poi recommendation. In *IJCAI*, 2015.

[9] H. Gao, J. Tang, X. Hu, and H. Liu. Exploring temporal effects for location recommendation on location-based social networks. In *RecSys*, pages 93–100, 2013.

[10] H. Gao, J. Tang, X. Hu, and H. Liu. Content-aware point of interest recommendation on location-based social networks. AAAI, 2015.

[11] E. Gilbert and K. Karahalios. Predicting tie strength with social media. In *SIGCHI*, pages 211–220. ACM, 2009.

[12] A. Gionis, T. Lappas, K. Pelechrinis, and E. Terzi. Customized tour recommendations in urban areas. In *WSDM*, pages 313–322, 2014.

[13] J. Hannon, M. Bennett, and B. Smyth. Recommending twitter users to follow using content and collaborative filtering approaches. In *RecSys*, pages 199–206, 2010.

[14] G. Heinrich. Parameter estimation for text analysis. *University of Leipzig, Tech. Rep*, 2008.

[15] B. Hu and M. Ester. Spatial topic modeling in online social media for location recommendation. In *RecSys*, pages 25–32, 2013.

[16] I. Kahanda and J. Neville. Using transactional information to predict link strength in online social networks. In *ICWSM*, pages 74–81, 2009.

[17] T. Kurashima, T. Iwata, T. Hoshide, N. Takaya, and K. Fujimura. Geo topic model: Joint modeling of user's activity area and interests for location recommendation. In *WSDM*, pages 375–384, 2013.

[18] K. W.-T. Leung, D. L. Lee, and W.-C. Lee. Clr: a collaborative location recommendation framework based on co-clustering. In *SIGIR*, pages 305–314, 2011.

[19] H. Li, R. Hong, S. Zhu, and Y. Ge. Point-of-interest recommender systems: A separate-space perspective. In *ICDM*, pages 231–240, 2015.

[20] M. Li, A. Ahmed, and A. J. Smola. Inferring movement trajectories from GPS snippets. In *WSDM*, pages 325–334, 2015.

[21] R.-H. Li, J. X. Yu, and J. Liu. Link prediction: the power of maximal entropy random walk. In *CIKM*, pages 1147–1156, 2011.

[22] X. Li, G. Cong, X.-L. Li, T.-A. N. Pham, and S. Krishnaswamy. Rank-geofm: A ranking based geographical factorization method for point of interest recommendation. In *SIGIR*, pages 433–442, 2015.

[23] D. Lian, Y. Ge, F. Zhang, N. J. Yuan, X. Xie, T. Zhou, and Y. Rui. Content-aware collaborative filtering for location recommendation based on human mobility data. In *ICDM*, pages 261–270, 2015.

[24] D. Lian, C. Zhao, X. Xie, G. Sun, E. Chen, and Y. Rui. GeoMF: Joint geographical modeling and matrix factorization for point-of-interest recommendation. In *KDD*, pages 831–840, 2014.

[25] D. Liben-Nowell and J. Kleinberg. The link prediction problem for social networks. In *CIKM*, pages 556–559, 2003.

[26] K. H. Lim, J. Chan, C. Leckie, and S. Karunasekera. Personalized tour recommendation based on user interests and points of interest visit durations. In *IJCAI*, 2015.

[27] B. Liu, Y. Fu, Z. Yao, and H. Xiong. Learning geographical preferences for point-of-interest recommendation. In *KDD*, pages 1043–1051, 2013.

[28] D. C. Liu and J. Nocedal. On the limited memory bfgs method for large scale optimization. *Mathematical programming*, 45(1-3):503–528, 1989.

[29] X. Liu, Y. Tian, M. Ye, and W.-C. Lee. Exploring personal impact for group recommendation. In *CIKM*, pages 674–683, 2012.

[30] T. Lou, J. Tang, J. Hopcroft, Z. Fang, and X. Ding. Learning to predict reciprocity and triadic closure in social networks. *TKDD*, 7(2):5, 2013.

[31] Z. Qiao, P. Zhang, Y. Cao, C. Zhou, L. Guo, and B. Fang. Combining heterogenous social and geographical information for event recommendation. In *AAAI*, 2014.

[32] D. M. Romero and J. M. Kleinberg. The directed closure process in hybrid social-information networks, with an analysis of link formation on twitter. In *ICWSM*, 2010.

[33] I. Ronen, I. Guy, E. Kravi, and M. Barnea. Recommending social media content to community owners. In *SIGIR*, pages 243–252, 2014.

[34] A. Sadilek, H. Kautz, and J. P. Bigham. Finding your friends and following them to where you are. In *WSDM*, pages 723–732, 2012.

[35] A. Salehi-Abari and C. Boutilier. Preference-oriented social networks: Group recommendation and inference. In *RecSys*, pages 35–42, 2015.

[36] R. Schifanella, A. Barrat, C. Cattuto, B. Markines, and F. Menczer. Folks in folksonomies: social link prediction from shared metadata. In *WSDM*, pages 271–280, 2010.

[37] S. Sintos and P. Tsaparas. Using strong triadic closure to characterize ties in social networks. In *KDD*, pages 1466–1475, 2014.

[38] D. Song, D. A. Meyer, and D. Tao. Top-k link recommendation in social networks. In *ICDM*, pages 389–398, 2015.

[39] K. Subbian, A. Banerjee, and S. Basu. PLUMS: predicting links using multiple sources. In *SDM*, pages 370–378, 2015.

[40] H. M. Wallach. Topic modeling: beyond bag-of-words. In *ICML*, pages 977–984, 2006.

[41] S. Wan, Y. Lan, J. Guo, C. Fan, and X. Cheng. Informational friend recommendation in social media. In *SIGIR*, pages 1045–1048, 2013.

[42] W. Wang, H. Yin, L. Chen, Y. Sun, S. Sadiq, and X. Zhou. Geo-sage: A geographical sparse additive generative model for spatial item recommendation. In *KDD*, pages 1255–1264.

[43] R. Xiang, J. Neville, and M. Rogati. Modeling relationship strength in online social networks. In *WWW*, pages 981–990, 2010.

[44] G. Yuan, P. K. Murukannaiah, Z. Zhang, and M. P. Singh. Exploiting sentiment homophily for link prediction. In *RecSys*, pages 17–24, 2014.

[45] Q. Yuan, G. Cong, and C.-Y. Lin. COM: A generative model for group recommendation. In *KDD*, pages 163–172, 2014.

[46] Q. Yuan, G. Cong, Z. Ma, A. Sun, and N. M. Thalmann. Time-aware point-of-interest recommendation. In *SIGIR*, pages 363–372, 2013.

[47] J. Zhang, X. Kong, and P. S. Yu. Transferring heterogeneous links across location-based social networks. In *WSDM*, pages 303–312, 2014.

[48] J. Zhang, C. Wang, P. S. Yu, and J. Wang. Learning latent friendship propagation networks with interest awareness for link prediction. In *SIGIR*, pages 63–72, 2013.

[49] J. Zhang, P. S. Yu, and Z.-H. Zhou. Meta-path based multi-network collective link prediction. In *KDD*, pages 1286–1295, 2014.

[50] J.-D. Zhang and C.-Y. Chow. Geosoca: Exploiting geographical, social and categorical correlations for point-of-interest recommendations. In *SIGIR*, pages 443–452, 2015.

[51] W. Zhang and J. Wang. A collective bayesian poisson factorization model for cold-start local event recommendation. In *KDD*, pages 1455–1464, 2015.

[52] W. Zhang, J. Wang, and W. Feng. Combining latent factor model with location features for event-based group recommendation. In *KDD*, pages 910–918, 2013.

[53] V. W. Zheng, Y. Zheng, X. Xie, and Q. Yang. Collaborative location and activity recommendations with GPS history data. In *WWW*, pages 1029–1038, 2010.

[54] Y. Zhong, N. J. Yuan, W. Zhong, F. Zhang, and X. Xie. You are where you go: Inferring demographic attributes from location check-ins. In *WSDM*, pages 295–304, 2015.

[55] W.-Y. Zhu, W.-C. Peng, L.-J. Chen, K. Zheng, and X. Zhou. Modeling user mobility for location promotion in location-based social networks. In *KDD*, pages 1573–1582, 2015.

A Utility Maximization Framework for Privacy Preservation of User Generated Content

Yi Fang
Department of Computer
Engineering
Santa Clara University
500 El Camino Real
Santa Clara, CA, 95053, USA
yfang@scu.edu

Archana Godavarthy
Department of Computer
Engineering
Santa Clara University
500 El Camino Real
Santa Clara, CA, 95053, USA
agodavarthy@gmail.com

Haibing Lu
Operations Management and
Information Systems
Santa Clara University
500 El Camino Real
Santa Clara, CA, 95053, USA
hlu@scu.edu

ABSTRACT

The prodigious amount of user-generated content continues to grow at an enormous rate. While it greatly facilitates the flow of information and ideas among people and communities, it may pose great threat to our individual privacy. In this paper, we demonstrate that the private traits of individuals can be inferred from user-generated content by using text classification techniques. Specifically, we study three private attributes on Twitter users: religion, political leaning, and marital status. The ground truth labels of the private traits can be readily collected from the Twitter bio field. Based on the tweets posted by the users and their corresponding bios, we show that text classification yields a high accuracy of identification of these personal attributes, which poses a great privacy risk on user-generated content.

We further propose a constrained utility maximization framework for preserving user privacy. The goal is to maximize the utility of data when modifying the user-generated content, while degrading the prediction performance of the adversary. The KL divergence is minimized between the prior knowledge about the private attribute and the posterior probability after seeing the user-generated data. Based on this proposed framework, we investigate several specific data sanitization operations for privacy preservation: add, delete, or replace words in the tweets. We derive the exact transformation of the data under each operation. The experiments demonstrate the effectiveness of the proposed framework.

Keywords

Privacy preservation; User generated content

1. INTRODUCTION

Social media has become an indispensable part of many lives. More and more people are using it to create their own content than ever before. According to [9], in 2014, 71% of

ICTIR '16, September 12-16, 2016, Newark, DE, USA

© 2016 ACM. ISBN 978-1-4503-4497-5/16/09. . . $15.00

DOI: http://dx.doi.org/10.1145/2970398.2970417

online adults use Facebook and 28%, 28%, 26%, and 23% for the other social network services LinkedIn, Pinterest, Instagram and Twitter respectively. 52% of online adults now use two or more social media sites, more than half of all online adults 65 and older use Facebook, and some 36% of Twitter users visit the site daily. The prodigious amount of user-generated content continues to grow at an unprecedented rate.

While it greatly facilitates the flow of information and ideas among people and communities, it may pose great threat to our individual privacy. Personal attributes may be derived from analysis of user-generated content, which could yield valid conclusions that the individual would not want to disclose. For example, an anonymous Twitter user may occasionally post tweets, e.g. describing some cosmetic products, praising services at some convenience store, mentioning his/her terrible birthday party. The comment on cosmetic products may suggest that person is female. The convenience store frequently patronized by that user would imply that the user lives in the neighborhood of that store. The posting date of the birthday party comment would suggest his/her date of birth. It was reported in [31] that 87% population in the United States could be uniquely identified based only on 5-digit zip, gender, and date of birth. Thus, the three seemingly irrelevant comments would reveal the identity of the user. Besides identity/anonymity, user-generated content may reveal confidential information that users want to keep to themselves. A user may comment on books that he/she recently read. The books could indicate his/her political opinion. Comments on youth sports center and education quality of local school districts could suggest the commenter is a soccer-mom. Discussion on some medicine could reveal a person's medical history. Posts on some ethnic restaurant could infer national origin of that user. Purchasing an infant bed could suggest this user is an expecting parent. Activities on weekend could reveal the user's religion.

Although many sites offer privacy controls that enable users to restrict how their data is viewed by other users, content analysis of seemingly innocuous user-generated text may reveal much personal information about the users. In this paper, we demonstrate that the private traits of individuals can be inferred from user-generated content by text classification techniques. Specifically, we study three private attributes on Twitter users: religion, political leaning, and marital status. The ground truth labels of the private traits can be readily collected from the Twitter bio field in an automatic fashion. Based on the tweets posted by the users and their corresponding bios, we show that a simple logistic regression model may yield a high accuracy of identification of these personal attributes, which poses a great privacy risk of user-generated content.

Privacy preservation on user-generated content has multiple challenges. First of all, user-generated content is typically in an unstructured form, i.e., text. Most of the existing privacy-preserving data publishing work has focused on structured data, which can be represented in a relational table that may include identifier (e.g., id) or quasi-identifier (e.g., zip code) attributes. Secondly, it is difficult to devise a good data sanitization strategy. The simplest solution would be deleting all user-generated data, which retains the perfect data privacy. Such a solution renders the data useless and hurts user experience the most. It is indeed against the spirit of the Internet and social media that is to share information. We have to find an effective data sanitization strategy to modify the data in some way such that an adversary cannot infer sensitive information while the sanitized data still carry semantic information and can be used for other legitimate uses. Possible data sanitization operations include deleting words, sentences, or whole records, replacing sensitive words with general words, publishing summary of data instead of complete data, and many others. Different operations would have different impacts on data utility and the amount of information that an adversary can infer. A unified private preservation strategy is needed for handling various data sanitization operations.

To tackle these challenges, we propose a utility maximization framework for preserving user privacy. The goal is to maximize the data utility when modifying the user-generated content, while degrading the prediction performance of the adversary as much as possible. The KL divergence is minimized between the prior knowledge about a private attribute and the posterior probability after seeing the user-generated data. In this way, the data reveals little or no information about the personal attribute. The main contributions of this paper can be summarized as follows:

- We demonstrate that private attributes of Twitter users can be inferred from tweets by using text classification techniques. We utilize the Twitter bio field to collect ground truth labels for training and testing. The experiments show that text classification would yield high accuracy of identification of personal attributes, which poses a great privacy risk on user-generated content.

- We propose a utility maximization framework with the constraint of minimizing the KL divergence between the prior and posterior probabilities of the personal attribute. This is a general framework applicable to various definitions of utilities (e.g., minimal modification, cost-sensitive, personal preference, etc.) and various data sanitization operations.

- Based on the proposed framework, we investigate several specific data sanitization operations for privacy preservation: add, delete, or replace words in the tweets, under the logistic regression model. We derive the exact closed-from data transformation for each operation.

- The experiments are conducted on three personal attributes of Twitter users: religion, political leaning, and marital status. The results demonstrate that the data transformations derived from the proposed framework can effectively degrade the prediction performance of adversaries especially when they are linear models.

2. RELATED WORK

Most existing privacy models are within the area of structured databases [12], also known as micro data, in which released data consist of records with attributes of individuals. A canonical example is census data. Sanitizing micro data by simply removing identifiers, e.g. social security number, cannot prevent privacy inference, because basic demographics can uniquely identify record owners. k-anonymity [32] is the privacy protection model ensuring that any record in the set must be indistinguishable from at least $k - 1$ other records in the same set. Although k-anonymity helps to minimize identity disclosure, it may not protect against confidential attribute disclosure. This is the case of a group of k-anonymous records that share the same confidential value (e.g., patients being or not AIDS-positive). In such a case, even though an attacker would not be able to identify a particular individual, he can learn the individual's confidential attribute because all records have the same attribute value. To fix the issue, several privacy protection models are proposed such as differential privacy [10].

While there exist a number of privacy models for structured data, much less attention has been paid to unstructured data (e.g., plain text documents). To find semantic identifying data in textual documents (e.g., ID numbers, addresses, ages, dates, etc.), some automatic methods exploit the regular structure of documents by means of rules, patterns, or trained classifiers [20]. As stated in the current legislation of the Health Insurance Portability and Accountability Act (HIPAA) [21], identifiers should be directly removed/redacted in order to preserve the anonymity. Douglass et al. [8] presents schemes, which consist of techniques such as pattern matching, lexical matching, and heuristics, to identify protected identifiers from free-text nursing notes. Ruch et al. [24] uses a specialized medical semantic lexicon for finding personally identifying information in patient records. Atallah et al. [4] uses an ontological representation of a text document to find and remove sensitive sentences. Chakaravarthy et al. [6] assumes the existence of an external database containing demographic information. Abril et al. [1] use some named entity recognition techniques (e.g. Stanford Named Entity Recognizer [11]) to identify the entities of the documents that require protection. Named identity recognition techniques may not necessarily identify sensitive terms in a text. Staddon et al. [29] proposes a web-based inference detection method. It first extracts salient keywords from the private data, and then issues search queries for documents that match subsets of these keywords within the public web, and finally parses the documents returned by the search queries for keywords not present in the original private data. These additional keywords are used to estimate the likelihood of certain inferences. The idea of using a corpus, like the public web, to detect sensitive information is also found in [25, 26, 22]. Some prior work investigated the privacy issues on Twitter [13, 2].

To protect privacy in textual data, two common methods are removing sensitive entities, referred to as redaction, and

Table 1: Bio examples on Twitter

happily married to my wonderful husband and best friend and mother to our wonderful sweet baby boy, Brady. life couldn't be any more sweeter
I love music, my kid's and i'm from Brooklyn, birthday is Feb,28.1978.
I have a brain and I'll use it any way I want. Meanwhile, I wife, mother, knit, read, cook, garden, and work.
Love God, husband, animals, camping, beading, crocheting and friends
married, daughter, christian, hard worker, animals, antiques, travel, cookout

obfuscation by replacing sensitive pieces with appropriate generalizations (e.g., replacing AIDS by disease) that is also referred to as sanitization. One disadvantage of redaction is the loss of data utility. The other disadvantage is that the existence of blacked-out parts in the released document can raise awareness of the document's sensitivity to potential attackers [5]. It is easier to perform redaction than obfuscation. There are a few obfuscation methods for textual data. Some studies [14, 3] use less sensitive information to replace sensitive information, such as changing marijuana to drug. The Scrub system [30] finds and replaces patterns of identifying information such as name, location, Social Security Number, medical terms, age, date, etc. The replacement strategy is to change the identified word to another word of similar type, and it is not clear whether the semantics of the reports themselves reveal the individuals. Tveit et al. [33] provide a six-step anonymization scheme that finds and replaces identifying words in (Norwegian) patient records with pseudonyms. Saygin et al. [27] propose a two-phase scheme that employs both sanitization and anonymization. There are attempts of adapting the notion of k-anonymity in structured databases to unstructured data, such as k-safety [6], k-confusability ([7]), and k-plausibility [14, 3]. Li et al. [16] performed iterative classification to learn sensitive words by assuming the attacker would choose an optimal classifier from a set of classification models.

In the recent years, SIGIR has hosted workshops on Privacy Preserving IR (PIR) [28, 35, 36]. They aim at exploring and understanding the privacy and security risks in information retrieval. The workshops cover privacy issues in various IR subfields including sentiment analysis [34], document summarization [19], passage retrieval [18], and query log analysis [37].

3. PRIVATE ATTRIBUTE IDENTIFICATION

Given a set of user-generated content for a particular user, we want to know whether we can automatically infer personal sensitive information from the data. In this section, we look at Twitter with one personal attribute that may be regarded as sensitive information for some people: marital status. We formulate the task of identification of marital status as a binary classification problem, i.e., whether a user is married or not given the tweets posted by the user. Thus, it can be viewed as a text classification problem with individual words as features. To obtain a set of training data with known marital status, we utilize the bio box on Twitter where users can give some information about themselves in fewer than 160 characters. Based on our observations,

this bio box may contain some personal information such as marital status, age, location, occupation, etc. Table 1 shows some examples of bios that indicate marital status. Some of them also reveal birthday (2nd Tweet) and religion (4th and 5th tweets). The public tweets and user bios can be collected from Twitter Streaming API[1]. We use a list of marital status related keywords (e.g., "wife", "husband", "married", etc.) to match against the bios. We assume that the bios that contain any of these keywords indicate the user is married. Based on our preliminary study, this keyword-matching approach yields very high precision, probably due to the fact that the bios are in a limited length and lack variations in expressions. Section 5.1 presents the details about the data that we collected. We find that over 50% of Twitter users have filled out their bios and about 2% of the bios indicate marital status. Given the huge user base of Twitter, we would expect to obtain a large number of users with marital status by this automatic keyword-matching approach. Similarly, we can collect the negative labels (i,e. unmarried users) using keywords which reveal unmarried status (e.g., "single", "in a relationship", "unmarried", etc.).

After collecting both positive and negative labels along with the tweets posted by users, we can apply text categorization techniques to train a model and predict the marital status of a new user based on her posted tweets. The experiments in Section 6.1 demonstrate that just using conventional text classification models such as logistic regression or Support Vector Machine (SVM) would yield high accuracy of identification of personal attributes. These results would raise severe privacy concerns. The publicly available user-generated content constitutes a large knowledge base that allows an adversary to mine relations between content and personal attributes. Those learned relationships can then be used to infer the personal attributes of users who did not intentionally disclose such information and did not anticipate such disclosure either.

4. A UTILITY MAXIMIZATION FRAMEWORK

4.1 Privacy Model

A privacy model defines what type of privacy is guaranteed, which forms a basis on how privacy protection methods should be designed. In our setting, privacy is the true class (personal attribute) of a user, which might be inferred by some adversary/classifier. The goal of our privacy model is to hide the true user attribute value by degrading the classifier's performance. We argue that a classifier has degraded performance if it does not enhance one's prediction accuracy. In other words, a sanitized text is considered safe if its class prediction result by a classifier is the same as or close enough to random guessing based on the prior knowledge. To formalize the privacy problem, we denote $P(C|D)$ as the trained classifier, which outputs a probability distribution of predicted classes C. D is the original text and $\widetilde{D}$ is the sanitized text . We define the privacy as follows.

DEFINITION 1 (STRONG PRIVACY). *The sanitized document $\widetilde{D}$ is considered strongly private if releasing $\widetilde{D}$ does not improve one's chance in guessing the true class of D than without disclosing D.*

---
[1]https://dev.twitter.com/streaming/

The above definition is strong in the sense that releasing the sanitized document does not provide any information about the true class of D. If we know what kind of information are correlated with the true class of D, we can simply remove such information and only retain irrelevant information, or perturb D by adding noise to dilute the relevant features. In practice, we can often tolerate certain degree of predictability of the sanitized document as long as the prediction is not of high confidence. Intuitively, we aim to have the posterior probability $P(C|\widetilde{D})$ of the personal attribute C after seeing the sanitized document $\widetilde{D}$ close enough to the prior probability $P(C)$ of the class. In this way, the sanitized document $\widetilde{D}$ does not reveal much information about the attribute C. Mathematically, we can use the KL divergence $KL\big(P(C)||P(C|\widetilde{D})\big)$ to measure the closeness between the two probability distributions. Thus, we give another privacy definition.

DEFINITION 2 (WEAK PRIVACY). *The sanitized document* $\widetilde{D}$ *is considered private if* $KL\big(P(C)||P(C|\widetilde{D})\big) \leq \epsilon$ *where ϵ is the privacy tolerance threshold.*

4.2 Sanitization Operations

Sanitization of a document involves modifying the information that may help a classifier perform accurate prediction on the document. Common text sanitization operations can be divided into two categories: suppression and generalization. Suppression is widely used for protecting privacy for structured database. On the other hand, the generalization operation attempts to generalize the key terms so that they are not indicative any more. Different operations would have different impacts on user experience and usefulness of sanitized data. Some utility function can be built to quantify the effects of various types of operations. One can also allow the use of personalized perceptions on sanitized data utility to enable individualized sanitization decision.

4.3 Utility Maximization

While we know what to protect and the tools (operations) used for protection, we need to find out how to effectively use those tools and achieve a balance between privacy and utility. The level of privacy would depend on the ability of adversaries on inferring the true class of a document, while utility can be measured by how much a sanitized text $\widetilde{D}$ differs from the original text D. Mathematically, we propose the following constrained utility maximization objective:

$$\max U(\widetilde{D}, D) \qquad (1)$$
$$s.t. \qquad KL\big(P(C)||P(C|\widetilde{D})\big) \leq \epsilon \qquad (2)$$

where $U(\widetilde{D}, D)$ measures the utility of the sanitized document $\widetilde{D}$ with respect to the original document D. For example, it can be defined as the total number of changes done on the original document D, i.e., $U(\widetilde{D}, D) = -(E + F + G)$ where E, F, G is the number of terms added, deleted, or replaced, respectively. The utility could also be cost-sensitive since some operations may be less desirable than others. For example, some users may not want any terms in the tweets to be deleted, while adding some words may be fine. Thus, a utility function can be defined as $U(\widetilde{D}, D) = -(w_e \times E + w_f \times F + w_g \times G)$ where w_e, w_f, and w_g are the weights for the corresponding operations. To achieve perfect privacy,

the extreme solution is to remove the whole text, which is not a desired solution as no data utility is retained. A good privacy protection strategy should allow a trade-off between utility and privacy.

4.4 Privacy Preservation

If we specify in the proposed framework the utility function, prediction model, the privacy threshold, and the type of sanitization operation (e.g., Add/Delete), we can obtain the exact actions that we need to perform (e.g., what words to delete and how many of them to be deleted) by solving the optimization problem in Eqn.(1). In this section, we use logistic regression as the text classification model and show how to preserve user private attributes based on the proposed framework. In practice, it is infeasible to know the prediction model that adversary will use. However, the experiments in Section 6 show that the sanitization operations based on logistic regression can still substantially degrade the performance of other linear prediction models. This may be explained by the fact that the terms identified by logistic regression to be added/deleted/replaced are indicative and predictive of the personal attributes and thus modifying them would also largely affect the results of other classifiers.

We concatenate all the tweets posted by a given user u in a single document represented as a v-dimensional feature vector $u = (f_1, f_2, ..., f_v)$ where v is the vocabulary size. Here, we use TF-IDF weighting scheme $f_j = tf_j \times idf_j$ where tf_j is the term frequency of the j-th word in the vocabulary and idf_j is the inverse document frequency of the word. In logistic regression, the probability of being the positive personal attribute/class given the feature vector is modeled by:

$$P(C = 1|u) = \frac{1}{1 + \exp(-\sum_{j=1}^{v} \beta_j f_j - b)} \qquad (3)$$

where β_j are b are the weight and bias parameters respectively, and are learned from the training data.

Let us assume strong privacy by setting the privacy threshold $\epsilon = 0$.

$$KL(P(C)||P(C|\widetilde{D})) = 0$$
$$\Rightarrow \sum_C P(C) \log \frac{P(C)}{P(C|\widetilde{D})} = 0$$
$$\Rightarrow P(C|\widetilde{D}) = P(C)$$
$$\Rightarrow \frac{1}{1 + \exp(-\sum_{j=1}^{v} \beta_j f_j - b)} = P(C)$$
$$\Rightarrow \sum_{j=1}^{v} \beta_j f_j + b = \log \frac{P(C)}{1 - P(C)} \qquad (4)$$

where $P(C)$ comes from the prior knowledge about the personal attribute. For example, based on the demographics of Twitter users, one can roughly estimate the percentage of married people, or just use $P(C = 1) = 0.5$ if we do not have any prior knowledge. For a trained model, the parameters β_j and b are constant in the equation. Thus, any reasonable data sanitization operation can be boiled down to change f_j so that Eqn.(4) is satisfied and consequently the user data $\widetilde{D}$ does not improve one's chance in guessing the true class C over the prior knowledge. For weak privacy with nonzero ϵ, we can similarly derive the condition to be satisfied but there may exist no simple and closed form as Eqn.(4). This is a general framework applicable to various definitions of utilities (e.g., minimal modification, cost-sensitive, personal preference, etc.), various sanitization operations, and various learning models. In the subsections below, we derive the specific actions for each sanitization operation based on the privacy condition in Eqn.(4).

4.4.1 Delete or Add Operation

Assume we want to delete x_k number of the k-th word in the vocabulary. f_k is the original TF-IDF feature value of word k. After the delete operation, Eqn.(4) must be satisfied. Thus, we have

$$\beta_k(f_k - x_k \times idf_k) + \sum_{j \neq k}^{v} \beta_j f_j + b = \log \frac{P(C)}{1 - P(C)}$$

$$\Rightarrow -\beta_k x_k idf_k + \sum_{j=1}^{v} \beta_j f_j + b = \log \frac{P(C)}{1 - P(C)}$$

$$\Rightarrow -\beta_k idf_k x_k = \log \frac{P(C)}{1 - P(C)} - \sum_{j=1}^{v} \beta_j f_j - b$$

$$\Rightarrow x_k = \frac{\sum_{j=1}^{v} \beta_j f_j + b - \log \frac{P(C)}{1 - P(C)}}{\beta_k idf_k} \quad (5)$$

Eqn.(5) specifies the exact action if we want to add or delete the word k. If $\sum_{j=1}^{v} \beta_j f_j + b \geq \log \frac{P(C)}{1 - P(C)}$, x_k is positive and we will delete x_k occurrences of the word. If it is negative, we will add x_k occurrences of the word.

If the utility function is $U(\widetilde{D}, D) = -E$, i.e., minimizing the number of times the word to be added or deleted, we can solve the constrained optimization problem (Eqn.(1)) by calculating x_k for each word k and choose the word that has the smallest x_k, which indicates the minimum changes to the original document. The proposed framework is also applicable to Add/Delete multiple words. Similar formulas can be derived based on Eqn.(4) which specifies the condition when KL divergence is minimized to zero.

4.4.2 Replace Operation

If we want to replace the word k by the word s, we can derive the exact number of such replacements, denoted by y_{ks}, that are needed. Denote the original TF-IDF feature values of the word k and s by f_k and f_s, and the sanitized feature values by $\widetilde{f_k}$ and $\widetilde{f_s}$, respectively, and the corresponding learned weights by β_k and β_s. Based on Eqn.(4), we have

$$\beta_k \widetilde{f_k} + \beta_s \widetilde{f_s} + \sum_{j \neq k,s}^{v} \beta_j f_j + b = \log \frac{P(C)}{1 - P(C)}$$

$$\Rightarrow \beta_k(f_k - y_{ks} \times idf_k) + \beta_s(f_s + y_{ks} \times idf_s)$$

$$= \log \frac{P(C)}{1 - P(C)} - \sum_{j \neq k,s}^{v} \beta_j f_j - b$$

$$\Rightarrow (\beta_s idf_s - \beta_k idf_k)y_{ks} = \log \frac{P(C)}{1 - P(C)} - \sum_{j=1}^{v} \beta_j f_j - b$$

$$\Rightarrow y_{ks} = \frac{\sum_{j=1}^{v} \beta_j f_j + b - \log \frac{P(C)}{1 - P(C)}}{\beta_k idf_k - \beta_s idf_s} \quad (6)$$

Based on Eqn.(6), if y_{ks} is a positive number, we will replace the word k by the word s in y_{ks} number of times. If y_{ks} is a negative number, we will replace the word s by the word k in y_{ks} number of occurrences.

4.4.3 More Sophisticated Operations

The above Add, Delete, and Replace are just simple operations to illustrate the usage of the proposed utility maximization framework. More sophisticated sanitization operations can be defined based on the general framework. For example, we may not want to replace word k by any word s. Otherwise, it may lead to grammatical errors or alter the meaning of the text. We can enforce constraints on the data transformation, e.g., requiring the word s has the same part-of-speech with the word k or it is a generalized concept of the work k (referred to as obfuscation as introduced in Section 2). The candidate words to replace can be chosen based on WordNet[2]. In addition, we can further add semantic preservation into the utility function so that the sanitized text retains the semantics of the original text as much as possible. Distributed representation of text such as Doc2Vec [15] can be used to measure the semantic similarity between the texts. This paper is just an initial step to demonstrate the proposed privacy preservation framework. We will study more sophisticated sanitization operations in the future work.

5. EXPERIMENTAL SETUP

5.1 Data Collection and Preprocessing

We used Twitter data as our testbed. We collected the user ids through Twitters Streaming API in the period of December, 2015 to March, 2016. and then identified the user profiles using Tweepy[3] get_user API. In the experiments, we focus on three categories, i.e., political leaning (Democratic vs Republican), religious affiliation (Christian vs non-Christian) and marital status (married vs unmarried). To collect the ground truth labels for users of different categories, we employ the keyword-matching approach as introduced in Section 3 to identify positive and negative users for each category. Table 2 contains the list of the keywords. The tweets were then collected for these users using Tweepy user_timeline() API. We only included the users who posted at least 100 tweets. Table 3 shows the data statistics. We preprocessed these tweets by removing stop words, punctuation, user ids, urls, and non-ascii characters. The top 10,000 terms with the highest TF-IDF values in each category were selected as word features. The whole data was randomly split into 80% for training and the rest 20% for testing.

We use standard evaluation metrics for classification including Precision, Recall, F-score, and Accuracy [17] to determine to what extent the model can correctly classify the instances. We evaluated the results using these metrics on the data before and after the sanitization transformations based on our proposed framework.

5.2 Research Questions

We performed an extensive set of experiments to address the following questions related to the proposed research:

- Can the users' private traits be inferred with high accuracy using off-the-shelf machine learning algorithms like logistic regression? (Section 6.1)

- Can these operations be applied in order to maximize the data utility? (Section 6.2.2)

---

[2]https://wordnet.princeton.edu/
[3]http://www.tweepy.org/

Table 2: Keywords for matching personal attributes in Twitter user bios

Christian
christian, jesus, christ, church, bible

Non-Christian
islam, hindu, buddhist, sikh, quran, jew, atheist

Democratic
democrat, liberal, left-leaning, progressives

Republican
republican, gop, conservative, right-leaning, pro-life, pro-gun

Married
marriage, married, wife, husband, dad, mom, father, mother, parent, family

Unmarried
single, i am available, looking for a relationship, dating, boyfriend, girlfriend, bachelor

Table 3: Statistics of the testbed

	Religious	Political	Marital
Positive	1,001	801	3,500
Negative	745	772	3,400
Average # of tweets / user	2,831	2,834	2,861
Average # of words / user	41,672	43,573	40,839

- Given the risk of exposure of the private traits, what kind of measures can be taken to protect the privacy of the user? (Section 6.2.1)

- Can we monitor the user tweet stream to detect sensitive tweets in real time? Would suppressing selected tweets help protect the privacy? (Section 6.3)

6. EXPERIMENTS

In this section, we present both quantitative and qualitative experiments to address the above research questions in Section 5.2.

6.1 Privacy Risk Analysis

We show the effectiveness of a simple off-the-shelf machine learning algorithm like logistic regression in predicting the private traits of a user. With the ground truth data, we train the model and apply it to predict the class labels of the test users. Table 4 contains the prediction results. In general, the model yielded high accuracy on all the three categories with the best results on the religious category. Based on the results in Accuracy, at least more than 70% of the users in each category have their personal attributes correctly identified. Given the fact that we only used a linear model with a modest size of training data, these results raise a significant privacy concern on the user-generated content.

Table 4: Prediction results on the test users by logistic regression

	Precision	Recall	F-Score	Accuracy
Religious	0.938	0.829	0.880	0.835
Political	0.796	0.704	0.747	0.741
Marital	0.746	0.739	0.743	0.726

Table 5: Average changes in term frequency over the users under different sanitization operations for the three categories.

	Add/Delete Random	Add/Delete Minimum	Replace Random	Replace Minimum
Religious	32,825	85	8,834	39
Political	2,251	85	2,767	38
Marital	2,719	19	10,204	8

6.2 Privacy Protection

6.2.1 Utility Maximization

Given the privacy risk exposed in Section 6.1, we apply the proposed privacy preservation framework in Section 4, which is based on maximizing the utility of user data given a transformation. Here we define the utility as the negative amount of change we make on the user data. For example, deleting or adding m words will yield the utility of $-m$. In other words, the objective is to minimize the amount of change on the data. As shown in Section 4, in order to preserve user privacy, we minimize the KL divergence between prior knowledge about the personal attribute and the posterior probability as the constraint. The prior probabilities are assumed to be 0.5.

Specifically, we investigate the Add/Delete operation and the Replace operation introduced in Section 4.4.1 and 4.4.2. For each operation, we have two variants: *Random* and *Minimum*. For Add/Delete, *Random* is to randomly pick a term in the user tweets to add/delete and then solve Eqn.(5) to obtain the number of the term occurrences to add/delete. On the other hand, the *Minimum* operation is to pick the term that causes the minimum number of changes on the tweets, by solving Eqn.(5) for each vocabulary term and finding the minimum of x_k. Similarly *Random* and *Minimum* procedures are defined for the Replace operation based on Eqn.(6). In other words, the *Random* procedure only minimizes the KL divergence without considering data utility, while the *minimum* procedure applies the full proposed utility maximization framework.

Table 5 contains the results of the average changes in term frequency over all the users for different operations. As we can see, the average changes in term frequency for the *Minimum* procedure are significantly smaller than for the *Random* procedure across all the three categories. These results demonstrate that the data utility preserved by the proposed utility maximization framework is much higher under the *Minimum* procedure. The average changes for religious and political categories are comparable while they are much less for the marital category. This may be due to the different numbers of training instances in different categories. Moreover, we can find that the frequency change for the Replace operation is generally smaller than for Add/Delete, which may be explained by the involvement of two terms in the Replace operation while only one term in Add/Delete.

6.2.2 Privacy Preservation

Table 6 shows the evaluation metrics on various classifiers before (Pre) and after (Post) applying the proposed sanitization operations. In these experiments, we only look at the users whose attributes were correctly identified by the logistic regression model, since these users are at high privacy risk. As a result, the Pre-transformation metrics for the

Table 6: Performance of various classifiers before (Pre) and after (Post) applying the privacy preservation operations Add/Delete *Minimum* (A/D-Min) and Replace *Minimum* (Rep-Min)

Category	Classifier	Operation		Precision	Recall	F-Score	Accuracy
Religious	Logistic	Pre		1.0	1.0	1.0	1.0
		Post	A/D-Min	0.698	0.413	0.519	0.444
			Rep-Min	0.753	0.446	0.560	0.492
	Linear-SVM	Pre		0.987	0.949	0.968	0.954
		Post	A/D-Min	0.325	0.163	0.217	0.146
			Rep-Min	0.528	0.300	0.383	0.298
	KNN	Pre		0.914	0.889	0.901	0.859
		Post	A/D-Min	0.911	0.886	0.898	0.855
			Rep-Min	0.910	0.877	0.893	0.848
	Nonlinear-SVM	Pre		0.968	0.928	0.948	0.926
		Post	A/D-Min	0.959	0.916	0.937	0.911
			Rep-Min	0.959	0.916	0.937	0.911
Political	Logistic	Pre		1.0	1.0	1.0	1.0
		Post	A/D-Min	0.561	0.457	0.504	0.536
			Rep-Min	0.480	0.387	0.429	0.468
	Linear-SVM	Pre		0.924	0.945	0.934	0.932
		Post	A/D-Min	0.403	0.403	0.403	0.384
			Rep-Min	0.631	0.705	0.666	0.636
	KNN	Pre		0.774	0.744	0.758	0.756
		Post	A/D-Min	0.75	0.744	0.747	0.74
			Rep-Min	0.761	0.744	0.752	0.748
	Nonlinear-SVM	Pre		0.887	0.852	0.869	0.868
		Post	A/D-Min	0.755	0.790	0.772	0.76
			Rep-Min	0.863	0.837	0.850	0.848
Marital	Logistic	Pre		1.0	1.0	1.0	1.0
		Post	A/D-Min	0.582	0.538	0.559	0.539
			Rep-Min	0.610	0.601	0.606	0.574
	Linear-SVM	Pre		0.935	0.901	0.917	0.912
		Post	A/D-Min	0.562	0.528	0.545	0.520
			Rep-Min	0.631	0.705	0.666	0.636
	KNN	Pre		0.780	0.781	0.780	0.761
		Post	A/D-Min	0.771	0.776	0.773	0.753
			Rep-Min	0.776	0.776	0.776	0.756
	Nonlinear-SVM	Pre		0.809	0.833	0.821	0.803
		Post	A/D-Min	0.697	0.760	0.728	0.690
			Rep-Min	0.756	0.762	0.759	0.737

logistic regression model are all 1.0. We apply both linear and nonlinear classifiers including logistic regression (LR), linear SVM, nonlinear SVM (with quadratic kernel), and K-Nearest Neighborhood (KNN) (where $K = 20$) to test the effect of the proposed transformations. We utilize the Scikit-learn machine learning library [23] for these classifiers. We have a number of observations from the table.

First of all, the proposed sanitization operations reduce the predictive performance of all the classifiers across all the metrics. The transformations are much more effective on the linear classifiers (LR and Linear-SVM) than the non-linear ones (nonlinear SVM and KNN) across all the categories. For logistic regression, the accuracy has reduced to be around 0.5 for all the three categories, which is close to random guessing. This is expected since the transformations are based on logistic regression. However, Linear-SVM also has much degraded predictive performance after the data transformations. These results show that even when the adversary uses a different or unknown prediction model, we may still be able to preserve user privacy based on the proposed sanitization operations.

Secondly, the nonlinear classifiers are affected to a much lesser extent, which may be due to the fact that the transformations are based on a linear model. A noticeable performance drop can be observed on Nonlinear-SVM in the marital category. This may be explained by the fact that this category has much more training data than the other two categories.

Thirdly, for the linear classifiers, the performance seems to be affected more by the Add/Delete operation than the Replace operation. However, as shown in Table 5, this comes at the expense of doing more changes to the user generated data. As we can see in the table, the Replace *Min* operation only caused half of the changes than the Add/Delete operation did. Therefore, the data utility is much higher in Replace *Min*. Considering the fact that the performance drops based on these two operations are quite similar, we may prefer the Replace *Min* operation.

The above observations demonstrate the effectiveness of our proposed framework in dampening the prediction accuracy and thus retaining the privacy of the users, especially when the adversary uses a linear model. In the future work, we will study nonlinear prediction models under the proposed framework and derive the corresponding data transformation operations.

6.2.3 Term Sanitization

To gain a further insight into the proposed utility maximization framework, we take a closer look at the specific terms that are selected by the proposed Add/Delete operation for data sanitization. Table 7 includes the probabilities on the personal attributes before (Pre) and after (Post) the Add/Delete *Minimum* operation for some example users. We can see that the terms picked by the proposed approach are quite indicative of the corresponding personal attributes. For example, the term *dnc2012* (i.e., 2012 Democratic National Convention) was identified for a user who is predicted to be democratic. A total of 19 *dnc2012* occurrences are deleted so that the Post transformation probability is decreased to 0.5, which was set as the prior probability on the attributes. When the model predicts a user to be Republican, the term *conservative* is deleted for 18 occurrences to keep the tweets less indicative. Similarly for the user predicted to be married, the proposed approach adds 10 occurrences of *bffs* to confuse the classifier. In sum, the terms identified by the proposed approach under logistic regression seem quite important and predictive of the user attributes. This explains why these operations also affect other prediction models, which makes privacy preservation possible even when the adversary model is unknown.

Table 7: Attribute probabilities before (Pre) and after (Post) the Add/Delete *Minimum* operation for some example users

User Attribute	Term	Freq change	Pre	Post
Democratic	*dnc2012*	19	[0.054,0.946]	[0.5,0.5]
Republican	*conservative*	18	[0.903,0.097]	[0.5,0.5]
Christian	*vote*	-21	[0.002,0.998]	[0.5,0.5]
Christian	*praying*	742	[0.000,1.000]	[0.5,0.5]
Married	*bffs*	-10	[0.004,0.996]	[0.5,0.5]
Married	*agreement*	18	[0.003,0.997]	[0.5,0.5]

6.2.4 ROC Curves

To further investigate the effect of the proposed operations for privacy preservation, we plot in Figure 1 the ROC (Receiver Operating Characteristic) curves of different classification results for users at high privacy risk (whose personal attributes have been correctly identified in Section 6.1) in three categories. Three classification models are compared including logistic regression (LR), linear SVM (LNR-SVM), and SVM with quadratic kernel (SVM-Poly). Pre and Post transformations are investigated. Two data sanitization operations are shown: Add/Delete (A) and Replace (R), with the *Minimum* procedure (minimizing the amount of changes). Figure 2 shows the similar ROC curves for the entire test users. We can see from the graphs that the Post ROC curve of logistic regression nearly lies on the random-prediction line, which indicates the predictions after the transformations are very poor. Moreover, Linear-SVM clearly responds to the transformations. It is worth noting that Linear-SVM shows different patterns for different categories. For the religious category, both Add/Delete and Replace operations move the predictions to the other side of

the random-prediction line. For the political category, they are on either side of the line. For the marital category, both operations are mostly around the random-prediction line. On the other hand, the nonlinear models are not much affected by the data transformations. These observations are generally consistent in the two figures.

6.3 Monitoring Indicative Tweets

Tweets appear in a streaming fashion and sensitive tweets may emerge unexpectedly. We can develop a temporal based privacy preservation strategy by monitoring the real-time stream of user tweets. In the previous section, the methods were based on changing the frequency of words in tweets to disguise user private traits. These operations may change the syntactic structure of the sentences. This may not be as a serious issue as that in regular documents since tweets usually do not follow very strict syntactic rules. An alternative operation is to suppress an entire new tweet that might expose too much personal information when combined with the prior tweets. The prediction model can compute on the regular basis the KL divergence $KL\big(P(C)\|P(C|\widetilde{D})\big)$ between the prior probability and posterior probability of the user attribute based on the currently observed tweets. If the KL divergence exceeds a certain threshold, it would generate an alarm for raising a privacy concern for the user.

We randomly select one user from each category for case studies. Figure 3 shows how the predicted probability of the correct attribute changes over time before and after suppressing the new tweets. As we can see for the religious category, there are spikes around the tweets related to Christianity, e.g., *"Love my CG! God is doing cool stuff!"* and *"8:36am and my day has already been made by a simple text from a friend who experienced God's grace in a real way. Thank you Jesus for grace."* Here the terms like *Love, God, Jesus,* and *grace* are all related to Christianity. The prediction accuracy spiked around the appearance of these tweets. When we detect such tweets and suppress them, it lowers the prediction accuracy, and thus preserves privacy. Similarly in the political category, there were spikes at the beginning related to tweets such as *"RT @GKMTNtwits: MSM Misinforms/Polls/Reports"* outcomes. @AymanM *"...See Hillary "Liar" Poll/A Joke"* and *"@DWStweets needs to be stripped of the DNC Chair title then voted out of office aTRAITOR ;Pro-Israel first over USA"*. The terms like *Hillary, DNC, Pro-Israel* are related to Democrats. When we suppress them, it degrades the prediction. There might be more tweets related to Democrats, but when we suppress the tweet early, it may cause future prediction ineffective, until the appearance of some strongly indicative tweets. For the marital category, although it started out with low prediction accuracy, it slowly gained accuracy around the tweets *"Children don't stress they only want to laugh - Children don't stress they just want to have fun and laugh..."* and *"10 Seconds That Will Change Your Life - 10 Seconds That Will Change Your Life. For most people we never..."*. The terms like *Children, stress, fun,* and *laugh* are associated with marriage, although they are not as strong indicators as in the previous two cases. Therefore, the prediction accuracy is just slightly above 0.5 in this case. By conducting the proposed operation in an online fashion, we can monitor user tweets in real time and generate alarms so that users are aware of the privacy risk associated with their posts.

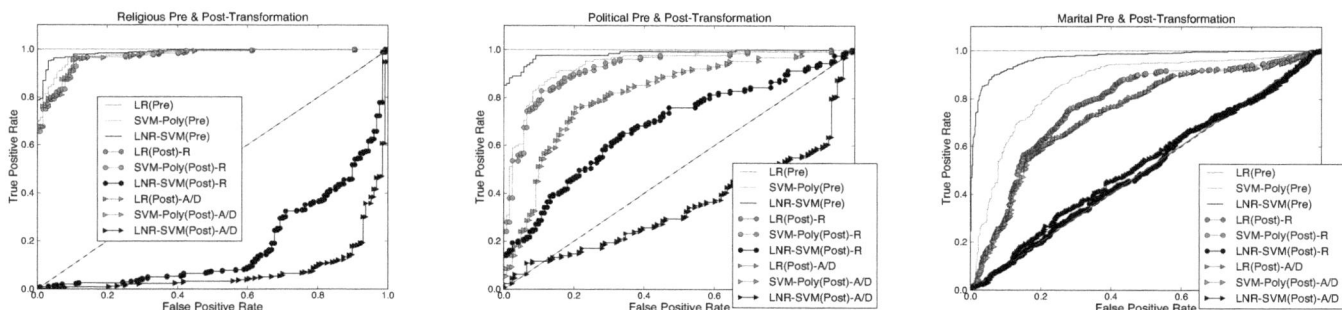

Figure 1: ROC curves of various classifiers for the test users who are at privacy risk

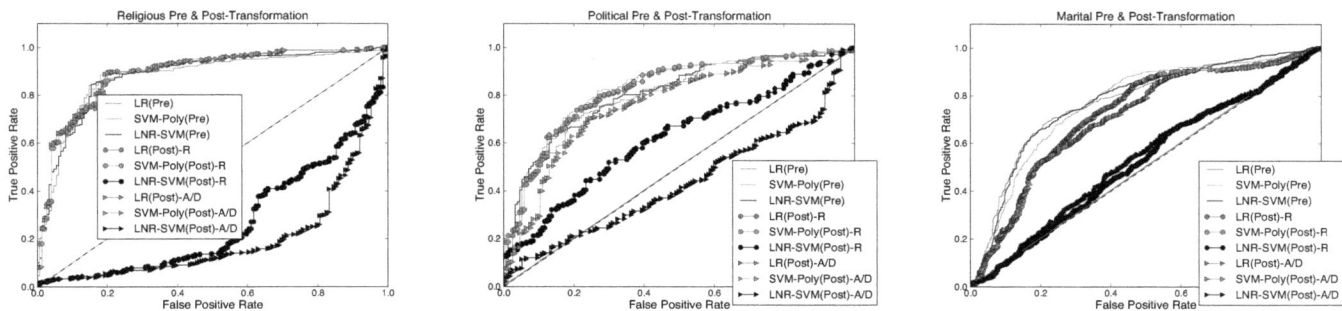

Figure 2: ROC curves of various classifiers for all the test users

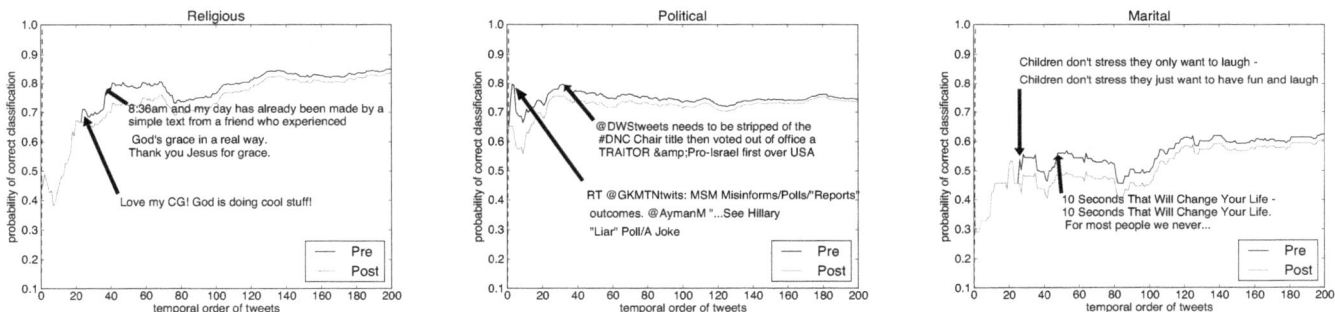

Figure 3: Temporal detection of sensitive tweets

7. CONCLUSION AND FUTURE WORK

We demonstrate that private attributes of Twitter users can be accurately inferred by simple text categorization with the labels automatically extracted from the bio fields. We propose a general utility maximization framework to preserve user privacy while maximizing data utility. Specific data sanitization transformations are derived based on the framework.

This work is an initial step towards a promising research direction, as there exists few work on privacy preservation of user-generated content. First of all, the simple sanitization operations presented in this paper may lead to grammatical errors or hamper the meaning of the user tweets. In future

work, we plan to explore semantic preserving operations to produce meaningful tweets in practice. This may require to enforce constraints on the transformation and proper definition of utility function as discussed in Section 4.4.3. Secondly, we will make more relaxed assumptions about the adversary by allowing uncertainties, which can be be modeled by probability distributions over a wide range of models and features that the attacker might use. We can extend the proposed utility maximization framework with probabilistic inference. Last but not the least, we will investigate the user interface of the proposed privacy preservation operations, e.g., when to alarm users about the privacy risk and how to suggest the changes on the user generated content.

ACKNOWLEDGMENTS

We thank the anonymous reviewers for their valuable comments.

8. REFERENCES

[1] D. Abril, G. Navarro-Arribas, and V. Torra. On the declassification of confidential documents. In *MDAI*. 2011.

[2] H. Almuhimedi, S. Wilson, B. Liu, N. Sadeh, and A. Acquisti. Tweets are forever: a large-scale quantitative analysis of deleted tweets. In *CSCW*, 2013.

[3] B. Anandan, C. Clifton, W. Jiang, M. Murugesan, P. Pastrana-Camacho, and L. Si. t-plausibility: Generalizing words to desensitize text. *Transactions on Data Privacy*, 2012.

[4] M. J. Atallah, C. J. McDonough, V. Raskin, and S. Nirenburg. Natural language processing for information assurance and security: an overview and implementations. In *NSPW*, 2001.

[5] E. Bier, R. Chow, P. Golle, T. H. King, and J. Staddon. The rules of redaction: Identify, protect, review (and repeat). *W2SP*, 2009.

[6] V. T. Chakaravarthy, H. Gupta, P. Roy, and M. K. Mohania. Efficient techniques for document sanitization. In *CIKM*, 2008.

[7] C. M. Cumby and R. Ghani. A machine learning based system for semi-automatically redacting documents. In *IAAI*, 2011.

[8] M. Douglass, G. Clifford, A. Reisner, W. Long, G. Moody, and R. Mark. De-identification algorithm for free-text nursing notes. In *CINC*, 2005.

[9] M. Duggan, N. B. Ellison, C. Lampe, A. Lenhart, and M. Madden. Social media update 2014. *Pew Research Center*, 2015.

[10] C. Dwork. Differential privacy. In *ICALP*, 2006.

[11] J. R. Finkel, T. Grenager, and C. Manning. Incorporating non-local information into information extraction systems by gibbs sampling. In *ACL*, 2005.

[12] B. C. M. Fung, K. Wang, R. Chen, and P. S. Yu. Privacy-preserving data publishing: A survey of recent developments. *ACM Computing Survey*, 2010.

[13] L. Humphreys, P. Gill, and B. Krishnamurthy. How much is too much? privacy issues on twitter. In *ICA*, 2010.

[14] W. Jiang, M. Murugesan, C. Clifton, and L. Si. t-plausibility: Semantic preserving text sanitization. In *ICSE*, 2009.

[15] Q. V. Le and T. Mikolov. Distributed representations of sentences and documents. In *ICML*, 2014.

[16] B. Li, Y. Vorobeychik, M. Li, and B. Malin. Iterative classification for sanitizing large-scale datasets. In *ICDM*, 2015.

[17] C. D. Manning, P. Raghavan, H. Schütze, et al. *Introduction to information retrieval*. Cambridge university press, 2008.

[18] L. Marujo, J. Portêlo, D. M. De Matos, J. P. Neto, A. Gershman, J. Carbonell, I. Trancoso, and B. Raj. Privacy-preserving important passage retrieval. In *SIGIR Workshop on PIR*, 2014.

[19] L. Marujo, J. Portêlo, W. Ling, D. M. de Matos, J. P. Neto, A. Gershman, J. Carbonell, I. Trancoso, and B. Raj. Privacy-preserving multi-document summarization. In *SIGIR Workshop on PIR*, 2015.

[20] S. M. Meystre, F. J. Friedlin, B. R. South, S. Shen, and M. H. Samore. Automatic de-identification of textual documents in the electronic health record: a review of recent research. *BMC Medical Research Methodology*, 10, 2010.

[21] U. D. of Health, H. Services, et al. Summary of the HIPAA privacy rule. *HHS*, 2003.

[22] S. T. Peddinti, A. Korolova, E. Bursztein, and G. Sampemane. Cloak and swagger: Understanding data sensitivity through the lens of user anonymity. In *IEEE Symposium on Security and Privacy*, 2014.

[23] F. Pedregosa, G. Varoquaux, A. Gramfort, V. Michel, B. Thirion, O. Grisel, M. Blondel, P. Prettenhofer, R. Weiss, V. Dubourg, et al. Scikit-learn: Machine learning in python. *JMLR*, 12, 2011.

[24] P. Ruch, R. H. Baud, A.-M. Rassinoux, P. Bouillon, and G. Robert. Medical document anonymization with a semantic lexicon. In *AMIA Symposium*, 2000.

[25] D. Sánchez, M. Batet, and A. Viejo. Detecting sensitive information from textual documents: an information-theoretic approach. In *MDAI*. 2012.

[26] D. Sánchez, M. Batet, and A. Viejo. Minimizing the disclosure risk of semantic correlations in document sanitization. *Information Sciences*, 2013.

[27] Y. Saygin, D. Hakkani-Tur, and G. Tur. Sanitization and anonymization of document repositories. *Web and information security*, 2005.

[28] L. Si and H. Yang. Privacy-preserving IR 2014: When information retrieval meets privacy and security. In *SIGIR Workshop on PIR*, 2014.

[29] J. Staddon, P. Golle, and B. Zimny. Web-based inference detection. In *USENIX Security*, 2007.

[30] L. Sweeney. Replacing personally-identifying information in medical records, the scrub system. In *AMIA*, 1996.

[31] L. Sweeney. Simple demographics often identify people uniquely. *Health*, 2000.

[32] L. Sweeney. k-anonymity: A model for protecting privacy. *IJUFKS*, 2002.

[33] A. Tveit, O. Edsberg, T. Rost, A. Faxvaag, O. Nytro, M. Nordgard, M. T. Ranang, and A. Grimsmo. Anonymization of general practioner medical records. In *HelsIT*, 2004.

[34] S. S. Woo and H. Manjunatha. Empirical data analysis on user privacy and sentiment in personal blogs. In *SIGIR Workshop on PIR*, 2015.

[35] H. Yang and I. Soboroff. Privacy-preserving IR 2015: When information retrieval meets privacy and security. In *SIGIR Workshop on PIR*, 2015.

[36] H. Yang, I. Soboroff, L. Xiong, C. L. Clarke, and S. L. Garfinkel. Privacy-preserving IR 2016: Differential privacy, search, and social media. In *SIGIR Workshop on PIR*, 2016.

[37] S. Zhang, H. Yang, and L. Singh. Applying epsilon-differential private query log releasing scheme to document retrieval. In *SIGIR Workshop on PIR*, 2015.

Joint Estimation of Topics and Hashtag Relevance in Cross-Lingual Tweets

Procheta Sen
CVPR Unit
Indian Statistical Institute
Kolkata, India
senprocheta@gmail.com

Debasis Ganguly
ADAPT Centre
School of Computing
Dublin City University
Dublin, Ireland
dganguly@computing.dcu.ie

Gareth J.F. Jones
ADAPT Centre
School of Computing
Dublin City University
Dublin, Ireland
gjones@computing.dcu.ie

ABSTRACT

Twitter is a widely used platform for sharing news articles. An emerging trend in multi-lingual communities is to share non-English news articles using English tweets in order to spread the news to a wider audience. In general, the choice of relevant hashtags for such tweets depends on the topic of the non-English news article. In this paper, we address the problem of automatically detecting the relevance of the hashtags of such tweets. More specifically, we propose a generative model to jointly model the topics within an English tweet and those within the non-English news article shared from it to predict the relevance of the hashtags of the tweet. For conducting experiments, we compiled a collection of English tweets that share news articles in Bengali (a South Asian language). Our experiments on this dataset demonstrate that this joint estimation based approach using the topics from both the non-English news articles and the tweets proves to be more effective for relevance estimation than that of only using the topics of a tweet itself.

CCS Concepts

•Computing methodologies → Natural language processing;

Keywords

Cross-lingual Tweet tagging; bilingual topic modelling; joint estimation of topic and tag relevance

1. INTRODUCTION

In recent years, social media has played a major role in distributing news among people, often crossing language barriers. For example, a significant number of news articles are shared with the help of Twitter, a micro blogging platform. Sometimes, non-native English speakers compose tweets in English in order to share a news article published in their own native language. The most likely motive for this *cross-lingual* news sharing across the social media is to allow a non-English news article to receive wider visibility outside its own local community.

ICTIR '16, September 12-16, 2016, Newark, DE, USA

© 2016 ACM. ISBN 978-1-4503-4497-5/16/09. . . $15.00

DOI: http://dx.doi.org/10.1145/2970398.2970425

(a) Tweet (b) News article

Figure 1: A sample tweet in English that contains a link to a foreign language (Bengali, in this example) news article.

The widespread generation of such user generated *cross-lingual* tweets has given rise to the problem of selecting the appropriate hashtags for these tweets (which we call *cross-lingual* tweets), so that they can effectively be retrieved at a later period of time. More often than not Twitter users do not select hashtags that effectively describe the core concepts of their tweet. This observation has motivated research into constructing automated approaches for identifying the relevant tags of a tweet [4], or recommending alternative potentially relevant hashtags to users [2, 7].

In general, it is difficult to model the relevance of hashtags with the tweet text alone, because of their short length. The motivation of our work in this paper is to make use of the text of the related news article to improve the relevance estimation of the tags. Our motivation is that intuitively speaking, it is the *aboutness* of the shared article which should influence the choice of appropriate hashtags for the tweet. Since the language of a news document (say F) shared from a tweet is different from that of the tweet itself (say E)[1], the problem of joint topic modeling is more challenging.

An example of a cross-lingual tweet is shown in Figure 1. The word '#CBI' ('Central Bureau of Investigation') is a relevant tag for the tweet shown in Figure 1. However, it is difficult to predict this word as a relevant tag, since the only word in the tweet topically related to the word 'CBI' is 'investigation'. Contrastingly, the Bengali news article, shown in Figure 1, contains more words that are topically related to the word 'CBI', such as 'mrityur'[2] (of death), 'court', 'nihoto' (dead), 'mamla' (case), 'abhijoger' (of accusation), 'abhijukto' (accused), etc. The key idea of our proposed approach is to use these additional topically relevant words in a news document to improve relevance estimation of the tweet hashtags. Our experimental results show that our method improves the F-score of the relevance of tags by 1.79% and the perplexity of the topic model by 23.9% compared to a mono-lingual baseline [4].

---

[1]We follow this naming convention for the rest of the paper.
[2]We use Roman transliteration to represent Bengali words.

2. RELATED WORK

A graphical model for hashtag relevance prediction for microblogs (such as Flickr, Hatena) was proposed in [4]. This first estimates the topic distribution of the content words and the tags of a document, similar to LDA [1], and then models the likelihood of relevance of the tags based on the topics. The major limitation of this model is that it only works for monolingual documents, and not on cross-lingual document pairs, which we address in this paper. Our work extends the work in [4] to model the relevance of hashtags using documents in a language different from that of the tweets.

The work in [2] suggests hashtags by using topic models to disambiguate the sense of the content words that are candidate tags. The main disadvantage of a word alignment based model is that its effectiveness largely depends on the availability of a parallel corpus. In contrast, we propose a generative approach which does not depend on any linguistic resources. A convolutional neural network model for predicting hashtags was proposed in [7]. The main difficulty with such a deep learning based approach is that a large training set is required for its effective training. A personalized hashtag recommendation method for tweets, based on the tweet content and user preferences, was proposed in [6].

3. PROPOSED METHOD

Our model is motivated by the mono-lingual model of hashtag relevance prediction [4], which we name mono-lingual tag relevance (MTR) model. Before discussing our proposed method, we briefly introduce the MTR model.

Overview of MTR. The solidly outlined circles in Figure 2 represent the variables of the MTR model [4]. The observed variables (shown shaded) in this model correspond to words and tags of a tweet. The topic assigned to a tweet word, w^E, is sampled from the latent topic variables z^E. The generative process of an observed hashtag t is more involved, because in order to jointly model the topics and relevance of a tag, the model assumes the existence of a latent variable r. A value of $r = 1$ indicates relevance of a tag t to the content of a tweet, in which case, t is sampled from a latent topic distribution c^E, which in turn depends on z^E (topics of the content words of the tweet). Otherwise, $r = 0$ indicates that a tag is not related to the content, in which case, t is drawn from a global distribution not related to the content of the tweet. Note that the dimension of τ is $K + 1$ to account for one additional global topic distribution unrelated to the content of a tweet.

Extending MTR to BTR. We now describe the latent variables that we propose to add to the MTR so as to model the relevance of cross-lingual tweets, in our bilingual tweet relevance (BTR) model. The additional variables are shown with a dotted outline. The key difference between this and the MTR model is that in the scenario of cross-lingual tweets, we have a document pair (a tweet with its shared article) instead of only a single document (the tweet itself).

In our proposed BTR model, a shared document-topic distribution, θ, generates the topics of the news document in language F and the tweet in language E. The additional latent variable representing the topics of the news document is z^F, the words of which (denoted by w^F), are drawn from an additional multinomial distribution from the vocabulary of language F, shown as ϕ^F. Moreover, in order to model the fact that the relevance of a hashtag t for a cross-lingual tweet also depends on the topical content of the shared news document, we introduce a latent variable c^F which depends on z^F in a similar way as c^E depends on z^E in MTR. To see the dependence between c^F and t note that the topic distribution of the non-English words contributes to modifying the sampling probability of the relevance variables, r_is, as shown in Equation 5.

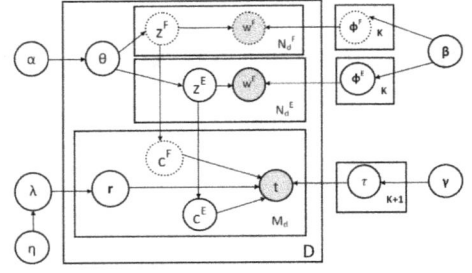

Figure 2: Plate diagram of our proposed generative model for jointly modeling relevance of hashtags of cross-lingual tweets.

BTR Estimation. After describing the key extensions of BTR with respect to MTR, we now provide the estimation details of the BTR model. From Figure 2, it can be seen that the joint distribution of the observed variables, i.e. the words and tags of a tweet in language E (d^E) and those of the document it shares in language F (d^F), depend on the latent variables and the hyper-parameters shown in Equation 1.

$$P(W^F, W^E, T, Z^F, Z^E, C^F, C^E, R, \alpha, \beta, \gamma, \eta) =$$
$$P(Z^F|\alpha)P(Z^E|\alpha)P(W^F|Z^F, \beta)P(W^E|Z^E, \beta) \quad (1)$$
$$P(T|C^F, C^E, R, \gamma)P(R|\eta)P(C^F|Z^F)P(C^E|Z^E)$$

The latent topics Z^E and Z^F, given the content words W^E, W^F and the hashtags T, are computed using Gibbs sampling [3]. Following the standard Gibbs sampling exposition for polylingual topic models [5], and using the conditional dependence of C^E on Z^E and that of C^F on Z^F, the sampling probabilities for the latent topic of the jth word of the dth document pair d^E (i.e. z_j^E) and d^F (i.e. z_j^F) are calculated as shown in Equations 2 and 3, where M_{kd}^E and M_{kd}^F denote the number of tags that are assigned to topic k using d^E and d^F respectively.

$$P(z_j^E = k|Z_{\backslash j}^E) \propto \frac{N_{kd\backslash j}^E + N_{kd}^F + \alpha}{N_{d\backslash j}^E + N_d^F + \alpha K} \frac{N_{kw_j\backslash j}^E + \beta}{N_{k\backslash j}^E + \beta W^E} \left(\frac{N_{kd\backslash j}^E}{N_{d\backslash j}^E} \right)^{M_{kd}^E} \quad (2)$$

$$P(z_j^F = k|Z_{\backslash j}^F) \propto \frac{N_{kd}^E + N_{kd\backslash j}^F + \alpha}{N_d^E + N_{d\backslash j}^F + \alpha K} \frac{N_{kw_j\backslash j}^F + \beta}{N_{k\backslash j}^F + \beta W^F} \left(\frac{N_{kd\backslash j}^F}{N_{d\backslash j}^F} \right)^{M_{kd}^F} \quad (3)$$

Equations 2 and 3 allow joint modeling of the topics from the content of a document pair.

Equations 4 and 5 show how the latent variable for hashtag-topic relevance r_i (i.e relevance of the ith tag of the dth document d^E) are sampled. It can be seen from Equation 5 that the probability of relevance of a tag increases with the likelihood of the co-occurrence of that tag with a topic, which is estimated by the global tag-topic co-occurrence counts for the corresponding languages E and F, denoted respectively by $M_{c,t}^E$ and $M_{c,t}^F$. $M_{0\backslash i}$ in 4 and 5 denotes the number of non-relevant tags in the tweet collection excluding the ith tag of the dth document d^E.

$$P(r_i = 0|R_{\backslash i}) \propto \frac{M_{0\backslash i} + \eta}{M_{\backslash i} + 2\eta} \frac{M_{0t_i\backslash i} + \gamma}{M_{0\backslash i} + \gamma T} \quad (4)$$

$$P(r_i = 1|R_{\backslash i}) \propto \frac{M_{\backslash i} - M_{0\backslash i} + \eta}{M_{\backslash i} + 2\eta} \frac{M_{c_i t_i\backslash i}^E + M_{c_i t_i\backslash i}^F + \gamma}{M_{c_i\backslash i}^E + M_{c_i\backslash i}^F + \gamma T} \quad (5)$$

The assignment of a topic to a content unrelated hashtag is given by the maximum likelihood estimates from the corresponding documents, i.e. $P(c_i^E = k | r_i = 0, C_{\backslash i}^E, R_{\backslash i}) = N_{kd}^E / N_d^E$ and a similar expression with the corresponding variables for d^F. On the other hand, the assignment of a topic to a content related hashtag is estimated according to Equation 6 and 7.

$$P(c_i^E = k | r_i = 1, C_{\backslash i}, R_{\backslash i}) \propto \frac{M_{kt_i \backslash i}^E + \gamma}{M_{k \backslash i}^E + \gamma T} \frac{N_{kd}^E}{N_d^E} \quad (6)$$

$$P(c_i^F = k | r_i = 1, C_{\backslash i}, R_{\backslash i}) \propto \frac{M_{kt_i \backslash i}^F + \gamma}{M_{k \backslash i}^F + \gamma T} \frac{N_{kd}^F}{N_d^F} \quad (7)$$

$M_{kt_i \backslash i}^F$ of Equation 7 denotes the number of times tag t_i is assigned the topic k, using the documents in F (and similarly $M_{kt_i \backslash i}^E$ for the documents in E). Hence, Equations 6 and 7 make a tag-topic association more likely if the topic itself occurs frequently in both d^F and d^E (instead of d^E alone as in MTR).

The values of the latent variables of the model, i.e. the topics of the English tweets and the non-English news documents along with the relevance of the tags, i.e. the r_i variables are estimated by executing Gibbs sampling iterations. The r values are eventually used to measure how effectively the relevance of the tags are predicted.

4. EXPERIMENTAL SETUP

DataSet. One of the difficulties in collecting a dataset of cross-lingual tweets is that despite the presence of numerous bilingual Twitter users, due to the limitations of the Twitter streaming API, it is difficult to implement a streaming service that can automatically track such tweets. A much simpler solution is to track a particular Twitter account that is known to post such cross-lingual tweets. Consequently, for the purpose of building the dataset for our investigation, we collected tweets from the Twitter account of a leading Bengali (a South Asian language) news daily Anandabazar Patrika (ABP)[3]. The Twitter account of ABP[4] is a bilingual account that posts tweets sharing Bengali news articles both in Bengali and English. For our research, we collected only the English tweets posted by the ABP twitter account by making use of the language identifier settings of the Twitter API. To collect the data, Twitter data streaming was executed for about 3 months[5]. Out of a total of 13,299 tweets collected from this account, 1,370 tweets were cross-lingual and hence used for our experiments (see Table 1).

A filtering step ensured that each tweet in our dataset has a relevant news article (in Bengali) linked to it. Tweets with no linked news articles were discarded. The characteristics of the cross-lingual tweet dataset used for our experiments are shown in Table 1. To measure the effectiveness of BTR, we need a reference set of relevant tags for each tweet. Since all of the tweets in our dataset were posted by a news publisher, the tags are mostly carefully selected according to content relevance. However, to make a more realistic dataset where tweets have a mixture of both relevant and non-relevant tags, we randomly assigned a number of tags to each tweet. These tags are considered to be the non-relevant during evaluation, i.e. the objective of the model is to predict that these additional tags are non-relevant. The source of these randomly assigned tags is the entire tag vocabulary of the dataset, which makes the chance of adding a truly relevant tag to a tweet very unlikely.

Baseline. The objective of our experiments is to show that jointly modeling hashtag relevance by additionally using the content of the

Table 1: Characteristics of the cross-lingual tweet dataset.

Attribute	Value
# English Tweets and corresponding Bengali news articles	1370
Vocabulary size of English tweets	4550
Tag vocabulary size of tweets	1325
Vocabulary size of Bengali news articles	55201
Avg. # words in an English tweet (without URLs and stopwords)	3.32
Avg. # words in a Bengali news article	40.29
Avg. # tags per tweet	2.05
Overlap between tweet words and tag words	39.40%

document shared from a tweet can improve relevance prediction effectiveness. Consequently, as a baseline for our experiments, we use the MTR model, which makes use of the tweet text only to predict hashtag relevance. Bilingual LDA [5] cannot be used as a baseline because it is a model for generating only the content words in two languages with latent topic distributions for each language. It does not however model tag relevance.

Machine translation (MT) is one way of bridging the vocabulary gap, with which one would be able to apply the mono-lingual tag relevance prediction model. However, there are two main reasons for not using MT in our experiments. Firstly, the availability of parallel corpora for Bengali-English translation is limited. The only parallel corpus that we are aware of comprises 48K parallel sentences in health and tourism[6]. Secondly, the key motivation of our approach is to be able to bridge the vocabulary gap with the help of a completely unsupervised approach even without the presence of any translation resource at all.

Parameters. For collapsed Gibbs sampling of both BTR and MTR, we use 1000 iterations as prescribed in [3]. The LDA hyper-parameters for the Dirichlet priors of the document-topic and the topic-term distributions were set to $50/K$ (K being the number of topics) and 0.01 respectively according to [3]. For BTR, the topic-term distribution priors for both E and F, were set to 0.01. The hyper-parameters η and γ were set to 0.01 for both BTR and MTR.

Evaluation Metrics. To compare BTR against MTR, we use two standard evaluation measures. The first measure, called *perplexity* (shown in Equation 8), uses the posterior document-topic (θ) and the topic-tag distributions (τ) to measure how stable the posterior estimates are. A lower value of perplexity indicates higher posterior likelihood of the observed variables, i.e. the content words and tag words. Our second evaluation measure is targeted towards directly measuring the effectiveness of the hashtag relevance prediction. We calculate the *F-score* by comparing the estimated r_i values for both the relevant and the non-relevant tags with their true values. A higher F-score indicates that there is a better agreement between the true r_i values and the estimated ones, and that the model is more effective in distinguishing relevant tags from non-relevant ones.

$$H = \exp\left(-\frac{\sum_{d=1}^{M} log(P_d(t_1 \ldots t_{M_d} | \theta, \tau))}{\sum_{d=1}^{M} N_d}\right), P_d(t) = \sum_{k=1}^{K} \theta_{dk} \tau_{kt} \quad (8)$$

5. RESULTS

In our initial experiments, we set the number of topics (K), used for estimating both MTR and BTR, to 10. To evaluate tag relevance, we artificially add one non-relevant hashtag to each tweet. Table 2 shows the results with this settings. Firstly, it can be seen that BTR produces a lower perplexity score in comparison to MTR in Table 2), which indicates that the posterior distributions are more

---

[3]http://www.anandabazar.com/

[4]https://twitter.com/MyAnandaBazar

[5]For dataset and code see https://bitbucket.org/procheta/cltagrel

[6]http://sanskrit.jnu.ac.in/projects/ilci.jsp?proj=ilci

Method	Evaluation Metrics	
Name	Perplexity	F-score
MTR	585.76	0.7311
BTR	**472.51**	**0.7442**

Table 2: Relevance prediction effectiveness (F-score) of cross-lingual tweets. #topics was set to 10. One non-relevant hashtag was added for each tweet.

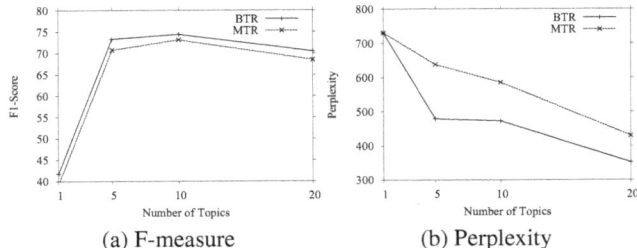

(a) F-measure (b) Perplexity

Figure 3: Sensitivity of F-score and perplexity on #topics.

stable for BTR. Secondly, in terms of predicting the relevance of tags, we see that BTR achieves a higher F-score than MTR. The improvements in F-score are statistically significant as measured by the Wilcoxon test with 95% confidence measure. This verifies our hypothesis that making use of the shared news article helps to provide the additional context for the tag relevance to perform better. The topics estimated jointly over each document pair (i.e. the tweet and the news) are more robust than those estimated over a single tweet, because in BTR, the distribution $P(C^F|Z^F)$ (see Figure 2) improves the prediction of hashtag relevance. In contrast to MTR, this additional factor helps to identify more relevant tags, which is also evident from the higher F-score.

Sensitivity to the number of Topics. For our next set of experiments, we vary the number of topics to see how this affects the perplexity and the F-score values of the hashtag relevance models. The results are shown in Figure 3. It can be seen from Figure 3a that with a degenerate case of only 1 topic, the performance of both MTR and BTR is low. In fact, with a lower number of topics, MTR yields better results than BTR. However, it can be seen from Figure 3a, that the results improve when the number of topics in BTR is increased. It can also be seen that the effectiveness of BTR is optimal with $K = 10$, i.e. when 10 topics are used to estimate the model. A further increase in the number of topics exhibits a steady decrease in F-score for both the models. The effect of the number of topics on perplexity is shown in Figure 3b. We observe that the perplexity of BTR is consistently lower than that of MTR.

Sensitivity to the number of non-relevant tags. For our next set of experiments, we added an increasing number of non-relevant tags to the tweets. The purpose of this set of experiments was to examiner the robustness of the models in the presence of noisy data. The results are shown in Figure 4. As expected, the effectiveness of both the models decreases with an increasing number of non-relevant tags. However, it can be seen from Figure 4a that BTR consistently outperforms MTR even with an increasing number of non-relevant tags, which indicates that BTR is able to recognize relevant tags more effectively than its monolingual counterpart in the presence of non-relevant tags. Figure 4b shows that the perplexity of both the models increases with an increasing number of non-relevant tags. For MTR, this perplexity variation effect with

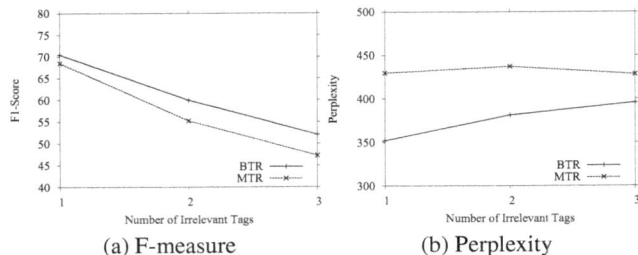

(a) F-measure (b) Perplexity

Figure 4: Sensitivity to the number of non-relevant tags.

increasing noise is consistent with the observations reported in [4] on different datasets such as Hatena, Delicious and Flickr.

6. CONCLUSIONS AND FUTURE WORK

In this paper, we addressed the problem of predicting the relevance of hashtags for a tweet which shares an article in a language different from the language of the tweet itself (we call such tweets cross-lingual tweets). We hypothesize that the relevance of hashtags of cross-lingual tweets depends on the topical content of the articles that they share. We proposed a generative model to jointly model the topics in each document pair comprised of the tweet and the shared article in two different languages. The key idea is that the topics extracted from the content words of the foreign language article can improve on the hashtag relevance prediction performance of the tweets. Our experiments, conducted on a set of cross-lingual tweets, verify this claim. Our proposed model (BTR) consistently outperforms its monolingual counterpart (MTR) over a varying range of number of topics and non-relevant tags. As a part of our future work, we would like to extend our proposed model to a non-parametric version that would not require a preset number of topics. Another idea is to incorporate other user generated signals, such as retweet count, favourites count etc. as a part of the generative model to improve modeling relevance of hashtags.

Acknowledgements: This research is supported by Science Foundation Ireland (SFI) as a part of the ADAPT Centre at DCU (Grant No: 13/RC/2106).

7. REFERENCES

[1] D. M. Blei, A. Y. Ng, and M. I. Jordan. Latent Dirichlet allocation. *J. Mach. Learn. Res.*, 3:993–1022, 2003.

[2] Z. Ding, Q. Zhang, and X. Huang. Automatic hashtag recommendation for microblogs using topic-specific translation model. In *Proc. of COLING'12*, pages 265–274, 2012.

[3] T. L. Griffiths and M. Steyvers. Finding scientific topics. *PNAS*, 101:5228–5235, 2004.

[4] T. Iwata, T. Yamada, and N. Ueda. Modeling social annotation data with content relevance using a topic model. In *Proc. of NIPS '09*, pages 835–843, 2009.

[5] D. Mimno, H. M. Wallach, J. Naradowsky, D. A. Smith, and A. McCallum. Polylingual topic models. In *Proceedings of the EMNLP '09*, pages 880–889, 2009.

[6] E.-P. L. Su Mon Kywe, Tuan-Anh Hoang and F. Zhu. On recommending hashtags in twitter networks. In *Proceedings of ICSI 2012*, pages 337–350, 2012.

[7] J. Weston, S. Chopra, and K. Adams. #tagspace: Semantic embeddings from hashtags. In *Proc. of EMNLP '14*, pages 1822–1827, 2014.

Temporal Query Expansion Using a Continuous Hidden Markov Model

Jinfeng Rao
Department of Computer Science
University of Maryland, College Park
jinfeng@cs.umd.edu

Jimmy Lin
Cheriton School of Computer Science
University of Waterloo
jimmylin@uwaterloo.ca

ABSTRACT

In standard formulations of pseudo-relevance feedback, document timestamps do not play a role in identifying expansion terms. Yet we know that when searching social media posts such as tweets, relevant documents are bursty and usually occur in temporal clusters. The main insight of our work is that term expansions should be biased to draw from documents that occur in bursty temporal clusters. This is formally captured by a continuous hidden Markov model (cHMM), for which we derive an EM algorithm for parameter estimation. Given a query, we estimate the parameters for a cHMM that best explains the observed distribution of an initial set of retrieved documents, and then use Viterbi decoding to compute the most likely state sequence. In identifying expansion terms, we only select documents from bursty states. Experiments on test collections from the TREC 2011 and 2012 Microblog tracks show that our approach is significantly more effective than the popular RM3 pseudo-relevance feedback model.

1. INTRODUCTION

A longstanding challenge in information retrieval is the issue of vocabulary mismatch, where query terms are not present in relevant documents. This problem is especially severe in searching social media posts such as tweets due to their short lengths and frequent use of informal language. Query expansion techniques, especially those based on pseudo-relevance feedback, are effective in addressing this problem. The main idea is to augment the user's query with terms that appear in the initial top k retrieved documents. In this paper, we extend this idea to consider the temporal dimension in the term expansion process.

We are motivated by Efron et al.'s temporal cluster hypothesis [7], which stipulates that in search tasks where time plays an important role (such as tweet search), relevant documents tend to cluster together in time, and that this property can be exploited to improve search effectiveness. Just as van Rijsbergen's "classic" cluster hypothesis suggests that

documents relevant to a query form clusters in term space, Efron et al. suggest that documents relevant to a query will form clusters along a timeline.

The temporal cluster hypothesis is illustrated by the visualizations in Figure 1, similar to those presented by Efron et al. [7], which help illustrate the intuition behind our techniques. These visualizations show three topics from the TREC 2011 Microblog track. In each timeline, the query time (the time at which the query was issued) is anchored to the right edge; the x-axis shows time prior to the query time, in days. Dots show tweets that were retrieved by participating teams and evaluated by assessors (i.e., the pools): green dots are relevant, red dots are highly relevant, and gray dots are not relevant. The underlying blue bars show the distribution of relevant and highly-relevant tweets as a histogram. As we can see, relevant tweets for topics 14 and 30 tend to cluster together in time, while relevant tweets for topic 6 are more evenly distributed. Across all topics from the TREC test collections, we observe many timelines that exhibit temporal clustering (like topics 14 and 30).

In standard formulations of pseudo-relevance feedback, the timestamp of a document is not considered in identifying expansion terms—yet we know from Figure 1 that relevant documents are bursty and usually occur in temporal clusters, and that this signal should be incorporated into the relevance feedback model. The main insight of our work is that term expansions should be biased to draw from documents that occur in the bursty temporal clusters. This is formally captured by a continuous hidden Markov model (cHMM), in which the temporal distribution of documents (not necessarily relevant) is represented by a sequence of hidden states; the probability of generating a particular number of documents from each state follows a Gaussian distribution. We present the derivation of an EM algorithm to estimate the parameters of such a cHMM. Given a query, we first perform an initial retrieval, estimate the parameters for a cHMM that best explains the observed distribution of retrieved documents, and then use Viterbi decoding to compute the most likely state sequence. In identifying term expansions, we only select documents from bursty states. Experimental evaluations on test collections from the TREC 2011 and 2012 Microblog tracks show that our approach is significantly more effective than the popular RM3 pseudo-relevance feedback model [10, 1].

2. RELATED WORK

There is a long thread of research exploring the role of temporal signals in search [11, 6, 5, 7, 9], and it is well estab-

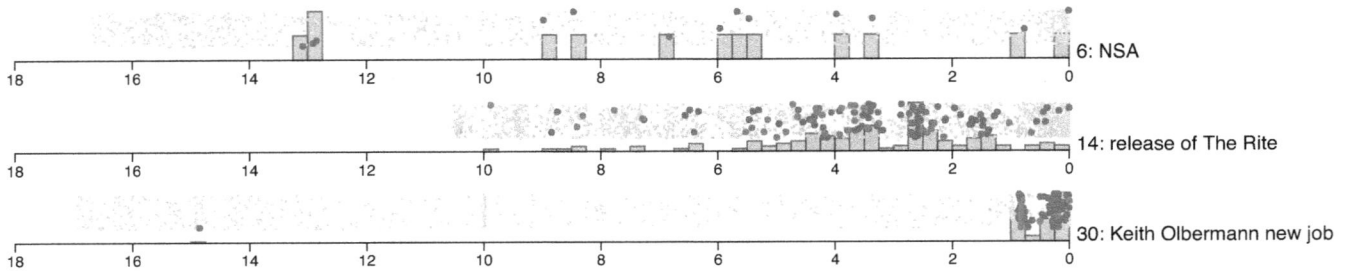

Figure 1: Temporal distribution of relevant (green) and highly-relevant (red) tweets for three topics from the TREC 2011 Microblog track.

lished that for certain tasks, better modeling of the temporal characteristics of queries and documents can lead to higher retrieval effectiveness. For example, Li and Croft [11] introduced recency priors that favor more-recent documents; Efron et al. [6] presented several language model variants that incorporate temporal evidence; Dakka et al. [5] proposed a moving window-based approach to integrate query-specific temporal evidence with lexical evidence.

More recently, Efron et al. [7] introduced the temporal cluster hypothesis (as discussed above), which was operationalized in retrieval models based on kernel density estimation. This work was subsequently expanded upon by Rao et al. [13]. We further build on this work using cHMMs to capture temporal evidence in the form of bursty documents. As such, our technique is most directly related to the work of Kleinberg [9], who proposed a weighted-automaton model to uncover bursty and hierarchical structure in document streams of email and news articles.

There have been several other works that studied temporal query expansion [8, 4, 3, 12]. Keikha et al. [8] represented queries and documents with their normalized term frequencies in the time dimension and used a time-based similarity metric to measure relevance. Craveiro et al. [4] exploited the temporal relationship between words for query expansion. Choi et al. [3] presented a method to select time periods for expansion based on users' behaviors (i.e., retweets). Our work is related to that of Peetz et al. [12], who identified temporal bursts through heuristics by setting hard thresholds on the distribution of document counts within a time window. Their approach showed improvements over a query-likelihood baseline and an exponential-decay baseline. We believe our cHMM approach represents a more formal and flexible way to capture bursty document behavior.

3. APPROACH

Previous work has established the importance of temporal signals in searching social media posts, and in this paper we apply this basic idea to pseudo-relevance feedback. Our main insight is that term expansions should be biased to draw from documents that occur in bursty temporal clusters of documents. We use a continuous hidden Markov model to identify such temporal clusters based on top-ranked documents from the user's initial query, and then compute the most likely underlying state sequence. Documents in the bursty state are then selected for query expansion. In this section, we present our formal model, describe an EM algorithm for estimating parameters, and explain how term expansions are computed.

3.1 Continuous Hidden Markov Model

We begin with the standard definition of an HMM for modeling a discrete observation sequence O of length T with a fixed number of hidden states. An HMM is parameterized by (A, B, π), where A is the transition matrix with A_{ij} denoting the transition probability from state i to state j at each time step, B is the emission matrix with each $B_i(O)$ denoting the probability of generating observation O from state i, and π is the initial state distribution vector.

Our approach is a variant of classic HMMs. In classic HMMs each observation is a discrete symbol drawn from a finite alphabet, while in our case the observation is an integer that denotes the document count at time interval t. That is, we assume the probability of generating an observation count O_t in state i is as follows:

$$B_i(O_t) = P(O_t|q_t = i) \sim N(u_i, \sigma_i)$$

The underlying states in our cHMM capture the burstiness of tweets during a particular time interval. A bursty state might correspond to a time when there are lots of users postings tweets (for example, when something newsworthy is taking place). A quiet state would correspond to times when nothing interesting is happening. In our current implementation, our cHMM uses three hidden states, but the model can be extended to capture arbitrarily many gradations of burstiness. The state transitions in our cHMM model sequential dependencies in these states—for example, a burst "dies down" when a newsworthy event passes. In each state, the mean u controls the "intensity" of the burst (i.e., how many documents are generated), and σ controls variations in different instances of the same state.

Figure 2 shows the three-state cHMM in our current implementation: circles represent states and arrows represent transitions. The blue circle denotes a "bursty" state as it has the largest mean, while the white circle can be interpreted as an "inactive" state since it has the smallest mean; the gray circle might be interpreted as an intermediate state.

Thus, our cHMM is parameterized as $\lambda = (A, u, \sigma, \pi)$. Given a sequence of observations (document counts within a fixed time window), we can derive an EM algorithm to estimate the parameters iteratively.

In the E-step, the expectation of the complete-data log-likelihood $\log P(O, q|\lambda)$, namely the Q function, is:

$$Q(\lambda, \lambda') \propto \sum_q \log P(O, q|\lambda) P(O, q|\lambda') \quad (1)$$

where λ' represents estimates of parameters in the previous iteration that are known in the calculation and λ represents

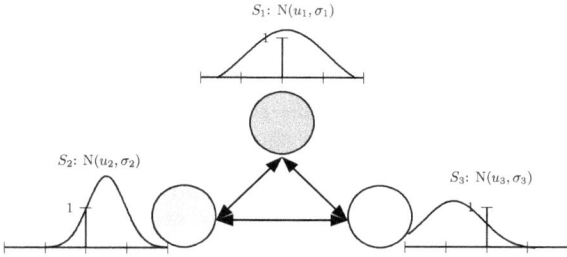

Figure 2: An illustration of a three-state cHMM. Each circle represents a state and arrows represent transitions. The Gaussians represent emissions (count of documents) from each state.

unknown parameters that we are trying to estimate for maximizing the Q function.

From the independence assumptions of HMMs (namely, that the observation O_t is only dependent on state q_t; state q_t is only dependent on the previous state q_{t-1}), we can compute the joint probability $P(O, q|\lambda)$ as follows:

$$P(O, q|\lambda) = P(q|\lambda)P(O|q, \lambda)$$
$$= \pi_{q_1} \prod_{t=2}^{T} A_{q_{t-1}q_t} \prod_{t=1}^{T} B_{q_t}(O_t) \quad (2)$$

Substituting $P(O, q|\lambda)$ in Equation (2) into Equation (1):

$$Q(\lambda, \lambda') = \sum_q \log \pi_{q_1} P(O, q|\lambda')$$
$$+ \sum_q \left(\sum_{t=2}^{T} \log A_{q_{t-1}q_t} \right) P(O, q|\lambda')$$
$$+ \sum_q \left(\sum_{t=1}^{T} \log B_{q_t}(O_t) \right) P(O, q|\lambda') \quad (3)$$

We have broken the overall objective into three independent parts that we can optimize individually in the M-step. Since the optimization shares similarities with discrete HMMs (we recommend the tutorial by Bilmes [2] for more details), we skip the detailed derivations here and provide the final solutions as follows:

$$\pi_i = \frac{P(O, q_1 = i|\lambda')}{P(O|\lambda')} \quad (4)$$

$$A_{ij} = \frac{\sum_{t=2}^{T} P(O, q_{t-1} = i, q_t = j)}{\sum_{t=2}^{T} P(O, q_{t-1} = i|\lambda')} \quad (5)$$

$$u_i = \frac{\sum_{t=1}^{T} O_t \cdot P(O, q_t = i|\lambda')}{\sum_{t=1}^{T} P(O, q_t = i|\lambda')} \quad (6)$$

$$\sigma_i^2 = \frac{\sum_{t=1}^{T} (O_t - u_i)^2 \cdot P(O, q_t = i|\lambda')}{\sum_{t=1}^{T} P(O, q_t = i|\lambda')} \quad (7)$$

As with any EM algorithm, we iteratively update the parameters using above derivations until convergence. After arriving at the final parameter estimates $\lambda_f(A, u, \sigma, \pi)$, we

can then use the Viterbi algorithm to find the sequence of states q_{opt} that maximizes $P(O|\lambda_f)$. Expansion terms are then computed from this state sequence, explained next.

3.2 Temporal Query Expansion

Given a query Q consisting of n query terms $\{t_1, t_2, ...t_n\}$, we use the above continuous hidden Markov model to find the state sequence that best describes the temporal distribution of the top k documents collected by an initial retrieval. We consider the state with the largest mean as the bursty state, and only select documents whose timestamps fall in the bursty state for query expansion. For convenience, we call these documents *bursty documents*. We then estimate a relevance model $P(w|R)$ [10] as follows:

$$P(w|R) = \sum_{D \in C} P(D)P(w|D) \prod_{i=1}^{n} P(t_i|D) \quad (8)$$

where C is the set of bursty documents. We assume uniform priors $P(D)$, so the relevance model is simply a weighted average of the terms in the documents, where the weights are the query likelihood scores.

Finally, just as in RM3, we interpolate the estimated relevance model with the original query model:

$$P'(w|R) = \alpha \cdot P(w|R) + (1 - \alpha) \cdot P(w|Q) \quad (9)$$

The interpolation parameter α is set to 0.5 by default. Following common parameter settings, we estimated the relevance models from $k = 50$ pseudo-relevant documents and selected $m = 20$ feedback terms.

4. EXPERIMENTS

We evaluated our model on the Tweets2011 corpus using test collections from the Microblog tracks at TREC 2011 and 2012. The Tweets2011 corpus contains ~1% of all tweets from January 23, 2011 to February 7, 2011, totaling around 16 million tweets. There are 49 topics in TREC 2011 and 60 topics in TREC 2012, with relevance judgments assigned one of three grades: not relevant, relevant, and highly relevant. In our experiments, we considered both relevant and highly-relevant tweets as relevant. We removed retweets in the query expansion and final results, as the track guidelines consider them not relevant by fiat.

Our experimental procedure was as follows: We first performed initial retrieval using query-likelihood to gather ranked lists of tweets from the corpus. We then trained our cHMM on the top 50 tweets for each topic as described in Section 3.1, with three states and the number of time intervals T set to 30. After the cHMM parameters have been estimated via EM, we apply Viterbi decoding to extract the most likely state sequence, which is then used for temporal query expansion as described in Section 3.2. Note that this experimental procedure does not require a training/test split of the topics.

Our cHMM temporal pseudo-feedback technique is compared against the RM3 pseudo-feedback technique [10, 1] as a baseline. We also implemented the KDE variant of RM3 [7, 13], which includes four different ways to estimate feedback parameters: uniform, score-based, rank-based, and oracle. The first three are based on pseudo-feedback because they do not rely on user relevance judgments in the initial retrieved hits (which is the same as with RM3 and cHMM), while the oracle method requires explicit relevance

Method	P5	P15	P30	MAP
QL	0.465	0.411	0.354	0.268
RM3	0.500	0.433	0.378	0.302
RM3 + KDE (score)	0.494	0.436	0.379	0.300
RM3 + KDE (rank)	0.490	0.425	0.376	0.292
RM3 + KDE (oracle)	0.548$^\bullet$	0.492$^\bullet$	0.422$^\bullet$	0.319$^\bullet$
cHMM	**0.528$^\bullet$**	**0.444$^\bullet$**	**0.391°**	**0.310°**

Table 1: Experimental results comparing the effectiveness of cHMMs against RM3 and KDE variants.

judgments. The oracle, naturally, is not realistic, but is nevertheless useful to illustrate upper bound effectiveness. Here, we include results for the score-based, rank-based, and oracle conditions. We follow the same parameter tuning procedure in Rao et al. [13], where the parameters were learned using test data from TREC 2013 and 2014 topics. For completeness, we show the results of the initial query-likelihood (QL) retrieval without any feedback (this, of course, is a weak condition to compare against). In terms of evaluation metrics, we computed mean average precision (MAP) to 1000 hits and precision at ranks 5, 15 and 30 (P5, P15, P30), computed using `trec_eval`.

Experimental results are reported in Table 1. The symbols $\circ$ and $\bullet$ indicate that differences with respect to the RM3 baseline are statistically significant at $p < 0.10$ and $p < 0.05$ based on Fisher's two-sided, paired randomization test [14], respectively. We observe that QL is relatively ineffective as all other models outperform it by a large margin (all differences are statistically significant at $p < 0.01$). This replicates the robust finding that query expansion is effective for searching tweets.

Consistent with the findings in Efron et al. [13], the KDE (score) and KDE (rank) approaches do not improve upon the effectiveness of RM3 by itself. However, our cHMM approach significantly outperforms RM3, confirming our initial intuitions—we obtain higher-quality expansion terms from bursty documents, and that bursty states can be captured with our cHMM. The results of the KDE (oracle) condition are not surprising, since it exploits users' explicit relevance feedback. This condition can be viewed as an upper bound on how much temporal signal can be extracted to improve relevance ranking (at least with this broad class of techniques)—and results show that our cHMM achieves effectiveness that is pretty close to this upper bound.

As a specific example of how our cHMM helps, we took a closer look at topic 14 "release of The Rite", which achieves an improvement of 0.22 (MAP) and 0.57 (P30) against the RM3 baseline. We visualized the estimated cHMM state sequence from day 6 to day 1 in Figure 3. As there are too many states to show if we follow the setting of $T = 30$ in our experiments above, we reduced the number of states to one per day for illustrative purposes. The blue circle denotes a bursty state, the gray circles denote an intermediate (less bursty) state, and the white circle denotes an inactive state. As we can see, the bursty state reflects the cluster of documents at day 3 in the distribution of relevant documents (topic 14 in Figure 1). From day 6 to day 1, the inferred states reflect the density of the documents along the timeline. Overall, this example suggests that our cHMM is able to capture sequential dependencies in the temporal distribution of relevance, which is essential for identifying those bursty and expressive terms for expansion.

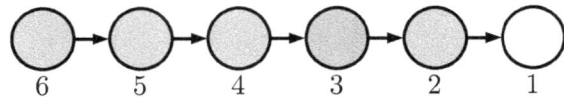

Figure 3: State evolution of topic 14 "release of The Rite" from day 6 to day 1 (each circle = one day). The blue circle represents a bursty state, the gray circles represent an intermediate state, and the white circle represents an inactive state.

5. CONCLUSIONS

This work contributes to a long thread of research on exploiting temporal signals for relevance ranking. We focus on query expansion via pseudo-relevance feedback, exploring the idea that expansion terms should be drawn from bursty documents. This is formalized via a continuous hidden Markov model to identify such documents, and our technique leads to significant effectiveness improvements over the popular RM3 model on standard TREC data. Our cHMM, however, represents only one possible model, and we are interested in exploring alternative approaches for capturing the temporal evolution of documents.

Acknowledgments. This work was supported by the U.S. National Science Foundation (NSF) under IIS-1218043 and CNS-1405688 and the Natural Sciences and Engineering Research Council of Canada (NSERC). Any opinions, findings, conclusions, or recommendations expressed are solely those of the authors.

6. REFERENCES

[1] N. Abdul-Jaleel, J. Allan, W. B. Croft, F. Diaz, L. Larkey, X. Li, D. Metzler, M. D. Smucker, T. Strohman, H. Turtle, and C. Wade. UMass at TREC 2004: Novelty and HARD. *TREC*, 2004.

[2] J. A. Bilmes. A gentle tutorial of the EM algorithm and its application to parameter estimation for Gaussian mixture and hidden Markov models. Technical report, International Computer Science Institute, 1998.

[3] J. Choi and W. B. Croft. Temporal models for microblogs. *CIKM*, 2012.

[4] O. Craveiro, J. Macedo, and H. Madeira. Query expansion with temporal segmented texts. *ECIR*, 2014.

[5] W. Dakka, L. Gravano, and P. G. Ipeirotis. Answering general time-sensitive queries. *TKDE*, 24(2):220–235, 2012.

[6] M. Efron and G. Golovchinsky. Estimation methods for ranking recent information. *SIGIR*, 2011.

[7] M. Efron, J. Lin, J. He, and A. de Vries. Temporal feedback for tweet search with non-parametric density estimation. *SIGIR*, 2014.

[8] M. Keikha, S. Gerani, and F. Crestani. TEMPER: A temporal relevance feedback method. *ECIR*, 2011.

[9] J. Kleinberg. Bursty and hierarchical structure in streams. *KDD*, 2003.

[10] V. Lavrenko and W. B. Croft. Relevance based language models. *SIGIR*, 2001.

[11] X. Li and W. B. Croft. Time-based language models. *CIKM*, 2003.

[12] M.-H. Peetz, E. Meij, M. de Rijke, and W. Weerkamp. Adaptive temporal query modeling. *ECIR*, 2012.

[13] J. Rao, J. Lin, and M. Efron. Reproducible experiments on lexical and temporal feedback for tweet search. *ECIR*, 2015.

[14] M. D. Smucker, J. Allan, and B. Carterette. A comparison of statistical significance tests for information retrieval evaluation. *CIKM*, 2007.

Nearest Neighbour based Transformation Functions for Text Classification: A case study with StackOverflow

Piyush Arora, Debasis Ganguly and Gareth J.F.Jones
ADAPT Centre, School of Computing
Dublin City University, Dublin, Ireland
{parora,dganguly,gjones}@computing.dcu.ie

ABSTRACT

The significant growth in the number of questions in question answering forums has led to increasing interest in text categorization methods for classifying *newly* posted questions as *good* (suitable) or *bad* (otherwise) for the forum. Standard text categorization approaches, e.g. multinomial Naive Bayes, are likely to be unsuitable for this classification task because of: i) the lack of sufficient informative content in the questions due to their relatively short length; and ii) considerable vocabulary overlap between the classes. To increase the robustness of this classification task, we propose to use the *neighbourhood* of existing questions which are similar to the newly asked question. Instead of learning the classification boundary from the questions alone, we *transform* each question vector into a different one in the feature space. We explore two different neighbourhood functions using: the discrete term space, the continuous vector space of real numbers obtained from vector embeddings of documents. Experiments conducted on StackOverflow data show that our approach of using this neighborhood transformation can improve classification accuracy by up to about 8%. as compared to using just unigram textual features.

CCS Concepts

•**Information systems** → **Question answering;** *Query representation; Clustering and classification;*

Keywords

Neighbourhood based transformation; Document embedding; Question quality prediction

1. INTRODUCTION

Community question answering (CQA) platforms provide forums for knowledge exchange between individuals interested in a wide range of topics. The success of forums such as StackOverflow (SO) which currently contains around 11M questions in the area of software programming, make manual moderation of question quality a daunting task. CQA forums generally use a voting

mechanism to obtain feedback from the community about the usefulness or suitability of each question. Based on this feedback, poorly scoring questions might be deleted or closed from the community. However, obtaining community feedback on questions takes time. Thus, it does not provide an indication of the quality of *newly* posted questions, which would for example enable them to be prioritised for attention or for deletion. A text categorization method that classifies such questions into: *good* (a question conforming to the community guidelines) or *bad* (a vague, imprecise, controversial question) would thus form a valuable component in the question moderation process. Despite the practical issue of the unavailability of community feedback for newly posted questions, to the best of our knowledge all prior work, e.g. [2], on CQA question classification has made use of community feedback, such as the number of votes, comments etc. Our work in this paper uses bag-of-words features from the questions, similar to [6] to address the problem of new question classification in CQA forums. Moreover, using only the text makes the approach generic enough to be applied to CQA forums which do not support community feedback, e.g. Ubuntu forums and Yahoo answers.

Carrying out this question classification task in the absence of community feedback faces two significant challenges: the relatively short length of the questions as compared to traditional web documents, and the considerable vocabulary overlap that exists between the *good* and *bad* questions. The complete SO question dataset, comprising $1.3M$ positive and $30K$ negative questions (see Table 1), has a high vocabulary overlap of 59.5% between the two classes. The sampled data for our experiments constituting 1000 samples from each class also has a high vocabulary overlap of 34.6%. In SO, the average length of questions in positive and negative classes is about 72 and 66 words, respectively. This high vocabulary overlap and relatively short length of questions indicates that a question by itself lacks sufficient informative and discriminative content for the classification task.

One obvious solution to this problem is to increase the number of training examples so as to incorporate more information into the classifier. However, this could lead to a strong imbalance in the number of samples between the positive and the negative class, because the number of down-voted questions in SO is much lower than the number of positively voted questions (see Table 1 and [6]). In this situation, adding more training examples is likely to bias the classifier towards predicting every question as *good*. The results of an exploratory investigation that we carried our on this imbalanced dataset (considering questions with at least 1000 views as in [6]) are shown in Table 2. These results indicate that increasing the number of training samples is not a good solution, because despite giving high accuracy, the average F-score (see Table 2) is close to that of random classification due to the strong class imbalance.

Class name	Questions	
	All	#Views $\geq$ 1000
Bad (net score < 0)	380800	30163
Good (net score > 0)	3780301	1315731

Table 1: Frequency distribution for the two classes of SO questions (overall and the subset of questions with #views $\geq$ 1000). The net score of an SO question is the difference between the number of positive and negative votes.

Method	Accuracy	F-Measure (Macro average)
Only title content	0.9707	0.503
Title + Body content	0.9735	0.503

Table 2: Classification effectiveness for all SO questions with #views > 1000, #neg and #pos samples being 30,163 and 1,315,731, respectively (see Table 1) using MNB classifier.

To alleviate this problem of the lack of sufficient discriminative content in the questions, we propose to make use of other existing questions previously asked in the forum, to enrich the informative content of the question vectors. Since the previous questions asked on the forum already have votes, they can be treated as labelled samples and one may make use of a simple non-parametric classifier such as the K-NN. In the context of our problem, this simply refers to the process of retrieving other similar (in terms of text content) questions and classifying a question as *good* if it is surrounded by a higher number of positively voted questions than negatively voted ones. Unfortunately, such a simple classifier does not yield satisfactory results for our problem, as shown in Table 3. This motivates us to pursue the proposed method of transforming the data points before classification throughout the rest of the paper.

In contrast to using the class labels of other similar questions for K-NN classification, we propose to make selective use of other samples (whose labels we do not consider) for the purpose of transforming the current labelled sample in the training set. The objective is to obtain a different decision boundary than that obtained with the original training samples. Indeed, on each training instance vector (comprised of discrete terms or real numbers), $\mathbf{x}$, we propose to apply a *transformation* function ϕ to obtain a modified training sample $\phi(\mathbf{x})$. Recent research has shown that supervised learning on distributions rather than fixed training points proves to be effective, e.g, the support measure machine model proposed in [5]. Conceptually, the proposed transformation methods provide additional information from the neighbourhood which can be further used to form more descriptive features using kernel methods. The focus of this paper is to compare and explore the use of a transformation functions for the task of SO question classification. In the next section, we investigate the characteristics of this transformation function.

2. TRANSFORMATION FUNCTION

Our main hypothesis is that the transformation function ϕ operating on a vector $\mathbf{x}$ depends on the neighbourhood of $\mathbf{x}$. More specifically, ϕ is a function, say Φ, of the current point $\mathbf{x}$ and its neighborhood $N(\mathbf{x})$ as shown in Equation 1.

$$\phi(\mathbf{x}) = \Phi(\mathbf{x}, N(\mathbf{x})), \ N(\mathbf{x}) = \{\mathbf{x_i} : d(\mathbf{x}, \mathbf{x_i}) \leq r\} \quad (1)$$

The transformation function shown in Equation 1 is a non-parametric

k	Accuracy	F-score
1	0.4668	0.4766
3	0.4594	0.4548
5	0.4599	0.4523

Table 3: K-NN classifier fails to yield satisfactory results on a 50-50 train-test split of $1,000$ questions from each class.

one in the sense that this function solely depends on the current vector $\mathbf{x}$ and its neighbourhood, and cannot be expressed in a parametric form. In principle, the transformation function $\Phi(\mathbf{x}, N(\mathbf{x}))$ is somewhat similar to document expansion in information retrieval (IR), where a short document is expanded with the textual content from other documents in order to improve its informativeness and retrievability [3]. Further, from Equation 1, we can observe that the effectiveness of the transformation approach largely depends on the choice of the distance function $d(\mathbf{x}, \mathbf{x_i})$, the distance between a given training vector $\mathbf{x}$ and other vectors $\mathbf{x_i}$ that are not a part of the training set. An optimal choice of the distance function depends on the type of the vector $\mathbf{x}$, i.e. $\mathbf{x}$ is a real-valued or a categorical (e.g. composed of bag of words) vector. In particular for our study, we consider two different types of vector representations, namely the discrete term space representation of the SO questions (documents) (Section 4), and the finite dimensional vector representation learnt using neural network based embedding techniques such as [4] (Section 5).

3. EXPERIMENT SETUP

As introduced in Section 1, we used the 2014 StackOverflow data dump for our experiments. For all our classification experiments, in order to create a training set with reliable community feedback, we selected questions with at least a $1,000$ views, as prescribed in [6] and explored in our earlier work [1] . For the two classes in this classification task, we labeled questions with net positive scores (more up and then down votes) (*good*) and those with net negative scores (*bad*), as shown in Table 1. Due to the strong class frequency imbalance, using the whole dataset for training does not produce satisfactory classification effectiveness (Table 2 shows that despite high accuracy, the F-score values are close to random). Hence, we down-sampled the dataset by randomly selecting $1,000$ questions from each class to conduct our experiments.

In order to efficiently compute the neighbourhood (see Equation 1) for applying the transformation function of each question vector, each question in the SO dump, comprised of the title, body and the tags, was indexed with Lucene. For the neighbourhood set, we only consider questions that have non-zero scores. In total, the number of documents in the index (the questions with net zero scores were not indexed) is about 1.35M. For our text-based classification experiments, we use a Multinomial Naive Bayes (MNB) classifier with additive smoothing [7]. For document embedded vector based experiments, we use an SVM classifier (Gaussian kernel with default parameters $C = 1$ and $\gamma = 0.005$[1]). For all our experiments, we performed 10 fold stratified cross-validation over our dataset to avoid over-fitting. We evaluated classification performance using accuracy and F-score measures.

4. TERM BASED CLASSIFICATION

Neighbourhood selection using whole documents. We first performed standard text based classification with the help of the

---

[1]http://scikit-learn.org/stable/

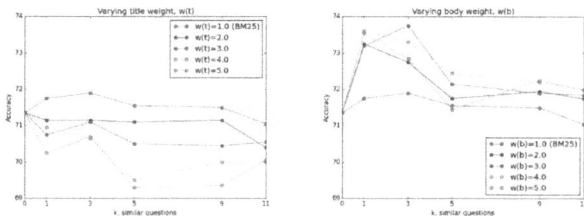

Figure 1: Accuracies obtained with different neighbourhood transformations and weights for the title (left, $w(B) = 1$) and the body (right, $w(T) = 1$) fields of SO questions.

Table 4: Multinomial Naive Bayes classification with BM25 based neighbourhood transformation.

k	Accuracy	F-Measure
0	0.713	0.704
1	0.718	0.710
3	**0.719**	**0.713**
5	0.715	0.710
9	0.715	0.711
11	0.710	0.706

MNB classifier by making use of text of each question in the training set. This amounts to simply using the original training vectors **x** for learning a decision boundary (reported as the result $k = 0$ in Table 4). Next in order to test our hypothesis that enhancing the informative content of a question improves classification effectiveness (see Section 2), we undertook a simple approach of finding $N(\mathbf{x})$, the neighbourhood of a data point **x**. We considered the title of a question as a query and retrieved a ranked list of related questions from our SO index. For retrieval we used BM25, with parameters $k = 1.2$ and $b = 0.75$. The BM25 similarity measure acts as the inverse distance metric d of Equation 1. The top k documents from this list yields the desired neighbourhood. As the transformation function $\Phi(\mathbf{x}, N(\mathbf{x}))$, we concatenate (denoted by the $\oplus$ operator) the text of each $\mathbf{x_i} \in N(\mathbf{x})$ to **x**.

$$\Phi(\mathbf{x}, N(\mathbf{x})) = \mathbf{x} \oplus (\oplus_{x_i \in N(\mathbf{x})} \mathbf{x_i}) \quad (2)$$

We also varied the parameter k, i.e. the number of top most similar documents (SO questions), used to define the neighbourhood for transforming the current document (SO question) before MNB classifier training. $k = 0$ refers to the 'no transformation' case. The results in Table 4 show improvement in classification effectiveness (compare the F-scores with the baseline case, i.e. when $k = 0$ and those of Table 2). This empirically proves the hypothesis that it is possible to achieve a better decision boundary between the two classes of SO questions by transforming each training vector **x** to a different point $\Phi(\mathbf{x}, N(\mathbf{x}))$ similar to the results shown in our earlier work [1]. Another interesting observation is that with $k = 11$, classification effectiveness decreases. This happens because too large a neighbourhood is prone to attract noisy information for classifier training.

Neighbourhood selection using individual document fields. After observing improvements in classification results with the use of neighbourhood, we now explore alternative ways of obtaining potentially better neighbourhoods and transformation functions by leveraging the content of the individual fields of a question, namely its title and body. Instead of using BM25 (as used for selecting

Table 5: Multinomial Naive Bayes classification with BM25F based neighbourhood transformation.

k	Neighborhood	Accuracy	F-Measure
0	N/A	0.713	0.704
3	BM25	0.719	0.713
3	BM25F	**0.738**	**0.733**

neighbourhoods based on the whole question text), for the field based neighbourhood selection, we applied BM25F [8] which makes provision to associate relative importance to each field by assigning individual weights to each. To search for the optimal neighbourhood for a question, a query was formulated by using the terms from the 'title' field and retrieval was performed over documents comprised of two fields - the 'title' and the 'body'. To find the optimal settings for the relative weights, denoted $w(B)$ and $w(T)$ corresponding to the body and the title respectively, we performed a two-step grid search as shown in Figure 1. We fixed one of the weights and varied the other in the range $[1, 5]$. The best results were obtained with $(w(T), w(B)) = (1, 3)$ with $k = 3$.

Setting a higher weight for w_T (the weight of the title field) degrades classification accuracy. The most likely reason is that the top ranked retrieved questions defining the neighbourhood of **x** may only have a few matching terms with the current document from the title field only. A few matching terms in the title may not necessarily mean that the current question and those in the neighbourhood are topically related to each other. On the other hand, the main informative content of a SO question is likely to be present in the body field. Matching the title terms of the query (a new question) with those in the body of previous questions proves to be more effective in retrieving topically related questions.

Table 5 compares the results obtained with optimal BM25F parameter settings (as per Figure 1) with the BM25 based neighbourhood (reproduced from Table 4). We find that the accuracy obtained with BM25 based neighborhood transformation increases by 2.6% and the F-score by 2.8% in comparison to the BM25 one. This not only shows that BM25F is a better (inverse) distance measure for choosing the neighbourhood function $N(\mathbf{x})$ more effectively, but also indicates that the neighbourhood function plays a crucial part in estimating the decision boundary for this classification problem.

5. EMBEDDING BASED CLASSIFICATION

In this section, we approach the SO question classification using vector embeddings of documents [4]. Embedded representations have shown to outperform text based approaches for various NLP tasks, such as sentiment analysis [4]. The document vector embedding process learns a one-hot vector representation of a word or sentence. These vectors can then be used as inputs to a classifier.

5.1 Embedding SO questions as vectors

In the context of our classification task, the purpose of document embeddings is to represent the semantic relatedness between documents with the help of distances between real valued vector. An interesting question for our study is then: how may we choose the neighbourhood and the transformation functions for real valued vectors rather than text? In particular, we used the model of distributed representation of sentences and documents [4] to learn embeddings for questions. We used gensim implementation[2] of *doc2vec* for training the model and learning question embeddings.

---

[2]https://radimrehurek.com/gensim/models/doc2vec.html

For each of the question q in our data set, we learned a real-valued vector with the component values ranging between $[-1, 1]$. For real-valued vectors, one cannot use Multinomial Naive Bayes (MNB) for classification as it uses MLE estimates of categorical features, such as terms of a document. For classification experiments with the document vector representations, we used the SVM classifier. As a baseline approach we applied the SVM classifier on the vector embeddings of documents to obtain the decision boundary. To obtain the document embedded vectors, we experimented with both the 'distributed bag of words' (*dbow*) model and the 'distributed memory model' (*dmm*) as described in [4]. The SVM classification effectiveness obtained with the *dbow* document vectors outperforms those obtained with the *dmm* model, as a result of which, all the subsequent results reported in this section used the *dbow* model trained document vectors for classifier training. Another parameter for the document vector embedding process is the dimensionality of the vectors (i.e. the number of nodes in the output layer of the neural network). We varied this number from 100 to 500 with a step size of 100. We obtained the best classification results with 200 dimensional embeddings. The 'window size' parameter for the document embedding process was set to 10 as prescribed in [4].

5.2 Neighbourhood and Transformation

For document embedded vectors, we applied the most common notion of similarity, the inner product between two vectors, as the (inverse) distance metric for choosing the neighbourhood around a vector $\mathbf{x}$ (see Equation 1). Note that for real-valued vectors we cannot make use of BM25 similarity as used in the experiments of Section 4. After obtaining the neighbourhood set $N(\mathbf{x})$, the next step is to apply the Φ function, which defines how to use the information contained in the neighbourhood set to enrich the current data point. A standard way to combine a set of vectors in $\mathbb{R}^P$ is to compute the centroid vector. We considered the more generalized approach for computing the weighted centroid, where each point $\mathbf{x_i}$ from the neighbourhood set is weighted by its distance from the current point $\mathbf{x}$, as shown in Equation 3.

$$\Phi(\mathbf{x}, N(\mathbf{x})) = \mathbf{x} + \sum_{\mathbf{x_i} \in N(\mathbf{x_i})} (\mathbf{x} \cdot \mathbf{x_i}) \mathbf{x_i} \tag{3}$$

It can be seen that the dot product between $\mathbf{x}$ and its neighbour $\mathbf{x_i}$, which is a real number, acts as the weight to define the relative contribution of $\mathbf{x_i}$ in the transformation function. Unlike the transformation function for the text space (Equation 2), the weighted neighbourhood for document embedded vectors (Equation 3) is able to capture the contributions from each individual point of the neighbourhood in variable quantities.

Table 6 shows the results after applying the transformation function Φ, as defined in Equation 3, on the embedded document vectors after training with SVM. The baseline case, i.e., when no transformation is applied, is shown with $k = 0$. Similar to the text based classification, we varied the neighbourhood size to see its effect on classification performance. From Table 6, we observe that the application of the transformation function shows consistent improvement for the document embedded vectors as was the case for the text vectors (see Table 5). The best classification effectiveness achieved with the vector embeddings of SO questions is higher than that obtained with the text features (compare Table 6 with Table 5).

6. CONCLUSIONS AND FUTURE WORK

In this paper, we proposed a general framework for applying a non-parametric based transformation function on a given set of training examples before training a parametric classifier. The transformation function decides what information to use from the local

Table 6: SVM classification after applying neighborhood based transformation on document vector embeddings.

k	Accuracy	F-Measure
0	0.743	0.743
1	0.740	0.739
3	0.747	0.746
5	0.750	0.749
9	**0.769**	**0.768**
11	0.765	0.764

neighbourhood of a training point so as to enrich the representation of the current point. The task that we address is the classification of a newly posted StackOverflow question as good or bad for its community. The considerable vocabulary overlap between the classes and short length of questions make this a challenging classification task, which is an ideal candidate for the transformation function based approach to classification. We study two different classification approaches, one with text and the other with document vector embeddings. We find empirically that selecting a good neighbourhood is important for achieving good classification results. Results show that the use of BM25F with more importance given to the match in the 'body' field of a question results in a better neighbourhood estimation with improved classification. For the text based approach, we applied concatenation as a transformation function. The neighbourhood is computed using BM25 similarity. For the document vector space, the neighbourhood is computed using dot products coupled with a weighted centroid transformation function. Consistent trends in improvements of classification results are observed with the transformation function applied on both text and document vector embeddings. The improvements in classification F-scores obtained with the transformation function on the text and on the document embedded vectors are up to 4.1% and 3.4%, respectively. As a part of future work, we would like to explore alternative transformation functions, and different ways of combining the neighbourhood and the transformation functions of the textual and the document vector spaces.

Acknowledgment: This research is supported by Science Foundation Ireland (SFI) as a part of the ADAPT Centre at Dublin City University (Grant No: 12/CE/I2267 and 13/RC/2106).

7. REFERENCES
[1] P. Arora, D. Ganguly, and G. J. Jones. The good, the bad and their kins: Identifying questions with negative scores in stackoverflow. In *Proceedings of ASONAM '15*, pages 1232–1239. ACM, 2015.

[2] D. Correa and A. Sureka. Chaff from the wheat: characterization and modeling of deleted questions on stack overflow. In *Proceedings of WWW '14*, pages 631–642, 2014.

[3] M. Efron, P. Organisciak, and K. Fenlon. Improving retrieval of short texts through document expansion. In *Proceedings of the SIGIR '12*, pages 911–920, 2012.

[4] Q. V. Le and T. Mikolov. Distributed representations of sentences and documents. In *Proceedings of ICML '14*, pages 1188–1196, 2014.

[5] K. Muandet, K. Fukumizu, F. Dinuzzo, and B. Schölkopf. Learning from distributions via support measure machines. In *Proc. of NIPS '12*, pages 10–18, 2012.

[6] S. Ravi, B. Pang, V. Rastogi, and R. Kumar. Great Question! Question Quality in Community Q&A. In *Proc. of ICWSM '14*, 2014.

[7] J. D. Rennie, L. Shih, J. Teevan, and D. R. Karger. Tackling the poor assumptions of naive bayes text classifiers. In *Proc. of ICML '03*, pages 616–623, 2003.

[8] S. E. Robertson, H. Zaragoza, and M. J. Taylor. Simple BM25 extension to multiple weighted fields. In *Proceedings of CIKM '04*, pages 42–49, 2004.

Cross-Language Microblog Retrieval using Latent Semantic Modeling

Archana Godavarthy
Department of Computer Engineering
Santa Clara University
500 El Camino Real
Santa Clara, CA, 95053
agodavarthy@gmail.com

Yi Fang
Department of Computer Engineering
Santa Clara University
500 El Camino Real
Santa Clara, CA, 95053
yfang@scu.edu

ABSTRACT

Microblogging has become one of the major tools of sharing real-time information for people around the world. Finding relevant information across different languages on microblogs is highly desirable especially for the large number of multilingual users. However, the characteristics of microblog content pose great challenges to the existing cross-language information retrieval approaches. In this paper, we address the task of retrieving relevant tweets given another tweet in a different language. We build parallel corpora for tweets in different languages by bridging them via shared hashtags. We propose a latent semantic approach to model the parallel corpora by mapping the parallel tweets to a low-dimensional shared semantic space. The relevance between tweets in different languages is measured in this shared latent space and the model is trained on a pairwise loss function. The preliminary experiments on a Twitter dataset demonstrate the effectiveness of the proposed approach.

Keywords

Cross Language Information Retrieval; Microblog Retrieval; Latent Semantic Modeling

1. INTRODUCTION

Microblogging platforms such as Twitter have emerged as a powerful source of real-time information sharing for people around the world. Its popularity is witnessed in different parts of the world such as Brazil, Japan, India, France and Turkey[1]. As a result, the content on Twitter is highly multilingual. One study[2] shows that only about 50% of the Twitter messages are in English and other popular languages on Twitter include Japanese, Portuguese, Malay and Spanish.

---

[1]http://www.forbes.com/sites/victorlipman20140524top-twitter-trends-what-countries-are-most-active-whos-most-popular

[2]http://techcrunch.com/2010/02/24/twitter-languages

ICTIR '16, September 12-16, 2016, Newark, DE, USA
© 2016 ACM. ISBN 978-1-4503-4497-5/16/09. . . $15.00
DOI: http://dx.doi.org/10.1145/2970398.2970436

Table 1: An Example of parallel tweets sharing a common hashtag

HashTag: #Immigration
English Tweet: *Our overall #immigration policy is focus enfrcmnt resources more effectively on threats to pub safety & border security*
Spanish Tweet: *Por qué importa una reforma migratoria integral en EU: "US #immigration: Help wanted" http fb.me/81l8JGJWI , vía FT*
Google Translate [3] : *Why not give a comprehensive immigration reform in the US , "US #immigration: Help wanted" http fb.me 81l8JGJWI via FT*

Microblogging services played a crucial role in quickly spreading the news about important international events such as Arab Springs. The news on microblogs is sometimes ahead of the major news media. It is very desirable to provide rapid cross-lingual data access for the huge number of multilingual users on microblogs. One solution is to deploy traditional cross-language information retrieval techniques (CLIR) such as machine translation. However, microblog content is quite different from the traditional textual data. For example, the tweets are short text with limitation of 140 characters. Some of the shortcomings of the tweets include informal usage of language, poor spelling and grammatical quality, and inclusion of symbols and diacritics. The existing CLIR approaches focus on regular text documents and may not be directly applicable to microblog data.

In this paper, we study cross-language microblog retrieval. We tackle a specific retrieval problem on microblogs: given a tweet in one language (e.g., English), retrieve a ranked list of relevant tweets in another language (e.g., Spanish). This retrieval task can also be used for recommending interesting tweets in different languages for multilingual users.

We build parallel corpora for tweets in different languages by bridging them via common hashtags. The intuition is that if two tweets share the same hashtag, they are semantically related. Due to the prevalence of hashtags on microblogs, we could find a large amount of parallel texts for tweets in different languages in an automatic manner. Table 1 contains an example of parallel tweets in English and in Spanish sharing a common hashtag. As we can see, the two tweets may not talk about exactly the same issue, but they are semantically related.

The traditional translation based approaches may not be

---

[3]https://translate.google.com/

effective for cross-language microblog retrieval because tokens on microblogs are often irregular and noisy. Having a good translation on microblogs is a challenging research problem in itself [1]. In contrast, we model the latent semantics of the parallel tweets by mapping the original high-dimensional tweets to the low-dimensional semantic space and measuring their similarity in this shared semantic space. The mappings are learned from the parallel corpora in a pairwise manner. It is more reasonable than using pointwise loss function because the negative relevance judgments cannot be reliably obtained in this task. The model is trained by stochastic gradient descent (SGD). We conduct experiments on a dataset from Twitter for Spanish and English tweets. The preliminary results demonstrate the effectiveness of the proposed approach over the translation based approach.

2. RELATED WORK

Cross-language information retrieval (CLIR) is a well studied field in the IR community. The major IR evaluation platforms including CLEF[4], NTCIR[5], and TREC[6] have frequently organized the CLIR benchmark evaluations. Dumais et al. [2] is a classic work on general-purpose cross-language IR, which uses latent semantic features to retrieve relevant cross script documents. Our work differs from this work in utilizing the pairwise training of the latent semantic features, instead of pointwise training. Tang et al. [10] apply latent factor models for cross-language citation recommendations.

Microblog retrieval has recently attracted increased attention. TREC has hosted the Microblog track since 2011 [7] to study the retrieval tasks on microblogs. The characteristics of microblogs are investigated, but the TREC tasks have been exclusively focused on English content while a noticeable portion of tweets in the corpus are in other languages [9]. TweeMT[7] is a workshop and shared task on machine translation applied to tweets. Jehl et al. [4] propose probabilistic translation-based approach for Arabic tweets. They utilize the retrieved results to build parallel corpora between different languages. Hu et al.[3] use crowdsourcing methods to translate SMS messages between different languages. Ling et al. [5] build parallel corpora by identifying the presence of multiple languages in the same tweet. They also utilize retweets to identify parallel text. To the best of our knowledge, no prior work has utilized latent semantic modeling for cross-language microblog retrieval.

3. LATENT SEMANTIC MODELING

We utilize the parallel tweets in different languages by assuming that if two tweets in different languages share the same hashtag, they are semantically related. In this paper, we focus on English and Spanish tweets, but the model can be applied to any other languages. Without resorting to language translation, we model the latent semantics of the parallel tweets by projecting the original high-dimensional tweets into a low-dimensional semantic space. The projections are learned from the parallel corpora. The proposed approach is named as **C**ross-language **L**atent semantic **M**odel (CLM).

[4] http://www.clef-campaign.org/
[5] http://research.nii.ac.jp/ntcir/index-en.html
[6] http://trec.nist.gov/
[7] http://komunitatea.elhuyar.eus/tweetmt/

It is worth noting that the tweets that do not share the same hashtag could still be semantically related. Therefore, instead of doing pointwise relevance judgment (which would assume tweets that do not share the same hashtag are not relevant), we use a pairwise ranking approach by assuming that the tweets that share the same hashtag are more relevant than those that do not. This is a more reasonable assumption for our task than the pointwise relevance judgment.

Formally, let $\mathbf{e}_i \in R^n$ denote the ith English tweet in the parallel corpus by using vector representation such as TF-IDF. Similarly, let $\mathbf{s}_j \in R^p$ be the vector of the jth Spanish tweet. Given an English tweet $\mathbf{e}_i$, if the Spanish tweet $\mathbf{s}_j$ has a common hashtag with $\mathbf{e}_i$ while $\mathbf{s}_m$ does not, we have a pairwise triple $(\mathbf{e}_i, \mathbf{s}_j^+, \mathbf{s}_m^-)$ indicating the Spanish tweet $\mathbf{s}_j^+$ is more relevant than $\mathbf{s}_m^-$. We then learn the mapping from TF-IDF feature space to the joint space with reduced dimensionality of K. $\phi_e : R^n \to R^K, \phi_s : R^p \to R^K$.

We apply linear mapping for both ϕ_e and ϕ_s as

$$\phi_e = \mathbf{e}_i^T \mathbf{W} \tag{1}$$

$$\phi_s = \mathbf{s}_j^T \mathbf{Q} \tag{2}$$

where $\mathbf{W}$ and $\mathbf{Q}$ are the projection matrices for English and Spanish tweets respectively. The relevance score $r(\mathbf{e}_i, \mathbf{s}_j)$ between the English and Spanish tweets can be measured by the inner product in the shared space:

$$r(\mathbf{e}_i, \mathbf{s}_j) = \phi_e \phi_s^T = \mathbf{e}_i^T \mathbf{W}(\mathbf{s}_j^T \mathbf{Q})^T = \mathbf{e}_i^T \mathbf{W} \mathbf{Q}^T \mathbf{s}_j \tag{3}$$

We sample $\mathbf{e}_i$, $\mathbf{s}_j^+$, and $\mathbf{s}_m^-$ to form the pairwise triples from the corpus based on the presence of common hashtags. Section 4.2 provides the details of our sampling strategy in the experiments. Given all the pairwise triples $(\mathbf{e}_i, \mathbf{s}_j^+, \mathbf{s}_m^-)$, we define the pair-wise loss function as follows:

$$L = \sum_{\mathbf{e}_i} \sum_{\mathbf{s}_j^+, \mathbf{s}_m^-} - \log \sigma \left(h(\mathbf{e}_i, \mathbf{s}_j^+, \mathbf{s}_m^-) \right) \tag{4}$$

where $h(\mathbf{e}_i, \mathbf{s}_j^+, \mathbf{s}_m^-) = r(\mathbf{e}_i, \mathbf{s}_j^+) - r(\mathbf{e}_i, \mathbf{s}_m^-) = \mathbf{e}_i^T \mathbf{W} \mathbf{Q}^T (\mathbf{s}_j^+ - \mathbf{s}_m^-)$ and $\sigma(x)$ is the sigmoid function defined as: $\sigma(x) = \frac{1}{1+\exp(-x)}$.

As we can see, this loss function maximizes the difference between the ranking scores $r(\mathbf{e}_i, \mathbf{s}_j^+)$ and $r(\mathbf{e}_i, \mathbf{s}_m^-)$ by using $\log \sigma(x)$ which is a monotonically increasing function. As a result, the tweet $\mathbf{s}_j^+$ becomes more relevant than the tweet $\mathbf{s}_m^-$. This optimization criterion is similar to Bayesian Personalized Ranking [8] that has demonstrated success in recommender systems with implicit feedback.

We learn the parameters $\mathbf{W}$ and $\mathbf{Q}$ by minimizing the loss function Eqn.(4) on the training data. The model is trained by Stochastic Gradient Descent (SGD). For each triple $(\mathbf{e}_i, \mathbf{s}_j^+, \mathbf{s}_m^-)$ in the training data, the gradients of the loss function L with respect to the parameters $\mathbf{W}$ and $\mathbf{Q}$ are computed as follows:

$$\frac{\partial L}{\partial \mathbf{W}} = \frac{\partial L}{\partial h} \frac{\partial h}{\partial \mathbf{W}} = \left(\sigma \left(h(\mathbf{e}_i, \mathbf{s}_j^+, \mathbf{s}_m^-) \right) - 1 \right) \mathbf{e}_i (\mathbf{s}_j^+ - \mathbf{s}_m^-)^T \mathbf{Q}$$

$$\frac{\partial L}{\partial \mathbf{Q}} = \frac{\partial L}{\partial h} \frac{\partial h}{\partial \mathbf{Q}} = \left(\sigma \left(h(\mathbf{e}_i, \mathbf{s}_j^+, \mathbf{s}_m^-) \right) - 1 \right) (\mathbf{s}_j^+ - \mathbf{s}_m^-) \mathbf{e}_i^T \mathbf{W}$$

For each triple, the parameters are updated as follows:

$$\mathbf{W}_{t+1} = \mathbf{W}_t - \alpha \frac{\partial L}{\partial \mathbf{W}}$$

$$\mathbf{Q}_{t+1} = \mathbf{Q}_t - \alpha \frac{\partial L}{\partial \mathbf{Q}} \qquad (5)$$

where α is the learning rate. The converged values of $\mathbf{W}$ and $\mathbf{Q}$ are then used to rank all the candidate Spanish tweets $\mathbf{s}_j$ given any new English tweet $\mathbf{e}_i$ in the test data based on the descending order of ranking score $r(\mathbf{e}_i, \mathbf{s}_j)$ in Eqn.(3).

4. EXPERIMENTS

4.1 Data Collection

We collected English and Spanish tweets from Twitter streaming API via tweepy[8]. Between Nov. 11 to Dec. 5, 2015, we gathered about 1 million English tweets and 400,000 Spanish tweets for our experiments. We preprocess the tweets by removing the Retweets, URLs, usernames, punctuations, and stopwords. Since our approach is based on matching the tweets in different languages using hashtags, we filtered out the tweets that do not have any hashtag. Additionally, we pair each tweet with a single hashtag and remove the most & least frequent terms occurring in the corpus. After preprocessing, we obtained 167,203 English tweets with 35,305 unique tokens and 198,690 Spanish tweets with 30,531 tokens. We obtained 5,880 common hashtags shared by both English and Spanish tweets. We randomly form pairwise triples for each of the English tweet pairing with a positive Spanish tweet, $\mathbf{s}_j^+$ and a negative Spanish tweet, $\mathbf{s}_m^-$. We used 80% of these triples for the training and the remaining 20% for testing.

4.2 Baselines and Settings

To evaluate the performance of the proposed approach, we randomly picked 30 English tweets from the test set as queries. These 30 tweets cover a variety of topics in entertainment, sports, politics, technology, etc. Given each test English tweet $\mathbf{e}_i$, each of the baselines retrieves a ranked list of Spanish tweets from the whole corpus. Jaccard and BM25 are the baselines we used. They are Translation based, i.e. given an English tweet $\mathbf{e}_i$, we obtain its Spanish translation, $\mathbf{s}_t$ using Google Translate. Using $\mathbf{s}_t$, we apply different similarity based retrieval methods to retrieve the Spanish tweets that are most similar to $\mathbf{s}_t$.

- Jaccard: The translated tweet $\mathbf{s}_t$ is used to rank all the candidate Spanish tweets based on Jaccard similarity [6].

- BM25: Similarly we compute the scores of the Spanish tweets using BM25 [6] for each query term $\mathbf{s}_{ti} \in \mathbf{s}_t$. For parameters in BM25, we use default values ($k = 1.5$, $b = 0.75$).

- CLM: our proposed model. For the given $\mathbf{e}_i$, we compute the relevance score as defined in Eqn.(3) using the converged $\mathbf{W}$ and $\mathbf{Q}$.

- Hybrid (CLM+BM25): We normalize the ranking scores of CLM and translation approaches respectively using the min-max normalization $(x - x_{min})/(x_{max} - x_{min})$,

[8]http://www.tweepy.org

Table 2: Experimental results for different methods.

Method	P@5	P@10	AP@10	NDCG@10
Jaccard	0.060	0.110	0.157	0.074
BM25	0.080	0.100	0.170	0.075
CLM	**0.493**	**0.463**	0.536	**0.485**
Hybrid	**0.493**	0.460	**0.572**	0.479

for feature scaling. The two scores are combined as follows:

$$\lambda \widehat{r}(\mathbf{e}_i, \mathbf{s}_j) + (1 - \lambda)\widehat{bm}(\mathbf{s}_t, \mathbf{s}_j) \qquad (6)$$

where $\widehat{r}(\mathbf{e}_i, \mathbf{s}_j)$ and $\widehat{bm}(\mathbf{e}_i, \mathbf{s}_j)$ are the normalized scores from the respective approaches. λ is the combination weight which is set to be 0.5 in the experiments, giving equal weightage to both methods.

We randomly form the pairwise triples $(\mathbf{e}_i, \mathbf{s}_j^+, \mathbf{s}_m^-)$ for training the CLM model by SGD. Specifically, we first randomly select an English tweet $\mathbf{e}_i$ with a hashtag $\mathbf{g}$, and then randomly sample a positive tweet $\mathbf{s}_j^+ \in \mathbf{I}_g^+$ from the pool of Spanish tweets $\mathbf{I}_g^+$ that have the same hashtag $\mathbf{g}$. For the negative tweet, we randomly sample $\mathbf{s}_m^-$ from the pool of Spanish tweets that excludes $\mathbf{I}_g^+$, i.e., $\mathbf{V} \setminus \mathbf{I}_g^+$, where $\mathbf{V}$ is the set of all Spanish tweets. Once a sufficient number of triples are sampled, we randomly shuffle them to avoid bias for certain hashtags. The model is then trained on these permuted instances by SGD.

The initial values of the parameters $\mathbf{W}$ and $\mathbf{Q}$ in the SGD algorithm are uniformly randomly sampled from $[0, 1]$ and the stopping criteria is when the relative change of the loss function in Eqn.(4) is less than 0.1%. The learning rate (α in Eqn.(5)) is set to be 0.1. The default dimension of the latent semantic space is $K = 500$ (we investigate the impact of K in Section 4.4).

4.3 Evaluation Metrics

Given the English tweets as queries, the retrieved Spanish tweets are manually judged based on binary relevance, i.e., relevant or not. We evaluate the results obtained from all the baselines mentioned above. We use Google Translate and Twitter to judge the relevance of the results. We used evaluation metrics like P@5, P@10, AP@10 and NDCG@10 which are widely used to evaluate the results of ranked lists [6]. To calculate NDCG@10, we assume that there are at least 10 relevant Spanish tweets for each query, so the ideal ranking has all of the top 10 results as relevant.

4.4 Results

Table 2 contains the experimental results for different methods. All the values are averaged over the 30 queries. As we can see, our proposed CLM model yields substantial improvement over the two baselines: Jaccard and BM25, which are Translation based methods. We found that the improvement is statistically significant at 0.99 confidence level by the paired t-test. As mentioned in Section 4.2, we based our Hybrid model on CLM and BM25. The improvement of the Hybrid model over CLM is not as significant as the improvement of CLM over the Translation methods. We can see that P@5 is high for CLM and Hybrid. NDCG is higher for the CLM model, as the Hybrid model is affected by the poor performance of BM25 for some queries. The AP@10 of the Hybrid is higher than CLM model, as the performance

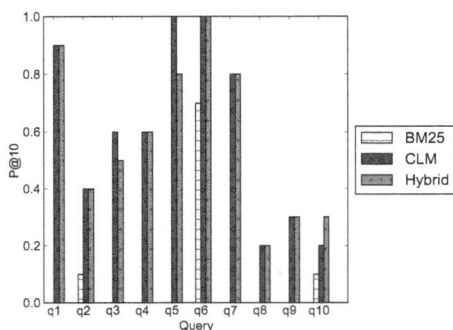

Figure 1: P@10 per query (we only show 10 out of the total 30 queries.)

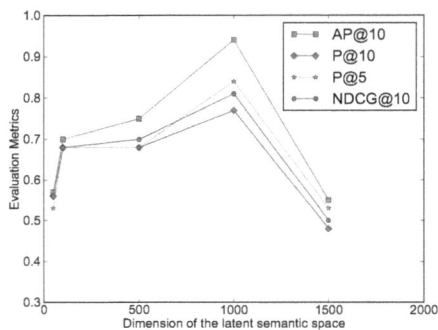

Figure 2: Performance of *CLM* with different dimensionality (K) of the latent semantic space.

of some of the queries improved by utilizing the relevant retrievals by BM25.

To gain further insight into the proposed model, we investigate the performance of different methods using P@10 metric on the per query basis. Due to lack of space we only show 10 out of the total 30 queries. As we can see, for most of the queries, CLM outperforms Translation methods with a large margin. We find there exist several reasons. First of all, many tokens in the tweets are not translated correctly in the Translation methods. This is a challenging issue because words on microblogs are often quite noisy. Secondly, the Translation methods rely on the match of the words in the tweets. If two tweets do not have overlap of tokens, the similarity by translation would be zero. Our proposed CLM model tackles these challenges by modeling the latent semantic space instead. The relations between tweets in different languages are automatically learned via the presence of common hashtags. Consequently, no translation is needed and fuzzy match is possible.

For many queries the performance improvement of the Hybrid model comes directly from the CLM. The CLM model retrieved tweets that do not have exact terms in the query. For example, for query q5 with text: "2025 facebook?", having the same text after Spanish transaltion, the CLM model retrieved tweets like "snapchat redessociales" and "elimina botón redessociales feedly" with the Google translation of "Snapchat social networks" and "delete button social networks feedly" respectively. Even though the term "facebook" does not appear in the Spanish tweets, our model learned the latent semantic to determine these as relevant tweets for social networks like facebook.

However there are few cases where Hybrid utilizes the high performance of both CLM and BM25. For example consider query q10 with query text: "urbana christmasgift", with its corresponding translation "christmasgifts Urbana". BM25 retrieves a relevant tweet: "urbana calzado" (urban footwear in English) which was not retrieved by CLM. In a couple of cases the Hybrid performs worse than CLM, owing to the poor retrievals of BM25. These observations indicate further improvement could be achieved if we use adaptive weights (e.g., high $1 - \lambda$ for popular topic queries) to combine Translation and CLM instead of the fixed weight. We will explore this idea in future work.

Figure 2 shows the impact of the dimensionality of the latent semantic space on the CLM model, with $K = 50, 100,$

500, 1000, 1500, respectively. We can see that the model performance peaks at $K = 1000$ in all the metrics. As K is further increased to 1500, the performance quickly deteriorates, probably due to model overfitting.

5. CONCLUSIONS AND FUTURE WORK

In this paper, we investigate the task of cross-language microblog retrieval. We propose a pairwise latent semantic learning approach that models the low-dimensional shared semantic space between tweets in different languages. The experimental results demonstrate the effectiveness of the proposed approach over the traditional translation baseline. This work is an initial step towards a promising research direction. In future work, we plan to conduct more extensive experiments to validate the proposed approach, including different losses and different learning-to-rank approaches. We also plan to expand our evaluation by including the tweets without hashtags.

6. REFERENCES

[1] I. Alegria, N. Aranberri, C. España Bonet, P. Gamallo, H. Gonçalo Oliveira, E. Martínez Garcia, I. S. V. Roncal, A. Toral, and A. Zubiaga. Overview of tweetmt: a shared task on machine translation of tweets. 2015.

[2] S. T. Dumais, T. A. Letsche, M. L. Littman, and T. K. Landauer. Automatic cross-language retrieval using latent semantic indexing. In *AAAI*, 1997.

[3] C. Hu, P. Resnik, Y. Kronrod, V. Eidelman, O. Buzek, and B. B. Bederson. The value of monolingual crowdsourcing in a real-world translation scenario: Simulation using haitian creole emergency sms messages. In *SMT*, 2011.

[4] L. Jehl, F. Hieber, and S. Riezler. Twitter translation using translation-based cross-lingual retrieval. In *SMT*, 2012.

[5] W. Ling, G. Xiang, C. Dyer, A. W. Black, and I. Trancoso. Microblogs as parallel corpora. In *ACL*, 2013.

[6] C. D. Manning, P. Raghavan, H. Schütze, et al. *Introduction to information retrieval.* 2008.

[7] I. Ounis, C. Macdonald, J. Lin, and I. Soboroff. Overview of the trec-2011 microblog track. In *TREC*, 2011.

[8] S. Rendle, C. Freudenthaler, Z. Gantner, and L. Schmidt-Thieme. Bpr: Bayesian personalized ranking from implicit feedback. In *UAI*, 2009.

[9] I. Soboroff, I. Ounis, C. Macdonald, and J. Lin. Overview of the trec-2012 microblog track. In *TREC*, 2012.

[10] X. Tang, X. Wan, and X. Zhang. Cross-language context-aware citation recommendation in scientific articles. In *SIGIR*. ACM, 2014.

Author Index

www.ingramcontent.com/pod-product-compliance
Lightning Source LLC
Chambersburg PA
CBHW080932220326

41598CB00034B/5765